THE STRATEGY PROCESS

Concepts, Contexts, Cases

—THIRD EDITION—

HENRY MINTZBERG
McGill University

JAMES BRIAN QUINN
Dartmouth College

PRENTICE HALL
Upper Saddle River, New Jersey 07458

Library of Congress Cataloging-in-Publication Data

Mintzberg, Henry.
  The strategy process: concepts, contexts, and cases/**Henry
Mintzberg** and **James Brian Quinn**—3rd ed.
    p.   cm.
  Includes bibliographical references and index.
  ISBN 0-13-234030-5
  1. Strategic planning.   2. Strategic planning—Case studies.
  I. Quinn, James Brian, [date].   II. Title.
HD30.28.Q53   1996
658.4'012—dc20   95-32626

Acquisitions Editor: David A. Shafer
Associate Editor: Lisamarie Brassini
Project Management: Edie Riker
Design Director: Patricia Wosczyk
Interior and Cover Design: Lorraine Castellano
Marketing Manager: Jo-Ann DeLuca
Buyer: Vincent Scelta
Editorial Assistant: Nancy Kaplan

© 1996, 1991, 1988 by Prentice-Hall, Inc.
A Simon & Schuster Company
Upper Saddle River, New Jersey 07458

Printed in the United States of America

10 9 8 7 6 5 4 3 2 1

ISBN 0-13-234030-5

Prentice-Hall International (UK) Limited, *London*
Prentice-Hall of Australia Pty. Limited, *Sydney*
Prentice-Hall Canada Inc., *Toronto*
Prentice-Hall Hispanoamericana, S.A., *Mexico*
Prentice-Hall of India Private Limited, *New Delhi*
Prentice-Hall of Japan, Inc., *Tokyo*
Simon & Schuster Asia Pte. Ltd., *Singapore*
Editora Prentice-Hall do Brasil, Ltda., *Rio de Janeiro*

CONTENTS

ACKNOWLEDGMENTS   ix

INTRODUCTION   xi

SECTION 1   STRATEGY   **1**

▼ CHAPTER 1   THE STRATEGY CONCEPT   **2**

1-1   Strategies for Change   3
James Brian Quinn

1-2   Five Ps for Strategy   10
Henry Mintzberg

▼ CHAPTER 2   THE STRATEGIST   **18**

2-1   The Manager's Job   19
Henry Mintzberg

2-2   Good Managers Don't Make Policy Decisions   35
H. Edward Wrapp

2-3   Strategic Intent   41
Gary Hamel and C.K. Prahalad

▼ CHAPTER 3   FORMULATING STRATEGY   **46**

3-1   The Concept of Corporate Strategy   47
Kenneth R. Andrews

3-2   Evaluating Business Strategy   55
Richard R. Rumelt

3-3   Core Competencies and Strategic Outsourcing   63
James Brian Quinn and Frederick G. Hilmer

iii
▼

▼ CHAPTER 4   STRATEGY ANALYSIS   74

4-1 How Competitive Forces Shape Strategy   75
Michael E. Porter

4-2 Generic Business Strategies   83
Henry Mintzberg

▼ CHAPTER 5   STRATEGY FORMATION   93

5-1 Logical Incrementalism: Managing Strategy Formation   95
James Brian Quinn and John Voyer

5-2 Crafting Strategy   101
Henry Mintzberg

5-3 The Honda Effect   110
Richard T. Pascale

SECTION I   CASES

I-1 Edward Marshall Boehm, Inc.   119

I-2 Genentech, Inc.   121

I-3 MacArthur and the Philippines   127

I-4 New Steel Corporation   142

I-5 Intel Corporation   149

I-6 Apple Computer, Inc. (A)   168

I-7 Apple Computer 1992   173

I-8 Microsoft Corporation (A)   193

I-9 E & J Gallo Winery   209

I-10 The IBM 360 Decision: From Triumph to a New Industry   220

I-11 The Transformation of AT&T   239

I-12 Nintendo Co., Ltd.   254

I-13 Magnetic Levitation Train   272

I-14 Ford: Team Taurus   289

I-15 Argyle Diamonds   309

SECTION II ORGANIZATION

▼ **CHAPTER 6 DEALING WITH STRUCTURE AND SYSTEMS   320**

6-1 Strategy and Organization Planning   322
Jay R. Galbraith

6-2 The Structuring of Organizations   331
Henry Mintzberg

6-3 New Forms of Organizing   350
James Brian Quinn, Philip Anderson, and Sydney Finkelstein

6-4 Collaborating to Compete   362
Joel Bleeke and David Ernst

▼ **CHAPTER 7 DEALING WITH CULTURE AND POWER   367**

7-1 Ideology and the Missionary Organization   370
Henry Mintzberg

7-2 Building Structure in Managers' Minds   375
Christopher A Bartlett and Sumantra Ghoshal

7-3 Politics and the Political Organization   382
Henry Mintzberg

7-4 Competitive Maneuvering   387
Bruce Henderson

7-5 Who Should Control the Corporation?   391
Henry Mintzberg

▼ **CHAPTER 8 MANAGERIAL STYLES   406**

8-1 Artists, Craftsmen, and Technocrats   407
Patricia Pitcher

8-2 The Leader's New Work:
Building Learning Organizations   413
Peter M. Senge

8-3 Middle Managers to "Do Things Right"   422
Leonard R. Sayles

SECTION II   CASES

II-1 The New York Times Company   428

II-2 Matsushita Electric Industrial Company 1994   457

II-3 The Hewlett Packard Company   469

II-4 TCG, Ltd./Thermo Electron Corporation   489

II-5 Microsoft Corporation (B)   503

II-6 NovaCare, Inc.   517

II-7 Orbital Engine Company   530

II-8 Andersen Consulting (Europe):
Entering the Business of Business Integration   541

II-9 Polaroid Corporation   558

II-10 Exxon Corporation 1994   576

II-11 Sony Corporation: Innovation System   595

SECTION III CONTEXTS

▼ CHAPTER 9   THE ENTREPRENEURIAL CONTEXT   612

9-1 The Entrepreneurial Organization   614
Henry Mintzberg

9-2 Competitive Strategy in Emerging Industries   623
Michael E. Porter

9-3 How Entrepreneurs Craft Strategies that Work   626
Amar Bhide

▼ CHAPTER 10   THE MATURE CONTEXT   634

10-1 The Machine Organization   635
Henry Mintzberg

10-2 Cost Dynamics: Scale and Experience Effects   649
Derek F. Abell and John S. Hammond

▼ CHAPTER 11   THE PROFESSIONAL CONTEXT   657

11-1 The Professional Organization   658
Henry Mintzberg

11-2 Balancing the Professional Service Firm   669
David H. Maister

▼ CHAPTER 12   THE INNOVATION CONTEXT   678

12-1 The Innovative Organization   679
Henry Mintzberg

12-2 Managing Innovation: Controlled Chaos   693
James Brian Quinn

▼ CHAPTER 13   THE DIVERSIFIED CONTEXT   704

13-1 The Diversified Organization   705
Henry Mintzberg

13-2 Generic Corporate Strategies   717
Henry Mintzberg

13-3 Managing Large Groups in the East and West   721
Philippe Lasserre

13-4 From Competitive Advantage to Corporate Strategy   727
Michael E. Porter

▼ CHAPTER 14   THE INTERNATIONAL CONTEXT   737

14-1 Global Strategy . . . In a World of Nations?   738
George S. Yip

14-2 Managing Across Borders:
New Organizational Responses   748
Christopher A. Bartlett and Sumantra Ghoshal

▼ CHAPTER 15   MANAGING CHANGE   755

15-1 Beyond Configuration   757
Henry Mintzberg

15-2 Convergence and Upheaval   764
Michael L. Tushman, William H. Newman, and Elaine Romanelli

15-3 The Crescendo Model of Rejuvenation   771
Charles Baden-Fuller and John M. Stopford

SECTION III   CASES

III-1 Sony Entertainment   781

III-2 The Vanguard Group, Inc. (A)   804

III-3   The Battle for Paramount Communications, Inc.   819

III-4   Honda Motor Company 1994   849

III-5   The Pillsbury Company   867

III-6   Cadbury Schweppes, P.L.C.   887

III-7   SAS and the European Airline Industry   894

III-8   Peet, Russ, Anderson, & Detroit   915

III-9   Nintendo of America   922

III-10   Mountbatten and India   935

CASE NOTES   956

BIBLIOGRAPHY FOR READINGS   964

NAME INDEX   974

SUBJECT INDEX   978

ACKNOWLEDGMENTS

We have been involved in the teaching and practice of strategy formation since the 1960s. What originally brought this book together was our firm belief that this field badly needed a new kind of text. We wanted one that looked at process issues as well as analysis; one that was built around dynamic strategy concepts and contexts instead of overworked analytical rigidities and the dichotomy of formulation and implementation— and one that accomplished these aims in an intelligent, eclectic, and lively style. We sought to combine theory and practice, description and prescription, in new ways that offered insights none could achieve alone. All of these goals remain exactly the same in this third edition, except that here we set out to fine tune a basic formula that we feel worked well in the first two. Our own work on previous editions took far longer and was more difficult than we could have imagined, and the same holds true for this edition. We hope that good students of management will think it worthwhile.

In any work of this scope, there are far too many people involved to thank each one individually. We would, however, like to acknowledge the special assistance given us by those who went especially out of their way to be helpful. In the academic community, several people deserve special mention. Deans Hennessey, Blaydon, and Fox at the Tuck School kindly arranged for time and funding support to develop many of the complex cases contained in the book. Mr. Hiroshi Murakami and Dean Melvyn Copen of the International University of Japan generously contributed funding and contacts for cases made in Japan. While at INSEAD, Sumantra Ghoshal offered especially valuable advice on new readings and cases to consider, in this edition even more than the last.

The people who really make such a major product as this happen are the competent research associates and secretaries who have undertaken the major burden of the work. At the Amos Tuck School of Business Administration, Penny C. Paquette, Suzanne Sweet, and Tammy Stebbins deserve special praise. Ms. Paquette was researcher and co-author of many of the cases for the book and oversaw the endless problems of coordinating clearances and production logistics for major portions of the book. Mrs. Sweet and Stebbins very professionally managed thousands of pages of original text and revisions with secretarial and computer skills that were invaluable. At McGill, Kate Maguire-Devlin's untold numbers of little contributions, important though they were, do not stand up to her big one— to provide a good-natured order without which the readings portion of this book could never have been finished.

At Prentice Hall, we thank David Shafer who took over this book with skill and energy, and Lisamarie Brassini who has been working on it helpfully for some time. Edie Riker, of East End Publishing Services, made sure the production of this edition was orderly and timely, despite its complexities.

A special thanks must also be offered to those who worked with the book in both its preliminary stages and in the various revisions and provided invaluable feedback: the many classes of "guinea pig" McGill and Tuck MBA students and our many professional and academic colleagues who have made useful suggestions for new readings and cases, taught both cases and readings on an experimental basis, and thoughtfully commented on how to improve this text. In particular: Bill Joyce, Rich D'Aveni, Philip Anderson, and Sydney Finkelstein at Tuck; John Voyer at University of

Southern Maine; Sumantra Ghoshal at LBS; Bill Davidson at the University of Southern California; Pierre Brunet and Bill Taylor at Concordia; Fritz Reiger at Windsor; Jan Jorgensen, Cynthia Hardy, and Tom Powell at McGill; Robert Burgelman at Stanford; and Franz Lohrke and Gary Castrogiovanni at Louisiana State University.

Among those who provided invaluable help on individual cases were Helen Boehm of The Studios of Edward Marshall Boehm; Fred Middleton and Robert Swanson of Genentech, Inc.; Dr. Robert Noyce and Dr. Gordon Moore of Intel Corporation; Peter Neupert and Nathan Myrvold of Microsoft Corporation; Bob O. Evans and Vincent Learson of IBM Corporation; Mr. Hiroshi Yamauchi of Nintendo Co., Ltd.; Hirachi Tanaka, Yuji Nishie, and Hachiro Saito of Japan Railways Research Institute; Lew Veraldi and Charles Gumushian at Ford Motor Company; Arthur Sulzberger (Sr. and Jr.) and Warren Hoge of The New York Times Company; Mr. John Foster at NovaCare, Inc.; Dr. Richard Young, William McCune, and Peter Wensberg of Polaroid Corporation; Dr. Norton Belknap, Thomas Barrow, and George Piercy of Exxon Corporation; Masura Ibuka, Akoi Morita, Dr. Nobutoshi Kihara, Dr. Makato Kikuchi, Norio Ohga and Kenji Wada of Sony Corporation; Mr. Michael Schulhof and Susan D'Agostino of Sony USA; Nobuhiko Kawamoto, Yasuhito Sato, T. Yashiki, and F. Kikuchi of Honda Motor Company, Ltd.; William Spoor, Jack Stafford, E.H. Wingate, and G. Dunhowe of The Pillsbury Company; and Howard Lincoln of Nintendo of America.

One last word; this book is not "finished." Our text, like the subject of so much of its content, is an ongoing process, not a static statement. So much of this book is different from conventional strategy textbooks, indeed from our own text last time, that there are bound to be all kinds of opportunities for improvement. We would like to ask you to help us in this regard. Please write to any of us with your suggestions on how to improve the readings, the case, and the organization of the book at large and its presentation. Strategy making, we believe, is a learning process; we are also engaged in a learning process. And for that we need your feedback. Thank you and enjoy what follows.

Henry Mintzberg
James Brian Quinn

INTRODUCTION

In our first edition, we set out to produce a different kind of textbook in the field of business policy or, as it is now more popularly called, strategic management. We tried to provide the reader with a richness of theory, a richness of practice, and a strong basis for linkage between the two. We rejected the strictly case study approach, which leaves theory out altogether, or soft-pedals it, and thereby denies the accumulated benefits of many years of careful research and thought about management processes. We also rejected an alternate approach that forces on readers a highly rationalistic model of how the strategy process *should* function. We collaborated on this book because we believe that in this complex world of organizations a range of concepts is needed to cut through and illuminate particular aspects of that complexity.

There is no "one best way" to create strategy, nor is there "one best form" of organization. Quite different forms work well in particular contexts. We believe that exploring a fuller variety systematically will create a deeper and more useful appreciation of the strategy process. In this revised edition, we remain loyal to these beliefs and objectives, having concentrated our efforts on improving the material we have included to reflect them. While maintaining the basic outline of the book, we have replaced, added, and revised a great many of its specific components. In particular, thirteen of the readings are new to this edition and six more have been significantly reworked. Since the second edition, seventeen of the cases are also new, while another nine more have been shortened, revised, or updated. Both cases and readings emphasize the new concepts generated by theorists and managers in the last five years. While keeping some of the classics, there are a variety of new

materials on core competency and outsourcing strategies, international strategies, new organization forms, competitive maneuvering, professional enterprises, global strategic considerations, and the implications of the new information and communications technologies. Both cases and readings from Europe, Japan, and Austronesia have been significantly expanded.

A host of new cases provide rich analytical vehicles for discussing the value and limits of new management approaches and the dimensions of new management issues. There is a conscious balance among small, medium, and large-scale companies; entrepreneurial, innovative, and maturing companies; and basic, high-technology, and consumer products industries. However, representing the more exciting and rapidly growing components of the economy, we have expanded the cases on computers, software, services, entertainment industries, and international operations. Companies such as Apple Computer, Microsoft, Nintendo, Argyle Diamonds, Arthur Andersen, NovaCare, TCG, Ltd., Thermo Electron, The Vanguard Group, and Paramount Communications, represent some of the most exciting experiments in products, services, and management concepts in business today. However, both the cases and readings continue to emphasize the full dimensions of the strategy process, corporate style, culture, historical backdrop, complete financial information, industry economics, competitive posture, change processes, technology impacts, and business-government interactions.

This text, unlike most others, is therefore eclectic. Presenting published articles and portions of other books in their original form, rather than filtered through our minds and pens, is one way to reinforce this variety. Each author has his or her ideas and his or her own best way of expressing them (ourselves included!). Summarized by us, these readings would lose a good deal of their richness.

We do not apologize for contradictions among the ideas of leading thinkers. The world is full of contradictions. The real danger lies in using pat solutions to a nuanced reality, not in opening perspectives up to different interpretations. The effective strategist is one who can live with contradictions, learn to appreciate their causes and effects, and reconcile them sufficiently for effective action. The readings have, nonetheless, been ordered by chapter to suggest some ways in which reconciliation can be considered. Our own chapter introductions are also intended to assist in this task and to help place the readings in perspective.

ON THEORY

A word on theory is in order. We do not consider theory a dirty word, nor do we apologize for making it a major component of this book. To some people, to be theoretical is to be detached and impractical. But a bright social scientist once said, "There is nothing so practical as a good theory." And every successful doctor, engineer, and physicist would have to agree: They would be unable to practice their modern work without theories. Theories are useful because they shortcut the need to store masses of data. It is easier to remember a simple framework about some phenomenon than it is to consider every small detail you ever observed. In a sense theories are a bit like cataloging systems in libraries: The world would be impossibly confusing without them. They enable you to store and conveniently access your own experiences as well as those of others.

One can, however, suffer not just from an absence of theories but also from being dominated by them without realizing it. To paraphrase the words of John Maynard Keynes, most "practical men" are the slaves of some defunct theory . Whether we realize it or not, our behavior is guided by the systems of ideas that we have internalized over the years. Much can be learned by bringing these out in the open, examining them more carefully, and comparing them with alternative ways to view the world—including ones based on systematic study (that is, research). One of our prime intentions in this book is to expose the limitations of conventional theories and to offer alternate explanations that can be superior guides of understanding and taking action in specific contexts.

PRESCRIPTIVE THEORY VERSUS DESCRIPTIVE THEORY

Unlike many textbooks in this field, this one tries to explain the world as it is rather than as someone thinks it is *supposed* to be. Although there has sometimes been a tendency to disdain such *descriptive* theories, *prescriptive* (or normative) ones have often been the problem, rather than the solution, in the field of management. There is no one best way in management; no prescription works for all organizations. Even when a prescription seems effective in some context, it requires a sophisticated understanding of exactly what that context is and how it functions. In other words, one cannot decide reliably what should be done in a system as complicated as a contemporary organization without a genuine understanding of how that organization really works. In engineering, no student ever questions having to learn physics, in medicine, having to learn anatomy. Imagine an engineering student's hand shooting up in physics class: "Listen, prof, it's fine to tell us how the atom does work. But what we really want to know is how the atom *should* work." Why should a management student's similar demand in the realm of strategy or structure be considered any more appropriate? How can people manage complex systems they do not understand?

Nevertheless, we have not ignored prescriptive theory when it appears useful. A number of prescriptive techniques (industry analysis, experience curves, and so on) are discussed. But these are associated both with other readings and with cases that will help you understand the context and limitations of their usefulness. Both readings and cases offer opportunities to pursue the full complexity of strategic situations. You will find a wide range of issues and perspectives addressed. One of our main goals is to integrate a variety of views, rather than allow strategy to be fragmented into just "human issues" and "economics issues." The text and cases provide a basis for treating the full complexity of strategic management.

ON SOURCES

How were the readings selected and edited? Some textbooks boast about how new all their readings are. We make no such claim; indeed we would like to make a different boast; many of our readings have been around quite a while, long enough to mature, like fine wine. Our criterion for inclusion was not the newness of the article so much as the quality of its insight—that is, its ability to explain some aspect of the strategy process better than any other article. Time does not age the really good articles. Quite the opposite—it distinguishes their quality (but sometimes brings us back to the old habits of masculine gender; we apologize to our readers for this). We are, of course, not biased toward old articles—just toward good ones. Hence, the materials in this book range from classics of the 1960s to some published just before our final selection was made (as well as a few hitherto unpublished pieces). You will find articles from the most serious academic journals, the best practitioner magazines, books, and some very obscure sources. The best can sometimes be found in strange places!

We have tried to include many shorter readings rather than fewer longer ones, and we have tried to present as wide a variety of good ideas as possible while maintaining clarity. To do so we often had to cut within readings. We have, in fact, put a great deal of effort into the cutting in order to extract the key messages of each reading in as brief, concise, and clear a manner as possible. Unfortunately, our cutting sometimes forced us to eliminate interesting examples and side issues. (In the readings, as well as some of the case materials from published sources, dots . . . signify portions that have been deleted from the original, while square brackets [ ] signify our own insertions of minor clarifications into the original text). We apologize to you, the reader, as well as to the authors, for having done this, but hope that the overall result has rendered these changes worthwhile.

We have also included a number of our own works. Perhaps we are biased, having less objective standards by which to judge what we have written. But we have messages to convey, too, and our own writings do examine the basic themes that we feel are important in policy and strategy courses today.

ON CASES

A major danger of studying the strategy process—probably the most enticing subject in the management curriculum, and at the pinnacle of organizational processes—is that students and professors can become detached from the basics of the enterprise. The "Don't bore me with the operating details; I'm here to tackle the really big issues" syndrome has been the death of many business policy or strategy courses (not to mention managerial practices!). The big issues *are* rooted in little details. We have tried to

recognize this in both the readings and the cases. Effective strategy processes always come down to specifics. The cases and the industry notes provide a rich soil for investigating strategic realities. Their complexities always extend well below the surface. Each layer peeled back can reveal new insights and rewards.

As useful as they are, however, cases are not really the ideal way to understand strategy: Involving oneself in the hubbub of life in a real organization is. We harbor no illusions that reading twenty pages on an organization will make you an expert. But cases remain the most convenient way to introduce practice into the classroom, to tap a wide variety of experiences, and to involve students actively in analysis and decision making. Our cases consciously contain both their prescriptive and descriptive aspects. On the one hand, they provide the data and background for making a major decision. Students can appraise the situation in its full context, suggest what future directions would be best for the organization in question, and discuss how their solutions can realistically be implemented. On the other hand, each case is also an opportunity to understand the dynamics of an organization—the historical context of the problems it faces, the influence of its culture, its probable reactions to varying solutions, and so on. Unlike many cases which focus on only the analytical aspects of a decision, ours constantly force you to consider the messy realities of arriving at decisions in organizations and obtaining a desired response to any decision. In these respects, case study involves a good deal of descriptive *and* prescriptive analysis.

LINKING CASES AND READINGS

The cases in this book are not intended to emphasize any particular theories, any more than the theoretical materials are included because they explain particular cases. Each case presents a slice of some specific reality, each reading a conceptual interpretation of some phenomenon. The readings are placed in particular groupings because they approach some common aspects or issues in theory.

We have provided some general guidelines for relating particular cases to sets of readings. But do not push this too far: Analyze each case for its own sake. Cases are intrinsically richer than readings. Each contains a wide variety of issues—many awfully messy—in no particular order. The readings, in contrast, are usually neat and tidy, professing one or a few basic conceptual ideas, and providing some specific vocabulary. When the two connect—sometimes through direct effort, more often indirectly as conceptual ideas are recalled in the situation of a particular case—some powerful learning can take place in the form of clarification and, we hope, revelation.

Try to see how particular theories can help you to understand some of the issues in the cases and provide useful frameworks for drawing conclusions. Perhaps the great military theorist, Von Clausewitz, said it best over a century ago (to borrow a quotation from one of our readings of Chapter 1):

> All that theory can do is give the artist or soldier points of reference and standards of evaluation . . . with the ultimate purpose not of telling him how to act but of developing his judgment. (1976:15)

In applying the theory to cases, please do not assume that it is only the readings cross referenced with the case that matter. We have designed the book so that the textual materials develop as the chapters unfold. Concepts introduced in earlier chapters become integrated in the later ones. And early cases tend to build knowledge for those appearing later. Problems and their organizational context move from the simple to the more complex. Space limitations and the structured nature of theories require some compartmentalization. But don't take that compartmentalization too literally. In preparing each case, use whatever concepts you find helpful both from chapters of this book and from your personal knowledge. The cases themselves deal with real people in real companies. The reality they present is enormously complicated; their dynamics extend to today's newspaper, and *Who's Who*, or any other reference you can imagine. Use any sound source of information that helps you to deal with them. Part of the fun of policy or strategy courses is understanding how major decisions happened to be made and what were their subsequent consequences—local, national, and international.

These are all living cases. In the strictest sense they have no beginning or end. They have been written in as lively a style as possible; we do not believe business school cases need be dull! Each case deals with a major transition point in the history of the enterprise. Each can be used in a variety of ways to emphasize a particular set of concepts at a particular time in the course. Many lend themselves to sophisticated financial, industry, portfolio, and competitive analyses as well as discerning organizational,

behavioral, and managerial practice inquiries. And many contain entrepreneurial and technological dimensions rarely found in strategy cases. Trying to figure out what is going on should be challenging as well as fun!

CASE DISCUSSION

Management cases provide a concrete information base for students to analyze and share as they discuss management issues. Without this focus, discussions of theory can become quite confusing. You may have in mind an image of an organization or a situation that is very different from that of other discussants. As a result, what appears to be a difference in theory will—after much argument—often turn out to be simply a difference in perception of the realities surrounding these examples.

In this text we try to provide three levels of learning: *first*, a chance to share the generalized insights of leading theoreticians (in the readings); *second*, an opportunity to test the applicability and limits of these theories in specific (case) situations; *third*, the capacity to develop one's own special amalgam of insights based upon empirical observations and inductive reasoning (from case analyses). All are useful approaches; some students and professors will find one mix more productive for their special level of experience or mind set. Another will prefer a quite different mix. Hence, we include a wide selection of cases and readings.

The cases are not intended as *examples* of either weak or exceptionally good management practices. Nor, as we noted, do they provide *examples* of the concepts of a particular reading. They are discussion vehicles for probing the benefits and limits of various approaches. And they are analytical vehicles for applying and testing concepts and tools developed in your education and experience. Almost every case has its marketing, operations, accounting, financial, human relations, planning and control, external environmental, ethical, political, and quantitative dimensions. Each dimension should be addressed in preparations and classroom discussions, although some aspects will inevitably emerge as more important in one situation than another.

In each case you should look for several sets of issues. First, you should understand what went on in that situation. Why did it happen this way? What are the strong or weak features of what happened? What could have been changed to advantage?

How? Why? Second, there are always issues of what should be done next. What are the key issues to be resolved? What are the major alternatives available? What outcomes could the organization expect from each? Which alternative should it select? Why? Third, there will almost always be "hard" quantitative data and "soft" qualitative impressions about each situation. Both deserve attention. Because the cases deal with real companies, and real people, in real situations, their databases can be *extended* as far as students and professors wish. They only have to consult their libraries and daily newspapers.

But remember, no realistic strategy situation is *just* an organization behavior problem or *just* a financial or economic analytical one. Both sets of information should be considered, and an *integrated* solution developed. Our cases are consciously constructed for this. Given their complexity we have tried to keep the cases as short as possible. And we have tried to capture some of the flavor of the real organization. Moreover, we have sought to mix product and services cases, technological and "non-tech" cases, entrepreneurial, small company, and large enterprise situations. In this cross section, we have tried to capture some of the most important and exciting issues, concepts, and products of our times. We believe management is fun and important. The cases try to convey this.

There is no "correct" answer to any case. There may be several "good" answers and many poor ones. The purpose of a strategy course should be to help you understand the nature of these "better" answers, what to look for, how to analyze alternatives, and how to see through the complexities of reaching solutions and implanting them in real organizations. A strategy course can only improve your probability of success, not ensure it. The total number of variables in a real strategy situation is typically beyond the control of any one person or group. Hence another caveat; don't rely on what a company actually did as a guide to effective action. The company may have succeeded or failed not because of its specific decisions, but because of luck, an outstanding personality, the bizarre action of an opponent, international actions over which it had no control, and so on. One of the products of a successful strategy course should be a little humility.

CASE STUDY GUIDES

We have posed a few questions at the end of each case as discussion guides. Students have generally found these helpful in organizing their thinking about each case. If you answer these questions well, you can probably deal with anything that comes up in class. But each professor may conduct his or her class in a quite different fashion. The questions should help you see relevant issues, but they should not limit your thinking. From time to time there are intermediate "decision points" in a case. Work on the material up to that point just as you would a short case. The case materials immediately following these decision points consciously leave out much detail on what might have happened so that you can arrive at your own specific solutions. Later you can see them in the context of a longer time horizon, much like a mystery story unfolding in phases. Analyze the specific situations, consider alternatives, and arrive at specific conclusions —understanding that later events might have looked a bit different if your solution had been implemented. Like any good mystery story, a case provides many clues, never all, but, surprisingly, sometimes more than executives might have had time to absorb in the real situation.

Believing that no "canned approach" is viable for all strategic situations, we have selected cases that cut across a variety of issues and theoretical constructs. Almost any of these cases is so complex that it can be positioned at a number of different spots in a good strategy course. We have clustered them around the three major segments of the text for convenience to students and professors. But the cases could equally well be taught in a number of other sequences. We leave the final case selection to the style and wisdom of the professor and his or her students.

THIS BOOK'S STRUCTURE

NOT FORMULATION, THEN IMPLEMENTATION

The first edition of this text offered a chapter format that was new to the policy or strategy field. Unlike most others, it had no specific chapter or section devoted to "implementation" per se. The assumption in other texts is that strategy is formulated and then

STRATEGY PROCESS THEME DIAGRAM

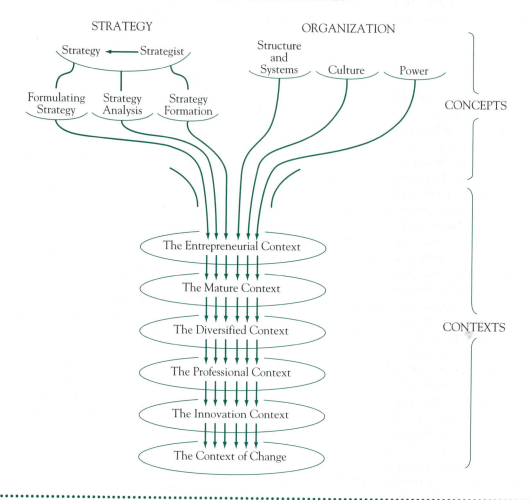

BUT CONCEPTS, THEN CONTEXTS

implemented, with organizational structures, control systems, and the like following obediently behind strategy. In this text, as in reality, formulation and implementation are intertwined as complex interactive processes in which politics, values, organizational culture, and management styles determine or constrain particular strategic decisions. And strategy, structure, and systems mix together in complicated ways to influence outcomes. While strategy formulation and implementation may be separated in some situations—perhaps in crises, in some totally new ventures, as well as in organizations facing predictable futures—these events are far from typical. We certainly do not believe in building a whole book (let alone a whole field) around this conceptual distinction.

The readings are divided roughly into two different parts. The first deals with *concepts*, the second with *contexts*. We introduce strategy and structure as well as power, culture, and several other concepts early in the text as equal partners in the complex web of ideas that make up what we call "the strategy process." In the second half of the text we weave these concepts together in a number of distinct situations, which we call *contexts*.

Our theme diagram illustrates this. Concepts, shown on top, are divided into two groups—strategy and organization—to represent the first two sections of the book. Contexts draw all these concepts together, in a variety of situations—covered in the third section—which we consider the key ones in the field of strategy today (though hardly the only ones). The outline of the text, chapter by chapter, proceeds as follows:

SECTION I: STRATEGY

The first section is called *Strategy*; it comprises five chapters (two introductory in nature and three on the processes by which strategy making takes place). Chapter 1 introduces *the strategy concept* and probes the meaning of this important word to broaden your view of it. Here the pattern is set of challenging you to question conventional views, especially when these act to narrow perspectives. The themes introduced in this chapter carry throughout the book and are worth care in understanding.

Chapter 2 introduces a very important character in this book, *the strategist* as general manager. This person may not be the only one who makes strategy in an organization, but he or she is clearly a key player. In examining the work of the general manager and the character of his or her job, we shall perhaps upset a number of widely accepted notions. We do this to help you understand the very real complexities and difficulties of making strategy and managing in contemporary organizations.

Chapters 3, 4, and 5 take up a theme that is treated extensively in the text—to the point of being reflected in its title: the development of an understanding of the *processes* by which strategies are made. Chapter 3 looks at *formulating strategy*, specifically at some widely accepted prescriptive models for how organizations should go about developing their strategies. Chapter 4 extends these ideas to more formal ways of doing *strategy analysis* and considering what, if any, "generic" forms a strategy can take. While readings in later chapters will challenge some of these precepts, what will not be questioned is the importance of having to understand them. They are fundamental to appreciating the strategy process today.

Chapter 5 switches from a prescriptive to a descriptive approach. Concerned with understanding *strategy formation*, it considers how strategies actually *do* form in organizations (not necessarily by being formulated) and *why* different processes may be effective in specific circumstances. This text takes an unconventional stand by viewing planning and other formal approaches as not the only—and often indeed not even the most desirable—ways to make strategy.

You will find our emphasis on the descriptive process—as an equal partner with the more traditional concerns for technical and analytical issues—to be one of the unifying themes of this book.

SECTION II: ORGANIZATION

In Section I, the readings introduced strategy, the strategist, and various ways in which strategy might be formulated and does in fact form. In Section II, entitled *Organization*, we introduce other concepts that constitute part of the strategy process.

In Chapter 6, we consider structure and systems, where particular attention is paid to the various forms that structure can take as well as the mechanisms that comprise it. In Chapter 7, we consider culture and power, especially how strong systems of beliefs, called "ideologies," impact on organizations and their strategies and so influence their effectiveness. We also view how power distributes itself among the various actors within the organization and how the organization acts as a political entity in its own right, whether or not responsibly, in the face of opposing forces in society. Both aspects will be seen to influence significantly the processes by which strategies are formulated or form. Then Chapter 8 (new to this edition of the book) takes a hard look at managerial styles as they impact strategy and operations, and introduces an especially important actor, the middle manager.

SECTION III: CONTEXTS

Section III is called *Contexts*. We consider how all of the elements introduced so far—strategy, the processes by which it is formulated and gets formed, the strategist, structure, systems, culture, power, and style—combine to suit particular contexts, seven in all.

Chapter 9 deals with the entrepreneurial context, where a rather simple organization comes under the close control of a strong leader, often a person with vision. Chapter 10 examines the mature context, one common to many large business and government organizations involved in the mass production or distribution of goods and services.

Chapters 11 and 12 develop the contexts of professionalism and innovation, both involving organizations of high expertise. In the professional context, the experts work relatively independently in rather stable conditions, while in the innovation context, they combine in project teams under more dynamic conditions. What these two contexts have in common, however, is that they act in ways that upset many of the widely accepted notions about how organizations should be structured and make strategy.

Chapter 13 introduces the diversified context, and deals with organizations that have diversified their product or service line and usually divisionalized their structures to deal with the greater varieties of environments they face. In Chapter 14, we take a look at an increasingly important and popular aspect of the diversified context, that of geography—namely the international or so-called global context.

In considering each of these widely different contexts we seek to discuss (where appropriate material is available) the situation in which each is most likely to be found, the structures most suited to it, the kinds of strategies that tend to be pursued, the processes by which these strategies tend to be formed and might be formulated, and the social issues associated with the context.

Chapter 15 is devoted not so much to a specific context as to managing change between contexts, or within a context (which we can, of course, characterize as the context of change). The major concerns are how organizations can cope with crises, turnarounds, revitalizations, and new stages in their own life cycles or those of their key products.

Well, there you have it. We have worked hard on this book, in both the original and revised editions, to get it right. We have tried to think things through from the basics, with a resulting text that in style, format, and content is unusual for the field of policy or strategy. Our product may not be perfect, but we believe it is good—indeed better than any other text available. Now it's your turn to find out if you agree. Have fun doing so!

Henry Mintzberg
James Brian Quinn

STRATEGY

THE STRATEGY CONCEPT

We open this text on its focal point: strategy. The first section is called "Strategy," the first chapter, "The Strategy Concept." Later chapters in this section describe the role of the general manager as strategist and consider the processes by which strategies develop from three perspectives: deliberate formulation, systematic analysis, and emergent formation. But in this opening chapter, we consider the central concept—strategy itself.

What is strategy? There is no single, universally accepted definition. Different authors and managers use the term differently; for example, some include goals and objectives as part of strategy while others make firm distinctions between them. Our intention in including the following readings is not to promote any one view of strategy, but rather to suggest a number that seem useful. As will be evident throughout this text, our wish is not to narrow perspectives but to broaden them by trying to clarify issues. In pursuing these readings, it will be helpful to think about the meaning of strategy, to try to understand how different people have used the term, and later to see if certain definitions hold up better in particular contexts.

We have taken the opportunity to include in this first chapter readings by each of us, the coauthors of the book. They set the tone for the material that follows and provide an indication of our own thinking. As you will see, our views are similar but certainly not identical; indeed in places we differ somewhat (for example, on the word "tactics"). But overall, we believe you will find these views complementary.

The first reading, by James Brian Quinn of the Amos Tuck School at Dartmouth College, provides a general overview by clarifying some of the vocabulary in this field and introducing a number of the themes that will appear throughout the text. In this reading from his book *Strategies for Change: Logical Incrementalism,* Quinn places special emphasis on the military uses of the term "strategy" and draws from this domain a set of essential "dimensions" or criteria for successful strategies. To derive these, he goes back to Philip and Alexander of Macedonia for his main example; he also provides a brief kaleidoscope of how similar concepts have influenced later military and diplomatic strategists.

Discussion of the military aspects of strategy must surely be among the oldest continuous literatures in the world. In fact, the origins of the word "strategy" go back even farther than this experience in Macedonia, to the Greeks whom Alexander and his father defeated. As Quinn notes and Roger Evered, in another article, elaborates,

> Initially *strategos* referred to a role (a general in command of an army). Later it came to mean "the art of the general," which is to say the psychological and behavioral skills with which he occupied the role. By the time of Pericles (450 B.C.) it came to mean managerial skill (administration, leadership, oration, power). And by Alexander's time (330 B.C.) it referred to the skill of employing forces to overcome opposition and to create a unified system of global governance. (1980:3)

The second reading, by Henry Mintzberg who is professor of management in the Faculty of Management at McGill University in Montreal and at INSEAD in France, serves to open up the concept of strategy to a variety of views, some very different from traditional military or business writings (but suggested briefly in the Quinn reading). Mintzberg focuses on various distinct definitions of strategy—as plan (as well as ploy), pattern, position, and perspective. He uses the first two of these definitions to take us beyond deliberate strategy—beyond the traditional view of the term—to the notion of *emergent* strategy. This introduces the idea that strategies can *form* in an organization without being consciously intended, that is, without being *formulated*. This may seem to run counter to the whole thrust of the strategy literature, but Mintzberg argues that many people implicitly use the term this way even though they would not so define it.

Upon completion of these readings, we hope that you will be less sure of the use of the word "strategy" but more ready to tackle the study of the strategy process with a broadened perspective and an open mind. There are no universally right answers in this field (any more than there are in most other fields), but there are interesting and constructive orientations.

Several cases relate well to the concepts developed in this chapter. The MacArthur, Apple, and Gallo cases pick up the military and formally derived concepts of strategy discussed in the two articles. Cases such as Edward Marshall Boehm, Inc., Intel Corporation, New Steel Corporation, and Genentech, Inc. (B) offer opportunities to consider the concepts of strategy analytically, while The IBM 360 Decision, Honda Motor Company 1994, Microsoft Corporation (A), and Ford: Team Taurus deal with the processes through which organizations arrive at strategies.

▼ READING 1.1   STRATEGIES FOR CHANGE*

by James Brian Quinn

Some Useful Definitions

Because the words *strategy, objectives, goals, policy,* and *programs* have different meanings to individual readers or to various organizational cultures, I [try] to use certain definitions consistently . . . For clarity—not pedantry—these are set forth as follows:

A **strategy** is the *pattern* or *plan* that *integrates* an organization's *major* goals, policies, and action sequences into a *cohesive* whole. A well-formulated strategy helps to *marshal* and *allocate* an organization's resources into a *unique and viable posture* based on its relative *internal competencies* and *shortcomings,* anticipated *changes in the environment,* and contingent moves by *intelligent opponents.*

Goals (or **objectives**) state *what* is to be achieved and *when* results are to be accomplished, but they do not state *how* the results are to be achieved. All organizations have multiple goals existing in a complex hierarchy (Simon, 1964): from value objectives, which express the broad value premises toward which the company is to strive; through overall organizational objectives, which establish the intended *nature* of the enterprise and the *directions* in which it should move; to a series of less permanent goals that define targets for each organizational unit, its subunits, and finally all major program activities within each subunit. Major goals—those that affect the entity's overall direction and viability—are called *strategic goals.*

---

* Excerpted from James Brian Quinn, *Strategies for Change: Logical Incrementalism* (copyright © Richard D. Irwin, Inc. 1980), Chaps. 1 and 5; reprinted by permission of the publisher.

Policies are rules or guidelines that express the *limits* within which action should occur. These rules often take the form of contingent decisions for resolving conflicts among specific objectives. For example: "Don't exceed three months' inventory in any item without corporate approval." Like the objectives they support, policies exist in a hierarchy throughout the organization. Major policies—those that guide the entity's overall direction and posture or determine its viability—are called *strategic policies*.

Programs specify the *step-by-step sequence of actions* necessary to achieve major objectives. They express *how* objectives will be achieved within the limits set by policy. They ensure that resources are committed to achieve goals, and they provide the dynamic track against which progress can be measured. Those major programs that determine the entity's overall thrust and viability are called *strategic programs*.

Strategic decisions are those that determine the overall direction of an enterprise and its ultimate viability in light of the predictable, the unpredictable, and the unknowable changes that may occur in its most important surrounding environments. They intimately shape the true goals of the enterprise. They help delineate the broad limits within which the enterprise operates. They dictate both the resources the enterprise will have accessible for its tasks and the principal patterns in which these resources will be allocated. And they determine the effectiveness of the enterprise—whether its major thrusts are in the right directions given its resource potentials—rather than whether individual tasks are performed efficiently. Management for efficiency, along with the myriad decisions necessary to maintain the daily life and services of the enterprise, is the domain of operations.

STRATEGIES VERSUS TACTICS

Strategies normally exist at many different levels in any large organization. For example, in government there are world trade, national economic, treasury department, military spending, investment, fiscal, monetary supply, banking, regional development, and local reemployment strategies—all related to each other somewhat hierarchically yet each having imperatives of its own. Similarly, businesses have numerous strategies from corporate levels to department levels within divisions. Yet if strategies exist at all these levels, how do strategies and tactics differ? Often the primary difference lies in the scale of action or the perspective of the leader. What appears to be a "tactic" to the chief executive officer (or general) may be a "strategy" to the marketing head (or lieutenant) if it determines the ultimate success and viability of his or her organization. In a more precise sense, tactics can occur at either level. They are the short-duration, adaptive, action-interaction realignments that opposing forces use to accomplish limited goals after their initial contact. Strategy defines a continuing basis for ordering these adaptations toward more broadly conceived purposes.

A genuine strategy is always needed when the potential actions or responses of intelligent opponents can seriously affect the endeavor's desired outcome—regardless of that endeavor's organizational level in the total enterprise. This condition almost always pertains to the important actions taken at the top level of competitive organizations. However, game theorists quickly point out that some important top-level actions—for example, sending a peacetime fleet across the Atlantic—merely require elaborate coordinative plans and programs (Von Neumann and Morgenstern, 1944; Shubik, 1975; McDonald, 1950). A whole new set of concepts, a true strategy, is needed if some people or nations decide to oppose the fleet's purposes. And it is these concepts that in large part distinguish strategic formulation from simpler programmatic planning.

Strategies may be looked at as either a priori statements to guide action or a posteriori results of actual decision behavior. In most complex organizations . . . one would be hard pressed to find a complete a priori statement of a total strategy that actually is followed. Yet often the existence of a strategy (or strategy change) may be clear to an objective observer, although it is not yet apparent to the executives making critical decisions. One, therefore, must look at the actual emerging *pattern* of the enterprise's operant goals, policies, and major programs to see what its true strategy is (Mintzberg, 1972). Whether it is consciously set forth in advance or is simply a widely held understanding resulting from a stream of decisions, this pattern becomes the real strategy of the enterprise. And it is changes in this pattern—regardless of what any formal strategic documents may say—that either analysts or strategic decision makers must address if they wish to comprehend or alter the concern's strategic posture. . . .

The Classical Approach to Strategy

Military-diplomatic strategies have existed since prehistoric times. In fact, one function of the earliest historians and poets was to collect the accumulated lore of these successful and unsuccessful life-and-death strategies and convert them into wisdom and guidance for the future. As societies grew larger and conflicts more complex, generals, statesmen, and captains studied, codified, and tested essential strategic concepts until a coherent body of principles seemed to emerge. In various forms these were ultimately distilled into the maxims of Sun Tzu (1963), Machiavelli (1950), Napoleon (1940), Von Clausewitz (1976), Foch (1970), Lenin (1927), Hart (1954), Montgomery (1958), or Mao Tse-Tung (1967). Yet with a few exceptions—largely introduced by modern technology—the most basic principles of strategy were in place and recorded long before the Christian era. More modern institutions primarily adapted and modified these to their own special environments.

Although one could choose any number of classical military-diplomatic strategies as examples, Philip and Alexander's actions at Chaeronea (in 338 B.C.) contain many currently relevant concepts (Varner and Alger, 1978; Green, 1970). . . .

A CLASSICAL STRATEGY

A Grand Strategy
Philip and his young son, Alexander, had very *clear goals*. They sought to rid Macedonia of influence by the Greek city-states and to *establish dominance* over what was then essentially northern Greece. They also wanted Athens to join a coalition with them against Persia on their eastern flank. *Assessing their resources*, they *decided to* avoid the overwhelming superiority of the Athenian fleet and *chose to forego* attack on the powerful walled cities of Athens and Thebes where their superbly trained phalanxes and cavalry would not *have distinct advantages*.

Philip and Alexander *used an indirect approach* when an invitation by the Amphictyonic Council brought their army south to punish Amphissa. In a *planned sequence of actions and deceptive maneuvers*, they cut away from a direct line of march to Amphissa, *bypassed the enemy*, and *fortified a key base*, Elatea. They then took steps to *weaken their opponents politically and morally* by pressing restoration of the Phoenician communities earlier dispersed by the Thebans and by having Philip declared a champion of the Delphic gods. Then *using misleading messages* to make the enemy believe they had moved north to Thrace and also *using developed intelligence sources*, the Macedonians in a *surprise attack* annihilated the Greeks' positions near Amphissa. This *lured their opponents away from their defensive positions* in the nearby mountain passes to *consolidate their forces* near the town of Chaeronea.

There, *assessing the relative strengths* of their opponents, the Macedonians first *attempted to negotiate* to achieve their goals. When this was unsuccessful they had a *well-developed contingency plan* on how to *attack and overwhelm* the Greeks. Prior to this time, of course, the Macedonians had *organized* their troops into the famed phalanxes, and had *developed the full logistics* needed for their field support including a longer spear, which helped the Macedonian phalanxes penetrate the solid shield wall of the heavily massed Greek formations. *Using the natural advantages* of their terrain, the Macedonians had developed cavalry support for their phalanxes' movements far beyond the Greek capability. Finally, using a *relative advantage*—the *command structure* their hierarchical *social system* allowed—against the more democratic Greeks, the Macedonian nobles had *trained their personnel* into one of the most *disciplined and highly motivated forces* in the world.

The Battle Strategy

Supporting this was the battle strategy at Chaeronea, which emerged as follows. Philip and Alexander first *analyzed their specific strengths and weaknesses and their opponents' current alignments and probable moves*. The Macedonian strength lay in their new spear technology, the *mobility* of their superbly disciplined phalanxes, and the powerful cavalry units led by Alexander. Their weaknesses were that they were badly outnumbered and faced—in the Athenians and the Theban Band—some of the finest foot troops in the world. However, their opponents had two weak points. One was the Greek left flank with lightly armed local troops placed near the Chaeronean Acropolis and next to some more heavily armed—but hastily assembled—hoplites bridging to the strong center held by the Athenians. The famed Theban Band anchored the Greek right wing near a swamp on the Cephissus River. [See Figure 1.]

Philip and Alexander *organized their leadership to command key positions,* Philip took over the right wing and Alexander the cavalry. They *aligned their forces* into *a unique posture* which *used their strengths* and *offset their weaknesses*. They decided on those spots at which they would *concentrate their forces*, what *positions to concede,* and what *key points* they *must take and hold*. Starting with their units angled back from the Greek lines (see map), they developed a *focused major thrust* against the Greek left wing and *attacked their opponents' weaknesses*—the troops near Chaeronea—with the most disciplined of the Macedonian units, the guards' brigade. After building up pressure and stretching the Greek line to its left, the guards' brigade abruptly began a *planned withdrawal*. This *feint* caused the Greek left to break ranks and rush forward, believing the Macedonians to be in full retreat. This *stretched the opponents' resources* as the Greek center moved left to *maintain contact* with its flank and to attack the "fleeing" Macedonians.

Then *with predetermined timing,* Alexander's cavalry *attacked the exposure* of the stretched line at the same moment Philip's phalanxes *re-formed as planned* on the high ground at the edge of the Heamon River. Alexander *broke through* and *formed a bridgehead* behind the Greeks. He *refocused his forces against a segment* of the opponents' line; his cavalry *surrounded and destroyed* the Theban Band

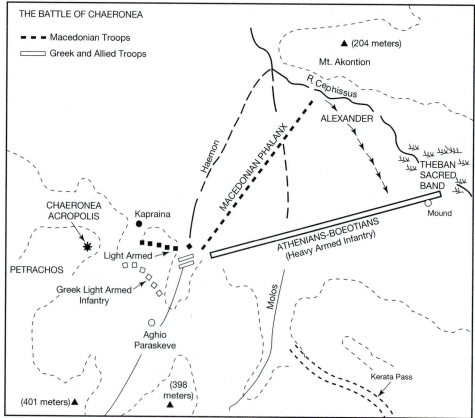

FIGURE 1
The Battle of Chaeronea
Source: Modified with permission from P. Green, *Alexander the Great,* Praeger Publishers, New York (1970).

THE BATTLE OF CHAERONEA

- - - Macedonian Troops
▭ Greek and Allied Troops

▲ (204 meters)

Mt. Akontion

R. Cephissus

ALEXANDER

Haemon

MACEDONIAN PHALANX

THEBAN SACRED BAND

Mound

CHAERONEA ACROPOLIS

Kapraina

Light Armed

PETRACHOS

ATHENIANS-BOEOTIANS (Heavy Armed Infantry)

Greek Light Armed Infantry

Molos

Aghio Paraskeve

Kerata Pass

(401 meters)▲

(398 meters)▲

as the *overwhelming power* of the phalanxes poured through the gap he had created. From its *secured position*, the Macedonian left flank then turned and *attacked the flank* of the Athenians. With the help of Philip's *planned counterattack*, the Macedonians *expanded their dominance and overwhelmed the critical target*, i.e., the Greek center. . . .

MODERN ANALOGIES

Similar concepts have continued to dominate the modern era of formal strategic thought. As this period begins, Scharnhorst still points to the need to *analyze social forces and structures* as a basis for *understanding effective command styles* and *motivational stimuli* (Von Clausewitz, 1976:8). Frederick the Great proved this point in the field. Presumably based on such analyses, he adopted *training*, *discipline*, and *fast maneuvers* as the central concepts for a tightly disciplined German culture that had to be constantly ready to fight on two fronts (Phillips, 1940). Von Bülow (1806) continued to emphasize the dominant strategic roles of *geographical positioning* and *logistical support systems* in strategy. Both Jomini (1971) and Von Bülow (1806) stressed the concepts of *concentration*, *points of domination*, and *rapidity of movement* as central strategic themes and even tried to develop them into mathematically precise principles for their time.

Still later Von Clausewitz expounded on the paramountcy of *clear major objectives* in war and on developing war strategies as a component of the nation's *broader goals* with *time horizons* extending beyond the war itself. Within this context he postulated that an effective strategy should be focused around a relatively *few central principles* which can *create*, *guide*, and *maintain dominance* despite the enormous frictions that occur as one tries to position or maneuver large forces in war. Among these he included many of the concepts operant in Macedonian times: *spirit or morale*, *surprise*, *cunning*, *concentration in space*, *dominance of selected positions*, *use of strategic reserves*, *unification over time*, *tension and release*, and so on. He showed how these broad principles applied to a number of specific attack, defense, flanking, and retreat situations; but he always stressed the intangible of *leadership*. His basic positioning and organizational principles were to be mixed with boldness, perseverance, and genius. He constantly emphasized—as did Napoleon—the need for *planned flexibility* once the battle was joined.

Later strategic analysts adapted these classic themes for larger-scale conflicts. Von Schlieffen linked together the huge numerical and production *strengths* of Germany and the vast *maneuvering capabilities* of Flanders fields to pull the nation's might together conceptually behind a *unique alignment of forces* ("a giant hayrake"), which would *outflank* his French opponents, *attack weaknesses* (their supply lines and rear), capture and *hold key political centers* of France, and *dominate or destroy* its weakened army in the field (Tuchman, 1962). On the other side, Foch and Grandmaison saw *morale* ("élan"), *nerve* ("cran"), and continuous *concentrated attack* ("attaque à outrance") as *matching the values* of a volatile, recently defeated, and vengeful French nation, which had decided (for both moral and *coalition* reasons) to *set important limits* on its own actions in World War I—that is, not to attack first or through Belgium.

As these two strategies lost shape and became the head-on slaughter of trench warfare, Hart (1954) revitalized the *indirect approach*, and this became a central theme of British strategic thinking between the wars. Later in the United States, Matloff and Snell (1953) began to stress planning for *large-scale coalitions* as the giant forces of World War II developed. The Enigma group *moved secretly to develop the intelligence network* that was so crucial in the war's outcome (Stevenson, 1976). But once engaged in war, George Marshall still saw the only hope for Allied victory in *concentrating overwhelming forces* against one enemy (Germany) first, then after *conceding early losses* in the Pacific, *refocusing Allied forces* in a gigantic *sequential coordinated movement* against Japan. In the eastern theater, MacArthur first *fell back, consolidated a base* for operations, *built up his logistics, avoided his opponent's strengths, bypassed* Japan's established defensive positions, and in a *gigantic flanking maneuver* was ready to invade Japan after *softening its political and psychological will* through saturation bombing (James, 1970).

All these modern thinkers and practitioners utilized classical principles of strategy dating back to the Greek era, but perhaps the most startling analogies of World War II lay in Patton's and Rommel's battle strategies, which were almost carbon copies of the Macedonians' concepts of planned concentration, rapid breakthrough, encirclement, and attack on the enemy's rear (Essame, 1974; Farago, 1964; Irving, 1977; Young, 1974).

Similar concepts still pervade well-conceived strategies—whether they are government, diplomatic, military, sports, or business strategies. What could be more direct than the parallel between Chaeronea and a well-developed business strategy that first probes and withdraws to determine opponents' strengths, forces opponents to stretch their commitments, then concentrates resources, attacks a clear exposure, overwhelms a selected market segment, builds a bridgehead in that market, and then regroups and expands from that base to dominate a wider field? Many companies have followed just such strategies with great success. . . .

Dimensions of Strategy

Analysis of military-diplomatic strategies and similar analogies in other fields provides some essential insights into the basic dimensions, nature, and design of formal strategies.

First, effective formal strategies contain three essential elements: (1) the most important *goals* (or objectives) to be achieved, (2) the most significant *policies* guiding or limiting action, and (3) the major *action sequences* (or programs) that are to accomplish the defined goals within the limits set. Since strategy determines the overall direction and action focus of the organization, its formulation cannot be regarded as the mere generation and alignment of programs to meet predetermined goals. Goal development is an integral part of strategy formulation. . . .

Second, effective strategies develop around a *few key concepts and thrusts,* which give them cohesion, balance, and focus. Some thrusts are temporary; others are carried through to the end of the strategy. Some cost more per unit gain than others. Yet resources must be *allocated in patterns* that provide sufficient resources for each thrust to succeed regardless of its relative cost/gain ratio. And organizational units must be coordinated and actions controlled to support the intended thrust pattern or else the total strategy will fail. . . .

Third, strategy deals not just with the unpredictable but also with the *unknowable.* For major enterprise strategies, no analyst could predict the precise ways in which all impinging forces could interact with each other, be distorted by nature or human emotions, or be modified by the imaginations and purposeful counteractions of intelligent opponents (Braybrooke and Lindblom, 1963). Many have noted how large-scale systems can respond quite counterintuitively (Forrester, 1971) to apparently rational actions or how a seemingly bizarre series of events can conspire to prevent or assist success (White, 1978; Lindblom, 1959). . . .

Consequently, the essence of strategy—whether military, diplomatic, business, sports, (or) political . . . —is to *build a posture* that is so strong (and potentially flexible) in selective ways that the organization can achieve its goals despite the unforeseeable ways external forces may actually interact when the time comes.

Fourth, just as military organizations have multiple echelons of grand, theater, area, battle, infantry, and artillery strategies, so should other complex organizations have a number of hierarchically related and mutually supporting strategies (Vancil and Lorange, 1975; Vancil, 1976). Each such strategy must be more or less complete in itself, congruent with the level of decentralization intended. Yet each must be shaped as a cohesive element of higher-level strategies. Although, for reasons cited, achieving total cohesion among all of a major organization's strategies would be a superhuman task for any chief executive officer, it is important that there be a systematic means for testing each component strategy and seeing that it fulfills the major tenets of a well-formed strategy.

The criteria derived from military-diplomatic strategies provide an excellent framework for this, yet too often one sees purported formal strategies at all organizational levels that are not strategies at all. Because they ignore or violate even the most basic strategic principles, they are little more than aggregates of philosophies or agglomerations of programs. They lack the cohesiveness, flexibility, thrust, sense of positioning against intelligent opposition, and other criteria that historical analysis suggests effective strategies must contain. Whether formally or incrementally derived, strategies should be at least intellectually tested against the proper criteria.

CRITERIA FOR EFFECTIVE STRATEGY

In devising a strategy to deal with the unknowable, what factors should one consider? Although each strategic situation is unique, are there some common criteria that tend to define a good strategy? The fact that a strategy worked in retrospect is not a sufficient criterion for judging any strategy. Was Grant really a greater strategist than Lee? Was Foch's strategy better than Von Schlieffen's? Was Xerxes's strategy superior to that of Leonidas? Was it the Russians' strategy that allowed them to roll over the Czechoslovaks in 1968? Clearly other factors than strategy—including luck, overwhelming resources, superb or stupid implementation, and enemy errors—help determine ultimate results. Besides, at the time one formulates a strategy, one cannot use the criterion of ultimate success because the outcome is still in doubt. Yet one clearly needs some guidelines to define an effective strategic structure.

A few studies have suggested some initial criteria for evaluating a strategy (Tilles, 1963; Christensen et al., 1978). These include its clarity, motivational impact, internal consistency, compatibility with the environment, appropriateness in light of resources, degree of risk, match to the personal values of key figures, time horizon, and workability. . . . In addition, historical examples—from both business and military-diplomatic settings—suggest that effective strategies should at a minimum encompass certain other critical factors and structural elements. . . .

▼ *Clear, decisive objectives:* Are all efforts directed toward clearly understood, decisive, and attainable overall goals? Specific goals of subordinate units may change in the heat of campaigns or competition, but the overriding goals of the strategy for all units must remain clear enough to provide continuity and cohesion for tactical choices during the time horizon of the strategy. All goals need not be written down or numerically precise, but they must be understood and be decisive—that is. if they are achieved they should ensure the continued viability and vitality of the entity vis-à-vis its opponents.

▼ *Maintaining the initiative:* Does the strategy preserve freedom of action and enhance commitment? Does it set the pace and determine the course of events rather than reacting to them? A prolonged reactive posture breeds unrest, lowers morale, and surrenders the advantage of timing and intangibles to opponents. Ultimately such a posture increases costs, decreases the number of options available, and lowers the probability of achieving sufficient success to ensure independence and continuity.

▼ *Concentration:* Does the strategy concentrate superior power at the place and time likely to be decisive? Has the strategy defined precisely what will make the enterprise superior in power—that is, "best" in critical dimensions—in relation to its opponents. A distinctive competency yields greater success with fewer resources and is the essential basis for higher gains (or profits) than competitors. . . .

- ▼ *Flexibility:* Has the strategy purposely built in resource buffers and dimensions for flexibility and maneuver? Reserved capabilities, planned maneuverability, and repositioning allow one to use minimum resources while keeping opponents at a relative disadvantage. As corollaries of concentration and concession, they permit the strategist to reuse the same forces to overwhelm selected positions at different times. They also force less flexible opponents to use more resources to hold predetermined positions, while simultaneously requiring minimum fixed commitment of one's own resources for defensive purposes.
- ▼ *Coordinated and committed leadership:* Does the strategy provide responsible, committed leadership for each of its major goals? . . . [Leaders] must be so chosen and motivated that their own interests and values match the needs of their roles. Successful strategies require commitment, not just acceptance.
- ▼ *Surprise:* Has the strategy made use of speed, secrecy, and intelligence to attack exposed or unprepared opponents at unexpected times? With surprise and correct timing, success can be achieved out of all proportion to the energy exerted and can decisively change strategic positions. . . .
- ▼ *Security:* Does the strategy secure resource bases and all vital operating points for the enterprise? Does it develop an effective intelligence system sufficient to prevent surprises by opponents? Does it develop the full logistics to support each of its major thrusts? Does it use coalitions effectively to extend the resource base and zones of friendly acceptance for the enterprise? . . .

These are critical elements of strategy, whether in business, government, or warfare.

▼ READING 1.2   FIVE Ps FOR STRATEGY*

by Henry Mintzberg

Human nature insists on *a* definition for every concept. But the word *strategy* has long been used implicitly in different ways even if it has traditionally been defined in only one. Explicit recognition of multiple definitions can help people to maneuver through this difficult field. Accordingly, five definitions of strategy are presented here—as plan, ploy, pattern, position, and perspective—and some of their interrelationships are then considered.

Strategy As Plan

To almost anyone you care to ask, **strategy is a plan**—some sort of *consciously intended* course of action, a guideline (or set of guidelines) to deal with a situation. A kid has a "strategy" to get over a fence, a corporation has one to capture a market. By this definition, strategies have two essential characteristics: they are made in advance of the actions to which they apply, and they are developed consciously and purposefully. A host of definitions in a variety of fields reinforce this view. For example:

- ▼ in the military: Strategy is concerned with "draft[ing] the plan of war . . . shap[ing] the individual campaigns and within these, decid[ing] on the individual engagements" (Von Clausewitz, 1976:177).
- ▼ in game theory: Strategy is "a complete plan: a plan which specifies what choices [the player] will make in every possible situation" (von Newman and Morgenstern, 1944:79).

* Originally published in the *California Management Review* (Fall 1987), © 1987 by the Regents of the University of California. Reprinted with deletions by permission of the *California Management Review*.

▼ in management: "Strategy is a unified, comprehensive, and integrated plan . . . designed to ensure that the basic objectives of the enterprise are achieved" (Glueck, 1980:9).

As plans, strategies may be general or they can be specific. There is one use of the word in the specific sense that should be identified here. As plan, **a strategy can be a ploy,** too, really just a specific "maneuver" intended to outwit an opponent or competitor. The kid may use the fence as a ploy to draw a bully into his yard, where his Doberman pinscher awaits intruders. Likewise, a corporation may threaten to expand plant capacity to discourage a competitor from building a new plant. Here the real strategy (as plan, that is, the real intention) is the threat, not the expansion itself, and as such is a ploy.

In fact, there is a growing literature in the field of strategic management, as well as on the general process of bargaining, that views strategy in this way and so focuses attention on its most dynamic and competitive aspects. For example, in his popular book, *Competitive Strategy*, Porter (1980) devotes one chapter to "Market Signals" (including discussion of the effects of announcing moves, the use of "the fighting brand, " and the use of threats of private antitrust suits) and another to "Competitive Moves" (including actions to preempt competitive response). And Schelling (1980) devotes much of his famous book, *The Strategy of Conflict*, to the topic of ploys to outwit rivals in a competitive or bargaining situation.

Strategy As Pattern

But if strategies can be intended (whether as general plans or specific ploys), surely they can also be realized. In other words, defining strategy as a plan is not sufficient; we also need a definition that encompasses the resulting behavior. Thus a third definition is proposed: **strategy is a pattern**—specifically, a pattern in a stream of actions (Mintzberg and Waters, 1985). By this definition, when Picasso painted blue for a time, that was a strategy, just as was the behavior of the Ford Motor Company when Henry Ford offered his Model T only in black. In other words, by this definition, strategy is *consistency* in behavior, *whether or not* intended.

This may sound like a strange definition for a word that has been so bound up with free will ("strategos" in Greek, the art of the army general [Evered 1983]). But the fact of the matter is that while hardly anyone defines strategy in this way, many people seem at one time or another to so use it. Consider this quotation from a business executive: "Gradually the successful approaches merge into a pattern of action that becomes our strategy. We certainly don't have an overall strategy on this" (quoted in Quinn, 1980:35). This comment is inconsistent only if we restrict ourselves to one definition of strategy: what this man seems to be saying is that his firm has strategy as pattern, but not as plan. Or consider this comment in *Business Week* on a joint venture between General Motors and Toyota:

> The tentative Toyota deal may be most significant because it is another example of how GM's strategy boils down to doing a little bit of everything until the market decides where it is going. (*Business Week*, October 31, 1983)

A journalist has inferred a pattern in the behavior of a corporation and labeled it strategy.

The point is that every time a journalist imputes a strategy to a corporation or to a government, and every time a manager does the same thing to a competitor or even to the senior management of his own firm, they are implicitly defining strategy as pattern in action—that is, inferring consistency in behavior and labeling it strategy. They may, of course, go further and impute intention to that consistency—that is, assume there is a plan behind the pattern. But that is an assumption, which may prove false.

Thus, the definitions of strategy as plan and pattern can be quite independent of each other: plans may go unrealized, while patterns may appear without preconception. To paraphrase Hume, strategies may result from human actions but not human designs (see Majone, 1976–77). If we label the first definition *intended* strategy and the second *realized* strategy, as shown in Figure 1, then we can distinguish *deliberate* strategies, where intentions that existed previously were realized, from *emergent* strategies, where patterns developed in the absence of intentions, or despite them (which went *unrealized*).

For a strategy to be truly deliberate—that is, for a pattern to have been intended *exactly* as realized—would seem to be a tall order. Precise intentions would have had to be stated in advance by the leadership of the organization; these would have had to be accepted as is by everyone else, and then realized with no interference by market, technological, or political forces and so on. Likewise, a truly emergent strategy is again a tall order, requiring consistency in action without any hint of intention. (No consistency means *no* strategy, or at least unrealized strategy.) Yet some strategies do come close enough to either form, while others—probably most—sit on the continuum that exists between the two, reflecting deliberate as well as emergent aspects. Table 1 lists various kinds of strategies along this continuum.

STRATEGIES ABOUT WHAT?

Labeling strategies as plans or patterns still begs one basic question: *strategies about what?* Many writers respond by discussing the deployment of resources, but the question remains: which resources and for what purposes? An army may plan to reduce the number of nails in its shoes, or a corporation may realize a pattern of marketing only products painted black, but these hardly meet the lofty label "strategy." Or do they?

As the word has been handed down from the military, "strategy" refers to the important things, "tactics" to the details (more formally, "tactics teaches the use of armed forces in the engagement, strategy the use of engagements for the object of the war," von Clausewitz, 1976:128). Nails in shoes, colors of cars; these are certainly details. The problem is that in retrospect details can sometimes prove "strategic." Even in the military: "For want of a Nail, the Shoe was lost; for want of a Shoe the Horse was lost . . . ," and so on through the rider and general to the battle, "all for want of Care about a Horseshoe Nail" (Franklin, 1977:280). Indeed one of the reasons Henry Ford lost his war with General Motors was that he refused to paint his cars anything but black.

FIGURE 1
Deliberate and Emergent Strategies

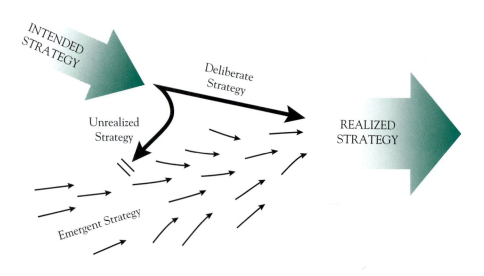

TABLE 1
Various Kinds of Strategies, from Rather Deliberate to Mostly Emergent*

Planned Strategy: Precise intentions are formulated and articulated by a central leadership, and backed up by formal controls to ensure their surprise-free implementation in an environment that is benign, controllable, or predictable (to ensure no distortion of intentions); these strategies are highly deliberate.

Entrepreneurial Strategy: Intentions exist as the personal, unarticulated vision of a single leader, and so are adaptable to new opportunities; the organization is under the personal control of the leader and located in a protected niche in its environment; these strategies are relatively deliberate but can emerge too.

Ideological Strategy: Intentions exist as the collective vision of all the members of the organization, controlled through strong shared norms; the organization is often proactive vis-à-vis its environment; these strategies are rather deliberate.

Umbrella Strategy: A leadership in partial control of organizational actions defines strategic targets or boundaries within which others must act (for example, that all new products be high priced and at the technological cutting edge, although what these actual products are to be is left to emerge); as a result, strategies are partly deliberate (the boundaries) and partly emergent (the patterns within them); this strategy can also be called deliberately emergent, in that the leadership purposefully allows others the flexibility to maneuver and form patterns within the boundaries.

Process Strategy: The leadership controls the process aspects of strategy (who gets hired and so gets a chance to influence strategy, what structures they work within, etc.), leaving the actual content of strategy to others; strategies are again partly deliberate (concerning process) and partly emergent (concerning content), and deliberately emergent.

Disconnected Strategy: Members or subunits loosely coupled to the rest of the organization produce patterns in the streams of their own actions in the absence of, or in direct contradiction to the central or common intentions of the organization at large; the strategies can be deliberate for those who make them.

Consensus Strategy: Through mutual adjustment, various members converge on patterns that pervade the organization in the absence of central or common intentions; these strategies are rather emergent in nature.

Imposed Strategy: The external environment dictates patterns in actions, either through direct imposition (say, by an outside owner or by a strong customer) or through implicitly preempting or bounding organizational choice (as in a large airline that must fly jumbo jets to remain viable); these strategies are organizationally emergent, although they may be internalized and made deliberate.

*Adapted from Mintzberg and Waters (1985:270).

Rumelt (1979) notes that "one person's strategies are another's tactics—that what is strategic depends on where you sit." It also depends on *when* you sit; what seems tactical today may prove strategic tomorrow. The point is that labels should not be used to imply that some issues are *inevitably* more important than others. There are times when it pays to manage the details and let the strategies emerge for themselves. Thus there is good reason to refer to issues as more or less "strategic," in other words, more or less "important" in some context, whether as intended before acting or as realized after it. Accordingly, the answer to the question, strategy about what, is: potentially about anything. About products and processes, customers and citizens, social responsibilities and self interests, control and color.

Two aspects of the content of strategies must, however, be singled out because they are of particular importance.

Strategy As Position

The fourth definition is that **strategy is a position**—specifically, a means of locating an organization in what organization theorists like to call an "environment." By this definition, strategy becomes the mediating force—or "match," according to Hofer and Schendel

(1978:4)—between organization and environment, that is, between the internal and the external context. In ecological terms, strategy becomes a "niche"; in economic terms, a place that generates "rent" (that is "returns to [being] in a 'unique' place" (Bowman, 1974:47)); in management terms, formally, a product-market "domain" (Thompson, 1967), the place in the environment where resources are concentrated.

Note that this definition of strategy can be compatible with either (or all) of the preceding ones; a position can be preselected and aspired to through a plan (or ploy) and/or it can be reached, perhaps even found, through a pattern of behavior.

In military and game theory views of strategy, it is generally used in the context of what is called a "two-person game," better known in business as head-on competition (where ploys are especially common). The definition of strategy as position, however, implicitly allows us to open up the concept, to so-called n-person games (that is, many players), and beyond. In other words, while position can always be defined with respect to a single competitor (literally so in the military, where position becomes the site of battle), it can also be considered in the context of a number of competitors or simply with respect to markets or an environment at large. But strategy as position can extend beyond competition too, economic and otherwise. Indeed, what is the meaning of the word "niche" but a position that is occupied to *avoid* competition. Thus, we can move from the definition employed by General Ulysses Grant in the 1860s, "Strategy [is] the deployment of one's resources in a manner which is most likely to defeat the enemy," to that of Professor Richard Rumelt in the 1980s, "Strategy is creating situations for economic rents and finding ways to sustain them,"(Rumelt, 1982) that is, any viable position, whether or not directly competitive.

Astley and Fombrun (1983), in fact, take the next logical step by introducing the notion of "collective" strategy, that is, strategy pursued to promote cooperation between organizations, even would-be competitors (equivalent in biology to animals herding together for protection). Such strategies can range "from informal arrangements and discussions to formal devices such as interlocking directorates, joint ventures, and mergers" (p. 577). In fact, considered from a slightly different angle, these can sometimes be described as *political* strategies, that is strategies to subvert the legitimate forces of competition.

Strategy As Perspective

While the fourth definition of strategy looks out, seeking to locate the organization in the external environment, and down to concrete positions, the fifth looks inside the organization, indeed inside the heads of the collective strategist, but up to a broader view. Here, **strategy is a perspective,** its content consisting not just of a chosen position, but of an ingrained way of perceiving the world. There are organizations that favor marketing and build a whole ideology around that (an IBM); Hewlett-Packard has developed the "H-P way," based on its engineering culture, while McDonald's has become famous for its emphasis on quality, service, and cleanliness.

Strategy in this respect is to the organization what personality is to the individual. Indeed, one of the earliest and most influential writers on strategy (at least as his ideas have been reflected in more popular writings) was Philip Selznick (1957:47), who wrote about the "character" of an organization—distinct and integrated "commitments to ways of acting and responding" that are built right into it. A variety of concepts from other fields also capture this notion; anthropologists refer to the "culture" of a society and sociologists to its "ideology"; military theorists write of the "grand strategy" of armies; while management theorists have used terms such as the "theory of the business" and its "driving force" (Drucker, 1974; Tregoe and Zimmerman, 1980); and Germans perhaps capture it best with their word "Weltanschauung, " literally "world view," meaning collective intuition about how the world works.

This fifth definition suggests above all that strategy is a *concept*. This has one important implication, namely, that all strategies are abstractions which exist only in the minds of interested parties. It is important to remember that no one has ever seen a strategy or touched one; every strategy is an invention, a figment of someone's imagination, whether conceived of as intentions to regulate behavior before it takes place or inferred as patterns to describe behavior that has already occurred.

What is of key importance about this fifth definition, however, is that the perspective is *shared*. As implied in the words Weltanschauung, culture, and ideology (with respect to a society), but not the word personality, strategy is a perspective shared by the members of an organization, through their intentions and/or by their actions. In effect, when we are talking of strategy in this context, we are entering the realm of the *collective mind*—individuals united by common thinking and/or behavior. A major issue in the study of strategy formation becomes, therefore, how to read that collective mind—to understand how intentions diffuse through the system called organization to become shared and how actions come to be exercised on a collective yet consistent basis.

Interrelating the Ps

As suggested above, strategy as both position and perspective can be compatible with strategy as plan and/or pattern. But, in fact, the relationships between these different definitions can be more involved than that. For example, while some consider perspective to *be* a plan (Lapierre, 1980, writes of strategies as "dreams in search of reality"), others describe it as *giving rise* to plans (for example, as positions and/or patterns in some kind of implicit hierarchy). But the concept of emergent strategy is that a pattern can emerge and be recognized so that it gives rise to a formal plan, perhaps within an overall perspective.

We may ask how perspective arises in the first place. Probably through earlier experiences: the organization tried various things in its formative years and gradually consolidated a perspective around what worked. In other words, organizations would appear to develop "character" much as people develop personality—by interacting with the world as they find it through the use of their innate skills and natural propensities. Thus pattern can give rise to perspective too. And so can position. Witness Perrow's (1970:161) discussion of the "wool men" and "silk men" of the textile trade, people who developed an almost religious dedication to the fibers they produced.

No matter how they appear, however, there is reason to believe that while plans and positions may be dispensable, perspectives are immutable (Brunsson, 1982). In other words, once they are established, perspectives become difficult to change. Indeed, a perspective may become so deeply ingrained in the behavior of an organization that the associated beliefs can become subconscious in the minds of its members. When that happens, perspective can come to look more like pattern than like plan—in other words, it can be found more in the consistency of behaviors than in the articulation of intentions.

Of course, if perspective is immutable, then change in plan and position within perspective is easy compared to change of perspective. In this regard, it is interesting to take up the case of Egg McMuffin. Was this product when new—the American breakfast in a bun—a strategic change for the McDonald's fast-food chain? Posed in MBA classes, this earth-shattering (or at least stomach-shattering) question inevitably evokes heated debate. Proponents (usually people sympathetic to fast food) argue that of course it was: it brought McDonald's into a new market, the breakfast one, extending the use of existing facilities. Opponents retort that this is nonsense; nothing changed but a few ingredients: this was the same old pap in a new package. Both sides are, of course, right—and wrong. It simply depends on how you define strategy. Position changed; perspective remained the same.

Indeed—and this is the point—the position could be changed easily because it was compatible with the existing perspective. Egg McMuffin is pure McDonald's, not only in product and package, but also in production and propagation. But imagine a change of position at McDonald's that would require a change of perspective—say, to introduce candlelight dining with personal service (your McDuckling à l'Orange cooked to order) to capture the late evening market. We needn't say more, except perhaps to label this the "Egg McMuffin syndrome."

The Need for Eclecticism in Definition

While various relationships exist among the different definitions, no one relationship, nor any single definition for that matter, takes precedence over the others. In some ways, these definitions compete (in that they can substitute for each other), but in perhaps more important ways, they complement. Not all plans become patterns nor are all patterns that develop planned; some ploys are less than positions, while other strategies are more than positions yet less than perspectives. Each definition adds important elements to our understanding of strategy, indeed encourages us to address fundamental questions about organizations in general.

As plan, strategy deals with how leaders try to establish direction for organizations, to set them on predetermined courses of action. Strategy as plan also raises the fundamental issue of cognition—how intentions are conceived in the human brain in the first place, indeed, what intentions really mean. The road to hell in this field can be paved with those who take all stated intentions at face value. In studying strategy as plan, we must somehow get into the mind of the strategist, to find out what is really intended.

As ploy, strategy takes us into the realm of direct competition, where threats and feints and various other maneuvers are employed to gain advantage. This places the process of strategy formation in its most dynamic setting, with moves provoking countermoves and so on. Yet ironically, strategy itself is a concept rooted not in change but in stability—in set plans and established patterns. How then to reconcile the dynamic notions of strategy as ploy with the static ones of strategy as pattern and other forms of plan?

As pattern, strategy focuses on action, reminding us that the concept is an empty one if it does not take behavior into account. Strategy as pattern also introduces the notion of convergence, the achievement of consistency in an organization's behavior. How does this consistency form, where does it come from? Realized strategy, when considered alongside intended strategy, encourages us to consider the notion that strategies can emerge as well as be deliberately imposed.

As position, strategy encourages us to look at organizations in their competitive environments—how they find their positions and protect them in order to meet competition, avoid it, or subvert it. This enables us to think of organizations in ecological terms, as organisms in niches that struggle for survival in a world of hostility and uncertainty as well as symbiosis.

And finally as perspective, strategy raises intriguing questions about intention and behavior in a collective context. If we define organization as collective action in the pursuit of common mission (a fancy way of saying that a group of people under a common label—whether a General Motors or a Luigi's Body Shop—somehow find the means to cooperate in the production of specific goods and services), then strategy as perspective raises the issue of how intentions diffuse through a group of people to become shared as norms and values, and how patterns of behavior become deeply ingrained in the group.

Thus, strategy is not just a notion of how to deal with an enemy or a set of competitors or a market, as it is treated in so much of the literature and in its popular usage. It also draws us into some of the most fundamental issues about organizations as instruments for collective perception and action.

To conclude, a good deal of the confusion in this field stems from contradictory and ill-defined uses of the term strategy. By explicating and using various definitions, we may be able to avoid some of this confusion, and thereby enrich our ability to understand and manage the processes by which strategies form.

THE STRATEGIST

Every conventional strategy or policy textbook focuses on the job of the general manager as a main ingredient in understanding the process of strategy formation. The discussion of emergent strategy in the last chapter suggests that we do not take such a narrow view of the strategist. Anyone in the organization who happens to control key or precedent-setting actions can be a strategist; the strategist can be a collection of people as well. Nevertheless, managers—especially senior general managers—are obviously prime candidates for such a role because their perspective is generally broader than any of their subordinates' and because so much power naturally resides with them. Hence, in this chapter we focus on the general manager as strategist.

We present three readings that describe the work of the manager. The one by Mintzberg challenges the conventional view of the manager. The image presented in this article is a very different one: of a job characterized by pressure, interruption, orientation to action, oral rather than written communication, and working with outsiders and colleagues as much as with so-called subordinates. These findings pertain to the characteristics of managerial work, described as they appeared in Mintzberg's original study of managerial work some years ago. The reading then goes on to describe the content of managerial work as Mintzberg has developed that in his more recent research. This part of the reading draws on a paper he published in the *Sloan Management Review* in 1994. Here managerial work is characterized as taking place on three levels—a rather abstract information level, an in-between people level, and a concrete action level. The roles the manager performs can be seen to fit into these levels, but, as emphasized, all managers must ultimately deal with all levels, in an integrated fashion, although most will favor one level or another.

While the issue is not addressed at this point in any detail, one evident and important conclusion is that managers who work in such ways cannot possibly function as traditionally depicted strategists supposedly do—as leaders directing their organizations the way conductors direct their orchestras (at least the way it looks on the podium). We shall develop this point further in Chapter 5, when we consider how strategies really are formed in organizations. The article by Edward Wrapp, of the University of Chicago, provides at least one widely referenced model illustrating how this does happen in large organizations. He depicts managers as somewhat political animals, providing broad guidance, but facilitating or pushing through their strategies, bit by bit, in rather unexpected ways. They rarely state specific goals. They practice "the art of imprecision," trying to "avoid policy strait-jackets," while concentrating on only a few really significant issues. They move whenever possible through "corridors of comparative indifference" to avoid undue opposition; at the same time they are trying to ensure that the organization has a cohesive sense of direction. Wrapp's observations challenge the more prescriptive views of strategy formulation, but elements of them can be observed in many of the cases, notably The IBM 360 Decision, Apple Computer Inc. (A), MacArthur in the Philippines, The Transformation of AT&T, The Pillsbury Company, and Mountbatten and India.

The article by Gary Hamel and C. K. Prahalad of the University of Michigan presents a view of the management role that is consistent with the military analogy of strategy in Quinn's article in the preceding chapter. The challenge of building global leadership, according to Hamel and Prahalad, is to embed the ambitions for such leadership through-out the company and to create "an obsession with winning" which will energize the collective action of all employees. The role is to build such an ambition, to help people develop faith in their own ability to deliver on tough goals, to motivate them to do so, and to channel their energies into a step-by-step progression that they compare with "running the marathon in 400-meter sprints."

How do you reconcile these different views on the role of the strategist? At one level, perhaps you do not need a grand theory that integrates across all of them. There are different kinds of managers, different beliefs and styles, and different kinds of authors—different lenses capture different aspects of managerial work. Some of you may also observe many similarities in the roles and tasks of the strategist described in these readings, despite the very different languages the authors use. You may, for instance, think about how the advocacies of Hamel and Prahalad relate to the managerial roles Mintzberg describes. You may like to carry over the debate in any of these readings to later sessions, testing these views against the roles played by senior managers in some of the cases you will discuss. In Chapter 8, we shall return to a broader discussion of managerial styles.

The impact of values in strategic decision making shows up most clearly in the following cases: NovaCare, Inc., Microsoft Corporation (B), E & J Gallo Winery, The New York Times Company, The Hewlett Packard Company, Genentech, Inc. (B), Sony Corporation: Innovation System, and Matsushita Electric Industrial Company 1994.

▼ READING 2.1   THE MANAGER'S JOB*

by Henry Mintzberg

Tom Peters tells us that good managers are doers. (Wall Street says they "do deals.") Michael Porter suggests that they are thinkers. Not so, argue Abraham Zaleznik and Warren Bennis: good managers are really leaders. Yet, for the better part of this century, the classical writers—Henri Fayol and Lyndell Urwick, among others—keep telling us that good managers are essentially controllers.

It is a curiosity of the management literature that its best-known writers all seem to emphasize one particular part of the manager's job to the exclusion of the others. Together, perhaps, they cover all the parts, but even that does not describe the whole job of managing.

Moreover, the image left by all of this of the manager's job is that it is a highly systematic, carefully controlled job. That is the folklore. The facts are quite different.

We shall begin by reviewing some of the early research findings on the *characteristics* of the manager's job, comparing that folklore with the facts, as I observed them in my first study of managerial work (published in the 1970s), reinforced by other research. Then we shall present a new framework to think about the *content* of the job—what managers really do—based on some recent observations I have made of managers in very different situations.

---

* This paper combines excerpts from "The Manager's Job: Folklore and Fact" which appeared in the *Harvard Business Review* (July-August 1975) on the characteristics of the job, with the framework of the context of the job which was published as "Rounding Out the Manager's Job" in the *Sloan Management Review* (Fall 1994).

Some Folklore and Facts About Managerial Work

There are four myths about the manager's job that do not bear up under careful scrutiny of the facts.

Folklore: The manager is a reflective, systematic planner. The evidence on this issue is overwhelming, but not a shred of it supports this statement.

Fact: Study after study has shown that managers work at an unrelenting pace, that their activities are characterized by brevity, variety, and discontinuity, and that they are strongly oriented to action and dislike reflective activities. Consider this evidence:

▼ Half the activities engaged in by the five [American] chief executives [that I studied in my own research (Mintzberg, 1973a)] lasted less than nine minutes, and only 10% exceeded one hour. A study of 56 U.S. foremen found that they averaged 583 activities per eight-hour shift, an average of 1 every 48 seconds (Guest, 1956:478). The work pace for both chief executives and foremen was unrelenting. The chief executives met a steady stream of callers and mail from the moment they arrived in the morning until they left in the evening. Coffee breaks and lunches were inevitably work related, and ever-present subordinates seemed to usurp any free moment.

▼ A diary study of 160 British middle and top managers found that they worked for a half hour or more without interruption only about once every two days (Stewart, 1967).

▼ Of the verbal contacts of the chief executives in my study, 93% were arranged on an ad hoc basis. Only 1% of the executives' time was spent in open-ended observational tours. Only 1 out of 368 verbal contacts was unrelated to a specific issue and could be called general planning. Another researcher finds that "in *not one single case* did a manager report the obtaining of important external information from a general conversation or other undirected personal communication" (Aguilar, 1967:102).

▼ No study has found important patterns in the way managers schedule their time. They seem to jump from issue to issue, continually responding to the needs of the moment.

Is this the planner that the classical view describes? Hardly. How, then, can we explain this behavior? The manager is simply responding to the pressures of the job. I found that my chief executives terminated many of their own activities, often leaving meetings before the end and interrupted their desk work to call in subordinates. One president not only placed his desk so that he could look down a long hallway but also left his door open when he was alone—an invitation for subordinates to come in and interrupt him.

Clearly, these managers wanted to encourage the flow of current information. But more significantly, they seemed to be conditioned by their own work loads. They appreciated the opportunity cost of their own time, and they were continually aware of their ever-present obligations—mail to be answered, callers to attend to, and so on. It seems that no matter what he or she is doing, the manager is plagued by the possibilities of what he or she might do and must do.

When the manager must plan, he or she seems to do so implicitly in the context of daily actions, not in some abstract process reserved for two weeks in the organization's mountain retreat. The plans of the chief executives I studied seemed to exist only in their heads—as flexible, but often specific, intentions. The traditional literature notwithstanding, the job of managing does not breed reflective planners; the manager is a real-time responder to stimuli, an individual who is conditioned by his or her job to prefer live to delayed action.

Folklore: The effective manager has no regular duties to perform. Managers are constantly being told to spend more time planning and delegating, and less time on operating details. These are not, after all, the true tasks of the manager. To use the popular analogy, the good manager, like the good conductor, carefully orchestrates everything in advance, then sits back to enjoy the fruits of his or her labor, responding occasionally to an unforeseeable exception. . . .

Fact: In addition to handling exceptions, managerial work involves performing a number of regular duties, including ritual and ceremony, negotiations, and processing of soft information that links the organization with its environment. Consider some evidence from the early research studies:

▼ A study of the work of the presidents of small companies found that they engaged in routine activities because their companies could not afford staff specialists and were so thin on operating personnel that a single absence often required the president to substitute (Choran in Mintzberg, 1973a).

▼ One study of field sales managers and another of chief executives suggest that it is a natural part of both jobs to see important customers, assuming the managers wish to keep those customers (Davis, 1957; Copeman, 1963).

▼ Someone, only half in jest, once described the manager as that person who sees visitors so that everyone else can get his or her work done. In my study, I found that certain ceremonial duties—meeting visiting dignitaries, giving out gold watches, presiding at Christmas dinners—were an intrinsic part of the chief executive's job.

▼ Studies of managers' information flow suggest that managers play a key role in securing "soft" external information (much of it available only to them because of their status) and in passing it along to their subordinates.

Folklore: The senior manager needs aggregated information, which a formal management information system best provides. In keeping with the classical view of the manager as that individual perched on the apex of a regulated, hierarchical system, the literature's manager was to receive all important information from a giant, comprehensive MIS.

But this never proved true at all. A look at how managers actually process information makes the reason quite clear. Managers have five media at their command—documents, telephone calls, scheduled and unscheduled meetings, and observational tours.

Fact: Managers strongly favor the verbal media—namely, telephone calls and meetings. The evidence comes from every one of the early studies of managerial work: Consider the following:

▼ In two British studies, managers spent an average of 66% and 80% of their time in verbal (oral) communication (Stewart, 1967; Burns, 1954). In my study of five American chief executives, the figure was 78%.

▼ These five chief executives treated mail processing as a burden to be dispensed with. One came in Saturday morning to process 142 pieces of mail in just over three hours, to "get rid of all the stuff." This same manager looked at the first piece of "hard" mail he had received all week, a standard cost report, and put it aside with the comment, "I never look at this."

▼ These same five chief executives responded immediately to 2 of the 40 routine reports they received during the five weeks of my study and to four items in the 104 periodicals. They skimmed most of the periodicals in seconds, almost ritualistically. In all, these chief executives of good-sized organizations initiated on their own—that is, not in response to something else—a grand total of 25 pieces of mail during the 25 days I observed them.

An analysis of the mail the executives received reveals an interesting picture—only 13% was of specific and immediate use. So now we have another piece of the puzzle: not much of the mail provides live, current information—the action of a competitor, the mood of a government legislator, or the rating of last night's television show. Yet this is the information that drove the managers, interrupting their meetings and rescheduling their workdays.

Consider another interesting finding. Managers seem to cherish "soft" information, especially gossip, hearsay, and speculation. Why? The reason is its timeliness; today's gossip may be tomorrow's fact. The manager who is not accessible for the telephone call informing him or her that the firm's biggest customer was seen golfing with its main competitor may read about a dramatic drop in sales in the next quarterly report. But then it's too late.

Consider the words of Richard Neustadt, who studied the information-collecting habits of Presidents Roosevelt, Truman, and Eisenhower.

> It is not information of a general sort that helps a President see personal stakes; not summaries, not surveys, not the *bland amalgams*. Rather . . . it is the odds and ends of *tangible detail* that pieced together in his mind illuminate the underside of issues put before him. To help himself he must reach out as widely as he can for every scrap of fact, opinion, gossip, bearing on his interests and relationships as President. He must become his own director of his own central intelligence (1960:153–154; italics added).

The manager's emphasis on the verbal media raises two important points:

First, verbal information is stored in the brains of people. Only when people write this information down can it be stored in the files of the organization—whether in metal cabinets or computer memory—and managers apparently do not write down much of what they hear. Thus the strategic data bank of the organization is not in the memory of its computers but in the minds of its managers.

Second, the managers' extensive use of verbal media helps to explain why they are reluctant to delegate tasks. When we note that most of the managers' important information comes in verbal form and is stored in their heads, we can well appreciate their reluctance. It is not as if they can hand a dossier over to someone; they must take the time to "dump memory"—to tell that someone all they know about the subject. But this could take so long that the managers find it easier to do the task themselves. Thus the managers are damned by their own information systems to a "dilemma of delegation"—to do too much themselves or to delegate to their subordinates with inadequate briefing.

Folklore: Management is, or at least is quickly becoming, a science and a profession. By almost any definitions of *science* and *profession*, this statement is false. Brief observation of any manager will quickly lay to rest the notion that managers practice a science. A science involves the enaction of systematic, analytically determined procedures or programs. If we do not even know what procedures managers use, how can we prescribe them by scientific analysis? And how can we call management a profession if we cannot specify what managers are to learn?

Fact: The managers' programs—to schedule time, process information, make decisions, and so on—remain locked deep inside their brains. Thus, to describe these programs, we rely on words like judgment and intuition, seldom stopping to realize that they are merely labels for our ignorance.

I was struck during my study by the fact that the executives I was observing—all very competent by any standard—are fundamentally indistinguishable from their counterparts of a hundred years ago (or a thousand years ago, for that matter). The information they need differs, but they seek it in the same way—by word of mouth. Their decisions concern modern technology, but the procedures they use to make them are the same as the procedures of the nineteenth-century manager. In fact, the manager is in a kind of loop, with increasingly heavy work pressures but no aid forthcoming from management science.

Considering the facts about managerial work, we can see that the manager's job is enormously complicated and difficult. The manager is overburdened with obligations; yet he or she cannot easily delegate tasks. As a result, he or she is driven to overwork and is forced to do many tasks superficially. Brevity, fragmentation, and verbal communication characterize the work. Yet these are the very characteristics of managerial work that have impeded scientific attempts to improve it. As a result, the management scientists have concentrated their efforts on the specialized functions of the organization, where they could more easily analyze the procedure and quantify the relevant information. Thus the first step in providing managers with some help is to find out what their job really is.

Toward a Basic Description of Managerial Work

Now let us try to put some of the pieces of this puzzle together. The manager can be defined as that person in charge of an organization or one of its units. Besides chief executive officers, this definition would include vice presidents, head nurses, hockey coaches, and prime ministers. Can all of these people have anything in common? Indeed, they can. Our description takes the form of a model, building the image of the manager's job from the inside out, beginning at the center with the person and his or her frame and working out from there, layer by layer.

THE PERSON IN THE JOB

We begin at the center, with the person who comes to the job. People are not neutral when they take on a new managerial job, mere putty to be molded into the required shape. Figure 1 shows that an individual comes to a managerial job with a set of *values*, by this stage in life probably rather firmly set, also a body of *experience* that, on the one hand, has forged a set of skills or *competencies*, perhaps honed by training, and, on the other, has provided a base of *knowledge*. That knowledge is, of course, used directly, but it is also converted into a set of *mental models*, key means by which managers interpret the world around them—for example, how the head nurse on a hospital ward perceives the behavior of the surgeons with whom she must work. Together, all these characteristics greatly determine how any manager approaches a given job—his or her *style* of managing. Style will come to life as we begin to see *how* a manager carries out *what* his or her job requires.

THE FRAME OF THE JOB

Embed the person depicted in a given managerial job and you get managerial work. At the core of it is some kind of *frame* for the job, the mental set the incumbent assumes to carry it out. Frame is strategy, to be sure, possibly even vision, but it is more than that. It is purpose, whether to create something in the first place, maintain something that has already been created or adapt it to changes, or else recreate something. Frame is also *perspective*—the broad view of the organization and its mission—and *positions*—concerning specific products, services, and markets.

Alain Noël, who studied the relationship between the frames and the work of the chief executives of three small companies, has said that managers have "occupations" and they have "preoccupations," (Noël, 1989). Frame describes the preoccupations, while roles (discussed below) describe the occupations. But frame does give rise to a first role in this model as well, which I call **conceiving**, namely thinking through the purpose, perspective, and positions of a particular unit to be managed over a particular period of time.

THE AGENDA OF THE WORK

Given a person in a particular managerial job with a particular frame, the question arises of how this is manifested in the form of specific activities. That happens through the *agenda* to carry out the work, and the associated role of **scheduling**, which has received consider-

FIGURE 1
The Person in the Job

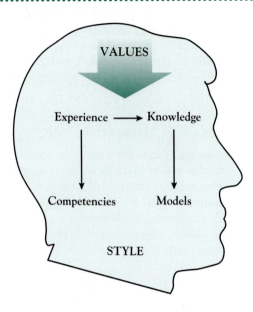

able attention in the literature of management. Agenda is considered in two respects here. First, the frame gets manifested as a set of current *issues*, in effect, whatever is of concern to the manager, broken down into manageable units—what Tom Peters likes to call "chunks." Ask any manager about his or her work, and the almost inevitable first reply will be about the "issues" of central concern, those things "on the plate," as the saying goes. Or take a look at the agendas of meetings and you will likewise see a list of issues (rather than decisions). These, in effect, operationalize the frame (as well as change it, of course, by feeding in new concerns).

The sharper the frame, the more integrated the issues. The more realizable they may be as well, since it is a vague frame that gives rise to that all-too-common phenomenon of the unattainable "wishlist" in an organization. Sometimes a frame can be so sharp, and the issues therefore so tightly integrated, that they all reduce to what Noël has called one "magnificent obsession" (Noël, 1989). In effect, all the concerns of the manager revolve around one central issue, for example, making a new merger work.

Second, the frame and the issues get manifested in the more tangible *schedule*, the specific allocations of managerial time on a day-to-day basis. Also included here, however implicitly, is the setting of priorities among the issues. The scheduling of time and the prioritization of issues are obviously of great concern to all managers, and, in fact, are themselves significant consumers of managerial time. Accordingly, a great deal of attention has been devoted to these concerns, including numerous courses on "time management."

THE CORE IN CONTEXT

If we label the person in the job with a frame manifested by an agenda, the central *core* of the manager's job (shown by the concentric circles in Figure 2), then we turn next to the context in which this core is embedded, the milieu in which the work is practiced.

The context of the job is depicted in Figure 2 by the lines that surround the core. Context can be split into three areas, labeled inside, within, and outside on Figure 2.

FIGURE 2
The Core in Context

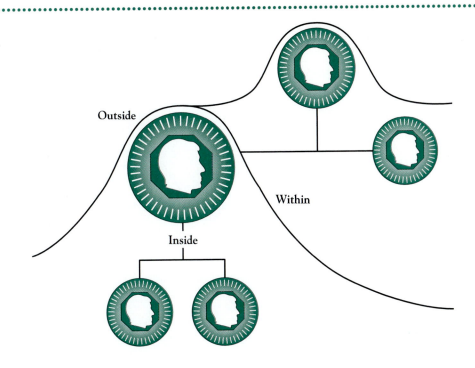

Inside refers to the unit being managed, shown below the manager to represent his or her formal authority over its people and activities—the hospital ward in the case of the head nurse, for example. *Within*, shown to the right, refers to the rest of the organization—other members and other units with which the manager must work but over which he or she has no formal authority, for example, the doctors, the kitchen, the physiotherapists in the rest of the hospital, to continue with the same example. (Of course, in the case of the chief executive, there is no inside separate from within: that person has authority over the entire organization.) And *outside* refers to the rest of the context not formally part of the organization with which the manager must work—in this example, patients' relatives, long-term care institutions to which some of the unit's patients are discharged, nursing associations, and so on. The importance of this distinction (for convenience, we shall mostly refer to inside versus outside) is that much of managerial work is clearly directed either to the unit itself, for which the manager has official responsibility, or at its various boundary contexts, through which the manager must act without that responsibility.

Managing on Three Levels

We are now ready to address the actual behaviors that managers engage in to do their jobs. The essence of the model, designed to enable us to "see" managerial work comprehensively, in one figure, is that these roles are carried out on three successive levels, each inside and outside the unit. This is depicted by concentric circles of increasing specificity, shown in Figure 3.

From the outside (or most tangible level) in, managers can manage *action* directly, they can manage *people* to encourage them to take the necessary actions, and they can manage *information* to influence the people in turn to take their necessary actions. In other words,

FIGURE 3
Three Levels of
Evoking Action

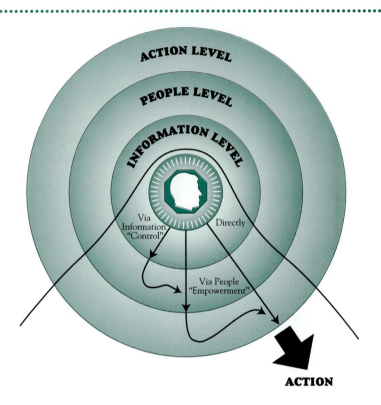

the ultimate objective of managerial work, and of the functioning of any organizational unit, the taking of action, can be managed directly, indirectly through people, or even more indirectly by information through people. The manager can thus choose to intervene at any of the three levels, but once done, he or she must work through the remaining ones. Later we shall see that the level a given manager favors becomes an important determinant of his or her managerial style, especially distinguishing so-called "doers" who prefer direct action, "leaders" who prefer working through people, and "administrators" who prefer to work by information.

MANAGING BY INFORMATION

To manage by information is to sit two steps removed from the purpose of managerial work. The manager processes information to drive other people who, in turn, are supposed to ensure that necessary actions are taken. In other words, here the managers' own activities focus neither on people nor on actions per se, but rather on information as an indirect way to make things happen. Ironically, while this was the classic perception of managerial work for the first half of this century, in recent years it has also become a newly popular, in some quarters almost obsessional, view, epitomized by the so-called "bottom line" approach to management.

The manager's various informational behaviors may be grouped into two broad roles, here labeled communicating and controlling, shown in Figure 4.

Communicating refers to the collection and dissemination of information. In Figure 4, communicating is shown by double arrows to indicate that managers devote a great deal of effort to the two-way flow of information with the people all around them—employees

FIGURE 4
The Information Roles

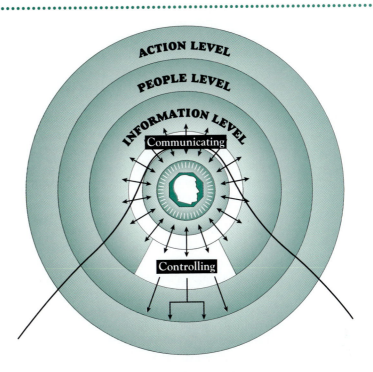

inside their own units, others in the rest of the organization, and especially, as the empirical evidence makes abundantly clear, a great number of outsiders with whom they maintain regular contact. Thus the head of one regional division of the national police force spent a good part of the day I observed him passing information back and forth between the central headquarters and the people on his staff.

Managers "scan" their environments, they monitor their own units, and they share with and disseminate to others considerable amounts of the information they pick up. Managers can be described as "nerve centers" of their units, who use their status of office to gain access to a wide variety of informational sources. Inside the unit, everyone else is a specialist who generally knows more about his or her specialty than the manager. But, because the manager is connected to all those specialists, he or she should have the broadest base of knowledge about the unit in general. This should apply to the head of a huge health care system, with regard to broad policy issues, no less than to the clinical director of one of its hospital units, with regard to the service rendered there. And externally, by virtue of their status, managers have access to other managers who are themselves nerve centers of their own units. And so they tend to be exposed to powerful sources of external information and thus emerge as external nerve centers as well. The health care chief executive can thus talk to people running health care systems in other countries and so gain access to an array of information perhaps inaccessible even to his most influential reports.

The result of all this is that a considerable amount of the manager's information turns out to be privileged, especially when we consider how much of it is oral and nonverbal. Accordingly, to function effectively with the people around them, managers have to spend considerable time sharing their information, both with outsiders (in a kind of spokesperson role) and with insiders (in a kind of disseminator role).

I found in my initial study of chief executives that perhaps 40 percent of their time was devoted almost exclusively to the communicating role—just to gaining and sharing information—leaving aside the information processing aspects of all the other roles. In other words, the job of managing is fundamentally one of processing information, notably by talking and especially listening. Thus Figure 4 shows the inner core (the person in the job, conceiving and scheduling) connected to the outer rings (the more tangible roles of managing people and action) through what can be called the membrane of information processing all around the job.

What can be called the **controlling** role describes the managers' efforts, not just to gain and share information, but to use it in a directive way inside their units: to evoke or provoke general action by the people who report to them. They do this in three broad ways: they develop systems, they design structures, and they impose directives. Each of these seeks to control how other people work, especially with regard to the allocation of resources, and so what actions they are inclined to take.

First, developing systems is the most general of these three, and the closest to conceiving. It uses information to control peoples' behaviors. Managers often take charge of establishing and even running such systems in their units, including those of planning and performance control (such as budgeting). Robert Simons has noted how chief executives tend to select one such system and make it key to their exercise of control, in a manner he calls "interactive" (Simons, 1990, 1991).

Second, managers exercise control through designing the structures of their units. By establishing responsibilities and defining hierarchical authority, they again exercise control rather passively, through the processing of information. People are informed of their duties, which in turn is expected to drive them to carry out the appropriate actions.

Third is imposing directives, which is the most direct of the three, closest to the people and action, although still informational in nature. Managers pronounce: they make specific choices and give specific orders, usually in the process of "delegating" particular responsibilities and "authorizing" particular requests. In effect, managers manage by transmitting information to people so that they can act.

If a full decision-making process can be considered in the three stages of diagnosing, designing, and deciding—in other words, identifying issues, working out possible solutions, and selecting one—then here we are dealing with a restricted view of decision making. Delegating means mostly diagnosing ("Would you please handle this problem in this context"), while authorizing means mostly deciding ("OK, you can proceed"). Either way, the richest part of the process, the stage of designing possible solutions, resides with the person being controlled rather than with the manager him or herself, whose own behavior remains rather passive. Thus the manager as controller seems less an *actor* with sleeves rolled up, digging in, than a *reviewer* who sits back in the office and passes judgment. That is why this role is characterized as informational; I will describe a richer approach to decision making in the section on action roles.

The controlling role is shown in Figure 4 propelling down into the manager's own unit, since that is where formal authority is exercised. The single-headed arrows represent the imposed directives, while the pitchfork shape symbolizes both the design of structure and the development of systems. The proximity of the controlling role in Figure 4 to the manager's agenda reflects the fact that informational control is the most direct way to operationalize the agenda, for example, by using budgets to impose priorities or delegation to assign responsibilities. The controlling role is, of course, what people have in mind when they refer to the "administrative" aspect of managerial work.

MANAGING THROUGH PEOPLE

To manage through people, instead of by information, is to move one step closer to action, but still to remain removed from it. That is because here the focus of managerial attention becomes affect instead of effect. Other people become the means to get things done, not the manager him or herself, or even the substance of the manager's thoughts.

If the information roles (and controlling in particular) dominated our early thinking about managerial work, then after that, people entered the scene, or at least they entered the textbooks, as entities to be "motivated" and later "empowered." Influencing began to replace informing, and commitment began to vie with calculation for the attention of the manager. Indeed, in the 1960s and 1970s especially, the management of people, quite independent of content—of the strategies to be realized, the information to be processed, even the actions to be taken—became a virtual obsession of the literature, whether by the label of "human relations," "Theory Y," or "participative management" (and later "quality of work life," to be replaced by "total quality management").

For a long time, however, these people remained "subordinates" in more ways than one. "Participation" kept them subordinate, for this was always considered to be granted at the behest of the managers still fully in control. So does the currently popular term "empowerment," which implies that power is being granted, thanks to the managers. (Hospital directors do not "empower" physicians!) People also remained subordinates because the whole focus was on those inside the unit, not outside it. Not until serious research on managerial work began did it become evident how important to managers were contacts with individuals outside their units. Virtually every single study of how all kinds of managers spent their time has indicated that outsiders, of an enormously wide variety, generally take as much of the managers' attention as so-called "subordinates." We shall thus describe two people roles here, shown in Figure 5, one internal, called leading, and one external, called linking.

The **leading** role has probably received more attention in the literature of management than all the other roles combined. And so we need not dwell on it here. But neither can we ignore it: managers certainly do much more than lead the people in their own units, and leading certainly infuses much else of what managers do (as, in fact, do all the roles, as we have already noted about communicating). But their work just as certainly cannot be understood without this dimension. We can describe the role of leading on three levels, as indicated in Figure 5.

First, managers lead on the *individual* level, "one on one," as the expression goes. They encourage and drive the people of their units—motivate them, inspire them, coach them, nurture them, push them, mentor them, and so on. All the managers I observed, from the chief executive of a major police force to the front-country manager in a mountain park, stopped to chat with their people informally during the day to encourage them in their work. Second, managers lead on the *group* level, especially by building and managing teams, an effort that has received considerable attention in recent years. Again, team meetings, including team building, figured in many of my observations; for example, the head of a London film company who brought film-making teams together for both effective and affective purposes. And third, they lead on the *unit* level, especially with regard to the creation and maintenance of culture, another subject of increasing attention in recent years (thanks especially to the Japanese). Managers, for example, engage in many acts of symbolic nature ("figurehead" duties) to sustain culture, as when the head of the national police force visited its officer training institute (as he did frequently) to imbue the force's norms and attitudes in its graduating class.

All managers seem to spend time on all three levels of leadership, although, again, styles do vary according to context and personality. If the communicating role describes the manager as the nerve center of the unit, then the leading role must characterize him or her as its "energy center," a concept perhaps best captured in Maeterlinck's wonderful description of the "spirit of the hive" (Maeterlinck, 1918). Given the right managerial "chemistry" (in the case of Maeterlinck's queen bee, quite literally!), it may be the manager's mere presence that somehow draws things together. By exuding that mystical substance, the leader

FIGURE 5
The People Roles

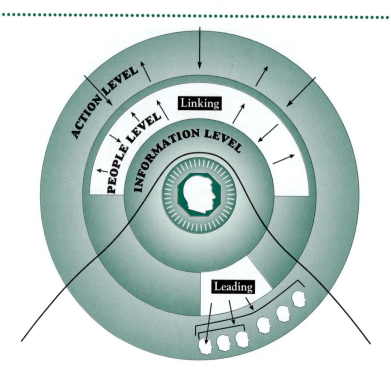

unites his or her people, galvanizing them into action to accomplish the unit's mission and adapt it to a changing world.

The excess attention to the role of leading has probably been matched by the inadequate attention to the role of **linking**. For, in their sheer allocation of time, managers have been shown to be external linkers as much as they are internal leaders, in study after study. Yet, still the point seems hardly appreciated. Indeed, now more than ever, it must be understood, given the great growth of joint ventures and other collaborating and networking relationships between organizations, as well as the gradual reconception of the "captive" employee as an autonomous "agent" who supplies labor.

Figure 5 suggests a small model of the linking role. The arrows go in and out to indicate that the manager is both an advocate of its influence outside the unit and, in turn, a recipient of much of the influence exerted on it from the outside. In the middle are two parallel lines to represent the buffering aspect of this role—that managers must regulate the receipt of external influence to protect their units. To use a popular term, they are the "gatekeepers" of influence. Or, to add a metaphor, the manager acts as a kind of valve between the unit and its environment. Nowhere was this clearer than in my observation of three levels of management in a national park system—a regional director, the head of one mountain park, and the front-country manager of that park. They sit in an immensely complex array of forces—developers who want to enhance their business opportunities, environmentalists who want to preserve the natural habitat, tourists who want to enjoy the beauty, truckers who want to drive through the park unimpeded, politicians who want to avoid negative publicity, etc. It is a delicate balancing, or buffering, act indeed!

All managers appear to spend a great deal of time "networking"—building vast arrays of contacts and intricate coalitions of supporters beyond their own units, whether within the rest of the organization or outside, in the world at large. To all these contacts, the manager represents the unit externally, promotes its needs, and lobbies for its causes. In response, these people are expected to provide a steady inflow of information to the unit as well as various means of support and specific favors for it. This networking was most evident in the case of the film company managing director I observed, who exhibited an impressive network of contracts in order to negotiate her complex contracts with various media in different countries.

In turn, people intent on influencing the behavior of an organization or one of its subunits will often exercise pressure directly on its manager, expecting that person to transmit the influence inside, as was most pointedly clear in the work of the parks manager. Here, then, the managerial job becomes one of delicate balance, a tricky act of mediation. Those managers who let external influence pass inside too freely—who act like sieves—are apt to drive their people crazy. (Of course, those who act like sponges and absorb all the influence personally are apt to drive themselves crazy!) And those who block out all influence—who act like lead to x-rays—are apt to detach their units from reality (and so dry up the sources of external support). Thus, what influence to pass on and how, bearing in mind the quid pro quo that influence exerted out is likely to be mirrored by influence coming back in, becomes another key aspect of managerial style, worthy of greatly increased attention in both the study of the job and the training of its occupants.

MANAGING ACTION

If managers manage passively by information and affectively through people, then they also manage actively and instrumentally by their own direct involvement in action. Indeed, this has been a long-established view of managerial work, although the excess attention in this century, first to controlling and then to leading, and more recently to conceiving (of planned strategy), has obscured its importance. Leonard Sayles, however, has long and steadily insisted on this, beginning with his 1964 book and culminating in *The Working Leader* (published in 1993), in which he makes his strongest statement yet, insisting that managers must be the focal points for action in and by their units (Sayles 1964, 1993). Their direct involvement must, in his view, take precedence over the pulling force of leadership and the pushing force of controllership.

I shall refer to this involvement as the **doing** role. But, in using this label—a popular one in the managerial vernacular ("Mary Ann's a doer")—it is necessary to point out that managers, in fact, hardly ever "do" anything. Many barely even dial their own telephones! Watch a manager and you will see someone whose work consists almost exclusively of talking and listening, alongside, of course, watching and "feeling." (That, incidentally, is why I show the manager at the core of the model as a head and not a full body!)

What "doing" presumably means, therefore, is getting closer to the action, ultimately being just one step removed from it. Managers as doers manage the carrying out of action directly, instead of indirectly through managing people or by processing information. In effect, a "doer" is really someone who gets it done (or, as the French put it with their expression *faire faire*, to "make" something "get made"). And the managerial vernacular is, in fact, full of expressions that reflect just this: "doing deals," "championing change," "fighting fires," "juggling projects." In the terms of decision making introduced earlier, here the manager diagnoses and designs as well as decides: he or she gets deeply and fully involved in the management of particular activities. Thus, in the day I spent with the head of the small retail chain, I saw a steady stream of all sorts of people coming and going, most involved with some aspect of store development or store operations, and there to get specific instructions on how to proceed next. He was not delegating or authorizing, but very clearly managing specific development projects step by step.

Just as they communicate all around the circle, so too do managers "do" all around it, as shown in Figure 6. *Doing inside* involves projects and problems. In other words, much "doing"

FIGURE 6
The Action Roles

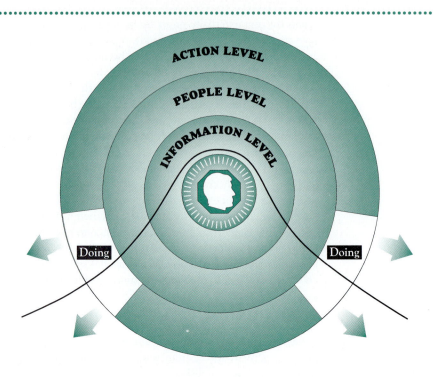

has to do with changing the unit itself, both proactively and reactively. Managers champion change to exploit opportunities for their units, and they handle its problems and resolve its crises, often with "hands on" involvement. Indeed, the president I observed of a large French systems company spent part of his day in a meeting on a very specific customer contract. Asked why he attended, he said it was a leading-edge project that could well change his company. He was being informed, to be sure, but also "doing" (more than controlling): he was an active member of the team. Here, then, the manager becomes a true designer (or, in the example above, a partner in the design), not of abstract strategies or of generalized structures, but of tangible projects of change. And the evidence, in fact, is that managers at all levels typically juggle many such projects concurrently, perhaps several dozen in the case of chief executives. Hence the popularity of the term "project management."

Some managers continue to do regular work after they have become managers as well. For example, a head nurse might see a patient, just as the Pope leads prayers, or a dean might teach a class. Done for its own sake, this might be considered separate from managerial work. But such things are often done for very managerial reasons as well. This may be an effective way of "keeping in touch" with the unit's work and finding out about its problems, in which case it falls under the role of communicating. Or it may be done to demonstrate involvement and commitment with others in the unit, in which case it falls under the role of culture building in the role of leading.

Doing outside takes place in terms of deals and negotiations. Again, there is no shortage of evidence on the importance of negotiating as well as dealing in managerial work. Most evident in my observations was the managing director of the film company, who was working on one intricate deal after another. This was a small company, and making deals was a key part of her job. But even in larger organizations, senior managers have to spend considerable time on negotiations themselves, especially when critical moments arise. After all, they are the ones who have the authority to commit the resources of their unit, and it is they who are the nerve centers of its information as well as the energy centers of its activity, not to mention the conceptual centers of its strategy. All around the circles, therefore, action connects to people who connect to information, which connects to the frame.

The Well-Rounded Job of Managing

I opened this article by noting that the best-known writers of management all seem to emphasize one aspect of the job—in the terms we now have, "doing" for Tom Peters, "conceiving" for Michael Porter, "leading" for Abraham Zaleznik and Warren Bennis, "controlling" for the classical writers. Now it can be appreciated why all may well be wrong: heeding the advice of any one of them must lead to the lopsided practice of managerial work. Like an unbalanced wheel at resonant frequency, the job risks flying out of control. That is why it is important to show all of the components of managerial work on a single integrated diagram, as in Figure 7, to remind people, at a glance, that these components form one job and cannot be separated.

Acceptance of Tom Peters' urgings—"'Don't think, do' is the phrase I favor"—could lead to the centrifugal explosion of the job, as it flies off in all directions, free of a strong frame anchoring it at the core. But acceptance of the spirit of Michael Porter's opposite writings—that what matters most is conception of the frame, especially of strategic positions—could produce a result no better: centripetal implosion, as the job closes in on itself cerebrally, free of the tangible connection to its outer actions. Thinking is heavy and can

FIGURE 7
Managerial Work
Rounded Out

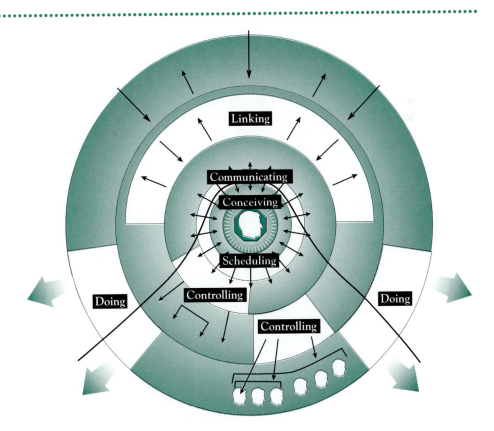

wear down the incumbent, while acting is light and cannot keep him or her in place. Only together do they provide the balance that seems so characteristic of effective management.

Too much leading produces a job free of content—aimless, frameless, and actionless—while too much linking produces a job detached from its internal roots—public relations instead of public service. The manager who only communicates or only conceives never gets anything done, while the manager who only "does" ends up doing it all alone. And, of course, we all know that happens to managers who believe their job is merely to control. A bad pun may thus make for good practice: the manager must practice a well-rounded job.

In fact, while we may be able to separate the components of this job conceptually, I maintain that they cannot be separated behaviorally. In other words, it may be useful, even necessary, to delineate the parts for purposes of design, selection, training, and support. But this job cannot be practiced as a set of independent parts. The core is a kind of magnet that holds the rest together, while the communication ring acts as a membrane that allows the flow of information between inner thinking and outer behaviors, which themselves tie people to action.

Indeed, the most interesting aspects of this job may well fall on the edges, between the component parts. For example, Andrew Grove, president of Intel, likes to describe what he does as "nudging," a perfect blend of controlling, leading, and doing (Grove, 1983). This can mean pushing people, tangibly but not aggressively, as might happen with pure doing, and not coldly, as with pure controlling, but with a sense of leading. There are similar edges between the inside and the outside, thinking and behaving, and communicating and controlling, as we shall see.

Managers who try to "do" outside without "doing" inside inevitably get themselves into trouble. Just consider all those chief executives who "did the deal," acquired the company or whatever, and then dropped it into the laps of others for execution. Likewise, it makes no more sense to conceive and then fail to lead and do (as has been the tendency in so-called "strategic planning," where controlling has often been considered sufficient for "implementation") than it makes sense to do or to lead without thinking through the frame in which to embed these activities. A single managerial job may be carried out by a small team, but only if its members are so tightly knitted together—especially by that ring of communication—that they act as a single entity. This is not to argue, of course, that different managers do not emphasize different roles or different aspects of the job. For example, we can distinguish a *conceptual* style of management, which focuses on the development of the frame, an *administrative* style, which concerns itself primarily with controlling, an *interpersonal* style, which favors leading on the inside or linking on the outside, and an *action* style, which is concerned mainly with tangible doing. And as we move out in this order, the overall style of managing can be described as less *opaque*, more *visible*.

A final aspect of managerial style has to do with the interrelationships among the various components of managerial work. For example, an important distinction can be made between *deductive* and *inductive* approaches to managerial work. The former proceeds from the core out, as the conceived frame is implemented through scheduling that uses information to drive people to get action done. We can call this a *cerebral* style of managing—highly deliberate. But there is an alternate, emergent view of the management process as well, which proceeds inductively, from the outer surface to the inner core. We might label it an *insightful* style. As Karl Weick puts it, managers act in order to think. They try things to gain experience, retain what works, and then, by interpreting the results, gradually evolve their frames (Weick, 1979).

Clearly, there is an infinity of possible contexts within which management can be practiced. But just as clearly, perhaps, a model such as the one presented here can help to order them and so come to grips with the difficult requirements of designing managerial jobs, selecting the right people to fill them, and training people accordingly.

by H. Edward Wrapp

The upper reaches of management are a land of mystery and intrigue. Very few people have ever been there, and the present inhabitants frequently send back messages that are incoherent both to other levels of management and to the world in general. This may account for the myths, illusions, and caricatures that permeate the literature of management—for example, such widely held notions as these:

▼ Life gets less complicated as a manager reaches the top of the pyramid.

▼ The manager at the top level knows everything that's going on in the organization, can command whatever resources he may need, and therefore can be more decisive.

▼ The general manager's day is taken up with making broad policy decisions and formulating precise objectives.

▼ The top executive's primary activity is conceptualizing long-range plans.

▼ In a large company, the top executive may be seen meditating about the role of his organization in society.

I suggest that none of these versions alone, or in combination, is an accurate portrayal of what a general manager does. Perhaps students of the management process have been overly eager to develop a theory and a discipline. As one executive I know puts it, "I guess I do some of the things described in the books and articles, but the descriptions are lifeless, and my job isn't."

What common characteristics, then, do successful executives exhibit *in reality?* I shall identify five skills or talents which, in my experience, seem especially significant. . . .

Keeping Well Informed

First, each of my heroes has a special talent for keeping himself informed about a wide range of operating decisions being made at different levels in the company. As he moves up the ladder, he develops a network of information sources in many different departments. He cultivates these sources and keeps them open no matter how high he climbs in the organization. When the need arises, he bypasses the lines on the organization chart to seek more than one version of a situation.

In some instances, especially when they suspect he would not be in total agreement with their decision, his subordinates will elect to inform him in advance, before they announce a decision. In these circumstances, he is in a position to defer the decision, or redirect it, or even block further action. However, he does not insist on this procedure. Ordinarily he leaves it up to the members of his organization to decide at what stage they inform him.

Top-level managers are frequently criticized by writers, consultants, and lower levels of management for continuing to enmesh themselves in operating problems, after promotion to the top, rather than withdrawing to the "big picture." Without any doubt, some managers do get lost in a welter of detail and insist on making too many decisions. Superficially, the good manager may seem to make the same mistake—but his purposes are different. He knows that only by keeping well informed about the decisions being made can he avoid the sterility so often found in those who isolate themselves from operations. If he follows the advice to free himself from operations, he may soon find himself subsisting on a diet of

* Originally published in the *Harvard Business Review* (September–October 1967) and winner of the McKinsey prize for the best article in the *Review* in 1967. Copyright © 1967 by the President and Fellows of Harvard College; all rights reserved. Reprinted with deletions by permission of the *Harvard Business Review*.

abstractions, leaving the choice of what he eats in the hands of his subordinates. As Kenneth Boulding puts it, "The very purpose of a hierarchy is to prevent information from reaching higher layers. It operates as an information filter, and there are little wastebaskets all along the way" (in *Business Week*, February 18, 1967:202). . . .

Focusing Time and Energy

The second skill of the good manager is that he knows how to save his energy and hours for those few particular issues, decisions, or problems to which he should give his personal attention. He knows the fine and subtle distinction between keeping fully informed about operating decisions and allowing the organization to force him into participating in these decisions or, even worse, making them. Recognizing that he can bring his special talents to bear on only a limited number of matters, he chooses those issues which he believes will have the greatest long-term impact on the company, and on which his special abilities can be most productive. Under ordinary circumstances he will limit himself to three or four major objectives during any single period of sustained activity.

What about the situations he elects *not* to become involved in as a decision maker? He makes sure (using the skill first mentioned) that the organization keeps him informed about them at various stages; he does not want to be accused of indifference to such issues. He trains his subordinates not to bring the matters to him for a decision. The communication to him from below is essentially one of. "Here is our sizeup, and here's what we propose to do." Reserving his hearty encouragement for those projects which hold superior promise of a contribution to total corporate strategy, he simply acknowledges receipt of information on other matters. When he sees a problem where the organization needs his help, he finds a way to transmit his know-how short of giving orders—usually by asking perceptive questions.

Playing the Power Game

To what extent do successful top executives push their ideas and proposals through the organization? The rather common notion that the "prime mover" continually creates and forces through new programs, like a powerful majority leader in a liberal Congress, is in my opinion very misleading.

The successful manager is sensitive to the power structure in the organization. In considering any major current proposal, he can plot the position of the various individuals and units in the organization of a scale ranging from complete, outspoken support down to determined, sometimes bitter, and oftentimes well cloaked opposition. In the middle of the scale is an area of comparative indifference. Usually, several aspects of a proposal will fall into this area, and *here is where he knows he can operate*. He assesses the depth and nature of the blocs in the organization. His perception permits him to move through what I call *corridors* of comparative indifference. He seldom challenges when a corridor is blocked, preferring to pause until it has opened up.

Related to this particular skill is his ability to recognize the need for a few trial-balloon launchers in the organization. He knows that the organization will tolerate only a certain number of proposals which emanate from the apex of the pyramid. No matter how sorely he may be tempted to stimulate the organization with a flow of his own ideas, he knows he must work through idea men in different parts of the organization. As he studies the reactions of key individuals and groups to the trial balloons these men send up, he is able to make a better assessment of how to limit the emasculation of the various proposals. For seldom does he find a proposal which is supported by all quarters of the organization. The emergence of strong support in certain quarters is almost sure to evoke strong opposition in others.

VALUE OF SENSE OF TIMING

Circumstances like these mean that a good sense of timing is a priceless asset for a top executive. . . . As a good manager stands at a point in time, he can identify a set of goals he is interested in, albeit the outline of them may be pretty hazy. His timetable, which is also pretty hazy, suggests that some must be accomplished sooner than others, and that some may be safely postponed for several months or years. He has a still hazier notion of how he can reach these goals. He assesses key individuals and groups. He knows that each has its own set of goals, some of which he understands rather thoroughly and others about which he can only speculate. He knows also that these individuals and groups represent blocks to certain programs or projects, and that these points of opposition must be taken into account. As the day-to-day operating decisions are made, and as proposals are responded to both by individuals and by groups, he perceives more clearly where the corridors of comparative indifference are. He takes action accordingly.

The Art of Imprecision

The fourth skill of the successful manager is knowing how to satisfy the organization that it has a sense of direction *without ever actually getting himself committed to a specific set of objectives.* This is not to say that he does not have objectives—personal and corporate, long-term and short-term. They are significant guides to his thinking, and he modifies them continually as he better understands the resources he is working with, the competition, and the changing market demands. But as the organization clamors for statements of objectives, these are samples of what they get back from him:

> "Our company aims to be number one in its industry."
> "Our objective is growth with profit."
> "We seek the maximum return on investment."
> "Management's goal is to meet its responsibilities to stockholders, employees, and the public."

In my opinion, statements such as these provide almost no guidance to the various levels of management. Yet they are quite readily accepted as objectives by large numbers of intelligent people.

MAINTAINING VIABILITY

Why does the good manager shy away from precise statements of his objectives for the organization? The main reason is that he finds it impossible to set down specific objectives which will be relevant for any reasonable period into the future. Conditions in business change continually and rapidly, and corporate strategy must be revised to take the changes into account. The more explicit the statement of strategy, the more difficult it becomes to persuade the organization to turn to different goals when needs and conditions shift.

The public and the stockholders, to be sure, must perceive the organization as having a well-defined set of objectives and clear sense of direction. But in reality the good top manager is seldom so certain of the direction which should be taken. Better than anyone else, he senses the many, many threats to his company—threats which lie in the economy, in the actions of competitors, and, not least, within his own organization.

He also knows that it is impossible to state objectives clearly enough so that everyone in the organization understands what they mean. Objectives get communicated only over time by a consistency or pattern in operating decisions. Such decisions are more meaningful than words. In instances where precise objectives are spelled out, the organization tends to interpret them so they fit its own needs.

Subordinates who keep pressing for more precise objectives are in truth working against their own best interests. Each time the objectives are stated more specifically, a subordinate's range of possibilities for operating are reduced. The narrower field means less room to roam and to accommodate the flow of ideas coming up from his part of the organization.

AVOIDING POLICY STRAITJACKETS

The successful manager's reluctance to be precise extends into the area of policy decisions. He seldom makes a forthright statement of policy. He may be aware that in some companies there are executives who spend more time in arbitrating disputes caused by stated policies than in moving the company forward. The management textbooks contend that well-defined policies are the sine qua non of a well-managed company. My research does not bear out this contention. For example,

> The president of one company with which I am familiar deliberately leaves the assignments of his top officers vague and refuses to define policies for them. He passes out new assignments with seemingly no pattern in mind and consciously sets up competitive ventures among his subordinates. His methods, though they would never be sanctioned by a classical organization planner, are deliberate—and, incidentally, quite effective.

Since able managers do not make policy decisions, does this mean that well-managed companies operate without policies? Certainly not. But the policies are those which evolve over time from an indescribable mix of operating decisions. From any single operating decision might have come a very minor dimension of the policy as the organization understands it; from a series of decisions comes a pattern of guidelines for various levels of the organization.

The skillful manager resists the urge to write a company creed or to compile a policy manual. Preoccupation with detailed statements of corporate objectives and departmental goals and with comprehensive organization charts and job descriptions is often the first symptom of an organization which is in the early stages of atrophy.

The "management by objectives" school, so widely heralded in recent years, suggests that detailed objectives be spelled out at all levels in the corporation. This method is feasible at lower levels of management, but it becomes unworkable at the upper levels. The top manager must think out objectives in detail, but ordinarily some of the objectives must be withheld, or at least communicated to the organization in modest doses. A conditioning process which may stretch over months or years is necessary in order to prepare the organization for radical departures from what it is currently striving to attain.

Suppose, for example, that a president is convinced his company must phase out of the principal business it has been in for 35 years. Although making this change of course is one of his objectives, he may well feel that he cannot disclose the idea even to his vice presidents, whose total know-how is in the present business. A blunt announcement that the company is changing horses would be too great a shock for most of them to bear. And so he begins moving toward this goal but without a full disclosure to his management group.

A detailed spelling out of objectives may only complicate the task of reaching them. Specific, detailed statements give the opposition an opportunity to organize its defenses.

Muddling with a Purpose

The fifth, and most important, skill I shall describe bears little relation to the doctrine that management is (or should be) a comprehensive, systematic, logical, well-programmed science. Of all the heresies set forth here, this should strike doctrinaires as the rankest of all!

The successful manager, in my observation, recognizes the futility of trying to push total packages or programs through the organization. He is willing to take less than total acceptance in order to achieve modest progress toward his goals. Avoiding debates on principles, he tries to piece together particles that may appear to be incidentals into a program that moves at least part of the way toward his objectives. His attitude is based on optimism and persistence. Over and over he says to himself, "There must be some parts of this proposal on which we can capitalize."

Whenever he identifies relationships among the different proposals before him, he knows that they present opportunities for combination and restructuring. It follows that he is a man of wide-ranging interests and curiosity. The more things he knows about, the more opportunities he will have to discover parts which are related. This process does not require great intellectual brilliance or unusual creativity. The wider ranging his interests, the more likely that he will be able to tie together several unrelated proposals. He is skilled as an analyst, but even more talented as a conceptualizer.

If the manager has built or inherited a solid organization, it will be difficult for him to come up with an idea which no one in the company has ever thought of before. His most significant contribution may be that he can see relationships which no one else has seen. . . .

CONTRASTING PICTURES

It is interesting to note, in the writings of several students of management, the emergence of the concept that, rather than making decisions, the leader's principal task is maintaining operating conditions which permit the various decision-making systems to function effectively. The supporters of this theory, it seems to me, overlook the subtle turns of direction which the leader can provide. He cannot add purpose and structure to the balanced judgments of subordinates if he simply rubberstamps their decisions. He must weigh the issues and reach his own decision. . . .

Many of the articles about successful executives picture them as great thinkers who sit at their desks drafting master blueprints for their companies. The successful top executives I have seen at work do not operate this way. Rather than produce a full-grown decision tree, they start with a twig, help it grow, and ease themselves out on the limbs only after they have tested to see how much weight the limbs can stand.

In my picture, the general manager sits in the midst of a continuous stream of operating problems. His organization presents him with a flow of proposals to deal with the problems. Some of these proposals are contained in voluminous, well-documented, formal reports; some are as fleeting as the walk-in visit from a subordinate whose latest inspiration came during the morning's coffee break. Knowing how meaningless it is to say, "This is a finance problem," or, "That is a communications problem," the manager feels no compulsion to classify his problems. He is, in fact, undismayed by a problem that defies classification. As the late Gary Steiner, in one of his speeches, put it, "He has a high tolerance for ambiguity."

In considering each proposal, the general manager tests it against at least three criteria:

1. Will the total proposal—or, more often, will some part of the proposal—move the organization toward the objectives which he has in mind?

2. How will the whole or parts of the proposal be received by the various groups and sub-groups in the organization? Where will the strongest opposition come from, which group will furnish the strongest support, and which group will be neutral or indifferent?

3. How does the proposal relate to programs already in process or currently proposed? Can some parts of the proposal under consideration be added on to a program already under way, or can they be combined with all or parts of other proposals in a package which can be steered through the organization? . . .

Conclusion

To recapitulate, the general manager possesses five important skills. He knows how to:

1. *Keep open many pipelines of information*—No one will quarrel with the desirability of an early warning system which provides varied viewpoints on an issue. However, very few managers know how to practice this skill, and the books on management add precious little to our understanding of the techniques which make it practicable.

2. *Concentrate on a limited number of significant issues*—No matter how skillful the manager is in focusing his energies and talents, he is inevitably caught up in a number of inconsequential duties. Active leadership of an organization demands a high level of personal involvement, and personal involvement brings with it many time-consuming activities which have an infinitesimal impact on corporate strategy. Hence this second skill, while perhaps the most logical of the five, is by no means the easiest to apply.

3. *Identify the corridors of comparative indifference*—Are there inferences here that the good manager has no ideas of his own, that he stands by until his organization proposes solutions, that he never uses his authority to force a proposal through the organization? Such inferences are not intended. The message is that a good organization will tolerate only so much direction from the top; the good manager therefore is adept at sensing how hard he can push.

4. *Give the organization a sense of direction with open-ended objectives*—In assessing this skill, keep in mind that I am talking about top levels of management. At lower levels, the manager should be encouraged to write down his objectives, if for no other reason than to ascertain if they are consistent with corporate strategy.

5. *Spot opportunities and relationships in the stream of operating problems and decisions*—Lest it be concluded from the description of this skill that the good manager is more an improviser than a planner, let me emphasize that he is a planner and encourages planning by his subordinates. Interestingly, though, professional planners may be irritated by a good general manager. Most of them complain about his lack of vision. They devise a master plan, but the president (or other operating executive) seems to ignore it, or to give it minimum acknowledgment by borrowing bits and pieces for implementation. They seem to feel that the power of a good master plan will be obvious to everyone, and its implementation automatic. But the general manager knows that even if the plan is sound and imaginative, the job has only begun. The long, painful task of implementation will depend on his skill, not that of the planner. . . .

*by Gary Hamel and
C. K. Prahalad*

Today managers in many industries are working hard to match the competitive advantages of their new global rivals. They are moving manufacturing offshore in search of low labor costs, rationalizing product lines to capture global scale economies, instituting quality circles and just-in-time production, and adopting Japanese human resource practices. When competitiveness still seems out of reach, they form strategic alliances, often with the very companies that upset the competitive balance in the first place.

Important as these initiatives are, few of them go beyond mere imitation. . . .For these executives and their companies, regaining competitiveness will mean rethinking many of the basic concepts of strategy. . . . The new global competitors approach strategy from a perspective that is fundamentally different from that which underpins Western management thought. . . .

Companies that have risen to global leadership over the past 20 years invariably began with ambitions that were out of all proportion to their resources and capabilities. But they created an obsession with winning at all levels of the organization and then sustained that obsession over the 10- to 20-year quest for global leadership. We term this obsession "strategic intent."

On the one hand, strategic intent envisions a desired leadership position and establishes the criteria the organization will use to chart its progress. Komatsu set out to "Encircle Caterpillar." Canon sought to "Beat Xerox." Honda strove to become a second Ford—an automotive pioneer. All are expressions of strategic intent.

At the same time, strategic intent is more than simply unfettered ambition. (Many companies possess an ambitious strategic intent yet fall short of their goals.) The concept also encompasses an active management process that includes: focusing the organization's attention on the essence of winning; motivating people by communicating the value of the target; leaving room for individual and team contributions; sustaining enthusiasm by providing new operations definitions as circumstances change; and using intent consistently to guide resource allocations.

Strategic intent captures the essence of winning. The Apollo program—landing a man on the moon ahead of the Soviets—was as competitively focused as Komatsu's drive against Caterpillar. The space program became the scorecard for America's technology race with the USSR. . . . For Coca-Cola, strategic intent has been to put Coke within "arms reach" of every consumer in the world.

Strategic intent is stable over time. In battles for global leadership, one of the most critical tasks is to lengthen the organization's attention span. Strategic intent provides consistency to short-term action, while leaving room for reinterpretation as new opportunities emerge. . . .

Strategic intent sets a target that deserves personal effort and commitment. Ask the chairmen of many American corporations how they measure their contributions to their companies' success and you've likely to get an answer expressed in terms of shareholder wealth. In a company that possesses a strategic intent, top management is more likely to talk in terms of global market leadership. Market share leadership typically yields shareholder wealth, to be sure. But the two goals do not have the same motivational impact. It is hard to imagine middle managers, let alone blue-collar employees, waking up each day with the sole thought of creating more shareholder wealth. But mightn't they feel different given the challenge to "Beat Benz"—the rallying cry at one Japanese auto producer? Strategic intent gives employees the only goal that is worthy of commitment: to unseat the best or remain the best, worldwide. . . .

Just as you cannot plan a 10- to-20-year quest for global leadership, the chance of falling into a leadership position by accident is also remote. We don't believe that global leadership comes from an undirected process of intrapreneurship. Nor is it the product of a skunkworks or other techniques for internal venturing. Behind such programs lies a nihilistic assumption: the organization is so hide-bound, so orthodox ridden that the only way to innovate is to put a few bright people in a dark room, pour in some money, and hope that something wonderful will happen. In the "Silicon Valley" approach to innovation, the only role for top managers is to retrofit their corporate strategy to the entrepreneurial successes that emerge from below. Here the value added of top management is low indeed. . . .

In companies that overcame resource constraints to build leadership positions, we see a different relationship between means and ends. While strategic intent is clear about ends, it is flexible as to means—it leaves room for improvisation. Achieving strategic intent requires enormous creativity with respect to means. . . . But this creativity comes in the service of a clearly prescribed end. Creativity is unbridled, but not uncorraled, because top management establishes the criterion against which employees can pretest the logic of their initiatives. Middle managers must do more than deliver on promised financial targets; they must also deliver on the broad direction implicit in their organization's strategic intent.

Strategic intent implies a sizable stretch for an organization. Current capabilities and resources will not suffice. This forces the organization to be more inventive, to make the most of limited resources. Whereas the traditional view of strategy focuses on the degree of fit between existing resources and current opportunities, strategic intent creates an extreme misfit between resources and ambitions. Top management then challenges the organization to close the gap by systematically building new advantages. For Canon this meant first understanding Xerox's patents, then licensing technology to create a product that would yield early market experience, then gearing up internal R&D efforts, then licensing its own technology to other manufacturers to fund further R&D, then entering marketing segments in Japan and Europe where Xerox was weak, and so on.

In this respect, strategic intent is like a marathon run in 400-meter sprints. No one knows what the terrain will look like at mile 26, so the role of top management is to focus the organization's attention on the ground to be covered in the next 400 meters. In several companies, management did this by presenting the organization with a series of corporate challenges, each specifying the next hill in the race to achieve strategic intent. One year the challenge might be quality, the next total customer care, the next entry into new markets, the next a rejuvenated product line. As this example indicates, corporate challenges are a way to stage the acquisition of new competitive advantages, a way to identify the focal point for employees' efforts in the near to medium term. As with strategic intent, top management is specific about the ends (reducing product development times by 75%, for example) but less prescriptive about the means.

Like strategic intent, challenges stretch the organization. To preempt Xerox in the personal copier business, Canon set its engineers a target price of $1,000 for a home copier. At the time, Canon's least expensive copier sold for several thousand dollars. . . . Canon engineers were challenged to reinvent the copier—a challenge they met by substituting a disposable cartridge for the complex image-transfer mechanism used in other copiers. . . .

For a challenge to be effective, individuals and teams throughout the organization must understand it and see its implications for their own jobs. Companies that set corporate challenges to create new competitive advantages (as Ford and IBM did with quality improvement) quickly discover that engaging the entire organization requires top management to:

Create a sense of urgency, or quasi crisis, by amplifying weak signals in the environment that point up the need to improve, instead of allowing inaction to precipitate a real crisis. . . .

Develop a competitor focus at every level through widespread use of competitive intelligence. Every employee should be able to benchmark his or her efforts against best-in-class competitors so that the challenge becomes personal. . . .

Provide employees with the skills they need to work effectively—training in statistical tools, problem solving, value engineering, and team building, for example.

Give the organization time to digest one challenge before launching another. When competing initiatives overload the organization, middle managers often try to protect their people from the whipsaw of shifting priorities. But this "wait and see if they're serious this time" attitude ultimately destroys the credibility of corporate challenges.

Establish clear milestones and review mechanisms to track progress and ensure that internal recognition and rewards reinforce desired behavior. The goal is to make the challenge inescapable for everyone in the company. . . .

Reciprocal responsibility means shared gain and shared pain . . . at Nissan when the yen strengthened: top management took a big pay cut and then asked middle managers and line employees to sacrifice relatively less. In too many companies, the pain of revitalization falls almost exclusively on the employees least responsible for the enterprise's decline. . . . This one-sided approach to regaining competitiveness keeps many companies from harnessing the intellectual horsepower of their employees.

Creating a sense of reciprocal responsibility is crucial because competitiveness ultimately depends on the pace at which a company embeds new advantages deep within its organization, not on its stock of advantages at any given time. Thus we need to expand the concept of competitive advantage beyond the scorecard many managers now use: Are my costs lower? Will my product command a price premium?

Few competitive advantages are long lasting. Uncovering a new competitive advantage is a bit like getting a hot tip on a stock: the first person to act on the insight makes more money than the last. . . .

Keeping score of existing advantages is not the same as building new advantages. The essence of strategy lies in creating tomorrow's competitive advantages faster than competitors mimic the ones you possess today. In the 1960s, Japanese producers relied on labor and capital cost advantages. As Western manufacturers began to move production offshore, Japanese companies accelerated their investment in process technology and created scale and quality advantages. Then as their U.S. and European competitors rationalized manufacturing, they added another string to their bow by accelerating the rate of product development. Then they built global brands. Then they deskilled competitors through alliances and outsourcing deals. The moral? An organization's capacity to improve existing skills and learn new ones is the most defensible competitive advantage of all.

To achieve strategic intent, a company must usually take on larger, better financed competitors. That means carefully managing competitive engagements so that scarce resources are conserved. Managers cannot do that simply by playing the same game better—making marginal improvement to competitor's technology and business practices. Instead, they must fundamentally change the game in ways that disadvantage incumbents—designing novel approaches to market entry, advantage building, and competitive warfare. For smart competitors, the goal is not competitive imitation but competitive innovation, the art of containing competitive risks within manageable proportions.

Four approaches to competitive innovation are evident in the global expansion of Japanese companies. These are: building layers of advantage, searching for loose bricks, changing the terms of engagement, and competing through collaboration.

The wider a company's portfolio of advantages, the less risk it faces in competitive battles. New global competitors have built such portfolios by steadily expanding their arsenals of competitive weapons. They have moved inexorably from less defensible advantages such as low wage costs to more defensible advantages like global brands. . . .

Business schools have perpetuated the notion that a manager with new present value calculations in one hand and portfolio planning in the other can manage any business anywhere.

In many diversified companies, top management evaluates line managers on numbers alone because no other basis for dialogue exists. Managers move so many times as part of their "career development" that they often do not understand the nuances of the businesses they are managing. At GE, for example, one fast-track manager heading an important new venture had moved across five businesses in five years. His series of quick successes finally came to an end when he confronted a Japanese competitor whose managers had been plodding along in the same business for more than a decade.

Regardless of ability and effort, fast-track managers are unlikely to develop the deep business knowledge they need to discuss technology options, competitors' strategies, and global opportunities substantively. Invariably, therefore, discussions gravitate to "the numbers," while the value added of managers is limited to the financial and planning savvy they carry from job to job. Knowledge of the company's internal planning and accounting systems substitutes for substantive knowledge of the business, making competitive innovation unlikely.

When managers know that their assignments have a two- to three-year time frame, they feel great pressure to create a good track record fast. This pressure often takes on one of two forms. Either the manager does not commit to goals whose time line extends beyond his or her expected tenure. Or ambitious goals are adopted and squeezed into an unrealistically short time frame. Aiming to be number one in a business is the essence of strategic intent; but imposing a three- to four-year horizon on that effort simply invites disaster. Acquisitions are made with little attention to the problems of integration. The organization becomes overloaded with initiatives. Collaborative ventures are formed without adequate attention to competitive consequences.

Almost every strategic management theory and nearly every corporate planning system is premised on a strategy hierarchy in which corporate goals guide business unit strategies and business unit strategies guide functional tactics. In this hierarchy, senior management makes strategy and low levels execute it. The dichotomy between formulation and implementation is familiar and widely accepted. But the strategy hierarchy undermines competitiveness by fostering an elitist view of management that tends to disenfranchise most of the organization. Employees fail to identify with corporate goals or involve themselves deeply in the work of becoming more competitive.

The strategy hierarchy isn't the only explanation for an elitist view of management, of course. The myths that grow up around successful top managers. . . perpetuate it. So does the turbulent business environment. Middle managers buffeted by circumstances that seem to be beyond their control desperately want to believe that top management has all the answers. And top management, in turn, hesitates to admit it does not for fear of demoralizing lower level employees. . . .

Unfortunately, a threat that everyone perceives but no one talks about creates more anxiety that a threat that has been clearly identified and made the focal point for the problem-solving efforts of the entire company. That is one reason honesty and humility on the part of top management may be the first prerequisite of revitalization. Another reason is the need to make participation more than a buzzword.

Programs such as quality circles and total customer service often fall short of expectations because management does not recognize that successful implementation requires more than administrative structures. Difficulties in embedding new capabilities are typically put down to "communication" problems, with the unstated assumption that if only downward communication were more effective—"if only middle management would get the message straight"—the new program would quickly take root. The need for upward communication is often ignored, or assumed to mean nothing more than feedback. In contrast, Japanese companies win, not because they have smarter managers, but because they have developed ways to harness the "wisdom of the anthill." They realize the top managers are a bit like the astronauts who circle the earth in the space shuttle. It may be the astronauts who get all the glory, but everyone knows that the real intelligence behind the mission is located firmly on the ground. . . .

Developing faith in the organization's ability to deliver on tough goals, motivating it to do so, focusing its attention long enough to internalize new capabilities—this is the real challenge for top management. Only by rising to this challenge will senior managers gain the courage they need to commit themselves and their companies to global leadership.

FORMULATING STRATEGY

Most of what has been published in this field deals with how strategy *should* be designed or consciously *formulated*. On the prescription of how this should be accomplished, there has been a good deal of consensus, although, as we shall see later, this is now eroding. Perhaps we should more properly conclude that there have been two waves of consensus. The first, which developed in the 1960s, is presented in this chapter; the second, which emerged around 1980, did not challenge the first so much as build on it. This is presented in Chapter 4.

Ken Andrews of the Harvard Business School is the person most commonly associated with the first wave, although Bill Newman of Columbia wrote on some of these issues much earlier and Igor Ansoff simultaneously outlined very similar views while he was at Carnegie-Mellon. But the Andrews text became the best known, in part because it was so simply and clearly written, in part because it was embodied in a popular textbook (with cases) emanating from the Harvard Business School.

We reproduce parts of the Andrews text (as revised in its own publication in 1980, but based on the original 1965 edition). These serve to introduce the basic point that strategy ultimately requires the achievement of fit between the external situation (opportunities and threats) and internal capability (strengths and weaknesses). Note how the Andrews approach builds directly on some of the military concepts outlined earlier. Both seek to leverage the impact of resources by concentrating efforts within a defined zone of dominance while attempting to anticipate the effects of potentially damaging external forces.

As you read the Andrews text, a number of basic premises will quickly become evident. Among these are: the clear distinction made between strategy formulation and strategy implementation (in effect, between thinking and action); the belief that strategy (or at least intended strategy) should be made explicit; the notion that structure should follow strategy (in other words, be designed in accordance with it); and the assumption that strategy emanates from the formal leadership of the organization. Similar premises underlie most of the prescriptive literature of strategic management.

This model (if we can call it that) has proven very useful in many circumstances as a broad way to analyze a strategic situation and to think about making strategy. A careful strategist should certainly touch all the bases suggested in this approach. But in many circumstances the model cannot or should not be followed to the letter, as shall be discussed in Chapter 5 and later ones.

The Rumelt reading (an updated version for this text) elaborates on one element in this traditional model—the evaluation of strategies. While the Andrews text contains a similar discussion, Rumelt, a graduate of the Harvard Business School and strategy professor at INSEAD, develops it in a particularly elegant way, helping to round out this chapter on the classical view of formulating strategy.

One more reading, by Quinn and Hilmer, combines two crucial concepts that have taken center stage in the strategy formation literature in recent years. One is "core competency," the idea that companies have to build, sustain, and use in their formulation of strategy fundamental competencies where they contribute unique value to customers by performing at "best in world" levels, to quote the authors. The authors develop this concept in a rich way. The second is strategic outsourcing. If companies are to focus on their core competencies, then they have to consider shedding much else, where they do not have distinct advantages. If they perform in-house activities that others could perform better, they sacrifice competitive edge. Hence, these two concepts must be linked together, as this article does elegantly, being careful to point out the pitfalls.

A number of cases allow us to apply and understand the value and limitations of this approach. The Apple Computer, Inc. (A), Argyle Diamonds, Ford: Team Taurus, Nintendo Co., Ltd., and Honda Motor Company 1994 cases provide particularly useful examples of where it has a high payoff as well as suggesting its limitations.

▼ READING 3.1   THE CONCEPT OF CORPORATE STRATEGY*

by Kenneth R. Andrews

The Strategy Concept

WHAT STRATEGY IS

Corporate strategy is the pattern of decisions in a company that determines and reveals its objectives, purposes, or goals, produces the principal policies and plans for achieving those goals, and defines the range of business the company is to pursue, the kind of economic and human organization it is or intends to be, and the nature of the economic and noneconomic contribution it intends to make to its shareholders, employees, customers, and communities. . . .

The strategic decision contributing to this pattern is one that is effective over long periods of time, affects the company in many different ways, and focuses and commits a significant portion of its resources to the expected outcomes. The pattern resulting from a series of such decisions will probably define the central character and image of a company, the individuality it has for its members and various publics, and the position it will occupy in its industry and markets. It will permit the specification of particular objectives to be attained through a timed sequence investment and implementation decisions and will govern directly the deployment or redeployment of resources to make these decisions effective.

Some aspects of such a pattern of decision may be in an established corporation unchanging over long periods of time, like a commitment to quality, or high technology, or certain raw materials or good labor relations. Other aspects of strategy must change as or before the world changes, such as product line, manufacturing process, or merchandising and styling practices. The basic determinants of company character, if purposefully institutionalized, are likely to persist through and shape the nature of substantial changes in product-market choices and allocation of resources. . . .

It is important, however, not to take the idea apart in another way, that is, to separate goals from the policies designed to achieve those goals. The essence of the definition of strategy I have just recorded is *pattern*. The interdependence of purposes, policies, and organized action is crucial to the particularity of an individual strategy and its opportunity to

* Excerpted from Kenneth R. Andrews, *The Concept of Corporate Strategy*, rev. ed. (copyright © by Richard D. Irwin, Inc., 1980), Chaps. 2 and 3; reprinted by permission of the publisher.

identify competitive advantage. It is the unity, coherence, and internal consistency of a company's strategic decisions that position the company in its environment and give the firm its identity, its power to mobilize its strengths, and its likelihood of success in the marketplace. It is the interrelationship of a set of goals and policies that crystallizes from the formless reality of a company's environment a set of problems an organization can seize upon and solve.

What you are doing, in short, is never meaningful unless you can say or imply what you are doing it for: the quality of administrative action and the motivation lending it power cannot be appraised without knowing its relationship to purpose. Breaking up the system of corporate goals and the character-determining major policies for attainment leads to narrow and mechanical conceptions of strategic management and endless logic chopping. . . .

SUMMARY STATEMENTS OF STRATEGY

Before we proceed to clarification of this concept by application, we should specify the terms in which strategy is usually expressed. A summary statement of strategy will characterize the product line and services offered or planned by the company, the markets and market segments for which products and services are now or will be designed, and the channels through which these markets will be reached. The means by which the operation is to be financed will be specified, as will the profit objectives and the emphasis to be placed on the safety of capital versus level of return. Major policy in central functions such as marketing, manufacturing, procurement, research and development, labor relations, and personnel, will be stated where they distinguish the company from others, and usually the intended size, form, and climate of the organization will be included.

Each company, if it were to construct a summary strategy from what it understands itself to be aiming at, would have a different statement with different categories of decision emphasized to indicate what it wanted to be or do. . . .

FORMULATION OF STRATEGY

Corporate strategy is an organization process, in many ways inseparable from the structure, behavior, and culture of the company in which it takes place. Nevertheless, we may abstract from the process two important aspects, interrelated in real life but separable for the purposes of analysis. The first of these we may call *formulation*, the second *implementation*. Deciding what strategy should be may be approached as a rational undertaking, even if in life emotional attachments . . . may complicate choice among future alternatives. . . .

The principal subactivities of strategy formulation as a logical activity include identifying opportunities and threats in the company's environment and attaching some estimate or risk to the discernible alternatives. Before a choice can be made, the company's strengths and weaknesses should be appraised together with the resources on hand and available. Its actual or potential capacity to take advantage of perceived market needs or to cope with attendant risks should be estimated as objectively as possible. The strategic alternative which results from matching opportunity and corporate capability at an acceptable level of risk is what we may call an *economic strategy*.

The process described thus far assumes that strategists are analytically objective in estimating the relative capacity of their company and the opportunity they see or anticipate in developing markets. The extent to which they wish to undertake low or high risk presumably depends on their profit objectives. The higher they set the latter, the more willing they must be to assume a correspondingly high risk that the market opportunity they see will not develop or that the corporate competence required to excel competition will not be forthcoming.

So far we have described the intellectual processes of ascertaining what a company *might do* in terms of environmental opportunity, of deciding what it *can do* in terms of ability and power, and of bringing these two considerations together in optimal equilibrium. The determination of strategy also requires consideration of what alternatives are preferred by the chief executive and perhaps by his or her immediate associates as well, quite apart from economic considerations. Personal values, aspirations, and ideals do, and in our judgment quite properly should, influence the final choice of purposes. Thus what the executives of a company *want to do* must be brought into the strategic decision.

Finally strategic choice has an ethical aspect—a fact much more dramatically illustrated in some industries than in others. Just as alternatives may be ordered in terms of the degree of risk that they entail, so may they be examined against the standards of responsiveness to the expectations of society that the strategist elects. Some alternatives may seem to the executive considering them more attractive than others when the public good or service to society is considered. What a company *should do* thus appears as a fourth element of the strategic decision. . . .

THE IMPLEMENTATION OF STRATEGY

Since effective implementation can make a sound strategic decision ineffective or a debatable choice successful, it is as important to examine the processes of implementation as to weigh the advantages of available strategic alternatives. The implementation of strategy is comprised of a series of subactivities which are primarily administrative. If purpose is determined, then the resources of a company can be mobilized to accomplish it. An organizational structure appropriate for the efficient performance of the required tasks must be made effective by information systems and relationships permitting coordination of subdivided activities. The organizational processes of performance measurement, compensation, management development—all of them enmeshed in systems of incentives and controls—must be directed toward the kind of behavior required by organizational purpose. The role of personal leadership is important and sometimes decisive in the accomplishment of strategy. Although we know that organization structure and processes of compensation, incentives, control, and management development influence and constrain the formulation of strategy, we should look first at the logical proposition that structure should follow strategy in order to cope later with the organizational reality that strategy also follows structure. When we have examined both tendencies, we will understand and to some extent be prepared to deal with the interdependence of the formulation and implementation of corporate purpose. Figure 1 may be useful in understanding the analysis of strategy as a pattern of interrelated decisions. . . .

Relating Opportunities to Resources

Determination of a suitable strategy for a company begins in identifying the opportunities and risks in its environment. This [discussion] is concerned with the identification of a range of strategic alternatives, the narrowing of this range by recognizing the constraints imposed by corporate capability, and the determination of one or more economic strategies at acceptable levels of risk. . . .

THE NATURE OF THE COMPANY'S ENVIRONMENT

The environment of an organization in business, like that of any other organic entity, is the pattern of all the external conditions and influences that affect its life and development. The environmental influences relevant to strategic decision operate in a company's industry, the total business community, its city, its country, and the world. They are technological, economic, physical, social, and political in kind. The corporate strategist is usually at

FIGURE 1

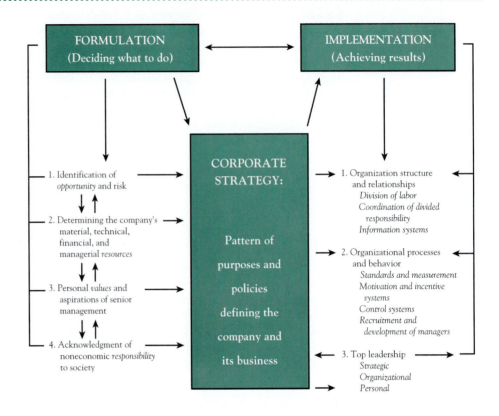

least intuitively aware of these features of the current environment. But in all these categories change is taking place at varying rates—fastest in technology, less rapidly in politics. Change in the environment of business necessitates continuous monitoring of a company's definition of its business, lest it falter, blur, or become obsolete. Since by definition the formulation of strategy is performed with the future in mind, executives who take part in the strategic planning process must be aware of those aspects of their company's environment especially susceptible to the kind of change that will affect their company's future.

Technology
From the point of view of the corporate strategist, technological developments are not only the fastest unfolding but the most far-reaching in extending or contracting opportunity for an established company. They include the discoveries of science, the impact of related product development, the less dramatic machinery and process improvements, and the progress of automation and data processing. . . .

Ecology
It used to be possible to take for granted the physical characteristics of the environment and find them favorable to industrial development. Plant sites were chosen using criteria like availability of process and cooling water, accessibility to various forms of transportation, and stability of soil conditions. With the increase in sensitivity to the impact on the physical

environment of all industrial activity, it becomes essential, often to comply with law, to consider how planned expansion and even continued operation under changing standards will affect and be perceived to affect the air, water, traffic density, and quality of life generally of any area which a company would like to enter. . . .

ECONOMICS

Because business is more accustomed to monitoring economic trends than those in other spheres, it is less likely to be taken by surprise by such massive developments as the internationalization of competition, the return of China and Russia to trade with the West, the slower than projected development of the Third World countries, the Americanization of demand and culture in the developing countries and the resulting backlash of nationalism, the increased importance of the large multinational corporations and the consequences of host-country hostility, the recurrence of recession, and the persistence of inflation in all phases of the business cycle. The consequences of world economic trends need to be monitored in much greater detail for any one industry or company.

INDUSTRY

Although the industry environment is the one most company strategists believe they know most about, the opportunities and risks that reside there are often blurred by familiarity and the uncritical acceptance of the established relative position of competitors. . . .

SOCIETY

Social developments of which strategists keep aware include such influential forces as the quest for equality for minority groups, the demand of women for opportunity and recognition, the changing patterns of work and leisure, the effects of urbanization upon the individual, family, and neighborhood, the rise of crime, the decline of conventional morality, and the changing composition of world population.

POLITICS

The political forces important to the business firm are similarly extensive and complex— the changing relations between communist and noncommunist countries (East and West) and between prosperous and poor countries (North and South), the relation between private enterprise and government, between workers and management, the impact of national planning on corporate planning, and the rise of what George Lodge (1975) calls the communitarian ideology. . . .

Although it is not possible to know or spell out here the significance of such technical, economic, social, and political trends, and possibilities for the strategist of a given business or company, some simple things are clear. Changing values will lead to different expectations of the role business should perform. Business will be expected to perform its mission not only with economy in the use of energy but with sensitivity to the ecological environment. Organizations in all walks of life will be called upon to be more explicit about their goals and to meet the needs and aspirations (for example, for education) of their membership.

In any case, change threatens all established strategies. We know that a thriving company—itself a living system—is bound up in a variety of interrelationships with larger systems comprising its technological, economic, ecological, social, and political environment. If environmental developments are destroying and creating business opportunities, advance notice of specific instances relevant to a single company is essential to intelligent planning. Risk and opportunity in the last quarter of the twentieth century require of executives a keen interest in what is going on outside their companies. More than that, a practical means of tracking developments promising good or ill, and profit or loss, needs to be devised. . . .

For the firm that has not determined what its strategy dictates it needs to know or has not embarked upon the systematic surveillance of environmental change, a few simple questions kept constantly in mind will highlight changing opportunity and risk. In examining your own company or one you are interested in, these questions should lead to an estimate of opportunity and danger in the present and predicted company setting.

1. What are the essential economic, technical, and physical characteristics of the industry in which the company participates? . . .
2. What trends suggesting future change in economic and technical characteristics are apparent? . . .
3. What is the nature of competition both within the industry and across industries? . . .
4. What are the requirements for success in competition in the company's industry? . . .
5. Given the technical, economic, social, and political developments that most directly apply, what is the range of strategy available to any company in this industry? . . .

IDENTIFYING CORPORATE COMPETENCE AND RESOURCES

The first step in validating a tentative choice among several opportunities is to determine whether the organization has the capacity to prosecute it successfully. The capability of an organization is its demonstrated and potential ability to accomplish, against the opposition of circumstance or competition, whatever it sets out to do. Every organization has actual and potential strengths and weaknesses. Since it is prudent in formulating strategy to extend or maximize the one and contain or minimize the other, it is important to try to determine what they are and to distinguish one from the other.

It is just as possible, though much more difficult, for a company to know its own strengths and limitations as it is to maintain a workable surveillance of its changing environment. Subjectivity, lack of confidence, and unwillingness to face reality may make it hard for organizations as well as for individuals to know themselves. But just as it is essential, though difficult, that a maturing person achieve reasonable self-awareness, so an organization can identify approximately its central strength and critical vulnerability. . . .

To make an effective contribution to strategic planning, the key attributes to be appraised should be identified and consistent criteria established for judging them. If attention is directed to strategies, policy commitments, and past practices in the context of discrepancy between organization goals and attainment, an outcome useful to an individual manager's strategic planning is possible. The assessment of strengths and weaknesses associated with the attainment of specific objectives becomes in Stevenson's (1976) words a "key link in a feedback loop" which allows managers to learn from the success or failures of the policies they institute.

Although [a] study by Stevenson did not find or establish a systematic way of developing or using such knowledge, members of organizations develop judgments about what the company can do particularly well—its core of competence. If consensus can be reached about this capability, no matter how subjectively arrived at, its application to identified opportunity can be estimated.

SOURCES OF CAPABILITIES

The powers of a company constituting a resource for growth and diversification accrue primarily from experience in making and marketing a product line or providing a service. They inhere as well in (1) the developing strengths and weaknesses of the individuals comprising the organization, (2) the degree to which individual capability is effectively applied to the common task, and (3) the quality of coordination of individual and group effort.

The experience gained through successful execution of a strategy centered upon one goal may unexpectedly develop capabilities which could be applied to different ends. Whether they should be so applied is another question. For example, a manufacturer of salt can strengthen his competitive position by offering his customers salt-dispensing equipment. If, in the course of making engineering improvements in this equipment, a new solenoid principle is perfected that has application to many industrial switching problems, should this patentable and marketable innovation be exploited? The answer would turn not only on whether economic analysis of the opportunity shows this to be a durable and profitable possibility, but also on whether the organization can muster the financial, manufacturing, and marketing strength to exploit the discovery and live with its success. The former question is likely to have a more positive answer than the latter. In this connection, it seems important to remember that individual and unsupported flashes of strength are not as dependable as the gradually accumulated product and market-related fruits of experience.

Even where competence to exploit an opportunity is nurtured by experience in related fields, the level of that competence may be too low for any great reliance to be placed upon it. Thus a chain of children's clothing stores might well acquire the administrative, merchandising, buying, and selling skills that would permit it to add departments in women's wear. Similarly, a sales force effective in distributing typewriters might gain proficiency in selling office machinery and supplies. But even here it would be well to ask what *distinctive* ability these companies could bring to the retailing of soft goods or office equipment to attract customers away from a plethora of competitors.

IDENTIFYING STRENGTHS

The distinctive competence of an organization is more than what it can do; it is what it can do particularly well. To identify the less obvious or by-product strengths of an organization that may well be transferable to some more profitable new opportunity, one might well begin by examining the organization's current product line and by defining the functions it serves in its markets. Almost any important consumer product has functions which are related to others into which a qualified company might move. The typewriter, for example, is more than the simple machine for mechanizing handwriting that it once appeared to be when looked at only from the point of view of its designer and manufacturer. Closely analyzed from the point of view of the potential user, the typewriter is found to contribute to a broad range of information processing functions. Any one of these might have suggested an area to be exploited by a typewriter manufacturer. Tacitly defining a typewriter as a replacement for a fountain pen as a writing instrument rather than as an input-output device for word processing is the explanation provided by hindsight for the failure of the old-line typewriter companies to develop before IBM did the electric typewriter and the computer-related input-output devices it made possible. The definition of product which would lead to identification of transferable skills must be expressed in terms of the market needs it may fill rather than the engineering specifications to which it conforms.

Besides looking at the uses or functions to which present products contribute, the would-be diversifier might profitably identify the skills that underlie whatever success has been achieved. The qualifications of an organization efficient at performing its long-accustomed tasks come to be taken for granted and considered humdrum, like the steady provision of first-class service. The insight required to identify the essential strength justifying new ventures does not come naturally. Its cultivation can probably be helped by recognition of the need for analysis. In any case, we should look beyond the company's capacity to invent new products. Product leadership is not possible for a majority of companies, so it is fortunate that patentable new products are not the only major highway to new opportunities. Other avenues include new marketing services, new methods of distribution, new values in quality-price combinations, and creative merchandising. The effort to find or to create a competence that is truly distinctive may hold the real key to a company's success or even to its future development. For example, the ability of a cement manufacturer to run a truck fleet more effectively than its competitors may constitute one of its principal competitive strengths in selling an undifferentiated product.

MATCHING OPPORTUNITY AND COMPETENCE

The way to narrow the range of alternatives, made extensive by imaginative identification of new possibilities, is to match opportunity to competence, once each has been accurately identified and its future significance estimated. It is this combination which establishes a company's economic mission and its position in its environment. The combination is designed to minimize organizational weakness and to maximize strength. In every case, risk attends it. And when opportunity seems to outrun present distinctive competence, the willingness to gamble that the latter can be built up to the required level is almost indispensable to a strategy that challenges the organization and the people in it. Figure 2 diagrams the matching of opportunity and resources that results in an economic strategy.

FIGURE 2

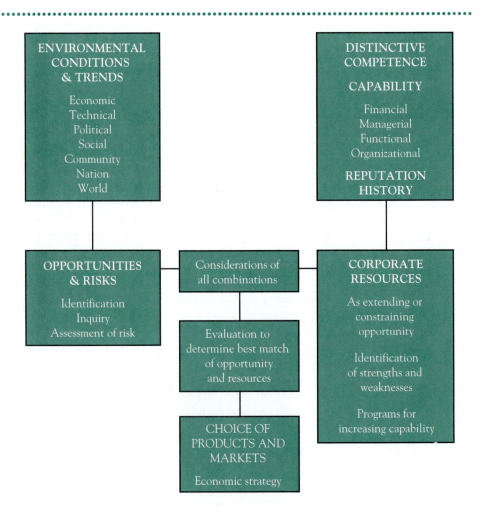

Before we leave the creative act of putting together a company's unique internal capability and opportunity evolving in the external world, we should note that—aside from distinctive competence—the principal resources found in any company are money and people—technical and managerial people. At an advanced stage of economic development, money seems less a problem than technical competence, and the latter less critical than managerial ability. Do not assume that managerial capacity can rise to any occasion. The diversification of American industry is marked by hundreds of instances in which a company strong in one endeavor lacked the ability to manage an enterprise requiring different skills. The right to make handsome profits over a long period must be earned. Opportunism without competence is a path to fairyland.

Besides equating an appraisal of market opportunity and organizational capability, the decision to make and market a particular product or service should be accompanied by an identification of the nature of the business and the kind of company its management desires. Such a guiding concept is a product of many considerations, including the managers' personal values. . . .

UNIQUENESS OF STRATEGY

In each company, the way in which distinctive competence, organizational resources, and organizational values are combined is or should be unique. Differences among companies are as numerous as differences among individuals. The combinations of opportunity to which distinctive competencies, resources, and values may be applied are equally extensive. Generalizing about how to make an effective match is less rewarding than working at it. The effort is a highly stimulating and challenging exercise. The outcome will be unique for each company and each situation.

▼ READING 3.2   EVALUATING BUSINESS STRATEGY*

by Richard R. Rumelt

Strategy can neither be formulated nor adjusted to changing circumstances without a process of strategy evaluation. Whether performed by an individual or as part of an organizational review procedure, strategy evaluation forms an essential step in the process of guiding an enterprise.

For many executives strategy evaluation is simply an appraisal of how well a business performs. Has it grown? Is the profit rate normal or better? If the answers to these questions are affirmative, it is argued that the firm's strategy must be sound. Despite its unassailable simplicity, this line of reasoning misses the whole point of strategy—that the critical factors determining the quality of current results are often not directly observable or simply measured, and that by the time strategic opportunities or threats do directly affect operating results, it may well be too late for an effective response. Thus, strategy evaluation is an attempt to look beyond the obvious facts regarding the short-term health of a business and appraise instead those more fundamental factors and trends that govern success in the chosen field of endeavor.

---

* This paper is a revised and updated version for this book. "The Evaluation of Business Strategy" was originally published in W. F. Glueck, *Strategic Management and Business Policy* (New York: McGraw-Hill, 1980). New version printed here by permission of the author.

The Challenge of Evaluation

However it is accomplished, the products of a business strategy evaluation are answers to these three questions:

▼ Are the objectives of the business appropriate?
▼ Are the major policies and plans appropriate?
▼ Do the results obtained to date confirm or refute critical assumptions on which the strategy rests?

Devising adequate answers to these questions is neither simple nor straightforward. It requires a reasonable store of situation-based knowledge and more than the usual degree of insight. In particular, the major issues which make evaluation difficult and with which the analyst must come to grips are these:

▼ Each business strategy is unique. For example, one paper manufacturer might rely on its vast timber holdings to weather almost any storm while another might place primary reliance in modern machinery and an extensive distribution system. Neither strategy is "wrong" nor "right" in any absolute sense; both may be right or wrong for the firms in question. Strategy evaluation must, then, rest on a type of situational logic that does not focus on "one best way" but which can be tailored to each problem as it is faced.
▼ Strategy is centrally concerned with the selection of goals and objectives. Many people, including seasoned executives, find it much easier to set or try to achieve goals than to evaluate them. In part this is a consequence of training in problem solving rather than in problem structuring. It also arises out of a tendency to confuse values, which are fundamental expressions of human personality, with objectives, which are devices for lending coherence to action.
▼ Formal systems of strategic review, while appealing in principal, can create explosive conflict situations. Not only are there serious questions as to who is qualified to give an objective evaluation, the whole idea of strategy evaluation implies management by "much more than results" and runs counter to much of currently popular management philosophy.

The General Principles of Strategy Evaluation

The term "strategy" has been so widely used for different purposes that it has lost any clearly defined meaning. For our purposes a strategy is a set of objectives, policies, and plans that, taken together, define the scope of the enterprise and its approach to survival and success. Alternatively, we could say that the particular policies, plans, and objectives of a business express its strategy for coping with a complex competitive environment.

One of the fundamental tenets of science is that a theory can never be proven to be absolutely true. A theory can, however, be declared absolutely false if it fails to stand up to testing. Similarly, it is impossible to demonstrate conclusively that a particular business strategy is optimal or even to guarantee that it will work. One can, nevertheless, test it for critical flaws. Of the many tests which could be justifiably applied to a business strategy, most will fit within one of these broad criteria:

▼ *Consistency*: The strategy must not present mutually inconsistent goals and policies.
▼ *Consonance*: The strategy must represent an adaptive response to the external environment and to the critical changes occurring within it.
▼ *Advantage*: The strategy must provide for the creation and/or maintenance of a competitive advantage in the selected area of activity.

▼ *Feasibility*: The strategy must neither overtax available resources nor create unsolvable sub problems.

A strategy that fails to meet one or more of these criteria is strongly suspect. It fails to perform at least one of the key functions that are necessary for the survival of the business. Experience within a particular industry or other setting will permit the analyst to sharpen these criteria and add others that are appropriate to the situation at hand.

CONSISTENCY

Gross inconsistency within a strategy seems unlikely until it is realized that many strategies have not been explicitly formulated but have evolved over time in an ad hoc fashion. Even strategies that are the result of formal procedures may easily contain compromise arrangements between opposing power groups.

Inconsistency in strategy is not simply a flaw in logic. A key function of strategy is to provide coherence to organizational action. A clear and explicit concept of strategy can foster a climate of tacit coordination that is more efficient than most administrative mechanisms. Many high-technology firms, for example, face a basic strategic choice between offering high-cost products with high custom-engineering content and lower-cost products that are more standardized and sold at higher volume. If senior management does not enunciate a clear consistent sense of where the corporation stands on these issues, there will be continuing conflict between sales, design, engineering, and manufacturing people. A clear consistent strategy, by contrast, allows a sales engineer to negotiate a contract with a minimum of coordination—the trade-offs are an explicit part of the firm's posture.

Organizational conflict and interdepartmental bickering are often symptoms of a managerial disorder but may also indicate problems of strategic inconsistency. Here are some indicators that can help sort out these two different problems:

▼ If problems in coordination and planning continue despite changes in personnel and tend to be issue- rather than people-based, they are probably due to inconsistencies in strategy.

▼ If success for one organizational department means, or is interpreted to mean, failure for another department, either the basic objective structure is inconsistent or the organizational structure is wastefully duplicative.

▼ If, despite attempts to delegate authority, operating problems continue to be brought to the top for the resolution of policy issues, the basic strategy is probably inconsistent.

A final type of consistency that must be sought in strategy is between organizational objectives and the values of the management group. Inconsistency in this area is more of a problem in strategy formulation than in the evaluation of a strategy that has already been implemented. It can still arise, however, if the future direction of the business requires changes that conflict with managerial values. The most frequent source of such conflict is growth. As a business expands beyond the scale that allows an easy informal method of operation, many executives experience a sharp sense of loss. While growth can of course be curtailed, it often will require special attention to a firm's competitive position if survival without growth is desired. The same basic issues arise when other types of personal or social values come into conflict with existing or apparently necessary policies: the resolution of the conflict will normally require an adjustment in the competitive strategy.

CONSONANCE

The way in which a business relates to its environment has two aspects: the business must both match and be adapted to its environment and it must at the same time compete with other firms that are also trying to adapt. This dual character of the relationship between the firm and its environment has its analog in two different aspects of strategic choice and two different methods of strategy evaluation.

The first aspect of fit deals with the basic mission or scope of the business and the second with its special competitive position or "edge." Analysis of the first is normally done by looking at changing economic and social conditions over time. Analysis of the second, by contrast, typically focuses on the differences across firms at a given time. We call the first the *generic* aspect of strategy and the second *competitive* strategy. Generic strategy deals with the creation of social value—with the question of whether the products and services being created are worth more than their cost. Competitive strategy, by contrast, deals with the firm's need to capture some of the social value as profit. Exhibit 1 summarizes the differences between these concepts.

The notion of consonance, or matching, therefore, invites a focus on generic strategy. The role of the evaluator in this case is to examine the basic pattern of economic relationships that characterize the business and determine whether or not sufficient value is being created to sustain the strategy. Most macroanalysis of changing economic conditions is oriented toward the formulation or evaluation of generic strategies. For example, a planning department forecasts that within six years flat-panel liquid crystal displays will replace CRT-based video displays in computers. The basic message here to makers of CRT-based video displays is that their generic strategies are becoming obsolete. Note that the threat in this case is not to a particular firm, competitive position, or individual approach to the marketplace but to the basic generic mission.

One major difficulty in evaluating consonance is that most of the critical threats to a business are those which come from without, threatening an entire group of firms. Management, however, is often so engrossed in competitive thinking that such threats are only recognized after the damage has reached considerable proportions.

Another difficulty in appraising the fit between a firm's mission and the environment is that trend analysis does not normally reveal the most critical changes—they are the result of interactions among trends. The supermarket, for example, comes into being only when home refrigeration and the widespread use of automobiles allow shoppers to buy in significantly larger volumes. The supermarket, the automobile, and the move to suburbia together form the nexus which gives rise to shopping centers. These, in turn, change the nature of retailing and, together with the decline of urban centers, create new forms of enterprise, such as the suburban film theater with four screens. Thus, while gross economic or demographic trends might appear steady for many years, there are waves of change going on at the institutional level.

EXHIBIT 1
Generic versus Competitive Strategy

	GENERIC STRATEGY	COMPETITIVE STRATEGY
Value Issue	Social value	Corporate value
Value Constraint	Customer value > Cost	Price > Cost
Success Indicator	Sales growth	Increased corporate worth
Basic Strategic Task	Adapting to change	Innovating, impeding imitation, deterring rivals
How Strategy Is Expressed	Product-market definition	Advantage, position, and policies supporting them
Basic Approach to Analysis	Study of an industry over time	Comparison across rivals

The key to evaluating consonance is an understanding of why the business, as it currently stands, exists at all and how it assumed its current pattern. Once the analyst obtains a good grasp of the basic economic foundation that supports and defines the business, it is possible to study the consequences of key trends and changes. Without such an understanding, there is no good way of deciding what kinds of changes are most crucial and the analyst can be quickly overwhelmed with data.

ADVANTAGE

It is no exaggeration to say that competitive strategy is the art of creating or exploiting those advantages that are most telling, enduring, and most difficult to duplicate.

Competitive strategy, in contrast with generic strategy, focuses on the differences among firms rather than their common missions. The problem it addresses is not so much "how can this function be performed" but "how can we perform it either better than, or at least instead of, our rivals?" The chain supermarket, for example, represents a successful generic strategy. As a way of doing business, of organizing economic transactions, it has replaced almost all the smaller owner-managed food shops of an earlier era. Yet a potential or actual participant in the retail food business must go beyond this generic strategy and find a way of competing in this business. As another illustration, IBM's early success in the PC industry was generic—other firms soon copied the basic product concept. Once this happened, IBM had to try to either forge a strong competitive strategy in this area or seek a different type of competitive arena.

Competitive advantages can normally be traced to one of three roots:

▼ Superior skills

▼ Superior resources

▼ Superior position

In examining a potential advantage, the critical question is "What sustains this advantage, keeping competitors from imitating or replicating it?" A firm's skills can be a source of advantage if they are based on its own history of learning-by-doing and if they are rooted in the coordinated behavior of many people. By contrast, skills that are based on generally understood scientific principles, on training that can be purchased by competitors, or which can be analyzed and replicated by others are not sources of sustained advantage.

The *skills* which compose advantages are usually organizational, rather than individual, skills. They involve the adept coordination or collaboration of individual specialists and are built through the interplay of investment, work, and learning. Unlike physical assets, skills are enhanced by their use. Skills that are not continually used and improved will atrophy.

Resources include patents, trademark rights, specialized physical assets, and the firm's working relationships with suppliers and distribution channels. In addition, a firm's reputation with its employees, suppliers, and customers is a resource. Resources that constitute advantages are specialized to the firm, are built up slowly over time through the accumulated exercise of superior skills, or are obtained through being an insightful first mover, or by just plain luck. For example, Nucor's special skills in mini-mill construction are embodied in superior physical plants. Goldman Sachs' reputation as the premier U.S. investment banking house has been built up over many years and is now a major resource in its own right.

A firm's *position* consists of the products or services it provides, the market segments it sells to, and the degree to which it is isolated from direct competition. In general, the best positions involve supplying very uniquely valuable products to price insensitive buyers, whereas poor positions involve being one of many firms supplying marginally valuable products to very well informed, price sensitive buyers.

Positional advantage can be gained by foresight, superior skill and/or resources, or just plain luck. Once gained, a good position is defensible. This means that it (1) returns enough value to warrant its continued maintenance and (2) would be so costly to capture that rivals are deterred from full-scale attacks on the core of the business. Position, it must be noted, tends to be self-sustaining as long as the basic environmental factors that underlie it remain stable. Thus, entrenched firms can be almost impossible to unseat, even if their raw skill levels are only average. And when a shifting environment allows position to be gained by a new entrant or innovator, the results can be spectacular.

Positional advantages are of two types: (1) first mover advantages and (2) reinforcers. The most basic *first mover advantage* occurs when the minimum scale to be efficient requires a large (sunk) investment relative to the market. Thus, the first firm to open a large discount retail store in a rural area precludes, through its relative scale, close followers. More subtle first mover advantages occur when standardization effects "lock-in" customers to the first mover's product (e.g., Lotus 1-2-3). Buyer learning and related phenomena can increase the buyer's switching costs, protecting an incumbent's customer base from attack. Frequent flyer programs are aimed in this direction. First movers may also gain advantages in building distribution channels, in tying up specialized suppliers, or in gaining the attention of customers. The first product of a class to engage in mass advertising, for example, tends to impress itself more deeply in people's minds than the second, third, or fourth. In a careful study of frequently purchased consumer products, Urban et al. (1986) found that (other things being equal) the first entrant will have a market share that is $\sqrt{n}$ times as large as that of the nth entrant.

Reinforcers are policies or practices acting to strengthen or preserve a strong market position and which are easier to carry out because of the position. The idea that certain arrangements of one's resources can enhance their combined effectiveness, and perhaps even put rival forces in a state of disarray, is at the heart of the traditional notion of strategy. It is reinforcers which provide positional advantage, the strategic quality familiar to military theorists, chess players, and diplomats.

A firm with a larger market share, due to being an early mover or to having a technological lead, can typically build a more efficient production and distribution system. Competitors with less demand simply cannot cover the fixed costs of the larger more efficient facilities, so for them larger facilities are not an economic choice. In this case, scale economies are a reinforcer of market position, not the cause of market position. The firm that has a strong brand can use it as a reinforcer in the introduction of related brands. A company that sells a specialty coating to a broader variety of users may have better data on how to adapt the coating to special conditions than a competitor with more limited sales—properly used, this information is a reinforcer. A famous brand will appear on TV and in films because it is famous, another reinforcer. An example given by Porter (1985: 145) is that of Steinway and Sons, the premier U.S. maker of fine pianos. Steinway maintains a dispersed inventory of grand pianos that approved pianists are permitted to use for concerts at very low rental rates. The policy is less expensive for a leader than for a follower and helps maintain leadership.

The positive feedback provided by reinforcers is the source of the power of position-based advantages—the policies that act to enhance position may not require unusual skills; they simply work most effectively for those who are already in the position in the first place.

While it is not true that larger businesses always have the advantages, it is true that larger businesses will tend to operate in markets and use procedures that turn their size to advantage. Large national consumer-products firms, for example, will normally have an advantage over smaller regional firms in the efficient use of mass advertising, especially network TV. The larger firm will, then, tend to deal in those products where the marginal effect of advertising is most potent, while the smaller firms will seek product/market positions that exploit other types of advantage.

Other position-based advantages follow from such factors as:

▼ The ownership of special raw material sources or advantageous long-term supply contracts
▼ Being geographically located near key customers in a business involving significant fixed investment and high transport costs
▼ Being a leader in a service field that permits or requires the building of a unique experience base while serving clients
▼ Being a full-line producer in a market with heavy trade-up phenomena
▼ Having a wide reputation for providing a needed product or service trait reliably and dependably

In each case, the position permits competitive policies to be adopted that can serve to reinforce the position. Whenever this type of positive-feedback phenomena is encountered, the particular policy mix that creates it will be found to be a defensible business position. The key factors that sparked industrial success stories such as IBM and Eastman Kodak were the early and rapid domination of strong positions opened up by new technologies.

FEASIBILITY

The final broad test of strategy is its feasibility. Can the strategy be attempted within the physical, human, and financial resources available? The financial resources of a business are the easiest to quantify and are normally the first limitations against which strategy is tested. It is sometimes forgotten, however, that innovative approaches to financing expansion can both stretch the ultimate limitations and provide a competitive advantage, even if it is only temporary. Devices such as captive finance subsidiaries, sale-leaseback arrangements, and tying plant mortgages to long-term contracts have all been used effectively to help win key positions in suddenly expanding industries.

The less quantifiable but actually more rigid limitation on strategic choice is that imposed by the individual and organization capabilities that are available.

In assessing the organization's ability to carry out a strategy, it is helpful to ask three separate questions:

1. Has the organization demonstrated that it possesses the problem-solving abilities and/or special competencies required by the strategy? A strategy, as such, does not and cannot specify in detail each action that must be carried out. Its purpose is to provide structure to the general issue of the business' goals and approaches to coping with its environment. It is up to the members and departments of the organization to carry out the tasks defined by strategy. A strategy that requires tasks to be accomplished which fall outside the realm of available or easily obtainable skill and knowledge cannot be accepted. It is either unfeasible or incomplete.

2. Has the organization demonstrated the degree of coordinative and integrative skill necessary to carry out the strategy? The key tasks required of a strategy not only require specialized skill, but often make considerable demands on the organization's ability to integrate disparate activities. A manufacturer of standard office furniture may find, for example, that its primary difficulty in entering the new market for modular office systems is a lack of sophisticated interaction between its field sales offices and its manufacturing plant. Firms that hope to span national boundaries with integrated worldwide systems of production and marketing may also find that organizational process, rather than functional skill per se or isolated competitive strength, becomes the weak link in the strategic posture.

3. Does the strategy challenge and motivate key personnel and is it acceptable to those who must lend their support? The purpose of strategy is to effectively deploy the unique

and distinctive resources of an enterprise. If key managers are unmoved by a strategy, not excited by its goals or methods, or strongly support an alternative, it fails in a major way.

The Process of Strategy Evaluation

Strategy evaluation can take place as an abstract analytic task, perhaps performed by consultants. But most often it is an integral part of an organization's processes of planning, review, and control. In some organizations, evaluation is informal, only occasional, brief, and cursory. Others have created elaborate systems containing formal periodic strategy review sessions. In either case, the quality of strategy evaluation, and ultimately, the quality of corporate performance, will be determined more by the organization's capacity for self-appraisal and learning than by the particular analytic technique employed.

In their study of organizational learning, Argyris and Schon distinguish between single-loop and double-loop learning. They argue that normal organizational learning is of the feedback-control type-deviations between expected and actual performance lead to problem solving which brings the system back under control. They note that

> [Single-loop learning] is concerned primarily with effectiveness—that is, with how best to achieve existing goals and objectives and how best to keep organizational performance within the range specified by existing norms. In some cases, however, error correction requires a learning cycle in which organizational norms themselves are modified. . . . We call this sort of learning "double-loop." There is . . . a double feedback loop which connects the detection of error not only to strategies and assumptions for effective performance but to the very norms which define effective performance. [1978:20]

These ideas parallel those of Ashby, a cyberneticist. Ashby (1954) has argued that all feedback systems require more than single-loop error control for stability; they also need a way of monitoring certain critical variables and changing the system "goals" when old control methods are no longer working.

These viewpoints help to remind us that the real strategic processes in any organization are not found by looking at those things that happen to be labeled "strategic" or "long range." Rather, the real components of the strategic process are, by definition, those activities which most strongly affect the selection and modification of objectives and which influence the irreversible commitment of important resources. They also suggest that appropriate methods of strategy evaluation cannot be specified in abstract terms. Instead, an organization's approach to evaluation must fit its strategic posture and work in conjunction with its methods of planning and control.

In most firms comprehensive strategy evaluation is infrequent and, if it occurs, is normally triggered by a change in leadership or financial performance. The fact that comprehensive strategy evaluation is neither a regular event nor part of a formal system tends to be deplored by some theorists, but there are several good reasons for this state of affairs. Most obviously, any activity that becomes an annual procedure is bound to become more automatic. While evaluating strategy on an annual basis might lead to some sorts of efficiencies in data collection and analysis, it would also tend to strongly channel the types of questions asked and inhibit broad-ranging reflection.

Second, a good strategy does not need constant reformulation. It is a framework for continuing problem solving, not the problem solving itself. One senior executive expressed it this way: "If you play from strength you don't always need to be rethinking the whole plan; you can concentrate on details. So when you see us talking about slight changes in tooling, it isn't because we forgot the big picture, it's because we took care of it."

Strategy also represents a political alignment within the firm and embodies the past convictions and commitments of key executives. Comprehensive strategy evaluation is not just an analytical exercise, it calls into question this basic pattern of commitments and policies. Most organizations would be hurt rather than helped to have their mission's validity called into question on a regular basis. Zero-base budgeting, for example, was an attempt to get agencies to re-justify their existence each time a new budget is drawn up. If this were literally true, there would be little time or energy remaining for any but political activity.

Finally, there are competitive reasons for not reviewing the validity of a strategy too freely! There are a wide range of rivalrous confrontations in which it is crucial to be able to convince others that one's position, or strategy, is fixed and unshakable. Schelling's (1963) analysis of bargaining and conflict shows that a great deal of what is involved in negotiating is finding ways to bind or commit oneself convincingly. This is the principle underlying the concept of deterrence and what lies behind the union leader's tactic of claiming that while he would go along with management's desire for moderation, he cannot control the members if the less moderate demands are not met. In business strategy, such situations occur in classic oligopoly, plant-capacity duels, new-product conflicts, and other situations in which the winner may be the party whose policies are most credibly unswayable. Japanese electronics firms, for example, have gained such strong reputations as low-cost committed players that their very entry into a market has come to induce rivals to give up. If such firms had instead the reputation of continually reviewing the advisability of continuing each product, they would be much less threatening, and thus less effective, competitors. . . .

CONCLUSIONS

Strategy evaluation is the appraisal of plans and the results of plans that centrally concern or affect the basic mission of an enterprise. Its special focus is the separation between obvious current operating results and those factors which underlie success or failure in the chosen domain of activity. Its result is the rejection, modification, or ratification of existing strategies and plans. . . .

In most medium- to large-size firms, strategy evaluation is not a purely intellectual task. The issues involved are too important and too closely associated with the distribution of power and authority for either strategy formulation or evaluation to take place in an ivory tower environment. In fact, most firms rarely engage in explicit formal strategy evaluation. Rather, the evaluation of current strategy is a continuing process and one that is difficult to separate from the normal planning, reporting, control, and reward systems of the firm. From this point of view, strategy evaluation is not so much an intellectual task as it is an organizational process.

Ultimately, a firm's ability to maintain its competitive position in a world of rivalry and change may be best served by managers who can maintain a dual view of strategy and strategy evaluation—they must be willing and able to perceive the strategy within the welter of daily activity and to build and maintain structures and systems that make strategic factors the object of current activity.

▼ READING 3.3 CORE COMPETENCIES AND STRATEGIC OUTSOURCING*

by James Brian Quinn and Frederick G. Hilmer

Two new strategic approaches, when properly combined, allow managers to leverage their companies' skills and resources well beyond levels available with other strategies:

---

* Originally published as "Strategic Outsourcing," reprinted from *Sloan Management Review* (Summer 1994) by permission of the publisher. Copyright by the Sloan Management.

▼ Concentrating the firm's own resources on a set "of core competencies" where it can achieve definable preeminence and provide unique value for customers (Quinn, Doorley, Paquette 1990).

▼ Strategically outsourcing other activities—including many traditionally considered integral to any company—where the firm has neither a critical strategic need nor special capabilities (Quinn, 1992).

The benefits of successfully combining the two approaches are significant. Managers can leverage their company's resources in four ways. First, they maximize returns on internal resources by concentrating investments and energies on what the enterprise does best. Second, well developed core competencies provide formidable barriers against present and future competitors seeking to expand into the company's areas of interest thus facilitating and protecting the strategic advantages of market share. Third, perhaps the greatest leverage of all is the full utilization of external suppliers' investments, innovations, and specialized professional capabilities that would be prohibitively expensive or even impossible to duplicate internally. Fourth, in rapidly changing marketplaces and technological situations, this joint strategy decreases risks, shortens cycle times, lowers investments, and creates better responsiveness to customer needs. Two examples from our studies of Australian and U.S. companies illustrate our point:

▼ Nike, Inc., is the largest supplier of athletic shoes in the world. Yet it outsources 100% of its shoe production and manufactures only key technical components of its "Nike Air" system. Athletic footwear is technology- and fashion-intensive, requiring high flexibility at both the production and marketing levels. Nike creates maximum value by concentrating on preproduction (research and development) and post production activities (marketing, distribution and sales) linked together by perhaps the best marketing information system in the industry. Using a carefully developed, on-site "expatriate" program to coordinate its foreign-based suppliers, Nike even outsourced the advertising component of its marketing program to Weiden and Kennedy, whose creative efforts drove Nike to the top of the product recognition scale. Nike grew at a compounded 20% growth rate and earned a 31% ROE for its shareholders through most of the last decade.

▼ Knowing it could not be the best at making chips, boxes, monitors, cables, keyboards, and so on for its explosively successful Apple II, Apple Computer outsourced 70% of its manufacturing costs and components. Instead of building internal bureaucracies where it had no unique skills, Apple outsourced critical items like design (to Frogdesign), printers (to Tokyo Electric), and even key elements of marketing (to Regis McKenna, which achieved a "$100 million image" for Apple when it had only a few employees and about $1 million to spend). Apple focused its internal resources on its own Apple DOS (disk operating system) and the supporting macro software to give Apple products their unique look and feel. Its open architecture policy stimulated independent developers to write the much-needed software that gave Apple II's customers uniquely high functionality. Apple thus avoided unnecessary investments, benefited from its vendors' R&D and technical expertise, kept itself flexible to adopt new technologies as they became available, and leveraged its limited capital resources to a huge extent. Operating with an extremely flat organization, Apple enjoyed three times the capital turnover and the highest market value versus fixed investment ratio among major computer producers throughout the 1980s.

How can managers combine core competency concepts and strategic outsourcing for maximum effectiveness? To achieve benefits like Nike's or Apple's requires careful attention to several difficult issues, each of which we discuss in turn:

1. What exactly is a "core competency"? Unfortunately, most of the literature on this subject is tautological—"core" equals "key" or "critical" or "fundamental." How can man-

agers analytically select and develop the core competencies that will provide the firm's uniqueness, competitive edge, and basis of value creation for the future?

2. Granting that the competencies defining the firm and its essential reasons for existence should be kept in house, should all else be outsourced? In most cases, common sense and theory suggest a clear "no." How then can managers determine strategically, rather than in a short term or *ad hoc* fashion, which activities to maintain internally and which to outsource?

3. How can managers assess the relative risks and benefits of outsourcing in particular situations? And how can they contain critical risks—especially the potential loss of crucial skills or control over the company's future directions—when outsourcing is desirable?

Core Competency Strategies

The basic ideas behind core competencies and strategic outsourcing have been well supported by research extending over a 20-year period. In 1974, Rumelt noted that neither of the then-favored strategies—unrelated diversification or vertical integration—yielded consistently high returns. Since then, other carefully structured research has indicated the effectiveness of disaggregation strategies in many industries (Rumelt 1974; D'Aveni and Illinich 1992; Batteyri 1988). Noting the failures of many conglomerates in the 1960s and 1970s, both financial theorists and investors began to support more focused company concepts. Generally this meant "sticking to your knitting" by cutting back to fewer product lines. Unfortunately, this also meant a concomitant increase in the "systematic risk" these narrower markets represented.

However, some analysts noticed that many highly successful Japanese and American companies had very wide product lines yet were not very vertically integrated (Maloney 1992; Miles and Show 1986). Japanese companies, like Sony, Mitsubishi, Matsushita, or Yamaha, had extremely diverse product offerings, as did 3M or Hewlett Packard in the United States. Yet, they were not conglomerates in the normal sense. They were first termed "related conglomerates," redeploying certain key skills from market to market. At the same time these companies also contracted out significant support activities.

The term "core competency strategies" was later used to describe these and other less diversified strategies developed around a central set of corporate skills (Prahalad and Hamel 1990). However, there has been little theory or consistency in the literature about what "core" really means. Consequently, many executives have been understandably confused about the topic. They need not be if they think in terms of the specific skills the company has or must have to create unique value for customers. However, their analyses must go well beyond looking at traditional product or functional strategies to the fundamentals of what the company can do better than anyone else.

▼ For example, after some difficult times, it was easy enough for a "beer company" like Foster's to decide that it should not be in the finance, forest products, and pastoral businesses into which it had diversified. It has now divested these peripheral businesses and is concentrating on beer. However, even within this concept, Foster's true competencies are in brewing and marketing beer. Many of its distribution, transportation, and can production activities, for example, might actually be more effectively contracted out. Within individual functions like production, Foster's could further extend its competitive advantage by outsourcing selected activities—such as maintenance or computing—where it has no unique capabilities.

THE ESSENCE OF CORE COMPETENCIES

What then is really core? And why? The concept requires that managers think much more carefully about which of the firm's activities really do—or could—create unique value and what activities could more effectively be bought externally. Careful study of both successful and unsuccessful corporate examples suggests that effective core competencies are:

1. SKILL OR KNOWLEDGE SETS, NOT PRODUCTS OR FUNCTIONS. Executives need to look beyond the company's products to the intellectual skills or management systems that actually create a maintainable competitive edge. Products, even those with valuable legal protection, can be too easily back engineered, duplicated, or replaced by substitutes. Nor is a competency typically one of the traditional functions such as production, engineering, sales, or finance around which organizations were formed in the past. Instead, competencies tend to be sets of skills which cut across traditional functions. This interaction allows the organization to consistently perform an activity better than functional competitors and to continually improve on the activity as markets, technology and competition evolve. Competencies thus involve activities such as product or service design, technology creation, customer service, or logistics—that tend to be based on knowledge rather than ownership of assets or intellectual property per se. Knowledge-based activities generate most of the value in services and manufacturing. In services, which account for 79% of all jobs and 76% of all value added in the United States, intellectual inputs create virtually all of the value added. Banking, financial services, advertising, consulting, accounting, retailing, wholesaling, education, entertainment, communications, and health care are clear examples. In manufacturing, knowledge-based activities—like R&D, product design, process design, logistics, marketing research, marketing, advertising, distribution, and customer service—also dominate the value-added chain of most companies (see Figure 1). [Editors note: See Chapter 4 of this text for discussion of the value chain.]

2. FLEXIBLE, LONG-TERM PLATFORMS—CAPABLE OF ADAPTATION OR EVOLUTION. Too many companies try to focus on the narrow areas where they currently excel, usually on some product-oriented skills. The real challenge is to consciously build dominating skills in areas that the customer will continue to value over time, as Motorola is doing with its focus on "superior quality, portable communications." The uniqueness of Toys "R" Us lies in its powerful information and distribution systems for toys; and that of State Street Boston in its developing advanced information and management systems for large custodial accounts. Problems occur when managers choose to concentrate too narrowly on products (as computer companies did on hardware) or too inflexibly on formats and skills that no longer match customer needs (as FotoMat and numerous department stores did). Flexible skill sets and constant, conscious reassessment of trends are hallmarks of successful core competency strategies.

3. LIMITED IN NUMBER. Most companies target two or three (not one or more than five) activities in the value chain most critical to future success. For example, 3M concentrates on four critical technologies in great depth and supports these with a peerless innovative system. As work becomes more complex, and the opportunities to excel in many detailed activities proliferate, managers find they cannot be best in every activity in the value chain. As they go beyond three to five activities or skill sets, they are unable to match the performance of their more focused competitors or suppliers. Each skill set requires intensity and management dedication that cannot tolerate dilution. It is hard to imagine Microsoft's top managers taking their enthusiasm and skills in software into, say, chip design or even large-

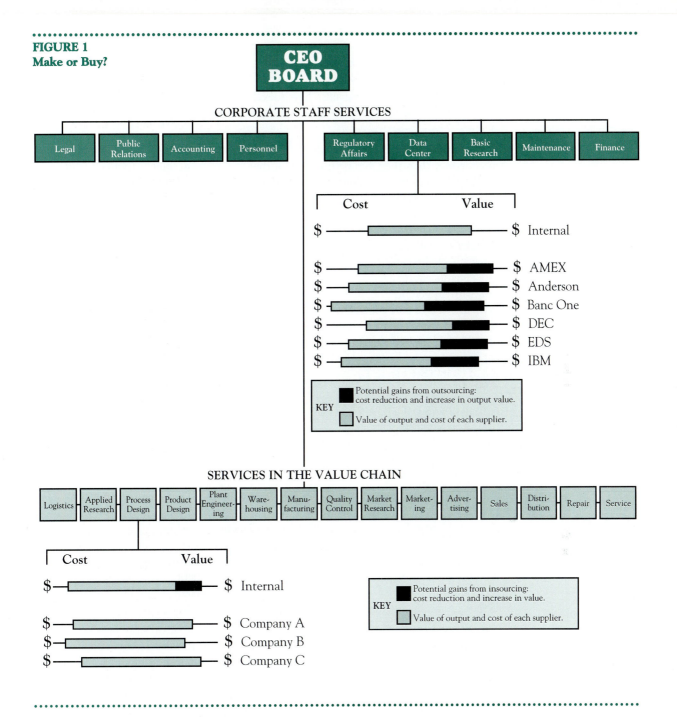

FIGURE 1
Make or Buy?

CEO BOARD

CORPORATE STAFF SERVICES

| Legal | Public Relations | Accounting | Personnel | | Regulatory Affairs | Data Center | Basic Research | Maintenance | Finance |

Cost   Value

$ —— $ Internal

$ —— $ AMEX
$ —— $ Anderson
$ —— $ Banc One
$ —— $ DEC
$ —— $ EDS
$ —— $ IBM

KEY
■ Potential gains from outsourcing: cost reduction and increase in output value.
▢ Value of output and cost of each supplier.

SERVICES IN THE VALUE CHAIN

| Logistics | Applied Research | Process Design | Product Design | Plant Engineering | Ware-housing | Manu-facturing | Quality Control | Market Research | Market-ing | Adver-tising | Sales | Distri-bution | Repair | Service |

Cost   Value

$ —— $ Internal

$ —— $ Company A
$ —— $ Company B
$ —— $ Company C

KEY
■ Potential gains from insourcing: cost reduction and increase in value.
▢ Value of output and cost of each supplier.

scale training in software usage. And if they did, what would be the cost of their loss of attention to software development?

4. UNIQUE SOURCES OF LEVERAGE IN THE VALUE CHAIN. Effective strategies seek out places where there are market imperfections or knowledge gaps that the company is uniquely qualified to fill and where investments in intellectual resources can be highly leveraged. Raychem and Intel concentrate on depth-in-design and on highly specialized test-feedback systems supporting carefully selected knowledge-based products—not on volume production of standardized products—to jump over the experience curve advantages of their larger competitors. Morgan Stanley, through its TAPS system and Bear Stearns, through its integrated bond-trading programs, have developed in-depth knowledge bases creating unique intellectual advantages in their highly competitive markets.

5. AREAS WHERE THE COMPANY CAN DOMINATE. Companies make consistently more money than their competitors only if they can perform some activities—which are important to customers—more effectively than anyone else. True focus in strategy means the capacity to bring more power to bear on a selected sector than any competitior can. Once, this meant owning and managing all the elements in the value chain supporting a specific product or service in a selected market position. Today, however, some outside supplier, by specializing on the specific skills and technologies underlying a single element in the value chain, can become more proficient at that activity than virtually any company spreading its efforts over the whole value chain. In essence, each company is in competition with all potential suppliers of each activity in its value chain. Hence, it must benchmark its selected core competencies against all other potential suppliers of that activity and continue to build these core capabilities until it is demonstrably best. Thus the basic nature of strategic analysis changes from an industry analysis perspective to a horizontal analysis of capabilities across *all potential providers of an activity* regardless of which industry the provider might be in. (See Figure 1.)

6. ELEMENTS IMPORTANT TO CUSTOMERS IN THE LONG RUN. At least one of the firm's core competencies should normally relate directly to understanding and serving its customers. High tech companies with the world's best state-of-the-art technology often fail when they ignore this caveat. . . .

7. EMBEDDED IN THE ORGANIZATION'S SYSTEMS. Maintaining competencies cannot depend on one or two talented stars—such as Steven Jobs and Stephen Wozniak at Apple or Herbert Boyer and Arthur D. Riggs at Genentech—whose departure could destroy a company's success. Instead the firm must convert these into a corporate reputation or culture that outlives the stars. Especially when a strategy is heavily dependent on creativity, personal dedication, and initiative, or on attracting top-flight professionals, core competency must be captured within the company's systems—broadly defined to include its values, organization structures, and management systems. . . (Turner and Crawford 1992).

PREEMINENCE: THE KEY STRATEGIC BARRIER. For its selected core competencies, the company must ensure that it maintains absolute preeminence. It may also need to surround these core competencies with defensive positions, both upstream and downstream. In some cases, it may have to perform some activities where it is not best-in-world, just to keep existing or potential competitors from learning, taking over, eroding, or bypassing elements of its special competencies. In fact, managers should consciously develop their core competencies to strategically block competitors and avoid outsourcing these or giving suppliers access to the knowledge bases or skills critical to their core competencies. Honda, for example, does all its engine R&D in-house and makes all the critical parts for its small motor design core competency in closely controlled facilities in Japan. It will consider outsourcing any other noncritical elements in its products, but builds a careful strategic block around this most essential element for all its businesses.

Most important, as a company's preeminence in selected fields grows, its knowledge-based core competencies become ever harder to overtake. Knowledge bases tend to grow exponentially in value with investment and experience. Intellectual leadership tends to attract the most talented people, who then work on and solve the most interesting problems. The combination in turn creates higher returns and attracts the next round of outstanding talent. . . .

Some executives regard core activities as those the company is continuously engaged in, while peripheral activities are those which are intermittent and therefore can be outsourced. From the viewpoint of outsourcing strategy, however, core competencies are the activities that offer long-term competitive advantage and thus must be rigidly controlled and protected. Peripheral activities are those not critical to the company's competitive edge.

Strategic Outsourcing

If supplier markets were totally reliable and efficient, rational companies would outsource everything except those special activities where they could achieve a unique competitive edge, i.e., their core competencies. Unfortunately, most supplier markets are imperfect and do entail some risks for both buyer and seller with respect to price, quality, time, or other key terms. Moreover, outsourcing entails unique transaction costs—searching, contracting, controlling, and recontracting—that at times may exceed the transaction costs of having the activity directly under management's in-house control.

To address these difficulties managers must answer three key questions about any activity considered for outsourcing. First, what is the potential for obtaining competitive advantage in this activity, taking account of transaction costs? Second, what is the potential vulnerability that could arise from market failure if the activity is outsourced? These two factors can be arrayed in a simple matrix (see Figure 2). Third, what can we do to alleviate our vulnerability by structuring arrangements with suppliers to provide appropriate controls yet provide for necessary flexibilities in demand?

The two extremes on the matrix are relatively straightforward. When the potentials for both competitive edge and strategic vulnerability are high, the company needs a high degree of control, usually entailing production internally, through joint ownership arrangements, or through tight long-term contracts (explicit or implicit). . . .

At each intervening point the question is not just whether to make or buy, but how to implement a desired balance between independence and incentives for the supplier versus control and security for the buyer. Most companies will benefit by extending outsourcing first in less critical areas— or parts of activities like payroll, rather than all of accounting. As they gain experience, they may increase profit opportunities greatly by outsourcing more critical activities to noncompeting firms that can perform them more effectively. In a few cases, more complex alliances with competitors may be essential to garner specialized skills that cannot be obtained in other ways. At each level, the company must isolate and rigorously control strategically critical relationships between its suppliers and its customers.

COMPETITIVE EDGE

The key strategic issue in insourcing versus outsourcing is whether a company can achieve a maintainable competitive edge by performing an activity internally—usually cheaper, better, in a more timely fashion, or with some unique capability—on a continuing basis. If one or more of these dimensions is critical to the customer and if the potential buyer can perform that function uniquely well, the activity should normally be kept in-house. Many companies unfortunately assume that because they have performed an activity internally, or because it seems integral to their business, the activity should be insourced. However, on closer investigation and with careful benchmarking, its internal capabilities may turn out

FIGURE 2
Competitive Advantage
vs. Strategic Vulnerability

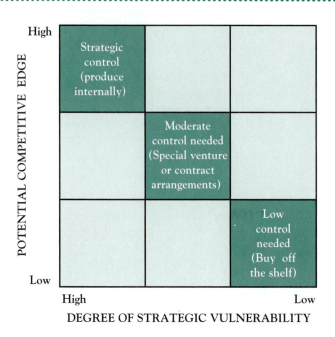

to be significantly below those of best-in-world suppliers. For example, Ford Motor Company found that many of its internal suppliers' quality practices and costs were nowhere near those of external suppliers when it began its famous "best in class" worldwide benchmarking studies on 400 subassemblies for the new Taurus-Sable line. . . . In interviews with top operating managers in both service and manufacturing companies concerning benchmarking, we frequently encountered a paraphrase of, "We thought we were best in the world at many activities. But when we benchmarked against the best external suppliers, we found we were not even up to the worst of the benchmarking cases."

TRANSACTION COSTS

In all calculations, analysts must include both internal transaction costs as well as those associated with external sourcing. If the company is to produce the item or service internally on a long-term basis, it must be prepared to back up its decision with continuing R&D, personnel development, and infrastructure investments which at least match those of the best external supplier. Otherwise, it will lose its competitive edge over time. Managers often tend to overlook such backup costs, as well as the losses from laggard innovation and nonresponsiveness from internal groups who know they have a guaranteed market. Finally, there are the headquarters and support costs of constantly managing the insourced activity. One of the great gains of outsourcing is the decrease in executive time for managing peripheral activities—freeing top management to focus more on the core of its business.

Various studies have shown that, when these internal transaction costs are thoroughly analyzed, they can be extremely high (D'Aveni and Ravenscraft, 1994). Since it is easier to identify the explicit transaction costs of dealing with external suppliers, these generally tend to be included in analyses. Harder-to-identify internal transaction costs are often not included, thus biasing results.

VULNERABILITY

When there are a large number of suppliers (with adequate but not dominating scale) and mature market standards and terms, a potential buyer is unlikely to be more efficient than the best available supplier. If, on the other hand, there is not sufficient depth in the market, overly powerful suppliers can hold the company to ransom. Conversely, if the number of suppliers is limited or individual suppliers are too weak, they may be unable to supply innovative products or services as well as a much larger buyer could by performing the activity in house. . . .

Another form of vulnerability is a lack of information available in the marketplace or from individual suppliers. For example, a supplier may secretly expect labour disruptions or raw material problems but hide these until it is too late for the customer to go elsewhere. A related problem occurs when a supplier has unique information capabilities; for example, large wholesalers or retailers, market research firms, software companies, or legal specialists may have information or fact-gathering systems that would be impossible for the buyer or any other single supplier to reproduce efficiently. Such suppliers may be able to charge essentially monopoly prices, but this could still be less costly than reproducing the service internally. In other cases, there may be many capable suppliers (e.g., of R&D or software), but the costs of adequately monitoring progress on the suppliers' premises might make outsourcing prohibitive. . . .

DEGREE OF SOURCING CONTROL

There is a full spectrum of outsourcing arrangements, depending on the buyer's control versus flexibility needs. (See Figure 3.) The issue is less whether to make or buy an activity than it is how to structure internal versus external sourcing on an optimal basis. Companies are outsourcing much more of what used to be considered either integral elements of their value chains or necessary staff activities. Because of greater complexity, higher specialization, and new technological capabilities, outside suppliers can now perform many such activities at lower cost and with higher value added than a fully integrated buying company can. . . .

STRATEGIC RISKS

Outsourcing complete or partial activities creates great opportunities but also new types of risks. Managements' main strategic concerns are: (1) loss of critical skills or developing the wrong skills, (2) loss of cross-functional skills, and (3) loss of control over a supplier.

1. LOSS OF CRITICAL SKILLS OR DEVELOPING THE WRONG SKILLS. Unfortunately, many U.S. companies have outsourced manufacture of what, at the time, seemed to be only minor componentry, like semiconductor chips or a bicycle frame, and taught suppliers how to build them to needed quality standards. Later these companies found their suppliers were unable or unwilling to supply the company as required. By then, the buying company had lost the skills it needed to reenter manufacture and could not prevent its suppliers from either assisting competitors or entering downstream markets on their own. In some cases, by outsourcing a key component, the company had lost its own strategic flexibility to introduce new designs when it wanted, rather than when the vendor permitted it. . . .

2. LOSS OF CROSS-FUNCTIONAL SKILLS. The interactions among skilled people in different functional activities often develop unexpected new insights or solutions. Companies fear outsourcing will make such cross-functional serendipity less likely. However, if the company consciously ensures that its remaining employees interact constantly and closely

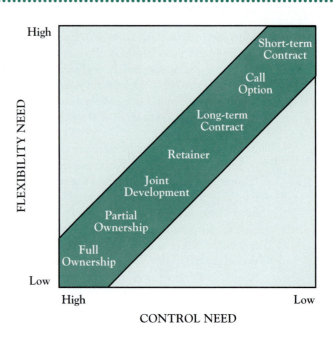

FIGURE 3
Potential Contract Relationships

with its outsourced experts, its employees' knowledge base can be much higher than if production were in-house, and the creativity benefits can be even greater.

3. LOSS OF CONTROL OVER A SUPPLIER. Real problems can occur when the supplier's priorities do not match the buyer's. The most successful outsourcers find it absolutely essential to have both close personal contact and rapport at the floor level and political clout and understanding with the supplier's top management. For this reason, Nike both has full-time "production expatriates" on its suppliers' premises and frequently brings the suppliers' top people to Beaverton, Oregon, to exchange details about future capabilities and prospects. . . .

NEW MANAGEMENT APPROACHES

Most large companies have already developed very sophisticated techniques for traditional purchasing of parts, subassemblies, supplies, equipment, construction, or standard services. And models from the natural resources, real estate/construction, and finance/insurance industries—where joint ventures have been common for years—can provide useful guides for more complex partnering relationships. In addition to seeking out these experiences, the main management adjustments for most companies are those needed for coping with the increased scale, diversity, and service-oriented nature of the activities potentially outsourced. These center on (1) a much more professional and highly-trained purchasing and contract management group (as compared with the lowly purchasing groups of the past); and (2) a greatly enhanced logistics-information system (to track and evaluate vendors, coordinate transportation activities, and manage service transactions and materials movements from vendors' hands through to the customers'). . . .

Conclusion

Most companies can substantially leverage their resources through strategic outsourcing by: (1) developing a few well-selected core competencies of significance to customers and in which the company can be best-in-world; (2) focusing investment and management attention on them; and (3) strategically outsourcing many other activities where it cannot be or need not be best. There are always some inherent risks in outsourcing, but there are also risks and costs of insourcing. When approached with a genuinely strategic framework, using the variety of outsourcing options available and analyzing the strategic issues developed here, companies can overcome many of the costs and risks. When intelligently combined, core competency and extensive outsourcing strategies provide improved returns on capital, lowered risk, greater flexibility, and better responsiveness to customer needs at lower costs.

STRATEGY ANALYSIS

As noted in the introduction to Chapter 3, there is a second prescriptive view of the way strategy should be formulated, which developed in the 1980s. Its contribution is less as a new conceptual model—in fact it embraces most of the premises of the traditional model—than in carefully structuring the kinds of formal analyses that should be undertaken to develop a successful strategy. One outcome of this more formal approach is that many of its adherents came to see strategies as fitting certain "generic" classifications—not being created so much individually as selected from a limited set of options based on systematic study of the firm and the industry conditions it faces. This approach has proved to be powerful and useful in specific situations.

A leader of this approach is Michael Porter of the Harvard Business School, who studied at the doctoral level in Harvard's economics department. By building intellectual bridges between the fields of management policy and industrial organization—the latter a branch of economics concerned with the performance of industries as a function of their competitive characteristics—Porter elaborated on the earlier views of Andrews, Ansoff, Newman, and the like.

We open this chapter with Porter's basic model of competitive and industry analysis, probably his best-known work in the area of strategy analysis. As presented in this award-winning *Harvard Business Review* article, it proposes a framework of five forces which in his view define the basic posture of competition in an industry—the bargaining power of existing suppliers and buyers, the threat of substitutes and new entrants, and the intensity of existing rivalry. The model is a powerful one, as you shall see in references to it in subsequent readings as well as in applications of it in the case studies.

Porter is known for several other frameworks as well: for example, his concept of "generic strategies," of which he argues there are three in particular—cost leadership, differentiation, and focus (or scope); his discussion of the "value chain" as a way of decomposing the activities of a business to apply strategy analyses of various kinds; his notion of strategic groups, where firms with like sets of strategies compete in subsegments of an industry; and his concept of "generic industry environments," such as "fragmented" or "mature," which reflect similar characteristics.

We shall hear from Porter again on the last of these in our context section. But his three generic strategies as well as his value chain concept will be summarized in a second reading in this chapter, by Mintzberg, that seeks to present a more comprehensive picture of the various strategies that firms commonly pursue at the so-called "business" level—that is for their individual businesses (as opposed to the "corporate" level, which concerns itself with strategies for the set of businesses a "diversified" company operates in; a companion reading in Chapter 13 discusses corporate-level generic strategies). These generic business strategies are described at three levels—strategies concerned with locating the core business, with distinguishing the core business by means of "differentiation" and "scope," and with elaborating the core business.

In some ways, the strategy analysis frameworks of this chapter parallel those of Andrews. But these authors add a number of new systematic and analytical elements, often creating a result that is less broad and more focused. You should consider which approach will be more effective, at least under specific circumstances.

The New Steel Corporation, Intel Corporation, Apple Computer 1992, and E & J Gallo Winery cases offer excellent opportunities for industry analysis. The Honda Motor Company 1994, Ford: Team Taurus, and Microsoft Corporation (A) cases present powerful vehicles for competitive analysis. And the Exxon Corporation 1994, The New York Times Company, Ford: Team Taurus, Honda Motor Company 1994, The IBM 360 Decision, Matsushita Electric Industrial Company 1994, Sony Corporation: Innovation System, and Genentech, Inc. (B) cases raise many issues about the value chain and outsourcing strategy concepts. We hope these cases will teach you how to conduct such analyses but at the same time will create some doubts about any specific analytical framework's capacity to capture the full richness of a major corporation's total strategy.

▼ READING 4.1 HOW COMPETITIVE FORCES SHAPE STRATEGY*

by Michael E. Porter

The essence of strategy formulation is coping with competition. Yet it is easy to view competition too narrowly and too pessimistically. While one sometimes hears executives complaining to the contrary, intense competition in an industry is neither coincidence nor bad luck.

Moreover, in the fight for market share, competition is not manifested only in the other players. Rather, competition in an industry is rooted in its underlying economics, and competitive forces exist that go well beyond the established combatants in a particular industry. Customers, suppliers, potential entrants, and substitute products are all competitors that may be more or less prominent or active depending on the industry.

The state of competition in an industry depends on five basic forces, which are diagrammed in Figure 1. The collective strength of these forces determines the ultimate profit potential of an industry. It ranges from *intense* in industries like tires, metal cans, and steel, where no company earns spectacular returns on investment, to *mild* in industries like oil field services and equipment, soft drinks, and toiletries, where there is room for quite high returns.

In the economists' "perfectly competitive" industry, jockeying for position is unbridled and entry to the industry very easy. This kind of industry structure, of course, offers the worst prospect for long-run profitability. The weaker the forces collectively, however, the greater the opportunity for superior performance.

Whatever their collective strength, the corporate strategist's goal is to find a position in the industry where his or her company can best defend itself against these forces or can influence them in its favor. The collective strength of the forces may be painfully apparent to all the antagonists; but to cope with them, the strategist must delve below the surface and analyze the sources of each. For example, what makes the industry vulnerable to entry? What determines the bargaining power of suppliers?

Knowledge of these underlying sources of competitive pressure provides the groundwork for a strategic agenda of action. They highlight the critical strengths and weaknesses of the company, animate the positioning of the company in its industry, clarify the areas where strategic changes may yield the greatest payoff, and highlight the places where industry trends promise to hold the greatest significance as either opportunities or threats. Understanding these sources also proves to be of help in considering areas for diversification.

---

* Originally published in the *Harvard Business Review,* (March–April, 1979) and winner of the McKinsey prize for the best article in the *Review* in 1979. Copyright ©1979 by the President and Fellows of Harvard College; all rights reserved. Reprinted with deletions by permission of the *Harvard Business Review.*

FIGURE 1
Elements of Industry Structure

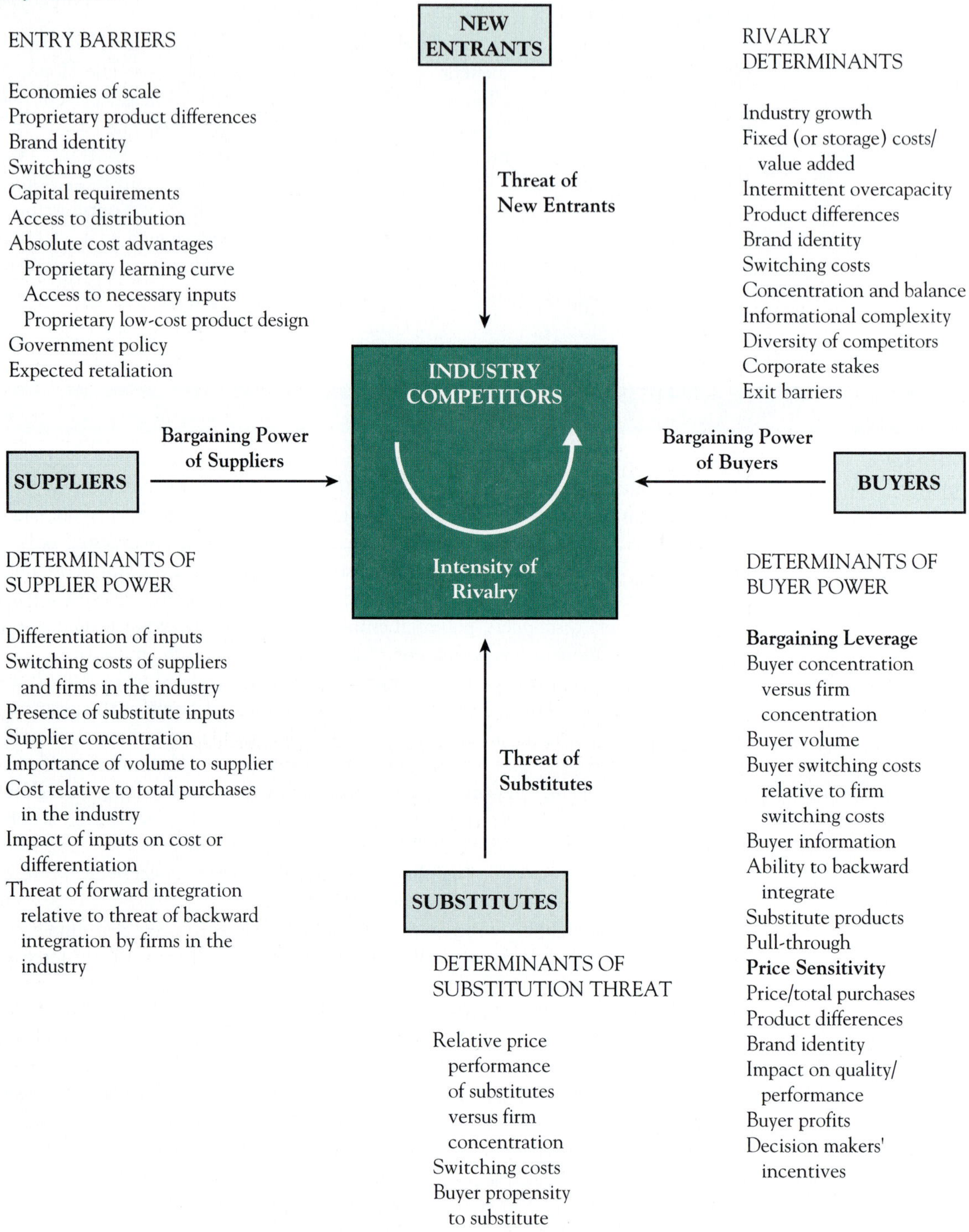

ENTRY BARRIERS
Economies of scale
Proprietary product differences
Brand identity
Switching costs
Capital requirements
Access to distribution
Absolute cost advantages
Proprietary learning curve
Access to necessary inputs
Proprietary low-cost product design
Government policy
Expected retaliation
NEW ENTRANTS
Threat of New Entrants
RIVALRY DETERMINANTS
Industry growth
Fixed (or storage) costs/ value added
Intermittent overcapacity
Product differences
Brand identity
Switching costs
Concentration and balance
Informational complexity
Diversity of competitors
Corporate stakes
Exit barriers
SUPPLIERS
Bargaining Power of Suppliers
INDUSTRY COMPETITORS
Intensity of Rivalry
Bargaining Power of Buyers
BUYERS
DETERMINANTS OF SUPPLIER POWER
Differentiation of inputs
Switching costs of suppliers and firms in the industry
Presence of substitute inputs
Supplier concentration
Importance of volume to supplier
Cost relative to total purchases in the industry
Impact of inputs on cost or differentiation
Threat of forward integration relative to threat of backward integration by firms in the industry
Threat of Substitutes
SUBSTITUTES
DETERMINANTS OF SUBSTITUTION THREAT
Relative price performance of substitutes versus firm concentration
Switching costs
Buyer propensity to substitute
DETERMINANTS OF BUYER POWER
Bargaining Leverage
Buyer concentration versus firm concentration
Buyer volume
Buyer switching costs relative to firm switching costs
Buyer information
Ability to backward integrate
Substitute products
Pull-through
Price Sensitivity
Price/total purchases
Product differences
Brand identity
Impact on quality/ performance
Buyer profits
Decision makers' incentives

Used with permission of the The Free Press, a Division of Macmillan, Inc., from *Competitive Strategy: Techniques for Analyzing Industries and Competitors* by Michael E. Porter. Copyright © 1980 by The Free Press. [used in place of article's Figure 1 as it contains more detail]

Contending Forces

The strongest competitive force or forces determine the profitability of an industry and so are of greatest importance in strategy formulation. For example, even a company with a strong position in an industry unthreatened by potential entrants will earn low returns if it faces a superior or lower-cost substitute product—as the leading manufacturers of vacuum tubes and coffee percolators have learned to their sorrow. In such a situation, coping with the substitute product becomes the number one strategic priority.

Different forces take on prominence, of course, in shaping competition in each industry. In the oceangoing tanker industry the key force is probably the buyers (the major oil companies), while in tires it is powerful OEM buyers coupled with tough competitors. In the steel industry the key forces are foreign competitors and substitute materials.

Every industry has an underlying structure, or a set of fundamental economic and technical characteristics, that gives rise to these competitive forces. The strategist, wanting to position his company to cope best with its industry environment or to influence that environment in the company's favor, must learn what makes the environment tick.

This view of competition pertains equally to industries dealing in services and to those selling products. To avoid monotony in this article, I refer to both products and services as "products." The same general principles apply to all types of business.

A few characteristics are critical to the strength of each competitive force. I shall discuss them in this section.

THREAT OF ENTRY

New entrants to an industry bring new capacity, the desire to gain market share, and often substantial resources. Companies diversifying through acquisition into the industry from other markets often leverage their resources to cause a shakeup, as Philip Morris did with Miller beer.

The seriousness of the threat of entry depends on the barriers present and on the reaction from existing competitors that the entrant can expect. If barriers to entry are high and a newcomer can expect sharp retaliation from the entrenched competitors, obviously he will not pose a serious threat of entering.

There are six major sources of barriers to entry:

1. *Economies of scale*—These economies deter entry by forcing the aspirant either to come in on a large scale or to accept a cost disadvantage. Scale economies in production, research, marketing, and service are probably the key barriers to entry in the mainframe computer industry, as Xerox and GE sadly discovered. Economies of scale can also act as hurdles in distribution, utilization of the sales force, financing, and nearly any other part of a business.

2. *Product differentiation*—Brand identification creates a barrier by forcing entrants to spend heavily to overcome customer loyalty. Advertising, customer service, being first in the industry, and product differences are among the factors fostering brand identification. It is perhaps the most important entry barrier in soft drinks, over-the-counter drugs, cosmetics, investment banking, and public accounting. To create high fences around their businesses, brewers couple brand identification with economies of scale in production, distribution, and marketing.

3. *Capital requirements*—The need to invest large financial resources in order to compete creates a barrier to entry, particularly if the capital is required for unrecoverable expenditures in up-front advertising or R&D. Capital is necessary not only for fixed facilities but also for customer credit, inventories, and absorbing start-up losses. While major corporations have the financial resources to invade almost any industry, the huge cap-

ital requirements in certain fields, such as computer manufacturing and mineral extraction, limit the pool of likely entrants.

4. *Cost disadvantages independent of size*—Entrenched companies may have cost advantages not available to potential rivals, no matter what their size and attainable economies of scale. These advantages can stem from the effects of the learning curve (and of its first cousin, the experience curve), proprietary technology, access to the best raw materials sources, assets purchased at preinflation prices, government subsidies, or favorable locations. Sometimes cost advantages are legally enforceable, as they are through patents. . . .

5. *Access to distribution channels*—The new boy on the block must, of course, secure distribution of his product or service. A new food product, for example, must displace others from the supermarket shelf via price breaks, promotions, intense selling efforts, or some other means. The more limited the wholesale or retail channels are and the more that existing competitors have these tied up, obviously the tougher that entry into the industry will be. Sometimes this barrier is so high that, to surmount it, a new contestant must create its own distribution channels, as Timex did in the watch industry in the 1950s.

6. *Government policy*—The government can limit or even foreclose industries with such controls as license requirements and limits on access to raw materials. Regulated industries like trucking, liquor retailing, and freight forwarding are noticeable examples; more subtle government restrictions operate in fields like ski-area development and coal mining. The government also can play a major indirect role by affecting entry barriers through controls such as air and water pollution standards and safety regulations.

The potential rival's expectations about the reaction of existing competitors also will influence its decision on whether to enter. The company is likely to have second thoughts if incumbents have previously lashed out at new entrants or if:

▼ The incumbents possess substantial resources to fight back, including excess cash and unused borrowing power, productive capacity, or clout with distribution channels and customers.

▼ The incumbents seem likely to cut prices because of a desire to keep market shares or because of industrywide excess capacity.

▼ Industry growth is slow, affecting its ability to absorb the new arrival and probably causing the financial performance of all the parties involved to decline.

CHANGING CONDITIONS

From a strategic standpoint there are two important additional points to note about the threat of entry.

First, it changes, of course, as these conditions change. The expiration of Polaroid's basic patents on instant photography, for instance, greatly reduced its absolute cost entry barrier built by proprietary technology. It is not surprising that Kodak plunged into the market. Product differentiation in printing has all but disappeared. Conversely, in the auto industry economies of scale increased enormously with post–World War II automation and vertical integration—virtually stopping successful new entry.

Second, strategic decisions involving a large segment of an industry can have a major impact on the conditions determining the threat of entry. For example, the actions of many U.S. wine producers in the 1960s to step up product introductions, raise advertising levels, and expand distribution nationally surely strengthened the entry roadblocks by raising economies of scale and making access to distribution channels more difficult. Similarly, decisions by members of the recreational vehicle industry to vertically integrate in order to lower costs have greatly increased the economies of scale and raised the capital cost barriers.

POWERFUL SUPPLIERS AND BUYERS

Suppliers can exert bargaining power on participants in an industry by raising prices or reducing the quality of purchased goods and services. Powerful suppliers can thereby squeeze profitability out of an industry unable to recover cost increases in its own prices. By raising their prices, soft drink concentrate producers have contributed to the erosion of profitability of bottling companies because the bottlers, facing intense competition from powdered mixes, fruit drinks, and other beverages, have limited freedom to raise *their* prices accordingly. Customers likewise can force down prices, demand higher quality or more service, and play competitors off against each other—all at the expense of industry profits.

The power of each important supplier or buyer group depends on a number of characteristics of its market situation and on the relative importance of its sales or purchases to the industry compared with its overall business.

A *supplier* group is powerful if:

▼ It is dominated by a few companies and is more concentrated than the industry it sells to.

▼ Its product is unique or at least differentiated, or if it has built up switching costs. Switching costs are fixed costs buyers face in changing suppliers. These arise because, among other things, a buyer's product specifications tie it to particular suppliers, it has invested heavily in specialized ancillary equipment or in learning how to operate a supplier's equipment (as in computer software), or its production lines are connected to the supplier's manufacturing facilities (as in some manufacture of beverage containers).

▼ It is not obliged to contend with other products for sale to the industry. For instance, the competition between the steel companies and the aluminum companies to sell to the can industry checks the power of each supplier.

▼ It poses a credible threat of integrating forward into the industry's business. This provides a check against the industry's ability to improve the terms on which it purchases.

▼ The industry is not an important customer of the supplier group. If the industry *is* an important customer, suppliers' fortunes will be closely tied to the industry, and they will want to protect the industry through reasonable pricing and assistance in activities like R&D and lobbying.

A *buyer* group is powerful if:

▼ It is concentrated or purchases in large volumes. Large-volume buyers are particularly potent forces if heavy fixed costs characterize the industry—as they do in metal containers, corn refining, and bulk chemicals, for example—which raise the stakes to keep capacity filled.

▼ The products it purchases from the industry are standard or undifferentiated. The buyers, sure that they can always find alternative suppliers, may play one company against another, as they do in aluminum extrusion.

▼ The products it purchases from the industry form a component of its product and represent a significant fraction of its cost. The buyers are likely to shop for a favorable price and purchase selectively. Where the product sold by the industry in question is a small fraction of buyers' costs, buyers are usually much less price sensitive.

▼ It earns low profits, which create great incentive to lower its purchasing costs. Highly profitable buyers, however, are generally less price sensitive (that is, of course, if the item does not represent a large fraction of their costs).

▼ The industry's product is unimportant to the quality of the buyers' products or services. Where the quality of the buyers' products is very much affected by the industry's product, buyers are generally less price sensitive. Industries in which this situation includes oil field equipment, where a malfunction can lead to large losses, and enclosures for electronic medical and test instruments, where the quality of the enclosure can influence the user's impression about the quality of the equipment inside.

▼ The industry's product does not save the buyer money. Where the industry's product or service can pay for itself many times over, the buyer is rarely price sensitive; rather, he is interested in quality. This is true in services like investment banking and public accounting, where errors in judgment can be costly and embarrassing, and in businesses like the logging of oil wells, where an accurate survey can save thousands of dollars in drilling costs.

▼ The buyers pose a credible threat of integrating backward to make the industry's product. The Big Three auto producers and major buyers of cars have often used the threat of self-manufacture as a bargaining lever. But sometimes an industry engenders a threat to buyers that its members may integrate forward.

Most of these sources of buyer power can be attributed to consumers as a group as well as to industrial and commercial buyers; only a modification of the frame of reference is necessary. Consumers tend to be more price sensitive if they are purchasing products that are undifferentiated, expensive relative to their incomes, and of a sort where quality is not particularly important.

The buying power of retailers is determined by the same rules, with one important addition. Retailers can gain significant bargaining power over manufacturers when they can influence consumers' purchasing decisions, as they do in audio components, jewelry, appliances, sporting goods, and other goods.

STRATEGIC ACTION

A company's choice of suppliers to buy from or buyer groups to sell to should be viewed as a crucial strategic decision. A company can improve its strategic posture by finding suppliers or buyers who possess the least power to influence it adversely.

Most common is the situation of a company being able to choose whom it will sell to—in other words, buyer selection. Rarely do all the buyer groups a company sells to enjoy equal power. Even if a company sells to a single industry, segments usually exist within that industry that exercise less power (and that are therefore less price sensitive) than others. For example, the replacement market for most products is less price sensitive than the overall market.

As a rule, a company can sell to powerful buyers and still come away with above-average profitability only if it is a low-cost producer in its industry or if its product enjoys some unusual, if not unique, features. In supplying large customers with electric motors, Emerson Electric earns high returns because its low-cost position permits the company to meet or undercut competitors' prices.

If the company lacks a low-cost position or a unique product, selling to everyone is self-defeating because the more sales it achieves, the more vulnerable it becomes. The company may have to muster the courage to turn away business and sell only to less potent customers.

Buyer selection has been a key to the success of National Can and Crown Cork & Seal. They focus on the segments of the can industry where they can create product differentiation, minimize the threat of backward integration, and otherwise mitigate the awesome power of their customers. Of course, some industries do not enjoy the luxury of selecting "good" buyers.

As the factors creating supplier and buyer power change with time or as a result of a company's strategic decisions, naturally the power of these groups rises or declines. In the ready-to-wear clothing industry, as the buyers (department stores and clothing stores) have become more concentrated and control has passed to large chains, the industry has come under increasing pressure and suffered falling margins. The industry has been unable to differentiate its product or engender switching costs that lock in its buyers enough to neutralize these trends.

SUBSTITUTE PRODUCTS

By placing a ceiling on prices it can charge, substitute products or services limit the potential of an industry. Unless it can upgrade the quality of the product or differentiate it somehow (as via marketing), the industry will suffer in earnings and possibly in growth.

Manifestly, the more attractive the price-performance trade-off offered by substitute products, the firmer the lid placed on the industry's profit potential. Sugar producers confronted with the large-scale commercialization of high-fructose corn syrup, a sugar substitute, are learning this lesson today.

Substitutes not only limit profits in normal times; they also reduce the bonanza an industry can reap in boom times. In 1978 the producers of fiberglass insulation enjoyed unprecedented demand as a result of high energy costs and severe winter weather. But the industry's ability to raise prices was tempered by the plethora of insulation substitutes, including cellulose, rock wool, and styrofoam. These substitutes are bound to become an even stronger force once the current round of plant additions by fiberglass insulation producers has boosted capacity enough to meet demand (and then some).

Substitute products that deserve the most attention strategically are those that (1) are subject to trends improving their price-performance trade-off with the industry's product, or (2) are produced by industries earning high profits. Substitutes often come rapidly into play if some development increases competition in their industries and causes price reduction or performance improvement.

JOCKEYING FOR POSITION

Rivalry among existing competitors takes the familiar form of jockeying for position—using tactics like price competition, product introduction, and advertising slugfests. Intense rivalry is related to the presence of a number of factors:

▼ Competitors are numerous or are roughly equal in size and power. In many U.S. industries in recent years foreign contenders, of course, have become part of the competitive picture.

▼ Industry growth is slow, precipitating fights for market share that involve expansion-minded members.

▼ The product or service lacks differentiation or switching costs, which lock in buyers and protect one combatant from raids on its customers by another.

▼ Fixed costs are high or the product is perishable, creating strong temptation to cut prices. Many basic materials businesses, like paper and aluminum, suffer from this problem when demand slackens.

▼ Capacity is normally augmented in large increments. Such additions, as in the chlorine and vinyl chloride businesses, disrupt the industry's supply-demand balance and often lead to periods of overcapacity and price cutting.

▼ Exit barriers are high. Exit barriers, like very specialized assets or management's loyalty to a particular business, keep companies competing even though they may be earning low or even negative returns on investment. Excess capacity remains functioning, and the profitability of the healthy competitors suffers as the sick ones hang on. If the entire industry suffers from overcapacity, it may seek government help—particularly if foreign competition is present.

▼ The rivals are diverse in strategies, origins, and "personalities." They have different ideas about how to compete and continually run head on into each other in the process. . . .

While a company must live with many of these factors—because they are built into industry economics—it may have some latitude for improving matters through strategic shifts. For example, it may try to raise buyers' switching costs or increase product differentiation. A focus on selling efforts in the fastest-growing segments of the industry or on market areas with the lowest fixed costs can reduce the impact of industry rivalry. If it is feasible, a company can try to avoid confrontation with competitors having high exit barriers and can thus sidestep involvement in bitter price cutting.

Formulation of Strategy

Once the corporate strategist has assessed the forces affecting competition in his industry and their underlying causes, he can identify his company's strengths and weaknesses. The crucial strengths and weaknesses from a strategic standpoint are the company's posture vis-a-vis the underlying causes of each force. Where does it stand against substitutes? Against the sources of entry barriers?

Then the strategist can devise a plan of action that may include (1) positioning the company so that its capabilities provide the best defense against the competitive force; and/or (2) influencing the balance of the forces through strategic moves, thereby improving the company's position; and/or (3) anticipating shifts in the factors underlying the forces and responding to them, with the hope of exploiting change by choosing a strategy appropriate for the new competitive balance before opponents recognize it. I shall consider each strategic approach in turn.

POSITIONING THE COMPANY

The first approach takes the structure of the industry as given and matches the company's strengths and weaknesses to it. Strategy can be viewed as building defenses against the competitive forces or as finding positions in the industry where the forces are weakest.

Knowledge of the company's capabilities and of the causes of the competitive forces will highlight the areas where the company should confront competition and where avoid it. If the company is a low-cost producer, it may choose to confront powerful buyers while it takes care to sell them only products not vulnerable to competition from substitutes. . . .

INFLUENCING THE BALANCE

When dealing with the forces that drive industry competition, a company can devise a strategy that takes the offensive. This posture is designed to do more than merely cope with the forces themselves; it is meant to alter their causes.

Innovations in marketing can raise brand identification or otherwise differentiate the product. Capital investments in large-scale facilities or vertical integration affect entry barriers. The balance of forces is partly a result of external factors and partly in the company's control.

EXPLOITING INDUSTRY CHANGE

Industry evolution is important strategically because evolution, of course, brings with it changes in the sources of competition I have identified. In the familiar product life-cycle pattern, for example, growth rates change, product differentiation is said to decline as the business becomes more mature, and the companies tend to integrate vertically.

These trends are not so important in themselves; what is critical is whether they affect the sources of competition. . . .

Obviously, the trends carrying the highest priority from a strategic standpoint are those that affect the most important sources of competition in the industry and those that elevate new causes to the forefront. . . .

The framework for analyzing competition that I have described can also be used to predict the eventual profitability of an industry. In long-range planning the task is to examine each competitive force, forecast the magnitude of each underlying cause, and then construct a composite picture of the likely profit potential of the industry. . . .

The key to growth—even survival—is to stake out a position that is less vulnerable to attack from head-to-head opponents, whether established or new, and less vulnerable to erosion from the direction of buyers, suppliers, and substitute goods. Establishing such a position can take many forms—solidifying relationships with favorable customers, differentiating the product either substantively or psychologically through marketing, integrating forward or backward, establishing technological leadership.

▼ READING 4.2   GENERIC BUSINESS STRATEGIES*

by Henry Mintzberg

Almost every serious author concerned with "content" issues in strategic management, not to mention strategy consulting "boutiques," has his, her, or its own list of strategies commonly pursued by different organizations. The problem is that these lists almost always either focus narrowly on special types of strategies or else aggregate arbitrarily across all varieties of them with no real order.

In 1965, Igor Ansoff proposed a matrix of four strategies which became quite well known—market penetration, product development, market development, and diversification (1965: 109). But this was hardly comprehensive. Fifteen years later, Michael Porter (1980) introduced what became the best-known list of "generic strategies": cost leadership, differentiation, and focus. But the Porter list was also incomplete: while Ansoff focused on *extensions* of business strategy, Porter focused on *identifying* business strategy in the first place.

We believe that families of strategies may be divided into five broad groupings. These are:

1. Locating the core business.

2. Distinguishing the core business.

3. Elaborating the core business.

4. Extending the core business.

5. Reconceiving the core business.

This reading examines the first three, locating, distinguishing, and elaborating the core business, since they are more relevant for business-level strategy. A companion reading in

---

* Abbreviated version prepared for this book of an article by Henry Mintzberg, "Generic Strategies Toward a Comprehensive Framework," originally published in *Advances in Strategic Management*, Vol. 5 (Greenwich, CT: JAI Press, 1988), pp. 1–67.

Chapter 13 discusses the two more relevant for corporate-level strategy—extending and reconceiving the core business. These five groupings of strategies are presented as a logical hierarchy, although it should be emphasized that strategies do not necessarily develop that way in organizations.

Locating the Core Business

A business can be thought to exist at a junction in a network of industries that take raw materials and through selling to and buying from each other produce various finished products (or services). Figure 1, for example, shows a hypothetical canoe business in such a network. Core location strategies can be described with respect to the stage of the business in the network and the particular industry in question.

STRATEGIES OF STAGE OF OPERATIONS

Traditionally, industries have been categorized as being in the primary (raw materials extraction and conversion), secondary (manufacturing) or tertiary (delivery or other ser-

FIGURE 1
Locating a Core Business as a Junction in a Network of Industries

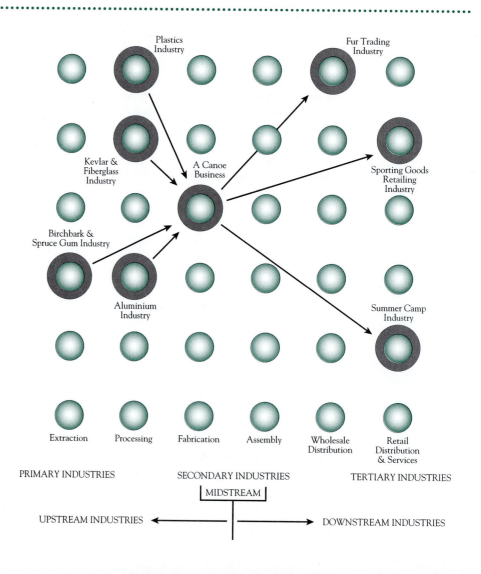

vice) stage of operations. More recently, however, state in the "stream" has been the favored form of description:

UPSTREAM BUSINESS STRATEGY

Upstream businesses function close to the raw material. The flow of product tends to be divergent, from a basic material (wood, aluminum) to a variety of uses for it. Upstream business tends to be technology- and capital-intensive rather than people-intensive, and more inclined to search for advantage through low costs than through high margins and to favor sales push over market pull (Galbraith, 1983: 65–66).

MIDSTREAM BUSINESS STRATEGY

Here the organization sits at the neck of an hour-glass, drawing a variety of inputs into a single production process out of which flows the product to a variety of users, much as the canoe business is shown in Figure 1.

DOWNSTREAM BUSINESS STRATEGY

Here a wide variety of inputs converge into a narrow funnel, as in the many products sold by a department store.

STRATEGIES OF INDUSTRY

Many factors are involved in the identification of an industry, so many that it would be difficult to develop a concise set of generic labels. Moreover, change continually renders the boundaries between "industries" arbitrary. Diverse products get bundled together so that two industries become one, while traditionally bundled products get separated so that one industry becomes two. Economists in government and elsewhere spend a great deal of time trying to pin these things down, via Standard Industrial Classification codes and the like. In effect, they try to fix what strategists try to change: competitive advantage often comes from reconceiving the definition of an industry.

Distinguishing the Core Business

Having located the circle that identifies the core business, the next step is to open it up— to distinguish the characteristics that enable an organization to achieve competitive advantage and so to survive in its own context.

THE FUNCTIONAL AREAS

This second level of strategy can encompass a whole host of strategies in the various functional areas. As shown in Figure 2, they may include input "sourcing" strategies, throughput "processing" strategies, and output "delivery" strategies, all reinforced by a set of "supporting" strategies.

It has been popular to describe organizations in this way, especially since Michael Porter built his 1985 book around the "generic value chain," shown in Figure 3. Porter presents it as "a systematic way of examining all the activities a firm performs and how they interact . . . for analyzing the sources of competitive advantage" (1985: 33). Such a chain, and how it performs individual activities, reflects a firm's "history, its strategy, its approach to implementing its strategy, and the underlying economies of the activities themselves" (p. 36). According to Porter

FIGURE 2
Functional Areas,
in Systems Terms

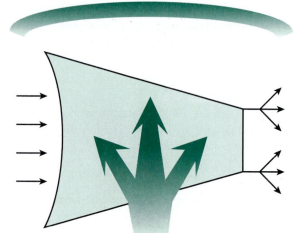

SUPPORTING STRATEGIES
- Legal
- Control
- Training
- Etc.

SOURCING STRATEGIES
- Procurement
- People
- Finance

DELIVERING STRATEGIES
- Marketing
  - market/ channel
  - pricing
  - promotion
- Sales
- Distribution
- Service

PROCESSING STRATEGIES
- Process development
- Operations
  (including productivity)
  - fabrication
  - assembly

DESIGNING   STRATEGIES
- Product research
- Product development

"the goal of any generic strategy" is to "create value for buyers" at a profit. Accordingly, the value chain displays total value, and consists of *value activities* and *margin*. Value activities are the physically and technologically distinct activities a firm performs. These are the building blocks by which a firm creates a product valuable to its buyers. Margin is the difference between total value and the collective cost of performing the value activities. . . .

Value activities can be divided into two broad types, *primary* activities and *support* activities. Primary activities, listed along the bottom of Figure 3, are the activities involved in the physical creation of the product and its sale and transfer to the buyer as well as after-sale assistance. In any firm, primary activities can be divided into the five generic categories shown in Figure 3. Support activities support the primary activities and each other by providing purchased inputs, technology, human resources, and various firmwide functions. (p. 38)*

---

* In other words, it is the differentiation of price that naturally drives the functional strategy of reducing costs just as it is the differentiation of product that naturally drives the functional strategies of enhancing quality or creating innovation. (To be consistent with the label of "cost leadership," Porter would have had to call his differentiation strategy "product leadership.") A company could, of course, cut costs while holding prices equivalent to competitors'. But often that means less service, lower quality, fewer features, etc., and so the customers would have to be attracted by lower prices. (See Mintzberg (1988: 14–17) for a fuller discussion of this point.)

FIGURE 3
The Generic Value Chain
Source: *Porter* (1983:3)

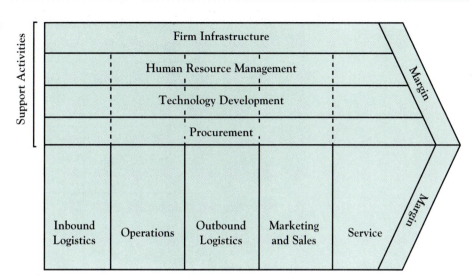

Primary Activities

PORTER'S GENERIC STRATEGIES

Porter's framework of "generic strategies" has also become quite widely used. In our terms, these constitute strategies to distinguish the core business. Porter believes there are but two "basic types of competitive advantage a firm can possess: low costs or differentiation" (1985:11). These combine with the "scope" of a firm's operation (the range of market segments targeted) to produce "three *generic strategies* for achieving above-average performance in an industry: cost leadership, differentiation, and focus" (namely, narrow scope), shown in Figure 4.

To Porter, firms that wish to gain competitive advantage must "make a choice" among these: "being 'all things to all people' is a recipe for strategic mediocrity and below-average performance" (p. 12). Or in the words that have become more controversial, "a firm that engages in each generic strategy but fails to achieve any of them is 'stuck in the middle'" (p. 16). Gilbert and Strebel (1992), however, have disagreed with this, arguing that highly successful companies, such as some of the Japanese automobile manufacturers, have adopted "outpacing strategies." First they use a low cost strategy to secure markets, and then, by "proactive" differentiation moves (say an increase in quality), they capture certain important market segments. Or else firms begin with value differentiation and follow that up with "preemptive" price cutting. In effect, the authors argue that companies can achieve both forms of Porter's competitive advantage simultaneously.

The strategies we describe in this section take their lead from Porter, but depart in some respects. We shall distinguish scope and differentiation, as Porter did in his 1980 book (focus being introduced as narrow scope in his later book), but we shall include cost leadership as a form of differentiation (namely, with regard to low price). If, as Porter argues, the intention of generic strategies is to seize and sustain competitive advantage, then it is not

FIGURE 4
Porter's Generic Strategies
Source: *Porter* (1983:3).

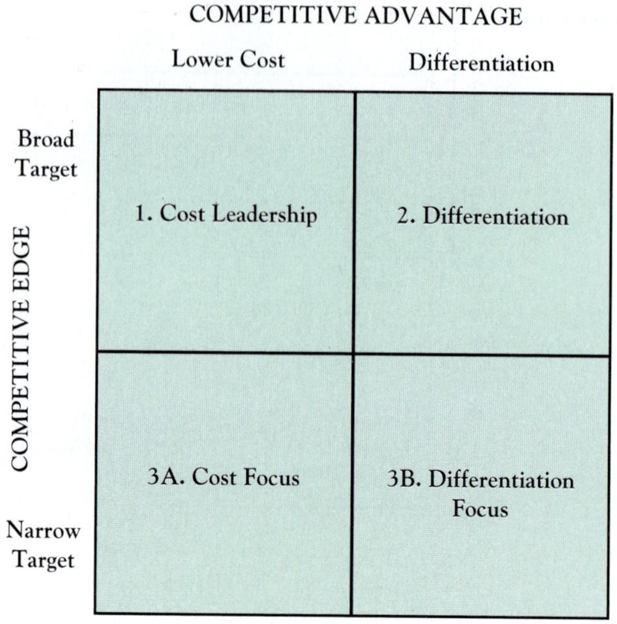

COMPETITIVE ADVANTAGE

Lower Cost   Differentiation

	Lower Cost	Differentiation
Broad Target	1. Cost Leadership	2. Differentiation
Narrow Target	3A. Cost Focus	3B. Differentiation Focus

COMPETITIVE EDGE

just taking leadership on cutting costs that matters so much as using that cost leadership to underprice competitors and so to attract buyers.*

Thus two types of strategy for distinguishing a core business are presented here. First is a set of increasingly extensive strategies of *differentiation*, shown on the face of the circle. These identify what is fundamentally distinct about a business in the marketplace, in effect as perceived by its customers. Second is a set of decreasingly extensive strategies of *scope*. These identify what markets the business is after, as perceived by itself.

STRATEGIES OF DIFFERENTIATION

As is generally agreed in the literature of strategic management, an organization distinguishes itself in a competitive marketplace by differentiating its offerings in some way—by acting to distinguish its product and services from those of its competitors. Hence, differentiation fills the face of the circle used to identify the core business. An organization can differentiate its offerings in six basic ways:

---

* Our figure differs from Porter's in certain ways. Because he places his major emphasis on the flow of physical materials (for example, referring to "inbound logistics" as encompassing materials handling, warehousing, inventory control, vehicle scheduling, and returns to suppliers), he shows procurement and human resource management as support activities, whereas by taking more of a general system orientation, our Figure 2 shows them as inputs, among the sourcing strategies. Likewise, he considers technology development as support whereas Figure 2 considers it as part of processing. (Among the reasons Porter gives for doing this is that such development can pertain to "outbound logistics" or delivery as well as processing. While true, it also seems true that far more technology development pertains to operations than to delivery, especially in the manufacturing firms that are the focus of Porter's attention. Likewise, Porter describes procurement as pertaining to any of the primary activities, or other support activities for that matter. But in our terms that does not make it any less an aspect of sourcing on the inbound side.) In fact, Porter's description would relegate engineering and product design (not to mention human resources and purchasing) to staff rather than line activities, a place that would certainly be disputed in many manufacturing firms (with product design, for example, being mentioned only peripherally in his text (p. 42) alongside other "technology development" activities such as media research and servicing procedures).

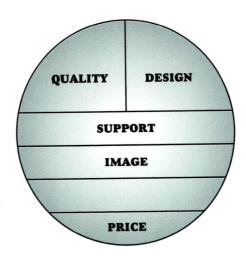

PRICE DIFFERENTIATION STRATEGY

The most basic way to differentiate a product (or service) is simply to charge a lower price for it. All things being equal, or not too unequal, some people at least will always beat a path to the door of the cheaper product. Price differentiation may be used with a product undifferentiated in any other way—in effect, a standard design, perhaps a commodity. The producer simply absorbs the lost margin, or makes it up through a higher volume of sales. But other times, backing up price differentiation is a strategy of design intended to create a product that is intrinsically cheaper.

IMAGE DIFFERENTIATION STRATEGY

Marketing is sometimes used to feign differentiation where it does not otherwise exist—an image is created for the product. This can also include cosmetic differences to a product that do not enhance its performance in any serious way, for example, putting a fancier package around yogurt. (Of course, if it is the image that is for sale, in other words if the product is intrinsically cosmetic, as, say, in "designer" jeans, then cosmetic differences would have to be described as design differentiation.)

SUPPORT DIFFERENTIATION STRATEGY

More substantial, yet still having no effect on the product itself, is to differentiate on the basis of something that goes alongside the product, some basis of support. This may have to do with selling the product (such as special credit or 24-hour delivery), servicing the product (such as exceptional after-sales service), or providing a related product or service alongside the basic one (paddling lessons with the canoe you buy). In an article entitled "Marketing Success Through Differentiation—of Anything," Theodore Levitt has argued the interesting point that "there is no such thing as a commodity" (1980: 8). His basic point is that no matter how difficult it may be to achieve differentiation by design, there is always a basis to achieve another substantial form of differentiation, especially by support.

QUALITY DIFFERENTIATION STRATEGY

Quality differentiation has to do with features of the product that make it better—not fundamentally different, just better. The product performs with (1) greater initial reliability, (2) greater long-term durability, and/or (3) superior performance.

DESIGN DIFFERENTIATION STRATEGY

Last but certainly not least is differentiation on the basis of design—offering something that is truly different, that breaks away from the "dominant design" if there is one, to provide unique features. When everyone else was making cameras whose pictures could be seen next week, Edward Land made one whose pictures could be seen in the next minute.

UNDIFFERENTIATION STRATEGY

To have no basis for differentiation is a strategy: indeed by all observation a common one, and in fact one that may be pursued deliberately. Hence there is a blank space in the circle. Given enough room in a market, and a management without the skill or the will to differentiate what it does, there can be a place for copycats.

SCOPE STRATEGIES

The second dimension to distinguish the core business is by the *scope* of the products and services offered, in effect the extent of the markets in which they are sold. Scope is essentially a demand-driven concept, taking its lead from the market for what exists out there. Differentiation, in contrast, is a supply-driven concern, rooted in the nature of the product itself—what is offered to the market (W. E. Smith, 1956). Differentiation, by concentrating on the product offered, adopts the perspective of the customer, existing only when that person perceives some characteristic of the product that adds value. And scope, by focusing on the market served, adopts the perspective of the producer, existing only in the collective mind of the organization—in terms of how it diffuses and disaggregates its markets (in other words, what marketing people call segmentation).

UNSEGMENTATION STRATEGY

"One size fits all": the Ford Model T, table salt. In fact, it is difficult to think of any product today that is not segmented in some way. What the unsegmented strategy really means then is that the organization tries to capture a wide chunk of the market with a basic configuration of the product.

SEGMENTATION STRATEGIES

The possibilities for segmentation are limitless, as are the possible degrees. We can, however, distinguish a range of this, from a simple segmentation strategy (three basic sizes of paper clips) to a hyperfine segmentation strategy (as in designer lighting). Also, some organizations seek to be *comprehensive*, to serve all segments (department stores, large cereal manufacturers), others to be *selective*, targeting carefully only certain segments (e.g., "clean" mutual funds).

NICHE STRATEGY

Niche strategies focus on a single segment. Just as the panda bear has found its biological niche in the consumption of bamboo shoots, so too is there the canoe company that has found its market niche in the fabrication of racing canoes, or the many firms which are distinguished only by the fact that they provide their highly standardized offerings in a unique place, a geographical niche—the corner grocery store, the regional cement producer, the national Red Cross office. All tend to follow "industry" recipes to the letter, providing them to their particular community. In a sense, all strategies are in some sense niche, characterized as much by what they exclude as by what they include. No organization can be all things to all people. The all-encompassing strategy is no strategy at all.

CUSTOMIZING STRATEGIES

Customization is the limiting case of segmentation: disaggregation of the market to the point where each customer constitutes a unique segment. *Pure* customization, in which the product is developed from scratch for each customer, is found in the architecturally designed house and the special purpose machine. It infiltrates the entire value chain: the product is not only delivered in a personalized way, not only assembled and even fabricated to order, but is also designed for the individual customer in the first place. Less ambitious but probably more common is *tailored* customization: a basic design is modified, usually in the fabrication stage, to the customer's needs or specifications (certain housing, prostheses modified to fit the bone joints of each customer, and so on). *Standardized customization* means that final products are assembled to individual request for standard components—as in automobiles in which the customer is allowed to choose color, engine and various accessories. Advances in computer-aided design and manufacturing (CAD, CAM) have caused a proliferation of standardized customization, as well as tailored customization.

Elaborating the Core Business

An organization can elaborate a business in a number of ways. It can develop its product offerings within that business, it can develop its market via new segments, new channels or new geographical areas, or it can simply push the same products more vigorously through the same markets. Back in 1965, Igor Ansoff showed these strategies (as well as one to be discussed in Chapter 13) as presented in Figure 5.

PENETRATION STRATEGIES

Penetration strategies work from a base of existing products and existing markets, seeking to penetrate the market by increasing the organization's share of it. This may be done by straight *expansion* or by the *takeover* of existing competitors. Trying to expand sales with no fundamental change in product or market (buying market share through more promotion, etc.) is at one and the same time the most obvious thing to do and perhaps the most difficult to succeed at, because, at least in a relatively stable market, it means extracting market share from other firms, which logically leads to increased competition. Takeover, where possible, obviously avoids this, but perhaps at a high cost. The harvesting strategy, popularized in the 1970s by the Boston Consulting Group, in some ways represents the opposite of the penetration strategies. The way to deal with "cash cows"—businesses with high market shares but low growth potential—was to harvest them, cease investment and exploit whatever potential remained. The mixing of the metaphors may have been an indication of the dubiousness of the strategy since to harvest a cow is, of course, to kill it.

MARKET DEVELOPMENT STRATEGIES

A predominant strategy here is *market elaboration*, which means promoting existing products in new markets—in effect broadening the scope of the business by finding new market segments, perhaps served by new channels. Product substitution is a particular case of market elaboration, where uses for a product are promoted which enable it to substitute for

FIGURE 5
Ways to Elaborate a Given Business
Source: *Ansoff* (1965:109) with minor modifications; see also Johnson and Jones (1957:52).

	EXISTING PRODUCT	NEW PRODUCT
EXISTING MARKET	Penetration Strategies	Product Development Strategies
NEW MARKET	Market Development Strategies	Diversification Strategies

other products. *Market consolidation* is the inverse of market elaboration, namely reducing the number of segments. But this is not just a strategy of failure. Given the common tendency to proliferate market segments, it makes sense for the healthy organization to rationalize them periodically, to purge the excesses.

GEOGRAPHIC EXPANSION STRATEGIES

An important form of market development can be geographic expansion—carrying the existing product offering to new geographical areas, anywhere from the next block to across the world. When this also involves a strategy of geographic rationalization—locating different business functions in different places—it is sometimes referred to as a "global strategy." The IKEA furniture company, for example, designs in Scandinavia, sources in Eastern Europe among other places, and markets in Western Europe and North America.

PRODUCT DEVELOPMENT STRATEGIES

Here we can distinguish a simple *product extension* strategy from a more extensive *product line proliferation* strategy, and their counterparts, *product line rationalization*. Offering new or modified products in the same basic business is another obvious way to elaborate a core business—from cornflakes to bran flakes and rice crispies, eventually offering every permutation and combination of the edible grains. This may amount to differentiation by design, if the products are new and distinctive, or else to no more than increased scope through segmentation, if standardized products are added to the line. Product line proliferation means aiming at comprehensive product segmentation—the complete coverage of a given business. Rationalization means culling products and thinning the line to get rid of overlaps or unprofitable excesses. Again we might expect cycles of product extension and rationalization, at least in businesses (such as cosmetics and textiles) predisposed to proliferation in their product lines.

We shall take this analysis beyond generic business strategies to generic corporate ones in Chapter 13.

STRATEGY FORMATION

The readings of the last two chapters described how strategies are supposed to be made and thereby illustrate the *prescriptive* side of the field. This chapter presents readings that describe how strategies really do seem to be made, the *descriptive* side. We title this chapter "Strategy Formation" to emphasize the point introduced in Chapter 1 that strategies can *form* implicitly as well as be *formulated* explicitly.

The preceding chapters may seem to deal with an unreachable utopia, this one with an imperfect reality. But there may be a better conclusion: that *prescription* offers useful guidelines for thinking about ends and how to order physical resources efficiently to achieve them, while *description* provides a useful frame of reference for considering how this must be related to real-world patterns of behavior in organizations. Another way to say this is that while the analytical tools and models prescribed earlier are vital to thinking about strategy intelligently, they must also be rooted in a genuine understanding of the realities of organizations. Unfortunately, management writers, especially in traditional strategy textbooks, have often been quick to prescribe without offering enough appreciation of why managers and organizations act in the ways they do.

Brian Quinn and John Voyer (of the University of Southern Maine) open with a sharp focus on how managers really do seem to behave when they create strategy. This reading is drawn from Quinn's book *Strategies for Change: Logical Incrementalism*, and it develops a particular view of the strategy-making process based on intensive interviews in some of America's and Europe's best-known corporations. Planning does not capture the essence of strategy formation, according to Quinn and Voyer, although it does play an important role in developing new data and in confirming strategies derived in other ways. The traditional view of incrementalism does not fit observed behavior patterns either. The processes may seem randomly incremental on the surface, but a powerful logic underlies them. And, unlike the other incremental processes, these are not so much *reactive* as subtly *proactive*. Executives use incremental approaches to deal simultaneously with the informational, motivational, and political aspects of creating a strategy.

Above all, Quinn and Voyer depict strategy formation as a managed interactive *learning* process in which the chief strategist gradually works out strategy in his or her own mind and orchestrates the organization's acceptance of it. In emphasizing the role of a central strategist—or small groups managing "subsystems" of strategy—Quinn and Voyer often seem close to Andrews' views. But the two differ markedly in other important respects. In their emphasis on the political and motivational dimensions of strategy, they may be closer to Wrapp, whose managers "don't make policy decisions." In fact, Quinn and Voyer attempt to integrate their views with the traditional one, noting that while the strategies themselves "emerge" from an incremental process, they have many of the characteristics of the highly deliberate ones of Andrews' strategists. This reading ends with practical advice on how to manage strategy making as an incremental process. A number of cases, notably MacArthur in the Philippines, Sony Corporation: Innovation System, Microsoft Corporation (A), The IBM 360 Decision, Nintendo Co., Ltd., The Pillsbury Company, The Transformation of AT&T, SAS and the European Airline Industry, Andersen Consulting (Europe), and Mountbatten and India offer opportunities to investigate the interaction of analytical and incremental processes in strategy formation.

The following reading by Mintzberg complements the first one. Called "Crafting Strategy," it shows how managers mold strategies the way craftsmen mold their clay. This reading also builds on Mintzberg's reading of Chapter 1 on the different forms of strategy, developing further the concept of emergent strategy.

As you will see, the two authors of this book share a basic philosophy about how organizations must go about the difficult process of setting basic direction in a complex world. They also share a basic belief in the key role of the actual strategy-making process in organizations. Hence the title of the book, *The Strategy Process*, and the particular importance of this chapter in it.

In a chapter that challenges many of the accepted notions about how strategy should be made, the next reading may be the most upsetting of all. In it Richard Pascale, a well-known consultant, writer, and lecturer at Stanford Business School, challenges head-on not only the whole approach to strategy analysis (as represented in the last chapter), especially as practiced by the Boston Consulting Group (one of the better-known "strategy boutiques" whose ideas will be discussed in Chapter 10), but also the very concept of strategy formulation itself.

As his point of departure, Pascale describes a BCG study carried out for the British government to explain how manufacturers in that country lost the American motorcycle market to the Japanese, and to the Honda Company in particular. The analysis seems impeccable and eminently logical: the Japanese were simply more clever, by thinking through a brilliant strategy before they acted. But then Pascale flew to Japan and interviewed those clever executives who pulled off this coup. We shall save the story for Pascale, who tells it with a great deal of color, except to note here its basic message: an openness to learning and a fierce commitment to an organization and its markets may count for more in strategy making than all the brilliant analysis one can imagine. (Ask yourself while reading these accounts how the strategic behavior of the British motorcycle manufacturers who received the BCG report might have differed if they had instead received Pascale's second story.) Pascale in effect takes the arguments for incrementalism and strategy making as a crafting and learning process to their natural conclusions (or one of them, at least).

No one who reads Pascale's account can ever feel quite so smug about rational strategy analysis again. We include this reading, however, not to encourage rejection of that type of analysis or the very solid thinking that has gone into the works of Porter, Ansoff, and others. Rather, we wish to balance the message conveyed in so much of the strategy literature with the practical lessons from the field. The point is that successful strategies can no more rely exclusively on such analysis than they can do without it. Effective strategy formation, one must conclude from all these readings, is a sometimes deceptive and multifaceted affair, its complexity never to be underestimated.

We have mentioned the complementarity of the Quinn and Mintzberg views of strategy making. But there is one difference that is worth addressing. While both view the process as one of evolution and learning, Quinn tends to place greater emphasis on the role of the chief executive, and the senior management team in general, as central strategist, while Mintzberg tends to place a little more emphasis on others who can feed strategy up the hierarchy, especially in his discussion of a "grass-roots" approach to the process. In effect, organizations may have senior managers sending their strategic visions down the hierarchy, while creative people below may be sending strategic initiatives back up.

Effective organizations seem to do both, but that raises a major problem in the strategy process: the middle managers may get caught in the middle, between these two. How can one reconcile the two opposing pressures? The Andersen Consulting (Europe), The Transformation of AT&T, Microsoft Corporation (B), SAS and the European Airline Industry, and Nintendo of America cases give some indication of the issues and how managers may deal with them. In the Sayles reading of Chapter 8, we shall return to this important issue.

▼ READING 5.1 LOGICAL INCREMENTALISM: MANAGING STRATEGY FORMATION*

*by James Brian Quinn
and John Voyer*

The Logic of Logical Incrementalism

Strategy change processes in well-managed major organizations rarely resemble the rational-analytical systems touted in the literature. Instead, strategic change processes are typically fragmented, evolutionary, and intuitive. Real strategy *evolves* as internal decisions and external events flow together to create a new, widely shared consensus for action.

THE FORMAL SYSTEMS PLANNING APPROACH

There is a strong literature stating which factors *should* be included in a systematically planned strategy. This systems-planning approach focuses on quantitative factors, and underemphasizes qualitative, organizational, and power factors. Systems planning *can* make a contribution, but it should be just one building block in the continuous stream of events that creates organizational strategy.

THE POWER-BEHAVIORAL APPROACH

Another body of literature has enhanced our understanding of *multiple goal structures*, the *politics* of strategic decisions, *bargaining* and *negotiation* processes, *satisficing* in decision making, the role of *coalitions*, and the practice of *"muddling"* in public sector management. The shortcomings of this body of literature are that it has typically been far-removed from strategy making, it has ignored the contributions of useful analytical approaches, and it has offered few practical recommendations for the strategist.

SUMMARY FINDINGS FROM STUDY OF ACTUAL CHANGE PROCESSES

Recognizing the strengths and weaknesses of each of these approaches, the change processes in ten major organizations were documented. Several important findings emerged from these investigations.

▼   Neither approach above adequately describes strategy processes.

---

* Originally published in the collegiate edition of *The Strategy Process*, Prentice Hall, 1994. Based on James Brian Quinn, "Strategic Change: Logical Incrementalism," *Sloan Management Review*, Fall 1978, pp. 1–21, and James Brian Quinn, "Managing Strategies Incrementally," *Omega: The International Journal of Management Science*, 1982, drawn from his book *Strategies for Change: Logical Incrementalism* (Irwin, 1980).

▼ Effective strategies tend to emerge incrementally and opportunistically, as subsystems of organizational activity (e.g., acquisitions, divestitures, major reorganizations, even formal plans) are blended into a coherent pattern.

▼ The logic behind this process is so powerful that it may be the best approach to recommend for strategy formation in large companies.

▼ Because of cognitive and process limits, this approach must be managed and linked together in a way best described as "logical incrementalism."

▼ Such incrementalism is not "muddling." It is a purposeful, effective, active management technique for improving and integrating *both* the analytical and behavioral aspects of strategy formation.

CRITICAL STRATEGIC ISSUES

Though "hard data" decisions dominate the literature, there are various "soft" kinds of changes that affect strategy:

▼ The design of an organization's structure
▼ The characteristic management style in the firm
▼ A firm's external (especially government) relations
▼ Acquisitions, divestitures, or divisional control issues
▼ A firm's international posture and relationships
▼ An organization's innovative capabilities
▼ The effects of an organization's growth on the motivation of its personnel
▼ Value and expectation changes, and their effects on worker and professional relationships in the organization
▼ Technological changes that affect the organization.

Top executives made several important points about these kinds of changes. Few of these issues lend themselves to quantitative modeling or financial analysis. Most firms use different subsystems to handle different types of strategic changes, yet the subsystems were similar across firms. Lastly, no single formal analytical process could handle all strategic variables simultaneously using a planning approach.

Precipitating Events and Incremental Logic

Executives reported that various events often resulted in interim decisions that shaped the company's future strategy. This was evident in the decisions forced on General Motors by the 1973–74 oil crisis, in the shift in posture pressed upon Exxon by the Prince William Sound oil spill, or in the dramatic opportunities allowed for Haloid Corporation and Pilkington Brothers by the unexpected inventions of xerography and float glass. No organization—no matter how brilliant, rational, or imaginative—could possibly have foreseen the timing, severity, or even the nature of all such precipitating events.

Recognizing this, top executives tried to respond incrementally. They kept early commitments broadly formative, tentative, and subject to later review. Future implications were too hard to understand, so parties wanted to test assumptions and have an opportunity to learn. Also, top executives were sensitive to social and political structures in the organization; they tried to handle things in a way that would make the change process a good one.

The Diversification Subsystem

Strategies for diversification provide excellent examples of the value of proceeding incrementally. Incremental processes aid both the formal aspects of diversification (price and strategic fit, for example), and the psychological and political aspects. Most important among the latter are generating a genuine, top-level psychological commitment to diversification, consciously preparing the firm to move opportunistically, building a "comfort factor" for risk taking, and developing a new ethos based on the success of new divisions.

THE MAJOR REORGANIZATION SUBSYSTEM

Large-scale organizational moves may have negative effects on organizational politics and social structure. Logical incrementalism makes it easier to avoid those negative effects. As the organization proceeds incrementally, it can assess the new roles, capabilities, and individual reactions of those involved in the restructuring. It allows new people to be trained and tested, perhaps for extended periods. Logical incrementalism allows organizational actors to modify the idea behind the reorganization as more is learned. It also gives executives the luxury of making final commitments as late as possible. Executives may move opportunistically, step-by-step, selectively moving people as developments warrant (events seldom come together at one convenient time). They may also articulate the broad organizational concept in detail only when the last pieces fit together. Lastly, logical incrementalism works well in large-scale reorganization because it allows for testing, flexibility, and feedback.

FORMAL PLANNING IN CORPORATE STRATEGY

Formal planning techniques do serve some essential functions. They discipline managers to look ahead, and to express goals and resource allocations. Long-term planning encourages longer time horizons, and eases the evaluation of short-term plans. Long-term plans create a psychological backdrop and an information framework about the future against which managers can calibrate short-term or interim decisions. Lastly, "special studies," like the white papers used at Pillsbury to inform the chicken-business divestiture decision, have a large effect at key junctures for specific decisions.

Planning may make incrementalism standard organizational practice, for two reasons. First, most planning is "bottom up," and the people at the bottom have an interest in their existing products and processes. Second, executives want most plans to be "living" or "ever green," intended to be only frameworks, providing guidance and consistency for incremental decisions. To do otherwise would be to deny that further information could have value. Thus, properly used formal planning can be part of incremental logic.

TOTAL POSTURE PLANNING

Occasionally, managements did attempt very broad assessments of their companies' total posture. But these major product thrusts were usually unsuccessful. Actual strategies *evolved*, as each company overextended, consolidated, made errors, and rebalanced various thrusts over time. The executives thought that this was both logical and expected.

LOGICAL INCREMENTALISM

Strategic decisions cannot be aggregated into a single decision matrix, with factors treated simultaneously to achieve an optimum solution. There are cognitive limits, but also "process limits"—timing and sequencing requirements, the needs to create awareness, to build comfort levels, to develop consensus, to select and train people, and so forth.

A STRATEGY EMERGES

Successful executives connect and sequentially arrange a series of strategic processes and decisions over a period of years. They attempt to build a resource base and posture that are strong enough to withstand all but the most devastating events. They constantly reconfigure corporate structure and strategy as new information suggests better—but never perfect—alignments. The process is dynamic, with no definite beginning or end.

CONCLUSIONS

Strategy deals with the unknowable, not the uncertain. It involves so many forces, most of which have great strength and the power to combine, that one cannot, in a probabilistic sense, predict events. Therefore, logic dictates that one proceed flexibly and experimentally from broad ideas toward specific commitments. Making the latter concrete as late as possible narrows the bands of uncertainty, and allows the firm to benefit from the best available information. This is the process of "logical incrementalism." It is not "muddling." Logical incrementalism is conscious, purposeful, active, good management. It allows executives to blend analysis, organizational politics, and individual needs into a cohesive new direction.

Managing Incrementally

How can one actively manage the logical incremental process? The study discussed here shows that executives tend to use similar incremental processes as they manage complex strategy shifts.

BEING AHEAD OF THE FORMAL INFORMATION SYSTEM

The earliest signals for strategy change rarely come from formal company systems. Using multiple internal and external sources, managers "sense" the need for change before the formal systems do. T. Vincent Learson at IBM drove the company to develop the 360 series of computers based on his feeling that, despite its current success, IBM was heading toward market confusion. IBM's formal intelligence system did not pick up any market signals until three years after Learson launched the development process.

BUILDING ORGANIZATIONAL AWARENESS

This is essential when key players lack information or psychological stimulation to change. At early stages, management processes are broad, tentative, formative, information-seeking, and purposely avoid irreversible commitments. They also try to avoid provoking potential opponents of an idea.

BUILDING CREDIBILITY/CHANGING SYMBOLS

Symbols may help managers signal to the organization that certain types of changes are coming, even when specific solutions are not yet in hand. Highly visible symbolic actions can communicate effectively to large numbers of people. Grapevines can amplify signals of pending change. Symbolic moves often verify the intention of a new strategy, or give it credibility in its early stages. Without such actions, people may interpret even forceful verbiage as mere rhetoric and delay their commitment to new strategic ideas.

LEGITIMIZING NEW VIEWPOINTS

Planned delays allow the organization to debate and discuss threatening issues, work out implications of new solutions, or gain an improved information base. Sometimes, strategic ideas that are initially resisted can gain acceptance and commitment simply by the passage of time and open discussion of new information. Many top executives, planners and change agents consciously arrange such "gestation periods." For example, William Spoor at

Pillsbury allowed more than a year of discussion and information-gathering before the company decided to divest its chicken business.

TACTICAL SHIFTS AND PARTIAL SOLUTIONS

These are typical steps in developing a new strategic posture, especially when early problem resolutions need to be partial, tentative or experimental. Tactical adjustments, or a series of small programs, typically encounter little opposition, while a broad strategic change could encounter much opposition. These approaches allow the continuation of ongoing strengths while shifting momentum at the margin. Experimentation can occur with minimized risk, leading to many different ways to succeed.

As events unfurl, the solutions to several problems, which may initially have seemed unrelated, tend to flow together into a new combination. When possible, strategic logic (risk minimization) dictates starting broad initiatives that can be flexibly guided in any of several possible desirable directions.

BROADENING POLITICAL SUPPORT

This is an essential and consciously-active step in major strategy changes. Committees, task forces or retreats tend to be favored mechanisms. By selecting such groups' chairpersons, membership, timing, and agenda the guiding executives can largely influence and predict a desired outcome, yet nudge other executives toward a consensus. Interactive consensus building also improves the quality of decisions, and encourages positive and innovative help when things go wrong.

OVERCOMING OPPOSITION

Unnecessary alienation of managers from an earlier era in the organization's history should be avoided; their talents may be needed. But overcoming opposition is usually necessary. Preferred methods are persuasion, co-optation, neutralization, or moving through zones of indifference (i.e., pushing those portions of a project that are non-controversial to most of the interested parties). To be sure, successful executives honor and even stimulate legitimate differences. Opponents sometimes thoughtfully shape new strategies into more effective directions; sometimes they even change their views. Occasionally, though, strong-minded executives may need to be moved to less-influential positions, or be stimulated to leave.

CONSCIOUSLY STRUCTURED FLEXIBILITY

Flexibility is essential in dealing with the many "unknowables" in the environment. Successful organizations actively create flexibility. This requires active horizon scanning, creating resource buffers, developing and positioning champions, and shortening decision lines. These are the keys to *real* contingency planning, not the usual pre-capsuled (and shelved) programs designed to respond to stimuli that never occur quite as expected.

TRIAL BALLOONS AND SYSTEMATIC WAITING

Strategists may have to wait patiently for the proper option to appear or precipitating event to occur. For example, although he wanted to divest Pillsbury's chicken business, William Spoor waited until his investment bankers found a buyer at a good price. Executives may also consciously launch trial ideas, like Spoor's "Super Box" at Pillsbury, to attract options and concrete proposals. Without making a commitment to any specific solution, the executive mobilizes the organization's creative abilities.

CREATING POCKETS OF COMMITMENT

Executives often need this tactic when they are trying to get organizations to adopt entirely new strategic directions. Small projects, deep within the organization, are used to test options, create skills, or build commitments for several possible options. The executive provides broad goals, proper climate, and flexible resource support, without public commitment. This avoids attention on, and identification with, any project. Yet executives can stimulate the good options, make life harder for the poorer options, or even kill the weakest ones.

CRYSTALLIZING THE FOCUS

At some point, this becomes vital. Early commitments are necessarily vague, but once executives develop information or consensus on desirable ways to proceed, they may use their prestige or power to push or crystallize a particular formulation. This should not be done too early, as it might inadvertently centralize the organization or preempt interesting options. Focusing too early might also provide a common target for otherwise fragmented opposition, or cause the organization to undertake undesirable actions just to carry out a stated commitment. When to crystallize viewpoints and when to maintain open options is a true art of strategic management.

FORMALIZING COMMITMENT

This is the final step in the logical incremental strategy formation process. It usually occurs after general acceptance exists, and when the timing is right. Typically, the decision is announced publicly, programs and budgets are formed, and control and reward systems are aligned to reflect intended strategic emphases.

CONTINUING THE DYNAMICS AND MUTATING THE CONSENSUS

Advocates of the "new" strategy can become as strong a source of inflexible resistance to new ideas as were the advocates of the "old" strategy. Effective strategic managers immediately introduce new ideas and stimuli at the top, to maintain the adaptability of the strategic thrusts they have just solidified. This is a most difficult, but essential, psychological task.

NOT A LINEAR PROCESS

While generation of a strategy generally flows along the sequence presented above, the stages are usually not ordered or discrete. The process is more like fermentation in biochemistry, instead of being like an industrial assembly line. Segments of major strategies are likely to be at different stages of development. They are usually integrated in the minds of top executives, each of whom may nevertheless see things differently. Lastly, the process is so continuous that it may be hard to discern the particular point in time when specific clear-cut decisions are made.

An important point to remember is that the validity of a strategy lies not in its pristine clarity or rigorously maintained structure. Its value lies in its capacity to capture the initiative, to deal with unknowable events, and to redeploy and concentrate resources as new opportunities and thrusts emerge. This allows the organization to use resources most effectively toward selected goals.

INTEGRATING THE STRATEGY

The process described above may be incremental, but it is not piecemeal. Effective executives constantly reassess the total organization, its capacities, and its needs as related to the surrounding environment.

CONCENTRATING ON A FEW KEY THRUSTS

Effective strategic managers constantly seek to distill a few (six to ten) "central themes" that draw the firm's actions together. These maintain focus and consistency in the strategy. They make it easier to discuss and monitor intended directions. By contrast, formal models, designed to keep track of divisional progress toward realizing strategy, tend to become bound up in red tape, procedure, and rigid bureaucracy.

COALITION MANAGEMENT

The heart of all controlled strategy development is coalition management. Top managers act at the confluence of pressures from all stakeholders. These stakeholders will form coalitions, so managers must be active in forming their own. People selection and coalition management are the ultimate controls top executives have in guiding and coordinating their companies' strategies.

CONCLUSIONS

Many recent attempts to devise strategy using approaches that emphasize formal planning have failed because of poor implementation. This results from the classic trap of thinking about strategy formulation and implementation as separate and sequential processes. Successful managers who operate logically and actively, in an *incremental* mode, build the seeds of understanding, identity and commitment into the very processes that create their strategies. Strategy "formulation" and strategy "implementation" interact in the organization's continuing stream of events.

CRAFTING STRATEGY*

by Henry Mintzberg

Imagine someone planning strategy. What likely springs to mind is an image of orderly thinking: a senior manager, or a group of them, sitting in an office formulating courses of action that everyone else will implement on schedule. The keynote is reason—rational control, the systematic analysis of competitors and markets, of company strengths and weaknesses, the combination of these analyses producing clear, explicit, full-blown strategies.

Now imagine someone *crafting* strategy. A wholly different image likely results, as different from planning as craft is from mechanization. Craft evokes traditional skill, dedication, perfection through the mastery of detail. What springs to mind is not so much thinking and reason as involvement, a feeling of intimacy and harmony with the materials at hand, developed through long experience and commitment. Formulation and implementation merge into a fluid process of learning through which creative strategies evolve.

My thesis is simple: the crafting image better captures the process by which effective strategies come to be. The planning image, long popular in the literature, distorts these processes and thereby misguides organizations that embrace it unreservedly.

In developing this thesis, I shall draw on the experiences of a single craftsman, a potter, and compare them with the results of a research project that tracked the strategies of a number of corporations across several decades. Because the two contexts are so obviously different, my metaphor, like my assertion, may seem far-fetched at first. Yet if we think of a craftsman as an organization of one, we can see that he or she must also resolve one of the great challenges the corporate strategist faces: knowing the organization's capabilities well enough

* Originally published in the *Harvard Business Review* (July–August 1987) and winner of McKinsey prize for second best article in the *Review* 1987. Copyright © 1987 by the President and Fellows of Harvard College; all rights reserved. Reprinted with deletions by permission of the *Harvard Business Review*.

to think deeply enough about its strategic direction. By considering strategy making from the perspective of one person, free of all the paraphernalia of what has been called the strategy industry, we can learn something about the formation of strategy in the corporation. For much as our potter has to manage her craft, so too managers have to craft their strategy.

At work, the potter sits before a lump of clay on the wheel. Her mind is on the clay, but she is also aware of sitting between her past experiences and her future prospects. She knows exactly what has and has not worked for her in the past. She has an intimate knowledge of her work, her capabilities, and her markets. As a craftsman, she senses rather than analyzes these things; her knowledge is "tacit." All these things are working in her mind as her hands are working the clay. The product that emerges on the wheel is likely to be in the tradition of her past work, but she may break away and embark on a new direction. Even so, the past is no less present, projecting itself into the future.

In my metaphor, managers are craftsmen and strategy is their clay. Like the potter, they sit between the past of corporate capabilities and a future of market opportunities. And if they are truly craftsmen, they bring to their work an equally intimate knowledge of the materials at hand. That is the essence of crafting strategy.

1. Strategies Are Both Plans for the Future and Patterns from the Past

Ask almost anyone what strategy is, and they will define it as a plan of some sort, an explicit guide to future behavior. Then ask them what strategy a competitor or a government or even they themselves have actually pursued. Chances are they will describe consistency in *past* behavior—a pattern in action over time. Strategy, it turns out, is one of those words that people define in one way and often use in another, without realizing the difference.

The reason for this is simple. Strategy's formal definition and its Greek military origins not withstanding, we need the word as much to explain past actions as to describe intended behavior. After all, if strategies can be planned and intended, they can also be pursued and realized (or not realized, as the case may be). And pattern in action, or what we call realized strategy, explains that pursuit. Moreover, just as a plan need not produce a pattern (some strategies that are intended are simply not realized), so too a pattern need not result from a plan. An organization can have a pattern (or realized strategy) without knowing it, let alone making it explicit.

Patterns, like beauty, are in the mind of the beholder, of course. But finding them in organizations is not very difficult. But what about intended strategies, those formal plans and pronouncements we think of when we use the term *strategy*? Ironically, here we run into all kinds of problems. Even with a single craftsman, how can we know what her intended strategies really were? If we could go back, would we find expressions of intention? And if we could, would we be able to trust them? We often fool ourselves, as well as others, by denying our subconscious motives. And remember that intentions are cheap, at least when compared with realizations.

READING THE ORGANIZATION'S MIND

If you believe all this has more to do with the Freudian recesses of a craftsman's mind than with the practical realities of producing automobiles, then think again. For who knows what the intended strategies of an organization really mean, let alone what they are? Can we simply assume in this collective context that the company's intended strategies are represented by its formal plans or by other statements emanating from the executive suite? Might these be just vain hopes or rationalizations or ploys to fool the competition? And even if expressed intentions do exist, to what extent do various people in the organization share them? How do we read the collective mind? Who is the strategist anyway?

The traditional view of strategic management resolves these problems quite simply, by what organizational theorists call attribution. You see it all the time in the business press. When General Motors acts, it's because its CEO has made a strategy. Given realization, there must have been intention, and that is automatically attributed to the chief.

In a short magazine article, this assumption is understandable. Journalists don't have a lot of time to uncover the origins of strategy, and GM is a large, complicated organization. But just consider all the complexity and confusion that gets tucked under this assumption—all the meetings and debates, the many people, the dead ends, the folding and unfolding of ideas. Now imagine trying to build a formal strategy-making system around that assumption. Is it any wonder that formal strategic planning is often such a resounding failure?

To unravel some of the confusion—and move away from the artificial complexity we have piled around the strategy-making process—we need to get back to some basic concepts. The most basic of all is the intimate connection between thought and action. That is the key to craft, and so also to the crafting of strategy.

2. Strategies Need Not Be Deliberate—They Can Also Emerge, More or Less

Virtually everything that has been written about strategy making depicts it as a deliberate process. First we think, then we act. We formulate, then we implement. The progression seems so perfectly sensible. Why would anybody want to proceed differently?

Our potter is in the studio, rolling the clay to make a waferlike sculpture. The clay sticks to the rolling pin, and a round form appears. Why not make a cylindrical vase? One idea leads to another, until a new pattern forms. Action has driven thinking: a strategy has emerged.

Out in the field, a salesman visits a customer. The product isn't quite right, and together they work out some modifications. The salesman returns to his company and puts the changes through; after two or three more rounds, they finally get it right. A new product emerges, which eventually opens up a new market. The company has changed strategic course.

In fact, most salespeople are less fortunate than this one or than our craftsman. In an organization of one, the implementor is the formulator, so innovations can be incorporated into strategy quickly and easily. In a large organization, the innovator may be ten levels removed from the leader who is supposed to dictate strategy and may also have to sell the idea to dozens of peers doing the same job.

Some salespeople, of course, can proceed on their own, modifying products to suit their customers and convincing skunkworks in the factory to produce them. In effect, they pursue their own strategies. Maybe no one else notices or cares. Sometimes, however, their innovations do get noticed, perhaps years later, when the company's prevalent strategies have broken down and its leaders are groping for something new. Then the salesperson's strategy may be allowed to pervade the system, to become organizational.

Is this story farfetched? Certainly not. We've all heard stories like it. But since we tend to see only what we believe, if we believe that strategies have to be planned, we're unlikely to see the real meaning such stories hold.

Consider how the National Film Board of Canada (NFB) came to adopt a feature-film strategy. The NFB is a federal government agency, famous for its creativity and expert in the production of short documentaries. Some years back, it funded a filmmaker on a project that unexpectedly ran long. To distribute his film, the NFB turned to theaters and so inadvertently gained experience in marketing feature-length films. Other filmmakers caught onto the idea, and eventually the NFB found itself pursuing a feature-film strategy—a pattern of producing such films.

My point is simple, deceptively simple: strategies can *form* as well as be *formulated*. A realized strategy can emerge in response to an evolving situation, or it can be brought about deliberately, through a process of formulation followed by implementation. But when these planned intentions do not produce the desired actions, organizations are left with unrealized strategies.

Today we hear a great deal about unrealized strategies, almost always in concert with the claim that implementation has failed. Management has been lax, controls have been loose, people haven't been committed. Excuses abound. At times, indeed, they may be valid. But often these explanations prove too easy. So some people look beyond implementation to formulation. The strategists haven't been smart enough.

While it is certainly true that many intended strategies are ill conceived, I believe that the problem often lies one step beyond, in the distinction we make between formulation and implementation, the common assumption that thought must be independent of and precede action. Sure, people could be smarter—but not only by conceiving more clever strategies. Sometimes they can be smarter by allowing their strategies to develop gradually, through the organization's actions and experiences. Smart strategists appreciate that they cannot always be smart enough to think through everything in advance.

HANDS AND MINDS

No craftsman thinks some days and works others. The craftsman's mind is going constantly, in tandem with her hands. Yet large organizations try to separate the work of minds and hands. In so doing, they often sever the vital feedback linking between the two. The salesperson who finds a customer with an unmet need may possess the most strategic bit of information in the entire organization. But that information is useless if he or she cannot create a strategy in response to it or else convey the information to someone who can—because the channels are blocked or because the formulators have simply finished formulating. The notion that strategy is something that should happen way up there, far removed from the details of running an organization on a daily basis, is one of the great fallacies of conventional strategic management. And it explains a good many of the most dramatic failures in business and public policy today.

Strategies like the NFB's that appear without clear intentions—or in spite of them—can be called emergent. Actions simply converge into patterns. They may become deliberate, of course, if the pattern is recognized and then legitimated by senior management. But that's after the fact.

All this may sound rather strange, I know. Strategies that emerge? Managers who acknowledge strategies already formed? Over the years we have met with a good deal of resistance from people upset by what they perceive to be our passive definition of a word so bound up with proactive behavior and free will. After all, strategy means control—the ancient Greeks used it to describe the art of the army general.

STRATEGIC LEARNING

But we have persisted in this usage for one reason: learning. Purely deliberate strategy precludes learning once the strategy is formulated; emergent strategy fosters it. People take actions one by one and respond to them, so that patterns eventually form.

Our craftsman tries to make a freestanding sculptural form. It doesn't work, so she rounds it a bit here, flattens it a bit there. The result looks better, but still isn't quite right. She makes another and another and another. Eventually, after days or months or years, she finally has what she wants. She is off on a new strategy.

In practice, of course, all strategy making walks on two feet: one deliberate, the other emergent. For just as purely deliberate strategy making precludes learning, so purely emergent strategy making precludes control. Pushed to the limit, neither approach makes much sense. Learning must be coupled with control. That is why we use the word *strategy* for both emergent and deliberate behavior.

Likewise, there is no such thing as a purely deliberate strategy or a purely emergent one. No organization—not even the ones commanded by those ancient Greek generals—knows enough to work everything out in advance, to ignore learning en route. And no one—not even a solitary potter—can be flexible enough to leave everything to happenstance, to give up all control. Craft requires control just as it requires responsiveness to the material at hand. Thus deliberate and emergent strategy form the end points of a continuum along which the strategies that are crafted in the real world may be found. Some strategies may approach either end, but many more fall at intermediate points.

3. Effective Strategies Develop in All Kinds of Strange Ways

Effective strategies can show up in the strangest places and develop through the most unexpected means. There is no one best way to make strategy.

The form for a ceramic cat collapses on the wheel, and our potter sees a bull taking shape. Clay sticks to a rolling pin, and a line of cylinders results. Wafers come into being because of a shortage of clay and limited kiln space while visiting a studio in France. Thus errors become opportunities, and limitations stimulate creativity. The natural propensity to experiment, even boredom, likewise stimulates strategic change.

Organizations that craft their strategies have similar experiences. Recall the National Film Board with its inadvertently long film. Or consider its experiences with experimental films, which made special use of animation and sound. For 20 years, the NFB produced a bare but steady trickle of such films. In fact, every film but one in that trickle was produced by a single person, Norman McLaren, the NFB's most celebrated filmmaker. McLaren pursued a *personal strategy* of experimentation, deliberate for him perhaps (though who can know whether he had the whole stream in mind or simply planned one film at a time?) but not for the organization. Then 20 years later, others followed his lead and the trickle widened, his personal strategy becoming more broadly organizational.

While the NFB may seem like an extreme case, it highlights behavior that can be found, albeit in muted form, in all organizations. Those who doubt this might read Richard Pascale's account of how Honda stumbled into its enormous success in the American motorcycle market [the following article in this book].

GRASS-ROOTS STRATEGY MAKING

These strategies all reflect, in whole or part, what we like to call a grass-roots approach to strategic management. Strategies grow like weeds in a garden. They take root in all kinds of places, wherever people have the capacity to learn (because they are in touch with the situation) and the resources to support that capacity. These strategies become organizational when they become collective, that is, when they proliferate to guide the behavior of the organization at large.

Of course, this view is overstated. But it is no less extreme than the conventional view of strategic management, which might be labeled the hothouse approach. Neither is right. Reality falls between the two. Some of the most effective strategies we uncovered in our research combined deliberation and control with flexibility and organizational learning.

Consider first what we call the *umbrella strategy*. Here senior management sets out broad guidelines (say, to produce only high-margin products at the cutting edge of technology or to favor products using bonding technology) and leaves the specifics (such as what these products will be) to others lower down in the organization. This strategy is not only deliberate (in its guidelines) and emergent (in its specifics), but it is also deliberately emergent, in that the process is consciously managed to allow strategies to emerge en route. IBM used the umbrella strategy in the early 1960s with the impending 360 series, when its senior management approved a set of broad criteria for the design of a family of computers later developed in detail throughout the organization. [See the IBM case in this section.]

Deliberately emergent, too, is what we call the *process strategy*. Here management controls the process of strategy formation—concerning itself with the design of the structure, its staffing, procedures, and so on—while, leaving the actual content to others.

Both process and umbrella strategies seem to be especially prevalent in businesses that require great expertise and creativity—a 3M, a Hewlett-Packard, a National Film Board. Such organizations can be effective only if their implementors are allowed to be formulators, because it is people way down in the hierarchy who are in touch with the situation at hand and have the requisite technical expertise. In a sense, these are organizations peopled with craftsmen, all of whom must be strategists.

4. Strategic Reorientations Happen in Brief, Quantum Leaps

The conventional view of strategic management, especially in the planning literature, claims that change must be continuous: the organization should be adapting all the time. Yet this view proves to be ironic because the very concept of strategy is rooted in stability, not change. As this same literature makes clear, organizations pursue strategies to set direction, to lay out courses of action, and to elicit cooperation from their members around common, established guidelines. By any definition, strategy imposes stability on an organization. No stability means no strategy (no course to the future, no pattern from the past). Indeed, the very fact of having a strategy, and especially of making it explicit (as the conventional literature implores managers to do), creates resistance to strategic change!

What the conventional view fails to come to grips with, then, is how and when to promote change. A fundamental dilemma of strategy making is the need to reconcile the forces for stability and for change—to focus efforts and gain operating efficiencies on the one hand, yet adapt and maintain currency with a changing external environment on the other.

QUANTUM LEAPS

Our own research and that of colleagues suggest that organizations resolve these opposing forces by attending first to one and then to the other. Clear periods of stability and change can usually be distinguished in any organization: while it is true that particular strategies may always be changing marginally, it seems equally true that major shifts in strategic orientation occur only rarely.

In our study of Steinberg, Inc., a large Quebec supermarket chain headquartered in Montreal, we found only two important reorientations in the 60 years from its founding to the mid-1970s: a shift to self-service in 1933 and the introduction of shopping centers and public financing in 1953. At Volkswagenwerk, we saw only one between the late 1940s and the 1970s, the tumultuous shift from the traditional Beetle to the Audi-type design. And at Air Canada, we found none over the airline's first four decades, following its initial positioning.

Our colleagues at McGill, Danny Miller and Peter Friesen (1984), found this pattern of change so common in their studies of large numbers of companies (especially the high-performance ones) that they built a theory around it, which they labeled the quantum theory of strategic change. Their basic point is that organizations adopt two distinctly different modes of behavior at different times.

Most of the time they pursue a given strategic orientation. Change may seem continuous, but it occurs in the context of that orientation (perfecting a given retailing formula, for example) and usually amounts to doing more of the same, perhaps better as well. Most organizations favor these periods of stability because they achieve success not by changing strategies but by exploiting the ones they have. They, like craftsmen, seek continuous improvement by using their distinctive competencies on established courses.

While this goes on, however, the world continues to change, sometimes slowly, occasionally in dramatic shifts. Thus gradually or suddenly, the organization's strategic orientation moves out of sync with its environment. Then what Miller and Friesen call a strategic revolution must take place. That long period of evolutionary change is suddenly punctuated by a brief bout of revolutionary turmoil in which the organization quickly alters many of its established patterns. In effect, it tries to leap to a new stability quickly to reestablish an integrated posture among a new set of strategies, structures, and culture.

But what about all those emergent strategies, growing like weeds around the organization? What the quantum theory suggests is that the really novel ones are generally held in check in some corner of the organization until a strategic revolution becomes necessary. Then, as an alternative to having to develop new strategies from scratch or having to import generic strategies from competitors, the organization can turn to its own emerging patterns to find its new orientation. As the old, established strategy disintegrates, the seeds of the new one begin to spread.

This quantum theory of change seems to apply particularly well to large established, mass-production companies, like a Volkswagenwerk. Because they are especially reliant on standardized procedures, their resistance to strategic reorientation tends to be especially fierce. So we find long periods of stability broken by short disruptive periods of revolutionary change. Strategic reorientations really are cultural revolutions.

In more creative organizations we see a somewhat different pattern of change and stability, one that is more balanced. Companies in the business of producing novel outputs apparently need to run off in all directions from time to time to sustain their creativity. Yet they also need to settle down after such periods to find some order in the resulting chaos—convergence following divergence.

Whether through quantum revolutions or cycles of convergence and divergence, however, organizations seem to need to separate in time the basic forces for change and stability, reconciling them by attending to each in turn. Many strategic failures can be attributed either to mixing the two or to an obsession with one of these forces at the expense of the other.

The problems are evident in the work of many craftsmen. On the one hand, there are those who seize on the perfection of a single theme and never change. Eventually the creativity disappears from their work and the world passes them by—much as it did Volkswagenwerk until the company was shocked into its strategic revolution. And then there are those who are always changing, who flit from one idea to another and never settle down. Because no theme or strategy ever emerges in their work, they cannot exploit or even develop any distinctive competence. And because their work lacks definition, identity crises are likely to develop, with neither the craftsmen nor their clientele knowing what to make of it. Miller and Friesen (1978: 921) found this behavior in conventional business too; they label it "the impulsive firm running blind." How often have we seen it in companies that go on acquisition sprees?

5. To Manage Strategy, Then, Is to Craft Thought and Action, Control and Learning, Stability and Change

The popular view sees the strategist as a planner or as a visionary, someone sitting on a pedestal dictating brilliant strategies for everyone else to implement While recognizing the importance of thinking ahead and especially of the need for creative vision in this pedantic world, I wish to propose an additional view of the strategist—as a pattern recognizer, a learner if you will—who manages a process in which strategies (and visions) can emerge as well as be deliberately conceived. I also wish to redefine that strategist, to extend that someone into the collective entity made up of the many actors whose interplay speaks an organization's mind. This strategist *finds* strategies no less than creates them, often in patterns that form inadvertently in his or her own behavior.

What, then, does it mean to craft strategy? Let us return to the words associated with craft: dedication, experience, involvement with the material, the personal touch, mastery of detail, a sense of harmony and integration. Managers who craft strategy do not spend much time in executive suites reading MIS reports or industry analyses. They are involved, responsive to their materials, learning about their organizations and industries through personal touch. They are also sensitive to experience, recognizing that while individual vision may be important, other factors must help determine strategy as well.

MANAGE STABILITY

Managing strategy is mostly managing stability, not change. Indeed, most of the time senior managers should not be formulating strategy at all; they should be getting on with making their organizations as effective as possible in pursuing the strategies they already have. Like distinguished craftsmen, organizations become distinguished because they master the details.

To manage strategy, then, at least in the first instance, is not so much to promote change as to know *when* to do so. Advocates of strategic planning often urge managers to plan for perpetual instability in the environment (for example, by rolling over five-year plans annually). But this obsession with change is dysfunctional. Organizations that reassess their strategies continuously are like individuals who reassess their jobs or their marriages continuously—in both cases, they will drive themselves crazy or else reduce themselves to inaction. The formal planning process repeats itself so often and so mechanically that it desensitizes the organization to real change, programs it more and more deeply into set patterns, and thereby encourages it to make only minor adaptations.

So-called strategic planning must be recognized for what it is: a means, not to create strategy, but to program a strategy already created—to work out its implications formally. It is essentially analytic in nature, based on decomposition, while strategy creation is essentially a process of synthesis. That is why trying to create strategies through formal planning most often leads to extrapolating existing ones or copying those of competitors.

This is not to say that planners have no role to play in strategy formation. In addition to programming strategies created by other means, they can feed ad hoc analyses into the strategy-making process at the front end to be sure that the hard data are taken into consideration. They can also stimulate others to think strategically. And of course people called planners can be strategists too, so long as they are creative thinkers who are in touch with what is relevant. But that has nothing to do with the technology of formal planning.

DETECT DISCONTINUITY

Environments don't change on any regular or orderly basis. And they seldom undergo continuous dramatic change, claims about our "age of discontinuity" and environmental "turbulence" notwithstanding. (Go tell people who lived through the Great Depression or survivors of the siege of Leningrad during World War II that ours are turbulent times.) Much of the time, change is minor and even temporary and requires no strategic response. Once in a while there is a truly significant discontinuity or, even less often, a gestalt shift in the environment, where everything important seems to change at once. But these events, while critical, are also easy to recognize.

The real challenge in crafting strategy lies in detecting the subtle discontinuities that may undermine a business in the future. And for that, there is no technique, no program, just a sharp mind in touch with the situation. Such discontinuities are unexpected and irregular, essentially unprecedented. They can be dealt with only by minds that are attuned to existing patterns yet able to perceive important breaks in them. Unfortunately, this form of strategic thinking tends to atrophy during the long periods of stability that most organizations experience. So the trick is to manage within a given strategic orientation most of the time yet be able to pick out the occasional discontinuity that really matters. The ability to make that kind of switch in thinking is the essence of strategic management. And it has more to do with vision and involvement than it does with analytic technique.

KNOW THE BUSINESS

Note the kind of knowledge involved in strategic thinking: not intellectual knowledge, not analytical reports or abstracted facts and figures (though these can certainly help), but personal knowledge, intimate understanding, equivalent to the craftsman's feel for the clay. Facts are available to anyone; this kind of knowledge is not. Wisdom is the word that captures it best. But wisdom is a word that has been lost in the bureaucracies we have built for ourselves, systems designed to distance leaders from operating details. Show me managers who think they can rely on formal planning to create their strategies, and I'll show you managers who lack intimate knowledge of their businesses or the creativity to do something with it.

Craftsmen have to train themselves to see, to pick up things other people miss. The same holds true for managers of strategy. It is those with a kind of peripheral vision who are best able to detect and take advantage of events as they unfold.

MANAGE PATTERNS

Whether in an executive suite in Manhattan or a pottery studio in Montreal, a key to managing strategy is the ability to detect emerging patterns and help them take shape. The job of the manager is not just to preconceive specific strategies but also to recognize their emergence elsewhere in the organization and intervene when appropriate.

Like weeds that appear unexpectedly in a garden, some emergent strategies may need to be uprooted immediately. But management cannot be too quick to cut off the unexpected, for tomorrow's vision may grow out of today's aberration. (Europeans, after all, enjoy salads made from the leaves of the dandelion, America's most notorious weed.) Thus some patterns are worth watching until their effects have more clearly manifested themselves. Then those that prove useful can be made deliberate and be incorporated into the formal strategy, even if that means shifting the strategic umbrella to cover them.

To manage in this context, then, is to create the climate within which a wide variety of strategies can grow. In more complex organizations, this may mean building flexible structures, hiring creative people, defining broad umbrella strategies and watching for the patterns that emerge.

RECONCILE CHANGE AND CONTINUITY

Finally, managers considering radical departures need to keep the quantum theory of change in mind. As Ecclesiastes reminds us, there is a time to sow and a time to reap. Some new patterns must be held in check until the organization is ready for a strategic revolution, or at least a period of divergence. Managers who are obsessed with either change or stability are bound eventually to harm their organizations. As pattern recognizer, the manager has to be able to sense when to exploit an established crop of strategies and when to encourage new strains to displace the old.

While strategy is a word that is usually associated with the future, its link to the past is no less central. As Kierkegaard once observed, life is lived forward but understood backward. Managers may have to live strategy in the future, but they must understand it through the past.

Like potters at the wheel, organizations must make sense of the past if they hope to manage the future. Only by coming to understand the patterns that form in their own behavior do they get to know their capabilities and their potential. Thus crafting strategy, like managing craft, requires a natural synthesis of the future, present, and past.

▼ READING 5.3   THE HONDA EFFECT*

by Richard T. Pascale

At face value, "strategy" is an innocent noun. Webster defines it as the large-scale planning and direction of operations. In the business context, it pertains to a process by which a firm searches and analyzes its environment and resources in order to (1) select opportunities defined in terms of markets to be served and products to serve them and (2) make discrete decisions to invest resources in order to achieve identified objectives. (Bower, 1970: 7–8).

But for a vast and influential population of executives, planners, academics, and consultants, strategy is more than a conventional English noun. It embodies an implicit model of how organizations should be guided and consequently, preconfigures our way of thinking. Strategy formulation (1) is generally assumed to be driven by senior management whom we expect to set strategic direction, (2) has been extensively influenced by empirical models and concepts, and (3) is often associated with a laborious strategic planning process that, in some companies, has produced more paper than insight.

A $500-million-a-year "strategy" industry has emerged in the United States and Europe comprised of management consultants, strategic planning staffs, and business school academics. It caters to the unique emphasis that American and European companies place upon this particular aspect of managing and directing corporations.

Words often derive meaning from their cultural context. *Strategy* is one such word and nowhere is the contrast of meanings more pronounced than between Japan and the United States. The Japanese view the emphasis we place on "strategy" as we might regard their enthusiasm for Kabuki or sumo wrestling. They note our interests not with an intent of acquiring similar ones but for insight into our peculiarities. The Japanese are somewhat distrustful of a single "strategy" for in their view any idea that focuses attention does so at the expense of peripheral vision. They strongly believe that *peripheral vision* is essential to discerning changes in the customer, the technology or competition, and is the key to corporate survival over the long haul. They regard any propensity to be driven by a single-minded strategy as a weakness.

The Japanese have particular discomfort with strategic concepts. While they do not reject ideas such as the experience curve or portfolio theory outright they regard them as a stimulus to perception. They have often ferreted out the "formula" of their concept-driven American competitors and exploited their inflexibility. In musical instruments, for example (a mature industry facing stagnation as birthrates in the United States and Japan declined), Yamaha might have classified its products as "cash cows" and gone on to better things (as its chief U.S. competitor, Baldwin United, had done). Instead, beginning with a negligible share of the U.S. market, Yamaha plowed ahead and destroyed Baldwin's seemingly unchallengeable dominance. YKK's success in zippers against Talon (a Textron division) and Honda's outflanking of Harley-Davidson (a former AMF subsidiary) in the motorcycle field provide parallel illustrations. All three cases involved American conglomerates,

*Excerpted from an article originally entitled "Perspectives on Strategy: The Real Story Behind Honda's Success," *California Management Review* XXVI, no. 3, pp. 47–72. Copyright © 1994 by the Regents of the University of California. Reprinted by permission of the Regents.

wedded to the portfolio concept, that had classified pianos, zippers, and motorcycles as mature businesses to be harvested rather than nourished and defended. Of course, those who developed portfolio theory and other strategic concepts protest that they were never intended to be mindlessly applied in setting strategic direction. But most would also agree that there is a widespread tendency in American corporations to misapply concepts and to otherwise become strategically myopic—ignoring the marketplace, the customer, and the problems of execution. This tendency toward misapplication, being both pervasive and persistent over several decades, is a phenomenon that the literature has largely ignored [for exceptions, see Hayes and Abernathy, 1980:67; Hayes and Garvin, 1982:71]. There is a need to identify explicitly the factors that influence how we conceptualize strategy—and which foster its misuse.

Honda: The Strategy Model

In 1975, Boston Consulting Group (BCG) presented the British government its final report: *Strategy Alternatives for the British Motorcycle Industry*. This 120-page document identified two key factors leading to the British demise in the world's motorcycle industry:

▼ Market share loss and profitability declines
▼ Scale economy disadvantages in technology, distribution, and manufacturing

During the period 1959 to 1973, the British share of the U.S. motorcycle industry had dropped from 49% to 9%. Introducing BCG's recommended strategy (of targeting market segments where sufficient production volumes could be attained to be price competitive) the report states:

> The success of the Japanese manufacturers originated with the growth of their domestic market during the 1950s. As recently as 1960, only 4 percent of Japanese motorcycle production was exported. By this time, however, the Japanese had developed huge production volumes in small motorcycles in their domestic market, and volume-related cost reductions had followed. This resulted in a highly competitive cost position which the Japanese used as a springboard for penetration of world markets with small motorcycles in the early 1960s (BCG, 1975:xiv).

The BCG study was made public by the British government and rapidly disseminated in the United States. It exemplifies the necessary (and, I argue, insufficient) strategist's perspective of:

▼ examining competition primarily from an intercompany perspective,
▼ at a high level of abstraction,
▼ with heavy reliance on macroeconomic concepts (such as the experience curve).

Case writers at Harvard Business School, UCLA, and the University of Virginia quickly condensed the BCG report for classroom use in case discussions. It currently enjoys extensive use in first-term courses in business policy.

Of particular note in the BCG study, and in the subsequent Harvard Business School rendition, is the historical treatment of Honda.

> The mix of competitors in the U.S. motorcycle market underwent a major shift in the 1960s. Motorcycle registrations increased from 575,000 in 1960 to 1,382,000 in 1965. Prior to 1960 the U.S. market was served mainly by Harley-Davidson of U.S.A., BSA, Triumph and Norton of U.K. and Moto-Guzzi of Italy. Harley was the market leader with total 1959 sales of $16.6 million. After the second world war, motorcycles in the U.S.A. attracted a very limited group of people other than police and army personnel who used motorcycles on the job. While most motorcyclists were no doubt decent people, groups of rowdies who went around on motorcycles and called themselves by such names as "Hell's Angels," "Satan's Slaves" gave motorcycling a

bad image. Even leather jackets which were worn by motorcyclists as a protective device acquired an unsavory image. A 1953 movie called "The Wild Ones" starring a 650cc Triumph, a black leather jacket and Marlon Brando gave the rowdy motorcyclists wide media coverage. The stereotype of the motorcyclist was a leather-jacketed, teenage troublemaker.

Honda established an American subsidiary in 1959—American Honda Motor Company. This was in sharp contrast to other foreign producers who relied on distributors. Honda's marketing strategy was described in the 1963 annual report as "With its policy of selling, not primarily to confirmed motorcyclists but rather to members of the general public who had never before given a second thought to a motorcycle. . . ." Honda started its push in the U.S. market with the smallest, lightweight motorcycles. It had a three-speed transmisson, an automatic clutch, five horsepower (the American cycle only had two and a half), an electric starter and step through frame for female riders. And it was easier to handle. The Honda machines sold for under $250 in retail compared with $1,000–$1,500 for the bigger American or British machines. Even at that early date Honda was probably superior to other competitors in productivity.

By June 1960 Honda's Research and Development effort was staffed with 700 designers/engineers. This might be contrasted with 100 engineers/draftsmen employed by . . . (European and American competitors). In 1962 production per man-year was running at 159 units, (a figure not matched by Harley-Davidson until 1974). Honda's net fixed asset investment was $8170 per employee . . . (more than twice its European and American competitors). With 1959 sales of $55 million Honda was already the largest motorcycle producer in the world.

Honda followed a policy of developing the market region by region. They started on the West Coast and moved eastward over a period of four–five years. Honda sold 2,500 machines in the U.S. in 1960. In 1961 they lined up 125 distributors and spent $150,000 on regional advertising. Their advertising was directed to the young families, their advertising theme was "You Meet the Nicest People on a Honda." This was a deliberate attempt to dissociate motorcycles from rowdy, Hell's Angels type people.

Honda's success in creating demand for lightweight motorcycles was phenomenal. American Honda's sales went from $500,000 in 1960 to $77 million in 1965. By 1966 the market share data showed the ascendancy of Japanese producers and their success in selling lightweight motorcycles. [Honda had 63% of the market] . . . Starting from virtually nothing in 1960, the lightweight motorcycles had clearly established their lead (Purkayastha, 1981: 5, 10, 11, 12).

Quoting from the BCG report:

The Japanese motorcycle industry, and in particular Honda, the market leader, present a [consistent] picture. The basic philosophy of the Japanese manufacturers is that high volumes per model provide the potential for high productivity as a result of using capital intensive and highly automated techniques. Their marketing strategies are therefore directed towards developing these high model volumes, hence the careful attention that we have observed them giving to growth and market share.

The overall result of this philosophy over time has been that the Japanese have now developed an entrenched and leading position in terms of technology and production methods. . . . The major factors which appear to account for the Japanese superiority in both these areas are . . . (specialized production systems, balancing engineering and market requirements, and the cost efficiency and reliability of suppliers) (BCG, pp. 59, 40).

As evidence of Honda's strategy of taking position as low cost producer and exploiting economies of scale, other sources cite Honda's construction in 1959 of a plant to manufacture 30,000 motorcycles per month well ahead of existing demand at the time. (Up until then Honda's most popular models sold 2,000–3,000 units per month.) (Sakiya, 1982:119)

The overall picture as depicted by the quotes exemplifies the "strategy model." Honda is portrayed as a firm dedicated to being the low price producer, utilizing its dominant market position in Japan to force entry into the U.S. market, expanding that market by redefining a leisure class ("Nicest People") segment, and exploiting its comparative advantage via aggressive pricing and advertising. Richard Rumelt, writing the teaching note for the UCLA adaptation of the case states: "The fundamental contribution of BCG is not the

FIGURE 1
Source: BCG (1975),
"Strategy Alternatives for the
British Motorcycle Industry."

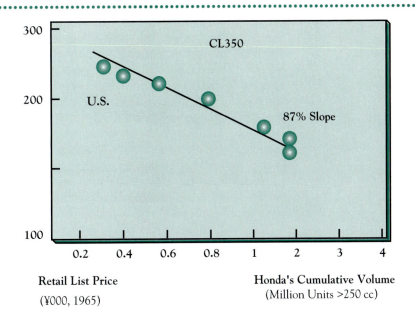

Retail List Price
(¥000, 1965)

Honda's Cumulative Volume
(Million Units >250 cc)

experience curve per se but the ever-present assumption that differences in cost (or efficiency) are the fundamental components of strategy." (Rumelt, 1980:2).

The Organizational Process Perspective

On September 10, 1982, the six Japanese executives responsible for Honda's entry into the U.S. motorcycle market in 1959 assembled in Honda's Tokyo headquarters. They had gathered at my request to describe in fine grain detail the sequence of events that had led to Honda's ultimate position of dominance in the U.S. market. All were in their sixties; three were retired. The story that unfolded, greatly abbreviated below, highlights miscalculation, serendipity, and organizational learning—counterpoints to the streamlined "strategy" version related earlier. . . .

Any account of Honda's successes must grasp at the outset the unusual character of its founder, Sochiro Honda, and his partner, Takeo Fujisawa. Honda was an inventive genius with a large ego and mercurial temperament, given to bouts of "philandering" (to use his expression) (Sakiya, 1979). . . .

Postwar Japan was in desperate need of transportation. Motorcycle manufacturers proliferated, producing clip-on engines that converted bicycles into makeshift "mopeds." Honda was among these but it was not until he teamed up with Fujisawa in 1949 that the elements of a successful enterprise began to take shape. Fujisawa provided money as well as financial and marketing strengths. In 1950 their first D-type motorcycle was introduced. They were, at that juncture, participating in a fragmented industry along with 247 other manufacturers. Other than its sturdy frame, this introductory product was unnoteworthy and did not enjoy great commercial success. (Sakiya, 1979, 1982).

Honda embodied a rare combination of inventive ability and ultimate self-confidence. His motivation was not primarily commercial. Rather, the company served as a vehicle to give expression to his inventive abilities. A successful company would provide a resource base to pursue, in Fujisawa's words, his "grandiose dream." Fujisawa continues, "There was no end to his pursuit of technology." (Sakiya, 1982).

Fujisawa, in an effort to save the faltering company, pressed Honda to abandon their noisy two-stroke engine and pursue a four-stroke design. The quieter four-stroke engines were appearing on competitive motorcycles, therefore threatening Honda with extinction. Mr. Honda balked. But a year later, Honda stunned Fujisawa with a breakthrough design that doubled the horsepower of competitive four-stroke engines. With this innovation, the firm was off and putting, and by 1951 demand was brisk. There was no organization, however, and the plant was chaotic (Sakiya, 1982). Strong demand, however, required early investment in a simplified mass production process. As a result, *primarily* due to design advantages, and secondarily to production methods, Honda became one of the four or five industry leaders by 1954 with 15 percent market share (data provided by company). . . .

For Fujisawa, the engine innovation meant increased sales and easier access to financing. For Mr. Honda, the higher horsepower engine opened the possibility of pursuing one of his central ambitions in life—to race his motorcycle and win. . . .

Fujisawa, throughout the fifties, sought to turn Honda's attention from his enthusiasm with racing to the more mundane requirements of running an enterprise. By 1956, as the innovations gained from racing had begun to pay off in vastly more efficient engines, Fujisawa pressed Honda to adapt this technology for a commercial motorcycle (Sakiya, 1979, 1982). Fujisawa had a particular segment in mind. Most motorcyclists in Japan were male and the machines were used primarily as an alternative form of transportation to trains and buses. There were, however, a vast number of small commercial establishments in Japan that still delivered goods and ran errands on bicycles. Trains and buses were inconvenient for these activities. The pursestrings of these small enterprises were controlled by the Japanese wife—who resisted buying conventional motorcycles because they were expensive, dangerous, and hard to handle. Fujisawa challenged Honda: Can you use what you've learned from racing to come up with an inexpensive, safe-looking motorcycle that can be driven with one hand (to facilitate carrying packages).

In 1958, the Honda 50cc Supercub was introduced—with an automatic clutch, three-speed transmission, automatic starter, and the safe, friendly look of a bicycle (without the stigma of the outmoded mopeds). Owing almost entirely to its high horsepower but *lightweight 50cc engine* (not to production efficiencies), it was affordable. Overnight, the firm was overwhelmed with orders. Engulfed by demand, they sought financing to build a new plant with a 30,000 unit per month capacity. "It wasn't a speculative investment," recalls one executive. "We had the proprietary technology, we had the market and the demand was enormous." (The plant was completed in mid-1960.) Prior to its opening, demand was met through makeshift, high cost, company-owned assembly and farmed-out assembly through subcontractors. By the end of 1959, Honda had skyrocketed into first place among Japanese motorcycle manufacturers. Of its total sales that year of 285,000 units, 168,000 were Supercubs.

Fujisawa utilized the Supercub to restructure Honda's channels of distribution. For many years, Honda had rankled under the two-tier distribution system that prevailed in the industry. These problems had been exacerbated by the fact that Honda was a late entry and had been carried as secondary line by distributors whose loyalties lay with their older manufacturers. Further weakening Honda's leverage, all manufacturer sales were on a consignment basis.

Deftly, Fujisawa had characterized the Supercub to Honda's distributors as "something much more like a bicycle than a motorcycle." The traditional channels, to their later regret, agreed. Under amicable terms Fujisawa began selling the Supercub directly to retailers—and primarily through bicycle shops. Since these shops were small and numerous (approximately 12,000 in Japan), sales on consignment were unthinkable. A cash-on-delivery system was installed, giving Honda significantly more leverage over its dealerships than the other motorcycle manufacturers enjoyed.

The stage was now set for exploration of the U.S. market. Mr. Honda's racing conquests in the late 1950s had given substance to his convictions about his abilities. . . .

Two Honda executives—the soon-to-be-named president of American Honda, Kihachiro Kawashima, and his assistant—arrived in the United States in late 1958. Their itinerary: San Francisco, Los Angeles, Dallas, New York, and Columbus. Mr. Kawashima recounts his impressions:

My first reaction after travelling across the United States was: how could we have been so stupid as to start a war with such a vast and wealthy country! My second reaction was discomfort. I spoke poor English. We dropped in on motorcycle dealers who treated us discourteously and in addition, gave the general impression of being motorcycle enthusiasts who, secondarily, were in business. There were only 3,000 motorcycle dealers in the United States at the time and only 1,000 of them were open five days a week. The remainder were open on nights and weekends. Inventory was poor, manufacturers sold motorcycles to dealers on consignment, the retailers provided consumer financing; after-sales service was poor. It was discouraging.

My other impression was that everyone in the United States drove an automobile—making it doubtful that motorcycles could ever do very well in the market. However, with 450,000 motorcycle registrations in the U.S. and 60,000 motorcycles imported from Europe each year it didn't seem unreasonable to shoot for 10 percent of the import market. I returned to Japan with that report.

In truth, we had no strategy other than the idea of seeing if we could sell something in the United States. It was a new frontier, a new challenge and it fit the "success against all odds" culture that Mr. Honda had cultivated. I reported my impressions to Fujisawa—including the seat-of-the-pants target of trying, over several years, to attain a 10 percent share of U.S. imports. He didn't probe that target quantitatively. We did not discuss profits or deadlines for breakeven. Fujisawa told me if anyone could succeed, I could and authorized $1 million for the venture.

The next hurdle was to obtain a currency allocation from the Ministry of Finance. They were extraordinarily skeptical. Toyota had launched the Toyopet in the U.S. in 1958 and had failed miserably. "How could Honda succeed?" they asked. Months went by. We put the project on hold. Suddenly, five months after our application, we were given the go-ahead—but at only a fraction of our expected level of commitment. "You can invest $250,000 in the U.S. market." they said, "but only $110,000 in cash." The remainder of our assets had to be in parts and motorcycle inventory.

We moved into frantic activity as the government, hoping we would give up on the idea, continued to hold us to the July 1959 start-up timetable. Our focus, as mentioned earlier, was to compete with the European exports. We knew our products at the time were good but not far superior. Mr. Honda was especially confident of the 250cc and 305cc machines. The shape of the handlebar on these larger machines looked like the eyebrow of Buddha, which he felt was a strong selling point. Thus, after some discussion and with no compelling criteria for selection, we configured our start-up inventory with 25 percent of each of our four products—the 50cc Supercub and the 125cc, 250cc, and 305cc machines. In dollar value terms, of course, the inventory was heavily weighted toward the larger bikes.

The stringent monetary controls of the Japanese government together with the unfriendly reception we had received during our 1958 visit caused us to start small. We chose Los Angeles where there was a large second and third generation Japanese community, a climate suitable for motorcycle use, and a growing population. We were so strapped for cash that the three of us shared a furnished apartment that rented for $80 per month. Two of us slept on the floor. We obtained a warehouse in a run-down section of the city and waited for the ship to arrive. Not daring to spare our funds for equipment, the three of us stacked the motorcycle crates three high—by hand, swept the floors, and built and maintained the parts bin.

We were entirely in the dark the first year. We were not aware the motorcycle business in the United States occurs during a seasonable April-to-August window—and our timing coincided with the closing of the 1959 season. Our hard-learned experiences with distributorships in Japan convinced us to try to go to the retailers direct. We ran ads in the motorcycle trade magazine for dealers. A few responded. By spring of 1960, we had forty dealers and some of our inventory in their stores—mostly larger bikes. A few of the 250cc and 305cc bikes began to sell. Then disaster struck.

By the first week of April 1960, reports were coming in that our machines were leaking oil and encountering clutch failure. This was our lowest moment. Honda's fragile reputation was being destroyed before it could be established. As it turned out, motorcycles in the United States are driven much farther and much faster than in Japan. We dug deeply into our precious cash reserves to air freight our motorcycles to the Honda testing lab in Japan. Through the dark month of April, Pan Am was the only enterprise in the U.S. that was nice to us. Our testing lab worked twenty-four-hour days bench testing the bikes to try to replicate the failure. Within a month, a redesigned head gasket and clutch spring solved the problem. But in the meantime, events had taken a surprising turn.

Throughout our first eight months, following Mr. Honda's and our own instincts, we had not attempted to move the 50cc Supercubs. While they were a smash success in Japan (and manufacturing couldn't keep up with demand there), they seemed wholly unsuitable for the U.S. market where everything was bigger and more luxurious. As a clincher, we had our sights on the import market—and the Europeans, like the American manufacturers, emphasized the larger machines.

We used the Honda 50s ourselves to ride around Los Angeles on errands. They attracted a lot of attention. One day we had a call from a Sears buyer. While persisting in our refusal to sell through an intermediary, we took note of Sears' interest. But we still hesitated to push the 50cc bikes out of fear they might harm our image in a heavily macho market. But when the larger bikes started breaking, we had no choice. We let the 50cc bikes move. And surprisingly, the retailers who wanted to sell them weren't motorcycle dealers, they were sporting goods stores.

The excitement created by the Honda Supercub began to gain momentum. Under restrictions from the Japanese government, we were still on a cash basis. Working with our initial cash and inventory, we sold machines, reinvested in inventory, and sunk the profits into additional inventory and advertising. Our advertising tried to straddle the market. While retailers continued to inform us that our Supercub customers were normal everyday Americans, we hesitated to target toward this segment out of fear of alienating the high margin end of our business—sold through the traditional motorcycle dealers to a more traditional "black leather jacket" customer.

Honda's phenomenal sales and share gains over the ensuing years have been previously reported. History has it that Honda *"redefined"* the U.S. motorcycle industry. In the view of American Honda's start-up team, this was an innovation they backed into—and reluctantly. It was certainly not the strategy they embarked on in 1959. As late as 1963, Honda was still working with its original Los Angeles advertising agency, its ad campaigns straddling all customers so as not to antagonize one market in pursuit of another.

In the spring of 1963, an undergraduate advertising major at UCLA submitted, in fulfillment of a routine course assignment, an ad campaign for Honda. Its theme: You Meet the Nicest People on a Honda. Encouraged by his instructor, the student passed his work on to a friend at Grey Advertising. Grey had been soliciting the Honda account—which with a $5 million a year budget was becoming an attractive potential client. Grey purchased the student's idea—on a tightly kept nondisclosure basis. Grey attempted to sell the idea to Honda.

Interestingly, the Honda management team, which by 1963 had grown to five Japanese executives, was badly split on this advertising decision. The president and treasurer favored another proposal from another agency. The director of sales, however, felt strongly that the Nicest People campaign was the right one—and his commitment eventually held sway. Thus, in 1963, through an inadvertent sequence of events, Honda came to adopt a strategy that directly identified and targeted that large untapped segment of the marketplace that has since become inseparable from the Honda legend.

The Nicest People campaign drove Honda's sales at an even greater rate. By 1964, nearly one out of every two motorcycles sold was a Honda. As a result of the influx of medium income leisure class consumers, banks and other consumer credit companies began to finance motorcycles—shifting away from dealer credit, which had been the traditional purchasing mechanism available. Honda, seizing the opportunity of soaring demand for its products, took a courageous and seemingly risky position. Late in 1964, they announced that thereafter, they would cease to ship on a consignment basis but would require cash on delivery. Honda braced itself for revolt. While nearly every dealer questioned, appealed, or complained, none relinquished his franchise. In one fell swoop, Honda shifted the power relationship from the dealer to the manufacturer. Within three years, this would become the pattern for the industry.

The "Honda Effect"

The preceding account of Honda's inroads in the U.S. motorcycle industry provides more than a second perspective on reality. It focuses our attention on different issues and raises different questions. What factors permitted two men as unlike one another as Honda and Fujisawa to function effectively as a team? What incentives and understandings permitted the Japanese executives at American Honda to respond to the market as it emerged rather than doggedly pursue the 250cc and 305 cc strategy that Mr. Honda favored? What decision process permitted the relatively junior sales director to overturn the bosses' preferences and choose the Nicest People campaign? What values or commitment drove Honda to take the enormous risk of alienating its dealers in 1964 in shifting from a consignment to cash? In hindsight, these pivotal events all seem ho-hum common sense. But each day, as organizations live out their lives without the benefit of hindsight, few choose so well and so consistently.

The juxtaposed perspectives reveal what I shall call the "Honda Effect." Western consultants, academics, and executives express a preference for oversimplifications of reality and cognitively linear explanations of events. To be sure, they have always acknowledged that the "human factor" must be taken into account. But extensive reading of strategy cases at business schools, consultants' reports, strategic planning documents as well as the coverage of the popular press, reveals a widespread tendency to overlook the process through which organizations experiment, adapt, and learn. We tend to impute coherence and purposive rationality to events when the opposite may be closer to the truth. How an organization deals with miscalculation, mistakes, and serendipitous events *outside its field of vision is often crucial to success over time*. It is this realm that requires better understanding and further research if we are to enhance our ability to guide an organization's destiny. . . .

An earlier section has addressed the shortcomings of the narrowly defined macroeconomic strategy model. The Japanese avoid this pitfall by adopting a broader notion of "strategy." In our recent awe of things Japanese, most Americans forget that the original products of the Japanese automotive manufacturers badly missed the mark. Toyota's Toyopet was square, sexless, and mechanically defective. It failed miserably, as did Datsun's first several entries into the U.S. market. More recently, Mazda miscalculated badly with its first rotary engine and nearly went bankrupt. Contrary to myth, the Japanese did not from the onset embark on a strategy to seize the high-quality small-car market. They manufactured what they were accustomed to building in Japan and tried to sell it abroad. Their success, as any Japanese automotive executive will readily agree, did not result from a bold insight by a few big brains at the top. On the contrary, success was achieved by senior managers humble enough not to take their initial strategic positions too seriously. What saved Japan's near-failures was the cumulative impact of "little brains" in the form of salesmen and dealers and production workers, all contributing incrementally to the quality and market position these companies enjoy today. Middle and upper management saw their primary task as guiding and orchestrating this input from below rather than steering the organization from above along a predetermined strategic course.

The Japanese don't use the term "strategy" to describe a crisp business definition or competitive master plan. They think more in terms of "strategic accommodation," or "adaptive persistence," underscoring their belief that corporate direction evolves from an incremental adjustment to unfolding events. Rarely, in their view, does one leader (or a strategic planning group) produce a bold strategy that guides a firm unerringly. Far more frequently, the input is from below. It is this ability of an organization to move information and ideas from the bottom to the top and back again in continuous dialogue that the Japanese value above all things. As this dialogue is pursued, what in hindsight may be "strategy" evolves. In sum, "strategy" is defined as "all the things necessary for the successful functioning of organization as an adaptive mechanism." . . .

EDWARD MARSHALL BOEHM, INC.

Edward Marshall Boehm—a farmer, veterinarian, and nature lover living near New York City—was convinced by his wife and friends to translate some of his clay animal sculptures into pieces for possible sale to the gift and art markets. Boehm recognized that porcelain was the best medium for portraying his creations because of its translucent beauty, permanence, and fidelity of color as well as form. But the finest of the porcelains, hard paste porcelain, was largely a secret art about which little technical literature existed. Boehm studied this art relentlessly, absorbing whatever knowledge artbooks, museums, and the few U.S. ceramic factories offered. Then after months of experimentation in a dingy Trenton (N.J.) basement, Boehm and some chemist friends developed a porcelain clay equal to the finest in the world.

Next Boehm had to master the complex art of porcelain manufacture. Each piece of porcelain sculpture is a technical as well as artistic challenge. A 52-step process is required to convert a plasticine sculpture into a completed porcelain piece. For example, one major creation took 509 mold sections to make 151 parts, and consumed 8 tons of plaster in the molds. Sculptural detail included 60,000 individually carved feather barbs. Each creation had to be kiln-fired to 2400° where heat could change a graceful detail into a twisted mass. Then it had to be painted, often in successive layers, and perhaps fired repeatedly to anneal delicate colors. No American had excelled in hard paste porcelains. And when Boehm's creations first appeared no one understood the quality of the porcelain or even believed it was hard paste porcelain.

But Boehm began to create in porcelain what he knew and loved best, nature—particularly the more

delicate forms of animals, birds, and flowers. In his art Boehm tried "to capture that special moment and setting which conveys the character, charm, and loveliness of a bird or animal in its natural habitat." After selling his early creations for several years during her lunch hours, his talented wife, Helen, left an outstanding opthalmic marketing career to "peddle" Boehm's porcelains full time. Soon Mrs. Boehm's extraordinary merchandising skills, promotional touch, and sense for the art market began to pay off. People liked Boehm's horses and dogs, but bought his birds. And Boehm agreeably complied, striving for ever greater perfection on ever more exotic and natural bird creations.

By 1968 some Boehm porcelains (especially birds) had become recognized as collectors items. An extremely complex piece like "Fondo Marino" might sell for $28,500 at retail, and might command much more upon resale. Edward Marshall Boehm, then 55—though flattered by his products' commercial success—considered his art primarily an expression of his love for nature. He felt the ornithological importance of portraying vanishing species like U.S. prairie chickens with fidelity and traveled to remote areas to bring back live samples of rare tropical birds for study and later rendering into porcelain. A single company, Minton China, was the exclusive distributor of Boehm products to some 175 retail outlets in the U.S. Boehm's line included (1) its "Fledgling" series of smaller somewhat simpler pieces, usually selling for less than $100, (2) its profitable middle series of complex sculptures like the "Snowy Owl" (see picture) selling from $800 to $5,000, and (3) its special artistic pieces (like "Fondo Marino" or "Ivory Billed Woodpeckers") which might sell initially for over $20,000.

Individual Boehm porcelains were increasingly being recognized as outstanding artistic creations and sought by some sophisticated collectors. Production of

Case copyright © 1976 by James Brian Quinn.
The generous cooperation of Edward Marshall Boehm, Inc. is gratefully acknowledged.

such designs might be sold out for years in advance, but it was difficult to anticipate which pieces might achieve this distinction. Many of the company's past policies no longer seemed appropriate. And the Boehms wanted to further position the company for the long run. When asked what they wanted from the company, they would respond, "to make the world aware of Mr. Boehm's artistic talent, to help world wildlife causes by creating appreciation and protection for threatened species, and to build a continuing business that could make them comfortably wealthy, perhaps millionaires." No one goal had great precedence over the others.

QUESTIONS

1. What strategy should the Boehms follow?
2. Why?

GENENTECH, INC.

In January 1976, Robert Swanson, a venture capitalist with Kleiner and Perkins in San Francisco, made a "cold call" to Dr. Herbert Boyer. He wanted to arrange a short (20 minute) meeting to discuss the commercial possibilities of recombinant DNA. Swanson had tried for several years to interest big biological and pharmaceutical laboratories in the commercial prospects for rDNA. They and all the many academic scientists Swanson contacted insisted the technology was too far from the marketplace to be of interest. Boyer was the only eminent scientist who thought the technology was ripe for exploitation.

Earlier, in 1972 at another chance meeting (over corned beef sandwiches during a conference in Hawaii) Boyer and Stanley Cohen, Stanford's brilliant biologist, had found that their research merged in a unique way. Cohen had been experimenting with the *E. coli* bacterium's plasmids which contained all the DNA of the bacterium in a much simpler form than chromosomes. Boyer, for his part, had found some restriction enzymes which would cut DNA structure precisely at predetermined points leaving some "sticky ends" on the DNA molecule—to which (the two reasoned) specific genes similarly cut from other living structures might attach themselves.

In 1973 Boyer's and Cohen's teams became the first to perfect the technique, now called gene splicing (or recombinant DNA). They transplanted a gene from a South African toad into a bacterium, which then reproduced itself—and the toad gene—in quantity. Although the structure of DNA had been deciphered by Watson and Crick in 1957, until 1973 no practical way had existed to produce selected genes or genetic material in volume. At the time of Swanson and Boyer's meeting in 1976 there was still no significant commercial application of this knowledge.

Case copyright © 1995 by James Brian Quinn.

However, after their 20 minute conversation had extended to 4 hours, Swanson and Boyer agreed to form a company for this purpose. Each put up $500—Boyer borrowed his—to start a new company which became Genentech, Inc. Between January and April 1976 they made more detailed evaluations of the specific commercial and technological opportunities possibly available for rDNA. The resulting business plan proposed that they take 25,000 common shares each, and that Kleiner and Perkins put up $100,000 of seed capital for 20,000 shares of convertible preferred stock, with a guarantee of $100,000 more when other outside capital came in. The initial business plan called for the following financial structure, with a new (private placement) investor putting up $500,000 in return for convertible preferred shares (see Table 1).

The money was to carry Genentech through laboratory development of its first product. The plan estimated 1980 sales at $15 million and profits at $3.1 million. The first two compounds to be attempted were: somatostatin, a relatively simple molecule (but very costly and in limited supply) with possible uses in the treatment of diabetes, gastric bleeding, and hormonal disorders; and human insulin. (See Exhibit 1 for an overview of the potential markets.)

GOALS FOR GENENTECH

In seeking these products, Mr. Swanson repeatedly affirmed Genentech's determination "to build one of the finest scientific teams in the world." Genentech's policy was to remain "a part of the scientific community with responsibilities to both its own scientists and to science at large." Mr. Swanson stressed a philosophy of integrating science and business. Genentech was not to be "just an innovative research and development organization that coordinates major research projects," he

TABLE 1

HOLDER	SHARES	AMOUNT INVESTED
Boyer	25,000	$500 Invested
Swanson	25,000	$500
2 key scientists	10,000	-0-
Kleiner & Perkins	20,000 convertible preferred	$100,000
New investor	10,000 convertible perferred	$500,000

said. That might be profitable in its own right, but shortsighted. "We were determined to be a fully integrated organization."

The plan further stated, "It is Genentech's goal to select products that are in great demand and to specifically engineer microorganisms to produce those products. We expect to be the first company to commercialize the technology, and we plan to build a major profitable corporation by manufacturing and marketing needed products that benefit mankind. . . . It is Genentech's initial strategy to design microorganisms that will synthesize products for which there is a large existing market and where economies of production will give the company very substantial cost advantages . . . . The future uses of genetic engineering are far reaching and many. With Genentech's technology, microorganisms could be engineered to produce protein to meet world food needs or to produce antibodies to fight viral infections. Any product produced by a living organism is eventually within the company's reach."

The plan also provided: a detailed explanation of the recombinant DNA technology itself, a schedule for the development of products, a broad description of the market opportunity, and more detailed descriptions of the intended first two products (somatostatin and insulin). (See Exhibit 2 for a simplified explanation of the technology.)

HUMAN INSULIN ACHIEVED

In August 1978 Genentech and City of Hope National Medical Center at Duart, California, jointly announced that they had produced human insulin by recombinant DNA technology. The announcement said, "This achievement may be the most significant advance in the treatment of diabetes since the development of animal insulin for human use in the 1920s. The insulin synthesis is the first laboratory production of a significant widely needed human hormone using recombinant DNA technology." The contributions of

Drs. Crea, Itakura, and Riggs at the City of Hope, as well as Drs. Goeddel and Cleid at Genentech, were specifically cited. The announcement noted that approximately 1.5 million diabetics took injections of expensive insulin every day. If successfully produced in quantity Genentech's insulin would be "human insulin," with a chemical structure exactly like the insulin naturally occurring within the human body. Unlike bovine or porcine insulin, "human insulin" was not expected to cause allergic reactions in certain individuals. Insulin represented a large existing market (more than $100 million worldwide, with over half the market in the United States). Eli Lilly Co. held over 80% of the domestic market, which at that time was growing at about 6% annually. The existing source for insulin was animal pancreas glands. As the market grew, these were coming into increasingly short supply and were very expensive to process.

Bovine and porcine pancreases had increased in price from 40¢ per pound in 1972 to over $1.25 per pound in 1978. Ten thousand pounds of pancreas were needed for one pound of insulin. Then, large-scale and complicated chemical processing techniques were needed to obtain purified insulin. Genentech's production process was expected to take place in a standard 750-liter laboratory fermentation vessel. A little over $800 worth of growth medium would produce approximately 15 kilograms (net weight) of bacterial cells coded for insulin within a 8-hour shift, and the process could be speeded so that cell mass doubled every 20 minutes. Early estimates were that about 30% of the total protein would be insulin. This would yield approximately one pound of purified insulin per production run. However, Mr. Swanson cautioned "the technology is a long way from being ready for commercial production."

Development and scale up costs would be "several million dollars" for each product. Clinical tests would require $3–20 million more. (See Exhibit 3 for the typical sequence of steps involved in the product development process.) Few pharmaceutical products then reached the market with less than $8–10 million in investment, with delays of 3–4 years being common. Even then Genentech would have to meet other potential genetic competitors, existing products in the market, and an unreliable world patent structure in which many countries did not recognize product patents on products for human health. To complicate things further Genentech was supporting other laboratory work which could lead to a highly diverse set of end products. But the company could not be sure which products could ultimately be achieved in the laboratory or cleared for commercial use. Nor did it know the precise sequence in which these events would occur.

QUESTIONS

1. What should the venture capitalists' strategy have been with their first $100,000 to $200,000 investment? Why is the company financed the way it is? Approximately what level of further financing will it need? For what? When? How should it finance its next steps? Why? How would you value Genentech at the time of the initial investment? Why?

2. What do you think of the goals Mr. Swanson has expressed? What are the major strategic options facing Genentech at the end of the case? What strategy should it follow? How much of its strategy should it disclose? Internally? Externally? Why?

3. What are the principal threats the company faces? What should it do about each? How should it organize itself? Why? How can it leverage its special competencies? How does a strategy in this situation differ from that in a more mature situation?

EXHIBIT 1
Potential Markets for
the Gene-Splicers

PRODUCT CATEGORY	NUMBER OF COMPOUNDS	CURRENT MARKET VALUE	SELECTED COMPOUND OR USE	TIME NEEDED TO IMPLEMENT GENETIC PRODUCTION
AMINO ACIDS	9	$1,703,000,000	Glutamate	5 years
			Tryptophan	5 years
VITAMINS	6	667,700,000	Vitamin C	10 years
			Vitamin E	15 years
ENZYMES	11	217,700,000	Pepsin	5 years
STEROID HORMONES	6	367,800,000	Cortisone	10 years
PEPTIDE HORMONES	9	269,700,000	Human growth hormone	5 years
			Insulin	5 years
VIRAL ANTIGENS	9	N/A	Hoof-and-mouth disease virus	5 years
			Influenza viruses	10 years
SHORT PEPTIDES	2	4,400,000	Aspartame	5 years
MISCELLANEOUS PROTEINS	2	300,000,000	Interferon	5 years
ANTIBIOTICS	4*	4,240,000,000	Penicillins	10 years
			Erythromycins	10 years
PESTICIDES	2*	100,000,000	Microbial	5 years
			Aromatics	10 years
METHANE	1	$12,572,000,000	Methane	10 years
ALIPHATICS (Other than methane)	24	2,737,500,000	Ethanol	5 years
			Ethylene glycol	5 years
			Propylene glycol	10 years
			Isobutylene	10 years
AROMATICS	10	1,250,900,000	Aspirin	5 years
			Phenol	10 years
INORGANICS	2	2,681,000,000	Hydrogen	15 years
			Ammonia	15 years
MINERAL LEACHING	5	N/A	Uranium	
			Cobalt	
			Iron	
BIODEGRADATION	N/A	N/A	Removal of organic phosphates	

N/A = not available.
Number indicates classes of compounds, rather than number of compounds.
Source: Industry Week, September 7, 1981.

FIGURE 2
Redesigning Bacteria

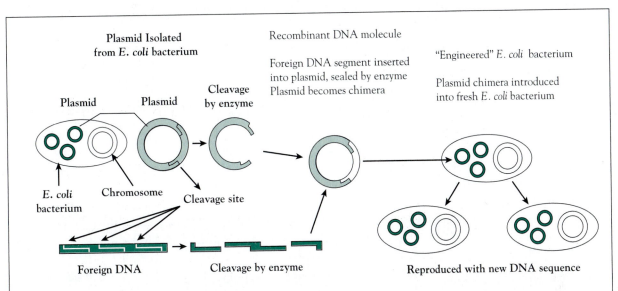

Plasmid Isolated from E. coli bacterium

Recombinant DNA molecule

Foreign DNA segment inserted into plasmid, sealed by enzyme
Plasmid becomes chimera

"Engineered" E. coli bacterium

Plasmid chimera introduced into fresh E. coli bacterium

Plasmid   Plasmid

Cleavage by enzyme

E. coli bacterium   Chromosome   Cleavage site

Foreign DNA   Cleavage by enzyme   Reproduced with new DNA sequence

The development of the recombinant DNA technique ushered in a new era of genetic engineering—with all of its promise and possible peril. The lowly organism that currently plays the largest role in the process is the E. coli bacterium. This microbe—a laboratory derivative of a common inhabitant of the human intestine—lends itself to being engineered because its genetic structure has been so well studied. In the first step of the process, scientists place the bacterium in a test tube with a detergent-like liquid. This dissolves the microbe's outer membrane, causing its DNA strands to spill out in a disorderly tangle. Most of the DNA is included in the bacterium's chromosome, in the form of a long strand containing thousands of genes. The remainder is found in several tiny, closed loops called plasmids, which have only a few genes each and are the most popular vehicles for the recombinant technique.

After the plasmids are separated from the chromosomal DNA in a centrifuge, they are placed in a solution with a chemical catalyst called a restriction enzyme. This enzyme cuts through the plasmids' DNA strips at specific points. It leaves overlapping, mortise-type breaks with "sticky" ends. The opened plasmid loops are then mixed in a solution with genes—also removed by the use of restriction enzymes—from the DNA of a plant, animal, bacterium or virus. In the solution is another enzyme called a DNA ligase, which cements the foreign gene into place in the opening of the plasmids. The result of these unions are new loops of DNA called plasmid chimeras because, like the Chimera—the mythical lion-goat-serpent after which they are named—they contain the components of more than one organism.

Finally, the chimeras are placed in a solution of cold calcium chloride containing normal E. coli bacteria. When the solution is suddenly heated, the membranes of the E. coli become permeable, allowing the plasmid chimeras to pass through and become part of the microbes' new genetic structure. When the E. coli reproduce, they create carbon copies of themselves, new plasmids—and DNA sequences—and all. Thus they become forms of life potentially different from what they had been before—imbued with characteristics dictated not only by their own E. coli genes, but also by genes from an entirely different species.

Source: "Tinkering With Life," *Time,* April 18, 1977. Copyright © 1977 Time, Inc. All rights reserved. Reprinted by permission from Time.

EXHIBIT 3
The Product
Development
Process

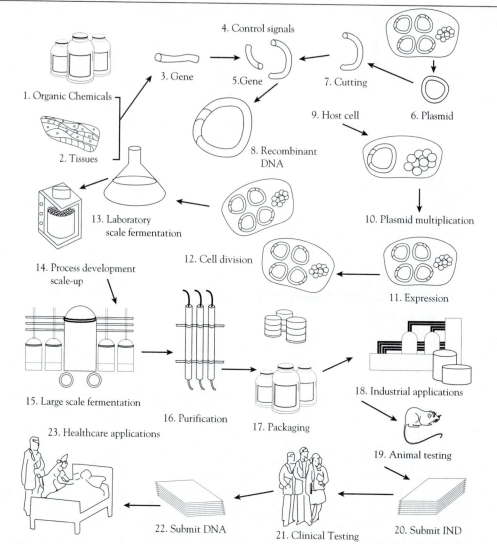

1. Organic Chemicals
2. Tissues
3. Gene
4. Control signals
5. Gene
6. Plasmid
7. Cutting
8. Recombinant DNA
9. Host cell
10. Plasmid multiplication
11. Expression
12. Cell division
13. Laboratory scale fermentation
14. Process development scale-up
15. Large scale fermentation
16. Purification
17. Packaging
18. Industrial applications
19. Animal testing
20. Submit IND
21. Clinical Testing
22. Submit DNA
23. Healthcare applications

The development process begins by obtaining DNA either through organic synthesis (1) or derived from biological sources such as tissues (2). The DNA obtained from one or both soures is tailored to form the basic "gene" (3) which contains the genetic information to "code" for a desired product, such as human interferon or human insulin. Control signals (4) containing instructions are added to this gene (5). Circular DNA molecules called plasmids (6) are isolated from micro-organisms such as E. coli, cut open (7) and spliced back (8) together with genes and control signals to form "recombinant DNA" molecules. These molecules are then introduced into a host cell (9).

Each plasmid is copied many times in a cell (10). Each cell then takes the information contained in these plasmids into the product, a process called "expression" (11). Cells divide (12) and pass on to their offspring the same genetic information contained in the parent cell.

Fermentation of large populations of genetically engineered micro-organisms is first done in shaker flasks (13), and then in small fermenters (14) to determine growth conditions, and eventually in larger fermentation tanks (15). Cellular extract obtained from the fermentation process is then separated, purified (16), and packaged (17) either for industrial use (18) or health care applications.

Health care products are first tested in animal studies (19) to demonstrate a product's pharmacological activity and safety. In the United States, an investigational new drug application (IND) (20) is submitted to begin human clinical trials to establish safety and efficacy. Following clinical testing (21), a new drug application (NDA) (22) is filed with the Food and Drug Administration (FDA). When the NDA has been reviewed and approved by the FDA the product may be marketed in the United States (23).

Source: Genentech, Inc.

MacArthur and the Philippines

The Americans never came. *They never came.* Month after month the embattled garrison awaited a blow in vain. . . . Truk was being devastated by Nimitz's carrier planes, but the sky over Rabaul was serene, and sentinels posted to sound the alarm when Allied patrols approached overland from Cape Gloucester and Arawe stared out at a mocking green silence. All they wanted was an opportunity to sell their lives dearly before they were killed or eviscerated themselves in honorable seppuku. They believed that they were entitled to a Nipponese gotterdammerung. . . . MacArthur was denying them it, and they were experiencing a kind of psychological hernia.[1]

Here they were, commanding an army larger than Napoleon's at Waterloo or Lee's at Gettysburg—or Wellington's or Meade's, for that matter—which was spoiling for a fight. Their sappers had thrown up ramparts, revetments, parapets, barbicans, and ravelins. Hull-down tanks were in position. Mines had been laid, Hotchkiss-type guns sited, Nambus cunningly camouflaged. Mortarmen had calculated precise ranges. Crack troops, designated to launch counterattacks, lurked in huge bunkers behind concertinas of barbwire. And there they remained, in an agony of frustration, for the rest of the war. . . .

"Bypass" or "Island Hop?"

This phenomenon was not confined to Rabaul. . . . . . Exactly who first suggested the stratagem is unclear.

MacArthur himself has been widely credited with it, largely on the basis of his own recollections and those of the men around him. In *Reminiscences* he writes:

> To push back the Japanese perimeter of conquest by direct pressure against the mass of enemy-occupied islands would be a long and costly effort. My staff worried about Rabaul and other strongpoints. . . . I intended to envelop them, incapacitate them, apply the "hit 'em where they ain't—let 'em die on the vine" philosophy. I explained that this was the very opposite of what was termed "island-hopping," which is the gradual pushing back of the enemy by direct frontal pressure, with the consequent heavy casualties which would certainly be involved. There would be no need for storming the mass of islands held by the enemy.

According to Huff, Willoughby, and Kenney, the General first unveiled this concept at a council of war attended by, among others, Halsey, Krueger, and Australia's Sir Thomas Blamey. Gesturing at the map, one of the conferees said, "I don't see how we can take these strongpoints with our limited forces." Tapping his cigarette on an ashtray, MacArthur said in a slow deliberate voice: "Well, let's just say that we don't take them. In fact, gentlemen, I don't want them." Turning to Kenney [head of Allied air forces in the area], he said: "You incapacitate them. . . ." He told the airman: "Starve Rabaul! The jungle! Starvation! They're my allies."[2]

But the notion that the isolation of Rabaul was the General's inspiration just won't wash. Apparently the first references to the possibility of such a bypass were made in March of 1943, during Washington talks which were attended by Sutherland, Kenney, and Stephen J. Chamberlin, the General's operations officer. If they mentioned it to MacArthur on their return, he was unimpressed. Eight months earlier the Joint Chiefs had instructed him to take Rabaul and Kavieng.

He hadn't protested then, and he didn't now. Indeed, when the Chiefs sounded him out in June, informing him that some Pentagon officers thought that Rabaul could be cut off and left to rot, he objected. He needed "an adequate forward naval base" there, he said, to protect his right flank; without it, his westward drive along the back of New Guinea's plucked buzzard "would involve hazards rendering success doubtful."

"THE STRATEGY WE HATED MOST"

The issue was resolved in August, at the Quadrant conference in Quebec. Ironically, this boldest stratagem of the Pacific war was decided, not on its merits, but because the Anglo-American Combined Chiefs were searching for a compromise. The British wanted more U.S. troops and more landing craft in the European theater. They didn't see why the American offensive against Japan couldn't be mounted on a single front—Nimitz's, in the central Pacific—and U.S. admirals were inclined to agree with them. Roosevelt and his political advisers demurred, however. They had to reckon with MacArthur's popularity at home. . . . In the end FDR sided with MacArthur's strongest supporter at the conference—George Marshall. MacArthur never acknowledged Marshall's strong support at Quebec and elsewhere, and it is possible that he never knew of it. . . .

However, the fact remains that MacArthur transformed the bypass maneuver into the war's most momentous strategic concept. Here the most impressive testimony comes from the Japanese. After the war Colonel Matsuichi Juio, a senior intelligence officer who had been charged with deciphering the General's intentions, told an interrogator that MacArthur's swooping envelopment of Nipponese bastions was "the type of strategy we hated most." The General, he said, repeatedly, "with minimum losses, attacked and seized a relatively weak area, constructed airfields and then proceeded to cut the supply lines to [our] troops in that area. . . . Our strongpoints were gradually starved out. The Japanese Army preferred direct [frontal] assault, after the German fashion, but the Americans flowed into our weaker points and submerged us, just as water seeks the weakest entry to sink a ship. We respected this type of strategy . . . because it gained the most while losing the least."[3]

Yet, while GIs would proudly identify themselves as members of his army, they disparaged their commander in chief, or rather the image of himself he had created. Distrust of great commanders by their troops is nothing new; the British rank and file loathed Wellington, and during the American Revolution, as Gore Vidal has pointed out, "the private soldiers disliked Washington as much as he disdained them." In MacArthur's case it was ironical, however, for had his bitter men understood the consequences of the General's strategy they would have taken a very different view. For every Allied serviceman killed, the General killed ten Japanese. Never in history, John Gunther wrote, had there been a commander so economical in the expenditure of his men's blood. In this respect certain comparisons with European Theater Operations campaigns are staggering. During the single Battle of Anzio, 72,306 GIs fell. In the Battle of Normandy, Eisenhower lost 28,366. Between MacArthur's arrival in Australia and his return to Philippine waters over two years later, his troops suffered just 27,684 casualties.[4]

THE HAWAIIAN CONFERENCE

The one great Pacific issue confronting American strategists that summer [1944] was where to strike next. MacArthur wanted to reconquer the Philippines. Admiral King recommended bypassing the archipelago and invading Formosa instead; he saw no reason to risk becoming mired in the great land masses of the islands. The dispute had been almost a year in the making. The previous October Eichelberger [field Commander of American Forces] had heard in Hawaii that once MacArthur had reached the equator, the admirals wanted the war against Japan to be "their show and no one else's." The decision could be deferred no longer.[5]

They needed each other, and the President, the more flexible of the two, recognized that. Therefore he decided, after MacArthur had dropped out of the presidential race, to meet him in Hawaii. The Joint Chiefs—to their discomfiture—would be left in Washington. Nimitz would represent the navy. The three of them, as power brokers, would hammer out the wisest way to defeat the Japanese, who, despite the vicissitudes of quadrennial politics, were after all, the real enemy.[6]

Roosevelt's military advisers were sharply divided on the subject. MacArthur was at one end of the spectrum; King at the other. Field commanders of all services in the Pacific tended to agree with the General, while George Marshall (chief of staff) and Hap Arnold leaned toward King, though individuals changed their minds from week to week. By the week of the Honolulu conference, Marshall was beginning to side with

MacArthur. Hap Arnold, eager for B-29 bases on Formosa, continued to support King. Admiral Nimitz, wavering, instructed his staff to draw up plans for assaults on all possible objectives, including the Japanese homeland.

If Roosevelt was already familiar with the Pentagon's views, vacillating as they were, he knew those of MacArthur and Nimitz, too. . . . The blunt fact is that he was running for a fourth term, and being photographed with MacArthur and Nimitz would be more impressive to his constituents than pictures of him politicking at the Democratic National Convention.

A GREAT ENTRANCE

Roosevelt knew how to make a great entrance; a huge crowd of Hawaiians, who had been alerted to his approach, cheered as the *Baltimore* docked at 3:00 P.M. on Wednesday, July 26, and fifty high-ranking military officers, led by Nimitz and Lieutenant General Robert C. Richardson, the commander of Nimitz's ground forces, mounted the gangboard. But MacArthur could be dramatic, too. Though [MacArthur's] B-17 had landed an hour earlier, . . . , he would be the last officer to board the cruiser. . . . Roosevelt had just asked Nimitz if he knew the General's whereabouts when "a terrific automobile siren was heard, and there raced on to the dock and screeched to a stop a motorcycle escort and the longest open car I have ever seen. . . . The car traveled some distance around the open space and stopped at the gangplank. When the applause died down, the General strode rapidly to the gangplank all alone."[7]

[Later the President] led MacArthur, Nimitz, and Leahy into [a large] room, one wall of which was covered by a huge map of the Pacific. Picking up a long bamboo pointer, the President touched the islands with it and suddenly spun his wheelchair around to face the General. "Well, Douglas," he said challengingly, "Where do we go from here?" MacArthur shot back, "Mindanao, Mr. President, then Leyte—and then Luzon."[8]

He and Nimitz took turns at the map arguing their cases forcefully while the President listened intently, interrupting now and then to ask a question or suggest another line of reasoning. Leahy thought he was "at his best as he tactfully steered the discussion from one point to another and narrowed down the areas of disagreement between MacArthur and Nimitz." Despite his earlier misgivings, the General found himself thoroughly enjoying the session. The President, he said

afterward, had conducted himself as a "chairman," and had remained "entirely neutral," while Nimitz displayed a "fine sense of fair play." . . . [But Nimitz] lacked the General's eloquence. He was arguing King's case, not his own; under FDR's skillful questioning he conceded that Manila Bay would be useful to him, and admitted that an attack on Formosa, instead of Luzon, would succeed only if anchorages and fighter strips had been established in the central and southern Philippines. Finally, he was unprepared or unwilling to discuss the political problems which would arise if the archipelago were bypassed.[9]

Here MacArthur was his most trenchant. The Filipinos, he said, felt that they had been betrayed in 1942—he did not add that he had shared the feeling, but FDR knew it—and they would not forgive a second betrayal. "Promises must be kept," he said forcefully, meaning his own vow to return at the head of an army of liberation, a pledge which, he believed, had committed the United States. . . . In the postwar world all Asian eyes would be on the emerging Philippine republic. If its people thought they had been sold out, the reputation of the United States would be sullied with a stain that could never be removed.[10]

Again and again he used the words "ethical" and "unethical," "virtue" and "shame." As Barbey later wrote, "General MacArthur approached the matter from a different point of view" than the Joint Chiefs; "he felt it was as much a moral issue as a military one." In addition, however, "He did not think the military conquest of the Philippines would be as costly, lengthy, or difficult as the conquest of Formosa, and yet the same military purposes would be accomplished." . . .

THE GREATER PRIZE?

Luzon was a greater [strategic] prize than Formosa . . . the Filipinos, unlike the Formosans, would provide the Americans with powerful guerrilla support. Last— and here Leahy thought he saw Nimitz nod—Luzon couldn't be enveloped. It was too big. Rabaul and Wewak could be bypassed because their land masses were smaller. Attempting to detour around Luzon would expose U.S. flanks to crippling attacks from the enemy's bomber bases there.[11]

Newspapers and even some correspondence of that summer support the premise that the issue had been resolved at Waikiki. After MacArthur had left Hickam Field, FDR told reporters that "we are going to get the Philippines back, and without question General MacArthur will take a part in it." There was more to it than that, however. Under the Constitution Roosevelt's power over the Pentagon was absolute, but in practice he couldn't act without the support of the military advisers who hadn't accompanied him to Hawaii. In effect, he, MacArthur, and Leahy had formed a coalition, the object of which was the conversion of the Joint Chiefs.

The Joint Chiefs continued the Luzon-or-Formosa debate through August and September. Leahy had briefed them on the Waikiki talks and told them that both he and Roosevelt were impressed by MacArthur's political and moral arguments. The Chiefs weren't. They insisted that the matter be decided wholly on the grounds of military merit. They agreed to a Leyte landing, but added that a "decision as to whether Luzon will be occupied before Formosa will be made later." King still wanted to land in southern Formosa, supported by American aircraft using Chiang Kai-shek's bases. . . . [Then over] the last weekend in September, Nimitz convinced him. The two admirals met in San Francisco, and Nimitz, pointing to recent Japanese successes against Chiang's troops, said the United States could no longer rely on his airdromes. An attack on Formosa, Nimitz said, would now be impossible unless Luzon were seized first. And back in Washington, King withdrew his objections to MacArthur's Philippine plans.

THE INVASION TIMETABLE

MacArthur, meanwhile, had been contemplating a continuation of his steady advance northward, with each amphibious thrust providing airfields for the next, so that Kenney could always fill the skies over the beaches with friendly fighters and bombers. Under this principle their schedule had called for vaults into Morotai (September 15), Mindanao (November 15), and Leyte (December 20). Then, in the waning days of summer, even before King's capitulation, Admiral Halsey gave the General a tremendous lift by proposing that the timetable be scrapped for a bolder leap.[12]

Halsey had been cruising off the Philippines, launching carrier strikes at Japanese bases. One of his pilots had been shot down over Leyte, the archipelago's midrib. Parachuting to safety and rescued by a submarine, he had reported that Leyte was held by far fewer Japanese troops than the Americans had thought. All week the admiral had noticed that his fleet was rarely challenged by land-based enemy aircraft. The rescued flier seemed to confirm his suspicion that, in his words, the central Philippines were "a hollow shell, with weak defense and skimpy facilities. In my opinion, this was the vulnerable belly of the imperial dragon." . . . Finally

on Wednesday, September 13, 1944, he radioed Nimitz in Pearl Harbor, suggesting that assaults on the Talauds, Mindanao, and the Palaus be canceled. In their place he urged the swift seizure of Leyte.[13]

At that moment two U.S. invasion convoys were at sea. MacArthur, aboard the cruiser *Nashville*, was bound for Morotai, the northeasternmost island of the Molucas, which would be needed to launch any blow at the Philippines. . . . Halsey's proposals were forwarded to Quebec, where the Combined Chiefs were attending a formal dinner as guests of Prime Minister W. L. Mackenzie King. As Hap Arnold later wrote, "Admiral Leahy, General Marshall, Admiral King, and I excused ourselves, read the message, and had a staff officer prepare an answer which naturally was in the affirmative." There was one small difficulty. MacArthur's approval was needed, and he couldn't be reached; the *Nashville*, in enemy waters, was observing radio silence. Thus the momentous message from Canada was handed to Sutherland [MacArthur's chief of staff. That normally impassive officer's hands trembled; he was, Kenney later recalled, "worried about what the General would say about using his name and making so important a decision without consulting him." After a long, tense pause, the chief of staff radioed back an endorsement in MacArthur's name.[14]

The General had gone ashore on Morotai after the first wave had hit the beach. His Higgins boat had grounded on a rock, and when he stepped off the ramp he found the water was chest deep, . . . [but] if his clothes were damp, his mood wasn't. The landing was unopposed; without losing a man, he had anchored his right flank for the next amphibious bound. By now he had evaded 220,000 enemy troops and was within three hundred miles of the Philippines. On hearing the news from Sutherland, he instantly approved.

THE PHILIPPINE INVASION

In the fall of 1944 the Philippines were inhabited by about 18,160,000 Filipinos, 80 percent of whom worshiped the Roman Catholic God, and some 400,000 Japanese soldiers, all of whom venerated their emperor and could imagine no greater honor than to die for him in battle. The twain seldom met. Except for chronic food shortages and the repressive regime, life in the thousand-mile chain of islands had for the most part been unaffected by enemy rule, now approaching the end of its third year. The hulk of [the giant island fortress of] Corregidor lay dead in the slate gray waters of Manila Bay. . . . An unwary stranger might have concluded that it was a land finished with fiery deeds, was now slum-

bering, indolent, indifferent. But the General knew better. He understood that the flames of ardor needed only a spark of hope to be rekindled. He had a better grasp of the Philippines than of the United States. It was his second homeland, and in some ways it was a metaphor of his intricate personality: dramatic, inconsistent, valiant, passionate, and primitive.[15]

No sparrow fell there but MacArthur knew of it; his files held everything from the transcripts of executive sessions in Malacanan to the guest lists of the Manila Hotel. His submarines brought the guerrillas equipment, technicians, transmitters, and commando teams, and he personally interviewed each partisan who escaped into his lines. . . . The resistance grew and grew. . . . The strategic information the partisans sent southward was priceless. Their eagerness to provide it was an index of their enthusiasm for the U.S. cause and their devotion was translated into loyalty to two men, MacArthur and Quezon. When Quezon died of tuberculosis at Saranac, New York, the day after the General returned from his Hawaii conference with Roosevelt, MacArthur became their sole idol. He was, quite simply, the symbol of their hopes for a better postwar world. American GIs ridiculed him. Filipinos didn't. Carlos Romulo wrote: "To me he represents America."[16]

LEYTE—THE GIANT MOLAR

Leyte Gulf, the chief anchorage in the central islands, is approachable through only two major entrances. Surigao Strait to the southwest and San Bernardino Strait to the northwest. These tropical waters were about to become the scene of the greatest naval battle in history, for the Japanese were now desperate. If they were unable to prevent MacArthur from retaking the Philippine archipelago, they knew they would no longer have access to the Indies' oil, the lifeblood of their generals and admirals.[17]

Imperial Japanese headquarters in Tokyo had drawn up a do-or-die plan encoded "Sho-Go," or "Operation Victory." Everything would be thrown into an attempt to prevent the General from establishing a foothold in the islands. . . . There would be no sense in saving the fleet at the expense of the loss of the Philippines.

When word reached [the Japanese] that a seven-hundred-ship, hundred-mile-long American armada was steaming toward Surigao Strait between Dinagat and Homonhon islands, they brimmed with confidence. Lieutenant General Sosaku Suzuki, commander of the Thirty-fifth Army in the Visayan Islands, the

central Philippines, told his staff: "We don't even need all the reinforcements they are sending us." His only worry, he said, was that the American leader might attempt to surrender just the troops participating in this operation: "We must demand the capitulation of MacArthur's entire forces, those in New Guinea and other places as well as the troops on Leyte."[18]

The most cheerful news, for many Japanese, was the identity of the new overall commander of Philippine defenses. He was Lieutenant General Tomoyuki Yamashita, the legendary "Tiger of Malaya" of the war's opening weeks. Jealous of his fame, Tojo had shunted him off to minor posts, but now Tojo was out of office, and Koiso needed someone in Manila in whom the country had faith. Yamashita seemed to be just the man; his appointment as MacArthur's adversary meant that two gifted generals, each at the height of his powers, would be pitted against each other. . . .

GUNS AT LEYTE

Leyte at that moment was under the awesome guns of two U.S. fleets, Halsey's Third and Tom Kinkaid's Seventh. Kinkaid was subordinate to MacArthur, but Halsey—whose force was faster and far more powerful—was answerable only to Nimitz in Honolulu. The split command worried MacArthur. He repeatedly urged the Joint Chiefs to designate one commander in chief, and had even offered to step down if they thought that necessary. They didn't believe he was serious, and they were probably right. In any event, shunting a national idol aside in the middle of a presidential campaign was unthinkable, especially when he belonged to the party out of power. George Marshall wouldn't agree to an admiral as supreme commander, so the flawed command structure remained. Presently it would lead the Allied cause in the Pacific to the brink of disaster.[19]

[MacArthur] had perfected a battle plan which he considered his best yet. After the war Vincent Sheean agreed: "His operations towards the end . . . were extremely daring, more daring and far more complicated than those of Patton in Europe, because MacArthur used not infantry alone but also air and seapower in a concerted series of jabbing and jumping motions designed to outflank and bypass the Japanese all through the islands. The operation in which he jumped from Hollandia to Leyte will remain, I believe, the most brilliant strategic conception and tactical execution of the entire war."[20]

He knew that his reputation was as imperiled as the lives of his men. Kenney had pointed out one glaring flaw in the plan—until Japanese landing strips had been captured, they would be fighting five hundred miles beyond the range of their fighter cover. Kenney recalls: "He stopped pacing the floor and blurted out, 'I tell you I'm going back there this fall if I have to paddle a canoe with you flying cover for me with that B-17 of yours.'"[21]

At daybreak, the U.S. warships opened fire on the beach. The General stood on the bridge. The shore was dimly visible through an ominous, rising haze shot with yellow flashes; inland, white phosphorus crumps were bursting among the thick, ripe underbrush of the hills. The light of the rising sun spread rapidly across the smooth green water of the gulf. . . . Halsey had been misinformed; the enemy was nowhere as weak as the admiral had thought. Imperial General Headquarters had been holding back, waiting until MacArthur committed himself. Even more alarming, Kenney would discover before the day was out that because of the island's unstable soil, airfields there were unusable during the rainy season, which had just begun. U.S. air support would be limited to carrier planes through most of the coming engagement.[22]

After lunch the General reappeared on deck wearing a freshly pressed khaki uniform, sun glasses, and his inimitable cap. He stood, akimbo, watching the diving enemy planes zooming overhead; then he looked shoreward, where the sand pits, palms, thick underbrush, and tin grass-thatched huts were obscured by the burst of exploding shells and tall columns of black smoke.

In his *Reminiscences* he writes that he went in with the third assault wave. Actually the invasion was four hours old when he descended ladder to a barge; his staff and war correspondents followed him aboard . . . Then, fifty yards from shore, they ran aground. . . . The General, impatient and annoyed, ordered the barge ramp lowered, stepped off into knee-deep brine, splashed forty wet strides to the beach, destroying the neat creases of his trousers. A news photographer snapped the famous picture of this.

His scowl, which millions of readers interpreted as a reflection of his steely determination, was actually a wrathful glare at the impertinent naval officer. When MacArthur saw a print of it, however, he instantly grasped its dramatic value, and the next day he deliberately waded ashore for cameramen on the 1st Cavalry Division's White Beach. By then the shore was safe there, and troopers watching him assumed that he had waited until Japanese snipers had been cleared out.

Later, seeing yesterday's photography, they condemned it as a phony. Another touch had been added to his antihero legend.[23]

"SIR, THERE ARE SNIPERS OVER THERE"

[But the facts were very different.] On Red Beach that first afternoon there were plenty of snipers, tied in trees or huddled in takotsubo—literally, "octopus traps," the Nipponese equivalent of foxholes. In his braided cap, pausing to relight his corncob from time to time, he once more made a conspicuous target. A Nambu opened up. He didn't even duck. As he strolled about, inspecting four damaged landing craft and looking for the 24th Division's command post, Kenney heard the General murmur to himself. "This is what I dreamed about." Kenney thought it was more like a nightmare. He could hear the taunts of enemy soldiers, speaking that broken English which was so familiar to soldiers and marines in the Pacific. . . .

The airman heard a GI crouched behind a coconut log gasp: "Hey, there's General MacArthur!" Without turning to look, the GI beside him drawled, "Oh, yeah? And I suppose he's got Eleanor Roosevelt along with him." . . . Hearing heavy fire inland, he strolled in that direction, jovially asked an astonished fire team of the 24th, "How do you find the Nip?" and, seeing several fresh Japanese corpses, kicked them over with his wet toe to read their insignia. He said with deep satisfaction: "The Sixteenth Division. They're the ones that did the dirty work on Bataan."

Back at the shore, he sat on a coconut log by four wrecked Higgins boats, his back to the surf. A nervous lieutenant pointed toward a nearby grove and said, "Sir, there are snipers over there." The General seemed not to have heard him. He continued to stare entranced at the Leyte wilderness.

[Sitting there] MacArthur scrawled a letter to President Roosevelt.[24] Granting the Filipinos independence swiftly, he predicted, would "place American prestige in the Far East at the highest pinnacle of all times." On "the highest plane of statesmanship" the General urged "that this great ceremony be presided over by you in person": such a step would "electrify the world and rebound immeasurably to the credit and honor of the United States for a thousand years." . . .

[But] Roosevelt's failing health, his global command responsibilities, and his campaign for reelection prevented him from agreeing to broadcast an address to the Filipinos, so their first vivid recollection of their liberation was the two minute address which the

General had edited on the Nashville and was now prepared to deliver.

"I HAVE RETURNED"

"People of the Philippines: I have returned," he said. His hands were shaking, and he had to pause to smooth out the wrinkles in his voice. He then continued, "By the grace of Almighty God, our forces stand again on Philippine soil—soil consecrated in the blood of our two peoples. . . . At my side is your President, Sergio Osmena, a worthy successor of that great patriot, Manuel Quezon. . . . The seat of your government is now, therefore, firmly re-established on Philippine soil. The hour of your redemption is here. . . . Rally to me. Let the indomitable spirit of Bataan and Corregidor lead on. As the lines of battle roll forward to bring you within the zone of operations, rise and strike. Strike at every favorable opportunity. For your homes and hearths, strike! For future generations of your sons and daughters, strike! In the name of your sacred dead, strike! Let no heart be faint. Let every arm be steeled. The guidance of Divine God points the way. Follow in His name to the Holy Grail of righteous victory." [25]

Next Osmena and then Romulo spoke briefly into the hand-held mike. That ended the little ceremony, and a small cluster of Filipinos, who had been trapped here since the beginning of Kinkaid's bombardment, cheered.

Later Kenney wanted to inspect an old Japanese airfield nearby. MacArthur decided to join him. Kenney recalled that "my enthusiasm cooled when I found that the west end of the field was being used as a firing range by the Japs on one side and our troops on the other . . . We had to halt a couple of times on the way, once until a Jap sniper had been knocked out of a tree about 75 yards off the road and again when we had to wait for about twenty minutes until a Jap tank headed in our direction had been hit and the crew disposed of. We passed the burning tank on the way to the airdrome."

Once there, MacArthur paced around the strip, asking Kenney how quickly it could be made operational. Ricochets of enemy bullets were whining around them. The airman afterward remembered, "I told him I'd like to look at it under more favorable conditions, when I could inspect all of it at the same time. I added that I would feel much better at that moment if I were inspecting the place from an airplane. MacArthur laughed and said it was good for me to find out 'how the other half of the world lives.'"[26]

SURIGAO STRAITS

Now that MacArthur had committed himself to Leyte, now that over 200,000 troops of Krueger's Sixth Army were pouring ashore, the Japanese navy made its great move. Admiral Toyoda, flying his flag on Formosa, had hatched a brilliant plan. His main fleet, led by seven battleships, thirteen heavy cruisers, and three light cruisers, was racing up from Singapore under Vice Admiral Takeo Kurita. Kurita was instructed to divide this force in two, with the smaller detachment, under Vice Admiral Teji Nishamura, entering Leyte Gulf through Surigao Strait while the main body commanded by Kurita himself knifed through San Bernardino Strait. Both jaws would then converge on MacArthur's troop transports and Kinkaid's obsolescent warships. Banzai.

Halsey's Task Force 34, the backbone of his Third Fleet, was guarding San Bernardino Strait. To divert him, a third Nipponese flotilla of four overage carriers and two battleships converted into carriers was steaming down from the Japanese homeland. The mission of its commander, Vice Admiral Jisaburo Ozawa, was to entice Task Force 34 away from Leyte Gulf.

On the night of Monday, October 23, 1944, two U.S. submarines, the *Darter* and the *Dace*, sighted Kurita's main force off the coast of Borneo. At first light Tuesday morning, they torpedoed three of his cruisers, sinking two of them, and warned Halsey and Kinkaid that trouble was on its way. . . . Ozawa, the decoy commander, learned of this development and tried to draw Halsey toward him by sending out uncoded messages. Halsey didn't pick up the signals, however, and his reconnaissance planes missed Ozawa because they were all flying westward, looking for Kurita's vanguard. Finding it, U.S. planes hit the massive *Musashi* thirty-six times, thereby sending to the bottom a vessel that the Japanese thought unsinkable. . . . Kurita turned his fleet away from Leyte Gulf, intending to sail beyond reach of U.S. naval planes until dark, when he could return. Halsey concluded that he was retreating and could now be ignored. But the American admiral noted that no enemy carriers had been sighted. Believing that there must be some in the vicinity, he sent up reconnaissance planes on broader searches. At 5:00 P.M. they finally discovered Ozawa's bait. Halsey went for it leaving San Bernardino Strait wide open.[27]

Tuesday night, under a roving moon, Admiral Nishimura, commanding Kurita's southern unit, entered the narrow waters of Surigao Strait. Rear Admiral Jesse Oldendorf, USN, had the strait corked.

As the enemy vessels came through one by one, Oldendorf "crossed their T"—raked them viciously with broadsides from all his ships. Nishimura drowned and his force was wiped out; at dawn there would be nothing left of it but wreckage and streaks of oil. . . . Now, to his horror, [Kinkaid, who was guarding the San Bernardino Strait learned that the returning] Kurita was almost upon him, and that the Japanese force was intact except for the sunken *Musashi*. Kurita had passed through San Bernardino Strait and was already training his mammoth guns on part of Kinkaid's fleet, six escort carriers and a group of destroyers covering MacArthur's beachheads. The fox was among the chickens.

At 8:30 A.M. Kinkaid radioed Halsey: "Urgently need fast battleships Leyte Gulf at once." There was no response. . . . At this point there occurred one of the most remarkable episodes in the history of naval warfare. Kurita was less than thirty miles from his objective. All that stood between his guns and Kinkaid's carriers was a screen of destroyers and [antisubmarine] escorts . . . The destroyers counterattacked Kurita's battleships, and then their gallant little escorts sprang toward the huge Japanese armada, firing their small-bore guns and launching torpedoes. Kurita's Goliaths milled around in confusion as the persistent Davids, some of them sinking, made dense smoke. Kinkaid's carriers sent up everything that could fly, and Kurita, with the mightiest Nipponese fleet since Midway, hesitated. [28]

"WHERE IS TASK FORCE 34?"

[Halsey] had gone so far in chasing the decoy that [his fleet] could not arrive until the next morning. By all the precedents of naval warfare but one, Kurita had won the battle. The exception was confusion. . . . He intercepted and misread two of Kinkaid's messages to Halsey. Believing that Halsey was approaching rapidly, and that he would soon bolt the door of San Bernardino Strait, Kurita turned tail. He passed through the strait a few minutes before 10:00 P.M.—unaware that Halsey's leading ships would not reach it for another three hours.

Thus ended the Battle of Leyte Gulf. It had involved 282 warships, compared with 250 at Jutland in 1916, until then the greatest naval engagement in history. And unlike Jutland, which neither side had won, this action had been decisive. The Americans had lost one light carrier, two escort carriers, and three destroyers. They had sunk four carriers, three battleships, six heavy cruisers, three light cruisers and eight destroyers. Except for sacrificial kamikaze fliers, who made their debut in this battle, Japanese air and naval strength would never again be serious instruments in the war.

"LEAVE THE BULL ALONE"

Thursday evening MacArthur was sitting down to dinner in the restored Price house when he heard staff officers at the other end of the table making recriminatory remarks about Halsey's action "in abandoning us" while he went after the Jap northern "decoy" fleet. The General slammed his bunched fist on the table. "That's enough!" he roared. "Leave the Bull alone! He's still a fighting admiral in my book."

[On the land] MacArthur had achieved strategic surprise. The troops of Shiro Makino's 16th Division were being slowly pushed back on Leyte's Highway 2, toward an eminence which American GIs had christened Breakneck Ridge . . . At the time MacArthur seemed to be just inching along. Unlike commanders of marines and Australians, the two other infantry forces in the Pacific, the General preferred to pause at enemy strongpoints, waiting until his artillery had leveled the enemy's defenses. When American newspapers fretted over this . . . MacArthur said, "If I like I can finish Leyte in two weeks, but I won't! I have too great a responsibility to the mothers and wives in America to do that to their men. I will not take by sacrifice what I can achieve by strategy." [29]

His greatest problem . . . was the weather, which erased the margin that superior naval and air power should have given him. He had called Leyte a springboard, but he was discovering that it could be a very soggy one. In forty days, thirty-four inches of rain fell, turning the island into one vast bog. The steady, drenching tropical monsoon made runway grading impossible. . . . Finally a new strip was built on relatively solid ground at Tanauan, nine miles south of Tacloban, and P-38s began flying in and out, but Leyte never became the air base the General needed. [30]

THE COMMAND STYLE

[MacArthur's] staff continued to seethe and churn with plots, counterplots, and intrigues which would have been more appropriate in Medicean Florence. Dr. Egeberg and Laurence E. "Larry" Bunker, like most survivors of it, blame Sutherland; "he divided the Gs—[G-1, administration; G-2, intelligence; G-3, operations; G-4, quartermaster]—against each other." But the chief of staff could hardly have pitted officers against one another without the knowledge, and even the encouragement, of the ironhanded commander in chief. What is extraordinary is the degree to which MacArthur convinced them that he knew nothing of the turmoil. . . .

MacArthur, like Roosevelt, was exploiting his position at the center of the staff. Kenney noted how "in a big staff meeting, or in conversation with a single individual, MacArthur has a wonderful knack of leading a discussion up to the point of a decision that each member present believes he himself originated. I have heard officers say many times, 'The Old Man bought my idea,' when it was something that weeks before I had heard MacArthur decide to do. . . . As a salesman, MacArthur had no superior and few equals." In other conferences, the General would identify a military target and invite suggestions on how it might be seized. Each officer would reply, he would ask broad questions, say "Thank you very much, gentlemen," and go off to ponder the problem himself.

Often an aide recalls "he would ask me questions and then answer them. From some of these interchanges I got a clear picture of the connection between chess and war. He might say, 'Now if we do this, which Steve suggested, they might do this, or if they were clever, they might do that. Now if they do this, we should answer them in one of three ways,' and he would outline the other alternatives, and then he would go to the Japanese answer to the six or seven possibilities. By the time he had done this for a day or a week, he would call his staff, establish the strategy which was amazingly frequently the opposite from the feeling of the majority, and which would seem always to have been right."[31]

He never lost an opportunity to remind his staff that while they were talking, other, younger men were dying. Before leaving Hollandia, each of the headquarters officers had chipped in twenty dollars apiece to buy liquor. The shipment had arrived after they had left for Leyte, and it could not be forwarded without the General's permission. They chose Dick Marshall as their spokesman. After mess that evening, he cleared his throat and explained the problem. MacArthur asked, "What about the men? Have they got anything?" Marshall explained that they had beer. The General thought awhile and then said: "If beer is good enough for the enlisted men, it's good enough for the officers."[32]

THE LAST STEPPINGSTONE

Altogether [at Luzon] MacArthur would command nearly a thousand ships, accompanied by three thousand landing craft, many of them new arrivals from Normandy, and 280,000 men—more than Eisenhower's U.S. strength in the campaigns of North Africa, Italy, or southern France; more than the total Allied force in the conquest of Sicily. But Yamashita was lying in wait for him with 275,000 men, the largest enemy to be encountered in the Pacific campaigns. . . .

Although [Yamashita] had thirty-six thousand men on the Lingayen beaches, he withdrew them, having concluded that American firepower made resistance at the shoreline pointless, that with Halsey roaming the seas the best could do was to prolong the struggle for the island, tying up MacArthur to buy time for the Japanese now furiously digging in on the home islands of Dai Nippon.

WALK ON WATER

Before dawn on Wednesday, January 10, the Americans lay to off the landing beaches, and a thousand anchors plummeted into the gulf. It was a calm sea; there was less surf than anyone could remember. A typhoon had darted away at the last moment, and the different reactions of Americans and Filipinos to that lucky circumstance says much about their views of the General. U.S. war correspondents wondered whimsically whether he would walk on the water. To the Filipinos it was no laughing matter; many of them believed then, and believe to this day, that the gentle waves lapping the white sands were a consequence of divine intervention. MacArthur was the last man to disillusion them. He knew the power of myth in the minds of the islands' people. If they thought him capable of miracles, their conviction added a powerful weapon to his arsenal, one which his showmanship would polish.

After Krueger's first four divisions had splashed ashore, the commander in chief followed in his Higgins boat. In his memoirs he writes: "As was getting to be a habit with me, I picked a boat that took too much draft to reach the beach, and I had to wade in. . . ." It should be added that a group of peasants watching on the shore cheered lustily and hurried inland to spread the word of his second coming. That, of course, was precisely what he wanted them to do.[33]

"GET TO MANILA"

The General had told Eichelberger that he wanted him to "undertake a daring expedition against Manila with a small mobile force," using tactics which "would have delighted Jeb Stuart." The implication was that such a maneuver was too difficult for Krueger, and while MacArthur was doubtless playing his two fighting generals against one another—as Napoleon did with his marshals, and as Stalin would soon do in encouraging Zhukov and Konev to race each other to Berlin—the General clearly regarded his senior field commander as unenterprising, and even timid.[34]

The amphitheater in which they were maneuvering, the island's central plain, is about 40 miles wide and 110 miles deep. . . . Though MacArthur had shown the defensive potential of Bataan and Corregidor, south of Manila, Yamashita preferred to withdraw the main body of his troops into the mountains to the east. And MacArthur somehow knew this. He was so sure of it that he saw no need to guard his left flank. "Get to Manila!" he told his field commanders. "Go around the Japs, bounce off the Japs, save your men, but get to Manila! Free the internees at Santo Tomas! Take Lalacanan and the legislative buildings!" But Krueger was haunted by the nightmare of a quarter-million Japanese driving in his flank pickets, cutting him off from the gulf, and "slicing him up like a pie." He wanted to spend two or three weeks consolidating his gains before advancing behind heavy artillery barrages toward the capital, which he assumed would be strongly defended.[35]

The General vehemently disagreed. Those, he said, were the tactics which had destroyed the flower of a generation in the trenches of World War I. Moreover, he pointed out, in his words . . . "I knew every wrinkle of the terrain, every foot of the topography." He saw no reason why flying columns shouldn't move swiftly down the fine roads leading southward between the rice paddies and neat little towns to Manila, which he believed would be undefended. MacArthur and Krueger [often] had words over this . . . . Yet MacArthur never pulled rank on him. Sutherland had frequently urged that Krueger be "sent home"—Sutherland wanted to lead the Sixth Army himself—and others wondered why he wasn't. The likeliest explanation was that the General knew his plodding subordinate was a useful counterweight to his own bravura.[36]

CONTROL THE STRATEGY

[George Marshall wrote in an official report to the secretary of war] "Yamashita's inability to cope with MacArthur's swift moves" and "his desired reaction to the deception measures" combined "to place the Japanese in an impossible situation." The enemy "was forced into a piecemeal commitment of his troops.". . . "They were unable to conduct an orderly retreat, in classic fashion, to fall back on inner perimeters with forces intact for a last defense. . . . It was a situation unique in modern war. Never had such large numbers of troops been so outmaneuvered, . . . and left tactically impotent to take an active part in the final battle for their homeland."[37]

While Krueger was investing Clark Field, his commander in chief was dazzling Yamashita with a series of lightning thrusts elsewhere. . . . Without losing a man, an expedition captured the invaluable port of Olangapo. Then he put a regiment ashore at Mariveles, on the peninsula's lower tip. Trapped in a double envelopment, Yamashita's Bataan garrison was isolated and impotent; the peninsula was taken in just seven days.[38]

The only remaining stronghold in the bay itself was Corregidor. In 1942 the Japanese had lost twice their landing force—several thousand men—to the gallant marines on the Rock's beaches. Now, with 5,200 enemy defenders in superb condition and provided with enormous stocks of ammunition, the fortress seemed far more formidable. MacArthur landed a regiment of airborne troops on Topside while an infantry battalion, with exquisite timing, leaped from Higgins boats to storm the Bottomside shore. After losing 1,500 men in a ten-day battle, the enemy commander holed up with the rest in Malinta Tunnel, where they committed suicide spectacularly by igniting a huge mass of explosives and blowing themselves up. The Americans' losses had been 210 men, 50 of them killed in that final blowup.

IN PERSONAL COMMAND

What makes [these events] all the more remarkable is that [MacArthur] was leaving his staff every morning to race around in his five-star jeep like a man forty years younger. "The Chief wanted to be in *personal* command," Eichelberger wrote, "and apparently he has done so." Willoughby wrote afterward: "Constantly on the front line—at times well ahead of it—his sheer physical endurance and his reckless exposure of himself excited the native population and even his own forces to a pitch of effort that became the dismay of the enemy." . . . He was everywhere, doing everything but digging the foxholes and loading the machine-gun belts. He watched the airborne drops from a B-17 overhead. On the central plain, he climbed on tanks to observe enemy patrols through field glasses. On Bataan he ventured five miles beyond American lines, hoping for a glimpse of Corregidor, and was almost strafed by a squadron of Kenny's fighters. He stood erect at an enemy roadblock, and when a nearby Nambu opened up and an American lieutenant said, "We're going after those fellows, but please get down sir; we're under fire," MacArthur replied crisply, without moving, "I'm not under fire. Those bullets are not intended for me."[39]

In late January he was inspecting the 161st Infantry when the regiment was struck by a tank led counterattack. The American lines buckled, and MacArthur personally rallied the men. When Stimson heard about it, the General was awarded his third Distinguished Service Cross.

On another occasion, just north of Manila, his jeep halted at a blown bridge. . . . Shortly thereafter, he made what he called a "personal reconnaissance" inside the enemy-held city itself, touring the Malacanan Palace grounds and returning to report, like a scout, that he believed GIs "could cross the river and clear all southern Manila with a platoon." . . . As MacArthur had predicted, Yamashita had withdrawn his troops from the city, declaring that "the capital of the republic and its law-abiding inhabitants should not suffer from the ravages of war." MacArthur's headquarters informed senior U.S. officers that plans were being made "for a great victory parade à la Champs Elysees."

"DESTRUCTION IS IMMINENT"

At 6:00 P.M. on Saturday, February 3, patrols of the lst Cavalry entered the city limits. Three days later, on Tuesday, MacArthur's communique announced: "Our forces are rapidly clearing the enemy from Manila. Our converging columns . . . entered the city and surrounded the Jap defenders. Their complete destruction is imminent."

Although the American public was unaware of the fact—the General's censors told correspondents they couldn't expose his victory communique as a lie—the fall of the capital was a month away . . . Eichelberger wrote on February 21, "the big parade has been called off." That was a shattering understatement. . . . The devastation of Manila was one of the great tragedies of World War II. Of Allied cities in those war years, only

Warsaw suffered more. Seventy percent of the utilities, 75 percent of the factories, 80 percent of the southern residential district, and 100 percent of the business district were razed. Nearly 100,000 Filipinos were murdered by the Japanese. Hospitals were set afire after their patients had been strapped to their beds. The corpses of males were mutilated, females of all ages were raped before they were slain, and babies' eyeballs were gouged out and smeared on walls like jelly.

MacArthur blamed the holocaust on [Yamashita] but the guilt lay elsewhere. Yamashita's orderly evacuation into the hills had left about thirty thousand Japanese sailors and marines under Rear Admiral Sanji Iwabuchi . . . Either Iwabuchi had not received the order from Yamashita declaring the capital an open city, or he chose to ignore it. Once he had decided to defend Manila, the atrocities began, and the longer the battle raged, the more the Japanese command structure deteriorated, until the uniforms of Nipponese sailors and marines were saturated with Filipino blood.

"THE ISLANDS ARE LIBERATED"

[Yet] the contrast between [MacArthur's] casualties and those of the enemy is, in fact, extraordinary. In his Philippine operations after Luzon he lost 820 GIs, while over 21,000 Japanese were slain. On July 5 he could announce: "The entire Philippine Islands are now liberated . . . The Japanese during the operations employed twenty-three divisions, all of which were practically annihilated. Our forces comprised seventeen divisions. This was one of the rare instances when in a long campaign a ground force superior in numbers was entirely destroyed by a numerically inferior opponent."

In these battles he continued to expose himself to danger at the front. At Brunei Bay and Balikpapan, he insisted on going in with the assault waves. . . . Ashore at Brunei Bay he walked along a road paralleling the beach, about a quarter of a mile inland, with the sound of snipers' shots and machine guns on both sides. Kenney remembers beginning "to feel all over again as I had when we landed in the Philippines at Leyte. A tank lumbered by, and fifty yards ahead, atop a small rise, a rifleman and a machine gunner exchanged bursts of fire. MacArthur walked there to see what was happening. Two dead Japanese lay in a ditch . . . An Australian army photographer appeared, hoping to take a picture of the General and the bodies. MacArthur refused, and the cameraman squared away to snap the two corpses. Just as his bulb flashed, the photographer fell with a sniper's bullet in his shoulder.[40]

ON TO JAPAN

[MacArthur] looked forward to Soviet entry into the Pacific war. By engaging a million Japanese and taking the sting out of their air force, he reckoned, Stalin would distract the enemy and save thousands of lives.

Meanwhile Hirohito's generals, grimly preparing for the invasion [of Japan] had not abandoned hope of saving their homeland. Although a few strategic islands had been lost, they told each other, most of their conquests, including the Chinese heartland, were firmly in their hands, and the bulk of their army was undefeated. Even now they could scarcely believe that any foe would have the audacity to attempt landings in Japan itself. Allied troops, they boasted, would face the fiercest resistance in history. Over ten thousand kamikaze planes were readied for "Ketsu-Go," Operation Decision. Behind the beaches, enormous connecting underground caves had been stocked with caches of food and thousands of tons of ammunition. Manning the nation's ground defenses were 2,350,000 regular soldiers, 250,000 garrison troops, and 32,000,000 civilian militiamen—a total of 34,600,000, more than the combined armies of the United States, Great Britain, and Nazi Germany. All males aged fifteen to sixty, and all females aged seventeen to forty-five, had been conscripted. Their weapons included ancient bronze cannon, muzzle-loading muskets, bamboo spears, and bows and arrows. Even little children had been trained to strap explosives around their waists, roll under tank treads, and blow themselves up. They were called "Sherman carpets."

FANATICS OR DOVES?

This was the enemy the Pentagon had learned to fear and hate—a country of fanatics dedicated to hara-kiri, determined to slay as many invaders as possible as they went down fighting. But there was another Japan, and MacArthur was one of the few Americans who suspected its existence. He kept urging the Pentagon and the State Department to be alert for conciliatory gestures. Kenney notes that the General predicted that "the break would come from Tokyo, not from the Japanese army." . . . A dovish coalition was forming in the Japanese capital, and it was headed by Hirohito himself, who had concluded in the spring of 1945 that a negotiated peace was the only way to end his nation's agony. Beginning in early May a six-man council of Japanese diplomats explored ways to accommodate the Allies.

Had Roosevelt been alive, his fine political antennae might have sensed the possibilities here. But Truman, new in office and less flexible in diplomacy, was swayed by such advisers as Dean Acheson, Archibald MacLeish, and Hopkins who believed that negotiations were pointless; that unless Hirohito was unthroned, the war would have been in vain. The upshot was the Potsdam declaration in July, demanding that Japan surrender unconditionally or face "prompt and utter destruction." MacArthur was appalled. He knew that the Japanese would never renounce their emperor, and that without him an orderly transition to peace would be impossible anyhow, because his people would never submit to Allied occupation unless he ordered it. Ironically, when the surrender did come, it was conditional, and the condition was a continuation of the imperial reign. Had the General's advice been followed, the resort to atomic weapons at Hiroshima and Nagasaki might have been unnecessary.[41]

In an implacable mood then, successive versions of "Downfall," the code word for the invasion of Dai Nippon, were drafted in Washington and revised in Manila. . . . "Downfall" would begin with "Operation Olympic," a frontal assault on Kyushu by 766,700 Allied troops under Krueger on November 1, 1945, whose purpose would be to secure, in the General's words "airfields to cover the main assault on Honshu." The second phase "Operation Coronet," the landing on Honshu, would follow on March 1, 1946. He himself probably with Eichelberger as his chief of staff would lead that.[42]

He had no illusions about the savagery that lay ahead—he told Stimson that Downfall would "cost over a million casualties to American forces alone"—but he was confident that with the tanks from Europe he could outmaneuver the defenders on the great Kanto Plain before Tokyo.

THE ATOMIC BOMB

With each passing day the General felt surer that peace was very near. Two weeks before Hiroshima he told Kenney that he believed the enemy would surrender "by September 1 at the latest and perhaps even sooner." On Sunday, August 5, a courier arrived from Washington with word that an atomic bomb would be dropped "on an industrial area south of Tokyo the following day." . . . Three days later President Truman suspended B-29 raids on Japan; three days after that, on Wednesday, August 15, Hirohito ordered an end to all hostilities at 4:00 P.M. Tokyo time, telling his people that they must "endure the unendurable and suffer the insufferable." Truman, with the approval of Clement Attlee, Stalin, and Chiang Kai-shek, appointed MacArthur Supreme Commander for the Allied Powers (SCAP).

THE OCCUPATION

One of his first acts, he told Bonner Fellers, would be to give women the vote. "The Japanese men won't like it," said Fellers, and indeed, as events would prove, many of them regarded it as worse than sexual assault. The General said, "I don't care. I want to discredit the military. Women don't like war." It was part of his enigmatic temperament that although he could be ungenerous toward American admirals and uncivil toward his superiors in Washington, he was an imaginative, magnanimous conqueror. He intended, he said, to "use the instrumentality of the Japanese government to implement the occupation." Sitting in front of a Quonset hut and puffing on his pipe, he told an aide that woman suffrage was only one point in his seven-point plan for Japan. The others were disarming Japanese soldiers, sending them home, dismantling war industry, holding free elections, encouraging the formation of labor unions, and opening all schools with no check on instruction except the elimination of military indoctrination and the addition of courses in civics.[43]

"OF ALL THE AMAZING DEEDS"

Later Winston Churchill said: "Of all the amazing deeds in the war, I regard General MacArthur's personal landing at Atsugi [Japan] as the bravest of the lot." John Gunther wrote: "Professors who studied Japan all their lives, military experts who knew every nook and cranny of the Japanese character, thought that 'MacArthur was taking a frightful risk.'" In Manila Sutherland remonstrated: "My God General, the emperor is worshipped as a real god, yet they still tried to assassinate him. What kind of target does that make you?" MacArthur replied that he believed the reported attempt on Hirohito's life was spurious—he was right, although there was no way of knowing it then—and when his C-54, with "Bataan" emblazoned on its nose, touched down for a brief stop on Okinawa, and he noticed that Kenney and the others were strapping on pistols in shoulder holsters, he said, "Take them off. If they intend to kill us, sidearms will be useless. And nothing will impress them like a show of absolute fear-

lessness. If they don't know they're licked, this will convince them."[44]

The General knew that word of everything he said and did would quickly spread throughout the country. He was determined that the occupation be benign from the outset. Moreover, remembering his tour of duty in Germany after the 1918 Armistice, he realized that in a war-torn, defeated country, food would be at a premium. . . . When the commander of the 11th Airborne ruefully reported that his division had searched all night and found exactly one egg for the Supreme Commander's breakfast, MacArthur immediately issued an order at odds with the whole history of conquering armies in Asia. Occupation troops were forbidden to consume local victuals; they would eat only their own rations. An hour later, he canceled the martial law and curfew decrees Eichelberger had imposed on the city. The first step in the reformation of Japan, he said, would be an exhibition of generosity and compassion of the occupying power.[45]

That evening he was sitting down to dinner in the hotel when an aide reported that he had a visitor outside: Lieutenant General Jonathan M. Wainwright. Liberated from his Manchurian prisoner-of-war camp by the Russians four days earlier . . . was the man the General had left in command [at Corregidor] in 1942 . . . [Wainwright] was haggard and aged. . . . He walked with difficulty and with the help of a cane. His eyes were sunken and there were pits in his cheeks. His hair was snow white and his skin looked like old shoe leather. . . . For three years he had imagined himself in disgrace for having surrendered Corregidor. He believed he would never again be given an active command. This shocked MacArthur. "Why, Jim," he said, "Your old corps is yours when you want it."[46] Wainwright said, "General . . ." Then his voice wavered and he burst into tears.

THE FINAL CEREMONY

Early Sunday morning, two days later, a destroyer took Wainwright out to the slate-gray, forty-five thousand ton battleship *Missouri*, on Tokyo Bay. . . .

[At the ceremony, MacArthur's] stance was a portrait of soldierly poise. Only his hand trembled slightly as he held a single sheet of paper before him and said: "We are gathered here, representatives of the major warring powers, to conclude a solemn agreement whereby peace may be restored. . . . Both the conquerors and the conquered must rise to that higher dignity which alone befits the sacred purposes we are about to serve. . . . To the Pacific basin has come the vista of a new emancipated world. Today, freedom is on the offensive, democracy is on the march. Today, in Asia, as well as in Europe, unshackled peoples are tasting the full sweetness of liberty, the relief from fear." He concluded: "And so, my fellow countrymen, today I report to you that your sons and daughters have served you well and faithfully with the calm, deliberate, determined fighting spirit of the American soldier and sailor. . . . Their spiritual strength and power has brought us through to victory. They are homeward bound—take care of them."[47]

QUESTIONS

1. What were the most important components of the Allies' strategy in the South Pacific? Why were these strategies chosen?
2. Were better strategies available? If so, what were they? Why?
3. What do you think of the way in which the Allies' strategy was arrived at? What made Douglas MacArthur a good (or poor) strategist?
4. What characteristics of a good military strategy have application in the business world? What "principles of strategy" can you derive from this case?

NEW STEEL CORPORATION

In the late 1970s, some young executives—their leader was 35—in a major steel company proposed to the top executive group a way of counteracting the increasingly heavy imports of foreign steel into the company's market places. They suggested that—despite many seemingly unfavorable cost factors in the United States—it would be possible to compete successfully, make high margins, and grow rapidly by producing steel in the United States in competition with foreign sources. Top management was interested but unpersuaded, and the team set out to develop its plan in greater depth and to implement it personally if necessary.

During the 1980s, hundreds of U.S. steel mills closed, over 200,00 workers were laid off, and whole regions of the country were economically devastated. While the major vertically integrated steel companies' share of the U.S. market shrank from 64% in 1979 (and to a projected 30% by the mid-1990s), New Steel Corporation—founded by these young executives—grew at an average compounded rate of 35% per year. The founders were "dedicated steel men determined to break all the rules" of the steel industry's past. It set out to be "the international low-cost supplier of quality steel." By 1990 it set a record of 1.4 labor hours per ton of steel—compared to an average of 2.2 for all mini-mills and 4.6 for big U.S. integrated mills. From its raw start-up in the '70s, New Steel had grown into a world leader in profitability and one of the eight largest steel companies in the United States. Its unique strategy was crucial to its success.

Until about 1960, the U.S. steel industry had been the world's leader in steel production, technology, and marketing. But in 1959 the United States became a net importer of steel, and technological leadership in basic carbon steels began to shift to Japan. The U.S. industry, mired in low profits, was unable to generate the capital to modernize. Meanwhile, the Japanese and Korean industries, with one-half the capital cost of the United States and much lower labor rates (see accompanying exhibits), were able to surge ahead in a wide range of steel products. In 1978 the Japanese had an average cost advantage of 10–15% against U.S. competitors, and this advantage increased as the exchange rate for the U.S. dollar rose against the yen. By the early 1980s, total U.S. capacity for raw steel was 155 million tons annually, with 76% being in the hands of the top 10 integrated producers. The industry's top 15 firms operating 36 integrated mills—located primarily in Pennsylvania, Ohio, Indiana, and Illinois—averaged about 3.2 million tons of steel per year and had plant investment levels of $30,000–45,000 per employee.

Although Japan led in many areas of steel technology, such technologies were generally available to others through licensing. By the early 1980s, the United States had dropped to second place in its steel R&D effort behind Japan, but still led in those special stocks and alloys the U.S. space and defense programs demanded. More detailed figures about the U.S. industry and its competitive posture are contained in the following exhibits.

QUESTIONS

1. How could the team best position the proposed new company for success against foreign competition?
2. What would be the critical factors for success? What target performance levels in these characteristics would ensure success? How could these be achieved?
3. How could the team implement a strategy which would be sure to win against foreign competition?

Case copyright © 1995 James Brian Quinn. Penny Paquette—research associate. New Steel Corporation is a real company whose name has been disguised.

EXHIBIT 1
U.S. Raw Steel Production by Grade, 1965–1993
(thousands of net tons)

	CARBON		ALLOY		STAINLESS		TOTAL
Year	Tonnage	Percentage of Total	Tonnage	Percentage of Total	Tonnage	Percentage of Total	
1965	116,651	88.80%	13,318	10.10%	1,493	1.10%	131,462
1970	117,411	89.3	12,824	9.70	1,279	1.00	131,514
1975	100,360	86.00	15,171	13.00	1,111	1.00	116,642
1980	94,689	84.70	15,445	13.80	1,701	1.50	111,835
1985	76,699	86.9	9,877	11.20	1,683	1.90	88,259
1990	86,590	87.50	10,279	10.40	2,037	2.00	98,906
1993	86,865	88.70	9,056	9.30	1,956	2.00	97,877

Source: American Iron and Steel Institute, *Annual Statistical Report,* various years.

EXHIBIT 2
Total Costs of Steel Production, 1982

	UNITED STATES		UNITED KINGDOM		FRANCE		JAPAN		WEST GERMANY	
Capacity utilization[a]	90%	48%	90%	58%	90%	61%	90%	58%	90%	55%
Labor	$172	—	$122	—	$150	—	$72	—	$133	-
Materials	291	372	386	370	299	296	254	285	283	290
Financial exp.[b]	34	74	42	77	84	98	61	101	46	64
Total pretax cost	580	695	493	585	465	546	411	490	430	513
Total pretax profit	23	—	11	—	28	—	72	—	45	—

[a]The first column for each country presents estimates of what production costs would have been if capacity utilization was 90 percent. The second column contains estimates of costs at the rate of capacity that actually existed in 1982.

[b]Depreciation, interest, and miscellaneous taxes.

Source: "World Steel Dynamics," Paine Webber Mitchell Hutchins, Inc., 1983, in *The Competitive Status of the U.S. Steel Industry,* National Academy Press, 1985.

EXHIBIT 3
Costs of Refining
(basis: 1 short ton of output)

COST CATEGORY	BOF[A]	EAF (DRI1)[B]	EAF (DRI2)[C]	EAF (SCRAP)[D]
Process materials	$207.59	$217.53	$186.30	$117.67
Energy	1.58	34.98	34.13	26.25
Direct labor	8.55	15.54	15.54	15.54
Capital	9.73	15.04	15.04	16.26
Other	5.26	7.28	6.90	6.33
Total	$232.71	$290.37	$257.91	$182.05

[A]BOF = Basic oxygen furnace.
[B]EAF (DRI1) = Electric arc furnace using direct reduced iron (gas-based).
[C]EAF (DRI2) = Electric arc furnace using direct reduced iron (coal-based).
[D]EAF (scrap) = Electric arc using scrap.

Source: The Competitive Status of the U.S. Steel Industry, National Academy Press, 1985.

EXHIBIT 4
Labor Productivity at Actual Operating Rates, 1964–1980 (employee hours required per short ton of carbon steel shipped)

YEAR	UNITED STATES	JAPAN	WEST GERMANY	UNITED KINGDOM	FRANCE
1964	12.32	26.03	22.39	25.43	25.61
1972	10.61	11.85	13.44	19.59	16.32
1973	10.15	9.49	12.08	18.40	15.36
1974	9.97	9.33	11.34	19.99	14.76
1975	10.63	10.08	12.64	23.17	17.15
1976	10.30	9.16	11.89	21.02	15.75
1977	10.62	8.91	11.87	21.69	14.85
1978	9.84	8.39	10.77	20.37	13.34
1979	9.97	7.58	9.79	18.86	12.07
1980	10.37	7.33	9.85	21.45*	11.59
Percentage of average annual change: 1964–1980	–1.08	–7.92	–5.13	–1.06	–4.96

*Estimates for 1990 are based on a comparison of the last 9 months of 1980 with the same period in 1979 because of nationwide work stoppage in January through March 1980.

Source: U.S. Department of Labor, Bureau of Labor Statistics, unpublished data, in *The Competitive Status of the U.S. Steel Industry*. National Academy Press, 1985.

EXHIBIT 5
Comparative International Materials Costs, 1969–1982

YEAR	UNITED STATES	JAPAN	WEST GERMANY	FRANCE	UNITED KINGDOM
1969	92	78	76	87	85
1970	100	82	86	90	92
1971	106	87	97	97	106
1972	110	90	102	103	109
1973	118	100	125	125	122
1974	157	.140	170	168	169
1975	186	167	210	212	213
1976	199	175	208	205	201
1977	215	194	223	211	229
1978	233	218	241	231	265
1979	262	220	262	268	319
1980	298	261	291	302	441
1981	329	290	286	298	387
1982	373	285	290	296	370

Note: This table shows comparative materials cost for the United States and four other major producing countries. An examination of Exhibit 3 reveals that materials costs represent between 50 and 70 percent of the total cost of making steel. The major components of materials costs are (1) iron ore and scrap, (2) coking coal, and (3) other forms of energy (fuel oil, electricity, noncoking coal, natural gas), representing about 45, 35, and 20 percent of the total, respectively.

Source: "World Steel Dynamics," Paine Webber Mitchell Hutchins, Inc., 1981 and 1983, in *The Competitive Status of the U.S. Steel Industry*, National Academy Press, 1985.

EXHIBIT 6
World Steel Production, 1974–1992
(thousands of tons)

COUNTRY	1974	1980	1992
United States	136,802	101,455	84,322
Japan	119,322	111,395	98,132
Germany	53,232	43,838	38,711
United Kingdom	26,594	11,227	16,050
France	27,021	23,176	17,961
Italy	23,804	26,501	24,904
Spain	11,502	12,643	12,295
Belgium	16,227	12,322	10,330
Canada	13,623	15,901	13,933
China	21,119	37,121	80,037
Brazil	7,515	15,309	23,898
South Korea	1,947	8,558	28,054
India	7,069	9,514	18,117
Taiwan	597	3,417	10,705
Mexico	5,138	7,156	8,436
Argentina	2,353	2,687	2,661
Venezuela	1,058	1,975	3,396
Turkey	1,590	2,536	10,254
Saudi Arabia	—	—	1,823
Iran	567	1,200	2,937
Egypt	500	800	1,400

Source: William T. Hogan, *Steel in the 21st Century*, Lexington Books, 1994, pp. 8–9.

EXHIBIT 7
U.S. Imports by Type of Steel, 1970–1993

Year	CARBON Tonnage	CARBON Percentage of Total	ALLOY Tonnage	ALLOY Percentage of Total	STAINLESS Tonnage	STAINLESS Percentage of Total
1970	12.83	96.10%	0.35	2.60%	0.18	1.30%
1975	11.39	94.90	0.45	3.70	0.17	1.40
1980	14.78	95.40	0.56	3.60	0.15	1.00
1985	22.86	94.27	1.12	4.62	0.27	1.11
1990	15.55	90.62	1.23	7.17	0.38	2.21
1993	16.65	85.38	2.18	11.18	0.67	3.44

Source: American Iron and Steel Institute, *Annual Statistical Report*, various years.

EXHIBIT 8
U.S. Steel Market
Forecast to 2010
(millions of tons unless
otherwise noted)

	AVERAGE 1988–1992	1995	2000	2005	2010
Gross Domestic Product (in billions of 1987 dollars)	$4,836	$5,380	$6,167	$6,949	$7,716
Steel per millions dollars of GNP	19.9	18.5	16.5	15.0	14.0
Steel demand	96.2	99.5	101.8	104.2	108.0
Steel imports	17.7	15.5	16.0	16.5	18.0
Steel exports	4.3	5.0	5.0	5.0	5.0
Steel shipments	82.8	89.0	90.8	92.7	95.0

Source: William T. Hogan, *Steel in the 21st Century*, Lexington Books, 1994, p. 97.

EXHIBIT 9
U.S. Carbon Steel
Production by
Furnace Type

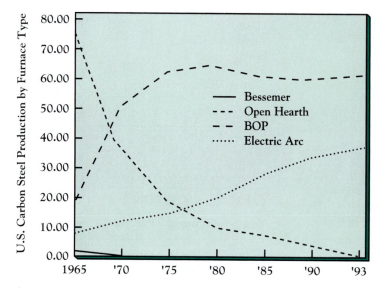

Source: American Iron and Steel Institute, *Annual Statistical Report*, various years.

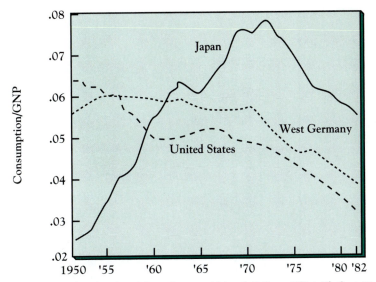

Source: *Steel: Upheaval in a Basic Industry*, Barnett and Schorsch, Ballinger, 1983, in *The Competitive Status of the U.S. Steel Industry*, National Academy Press, 1985.

EXHIBIT 11
The World Steel Market,
1989–1993

	1989			1992		
	Crude Steel Production (thousands of tons)	Apparent Crude Steel Consumption Per Capita	Apparent Finished Steel Consumption Per Capita	Crude Steel production (thousands of tons)	Apparent Crude Steel Consumption Per Capita	Apparent Finished Steel Consumption Per Capita
Africa-Total	11,445	22	17	12,302	20	16
Middle East-Total	5,726	96	84	8,068	113	101
Far East-Total	228,746	88	76	251,123	93	80
China	61,590	64	49	80,935	74	58
India	14,608	24	19	18,117	21	17
Japan	107,908	759	718	98,131	674	634
Rep. of Korea	21,873	424	393	28,054	522	491
Others	22,767	63	40	25,886	83	58
North America-Total	103,764	431	359	98,162	388	337
Canada	15,332	541	445	13,840	425	377
United States	88,432	420	350	84,322	380	333
Other America-Total	42,759	76	64	41,368	68	58
Oceania-Total	7,417	355	312	7,113	237	210
Europe-Total	384,945	444	358	304,718	319	267
EC-Total	139,492	391	336	132,050	349	312
EFTA-Total	13,926	411	351	12,884	316	304
Eastern Europe-Total	59,129	454	356	29,340	179	128
Former USSR-Total	160,096	583	445	118,514	394	301
WORLD	784,863	158	131	722,854	135	115

Source: Economic Commision for Europe, "The Steel Market in 1993 and Prospects for 1994," United Nations, 1994.

INTEL CORPORATION

In 1968 Robert N. Noyce (age 40) and Gordon E. Moore (age 39) broke away from Fairchild Semiconductor to form Intel Corporation. They concentrated on semiconductor memory components for the computer industry. When Intel started, no market existed for its principal product. By the late 1970s Intel's trailblazing technologies had irrevocably restructured the electronics, computer, and communications industries. In the 1980s semiconductors were affecting social changes many believed would be as profound as those of the industrial revolution. Not without cause did CEO Moore say, "We're in the business of revolutionizing society."[1] Opportunities seemed boundless. But in the early 1990s continuing technological advances and Japan's massive competitive capabilities presented unprecedented strategic challenges for this unique company.

BUDDING ENTREPRENEURS

Noyce and Moore made an unusual team. Although the future of this revolutionary technology was unknown at that time, Noyce—an inveterate young tinkerer from a small Iowa town—headed for

Case compilation copyright © 1995 by James Brian Quinn. The first part of the case is based on the Intel Corporation case written in 1985 and revised in 1995 by Professor Quinn. The generous support and cooperation of the Adolf H. Lundin Professorship at the International Management Institute, Geneva, Switzerland and the Intel Corporation in the development of this case is gratefully acknowledged. Numbers in parentheses indicate the reference and page number for material from a previously footnoted source. The second part of the case is based on the Intel Corporation case written in 1989 by George W. Cogan, under the supervision of Associate Professor Robert A. Burgelman, and edited in 1995 by Professor Quinn with permission from the author. Case Copyright © 1989 by The Trustees of Leland Stanford Jr. University. Revised 1991.

MIT to study about the new field only to find it had no courses on semiconductors. Taking his Ph.D. (in electron physics) at the top of his class, Noyce had joined Philco's semiconductor division. Two and a half years later, he got a call from William Shockley, the inventor of the transistor, who was starting a new semiconductor company in Palo Alto (California). Noyce and Moore, a Ph.D. chemist from Cal Tech, arrived there the same day.[2] Thus began one of the most successful technical partnerships of modern times.

FAIRCHILD SEMICONDUCTOR

The imaginative Shockley had assembled a group of bright young scientists, but the operation fell apart when eight of them left only a year later. Shockley's managerial shortcomings had totally alienated them.[3] Even while with Shockley, the group had looked upon Noyce as a leader. His enthusiasm—and his approach to everything with the idea that it was going to work— easily infected people. One of the members of the group wrote to a friend of his family who worked for Hayden Stone, the New York investment firm. Hayden Stone soon arranged to finance the new semiconductor company the young entrepreneurs wanted to organize. The eight young founders contributed about $500 apiece . . . but most of the start-up money came from Fairchild Camera and Instrument Corporation which also received an option to buy the group's budding company, known as Fairchild Semiconductor. (2,147)

BIG COMPANY BLUES

The company, which started in a rented building in Mountain View, California, grew fast. By 1968 Noyce was supervising nearly 15,000 employees in the United States and abroad. Both he and Moore achieved major technical advances in semiconductor technology at Fairchild (including the first planar integrated circuit and the first stable MOS transistor). But both men had begun to find big-company life less and less satisfying.

When Fairchild Camera had exercised its option to buy out Fairchild Semiconductor in 1959 and make it into an operating division, the originators each got about $250,000 worth of stock in Fairchild Camera. But Noyce and Moore began to feel that a company as big as Fairchild could not easily expand into new areas of semiconductor technology. Noyce said, "Fairchild was getting big and clumsy. LSI had been talked about a good deal, but there was no commitment behind it."[4] New ventures in such a complex field initially lose money—sometimes a lot of it—and it is often difficult to justify big losses to directors and stockholders. Moore and Noyce finally left Fairchild Semiconductor (in the summer of 1968). But not before they had built the company into a $150 million enterprise, one of the Big Three in its field along with Texas Instruments and Motorola.

A NEW COMPANY

"We figured LSI (Large Scale Integration) was the kind of business we'd be interested in. We both had started in technology, not in computers or finance. It would be fun for us," said Noyce. Noyce and Moore decided that their new company should try to establish itself as a specialist and leader in the computer memory field, a field where semiconductors had had very little impact and no larger companies were present. As Moore explains, "It's very tempting for a little company to run in all directions. We went the other way. It was our objective to dominate any market in which we participated."

VENTURE CAPITAL

The pair knew they would need quite a bit of money to start up. Fortunately, Noyce had already had considerable personal exposure to the investment community. Among his acquaintances was Arthur Rock, who had helped to arrange the original financing for Fairchild Semiconductor while he was at Hayden Stone.

"It was a very natural thing to go to Art and say, 'Incidentally, Art, do you have an extra $2.5 million you would like to put on the crap table?'" said Noyce. Rock had long before become convinced of Noyce's abilities as a manager. But he also knew that men who run big companies for others don't necessarily make

good entrepreneurs. So Rock, a cautious man, grilled Noyce on his goals and his emotional and financial commitment to the idea. "My way with people who want to start companies is to talk to them until they are exhausted—and then talk to them some more," said Rock. "Finally, I get an impression what their real objectives are, whether they have integrity, whether they are interested in running a big company, whether their goals are big enough. One of the things I'm interested in is whether the management puts a limit on the company they want. If they do, I get fearful." (2,149) Noyce wanted to grow to $100 million in 10 years.[3] Rock was pleased with Noyce's responses and by the fact that both Noyce and Moore were willing to invest substantial amounts of their own money, about $250,000 each.

Intel (a contraction of "integrated electronics") started in the enviable position of having so many would-be investors that it could choose those it preferred. "People had known Bob and were kind of lined up to invest in the company," said Rock. Rock purchased $300,000 worth of convertible debentures and brought in other investors who took an additional $2.2 million. Later Intel sold 154,000 shares of common stock in private placements for $2.2 million. The common was immediately oversubscribed.[5] Ultimately, paid-in capital for Intel amounted to about $17.5 million. But after its initial debenture issues, Intel did not find it necessary to borrow or to use its line of bank credit. During this period the company owned almost all its facilities.

Total sales growth of integrated circuits (I/Cs) in the 1970s would exceed 20% per year.[6] I/Cs would have even more impact on electronics than transistors had, although no one knew then precisely when or how. It cost millions to develop initial technologies, to build facilities, and to make the first successful chips. But production bugs made yields a miserable 1–5% of each run. Over 100 steps had to be performed perfectly in sequence. With tolerances of a few microns (millionths of a meter) required, a fleck of dust would cause a faulty device. And reliability testing of the circuits had to be meticulous, a million or more tests for each chip. Nevertheless, this miraculous technology, when mastered, would drive the cost of transistors down 10,000-fold or more. (2,151–152) Older vacuum tube companies couldn't cope with these uncertainties.[7] And customers, so-called "systems houses," were often afraid of trusting their design secrets to outside I/C suppliers.[8] This was the business Intel set its cap for.

A COMPLEX TECHNOLOGY

"The 1103 was a brand-new circuit-design concept, it brought about a brand-new systems approach to computer memories, and its manufacturing required a brand-new technology," added Andy Grove, then V.P. Operations. "Yet it became, over the short period of one year, a high-volume production item—high volume by any standards in this industry." Making the 1103 concept work at the technology level, at the device level, and at the systems level and successfully introducing it into high-volume manufacturing required . . . a fair measure of orchestrated brilliance. Everybody from technologists to designers to reliability experts had to work to the same schedule toward a different aspect of the same goal, interfacing simultaneously at all levels over quite a long period of time . . . Yet I would wake up at night, reliving some of the fights that took place during the day on how to accomplish various goals." (2,155)

"The operating style that evolved at Intel was based on the recognition of our own identity," said Grove. "The semiconductor industry consisted of companies that typically fell into one of two extremes: technology leaders and manufacturing leaders. Neither of these types of leadership would accomplish what we wanted to do. We wanted to capitalize on new technology and we wanted to sell our technology and our engineering over and over again. This meant high volume. We regarded ourselves as essentially a manufacturer of *high-technology jelly beans*."

EARLY ORGANIZATION

"A manufacturer of high-technology jelly beans needs a different breed of people. The wild-eyed, bushy-haired, boy geniuses that dominate the think tanks and the solely technology-oriented companies will never take their technology to the jelly-bean stage. Similarly, the other stereotype—the straight-laced, crewcut, and moustache-free manufacturing operators of conventional industry—will never generate the technology in the first place." A key question was how to find and mix the two talents. There weren't many experienced engineering or manufacturing people, and top young graduates were sought after by everyone. "In engineering we needed to orient toward market areas and specialized customer needs—such as computer mainframe memories, increasingly sophisticated peripheral capabilities, general purpose I/Cs, and timing circuits." Engineering had to come through *first* with a workable design for what the customer would need most.

But in manufacturing Intel needed to standardize as much as possible. In production, said Grove, "We actually borrowed from a very successful manufacturer of medium technology jelly beans—McDonald's hamburgers. When you thought about their standardized process and standardized module approach, it had much to offer in our technology." But there was also a sociological reason for what became known as the "McIntel" approach. Noyce was convinced that the day of the huge production unit was gone, that modern workers performed better in smaller, more informal production units. And by 1975 Intel had such units in various Santa Clara towns as well as in Oregon, the Philippines, and Malaysia. In each area Grove introduced perhaps the toughest quality control and monitoring systems in the industry and a system of rewards to match Intel's production philosophy.

Finally Intel realized that reliable delivery was perhaps the most important single issue in marketing its chips. Intel quickly evolved its well known motto, "Intel Delivers." But these words had to be backed by careful practices and dramatic policies to be credible to a skeptical market place. For example, at one point early in its history, Intel convinced Honeywell to give it a contract for a custom memory device. Honeywell had already placed contracts with six semiconductor manufacturers including Texas Instruments and Fairchild. "We started about six months later than the others," recalls Grove, "and we were the only ones to deliver the device, about a year later." (2,158)

LIVING ON THE BRINK OF DISASTER

"This business lived on the brink of disaster," explained Moore. "As soon as you could make a device with high yield, you calculated that you could decrease costs by trying to make something four times as complex, which brought your yield down again." Overeager technologists could easily miscalculate future yields and pledge deliveries they could not meet or set prices that turned out to be below their costs. Said Noyce, "If you look at our stuff and melt it down for silicon, that's a small fraction of cost—the rest is mistakes. Yet we chose to work on the verge of disaster because that meant doing the job with finesse, not brute strength." Early entry allowed Intel quick recovery of development costs through high prices for unique products. It also meant "experience curve" advantages in costs over those who entered later. Volumes were growing so rapidly that future plant space was a necessity, but the technology was moving so fast that one never knew two years ahead what products would be made in the plants. Still plant construction might easily take more than two years for planning and implementation.

The conflicting strategic requirements of production, engineering, marketing (plus international operations) required some unique policy and organizational solutions for the young Intel. Intel had an insatiable need for skilled personnel and tried some imaginative ways of meeting it. The company hired new employees for its wafer-processing facility at Livermore months before that plant went into operation and bused the employees 35 miles each way daily to Santa Clara to train them. To hang on to skilled people, Grove used a technique that he called "Peter Principle recycling."* Instead of firing foremen and other managers who flopped when promoted to more demanding jobs, he split their tasks, giving them smaller responsibilities. Some of these "recycled" people again advanced to higher positions; only a few left.

Middle managers at Intel were monitored carefully but had considerable operational freedom. "Lots of guys starting new companies are interested in keeping their fingers in every part of the pie" said Moore. "I think Bob and I were relatively willing to relinquish day-to-day details. For example, Intel had streamlined purchasing to the point where the engineer in charge of a project could buy a $250,000 tester, or whatever he needed, by simply signing for it—provided it was in his budget. . . . (In a big company) you would need seven different signatures on a piece of paper to spend any money," said Moore. Noyce and Moore also tried to keep operations as informal as they could. Spaces in the huge Intel parking lot were not marked with officials' names. . . . "If Bob gets to work late," said Moore, "he parks way out in the corner of the lot. I think this will continue. Sometimes it's a pain in the neck. But the other problem is, once you start marking parking spaces, where do you stop." (2,189-190) The rule still held in the 1980s.

DECISION POINT

What are the key factors for success in each functional area?

What specific policies should Intel develop to meet the conflicting requirements of manufacturing, engineering, and the market?

What specific organizational form should Intel undertake in its early years?

THE MICROPROCESSOR

Among the more exciting potentials of the mid-1970s was the emerging impact of another Intel invention—the microprocessor. By 1972 a number of LSI chips capable of significant computation had been produced or were in design for small calculators or intelligent terminals. A Japanese calculator company, Busicom, asked Intel to develop a 12-chip set for a high-performance programmable calculator series. ROM—read-only memory—chips would customize each model for specific uses. As he worked on the problem, Intel's M. E. "Ted" Hoff concluded that Busicom's design was too complex to be cost effective. Hoff had been utilizing a DEC PDP8 and was struck by its lean architecture versus the complexity of the Busicom design. With a relatively primitive instruction set, the PDP8 could perform highly complex control and arithmetic functions because of its large program memory. Hoff proposed to Intel management a program to design a simpler, more general-purpose, more powerful single-chip processor. If successful, such a device might have applications well beyond just calculators.

Intel's management responded quickly and enthusiastically. A small team soon defined a 3-chip design: a 4-bit CPU, a ROM program memory, and a RAM (random access memory) data memory. This design was vastly aided by the concurrent invention of the EPROM (erasable programmable read-only memory) by Dov Frohman at Intel. But it still languished for lack of staffing until Federico Faggin—later cofounder of Zilog—arrived from Fairchild in early 1970. Faggin worked furiously on the silicon design, and in only nine months produced working samples of the chips that would become the MCS-4 microprocessor, the world's first "micro" computer.

In some complex negotiations with Busicom, Intel won the right to sell the MCS-4 chips to others for non-calculator applications. The marketing department saw microprocessors as possibly a 10% slice of the minicomputer market, then at 20,000 units per year. While Intel management thought it might obtain as much as 90% of this market in its early stages, there was widespread skepticism about the microprocessor in the industry. Many saw it as too slow and small to be of much use. But Intel went ahead.

---

* The Peter Principle said that an organization kept on promoting its people until they reached a level beyond their competency, where they were held. Thus managements of all organizations became incompetent.

Even as Intel was working on the MSC-4, a parallel development was underway that would lead to its first 8-bit processor, the 8008. Then in 1974 Intel introduced its much more powerful 8080, which quickly became accepted as the 8-bit standard and was widely second sourced. Faggin, Hoff, and Mazor carefully designed the 8080 to be compatible in software with the earlier 8008. This policy of upward compatibility had been followed for all Intel machines thereafter. The 8080 was the first Intel microprocessor announced before it was actually available, "to give customers lead time to design the part into new products." Now things were moving fast. In only three years, microcomputers had exceeded the population of both minis and mainframe computers combined. (2,189-190) The first 8-bit single-chip computer (CPU, I/O, RAM, and ROM) was Intel's 8048, introduced in 1976. With it a whole new era of computers and automation began.

PRACTICES ATTUNED TO THE TIMES

The company had grown larger and more complex in the 1970s and '80s. But it worked hard to keep its management systems attuned to the times. A few key elements in its approach follow.

THE TOP TEAM

By 1982 Intel's "two-headed monster"—Noyce and Moore—had become a three-headed "executive office." Chairman Moore—pensive and more reserved in his habits—was the company's long-range thinker, charting overall product strategies. The more gregarious Noyce, now vice chairman, had become Intel's Mr. Outside and was increasingly recognized as one of the industry's major spokesmen. Andy Grove (then age 45) was president and chief operating officer. Although less visible than Noyce and Moore in the early years, Grove was increasingly recognized as the personality driving Intel's internal affairs. "Grove has to be the world's most organized guy," said an admiring Moore. "He sees problems developing much sooner than other people, and he's interested in the people and people interactions needed to solve them."

The three worked well together, respecting each other's technical abilities, and arguing openly and without rancor when they disagreed. To maintain a close touch with the organization each man was in a separate area of Intel's Santa Clara complex. Their offices were indistinguishable from all the other cubicles that secretaries and junior executives worked in. All office walls in Intel were only shoulder high partitions, there were no doors on any offices (including Moore's), no limousines, and no executive dining rooms. Any of the top three was likely to plop down at a table in their building's cafeteria and join in a lunch chat with whomever was there. Said one group of employees, "It's exciting to know you may see and talk to the very top guy at any time. You feel a real part of things."

COUNCILS AND CONFRONTATION

Intel had tried hard to avoid communications barriers and structural bureaucracies. While the company was decentralized into relatively small operating units, people might still have several bosses, depending on the problems at hand. Virtually all staff functions—purchasing, operating procedures, employee compensation, and so on—were handled by "councils" of line managers. There were usually several dozen—ninety were once counted—of such councils operating at one time. On the councils all people participated as equals, with new members free to openly challenge top managers. "The idea," said Grove, "is to remove authority from an artificial spot at the top and place it where the most knowledgeable people are. . . . I can't pretend to know the shape of the next generation of silicon or computer technology any more. People like me need information from those closest to the technology. We can't afford the hierarchical barriers to the exchange of ideas that so many corporations have. The technology is moving too fast."

This free exchange of ideas was reinforced by a policy of "constructive confrontation." Each member of a team was expected to challenge *ideas* openly and aggressively, but never to attack an individual's motives for presenting an idea. Employees said, "Things can get very rough in a meeting. You'd be surprised at the things people can say. But if you are seeking a solution, it's OK." Grove himself set the tone. "When he walks into the room, things can get electric. . . . I've seen him listen to a carefully prepared report for a while and shatter the room with 'I've never heard so much bullshit in my life.'" The company has courses on "constructive confrontation" for all its rising executives and includes the concept in its early training of people in Intel's philosophy.

THE WORLD OF HIGH ACHIEVERS

Like all other groups and individuals in Intel, the councils were required to set performance objectives and be measured against them. Assignments were set by the council and agreed to by each employee and his supervisor. Grove said, "This takes a lot of time but everyone knows exactly whom they report to on each item—and so do their supervisors. We can't afford to leave anything to chance as we grow larger." Performance measurement pervaded everything. When Noyce had joined Shockley, he had said, "I had to test myself, to know if I could hold my own with the best." In 1982 the attitude persisted: "We are seeking high achievers. And high achievers love to be measured because otherwise they can't prove to themselves that they're achieving. Measuring them says that you care about them. . . . (But it must be an honest review.) Many people have never had an honest review before. They've been passed along by school systems and managements that don't want to tell people when they don't measure up. We tell them, 'Here are the things you did poorly. And here are the things you did well.'"

Intel had MBO (management by objectives) everywhere. Each person had multiple objectives. All employees wrote down what they were going to do, got their bosses' agreements and reviewed how well they performed with both their management *and* peer groups. This made the review a communication device among various groups as well. A key to the system was the "one-on-one" meetings between a supervisor and subordinate. The meeting belonged to the subordinate who went to the boss, provided the agenda, told the boss what he was doing, and saw whether there was any assistance the boss could offer. These meetings were required for everyone on a regular basis. They might occur weekly for newcomers, but they were seldom less than monthly for anyone. In any meeting at Intel problems were put forward first, and everyone dug in to solve them.[9]

FORMAL ORGANIZATION

There was no large corporate staff in the usual sense. Instead the top division managers formed the "executive staff" whose job was to worry about the whole business, not just their individual portions of it. Expectedly, Intel was leery of formal organization charts. Within its structure "flexibility" dominated. Teams were formed for special problems. And planning was performed across all divisions toward a selected set of strategic business segments (SBSs), Intel's version of the strategic business units (SBUs) used in other companies. Noyce said, "Strategic planning is imbedded into the organization. It is one of the primary functions of line managers. They buy into the program. They carry it out. They're determining their own future."[10]

An interesting example of this was the bubble memory group established as a separate entrepreneurial division within Intel. In 1970 Bell Laboratories discovered that in certain materials, it was possible to create small densely packed magnetic bubbles whose location and polarity could be controlled to store enormous quantities of information in a very small space. Although greeted with enthusiasm at first, the technology was difficult to reduce to practice, and most larger companies gave up on it in the late 1970s. A few small entrepreneurial concerns persisted, however; and in 1978 one of these came to Intel with a promising approach ready for scale up and possible introduction. Intel brought the company in as a separate division with a very unusual incentive program to maintain its management's enthusiasm and entrepreneurial flair. In 1982, Intel bubble memories with 1 million bits per chip capacity were commercial and a 4 million-bit chip was announced for release late in the year.

THE INTEL CULTURE

Many observers felt that the "Intel culture" was a major determinant of its success in the wild world of the 1980s. This "culture" was an odd mixture of discipline and flexibility that pervaded the company. So important was this "culture" that all employees were put through a course on it soon after they arrived. This was especially important in a company like Intel where half of the people might have been present only a year or less. The top three executives consistently taught in this course as they did in the complex of other courses set up to maintain Intel's competitiveness. Grove said, "Management must teach to have the courses believed. . . . It takes a lot of time. But nothing could be more important than understanding how we operate and what makes Intel unique. Intel is a complete philosophy not just a job."

At Intel people were expected to be disciplined, to work hard. There are clocks and "sign-in sheets" for all people who arrived after the rigorous 8:00 A.M. starting hour. Even top executives followed this rule. Someone once said, "Intel is the only place I've ever seen where 8 A.M. meetings start at 8." Many people don't like the demands Intel makes and its lack of structure. Some employees said, "Some people can't understand that no one will tell them what to do. They have to define what they are going to do and then live up to it. We've seen lots of people quit in the first month because they can't take the pressure." But those who stay like the atmosphere. "It's great to say you work at Intel. You know you're the best. . . . I guess it's a real pride in being first, in being on the frontier. You know you're really a part of something very big—very important." At Intel employees had put over $60 million of their own money into its stock, which had never paid a dividend.[11] Perhaps this was why Intel was able to meet the mid-1980s downturn with its "20% solution." Under this program many of the professional staff agreed to work an extra day a week—without extra pay—to get out new products and to break production bottlenecks as necessary, allowing Intel to rocket out of the recession with a momentum of new products and processes few enjoyed.

"Quality Circles," Total Quality Control, and Quality Assurance programs had long been present in Intel, along with a monthly cash bonus system for quantity and quality of production output. The latter was announced at a monthly bonus meeting in which performance, suggestions, and solutions were discussed directly with the people doing the job on the production line. But noted Noyce, "In a larger organization there is a frustration. It takes longer to see the results of what you're doing. You push on one thing a year and see some movement. In a small organization you can turn on a dime and change direction. With 10,000 people, you break the organization into small manageable units, so you can change the direction of one unit at a time. . . ."

"But in development you can't afford that. You have to move fast, to be first. But you're in a realm where no one has done before what you're trying to do. You have to measure absolutely everything, so when something goes wrong, you have some idea of what went wrong. You don't change something unless you've proved it on a pilot basis first, so that it won't louse up something else. . . . Yet you have to compete against other people who may not know this—and get lucky. You also have to compete against the massive capacities of the large Japanese companies to change the whole market place if they make a right decision and you don't. None of us—no one—has managed a company in this kind of technology and this competition before. We have to write the book for the future. It's quite a challenge."

Moore had stated the ultimate challenge in these terms, "We intend to be the outstandingly successful company in this industry. And we intend to continue to be a leader in the revolutionary technology that is changing the way the world is run."[11] The question was how to do this in an era in which many saw the once almost mystically high technology chip business moving into a commodity era.

INTEL IN THE 1990s

Intel's revenues had fallen during the mid-1980s as its top management discontinued several low-margin product lines and reduced its work force of 25,400 by 7,200. Intel's losses for 1986 exceeded $200 million, as the entire industry suffered while it adjusted to the new Japanese capacity and slackening demand. In 1987, Intel began to emerge from the recession. While the company adopted a sole sourcing strategy for its microprocessor products, demand grew dramatically for its 386 microprocessor* product line. In the middle of 1989, the company's expected sales had nearly tripled to $3.1 billion. By 1989, it had the highest return on sales of any major semiconductor company in the world. (See Exhibits 1–4.)

In 1984 Intel had left the direct random access memory (DRAM) market. Intel's experience in the DRAM marketplace mirrored that of several other U.S. competitors who also exited during the 1985–1986 recession. In 1985, the entire DRAM market shrank by over 50% to $1.4 billion. However, by late 1987, demand once again began to outpace supply, and DRAM suppliers enjoyed market growth and renewed profitability. By 1987, Japanese companies controlled the overwhelming majority of the DRAM market since only two U.S. manufacturers, Texas Instruments and Micron Technology, remained. [Although IBM does not sell DRAMs, it is one of the world's largest producers for its own use.]

By 1990, Japanese companies commanded 87% of the $8 billion DRAM market, U.S. companies held about 8%, and Korean companies held the remaining 5%.[12] Korean market share was likely to increase as Korean firms announced investment plans of over $4 billion by the early 1990s. In order to address marketing concerns that the company have a full product line, Intel, in 1987, had signed a long-term sourcing agreement with Samsung Semiconductor for DRAM chips under which Intel would market the Korean chips under its own name. *Electronic Buyers News* reported that Intel had sold more than 10 million 256K and 1-megabit DRAMs during 1988 through its commodity operation. Prevailing prices suggested that the DRAM reseller business generated well over $100 million in revenue by 1990.

The dramatic decline in U.S. position led some industry observers to predict the eventual downfall of

---

* 386, 486, and 860 are all trademarks of the Intel Corporation.

the entire U.S. semiconductor industry. The concern over U.S. competitiveness and dependence on foreign suppliers led several companies to announce plans to form a joint DRAM venture. A group of semiconductor and computer companies (including Hewlett Packard, Intel, IBM Corp., Digital Equipment Corp., LSI Logic Corp., National Semiconductor, and Advanced Micro Devices) agreed in June 1989 to form U.S. Memories, Inc., investing an initial $50,000 each. The venture required $1 billion in capitalization over several years and intended to use IBM's design for a 4-megabit DRAM as its introductory product offering early in 1991. The unusual arrangement between competitors required federal antitrust clearance[13] and faced opposition from some vocal critics.

NEW TECHNOLOGY DRIVERS

Until 1985, Intel managers thought of DRAMs as the company's technology driver. Historically, DRAMs had always been the first products to employ new technology. Even though it never went into production, the 1-megabit DRAM was Intel's first attempt at a 1-micron geometry. Sun Lin Chou, then the leader of the DRAM technology development group, said it was typical for DRAMs to precede logic products in linewidth reduction by at least one year.

In 1990, Sun Lin Chou expressed some skepticism in discussing the cumulative volume model for learning in the semiconductor industry:

The traditional model of a technology driver says that the more you do, the more high-volume products you run, the more productive you get. That means in order to stay on the leading edge, you need a product you can ramp into high-volume production rapidly. There is some truth to the model, but it can be carried to an extreme.

There are certainly ways of learning that can be carried out at much lower volumes. Our recent experience suggests that you can learn without massive volumes. If so, that takes away the requirement or urgency to have a traditional technology driver. We think it is possible to achieve mature yields by processing only about 10,000 wafers versus the old model's predicted requirement of 1,000,000 wafers. But you have to use intelligence.

You don't learn quickly when you increase volume by brute force. You have to learn by examining wafers. Learning is based on the number of wafers looked at, analyzed, and the number of effective corrective actions taken. Even if you have processed 1,000 wafers, the technical learning probably only came from the 10 wafers you analyzed. Technical learning is time and engineering constrained, not number of wafers constrained.

There are also a great number of things you can do in an open loop system. For example, you can see or guess where particles are coming from and remove them without really knowing for sure whether they are a yield limiter. You don't take the time to get the data to justify the fix; you don't do a detailed study; you just fix what seems broken. You have an intuition about what to do. The Japanese have really led the way on this. You don't undertake an ROI analysis to figure out the cost/benefit for every little improvement. You just fix everything you can think of. Everyone can participate.

Craig Barrett, Executive Vice President and General Manager of the Microcomputer Components Group, believed the importance of DRAMs to technology leadership had been overestimated by most industry observers:

At one time DRAMs really were a technology driver for Intel. DRAMs are still the single biggest product in the industry as a whole. They are about $8-10 billion of a $50 billion market. And they are certainly a learning vehicle for some.

When we got out of DRAMs we were concerned that we might suffer from the lack of volume. We tried to address that concern by selectively staying in the EPROM business. Even though the EPROM volume is not as big, it is a volume product. But I would have to conclude that after two generations post-DRAM we do not miss it as a technology driver.

I think that the industry used the notion of technology driver as a crutch. We were late waking up to the fact that we did not need to run volume in order to learn. There are other ways to be intelligent. You don't have to depend on volume if you depend on good engineering.

We have data to show that our learning as represented by lowering defect density has actually accelerated in the past two generations when plotted as a function of time or as a function of cumulative wafers put through the fab. For each generation since 1985, 1.5 micron, 1 micron, and most recently 0.8 micron, each defect density trend line is downward sloping with the most recent generations having the steepest slopes.

While we have some volume from our EPROM line and we make lots of efforts to transfer learning from one facility to another, we focus on basic techniques to accelerate learning: design of experiments, statistical process control, and just plain good engineering.

While we do have a lot of high-margin wafer starts, we still have a significant mixture of products. We have 256K EPROMs, 1 meg, 2 meg, and just recently, 4 meg in addition to our microcontrollers which are all very cost sensitive. We chose to stay in those commodity businesses partly because it does "keep us honest." Of course, it also represents a significant part of our revenue and it helps to amortize R&D expenditures.

Gerry Parker, Vice President of Technology Development, had a slightly different perspective on the issue of technology drivers:

There is no single technology driver at Intel. We focus our technology development on logic and nonvolatile memory products. More than ever before, we watch what the rest of the industry is doing and try to follow trends. The DRAM is the industry's driver, because it is the highest-volume product and DRAM suppliers are the biggest equipment purchasers. There have been some really fascinating developments in the industry. I think that the entire industry paradigm has shifted in the past several years.

A great deal of the know-how is now generated at the equipment suppliers. We try to stay in the mainstream by purchasing the most advanced equipment, but then we optimize it to maximum advantage for our products.

For example, I know that a certain stepper vendor is developing a new tool that will accommodate a certain maximum chip size. It will not be able to process larger chips. The size is driven by the needs of Toshiba's next generation DRAM. They are building the equipment to satisfy the demands of their largest customer.

You can bet that all of Intel's next generation parts will be designed to capitalize on the DRAM tool. We will put that constraint on our designers. The equipment vendor will be ready to produce those steppers in volume and will be happy to supply us with a few machines. We could ask them to design a special tool for us, but it would be inferior because we wouldn't command the same level of attention that Toshiba gets.

Attitude is important and has led to the changes. The Japanese really have taught us something. They expect excellence from equipment vendors and make *them* develop the expertise to provide the best possible equipment. If a piece of equipment has a problem, the vendor is right there in the fab area fixing it, and he can make appropriate changes on the next generation.

In Japan, all the technicians set the machines to the exact settings that are specified by Applied Materials. If the process doesn't work, Applied Materials gets blamed. In the United States, we tend to be more inventive: each technician sets the machine to an optimum that he has determined. When you operate like that, it becomes more difficult to blame the vendor when the yields are down.

As a result of this fundamental change in the equipment suppliers' role, learning now resides in the industry not just in the company. That is a complete shift. Just to prove it, look at this example. A Japanese ball bearing company, NMB, with no expertise in the semiconductor industry, had $500 million in excess cash and decided to get into the DRAM business. They got vendors to sell them equipment and set it up, and they contracted with

consultants to sell them a process and get it running. In a short time they were the most automated semiconductor factory in the world. That could never have happened even five years ago. . . . The latest equipment is essential to getting the highest yields. Equipment vendors allow Intel and even new start ups to keep up with the latest industry advances.

EPROM AND FLASH

By the end of 1986, Intel had also exited the static random-access memory (SRAM) businesses, stopped development of electrically erasable programmable read-only memory (E^2PROM), sold its memory systems division, and sold its bubble memory subsidiary. Intel's only remaining position in memory businesses was in EPROMs. In 1986, Intel commanded a 21% share of the $910 million market versus 17% of an $860 million market two years earlier. In 1989, EPROMs were manufactured in five of Intel's fabrication sites.

Intel's continued dominance in the EPROM business arose partly from a successful legal battle against Hitachi and other Japanese companies accused of selling EPROMs below cost in the United States. Intel successfully fended off the attack through actions taken by the U.S. government.

In September 1986, Intel top management requested a middle-level manager to prepare a study of each memory business and make recommendations for Intel's long-term strategy. The manager recommended that Intel maintain its position in the EPROM business.

Intel top management decided to keep the EPROM operation as a relatively high-volume product to drive learning, but primarily as an enabling technology for the microcontroller business. Intel's microcontrollers integrate EPROM functionality and use an EPROM process technology. In 1989, Intel remained the EPROM market leader, with 21% market share of a billion-dollar market.

FLASH

The middle manager also recommended that the company devote resources to a new memory technology called Flash. He said:

Flash is very similar to E^2PROM, in functionality, but it is much cheaper to make. Basically, it costs less than EPROM, but you can erase it electrically instead of with light. This is a major cost-functionality discontinuity in EPROM semiconductor technology and has significant implications. One can envision low-end solid-state reprogrammable systems for instance, as well as simpler field service for ROM/EPROM-based systems.

Contrasting Flash to DRAM reveals some interesting perspectives. Flash does not have the flexible write functionality of DRAM, but it is nonvolatile. Additionally, Flash is actually a simpler-to-manufacture read-write technology because it is not constrained by the need for a large capacitor in each memory cell. About 80% of the current DRAM cell is active, whereas only 5% of the Flash cell is. That means that Flash can shrink like mad.

Another paradigm change has resulted in our working on a truly parallel processor, or neural network, that uses a version of Flash technology. By making an analog instead of a digital device, we can develop a low precision but very high performance "trainable analog-memory processor." It remains to be seen what applications will evolve from this capacity but it has exciting possibilities.

If Flash leads to miniaturization of computers from portable to hand-held units, neural nets may solve handwriting recognition. This combined with a notebook computer would result in a very user-friendly tool for a large market.

By 1990, some industry observers began to recognize the potential for Flash as a replacement for conventional magnetic disk drives in laptop or portable computers.* Some industry specialists noted that solid-state disks, when compared to traditional Winchester drives, can consume up to 300 times less power, are 15 times more durable, can withstand much more heat, and are up to 100 times faster. Other industry specialists, however, noted that there has been a 100-fold "shrink" in the size of 20–40 MB drives since the late 1970s (from 2,300 cubic inches for the 14-inch drive to 23 cubic inches for the current 1-inch drive) and that during that time, price has decreased by a factor of 10 and access time improved by a factor of 2.[14] Exhibit 5 shows projections of prices for various 2.5-inch disk drive capacities.

While the current installed base of portables was fewer than 5 million units, the future potential is estimated in the tens of millions.[14] Although Flash was still more expensive than traditional magnetics, its learning curve was much steeper. Exhibit 6 shows price projections for different storage technologies.

In 1990, Intel announced a credit card size "Flash memory card," available in 1- and 4-megabyte storage units and priced at $298 and $1,198, respectively. The new storage system would offer an important alternative to floppy and hard disk drives in portable comput-

ers because it used less power and offered improved performance. The reduced power demands, for instance, extended battery life between 10 and 100 times for portable computers.

By 1994, Intel predicted it would have a 16-megabit Flash chip. The chip would enable a cost-competitive alternative to the industry standard 50-megabyte hard drive on a credit card size format.

Western Digital was reportedly developing Flash subsystems that could be managed like magnetic media and could be interfaced into a system like a disk drive.[14] Texas Instruments was also developing its own Flash technology, which reportedly used less power than Intel's during data writing.

NEW MICROPROCESSOR STRATEGY

During the same week in 1985 when Intel made the decision to close Fab 5 in Oregon for DRAM production, it announced shipment of the 32-bit 80386. The electronics industry received the 386 microprocessor with great enthusiasm. Just one year later, in the third quarter of 1986, customers had completed development of new products, and the first products to contain the 386 were shipped. The power of the 386 to leverage previous software led to the most rapid ramp-up of production for any microprocessor in Intel's history. By the end of 1987, just two years after the 386's introduction, Intel had shipped an estimated 800,000 units as compared to 50,000 for the earlier 8086 at two years after its introduction. By 1989, some analysts believed that Intel was too dependent on the 386 and its support chips, estimating that they generated nearly $1 billion, or between 30% and 40% of the company's revenues during fiscal 1988.

A new corporate strategy added to Intel's early success with the 80386. During previous generations, Intel supported a cross-licensing agreement with AMD (Advanced Micro Devices) in which AMD acted as a second source and provided development of support chips. Intel's top management made the decision to make AMD perform under the existing agreement or be prepared to act as a sole source for the 386. [Intel believed that AMD did not earn rights to the 386 design under the existing licensing agreements. Intel's decision led to a widely publicized dispute with AMD that was still unresolved at the time of case development.]

Craig Barrett described some of the factors that figured in the decision:

---

* Microsoft had decided to support the technology by releasing file management software that lets MS-DOS treat Flash like disk drives.

Basically, Intel got to the point where it could generate enough customer confidence to pull it off. There were at least several forces at work.

Our quality thrust of the early 1980s began to pay off in improved consistency on the manufacturing line and overall better product quality. In addition, customer-vendor partnerships became more prevalent throughout our business. For example, we had recently started selling Ford a microcontroller product, the 8061. They proclaimed that total cost was more important than purchase price alone and decided to work with us closely and exclusively—sort of on the Japanese model. We learned a great deal from that which carried into our other customers and to our vendors.

We had also decided to pursue a "vendor of choice" strategy in 1984 which led to improved customer satisfaction. Finally, the experience with earlier x86 generations led us to believe that we could accurately forecast demand for the 386 and put sufficient manufacturing capacity in place.

With improved manufacturing consistency and better forecast accuracy, we realized that it wasn't always necessary to have a second source to keep the customer satisfied. As our second source deal with AMD came unraveled, we put in the capability to never miss a shipment by adding strategic inventory and redundant capacity. Since then we have never missed an 80386 customer commitment.

The pitfalls of our strategy are obvious. You can fall on your sword. And it only takes once to lose the confidence of your customers. Also, the business is sufficiently profitable that everyone is gunning for you. They try to make clones of your product or substitutes.

Bob Reed, Chief Financial Officer, underlined the importance of intellectual property to Intel and to the semiconductor industry:

Intel has looked around for an edge against competitors. When we look back 10 years from now we may see that intellectual property protection saved the U.S. semiconductor market.* The protection will essentially lead to a segmentation of the semiconductor industry into maybe 10 industries, all with leaders. Intel's sole source strategy for the 386 is a good example of a winning strategy. Now Motorola is also a sole source.

This does not imply much more complicated contractual relationships with customers. For example, Intel has no penalty clauses for nondelivery of parts; however, we never miss a delivery. The stakes have been raised on both sides of the table. At Intel, the legal department has grown from 5 to 20 internal people in the past 5 years. In addition, we retain outside counsel. We vigorously pursue anyone who infringes on our intellectual property rights.

In order to support the sole sourcing strategy, the Portland technology development group began developing a 1-micron version of the 386, a significant reduction in chip size from the original 1.5-micron geometry. Increased functionality and integration depend on the ability to "shrink" the microprocessor, allowing more space to integrate new features. Jack Carsten, formerly an Intel senior vice president, said:

Lots of people talk about the design team that developed Intel's 386 chip. It's a great product. But, the great unsung heroes at Intel are the people who successfully developed the "shrink" technology for the 386. That reduction in geometry led to higher-performance parts as well as greatly increased yields.

Exhibit 7 shows the evolution as the result of the shrinking CPU technology.

Sun Lin Chou discussed the role of the Portland Technology Development Group:

In the past 2 years the situation has changed significantly. We don't just do process development in Portland. We have designers in Portland who leverage our ability to make use of leading-edge technology sooner. Some of those designers are old DRAM designers who have been retrained.

In the old days, memory was always the first product to use a new process. First, we would get the yields up on memory, then a couple of years later the logic product would use the process. We stabilized the process on memory, then did logic. Since logic takes longer to design, it is easier to do it that way. Now we have no DRAMs; the concept of technology driver has changed.

Our challenge is to get logic products up on new processes sooner than we ever have before. To do that, we have accelerated and integrated the design process. We use the Portland designers to design standard cells which can then be used by chip designer groups. We also take existing logic parts that have proven designs and use the new standard cells to generate "shrink" designs. Instead of using memory to ramp production, we are now using logic products redesigned with smaller geometrics.

The 80486 was introduced in April 1989. With over 1 million transistors, the 486 microprocessor contained nearly four times the circuit elements in the 386. The 486 had taken a total of 130 person-years in design effort compared to 80 for the 386. It had benefited from a fourfold increase in proprietary specialized design tools created by Intel. The overall investment in the 486 development had been more than $200 million. In keeping with its strategy of upward compatibil-

---

* In a landmark decision in 1986, the U.S. courts agreed with Intel that computer code embedded in silicon is covered by U.S. copyright laws, thus affording protection for Intel's chip designs.

ity, Intel had designed the new offering to run software developed for its predecessors. The 486 was expected to be especially important in the growing market for a new class of "servers," which could store information for an entire corporation and send it out as needed to PCs in response to queries from different types of users.

RISC VERSUS CISC

By the early 1990s, Intel had established a dominant position in the personal computer microprocessor business based on complex instruction set computer (CISC) design. Every manufacturer of advanced IBM-compatible personal computers had to purchase a 386 or 486 microprocessor from Intel. Similarly, those manufacturers or their customers had to purchase operating system software from Microsoft Corporation in order to maintain backward compatibility with the thousands of programs already developed for the PC market. [Microsoft was the sole source for the IBM PC operating system, MS-DOS. In conjunction with IBM, Microsoft also developed a new operating system, OS/2, which took advantage of the 286 and 386's multitasking features, while maintaining upward compatibility.] (See Exhibit 8 for forecasts.)

The engineering workstation market—characterized by high-performance graphics and computation ability—was pioneered by Sun Microsystems. In some of its earlier systems, Sun used the Intel 386 chip, but instead of MS-DOS chose the UNIX operating system. [Unlike MS-DOS, the UNIX operating system is capable of taking advantage of the multiprocessing feature of the 386. In addition, UNIX is an "open" program and available from multiple sources—although many of the versions are not compatible.]

Sun Microsystems' president, Scott McNealy, believed that Intel was charging too much for its processor, so he initiated the development* of a new

---

* While Sun designed the chip, it did not have chip-making expertise and farmed out the actual manufacturing of the chip to several silicon foundries.

**The RISC actually preceded the CISC architecture. Instructions are the lowest-level commands a microprocessor responds to (such as "retrieve from memory" or "compare two numbers"). CISC microprocessors support between 100 and 150 instructions while RISC chips support 70 to 80. As a result of supporting few instructions, RISC chips have superior performance over a narrow range of tasks and can be optimized for a specific purpose. Through combinations of the reduced instruction set, the RISC architecture can be made to duplicate the more complex instructions of a CISC chip, but at a performance penalty.

processor using a competing architecture called RISC (reduced instruction set computer).** Following a strategy of "open" standards, McNealy made the Sun RISC chip design (SPARC) available to his competitors. In addition to the SPARC chip, several other RISC chips appeared from MIPS and Motorola, capable of supporting some version of the UNIX operating system environment. While RISC microprocessors were simpler than CISCs, the system logic that surrounds the RISC microprocessor is more complex; all that RISC does is to transfer system complexity from the microprocessor to the system logic. RISC was far behind CISC on the learning curve. In 1990, Intel shipped over 8 million 32-bit CISC microprocessors, while the 10 RISC suppliers combined shipped no more than 200,000 units.[15]

THE i860 STORY

Intel's initial response to RISC architecture was to call it "the technology of the have nots." As several companies announced new RISC chips, Intel developed an internal jargon referring to the competitor chips as YARPs, or "yet another RISC processor."

Yet, within the Intel design organization, a designer named Les Kohn had been trying for several years to initiate a RISC program:

> It was very difficult to see from Intel's perspective on the x86 architecture [that RISC had some definite technical advantages]. Between 1982 and 1986, I made several proposals for RISC projects through the Intel product planning system, but I wasn't successful. RISC was not an existing business, people were not convinced that the market was there, and the design would have been way too big to do in a skunkworks.
>
> In 1986, I saw that our next generation processors would have 1 million transistor chips, and I started working on the idea of a RISC-based processor that would take full advantage of that technology. We drafted a product requirement document that outlined market size, pricing, and rough development cost. We positioned it as a coprocessor to the 80486 and made sure that it could be justified on that basis. We designed it as a stand-alone processor, but made it very useful as an accessory to the 486. We made sure it was very different from the x86 family so that there would be no question in the customer's mind of which product to use. The really fortuitous part came when presentations to several large customers generated a lot of positive feedback to senior management. There was also a whole group of customers who did not previously talk to Intel because they were more interested in performance than compatibility. 3D graphics, workstation, and minicomputer accounts all

got very interested. In the end, it looked like the 860 would generate a whole new business for Intel.

Kohn's new chip had a 64-bit architecture with floating point and integer processing as well as enhanced graphics capability. The chip utilized design concepts found in supercomputers, and its design team of 50 wore tee shirts with a miniaturized CRAY supercomputer icon resting on a chip. But top management saw it as a coprocessor for the 486. Kohn commented on Intel's unique position to produce a 1 million transistor RISC chip:

> Intel has historically led the industry in having the most transistors—at least in terms of widely used, commercial microprocessors. To do it on the schedule we did required a very close working relationship between technology development and the design teams.
>
> In a lot of cases, RISC companies worked with external vendors for the fabrication of parts so they either had to design for the lowest common denominator of those technologies or they wouldn't necessarily get access to the most advanced technology.
>
> Another factor was the design tools. Intel made a strategic decision to invest in advanced CAD tools. Our new data base manager allowed us to manage the several thousand files that go into this chip. It made sure that people didn't make changes that got lost or that two different people weren't making changes to the same file at the same time. We also used a new generation of workstation-based circuit design that was very graphic, allowing the engineers to work directly with schematics and display results graphically.

In February 1989, Intel announced the 860 not as a coprocessor, but rather as a stand-alone RISC processor. Top management decided to join the RISC processor race. Grove said:

> We had our own marketing story for the chip, but our customers changed it. They said, "Listen, this isn't just a coprocessor chip. This could be the central processor of a supertechnical workstation." Occasional sarcastic jibes aside, we were in no position now to dump on RISC as a technology. Our chip showed what the real potential of RISC was.[16]

SYSTEMS BUSINESS

In 1985 Les Vadasz became senior vice president and general manager of the Intel Systems Business which by 1990, was expected to contribute over $1 billion to sales. Originally, the Systems Business provided technology to enable the growth of Intel's semiconductor business. For example, development systems, which allowed customers to design their own systems and to write software for microprocessor applications, provided a significant portion of revenue. Vadasz said:

> We were providing customers multiple choices at different levels of integration. If they wanted microprocessors or board-level products, we could provide either. Now we are more like an independent business. We make a range of products: PC-compatibles for OEMs, mainframes through a joint venture, and even parallel supercomputers based on the 386 and 860 processors. We also make PC enhancement boards and sell them through retail channels.
>
> We have organized around segmented strategies for each market. We must recognize that each of our segments requires a different business structure. For example, supercomputers and PCs require entirely different manufacturing disciplines. The PC enhancement business requires a retail understanding, its own sales force, a different kind of documentation, and, of course, its own product engineering. Each new capability can then be deployed into other areas. But you must exercise discipline in how you use your capabilities.

Several of the businesses started as ventures in the Intel Development Organization (IDO), which Vadasz also headed. Vadasz continued:

> IDO looks a bit like an internal venture capital fund. It is funded by the corporation and has its own miniboard of Gordon Moore, Bob Reed, and me. It serves to isolate a new idea from the quarterly cycles of Intel's business. We create an isolated investment unit and see how it does. These units are managed with an iron hand, but on their own merits.
>
> The guiding question at Intel is: Where can we add intellectual value? Some semiconductor people used to grow crystal ingots [raw material for semiconductors], but they found they could not add value there. Others, specializing in crystal growth, became more effective suppliers. DRAMs were like that, the lowest value added component in the chain always tends to spread, so you get perfect competition in that area.

Some industry observers believed Intel's Systems Business represented a bold strategy which might alienate its customers. Not only did Intel have a sole source position, it could become a potential competitor to some of its customers—companies like Compaq, Tandy, or Olivetti.

ISSUES FOR THE 1990s

In reviewing the recent history of the company, Mr. Grove wondered how to top the "awesome new $3 billion Intel." Among the U.S. semiconductor companies, Intel was clearly a leading performer in 1990, but what steps would be necessary to continue that performance?

In particular, Grove wondered about the future role of the relatively low-margin EPROMs in what was now "the microprocessor company." Should Intel get out of EPROMs to free resources for microprocessors, or should they be continued? This was particularly important in light of the potential future of Flash. He also questioned the role of RISC and the implications of Intel's endorsement of that technology. Was RISC a distortion of Intel's microprocessor strategy or part of it? What options could Intel pursue? Finally, he wondered what larger environmental forces might help or inhibit Intel in sustaining its current growth and profitability throughout the 1990s.

QUESTIONS

1. Evaluate Intel's early entrepreneurial strategy. What makes Intel continuously innovative? What elements of its strategy and culture should continue in the future?

2. Should Intel exit the EPROM business now that it no longer produces DRAMs? Compare and contrast the arguments of Chou, Parker, and Barrett regarding "technology drivers." What are the implications for Intel's technology strategy? Should Intel continue to invest in Flash? As the Flash manager, how would you defend your position to senior management?

3. What new forces should most concern Grove? What should he do about these? What should the broad lines of Intel's new strategy be? Why?

EXHIBIT 1
Major Worldwide Semiconductor Forms (ranked by annual sales)

	1994	1991	1986	1981
Intel	9,850	3,800	880	500
NEC	8,830	5,335	2,560	9,828
Toshiba	8,250	5,330	2,270	768
Motorola	7,005	3,850	1,960	1,185
Hitachi	6,755	4,250	2,160	824
Texas Instruments	5,560	2,820	1,800	1,295
Samsung	5,005	—	—	—
Mitsubishi	3,805	2,685	—	308
Fujitsu	3,335	3,150	1,145	482
Matsushita	2,925	2,125	1,145	379

Source: Integrated Circuit Engineering Corporation.

EXHIBIT 2
Semiconductor Markets and Competitors

	Total Sales	Total Discretes	Total Integrated Circuits	32/64 Bit Micro-Processors	MCUs	Total Micro-components	MOS MEMORIES							MOS LOGIC		
							DRAM	SRAM	EPROM	EEPROM	Flash	ROM	MOS Memories Total	Analog	Standard Cell	Gate Arrays
Intel	9,850	0	9,850	8,390	825	9,450					353					
NEC	8,830	975	7,885		900	1,775		330				455	3,440	765	280	610
Toshiba	8,250	1,670	6,580		375	735		370					3,400	925	230	560
Motorola	7,005	1,159	6,580	510	1,500	2,365		330						920		185
Hitachi	6,755	1,025	5,730		600	990		575				255	2,935			250
Texas Instruments	5,560	60	5,500	100		1,005		30	190					810	445	
Samsung	5,005	640	4,365					225				335	3,940			
Mitsubishi	3,805	585	3,220		600	640		220					1,755			
Fujitsu	3,335	360	2,975		225	510		195				190		920	180	595
Matsushita	2,925	780	2,145		525											140
Other	44,060	6,646	36,650	1,315	1,950	6,530	23,050	1,835	1,220	500	507	840	16,535	9,905	2,795	2,200
1994 TOTAL	105,380	13,900	91,480	10,315	7,500	24,000	23,050	4,110	1,410	500	860	2,075	32,005	14,245	3,930	4,540

Source: Integrated Circuit Engineering Corporation.

EXHIBIT 3
Intel Corporation
Historical Financial
Summary
(millions of dollars,
unless otherwise noted)

	1994	1989	1984	1979
Sales	11,521	3,127	1,629	663
Cost of goods sold	5,576	1,721	883	313
Gross margin	5,945	1,406	746	350
R & D	1,111	365	180	67
SG & A	1,447	483	315	131
Operating profit	3,387	557	251	152
Profit before tax	3,603	583	298	149
Income tax	1,315	192	100	71
Net income	2,288	391	198	78
Depreciation	1,028	190	114	40
Capital investment	2,441	351	388	97
Working capital	875	1,242	568	115
Fixed assets	5,367	1,284	778	217
Total assets	13,816	3,994	2,029	500
Long-term debt	392	412	146	0
Equity	9,267	2,549	1,360	303
Employees (thousands)	32,600	22,000	25,400	14,300
Revenue per employee ($)	353,405	142,136	64,134	46,364
Return on sales (%)	19.86%	12.50%	12.20%	11.80%
Return on assets (%)	16.56%	9.80%	11.80%	21.90%
Return on equity (%)	24.69%	15.30%	17.60%	38.00%

Source: Intel Corporation, various Annual Reports.

	INTEL	MOTOROLA	TEXAS INSTRUMENTS
Total sales	8,782	16,963	8,523
Cost of goods sold	2,535	10,351	5,657
SG & A	2,138	3,776	1,247
Net income	2,295	1,022	456
Capital expenditures	1,933	2,187	730
Research & development	970	1,521	590
Depreciation	717	1,170	617
Total assets	11,344	13,498	5,756
Shareholders' equity	7,500	6,409	2,315
Long-term debt	426	1,360	694
Employees (thousands)	30	120	59

Source: Compustat Worldscope database and individual company annual reports.

EXHIBIT 5
Cost per 2.5-Inch Drive,
1988–1994
(20–200 megabyte drives,
midyear OEM quantities)

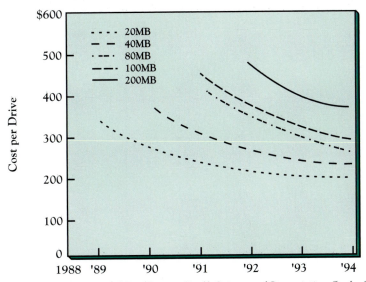

Source: "You Can Take It With You," *Forum on Portable Computers and Communications.* October 2-3, 1990, Bear Stearns & Co., New York.

NEC	TOSHIBA	HITACHI	MATSUSHITA
35,096	44,960	71,847	64,307
24,153	32,477	51,573	44,407
10,183	11,823	18,202	18,214
65	118	633	238
2,108	2,743	5,762	2,588
2,565	3,024	4,699	3,706
2,092	2,481	4,817	3,080
39,606	51,948	86,710	79,540
7,667	10,852	28,730	31,932
9,376	9,810	9,954	12,237
148	175	332	254

EXHIBIT 6
IPC Card Cost Projection,
1990–1993

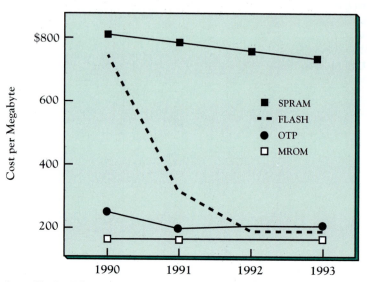

Source: "You Can Take It With You," *Forum on Portable Computers and Communications*. October 2-3, 1990, Bear Stearns & Co., New York.

EXHIBIT 7
Silicon Trends and
PC Integration

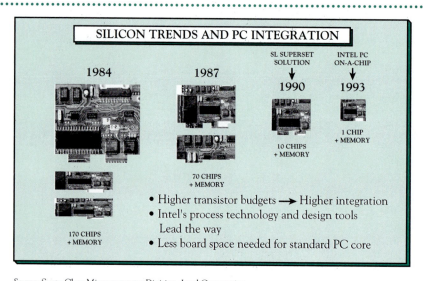

Source: Santa Clara Microcomputer Division, Intel Corporation.

EXHIBIT 8
Intel X86-Compatible
Computers Will Dominate
PCs, Workstations,
Midrange, and Eventually
All Computing

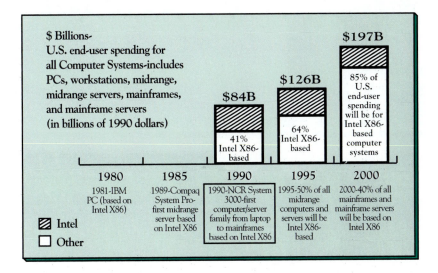

$ Billions-
U.S. end-user spending for
all Computer Systems-includes
PCs, workstations, midrange,
midrange servers, mainframes,
and mainframe servers
(in billions of 1990 dollars)

$84B
41% Intel X86-based

$126B
64% Intel X86-based

$197B
85% of U.S. end-user spending will be for Intel X86-based computer systems

1980	1985	1990	1995	2000
1981-IBM PC (based on Intel X86)	1989-Compaq System Pro-first midrange server based on Intel X86	1990-NCR System 3000-first computer/server family from laptop to mainframes based on Intel X86	1995-50% of all midrange computers and servers will be Intel X86-based	2000-40% of all mainframes and mainframe servers will be based on Intel X86

Intel
Other

Source: Intel company records.

APPLE COMPUTER, INC. (A)

Steve Jobs and Steve Wozniak had both dropped out of college to work in Silicon Valley, Jobs at Atari and Wozniak at Hewlett-Packard. Their spare time was spent in a Los Altos garage experimenting with video games and electronic circuits. Wozniak was particularly intrigued by the potential power of the microprocessor, a programmable computer-on-a-chip invented by Intel in the early 1970s. His curiosity led him to build a home-made computer system around a microprocessor purchased off the shelf. The machine that emerged was crude but effective. Jobs' first sale of the computer was to the Byte Shop in Palo Alto, the only known store of its time that sold kits for microprocessor-based computers. Wozniak's machine was only a stuffed and wired circuit board; but when Jobs asked if they were interested in buying, Byte Shop replied they would take a hundred. Not quite believing, Jobs quoted a price of $666.66 each, COD, to be delivered in 30 days. They agreed, and the deal was done.

Jobs and Wozniak had almost no cash, no components, and no one to assemble the boards. Wozniak sold his H-P calculator and Jobs his VW van to raise $1300. Jobs' next step was to call component suppliers to ask for credit on parts purchases. One supplier offered him net 30 terms. Jobs agreed, not quite knowing what net 30 meant, but the firm had its components within a week; and Jobs, Wozniak, and Jobs' sister furiously stuffed circuit boards for the next three weeks. They delivered 100 completed boards to the Byte Shop in 30 days, deposited Byte's check for $66,666, and paid their

creditors within terms. Jobs and Wozniak were profitable from the time of their first sale.

WE DIDN'T KNOW WHAT WE WERE DOING

Jobs sensed the market potential of what they had started, but he also acknowledged "we didn't know what the hell we were doing," and sought outside advice. Wozniak presented his computer to people at Hewlett-Packard, but they turned the design down. Jobs approached Nolan Bushnell, founder of Atari. Bushnell declined any direct involvement, but referred Jobs to a local public relations firm, Regis McKenna, for help. After turning Jobs down twice, the company finally agreed to accept the venture as a client on a pay-later basis. While doing the rounds of Bay area venture capitalists, they soon met A. C. "Mike" Markkula, a successful marketing executive who had recently left Intel. He put up $91,000 of his own funds, helped create a business plan, and secured a line of credit with the Bank of America. In return, Markkula received 20% of the equity in the fledgling company. He later raised $600,000 in venture capital from Venrock Associates and Henry Singleton of Teledyne. Markkula also negotiated terms so that Apple received payment from its dealers in 15 days, yet paid its suppliers after 60 days.

Jobs, Wozniak, and Markkula formed their new venture on April Fool's Day, 1976. However, as the (January 1977) deadline for filing their incorporation papers approached, they still had no name for the company. Finally, Jobs, looking at the apple he was eating, said that if no one could think of anything better, they would call it Apple. Thus, Apple Computer, Inc., was born. Jobs and Markkula used the $600,000 in venture capital equity funds, not for product development, but for promotion. Regis McKenna created the colorful

Apple logo and the 4-color glossy ads that began appearing in magazines. They gave Apple the image of a $100 million company at a time when it had 12 employees. Markkula described this effort as critical because:

> We had to gain recognition in the market fast. We could not start small. We had to dominate the business or go bankrupt trying.

Apple's distribution and promotion policies contributed greatly to its rapid growth. Markkula's marketing plan depended on independent distributors rather than Apple's own salespeople. Apple encouraged electronics retailers and specialized chains like Computerland to carry its computers by offering high (45%) margins, dealer training, cooperative advertising, and point of sale displays. Apple relied on third party wholesalers until 1981, when the company took over its own distribution and service operations.

THE APPLE II

They used Markkula's $91,000 for tooling of the high-quality, attractive looking outer case Jobs insisted on using and concentrated their other energies on the user-friendly graphics and screen-interface software that would become the hallmark of Apple computers. In May of 1977, Apple introduced the Apple II, the first personal computer with a built-in operating system. Apple II users did not have to program the computer themselves. Instead, they could simply buy software and run programs that had already been written for the Apple.

The early customers for the Apple were hobbyists already familiar with computers, but they lacked applications software. Jobs and Markkula both realized there were many hobbyists and enthusiasts, known in the industry as "hackers," who had bought Apples and wanted to write their own programs. Further, they realized that the Apple II would be useful to large numbers of people only if they could choose from a selection of high quality software. Recognizing this, they revealed the secrets of the Apple II by publishing its technical specifications. This was an unprecedented step in the computer industry, where the inner workings of computers had always been cloaked in secrecy. Programmers could see how the Apple worked and could easily write their own software applications. New programs and applications for the Apple soon poured in from every imaginable source. Apple assisted the authors of the more promising software with documentation and publication of their products.

In 1978 Daniel Bricklin, a Harvard Business School graduate, and Robert Frankston wrote a program that used a computer to perform lengthy and tedious calculations involved in creating and altering financial spreadsheets. They wrote their program, called Visicalc, for the Apple II. For 11 months, Apple was the only computer that supported Visicalc. Suddenly, the Apple II had the first broadly-based, tangibly valuable application for personal computing, and sales of Apple and Visicalc soared. By the end of 1980, over 100,000 Apple IIs had been sold. The Apple II was positioned as a personal computer that was easy to use and friendly to the user, whoever the user happened to be. It was small, compact, and neat in appearance. The logo was bright and attractive, and the name connoted a friendly product. Nowhere in the ad copy and promotional material was there the high-technology image and jargon that frightened most people when the word "computer" came to mind.

The written documentation, or instructions and references, that accompanied the Apple II and its software represented a major innovation in the computer industry. The graphics were attractive, the type large and well laid out, the text friendly and humorous, and most importantly, comparatively easy to understand. In January 1983, the Apple II had the largest installed base of any personal computer priced over $1000. The Apple II enjoyed phenomenal sales growth despite obvious shortcomings. The keyboard was limited to upper case letters, did not contain the full set of characters used in computer programs, and had no up and down arrow key to move the cursor. And the Apple II could display only 40 columns on the video monitor, while 80 columns was the standard display. Yet, capacity constraints had limited sales of Apple II systems throughout its life cycle.

EARLY MANUFACTURING

Apple's early manufacturing operations were based in a modern 250,000 square foot plant in Dallas. Operations were oriented towards minimizing cost and maintaining strict quality control. Significant emphasis was also placed on just-in-time inventory management. The Dallas plant was primarily an assembly operation; Apple relied heavily on external suppliers. Printed circuit boards were assembled by subcontractors in Singapore. Apple sourced microprocessors from Synertek, other chips from Hitachi, Texas Instruments, and Motorola, video monitors from Hitachi, power supplies from Astec in Hong Kong, and printers from Tokyo Electric and Qume. Reliance on outsiders became an Apple characteristic. Michael Scott, Chief Financial Officer, stated:

> Fast-growing companies should rely on outside help for the manufacture of non-proprietary components and systems. As long as cost-efficient outside alternatives exist, we won't worry about being innovative in such areas as production procedures. As long as we are protected in terms of quality assurance, there are better things to do with our time here. Our scarcest commodity at Apple isn't cash, it's time.

The Apple II, which retailed for about $2000, contained about $350 in purchased components. Industry observers estimated that the Apple II cost less than $500 to build. (Exhibit 1 shows the cost structure of major companies in the early '80s; Exhibit 2 gives financial and operating statistics for Apple Computer from 1978 through 1982.)

EARLY DISTRIBUTION CHANNELS

Distribution channels evolved together with the personal computer industry. Many retail outlets were owned by independent entrepreneurs, but computer retail chains expanded rapidly. The largest of these, Computerland, soon had over 250 outlets in the U.S. Some nationwide department store chains, like Macy's and Sears, opened personal computer centers in many of their outlets. Computer manufacturers competed vigorously for shelf space in these stores. IBM Product Centers sold only IBM products, while the Xerox Stores carried several brands. Most stores carried no more than four or five brands.

Retail margins ranged from 25% to over 50%. Retailers relied heavily on the manufacturer for train-ing materials, point of sale displays, brochures, co-op advertising, and repair service. Some manufacturers, including Apple and IBM, devoted a great deal of time and effort to educating dealers about their products. Availability of software and accessories was considered important to dealers, because often a prospective customer would approach a retailer with several applications in mind, and rely on the salesman's recommendation in his purchase decision. Margins on software products tended to be higher than for hardware, and dealers would tend to prefer systems with extensive software over a machine with more limited software. Early personal computers were also distributed through other channels. For example, companies like Atari, TI and Commodore sold through mass merchandise outlets, and mail order also accounted for a share of the business. But Apple, IBM, and Tandy did not authorize sales of their products through the mail.

QUESTIONS

1. What were the critical factors in Apple Computer's start-up? What were its core competencies? How did it leverage these for greatest benefit?
2. What were the benefits and risks of this strategy? How would you measure them? How would you offset these risks?
3. If you were a venture capitalist how could you have evaluated the potentials of Apple in its early stages? How would you have "priced the deal" for your investment? How should Apple have been organized at this stage?

EXHIBIT 1
Leading U.S. Companies Key Financial and Operating Ratios—1982

	GROSS MARGIN/ SALES %	R & D/ SALES %	SELLING & GEN. ADMIN./ SALES %	P, P & E/ SALES %	DEBT/ EQUITY %	INVENTORY/ SALES %	SALES/ EMPLOYEE	CASH & SECUR./ TOTAL ASSETS %	PROFIT BEFORE TAX/ SALES %	PROFIT/ TOTAL ASSETS %	DIVIDENDS/ PROFIT %	AR-AP/ SALES %
Apple	50.6	6.5	26.5	5.9	7.8	13.9	171,944	42.8	20.0	32.7	0	7.95
Burroughs	34.8	5.4	25.6	20.0	37.8	13.5	66,053	1.3	1.8	1.8	146.0	14.9
Commodore	47.8	5.8	23.2	16.2	41.8	30.3	121,800	2.9	16.7	21.6	0	9.7
Data General	43.8	10.5	28.3	19.4	32.4	32.6	53,019	24.4	4.5	4.6	0	15.2
DEC	43.6	9.0	19.5	29.5	2.9	29.3	57,836	19.0	17.3	16.7	0	17.2
Hewlett Packard	52.0	10.0	26.4	27.6	1.7	15.5	62,426	19.7	15.9	19.5	4.4	14.9
IBM	60.2	9.0	27.9	25.5	13.4	10.2	94,201	10.1	23.1	24.4	25.9	12.9
Prime	57.4	8.5	33.2	27.5	7.3	13.2	82,056	7.9	15.0	17.4	0	27.7

Source: Compiled by author from annual reports and other published corporate documents.

EXHIBIT 2
**Apple Computer
Company Financial and
Operating Statistics**

	1978	1979	1980	1981	1982
Sales	$7,883	$47,867	$117,126	$334,783	$583,061
Cost of sales	3,960	27,450	66,490	170,124	288,001
Gross margin	3,923	20,417	50,636	164,659	295,060
Marketing and distribution	1,170	8,802	12,619	55,369	119,945
Research and development	597	3,601	7,282	20,956	37,979
General and administrative	609	2,080	7,150	22,191	34,927
Operating income	1,547	5,933	23,585	66,143	102,209
Interest income	0	0	567	10,400	14,563
Net income	793	3,023	11,698	39,420	61,306
Cash and investments	775	562	2,500	72,834	153,056
Accounts receivable	1,379	5,006	17,400	42,330	71,470
Inventories	1,063	6,348	34,200	103,873	81,229
Net plant and equipment	268	900	4,000	8,453	22,811
Total assets	4,341	17,070	65,400	254,838	357,787
Accounts payable	996	5,411	18,400	26,613	25,125
Notes payable	0	0	0	10,745	4,185
Long term debt	0	200	700	0	0
Shareholders equity	1,916	8,155	25,900	177,387	259,402
Apple II unit sales	7,600	35,090	78,100	192,000	350,000
Installed base	8,170	43,260	121,360	313,360	663,360

Source: Apple Computer, Inc. financial statements.

APPLE COMPUTER 1992

John Sculley, Apple Computer's charismatic CEO, sat in his small, interior glass office in Cupertino, California reading the year-end results for 1991. The computer industry had just experienced its worst year in history. Average return on sales plummeted to under 4% and the ROE was under 11%, For the first time, worldwide PC revenues actually dropped by almost 10%, despite rising unit volume. Although Apple continued to outperform the industry, the intensity of competition was putting acute pressure on Apple's margins. "Our challenge," noted Sculley, "is not only to stay ahead of our competition, but we have to find some way to change the rules of the game. If computer manufacturers continue to make and sell commodities, everyone in our business will suffer." Changing a $50 billion global industry, however, was no easy task. Yet Sculley believed that Apple was one of the only companies that could do it. For Apple's next strategy session, he asked his staff to address two key questions: (1) could Apple change the structure of the industry, and if so how? and (2) what other alternatives are available?

A Brief History of Apple

Apple's legendary story began when Steve Wozniak (Woz) and Steve Jobs joined forces to produce the Apple I computer in the Jobs family garage in Cupertino. [For details of Apple's startup, see the Apple Computer, Inc. (A) case.] After selling 200 Apple I computers, mainly to hobbyists, they managed to obtain venture capital. Jobs sold his vision of making the personal computer easy to use for non-technical people. His stated mission, which permeated the firm through

1992, was "to change the world through technology." The concept was one computer for every man, woman, and child. When Jobs and Wozniak announced the Apple II in March 1977, they began a revolution in computing, which changed the company and the world. Apple sold over 100,000 Apple IIs by the end of 1980, generating revenues over $100 million. Primarily selling to homes and schools, Apple was recognized as the industry leader. The company went public in December 1980, making the founders multi-millionaires.

Apple's competitive position had changed fundamentally when IBM entered the personal computer market in 1981. While Apple's revenues continued to grow rapidly, market share and margins fell precipitously. Apple responded to IBM with two new products, the Lisa and Macintosh (Mac). These innovative computers featured a graphical interface and a windowing operating system that allowed the user to view and switch between several applications at once. They also used a mouse to move and point to positions on the screen, making applications easier to use. However, both computers were incompatible with the IBM standard and even with the Apple II. The technologically sophisticated, but expensive ($10,000) Lisa Computer was soon dropped. The Macintosh fared better, but suffered because of limited software and low performance. By 1984, the company was in crisis.

A year before the introduction of the Lisa and Macintosh, Apple hired John Sculley to be its president and CEO. Sculley, 44, an MBA from Wharton and previously president of Pepsi's beverage operations, had spent most of his career in marketing and advertising. Sculley was to provide the operational expertise, and Steve Jobs the technical direction and vision. But Jobs resigned from Apple in September 1985 after a well publicized dispute with Sculley and Apple's board of directors.

After its slow start, Apple's new Mac computer picked up steam. Between 1986 and 1990, Apple's sales exploded (see Exhibit 1). It introduced new, more powerful Macs that roughly matched the newest IBM personal computers in speed. Even more important, the Mac offered superior software and a variety of peripherals (e.g., laser printers) that gave Apple a unique market niche—the easiest computer to use in the industry with unmatched capabilities at desktop publishing. Apple's strategy of being the only manufacturer of its hardware and software made Apple's profitability the envy of the industry. By 1990, Apple had $1 billion in cash and more than $5.5 billion in sales. Return on equity, at 32%, was one of the best in the industry. Market share had stabilized at around 10%.

But the industry environment was changing rapidly. Rather than basking in success, Apple's management became convinced in the spring of 1990 that their position was unsustainable. According to Dan Eilers, V.P. of Strategic Planning at the time, "the company was on a glide path to history."

THE EVOLVING PERSONAL COMPUTER INDUSTRY[1]

The personal computer was a revolution in information technology that spawned a $50 billion hardware business, with another $30 billion in software and peripherals by 1991. During its short 15 years, the industry evolved through three successive periods. During its first 5–6 years, it was characterized by explosive growth and multiple, small competitors vying for a piece of the market. IBM's introduction of the IBM PC in 1981 launched a second stage in desktop computing. Over the next five years, the industry became a battle for standards and retail shelf space. Three firms emerged as the clear leaders during this period: IBM, Compaq, and Apple. The third era was one of increasing fragmentation. From 1986 through 1991–92, new manufacturers of IBM clones from around the world grabbed share from the industry leaders as new channels of distribution emerged and product innovation as well as revenue growth slowed.

In some ways, the personal computer was a very simple device. Most PCs were composed of five, widely available components: memory storage, a microprocessor (the brains of the PC), a main circuit board called a mother board, a disk drive, and peripherals (e.g., display, keyboard, mouse, printer, etc.). Most manufacturers also bundled their PC hardware with critical software packages, especially an operating system (the software required to run applications). But from the beginning, PCs have been available in almost infinite variety. They could vary in speed, amounts of memory and storage, physical size, weight, functionality, and so on.

During the early years of the industry, venture capital in the United States encouraged the entry of new firms, which offered products in every conceivable shape and size. By 1980, new entrants flooded the market, promoting distinct standards and unique technical features. Almost every firm had a different configuration of hardware and software, making communication or sharing applications between machines virtually impossible. The first PCs introduced by Commodore and Apple had relatively little speed or memory. However, even these early computers allowed managers to perform tasks that were either very time consuming or reserved for expensive ($50,000 to >$1 million), multi-user mini and mainframe computers. For under $5,000, anyone could now do spreadsheet analysis and word processing.

Before IBM entered the market in 1981, most products were considered "closed" or proprietary systems. A closed system, like mainframes, minicomputers, and Apple's PCs, could not be copied or cloned because it was protected by patents or copyrights. However, closed systems typically rendered the computer incompatible with competitor's products. IBM's entry in 1981 changed the playing field by offering an "open" system. The specifications of IBM's PC were easily obtainable, allowing independent hardware companies to make compatible machines and independent software vendors (ISVs) to write applications that would run on different brands. Open systems had a big advantage for customers because they were no longer locked into a particular vendor's product, and they could mix and match hardware and software from different competitors to get the lowest system price. And as long as manufacturers could buy the key components, particularly Microsoft's DOS (disk operating system) and Intel's X86 family of microprocessors, they could manufacture a product that could piggyback on IBM's coattails. Between 1982 and 1986, the majority of the industry consolidated around IBM's MS-DOS/Intel X86 microprocessor standard. Among the various proprietary PC systems, which had included names like DEC, Xerox, and Wang, only Apple thrived.

Although IBM had created an open system that fostered imitators, few firms were capable of competing head-to-head with IBM. On the strength of its brand name and product quality, IBM captured almost 70% of the Fortune 1000 business market during its first four years. In addition, the personal computer was still a relatively new machine through the mid-1980s, and users were uncertain about quality, compatibility, service, and reliability. Concerns over the bankruptcies of companies, like Osborne and Leading Edge, as well as the occasional incompatible machine, led the majority of corporate buyers to buy brand name computers through respected, high service retail channels, such as ComputerLand. Most retailers, however, only had space on their shelves for four or five major brands. In the mid-1980s, the typical retailer carried three core, premium brands: Apple, which was the leader in user-friendliness and applications like desktop publishing; IBM, which was the premium priced, industry standard; and Compaq, which built IBM compatible machines with a strong reputation for quality and high performance. The multitude of smaller clone companies had to compete for the remaining one or two spaces an the retailer's shelf.

The early growth in PCs was built partly on rapidly changing innovative hardware and partly on existing software applications. In its first few years, IBM and compatibles went through four major hardware product generations—the PC (based on Intel 8088), PC XT (based on 8086 and a hard drive), PC AT (based on Intel 80286), and 80386 PCs; in the meantime, Apple went from the Apple II to Macintosh—a major breakthrough in user-friendliness and functionality. The PC explosion was also fueled by software applications. Programs like Lotus 1-2-3 and WordPerfect were nicknamed "killer apps" because they were so powerful compared to their predecessors, everyone wanted them. Most of the best programs for business applications were written for the IBM standard, while Apple dominated educational applications and graphics.

The late 1980s saw revolution turn into evolution in both hardware and software. On one front, the IBM PC standard became the MS-DOS/Intel compatible standard. IBM tried to make PCs more proprietary in 1987 with the introduction of its PS/2 line of computers. Old IBM PC boards could not be plugged into the PS/2. Many customers, however, did not want to give up any compatibility with their prior purchases. As a result IBM faltered, losing almost half its market share. Since Intel and Microsoft provided all manufacturers with identical parts, it was IBM's clones that offered compatibility with the installed base. A new generation of PC clone manufacturers such as Dell and Gateway also found that most customers could no longer distinguish between low priced and premium brands. Finally, the greatest differentiation in the industry had been between standards—IBM versus Apple. However, when Microsoft introduced its "Windows" 3.0 graphical user interface in 1990, the differences in user-friendliness between MS-DOS/Intel machines and Macs narrowed significantly.

By 1992, the PC business had changed from a high growth industry to an industry with a few high growth segments. The installed base of PCs approached 100 million units. New products, like notebook computers, and traditional products sold through new channels, like direct mail, continued to sell at double digit growth rates. But the economics of PC manufacturing, sales, R&D, and software, were fundamentally different compared to the early and mid-1980s.

MANUFACTURING AND R&D

A company could manufacture a personal computer box (with the most current, state of the art microprocessor, but without a keyboard and screen) for as little as $540 in 1992. That box would typically carry a wholesale price of $600. PC boxes with a last generation microprocessor (i.e., an 80396) wholesaled for about $500. Firms, however, had different cost structures which varied with their manufacturing strategy. Some were pure assembly operations, buying all of their components from independent vendors, while others designed and made their own computer boards. For under $1 million, an assembler could buy the equipment and lease enough space to make 200,000–300,000 PCs per year. It would cost that assembler about $480 for the boards, chassis, disk drives, and power supplies and another $60 in direct labor. If a firm designed and manufactured its own boards, the entry costs were somewhat higher. While you only needed one manufacturing line to be efficient, the initial capital costs for assembling computer boards was $5 million. One line would produce about 1000 boards per day. If the PC manufacturer produced its own boards, it could reduce the cost of the computer box by as much as $50. The price of the keyboard and monitor could add from $100 to more than $500 to the system's total costs, depending on the options. The costs of specialty PCs, like notebooks, were considerably higher. There were fewer standard components, the products required more special engineering, and there were only two major suppliers of LCD screens in the world, Japan's Sharp and Toshiba.

Location was another important variable in the manufacturing equation. Freight and duty costs for a complete system could be as much as 10%-15% of total cost. As a result, many companies manufactured their boards in low labor cost locations (like Southeast Asia), then did final assembly near their market. The lowest cost producers in the world in the early 1990s were probably the Taiwanese. Their advantages went beyond having lower labor. For instance, they designed their products for the lowest possible costs. Companies like Compaq, IBM, and Apple typically designed a PC to last up to 50 years, while Taiwanese engineers used a 10–15 year horizon. In addition, their overhead was usually minimal: manufacturing was often set up in warehouses rather than fancy air-conditioned factories.

R&D expenditures closely tracked a firm's manufacturing strategy. While the average R&D spending in computers was ~5%, PC manufacturers spent from 1% for a pure assembler to 8%–10% for companies like Apple, which designed their boards, chips, and even the ergonomics of the keyboards and boxes. Since R&D costs on many key technologies were rising, there was a growing trend in the industry in the early 1990s to license technology from third parties, work collectively in consortiums, and whenever possible, buy off-the-shelf components and software, rather than develop from scratch.

DISTRIBUTION AND BUYERS

Buyers of PCs could be roughly divided into three broad categories: business/government; education; and individual/home. Each customer had somewhat different criteria and different means for purchasing computers. The largest segment was business, with roughly 60% of the units and 70% of the total revenue. During the 1980s, personal computers were most often bought by individuals or small departments in corporations, without much input from a corporation's MIS staff. Individual business PC buyers were usually unsophisticated about the technology, and worried most about service, support, and compatibility. Brand name was especially important and full service computer dealers, such as Businessland and ComputerLand, built billion dollar businesses servicing these customers.

By the early 1990s, individual business consumers had become more knowledgeable about the PC; in addition, more computers were purchased by technically trained MIS staff, who were operating under tight budgets. (See Exhibit 2.) Full-service dealers suddenly became an expensive channel. Demand exploded at "superstores" like CompuAdd and Staples as well as at mail order outlets, which offered computers and peripherals at 30%-50% off list price. Even K-Mart, Costco, and other mass merchandisers started to sell large volumes of PCs. (See Exhibit 3.) Since business organizations were increasingly demanding that their PCs be networked, another channel evolved, called value-added resellers or VARS. Most VARs were low overhead operations that could buy computers in volume, package them with software or peripherals, and then configure the PCs into networks. Finally, some computer manufacturers bypassed third-party distribution entirely, selling directly through the mail with phone support for customer service.

The education and individual/home markets were driven by different channels and somewhat different criteria. In the early 1990s, education accounted for roughly 9% of units and 7% of revenues. While most schools had limited budgets for computers, the primary concern for most educators was the availability of appropriate software. The individual/home market comprised about 31% of units and 23% of revenues; however, the market was a complicated mixture of people who bought computers for business work at home, and those who bought the computer for home uses. Most of these consumers bought PCs through mail order or other high volume, low-priced channels.

Compaq. Compaq got its start by selling the first successful IBM clone portable. In its very first year, Compaq generated $100 million in sales, making it the fastest growing company in history. Compaq's subsequent growth and profitability was based on offering more power or features than comparable IBMs, usually at slightly higher prices. When Compaq launched the first PC with an Intel 80386 microprocessor, it became a trend-setter rather than just another clone. Compaq generally engineered its products from scratch, developing and manufacturing many custom components. However, Compaq did not make semiconductors, like IBM, nor did it develop software or manufacture peripherals, like Apple. Compaq was a pure PC hardware company that sold its products through full service dealers. In 1991, however, Compaq's position weakened considerably. Clones were quickly copying Compaq's PCs and even beating Compaq to market with some new products. The most damage was done by Dell Computer, which ran full page ads in newspapers around the world, suggesting that Dell offered comparable value at 50% off Compaq's list price. Although Compaq rarely sold its computers at list, the campaign had a devastating impact. Compaq was put on the defensive with its customers, causing it to cut prices and streamline costs. Compaq's board fired the CEO and embarked on a new strategy of reducing costs and offering low-priced products through lower cost channels.

Dell Computer. Michael Dell, a dropout from the University of Texas, started Dell Computer in Austin in 1984. The company's first product was an IBM PC/XT clone that it sold through computer magazines at one-half IBM's prices. From 1985 to 1990, Dell became the fastest growing computer company in the world. By 1991, it was a half billion dollar company, offering a full line of PCs through direct mail. What made Dell distinctive was its unconditional money back guarantee within 30 days, its toll-free customer service number, and a one year contract with Xerox to provide next day, on-site service, within 100 miles of nearly 200 locations. Dell could bypass dealers because, utilizing computer technology (i.e., running PCs with software tools that could tell the customer quickly how to fix a PC) it could offer customers comparable or better service at much lower prices than a local dealer. Moreover, Dell generally copied Compaq or IBM's basic design while assembling the products with standard components. Yet even Dell was feeling pressure from lower priced clones in 1992. Companies such as ALR, Packard Bell, and Gateway were doing to Dell what Dell had done to Compaq: copying the strategy with an even lower expense structure and lower prices. Packard Bell, for instance, grew larger than Dell in 1990 by selling cheap clones exclusively through mass merchandisers; in the meantime, ALR started offering Dell clones with similar service at lower prices. Since ALR's overhead was only 14% of sales, with R&D of only 1.5%, Dell was forced to look for new ways to differentiate its products. By 1992, Dell was introducing new PCs every three weeks; its oldest product was 11 months old. Dell also planned to offer on-site service within four hours.

SUPPLIERS

There were two categories of suppliers to the personal computer industry in the early 1990s: those supplying products that had multiple sources, like disk drives, CRT screens, keyboards, computer boards, and memory chips; and those supplying products that came from only one or two sources, particularly microprocessors and operating system software. The first category of suppliers were all producing products that had become commodities by 1992. Anyone in the world could buy memory chips or disk drives at highly competitive prices from a large number of companies, often from a wide variety of countries. Microprocessors and operating system software, on the other hand, were dominated by a small number of companies.

PC MANUFACTURERS

In 1991, the four largest PC manufacturers were IBM, Apple, NEC and Compaq, collectively accounting for roughly 37% of the world market. (See Exhibit 4.) But PCs were a truly global business, with more than 200 players from a dozen countries.[2] While U.S. firms had more than 60% of global revenues, small Taiwanese companies, like Acer, were gaining share in the very low end and Japanese firms were the biggest players in portable computers, the fastest growing PC segment. Toshiba, a huge Japanese conglomerate, dominated laptops (26% share in 1990), followed by NEC (15%). The United States was also the largest market for computers (39%), followed by Europe (36%) and Asia (25%).

In general, the majority of buyers could not easily distinguish between IBM and no-name brands in 1992. As a consequence, price competition had become the rule. For instance, on the same day in February of 1992, Apple and Dell Computer both slashed prices by almost 40%. Within a week, other competitors were cutting prices. "386" clones retailed for as little as $999.00 and "486" clones were selling for $1,600.00. Analysts repeatedly talked about a shake-out in the computer industry, yet there were no indications when and if a shake-out would occur. A few large mergers had taken place in the early 1990s, such as Groupe Bull's purchase of Zenith, and AT&T's purchase of NCR. But the worldwide PC business was more fragmented in 1992 than 1985. Despite the variety of competition, Apple's rivalry in the PC industry could be typified by three players: IBM—the worldwide leader; Compaq—the premium priced leader in the MS-DOS/Intel segment; and Dell, a low-priced clone.

IBM. IBM's position in PCs was characteristic of many broad line computer companies in the world, ranging from Digital Equipment to Siemens. Like its competitors in mainframes and minicomputers, IBM had a large installed base of customers that were tied to the company's highly profitable, proprietary technology. However, like most mini and mainframe companies, IBM was also a relatively high cost producer of PCs that was struggling to create a unique position for itself in the 1990s. Despite suffering its first loss in history in 1991, IBM was still the world leader in computers, with $64 billion in revenue and the #1 market share in PCs, minicomputers and mainframes (see Exhibit 5). IBM's trademark was its sweeping horizontal and vertical integration. One of the largest manufacturers of semiconductors, IBM had the largest direct sales forces in the computer industry, and sold more types of computers, software and peripherals than any company in the world. IBMs R&D budget of $6.6 billion exceeded the *revenues* of all but a few competitors. Nonetheless, IBM's market share had steadily declined in the PC business since 1984. IBM's products lost much of their differentiation, as clones successfully attacked IBM with cheaper (and in a few cases, technically superior) products; and after a dispute with Microsoft, IBM appeared to lose control over the operating system software (discussed below). To regain the initiative, IBM launched a blizzard of alliances in the 1990s, ranging from jointly developing the next generation memory chips with Siemens and flat panel displays with Toshiba, to working with Apple on a next generation operating system and with Motorola on microprocessors.

Every PC needed a microprocessor, which served as the brains of the computer. While several companies offered microprocessors, two companies dominated the industry: Intel, which was a sole source for the latest generation (386, 486, Pentiums) of chips for the MS-DOS standard; and Motorola, which supplied 100% of Apple's needs.[3] (See Exhibits 5 and 6.) Microprocessors were critical to the personal computer because in 1992, the leading software operating systems (OSs) could only run on specific chips. Most new OSs conceived since the late 1980s were developed for multiple microprocessors. But Apple's OS was originally written in the early 1980s and would only run on the Motorola chip, and Microsoft's MS-DOS would only work on Intel's X86.

Similarly, there were only two major suppliers of OSs for the PC market—Apple and Microsoft (see Exhibit 5). Since application programs like word processing or spreadsheets would have to be rewritten to run on a different operating system, even the huge PC market could not support a multitude of OS standards. In the early 1990s, analysts estimated that more than $40 billion in software was installed on the Intel/Microsoft standard and $4.5–$5.0 billion on the Motorola/Apple standard. For computer users to switch standards, they had to buy new hardware and software as well as incur substantial retraining costs. The economics of operating systems also made it difficult for multiple players to survive. While the marginal costs of producing software were negligible, it cost an estimated $500 million to develop a new generation operating system, plus substantial ongoing development cost.

Microsoft's dominance in this arena was based on its ability to sell to the huge installed base of Intel's X86 microprocessors, even though MS-DOS (and Windows) were widely acknowledged to be inferior to Apple's System 7. Microsoft typically received about $15 from a manufacturer for every PC sold with MS-DOS, and approximately another $15 if the PC was sold with Windows. Finally, OSs were of little value without application programs written by independent software vendors (ISVs). The market share of an OS was critical in influencing an ISV's decision. A program written for MS-DOS, for instance, had a potential market of more than 80 million PCs; a program written for Apple's OS had roughly one-tenth the potential; and programs written for some of the other OSs, discussed below, had only one-tenth of Apple's possible market.

Events in the early 1990s suggested that the configuration of players in both microprocessors and operating systems might be changing. First, several new players entered the microprocessor arena, including imitators of Intel's chips as well as new competitors, such as IBM (with its RS6000 chip), Sun Microsystems, MIPS, and DEC. Most of these chips were designed in special ways, called RISC, which gave them some initial performance advantages over Intel and Motorola's existing products.[4] These RISC chips, however, could not run software directly compatible with Intel or Motorola in 1992. Second, there was an emerging battle over new operating systems. Microsoft's graphical user interface (GUI), Windows 3.0, worked on top of MS-DOS. Windows sold 10 million copies from its introduction in June of 1990 through March 1992, and was selling one million copies per month. Since Windows mimicked Apple's operating system, the differences between the Apple environment and the Microsoft/Intel world were less obvious.[5] Windows was also attracting the greatest ISV attention in the early 1990s. In the meantime, several companies were trying to compete directly with Microsoft by rewriting their operating systems to work on Intel's X86 chips. These firms included Sun and Steve Jobs' new company, NeXT. In addition, after IBM broke with Microsoft, it spent $1 billion to offer its own OS in 1992, called OS/2 2.0. While other vendors were not offering OSs compatible with the installed base, IBM hoped to stall Microsoft's momentum with a superior OS that would maintain compatibility with MS-DOS and Windows. Finally, both Microsoft and Apple were developing new OSs. Microsoft promised that its next product, Windows

NT, would be available in late 1992. Microsoft claimed that Windows NT would match or exceed competitive products, be backward compatible with MS-DOS and Windows, and run on Intel, MIPS, and DEC microprocessors.[6] Apple's new OS, discussed below, was scheduled for release in 1994.

ALTERNATIVE TECHNOLOGIES

Like many high-technology businesses, there was a variety of substitutes either available or on the horizon. The most direct substitutes for PCs were technical workstations, powerful stand-alone computers that were used primarily by engineers for scientific applications, graphic-intensive applications, like designing airplane wings, and number-intensive applications, like financial transactions on Wall Street. Workstations comprised a highly competitive business, dominated by four companies: Sun, DEC, Hewlett-Packard, and IBM. Each of these companies used their own RISC chip and incompatible OS. Historically, workstations were not only more powerful than PCs, but they were also much more expensive. By the early 1990s, all of the major workstation vendors had proclaimed that they, too, wanted to sell cheap versions of their computers for the mass market. In 1992, prices of low-end workstations dropped to less than $5000, making them competitive with high-end PCs and Macs.

Many analysts thought that much faster growth would come from other alternative technologies, like pen-based computers, palm-top computers, and mobile-computing. All of these technologies were in their nascent stages in 1992. Pen-based computers allowed the user to point a stylus on a screen rather than use a keyboard. Both hardware and software innovations were required to make pen-based systems cost-effective. Microsoft had already announced a version of Windows for pen-based machines that was expected to compete with alternative OSs from a variety of start-up companies and Apple.

Hewlett-Packard and Japan's Sharp were the early entrants of the palm-top market. Their products were relatively primitive computers that could do very simple operations, like spreadsheets, word processing, as well as keep calendars and address books. Their advantage was size and price: these computers sold for a few hundred dollars and could be carried in a shirt pocket. Sony also announced that it would offer for under $1000 portable "computer players" in 1992: book size devices with CD audio capability that displayed text and video, and ran Microsoft's MS-DOS software.

Finally, several observers expected that all forms of computers would be networked in the 1990s, many with cellular phone connections. While analysts had talked about the merging of computer, telecommunications, and consumer electronics technologies for more than a decade, many industry executives believed that the integration of computers, phones and videos would be a reality by the mid-to-late 1990s. Many consumer electronic products, like televisions, were beginning to use digital technologies, while computers were becoming sufficiently powerful to encode and manipulate video, sound, and data.

APPLE'S POSITION IN OCTOBER 1990

Apple held a peculiar position in the computer industry as it entered the 1990s. It was the only existing alternative hardware and software standard for PCs other than the MS-DOS/Intel standard. It was also unique because it was more vertically and horizontally integrated than any other PC company, with the exception of IBM. Historically, Apple designed its products, usually from scratch, specifying unique chips, disk drives, monitors, and even unusual shapes for its chassis. While it never backward integrated into semiconductors, it manufactured and assembled most of its own products in state-of-the-art factories in California, considered among the most automated and modern in the industry. In addition, Apple developed its own operating systems software for the Mac, some of its applications software, and many of its peripherals, such as printers. About half of Apple's revenues came from overseas, and roughly half the U.S. sales were to education, where Apple had more than a 50% market share.

Analysts generally considered Apple's products to be easier to use, easier to network, and more versatile than comparable IBM machines. In many core software technologies like multimedia (integrating video, sound, and data), Apple had a two year lead on vendors such as Microsoft. Since Apple controlled all aspects of the computer, from board design to software, it could offer a better computer "system," where all the parts—software, hardware, and peripheral—interacted in a coherent way. If someone bought an IBM and a clone, they could never be sure if one computer could be easily connected to another or whether two software programs from different vendors would lead the system to crash. Apple, on the other hand, gave customers a complete desktop solution. Hardware and operating system software were sold as a package, bundled together. This made Apple's customers the most loyal in the industry.

As one analyst commented, "the majority of IBM and compatible users 'put up' with their machines, but Apple's customers 'love' their Macs."

Trouble started brewing, however, in the late 1980s. Apple had not aggressively lowered prices during the price war among competitors in the Microsoft/Intel standard. In addition, Apple's image as a performance leader was damaged in 1990 when Motorola, its sole source for microprocessors, was delayed in shipping its newest products. Suddenly Apple's computers looked overpriced and underpowered. And those were not the only problems, according to John Sculley:

> We were increasingly viewed as the "BMW" of the computer industry. Our portfolio of Macintoshes were almost exclusively high-end, premium-priced computers that our market research suggested would continue to have limited success in penetrating the corporate marketplace. Without lower prices, we would be stuck selling to our installed base. We were also so insular that we could not manufacture a product to sell for under $3000. We constantly fell into the trap of "creeping elegance" with our NIH—not invented here—mentality. We spent more than two years, for instance, designing a portable computer that had to be "perfect." But in the end, it was a disaster—it was 18 months late and 10 pounds too heavy. Our distribution was also an issue. Five large dealers were selling 80% of our products. Given the evolution of the computer industry, we concluded that drastic action was necessary; there could be no sacred cows. The result was a dramatic shift in Apple's strategy and culture. We still want to change the world, but we have to transform the company and industry for it to work. We cannot permit the commoditization of this industry to continue.

THE NEW APPLE

In October of 1990, Apple began a process of repositioning its entire business. This repositioning included new financial and manufacturing policies, a new marketing mix (new products, pricing, and distribution), and new relationships with other companies, including its own subsidiaries, IBM, and a variety of Japanese firms.

New marketing mix. The key to Apple's ongoing business, noted John Sculley, was that "Apple could no longer be a niche player. We were going to enter the mainstream with products and prices designed to regain market share." With that philosophy, Apple embarked on an ambitious strategy of expanding its product portfolio to include low-cost, low-priced computers for the larger business and individual market. With the introduction of the Mac Classic with a street

price of $999 in October of 1990, Apple would be competing head-on with the clones and go for volume (see Exhibit 4). Sales of Macs rose from 9.8% of U.S. computer stores' unit sales in Q2 1990 to 17% market share, one year later.

But Sculley did not believe that volume was enough. In 1990, he also appointed himself the chief technology officer, and made it a priority to get products out faster and extend the hardware and software product lines. "To build on our core differentiation," commented Sculley, "we will bring out a series of 'hit products' through the first half of the 1990s." "Hit products" were defined as new products and derivations of older products that could be produced with very rapid cycle times. Sculley believed that product turns would have to be every 6 to 12 months. By the end of 1991 he noted with pride that 80% of Apple volume was coming from products introduced in October of 1990. In the previous year, only 35% of revenue came from new products. Two more hit products were introduced in late 1991 and early 1992. The first were aggressively priced notebook computers, called Powerbooks. Notebook computers were the fastest growing segment of the computer market since 1989, but it was a segment where Apple had previously failed. When the Powerbook shipped in October 1991, it got rave reviews. Analysts predicted the Powerbook might generate a billion dollars in revenue in its first year. Sculley's second effort was unveiled shortly thereafter. In January 1992, Apple introduced a new software product, called Quicktime, which put Apple at the forefront of multimedia technology. One month later, Apple announced software that would allow Macs to respond to commands from the human voice, without special hardware or training. In both areas, Apple was probably 12–18 months ahead of the competition.

To complement the hit products strategy, Sculley also proclaimed that Apple would restructure its distribution strategy. Apple maintained a direct sales force of approximately 300, one-third covering large corporate accounts, two-thirds focused on education and other markets. Most products, however, were still sold through computer stores. Bob Puette, president of Apple USA, described the problem succinctly, "how do we move to the Dell model, without killing our existing business?" In late 1991, Apple decided that it would sell its products through superstores and started to offer limited direct end-user telephone support.

Finance and manufacturing. Apple's historical financial model was based on one simple principle, Sculley's

"50-50-50" rule: If Apple could sell 50,000 Macs a month, with a gross margin of 50%, Apple will have a stock price of $50. In 1987, Sculley wrote in his autobiography, "it was critical to have high gross margins to pay for the huge research and development expenses to support a proprietary technology." And until 1990, Apple followed these policies religiously, achieving all of Sculley's objectives.

New, low-end products designed to gain market share as well as "hit products" with short product life cycles could not operate on the same principle. Joe Graziano, Apple's CFO remarked, "we have no choice. We must bring down our expense structure, raise our productivity, and fundamentally alter the way we do business." If Apple wanted to match the computer hardware industry's average (see Exhibit 7), it would have to cut costs drastically. Yet Apple was also a software company, which meant that Apple had less flexibility than other PC companies in cutting certain expenditures, especially R&D. Sculley nonetheless decided to trim Apple's entire cost structure before a crisis emerged. In May of 1991, Apple reduced its work force by 10% or 1,560 people. But as Kevin Sullivan, S.V.P. Human Resources. explained, the cuts went much deeper:

> This was not a drive to lower expense rates in response to temporary market conditions, but rather to get cost out of the system permanently. We had to change the way we did our work . . . we attacked how we spent our money rather than reducing our expenses. Actions ranged from consolidating buildings, cutting away cafeteria subsidies, charging for the use of the Fitness Center, subcontracting the management of the Child Care Center, etc. . . . In addition, we cut some projects and activities that some people felt were important to us, especially in sales and marketing. We let people go who were very talented and doing great work, but we chose not to do that work any more. We also stated that we were going to be moving jobs out of California . . . The Campus was no longer the Center of the Universe. . . . Finally, we changed many of our relationships with the channel, large accounts, and developers. We got much tougher on selecting who they were and what kind of service or response they would get from us. We were building a new Apple that had to be leaner and swifter. Finally, we had to do layoffs, and layoffs are layoffs, any way you cut it.

Part of Apple's greatest challenge was in manufacturing, which historically was a centerpiece of Apple's sole source strategy. In the past, virtually *everything* was done in-house. But now manufacturing had new instructions: anything that could be bought on the out-side should be subcontracted rather than developed. NIH was no longer acceptable. At the same time, manufacturing facilities were expanded to build a greater variety of products that could be ramped faster to global volumes.

Relationships with other companies. To get a better understanding of the competitive environment, Sculley and his COO, Michal Spindler, spent nine months in 1990 visiting with the, senior executives of major computer companies, including Sun, Hewlett-Packard, IBM, DEC, as well as the large Japanese and European companies. Sculley said, "we discovered that we were out of touch. We did not really understand open systems, how to penetrate big corporations, and we did not realize that firms like IBM had big leads in semiconductor technology." Sculley's conclusion was that Apple should build a "federation" of alliances with partners that could help leverage Apple's strengths in software, especially user-friendliness, multi media, and networking. He said, "we have to have partners; we have to become more open; we have to penetrate a broader market or our application developers will abandon us; we have to license technologies in and be willing to license technologies out." A key to the federation concept was that the core Macintosh business would be largely separate from the new ventures and product groups. Spindler would run the Mac business, while Sculley could operate the alliances and federation like Silicon Valley start-ups. (See Exhibit 8.) However, Apple shocked the world when it chose its first significant alliance partner—its long-time nemesis, IBM.

The Apple-IBM joint ventures. During the summer of 1991, IBM and Apple formed two joint ventures—Taligent and Kaleida. Sculley listed four major objectives in working with IBM:

> First, we had to overcome the resistance of MIS managers in large corporations to buying Apple computers. We called this our Enterprise Systems effort. The alliance attacked this problem in three ways: (1) we got IBM's stamp of approval; (2) IBM' sales force would offer Mac communication products; and (3) we both committed to achieve "interoperability" (seamless connections between the varying IBM, and Apple computers). Second, our current microprocessor technology from Motorola would not carry us through the 1990s. We saw IBM's RS6000 RISC microprocessor as the best technology in the industry. Since IBM also agreed to work with Motorola as a second source for the technology, we reduced our vulnerability from being dependent on a sole source. We would call this new generation of computers

the "PowerPC." Third, we formed Taligent to develop our next generation OS, which we internally called Pink. Pink will be a major breakthrough in software technology.[7] However, to pay for Pink, we needed money and a broader market. IBM and Apple together would have the resources and large installed base. In addition, Pink would be written to run on Apple's installed base of Motorola chips, the new IBM chip, as well as the Intel X86 chips. Lastly, we formed Kaleida to create standards in multimedia technologies, like putting full motion video on the personal computer.[8]

The underlying concept of the IBM–Apple relationship was that both companies could share the costs and risks of developing new technologies, but ultimately, the parents would compete in the market place for computers. The JVs would operate independently, shipping their software products to both parents at agreed upon transfer prices. IBM would provide the semiconductor technology while Apple would provide most of the software technology and personnel. Six months after the JV was formed, the parents appointed a CEO from IBM and COO from Apple.

Claris. To help create a supply of applications for the Mac in the mid-1980s, Apple created a software subsidiary called Claris. Claris was responsible for many of the important programs for the Mac, like MacDraw and MacWrite. However, in an effort to reduce potential conflicts of interest with Apple's ISVs, Sculley decided to spin-off a portion of Claris to the public. Although Apple ultimately decided to keep 100% of Claris in 1990, it kept Claris operationally independent (see Exhibit 8). By 1992 Claris was the second leading supplier of applications to the Mac with 15% of the market (compared to Microsoft's 30% share of Mac applications) and was in the top 15 application software companies in the world. Analysts estimated that Claris had broken even on roughly $100 million in sales in 1991. As part of Sculley's strategy to be a more open computer company, Claris would not have to dedicate itself in the future to Mac applications. It could write applications for DOS, Windows, OS/2 as well as the Mac. Although Claris was behind other companies, like WordPerfect, Lotus, and Microsoft, its goal was to be in the top 5 software companies by the mid-1990s.

Alliances with Japanese firms. Beyond reinvigorating its core business with the IBM alliance and expanding its application software sales, Sculley believed that Apple had to break out of the mold set by other computer companies and look for major innovations that would change the way people used computers. In the near future, Sculley argued, computers would be pervasively networked. His vision of the year 2001 saw computers, telecommunications, consumer electronics, publishing, and a variety of other technologies merging together (see Exhibit 9). Apple, he believed, had unique software technology that could exploit these linkages. Rather than everyone using general purpose PCs in the future, computing would be increasingly specialized.

Sculley announced to the world at the Consumer Electronics Show in January of 1992 Apple's intention of creating a new era of "personal electronics" with "personal digital assistants (PDAs)." In describing the product concept, Sculley recalled the words of Dr. Edwin Land of Polaroid, who said, "we really don't invent new products, but the best ones are there already, only invisible, just waiting to be discovered." In this vein, Apple would introduce an executive organizer that would fit in the palm of your hand and keep track of telephone numbers, calendars, etc. It would have built-in wireless communications, and have the capability of displaying best selling book titles. Other products would include portable multimedia players that used computer and CD technology, and a portable pen-based computing product. Sculley even suggested at the public gathering that Apple would license its GUI and operating systems for other companies' consumer electronic products, possibly including digital television.

These types of computing and consumer electronics products, however, required expertise that exceeded Apple's core skills and competencies. While Apple could pioneer the computing hardware and software technologies, it lacked distribution and marketing expertise for consumer electronics, LCD display technology needed for hand-held computers, and very low-cost manufacturing for miniaturized products. For these new technologies to be successful, analysts speculated that they would have to be priced under $500. Given the ambitious nature of these projects, Sculley also believed that no one company could pursue all of these avenues by itself. Sony had already manufactured one of Apple's new portable computers, and a number of other Japanese companies might be candidate partners to work with Apple in this new realm.

GOING FORWARD IN 1992

Sculley told his sales force in late 1991, "the industry must once again become innovation drive, move away from commodity status, and provide value-added products and services. I believe Apple has a chance to make the difference. In fact, Apple may be one of the few great hopes for turning things around."

QUESTIONS

1. Could Apple's own actions to date achieve the objective of changing the industry structure? Would others steps be necessary?
2. Was it even required that Apple change the industry structure to be successful in the future? Were there other alternatives that Apple might consider?
3. How has Apple's competitive posture changed since the (A) case? What were the principle drivers of this change? How should Apple deal with each driver?

NOTES

1. The description of the industry will focus primarily on the U.S. market, which was the trendsetter in PCs in the 1980s. PC penetration was much deeper in the United States than Europe and Japan, and trends in areas such as software and distribution generally started in the United States and filtered to Europe, then Japan within 1-3 years.
2. Different geographic areas had different configurations of competitors: in North America, IBM, Apple, Compaq and Dell had approximately 70% market share. In Japan, NEC had a proprietary standard, with almost 50% of the market. NEC had a relatively low share outside of Japan. The European market was dominated by U.S. competitors, with national champions, such as Bull, Siemens, and Olivetti commanding large shares of their domestic markets.
3. Apple worked closely with Motorola to design their microprocessor. In addition, since Apple did not allow other vendors to make compatible products, Motorola was essentially a captive supplier to Apple.
4. RISC stood for reduced instruction set computing. RISC chips were designed for greater speed than the traditional chips made by Intel and Motorola, known as CISC or complex instruction set computing. Intel was investing aggressively to narrow the gap.
5. Apple had sued Microsoft over infringing its copyrights. Analysts did not expect Apple to win the lawsuit.
6. Microsoft helped form the "ACE"—advanced computing environment—consortium in 1991 to help generate a coalition around the Windows NT OS. More than 80 computer companies originally committed to the standard; 12 months later, however, several of the leading firms broke ranks, including DEC and Dell.
7. This new technology, known as "object-based systems," was so complicated that it would take several hundred million dollars and at least three years to complete the project. Pink promised to increase significantly a computer user's productivity by making the writing of customized software applications very easy. If on schedule, Pink would probably give IBM and Apple at least a two-year lead on Microsoft. In a parallel, independent effort, Apple was developing the follow-on OS to System 7. This follow-on OS could be designed to run on multiple microprocessors, such as the RS6000.
8. A fifth objective was highly technical—creating a joint Apple–IBM version of UNIX, which was another OS that both companies wanted to use for certain large corporate applications.

EXHIBIT 1
Detailed Financials of Apple Over Time

	1991	1990	1989	1988	1987	1986	1985	1984	1983	1982	1981
Total revenues ($ millions)	$6,309	$5,558	$5,284	$4,071	$2,661	$1,902	$1,918	$1,516	$983	$583	$334
Cost of sales	3,314	2,606	2,695	1,991	1,296	891	1,118	879	506	288	170
Research and development	583	478	421	273	192	128	72.5	71	60	38	21
Marketing and distribution	1,740	1,556	1,340	908	655	477	478	399	230	120	55
General and administrative	224	207	195	180	146	133	110	82	57	35	22
Operating income	447	712	634	620	371	274	103	86	130	102	66
Net income	310	475	454	400	218	154	61.3	64.1	77	61	39
Property, plant, equipment and other	275	321	284	186	121	67	66	53	64	30	NA
Depreciation and amortization	204	202	124	77	70	51	41	37	22	16	NA
Cash dividends paid	56	53	50	39	15	—	—	—	—	—	NA
Cash and temporary cash investment	893	997	809	546	565	576	337	115	143	153	73
Accounts receivable	907	762	793	639	406	263	220	258	136	72	42
Inventories	672	356	475	461	226	109	167	265	142	81	104
Property, plant and equipment	448	398	334	207	130	222	176	150	110	57	31
Total assets	3,494	2,976	2,744	2,082	1,478	1,160	936	789	557	358	255
Total current liabilities	1,217	1,027	895	827	479	138	90	255	129	86	70
Total shareholders' equity	1,767	1,447	1,486	1,003	837	694	550	465	378	257	177
Permanent employees	12,386	12,307	12,068	9,536	6,236	4,950	4,326	5,382	4,645	3,391	2,456
International sales/sales (%)	45	42	36	32	27	26	22	22	22	24	27
Gross margin/sales (%)	47	53	49	51	51	53	42	42	49	51	49
R&D/sales (%)	9	9	8	7	7	7	4	5	6	7	6
ROS[a] (%)	4.91	8.55	8.59	9.83	8.19	8.10	3.20	4.23	7.83	10.46	11.68
ROA[b] (%)	8.87	15.96	16.55	19.21	14.75	13.20	6.55	8.12	13.82	17.04	15.29
Return on equity (%)	19	32	36	44	28	28	12	15	24	28	44
Stock price range	40.5–73.3	24.3–47.8	32.5–50.4	35.5–47.75	20.3–59.8	10.8–22	7.3–15.6	10.8–17.25	8.6–31.6	5.5–7.5	6.8–7.3
PE/ratio	12.9	10.5	12.9	13.6	20.3	11.6	22.1	26.7	30.6	16.1	24.3
Market value[c]	6,751	4,150	5,166	5,033	4,914	2,004	1,360	1,694	2,368	742	1,320

[a]ROS—net income/total revenues.
[b]ROA—net income/total assets.
[c]Year-end stock price times the number of shares outstanding.
Sources: Apple Annual Reports and *Value Line.*

EXHIBIT 2
PC Consumer Preferences—Major Brands (Tier 1) versus Other Secondary Companies—Baseline Study
(March 1991–May 1991)

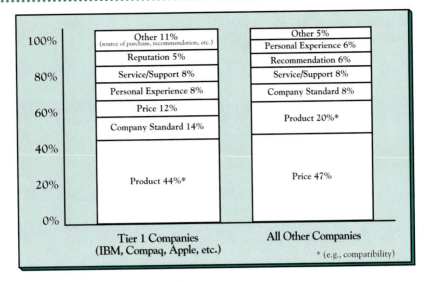

Source: Compiled from Intellitrack data, 1991.

EXHIBIT 3
PC Distribution Channel Breakdown[a]

	DIRECT	DEALER	SUPERSTORE	VAR	MASS MERCHANT	CONSUMER ELECTRONICS	MAIL ORDER
(%) of Total Unit Shipments							
1987	17.4	58.9	0	11.3	3.4	4.1	4.3
1988	12.3	61.7	0	12.4	3.9	4.3	4.8
1989	8.6	63.2	0	13.9	4.1	4.7	4.8
1990	8.0	58.3	1.1	14.7	5.2	5.2	6.1
1991	7.9	55.7	2.0	15.2	6.4	6.4	6.2
1992[b]	8.3	51.6	2.9	15.7	7.5	7.5	6.2
(%) of Total Value Shipments							
1987	31.0	49.0	0	13.2	1.4	1.8	2.3
1988	25.3	52.9	0	14.3	1.7	1.9	3.2
1989	17.3	56.9	0	17.1	1.9	2.1	3.7
1990	18.4	52.7	0.7	18.0	2.9	2.5	5.1
1991	14.7	51.7	1.6	18.7	3.9	3.7	4.6
1992[b]	14.4	50.0	2.5	19.0	4.1	4.0	4.9

[a]Estimated sales do not equal 100% because of rounding.

[b]Projected figures.

Source: Compiled from International Data Corporation data, 1991.

RANK	COMPANY	1981	1982	1983	1984
1	IBM	6.04%	11.47%	21.34%	29.96%
2	Apple	8.82	7.34	7.10	10.10
3	NEC	3.92	4.30	4.79	4.64
4	Compaq	0.00	0.00	0.73	1.52
5	Olivetti	2.27	2.08	1.76	1.28
6	Toshiba	0.60	1.68	0.94	0.46
7	Epson	0.00	0.01	0.41	0.62
8	Tandy	10.57	10.42	7.22	3.92
9	AT&T	0.63	0.35	0.39	0.98
10	Zenith	2.03	1.65	1.30	1.24
11	Philips	0.73	0.59	0.97	0.98
12	Siemens	0.00	0.00	0.01	0.05
13	HP	2.66	2.25	2.26	2.66
14	Acer	0.27	0.63	0.25	0.21
15	Packard Bell	0.00	0.00	0.00	0.00
16	Unisys	0.64	2.57	2.27	2.74
17	Dell	0.00	0.00	0.00	0.02
18	Other	60.83%	54.66%	48.26%	38.62%

COMPANY	1981	1982	1983	1984
IBM	1.35%	2.73%	4.60%	8.64%
Apple	8.85	6.65	6.09	7.80
NEC	4.28	3.55	3.77	4.53
Compaq	0.00	0.00	0.27	0.70
Olivetti	1.78	1.03	0.78	0.68
Toshiba	0.29	0.86	0.84	0.74
Epson	0.00	0.01	0.18	0.38
Tandy	0.00	0.00	0.00	0.00
AT&T	0.26	0.10	0.09	0.25
Zenith	0.98	0.66	0.53	0.56
Philips	0.20	0.19	0.22	0.25
Siemens	0.00	0.00	0.00	0.02
HP	1.29	1.00	0.96	1.08
Acer	0.21	0.20	0.13	0.16
Packard Bell	0.00	0.00	0.00	0.00
Unisys	0.18	0.33	0.36	0.46
Dell	0.00	0.00	0.00	0.01
Other	80.32%	82.69%	81.18%	73.73%

[a]Market share includes all computer sales under $12,000. Commodore and Sharp have been included In the "other" category even though their share exceeds 1%. However, both companies derive a large percentage of their revenues from nontraditional computer products (e.g., palmtop computers, organizers, and computers designed primarily for entertainment), which are not directly comparable to IBM PCs and Macs.

Source: Adapted from InfoCorp data.

1985	1986	1987	1988	1989	1990	1991
29.04%	25.28%	25.27%	21.54%	18.65%	17.94%	16.05%
8.78	7.98	7.99	8.83	9.98	10.22	10.49
6.33	6.70	7.11	6.04	5.65	5.81	5.79
2.25	2.48	3.47	4.93	5.36	4.77	4.44
2.63	3.37	3.14	3.12	2.79	2.92	3.10
0.24	0.74	1.32	1.58	1.68	2.44	2.72
0.66	0.96	1.26	1.81	2.11	2.39	2.67
4.32	3.66	3.14	2.81	3.28	2.38	2.57
3.18	3.24	2.95	2.70	2.13	1.92	2.09
1.71	2.31	2.78	3.05	2.60	1.70	1.79
1.33	1.70	1.45	1.25	1.60	1.83	1.75
0.26	0.62	1.14	1.45	1.51	1.58	1.62
2.70	2.20	1.44	1.74	1.81	1.67	1.58
0.28	0.53	0.92	1.28	1.29	1.34	1.30
0.00	0.01	0.04	0.13	0.72	1.05	1.20
2.87	2.27	2.01	1.81	1.58	1.36	1.11
0.11	0.23	0.46	0.63	0.74	0.99	1.10
33.30%	35.71%	34.13%	35.29%	36.54%	37.68%	38.18%

1985	1986	1987	1988	1989	1990	1991
11.09%	12.07%	13.12%	13.68%	13.68%	13.36%	12.81%
8.27	8.22	8.23	8.21	7.98	7.63	7.90
5.23	5.53	5.63	5.51	5.35	4.97	4.79
1.08	1.37	1.66	2.04	2.38	2.57	2.74
0.99	1.25	1.50	1.69	1.79	1.72	1.66
0.68	0.77	0.83	0.98	1.18	1.59	1.98
0.50	0.70	0.95	1.36	1.85	2.18	2.40
0.00	0.12	0.33	0.48	0.64	0.80	0.89
0.79	1.08	1.24	1.34	1.33	1.24	1.20
0.80	1.14	1.60	2.02	2.18	2.05	1.96
0.38	0.53	0.62	0.76	0.91	1.03	1.08
0.06	0.14	0.27	0.41	0.53	0.61	0.68
1.19	1.20	1.07	1.04	0.92	0.84	0.84
0.25	0.44	0.76	1.12	1.37	1.55	1.68
0.00	0.00	0.02	0.07	0.34	0.58	0.80
0.51	0.60	0.71	0.75	0.76	0.70	0.65
0.05	0.11	0.23	0.30	0.38	0.47	0.59
68.14%	64.73%	61.23%	58.24%	56.43%	56.12%	55.34%

	1991	1990	1988	1986	1984	1980
IBM						
Revenues	$64,792	$69,018	$59,681	$51,250	$45,937	$26,213
Cost of goods sold	32,474	30,723	25,648	22,706	18,919	10,149
R&D expense	6,644	6,554	5,925	5,221	4,200	1,520
Selling, general and administrative	24,732	20,709	19,362	15,464	11,587	8,804
Net income	−2,827	6,020	5,491	4,789	6,582	3,563
Total assets	92,473	87,568	73,037	63,020	42,808	26,703
Long-term debt	13,231	11,943	8,518	6,923	3,269	2,099
Stockholders' equity	37,006	42,832	39,509	34,374	26,489	16,453
ROS %[a]	−4.4	8.7	9.2	9.3	14.3	13.6
ROA %[b]	−3.1	6.8	7.5	7.6	15.4	13.3
ROE %[c]	−7.6	14.8	14.9	14.4	26.5	22.7
Stock prices ($/share)						
High	139.8	123.1	130	162	128.5	72.8
Low	92	94.5	104.5	119	99	50.4
P/E ratio	21.2	10.4	11.9	18	10.6	10.4
Market valuation[d]	50,285	64,523	70,210	72.720	75,399	39,115
Compaq						
Revenues	$3,271	$3,598	$2,066	$625	$329	
Cost of goods sold	2,054	2,058	1,233	361	232	
R&D expense	197	185	75	27	11	
Selling, general and administrative	721	706	397	152	66	
Net income	131	455	255	43	13	
Total assets	2,826	2,717	1,589	378	231	
Long-term debt	73	74	275	73	0	
Stockholders' equity	NA	1,859	815	183	109	
ROS %[a]	4	12.6	12.3	6.9	3.9	
ROA %[b]	4.6	16.7	16	11.3	5.6	
ROE %[c]	6.9	30	42	26.8	12.9	
Stock prices ($/share)						
High	74.3	68	33	10.8	7.3	
Low	29.9	35.5	21	5.8	1.8	
P/E ratio	28.2	10.3	8.9	11.7	14.5	
Market valuation[d]	2,244	4,859	4,312	1,026	325	

	1992	1991	1990	1989	1988	1987
Dell Computer[e]						
Revenues	$ 890	$ 546	$ 389	$ 258	$ 159	$70
Cost of goods sold	608	364	279	176	109	54
R&D expense	33	22	17	7	6	2
Selling, general and administrative	180	114	80	50	27	10
Net income	51	27	5	14	9	2
Total assets	560	264	172	167	56	24
Long-term debt	42	0	0	0	0	0
Stockholders' equity	274	112	80	75	9	3
ROS[a]	5.7	4.9	1.3	5.4	5.7	28.6
ROA[b]	11.9	10.2	2.9	8.4	16.1	8.3
ROE[c]	18.6	24.1	6.3	18.7	100	66.7
Stock prices ($/share)						
High	NA	36.3	18.8	10.6	12.6	NA
Low	NA	15.8	4.6	5	7.7	NA
P/E ratio	NA	13.2	8.3	26	12.5	NA
Market valuation[f]	900	614	339	108	187	NA

EXHIBIT 5
(cont'd)

	1991	1990	1988	1986	1984	1982
Intel						
Revenues	$4,778	$3,921	$2,875	$1.265	$1,629	900
Cost of goods sold	1,898	1,638	1,295	687	774	467
R&D expense	618	517	318	228	180	131
Selling, general and administrative	765	616	456	311	316	NA
Net income	818	650	453	-173	198	30
Total assets	6,292	5,276	3,550	2,080	2,029	1,056
Long-tem debt	363	345	479	287	146	197
Stockholders' equity	4,558	3,592	2,080	1,275	1,360	552
ROS %[a]	17.0	17.0	16.0	-14.0	12.0	3.0
ROA %[b]	13	12.3	12.8	-10.3	9.8	2.8
ROE %[c]	20.4	18.1	21.8	-16.3	14.6	5.4
Stock prices ($/share)						
High	59.3	52	37.3	21.5	29	13.8
Low	37.8	28	19.3	10.9	16.5	6.9
P/E ratio	11	12.3	11.4	NA	21.2	48.7
Market valuation[d]	10,045	7,600	4,344	3,717	4,788	5,032
Microsoft						
Revenues	$ 1,843	$1,183	$591	$197	$98	$25
Cost of goods sold	363	253	148	41	23	NA
R&D expense	235	181	70	21	11	NA
Selling, general and administrative	596	357	185	76	35	NA
Net income	463	279	124	39	16	4
Total assets	1,644	1,105	493	170	48	15
Long-tem debt	0	0	0	2	1	0
Stockholders' equity	1,350	1,105	493	171	31	8
ROS[a] (%)	25.1	23.6	20.9	19.1	16.3	16.0
ROA[b] (%)	28.2	25.2	25	22.9	33.3	23.3
ROE[c] (%)	40.8	37.7	40.3	40.5	70	62.1
Stock prices ($/share)						
High	115	53.9	23.5	8.5	NA	NA
Low	49	28	5.2	6.5	NA	NA
P/E ratio	22.6	19.9	25.2	19.5	NA	NA
Market valuation[d]	19,380	12,788	8,533	NA	NA	NA

[a]ROS - net income/total revenues.

[b]ROA - net income/total assets.

[c]ROE - net income/total stockholders' equity.

[d]Number of shares outstanding (*Value Line* 1992) times the year-end stock price
(NYSE and OTC daily stock price reports).

[e]Fiscal year ends in February.

[f]Market capitalization as of March 17th.

Sources: *Value Line* and companies' annual reports.

EXHIBIT 6
Shipments and Installed
Base of Various
Microprocessors,
1981–1991
(million units)

	1981	1982	1983	1984	1985	1986	1987	1988	1989	1990	1991
Intel X86 Microprocessors											
Units shipped	0	0.2	1	2.6	3.7	5.5	10.2	14	16.1	18.3	20.2
Installed base	0	0.2	1.2	3.7	7.4	12.9	23.1	37	53.1	71.4	91.6
Motorola Microprocessors											
Units shipped	0	0	0	0.5	0.7	0.9	1.2	1.6	1.8	2.9	3.3
Installed base	0	0	0.1	0.5	1.3	2.2	3.4	5	6.4	9.3	12.6
RISC											
Units shipped	0	0	0	0	0	0	0	0	0	0.2	0.4
Installed base	0	0	0	0	0	0	0	0	0.1	0.3	0.7

Source: Adapted from InfoCorp, 1992.

EXHIBIT 7
Average Operating
Ratios in 1990

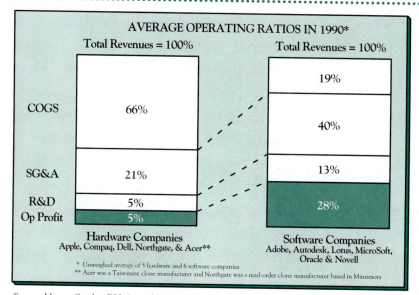

AVERAGE OPERATING RATIOS IN 1990*

Total Revenues = 100% — Hardware Companies (Apple, Compaq, Dell, Northgate, & Acer**)
COGS 66%; SG&A 21%; R&D 5%; Op Profit 5%

Total Revenues = 100% — Software Companies (Adobe, Autodesk, Lotus, MicroSoft, Oracle & Novell)
19%; 40%; 13%; 28%

* Unweighed average of 5 hardware and 6 software companies
** Acer was a Taiwanese clone manufacturer and Northgate was a mail-order clone manufacturer based in Minnesota

Sources: Morgan Stanley; DLJ; Annual Reports.

EXHIBIT 8
Apple's Federation
Concept

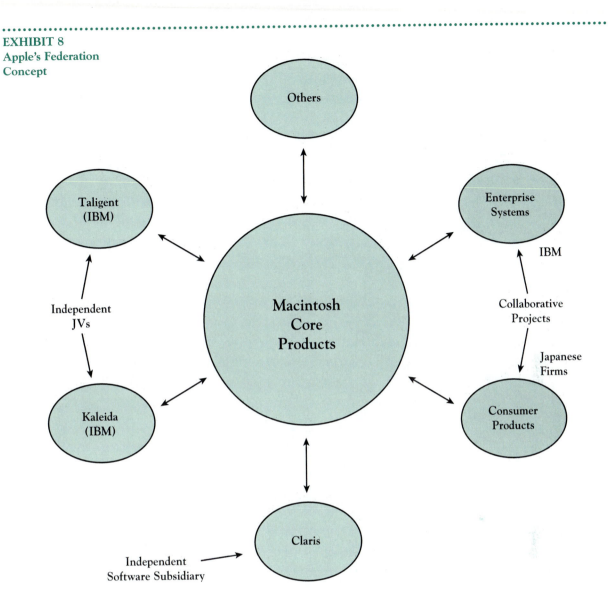

Source: Casewriter's Representation.

EXHIBIT 9

Info Industry, 2001: Fusion Powered

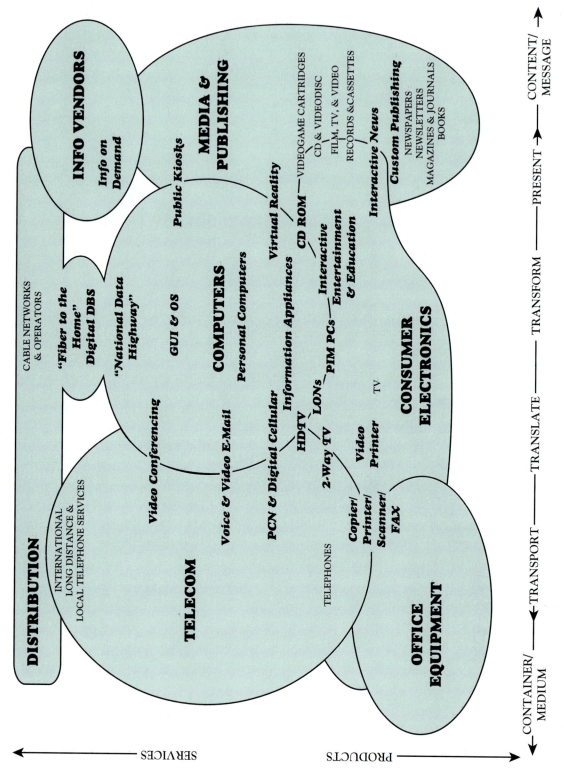

Source: Presentation by John Sculley at Harvard University—Program on Information Resources Policy, 1991.

In 1994, Bill Gates stood at the pinnacle of American success. He had become the youngest billionaire in U.S. history, with a net worth of more than $4 billion. In appearance, he was a most unlikely captain of industry. He looked as if he were 25 or younger, with an engaging boyish charm combined with the large round eyeglasses and energetic but highly focused look of the computer hacker reporters had once described as a nerd. In 1994, with among the highest market values on the stock exchange, Microsoft was both a distinguished success—and an increasing competitive and antitrust target. (See Exhibits 1–3 for Microsoft's historical, current, and comparative financial performance.) How had this phenomenon grown? What problems did it face? Where would it go from here?

THE EARLY YEARS

From the beginning, Bill Gates was a phenomenon, reading the encyclopedia from beginning to end when he was only 7 or 8 years old. He once memorized a 3-page monologue for a school play after a few seconds' glance at the material. From an early age, he worked all hours of the day and forced himself beyond anyone's expectations. When his grammar school teachers asked for a 4–5 page paper, Bill would respond with a 30-page treatise. Enrolled in Seattle's exclusive Lakeside School, Gates' competitive spirit was egged on by some of the finest young minds in the region. In the classroom, Gates became legendary for solving math and physics problems faster than anyone else— and a capacity to see uniquely efficient math solutions.

Case Copyright. James Brian Quinn. 1994. All rights reserved. Research Associates on this case were Allie Quinn and Penny C. Paquette. Sections reproduced by special permission from G. Danforth, R. McGrath, G. Castrogiovanni, *Microsoft Corp.* (case), Louisiana State University, 1992.

However, it was Lakeside's early acquisition of computers that changed his life. Gates and his friend Bob Allen became night and day users of a teletype machine that played into a PDP-10 DEC computer General Electric operated from a nearby Computer Center Corp. (CCC). Fortuitously, BASIC was the time sharing language the system used. Gates' group would wrestle with the computer all night to debug programs for CCC, surviving on Coca Cola and pizza—a style which Gates continued for years. Soon Gates and Allen formed other money making projects: Traf-O-Data to develop traffic statistics, payroll programs for local companies, and debugging systems for TRW. Before he left Lakeside and went to Harvard, Gates commented matter-of-factly, "I'm going to make my first million by the time I'm 25."[1]

THE BEGINNINGS OF MICROSOFT

Gates never graduated from Harvard, leaving in his junior year. He worked hard and did well in courses he cared about, but slouched through the rest. He spent many nights in the Aiken Computer Center working 36-hour stretches, collapsing for a few hours, and then with pizza and Coca Cola returning to work again. He also played lots of poker. His roommate said, "Bill had a monomaniacal quality. He would focus on something and really stick with it. He had a determination to master whatever it was he was doing . . . [He sort of decided] where he was going to put his energy and to hell with what anyone else thought."[2]

Then on a cold winter day in December 1974 Gates and Allen came across an announcement in *Popular Electronics* for the Altair 8080, stated to be the "world's first microcomputer kit to rival commercial models." The company making Altair was MITS operated by Ed Roberts, an enormous bear of a man, out of an abandoned restaurant in Albuquerque. In a prophetic event, Roberts had shipped his only working model of the Altair for *Popular Electronics* to test. It never arrived. The world's first home computer was lost in transit. The picture in *Popular Electronics* was of a metal shell with eye-catching lights and switches on the front, shipped empty to New York.

One week after reading the article on the Altair, Allen and Gates called MITS and claimed to have written a program that would allow the Altair to be programmed in BASIC. When Roberts expressed interest, Gates and Allen, lacking an Altair, wrote the BASIC program using a simulation based upon a manual about the 8080 chip it contained. They completed the project in eight weeks of night and day activity. But they had forgotten the "bootstrap" program to load BASIC on to the Altair. They wrote that on the plane to Albuquerque for a demonstration. Miraculously, the whole thing worked on the first demonstration for Roberts. The first software program ever run on what would become known as Microsoft BASIC was a "lunar landing" program Gates wrote on the spot, similar to one he had earlier programmed at Lakeside School. In July 1975, Gates and Allen formed a partnership called Microsoft (short for Microcomputer Software) with the intent of developing computer languages for the Altair and other microcomputers they were sure would follow. The Altair was inherently limited by the Intel 8080 chip, on which it was based.

LICENSING

Their very first agreement (with MITS) gave Gates and Allen royalties from the licensing of their BASIC, with or without the accompanying sale of MITS hardware. Under the terms of the contract they could earn only a maximum of $180,000 in royalties. They were willing to do this to obtain the distribution MITS had to offer. But from the beginning, Gates' mission in life was "to provide all the software for microcomputers." Later, Gates wrote—in five days—what would become known as DISKBASIC for the Altair. Then Microsoft encountered an early and important crisis. Computer hackers and clubs were making copies of BASIC and shipping it out to all their friends. Piracy was spreading like a virus, and no one was paying for the BASIC software. In frustration Gates offered to sell Roberts all rights to BASIC for about $6,500. Fortunately, Roberts declined. However, Microsoft's BASIC had become the *de facto* standard for microcomputers when they appeared in force.

In 1976, as National Cash Register, Citicorp, and GE signed lucrative contracts for Microsoft's BASIC. Gates assembled his famous "Micro Kids—high I.Q. insomniacs who wanted to join the personal computer crusade, kids with a passion for computers who would drive themselves to the limits of their ability and endurance, pushing the outside of the software envelope."[3] Gates himself would take only two vacations of a few days each over the next five years. But this energetic and talented group could make no real money from BASIC until it could crack the arrangement Gates and Allen had with MITS. At first ignored and scoffed at by his opponents, Gates personally masterminded and negotiated the strategy that beat the more expensive big company legal teams. In a complex out of court proceeding, Microsoft was determined the owner of BASIC and could market the product as it saw fit. This was the first of many transactions in which people underestimated Gates, "the skinny kid with the dandruff and uncombed mop haircut."[4]

INTERACTIONS WITH IBM

In 1980, when IBM covertly decided to enter the burgeoning microcomputer industry, with a machine based on Intel's new, more powerful 8086 chip, it inquired whether Microsoft could write a BASIC program for its 8-bit resident memory. IBM also asked Microsoft to furnish other languages for the machine, including FORTRAN, *Pascal*, and COBOL. To do this, Microsoft had to gain access to the operating system software on which they were based—Digital Research's CP/M. Both Gates and IBM representatives approached Digital Research about supplying CP/M, then the dominant operating system in the industry, to power the IBM machines. But in two classic miscalculations, Digital's President went on vacation when IBM's team arrived and Digital balked at IBM's restrictive contract provisions. With access, Microsoft would have continuously adapted its languages to Digital's emergent operating system and its Intel 8086 platform. Without access, Microsoft had to develop its own operating system.

Until this point, Digital Research had developed operating systems, and Microsoft had focused on programming languages; each had respected the other's domain. Frustrated, Bill Gates decided on a bold move. He told IBM that Microsoft could not only supply the languages for the IBM machine, but also the operating system. In August IBM, miffed over the snubs and inflexibility of Digital Research, accepted. In

September 1980, Tim Patterson showed Microsoft his 86 DOS operating system written for the Intel 8086 chip. For $50,000 Gates bought the rights to 86 DOS, then known as "dirty old system," which became the basis for Microsoft's MS-DOS.

Many proponents of CP/M argued that, as an industry standard, CP/M would have been best for linking existing languages, applications software, and hardware. Nonetheless, within less than a year after the announcement of the IBM PC, numerous microcomputer manufacturers signed contracts with Microsoft to make MS-DOS (Microsoft's operating system) their hardware's resident system. When IBM introduced the PC in 1981, Microsoft made short shrift of Digital Research in the MS-DOS-CP/M battle. CP/M was by all standards an excellent operating system, nearly all software and hardware systems had been tuned to it. But the quick and powerful emergence of the IBM PC as the industry standard catapulted MS-DOS and Microsoft to success. A whopping 99% of IBM compatibles carried MS-DOS as their operating system, although IBM later released a CP/M-86 operating system for PCs. Now holding a commanding position in operating systems software, Microsoft turned its attention to applications software.

THE ELECTRONIC SPREADSHEET[5]

In the early 1980s, many computer companies did not believe that microcomputers held significant potential for business applications. However, the appearance of the first electronic spreadsheet, VisiCalc, fulfilled a specific and important business need. VisiCalc enabled managers—previously confined to time consuming hand calculations or writing a specific program for the company's mainframe—to define their own models and to run countless alternative solutions. Initially, the program could be run only on an Apple II. This became a primary determinant of the Apple II's success. It was later adapted to run on the IBM PC. Sorcim developed another spreadsheet program, SuperCalc, to run on CP/M systems. The advent of spreadsheets created an unprecedented boom in both hardware and software sales to businesses.

SPREADING WITH THE SPREADSHEET

When Gates and Allen decided to enter the applications software market in 1980, the spreadsheet was a logical starting point. Because there was no hardware standard at the time, Gates decided to develop a spreadsheet that could be ported to all the operating systems on the market—including CP/M, Apple DOS, UNIX, and of course MS-DOS. The two dominant spreadsheet programs were limited in their portability. While Microsoft was developing its spreadsheet, dubbed Multiplan, IBM brought great pressure to assure that the new spreadsheet could run on its limited 64K PC models. Gates acquiesced to the computer giant, sacrificing many design attributes in order to stay in the good graces of Microsoft's primary customer.

When released in late 1982, Multiplan met with some initial success but then was quickly eclipsed when Lotus offered 1-2-3 in 1983. Unlike Multiplan, 1-2-3 was aimed at 256K machines and reflected the richness of capability that increased RAM storage afforded. Sales of Lotus 1-2-3 took off. In 1983, Lotus 1-2-3 became the top-selling applications software system, a position it held for the following six years. Fortunately Lotus 1-2-3 operated only on MS-DOS. Largely due to the phenomenal demand for 1-2-3, over 80% of all users became familiar with MS-DOS in 1984. With the extraordinary success of 1-2-3, Lotus became the largest independent software company—with annual sales of $157 million compared to $125 million for Microsoft. Microsoft's 64K Multiplan languished, but IBM's sales of 256K PCs skyrocketed that year. Lotus 1-2-3 did for the IBM PC what VisiCalc had done for the Apple II. And MS-DOS benefited.

THE MOVE TO EUROPE

However, the Multiplan project was not a complete loss. Microsoft had adeptly repositioned Multiplan in Europe. As early as 1982, Microsoft had begun to adapt Multiplan to each of the European languages. In addition, Gates decided to open up subsidiaries in each of Microsoft's three major European markets, England, France, and Germany. There Multiplan's ability to run on many different systems proved to be a decided advantage. Unlike the U.S. market, Apple controlled 50% of the European market and Commodore 30%. And when IBM's PC arrived in Europe in 1984, it included Multiplan rather than Lotus 1-2-3. By the time Lotus brought 1-2-3 to Europe in 1985, it was too late. In 1987, while Lotus held 80% of the American spreadsheet market to Multiplan's 6%, Multiplan dominated the European market, accounting for 60% in Germany and 90% in France. Because Multiplan was so successful overseas, Microsoft continued to distribute it. But Bill Gates would not forget why his package had failed in the United States while 1-2-3 had succeeded.

WORD PROCESSING

In 1983, Microsoft launched an offensive on a new front, word processing. At that time, WordStar, developed by MicroPro, was the most popular word processing software. Microsoft designers believed they could best WordStar by including in their program a number of additional features. Microsoft Word would be the first word processing software that displayed bold type, underlining, italics, subscripts, and superscripts on the screen. In addition, it would divide the screen into windows, allowing the user to work with more than one section of text at a time. Instead of requiring the user to format each document individually, Word would offer style sheets that stored formats created by the user for repeated use. Importantly, Word would print in any of the fonts available in the new state-of-the-art laser printers.

Microsoft introduced Word to the U.S. in a novel way. At great expense it sent out demonstration copies (which would do everything but save or print files) to the 100,000 subscribers of *PC World* in its November 1983 special edition. Many newspapers lauded the unique and imaginative marketing technique employed by Microsoft, but Word initially met with marginal response. Although extremely powerful, Word proved to be too complex for the average user. Improved versions in 1984 and 1985 steadily increased sales; however another small software publisher called WordPerfect again beat Microsoft in the marketplace.

WORD VERSUS WORDPERFECT

Jointly founded by a computer science professor and one of his students in 1979, WordPerfect's only employees were a group of students who helped with distribution tasks. Yet the fledgling enterprise was able to differentiate its program through a heavy emphasis on service. WordPerfect provided free telephone support to customers and followed up every inquiry until the customer was satisfied.

While Microsoft spent millions promoting Word, WordPerfect avoided sophisticated promotional campaigns, building a loyal following by word of mouth. Microsoft was at a loss as to how to respond to Word-Perfect's ingenious grass-roots campaign. WordPerfect's sales grew steadily, and it quickly became the top-selling word processing software, outselling 5th place Word (31% to Word's 11%) in 1986.

Just as Multiplan had succeeded by turning to the European market, so too would Word. When Word arrived in France in 1984 with mixed reviews, WordStar and Textor, produced by a French company, were already well positioned. Gates and his European staff decided on a three-prong penetration strategy. First, to encourage distributors to sell Word, Microsoft France provided distributors with free training and a free copy of Word. Second, Microsoft arranged to have all retailer demonstrations of Hewlett Packard's new LaserJet printer use Word. Microsoft France also convinced many printer manufacturers to promote Word because of its ability to be used in sophisticated, high-end multifont printers.

FIRST FRANCE, THEN THE WORLD

As a result of its aggressive marketing effort, Word began making inroads into the French market in 1985. After a much refined Word 3.0 was released in April 1986, sales of Word rose rapidly. In 1987, it was the highest-selling word processing software in France with sales of 28,700 copies compared to 10,300 for IBM Vision, 7,000 for Textor, 3,800 for WordPerfect, and 3,300 for WordStar.

The great improvements made in the 3.0 version of Word were also critical in increasing its U.S. market share. In this version, the previous problems experienced by users in learning Word were resolved by what was then an ingenious solution. Included with all 3.0 versions of Word was a step-by-step, on-line tutorial that replaced the traditional user's manual. U.S. sales of Word climbed substantially. By 1989, Word's sales had reached 650,000 compared to 937,000 of WordPerfect. Although Word was by many standards a superior product, WordPerfect had early on established itself as the word processing software of choice for PC users. Once customers learned and grew comfortable with a program, it was often difficult and orders of magnitude more costly for them to switch.

While Word was having problems in 1984 and 1985, Microsoft worked feverishly on a Word program for the Apple Macintosh computer, the only substantial challenger to IBM's standard. When Macintosh Word was released in 1985, there were no other word processing programs available for the Macintosh except Apple's own software (MacWrite), which was included with the sale of each machine. Although Word for the Mac had some bugs, it quickly gathered a following among Macintosh users. When the 3.0 version was released in 1986, it was a tremendous success. By 1988, with annual sales of 250,000 copies, it was second only to the PC versions of WordPerfect and

Word. WordPerfect released a version of its product for the Macintosh in 1988, but it was too late. As WordPerfect had beaten Microsoft to the U.S. PC market, so had Microsoft preempted WordPerfect in the Macintosh market. When Microsoft released Word 4.0 in 1989, it sold 100,000 copies immediately, establishing Word's preeminence through the Macintosh.

GRAPHICAL USER INTERFACES

As IBM's PC became the best-selling microcomputer in the industry, it was soon copied by other manufacturers. But due to its unique graphical user interfaces, Apple's Macintosh surpassed all other computers in user friendliness. While users of IBM PCs and compatibles had to interact with their machines using learned text commands such as *erase*, the Macintosh user could use a mouse to point to a file icon and pull it into a trash can icon. Both Gates and Apple's cofounder, Steve Jobs, believed that the future of microcomputing lay in graphical interface technologies because they opened up the world of computers to even the most unsophisticated users.

THE APPLE CORE

In 1981, Apple asked Microsoft to write applications programs for the Macintosh, realizing that the availability of high-demand software could determine the success of the Macintosh—just as the popularity of VisiCalc had launched the Apple II. Microsoft and Apple began a close collaboration aimed at designing an optimum match between the Macintosh configuration and Microsoft's applications programs. The agreement specified that Microsoft versions of Multiplan, Chart, and File would be shipped with each Macintosh machine and that Microsoft could not publish software with a graphical user interface until one year after the Macintosh was released or December 1983 at the latest.

Under this arrangement, Microsoft enjoyed tremendous successes with its various applications programs. In addition to Word for the Mac, Microsoft's new spreadsheet program, Excel, sold at a rapid rate in 1985, beating out Lotus's new integrated software for the Mac called Jazz. In 1986, Microsoft sold 160,000 copies of Excel to Mac users compared to 10,000 copies of Lotus's Jazz. By 1989, Lotus had decided to stay away from the Macintosh market altogether. Microsoft's success with Macintosh users made it the number one developer of applications software for the first time. And many thought virtually all of the PC market would inevitably move to graphical interfaces.

WINDOWS

Windows was Microsoft's attempt to convert MS-DOS into a graphical user interface. Although IBM had been successful in establishing its hardware and *operating* system software (MS-DOS) as industry standards, no such standardization applied to PC *applications* software. Each applications program written for the PC required its own unique methods to modify or print a file. In addition, different printers demanded different intermediary programs called drivers to enable printers to receive data from applications. In 1981 to address this problem, Microsoft decided to develop Windows as a layer between the operating system and applications software, interpreting the particular communications requirements of the printer and monitor being used. The second purpose of this program would be to place over MS-DOS a graphical interface that would standardize the appearance of applications and provide common commands for such actions as modifying texts or printing files.

OPENING NEW WINDOWS

While Microsoft was developing its "Windows" graphical interface system, other companies began to release their own versions. VisiCorp., for example, released VisiOn in 1983. More perturbing to Microsoft was that some industry analysts foresaw IBM developing its own version of a graphical interface. In the past, IBM had largely looked to Microsoft to develop its PC software. Gates suspected that Big Blue was intent on expanding its control to include standardization of the entire computer configuration—not just hardware, but software too. When IBM announced in 1983 that it was releasing TopView, a graphical interface to rest on top of DOS, it was a clear signal that IBM was no longer content to remain in the hardware domain. Recognizing that IBM was attempting to squeeze Microsoft out of future software sales, Gates acted quickly. He contacted the manufacturers of IBM-compatible computers and tried to persuade them to follow Microsoft's lead with Windows, and thus isolate IBM. When Windows was announced in November 1983, twenty-three hardware manufacturers supported it.

Many did not want IBM to monopolize standards further and were amenable to waiting for Microsoft's version of Windows rather than following IBM's lead by including TopView with their machines. Although direct competitors to Microsoft, many software companies also pledged their support to Microsoft Windows.

The support of Lotus was particularly important since it was a primary supplier of applications software for the PC and compatibles. Like others, Lotus did not relish the thought of a stronger, more influential IBM and was willing to accept Microsoft's lead to prevent it. The software producers were confident that Microsoft would create an interface environment into which they could easily port their applications programs. IBM, on the other hand, had released a version of TopView configured in such a way that, if successful, it would give Big Blue a significant advantage in the development of future applications.

Unfortunately the Windows project was characterized by lengthy and embarrassing delays. Although Gates repeatedly announced the imminent release of Windows, it did not actually hit the market until November 1985. Over 20 software publishers had to put their Windows-ported applications software on hold. Even then, Windows encountered constant problems in use. But Gates held on doggedly. It wasn't until Windows' 3.0 introduction in 1990 that these were overcome. Nevertheless, its earlier Windows 2.0 had offered an interface system approaching the user friendliness of the Macintosh. When Microsoft released its successful PC version of Excel along with 2.0, Windows' credibility increased, and many PC manufacturers began positioning their machines against Apple's Macintosh.

APPLE AND IBM

On March 17, 1988, Apple announced that it was suing Microsoft over Windows 2.03 and Hewlett Packard over New Wave, the latter's graphical interface environment. Apple announced the suit to the press before notifying Microsoft. Apple argued that it had spent millions creating a distinctive visual interface which had become the Macintosh's distinguishing feature and that Microsoft had illegally copied the "look and feel" of the Macintosh. Microsoft countered that its 1985 contract with Apple granted it license to use the visual interface already included in six Microsoft programs and that this license implicitly covered the 1987 version, Windows 2.03. In July 1989, Judge Schwarzer dropped 179 of the 189 items that Apple had argued were copyright violations. The 10 remaining items were related to the use of certain icons and the "overlapping windows" feature in Windows 2.03. In 1990, Judge Walker of the federal district court of San Francisco took over the case, having previously ruled against Xerox in its suit against Apple over the

same copyrights. In March 1990, Walker ruled that the portions of 2.03 under debate were not covered by the 1985 agreement between Apple and Microsoft. The stakes were enormous. If Apple were to lose the case on appeal, it would also lose a major competitive advantage in terms of its distinctive visual interface. If Microsoft should lose, it might have to take all current versions of Windows off the market and pay royalties on past sales to Apple.

As this war was going on, Microsoft started collaboration again with IBM in 1987 on the development of a new multi-tasking operating system called OS/2 and a new, more powerful graphical interface named Presentation Manager for PCs and PS/2 workstations designed around the new 80286 and 80386 chips. In late 1989, IBM released OS/2 version 1.2 for IBM PCs. Microsoft released OS/2 version 1.21 for IBM-compatible machines in mid-1990. But initial sales of OS/2 were far lower than had been hoped. Both IBM and Microsoft, as well as many industry observers, had assumed OS/2 would be the first logical replacement for DOS. But the introduction of OS/2 went poorly. The IBM team managing the project made decisions slowly and dictated compromises Microsoft did not always support. Independent software houses were reluctant to write applications for OS/2 when MS-DOS was so dominant. And it took an extra $2,000 in memory to make OS/2 run effectively on existing IBM machines. As these factors became apparent, Microsoft began to upgrade and push its MS-DOS and Windows programs ever harder. Many alleged that Microsoft moved key people to Windows at the expense of OS/2 and Presentation Manager to make sure its own products preempted the next generation of software.[6] Finally, perhaps feeling double-crossed, IBM took over most of the OS/2 development project and began to distance itself from Microsoft. It began to license workstation software from Steve Job's NeXt Corp. and pen-based technology from tiny GO Corp.

In June 1991, IBM and Apple began a joint venture—based around Motorola's powerful PowerPC chip Talagent—to develop an entirely new PC standard in which they would control the rights to both the operating system and the microprocessor. If successful, this cooperation between the two largest microcomputer manufacturers would tremendously influence the balance of power among software and hardware companies in the industry. Announced in late 1993 and early 1994 Apple's Power Mac and IBM's Power PC were designed to break the stranglehold Intel's X86 and Pentium chips and Microsoft's DOS Windows had on the world. Because the Power Macs were Apple's first new architecture in a decade, they would require new software. IBM would use its new Workplace OS software which could run Windows and DOS applications at OS/2 co-processing flexibility and speeds. Apple would offer a WinSoft emulation program that allowed its users to run Windows and DOS on the Power Macs at 486 speeds. Microsoft had been the biggest supplier of Macintosh applications.

The risks were high for both collaborating companies. John Sculley, then CEO of Apple, had said, "This is something only Apple and IBM could pull off. Still, it's a big gamble, and we're betting our whole company on it." In 1994 nearly all PC applications programs were being ported through Microsoft's MS-DOS or Windows environment. Bill Gates said, "Our position is being attacked on all sides. But that's not new. Customers will decide on all of this, and I think ours will thank us for preserving their current investment in PCs, while improving that technology. That has always been our strategy."

In the mid-1990s, the industry was changing radically along other dimensions. (See Exhibits 4–8 for selected software industry data.) Desktop computers were becoming so powerful that they were indistinguishable from what used to be mainframes. In any event mainframes and desktop computers, to be effective, increasingly had to be linked across both all a company's own offices and into the external linkages, databases, and systems popularly called the Information Superhighway. The network with all its nodes was becoming the computer itself. Desktop computers and applications—with 21% of operating system software sales and 62% of applications sales—were only a minor portion of all systems. Recognizing this, Gates had expanded his stated vision for Microsoft. "Our software will be used everywhere, in business, in the home, in the pocket, and in the car."[7]

Microsoft had a powerful base for its onslaught. It had almost 90% of the personal computer operation systems marketplace[8] (55 million Windows customers) and thousands of independents writing software to support its systems. But its recent upgrades of Windows (called 4.0 or Chicago) and NT (server operations) had been months late and lacked key intended components. Microsoft's attempts to reach beyond desktops—notably its LAN Manager (network operating system) co-developed with 3Com and NT—had made little headway against Unix or Novell's NetWare. And its Winpad (operating system for handhelds) and its software for "set-top boxes" in cable applications had yet to make a major dent in smaller non-PC support markets.[9] In databases, it had little experience on anything that did not run on desktops.

THE NETWORKED WORLD

In networking, Novell was the clear leader—67% of that $2.9 billion market (see Exhibit 9 for brief descriptions of Microsoft's principle competitors).[10] In 1993 Novell had bought UNIX System Labs from AT&T to increase its lead. Lotus's Lotus Notes ($100 million in sales) had grabbed a major share of the rapidly developing ($1 billion, 50% growth rate) "groupware" market for interactive business communications and team decision making.[11] Microsoft's Windows for Workgroups had yet to catch on in this market. Oracle was the pacesetter for minicomputer and server software. Oracle was also heavily engaged in software (n Cube) for supercomputers, which it saw playing an increasing role in large scale entertainment applications.

In the large scale network software market, Microsoft had worked on a three-way venture with TCI and Time Warner for interactive TV software. But this collapsed when Time Warner reportedly balked over the stiff terms Microsoft demanded. Others claimed that a major problem was combining the intense personalities of Gates and TCI's CEO Malone—"like putting two scorpions in a bottle together." Indeed the very tenacity, hard-nosed philosophy, and dominating technical competencies that had made Microsoft so successful ($4.5 billion in 1993 revenues with 25% margins) in the past might be an Achilles heel in the future. For example, a week before GO's announcement of its innovative "pen" software (for handwriting applications), Microsoft told the press it already had such software, and a few weeks later announced that 21 computer makers were considering designing around its Pen Windows. The press claimed that Microsoft often announced new products before they were ready to scare off competition. There was little doubt it aggressively matched all applications competitors' price reductions in its markets. And if small companies were unwilling to license key concepts in emerging markets, Microsoft moved quickly with end users or OEMs to co-design competing software.[12] Many of these practices were common complaints of defeated competitors.

ALLIANCES AND RIVALRIES

Some alliance partners—and many potential competitors—were becoming reluctant to risk their future by dealing with (or opposing) a party so powerful that it had repeatedly beaten world class companies in their very heartland.[13] Some companies (like HP and Sun Microsystems, or Lotus and Novell) had undertaken defensive alliances to counter Microsoft. And Microsoft's long-time ally, IBM, chose GO and Novell's NetWare as the pen-based and LAN technologies for its laptop and PC systems. Symbolic of the concern over Microsoft's growing power were a series of lawsuits—in addition to Apple's—alleging injury. In 1994 Star Electronics, a software company, won $120 million and a restraining order against Microsoft on some versions of MS-DOS. When the FTC abandoned its two-year antitrust probe of Microsoft, the Justice Department quickly picked up the investigation. The key issue was whether Microsoft used its dominant (77% to 90%) market share in personal computer operating systems to gain unfair competitive advantages in other markets.[14] There was little doubt that Microsoft currently enjoyed some significant advantages on the cost side. Once a program was widely accepted, it produced huge revenues with virtually no marginal costs—allowing its proprietary holder to invest or price with great flexibility.

But some rivals also claimed Microsoft's use of its licensing structure made it a monopolist. MS-DOS was currently standard on almost any PC; the manufacturer included it free, and paid Microsoft a royalty on each unit sold. Retailers who wanted to bundle Windows on one machine had to buy a copy for each machine offered in that series. Applications software producers and competitors like Sun Microsystems claimed that—despite the detailed maps of its operating systems Microsoft made available to assist others in writing applications—Microsoft always had more knowledge than others had about its operating systems and might (inadvertently or otherwise) fail to illuminate crucial details for others, giving Microsoft an unfair competitive advantage.[15] Microsoft vehemently denied this allegation. In fact it invited competitors to its headquarters to work with its programmers and even tipped off developers about forthcoming operating system changes so they could adapt in time. The Justice suit was settled in July with little impact on Microsoft; most agreed that the marketplace, not lawyers, would determine the industry structure.

Like many others, Microsoft was deeply aware of the huge and rapidly advancing software necessary to support interactive devices (in homes or offices), to compress or multiplex signals (to or from various devices), to support large scale systems (like stock and bond trading), and to expand the bandwidth and general utility of wireless, fiber optic, and other transmission systems. In 1994 there were over 180 million PCs worldwide, in the U.S. 7 million. Home computers accounted for $9 billion, or 40% of all PCs sold in 1994. By 2000 they would claim the highest percentage of the market for home appliances and have become more important in the home than the television set, according to AST Research, Inc.[15] Much new software would be needed for the "multimedia systems" many envisioned operating on PCs for voice interactive systems, and for "object oriented" parallel processing systems supporting highly decentralized operations, as well as the infinite variety of gizmos called "hand gear" people would carry, wear, or travel with in the new electronics era. No one doubted that there were endless possible horizons for electronics in all kinds of appliances, vehicles, office devices, and home products and that software—rather than hardware—would be the limiting factor in their development. One key issue in the mid '90s was where should Microsoft focus and how? Exhibits 10–12 provide data on some of the emerging markets.

Positioning the home marketplace was very complex because of the large number of small software developers who suddenly appeared to fulfill any apparent need. In this marketplace, it would be difficult, if not impossible, for Microsoft to achieve much of a timing advantage. It would be equally difficult to create a software platform that would become a powerful standard, as Microsoft DOS or Windows had. For its part, Microsoft was working on virtually all of the products which connected into the microprocessor. The hardware companies were of course trying to generate hardware solutions to problems like interactiveness among various systems and databases. A key question was where could solutions be better defined in software than in hardware.

As all this was occurring, the very microcomputer itself was changing. Computers were increasingly defined by the networks they attached to. Hardware capabilities continued to grow exponentially, typically with bandwidth, storage, and calculation capabilities doubling almost annually. Formerly dominant players like IBM, Apple, or AT&T found it increasingly hard to control architectures industry wide. Unlike applications, software architectures often took years to develop, but could provide a competitive edge for application and connecting programs for years. Selecting partners and implementing partnerships in ways that did not damage past relationships or inhibit future developments was particularly difficult. Such complexities compounded as Microsoft looked toward foreign markets. The issues of matching and pricing platforms versus application programs were profound, as were the issues of sharing benefits when Microsoft worked with selected hardware partners.

THE MICROSOFT STYLE

Another issue was whether Bill Gates' unique management style could. From its genesis in the early days of Microsoft—when Gates and Allen and a small coterie of programmers literally worked night and day for weeks at a time under incredible pressure—the Microsoft culture had gelled into a unique form. Its working atmosphere counterbalanced highly intensive activity with an offbeat emphasis on an unstructured and informal environment. Gates expected programmers to work as hard as he did—60–80 hour weeks. There was an unstated expectation that employees work evenings and weekends. No one wanted their car to be the first out of the parking lot. The Microsoft complex in Redmond, Washington, looked more like a college campus than the headquarters of a Fortune 500 company. At times its environment could be almost surrealistic. Most of its 10,000 employees had individual offices with windows, but the courtyards adjoining the principal structures were often rife with the activity of employees juggling, riding unicycles, or playing various musical instruments. Working hours were extraordinarily flexible. Dress and appearance were extremely casual. Many programmers worked in bare feet. It was not unknown for a team of programmers working on an intense project to take a break at 3 A.M. and spend 30 minutes making considerable racket with their electric guitars and synthesizers. Pranks were common. Offices would be filled with "bouncy balls" when their occupants were away. There were bouncy ball hockey games in the hallway and a special room just for juggling in the early days. [Microsoft Corporation (B) describes the 1995 organization and culture of Microsoft in some detail.]

THE GATES STYLE

Gates' personal style was legendary. He would challenge his programmers constantly. He wanted them to argue with him. If a programmer completed something (s)he thought was clever, Gates would suddenly challenge why it wasn't ready earlier, or why it wasn't done a different way. He was very aggressive and vocal in arguing an issue. But he was not afraid to change his mind if someone had a convincing argument. Observers said Gates turned everything into some form of competition. He even competed with Allen in the early years to see who could drive across Albuquerque faster. Gates still drove his Porsche, pushed to the limit, but always in control. Over the years, he had registered many run-ins with local traffic police and an incredible string of speeding fines. A former Microsoft top executive said, "Gates was competitive in all things. He was often so intense in negotiating sessions that he would push too hard and actually jeopardize the deal. There was 'almost a viciousness' to the intensity Gates displayed to secure a deal."

Gates' personal style became the subject of myths. He wore down both competitors and his own people by his tenacity and his formidable intellect. He had a reputation as the only entrepreneur in the industry with enormous personal technical acumen. He knew more about the industry and where it was going than anyone else. Being at the center of action was a vital attraction to good people. Technically, Gates had an uncanny ability to spot a weak link in the most logical argument or program. But he also could show a shocking lack of diplomacy. If angered, he could become "apoplectic," even throwing things when he was angry. Some felt he disagreed just to see if someone was strong in their beliefs. To others, it just appeared a portion of his style, as were his habits of firing off e-mail at all hours of the day or night and of meeting visitors or making public announcements in work clothes that had been his companions for days. For many, a technical staff meeting with Gates was like going through an oral examination with a verbal executioner. Once a flaw was pinpointed, he would rip the person to shreds, hurling his favorite expletives, "stupid," or "random." Rocking back and forth in his rocking chair, he would impose his own intellectual prowess and standards on all comers.[17]

Gates constantly conveyed his determination to be the dominant player in the industry. He not only wanted to beat his competition, but to eliminate them. As one executive said, "Bill learned early on that killing the competition is the name of the game. There just aren't as many people later to take you on." Gates' competitiveness had also led him to be a great sales person. He often overcommitted Microsoft and set unrealistic deadlines. He tended to press for a major sale and worry about the consequences later. As a result, among savants, Microsoft's first programs in a series were known for being a bit behind schedule and bug prone. But Gates never gave up. He approached every transaction with a zealotry of a true believer; from day one he continued to articulate the Microsoft mantra "a computer on every desktop and Microsoft software in every computer." Throughout Microsoft, employees were expected to display initiative, ambition, intelligence, expertise, and business judgment. Gates pushed his people hard because he wanted them to be better. Each day, he said, they should come to work thinking "I want to win." Gates thought this was the only way to stay ahead in an industry where he predicted, within twenty years, the software race would be over. Computers would then be writing better software than people.[18]

QUESTIONS

1. What were the critical factors in Microsoft's past success? Trace the crucial interactions with its customers, competitors, and other outside parties. How can these patterns be applied in the future? How do the strategies of hypercompetition fit this situation?
2. What are the major differences in strategic management in a company like Microsoft versus an Intel, IBM, or Sony? The major similarities? How does one form a strategy in this environment? What are the key trends Microsoft must deal with? How?
3. What are the keys to Microsoft's strategy in the future? What should they do to respond to the new joint venture between IBM and Apple? What role should government play in this industry? Why?

EXHIBIT 1
Microsoft Corporation
Selected Financial Data, 1989–1994
(in millions of dollars)

	1989	1991	1992	1993	1994
Net revenues	$804	$1,843	$2,759	$3,753	$4,649
Cost of revenues	$204	$362	$467	$633	$763
Research and development	110	235	352	470	610
Sales and marketing	219	534	854	1,205	1,384
General and administrative	28	62	90	119	166
Operating income	243	650	996	1,326	1,726
Net income	171	463	708	953	1,146
Working capital	310	735	1,323	2,287	3,399
Total assets	721	1,644	2,640	3,805	5,363
Stockholders' equity	562	1,351	2,193	3,242	4,450
Number of employees	4,037	8,226	11,542	14,430	15,257
Stock Price Range	10 1⁄8–19 7⁄8	32 1⁄2–74 5⁄8	65 3⁄4–95	70 3⁄8–98	n/a

Source: Microsoft Corporation, *Annual Report*, various years.

EXHIBIT 2
Microsoft Corporation
Segment Data, 1991–1994
(percentages)

	1991	1992	1993	1994
Products Groups				
Systems software	36%	48%	34%	33%
Applications software	51	49	58	63
Hardware	12	9	6	4
Books and others	1	2	2	—
Channels of Distribution				
U.S.	31	34	31	34
OEM	18	17	19	25
International	49	47	47	41
Press and other	2	2	3	—

Source: Microsoft Corporation, *Annual Report*, various years.

HISTORICAL FINANCIALS

	MICROSOFT	LOTUS	NOVELL	ORACLE	COMP.ASSOC	BORLAND
Net sales/revenues						
1989	$ 804	$ 556	$ 422	$ 584	$1,030	$ 91
1990	1,183	685	498	971	1,296	113
1991	1,843	829	640	1,028	1,348	227
1992	2,759	900	933	1,178	1,509	483
1993	3,753	981	1,123	1,503	1,841	464
Net income						
1989	$ 171	$ 68	$ 49	$ 82	$ 164	$ −3
1990	279	23	94	117	158	12
1991	463	43	162	−12	159	27
1992	708	80	249	62	163	−110
1993	953	56	−35	98	246	−49

1993 FINANCIALS

	MICROSOFT	LOTUS	NOVELL	ORACLE	COMP. ASSOC	BORLAND
Net sales/revenues	$ 3,753	$ 981	$ 1,123	$ 1,503	$ 1,841	$ 464
Gross margin	3,120	779	898	1,503	1,841	341
Operating expense	1,794	660	824	1,286	1,453	385
Net income	953	56	−35	98	246	−49
Total assets	3,805	905	1,344	1,184	2,349	342
Shareholders' equity	3,242	528	996	528	1,054	188

Source: Compiled by authors from corporation reports of named companies.

	1989	1991	1993
IBM	8,424	10,524	9,963
Microsoft	829	2,019	3,575
Computer Associates	1,484	1,589	1,845
Oracle	668	800	1,392
Novell	—	640	1,064
Hewlett-Packard	550	702	1,014
Digital Equipment	850	967	952
Lotus	534	716	846
Sun	150	531	692
AT&T Computer Systems	408	623	684
Unisys	700	740	655
WordPerfect	281	532	577
Bull	—	662	544
Borland	369	497	457
Apple	90	329	433

Source: International Data Corporation, 1993.

EXHIBIT 5
North American PC
Software Market
by Segment
(millions of dollars)

	PC/MS-DOS			WINDOWS			MACINTOSH			OTHER		
	1991	1992	1993	1991	1992	1993	1991	1992	1993	1991	1992	1993
Entertainment	$210.6	$267.2	$318.7	$12.2	$29.6	$39.3	$25.0	$31.4	$40.2	$16.3	$13.6	$3.9
Home education	76.0	104.3	109.5	**	12.4	88.5	13.8	22.6	41.4	9.6	6.7	2.4
Finance	188.5	220.3	213.0	13.9	45.0	131.1	23.7	30.9	42.6	**	**	**
Word processors	442.6	249.0	226.5	253.3	417.9	664.3	92.5	144.3	103.9	24.2	18.4	24.6
Spreadsheets	408.4	332.1	157.0	208.6	343.6	553.9	97.8	92.5	70.2	24.4	27.0	20.2
Databases	267.8	267.2	157.1	2.9	31.2	238.6	40.1	48.2	65.6	**	1.8	1.1
Integrated	84.8	66.4	32.1	11.2	28.9	60.0	24.7	47.6	54.3	7.3	5.3	2.0
Utilities	207.8	154.4	128.1	21.6	98.8	103.0	46.7	68.3	64.0	1.0	**	2.2
Presentation graphics	151.4	94.0	41.7	50.3	142.4	216.5	35.1	49.0	52.0	4.5	3.8	5.1
Drawing & painting	2.0	2.5	**	69.6	145.0	173.2	108.9	110.3	148.3	3.0	4.0	2.6
Desktop publishing	19.3	10.1	1.7	73.3	75.8	113.6	44.8	53.8	67.7	1.8	**	**

** Not meaningful or not available.

Source: Software Publishers Association.

EXHIBIT 6
Software Industry
Shipments by Product,
1993

	SHIPMENTS (000) UNITS	SHIPMENT MARKET SHARE
DOS Word Processing Software		
WordPerfect for DOS	1,800	80.4
Word for DOS	150	6.7
Other	290	12.9
Windows Word Processing Software		
Word for Windows	3,500	45.5
WordPerfect for Windows	2,800	36.4
Lotus Ami Pro	1,300	16.9
Wordstar for Windows	70	0.9
Other	25	0.3
Office Suite Software		
Microsoft Office	1,700	74.0
Lotus Smartsuite	500	21.7
Borland Office	100	4.3
Windows Spreadsheet Software		
Excel for Windows	3,900	48.8
1-2-3 for Windows	2,500	31.2
Quattro Pro for Windows	1,275	15.9
Improv for Windows	250	3.1
Other	80	1.0
Database Software		
Paradox (Borland)	852	38.3
Access (Microsoft)	800	36.0
FoxPro (microsoft)	412	18.5
DBase (Borland)	161	7.2

Source: International Data Corporation, 1994; *Computerworld,* January 17, 1994.

EXHIBIT 7
Network Software
Market

1990	
Total world sales	$580 million
Of which:	
Novell	60.0%
Microsoft	15.0%
Other	25.0%

1992	
Shares of U.S. market	
Novell	57%
Microsoft	8%
Apple	7%
IBM	7%
DEC	4%
Banyan Systems	11%

Source: Thompson Financial Networks, May 29, 1991 from Bear, Stearns & Co., Inc. and *Financial World,* April 12, 1992 from Shearson Lehman Brothers and Computer Intelligence.

EXHIBIT 8
World PC Population,
1981–1993
(millions)

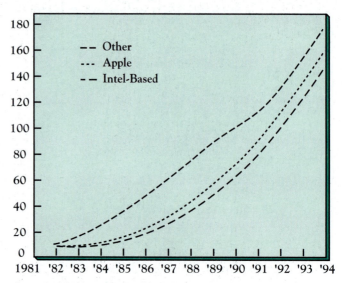

Source: PaineWebber in "Survey of the Computer Industry," *The Economist,* September 17, 1994, page 54.

EXHIBIT 10
Projections for Home
Computer Sales,
1993–1998

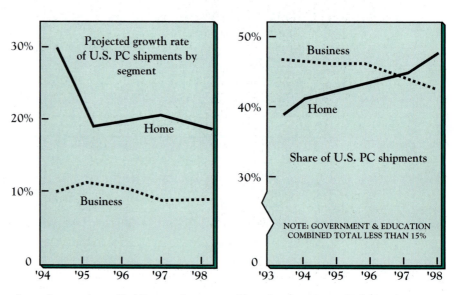

Sources: Dataquest, Inc., and Link Resources Corporation in "Home Computers," *Business Week,* November 28, 1994, page 89.

EXHIBIT 9
Brief Descriptions of
Microsoft's Principle
Competitors

LOTUS DEVELOPMENT CORPORATION

With its operating profits in 1991 and 1992 (excluding acquisition-related charges and profits from stock sales) dropping two years in a row and sales of its flagship spreadsheet program—Lotus 1-2-3, the most popular personal computer software application in the world with more than 20 million users—actually shrinking, Lotus is counting on its groupware product, Notes, to reverse its fortune. Lotus Notes, introduced first in 1989, experienced slow sales growth due to long customer learning curves and the fact that it worked only with the slow-selling OS/2 operating system. Notes 3.0 (introduced in spring 1993) works on Apple Macintoshs and workstations running the Unix operating systems as well. If Lotus wants Notes to become a software "platform" like Microsoft's MS-DOS and Windows operating software, it will need to attract hundreds of thousands of independent software developers. Recently Lotus and AT&T announced that they were negotiating an agreement to create a Notes Public Server Network, a corporate data network.

BORLAND INTERNATIONAL, INC.

Once powerful Borland International has suffered in the past several years but is now firmly focused on an "upsizing" strategy—an attempt to move its current base of Paradox (flat database) and dBase (relational database) users into the highly competitive client/server environment. Borland tried to enter the application suites business through a joint deal with WordPerfect (Office for Windows, marketed by Borland and including WordPerfect word processor, the Quattro Pro spreadsheet, and the Paradox database). Its innovative addition of a database component to the suite was quickly copied by its competitors Microsoft and Lotus. Novell's acquisition of WordPerfect and its purchase of Quattro Pro clearly signal the failure of this thrust which was plagued by insufficient integration among products and joint development by two geographically dispersed companies. It is now attempting to find a place in the market for groupware with its Obex technology which, rather than building a separate groupware application, allows end users to add their own connectivity between applications. As its resources have dwindled, Borland has had problems getting its important dBase for Windows product completed and is still embroiled in lawsuits with Lotus (over Quattro Pro) and several shareholders.

NOVELL INC.

The leader in networking software with NetWare—which has 65% of the market for local area networks, UnixWare (its recently acquired product line for Unix operating systems), and AppWare (a development tool for network-based distributed applications), Novell has been on an aggressive acquisition campaign over the past several years. This strategy may have been further fueled by the abortive merger talks between Microsoft and Novell that took place in 1989 and again in 1991. Its recent purchase of the word-processing king, WordPerfect (with its WordPerfect Office product, a combined electronic mail, scheduling, forms, and routing workgroup suite) is the most significant. The combination of Novell and WordPerfect creates another software giant, potentially able to compete with Microsoft, as it now has a postion in many of the key infrastructure components—desktop applications, workgroup applications, and network operating system. CEO Ray Noorda indicated that "the rationale behind the acquisition focused on redefining the applications business by helping drive the growing market transition to network applications. . . . Novell's objective is to accelerate this market transition by offering new generations of network applications. To complement the WordPerfect line, Novell purchased the Quattro Pro spreadsheet business.

Source: Compiled by authors from a wide variety of sources including articles, investment reports, and so on.

EXHIBIT 11
**Subscribers to Commercial
On-Line Services,
1990–1998**
(millions)

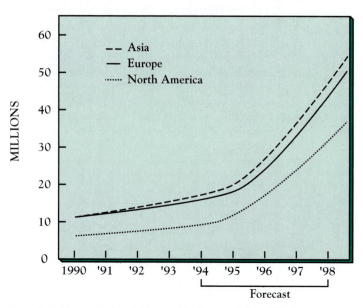

Source: Jupiter Communications, in "Survey of the Computer Industry," *The Economist,*
September 17, 1994, page 516.

EXHIBIT 12
**Global Growth in
Multimedia Hardware
and Software Sales**
(millions of CD-ROM drives
and thousands of titles)

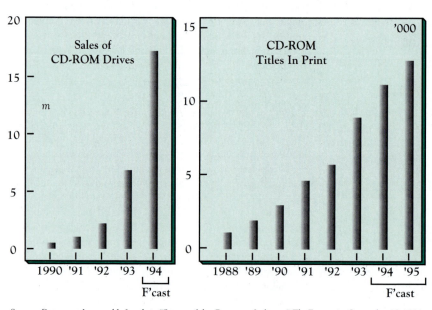

Sources: Dataquest, Inc., and Infotech in "Survey of the Computer Industry," *The Economist,* September 17, 1994, page 519.

E & J GALLO WINERY

"The winemaker is a warrior" begins an old Italian poem. For nearly 50 years, the two sons of an Italian immigrant have taken those words to heart. Ever since they pooled $5,900 in capital to set up their winery in Modesto, California, in 1933, the brothers have managed their enterprise with a discipline, precision, and success that few companies enjoy. But, in the late 1980s, Ernest and Julio, then in their 70s, had to worry about the future of their remarkable concern. In 1986, *Fortune* magazine published a rare and insightful article on the company. The article, quoted almost in its entirety, follows.

A WILL TO DOMINATE

When it comes to business, the brothers Ernest and Julio Gallo brook neither waste nor weakness. Just ask the scores of companies, large and small, that over the past five decades have made the mistake of venturing onto their turf. [Despite their ages, Ernest and Julio Gallo] have not lost their desperate will to dominate. . . . What is Gallo's secret? "A constant striving for perfection in every aspect of our business," says Ernest. That may sound self-serving, but it is in large part true. Plainly put, Ernest and Julio are better at the nuts and bolts of the wine business than anyone else in the world. They are more resourceful, more thorough, more exacting. And they are not afraid to exercise their power over grape growers, distributors, or anyone else. "I sometimes feel like an Olympic runner who gets mad at his coach," says David Terk, an independent distributor in Abilene,

Case copyright © 1989 James Brian Quinn. This case was prepared from secondary sources only with the help of professor Richard D'Aveni. Research associate on this case was Penny C. Paquette. Materials produced by special permission from "How Gallo Crushes The Competition," by Jaclyn Fierman, September 1, 1986. Copyright © 1986 *Fortune* magazine.

Texas. "Gallo pushes so hard you end up working more than you want."

Not that the Gallos face no challenges. The most unusual by far comes from their younger brother, Joseph, 66. In a drama worthy of the wine-country soap opera *Falcon Crest*, Joseph is suing for a one-third interest in the winery. He claims that the winery is an outgrowth of their father's wine-grape business and that his big brothers cheated him out of his rightful inheritance.

Ernest and Julio's other problems are more mundane. The national obsession with fitness and the crackdown on drunken driving have had a sobering effect on wine production, Gallo included. Americans drank 6.5% less table wine in 1985 than in 1984 and will probably cut consumption 5% more this year, according to *Impact*, an industry newsletter. The wine industry's smartest response to the new abstinence is coolers, fruity beverages with a splash of wine and roughly the alcohol content of beer. Gallo, in typical fashion, has outsmarted everyone: its year-old cooler, Bartles & Jaymes, is number one.

Further challenges come from another trend among wine drinkers—the swing to pricey table wines made from the finest grapes. Americans are demanding better quality than ever before, and premium wines have raised their share of the $8.3-billion-a-year business from 8% in 1980 to 20% today. Gallo sells more premium wine than any other producer, but its growth in this category is limited because it lacks snob appeal. The name Gallo, which means "rooster" in Italian, is associated with screw tops and bottles in paper bags (from its earlier marketing history). The brothers are battling to upgrade their image with the same vengeance they bring to every war they wage.

For now they can take heart in making the most, if not the best, wine in the world. The joke goes that Gallo spills more than anyone else sells. The truth is not far off. Last year Gallo shipped over 150 million gallons of wine, according to the *Gomberg-Fredrikson Report*, an authoritative industry newsletter. Its most popular brands are Chablis Blanc, Hearty Burgundy, Carlo Rossi, and other low-priced jug wines, which together account for a commanding 31% of the volume in that end of the market. The brothers also sell more champagne (André), brandy (E & J), sherry, vermouth, and port than anyone else. All told, they buy roughly 30% of California's annual wine-grape harvest and produce one of every four bottles of wine sold in the United States.

They also squeeze profits from the wine business while others come up dry. The winery is privately owned by Ernest, Julio, and their fecund families— between them the brothers have 4 children, 20 grand-children, and 6 great-grandchildren. Three children, a son-in-law, and 4 grandchildren work for the company, but share little of Ernest and Julio's power. . . . [Ernest and Julio] keep financial details tightly corked. Based on interviews with dozens of current and former employees, industry experts, and competitors, *Fortune* estimated that Gallo earns at least $50 million a year on sales of roughly $1 billion. By comparison, Seagram, the nation's largest distillery and second-largest winery, booked roughly $350 million in wine revenues [in 1984] and lost money on its best-selling table wines, Paul Masson and Taylor California Cellars. Gallo's other main competitors, Almadén, owned by National Distillers & Chemical Corp., and Inglenook, owned by Heublein, are making money, but not much.

Private ownership and staggering volume contribute to Gallo's success. The company can wrest market share from competitors by settling for paper-thin margins and occasional losses that stockholders of publicly held companies might not tolerate for long. Moreover, Gallo does not have disparate claims on its resources and can devote all its energy to wine. "Unlike our major competition," says Ernest, "wine is our only business."

[Few] other companies could afford to replicate the degree of vertical integration Gallo has built up over the years. The brothers own Fairbanks Trucking Co., one of the largest intrastate truckers in California. Its 200 semis and 500 trailers are constantly hauling wine out of Modesto and raw materials back in— including sand from around the state and lime from Gallo's quarry east of Sacramento. Alone among wine producers, Gallo makes bottles—2 million a day—and its Midcal Aluminum Co. spews out screw tops as fast as the bottles are filled.

CRUSHER POWER

Most of the country's 1,300 or so wineries concentrate on production to the neglect of marketing. They entrust their fate with consumers to independent distributors who work for several competing producers. Most distributors, in turn, figure their job is done once they take orders and make deliveries to grocery and liquor stores. Gallo, by contrast, participates in every aspect of selling short of whispering in the ear of each imbiber. The company owns its distributors in about a dozen markets and probably would buy many of the more than 300 independents who handle its wines if laws in most states did not prohibit doing so.

Gallo's power elicits emotions from admiration to hate from just about everyone touched by it. "The hate part," says a Sonoma Valley grower, "is getting rejected by Gallo at the crusher"—the place where growers bring their grapes to be graded, sold, and eventually crushed into juice and fermented. Distributors feel hatred or something near it if they are unceremoniously dumped, as many have been for failing to satisfy Ernest's demanding requirements. Competitors hate being singled out as the next rival to be vanquished. Says a cowed Stuart Bewley, who helped start California Cooler five years ago, "They aim all their guns at once." Bewley's brand was the market leader in wine coolers until Gallo stormed into the business. Bewley sold California Cooler to Brown-Forman (in 1984) but still manages the operation. Yet even competitors thank the Gallos for expanding the wine market. While the Gallos may not make the world's best wine, they have lifted the U.S. standard for low-priced table wine well above that served in Italy or France.

A DIVIDED KINGDOM

E & J Gallo Winery is a divided kingdom. Julio is president and oversees production. Big brother Ernest is chairman and rules over marketing, sales, and distribution. The two steer clear of each other, conducting business on separate floors. "We don't have everyday contact," says Julio, whose domain is the first floor at the neoclassic headquarters some natives call Parthenon West. Ernest holds court upstairs. The brothers mesh well despite the division: Julio's goal is to make more wine than Ernest can sell, Ernest's to sell more than Julio can make.

Thick fingered and full faced, Julio aptly describes himself as a farmer at heart. "I like to walk in the fields with the old-timers," he says. "I feel at home in the vineyards." Make no mistake, though, Julio is a patrician farmer dressed not in overalls and work boots but in linen trousers and slightly scuffed wing tips. His office is elegantly appointed, with a solid oak desk and inlaid wooden artworks depicting harvest scenes in the French countryside. His modern ranch house down the road from the winery is festooned with images of grapes, from jade carvings along the walls to the silverware and place mats on his table.

Ernest conducts business in a setting cluttered with mementos not from the fields but from the world of selling. He has a framed New Yorker cartoon that shows two couples drinking wine in a restaurant. The caption reads: "Surprisingly good, isn't it? It's Gallo. Mort and I simply got tired of being snobs." Expressions of fierce pride abound from the Gallo-green crushed-velvet couch to an ambitious collection of glass, metal, and ceramic statuettes of *galli*. Paler, grittier, and less courtly than his brother, Ernest cares little for social or decorative amenities. "We don't socialize much," says the more affable Julio. "There's not much to talk about."

Ernest wouldn't waste time schmoozing anyway. He would rather interrogate than converse. He bridles when questioned and has the habit of answering with questions of his own. He is after all the information he can get and is intolerant when someone does not deliver. "If you try to cover up, he'll expose you," says George Frank, who directed Gallo's East Coast sales for three decades and retired last year.

Ernest's employees toil much harder than most because they know the boss will try to catch them off guard. "I never knew if he was checking on the marketplace or on me," says Frank. On frequent trips around the country, Ernest orders a distributor to pick him up at eight in the morning, map in hand. Mindful of neither distance nor direction, he points to several towns where he wants to check the positioning of his products in stores. "Ernest doesn't want you to take him on a tour," says Laurence Weinstein, a distributor in Madison, Wisconsin. "If he sees you turning left, he'll tell you to turn right."

The distributors behave more like family members than independents because most owe their success to the winery. "Ernest picked distributors who were hungry," says Frank. "They knew if they failed with Gallo, they might be out on the street." Once Ernest chooses a distributor, he or his troops plan strategy with him down to the last detail, analyzing traffic patterns in every store in the district and the number of Gallo cases each should stock.

A REGIMENTED DISTRIBUTION SYSTEM

Ernest encourages distributors to hire a separate sales force to sell his products alone. When Texas distributor David Terk decided it wasn't worth the extra money to employ a special Gallo team, he and Ernest severed ties. Terk eventually came around to Gallo's way of thinking and has been reinstated. "If you follow Ernest's advice," Terk says, "he'll make you rich." Ernest also tries to persuade distributors to sell his wines exclusively. "We never told distributors to throw out Gallo competitors," says Frank. "But we might have asked them how they planned to do justice if they carried two competing brands."

The Federal Trade Commission objected to that friendly persuasion 10 years ago, charging Gallo with unfair competition. Gallo signed a consent order that prohibited it from punishing distributors for selling competing brands and from requiring them to disclose sales figures. The FTC set aside the order three years ago after Gallo argued that the market had grown more competitive and that the order was giving other wine makers an unfair advantage: they were freed to set up exclusive deals with distributors.

Now that Gallo can regiment its distributors once again, it rarely hears a grumble out of them. One bold exception: Ohio distributor Bernard Rutman sued Gallo last year, alleging that the company violated antitrust laws when it dumped him for no good reason after 40 years of loyal service. Without Gallo products, which Rutman referred to as "call items" or "door openers," he lost several retail accounts. Rutman claimed that Gallo's action had reduced competition because he could no longer afford the sales force needed to sell a broad range of products. Gallo fought the charges and won, arguing that it was not the winery's responsibility to open doors for competitors. Rutman is appealing.

Ernest finds distributors who will open doors for *him*. Aggressive salesmen are crucial to Gallo's success because they are the winery's link to retailers, and retailers have the last crack at influencing consumers. "Seagram," concedes Edgar Bronfman Jr., "has typically pushed everything to the distributor and left it to him to deal with the stores." Ernest makes certain that his distributors deal with the stores like no others. They build floor displays, lift cases, and dust the bottles on the shelves. "If you turn your back on a Gallo salesman," says a manager of a San Francisco liquor store, "he'll turn the place into a Gallo outlet."

Gallo leaves nothing to chance—and very little to the imagination. Required reading and rereading for new salesmen is Gallo's 300-page training manual. More graphic than the *Kama Sutra*, it describes and diagrams every conceivable angle of the wine business. "As a sales representative of Gallo wine," the tome begins, "you are the man that Ernest and Julio Gallo depend on to sell retailers the merchandising ideas that sell Gallo wine to consumers."

What follow are 16 dizzying chapters, each ending with a quiz. A section on how to display Gallo products in stores spells out which items to place at eye level (the most highly advertised ones) and which to position above the belt (impulse items). Another details how much shelf space Gallo brands should occupy (seven feet on each of five shelves, the largest area the eye can easily scan). Maintaining shelves the Gallo way requires a ten-point checklist (No. 7: "Wherever there is a decided price advantage in buying a larger size, the larger size should be placed to the right of the smaller size.") The "complete sales call" would be incomplete unless all ten steps from another checklist were taken (No. 6: "It's time to think . . . you should know what you'd like to say and how you're going to say it to this retailer").

Among the trove of sales tips: "An off-color joke may be great if you're selling pornography, but it's a little difficult to use this opener . . . to sell the retailer on cold-box placement for wine." The retail world is made up of six types of buyers, the manual explains. They range from "the silent type (he just listens)" to "the aggressive type (he's looking for a fight)." If you run into the silent type, "avoid embarrassing questions." When you meet up with an aggressive one, "let him win the battle, but you win the war."

Gallo hasn't lost a war yet. Even Coca-Cola, no wimp at marketing, surrendered in 1983 after six years of butting barrels with the wine Goliath. When Coke got into the wine business in 1977, consumption had been rising 7% a year. But that trend soon fizzled. The profit margins Coke was used to in soda never materialized for wine, not even close. By the time Coke sold its Wine Spectrum unit to Seagram for more than $200 million, it had overpromoted and underpriced its Taylor California Cellars.

FROM PLEBEIAN TO SNOB

Pleasing the plebeian palate in Podunk used to be all that mattered in the wine business, and no one did that better than Gallo. But today even Podunk has wine snobs. Having to prove themselves all over again is a nasty twist of fate for the Gallos, who have devoted decades to upgrading everyday drinking wine for

Americans. "We have varietals we think are the very best," Julio insists. Not Chateau Lafite, to be sure, but certainly respectable. Some wine connoisseurs compare Gallo's varietals to competing brands that sell for twice as much.

The screw-top stigma hurts, but the Gallo brothers learned early how bitter the wine business can be. They got their first taste as young boys, toiling in their father Joseph's Modesto vineyard in their spare time. After Julio finished high school and Ernest graduated from Modesto Junior College, they worked full time for their father. "He believed in hard work and no play," says Julio. "None at all."

An immigrant from the Piedmont region in northwest Italy, Joseph Gallo was a small-time grape grower and shipper. Prohibition did not put him out of work: the government permitted wine for medicinal and religious use. But the Depression took a tragic toll. The Gallo business almost went under, and in the spring of 1933 Joseph shot his wife and reportedly chased Ernest and Julio across his fields waving a shotgun. After they escaped, Joseph killed himself. Ernest is reminded of the tragedy daily: his childhood residence, a stucco house with a pillared porch, is on the road from the winery to his present home, a modest bungalow with a security guard out front. Julio relived the horror years later when his second son, Philip, then a teenager, committed suicide.

Prohibition ended the same year that their parents died, and the Gallos, then in their early 20s, decided to switch from growing grapes to producing wine. Problem was, they had no idea how to make the stuff. They found instructions in two thin pamphlets in the Modesto Public Library and, with $5,900.23 to their names, burst out of the post-Prohibition starting gate with 600 other newly formed wineries. "My confidence," recalls Ernest, "was unlimited."

Finding customers was the next hurdle, and Ernest was born with an instinct for that. A Chicago distributor wrote to newly licensed California wineries, inviting them to send him samples. Ernest went the extra mile. He boarded a plane for Chicago, met the man at his office, and sold him 6,000 gallons at 50 cents a gallon. Ernest continued east and sold the rest of the first year's production for a profit of $34,000. The Gallos initially sold wine in bulk to bottlers, but in 1938 they started doing their own bottling under the Gallo label, a far more profitable venture. Sales grew unabated for years.

"Success in life," says the insular Ernest, "depends on who your parents were and what circumstances you grew up in." Hard work was Joseph Gallo's ethic, and it became Ernest's as well. Driving himself and others is a survival instinct for Ernest. But perhaps because his father ultimately failed, Ernest also believes that hard work alone is not enough. "It boils down to luck," he says of his and Julio's success. "Circumstances could have been otherwise."

GROWING WITH THUNDER

As luck would have it, the Gallos had their first phenomenal success with a high alcohol, lemon-flavored beverage they began selling in the late 1950s. A radio jingle sent the stuff to the top of the charts on skid rows across the country: "What the word? Thunderbird. How's it sold? Good and cold. What's the jive? Bird's alive. What's the price? Thirty-twice." But Thunderbird also left Gallo with a gutter image it has been hard pressed to shake.

Each in his own way, the Gallos are fighting to change that. Julio may be more easygoing than Ernest, but he is no pushover when it comes to getting what he wants from growers. Says Frank, Gallo's former East Coast executive: "He works with grapes as if he's pursuing the Holy Grail." With the help of graduates from California's top oenology schools, Julio has experimented with hundreds of varieties over the years. In the 1960s he made an unprecedented offer of 15-year contracts to growers who would rip up their vineyards and replant better grapes. Julio got his better grapes, and he also got an assured supply of his most essential raw material. Unlike small wineries, which grow the bulk of their grapes, Gallo buys more than 95 percent of the grapes it crushes.

Growing for Gallo is a mixed blessing. The 1,500 Gallo growers know they have a home for their grapes every season because Gallo's needs are so vast. But they are never sure how much they will get paid until they get to one of Gallo's three grape-crushing and fermenting operations: the Frei Brothers winery in Sonoma County, which Gallo bought from the Frei family in 1977, or the Livingston and Fresno plants in San Joaquin Valley. If grapes do not meet standards for Gallo's top-quality wines—handpicked, the right color, the proper acid and sugar balance—the winery downgrades them for use in other products and slashes the price. The *Healdsburg Tribune*, a newspaper in Sonoma County, has condemned the Gallos and called for state regulation of grading. An editorial claimed growers had been victimized by "sudden devaluation or outright rejection of their grapes, always with the company's take-it-or-leave-it attitude. . . . Most growers have little choice but to take it."

One who chose not to take it was Steven Sommer, a Sonoma grower who filed a grievance with the California Department of Agriculture in 1984 after Gallo downgraded most of his 50-ton harvest from $475 a ton to $275. Gallo claimed the grapes were off color and therefore would not yield flavorful wine. "It was just the way the sun was shining on them," Sommer insisted. The state ruled in Gallo's favor: since the growers had no written contract stating otherwise, Gallo had the right to judge grapes however it chose. Sommer's protest served a purpose, though. Gallo now gives one-year contracts in Sonoma County that spell out its standards. "The old-timers always did business on a handshake," says Julio. "The young growers want things in writing." Sommer has gone into business for himself, producing wine from the grapes he grows.

Julio insists on rigorous standards in Modesto, where all Gallo products are blended, bottled, and tasted every morning at 11 o'clock. Gallo was among the first producers to store wine in stainless steel containers instead of the usual redwood or concrete casks that can breed bad-tasting bacteria. Like giant thermos bottles, tanks at Gallo's three crushers and at the Modesto headquarters protect 300 million gallons of wine from the searing heat. Passers-by could easily mistake the Modesto plant for an oil refinery. There's no sign anywhere that says Gallo. "We know where the place is," Julio explains.

The refinery image is a sore point with Julio. "It was never my ambition to run the biggest winery in the world," he says. "It doesn't impress me at all." Unlike other wineries, Gallo offers no tours to the public. [Although Gallo has a 3-million-gallon underground cask facility], changing Gallo's image is really an above-ground proposition, and Ernest is throwing more than $40 million into advertising this year to get the quality message to consumers. . . . It features sensuous, slow moving images of ethnic weddings, sunlit vineyards, and crystal goblets, to a mesmerizing score by Vangelis, the Academy Award-winning composer for the movie *Chariots of Fire*.

The new image is being crafted by Hal Riney, a San Francisco ad man with an agency bearing his name. Riney is also the genius behind those fictional farmers, Frank Bartles and Ed Jaymes, who told us in their early ads about how they put their orchard and vineyard together to make a premium wine cooler. "So Ed took out a second on his house," says poker-faced Frank, "and wrote to Harvard for an MBA." The pair was recently seen in New York City eating "big doughnuts" (the locals call them bagels).

Bartles & Jaymes has hurtled to the top of a high heap—there are over 100 coolers on the market. Cooler sales reached almost 40 million cases in 1984, and Marvin Shanken, publisher of *Impact*, predicted that consumption could swell to 90 million cases and constitute a third of the total wine market by 1990. The wine in most coolers is made from the cheapest grapes, and initially the mix was far more profitable than straight wine. But in typical fashion, Gallo devastated everyone else's profit margins when it entered the war. "We've had to double our ad spending and put our products on promotion a lot more often," says California Cooler's Bewley. Another major accomplishment for Riney has been getting along with Ernest Gallo. Before Riney, scores of agencies tried and failed to hack Ernest's ways. That kind of turnover is legendary at Gallo. A few employees, like Frank, stay forever, but many leave after a few years with whatever tricks they've managed to learn from one of America's best marketing minds.

A GENERATION GAP

A long-time Gallo executive puts his finger on a problem this has caused: "There's a whole level missing at Gallo in terms of age." The Gallos will not tolerate being crossed, even by family. Their battle with brother Joseph, who raises cattle and grows grapes, started when Joseph began selling cheese under the Gallo name. Ernest and Julio claimed Joseph was violating their trademark and, they say, offered him a royalty-free license to use the name. When Joseph refused, Ernest and Julio sued him for trademark infringement.

Joseph's lawyer says his research for that suit led to the discovery that the trademark dated back to the father's business. He then researched the father's estate to determine whether Joseph, who was 13 when his father killed himself, was an heir to the trademark. That search, the lawyer says, led to the discoveries that Joseph had inherited an interest in the father's business and that E & J Winery is an outgrowth of that business. Ernest and Julio say Joseph's claim is ridiculous, and that they started the winery with their own savings.

Ernest tries to recruit Ivy Leaguers and young MBAs—nearly all of them men. "We look for creativity, compatibility, and a sense of urgency," he says. But he doesn't give the whiz kids room to grow. Gallo graduates say the most frustrating thing about Ernest is his insistence on keeping everything secret. "I never saw a profit-and-loss statement," says Diana Kelleher, 39, who was marketing manager for several products in the early 1980s and one of the few women executives at Gallo. "Ernest wouldn't tell anyone the cost of raw materials, overhead, or packaging." Kelleher now runs a Los Angeles consulting firm.

Julio has begun to pass his scepter his son, Robert, 52, and son-in-law, James Coleman, 50, oversee much of the day-to-day production. Ernest refuses to give anyone an aerial view of his part of the kingdom. Both his sons, David, 47, and Joseph, 45, work on his side of the business, but neither is heir apparent. Though both graduated from Notre Dame and Joseph has an MBA from Stanford, they lack their father's drive and authority. Those who have worked closely with the family say that Joseph's judgment is uneven and David's behavior occasionally bizarre.

But if Ernest's sons are less prepared to run Gallo than they should be, the problem may have more to do with his management style than their deficiencies. Ernest claims he wants people to be daring, yet his intimidating manner usually produces sycophants. He governs by a committee consisting of his sons and a handful of top executives. On most policy matters, Ernest goes around the table and asks each man for his opinion. But he usually fails to elicit their best because they try to second-guess him. Ernest cannot bear to relinquish control. The deep-rooted need to hold on is understandable: in his world, events can get so wildly out of control that they produce the tragedies of his youth. Call his style shortsighted, even paranoid. Rest assured, though, Ernest has figured out how to sell Gallo products from the grave. He probably is well along on a manual outlining every conceivable war that could break out in the wine world and "ten steps to win each one."

THE CHANGING WINE MARKET

Although the U.S. market is growing, the U.S. total consumption of wines is still only sixth in the world, behind much smaller countries like Spain, Italy, and Argentina (see Exhibit 1). Moreover, the United States is a poor ninth in terms of per capita wine consumption among major countries, fortieth if all countries are included.

Production of wine has always been an international phenomenon (see Exhibit 2). France leads the world in quality wine exports, although individual wines from other areas (including a strong new representation from California) enjoy excellent individual reputations. Such wines usually come from individual vineyards, although starting in the mid-1970s, there were innumerable attempts to reproduce the qualities of the great wines—particularly French wines—by using the same varieties of grapes and similar soil conditions. Although the French have dominated with the concept of the "varietal" wines—those made from only one grape variety—the idea is beginning to spread to other areas. The Italians, in particular, are beginning to specialize, exploiting certain well-regarded grape stocks, their favorable growing climate, and low-cost labor.

New technology has also begun to affect the industry. Until recently, mass-produced wines were simply not stable enough to be transportable and had to be drunk within a few months of fermentation. Wines had to be aged in wood, distilled to kill destructive bacteria, or sweet enough to cope with storage and transport. However, modern technologies of wine processing and storage allow world transport of most varieties. But nearly half the cost of most imported wines is in excise duties and local taxes. Customs duties on wine in developed countries are generally specific to the particular wine and increase with the gradations of the wine and whether it is imported in bottles or bulk containers.

Many changes in technology have to do with the development of special grape varieties designed to appeal to the palates of modern consumers. The French call these varieties "noble," but they tend to be less productive per acre than some of the stronger wine grapes, yielding fewer grapes after more attention has been paid to them. Nevertheless, it is the fermentation process that has changed most. White dry wines formerly tended to be unstable unless they were treated with sulfur. The California industry, however, pioneered a revolution in which the juice is fermented at relatively cool temperatures in cylinders made of stainless steel. The temperature is much easier to control than in traditional wooden vats. And the wine can be kept firmly insulated from the air by means of inert gases. For red wines, tradition dictated that they be kept in wood storage for several years to stand the strains of travel and further storage. This led to stronger, tougher wines which provided energy for the drinker. Now stainless steel, temperature and atmosphere-controlled tanks, and careful measurement and control of the fermentation process allow production and shipment virtually anywhere for markets in which lightness is preferred, fruitiness is desirable, and nourishment is tertiary. (See Exhibit 3.)

THE AMERICAN MARKET

The American market for imported wine is the world's largest and most competitive. While wines were long the beverage of the elite, the large emerging class of professional people and the extended travel habits of Americans have led to a broad geographic and income distribution for imported wines. As the 1980s began, wine consumption was growing in the United States at an annual rate of 6-7%, with estimates for the 1985-1990 era being an average of 6.7% against an earlier growth rate of less than 4%. Wine purchases were growing at over twice the rate for soft drinks and beer, while sales of distilled spirits remained static. The U.S. wine industry responded by producing high-quality "jug wines" on a massive scale at prices which importers found hard to match. A number of well-to-do Californians also formed new boutique wineries to satisfy the emerging tastes for distinctiveness. Nevertheless, imports took over an increasing share of the total American market. In 1960 they accounted for 7% of the market, 10% in 1970, and 21% in 1980. By 1985 the figure was over 25%. The new market was still dominated by some very large players. In 1985 the approximate market shares were as follows:

E & J Gallo	26.1%	
Seagram and Sons	8.3%	
Canandaigua	5.4%	
Brown Forman	5.1%	
National Distillers	4.0%	
Heublein	3.7%	
Imports	25.0%	(approx.)
All others	22.6%	(approx.)

Source: Compiled from *Fortune,* September 1, 1986, and import data modified from world data sources.

An estimated 7% of the U.S. population consumed nearly two-thirds of all table wines sold, and nearly half these people lived in five states: California, New York, Florida, Illinois, and Texas. However, table wine was becoming much more widespread geographically in the mid-1980s. A saying persisted that "every time an old bourbon drinker dies, two wine drinkers come of age." The wine and spirits industry journal, *Impact,* estimated that per capita consumption would reach 5.4 gallons a year by 1990, translating into a sales increase of about 80% over the entire decade. While the mid- and low-priced wine markets became more competitive, the premium segment, which accounted for approximately 10% of the $5.5 billion California wine industry, boomed at a 12% growth rate. However, the resulting rush by the boutique vintners to satisfy this market produced a scattered and often inconsistent offering. Consumers who had earlier embraced common, inexpensive wines began to move to these wines, to imported beers, and to wine coolers. Growth of low-priced California wines had flattened since 1980 and actually fell 5% in 1985. In the mid-1980s, the U.S. wine-producing industry was beginning to undergo many mergers and consolidations as firms moved for scale economies and as foreign wineries and producers sought expanded access to U.S. distribution. For many, the industry was notoriously lacking in profits. As one executive of Christian Brothers said, "You want to know how to make a small fortune in the wine business? Start with a large one."

QUESTIONS

1. Why did Ernest and Julio Gallo choose their particular strategy? What are the strengths and weaknesses of their past strategy?

2. What important environmental and business changes must Gallo Winery deal with in the near future? What strategic alternatives exist?

3. If you were a consultant to the Gallos, how would you approach the issues of strategy implementation posed by the new strategy?

4. If you were competing against the Gallos, what actions would you take? What specific actions should the Gallos take in the near future? Why?

EXHIBIT 1
Wine Consumption
Comparison by Country

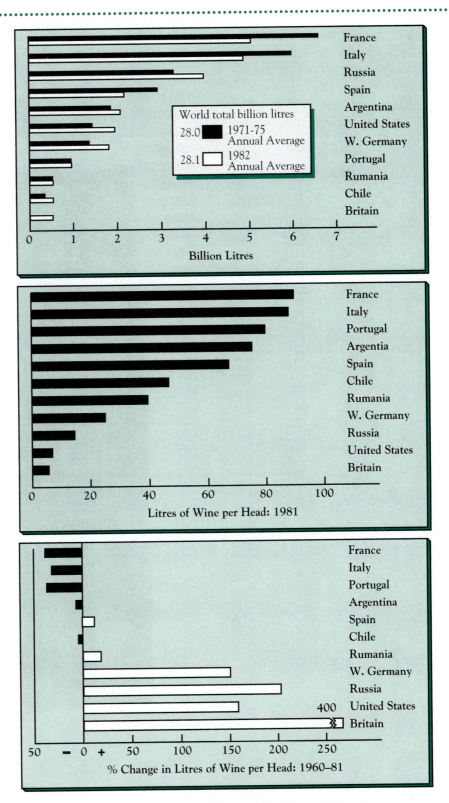

Note: 1971–81 annual average for the world was 28 billion litres; for 1982 it was 28.1 billion litres.
Source: "A Difficult Vintage: A Special Survey," *The Economist,* December 24, 1983.

EXHIBIT 2
The Big Producers

Area in production: 1982
(in thousands of hectares)

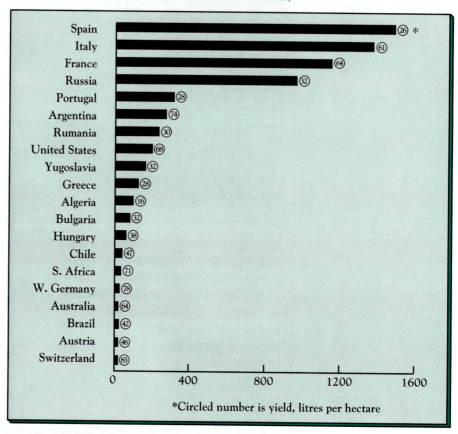

Source: "A Difficult Vintage: A Special Survey," The Economist, December 24, 1983.

EXHIBIT 3
French Wine Exports
(in millions of litres)

Defying All Comers

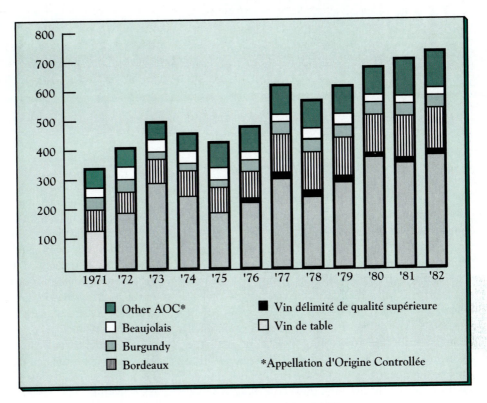

Other AOC*

Beaujolais

Burgundy

Bordeaux

Vin délimité de qualité supérieure

Vin de table

*Appellation d'Origine Controllée

Source: "A Difficult Vintage: A Special Survey," *The Economist*, December 24, 1983.

The decision by the management of the International Business Machines Corp. to produce a new family of computers, called the System/360, was one of the most crucial and portentous—as well as perhaps the riskiest—business judgments of recent times. The decision committed IBM to laying out money in sums that read like the federal budget of that time—some $5 billion over a period of four years. To launch the 360, IBM was forced into sweeping organizational changes, with executives rising and falling with the changing tides of battle. The very character of this large and influential company was significantly altered by the ordeal of the 360, and the way it thought about itself changed, too. Bob Evans, the line manager who had the major responsibility for designing this gamble of a corporate lifetime, was only half joking when he said: "We called this project 'You bet your company.'"

Evans insisted that the 360 "was a damn good risk, and a lot less risk than it would have been to do anything else, or to do nothing at all," and there is a lot of evidence to support him. . . . A long stride ahead in the technology of computers in commercial use was taken by the 360. So sweeping were the implications that it required ten years before there was enough data to evaluate the wisdom of the whole undertaking.

The new System/360 was intended to obsolete virtually all other existing computers—including those being offered by IBM itself. Thus, the first and most

Case compilation copyright © 1995 by James Brian Quinn. The first part of the case is drawn from a two-part series: T. A. Wise, "IBM's $5 Billion Gamble," and "The Rocky Road to the Marketplace," *Fortune*, September–October 1966. Copyright © 1966 Time, Inc. All rights reserved to original copyright holder. Reproduced by permission. The later part of the case is based on the 1983 IBM (C) case written by Professor Quinn and revised in 1995.

extraordinary point to note about this decision was that it involved a challenge to the marketing structure of the computer industry—an industry that the challenger itself had dominated overwhelmingly for nearly a decade. It was roughly as though General Motors had decided to scrap its existing makes and models and offer in their place one new line of cars, covering the entire spectrum of demand, with a radically redesigned engine and an exotic fuel. . . .

[In 1966] there were perhaps 35,000 computers in use, and it was estimated that there would be 85,000 by 1975. IBM sat astride this exploding market, accounting for something like two-thirds of the worldwide business—that is, the dollar value of general-purpose computers then installed or on order. IBM's share of this market [in 1965] represented about 77% of the company's $3.6 billion gross revenues [and $477 million of profits].

Several separate but interrelated steps were involved in the launching of System/360. Each one of the steps involved major difficulties, and taking them all meant that IBM was accepting a staggering challenge to its management capabilities. First, the 360 depended heavily on microcircuitry, [at the time] an advanced technology in the field of computers. IBM's second-generation machine, which used transistors instead of tubes, [had] 5,000 components per cubic foot. The System/360 model 75 computer, using hybrid microcircuitry, involved 30,000 components per cubic foot. . . .

Second was the provision for compatibility—that is, as the users' computer requirements grew they could move up from one machine to another without having to discard or rewrite already existing programs. Limited compatibility had already been achieved by IBM, and by some of its competitors too, for that matter, on machines of similar design but different power. But it had never been achieved on a broad line of computers with a wide range of powers, and achieving this compatibility depended as much on developing compatible programs or "software" as it did on the hardware. All the auxiliary machines—"peripheral equipment" as they are called in the trade—had to be designed so that they could feed information into or receive information from the central processing unit; this meant that the equipment had to have timing, voltage, and signal levels matching those of the central unit. In computerese, the peripheral equipment was to have "standard interface." The head of one competing computer manufacturing company acknowledges that at the time of the System/360 announcement he regarded the IBM decision as sheer folly and doubted that IBM would be able to produce or deliver a line that was completely compatible.

Finally—and this was the boldest and most perilous part of the plan—it was decided that six main units of the 360 line, originally designated models 30, 40, 50, 62, and 70, should be announced and made available simultaneously. (Models at the lower and higher ends of the line were to be announced later.) This meant that all parts of the company would have to adhere to a meticulous schedule.

UP IN MANUFACTURING, DOWN IN CASH

The effort involved in the program was enormous. IBM spent over half a billion dollars on research and development programs associated with the 360. This involved a tremendous hunt for talent: by the end of 1966, one-third of IBM's 190,000 employees had been hired since the new program was announced. Between that time—April 7, 1964—and the end of 1967, the company opened five new plants in the United States and abroad and had budgeted a total of $4.5 billion for rental machines, plant, and equipment. Not even the Manhattan Project, which produced the atomic bomb in World War II, cost so much (the government's costs up to Hiroshima are reckoned at $2 billion), nor, probably, had any other privately financed commercial project in history.*

Such an effort changed IBM's nature in several ways:

The company, which was essentially an assembler of computer components and a business-service organization, became a major manufacturing concern as well. It became the world's largest maker of integrated circuits, producing an estimated 150 million of the hybrid variety annually in the late 1960s.

* Editor's note: Multiply these figures by about 20 for 1990s comparability.

After some ambivalence, IBM abandoned any notion that it was simply another American company with a large foreign operation. The view became that IBM is a fully integrated international company, in which the managers of overseas units are presumed to have the same capabilities and responsibilities as those in the U.S. The company's World Trade subsidiary stopped trying to develop its own computers; instead, it marketed the 360 overseas, and helped in the engineering and manufacturing of the 360.

The company's table of organization was restructured significantly at least three times during the 360's development cycle. Several new divisions and their executives emerged, while others suffered total or partial eclipse. An old maxim of the IBM organization was that few men rose to line executive positions unless they had spent some time selling. A new group of technically oriented executives came to the forefront for the first time, diluting some of the traditional power of the marketing function in the corporation.

THE MISSIONARIES AND THE SCIENTISTS

Oddly enough, the upheaval at IBM went largely unnoticed. The company was able to make itself over more or less in private. It was able to do so partly because IBM was so widely assumed to be an organization in which the unexpected simply didn't happen. Outsiders viewing IBM presumed it to be a model of rationality and order—a presumption related to the company's products which are, of course, instruments that enable (and require) their users to think clearly about management.

This image of IBM, moreover, had been furthered over the years by the styles of the two Watsons. Tom Watson, Sr., combined an intense devotion to disciplined thinking with formal, rather Victorian attitudes about conduct, clothes, and courtesy. The senior Watson's hostility toward drinking, and his demand that employees dedicate themselves totally to the welfare of the corporation, created a kind of evangelical atmosphere. When Tom Watson, Jr., took over from his father in 1956, the manner and style shifted somewhat, but the missionary zeal remained—now overlaid by a new dedication to the disciplines of science. The overlay reinforced the image of IBM as a chillingly efficient organization, one in which plans were developed logically and executed with crisp efficiency. It was hard to envision the company in a gambling role.

The dimensions of the 360 gamble are difficult to state precisely. The company's executives, who are used to thinking of risks and payoffs in hard quantitative terms, insisted that no meaningful figure could ever be put on the gamble—that is, on the odds that the program would be brought off on schedule, or on the costs involved if it failed.

OUTSAILING THE BOSS

At the time, it scarcely seemed that any gamble at all was necessary. IBM was way out ahead of the competition, and looked as if it could continue smoothly in its old ways forever. Below the surface, though, IBM's organization didn't fit the changing markets so neatly anymore, and there really was, in Evans's phrase, a risk involved in doing nothing.

No one understood this more thoroughly, or with more sense of urgency, than one of the principal decision makers of the company, T. Vincent Learson. His entire career at IBM, which began in 1935, had been concerned with getting new products to market. In 1954 he was tapped by young Tom Watson as the man to spearhead the company's first big entry into the commercial computer field—with the 702 and 705 models. His success led to his promotion to vice president and group executive in 1956. In 1959 he took over both of the company's computer development and manufacturing operations, the General Products Division and the Data Systems Division.

Learson stood 6 foot 6 and was a tough and forceful personality. When he was managing any major IBM program, he tended to be impatient with staff reports and committees, and to operate outside the conventional chain of command; if he wanted to know why a program was behind schedule, he was apt to call directly on an executive at a much lower level who might help him find out. But he often operated indirectly, too, organizing major management changes without his own hands being visible to those involved. Though he lacked the formal scientific background that is taken for granted in many areas of IBM, Learson had a reputation as a searching and persistent questioner about any proposals brought before him; executives who had not done their homework might find their presentations falling apart under his questions—and might also find that he would continue the inquisition in a way that made their failure an object lesson to any spectators. And Learson was the most vigorous supporter of the company's attitude that a salesman who had lost an order without exhausting all the resources the company had to back him up deserved to be drawn and quartered.

At IBM, Learson was known as demanding, domineering, and direct—given to calling people anywhere in the company to find out firsthand what was going on. But Learson was also known as a friendly and whimsical man who was IBM's number one cheerleader. He delighted in showing up unannounced, whether in a hospital to cheer up one of his sick secretaries or at a retirement dinner in Boston for a lady who ran a course in keypunching there when Learson was a young salesman. For all the diverging views of Learson, the man, as a top executive the degree of loyalty that Learson inspired was remarkable. Said one former executive, who was forced out of IBM, "I admire the man. He's like General Patton—someone you follow into battle."

Learson's personal competitiveness was something of a legend at IBM. It was significantly demonstrated in the Newport-to-Bermuda yacht race, in which Learson entered his own boat, the *Thunderbird*. He boned up on the history of the race in past years, and managed to get a navigator who had been on a winning boat three different times. He also persuaded Bill Lapworth, the famous boat designer, to be a crewman. Learson traveled personally to California to get one of the best spinnaker men available. All these competitive efforts were especially fascinating to the people at IBM because Tom Watson, Jr., also had an entry in the Bermuda race; he'd, in fact, been competing in it for years. Before the race Watson good-humoredly warned Learson at a board meeting that he'd better not win if he expected to stay at IBM. Learson's answer was not recorded. But Learson won the race. Watson's *Palowan* finished twenty-fourth on corrected time.

When Learson took over the computer group he found himself supervising two major engineering centers that had been competing with each other for some time. The General Products Division's facility in Endicott, New York, produced the low-priced 1401 model, by far the most popular of all IBM's computers—or of anyone else's to that date; something like 10,000 of them had been installed by the mid-1960s. Meanwhile, the Data Systems Division in Poughkeepsie made the more glamorous 7000 series, of which the 7090 was the most powerful. Originally, IBM had intended that the two centers operate in separate markets, but as computer prices came down in the late 1950s and as more versions of each model were offered, their markets came to overlap—and they entered a period in which they were increasingly penetrating each other's markets, heightening the feeling of rivalry. Each had its own development program, although any decision to produce or market a new computer, of course, had to be ratified at corporate headquarters. The rivalry between the two divisions was to become an element in, and be exacerbated by, the decision to produce the 360.

Both the 1401 and the 7000 series were selling well in 1960. But computer engineers and architects are a restless breed; they are apt to be thinking of improvements in design or circuitry five minutes after the specifications of their latest machines are frozen. In the General Products Division, most such thinking in 1960 and 1961 was long term; it was assumed that the 1401 would be on the market until about 1968. The thinking at the Data Systems Division concerned both long-range and more immediate matters.

A $20 MILLION STRETCH

One of the immediate matters was the division's "Stretch" computer, which was already on the market but having difficulties. The computer had been designed to dwarf all others in size and power, and it was priced around $13,500,000. But it never met more than 70 percent of the promised specifications, and not many of them were sold. In May 1961, Tom Watson made the decision that the price of Stretch should be cut to $8 million to match the value of its performance—at which level Stretch was plainly uneconomic to produce. He had to make the decision, it happened, just before he was to fly to California and address an industry group on the subject of progress in the computer field.

Before he left for the coast, an annoyed Watson made a few tart remarks about the folly of getting involved in large and overambitious projects that you couldn't deliver on. In his speech, he admitted that Stretch was a flop. "Our greatest mistake in Stretch," he said, "is that we walked up to the plate and pointed at the left-field stands. When we swung, it was not a homer but a hard line drive to the outfield. We're going to be a good deal more careful about what we promise in the future." Soon after he returned the program was quietly shelved; only seven of the machines were ultimately put in operation. IBM's overall loss on the program was about $20 million.

The Stretch fiasco had two consequences. One was that the company practically ignored the giant-computer field during the next two years—and thereby enabled Control Data to get a sizable headstart in the

market. Customers were principally government and university research centers, where the most complex scientific problems are tackled and computers of tremendous power are required. Eventually, in 1963, Watson pointed out that his strictures against overambitious projects had not been meant to exclude IBM from this scientific market, and the company later tried to get back into it. Its entry was to be the 360-90, the most powerful machine of the new line.

A second consequence of the Stretch fiasco was that Learson and the people under him, especially those in the Data Systems Division, were under special pressure to be certain that the next big project was thought out more carefully and that it worked exactly as promised. As it happened, the project the division had in mind in 1960–1961 was a fairly ambitious one: it was for a line of computers, tentatively called the 8000 series, that would replace the 7000 series, and would also provide a limited measure of compatibility among the four models projected. The 8000 series was based on transistor technology, and therefore still belonged to the second generation; however, there had been so much recent progress in circuitry design and transistor performance that the series had considerably more capability than anything being offered by IBM at that time.

The principal sponsor of the 8000 concept was Fred Brooks, head of systems planning for the Poughkeepsie division. An imaginative, enthusiastic 29-year-old North Carolinian with a considerable measure of southern charm, Brooks became completely dedicated to the concept of the new series, and beginning in late 1960 he began trying to enlist support for it. He had a major opportunity to make his case for the 8000 program at a briefing for the division's management, which was held at Poughkeepsie in January 1961.

By all accounts, he performed well: he was relaxed, confident, informed on every aspect of the technology involved, and persuasive about the need for a change. Data Systems' existing product line, he argued, was a mixed bag. The capability of some models overlapped that of others, while still other capabilities were unavailable in any model. The 8000 series would end all this confusion. One machine was already built, cost estimates and a market forecast had been made, a pricing schedule had been completed, and Brooks proposed announcing the series late that year or early in 1962. It could be the division's basic product line until 1968, he added. Most of Brooks' audience found his case entirely persuasive.

ENTER THE MAN FROM HEADQUARTERS

Learson, however, was not ready to be sold so easily. The problems with Stretch must have been on his mind, and probably tended to make him look hard at any big new proposals. Beyond that, he was skeptical that the 8000 series would minimize the confusion in the division's product line, and he wondered whether the concept might not even *contribute* to the confusion. Learson had received a long memorandum from his chief assistant, Don Spaulding, on the general subject of equipment proliferation. Spaulding argued that there were already too many different computers in existence, and that they required too many supporting programs and too much peripheral equipment; some drastic simplification of the industry's merchandise was called for.

With these thoughts in mind, Learson was not persuaded that Brooks' concept was taking IBM in the right direction. Finally, he was not persuaded that the company should again invest heavily in second-generation technology. Along with a group of computer users, he had recently attended a special course on industrial dynamics that was being given at the Massachusetts Institute of Technology. Much of the discussion had been over his head, he later recalled, but from what his classmates were saying he came away with the clear conviction that computer applications would soon be expanding rapidly, and that what was needed was a bold move away from "record keeping" and toward more sophisticated business applications.

There was soon direct evidence of Learson's skepticism about the 8000 series. Shortly after the briefing Bob Evans, who was then manager of processing systems in the General Products Division, was dispatched to Poughkeepsie as head of Data Systems' planning and development. He brought along a number of men who had worked with him in Endicott. Given the rivalry between the two divisions, it is not very surprising that he received a cool welcome. His subsequent attitude toward the 8000 concept ensured that his relations with Brooks would stay cool.

Evans made several different criticisms of the concept. The main one was that the proposed line was "nonhomogeneous"—that is, it was not designed throughout to combine scientific and business applications. Further, he contended that it lacked sufficient compatibility within the line. It would compound the proliferation problem. He also argued that it was time to turn to the technologies associated with integrated circuits.

BLOOD ON THE FLOOR

For various reasons, including timing, Brooks was opposed, and he and Evans fought bitterly for several months. At one point Evans called him and quietly mentioned that Brooks was getting a raise in salary. Brooks started to utter a few words of thanks when Evans said flatly, "I want you to know I had nothing to do with it."

In March 1961, Brooks had a chance to make a presentation to the corporate management committee, a group that included Tom Watson, his brother, A. K. Watson, who headed the World Trade Corp., Albert Williams, who was then president of the corporation (later chairman of the executive committee), and Learson. Brooks made another effective presentation, and for a while he and his allies thought that the 8000 might be approved after all.

But early in May it became clear that Evans was the winner. His victory was formalized in a meeting, at the Gideon Putnam Hotel in Saratoga, of all the key people who had worked on the 8000. There, on May 15, Evans announced that the 8000 project was dead and that he now had the tough job of reassigning them all to other tasks. In the words of one participant, "There was blood all over the floor."

Evans now outlined some new programs for the Data Systems Division. His short-term program called for an extension of the 7000 line, both upward and downward. At the lower end of the line there would be two new models, the 7040 and 7044. At the upper end there would be a 7094 and a 7094 II. This program was generally noncontroversial, except for the fact that the 7044 had almost exactly the same capabilities as a computer called Scamp, which was being proposed by another part of IBM. It would obviously make no sense to build both computers; and, as it happened, Scamp had some powerful support.

Scamp was a small scientific computer developed originally for the European market. Its principal designer was John Fairclough, a young man (he was then 30) working in the World Trade Corp.'s Hursley Laboratory, sixty miles southwest of London. The subsidiary had a sizable stake in Scamp. It had been trying for many years to produce a computer tailored to the needs of its own markets, but had repeatedly failed, and had therefore been obliged to sell American-made machines overseas.

But Scamp looked especially promising, and the subsidiary's executives, including Fairclough and A. K. Watson, were confident that it would meet American standards. It had previously tested well and attracted a fair amount of attention in IBM's American laboratories. Evans himself came to Hursley to look at it, and was impressed. But its similarity to the 7044 finally took Fairclough and some associates to the United States to test their machine against a 7044 prototype.

MERE EQUALITY WON'T DO

As things turned out, Scamp did about as well as the 7044—but, also as things turned out, that wasn't good enough. Evans and Learson were resolved to stretch out the 7000 line, but opposed to anything that would add to proliferation. In principle, A. K. Watson, who had always run World Trade as a kind of personal fiefdom, could have stepped in and ordered the production of Scamp on his own authority. In practice, he decided the argument against proliferation was a valid one. And so, in the end, he personally gave the order to drop Scamp. Fairclough got the news one day soon after he had returned to England, and he found himself with a sizable staff that had to be reassigned. He says that he considered resigning, but instead worked off his annoyance by sipping Scotch and brooding much of the night.

Evans and Learson had also agreed that Data Systems should try its hand at designing a computer line that would blanket the market. The General Products Division was asked to play a role in the new design, but its response was lukewarm, so the bulk of the work at this stage fell to Data Systems. The project was dubbed NPL, for new product line; the name System/360 was not settled on until much later. To head the project, Evans selected his old adversary Brooks—a move that surprised a large number of IBM executives, including Brooks himself.

Still smarting over the loss of the 8000 project, and suspicious that the NPL was just a "window-dressing" operation, Brooks accepted the job only tentatively. To work with him, and apparently to ensure the NPL did not end up as the 8000 under a new name, Evans brought Gene Amdahl, a crack designer whom the company had called on to work on several earlier computers. However, Amdahl's influence was offset by that of another designer, Gerrit Blaauw, a veteran and past supporter of the 8000 project. Brooks' group received enough money to show that the company took NPL seriously (the first-year appropriation was $3,800,000), but Amdahl and Blaauw disagreed on design concepts, and the project floundered until November 1961.

Even to the trained eye IBM's main divisions appeared to be in excellent health in the summer of 1961. The General Products Division, according to Evans, was "fat and dumb and happy" in the lower end of the market, selling the 1401 at a furious rate, and still feeling secure about its line through about 1968. The World Trade Corp. was growing rapidly, although it had suffered its third major setback on getting a computer line of its own. The Data Systems Division was extending its old 7000 line to meet the competition, and working on the NPL.

THE PROLIFERATING PRODUCTS

But it was around this time that Tom Watson and Learson—then a group executive vice president, and nominally at least working under Albert Williams, the company president—developed several large concerns. There was the absence of any clear, overall concept of the company's product line; 15 or 20 different engineering groups scattered throughout the company were generating different computer products, and while the products were in most cases superior, the proliferation was putting overwhelming strains on the company's ability to supply programming for customers. The view at the top was that IBM required some major changes if it expected to stay ahead in the computer market when the third generation came along.

Between August and October 1961, Watson and Learson initiated a number of dialogues with their divisional lieutenants in an effort to define a strategy for the new era. By the end of October, though, neither of them believed that any strategy was coming into focus. At this point Learson made a crucial decision. He decided to set up a special committee, composed of representatives from every major segment of the company, to formulate some policy guidance. The committee was called SPREAD—an acronym for systems programming, research, engineering, and development. Its chairman was John Haanstra, then a vice president of the General Products Division. There were 12 other members, including Evans, Brooks, and Fairclough.

THE SPREAD COMMITTEE—FALL 1961

The SPREAD Committee was conducted informally, but with a good amount of spirited discussion. For the same purposes it broke up into separate committees, such as one on programming capability. Haanstra, as one member put it, acted as a hammer on the committee anvil, forcing ideas into debate and demanding definitions. Still, there was some feeling that Haanstra was bothered by the fact that the group was heavily represented by "big machine"-oriented managers.

The progress of the committee during November was steady, but it was also, in Learson's view, "hellishly slow." Suddenly Haanstra found himself promoted to the presidency of the General Products Division and Bob Evans took over as chairman of SPREAD. The committee meetings were held in the New Englander Motor Hotel, just north of Stamford, Connecticut. In effect, although not quite literally, Learson locked the doors and told the members that they couldn't get out until they had reached some conclusions.

While Evans accelerated the pace of the sessions somewhat, Fred Brooks increasingly emerged as the man who was shaping the direction of the committee recommendations. This was not very surprising, for he and his group had had a headstart in thinking out many of the issues. By December 28, 1961, the SPREAD Committee had hammered out an 80-page statement of its recommendations. On January 4, 1962, the committee amplified the report for the benefit of the 50 top executives of the corporation.

Brooks was assigned the role of principal speaker on this occasion. The presentation was split into several parts and took an entire day. The main points of the report were:

> There was a definite need for a single, compatible family of computers ranging from one with the smallest existing core memory, which would be below the 1401 line, to one as powerful as IBM's biggest—at that time the 7094. In fact, the needs were said to extend beyond the IBM range, but the report expressed doubt that compatibility could be extended that far.

> The new line should not be aimed simply at replacing the popular 1401 or 7000 series, but at opening up whole new fields of computer applications. At that time compatibility between those machines and the new line was not judged to be of major importance, because the original timetable on the appearance of the various members of the new family of computers stretched out for several years.

> The System/360 must have both business and scientific applications. This dual purpose was a difficult assignment because commercial machines accept large amounts of data but have little manipulative ability, while scientific machines work on relatively small quantities of data that are endlessly manipulated. To achieve duality the report decided that each machine in the new line would be made available with core memories of varying sizes. In addition, the machine would provide a variety of technical and esoteric features to handle both scientific and commercial assignments.

> Information input and output equipment, and all other peripheral equipment, must have "standard interface"—so that various types and sizes of peripheral equipment could be hitched to the main computer without missing a beat. This too was to become an important feature of the new line.

Learson recalled the reaction when the presentation ended. "There were all sorts of people up there and while it wasn't received too well, there were no real objections. So I said to them, 'All right, we'll do it.' The problem was, they thought it was too grandiose. The report said we'd have to spend $125 million on programming the system at a time when we were spending only about $10 million a year for programming. Everybody said you just couldn't spend that amount. The job just looked too big to the marketing people, the financial people, and the engineers. Everyone recognized it was a gigantic task that would mean all our resources were tied up in one project—and we knew that for a long time we wouldn't be getting anything out of it."

THE PUBLIC ANNOUNCEMENT

When Tom Watson, Jr., made what he called "the most important product announcement in the company's history," he created quite a stir. International Business Machines is not a corporation given to making earth-shaking pronouncements casually, and the declaration that it was launching an entirely new computer line, the System/360, was headline news. The elaborate logistics that IBM worked out in order to get maximum press coverage—besides a huge assembly at Poughkeepsie, IBM staged press conferences on the same day in 62 cities in the United States and in 14 foreign countries—underscored its view of the importance of the event. And the fact that the move until then had been a closely guarded secret added an engaging element of surprise. . . . In the scattered locations where IBM plans, builds, and sells its products, there was, on that evening of April 7, 1964, a certain amount of dancing in the streets. . . .

But the managerial and organizational changes that were brought about by the company's struggle to settle on, and then to produce and market, the new line [had very long-term] effects. In each of these several aspects, past, present, and future were closely intertwined.

THE RISING COST OF ASKING QUESTIONS

No part of the whole adventure of launching System/360 was as tough, as stubborn, or as enduring as the programming. Early in 1966, talking to a group of IBM customers, Tom Watson, Jr., said ruefully: "We are investing nearly as much in System/360 programming as we are in the entire development of System/360 hardware. A few months ago the bill for 1966 was going to be $40 million. I asked Vin Learson last night before I left what he thought it would be for 1966 and he said $50 million. Twenty-four hours later I met Watts Humphrey, who is in charge of programming production, in the hall here and said, "Is this figure about right? Can I use it?" He said it's going to be $60 million. You can see that if I keep asking questions we won't pay a dividend this year."

Watson's concern about programming went back to the beginnings of the System/360 affair. By late 1962 he was sufficiently aware of the proportions of the question to invite the eight top executives of IBM to his ski lodge in Stowe, Vermont, for a three-day session on programming. The session was conducted by Fred Brooks, the corporate manager for the design of the 360 project, and other experts; they went into the programming in considerable detail. While the matter can become highly technical, in general IBM's objective was to devise an "operating system" for its computer line, so that the computers would schedule themselves, without manual interruption, and would be kept working continuously at or near their capacity. At the time it announced System/360, IBM promised future users that it would supply them with such a command system.

Delivery on that promise was agonizingly difficult. Even though Tom Watson and the other top executives knew the critical importance of programming, the size of the job was seriously underestimated. The difficulty of coordinating the work of hundreds of programmers was enormous. The operating system IBM was striving for required the company to work out many new ideas and approaches; as one company executive said, "We were trying to schedule inventions, which is a dangerous thing to do in a committed project." Customers came up with more extensive programming tasks than the company had expected, and there were inevitable delays and slowdowns. The difficulties of programming prevented some users from getting the full benefits from their new machines for years. The company didn't have most of the bugs out of the larger systems' programming until at least mid-1967—well behind its expectations.

THE COLD REALITIES OF CHOICE

In technology, IBM was also breaking new ground. During the formative years of the decisions about the technology of System/360, a lengthy report on the subject was prepared by the *ad hoc* Logic Committee, headed by Erich Bloch, a specialist in circuitry for IBM. Eventually, the Logic Committee report led to the company's formal commitment to a new hybrid kind of integrated-circuit technology—a move that, like many other aspects of the 360 decision, is still criticized by some people in the computer industry, both inside and outside of IBM.

The move, though, was hardly made in haste. The whole computer industry had raced through two phases of electronic technology—vacuum tubes and transistors—between 1951 and 1960. By the late 1950s it was becoming apparent that further technological changes of sweeping importance were in the offing. At that time, however, IBM was not very much of a force in scientific research, its strengths lying in the assembling and marketing of computers, not in their advanced concepts. The company's management at the time had the wit to recognize the nature of the corporate deficiency, and to see the importance of correcting it. In 1956, IBM hired Dr. Emanuel Piore, formerly chief scientist of U.S. naval research. Piore became IBM's director of research and a major figure in the technological direction that the company finally chose for its System/360.

In the end, the choice narrowed to two technologies. One was monolithic integrated circuitry: putting all the elements of a circuit—transistors, resistors, and diodes—on one chip at one time. The other was hybrid integrated circuitry—IBM rather densely termed it "solid logic technology"—which means making transistors and diodes separately and then soldering them into place. In 1961 the Logic Committee decided that the production of monolithic circuits in great quantities would be risky, and in any case would not meet the schedule for any new line of computers to be marketed by 1964.

There was little opposition to this recommendation initially, except among a few engineering purists. Later, however, the opposition strengthened. The purists believed that monolithic circuits were sure to come, and that the company in a few years would find itself frozen into a technology that might be obsolete before the investment could be recovered. However, the Logic Committee's recommendation on the hybrid approach was accepted; since that time, Watson has referred to the acceptance as "the most fortunate decision we ever made."

THE SECRETS CIRCUITS HIDE

The decision to move into hybrid integrated technology accelerated IBM's push into component manufacturing, a basic change in the character of the company. In the day of vacuum tubes and transistors, IBM had designed the components for its circuits, ordered them from other companies (a principal supplier: Texas Instruments), then assembled them to its own specifications. But with the new circuitry, those specifications would have to be built into the components from the outset. "Too much proprietary information was involved in circuitry production," said Watson. "Unless we did it ourselves, we could be turning over some of the essentials of our business to another company. We had no intention of doing that." In addition, of course, IBM saw no reason why it should not capture some of the profit from the manufacturing that it was creating on such a large scale.

The company's turn to a new technology jibed neatly with a previous decision made in 1960 by Watson at the urging of the man who was then IBM president, Al Williams, that the company should move into component manufacturing. By the time the decision to go into hybrid circuits was made, IBM already had started putting together a component manufacturing division. Its general manager was John Gibson, a Johns Hopkins Ph.D. in electrical engineering. Under Gibson, the new division won the authority, hitherto divided among other divisions of the company, to designate and to buy the components for computer hardware, along with a new authority to manufacture them when Gibson thought it appropriate.

This new assignment of responsibility was resented by managers in the Data Systems and General Products divisions, since it represented a limitation of their authority. Also, they protested that they would be unable to compare the price and quality of inhouse components with those made by an outside supplier if they lost their independence of action. But Vincent Learson, then group executive vice president, feared that if they kept their independence they would continue to make purchases outside the company, and that IBM as a consequence would have no market for its own component output. He therefore put the power of decision in Gibson's hands. IBM's board, in effect, ruled in Gibson's favor when, in 1962, it authorized the construction of a new manufacturing plant, and the purchase of its automatic equipment, at a cost of over $100 million.

SYSTEMS DESIGN: WORLDWIDE

While IBM was making up its corporate mind about the technology for System/360, the delegation of specific responsibilities was going ahead. Learson designated Bob Evans, now head of the Federal Systems Division, to manage the giant undertaking. Under Evans, Fred Brooks was put in charge of all the System/360 work being done at Poughkeepsie, where four of the original models were designed; he was also made manager of the overall design of the central processors. The plant at Endicott was given the job of designing the model 30, successor to the popular 1401, which had been developed there. And John Fairclough, a systems designer at World Trade, was assigned to design the model 40 at the IBM lab at Hursley, England.

Out of the Hursley experience came an interesting byproduct that had significant implications for IBM's future. With different labs engaged in the 360 design, it was vital to provide for virtually instant communication between them. IBM therefore leased a special transatlantic line between its home offices and the engineers in England, and later in Germany. The international engineering group was woven together with considerable effectiveness, giving IBM the justifiable claim that the 360 computer was probably the first product of truly international design.

IN A TUG-OF-WAR, ENOUGH ROPE TO HANG YOURSELF

Even in a corporation inured to change, people resist change. By 1963, with the important decisions on the 360 being implemented, excitement about the new product line began to spread through the corporation—at least among those who were privy to the secret. But this rising pitch of interest by no means meant that the struggle inside the company was settled. The new family of computers cut across all the old lines of authority and upset all the old divisions. The System/360 concepts plunged IBM into an organizational upheaval.

Resistance came in only a mild form from the World Trade Corp., whose long-time boss was A. K. Watson, Tom's brother. World Trade managers always thought of European markets as very different from those in the United States, and as requiring special considerations that U.S. designers would not give them. Initially they had reservations about the concept of a single computer family, which they thought of as fitted only to U.S. needs. But when IBM laboratories in

Europe were included in the formulation of the design of some of the 360 models, the grumblings from World Trade were muted. Later A. K. Watson was made vice chairman of the corporation and Gilbert Jones, formerly the head of domestic marketing of computers for the company, took over World Trade. These moves further integrated the domestic and foreign operations, and gave World Trade assurance that its voice would be heard at the top level of the corporation.

The General Products Division, for its part, really bristled with hostility. Its output, after all, accounted for two-thirds of the company's revenues for data processing. It had a popular and profitable product in the field, the 1401, which the 360 threatened to replace. The executive in charge of General Products, John Haanstra, fought against some phases of the 360 program. Haanstra thought the new line would hit his division hard. He was concerned, from the time the System/360 program was approved, about the possibility that it would undermine his division's profits. Specifically, he feared that the cost of providing compatibility in the lower end of the 360 line (which would be General Products' responsibility) might price the machines out of the market. Later he was to develop some more elaborate arguments against the program.

Long after the company's SPREAD Committee had outlined the System/360 concept, and it had been endorsed by IBM's top management, there were numerous development efforts going on inside the company that offered continuing alternatives to the concept—and they were taken seriously enough, in some cases, so that there were fights for jurisdiction over them. Early in 1963, for example, there was a row over development work at IBM's San Jose Laboratory, which belonged to the General Products Division. It turned out that San Jose—which had been explicitly told to stop the work—was still developing a low-power machine similar to the one being worked on in World Trade's German lab. When he heard about the continuing effort, A. K. Watson went to the lab, along with Emanuel Piore, and seems to have angrily restated his demand that San Jose cut it out. Some people from San Jose were then transferred to Germany to work on the German machine, and the General Products effort was stopped. In the curious way of organizations, though, things turned out well enough in the end; the German machine proved to be a good one, and the Americans who came into the project contributed a lot to its salability. With some adaptations, the machine was finally incorporated into the 360 line,

and, as the model 20 it later sold better than probably any other in the series.

TOP MANAGEMENT SHIFTS

In the fall of 1963, Tom Watson . . . made some new management assignments that reflected the impact of the 360 program on the corporation. Learson was shifted away from supervising product development and given responsibility for marketing, this being the next phase of the 360 program. Gibson took over Learson's former responsibilities. The increasing development of IBM into a homogeneous international organization was reflected in the move up of A. K. Watson from World Trade to corporate vice chairman. He was succeeded by Gilbert Jones, former head of domestic marketing. Piore became a group vice president in charge of research and several other activities.

One reason for Watson's interest in speeding up the 360 program in late 1963 was an increasing awareness that the IBM product line was running out of steam. The company was barely reaching its sales goals in this period. Some of this slowdown, no doubt, was due to mounting rumors about the new line. But there was another, critical reason for the slowdown: major customers were seeking ways of linking separate data-processing operations on a national basis, and IBM had limited capability along that line. Finally, IBM got a distinctly unpleasant shock in December 1963, when the Honeywell Corp. announced a new computer. Its model 200 had been designed along the same lines as the 1401—a fact Honeywell cheerfully acknowledged—but it used newer, faster, and cheaper transistors than the 1401 and was therefore priced 30 percent below the IBM model. To make matters worse, Honeywell's engineers had figured out a means by which customers interested in reprogramming from an IBM 1401 to a Honeywell 200 could do so inexpensively. The vulnerability of the 1401 line was obvious, and so was the company's need for the new line of computers.

It was around this time that some IBM executives began to argue seriously for simultaneous introduction of the whole 360 family. There were several advantages to the move. One was that it would have a tremendous public relations impact and demonstrate the distinctive nature of IBM's new undertaking. Customers would have a clear picture of where and how they could grow with the computer product line, and so would be more inclined to wait for it. Finally, there might be an antitrust problem in introducing the various 360 models sequentially. The Justice Department might feel that an IBM salesman was improperly taking away competitors' business if he urged customers not to buy their products because of an impending announcement of his own company's new model. IBM had long had a company policy under which no employee was allowed to tell a customer of any new product not formally announced by the management. (Several employees have, in fact, been fired or disciplined for violating the rule.) Announcing the whole 360 line at once would dispose of the problem.

LEARSON STAGES A SHOOT-OUT

Beginning in late 1963, then, the idea of announcing and marketing the 360 family all at once gained increasing support. At the same time, by making the 360 program tougher to achieve, the idea gave Haanstra some new arguments against the program. His opposition now centered on two main points. First, he argued that the General Products manufacturing organization would be under pressure to build in a couple of years enough units of the model 30 to replace a field inventory of the 1401 that had been installed over a five-year period. He said that IBM was in danger of acquiring a huge backlog, one representing perhaps two or three years' output, and that competitors, able to deliver in a year or less, would steal business away.

But Haanstra's argument was countered to some extent by a group of resourceful IBM engineers. They believed that the so-called "read-only" storage device could be adapted to make the 360-30 compatible with the 1401. The read-only technique, which involved the storing of permanent electronic instructions in the computer, could be adapted to make the model 30 act like a 1401 in many respects: the computer would be slowed down, but the user would be able to employ his 1401 programs. IBM executives had earlier been exposed to a read-only device by John Fairclough, the head of World Trade's Hursley Laboratory in England, when he was trying (unsuccessfully) to win corporate approval for his Scamp computer.

Could the device really be used to meet Haanstra's objections to the 360-30? To find out, Learson staged a "shoot-out" in January 1964, between the 1401-S and the model 30. The test proved that the model 30, "emulating" the 1401, could already operate at 80% of the speed of the 1401-S—and could improve that figure with other adaptations. That was good enough for Learson. He notified Watson that he was ready to go, and said that he favored announcing the whole System/360 family at once.

"GOING . . . GOING . . . GONE!"

Haanstra was still not convinced. He persisted in his view that his manufacturing organization probably could not gear up to meet the production demand adequately. On March 18 and 19, a final "risk-assessment" session was held at Yorktown Heights to review once again every debatable point of the program. Tom Watson, Jr., President Al Williams, and 30 top executives of the corporation attended. This was to be the last chance for the unpersuaded to state their doubts or objections on any aspect of the new program—patent protection, policy on computer returns, the company's ability to hire and train an enormous new work force in the time allotted, and so on. Haanstra himself was conspicuously absent from this session. In February he had been relieved of his responsibilities as president of the General Products Division and assigned to special duty—monitoring a project to investigate the possibility of IBM's getting into magnetic tape. (He later became a vice president of the Federal Systems Division.) At the end of the risk-assessment meeting, Watson seemed satisfied that all the objections to the 360 had been met. Al Williams, who had been presiding, stood up before the group, asked if there were any last dissents, and then, getting no response, dramatically intoned, "Going . . . going . . . gone!"

The April 7, 1964, announcement of the program unveiled details of six separate compatible computer machines; their memories would be interchangeable, so that a total of nineteen different combinations would be available. The peripheral equipment was to consist of forty different input and output devices, including printers, optical scanners, and high-speed tape drives. Delivery of the new machines would start in April 1965.

THE NATURE OF THE RISK

The basic announcement of the new line brought a mixed reaction from the competition. The implication that the 360 line would make obsolete all earlier equipment was derided and minimized by some rival manufacturers, who seized every opportunity to argue that the move was less significant than it appeared . . . [or claimed it was unfeasible or uneconomic for customers].

But some of the competition was concerned enough about the System/360 to respond to its challenge on a large scale. During the summer of 1964, General Electric announced that its 600 line of computers would have time-sharing capabilities. The full import of this announcement hit IBM that fall, when

MIT, prime target of several computer manufacturers, announced that it would buy a G.E. machine. IBM had worked on a time-sharing program back in 1960 but had abandoned the idea when the cost of the terminals involved seemed to make it uneconomic. G.E.'s success caught IBM off base and in 1964 and 1965 it was scrambling madly to provide the same capability in the 360 line. Late in 1964, RCA announced it would use pure monolithic integrated circuitry (i.e., as opposed to IBM's hybrid circuitry) in some models of its new Spectra 70 line. This development probably led to a certain amount of soul-searching at IBM.

In the end, . . . the company felt that the turn to monolithic circuitry did not involve capabilities that threatened the 360 line; furthermore, if and when monolithic circuitry ever did prove to have decisive advantages over IBM's hybrid circuitry, the company was prepared— the computers themselves and some three quarters of the component manufacturing equipment could be adapted fairly inexpensively to monolithics. As for time sharing, any anxieties IBM had about that were eased in March 1965, when Watts Humphrey, a systems expert who had been given the assignment of meeting the time-sharing challenge, got the job done. . . .

IBM announced additions to the 360 line in 1964 and 1965. One was the model 90, a supercomputer type, designed to be competitive with Control Data's 6800. Another was the 360-44, designed for special scientific purposes. Also, there was the 360-67, a large time-sharing machine. Another, the 360-20, represented a pioneering push into the low end of the market. None of these were fully compatible with the models originally announced, but they were considered part of the 360 family.

System/360 underwent many changes after the concept was originally brought forth back in 1962 and even after Watson's announcement in 1964. More central processors were later offered in the 360 line; some of them had memories that were much faster than those originally offered. The number of input-output machines [increased several times]. . . .

"MAJOR RESHUFFLEMENTS"

IBM had several managers trying to keep the 360 program on track in 1964–1965. Gibson, who had succeeded Learson in the job, was replaced late in 1964. His successor, Paul Knaplund, lasted about another year. . . . [In 1965] the company suffered heavy setbacks at the high end of the 360 line—that is, in its efforts to bring forth a great supercomputer in the tradition of

Stretch. In 1964 it wrote off $15 million worth of parts and equipment developed specifically for the 360-90.

There were signs at about this time that the 360 program was still generating other reshufflements of divisions and personnel. Dr. Piore had been freed from operational duties and responsibilities and given a license to roam the company checking on just about all technical activities. Another change represented a comeback for Stephen Dunwell, who had managed the Stretch program and had been made the goat for its expensive failure to perform as advertised. When IBM got into the 360 program, its technical group discovered that the work done on Stretch was immensely valuable to them; and Watson personally gave Dunwell an award as an IBM fellow (which entitled him to work with IBM backing, for five years, on any project of his choosing).

In 1971 58-year-old Tom Watson, Jr., slowed by poor health, turned over the chairmanship of the company to T. Vincent Learson. While Learson was taking on the top job, computer makers were rattled by a recession and shaken by a series of corporate crises. [The years] 1970–1972 saw General Electric Co. and RCA withdraw from the field, cutting the number of U.S. computer makers from nine to seven. The industry was struck by a backlash from oversold customers, a new generation of computers, and a switch in government expenditures away from R&D and toward social services.

A GREAT SUCCESS

The success of the 360 line was greater than anyone had predicted. In 1964 (at the time of the 360 announcement) management expected to place roughly 2,700 of the five largest models by 1970 and projected that only a third of these would be ordered with remote terminal and communications gear. In fact, shipments approached the 5,000 level with more than half demanding extra peripheral equipment. IBM's revenues exploded from $3.5 billion in 1965 to $7.5 billion in 1970. Peripheral equipment represented a large percentage of the customers' hardware dollar in 1970, and the high margins on these sales helped cover further massive R&D expenditures for future mainframes.

Every five or six years IBM had traditionally introduced a new generation of computers that outmoded its existing series. To convince customers to trade up to the new line, the company usually offered new machines with a lot more performance for only a little more money. But the 360's very success threatened this carefully maintained structure, as independent leasing companies and "plug compatible" peripheral manufacturers (PCMs) moved in for the kill. To compound problems, the Justice Department filed an antitrust suit against IBM, charging in part that the entire 360 line represented an effort to reduce competition. The government's goal was nothing less than the breakup of IBM into several separate companies.

THE 370 RESPONSE

One of its responses was the 370 series of computers. The 370s were designed to be compatible with the 360 machines in terms of software so that the users' huge investments in programming would be protected. Typically a user would invest $3–$5 in software for each $1 in hardware. The 370 in essence was intended to make 360 programs run faster, and the transition to the new machines was intended to be painless compared to the disruptive way the 360 had been introduced.

Technical people at IBM would have preferred to equip the whole range of 370 computers with semiconductor memories at introduction. That would have made the 370 series much more versatile, more powerful, and technologically far ahead of any other computer. But IBM's marketing group pressed for earlier introduction with the first available quality product. "We had invested a few hundred million dollars in the 370," said Watson. "We might have been more prudent to upgrade the 360, but we thought a new line would be a stimulant for both the customer and the salesman." Unfortunately, the 370 strategy backfired. Customers often found they could replace two 360's with one 370 and save on monthly rental payments.

To compound difficulties, the medium- to large-sized mainframe market began to mature, and hardware prices dropped due to the rapid miniaturization of integrated circuits. To fill the gap in the low end of its line, IBM introduced the System/3, the result of an intensive development effort in the late 1960s headed up by the highest ranking line officer at IBM—Frank Cary, who later became IBM's chairman at age 52, when T. Vincent Learson stepped down. System/3 went on to become a best seller with more than 25,000 machines installed. But to achieve the breakthroughs in cost necessary to make it cheap enough for small users, the designers had to sacrifice compatibility with the 360/370 family. The System/3 spawned a new family of machines allowing all its new IBM users to trade up within the line. By 1983, the largest System/3 machines competed in price/performance with the smaller units in the 360/370 series.[1]

THE MINI-MARKET AND LINKAGES

The next major step in IBM's product development was the 1979 launch of the 4300, a family of medium-sized computers. According to many estimates, in the first three weeks customers sent in an astounding $10 billion worth of orders for 42,000 machines, twice as many as IBM had expected to manufacture over the entire life of the series. Some customers were assigned delivery dates four years into the future, and places near the head of the line were traded for up to $15,000 each.[2]

The 4300s were priced so low that one model exceeded the computing power of an existing $560,000 Series 360 machine, yet sold for only $69,000—an eightfold improvement in price/performance ratio. Users of bigger systems who assumed that IBM's future offerings at the high end of the market would be priced according to the same formula canceled orders for IBM's existing big machines, the 3030 series. Instead they turned to short-term leases which they could terminate when the new large-scale 3080 series computers came out. The result was a terrific cash crunch; the company had to go to the bond market in October 1979 with a $1 billion offering—the largest such public sale in history.

As hardware prices and sizes shrank in the 1970s, mini-computers became more powerful, more flexible, and much cheaper. IBM found that many of its customers started practicing "off-loading." When a large central mainframe was operating at capacity, instead of upgrading or replacing the existing machine, they pushed off the extra jobs onto minis. This trend finally forced IBM to get serious about this rapidly growing segment. IBM had had small business systems since 1970 when it came out with the System/3, but it didn't announce a true minicomputer until 1976.

DEC, Hewlett Packard, Data General, Texas Instruments, and others offered quantity discounts on their minis of 30–40% to "systems houses"—sophisticated middlemen who bought components in bulk and packaged them into systems for various users. IBM, on the other hand, was used to letting its highly disciplined blue-suited sales force contact and service end users directly and refused to consider discounts of more than 15% for large orders of minis. In the words of a former IBM executive, "You really had to love the machine to take it at that price."

As a result of such practices, in the early 1980s IBM was still fifth in minicomputer sales but was finally learning and moving up fast. Its division responsible for small systems began discounting. And the 4300 series, which was designed with distributed processing applications in mind, helped strengthen IBM's hand. The company also introduced a high level software package called System Network Architecture (SNA) to help link together its minis, mainframes, word processors, smart copiers, and communication devices into the much discussed decentralized "office of the future." (See Exhibits 1 and 2 for information on IBM's geographic and market segments in the early 1980s.)

IBM was also a partner in Satellite Business Systems, a joint venture (with Comsat and Aetna) that had three satellites providing interference-free data transmission capabilities. With the deregulation of the communications industry, both IBM and AT&T were free to move further in the direction of total systems services.

SHRINKING CHIPS

Perhaps the biggest threat to IBM's preeminence came not from any particular competitor, but from changes in the computer technology itself. Integrated circuit (IC) capabilities were radically altering the size, speed, reliability and cost of all computers and accessories. For instance, a circuit package used in a 1983 top-of-the-line machine measured 4" × 4" × 2" and contained over 100 chips interconnected through 33 layers. The same capacity had required a space the size of a refrigerator for a 370 System model produced in the early 1970s. The microprocessor, pioneered by Intel in the early 1970s, was the next logical challenge for IBM. The microprocessor was the engine driving the proliferation of electronic devices into home computers, "programmable" microwave ovens, "smart" machines, and so on worldwide. As one of the largest producers of ICs in the world—for its own use—IBM had to consider its possible role in such markets.

IBM's actions in the early 1980s indicated how seriously it took these challenges. Chairman Frank Cary said, "We've got to be price competitive, box by box (machine by machine). Nobody is going to pay us a 20% premium any more." Between 1977 and 1981 it added 22 million square feet of laboratory and manufacturing space, a staggering $10 billion in plant and equipment. Such additions accounted for roughly two-thirds of the gross asset value of plant and other property listed on IBM's balance sheet in 1983.

But these investments bucked two other important trends. In the 1970s, according to industry sources, the CPU represented 55% of a system's cost, the rest being terminals, printers, software, and other peripherals. By 1980, that share had declined to 35%. Furthermore, systems with big CPUs made up a large but declining share of the market. In the early 1980s IBM received only 29% of its revenue from the sale or rental of central processors. At the same time, software, which had been only 10% of development costs for early 1960s lines, became some 90% of such costs in the early 1980s.

ORGANIZING FOR THE FUTURE

In a fast-changing, high-technology industry—where small companies have very real advantages over larger, more bureaucratic firms—IBM was often likened to a whale in a pool with lots of aggressive sharks. IBM had developed some specific techniques for countering a large company's natural propensity to minimize risk. In IBM's early computer years, when Tom Watson, Jr., was CEO, he encouraged the fresh thinking of people he called "wild ducks." Bob Evans said, "Watson, Jr., always felt the world is full of people who just don't see it the way most people do. More times than not they are probably wrong, but sometimes they are right, and we ought to have some mechanism for the wild ducks to have their fling. Watson encouraged this 'wild duckism.' He encouraged people, who normally would not be inclined to just go along with a team, to know there was an avenue where—if they wanted to express a different view—they'd be heard and maybe funded to do something by themselves."

To help coordinate its rapidly diversifying lines and complex presence in the marketplace, IBM reorganized in the early 1980s. The most dramatic part of the shake-up occurred in IBM's three sales divisions which were folded into one integrated entity called the Information Systems Group. (See Exhibit 3.) This move was prompted in part by the confusion caused by IBM sales people from different divisions calling on the same company. The change streamlined IBM's manufacturing operation by grouping all the computer-related divisions together. It also set up 14 IBUs (independent business units) and SBUs (strategic business units) that could explore opportunities without the weight of the company's formal bureaucracy to hold them back. One of these new SBUs developed and built IBM's entry into the home or personal computer (PC) market.

While IBM had tightened its control over systems software for its large computers (to make it tougher for the plug compatible manufacturers), the PC designers adopted an "open architecture," opening the machines' technical specifications to the public. They commissioned an independent software house (Microsoft) to write the new operating system for the PC and quickly made it public too. Also breaking with tradition, many hardware components were standard units (including an Intel 8088 microprocessor CPU chip) sourced from outside vendors to ensure a faster start-up. Finally, instead of relying on IBM's sales force and 40-odd retail product centers, the PC's marketing people cut a deal with Sears and Computerland to sell IBM machines. The result—IBM's PC garnered 30% of the business microcomputer market in just two years. In late 1983 the PC manufacturing unit was allocating production by shipping only 1 unit for every 7 ordered—despite an assembly line that was so automated it took only 10 minutes of worker time to assemble a unit.[3]

IBM also had to deal with the small chip manufacturers who were integrating forward into computers as they developed more powerful microprocessors. But perhaps the biggest threat to IBM's long-term dominance in computers might come from the Japanese. By 1983 the Japanese had entered every major segment of the office equipment industry with particular strength in printers and copiers. In addition, Japanese companies held some 10–15% of the worldwide computer market, although their national goal was a 30% share by 1990. Fujitsu, Nippon Electric Co., and Hitachi were the largest computer makers. Fujitsu had surpassed IBM as the number one computer supplier in Japan. All the Japanese manufacturers had standardized their current products around IBM 360/370 architecture. Although they sold primarily to their own domestic market, Japanese companies were actively pursuing new world markets through joint ventures and other agreements. Fujitsu was the largest shareholder in Amdahl, which held a 56% share of the IBM plug-compatible mainframe market, and it distributed its own equipment through TRW. Hitachi had a joint distribution agreement with National Advanced Systems, the number two PCM.

QUESTIONS

1. What stimulated the change in strategy at the time of the 360? Evaluate the process by which change was brought about. Evaluate Mr. Learson as a change manager.
2. Hoes does the 1983 situation compare with that in the early 1960s?
3. What should IBM's strategy for the future be? Why? What should be the structure of its portfolio?
4. How should it organize for the new competition?

	CONSOLIDATED		U.S. ONLY	
	1983	1982	1983	1982
Information-Handling				
Processors				
Sales	9,046	7,784	4,908	4,203
Rentals	1,692	2,363	711	1,086
	10,738	10,147	5,619	5,289
Peripherals				
Sales	6,205	3,311	3,669	1,717
Rentals	4,778	5,371	2,533	2,917
	10,983	8,682	6,202	4,634
Office Systems/Workstations				
Sales	5,752	3,667	3,667	2,278
Rentals	2,275	2,778	1,295	1,498
	8,027	6,445	4,962	3,776
Program Products	2,302	2,693	1,288	935
Maintenance Services	4,577	3,940	2,633	2,230
Other				
Sales	1,181	1,238	778	768
Rental	485	609	278	372
Services	648	689	135	110
	2,314	2,536	1,191	1,250
Total for Information-Handling	38,941	33,443	21,895	18,114
Federal Systems				
Sales	1,028	753	1,028	753
Rentals	148	105	148	105
	1,176	858	1,176	858
Other Business				
Sales	62	62	55	55
Services	1	1	1	1
	63	63	63	63
	40,180	34,364	23,127	19,028

EXHIBIT 1
IBM Corporation
Gross Income by Industry Segments and Classes of Similar Products and Services
(in millions of dollars)

Source: IBM, *1983 Annual Report.*

EXHIBIT 2
IBM Corporation
Geographic Segment
Data for the
Early 1980s
(in millions of dollars)

	1983	1982	1981
United States			
Gross income-Customers	23,127	19,028	15,088
Interarea transfers	2,275	1,875	1,857
Total	25,402	20,903	16,945
Net earnings	3,296	2,766	2,094
Assets at December 31	23,083	19,028	16,022
Europe/Middle East/Africa			
Gross income—Customers	11,324	10,260	9,312
Interarea transfers	235	337	383
Total	11,559	10,597	9,695
Net earnings	1,580	1,196	1,074
Assets at December 31	10,011	9,197	8,981
Americas/Far East			
Gross income—Customers	5,729	5,076	4,670
Interarea transfers	728	651	659
Total	6,457	5,727	5,329
Net earnings	562	450	478
Assets at December 31	5,110	4,925	4,694
Eliminations			
Gross income	(3,238)	(2,863)	(2,899)
Net earnings	47	(3)	(36)
Assets at December 31	(961)	(609)	(590)
Consolidated			
Gross income	40,180	34,364	29,070
Net earnings	5,485	4,409	3,610
Assets at December 31	37,243	32,541	29,107

Source: IBM, *1983 Annual Report.*

EXHIBIT 3
IBM Organization in
the Early 1980s

To conduct its business throughout the world, IBM was organized into the following groups, divisions, and wholly owned subsidiaries:

Information Systems Group

Customer Service Division
Provides maintenance, related support and programming services within the United States and its territories for designated systems and products developed primarily by the Information Systems and Communications Group.

Federal Systems Division
Provides specialized information-handling and control systems to the Federal government for seaborne, spaceborne, airborne, and ground-based environments. Also participates in applied research and exploratory development.

Field Engineering Division
Provides maintenance and related services within the United States and its territories for all current IBM systems and products and designated new systems and products developed primarily by the Information Systems and Technology Group, as well as support for specified IBM program offerings. Has overall responsibility for the distribution of all hardware and software products and related publications. The division also provides maintenance, marketing support and central programming service for assigned products.

National Accounts Division
Has marketing and field administration responsibility within the United States and its territories for the full standard line of IBM products. Its assigned customers are selected large accounts with complex information processing needs.

National Marketing Division
Has marketing and field administration responsibility within the United States and its territories for the full standard line of IBM products. Its assigned customers are large, medium, and small accounts.

Systems Supplies Division
Has responsibility for formulating worldwide business strategy for information processing supplies and accessories; for manufacturing or procurement, and marketing within the United States and its territories of IBM supplies and services.

Information Systems and Technology Group

Data Systems Division
Has worldwide development and associated programming responsibility for large, complex systems, with primary emphasis on high-performance products, plus U.S. manufacturing responsibility for those systems.

General Products Division
Has worldwide development and U.S. manufacturing responsibility for storage systems, including tape units, disk products and mass storage systems, program products and product-related programming.

General Technology Division
Has worldwide development and product assurance and U.S. manufacturing responsibility for logic, memory, and special semiconductor devices and associated packaging. The division also procures components for the IBM World Trade Americas/Far East Corporation and U.S. operating units.

EXHIBIT 3
(continued)

Information Systems and Communications Group

Communication Products Division
Has worldwide development and U.S. manufacturing responsibility for telecommunications systems, office systems, display products, distribution industry systems and related programming. The division serves as the worldwide architectural and systems focal point for office systems and Systems Network Architecture activities.

Information Products Division
Has worldwide development and related programming and U.S. manufacturing responsibility for typewriters, copiers and systems for banking and manufacturing industries, and for peripheral equipment, including printers, copier systems, keyboards, diskettes and associated supplies.

System Products Division
Has worldwide development and U.S. manufacturing responsibility for small and intermediate-sized general purpose systems, robotic systems and related programming. Its responsibility for the IBM Personal Computer also includes U.S. marketing through retail channels.

Other Divisions

Real Estate and Construction Division
Manages the selection and acquisition of sites, the design and construction of buildings and the purchase or lease of facilities for all IBM operations in the United States. The division has responsibility for assessing real estate projects outside the United States, as well as for IBM's worldwide energy and environmental programs. It also provides facility services to selected headquarters locations.

Research Division
Brings scientific understanding to bear on areas of company interest through basic research and development of technologies of potential long-range importance.

Subsidiaries

IBM Credit Corporation
Offers term leases and finances installment payment agreements on IBM information-handling equipment in the United States.

IBM Instruments, Inc.
Has responsibility for IBM's efforts in the analytical instruments field, including marketing and servicing selected products in the United States.

Science Research Associates, Inc.
Has worldwide development, publication and marketing responsibility for a wide range of educational and testing materials, services, and microcomputer software designed for use in elementary and secondary schools, colleges, businesses, and the home.

IBM World Trade Americas/Far East Corporation
With a territory extending across four continents, this subsidiary is responsible for IBM operations in 46 countries, including Australia, Brazil, Canada, and Japan.

IBM World Trade Europe/Middle East/Africa Corporation
Through its subsidiary, IBM Europe, located in Paris, it is responsible for IBM operations in 85 countries.

IBM World Trade Corporation
Provides designated support to IBM World Trade organizational units.

Source: IBM, *Annual Report*, 1982.

In the early 1980s, two giant U.S. companies were embroiled in antitrust cases aimed at breaking them up. The first company effectively fought off the challenge, thereby managing to remain intact. The second company finally accepted a consent decree that required it to divest 70% of its assets, exit from the business that had yielded approximately half of its revenues, spin off 4000 scientists and engineers from its world-renowned research laboratories, and make available to its competitors the costly infrastructure it had built up over its hundred year history. To most external observers as well as to a vast majority of their employees, IBM had won and AT&T had lost.

Between 1989 and 1994, AT&T surprised everyone. During a period when one corporate giant after another was crumbling under its own weight—IBM, foremost among them—AT&T "defied gravity." Following a radical restructuring into 21 product-focused and relatively small business units—each challenged to operate as stand-alone businesses with full accountability for financial and market performance—the company achieved a spectacular turnaround that improved its return on equity from 10% to 28% and raised its stock price by over 200% to almost 5 times book value (see Exhibit 1 for financials). In 1993, AT&T's CEO, Bob Allen, was featured on the covers of many leading business journals.

BRIEF HISTORY

In 1984, in accordance with a consent decree with the U.S. Justice Department, AT&T divested its 22 local operating companies (the Regional Bell Operating Companies or RBOCs) while retaining its long distance

service (Long Lines), its equipment manufacturing (Western Electric) and the majority of its world-renowned research capability (Bell Labs). Prior to the breakup, $14 billion worth of network service equipment had been sold annually to the RBOCs by Western Electric. After the links were severed, AT&T no longer had an assured market for its networking and transmission systems; and other strong global competitors, particularly Northern Telecom, began aggressive marketing to the RBOCs.

Through 1986, AT&T seemed to founder in the new competitive storm created by divestiture. Realizing that AT&T was reaching a critical turning point which could determine if the company would ever truly succeed in the hostile world of competition, recently appointed CEO and President Jim Olson called together his 27 top executives in September 1986 to battle out a new vision and strategy for the company. After five days of intense and often emotional debate among the leaders of some very entrenched fiefdoms, the group emerged with a "single enterprise strategy" which aimed to make AT&T a slimmer and more seamless organization. The meeting ended with each executive giving his personal commitment to Olson that he would support the enterprise AT&T, above and beyond his own business. Helping Olson to implement this strategy would be Bob Allen who had been named President and Chief Operating Officer only seven months earlier.

Olson and Allen initiated stringent actions to reduce costs. Though AT&T had already reduced its workforce by 48,000 between 1984 and 1986, 27,000 more employees were released, offices and plants were rationalized, and half of the company's 900 retail phone stores were closed. Even while slashing costs, Olson made some strategic investments for the future. He made a major decision to arrest AT&T's slipping long distance market share by replacing the company's analog network over a period of several years with digital technology at a cost of $6 billion. On the international side of the business, he gave the Business Groups global responsibility for their product lines, and dissolved the International Group. Then in April 1988, tragedy struck. Olson died unexpectedly and within a day Bob Allen was appointed CEO of the company.

RATIONALIZING THE BUSINESS: 1989–1991

Allen found himself the leader of an organization in turmoil. Employees were dispirited, costs were still untenable, market share was continuing to slip, and its computer business did not yet command respect in the marketplace. Acting decisively to try to stem further erosion of the company's bread-and-butter long distance business, Allen accelerated the implementation of Olson's earlier decision to digitize the network. This move resulted in a $6.7 billion write-off and the company's first loss ever in 1988. Allen recounted the feeling of the time, "We had begun to lose our self-confidence—yet we had a lot of proud, competitive people. They needed to learn how to win again."

BUSINESS UNITS

One of Allen's first and most far-reaching actions was to break up AT&T's giant functional organization into manageable pieces to help drive responsibility and accountability into each unique business. Thus, twenty-one Business Units were formed, each with its own profit and loss statement and balance sheet. Within each BU, there were a number of smaller units also with their own financial reporting, giving AT&T over 100 distinct management units. The new BU managers' compensation was based primarily on the financial performance (measured operating income or MOI) of their Business Unit, and to a lesser extent on the financial achievement of the corporation.

The Business Units were grouped into Business Groups (BG) which carried out the role of planning, allocation of resources, and opportunity scouting, while the Business Units had almost total autonomy on factors that influenced their immediate performance, such as pricing, marketing and product development. (See Exhibit 2 for a description of the different Business Groups and their activities.) The only mechanism available for integrating and coordinating the BU strategies lay at the very top of the organization in the Operations Committee that Allen had created to look after corpo-

rate operations and to resolve inter-entity conflicts. It included the BG heads and the Chief Financial Officer. At the same time, Allen made a concerted effort to recruit a number of key new people at the top to bring in fresh ideas and spark a more aggressive culture.

STAFF FUNCTIONS

With the restructuring into BUs, there was a clear need to review the staff functions within AT&T, their reporting structure, their tasks and responsibilities, and the number of people required to perform these tasks in the new organization. Top management, including Bob Allen, spent substantial amounts of time determining how employees who were not directly focused on the BUs could add value. To assure that the staff functions provided effective service to the BUs, AT&T tried to adopt a customer-supplier relationship between line and staff units. At first the BUs had to sign contracts with their "suppliers" stating the terms and conditions of the service being supplied. But this was dropped when the process became too adversarial. The formal agreements were replaced by the philosophy—"The staffs are all good people—now how can they help us?" With this belief as the foundation for the relationship, units began gradually over time to adopt the customer-supplier idea in a more positive way.

An important part of the staff reorganization accompanying greater Business Unit accountability was in the finance function which had to track the new Units' performance. The finance staff of the company had always worked as a homogeneous, supportive community in which the members communicated frequently through a policy setting Steering Committee. With this trust among the members of the finance staff and a general agreement that something needed to be done, it was relatively easy to create a dual reporting structure for BU controllers which made them responsible both to the BU head and the corporate CFO.

BELL LABS

Bell Laboratories, the world-renowned research arm of AT&T, went through its own transformation. Shortly after the move to a business unit organization (when 4000 Lab people had been moved to Belcore to support the RBOCs), it became clear that many Bell Labs employees needed to become more customer-oriented. Management found that internal customers (the Business Units) were being bounced around throughout the organization rather than being served. Experiences in which the customer was told, "No, this is not a manufacturing issue, go see design. . . . No, this is not a design issue, go see someone else," were not uncommon. The resulting frustration led to the decision in 1989 to align Bell Labs more with the Business Units. Under the new structure, 80% of the Labs' employees were paid for directly by the Business Units they supported, thereby creating a tighter technology-market link. The other 20% remained in centralized, functional organizations which developed expertise or provided services to be used across all the Business Units. Contrary to external observers' expectations, the close alignment between Bell Labs and the Business Units did not cause the company to back off on research expenditures.

Nevertheless, there was some concern within the ranks of the world class scientists at Bell Labs that the new links with the Business Units would hurt the capabilities of the Labs in the long run. It seemed to some that the managers running the labs aligned to the Business Units spent "all their time hustling for money to feed their people." Further, the scientists who were left in the central research functions, while pleased with their freedom to work on what they liked, were unsure if their work would have immediate application. One of the risks some scientists feared was that if the pendulum swung too far toward commercial applications, Bell Labs researchers would find it harder to be a part of the scientific community and recruitment would suffer.

In the 1990s, the Labs retained a culture of completely open information sharing, cultivating and rewarding excellence, continual learning, and job mobility. However, while the Labs used to bring in 2000 new scientists each year in the early 1980s, due to productivity increases and the restructuring to support the Business Units, the number had been reduced to around 200. Both the growing power of the technology itself and the continuing pressure on costs would require on-going reduction of people. How to attract and retain the world's best scientific talent under such conditions remained as Bell Labs' President John Mayo's key challenge for the future.

IMPLEMENTING THE BUSINESS UNIT STRUCTURE

By 1991, the rationalization and restructuring at AT&T was well underway and the effect was dramatic. The new organization allowed the company to identify the key competitors in each of its markets, get closer to its customers, and foster a feeling of ownership and entrepreneurship within each unit. Importantly, in this new world of accountability, capital was no longer "free" and, within each unit, all investment projects required

convincing justification. For the first time, it became evident which businesses in AT&T were making money. The ability of the BUs to directly benchmark themselves against best-in-class competitors also resulted in the reduction of an additional 50,000 employees.

According to Allen, "The relative success of the moment was in part due to a pent-up drive for accountability and responsibility" by executives to run their own businesses. However, while the autonomy of the units stimulated numerous profit oriented actions, some negative behavior resulted as some of the BU heads focused almost solely on improving the financials of their own BU without regard for the larger corporate entity. As one manager expressed, "Some BU cowboys just strapped on their guns and said the hell with the rest of you."

REVITALIZING PEOPLE

By 1991, Allen had begun to realize that he must also address the softer side of the business: its vision, leadership skills, values, rewards and development processes. He spent many hours trying to communicate a new way of managing to his reports and down into the ranks. To some, Allen served as a role model of the revitalized AT&T manager. He believed strongly in empowered leadership teams and was known for not allowing his managers to push decisions into his lap. When asked his opinion about a BU issue or even a corporate issue, he was likely to say, "It doesn't matter what I think. What do you think?" He explained:

> I have never thought that I could be so knowledgeable and so current in our businesses and markets that I could make the decisions. I have always been an advocate of shared decision making. In fact, I believe this is one of the reasons I am CEO. . . . With the BU structure, we have divested a lot of responsibility by empowering people. This creates an environment where I could find myself completely useless unless I keep control over leadership, strategy, values and public policy. . . . Personnel and leadership decisions are very important and I need to be totally involved. Not because I am in any way wiser, but ultimately, leadership decisions are my responsibility.

NEW LEADERSHIP TEAM

Though Allen had filled a number of key top management positions from outside the company, 95% of the 130 corporate officers managing AT&T had been employees of the company since the breakup. As a group this team needed a new leadership style tuned to the company's mission of becoming a more nimble global competitor. The Strategy Forum was Allen's personal tool for developing his new management team's skills, values, and vision. He was directly involved in structuring each session's agenda. The two day meetings were attended by the company's top 60 managers, including all the Business Unit heads and key corporate staff members. Intentionally, Allen did not exclude the smaller BU heads because he wanted to stress openness in the new AT&T. The Forum was not a decision making body, though the meetings set the context for many important decisions taken at the corporate level such as the acquisition of NCR in 1991 and McCaw Cellular in 1993.

The first Strategy Forum meeting, held in 1991, was designed to help the top management develop a common view of what the industry might look like in the year 2000, the relative position AT&T would like to have in that industry, and a general vision of how the company could achieve that position. These discussions led the group to conclude that AT&T would have to begin a steady period of growth to succeed. This was only possible by entering markets and geographies in which it was not yet a major player. As expressed by Allen, AT&T's mission which would guide the company's strategic thinking became:

> To be the world's best at bringing people together—giving them easy access to each other and to the information and services they want and need—anytime, anywhere.

Later Forums discussed how AT&T would enter new markets and geographies. In one Forum, the wireless industry was reviewed as an example of a new market that AT&T might enter. In this meeting, six Business Units were asked to develop plans describing how the company might exploit the opportunity. When all six presented separate entry strategies, the limits of the Business Unit management structure became obvious to all present. This Forum prompted the group to conclude that better integration across the Business Units was a priority for AT&T's future growth. The Management Executive Committee (MEC)* later worked off-line to define six growth opportunities for AT&T's future to be addressed through specific cross-BU initiatives and supported by cross-BU teams.

As the Strategy Forum sessions continued at a pace of two or three each year, top management gradually began to bond as a team. Though initially the managers of larger BUs had felt less affiliation and need to meet as a group than managers of smaller BUs, this attitude

---

* The MEC was a larger group than the Operations Committee which included all BG heads and key corporate staff members to total around a dozen members responsible for strategy and policy issues.

changed. Likewise, some managers who had labeled the Forums as a control device began to change their views. One participant expressed, "There has been a definite change in attitude since the first Forum. Though I was not a big supporter at first, I don't know where we would be now if we weren't regularly bringing people together."

The Strategy Forums were not easy for the top management team because, by design, they questioned many of the longstanding beliefs of management about themselves and the company. But as one participant remarked, "The group was learning a different way of leading, although the results varied by individual." The tide was turning, albeit slowly. The succession planning process, which had begun in response to Olson's death, was starting to pay off by 1992 in terms of helping AT&T leaders to identify skill gaps in the next generation of managers.

While enlightening, the process was also quite painful for some when they realized that the successful profile for their job, in some cases, was in dramatic contrast to their own profile. For example, few of them had any significant international experience, while for most jobs the succession planning process highlighted this background to be important. Likewise, in the future, there would be a need for leaders who had spent significant periods of time in one business, enhancing and deepening their managerial skills, as opposed to the traditional AT&T senior manager who had been rotated through a number of businesses in one to two year stints. The future would also need leaders with significant experience in some of the high growth, emerging businesses such as multimedia. In some cases, the succession planning exercise revealed strategic gaps in the upper management lineup which needed to be filled immediately, causing the company to intensify its efforts to hire senior level managers from the outside. In 1993, about 50 managers were recruited from the outside into the top group of 80 managers.

OUR COMMON BOND

One of Allen's most important projects, on which he spent a lot of his own time and energy, was the creation of a values statement for AT&T, called *Our Common Bond*. The statement was a culmination of both top management input—within the Strategy Forum and outside—and a comprehensive program to solicit employee input through focus groups. Allen called these values the "rules of the game." They included respect for individuals, dedication to the customer, integrity, innovation, and team work (see Exhibit 3).

Our Common Bond was not to be a "plaque on the wall." Allen worked with great determination to assure that everyone within the company would live its values. He started at the top with himself and his immediate team by spending two full days in the Strategy Forum, probing how managers would use the values to guide their actions in the workplace on a daily basis. Allen saw *Our Common Bond* as a strong tool for pulling the Business Units together. In his opinion:

> One of the reasons why—and justifiably so—we're accused of short term thinking is that our Business Unit structure is relatively immature and we have a number of relatively inexperienced managers who, for the first time in their careers, are responsible for profits. Had we implemented that Business Unit structure with a strong surround of the values statement, we might have managed a little differently these last few years.

The existence of a substantial gap between the values and the way the management lived those values, as perceived by the employees, was brought home in a very emotional Strategy Forum meeting in 1992, one year after the values had been introduced. This meeting discussed the results of a recent survey in which only 17% of the employee population felt that top management encouraged and listened to employees at all levels and only 19% found management credible in their statements. To drive the point home, employees volunteered to have themselves videotaped describing specific examples in which management had not lived the values.

Allen set out to assure that this issue was addressed immediately and in a meaningful manner. He directed the MEC to develop an upward feedback mechanism to evaluate how well all the company's managers, on an individual basis, upheld AT&T's values as viewed by their subordinates. The MEC team identified 40 relevant behaviors on which the subordinates of the individual would be asked to evaluate their boss in a survey. A facilitator would then feed back the results to the manager and help subordinates discuss the findings with their manager, with the requirement that the manager must give the group a response on each issue raised in terms of the actions he or she would or would not take. Allen himself launched the process, which became known as Values Deployment, by having the MEC give him feedback on how he lived the 40 value-related measures.

A BALANCED SCORECARD

To support the values espoused in *Our Common Bond*, management performance was measured on a broader basis than before. In the words of the corporate compensation manager, "We aim to measure and compensate our managers on how well they are preparing

AT&T for the future." While in 1989 MOI (measured operating income) was the only criteria for evaluating the performance of a Business Unit and its management, in 1992 it was replaced by another financial measurement, EVA (Economic Value Added), a measure of return on capital employed—essentially net margin minus implicit capital cost. A year later, two other important measures were introduced which also affected management compensation: People Value Added (PVA), a measure of management's leadership skills as determined through employee surveys, and Customer Value Added (CVA), based on customer surveys of AT&T's product and service performance relative to the competition. Under the new system, the compensation of all employees, except hourly and non-U.S. employees, was tied to AT&T's corporate EVA, the Business Units' EVA, and their individual performance. For the top 800 managers of the company these factors were supplemented by PVA and CVA assessments. The newer PVA and CVA measurements were not yet well-refined or standardized enough to assure consistency between Business Units or from year to year. Thus they did not receive much weight in the 1993 compensation scheme. However, it was intended that eventually all three measures—EVA, PVA and CVA—would carry equal weight.

In spite of the broader performance measurement system, the early emphasis on immediate financial performance lingered over the Business Units. As one top manager said, "Though we consider Customer Value-Added and People Value-Added, EVA is the measure of goodness in reality." While acknowledging efforts to maintain a balance, most front-line managers echoed the concern that the short term remained clearly the dominant pressure.

PREPARING FOR THE FUTURE

To accomplish its corporate ambition of "anytime, anywhere," AT&T planned to exploit the disappearance of regulatory and technological boundaries driving the convergence of the telecommunications and information technology industries. A strong deregulation trend had been raging in the telecommunication business since the mid-1980s, as businesses pressured governments for more modern service and debt-laden foreign governments saw opportunities to raise cash through privatization. More than 100 countries were expected to privatize their telecommunications monopolies by the year 2000. Similarly, technological convergence was increasingly blurring the boundaries among many businesses—like cable television, information processing and computing, local telephone service, long distance service, and wireless communication—laying the foundation for a mammoth new industry, infocom. In the 1990s, traditional telephony, cable, satellite, cellular, fiber optics, and personal communications networks were all viable and competing technologies which could transport voice, data and video to homes, offices, automobiles, or individuals, wherever they might be. According to John Mayo, President of Bell Labs:

> The technology can provide more solutions than the customer wants. This is very different from the past when the market was hungry for anything we could do. Now, among the thousands of things we could do, the challenge is to choose the hundred that are worth doing.

Hundreds of companies, who played in any aspect of communications or information processing, were trying to increase their share of the business during this one-time, free-for-all period. The intense competition was expected to result in lower prices, thinner margins and commodization for the suppliers, but it would be a boon for both businesses and consumers in terms of access to new technologies at reasonable prices.

A NEW STRATEGIC FRAMEWORK

AT&T's strategy, as developed by Allen and the MEC, was geared to making the company a major player in all aspects of the infocom business. The company hoped to provide the means to generate, process, store, and transmit all forms of information within this framework. To begin with, the company concentrated its efforts on providing global "end-to-end" service to U.S.-based multinational corporations as well as providing service to the U.S.-based global traveler. After capturing this market, it hoped to expand beyond the U.S.-based customers into the global market for these services. At the same time, AT&T was working to leverage its computer expertise to provide integrated telecommunications solutions to businesses, as well as to invest in products and services for the entertainment industry.

Bob Allen recognized AT&T's crown jewel to be its core telecommunications network, an intricate web of wire, computers, optical fiber and software, and his strategy was to focus AT&T's expansion on only the areas which enhanced this core. In spite of the phenomenal success of AT&T's Universal Card, a combination calling card/credit card launched in 1991, AT&T had been unwilling to leverage this success to expand into other financial services as advocated by the President of the financial BU, because it exceeded the boundaries of the corporate strategy. Allen explained, "Everything we are doing is designed to put more traffic on our network, to enhance the value of our network," though these limits were relaxed somewhat by 1994.

DOMESTIC INDUSTRY LEADERSHIP

To achieve industry leadership, AT&T needed to choose the right highways to invest in as well as to combine forces with the winning complementary information technologies. Since the late 1980s, AT&T had been forging alliances and making acquisitions in order to attain leadership in all the key areas of infocom. (See Exhibit 4 for a listing of major alliances and acquisitions.) By 1991, it was clear that AT&T's attempt to develop a computer business internally had been unsuccessful in reaching the scale required to support its infocom strategy. Thus, the company's first major acquisition (a $7.5 billion stock deal) was aimed at building a foundation in data communication through the purchase of NCR, the world's fifth largest computer company.

Wireless communication was also important to AT&T's strategy. In 1993, cellular communication was commonplace, but double digit growth was still expected through the end of the decade—as wireless, data, and video transmission became available in developed countries and as many developing nations chose this technology as a fast, cost-effective alternative to building fiber or cable networks. While AT&T had been slow in recognizing the enormous potentials of this opportunity, in 1993 it made up for lost time through the acquisition of McCaw Cellular Communications (for $11.5 billion in stock) to capture 20% of the U.S. cellular market overnight. The purchase had caused serious concern among the RBOCs because the cellular capability could allow AT&T to connect its long distance customers by wireless means, bypassing the RBOCs and thereby avoiding the access fees that they charged. In retaliation, the RBOCs stepped up their lobbying efforts at the U.S. Justice Department to allow them to compete against AT&T in the equipment and long distance businesses.

Another new, thriving technology which could threaten the growth of cellular was personal communications services (PCS). This was a wireless technology similar to cellular which had the advantage of being lower in cost, as well as using lighter, smaller handsets. It was unclear if PCS would be a rival or complementary technology. AT&T was participating in this technology through the McCaw acquisition and an equity position in a start-up company called EO, Inc. But it would face tough competition from a number of other American and Japanese companies. AT&T, as well as the RBOCs, had also been seeking partnerships with cable television companies in order to participate in the interactive television and other multimedia communications markets. As with cellular, a strategic alliance of this type would give AT&T the ability to connect customers directly to its long distance service, bypassing the local operating companies.

AT&T's strategy to be an across-the-board player in all the profitable areas of the new infocom industry was generally acknowledged to be both aggressive and yet achievable. But some voices of dissent existed both inside and outside the company. First, the wisdom of AT&T's participation in the low profit equipment market was widely debated because the company was experiencing increasing tensions when it tried to sell equipment to the same companies with which it competed at a service level—e.g., the RBOCs and the national PTTs. Allen remained committed to playing in both the equipment and the service markets, believing that AT&T could understand its customers' needs better in this dual role. Second, some analysts predicted that AT&T might miss the interactive multimedia services market for the lack of a suitable partner in the cable television business. If cable companies chose to link with other telecommunications companies to form a national network, AT&T might be left with just an "alternate pipeline supplier" role in this huge, emerging industry. On the other hand, some within the company argued that AT&T had little to add in this type of a relationship because it was the cable companies which provided the real value—the entertainment—and that industry was better left to others. Finally, industry analysts questioned whether AT&T was trying to do too much in its broad-based strategy, with the risk that it would fall prey to companies who specialized in a given niche of the market and might thus be able to offer superior price performance.

INTERNATIONAL EXPANSION

While most segments of the American telecommunication equipment and services market were growing at 10% per year or less, the market in some lesser-developed countries, such as China and India, enjoyed annual growth rates of 30–80%. AT&T saw expansion outside the U.S. as a key to achieving its growth goals. Until 1980, when AT&T announced its desire to become a global company, its international activity had been limited for one hundred years to providing international long distance services to the U.S. population through cooperation with carriers in other countries. AT&T's international revenues of only 8% in 1984 increased to 24% in 1993, but much of the growth came from the

NCR acquisition. In 1993, AT&T laid claim to a presence in almost 120 countries, design facilities in 14 countries, and manufacturing operations in 35 countries around the world. The company employed over 50,000 people—16% of its workforce—outside the United States. However, in spite of these statistics, international expansion had, so far, been slower than the company would have liked, and Allen had publicly stated that he wanted to expand AT&T's share of non-U.S. revenues to something approaching 50% by the year 2000.

Within the developed countries of the world, AT&T found it difficult to promote its equipment sales against the many entrenched equipment suppliers already selling to the national PTTs. Most of AT&T's revenues in these markets came from the sale of its services to American companies and world travelers. In order to provide both its traditional and specialized services to these target markets, the company needed to achieve better linkages to all areas of the world, both industrialized and developing. This required alliances with the local phone companies in each country for access to their local networks and to provide platforms for various specialized services that AT&T could provide. The company had created alliances with phone companies in Singapore, Japan, Korea, Australia, and Canada to form the beginnings of a network it called "World Source." It had undertaken fruitless negotiations throughout 1992 and 1993 with the major European PTTs to further fill out this capability. AT&T found it difficult to develop such agreements in Europe because the large local operators—like France Telecom, British Telecom, and Deutsche Telecom—wanted to capture the same high-margin services for themselves.

AT&T's competitors appeared to have an advantage on this dimension. In 1993, British Telecom acquired a 20% shareholding in MCI—an American long distance carrier and AT&T's arch rival—to form the nucleus for a competitive network of worldwide alliances. A year later, Sprint, Deutsche Telecom, and France Telecom forged a partnership in which the two European companies would acquire a 20% equity position in Sprint. Meanwhile, AT&T continued its negotiations, which had begun in 1992, to form an alliance with Unisource, a consortium including the Swiss, Dutch, and Swedish PTTs. To some within AT&T, however, there seemed a lack of clear-cut strategic direction in the international arena, and they feared AT&T might be relegated to a minor player in Europe.

In the developing nations, AT&T concentrated on selling switches and other network hardware to the national phone companies. It had achieved significant successes in equipment sales in countries such as South Korea, Indonesia, Poland, the Ukraine, and Mexico. In 1993, AT&T signed an agreement with the government of China which identified AT&T as its chosen partner to help the country develop a world-class telecommunications infrastructure. This could mean billions of dollars in revenues for the company. The McCaw acquisition was expected to open up additional opportunities, allowing AT&T to sell its world-class wireless expertise to developing countries and then to expand these customers into wired networks joined with other AT&T offerings.

INTEGRATING DIVERSITY

The restructuring of the Business Units had driven a dramatic improvement in cost performance. But, by 1991, Allen recognized that the pendulum had swung far enough in the direction of autonomous entities. To avoid becoming a holding company, he began a sustained effort to integrate the Business Units behind certain critical strategic thrusts. In 1988 Allen had been surprised at the ease with which the BU management teams had welcomed the accountability and responsibility of the new system. Several years later, as he tried to align the BUs' efforts to support overall corporate ambitions, he was concerned about how difficult it was to balance the need for integration with the sense of autonomy and freedom the BU managers so cherished. A manager with the Global Business Communications systems business highlighted some issues he faced in trying to integrate the efforts of his group (a multibillion dollar telecommunications systems division) with those of AT&T Paradyne (a 500 million dollar unit selling data communications equipment like modems and multiplexers):

> We are supposed to give Paradyne sales leads. Our first problem is we don't want to recommend Paradyne products to our customers because if our customer should have a problem with the Paradyne equipment, we are held hostage until it gets fixed. Yet if it is a competitor's product, we are not vulnerable. Second, the asymmetry between the businesses makes it difficult. One of our salesmen gave Paradyne a lead recently for a $500,000 order. Yet Paradyne, in a whole year, gave us less than $500,000 in leads. . . . Unless Paradyne management finds a way to make it attractive for [our] salespeople to help them, they will get no help.

In an attempt to change this mindset, Allen personally spent a great deal of time meeting with various BU managers.

> I try to encourage people to do the right thing for AT&T—to do what makes sense. I cite examples of where people are doing the right thing—I spread the stories. And then I tell them, "If you do the right thing for the customer and you get grief from someone—tell them I told you to do it and then tell them to call me."

AT&T was also creating a number of other, more structured mechanisms to integrate conflicting interests among its organizations. For example, Allen asked MEC members to come to their meetings wearing two hats. The first hat was from their own business and the second hat was Allen's own, the hat of the CEO. Within Bell Labs, management was promoting the development of common processes and platforms in its research and development which it hoped all BUs would use to provide commonality and integration. However, in the end, it was the power of *Our Common Bond* that Allen most relied upon to motivate AT&T's diverse interests to work together for the corporate and customers' good.

CROSS-BUSINESS UNIT INITIATIVES

The Strategy Forums had revealed the need for steady growth if AT&T was to become a leader in the infocom industry. However, traditional telephony markets could not provide the required growth. Rather, in the 1990s and beyond, the "white spaces" between the traditional boundaries of the 21 Business Units would present most of the potential for high growth through creative combination of new technologies. To address this challenge, in 1992 the MEC created six cross-BU initiatives in: multimedia, wireless, data communication, voice recognition, messaging, and scalable computers (different size computers based on the same microprocessor). Special teams drawn from the appropriate Business Units and Bell Labs would drive these initiatives forward. Each team was headed by an AT&T executive who either was a BU head or reported to one. Some, like the Multimedia team, included 17 different Business Units, though 5 or 6 was closer to the norm.

These cross-BU teams had gotten off to a rocky start. Even though AT&T's leadership had transmitted a clear message that these initiatives were vital for the future, the importance given to them varied among individuals and groups. According to Bob Holder, Vice President for Corporate Strategy, "Some will say—these are the cornerstone of AT&T's future. Others will call them complementary to the BUs. That is part of the problem." By mid-1994, only two of the original six initiatives were still functioning as such. The other four had been absorbed into the existing BU structure. In Allen's opinion, "The senior team has to better clarify the strategic framework on which the BU and cross-BU initiatives work." No dedicated leadership was assigned to the teams, and limited money and people were available to build the initial "business cases" encouraging Business Units to fund these efforts. One manager said, "The teams have to beg, borrow, and steal to support themselves." According to Tim Stewart, who was supporting the Data Communications Initiative project (enabling the infrastructure to handle multimedia):

> Each decision that has any "teeth" can be adverse for someone in the room. Each BU on the team offers a different network management solution in terms of hardware and software. Some of this difference is necessary to address different customer needs. The ideal would be if the team could advocate one platform enabling a set of solutions which could support each BU. Yet this might require some BUs to change their software, hardware, or adjust their customer offering. And after investing money to do this, they may not see any additional returns.

According to John Berndt, President of Business Development, "The six projects were seen as principal growth initiatives that were supposed to engage the BU managers and change their mindsets. Now the issue is to which BU will we give the lead for the initiatives—this will determine their outcome."

TEAM MANAGEMENT

Empowerment of the teams and their busy leaders was another key issue. The key members were operating executives with numerous demands on their time, many of which took priority over team commitments. Don Moyer, Chief Financial Officer for the Business Development function, pointed out, "Some of the BUs are still trying to get well [i.e., profitable]. If everyone was well, collaborative working would be easier."

In spite of the problems, there were success stories as a result of the initiatives. The Wireless Initiative— perhaps driven by the developing potentials of one formidable, clearly identifiable competitor (Motorola)— had made commendable progress on standardizing the wireless platform technology. Another successful project was the ATM* team of Bell Labs researchers working for five BUs within the Network Systems Group. Its task was to develop an ATM platform for use across all Network Systems Group businesses. Prior to the cross-BU team, several BUs within Network Systems had been working and spending enormous sums of money on such a project independently for over 10 years.

---

* ATM (autosynchronous transfer mode) was an industry standard format for transferring packets of diverse types of data across networks.

Henry Bosco—an experienced project manager who had led important aspects of the development of AT&T's tremendously successful 5E switch—became the dedicated champion of the ATM project. After soliciting the resources from the BUs to build a strong business case, he created a work group consisting of 20 people who developed the vision and technical guidelines for the overall project. According to Bosco, "These 20 had credibility and power. These were people who wouldn't be questioned on their decisions when they went back to their organizations." Bosco then created an organization of 300 Bell Labs individuals dedicated to the project, located in three widely separated geographical areas, along with some marketing people from the BUs. In contrast to some of the other initiatives, this cross-BU team reported directly to Bosco. In spite of geographical, cultural, and operational differences, the team put out its first joint product in just 18 months, while a project of this type would normally have taken 38 to 40 months. A number of other products were planned to follow soon after.

In spite of the progress being made by cross-BU teams, which were widely publicized in the company, management believed it had a long way to go before cross-BU cooperation became a part of the day-to-day working norms within the company. In 1992 and 1993, AT&T's revenues had increased by 3% and 3.5%, while the global telecommunications industry grew at 10%, and the U.S. market grew at 8%. To try to give the cross-BU growth initiatives more support, they were strengthened in 1993 through a direct link to the Executive Vice President of the Multimedia Products and Services Group. This Group, previously called the Communications Products Group, was renamed in 1993 to symbolize its expanded mission.

REGIONAL GOVERNANCE

For the first four years following the BU restructuring, the BUs managed all international activity (except Network Systems) from their headquarters in the United States. Network Systems was managed from the Netherlands as the result of a Philips joint venture, officially terminated in 1990. Though AT&T had a number of sales offices and partnerships located across the world, its U.S. centers made all decisions of importance (and even many minor decisions in some people's minds). Both customers and AT&T employees working outside of the U.S. were often frustrated with the company's inability to respond to local challenges quickly and effectively. For example, when salespeople in Beijing identified an opportunity, they had to develop a requirements document which was sent to a U.S. office which generated the bid.

That would then be returned to China, but any revisions had to again go back and forth to the U.S. In the best case, it took the AT&T China office 24 hours to get even simple price information for its customers. If a decision involved multiple divisions, it took even longer.

In order to allow decision making on a local level, AT&T had begun to experiment with a regional management structure in Spain in 1992. In the experimental structure, the Spanish AT&T unit was run with profit and loss responsibility and overseen by a board consisting of officer-level representatives from the concerned BUs. The board had the responsibility to approve the annual business plan, but the execution of the plan was the job of the local country head.

In 1993, AT&T decided to make China a region to be managed by a CEO with profit and loss responsibility. AT&T's capability to marry a tremendous range of different technologies had been one of the primary reasons that the Chinese had decided to add AT&T as a partner while still maintaining their ongoing relationships with other competitors such as Alcatel or Siemens. The Chinese government expected AT&T to work as one enterprise to offer end-to-end solutions to the country's telecommunications needs. Allen appointed Bill Warwick, a mild-mannered, well-respected AT&T veteran, as the President and CEO of AT&T China, with full accountability for all aspects of the company's business within the Greater China region.* While the formal mandate gave him considerable strategic and operational autonomy, Warwick's principal challenge lay in gaining the trust and support of the corporate BU management. Warwick noted, "We need to set up an organization which doesn't involve [the BUs] in decision making but keeps them interested in the execution."

To assist in the coordination of AT&T interests across the world, in 1993 Allen renamed his Operations Committee as the Global Operations team, better known as the GO team, and gave it responsibility for "the effectiveness of AT&T's operations worldwide and leadership in the resolution of cross-business operations issues." It created new regional structures for Europe, Asia Pacific, China, and Latin America/Caribbean. AT&T recognized that the need for regional management varied across the world, and thus decided against uniformly structured "cookie cutter regions." Instead it allowed each region to organize to fit the needs of that market. Furthermore, regionalization did not necessarily equal integration. As Vic Pelson [Chairman of the GO Committee] explained, "We do not want to bring the parts of AT&T together

unless the customer believes it adds value. If not, we won't integrate." In 1994 AT&T restructured BU reporting and individual compensation practices at the regional level to create stronger incentives for cooperation through a "shared accountability" model.

However, lack of international experience within the company was proving one of the most severe handicaps AT&T faced as it tried to localize decision making in international markets. As one overseas manager commented, "AT&T has a problem with accepting a pedigree other than an American passport. If we don't correct this, we'll never succeed as a global competitor." In 1994, there were approximately 700 American expatriates working outside the U.S. (of 50,000 international employees), though the aim was to reduce this over time by replacing them with locals. However, the company had found that a local employee without any previous experience working in AT&T was at a significant disadvantage because personal networks were very important when trying to get the autonomous BUs to cooperate.

THE MANAGEMENT CHALLENGE

Few inside or outside AT&T would disagree that the company had the technical capability and the resources to be the leading player in the high potential infocom industry. There was no other company in the world which offered the breadth of telecommunications service, equipment, and computers that AT&T did. The company was a favorite of Wall Street due to its outstanding financial performance. And business academics and analysts across the world were looking to AT&T as a model of how an effective management team could keep a mega-corporation from going the way of IBM, General Motors, and other U.S. giants who were struggling for survival in 1994. The questions were how quickly and completely would AT&T follow through on its proposed redirections.

QUESTIONS

1. Evaluate the sequence of steps Mr. Allen has taken to reposition AT&T. What do you think of *Our Common Bond*? What could and should he have done differently? Test the various models of change in the readings against Mr. Allen's approach. What did he do well? Poorly?

2. Evaluate AT&T's strategy in terms of the criteria for good strategy provided in various articles. How would you compare the effectiveness of AT&T's strategy versus that of its implementation? What

---

* Including Taiwan, Hong Kong, and China.

are the key missing elements in both? What should be done about each?

3. What should be done about the "cross-business-unit" thrusts? The regional governance issues? The traditional lack of international focus in AT&T? Bell Labs' effectiveness and focus?

4. Why has AT&T done so well to date? What critical elements in its posture must it change? How? In what sequence? What should be its future core competencies at the corporate level? What does this mean in practical terms?

EXHIBIT 1
AT&T Financials[a]
Dollars in millions (except per share amounts)

	1993*	1992	1991*	1990	1989
Results of Operations					
Total revenues	$67,156	$64,904	$63,089	$62,191	$61,100
Research and development expenses	3,069	2,911	3,114	2,935	3,098
Operating income (loss)	6,238	6,269	1,358	5,496	5,024
Income before cumulative effects of accounting changes	3,974	3,807	522	3,104	3,109
Net income (loss)	(3,794)	3,807	522	3,104	3,109
Earnings (loss) per common share before cumulative effects of accounting changes	2.94	2.86	0.40	2.42	2.40
Earnings (loss) per common share	(2.80)	2.86	0.40	2.42	2.40
Dividends declared per common share	1.32	1.32	1.32	1.32	1.20
Assets and Capital					
Property, plant and equipment—net	$19,397	$19,358	$18,689	$18,661	$17,023
Total assets	60,766	57,188	53,355	48,322	42,187
Long-term debt including capital leases	6,812	8,604	8,494	9,354	8,377
Common shareowners' equity	13,850	18,921	16,228	15,883	14,723
Net capital expenditures	3,701	3,933	3,860	4,018	3,951
Other Information					
Operating income (loss) as a percentage of revenues	9.3%	9.7%	2.2%	8.8%	8.2%
Net income (loss) as a percentage of revenues	(5.6)%	5.9%	0.8%	5.0%	5.1%
Return on average common equity	(29.0)%	21.1%	3.1%	19.7%	21.9%
Stock price per share	$52.50	$51.00	$39.125	$30.125	$45.50
Book value per common share	$10.24	$14.12	$12.39	$12.46	$11.54
Debt ratio	56.1%	46.1%	48.9%	47.6%	43.0%
Debt ratio excluding financial services	28.3%	25.4%	34.7%	38.3%	36.3%
Employees	308,700	312,700	317,100	328,900	339,500

[a]Financial data for all years are adjusted to reflect AT&T and NCR as if they were always one company though the merger did not occur until 1991.

[b]Data at year end except for 1993.

*1993 data reflect a $7.8 billion net charge for three accounting changes. These changes involved new accounting rules which affected the way all U.S. companies book expenses for retiree benefits, separation payments and income taxes. Excluding these accounting changes, net income was at an all time high.

1991 data reflect $4.5 billion of business restructuring and other charges.

1988 data reflect a $6.7 billion charge due to accelerated digitization of the long distance network.

1986 data reflect $3.2 billion of charges for business restructuring, an accounting change and other items.

Source: AT&T 1993 Annual Report.

EXHIBIT 1 (cont'd)

	1988*	1987	1986*	1985	1994	JAN. 1. 1984
Results of Operations						
Total revenues	$61,756	$60,530	$61,906	$63,130	$60,318	
Research and development expenses	2,998	2,810	2,599	2,527	2,471	
Operating income (loss)	(2,275)	4,281	999	3,569	2,824	
Income before cumulative effects of accounting changes	(1.230)	2,463	651	1,872	1,713	
Net income (loss)	(1.230)	2,463	476	1,872	1,713	
Earnings (loss) per common share before cumulative effects of accounting changes	(0.94)	1.82	0.42	1.31	1.23	
Earnings (loss) per common share	(0.94)	1.82	0.29	1.31	1.23	
Dividends declared per common share	1.20	1.20	1.20	1.20	1.20	
Assets and Capital						
Property, plant and equipment—net	$16,394	$21,866	$22,061	$23,133	$22,167	$21,416
Total assets	39,869	44,014	43,617	44,683	43,418	39,156
Long-term debt including capital leases	8,350	8,027	7,789	8,026	8,943	9,462
Common shareowners' equity	13,705	16,617	15,946	16,951	15,839	14,413
Net capital expenditures	4,288	3,805	3,904	4,295	3,685	
Other Information						
Operating income (loss) as a percentage of revenues	(3.7)%	7.1%	1.6%	5.7%	4.7%	
Net income (loss) as a percentage of revenues	(2.0)%	4.1%	0.8%	3.0%	2.8%	
Return on average common equity	(7.2)%	15.0%	2.2%	10.7%	10.5%	
Stock price per share	$28.75	$27.00	$25.00	$25.00	$19.50	$17,875
Book value per common share	$10.55	$12.66	$11.91	$12.58	$12.00	$11.39
Debt ratio	41.6%	36.1%	34.4%	34.5%	36.5%	40.1%
Debt ratio excluding financial services	37.3%	32.5%	32.2%	32.9%	36.2%	40.1%
Employees	364,700	365,000	378,900	399,600	427,200	435,000

EXHIBIT 2

ABOUT AT&T

AT&T is a global company that provides communications services and products, as well as network equipment and computer systems, to businesses, consumers, telecommunications service providers and government agencies. Our worldwide intelligent network carries more than 140 million voice, data, video and facsimile messages every business day. AT&T Bell Laboratories engages in basic research as well as product and service development. AT&T also offers a general-purpose credit card and financial and leasing services. AT&T people work in more than 120 countries.

AT&T's business units are clustered in five groups.

Communication Services Group

Markets global long distance and electronic messaging services for business and residential customers. Manages the AT&T Worldwide Intelligent Network and private corporate networks. Installs undersea fiber-optic cable systems. Services include operator, directory and interpretation assistance; voice and electronic mail; teleconferencing; telephone-based marketing; and a consumer credit card.

Some familiar offerings: AT&T 800 Service. USA Direct®, Reach Out® World, AT&T Language Line® Service, AT&T Mail, AT&T Enhanced FAX Service and the AT&T Universal Card.

Communications Products Group

Develops, manufactures, markets and services telecommunications products for consumers, businesses and government entities around the world. Establishes business based on AT&T technology applications beyond the scope of existing business units. Products include corded, cordless and cellular phones; a videophone and a personal communicator; facsimile machines; answering systems; home security systems; modems; multiplexers and other data communications devices; business telephone systems; voice processing systems; and videoconferencing products. Some familiar names: AT&T Phone Centers, Trimline® telephones, AT&T VideoPhone 2500™, Definity® communications systems, Audix® voice messaging and Conversant® voice response systems, Partner® communications systems, Comsphere® data communications products.

Network Systems Group

Develops, manufactures, markets and services network software and equipment for telephone companies, governments, private network operators, cable television operators and wireless service providers. Offers cable, switching operations, transmission and wireless systems, and provides the engineering, installation and support services needed to build and operate networks. Develops and markets advanced microelectronic and photonic components and power supplies. Some familiar products: 5ESS® switching systems, Systemax® premises distribution systems, AccuRibbon® fiber-optic cable, Autoplex® wireless communications systems, and Hobbit™ microprocessors.

NCR

Develops, manufacutres, markets and services enterprise-wide information systems for customers worldwide. Links departments, buildings, campuses, and global locations through servers and client computers—from pen-based notepad computers to massively parallel systems. Also offers hardware, software and services for networking; imaging systems that convert paper-based information into electronic form; and industry-specific solutions for retail, financial, commercial, industrial, medical and educational institutions, and for government and the telecommunications industry.

Some familiar offerings: NCR System 3000 computers; WaveLAN and StarLAN networking systems; COOPERATION® software; NCR Document Management System™ and NCR automated teller machines and point-of-service terminals.

AT&T Capital Corporation

Provides commercial customers with leasing and financing services for a broad range of AT&T and non-AT&T products and services, including telecommunications equipment, complex computer systems, office and manufacturing equipment, automobiles and general business equipment. Some familiar names: AT&T Capital Corporation, AT&T Credit Corporation, NCR Credit Corp.

Source: AT&T *Annual Report,* 1992.

EXHIBIT 3

Our Common Bond

WE COMMIT TO THESE VALUES TO GUIDE OUR DECISIONS AND BEHAVIOR:

RESPECT FOR INDIVIDUALS

We treat each other with respect and dignity, valuing individual and cultural differences. We communicate frequently and with candor, listening to each other regardless of level or position. Recognizing that exceptional quality begins with people, we give individuals the authority to use their capabilities to the fullest to satisfy their customers. Our environment supports personal growth and continous learning for all AT&T people.

DEDICATION TO HELPING CUSTOMERS

We truly care for each customer. We build enduring relationships by understanding and anticipating our customers' needs and by serving them better each time than the time before. AT&T customers can count on us to consistently deliver superior products and services that help them achieve their personal or business goals.

HIGHEST STANDARDS OF INTEGRITY

We are honest and ethical in all our business dealings, starting with how we treat each other. We keep our promises and admit our mistakes. Our personal conduct ensures that AT&T's name is always worthy of trust.

INNOVATION

We believe innovation is the engine that will keep us vital and growing. Our culture embraces creativity, seeks different perspectives and risks pursuing new opportunities. We create and rapidly convert technology into products and services, constantly searching for new ways to make technology more useful to customers.

TEAMWORK

We encourage and reward both individual and team achievements. We freely join with colleagues across organizational boundaries to advance the interests of customers and shareowners. Our team spirit extends to being responsible and caring partners in the communities where we live and work.

By living these values, AT&T aspires to set a standard of excellence worldwide that will reward our shareowners, our customers, and all AT&T people.

Source: AT&T.

EXHIBIT 4
AT&T's Joint Ventures,
Equity Investments, and
Acquisitions

N. America

AG Communication Systems	JV	USA	Switching
AT&T Fitel	JV	USA	Fiber optic
3DO	Eqty	USA	Interactive Media
Eaton Financial	Eqty	USA	Financing
EO	JV	USA	Personal Communicators
General Magic	Eqty	USA	Personal Communicators
GO Corp	Eqty	USA	Handwriting recogn.
Knowledge Adventure	Eqty	USA	Multim. educ. s/w
Litespec	JV	USA	Fiber optic
McCaw	Acq.	USA	Cellular
NCR	Acq.	USA	Computers
Paradyne	Acq.	USA	Data communications
Shaye Communications	Acq	USA	Dig. cordless phones
Sierra Network	Eqty	USA	Interact. video game
Spectrum Holobyte	Eqty	USA	Computer games
Teradata	Acq.	USA	Computers
Unitel Comm.	Eqty	Canada	Long distance
Western Union Bus Services	Acq.	USA	Electr. messaging

Europe

ATP Italia	Eqty	Italy	Transmission
Atesia	JV	Italy	Telemarketing serv.
AT&T NS International BV	JV	Neth.	Network Equipment
AT&T Prague	JV	Czech	Transmission
AT&T St. Petersburg	JV	Russia	Transmission
Business Communi. Europ	JV	Italy	Sales/service
Compagnie Industr. Riu.	Eqty	Italy	Info. tech.
Dataid	Acq.	France	Software
Istel	Acq.	UK	Data services
Italtel	Eqty	Italy	Telecom Equipment
Lycom A/S	JV	Scand.	Fiber optic
Telfa S.A.	Eqty	Poland	Switching
Utel	JV	Ukraine	Network upgrde

Asia Pacific

AT&T of Beijing	JV	China	Fiber optic
AT&T of China	JV	China	Transmission
AT&T Japan Semic.	Eqty	Japan	Mkt. semiconductors
AT&T Jens	JV	Japan	Network Services
AT&T Network Tech.	JV	Thail.	Connectors
AT&T of Shanghai	JV	China	Transmission
AT&T Software Japan	Eqty	Japan	Software
AT&T Taiwan Telec.	JV	Taiwan	Switching/trans
Goldstar Fiber Opt.	JV	Korea	Fiber optic
Goldstar Info & Comm.	JV	Korea	Switch/transtICs
Hutchison AT&T Netwk	JV	HK	Network services
PT AT&T Netwk Systms	JV	Indon.	Switching
Trans-India Network Systems	JV	India	Transmission
United Fiber Optic	Eqty	Taiwan	Fiber optic/transm
Western Elec Saudi Arabia	Eqty	Saudi.	Install/maintenance

Caribbean/Mexico/S. America

AT&T Grupo ITSA	Eqty	Mexi.	Business services
Jamaica Digiport Intl	JV	Jamai.	Telecom services

In the early 1990s, Nintendo Co. Ltd. had quietly become one of the most successful companies in the world. Throughout the 1980s, the best performing companies on the Japanese stock market had been Toyota and Honda in terms of profits per employee and total profits. In 1992 the leading company was Nintendo. While Fujitsu and Sony with roughly 50,000 employees earned $94 million and $114 million respectively in 1992, Nintendo with approximately 850 people earned $763 million. In 1993, its sales ballooned to $6.2 billion and profits to $860 million. Approximately 37 million American homes then had Nintendo video game systems. Only 27 million American homes and 50–60 million users worldwide had PCs. Dozens of companies manufactured PCs, and the leader IBM had only 10% of the market. Nintendo held about 80% of its market and manufactured all its own systems. But 1993 turned into a crucial year for Nintendo as SEGA and 3DO reshaped the marketplace. (See exhibits at end of case for financial and market data.) How had Nintendo become so powerful and where might it go in the future? The implications were profound for both the entertainment and computer worlds.

EARLY HISTORY

Mr. Fusagiro Yamauchi had founded Nintendo Koppai in 1889 to produce playing cards for Hanafuda, a popular Japanese game. The kanji characters he chose to name his company—Nin–Ten–Do—connoted "leave luck to heaven."* Yamauchi expanded into Western-style playing cards in 1907 and by the time he retired, Nintendo was the largest Japanese playing card company. His grandson, Hiroshi Yamauchi, took over the company at age 21, after World War II, created a new distribution system, and expanded sales to record levels. Still, he wanted to expand faster. After some diversions the young Yamauchi, joined by Hiroshi Imanishi (a lawyer-administrator) and Gunpei Yokoi (an engineering tinkerer), moved the company into "games." He set up an R&D division, called simply Games, in a warehouse outside Kyoto in 1969.

Yamauchi asked Yokoi to create something for Christmas sales. "What should I make?" Yokoi asked. Yamauchi responded, "Something great."[1] Yokoi soon created "Ultra Hand" (a latticework extension that could grip things at a distance), "Ultra Machine" (a pitching machine that lobbed a light version of a baseball for indoor batting), a self-focusing periscope, and an electronic "Love Tester" that delighted buyers. Although he had no engineering background, Yamauchi demonstrated an uncanny sense about potential new products, giving Yokoi suggestions and challenging him to improve designs. The Chairman never sought a second opinion. If he liked the product, he instructed Imanishi to begin production.[1,22]

ELECTRONIC TOYS

Seeking to go beyond these products, Yamauchi pressed his engineers to investigate electronic toys. Yokoi's group soon built an electronic "Light Beam Gun" that led to a variety of "shooting games," includ-

© Copyright James Brian Quinn and Philip Anderson, 1995. All rights reserved. The generous financial support of International University of Japan and the kind cooperation of Nintendo Co., Nintendo of North America, and Technology Partners, Inc. are gratefully acknowledged. Research associates were Nobuo Okochi, Allie Quinn, and Penny Paquette.

*D. Scheff, *Game Over*, Random House, New York, 1993, provides an excellent history and insights into the game industry and Nintendo Co. References to this work are noted (1, pg. xx) in the text.

ing *Wild Gunman*, in which a homicidal maniac suddenly appeared on a screen and had to be blasted before he "shot" you. To exploit these, Yamauchi acquired a series of bowling alleys which had suddenly become mausoleums when Japan's bowling rage ended in the 1960s. He converted these into Nintendo Laser Clay Shooting Ranges, which became "in-group spots" for entertainment in the early 70s.

This phase of Nintendo's growth declined swiftly when the 70s oil shortages discouraged travel to the galleries. Yamauchi became intrigued by the rapidly falling prices of electronics and the new games like *Pong* that companies like Atari and Magnavox were beginning to sell for home television sets. He negotiated a license for Japan, but—lacking the electronic know-how to build games in volume—he teamed Nintendo with Mitsubishi to build its *Color TV Game 6* (offering six versions of *Pong* "light tennis"), *Block Buster*, and a racing game. Although these sold a few million units, they did not provide the revolutionary product Yamauchi was seeking. Yamauchi ordered his engineers to "throw away all your old ideas in order to come up with something new." The result was a tiny, superbly successful video game called *Game and Watch*, the size of a hand calculator. They also produced *Hell Fire*, *Sheriff*, *Sky Skipper*, and *Radar Scope* for arcades.

Mr. Yamauchi later modestly said of this era, "Just as many other industries were changed by the introduction of computer technologies, the entertainment industry for home use was revolutionized in a relatively short time. Because Nintendo had already been involved in many entertainment markets, we thought that in the near future the computer age would come for these industries, and thus Nintendo had to change. What Nintendo did was just very fortunate—to ride on the tide and make some products which happened to be attractive to customers and matched very large market forces, which we could not control."[2]

"SOMETHING NOTICEABLY MORE REALISTIC"

But Yamauchi continued to press for something really different. He insisted that Nintendo "develop something that other companies could not copy for at least one year. It must be so much better that there will be no question which system the customers will want."[1,29] And it also had to be cheap, less than $75, at a time when other machines were selling for $250–$350. Masayuki Uemura, who had been working with Yokoi, spent 18 hour days trying to compress arcade game intricacies onto a micro computer where one or two chips could control the entire action and interaction. He wanted a game that was "noticeably more realistic" than competitors' home video efforts.

His demands—for example, 52 colors instead of 8—required specific new chips, not just the chips mass produced for PCs. In addition to their more rigorous output requirements, the chips had to cost less than ¥2,000 (then about $7). Many chip manufacturers refused to cooperate at this price. Yamauchi insisted on both low prices and lower defect rates than any other customer. And most suppliers felt Nintendo could never reach the 3 million unit levels that would make production profitable. Fortunately, Ricoh's semiconductor division happened to be having difficult times and, although skeptical, took a risk and developed the chips. These initial contracts would lead to some of the most lucrative associations in the semiconductor and electronic industries. By 1993 Nintendo was spending well over $1 billion on semiconductors annually.

VAST NEW POTENTIALS

As componentry dropped in price, Yamauchi began to see vast new potentials. He saw his game platforms as "home computer systems disguised as toys."[1,29] But he never lost his focus on games. For his "computers disguised as toys" Yamauchi instructed Uemura to leave off all unnecessary frills—no keyboards; no modems or disk drives; cartridges, not disks; minimum memory, but more than competitors'. He feared frills would scare off game customers, especially computerphobes. Still Nintendo's friendlier cartridge contained 32 times more computer code than an Atari cartridge, and the machine's capabilities far exceeded Atari's most powerful games. Despite his caveats, Yamauchi insisted that even early models have circuitry and connectors that could send or receive modified signals to or from a central processor. This would pave the way for future peripherals (from modems to keyboards) and services if desirable. Nintendo built direct data communications functions into its systems from 1989 forward.

FAMICOM AND SOFTWARE

In May 1983 Yamauchi announced the name of Nintendo's new system, Family Computer, or "Famicom" for short. After a tidal wave of early sales, disaster hit around the Japanese New Year—the toy industry's busiest period. Certain games for the Famicom caused the system to freeze. Despite very expensive implications, Yamauchi instructed, "Recall them all." Although losing millions by missing the prime sales season, the success of Famicom was unprecedented. Eventually the 14 competing home video game machine companies were driven from the market, while kids camped out in front of stores to snap up copies of new Nintendo games before they were sold out. Once several million families had a Famicom, they desperately wanted games to play on it; and Yamauchi recognized that software, not hardware, was the key to the future.

A SPECIAL TALENT

In 1977, a special talent, Sigeru Miyamoto, arrived at Nintendo. He had come to show Yamauchi some bizarre but cheerful toy creations. Miyamoto's creative mind wondered why games couldn't draw on the great legends and fairy tales of fiction like King Kong or Jason and the Argonauts. Perhaps with King Kong in mind, he came up with a cute—but donkey-stubborn—ape as a main character in a game which became the improbably named *Donkey Kong*.

Although marketing people and American sales managers hated the name, millions of *Donkey Kong* games delighted their young users. In time (1984) Miyamoto was asked to head up a new division, R&D4, whose goal was to come up with the most imaginative video games ever seen. Given this challenge and direction by Yamauchi, Miyamoto converted the gentle Walter Mitty character from *Donkey Kong* into the delightful, round cartoon character, Mario. Soon he and his tall, thin brother, Luigi, were adventuring in new worlds of "dragons, serpents, flying turtles, fire-spitting daisies, and angel wings upon which they could hitch a ride."[1,50]

In an industry characterized by creative genius, Miyamoto is a Michelangelo. Miyamoto's early creations of *Super Mario* and the *Legend of Zelda* established a new standard for video games. Many of his games built on characters and skills the players had learned in preceding games. Each was a challenge, but with the comfort of not having to learn the entire game from scratch. His group worked in small teams (from 6 to 20 people) usually for 12 to 18 months. Miyamoto was said to be a terrible manager. He oversaw all aspects of the creation of his games, writing scripts, working with artists, editors, programmers, musical composers, etc. Miyamoto often spread out the blueprint of a game across a room full of tables that had been pushed together, determining points in the game

that were too frustrating or too easy, adding fillips of delight, or gimmicks to challenge the player's creative mind. Between 1985 and 1990 he produced eight *Mario* games. An astonishing 60–70 million were sold, making Miyamoto the most successful game designer in the world. *Mario Brothers* movies became a popular adjunct. *Mario* music became so popular that it was sold as separate CDs and records—and performed in symphony concerts.

When asked what guidance he gave to game designers or engineers inside Nintendo, Mr. Yamauchi responded, "If there were any specific rules which would allow you to make a very good game, we would like to know them. The interest for any one game or one person is very different. Some games will appeal to one group but not to others in each country or age group. There are many types of games. There are action games, role-playing games, situation games, and many other types. Some game creators like to make role-playing games because they like to play those games, while other designers prefer to play action games. But the big problem is that in most cases one game cannot be created or made up by a single designer. Game creation requires capable programmers, character designers, game designers, sound composers, and (for some games) scenario writers. Directors have to supervise these individuals and take care of the whole balance of each team and how the game can be made attractive to the customer. I, Yamauchi, cannot say much about these points. . . . I simply don't have any of these talents."

THE LICENSING PROGRAM

In the mid 1980s, with retailers turning away hordes of customers who wanted even more games, Yamauchi began a licensing program. For the privilege of being allowed to make games for Nintendo machines, developers granted Nintendo the right to approve their games, artwork, packaging, and advertising commercials. Nintendo could reject any games or portions of licensees' games it considered to be in bad taste. Once Nintendo approved a game, licensees had to place an order for at least 10,000 cartridges to be manufactured by Nintendo. These were sold back to the developers at $9–$14 per cartridge, about twice Nintendo's production cost. The charge included "manufacturing, printing, packaging, and a royalty for use of Nintendo's licensed intellectual property."[1,215] But its licensees prospered from Nintendo's endorsement and its distribution power, with sales often rocketing overnight from a few thousand to millions of units. One licensee, a start-up company called Enix, sold over 2 million copies of its first game, *Dragon Quest*; successors sold 2–3.5 million each, while *Dragon Quest 4* sold out its 1.3 million run within 1 hour after it was introduced.

After initially allowing its licensees to produce their own games, Nintendo moved to control the quality of its product. It became the sole manufacturer of games for the Famicom, and Nintendo insisted on cash in advance from its licensees. After a few years, Nintendo sometimes subcontracted licensees' orders to highly selected outside manufacturers, subject to its own rigid quality controls. In the early 90s, fearing a repeat of the Atari experience (where a proliferation of mediocre games had destroyed the entire games marketplace), Yamauchi moved to limit the number of games licensees could release each year.

When asked what guidance he gave to licensees, Mr. Yamauchi commented, "Basically we say nothing to our suppliers about the kinds of games we think will be successful or what they should design. All we do is inspect their software for quality and to protect [customers and ourselves] against issues of corporate morals; that is games which contain too much violence, contain any nudity, or have scenes of a pornographic sort that would not be acceptable for the family user."

COUNTERMEASURES

So successful were Nintendo's games that the chips at the heart of Famicom cartridges were often in short supply as consumer demand soared in 1988–1991. Nintendo was obliged to "ration" cartridges, a practice that infuriated retailers. Knowing that renegade companies would try to manufacture their own Famicom games, Uemura's engineers installed circuitry inside the Famicom that would reject non Nintendo approved games. Periodically, the code was updated to maintain the exclusion. Nintendo also exercised strong control of its distribution channels. In his excellent book about Nintendo, *Game Over*, David Sheff says, "It was almost impossible for an outsider, against Nintendo's wishes, to get distribution. Wholesalers refused to carry unauthorized products for fear of being cut off by Nintendo."[1,71] Both licensees and competitors complained, but were relatively helpless to take action.

There were a number of magazines devoted to Nintendo games, including its own *Nintendo World*, which sold more copies than any other magazine targeted to young readers. Those published by independent companies were almost completely dependent on Nintendo, which provided much of their editorial content and tips on how to be successful in certain difficult games. When one of the companies attempting to back-engineer Nintendo's "lock out" system tried to advertise in one of these magazines, Nintendo withdrew all of its advertising and support.[1,72] The offending "pirate" was refused space in the magazine. Other licensees or designers of successful games tried to compromise Nintendo's rigid licensing system. But none succeeded. Yamauchi was adamant that all agreements with licensees would be identical; there would be no exceptions.

EXPANSIONS INTO NETWORKS

In 1988, Yamauchi began another stage of Nintendo's development. The plan was called Family Computer Communications Network System. The Famicom was connected into a telephone line by a Communications Adapter (modem). Another cartridge allowed the Famicom to communicate with other terminals and mainframe computers. Customers could play interactive video games with other players throughout Japan. However, Yamauchi saw the system as a basis for "linking Nintendo households to create a communications network that provides users with new forms of recreation, and a new means of accessing information. From now on our purpose is not only to develop new exciting entertainment software, but to provide information that can be efficiently used in each household."[1,77] Through agreements with Nintendo and Nomura Securities Company, the largest Japanese brokerage firm, families could use the Famicom to buy, sell, trade, and monitor stocks and bonds. Soon other brokerage houses joined in. And new services were added, for buying stamps, betting on horse races, and exercise programs. In the early 1990s, however, only 15,000–20,000 had signed up for such programs.

THE AMERICAN ADVENTURE

In the meantime another major development had occurred. Headed by Minoru Arakawa (husband of Yamauchi's daughter, Yoko), Nintendo of America (NOA) had become a substantial power in its own right. Setting aside his biases against family members in the business, Yamauchi had been impressed by Arakawa's managerial and organization skills, as well as his perseverance and dedication.[1,92] Nintendo's American business was started by licensing its Japanese arcade games through a trading company to "coin-op" arcade businesses. During the early 1980s start up, Arakawa operated NOA on a shoestring. He hired kids he met at the video arcades, and ran the business from a run-down New Jersey warehouse—without heating or air conditioning and featuring enormous rats and a broken elevator. Everyone performed all tasks. Things moved slowly at first, but Hiroshi Yamauchi did not intervene since he had agreed to give Arakawa his head. The first games shipped in quantity to the U.S.—*Radar Scope* games from the Japanese arcades—took months to arrive in the U.S. By then, *Radar Scope* seemed very old and became a disaster that almost sank the fledgling Nintendo of America.

Seeking to shorten the cycle time of shipments and communications, Arakawa moved headquarters to Vancouver, Washington. Pleading with Yamauchi to obtain a superior game, Arakawa was assigned one from a new apprentice, Sigeru Miyamoto. When the game arrived and they saw that it was the then unknown *Donkey Kong*—with its strange title and improbable characters—some of the U.S. executives walked out saying, "It's over." Nevertheless Arakawa convinced some tavern owners to install the *Donkey Kong* game. It was an instant hit, gobbling up hundreds of quarters each night for the tavern owners. Arakawa trademarked the *Donkey Kong* name and copyrighted the game. With his young legal counsel, Howard Lincoln, Arakawa stubbornly stood off competitors who wanted to buy *Donkey Kong* and MCA-Universal who claimed its title violated their (non existent) copyright on the King Kong name. Arakawa's group sold 60,000 more *Donkey Kong* games, and NOA's second year ended up with more than $100 million in sales as other arcade games and Arakawa's Chuck E Cheese "food and entertainment" concept caught on.

CRASH AND REBIRTH

In 1983, Arakawa attempted to move from arcades into the toy business with Nintendo's *Game & Watch* game. But his timing was disastrous. In the early 1980s, companies like Atari, Mattel and Coleco had shared the multi-billion dollar U.S. video games business. Atari, the industry's leader, also led its decline. To build volume Atari had introduced a large number of games designed by outsiders and its own staff. Many had simplistic figures, unreliable software, and very poor definition of the game characters on the TV screen. Still Atari expanded rapidly, hitting $2 billion in sales in 1982, but the toys business was highly uncertain, and periodically imploded. Precipitously the $3 billion home video game industry of 1982 shrank to $100 million in 1983. Retailers lost millions on video games

they could not sell. Most of the earlier producers went bankrupt. No one welcomed the new entrant, Nintendo, to this disastrous scene.

As other companies collapsed in the home video games market, Minoru Arakawa noticed that video arcades featuring Miyamoto's games were still packed, bringing in more money than first-run movies. His conclusion, bad products and business practices in the home market were to blame for the industry fiasco. He decided he had to differentiate Nintendo from Atari, Coleco, and Mattel and broaden its merchandising base away from toy retailers. To support this, Arakawa had Nintendo engineers design an advanced (8 bit) video system—later called Nintendo Entertainment System or NES—with better graphics and a "lock and key system" that assured no one else could provide games for an NES without Nintendo's approval. Despite strongly negative market research findings in the U.S., Hiroshi Yamauchi agreed to a $50 million commitment to get the new home video game business rolling for NOA. But early sales were extremely discouraging. American retailers and consumers still associated video games with the earlier much more simplistic "stick like" products available on computers and Atari-like systems.

DECISION POINT

Given the negative consumer attitudes in 1983–1984, how could Nintendo of America crack the U.S. marketplace? How should Arakawa proceed step by step? How should NOA position its NES? Who will be its competition? How should it position against these competitors?

MORTAL COMBAT BEGINS

Some groups tried to bypass the "lock and key" system of Nintendo. One (Atari) broke the code by illegally getting access to Nintendo's copyrighted system from the U.S. Copyright Office.[1,248] It introduced some "Nintendo compatible systems" through its Tengen brand, but Nintendo shut off their distribution by threatening to sue any company carrying these games. Although Atari later claimed in a lawsuit that it had "reverse engineered" the lock and key system on its own, the court found to the contrary. Judge Fern Smith of the U.S. District Court for the northern district of California found against Atari in that case, prohibiting

Atari from copying, selling, or using Nintendo's copyrighted computer program in any way. Atari and others then brought suit against Nintendo for violation of antitrust laws. In the early 1990s some of these cases were wending their way slowly through the courts, but none had been resolved against Nintendo.

A major problem for Nintendo at this time was the burgeoning video game rental industry. Computer software producers had similar worries: that renting their software could become rampant. Nintendo pointed out that movies, which enjoyed a huge rental market, were protected against excessive use. Studios could decide if and when a movie would be made available to rental stores, and elaborate procedures were in place to capture royalties from this transaction. Nintendo sued Blockbuster and others who tried to rent its games and actively sought redress from software producers who made devices that would alter or bypass specific elements of a Nintendo game, claiming thereby to have created a whole new game. Of greatest concern to Nintendo were entire countries which refused to enforce Nintendo's property rights; in some cases governments actively benefited from deals with their national software producers who pirated copyrighted games. In some countries hardware suppliers willingly made "knock off" copies of game circuitry for unlicensed OEMs, claiming they could not know or be held responsible for how a circuit was used.

THE NEW TECHNOLOGIES' ATTACK[3]

In the fall of 1989, a small group of Americans decided that Nintendo had cracks in its armor. Working under the name of New Technologies Group (NTG) and in heavy secrecy, they set out to develop new video game technology that would incite a third revolution in the industry and challenge Nintendo's seemingly unassailable position in the American home.

One of NTG's founders, David Morse, had a unique track record as an entrepreneur. In 1982, he started a company called Amiga, to develop a computer with extraordinarily powerful graphics that would make possible games and graphic applications far beyond those available for any other personal computer. The computer was a technical success, but as the IBM Personal Computer emerged as an industry standard, it became clear Amiga would need $30–$40 million to bring its product to market. In 1984, Morse sold Amiga to Commodore, then the maker of the leading 8-bit home computer. Morse made a considerable

amount of money on the Amiga sale, but he watched in frustration as Commodore positioned the machine squarely against the entrenched IBM standard.

The Amiga turned out to be a niche product, and he thought it could have sold better had it been promoted that way. Under Morse, the Amiga was developed for the high-end home market, with heavy emphasis on its game-playing potential. It was optimized for superior graphics and sound, the critical elements in the video game market, and was intended to be marketed only incidentally as a home computer. To that end, Morse had cultivated support from important game developers, convinced that Amiga's customer was the software developer and the developer's customer was the consumer.

After selling Amiga, Morse had moved to Epyx, a game developer, where he was one of the driving forces behind a hand-held video game system called *Lynx*. *Lynx* was the world's first color hand-held video game. Epyx sold the Lynx system to Atari, where it was positioned against Nintendo's *Game Boy*.

Then Morse talked to Bill Hart (head of Technology Partners, venture capitalists, and a founding investor in Amiga) about the huge prospects of the video game business. He argued that there was always a market willing to pay for something new and different. Morse persuaded Hart that the only reason for the 1983–1986 downturn was that the existing generation of technology (exemplified by the Atari 2600 and the Commodore 64) had aged without something new coming along. It seemed that whenever a new technology did appear, the consumer had an almost insatiable appetite for it. In 1989, SEGA and NEC had introduced 16-bit game machines, and everyone was still skeptical of their success. Nevertheless, Morse believed firmly that consumers would put up money for next generation technology in an area where they had already shown interest. The one interactive market for high powered computing whose existence was indisputable was the market for games. He predicted that 16-bit systems would succeed, and that the market leader (Nintendo) would stay with the old technology too long, as had Atari when confronted with Nintendo's NES.

In the fall of 1989 when Morse was ready to launch New Technologies Group—aimed at creating a totally new generation of video game hardware that would represent a quantum leap over existing technology—he approached Hart for venture capital. Hart's Technology Partners agreed to back NTG with a $315,000 seed investment, an amount Morse thought sufficient to fund development through an early demonstration of the technology.

TECHNOLOGY. The introduction of 16-bit arcade systems by SEGA and NEC in 1989 initially had little impact on Nintendo. (The number of bits refers to the amount of data the processor can simultaneously call from registers and manipulate in a program.) Sixteen-bit machines could allow more colors, faster play, and the potential to accommodate richer, more complicated games. As Morse had predicted, Nintendo initially downplayed the advantages of a more powerful microprocessor but responded rapidly by upgrading its own system through imaginative data compression and later introducing its own 16-bit machine, "Super NES."

Morse felt that a new generation of genuinely superior games could be developed if real-looking and -sounding audio and video could be brought to a television screen. In his view, one didn't start by saying "the next generation will be a 32-bit machine" or "video discs are the wave of the future"; one started with a clean slate and asked "what would it take to design a system with near-TV or near-cartoon quality video and CD-quality audio?" and "could this be done at a cost the market will accept?" In 1989, nothing came close to providing this level of realism.

One key to providing cinema-level quality was a very large color value. The human eye can distinguish 30,000–40,000 colors, but at that time most games used only 256 colors. A prerequisite for a next-generation system was a huge increase in the number of colors available to the game developer. A second key was on-screen resolution. Televisions display images as a series of pixels, or tiny dots on the screen. To create a more realistic image from a pixel pattern, a new generation system would have to (1) avoid the step-like diagonals and edges of most computers' output, (2) blend the edges of objects together through certain types of filtering, and (3) use fractal geometry to assemble polygons that look rounded or irregular, as objects do in life.

A third key was improving animation. Many animation techniques had been developed in other arenas that were not being used in video games, most of which were as flat and dimensionless as comic strip cartoons. In order to create a three-dimensional object moving in space from a viewer's perspective, for example, one needed a consistent way to make objects increase or decrease in size, to change relative perspectives automatically, and to be able to flip everything on the screen upside down in a fraction of a second. Additionally, it was necessary to build a variety of "cor-

ner engines" to manipulate the corners of polygons independently as their shape changed. Texture mapping was also critical—a lot of machines could manipulate a solid-color polygon rapidly but new graphics engines could make it possible quickly to build very detailed and articulated polygons without jagged corners. The fourth key was compact-disk-quality sound; the machine needed to be able to *generate* high-fidelity sounds, not merely play back pre-recorded sounds.

It seemed clear that such a system would have to be built around a 32-bit Reduced Instruction Set Computing (RISC) chip of the type which typically powered high-performance engineering workstations. Morse located a very powerful RISC processor with a tiny instruction set that met NTG's needs at a much lower cost than the complex chips at the heart of workstations. To achieve high speed in specialized applications, NTG would design custom semiconductors to act as graphics engines. Similarly, NTG would have to create a new custom digital signal processor chip to produce the necessary sound performance. The last piece of the puzzle was memory—it was clear that the highest-speed memory available would put the game system into an unaffordable price range. The solution was to combine high-speed virtual random access memory (VRAM) with standard dynamic random access memory (DRAM) chips such as those used in personal computers.

Given the architecture of the game system, the clear choice for storing programs was a CD-ROM (compact disk read-only memory). It was becoming difficult for software developers to fit complex games into a cartridge format, and full-motion digitized video would require enormous amounts of additional storage. For Morse, the major technical challenge was providing enough processing power to take advantage of the richness and complexity that CD-ROMs made possible. But Morse's principal business concern was making the new game system an attractive environment for software developers. By providing games on compact disks, software providers could avoid the huge inventory investment required to make cartridges. It is far easier to make CD-ROMs in small batches than it is to fabricate chips for a cartridge. And dozens of manufacturers could press CD-ROMs at competitive prices.

STRATEGY. Hart was of the school of venture capitalists who bet on people first and business plans second. He believed that the team Morse had assembled at Amiga included some of the best hardware and software technologists on the globe. And working together at Amiga and Epyx, this team had become a secret weapon of sorts for Morse over the years. Morse felt that Japanese firms such as Nintendo "employed good engineers but did not invent anything truly new." In his view, taking a non-linear step forward, inventing genuinely new ways of doing things, required the kind of talent that existed only in Silicon Valley. Through March 1990, the NTG team designed the hardware specifications for the next-generation game system. Whenever a piece of the puzzle required something beyond the state-of-the-art, the specification contained a black box that said "invention required." For Morse, NTG's core competence was filling in the "invention required" boxes, which meant creating a new way of doing things that no one had thought of before.

NTG had started as a partnership of three men who had worked together since the Amiga days: Morse, Dave Needle, and R. J. Mical. Needle was a hardware engineer whose special talent lay in designing the architecture of low-cost computer systems and designing custom very-large-scale-integration (VLSI) semiconductor chips. Mical was a software engineer whose forté was designing operating systems that allowed game developers to tap the full power of the hardware. For Morse, one of NTG's key advantages was that Needle and Mical had a history of working together to create new systems in an industry whose structure tended to isolate such skills into separate companies.

Morse was the visionary and business architect— he saw his job as freeing the engineers to do engineering while he ensured that the system could be delivered at a cost the market would accept. NTG was shooting at a target four years in the future. Morse thought about what state-of-the-art in video gaming would look like in that time frame and how the cost/performance of critical technologies such as semiconductors and CD-ROMs would evolve. He had to manage critical technical choices with the marketplace in mind—for example, any design decisions that would commit NTG to a particular vendor or unchangeable solution. Since custom silicon chips were to be a true cornerstone of the game system, understanding and negotiating with very-large-scale-integrated circuit (VLSI) development and fabrication companies was perhaps the single most critical task Morse took on.

Technical superiority was to be the foundation of NTG's strategy. Morse's aim was to produce a machine that would offer at least ten times the performance of any other system that he projected would be available when the NTG system went to market, around 1993–1994. Morse was convinced that with such a per-

formance differential, enough developers would flock to the machine to make it a new standard, despite Nintendo's huge installed base. However, Morse realized that the success of his machine would hinge first and foremost on great software. Unlike Nintendo, NTG did not include a large in-house game development group. Nor could it rely on a Sigeru Miyamoto to give the new machine the sort of momentum *Super Mario Brothers* had given the NES. Morse was determined to keep NTG small, convinced that with the right people, a small development team was more productive than a large one.

NTG followed four basic strategies. The first was providing technology that would let software developers create spectacular new forms of entertainment. The second was providing a more flexible collaboration system, attacking Nintendo's greatest weakness by exploiting the frustration its licensing policies often generated.* Third, a sophisticated encryption scheme was built into the NTG system to defeat piracy. No one could produce an NTG-compatible CD-ROM without a license from NTG, although Morse intended to provide more liberal licensing terms than Nintendo. Fourth, Morse did not plan to enter game manufacturing, much less to control it as Nintendo had controlled cartridge production. The NTG team worked under a cloak of secrecy to avoid tipping off rivals that a new generation of game hardware was under development. It did not formally involve game companies in the development process. Morse relied on his Silicon Valley location and close personal contacts to keep the firm abreast of what software developers were looking for in a game system.

A CHOICE OF FUTURES

Experience had taught Morse and Hart that firms which spent too much money reaching their first major milestones tended to have few alternatives, and had to

---

* NTG's system was not "open" or "transparent" in the sense that Apple Computer's was. Because of the system's encryption, independent software firms would need NTG's explicit permission to write games for the system. But Morris' system offered some attractive features for licensees. (1) Pressing CD-ROMs was cheaper than cartridges. (2) Once approved, manufacturing was the licensee's business. (3) A licensee could produce as many games per year or units of approved games as it chose. (4) There were no restrictions on porting games to other platforms. (5) NTG did not seek to approve licensees' packaging or advertising, and third party reviewers did all ratings of games.

give up too much to obtain additional funding. Hence, Morse focused only on the technology—to limit the partnership's exposure and maximize its leverage when the time for the next step arrived. Said Hart, "You really have to think through where the goal line is in an industry where it takes $100 million to get a new product to the marketplace."

By mid-1990, the NTG development team had planned out the system architecture, projected its basic cost, and produced a crude videotape illustrating some of its animation capabilities. Actually simulating the machine would have required the power of a Cray supercomputer; it would be a year before a silicon prototype was ready. Instead, they took a model airplane, taped it against a blue background in dozens of positions, and put together hundreds of individual frames showing what the system's rotation, scaling and other capabilities would look like. Having nearly used up Technology Partners' initial $315,000 investment, they felt they had accomplished what they set out to do, demonstrate the feasibility of the technology. The time had arrived to take the next step, creating the custom chips and assembling components into a working system. Four alternative paths seemed feasible.

VENTURE CAPITAL

Hart estimated that the next round of financing to fund hardware development would require about $3 million. Technology Partners' policies would only allow it to put another $2.2 million into the start-up if necessary. Raising venture money elsewhere would not be difficult. The NTG partners had two home runs to their credit, the Amiga and the Lynx. Within Silicon Valley, knowledgeable people accepted that if this team laid out a plan, it was capable of executing it, and the best-known venture capital firm in the Valley, Kleiner Perkins, had repeatedly expressed interest in NTG. Raising capital from a syndicate including firms as prestigious as Kleiner Perkins would enhance the start-up's image, provide useful connections, and broaden the range of expertise available to NTG.

However, there would be a major dilution of the founders' stake in NTG. Hart judged that for $3 million, NTG's backers would demand at least 50% of the company. The additional funding would allow NTG to produce a prototype, but in a year or so the company would again face the same decision: i.e., to raise more venture capital, sell the company, sell the technology, or form a joint venture or partnership. On the other hand, one year further along, NTG might also be much more valuable and might have a much stronger bargaining position.

ELECTRONICS FIRMS

A second alternative would be to strike a deal with an electronics firm, possibly Nintendo, one of its video game competitors, or a company that was not presently in the game business. NTG might sell its technology, license it in return for development funding, or sell a stake in NTG—perhaps even 100%—to a partner with deep enough pockets to bring the system to the marketplace. In forming NTG, Morse and Hart's initial model assumed that one or more major players in video gaming or consumer electronics would pay NTG for its work and grant NTG a perpetual royalty if the start-up could push the technology far enough along to demonstrate its capability.

Nintendo itself was one possibility. From his Epyx days, Morse had some experience negotiating with Nintendo of America, and he came away with the impression that Nintendo saw itself as a marketing company, whose clout could overcome any technical advantage. However, it was widely rumored that Nintendo was going to introduce a new 16-bit machine in Japan during the fall, pushing the "Super Famicom" into the marketplace with a new *Mario Brothers* game from Miyamoto. It was reliably reported that Nintendo's new machine would not play old NES cartridges. If Nintendo was able to wean its loyal customers to a new system despite NES-incompatibility, the experience would be quite useful when the time came to replace 16-bit systems with 32-bit ones. Nintendo's name, position in distribution channels, and limitless capital would be major assets for any video game manufacturer.

NEC was another possibility. Its 16-bit system was floundering in the marketplace and the firm was beginning to experience severe difficulties in Japan's consumer electronics industry. NEC seemed to be retrenching, but its capital base was huge and it had a reputation for long-term thinking. NEC was the only consumer electronics company that was also a world leader in semiconductors; partnering with such a firm might give NTG a cost advantage, particularly in memory chips. Like NTG, it depended totally on third-party developers for game software, and was therefore more likely to endorse NTG's software strategy than Nintendo would be.

SEGA, the other Japanese company with a 16-bit system, was a third alternative. SEGA's founders were Americans. Although SEGA had not yet made serious inroads into Nintendo's overall market share, it was experiencing more success than NEC selling 16-bit systems. Earlier in 1990, NTG had helped SEGA with some technical problems on its 16-bit system, and SEGA's management clearly respected the talent of NTG's personnel. SEGA had developed a number of very successful coin-operated arcade games that incorporated advanced animation and displayed approximately 500 colors. SEGA's American distributor was Morse's old firm, Tonka, which gave it a strong position in the toy distribution channel. However, Morse thought that SEGA might be developing an advanced system of its own. He was concerned that if he signed a deal, SEGA might keep NTG's technology on the shelf.

A consumer electronics firm that was not in the video game business would bring not only the necessary funding but also the manufacturing capabilities and presence in distribution channels that NTG lacked. The following were major possibilities:

▼ **Philips** was a Dutch firm whose brand name was Magnavox. Philips had been working on an interactive compact-disk video system (CD-I) for years, but in fall 1990 its technology had not yet reached the marketplace. It was an open question whether Philips would back a system that might impinge on CD-I's market, even though CD-I did not have the capabilities NTG envisioned. Philips also had a long history of technical brilliance combined with poor marketing. Video recorders, compact disks, and camcorders were but a few of the technologies Philips had pioneered, only to lose out in the marketplace to imitators.

▼ **Sony** had a worldwide reputation for innovation, with a company culture that revolved around pioneering new frontiers in consumer electronics. It was a major force in both the CD-ROM and compact disk markets and was also rumored to be developing a portable video disk player. Sony was the only consumer electronics firm with a substantial position in the graphics workstation segment of the computer market. It had recently purchased Columbia Pictures for the express purpose of bringing both hardware and software competencies to the development of new multi-media applications. However, it was rumored that within a year Sony intended to bring out an inexpensive system with a CD-ROM player, meant to challenge Nintendo in the video game arena. As with Philips, it was open to question whether Sony would endorse a challenge to its own compact disk game-playing machine.

▼ **Matsushita,** whose labels included Panasonic and JVC, was the largest consumer electronics firm in the world. Through its JVC division, Matsushita had pioneered the VHS standard in video recorders, unseating Sony by putting together a cheaper design backed by a strong set of allies. Matsushita might bring competence in forging an industry standard, which would be of immeasurable assistance in attacking Nintendo. Through MCA it owned Universal Pictures. Its distribution channel strength was second to none. While Matsushita had a reputation in Japan as an imitator, not a pioneer, the firm was fixated on Sony and would invest almost any amount of money to match Sony's moves and defeat its rival in the marketplace.

ELECTRONIC ARTS

Another alternative had surfaced in May 1990 when Trip Hawkins, CEO of Electronic Arts (EA), approached Morse to see if there was a way to reverse-engineer SEGA or Nintendo cartridges so that EA could do its own manufacturing instead of relying on these licensees. A Stanford MBA and former Apple employee, Hawkins had founded Electronic Arts at about the same time Morse started Amiga. Electronic Arts was an entertainment software company that was structured like a movie studio; Hawkins hired star programmers as independent contractors, and promoted them as if they were movie stars. With this system, EA spawned hit after hit for the very significant personal computer segment of the market. Morse knew Hawkins well because Electronic Arts was the only game software company that had supported Amiga to any degree. EA had made a lot of money on Amiga games. Electronic Arts was also a leading distributor for other software companies, and it was considered a central actor in the game development community. Hawkins was frequently quoted in the press as a prominent industry spokesman and was a familiar figure at industry gatherings.

For all his prominence and success, many thought Hawkins had made one crucial mistake. Convinced that personal computers were better game-playing platforms than Nintendo machines, he had ignored the Nintendo market. Although a leader in games for PCs, Electronic Arts had been outstripped by Nintendo's licensees, whose sales seemed limited only by Nintendo's allocations. After suffering his first quarterly loss in 1989, Hawkins reversed course and took out a license from SEGA and Nintendo. Electronic Arts had made an initial public offering, partly to raise the capital needed to enter the Nintendo market with its huge inventory risks.

Hawkins' own frustration with Nintendo's licensing and manufacturing restrictions was what drove him to ask Morse in May if NTG could find a way to defeat

Nintendo's lock-out system. NTG was not prepared to undertake that challenge, but Hawkins pursued Morse further. He told Morse—through a person who served on both boards—that he had learned NTG had a very interesting hardware project underway. He thought they should talk because Electronic Arts might be able to make a major contribution. The NTG architecture plan soon found enthusiastic supporters inside Electronic Arts, and Hawkins began exploring the possibility of creating some form of partnership between his company and NTG.

Hawkins and Morse had exactly the same view of the games marketplace; both agreed that software developers were seriously constrained by the limitations of existing hardware. However, Hawkins also sketched a vision which placed the game-playing machine at the center of a new interactive multimedia system. In principle, a versatile CD-ROM player could be built into the machine that would not only play game software but could also play audio compact disks and possibly video disks, such as the photo CDs under development at Kodak. Thus the NTG system need not be only a game machine; it could serve as the heart of a complete home interactive entertainment system that could turn television into a device capable of delivering on-line movies, home shopping, banking, and a host of other services.

MERGER OR PARTNERSHIP?

To challenge Nintendo and ignite a revolution in interactive home entertainment, Hawkins argued, NTG would need to attract a broad range of world-class partners. Through Electronic Arts, Hawkins could not only strengthen NTG's links with the game development community, but also forge ties with major entertainment companies interested in multimedia, such as Time-Warner—owner of a magazine empire, a movie studio, services such as HBO, and the second biggest cable television network in the country.

One approach would have been to merge NTG into Electronic Arts. Flush with cash from its initial public offering, EA could fund NTG's development and possibly create synergies by linking its game developers to the evolving system. However, Morse believed that NTG's productivity depended on its independence and creative freedom. He strongly doubted that the small-team approach would work if NTG was folded into Electronic Arts, even as a quasi-independent venture.

Another possibility was forming a partnership to develop the system further. Hawkins proposed a deal that would create a new entity named Medio. Electronic Arts would put up the money for Medio— enough to fund development of a prototype machine— and would create a software development environment on top of the operating system that any programmer could use. Medio would receive all rights to NTG's system, but would not produce and market the system. As work progressed, other partners would be brought in to help foot the ultimate $100 million cost of commercializing the technology. NTG would remain a separate entity wholly owned by its partners, and would continue to develop the technology under Morse's leadership. Electronic Arts would receive a 75% stake in Medio and NTG would hold the other 25%. NTG would also receive an option to convert its equity into a stream of royalty payments. Should it exercise this option, it could choose between:

▼ A percentage of Medio net profits equal to NTG's percentage of ownership
▼ A royalty payment for each unit of hardware sold
▼ A royalty payment for each unit of software sold
▼ 2.5% of sales

FORM A CONSORTIUM?

Rather than form a partnership, with Electronic Arts receiving a 75% stake, NTG itself could assemble a consortium around its new machine. With Medio, as new partners were brought in, NTG's share would be diluted, and it could lose control over the way in which its technology would be brought to market. Hawkins clearly envisioned drawing together best-in-world capabilities in entertainment, electronics, communications, and software in such a formidable combination that others would then flock to the new standard his group promoted. In Hawkins' vision Electronic Arts would be the key software developer, but Morse and Hart worried that its dominance might discourage other developers from endorsing the NTG standard.

Morse and Hart thought it would take much more development of the technology to attract the caliber of partners that would be needed. Morse felt that to line up partners, one had to convince them both that what NTG had developed would work in the marketplace, *and* that the prospective partners could not duplicate the work themselves. He felt that it would be premature to show the concept to potential partners until it was clear they would find it very difficult to catch up with NTG. Down the road, however, it was clear Hawkins could bring a set of strong relationships neither Morse nor Hart had. Hawkins also had a considerable amount of personal credibility, and a real gift for selling a vision. Said Morse, "One of the big attractions of working with Trip is that we know when he gets committed to something, he's extremely hard to divert."

THE 1993 SITUATION

In 1993, the U.S. was by far the largest market for video games with a 50% share, followed by Japan with 30%, then Europe with 15%. SEGA Enterprises was the largest competitor for Nintendo. At first, in Japan, SEGA had been unable to persuade third party software producers to abandon Nintendo and had done all of its own development there. In the U.S., it was able to team up with independent developers like Electronic Arts (which had helped develop SEGA's Genesis software and its very realistic sports games, *John Madden Football* and *NHL Hockey*). These were based on actual players and teams and contained all the latest statistics and strategies. Their popularity had quickly made Electronic Arts the leading U.S. seller of video game software. SEGA's *Sonic The Hedgehog* made the Genesis system's sales soar. It was *Sonic*'s popularity that had forced Nintendo to introduce its 16-bit Super Nintendo System.

During the Christmas 1991 season, for the first time SEGA surpassed Nintendo in both U.S. and European sales.[4] These successes encouraged many of Nintendo's third-party suppliers to go over to SEGA. In late 1992 SEGA began selling a compact disc read-only memory (CD-ROM) player as a $299 add-on to the Genesis system. In September 1992, largely as a result of Morse and Hart's actions, 3DO Corporation came into being, with Trip Hawkins as its head. 3DO would exploit NTG's technologies and many of its strategic concepts. And in December 1993 the impossible happened; Nintendo's two decades of continued rapid growth stalled, and Nintendo had to rethink its positions rapidly.

WE ARE IN A SPECIAL SITUATION

In commenting on its competitors Mr. Yamauchi said, "Many so-called hardware companies are now trying to go into this market. They have many capable people, very strong marketing power, and their technology in terms of the hardware is just impeccable. But still, no hardware company has successfully entered this market and I don't think they can successfully survive. Those companies are designing in ways which just think in terms of hardware. . . . It is said that 3DO's hardware is going to (high density TV) HDTV: CD-ROM (High density TV: compact disk–read only memory) units. Naturally the cost of that hardware is very expensive, something like $600 or $700. Nintendo is selling Super Nintendo at $150."

In response to the CD-ROM threat Mr. Yamauchi noted, "CD-ROMs are actually much more vulnerable to piracy because CD-ROMs have standard formats for world-wide usage. Nintendo is taking every necessary counter-measure against piratings, but there are many professionals engaged in this practice. Unfortunately, Taiwan is the worst when it comes to pirating. It is not too much for me to say, I believe, that some governments and private entities are shaking hands to make copies of our copyrighted materials. I hope Taiwan and other countries will join the conventions supporting copyrights and property rights of others and try to seize any counterfeiters and to control these counterfeiting activities domestically.

"There are thousands of software-creating companies around the world, but according to our research there are only 20 to 30 such companies who are capable of coming up with an interesting idea and actually materializing the software. It takes a very long time to design and produce these interesting games. Introducing a game for even one hardware firm is very risky, introducing games for many is even more so. For each of the new systems, they will need extra time and money, but there is no guarantee that the new hardware formats will sell. So long as 3DO has not appeared on the market, I don't think any capable software licensee will be interested in working on 3DO's format. Once 3DO is successful, suppliers will start working on software.

"There are only two or three licensees who actually make large profits. Many have already quit, but there will always be someone else with a dream to create a million seller. In this kind of forum our license fee structure will not change very easily. We don't care whether the competition is 3DO, the electronic giants, or a movie company. They don't create any competition in the Japanese market. Someone has to come up with very good software, with an action that is very good, and one that is accepted by the audience. Then they have to be convinced that one of the other hardware systems can outnumber the total sales of Nintendo. The mere presence and entrance of these other (hardware or movie distribution) companies doesn't matter at all. For Nintendo as well, what we have to do is to produce games that can really attract world wide audiences. As in the case of color TV sets, nowadays there is no quality difference for the customer. They can buy any brand. But in the case of Nintendo, we are in a special situation. We are making both hardware and software, but we are saying that software is most important."

QUESTIONS

1. Evaluate Nintendo's past strategy. What are the critical factors for success in this business? Why had Nintendo made such high profits? Can it maintain them?

2. What should Nintendo's response be to entries like NTG/3DO? What are the biggest threats to Nintendo? How should it position for the future in its markets? Technologies? Globally?

3. Describe precisely what Nintendo's future strategy should be. Why? What issues would you anticipate? What antitrust, social, and international issues does Nintendo raise? Where should Nintendo go in the future?

EXHIBIT 1
Nintendo Co., Ltd.—
Historical Financial
Statistics, 1989–1993

Years Ended March 31, 1993, 1992, 1991 Seven Months Ended March 31, 1990, And Year Ended August 31, 1989		**YEN IN MILLIONS**				
		1993	**1992**	**1991**	**1990***	**1989**
For the Period	Net sales	¥634,669	¥561,843	¥471,417	¥240,234	¥291,201
	Income before income taxes	187,800	180,833	161,577	75,165	77,858
	Net income	88,609	87,104	68,886	32,930	34,271
At the Period-End	Total assets	608,769	517,205	425,372	342,619	279,073
	Property, plant & equip.–net	58,168	53,496	47,811	35,374	34,360
	Shareholders' equity	404,290	328,548	250,623	189,811	157,249
		Yen				
		1993	**1992**	**1991**	**1990***	**1989**
Amounts per Share	Net income	¥625.77	¥615.18	¥486.32	¥232.49	¥242.27
	Cash dividends	70	60	37	22	24

Years Ended March 31, 1993, 1992, 1991 Seven Months Ended March 31, 1990, And Year Ended August 31, 1989		**U.S. DOLLARS IN THOUSANDS**				
		1993	**1992**	**1991**	**1990***	**1989**
For the Period	Net sales	$5,471,289	$4,843,475	$4,063,940	$2,070,979	$2,510,353
	Income before income taxes	1,618,963	1,558,905	1,392,907	647,977	671,189
	Net income	763,870	750,898	593,843	283,876	295,443
At the Period-End	Total assets	5,248,012	4,458,664	3,667,004	2,953,610	2,405,806
	Property, plant & equip.–net	501,448	461,172	412,165	304,946	296,210
	Shareholders' equity	3,485,274	2,832,311	2,160,552	1,636,303	1,355,603
		U.S. Dollars				
		1993	**1992**	**1991**	**1990***	**1989**
Amounts per Share	Net income	$5.39	$5.30	$4.19	$2.00	$2.09
	Cash dividends	0.60	0.52	0.32	0.19	0.21

*The amounts for the fiscal period ended March 31, 1990 are for a seven-month period because of the change in the Company's fiscal year-end to March 31, from August 31.

Source: Nintendo Co., Ltd., *Annual Report* 1993.

EXHIBIT 2
SEGA Enterprises, Ltd.*
Historical Financial Summary

	MILLIONS OF YEN						THOUSANDS OF U.S. DOLLARS
	1988	1989	1990	1991	1992	1993	1993
Net sales:							
Consumer products	¥18,037	¥25,008	¥39,153	¥58,277	¥135,124	¥229,270	$1,971,367
Amusement center operations	11,265	12,240	17,325	24,627	41,410	58,914	506,569
Amusement machine sales	19,467	17,268	21,606	23,290	36,427	57,558	494,910
Royalties on game software	347	710	550	386	356	1,195	10,275
Total	49,116	55,226	78,634	106,580	213,317	346,937	2,983,121
Cost of sales	32,819	38,190	54,594	73,162	150,873	251,834	2,165,382
Gross profit	16,297	17,036	24,040	33,418	62,444	95,103	817,739
Selling, general & administrative expenses	9,501	9,762	11,854	15,548	23,153	32,563	279,992
Operating income	6,796	7,274	12,186	17,870	39,291	62,540	537,747
Net income	2,302	2,855	4,845	8,244	14,014	28,017	240,903
Depreciation & amortization	2,562	2,998	3,715	5,579	9,067	15,591	134,058
Total assets	44,522	65,956	98,450	115,512	226,065	295,153	2,537,859
Total shareholders' equity	29,769	45,640	69,090	77,075	90,318	116,511	1,001,814
Financial ratios:							
Return on average assets	6.3%	5.2%	5.9%	7.7%	8.2%	10.8%	
Return on average equity	10.2	7.6	8.4	11.3	16.7	27.1	
Payout ratio	7.7	4.6	4.2	6.5	8.9	8.7	

	Yen						U.S. Dollars
Net income per share	¥32.4	¥35.8	¥53.6	¥85.0	¥144.4	¥288.7	$2.48
Cash dividends per share (adjusted)	2.3	2.9	4.2	5.5	12.8	25.0	0.21
Number of employees	1,343	1,454	1,695	1,786	2,234	3,034	

*For the years ended April 30, 1988, 1989 and 1990, for the 11-month period ended March 31, 1991, and for the years ended March 31, 1992 and 1993.

Source: Sega Enterprises, Ltd., *Annual Report*, 1993.

EXHIBIT 3
Nintendo Co., Ltd.—
Statement of Income,
Year Ended
March 31, 1993
(millions of yen)

REVENUES	
Net sales	¥634,669
Interest income and other	18,043
	652,712
COSTS AND EXPENSES	
Cost of sales	387,113
Selling, general & admin. expenses	66,987
Foreign exchange loss, net	(415)
Other	10,812
	464,912
INCOME TAXES	
Current	100,117
Deferred	(489)
	99,628
NET INCOME	¥88,609
Per share of common stock	¥625.77
Cash dividends declared	70

Source: Nintendo Co. Ltd., *Annual Report*, 1993.

EXHIBIT 4
Nintendo Co., Ltd.—
Balance Sheet as of
March 31, 1993
(millions of yen)

ASSETS		LIABILITIES AND SHAREHOLDERS' EQUITY	
Current assets		Current liabilities	
Cash and cash equivalents	¥397,300	Trade notes and accounts payable	¥124,092
Receivables (net)	85,498	Accrued expenses	5,081
Inventories	50,033	Accrued income taxes	58,806
Other current assets	5,243	Other current liabilities	8,441
Total	538,074	Total	196,420
Propery, plant, and equipment		Retirement and severance benefits	1,896
Land	35,634	Deferred income taxes	975
Buildings and structures	20,765	Translation adjustments	5,188
Machinery and equipment	18,959	TOTAL LIABILITIES	204,479
Construction in progress	170	Shareholders' equity	
Accumulated depreciation	(17,360)	Common stock	10,065
Total	58,168	Additional paid-in capital	11,584
Investments and other assets		Legal reserves	2,516
Investments in securities	10,845	Retained earnings	380,648
Other assets	1,682	Treasury stock, at cost	(523)
Total	12,527	TOTAL SHAREHOLDERS' EQUITY	404,290
		TOTAL LIABILITIES AND	
TOTAL ASSETS	¥608,769	SHAREHOLDERS' EQUITY	¥608,769

Source: Nintendo Co. Ltd., *Annual Report*, 1993.

EXHIBIT 5
Nintendo Co., Ltd.—
Share Ownership as of
March 31, 1993

SHAREHOLDER'S NAME	NUMBER OF NINTENDO SHARES HELD	PERCENT OF TOTAL SHARES OUTSTANDING
Hiroshi Yamauchi	15,522,800	10.96
Daiwa Bank	7,075,800	4.99
Bank of Kyoto	7,075,700	4.99
Tokai Bank	7,075,700	4.99
Sanwa Bank	7,071,900	4.99
Toyo Trust Bank	6,333,400	4.47
Mitsubishi Bank	6,235,300	4.40
Total shares outstanding	141,669,000	
Number of shareholders	27,245	

Source: Nintendo Co. Ltd., *10K Report*, 1993.

EXHIBIT 6
Structure of the
Electronic Games
Industry

	CHIP DESIGN	SYSTEM MANUFACTURE	SOFTWARE DESIGN	AMUSEMENT PARKS	DISTRIBUTION RETAIL	ON-LINE
Nintendo	•	•	•		•	
Sega	•	•	•	•	•	•
Atari	•	•	•		•	
3DO	•					
Sony		•	•	•	•	•
Philips	•	•			•	
Matsushita		•	•	•	•	•
NEC	•	•			•	
Silicon Graphics	•					•
Time Warner			•			•
Disney			•	•	•	•

Source: Data compiled by authors from various corporate reports.

EXHIBIT 7
Game and Video
Game Market

1992 TOYS AND GAMES MARKET SHARES BY CATEGORY[a]

Video games	26%
Dolls/stuffed animals	15%
Vehicles	11%
Infant	9%
Activity toys	9%
Games/puzzles	8%
Other	22%

1992 U.S. VIDEO GAME HARDWARE MARKET[b]	**$1,236 MILLION**
Of which	
Super Nintendo 16-bit system	36.1%
Sega Genesis 16-bit system	26.0%
Games Boy portable system	16.3%
Nintendo 8-bit system	14.6%
Game Gear portable system	6.5%
Other	0.5%

1992 VIDEO GAME MARKET (HARDWARE AND SOFTWARE)[c]	**$5,800 MILLION**
Of which:	
Nintendo Entertainment Sy stems	79.0%
Sega	1.7%
Other	19.3%

[a]*Source:* USA Today, February 17, 1992 from Toy Manufacturers of America.
[b]*Source:* Thomson Financial Networks, April 16, 1992 from Johnson, Rice & Co.
[c]*Source:* Thomson Financial Networks, April 13, 1992 from Dean Witter Reynolds.

THE MAGNETIC LEVITATION TRAIN

On June 25, 1990, Japan's Minister of Transport approved the construction of a 42.8 kilometer-long experimental line at Yamanashi for a proposed magnetic levitation train. A press announcement later said, "Success or failure of the project to develop . . . a magnetic levitation (maglev) train [which can] travel at speeds of up to 500 kilometers per hour (310 mph) will depend on operational tests on the new 304 billion yen trial line scheduled for completion in 1995."[1] The proposed project could have profound implications for the competitiveness of corporations and nations throughout the world.

THE DREAM OF MAGNETIC LEVITATION

The dream of magnetic levitation had persisted since the science fiction era of the mid-1800s. Repelling magnetic forces would float objects in the air, while other magnets would pull them forward toward their destination; noiselessly, and at limitless speeds. For many this was dream enough. However, in the late 1980s two major developments added new dimensions to the dream.

First, energy consumption began to rise exponentially again after the temporary decreases of the 1970s. And burning of fossil fuels would later burgeon as less developed countries industrialized and populations continued to rise. Many scientists were convinced that by the year 2030 the world would encounter: (1) catastrophic levels of carbon monoxide in large urban centers, (2) significant increases in chemical pollutants (notably from increased ozone, acid rain, and dry par-

ticulate fallout), (3) slow but possibly devastating increases in earth temperatures from the "greenhouse effects" of CO_2 and other gasses, and (4) rapid depletion of the world's reserves of fossil fuels.

These trends would have strong negative effects on densely populated Japan, which both imported 104.9 million metric tons of coal and 4.18 million barrels per day of crude oil in 1991 and had frequent weather inversions trapping noxious pollutants throughout the urban areas between its mountains and the sea.

Second, in the late 1980s scientists discovered whole new classes of superconducting materials which could radically change the cost of operating superconducting magnets. Soon, many authorities envisioned fast, clean, efficient superconducting maglev trains carrying the bulk of traffic between centers less than 500 miles apart. They also foresaw superconductors making possible numerous other wonders like cost-efficient fusion power, low cost electrical power, new medical diagnostic and treatment techniques, and whole new industries based on portable computer and consumer products freed from the limitations of battery technologies. The developments associated with maglev were a dramatic example of the kinds of joint decisions—government-business actions—that would increasingly affect corporate and national growth and competitiveness. In the past, such interactions had been crucial in building the railroad, auto, aircraft, advanced materials, medical products, shipbuilding, computer, software, and even food products industries in advanced countries.

SUPERCONDUCTIVITY AND MAGNETIC LEVITATION

Early concepts of magnetic trains used the principle of magnetic repulsion. All physics students know that magnets with the same polarity will repel. A train

Case Copyright © James Brian Quinn, 1995. Allie Quinn and Penny C. Paquette were research associates. The generous cooperation of Japan's Railway Technical Research Institute is gratefully acknowledged. Case was developed with funding and arrangements provided by International University of Japan.

with strong built-in magnets could be made to fly by passing over a track containing magnets of the same polarity. Alternatively it could be lifted by magnets of opposite polarity. Neither design would require the ponderous wings an airplane needs to lift off. The train could be guided by other magnets (on the side of the track) to constrain its lateral movement. Forward propulsion could be provided either by magnets or by a jet engine. The ultimate dream was that *superconducting* magnets would lift, guide, and propel the train forward, thus saving enormously on energy.

Superconductivity is a physical phenomenon which occurs in some materials. When these "superconductive" materials are cooled to a certain "critical temperature," they lose all resistance to electricity. Consequently, once a current is put into a superconductor, it will continue to function, essentially indefinitely. Wrapping wires of superconducting materials around a magnet core creates a permanent electrical magnet using relatively little electrical current. Since there is no mechanical friction between a magnetically levitated body (such as a train car) and its surroundings, very little energy is needed to propel it. If magnets are used for levitation, propulsion, and guidance, no local pollution is created. The train could be extremely quiet, and there should be no upper bounds to speed not also encountered by aircraft. Maglev trains could be the largest commercial users of high powered superconducting magnets.

While such features made superconducting maglev trains appear very attractive, other aspects of their operation presented complexities. In the early 1990s useful superconducting magnets had to be kept extremely cold—i.e., between 4 Kelvin (K) and 22 K to keep them below their critical temperature. (Each degree Kelvin equals one degree Centigrade above absolute zero—which is −459.7°F or −273.2°C.) The dream of all electrical designers was to have a superconducting material that would operate above liquid nitrogen temperatures (77 K). Above 77 K, liquid nitrogen makes superconductors very inexpensive to cool. Room temperature superconductors—which would use no cooling at all—were also theoretically possible. A host of new materials had recently been found to superconduct at ever higher temperatures. (See Exhibit 1.) But in the early 1990s, these materials were neither available in commercial quantities nor with reliability and cost characteristics that made them attractive for operational purposes.

EXHIBIT 1
Record Transition
Temperatures over
the Years

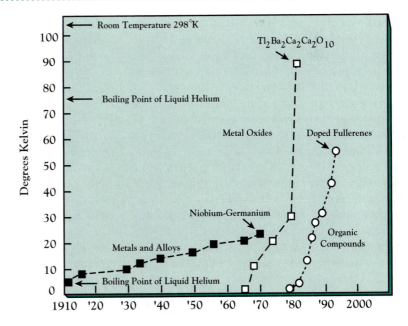

Source: Adapted from *The Economist*, February 13th, 1993.
Original Source: *Chemical and Engineering News* and *Scientific American*.

THE JAPANESE PROGRAM

Experiments with a maglev train system had been underway for some time by the Railway Technical Research Institute (RTRI) in Miyazaki Prefecture in southern Japan. Research had begun in Japan in 1962 to test various systems of vehicle propulsion, suspension, and guidance. In March 1972 the laboratories of Japanese National Railways (JNR) for the first time successfully achieved a self-levitating running speed of 50 kilometers per hour using a superconducting magnet. JNR—famous for its "bullet" trains—previously operated as a public corporation, was privatized in 1987. The privatized Japan Railways Group (JR) consisted of six passenger companies and one freight company. Its research center became a foundation, the Railway Technical Research Institute (RTRI), supported by contributions of 0.35 percent of passenger revenues and 0.035 percent of freight company revenues. RTRI, which could also raise money from other sources, had an early 1990s research budget (for about 600 people) of about 20 billion yen ($15.4 million at ¥130/$) per year.[2]

By 1979 a world record maglev speed of 517 kilometers per hour (kph) was attained on the Miyazaki test track (without passengers) over a distance of 7 kilometers. This early vehicle (ML500) verified the feasibility of operating a superconducting high-speed train on a maglev system.[3] A successor experimental unit (MLU001) was operated over 7500 times on the track and traveled a total of over 40,000 kilometers. In October 1991, the MLU002 was destroyed by fire in a freak experimental accident. (See Current Japanese Approach.) Its successor MLU002N began test runs in January 1993 on the Miyazaki track.

A new prototype vehicle for the proposed Yamanashi track would first run on a short distance maglev track in 1996 and perhaps on a longer distance version later. The test line to be built at Yamanashi would permit running at a maximum speed of over 550 kph (or 330 mph). It had a tunnel section accounting for about 35 kilometers (80% of its length) and a double track section where two trains could pass each other at very high speeds.[4] Maglev was considered a possible next generation system following two generations of Shinkansens or "bullet" trains. The conventional Shinkansen operated at 270 kph (169 mph). By 1996 advanced Shinkansens were targeted to operate at 350 kph. Researchers stated that to reach that speed would require new technology to reduce noise factors for the Shinkansens below the government's target of 75 decibels.

INFRASTRUCTURE ISSUES

The magnetic roadbeds for levitation trains were complex and costly. Several roadbed configurations had been tested. One was like a monorail which came up into the body of the train cars with magnets on the top and sides to levitate and guide the cars. Another was a U-shaped trough with magnets on the bottom and/or sides of the U. RTRI used this approach. The monorail configuration could be either "J-shaped" or "T-shaped." In the T-shaped configuration the car "wrapped around" the top flanges of the "T" and magnets pulled the car upward toward an iron rail embedded in the guide structure. (See Exhibit 2.) The German Transrapid system used this approach. Either the U shaped or the monorail type of infrastructure would be made of reinforced or prestressed concrete.

Because of the extremely high speed of the train, there could be no automobile or walkway crossings on the track. Consequently, it would either have to be in a tunnel (like a subway) or lifted—as are the bullet trains in Japan—above all traffic levels. The infrastructure had to contain control system electronics, electric power for magnets, and coolant systems if the magnets outside the train were superconductive. Because of the special materials superconducting magnets require, in the mid-1990s the cost of such magnets was too high for use as external magnets. The concrete infrastructure costs were expected to be somewhat less per mile in Japan than that of the Shinkansen "bullet train"—including its integrated power supply system. Land costs in Japan were extremely high and land owners could not be forced to sell their land. However, placing the train in tunnels could ameliorate this cost. Tunneling costs about 3–5 billion yen per kilometer in Japan.

Track infrastructures for fast trains had to be carefully controlled. Incline changes of more than a few degrees cause heavy gravitational (G) forces to pull on any humans in the train. These are similar to the effects one feels in an airplane or rollercoaster when it suddenly moves upward or downward. At certain levels of intensity, such "G" forces could be dangerous to health. Hence vertical changes were set to be less than on the Shinkansen, and G forces were less than those in an elevator. In addition, track curvatures had to be controlled carefully to keep people from being thrown against the side of the train and possibly injured. The target riding quality for maglev was to be at least as good as that of the Shinkansen.

EXHIBIT 2

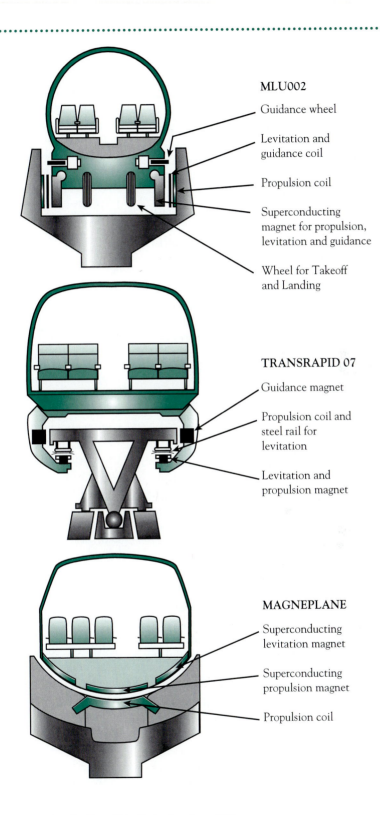

MLU002

Guidance wheel

Levitation and
guidance coil

Propulsion coil

Superconducting
magnet for propulsion,
levitation and guidance

Wheel for Takeoff
and Landing

TRANSRAPID 07

Guidance magnet

Propulsion coil and
steel rail for
levitation

Levitation and
propulsion magnet

MAGNEPLANE

Superconducting
levitation magnet

Superconducting
propulsion magnet

Propulsion coil

Source: Gary Stix, "Air Trains," *Scientific American*, August 1992.

WHY MAGLEV?

Why not stay with standard rail and "steel-wheel" designs? At very high speeds (above about 350 kph for general operating services) the friction coefficient between the wheel and the track tends to be smaller in inverse proportion to the speed. This causes the train to lose the friction it needs to drive forward against the "drag" of air resistance. In addition, small "fit" tolerances within the wheel and suspension systems tend to cause significant vibration at high speeds. Discomfort and even danger to passengers can result. The extreme vibration from "wheel on rail" trains also leads to high maintenance costs on trackbeds, tracks, cars, and other elements of infrastructure. Maintenance costs tended to be 20–30% of operating costs for "steel wheel" trains. For advanced countries like Japan or Germany heavily dependent on rail traffic all these were important limitations on further extending existing infrastructures. In many countries road and air traffic was becoming impossibly congested in populated areas with few opportunities to expand these existing infrastructures.

THE COMPETITIVE SITUATION

German companies had also pursued magnetic levitation for their rail systems. One company, Transrapid International, had used a standard electromagnet on its Transrapid 07 to levitate the train above a laminated iron rail in a T-shaped guideway. The electromagnet curled underneath the guideway and was attracted upward to within 10 mm (about 3/8 inch) of a steel rail in the guideway. This project appeared likely to obtain commercial backing for a maglev in Florida (1994) and in California-Nevada (1997). In Florida, a 13-mile maglev was planned between Orlando and the booming Disney resorts. The western line would run between Anaheim in southern California and Las Vegas, Nevada. The completed $5 billion line would carry passengers at up to 265 mph (442 kph) and cover the distance in 75 minutes.[5]

Transrapid had been operating a train for over 100,000 miles on its 20-mile prototype in Emsland (Germany) and was hoping to build a system between the Dusseldorf and Cologne-Bonn airports. Germany's transportation minister, Günther Krause, saw the maglev as an important emblem of renewal, a physical linkage that symbolized the connection of East and West Germany. "It was Krause's dream to spend $5 billion to make maglev into a twenty-first century version of the 'Flying Hamburger' [train] that connected Hamburg and Berlin in the 1930s . . . reaching speeds of more than 100 mph, faster than the trains that make the trip today."[6]

The Japanese approach, similar to a 1966 design first proposed at Brookhaven in the U.S., used coils of superconducting wire inside the vehicle to produce a magnetic field of the same polarity as in the coils embedded in a "U"-shaped guideway. The Japanese system had two advantages. The first was that the superconducting coils did not need the heavy iron core required by the Transrapid design. Secondly, the system lifted the cars 10 centimeters (approximately 4 inches) above the guideway as opposed to the 9.5 mm (3/8 inch) separation of the German Maglev. This gave the Japanese design greater flexibility and safety in earthquakes. The Japanese design (see Exhibit 3) had run successfully on its shorter test track, but was less thoroughly tested than Transrapid's system. In both Transrapid's and Japan Railway's maglevs, the vehicle was propelled by a linear synchronous motor, essentially an electric motor with its stator coils rolled out flat in the guideway. Each section of the stator was electronically activated long enough to pull the train upward and forward.

An American consortium (of Texas Accelerator Center, General Motors, Hughes Aircraft, and Bechtel) were considering commercializing a hybrid (superconducting and standard electromagnetic) design which shielded the magnetic coils in a way that reduced external magnetic radiation to a level lower than that produced by the earth's own magnetic field. The design had never been run at full scale. Another U.S. design (led by Grumman Corporation) was a hybrid of the German and Japanese designs. Like the German design, the vehicle wrapped around a guideway. Using superconducting magnets, pulling upward, the vehicle levitated at all speeds and thus did not need wheels for takeoff. The Grumman proposal avoided the tight rail clearances inherent in the German design by combining superconductivity with non-superconducting magnets which could be varied by a digital control system to preserve the separation between the vehicle and the guideway. The system allowed two inches of clearance to be maintained, rather than the few millimeter tolerances necessary on the Transrapid design.

THE U.S. LAG

Although Japanese institutions had poured $1 billion into maglev research and the West German government almost as much, the U.S. government had

EXHIBIT 3

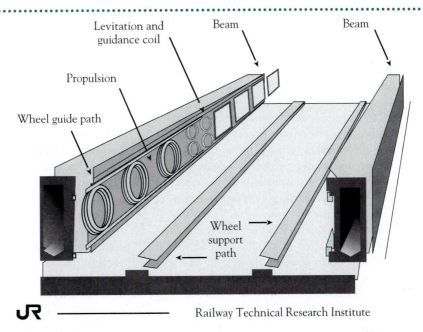

Source: Railway Technical Research Institute.

EXHIBIT 4
Passenger Travel and Energy Use by Rail for Selected Countries, 1970–1989

	PASSENGER TRAVEL (BILLIONS OF PASSENGER-MILES)					ENERGY USE (TRILLIONS OF BTUS)				
	1970	1975	1980	1985	1989	1970	1975	1980	1985	1989
Japan	178	200	194	204	228	54	58	60	61	70
France	29	35	38	44	46	20	21	21	23	23
Germany	30	30	31	32	31	30	26	28	27	28
United States	23	20	22	22	25	61	62	63	70	81
United Kingdom	23	20	22	22	25	33	33	35	34	n/a

Source: Lee Schipper, Steve Myers, et. al., "Energy Efficiency and Human Activity," Cambridge University Press, Cambridge, MA, 1992; and the "Proceedings of the ACEEE Conference on Automobiles and the Greenhouse Effect."

spent only $3 million on maglevs between 1966 and 1975 and nothing after that. Despite its much smaller size, in 1989 France had nearly twice as many railway passenger-miles as the U.S. and used less than one-third as much energy to do so (see Exhibit 4). In Fall 1988, Amtrak proudly announced that its Metroliner had averaged 100 mph on a special Boston to New York run—2 miles per hour slower than the mark set in 1893 by the Empire State Express #999 between Batavia and Buffalo, New York. Yet the proposed construction of maglev lines in Florida, Texas, and California by foreign companies in 1992 raised a great outcry in the United States. U.S. Senator Patrick Moynihan articulated the

fears: "At stake is preeminence in the production and sale of a revolutionary new mode of transportation . . . [likely to shape the future] just as the railroad defined the [nineteenth century] and the automobile and airplane have defined this century."[7]

A number of studies had indicated that maglev trains would be most effective at distances between 100–600 miles. These journeys made up the bulk of air travel in all countries, but represented the most inefficient use of jet aircraft and tended to clog airways and runways. Some estimates placed the annual cost of flight delays in the early 1990s at between $5 billion and $10 billion in the U.S.[8]

But these sums were small when compared to highway delays and proposed road construction costs. *Technology Review* noted: "When serious proposals are made for a 22-lane highway, you know something is wrong. Congestion, air pollution, and noise associated with highways and airways are steadily worsening. And the amount of petroleum used by transportation—64% of the country's total oil consumption [of 6,234 million barrels in 1992]—makes transportation a national security problem as well as an environmental problem." In addition to dealing with these problems, the same article stated that the maglev travel times (from city center to city center) would be less than those of jet aircraft for most flights of 500 miles or less and even for some cities as far apart as 1000 miles. Net travel times would generally be less than those of automobiles for distances as short as one hundred miles—and even 25 miles for dense urban centers. In accomplishing these time savings maglev vehicles used only 1/4 to 1/2 as much energy as jet aircraft or private automobiles. Exhibit 5 shows U.S. passenger travel and energy use by mode in 1990.[9] The final figure in Appendix A shows the relationship between time of day, volume of package pickup and deliveries, and cost per ton-mile.

In addition, there were safety advantages. The passenger fatality rate for the Japanese Shinkansen and the French Train à Grande Vitesse (TGV) was zero after billions of passenger miles. In 1991 fatality rates were 0.03 per 100 million passenger miles on scheduled airlines and intercity buses and 0.97 per 100 million passenger miles for passenger automobiles. Some estimates placed the initial capital cost of maglev in the U.S. at less than the $8–10 million per mile required for a TGV system or for new interstate highways in dense areas, while equipment and roadbed maintenance costs were expected to be substantially (2/3 or more) less than the TGV's cost of $2–$3 per train mile.[10] The big problem in the U.S. had been the unwillingness of either the government or private companies to make financial commitments sufficient to proceed beyond preliminary R&D. Through 1992, the Federal government had maintained that maglev must be developed by private industry, and that the only role of government would be to supply early R&D.

POLITICAL CHANGES

However, starting in 1991, various proposals were made for Congressional support of maglev trains. In December 1992, President Bush had signed—but did not budget for—a $151 billion authorization bill for surface transportation. This contained $725 million to develop and build a prototype American-designed maglev by the end of the decade. The authorized program was structured to attract private investment of an additional $250 million.

The Clinton Administration was more favorable to such ventures. Senator Patrick Moynihan became a major champion to raise the U.S. effort from a $20 million per year effort (under the supervision of the Federal Railroad Administration and the U.S. Army Corps of Engineers) into a program competitive with that of other nations. Senator Moynihan wanted to "give the U.S. a last-ditch chance to prevent yet another domestically nurtured technology from being ceded to foreign competitors." (Rocket scientist Robert Goddard had proposed an early tunnel designed version in 1909, while Powell of Brookhaven National Labs in 1969 had demonstrated the practical potentials of superconducting magnets for the purpose.) In 1993 French, German, and Swedish companies were actively selling their hardware to developers seeking to create new U.S. rail projects. Among these was a consortium, maglev Transit, organized by a group of Japanese, German, and U.S. investors to finance a package of more than $500 million for the 14-mile Orlando to Disneyland run. The most active plan was a consortium led by Morrison-Knudsen, an Idaho construction and engineering firm, to link five Texas cities with TGV technology. This project was to raise nearly $7 billion from private sources to connect major Southwestern cities in Texas, Louisiana, and Oklahoma. Existing and potential routes for high-speed trains in the U.S. and Europe are shown in Exhibit 6 A, B.

NATIONAL POLICY ANALYSIS

In 1993, no clear strategy for maglevs had emerged in the U.S. Studies varied widely on costs. Because system costs were substantially fixed, once maglev was installed, its costs per passenger mile traveled were largely a function of passenger density or demand. Models assumed that 150-passenger vehicles would travel on average half-full and consume 5 megawatts when traveling at 240 mph. If electricity cost $0.10 per kilowatt hour, the energy cost would be $0.03 per passenger mile or half that of air travel in the 100 to 1000 mile range. Vehicle and labor costs could be less than half of those for air travel since operating parameters were less complex and crew sizes were smaller, if existent at all. Many scenarios assumed that automated trains could operate without crews, as many airport trains already did.

Early 1990s coach air fares in the dense Northeast corridor (Washington DC to Boston) were about 50¢ per passenger mile. The projection for a maglev on the same route was less than 25¢ per passenger mile. Since at least 3/4 of all intercity passenger travel in these areas was by automobile with operating costs of at least 25¢ per mile, analysts thought maglev fares could compete economically, once sufficient demand developed. The colorful Senator Moynihan noted that interstate highways had actually exacerbated traffic congestions for the cities they were designed to relieve, "and the problem would only grow worse. By 2020, it will take 44 lanes to carry the traffic on I 95 from Miami to Ft. Lauderdale," Moynihan wrote, "Pretty soon there won't be anything left of Florida!"[11] Other political advocates saw the maglev as a possible substitute for high technology military expenditures. The cost of the proposed systems was a fraction of the cost of a single major weapon system like the B-2.

Fixed facilities accounted for about 90% of total maglev costs (exclusive of land). The guideway structure represented about 70% of these fixed costs. U.S models generally assumed total fixed facility costs of $16.5 million per mile for a single guideway, with second generation costs for guideways alone dropping to $8–$9 per mile. The most recent Shinkansen had cost $35–40 million per mile. In France the TGV had cost about $5 million per mile plus $2.5 million for electrification. The U.S. design consortium claimed that initial costs for its infrastructure would actually be $10–15 million per mile in the U.S., half their estimate for the cost of the Transrapid guideway. Vehicle costs for the Transrapid system were estimated at $3.6 million for an 80 seat car. The 60–70 passenger Japanese vehicle would be more expensive because of its superconducting magnet. For highly used routes vehicle costs would be about 11% of total capital costs in Western countries. Direct operating costs were generally agreed to be less than $.05 per passenger mile, depending on local energy costs. Land costs depended on location and whether existing superhighway right-of-ways could be used, but land costs in the U.S. (other than in dense cities) were not important factors.

A U.S. Office of Technology Assessment study estimated that a New York to Washington DC (300 mile) route for a maglev would have the highest capital costs of any U.S. system, approximately $7.4 billion for its vehicles and guideways. However, the maglev would have the lowest operating expenses for this distance—3.4¢ per mile, half the cost of a jetliner. A committee of the National Research Council tried to estimate possible demands for a high-speed ground transport system. It found that initially only the most traveled of the routes studied—San Francisco to Los Angeles—would generate enough revenues to exceed the system's capital and operating expenses. However, the experience of the Tokyo-Osaka Shinkansen run is instructive. Once available, Shinkansens increased ridership from 85 million in 1970 to 157 million in 1975.

In the U.S. there were few intercity passenger rail companies other than Amtrak. Most were a portion of city-operated metro systems. Although the U.S. government had earlier subsidized railroads, canals, and highways in various fashions, in 1993 no clear method existed for the U.S. to support the development of a major new transportation mode. States usually depended upon their gasoline taxes to pay for roadways and to contribute to other state expenditures, like education. The 14¢ of U.S. Federal tax paid on gasoline had traditionally been reserved for roadway use. While the Intermodal Surface Transportation Efficiency Act of 1991 allowed some of this money to be diverted to other transportation programs, the U.S. had no domestically owned railcar companies. Budd was owned by a West German company (Thysser), and Pullman had been acquired and broken up for its asset values. Total annual railcar production in the US. was only forecast at 450–550, without maglev. The New York City and Chicago Metro systems bought 77% of these.[12] Amtrak alone had a position as a national passenger rail carrier; and it was only planning a limited test of a 150 mph tilt-body fast train concept in 1993. See Appendix A for market and economic data.

The Japanese bullet trains and the French TGV were also genuinely competitive systems. The TGV had been designed to operate in the median strip of a superhighway. Since auto superhighways could tolerate grades up to 7%, so could the TGV. But the radius of curvature for a roadway for automobiles traveling at 70–80 mph could be 1/3 that of a train traveling at 210–250 mph. New versions of the TGV in 1990 attained speeds of 320 mph (515.3 kph) on a test run. Only the Japanese prototype maglev (517 kph) had exceeded that speed. Sections of the new TGV track were expected to handle trains running about 250 mph. While the original TGV was designed to ride smoothly enough to avoid spilling wine, this level of comfort was considered unlikely in a train moving 250–300 mph on rails, and constant maintenance would be critical.[13]

THE CURRENT JAPANESE APPROACH

In Japan the Railway Technical Research Institute's planned 27-mile test line in Yamanashi Prefecture would explore the commercial prospects of maglev trains. This track could be extended within 20 years' time into a system connecting Tokyo to Osaka, an extremely high density route within Japan. Japanese engineers envisioned that the train could carry 10,000 people per hour in trains up to 14 cars long. The Tokyo-Osaka maglev run would require only an hour, 1/3 the time taken by bullet trains. The Japanese team had made a number of important technical advances. Their train operated by a unique system of magnetic attraction. Magnets in the side of a "U"-shaped trough (1) "lifted" the train (more efficiently than repellent magnets would), (2) guided it effectively without wall contact, and (3) propelled the cars forward. Different magnets were used for the two functions. (See Exhibit 3.)[14]

The cars started moving on rubber-tired wheels. After the cars gained sufficient speed (about 100 mph), the wheels were retracted (like aircraft wheels) until they were needed again for the train to slow down. A single superconducting magnet was inside the cars. The levitation system is an electrodynamics suspension system. Magnets in the trough are ambient temperature magnets. The "figure 8" sidewall coils were energized by electromagnetic induction instantaneously as the train went by. The fire which destroyed the MLU002 advance prototype vehicle did not demonstrate any basic flaw in the magnetic levitation or propulsion scheme. A tire went flat and locked in place. The fire was caused when friction ignited the magnesium alloy wheel components (bought off the shelf from fighter aircraft manufacturers for lower costs) as they dragged on the support structure. The superconducting magnets in the car worked well and were so powerful that they sent a fire ax soaring from a fire fighter's hands almost an hour after the accident occurred.

A HIGH VISIBILITY PROGRAM

The Japanese maglev project was a high visibility program designed to solve next-generation transportation problems for the country, while keeping its technological capabilities at the frontier. The Railway Technical Research Institute's 7 kilometer test track at Miyazaki had been set up mainly to prove the feasibility of maglev technology and to test its safety, amenity, and computer features. The tests had also proved that maglev trains could be considerably lighter than Shinkansens; consequently, maglevs could handle steeper gradients than conventional trains, perhaps requiring fewer tunnels in mountainous Japan.[15]

Although experiments were successful for all elements tested at Miyazaki, a number of issues remained. What would happen when a maglev came roaring out of a tunnel at 500 kph (310 mph) into a strong wind? What would happen when two trains passed each other only a few meters apart at a combined speed of 1000 kph. Another problem was that maglevs could not rely on human drivers, human responses were simply not fast enough. Instead, speed was controlled from the ground by varying the frequency of the electric current sent from transformer substations to the track's electromagnets. Since each train was driven forward by changing the frequency and current of the electric transmissions to its particular magnets, each train had to be controlled separately, requiring entirely new high powered electronic controls.[16]

The newer U-shaped cross-section made it possible to manufacture a very strong (700 kA) superconducting coil to perform all the functions of suspension, guidance, and propulsion by interacting with lifting and propulsion coils mounted on the sides of the U-shaped trough. Still the Japanese system developed external magnetic fields of less than 20 Gauss, and no harmful health effects were known from such fields in 1993. The sidewall levitation system was much more efficient than the "repelling" of "facing levitation systems" used earlier. The superconducting magnets in the MLU002N were in the center of the car. In future designs, the superconducting magnets would be concentrated into the coupling position of an articulated structure (on the wheel bogies supporting the extreme ends of the cars).

Design of the trains had already led to a number of innovations in magnets, superconducting materials, switching techniques, computer controls, and methods of cooling superconductors.[17] But the Railway Technical Research Institute in August 1992 felt that the basic technology development stage was virtually completed. Already, the superconducting magnet to be employed for future operations had been tentatively built and submitted to stationery tests. Researchers anticipated experimentation with a number of new materials for the system. These would have special characteristics of light weight, superconductivity, low temperature resistance, thermal insulation, magnetic shielding, counter magnetic features, electrical insulation, weatherability, or high power conversion capability.[18] Exhibit 7 shows the expected impact of a $5.3 billion system on various industries in the U.S.

WHETHER AND HOW TO PROCEED

A U.S. report on "Application of Superconductivity to Transportation: Magnetically Levitated Train" in 1992 concluded: "The practical application of liquid helium refrigeration to superconducting magnets is [now] feasible. However, if high temperature superconductors become available, the structures of magnets and refrigerator systems will be drastically simplified. When high temperature superconductors become practically available, there will be no problem in replacing the liquid helium cooled magnets with these materials."

Despite the potentials of such technical advances, commercial development of operating maglev systems was likely to exceed the financial capabilities of any single train manufacturer. While many believed payoffs from a successful system could be extremely high, there were many uncertainties facing developers. And both countries and companies wondered how to position themselves in a technology many saw as essential to solving an urban transportation crisis in the future—when many of today's 1–3 million population cities begin to approach the 10 to 30 million sizes of Tokyo, London, New York, or Los Angeles.

QUESTIONS

1. Given these uncertainties, why should JR and the Ministry of Transport continue to support the maglev project? What strategic intent or figures of merit would make this project worthwhile? How should these be established?
2. What is the legitimate role of government in developing such large scale, high technology systems? Why shouldn't this be left to the marketplace? How can such government expenditures be justified in a "free enterprise" system?
3. Should the U.S. develop maglev trains? If so, how should they be supported? What role should the U.S. government, state and local governments, and private enterprise play? How does one analyze the various alternatives available (i.e., air, maglev, conventional train, advanced fast train)? Please note that all preceding transportation systems (dirt roads, canals, rivers, harbors, rail, highway, air, and steamship) have been heavily supported and subsidized by the Federal government.

EXHIBIT 5
Passenger Travel and Energy Use in the United States, 1990

	PASSENGER MILES (MILLIONS)	LOAD FACTOR (PERSONS/ VEHICLE)	ENERGY INTENSITY (BTU PER PASSENGER-MILE)	ENERGY USE (TRILLIONS OF BTUS)
Automobiles	2,424,992	1.6	3,750	9,066.3
Personal Trucks	444,237	1.5	6,042	2,694.0
Motorcycles	13,401	1.4	1,783	23.9
Buses	118,327	17.0	1,376	162.8
Transit	21,127	9.8	3,735	78.9
Intercity	23,600	23.2	944	21.7
School	74,200	19.5	836	62.2
Air	358,763	44.0	5,085	1,795.5
Certified route (domestic)	345,763	87.2	4,811	1,663.6
General aviation	13,000	3.1	10,146	131.9
Rail	25,310	23.5	3,125	79.1
Intercity	6,057	20.1	2,609	15.8
Transit	12,046	21.5	3,453	41.6
Commuter	7,207	33.8	3,011	21.7

Source: Oak Ridge National Laboratory (Martin Marietta Energy Systems, Inc.), *Transportation Energy Data Book: Edition 13,* pages 2–22 and 2–24.

EXAMPLES OF MAGLEV NETWORKS

Source: "Assessment of the Potential for Magnetic Levitation Transportation Systems in the United States," *Moving America: New Directions, New Opportunities,* June 1990.

EXHIBIT 6B
European High-Speed
Rail Links

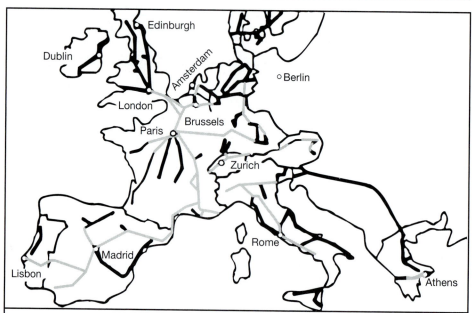

The projected high-speed steel-rail links throughout Europe. Darker lines are for routes already built or on the drawing boards. Lighter lines are for conventional track that will be upgraded for high-speed rail. Other links and extensions are also planned.

Source: Virginia Fairweather, "A Supertrain Solution?" *Civil Engineering,* February 1990.

About one-half of the budget goes to wages. Over the entire construction period, it will require 46,000 person-years of work with peak employment between 7,000 to 8,000. The rest of the funds go toward the purchase of equipment and construction materials directly. This means about $2.8 billion for steel, cement, stone, fabricating, equipment, communication systems, etc.

Expenditures for the various components of the project are:	**Millions**
Structures	$2,000
Track work	800
Roadway preparation	400
Electrification	450
Right of way	80
Signals and communications	120
Vehicles	220

The direct industry purchases are:	**Millions**
Primary metal products	$740
Quarry	99
Chemical and rubber	195
Fabricated metals	465
Transportation, communications and utilities	200
Wholesale and retail	295
Machinery	200

What the $5.7 billion really means, when the economic multiplier effects are taken into consideration, is at least $18 billion in total economic impact:

▼ Over 150,000 person-years of wages — 20,000 to 25,000 jobs in the peak year.

▼ $6 billion to $9 billion in purchases from industry. Hundreds of millions of tax dollars paid by industry and workers. For specific industries there are major implications; a few examples are:

For the chemical and rubber industry the $195 million in direct purchases increases to over $600 million of total impact.

The $200 million directly purchased from transportation, communications and utilities jumps to over $900 million.

$1.5 billion is generated for wholesale and retail trade.

Over $600 million is added to the finance, insurance and real estate industry.

The biggest impact is on households where about $4.5 billion is paid in wages, salaries and dividends.

Source: Advanced Rail Technology, report prepared by the Subcommittee on Transportation, Aviation and Materials; Transmitted to the Committee on Science and Technology, U.S. House of Representatives, Second Session, Washington, DC: U.S. Government Printing Office, September 1982.

TECHNOLOGY TYPE	SYSTEM	# PEOPLE PER CAR	EMPTY CAR WEIGHT (TONS)	OPERATING SPEED (MPH)	TESTING TOP SPEED (MPH)	MAX. GRADE	MIN. RADIUS (FT)	ENERGY (BTU/ SEAT-MILE)	NOISE (dB(A)@ 82 FT)	AIR QUALITY
MAGLEV	Birmingham (UK)	40	5	37		10%				Power plant emittance
	M-Bahn	80	9.5	25	50	15%			61 @ 25 mph	Power plant emittance
	JR (MLU-002)	44	17	260	260		19700 @ 310 mph	840 @ 260 mph		Liquid He Containment
	HSST (HSST-04)	70	30	124	204	6%	8200 @ 186 mph	275 @ 186 mph		Power plant emittance
	Transrapid (TRO7)	200	90	310	256	3.5% suggested 10% allowable	13100 @ 248 mph 21400 @ 310 mph	300 @ 185 mph 500 @ 260 mph	84 @ 186 mph	Power plant emittance
HIGH SPEED RAIL	ETR-500	46–78	40	171	186	1.8% outside 1.5% tunnels	17800 @ 186 mph 12100 @ 155 mph			Power plant emittance
	TGV	38–67	33	186	299.6	2% suggested 3.5% allowable	13,127 @ 186 mph	400 @ 186 mph	95 @ 186 mph	Power plant emittance
	ICE			186	253	5% allowable	16,700		93 @ 186 mph	Power plant emittance
	X-2	29–76	48	130–150	150+	5% allowable		250 @ 150 mph	70 @ 150 mph	Power plant emittance

Source: Gus Welty, "High Speed Race Heats Up," *Railway Age*, May 1990.

TECHNOLOGY TYPE	SYSTEM	HEALTH IMPACT	VISUAL	SAFETY	DEVELOPMENT LEVEL	CLIMATE EFFECTS	CAPITAL COST ($MILLION ML.)	OPERATING (CENTS PM)	RIGHT-OF-WAY NEEDED	OWNER OF TECHNOLOGY
MAGLEV	Birmingham	None	Elevated or at grade	493K revenue mi w/o injury	Completed	Gusts to 100 mph, up to 60 mph sustained				British rail PMG (4)
	M-Bahn	None	Elevated or at grade	50K testing in Berlin	Completed		16–27			AEG
	JR (MLU-002)	200 Gs field	U-shaped guideway		To be available in 1995		19–31 (1987$)		12 single 35 double	RTRI
	HSST (HSST-04)	None	Elevated or at grade		To be available in 1995					HSST
	Transrapid (TRO7)	None	Elevated or at grade	26K mi testing thru 7/88	To be available end 1990	Can run @ –13 to 104 deg. F, 50 mph wind	9–17 (1987$)	4–19 (1987$)	12 single 33 double	TRI
HIGH SPEED RAIL	ETR-500	None	At grade rail		Completed		9			Breda, Ansaldo, Fiat & TIBB
	TGV	None	At grade rail	17 M people per yr. w/o injury	Completed	–4 to 184 deg. F	5–10 (1987$)	6–29 (1987$)	26 single 45 double	French Nat. rail SNCF
	ICE	None	At grade rail		Completed		10–12			German Fed rail
	X-2	None	At grade rail		To be available 1990	–47 to 100 deg. F, snowproof			Standard intercity	ABB Traction

Source: Gus Welty, "High Speed Race Heats Up," *Railway Age*, May 1990.

APPENDIX A (cont'd.)
Volume of U.S. Intercity Passenger Traffic:
millions of revenue passenger-miles and percentage of total
(except private).

YEAR	RAILROADS[a]	PERCENT	BUSES	PERCENT	AIR CARRIERS	PERCENT	INLAND WATERWAYS	PERCENT	TOTAL (EXCEPT PRIVATE)	PRIVATE AUTOS	PRIVATE AIRPLANES	TOTAL (INCLUDING PRIVATE)
1929	33,965	77.1%	6,800	15.4%	—	—	3,300	7.5%	44,065	175,000	—	219,065
1939	23,669	67.7	9,100	26.0	683	2.0%	1,486	4.3	34,938	275,000	—	309,938
1944	97,705	75.7	26,920	20.9	2,177	1.7	2,187	1.7	128,989	181,000	1	309,990
1950	32,481	47.2	26,436	38.4	8,773	12.7	1,190	1.7	68,880	438,293	1,299	508,472
1960	21,574	28.6	19,327	25.7	31,730	42.1	2,688	3.6	75,319	706,079	2,228	783,626
1970	10,903	5.7	25,300	14.3	109,499	77.7	4,000	2.3	149,702	1,026,000	9,101	1,184,803
1974	10,475	5.9	26,700	15.1	135,469	76.7	4,000	2.3	178,644	1,143,440	11,000	1,331,044
1980[P]	11,500	4.6	27,700	11.2	204,400	82.6	4,000	1.6	247,600	1,200,000	15,000	1,583,000
1981[P]	11,800	4.8	27,200	11.1	102,200	82.5	4,000	1.6	244,300	1,344,000	14,700	1,603,000

NOTE: Air carrier data from reports of CAB and TAA; Great Lakes and rivers and canals from Corps of Engineers and TAA; all 1980 and 1981 figures are from TAA data, except rail freight traffic is by the AAR.

[a]Railroads of all classes, including electric railways, Amtrak and Auto-Train.

[P]These are preliminary estimates and are subject to frequent subsequent adjustments.

Source: *Yearbook of Railroad Facts, 1982* in *U.S. Passenger Rail Technologies* (Washington, D.C.: U.S. Congress, Office of Technology Assessment, OTA-STI-222, December 1983).

CALENDAR YEAR	RAILWAY			TROLLEY BUS (MILLIONS)	MOTOR BUS (MILLIONS)	DEMAND RESPONSE (MILLIONS)	OTHER (MILLIONS)	TOTAL PASSENGER RIDES/TRIPS (MILLIONS)
	LIGHT RAIL (MILLIONS)	HEAVY RAIL (MILLIONS)	COMMUTER RAIL (MILLIONS)					
1979	107	1,777	279	75	6,156	—	67	8,461
1980	133	2,108	280	142	5,837	—	67	8,567
1981	123	2,094	268	138	5,594	—	67	8,284
1982	136	2,115	259	151	5,324	—	67	8,052
1983	137	2,167	262	160	5,422	—	55	8,203
1984	135	2,231	267	165	5,908	62	61	8,829
1985	132	2,290	275	142	5,675	59	63	8,636
1986	130	2,333	306	139	5,753	63	53	8,777
1987	133	2,402	311	141	5,614	64	70	8,735
1988	154	2,308	325	136	5,590	73	80	8,666
1989	162	2,542	330	130	5,620	70	77	8,931
1990	175	2,346	328	126	5,677	68	79	8,799
1991	184	2,172	318	125	5,624	71	81	8,575
1992	189	2,207	314	127	5,525	79	78	8,519

NOTE: — Means data are not available.

[a]Total passenger rides for 1979 based on individual transit data collection procedures. Unlinked transit passenger trips beginning in 1980 based on data collection procedures as defined by the Federal Transit Act. Prior to 1984, the total excludes demand response and most rural and smaller systems. Series are not continuous between 1983 and 1984.

Source: American Public Transit Association, 1993 *Transit Fact Book*, Washington, D.C., 1993.

	NUMBER OF LOCOMOTIVES IN SERVICE	NUMBER OF PASSENGER CARS	REVENUE PASSENGER-MILES (MILLIONS)	AVERAGE TRIP LENGTH (MILES)	ENERGY USE (TRILLION BTU)
1975	355	1,913	3,753	224	13.8
1980	448	2,128	4,503	217	14.3
1985	382	1,818	4,785	238	13.4
1987	381	1,850	5,361	259	13.6
1989	312	1,742	5,859	274	16.0
1991	316	1,786	6,273	285	15.7

Source: Oak Ridge National Laboratory (Martin Marietta Energy Systems, Inc.), *Transportation Energy Data Book: Edition 13*, pages 6–29.

**APPENDIX A (cont'd.)
Inner City Congestion
and Costs per Ton Mile
versus Delivery of
Packages**

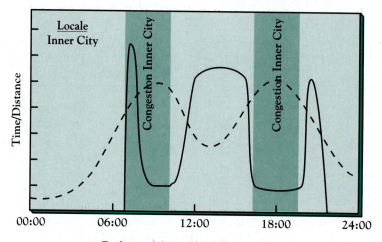

——— Packages delivered/picked up per hour

– – – Cost per ton-mile

In 1993, Ford's Taurus-Sable series was the highest selling auto brand in the U.S. and probably the most profitable car line in the world. Its history and current situation provide a catalog of the issues and management practices that accompany many turnarounds and later haunt their success. Its success was a source of both the strength and a challenge for Ford's new CEO, Alex Trotman.

FROM GREATNESS TO DECLINE

The Ford Motor Co., founded in 1903 by Henry Ford, was one of a very few large U.S. corporations where the top management position was traditionally held by a descendant of the founder. With his family owning 40% of the voting stock, Henry Ford II had led the company from 1945 until the early 1980s. As CEO, he had a management style that could best be described as "quite autocratic." While GM and the Japanese automakers had developed strategic decision-making processes that were intentionally depersonalized and based on a culture of consensus, Ford's strategic decisions had a highly personalized character because of Mr. Ford's presence.

One result was that in mid-1980, Ford Motor Company found itself with sales off 42% and a loss of $164 million for the quarter. Were it not for its profitable foreign operations, Ford's bottom line would have looked even worse. Although Ford had been the leading U.S. automaker in non-U.S. markets for the past three decades, its strategy was made primarily from a "Detroit viewpoint." The company did little to

Case copyright © 1995, James Brian Quinn. The cooperation of Ford Motor Co. is gratefully acknowledged. Penny C. Paquette was research associate on this case. The special contributions of Mr. Dan Dimancescu of Cambridge, Mass., are especially acknowledged.

import experience or gain U.S. advantages from its worldwide operations. What went on in the rest of the world seemed to have little to do with the North American market, where big cars had always been status symbols and customers expected cars to "feel and handle like sofas with seat belts." But in the late 1970s and early 1980s sales of small, fuel efficient, Japanese cars soared.

At Ford, the bottom line was all important. As in other old-line U.S. companies, blue-collar workers were generally considered as variable costs and laid off whenever cyclical downturns occurred. To obtain a measure of job security the unions resisted shifts among the very narrow job categories management itself had created to provide job ladders in the highly specialized mass production systems created by the "efficiency experts" of the past.

CHIMNEYS OF POWER

As in many other companies, Ford people were told what to do and were not expected to question it. Often when plants had met their quotas, workers would be told to "go home" and lose their pay for the rest of the day.

Workers on the line were allowed little active input. A manager once described the operating style as "Management by exception. Watch for an error and then dive on it. We barked and they reacted."[1] First-run yields might only be 70% in spec. When things were going well, management felt it could rebuild the rejects. The line was kept moving regardless of defects or machinery which might need repair. There never seemed to be enough money to maintain equipment or to improve the quality of Ford's cars, while advertising budgets seemed lush and marketing and finance executives earned considerably more than their manufacturing counterparts.[2]

The company gave suppliers minimal lead times, and the low-cost bidder usually won the job. This often meant that several different suppliers would receive contracts for various parts within one section or subsystem of the car. One engineer recalled spending almost a year working with a supplier to design and develop a part only to have the buyer in Ford's purchasing department, whose performance was judged on finding the cheapest supplier, give the contract to another company. Little trust existed between Ford and its suppliers, and communications with them usually began only after Ford's design teams had finalized the car's specifications and it was ready to go into production.

Within its major operational divisions—North American Automotive, International Automotive, and Diversified Products—Ford was vertically organized by function. These vertical organizations had become so powerful and self-contained that they were referred to as "chimneys" of power. Each stage of product development—from research to design, to product engineering, to manufacturing, to assembly, to sales, to the dealer, and finally to the service units—was dominated by an individual functional department which seemed to be obsessed with why the preceding group's design would not work. When a downstream group encountered a problem, it was always the "fault" of a preceding group. Redos and changes proliferated and continued even past "Job 1," when the first new car rolled off the assembly line.

NEWLY EMERGING TALENTS

In 1970, an up-and-coming engineer named Lewis Veraldi, whose career up to this point had been in design engineering, began a three-year stint in Ford's manufacturing group. Working double shifts in manufacturing he soon gained a very different perspective on the design and product development process from other Ford engineers who tended to avoid associating with people on "the line."

In 1973 when Ford embarked on its most expensive car program to date—the $840 million Fiesta small-car project in Germany—Philip Caldwell, then head of international operations, picked Veraldi to head the project. The car was to be a clean sheet project (not derived from an existing car platform). Ford's European engineering and manufacturing groups were then close to being at war with each other, and continuation of the internecine struggle could have been disastrous.[3] Since Veraldi had just experienced the frustration of taking an engineering design to the plant only to have manufacturing reject it "because it wasn't designed right," he decided the time had come to bring the manufacturing people upstream into the design process. Bringing the two disciplines together and executing the program simultaneously rather than sequentially turned out to avoid a plethora of changes and saved Ford "a bundle of money."

During the late '70s, as oil prices suddenly escalated to 10 times their original level, the nation tumbled into an inflationary recession that many thought might continue for a long time. In response Henry Ford cut capital spending by $2 billion, decided not to downsize as quickly as GM, and further postponed Ford's first small, front-wheel car then planned for introduction in 1978. Product design was elevated to the senior management level; and six more months were added to the implementation phase of Ford's already long product development cycle—then 5 to 6 years, as opposed to Japan's average of 43 months. The lengthy sequential progress of the car through the various functional groups is described in Exhibit 1. In addition, Henry Ford's own preferences overwhelmingly influenced outcomes, he often intervened after the design cycle was completed.

With big cars selling well, few of the company's top executives were in a hurry to design smaller cars. Even when Ford finally downsized its biggest cars, it reduced fuel consumption but kept the larger look and feel of an earlier era. In 1979, as gas lines reappeared and tastes suddenly shifted to smaller, fuel-efficient cars, Ford did not have them to sell. Its market share in the United States plummeted from 23.6% in 1978 to 17.3% by 1980. Finally, although Ford's Advanced Development Group had pioneered front wheel drive technology, in 1980 it belatedly introduced its first such cars, the Escort and Lynx. These helped Ford regain some market share, but they did not help its bottom line. Ford estimated that on a fully allocated basis it lost $400 every time it sold one. Ford ballyhooed the Escort as an example of a "world car," first designed in Europe. But it was reengineered in the United States by executives skeptical of their overseas counterparts, and the U.S. and European vehicles actually ended up with only one common part—a water pump seal![4]

In March 1980, Henry Ford II finally stepped down as chairman of the board while remaining a member of the board and chairman of the finance committee. He was succeeded as CEO by Caldwell and Donald E. Petersen was named president. Petersen had been executive vice president of the profitable International Automotive Operations. A mechanical

EXHIBIT 1
Typical Product
Development Cycle

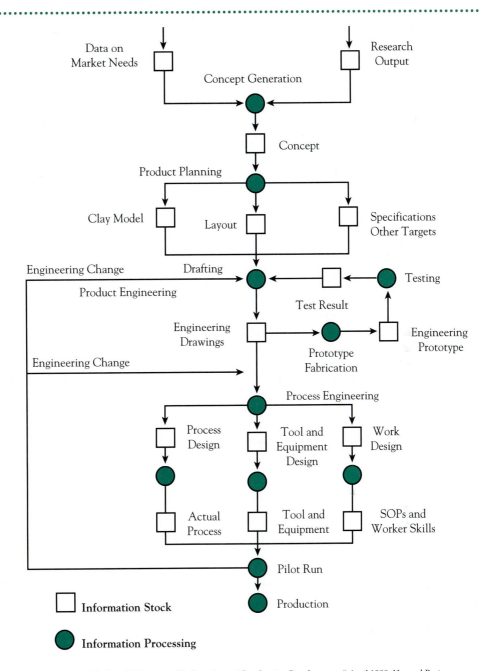

Source: Kim B. Clark and T. Fujimoto, Working Paper: "Overlapping Development, " April 1988, Harvard Business School.

engineer with a Stanford MBA, Petersen had started his career at Ford in 1949 as a financial and product planning analyst, but over the years, he had tried his hand at marketing, directed engineering and industrial design staffs, and managed truck operations. He had played a key part in developing the Mustang and got credit for Ford's Econoline, one of the most successful vans ever. During the 1970s, he served as head of Diversified Products as well as International Automotive Operations.

Harold A. "Red" Poling, who had been vice president of finance and later chairman of Ford Europe, became head of the ailing North American Automotive Operations. With its product plans largely committed through the 1983 model year, Ford tried to staunch its losses in North America with spending cuts. But the hemorrhaging continued, with losses of $1.5 billion in 1980 and $1 billion the next year. Poling slashed the payroll by 37,500 employees and permanently shut down two money-losing assembly plants.

MANAGEMENT, NOT TECHNOLOGY

About this time, a scene was being played out in Ford's corporate design center which exemplified some of the company's problems. A few consumers had been asked in to get their reactions to Ford's prototype cars for the future. The cars were very similar to GM's and almost identical to Ford's own boxy-looking 1980 models currently rusting on dealers' lots. One member of the audience stood up and said, "I know, these are all phony. The real car is behind the curtain back there, isn't it." The Ford people didn't know what to say because there were no other cars. When Petersen found his corporate designers were equally uninspired by the future models, the new management decided to turn the designers loose to develop ideas, without trying to second-guess their bosses or merely copying what the competition was doing. Ford's executives finally began to realize that fuel economy wasn't the only reason consumers were flocking to imports.

Ford simply wasn't competitive in quality and styling with many imports. During 1978 Ford United States had actually recalled more cars than it produced, and many thought it had become perhaps the worst U.S. producer in terms of quality. Caldwell and Petersen made quality a top priority. Manufacturing executives began to study the systems and technologies of automakers worldwide in an effort to make the company competitive again. They concluded that few major technical breakthroughs were either needed or

likely. They could gain most by concentrating on improving management methods to achieve three primary goals: improved quality, productivity, and quality of work life. Ford and the UAW signed a letter of understanding on employee involvement (EI) in which both formally agreed to give EI their total commitment in this effort. Ultimately this led to a new Mission Statement for Ford. (See Exhibit 2.)

EMPLOYEE INVOLVEMENT

In early 1980 Pete Pestillo was hired away from BF Goodrich Co. to be vice president of labor relations at Ford. A colorful figure, Pestillo spoke of the need for new ways to manage people. "Americans generally . . . have tended to rely upon their ability to manage and direct rather than what I see as the new need to motivate and lead." *Industry Week*[5] said, "Since the process of making a car offers 100,000 occasions for indifference, what Mr. Pestillo had in mind was a broad program that would involve everybody in the workplace on product quality—a system where everyone in an auto plant felt that the car at the end of the line bore a little part of him, so he wanted it done right." When Don Ephlin took over the Ford unit of UAW in May of the same year, the two of them saw a constructive opportunity to do things differently.

Neither Ford nor the UAW wanted to measure the economic results of EI, believing that "playing the numbers game" would kill the process.[6] In 1980, to prove its seriousness about employee involvement, Ford took the unprecedented step of sending drawings, parts, models, and mock-ups of its new Ranger truck to its Louisville plant, displaying them alongside the assembly lines, and inviting workers to comment on how to improve what they might one day be building. Through spring 1983, hourly employees had made 749 proposals, and Ford adopted 542 of them.[7]

After a joint trip to Japan in 1981 to look at how the competition did things, Pestillo and Ephlin, with the support of Chairman Caldwell, were able to negotiate a new Ford-UAW contract in only 13 days—six months before the old one expired. This had never happened in the industry's history. They hammered out such precedent-setting new contract innovations as lifetime employment security, coupled with changes in training, job classifications, and work rules. By 1982 some plants had even taken the then unprecedented step of allowing hourly workers to stop the line to correct defects. At one plant, within four months after the stop buttons were installed, defects dropped to fewer than 1 per car, down from 17.

EXHIBIT 2
Mission Statement

MISSION

Ford Motor Company is a worldwide leader in automotive and automotive-related products and services as well as in newer industries such as aerospace, communications, and financial services. Our mission is to improve continually our products and services to meet our customers' needs, allowing us to prosper as a business and to provide a reasonable return from our stockholders, the owners of our business.

VALUES

How we accomplish our mission is as important as the mission itself. Fundamental to success for the company are these basic values:

People—Our people are the source of our strength. They provide our corporate intelligence and determine our reputation and vitality. Involvement and teamwork are our core human values.

Products—Our products are the end result of our efforts, and they should be the best in serving customers worldwide. As our products are viewed, so are we viewed.

Profits—Profits are the ultimate measure of how efficiently we provide customers with the best products for their needs. Profits are required to survive and grow.

GUIDING PRINCIPLES

Quality comes first. To achieve customer satisfaction, the quality of our products and services must be our number-one priority.

Customers are the focus of everything we do. Our work must be done with our customers in mind, providing better products and services than our competition.

Continuous improvement is essential to our success. We must strive for excellence in everything we do: in our products, in their safety and value—and in our services, our human relations, our competitiveness and our profitability.

Employee involvement is our way of life. We are a team. We must treat each other with trust and respect.

Dealers and suppliers are our partners. The company must maintain mutually beneficial relationships with dealers, suppliers, and our other business associates.

Integrity is never compromised. The conduct of our company worldwide must be pursued in a manner that is socially responsible and commands respect for its integrity and for its positive contribution to society. Our doors are open to men and women alike without discrimination and without regard to ethnic origin or personal beliefs.

Source: Ford Motor Company, *Annual Report,* 1984.

QUALITY IMPROVEMENT

Ford's new team began other programs as well. It instigated business plans which (instead of focusing on a target return on investment) called for improving quality on the theory that returns would follow. Ford not only began rigorously applying the statistical process control techniques and quality attitudes popularized by W. Edwards Deming in Japan, it also adopted the newer approaches to quality management developed by Genichi Taguchi.

Taguchi methods start with the premise that the quality goal should be to continually reduce variability around well-defined target specifications, rather than simply to ensure that the production process stays within specification limits. His rationale is developed in a formula called the "loss function curve," which proposes that the cost of deviating from the target specification increases quadratically (by squares) the further one gets away from the target. This formula not only allows engineers to set cost-justified specification tolerances but to figure out how much money they can spend to reduce variation in a process or product. Taguchi's other theories involve ways to design a product to be robust enough to achieve high quality despite fluctuations on the production line. He developed a statistical procedure called the "signal-to-noise ratio" to vastly reduce the number of measurement and process options available by grouping them and changing several variables at a time. Once engineers define an efficient production process, they can also design the product itself to be less sensitive to expected variations—especially those that are difficult or costly for the factory to regulate.

Despite Mr. Poling's financial background and his diligence in cutting expenses, he emphasized that cutting costs and improving quality were not incompatible. In spite of formidable cost cutting, Ford North American spent around $3 billion during the early 1980s to completely renovate and expand its engine, transmission, stamping, and assembly plants. Ford's practice was to introduce new technology and new capacity in existing plants when new vehicles were introduced. This contrasted with GM's approach of bringing on new technology in new "green field" plants.

TAURUS RISES

In the midst of the pressures of meeting new environmental regulations, fuel cost increases, and cost cutting exigencies, Ford sought to replace its midsized cars with innovative new products that simultaneously would lure drivers back into the American fold and attack the heart of GM's market. The targeted segment, often called the "intermediate" car market, was the meat and potatoes of any full-line manufacturer's business. This was where volume sales and full profit margins met, and where Ford hoped that 40% of its sales would eventually lie.

The paper studies for what was to become the Taurus project began in earnest in 1979. The original designs were for a five-passenger, four-cylinder engine car about 170 inches long. It was to be a downsized replacement for the Ford LTD/Mercury Marquis as well as for the larger Crown Victoria/Marquis. In 1980, 64% of the U.S. market was in small cars. The product planning group was projecting fuel cost of $3 per gallon in the mid-1980s when the cars would go to market. When Lew Veraldi came back from Europe after the Fiesta project, he was assigned to Advanced Vehicle Development (AVD) where his job was to create advanced cars in hardware, not just on paper. He did his initial work on what became the Taurus/Sable cars there.

In the summer of 1980 Veraldi and others made a presentation to senior management. The meeting was to make basic decisions about the cars' specifications, let management look at various designs, and settle on the critical path the project would take. A key question was whether the new car would be the costly, radical, clean sheet design AVD had come up with, or a low-investment program, probably becoming a "muddle-through, parts bin car" liberally borrowing componentry from the Tempo and Topaz, which were to be introduced in 1983. Despite the fact that the company was treading water in red ink, Caldwell supported Veraldi's concept of a clean sheet project—a $3.25 billion project for a brand-new, unproven car design.

Starting at this point, Caldwell asked the key questions he was to repeat again and again during the program, "Why should I buy this car? Specifically, why will this car be a success? What will Ford have to do to make the car absolutely world class in terms of quality and customer satisfaction?" By October 1982 when the project went to the board of directors for final approval it had become clear that the LTD and Marquis were ill equipped to meet the needs of the "upper-middle" segment of the market. The board agreed that Ford had to become a world class leader in this key segment, and that was not possible with what Ford then had.

At the critical 1980 meeting senior management agreed to the creation of a management team, later known as Team Taurus, to implement the concept of *concurrent* rather than sequential car design and development. In a process Veraldi insisted upon, program representatives from *all* units—planning, design, engineering, manufacturing, marketing, and so on—would work together as a group and take final responsibility for the new vehicle. Veraldi even brought some team members over from Europe to help capture some of the luxury feel and nimble style of the European cars.

All decisions concerning the Taurus program would be made by the Team Taurus core group. The organization chart for Team Taurus resembled two large circular rings. (See Exhibit 3.) The inner ring contained the car program management (CPM) group of which Lew Veraldi was the head, with John Risk (Car Product Development planning director), A. L. Guthrie (chief engineer), John Telnack (chief designer), and Philip Benton (later president, Ford Automotive Group) among the other key players. In the various segments surrounding the inner CPM group were people from the various functional divisions within the company. Some of these worked full time with the Team Taurus core group. Others stayed in their respective functional divisions, but were committed to Team Taurus full time. The whole team was held together by common goals, keyed around the goal of Taurus being truly "world class in its segment."

Goals for the Team Taurus program management group eventually became

▼ Obtaining performance at "best in class"
▼ Getting 100% prototype parts on the first prototype in order to test designs and suppliers
▼ Improving key decision timing for development
▼ Reducing product complexity
▼ Eliminating avoidable changes

▼ Controlling late program modifications

▼ Creating an atmosphere like a small business unit with identity and commitment

SYSTEMATIC PLANNING AND TREMENDOUS TRIFLES

Little else was etched in granite at first. Instead the cooperative Team Taurus process was allowed to design the line. Before finalizing designs—and 4 1/2 years before the car was introduced—the team developed a "want list" from all the relevant constituencies—Ford designers, body and assembly engineers, line workers, marketing managers and dealers, legal and safety experts, parts suppliers, insurance companies, independent service people, ergonomics experts, and consumers. It asked each group, "Considering the kind of car we're planning, what would you want to see included, changed, or eliminated?" The want list eventually included some 1,400 items—of which Team Taurus concentrated on 500.

Mr. Veraldi described other cooperative measures followed in the Atlanta plant, chosen to assemble the Taurus:

> We met with the legal and safety people very early in the project. Since the cars were expected to be on the market for a seven- or eight-year life cycle, we asked them to tell us what changes or additions to the laws and emission and safety regulations we should anticipate and "bake in" to the design and specifications of the car.[8] We did this for both the United States and Europe so the car could be easily adapted to the European market.
>
> The Service Managers Council was helpful in telling us what steps we could take to make the cars easier to service. We also looked very carefully at bodywork repairability by talking to independent repairmen and insurance companies. The repairmen came in and told us where in any body structure it was best to design in body integrity, ease of repair, and so on. For example, they showed us where to cut the car to get structural integrity after an accident or other repairs.

While many auto companies talked about being "best in their field," Team Taurus attempted a systematic follow through on that goal. The CPM group scrapped Ford's traditional "Detroit-knows-best" or "Not Invented Here" attitudes. In early 1982, they methodically set out to identify 400 subsystems which comprised the world's best-designed and engineered automotive features, and tried to incorporate as many as possible into the Taurus. Seeking "best in class" capabilities for 1985 when the cars would be introduced they selected cars, subsystems, and components from

around the world with superior features and reverse engineered them to learn how they were designed, manufactured, and assembled. Mr. Veraldi continued:

> For Taurus, suppliers were asked to participate early. If they shared their expertise with us, they would be guaranteed the business if we used their designs. But under Team Taurus we also made them accountable for quality and fit before producing the part. We instituted what I called the "Must See Before" program under which suppliers were required to show the Team the parts they were making and how they would make sure they fit right, functioned right, felt right, and looked right in the final product. We also used "system sourcing" for Taurus purchasing; instead of having different companies supply, say, interior trim moldings (leading to confusion and difficulty in resolving fit problems), only one company supplied all the moldings.
>
> We tried to take time out of the project in ways that would take cost out as well. The car was sourced starting 3 1/2 years before Job 1. On average, sourcing was completed 26-29 months before production, letting suppliers plan their production and quality programs. We were even willing to make loans to qualified suppliers to help them get ready. Tooling was also planned far ahead for both stamping and assembly. Since we were always trying to come up with significant advantages for every component or feature in the car, we also tried to get suppliers to help us obtain "best-in-class" features for their products. We did this by getting the purchasing people to write long-term contracts with suppliers to create mutual trust.

MARKETING CONCENTRATION

Many critics felt this process could only lead to a "copycat" car, but Team Taurus was determined to create Ford's first really distinctive car of the 1980s. John Telnack is often given credit for Ford's new "aero look" first introduced in the 1983 LTD. To implement this in the new line, Team Taurus launched Ford's largest ever series of market studies to determine customers' preferences and to respond to top management's instruction "to break with tradition and give us something uniquely Ford." This helped in determining which features should have highest priority in the new design and brought out myriad ideas for "customer appreciation items"—"tremendous trifles" as Lew Veraldi began to call them—which the Team found created a "halo effect" about the quality and comfort in the rest of the car. Examples included a net in the trunk to hold grocery bags upright, oil dipsticks painted a bright yellow for fast identification, and more width and height (footroom) under the front seat to make the back-seat ride more comfortable. On a broader scale engineers

EXHIBIT 3
Team Taurus
Organizational Chart

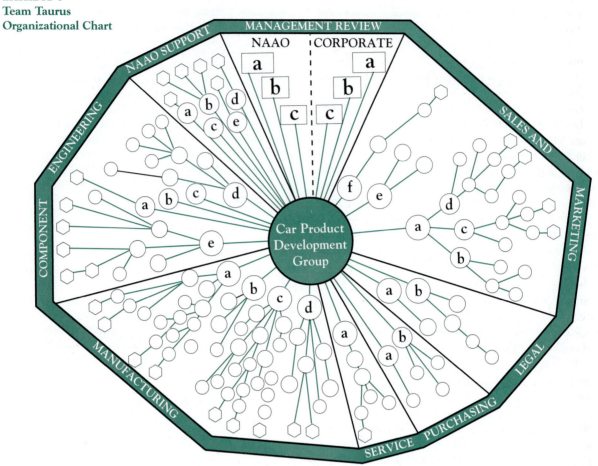

The Car Product Development Group is responsible for overall direction, design, development, control and final approval.

☐ Review committees
Corporate
a - Technical Affairs Subcommittee
b - Design Subcommittee
c - Product Planning Subcommittee
NAAO (North American Automotive Operations)
a - Taurus Program Control Meeting
b - Taurus Task Force
c - Taurus Sub-system Reviews

◯ Organization/operations
NAAO Support
a - Controller-Product Development
b - North American Design
c - Test Operations
d - Product Assurance
e - NAAO Timing
Component Engineering
a - Climate Control Division Engineering
b - Plastic/Paint/Vinyl Engineering
c - Electrical/Electronics Division Engineering
d - Body and Chassis Engineering
e - Powertrain Engineering

Manufacturing
a - Body and Assembly Operations/
   Engineering Operations
b - Engine Division
c - Diversified Products Operations
   Components
d - Transmission and Chassis Division
Service
a - Ford Parts and Service Division
Purchasing
a - Purchasing and Supply Staff
b - NAAO Purchasing
Legal
a - Office of General Counsel
b - Environmental and Safety Engineering
Sales and Marketing
a - NAAO Operations
b - NAAO Marketing
c - Lincoln-Mercury Division
d - Ford Division
e - Marketing Staff
f - Public Affairs
⬡ **Dedicated Taurus Personnel**

Source: "Team Taurus," *Ward's Auto World*, February 1985.

achieved a crisper, tauter, better tracking handling than other midsized U.S. cars. And a five-member ergonomics group undertook a systematic two-year task, scientifically studying ways to make the cars more comfortable and easier to operate.[9]

Based on the new inputs from consumers Team Taurus was able to reduce the marketing entities for Taurus (and the Mercury Division's version of the car, Sable) to the lowest number ever offered in this segment. Marketing entities are the models, series, or order specification groups production has to build. Taurus/Sable started out with about the same number of entities (188) the preceding line had, and ended up with 37. Within these 37 marketing entities, the average build repeatability increased to 13,000. For comparison, Ford's 1985 LTD build repeatability was a little over 1,000. Comparable figures were about 7,000 for Toyota's entry in this segment, 2,300 for GM's Celebrity, and 11,500 for Nissan's Maxima.[10] While Team Taurus designed about 4,000 totally new parts for its cars, the line had some 1,700 fewer parts than its predecessors.[11] Eventually, the line had 95% new parts, and only 5% holdovers.

From a design viewpoint Mr. Veraldi said the program's toughest moment was in April 1981 when Team Taurus decided to increase the line's wheelbase, tread, and length. Oil prices appeared to be adjusting dramatically downward. Although the Team felt a year had been wasted, changed circumstances dictated a larger car. "We changed our strategy and decided to let the Crown Victoria and Grand Marquis stay in place and to reorient the new car as a sophisticated, family-oriented car. It grew into a six-passenger, six-cylinder, 188-inch car as fuel prices began to stabilize in the $1 to $1.25 range." A 2.5-liter, 4-cylinder base engine had been locked in from the start, but the optional V-6 grew from 2.8 to 3.0 liters as Ford adjusted its road performance requirements upward.

THE TEAM TAURUS MANAGEMENT APPROACH

After the crucial positioning of the car and its main performance characteristics were decided, Veraldi said,

> We established a key events schedule. There were two levels of activity for this, direct responsibilities—including business planning, product planning, design, technical engineering, and so on—and indirect responsibilities where we only determined the "what and when" issues.

The line people determined the "who and how" issues. All the "key events" for each line function were set out on a chart with months across the top and functions down the side. A team member was assigned from each organization to sign off on the *entire* schedule on behalf of his department and to sign off on the *particulars of his own department's* key events schedule. The main program controls were getting these guys (1) to agree together on the overall schedule and (2) to agree to monitor it in their own organizations. There were over 1500 events on the way from concept to customer. The discipline of laying things down on the key events chart helped everyone to cut costs and increase value for each function. Team members were asked to sign off on these key events 3-4 years before production.

Involving all groups in the process although seemingly more complicated, actually lowered costs because each group was not optimizing at its own level. It was much easier to get people to talk about and come up with constructive changes when they couldn't pass off responsibility by saying, "that's really a manufacturing problem not a design one." There were no specific incentives set up for this project other than pride of workmanship. We found out that most people want to do the job right when they get a chance. When they are given that chance they have as much of an "equity" in the project as any designer does. We motivated people by making sure they had an equity in the product—and then listened to them carefully. At every stage of the process we had inputs from customers and users. Customers and users were considered to be those in the later stages of the design and introduction process—as well as actual consumers in the marketplace. We even had the media in to tell us what consumers told them about models of the car, their own desires, and so on two years before the release of the car.

My objective was to meet total returns on each design element. The only thing I looked at was total returns. When costs were higher than budgeted variable costs, the question was, "Could you price for the feature and meet 'returns' targets?" On earlier projects management used to give and get design targets as "less cost" for each element; now an element could cost more if value was added by the feature being introduced. We tried to put all members of the team in a position where they could measure themselves. If you measure yourself, you will be a lot tougher than your boss. We tried to indicate that arguments were okay—conflict and bargaining were permissible—as long as they increased the quality of the eventual output. Everything was done to direct ourselves toward the "best product." As the process went on, we tried to improve it each year by asking again how we could improve the product even more if we started over again from scratch.

THE MANUFACTURING PROCESS:
THE LIVONIA AND LIMA PLANTS

In 1981 designers decided a new front-wheel drive automatic overdrive (AXOD) transaxle was essential for the proposed 1986 family-sized cars. This transaxle would work as part of Ford's first electronically controlled powertrain, which would be used in the Taurus/Sable cars. With its existing operating procedures Ford's Powertrain and Chassis Division, which managed these plants, recognized how hard it would be to build the AXOD more efficiently than its Japanese competition. The 1,700 workers at the Livonia Transmission plant—which was currently building transmissions for Ford's rear-wheel cars—knew they could lose their jobs (and perhaps have their plant permanently closed in about five years) unless they could win the bid to build AXOD. Ford now made a regular practice of putting major new products out for bids both internally and externally.

Livonia's new manager and its union leader agreed that to win the contract away from Mazda (where Ford owned a 25% interest) they would have to work together to improve quality and cut costs sharply. Employee involvement became a keystone at Livonia—during 1982 employees there earned $600,000 in cash and new cars for ideas that saved Ford $3.7 million. The plant instituted a pilot program in which only two job classifications were used—"operator" and "manufacturing technician." The manufacturing technician was a new job classification—a multiskilled worker with extensive training for responsibilities both on and off the plant floor. As the pilot programs proved effective, Ford and the union negotiated a series of cost-saving work rule changes—and 91% of the local union members approved. Quality improved simultaneously; post-assembly repair rates dropped from 23% to 11% and continued to decrease, and with back-up investments of $1 billion, costs dropped 25%.

Ergonomics experts designed all the workstations and job functions; and hourly and salaried employees worked together to plan machinery layout, workstations, equipment and job designs, supplier selection, and personnel training. Mr. Veraldi said:

> I saw a dedication I had never seen before, especially when I visited the Livonia Transmission plant. The workers stayed until 8:00 P.M. to show me how they were building the parts. At each station the workers had small charts on easels or taped to desks—they were all different—and they would say, "This is how we are going to manufacture this part at this station—and this is how

we're going to make it perfect." They all had their own way of showing you how they were doing statistical process control; the methods were common, but their individual applications were all different since the plant manager had given them the latitude to run their own businesses in the way they thought best.

After the AXOD launch, the Livonia plant received daily deliveries of parts from suppliers in a "just-in-time" system. The revamped plant utilized the world's largest known collection of laser welding systems and a "local area network" (LAN) connecting 650 computer-controlled machines and production controlling PCs—considered one of the largest and most complex installations in the worldwide auto industry. Among other things, these provided real-time linkages to suppliers on their products' quality performance.

Management established a team approach for "consensus sourcing" in which the product engineering, manufacturing, and purchasing departments all had to agree on vendors selected. Each area represented its particular concerns: purchasing (price and availability), manufacturing (quality and ease of assembly), and engineering (design intent). The launch team made a complete mock-up of the engine assembly line (including details of each workstation) where many operations could be simulated, videotaped, and revised before any expensive equipment was installed. The Atlanta and Chicago (Taurus/Sable) assembly plants—laid out with the advice of ergonomics experts—contained power and free-overhead conveyors to get workers out of the pits they had previously occupied—reaching up to do their work.

Production lines were often half the size of a normal line. There were no extra parts between sequential steps—that is, worker A had to produce a part every time worker B needed it. Since workers needed adequate time to do a quality job, the line was non-synchronized—that is, each station was not directly connected to other stations. Each worker maintained control over his own world with a "hold" switch to keep the work in position longer if necessary, although the power rollers continued to move elsewhere, keeping the whole line from being stopped.

The rule was "only quality advanced." There were no repair bays along the line. To ensure quality further, dealers were given a hot-line to the Lima plant to report any engine problems so that manufacturing and suppliers could make needed corrections immediately and ensure that no more faulty engines were shipped. Previously, this feedback had come only from after-the-fact warranty data.

STAMPING AND VEHICLE ASSEMBLY

Taurus/Sable's outer body panels were designed on the CAD/CAM system. The design automatically produced an instruction tape which could be sent to the Buffalo stamping plant where it ran the milling machines making the dies from which panels would be stamped. Computers then checked the dies against the design specs before a single panel was struck. For final assembly, Team Taurus had some 100 "functional" cars built and tested with production parts, production tools, and processes to pretest the cars before full production. Previously, many major problems were discovered only after Job 1 rolled down the line.

In building Taurus/Sable, Ford made its most extensive use of automated, modular assembly. In modular assembly various subassemblies (or modules) are built on "feeder lines" connecting to the main line. This allows more fixed automation and hence tighter tolerances within each subsystem. Modular construction vastly simplifies the main line, allows a somewhat greater mix of flexibility in the subsystems, and creates added pockets of responsibility for cost and quality control. For example, doors and subframes were completed offline, allowing the interior to be completed with much easier access on the main line. Said Mr. Manoogian, quality control director, "Ten years ago 10-15 of every 100 cars built were diverted after assembly for repair. Now we have cut that to 1, and are shooting for 0." Both Taurus/Sable plants went from 53 to 63 cars per hour, with only about 24 hours of labor being required per assembly. Yet the plants were so flexible they could go from Taurus to Sable or from sedans to wagons each hour-on-the-hour, if necessary.[12] Still, Petersen attributed 85% of Taurus' gains to "managing smarter" and only 15% to the new technology.

THE LAUNCH

Ultimately, Team Taurus built prototypes of the new cars seven months earlier than Ford's system normally would have. Both as a tribute to retiring Chairman Caldwell and to precondition the public to the "revolutionary" look of the cars, Taurus and Sable were unveiled at a Hollywood gala in December 1984—some ten months before they were due to hit dealer showrooms. Job 1 for Taurus/Sable was initially planned for July 1985, but was delayed until mid-October. Even then production was slower than planned, as Ford worked to iron out problems with some of its new equipment (notably its new robotic welding machinery) in the plants.[13] But the delay perhaps served the function of hammering home management's priorities better than any number of "Quality Is Job 1" posters could have.[14]

In early 1985 Mr. Petersen took over as chairman and CEO, and Poling moved up to the presidency. *Fortune* later reported:

> Petersen and Poling are exemplars of Ford's new breed of manager. Both held big jobs overseas before landing top posts in the United States. . . . As the company's two top executives, they have done their jobs so well that Ford will make more money than GM and Chrysler combined this year, and Ford Division cars and trucks have passed Chevrolet's as the biggest-selling individual brand.[15]

THE NEW LINE

Ford's future rode on the success of the $3 billion Taurus/Sable program, carrying Ford's aerodynamic styling into the crucial family car market. Altogether Ford spent $100 million on its ad blitz for the introduction of Taurus/Sable;[16] and on the day they were first available Ford already had in hand more than 20,000 customer orders.[17] Taurus and Sable were the only domestically produced 1986 cars named by both *Car and Driver* and *Motor Trend* magazines as among the best cars available in the United States. Of the 400 "best-in-class" features studied, Ford claimed that 80% were met or exceeded in Taurus/Sable.

The cars gave Ford an aura of success, and they were good to Ford's earnings. (See Exhibits 4 and 5 for financial and sales data.) According to one analyst, Ford made $1,200 to $1,500 more on the Taurus and Sable than on the midsized cars they replaced. The cars, which offered "Japanese quality, European styling and ride for a modest price (of about $10,000)" lured the young professional market to Ford. The average age of the Ford Taurus buyer, for example was 47, compared to 59 for the replaced LTD. The buyers' median income was $38,000 for the Taurus owner versus $28,000 for the aged model; and a higher percentage (43%) had college degrees than the LTD buyers (29%). While only 5% of the trade-ins for a Marquis or LTD had come from former import owners, 15% did for the Taurus and Sable.[18]

The Team Taurus approach offered innumerable other benefits—including savings estimated at $250-$400 million on the cars' development. One key item was that design changes after the start of production cost only $35 million, compared with at least $150 million in recent cars.[19] By reducing the number of bodyside panels, from six to two, Ford got an unexpected benefit of being able to use the same front panel on both its sedans and the wagons. And the cars' improved repairability-after-accidents led Allstate and State Farm Mutual insurers to give 30% discounts to Taurus owners.

There were problems, however. Ford had to recall the new cars only a week after they were introduced to replace defective ignition switches that allowed the key to be removed without the ignition being locked. A second recall was necessary when some cars proved to have faulty window glass which broke into pieces too large to meet safety standards, because the glass had been improperly tempered. Other problems included a rotten egg smell coming from the catalytic converter and a minor engine surge which was corrected by replacing a microprocessor in the electronic engine control system. The most serious and publicized problem, however, was that the car scored poorly in 35 MPH crash tests.[20]

The gains established by the Taurus/Sable program, nevertheless, had set new standards that the rest of the domestic industry (and Ford itself in its future introductions) would be hard pressed to duplicate. (See Table 1.)

TABLE 1

BEFORE TAURUS	TAURUS
188 market models	37 market models
1,000 ave. run per model	13,000 ave. run per model
30% defect rate	Zero defect goal
5 to 6 year model turnaround	4-year model turnaround
6 days of inventory	4 hours of inventory
Little training	400,000 hours training 1984-85
3500 suppliers	2300 suppliers

As a basis for comparison, a group under Professor Kim B. Clark at Harvard Business School had made a study of worldwide automotive practices in product development. Their data indicated some striking differences in performance among U.S. groups and those elsewhere in the world. Professor Clark's group compared data on passenger vehicle development from 20 automobile companies in Japan, Europe, and the United States. A brief summary of some key data is included in Exhibits 6 and 7.

MID-1990s SITUATION

By 1993, the Taurus-Sable line had emerged as the highest selling single automobile line in the U.S. and perhaps the world. Ford reported record profits in 1987,

'88, and '89. Comparative data for Ford and its major competitors appears in Exhibit 8. However, in the late 1980s Ford's product development once again faltered. Design reverted to conservatism. Cars on the drawing board when Taurus and Sable were introduced did not take a big step forward. Reflecting the power still left in the old functional "chimneys," Ford reverted to its more traditional design processes. Costs escalated; the 1988 Thunderbirds and Cougars cost $1,000 more per vehicle than planned. Some commentators noted that the financial success of the Taurus masked troubles in other areas of Ford.

THE LATE '80S DOLDRUMS

Petersen, now CEO, became a public figure "spending less time running the business and more time aboard the corporate jet."[21] In 1989 Ford acquired Jaguar for $2.56 billion. And Ford began investing its record profits into financial services and defense, while it held capital spending steady at about 5% of sales. The board replaced Petersen with Poling as CEO in March 1990, just as the accumulated problems of Ford hit the marketplace; the company lost 1.5 points of market share in 1990 and fell $2.4 billion into the red a year later. Poling strongly pushed his philosophy of being the low cost producer, and Alex Trotman—Ford's new North American head—pushed through a 20% savings in salary costs, improved productivity, and upped capital returns on new capital deployed by 20%.

To conserve cash, Ford reemphasized its truck lines while only modestly redoing its Taurus-Sable. Two bright spots during this period were its Lincoln Continental and Town Car, designed by a process similar to Taurus-Sable. The 1988 Continental series was essentially sold out before the cars officially reached dealers' showrooms for display. However, it was Taurus with 272, 600 units and Sable with 88,200 units (compared to Accord's 298,600 units) that restored Ford's great strength, along with Poling's tight discipline over operations and wide-ranging overhead cuts. By 1992, aided by exchange rate changes, Ford reportedly had lower costs for its small car production than did the Japanese producers.[22]

In the late '80s, trucks—a category that includes minivans and sport-utility vehicles—actually produced more profit per unit than Ford's car divisions. Government fuel economy standards were more lenient for trucks and a 25% import duty on 2-door light trucks helped domestic producers. While Ford made about $3,000 on its Taurus-Sable units, it made

EXHIBIT 4
Eight-Year Financial Summary, 1985–1993, Ford Motor Company and Consolidated Subsidiaries

	1993	1991	1989	1987	1985
SUMMARY OF OPERATIONS					
Automotive					
Sales	$91,568	$72,051	$82,879	$71,797	$52,915
Operating income	1,432	(3,769)	4,252	6,256	2,902
Income (loss) before income taxes	1,291	(4,052)	5,155	6,499	3,154
Net income (loss)	940	(3,186)	3,175	3,767	2,012
Financial Services					
Revenues	$16,953	$16,235	$13,267	$8,096	$4,700
Income before income taxes	2,712	1,465	874	1,385	861
Net income (loss)	1,589	928	660	858	504
Total company					
Income (loss) before inome taxes	$4,003	$(2,587)	$6,030	$7,885	$4,015
Minority interests	124	66	82	34	13
Net income (loss)	2,529	(2,258)	3,835	4,625	2,515
TOTAL COMPANY DATA PER SHARE					
Income (loss) before cumulative effects of changes in accounting principles	$4.55	$(4.79)	$8.22	$9.05	$4.54
Income (loss), assuming full dillution	4.20	(4.79)	8.12	8.92	4.40
Cash dividends	1.60	1.95	3.00	1.58	0.80
Common stock price range (NYSE)	43/66⅛	23⅜/37¾	41⅜/56⅝	28½/56⅝	13⅜/19¾
Average number of shares outstanding (millions)	493	476	467	511	554
TOTAL COMPANY BALANCE SHEET DATA					
Assets					
Automotive	$61,737	$ 52,397	$ 45,819	$ 39,734	$29,297
Financial Services	137,201	122,032	115,074	76,260	45,797
Total	198,938	174,429	160,893	115,994	75,094
Long-term debt					
Automotive	$ 7,084	$ 6,539	$ 1,137	$ 2,058	$ 2,459
Financial Services	47,900	43,680	37,784	26,009	13,753
Stockholders' equity	$15,574	$22,690	$22,728	$18,493	$12,269

Source: Ford Motor Company, *Annual Report*, 1991 and 1993.

	1993	1991	1989	1987	1985	1983
U.S. AND CANADIAN CARS AND TRUCKS						
Cars						
United States	1,950,238	1,605,972	2,186,344	2,171,442	1,940,662	1,671,837
Canada	126,297	143,571	190,037	187,840	194,540	143,425
Total cars	**2,076,535**	**1,749,543**	**2,376,381**	**2,359,282**	**2,135,202**	**1,815,262**
Trucks						
United States	1,875,711	1,260,439	1,523,275	1,481,059	1,260,123	993,874
Canada	125,906	103,757	136,082	151,982	119,583	69,409
Total trucks	**2,001,617**	**1,364,196**	**1,659,357**	**1,633,041**	**1,379,706**	**1,063,283**
TOTAL CARS AND TRUCKS	4,078,152	3,113,739	4,035,738	3,992,323	3,514,908	2,878,545
CARS AND TRUCKS OUTSIDE THE U.S. AND CANADA						
Germany	831,216	969,003	1,023,380	899,609	769,883	833,119
Britain	421,939	481,794	515,520	484,057	422,003	414,018
Spain	211,413	340,796	310,481	276,448	265,783	228,150
Australia	126,753	108,986	158,740	134,222	177,108	138,394
Mexico	90,710	111,849	86,830	34,495	70,238	47,670
Other countries	203,403	219,390	205,665	230,220	330,577	394,335
TOTAL OUTSIDE U.S. AND CANADA	1,885,434	2,231,818	2,300,616	2,059,051	2,035,592	2,055,686
TOTAL WORLDWIDE CARS AND TRUCKS	5,963,586	5,345,557	6,336,354	6,051,374	5,550,500	4,934,231
TOTAL WORLDWIDE TRACTORS	a	13,243	71,690	63,914	83,848	67,318
TOTAL WORLDWIDE FACTORY SALES	5,963,586	5,358,800	6,408,044	6,115,288	5,634,348	5,001,549

aFord's Tractor operation, For New Holland, was sold in May 1991.

Source: Ford Motor Company, *Annual Report*, 1993

EXHIBIT 6
Selected Design Profiles
by Region

VARIABLES	TOTAL	JAPAN	UNITED STATES	EUROPE
Number of projects	29	12	6	11
Year of introduction	1980–87	1981–85	1984–87	1980–87
Engineering hours (thousands)				
Average	2,577	1,155	3,478	3,636
Minimum	426	426	1,041	700
Maximum	7,000	2,000	7,000	6,545
Lead time* (months)				
Average	54.2	42.6	61.9	62.6
Minimum	35.0	35.0	50.2	46.0
Maximum	97.0	91.0	77.0	97.0
Product complexity indicators				
Average price (thousand 1987 U.S. $)	13,591	9,238	13,193	19,720
Body size (% in number of projects)				
Micro-mini	10%	25%	0%	0%
Small	56%	67%	17%	64%
Medium-large	34%	8%	83%	36%
Number of body types (Average)	2.1	2.3	1.7	2.2
Project scope indicators (average)				
Common parts ratio	19%	12%	29%	21%
Carried-over parts ratio	10%	7%	9%	14%
Unique parts ratio	74%	82%	62%	71%
Supplier design percentage	38%	52%	15%	35%

*Lead time is the time elapsed between the start of the development project and market introduction.

Source: Kim B. Clark, W. Bruce Chew, and T. Fujimoto, "Product Development in the World Auto Industry: Strategy, Organization, and Performance," Working Paper, April 1988, Harvard Business School, Division of Research.

EXHIBIT 7
Average Project Lead
Time and Stage Length:
European, United States,
and Japanese
Automakers

DEVELOPMENT STAGE	JAPANESE			UNITED STATES			EUROPE		
	Begin	End	Stage Length	Begin	End	Stage Length	Begin	End	Stage Length
Concept study	42.6	34.3	8.3	61.9	44.0	18.0	62.6	49.6	13.1
Product planning	37.8	29.0	8.8	57.0	39.2	17.8	58.2	40.8	17.4
Advanced engineering	41.8	26.6	15.2	56.4	29.9	26.5	54.9	41.5	13.5
Product engineering	29.6	5.8	23.8	40.1	11.6	28.6	41.8	18.6	23.2
Process engineering	27.7	6.1	21.6	30.9	5.5	25.4	36.6	9.7	26.8
Pilot run	7.1	2.7	4.4	9.2	2.7	6.5	9.8	3.5	6.4
Total			82.2			122.6			100.3

Note: Data in months before Job 1

Sample size: Japan 12; United States 6; Europe 11

Source: Kim B. Clark and T. Fujimoto, "Overlapping Problem Solving in Product Development," Working Paper, April 1988, Harvard Business School, Division of Research.

about $6,000 on an Explorer sport-utility vehicle. Trucks had received far less attention than cars until Caldwell redesigned the line in the late 1960s and pushed it ahead of Chevrolet. During Caldwell's tenure as CEO, Ford's Aerostar, Bronco II, and Ranger pickup trucks boomed while the Japanese attacked the sub-compact and compact markets with costs $1,500-2,000 less than American vehicles. In August 1986, Lewis Ross, later head of Ford's technical staff, led the charge to redesign the truck line. Despite competing pressures for funds, the strategy group under Caldwell also pushed increased spending on engines and transmissions by 50 percent to provide Ford with much more competitive power plants for all its cars and trucks. By 1992 Americans were buying one light truck for every 1.8 cars produced, and pickups had become the number one seller in America (475,000 units). Ford had sold more trucks than cars since 1990 and commanded 30.3% of the U.S. market in 1992. However its market penetration among different lines was spotty (see Exhibit 9). Driven by these forces, Ford was the most profitable automobile company in the world in 1993 (see Exhibit 8).

TOMORROW THE MONDEO

Nevertheless, Ford was gearing up for the largest single investment in its history, a world car named Mondeo. Ford had twice tried the world car concept—in 1960 with an innovative little front-wheel drive economy car and in 1981 with the Ford Escort. Neither achieved its goals. Despite its 1980's engine investments, Ford still needed to create two new engines for the Mondeo. In Europe the early Mondeos were well received by the press. They reportedly performed and rode better than the Ford Tempo and Mercury Topaz they were to replace. But Mondeo's price was roughly $15,000, paralleling the bottom of the larger Taurus line and several thousand dollars higher than Tempo-Topaz. While there was wide agreement on the potential economies of design, scale, and marketing associated with a world car, there were also major problems in making it adaptable enough for all of the world's market-places and providing the tooling in local marketplaces where the car's volume might not justify full-scale production. The problem was, as *Business Week* stated in sepulcher tones, "With their existing cost structures and high volume production approach, the Big Three may not all survive if their market share erodes by six points in the 1990s as it did in the 1980s."[23] And many wondered whether they could survive if they met Japan's volume juggernaut head to head.

In a partial answer, in Fall 1991 Ford modestly restyled the six year old mid-sized Taurus to maintain its dominance of its crucial market—34% of the total car market, growing at an expected 4% per year. Unexpectedly, formerly conservative Ford became an innovation leader in marketing once again, with "no haggling" pricing and extensive safety features. For example, driver's airbags became standard, with an optional passenger-side airbag being purchased for an extra $400 on 80% of Tauruses. But both Honda's Accord and Toyota's Camry soon began targeting Ford's dominant share of the mid-size market and offering airbags as standard on many of their lines.

THE TROTMAN ERA

In 1990-1991, as the automobile industry went into one of its periodic downturns, Ford's North American Automotive Operations dropped deeply into the red. At this point Ford's board moved Alex Trotman—a Britisher with substantial international and domestic experience—into the role of President. Known as a penny-pinching operations man, Trotman quickly focused on the aging (nine year old) Tempo and Topaz and the Mustang last redesigned in 1979. Ford's design processes had slipped back to their old expensive and slow patterns (4-5 years for a major new product). Ford Europe, which had done well in 1988-1989, began to lose about $1 billion per year in 1991-1992 (according to industry estimates).[24]

Meanwhile experts noted that Ford, in its attempt to become a model "European corporation" setting up sales and operating units across Europe, had grown too fast, creating huge bureaucracies and internecine rivalries. Ford reportedly had invested a staggering $15 billion in its European operations between 1988-1993—part of which represented Ford Europe's project leadership on the Mondeo. Ford's Jaguar investment had also grown to $3.5 billion, but *Business Week* reported a turnaround was underway. Jaguar had earlier tolerated a stifling highly functionalized organization culture where "marketing didn't talk to engineers" and there was "gross inefficiency and indiscipline in manufacturing" with a breakeven point "higher than any number Jaguar had ever produced." By late 1992 Ford's management had boosted productivity by 35% and had broken some of Jaguar's worst work practices. However, Toyota's Lexus and Nissan's Infiniti luxury brands sold four times as many cars as Jaguar in its export markets, and by 1993 production had fallen from Jaguar's 1987 record of 49,000 to 27,500, well below its breakeven point. It lost $400 million—nearly $18,000 on every car

EXHIBIT 8

EXHIBIT 8
1993 Comparative Financial and Operating Statistics, Six of the Top Automakers
(in millions of dollars)

	GENERAL MOTORS	FORD	CHRYSLER	TOYOTA	NISSAN	HONDA
Net sales	138,220	108,521	43,600	84,400	53,428	35,533
Net income	2,466	2,529	(2,551)	1,454	(483)	329
Net income as percent of sales	1.78	2.33	(5.85)	1.72	(0.90)	0.93
Total assets	188,201	198,938	43,679	57,077	61,947	25,876
Shareholders' equity	5,598	15,574	6,836	38,242	14,839	8,913
Capital investment	6,471	6,714	2,972	2,630	4,830	1,446
Depreciation	9,442	5,456	1,524	3,118	3,078	1,494
Employees (thousands)	710,000	322,213	115,948	73,046	143,754	90,900
Vehicle factory sales (thousands)	7,785	5,964	2,476	3,883	2,813	1,793

Source: Compiled from corporate annual reports and Moody's *Industrial Manual* listings.

EXHIBIT 9A
Ford U.S. Car Sales by Segment, 1993

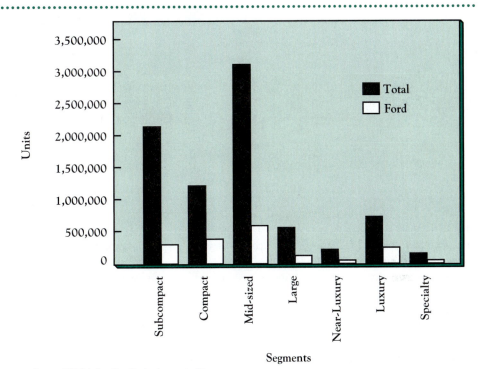

Source: 1993 Market Data Book, *Automotive News*.

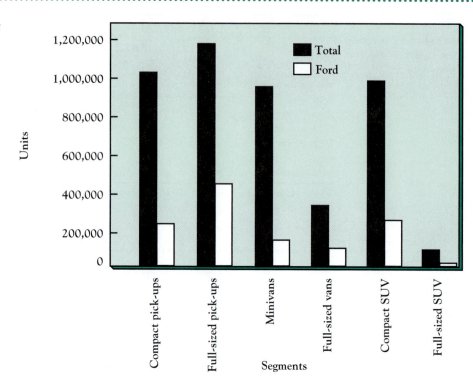

EXHIBIT 9B
Ford U.S. Truck Sales by
Segment, 1993

Source: 1993 Market Data Book, *Automotive News.*

it sold.[25] Jaguar's volume was only a tenth of Cadillac's and one-twentieth of Mercedes Benz'. Although sold as a premium performance car, the joke was "Jaguar owners need two cars: one to drive and one for spare parts." Despite chopping nearly 50% from its workforce, Ford had kept Jaguar's product development intact, hoping to regain a role in the high performance luxury niche.

THE WORLD SCENE

In 1992, Ford was still the number two volume producer of cars in the world (see Exhibit 10). But many powerful forces were at work. GM was ailing. The collapse of Tokyo's stock market and high exchange rates for the yen meant that Japan's long and short-term costs for domestic production were sky rocketing. Western Europe (with 170 million cars projected sales 1992-2002) and the U.S. and Canada (160 million projected sales) were still the world's largest auto marketplaces, but the main growth was expected to come from Asia, Eastern Europe, and Latin America. (See Exhibit 11.) The market was very competitive; U.S. producers had

lost a huge $7.3 billion in 1991, and Japanese producers had captured 30% of the American market and were continuing to build capacity there. Producers used to home markets that nearly always expanded would have a difficult time ahead, especially since most developing countries want to produce their own cars rather than import them. While comparative performance in car plants in Japan, the U.S., and Europe still varied considerably, widely available flexible manufacturing machines and systems would continue to eliminate many of these differences among major producers. (See Exhibit 12.) And, as these machines were introduced, many expected the capital intensity of automobiles, per unit produced, to drop rapidly. Several studies indicated that in the 1980s the number of machines in a typical factory was 150, during the 1990s the number would drop to about 50, and by the 2000s would be as low as 30—machines on which an infinite number of different models could be made.[26]

Against this background, Mr. Trotman had to determine how to strategically position the Ford Motor Company, its dominant Taurus-Sable line, and its numerous niched cars, trucks, and vans in the world-wide marketplace. Many wondered whether Alex Trotman would be the one to bring Ford back into its position as the number one car producer in the world, the spot it had occupied in the 1920s before Alfred P. Sloan's remarkable repositioning of General Motors changed the auto landscape.

QUESTIONS

1. What were the key elements or conditions that made the Ford Team Taurus process successful?
2. What problems would you have expected Ford to encounter in introducing its simultaneous design process? What were likely to be its main policy implications? How could the process have been improved?
3. Why did Ford regress in the late 1980s? What overall posture should it assume in the 1990s? How can it differentiate itself from all other motor car companies?

EXHIBIT 10
Summary of World Production, 1992
(millions of vehicles)

PRODUCTION BY REGION	TOTAL VEHICLES	PASSENGER CARS	COMMERCIAL VEHICLES
North American Companies	14.669	9.403	5.267
Japanese Companies	14.859	11.295	3.564
Western European Companies	12.205	10.896	1.309
Eastern European Companies	2.231	1.706	0.526
Korean Companies	1.555	1.204	0.351

TOP 15 MANUFACTURERS (IN DESCENDING ORDER OF TOTAL VEHICLE OUTPUT)	TOTAL VEHICLES	PASSENGER CARS	COMMERCIAL VEHICLES
1. General Motors–U.S.A.	6.866	4.990	1.876
2. Ford Motor–U.S.A.	5.744	3.685	2.059
3. Toyota–Japan	4.488	3.650	0.838
4. Volkswagen–Germany	3.288	3.120	0.166
5. Nissan–Japan	2.898	2.223	0.675
6. PSA–France	2.438	2.252	0.186
7. Renault–France	2.264	1.930	0.334
8. Chrysler–U.S.A.	1.983	0.728	1.255
9. Fiat–Italy	1.800	1.558	0.243
10. Honda–Japan	1.762	1.630	0.133
11. Mitsubishi–Japan	1.573	1.117	0.456
12. Mazda–Japan	1.449	1.205	0.244
13. Suzuki–Japan	0.888	0.536	0.352
14. Hyundai–South Korea	0.874	0.716	0.158
15. Daimler-Benz–Germany	0.799	0.531	0.268
Total 40 Manufacturers	45.738	34.711	11.026
Others	1.954	0.611	1.343
Total Production	47.692	35.322	12.369

Source: Compiled by the American Automotive Manufacturers Association (AAMA) from various sources.

EXHIBIT 11
Where Growth Will Be:
Extrpolation versus
Projection

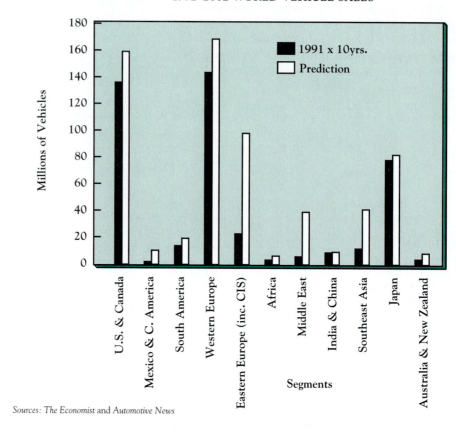

1992–2002 WORLD VEHICLE SALES

Sources: The Economist and Automotive News

EXHIBIT 12
Comparative Auto
Manufacturing by
Country

AVERAGE FOR CAR PLANTS IN:	JAPAN	UNITED STATES	EUROPE
Performance			
Productivity (hours per car)	16.8	25.1	36.2
Quality (defects per 100 cars)	60	82	97
Layout			
Factory space (per sq. ft. per car per year)	5.7	7.8	7.8
Size of repair area (as % of assembly space)	4.1	12.9	14.4
Stocks (for eight sample parts)	0.2	2.9	2
Employees			
Workforce in teams (%)	69.3	17.3	0.6
Suggestions (per employee per year)	61.6	0.4	0.4
Number of job classifications	12	67	15
Training of new workers (hours)	380	46	173
Automation (% of process automated)			
Welding	86	76	77
Painting	55	34	38
Assembly	2	1	3

Source: MIT; J.D. Power & Associates in "The Endless Road: A Survey of the Car Industry," *The Economist*, October 17, 1992.

ARGYLE DIAMONDS

In 1986, Argyle Diamond Sales (ADS) had entered into a five-year contract which required it to sell 75% of its production to the Central Selling Organization (CSO)—part of the De Beers group— leaving the remaining 25% for ADS to market itself.

In 1991, ADS had to decide whether it had the independent marketing power to break away from the London-based CSO, rather than relying on it so heavily for sales. The ADS general manager, Mike Mitchell, explained in 1990, "Next year leaves ADS with a tough choice—continue with the CSO as a major customer, or become a major competitor."[1]

On the subject of the contract renegotiation, CSO Director Anthony Oppenheimer was quoted: "They [Argyle] would be unwise if they did not look into the markets before coming to the negotiations so that they have an alternative plan. If I were in their place, I would have a plan so that if the negotiations did not come to an agreement, I would certainly want to see if I could sell my production in the markets."[2]

BACKGROUND

In 1976 the first significant diamond deposit in Australia was discovered in the Kimberley region, in the far north of the state of Western Australia. The find followed systematic exploration efforts throughout the Kimberley region by several organizations, notably, the Kalumburu Joint Venture, which was established in 1972. In 1976, Conzinc Riotinto of Australia (CRA), one of the largest mining groups in the country, became involved through CRA Exploration (CRAE). The Kalumburu Joint Venture was reformed as the Ashton Joint Venture, and CRA assumed the role of manager in 1977. CRA, with assets of A\$7,603* million in 1990, was listed on the Australian stock exchange and was active in the mining of iron ore, bauxite, copper, and gold in Australia and neighboring countries, as well as being a producer of aluminum metal. Its main shareholder at 49% was Tinto Holdings Australia Proprietary Limited.

EXPLORATION 1979

In September 1979 the joint venturers, led by CRAE, set up camp in the wild outback area 80 kilometers from the Argyle region for what was to be an "undercover" exploration mission. The tenements (claim options), which contained the diamond-rich AK1 (Argyle pipe), were held by other explorers, but were due to expire within weeks. The CRAE geologists avoided radio communication and developed secret codes for telephone messages to ensure that their presence remained hidden. Grant Boxer, Argyle Diamond Mines' senior geologist at the "secret camp," explained: "We had helicopters on standby so that as soon as we confirmed the find and the other tenement had expired, we could stake our claim."[3]

During September, the CRAE team uncovered many stones from the Smoke Creek alluvial diamond deposits before they discovered the 45-hectare AK1 pipe on October 2. The geologists needed to maintain their secrecy for a further six weeks, because another tenement had still not yet expired. However, to their relief, the CRAE cover was not blown, and after further investigation its geologists were confident that a mine could be economically developed on the site.

---

*All figures are in U.S. dollars unless otherwise indicated.

THE ARGYLE DIAMOND MINES JOINT VENTURE

In 1982 the Ashton Joint Venture established the Argyle Diamond Mines Joint Venture consisting of CRA with 56.8%, Ashton Mining Group with 38.2%, and the Western Australia state government through the WA Diamond Trust (WADT) with 5%. At a later stage, CRA and Ashton took over the WADT's interests, raising their share holdings to 59.7% and 40.3%, respectively.

The Argyle project was managed by a wholly owned CRA subsidiary, Argyle Diamond Mines Proprietary Ltd. (ADM), while marketing was done through Argyle Diamond Sales Ltd. (ADS), owned 60% by CRA and 40% by Ashton. The only other diamond mine in Australia, Bow River Diamonds, commenced alluvial (stream bed or wash) production in 1988 and yielded 0.58 million carats in the 1988–89 fiscal year (compared to 34 million carats produced by Argyle), after treating 2.5 million tons of ore.[4]

PRODUCTION AND OPERATIONS

Total proved ore reserves in 1990 amounted to 94.2 million tons at 4.0 carats per ton at the Argyle site with further probable reserves of 5.8 million tons at 2.8 carats per ton.[5] ADM commenced commercial mining of alluvial deposits downstream from the AK1 pipe in 1983 and continued until late 1985. Some 17.3 million carats of diamonds were recovered during this phase. ADM resumed alluvial mining in 1989 to augment production from the AK1 "pipe." A pipe is a vertical or steeply sloped concentration of minerals, usually caused by ancient volcanic action.

Following a feasibility study and the state government's approval of proposals for mining the ore body, construction and development work on the "pipe" mining phase of the Argyle project commenced in 1983. This involved the design and construction of the mine, the processing plant, an airstrip, and all the associated infrastructures at the mine site in the remote Argyle region, more than 2,000 kilometers (1,250 miles) from Perth, the capital of Western Australia, and 120 kilometers (75 miles) south of the nearest town, Kununurra. Virtually all the infrastructure development was contracted out to specialist suppliers. Capital investment in this stage of the project was on the order of $465 million.[6] Despite industrial relations problems associated with union protests against the company's proposed marketing association with De Beers of South Africa, the plant came into operation, ahead of schedule, in December 1985.

The plant processed ore mined from the pipe by open-cut methods. After crushing, screening, and heavy media concentration, diamonds were recovered through x-ray technology and were cleaned in acid before being sent to Perth for sorting and classifying prior to sale. Although the plant was designed to process throughput of 3 million tons a year, Table 1 indicates that this figure had been exceeded consistently. (See Exhibit 1 for photographs of the mining operations themselves.)

WORK FORCE ARRANGEMENTS

Argyle employed a work force of almost 850 people. Under its principles of equal employment opportunity, Argyle had achieved a level of female employment of more than 20%, which was the highest in the mining industry.

Most employees were Perth based and commuted to the mine on a "14-days" rotation system. Workers flew into the Argyle airport in chartered jet aircraft from Perth, and about 70 Kununurra-based employees commuted daily to the mine site by light aircraft. On-site accommodation consisted of single motel-style units with extensive recreational facilities. The Perth office contingent numbered about 250 and was responsible for the general administration, diamond sorting, cutting, polishing, and marketing.[7]

TABLE 1 Argyle Diamonds, 1985–1989 (approximate figures)	1989	1988	1987	1986	1985
Production (million carats)	33.9	34.1	30.3	29.2	7.1
AK1 ore (million tons)	4.9	4.6	3.5	3.2	0
Alluvial ore (million tons)	0.85	0	0	0	0
Sales (A$ million)	391	288	283	200	38.3

Source: Compiled by authors from various sources.

PILOTS' DISPUTE

The Argyle mine was dependent on air transport for its work force, and in 1989 its operations faced a serious threat when commercial pilots all over Australia began a protracted strike lasting many months. Faced with the prospect of having its workers isolated at the mine, as well as in Perth, Argyle managers hired a collection of smaller aircraft (15–18 seaters), and even a 49-year-old DC3, before they managed to track down two F27 aircraft which they employed on the shuttle service. Helen Mulroney, senior corporate affairs officer, described the earlier, uncomfortable trips on the smaller aircraft, "These were grueling trips, but, if anything, the hardship, rearrangement of schedules, the inconvenience and disruption were overshadowed by the sense of unity that beating the dispute engendered in employees and management alike."[8]

Argyle also assisted the local community in Kununurra by providing both F27 aircraft to fly children at boarding schools in Perth home for their holidays and returning them to Perth two weeks later.

SECURITY

Mining Monthly reported that workers could be subjected to random dressed or undressed body searches whenever on-site police or security officers thought it necessary. These searches could only be carried out by a doctor, in private, and only on police or security orders. Both the mine and Perth office contained top security areas, which were continually scanned by cameras and monitored from a control room. It further stated that three employees had been detected trying to conceal "souvenirs" from the mine.[9]

STAFF DEVELOPMENT AND TRAINING

Argyle Diamond Mines spent about 8% of wages on training. Managing Director David Karpin pointed out that, "In terms of the percentage of gross wages spent on training, Argyle led the way among the mining companies of Western Australia."[10] Argyle had introduced a "Skills Extension" training and development program, which identified key skills for different areas of the mine's operations, drawn up in a matrix. Through a combination of formal and on-the-job training, employees were given credit for each unit in the matrix, and as they gained more unit credits, their pay rate increased. Joanne Farrell, Argyle's employee relations manager, commented, "The company had created an appetite for learning and most of the work force was searching for opportunities to learn."[11]

THE WORLD DIAMOND INDUSTRY

From the late nineteenth century until 1954, the African continent was the only major diamond producer. The Soviet Union discovered its first significant Siberian pipe in 1954. The Argyle AKI pipe represented Australia's only major diamond discovery. The leading world producers are presented in Table 2. Although Argyle was ranked number one in the world as the leading volume supplier of diamonds, it was only fifth in terms of value, behind the USSR, Botswana, South Africa, and Namibia.[12]

While beauty and durability play key roles, a steady price which increases over the years is also an important part of the attraction of diamonds in the marketplace. In reality, diamonds are not scarce and the main role of the Central Selling Organization has been to bring stability to diamond markets. Before the late Sir Ernest Oppenheimer forged the CSO and its many trading arms early this century, there were several periods in which diamonds flooding into the markets had severely depressed prices.

About 80–90% of all rough diamonds marketed in the world were sold through the CSO, and its sales for 1986 (uncut production) amounted to $2,562 million.[13] De Beers, through the CSO, had maintained the price of diamonds by controlling supply and demand. In fact, De Beers had never announced a reduction in prices, although, in 1978, temporary surcharges were progressively removed.

The company's chairman, Mr. H. F. Oppenheimer, had defended De Beers against the accusation that it had created a classic monopoly:

> Whether this measure of control amounts to a monopoly, I would not know. But if it does, it is certainly a monopoly of the most unusual kind. There is no one concerned with diamonds, whether as producer, dealer, cutter, jeweler, or customer who does not benefit from it. It protects not only the shareholders in the big diamond companies but also the miners they employ and the communities that are dependent on their operations. The well-being of tens of thousands of individual diamond diggers of all races is dependent on its maintenances.[14]

The U.S. government had often held that De Beers and the CSO were in violation of its antitrust laws. While North America has always been one of De Beers' most important markets, it is said that to avoid

TABLE 2
World Diamond
Production, 1986

	Country	Carats (millions)	% of Total	APPROXIMATE VALUE		
				$ US (millions)	% of Total	Value Rank
1.	Australia	29.20	32.61%	204	6.9%	5
2.	Zaire	20.00	22.33	190	6.4	6
3.	Botswana	13.09	14.62	674	22.7	2
4.	USSR (estimated)	12.00	13.40	900	30.3	1
5.	South Africa	9.85	11.00	508	17.1	3
6.	Namibia	1.01	1.13	303	10.2	4
7.	South America (Brazil, Venezuela)	0.86	0.96	N/A	N/A	N/A
8.	Ghana	0.85	0.95	17	0.6	11
9.	Central African Republic	0.50	0.56	45	1.5	9
10.	Sierra Leone	0.40	0.45	46	1.6	8
11.	Liberia (mainly smuggled)	0.40	0.45	18	0.6	10
12.	Tanzania	0.34	0.24	N/A	N/A	N/A
13.	Guinea	0.20	0.22	53	1.8	7
14.	China	0.20	0.22	N/A	N/A	N/A
15.	Angola	0.18	0.20	8	0.3	12
16.	Other	0.47	0.0052	N/A	N/A	N/A
		89.55	100.00%	2966	100.0%	

N/A—Not available

Source: Prospect, Vol. 11, no. 1, March 1988.

the possibility of initiating a court case no executive or official from the group ever visits the United States.

THE CSO'S INFLUENCE OVER SUPPLY

During a major downturn in the diamond industry in the early 1980s, the CSO literally saved the industry from collapse when it withheld a stockpile valued at nearly $2 billion between 1983 and 1984, demonstrating its enormous power and financial resources.[15]

While the CSO's administration of rough diamond supplies provided stability benefitting all producers, most of these producers and their governments had sought to retain some control over national output by either the establishment of local polishing industries or by marketing a proportion of output independently. Producers who had attempted to split from the CSO cartel had not, generally, succeeded. Zaire, for example, in 1981–1983 failed to achieve any significant price benefit in spite of the efforts of many independent market dealers. Consequently, Zaire was obliged to return to the CSO fold. Similarly, Botswana tried to take an independent position, but was also forced to rejoin the

CSO by selling its $500 million stockpile to De Beers. In 1990 the then Soviet Union reaffirmed its links with De Beers in an exclusive five-year contract to sell its rough diamonds through the CSO. The value was estimated at $5 billion over the period of the contract.[16] These deals put the stamp of De Beers firmly on the diamond market. Output from the Aredor mine in Guinea had been marketed independently with some success, but its production was relatively modest and characterized by larger, high-quality diamonds, for which there is considerable demand.[17] The agreement between the CSO and Argyle Diamonds was unique in that ADS was able to sell a portion of Argyle's output on its own, while continuing to market the bulk of its production through the CSO.

The CSO also exercised strong control downstream in the diamond trade. The CSO supplied rough diamonds only to accredited dealers in a highly formalized procedure. Dealers were invited to inspect preselected parcels of diamonds, called "sights," at prices set by the CSO. No haggling over price was allowed, and the dealer either accepted or rejected the parcel. From there the rough diamonds proceeded to the diamond cutting industry and the jewelers who created the settings for the final customers.

THE CSO'S INFLUENCE OVER DEMAND

In addition to regulating supply, De Beers had also excelled in marketing by literally creating large demand for diamonds in markets where little existed before.

In the mid-1930s, as a result of the depression, De Beers was holding stock worth over four times its annual sales. In 1939, De Beers embarked on a marketing campaign to soak up its stockpiles. In effect, De Beers established the nearly universal tradition of diamond engagement rings. De Beers carried the whole diamond industry on its shoulders by popularizing the slogan "a diamond is forever." By the early 1960s, almost 80% of U.S. males "made it official" by buying a diamond engagement ring. This trend had matured in the United States, and in 1979 a slightly lower 79% of engaged U.S. males bought diamond engagement rings. The trend might further be reduced, as de facto life-styles become more popular and people marry later, perhaps being less subject to the sentimental appeal of a diamond engagement ring.[18]

However, De Beers' marketing accomplishments in the United States pale by comparison with its achievements in Japan and West Germany. Thirty years ago, there was no Japanese word for diamond. In 1966, only 5% of Japanese brides received a diamond engagement ring, which played little part in Japanese culture. But an advertising initiative by De Beers, through J. Walter Thompson, discovered a cultural niche called *yuino*—the exchange of gifts between bride and groom. As a result of marketing efforts, 60% of Japanese brides received diamond engagement rings in 1979. Much the same trend occurred in Germany, where there was a Teutonic tradition that two gold bands symbolized undying love. In 1967, De Beers introduced the concept of a third band, only this one studded with diamonds. West Germany became the third biggest market behind the United States and Japan. More recent marketing attempts by De Beers to increase diamond demand included the "eternity ring" and diamond-studded cuff links and tie pins for men.[19]

THE INVESTMENT MARKET

Because of the diamond's value, portability, and attractiveness, it had often been viewed as a promising medium for investment. The remarkable rise in the price of the "D-flawless" in the late 1970s could be largely attributed to a general lack of confidence in all paper currencies, encouraging investment in inflation shelters. However, smaller investors who paid a retail price for a diamond (often including sales taxes) frequently found on resale to the trade that they had to compete with similar gems freely available at wholesale prices from the CSO.

An important problem for investors was that diamonds are not a homogeneous commodity. While size and weight can be established unambiguously, each diamond is an individual gem with subtle differences in terms of color and lack of flaws. Even experts will disagree on the exact classification of a particular diamond. Thus diamonds which have investment value are largely confined to top quality and unusual stones which have scarcity value. Lower-quality diamond investments often rely on certification to determine a stone's grade. Yet, even at the most respected laboratories, diamond grading remains an inexact art.[20]

The diamond industry appears to be ambivalent about widespread development of the investment and resale markets. High prices paid for spectacular gems enhances the mystique and appeal of diamonds. However, as more polished diamonds enter investment portfolios, this stockpile could become a threat to the ability of De Beers to control the supply of diamonds. Major fluctuations in the prices for diamonds have occurred only in cases where De Beers temporarily lost control over the supply of diamonds, for example, due to investment market transactions and situations where the USSR dumped diamonds on the world market in order to secure much needed foreign exchange. In fact, it had been argued that De Beers had already lost control of the top-quality gem market (D-flawless), as a result of investor trading.

INDUSTRIAL DIAMONDS

The industrial market had been extremely competitive and characterized by high technology and product innovation. Prices of naturally occurring industrial diamonds faced ever-increasing competition from synthetics and consisted of about 20% of the industrial market in 1982.[21]

General Electric announced in 1954 that it had fully synthesized industrial diamonds, and by the 1960s both G.E. and De Beers were manufacturing large quantities of industrial diamonds. However, since 1954, the price of industrial diamonds (both natural and synthetic) had decreased almost annually,[22] and in dollar terms, the economic significance of industrials to the diamond industry had been greatly reduced.

Natural industrial diamonds are preferred in some applications for technical reasons, but in most applications they can only really compete against synthetics on price. The recession of the early 1980s, plus the defection of Zaire from the CSO at that time, caused a fall in the price of industrials. (Zaire later reestablished ties with De Beers.)

The mid-1980s had seen some major developments in the production of synthetic diamonds, particularly in the United States, USSR, and Japan. *Business Week* noted some of the uses for synthetic diamonds, which included abrasion-resistant drills and other cutting tools, as well as superfast diamond integrated circuits.[23]

Despite some reports, it was unlikely that synthetic diamonds could be sold as gems, because of their distinct yellow color. Imitation diamond gems such as glass and cubic zirconium had occasionally threatened the diamond gem industry, but had not caused significant damage.

MAJOR CENTERS FOR CUTTING, POLISHING, AND TRADING

The major centers for the processing of rough diamonds included Belgium (Antwerp), India (Surat and Bombay), Israel (Tel Aviv), and the United States (New York).

India was the world's largest diamond cutting and polishing center with an estimated 800,000 people employed in the industry.[24] Exports of cut and polished diamonds were India's second largest foreign exchange earner after textiles. Because of its low labor costs, India was cost effective at cutting and polishing the smaller, lower-quality stones.

Antwerp was widely acknowledged as the center for trading both rough and polished stones, and was the chief market for non-CSO sales. Antwerp's cutting industry numbered around 5,000 individuals who specialized in the better-quality diamonds, particularly those which were difficult to cut.

Israel employed around 12,000 cutters, and, as in India, the industry was an important source of foreign exchange for the country. Israel specialized in commercial quality, medium- to smaller-sized diamonds. The New York center employed about 400 cutters and, because of high labor costs, American cutters specialized in larger, better quality stones.

Due to their relative specialties, processing in India added 43–47% to the value of rough diamonds, processing in Israel added 22% value to its roughs, while Antwerp and New York added even less value.[25]

Diamond processing also took place to a lesser extent in other countries like the USSR, South Africa, and Brazil.

DIAMOND GRADING

Diamonds were graded according to weight, color, clarity, and proportion. Diamond sorting was a demanding occupation which required extensive training. In the end there also remained an element of subjectivity and judgment.

The first major factor affecting the price of a diamond was the carat weight, a carat being equal to 200 milligrams.

Second, the color of a diamond also greatly affected its value. When diamond graders discussed "color," they were in most cases referring to the relative "discoloration" or "tinges" of a white stone. There were several grades of color ranging from "D" a perfectly colorless tone—through to "Z"—a decidedly yellow or brown stone. The lower the letter, the lower the price of the diamond. The gems further down the color scale had been very difficult to sell in the United States, despite retailers' efforts to promote them as "champagne hued" or "honey colored."[26] Apart from the yellow and brown stones, there were also certain naturally occurring pink, red, green, and blue diamonds, which were extremely rare and very valuable.

Third, a diamond's "clarity" referred to its internal qualities, that is, the number, kind, size, location, and overall significance of flaws and imperfections within the stone. Diamonds were graded for clarity on an elaborate scale, ranging from "flawless" (top quality) to "imperfect" (industrial quality).

Finally, the cut of the diamond was determined by the proportions of the stone, and this also affected the weight of the final product.

To the ordinary eye, a one carat D flawless gem may look identical to a similarly sized SI (slight imperfect) stone. At wholesale price in 1981, though, the first sold for $40,000, while the latter cost $429.50.[27]

POLISHED DIAMOND TRADERS

The diamond processing centers (particularly Antwerp) had also been major centers for world trading. Due to the nature of the product, establishing trusting business relationships was vital in the diamond trade. After all, how could you be sure that the diamond you purchased was the same one which had been delivered? The following quotes by diamond traders illustrate some of the problems: "Yes, this is a business of trust, but that doesn't mean that it doesn't get vio-

Strategy and Organization

There has been a good deal of recent attention given to the match between strategy and organization. Much of this work consists of empirical tests of Chandler's ideas presented in *Strategy and Structure* (1962). Most of this material is reviewed elsewhere (Galbraith and Nathanson, 1978). However, some recent work and ideas hold out considerable potential for understanding how different patterns of strategic change lead to different organization structures, management systems, and company cultures. In addition, some good relationships with economic performance are also attained.

The ideas rest on the concept of an organization having a center of gravity or driving force. (Tregoe and Zimmerman, 1980). This center of gravity arises from the firm's initial success in the industry in which it grew up. Let us first explore the concept of center of gravity, then the patterns of strategic change that have been followed by American enterprises.

The center of gravity of a company depends on where in the industry supply chain the company started. In order to explain the concept, manufacturing industries will be used. Figure 2 depicts the stages of supply in an industry chain. Six stages are shown here. Each industry may have more or fewer stages. Service industries typically have fewer stages.

The chain begins with a raw material extraction stage which supplies crude oil, iron ore, logs, or bauxite to the second stage of primary manufacturing. The second stage is a variety-reducing stage to produce a standardized output (petrochemicals, steel, paper pulp, or aluminum ingots). The next stage fabricates commodity products from this primary material. Fabricators produce polyethylene, cans, sheet steel, cardboard cartons, and semiconductor components. The next stage is the product producers who add value, usually through product development, patents, and proprietary products. The next stage is the marketer and distributors. These are the consumer branded product manufacturers and various distributors. Finally, there are the retailers who have the direct contact with the ultimate consumer.

The line splitting the chain into two segments divides the industry into upstream and downstream halves. While there are differences between each of the stages, the differences between the upstream and downstream stages are striking. The upstream stages add value by reducing the variety of raw materials found on the earth's surface to a few standard commodities. The purpose is to produce flexible, predictable raw materials and intermediate products from which an increasing variety of downstream products are made. The downstream stages add value through producing a variety of products to meet varying customer needs. The downstream value is added through advertising, product positioning, marketing channels, and R&D. Thus, the upstream and downstream companies face very different business problems and tasks.

FIGURE 2
Supply Stages in an
Industry Chain

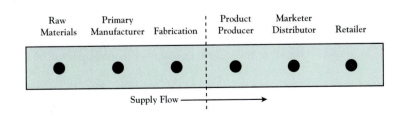

Raw Materials · Primary Manufacturer · Fabrication · Product Producer · Marketer Distributor · Retailer

Supply Flow ⟶

The reason for distinguishing between upstream and downstream companies is that the factors for success, the lessons learned by managers, and the organizations used are fundamentally different. The successful, experienced manager has been shaped and formed in fundamentally different ways in the different stages. The management processes are different, as are the dominant functions. In short, the company's culture is shaped by where it began in the industry chain. Listed are some fundamental differences that illustrate the contrast:

Upstream	*Downstream*
Standardize/homogenize	Customize/segment
Low-cost producer	High margins/proprietary positions
Process innovation	Product innovation
Capital budget	R&D/advertising budget
Technology/capital intensive	People intensive
Supply/trader/engineering	R&D/marketing dominated
Line driven	Line/staff
Maximize end users	Target end users
⋮	⋮
Sales push	Market pull

The mind set of the upstream manager is geared toward standardization and efficiency. They are the producers of standardized commodity products. In contrast, downstream managers try to customize and tailor output to diverse customer needs. They segment markets and target individual users. The upstream company wants to standardize in order to maximize the number of end users and get volume to lower costs. The downstream company wants to target particular sets of end users. Therefore, the upstreamers have a divergent view of the world based on their commodity. For example, the cover of the 1981 annual report of Intel (a fabricator of commodity semiconductors) is a listing of the 10,000 uses to which microprocessors have been put. The downstreamers have a convergent view of the world based on customer needs and will select whatever commodity will best serve that need. In the electronics industry there is always a conflict between the upstream component types and the downstream systems types because of this contrast in mind sets.

The basis of competition is different in the two stages. Commodities compete on price since the products are the same. Therefore, it is essential that the successful upstreamer be the low-cost producer. Their organizations are the lean and mean ones with a minimum of overheads. Low cost is also important for the downstreamer, but it is proprietary features that generate high margins. That feature may be a brand image, such as Maxwell House, a patented technology, an endorsement (such as the American Dental Association's endorsement of Crest toothpaste), customer service policy, and so on. Competition revolves around product features and product positioning and less on price. This means that marketing and product management sets prices. Products move by marketing pull. In contrast, the upstream company pushes the product through a strong sales force. Often salespeople negotiate prices within limits set by top management.

The organizations are different as well. The upstream companies are functional and line driven. They seek a minimum of staff, and even those staffs that are used are in supporting roles. The downstream company with multiple products and multiple markets learns to manage diversity early. Profit centers emerge and resources need to be allocated across products and markets. Larger staffs arise to assist top management in priority setting across competing product/market advocates. Higher margins permit the overhead to exist.

Both upstream and downstream companies use research and development. However, the upstream company invests in process development in order to lower costs. The downstream company invests primarily in product development in order to achieve proprietary positions.

The key managerial processes also vary. The upstream companies are driven by the capital budget and have various capital appropriations controls. The downstream companies also have a capital budget but are driven by the R&D budget (product producers) or the advertising budget (marketers). Further downstream it is working capital that becomes paramount. Managers learn to control the business by managing the turnover of inventory and accounts receivable. Thus, the upstream company is capital intensive and technological "know-how" is critical. Downstream companies are more people intensive. Therefore, the critical skills revolve around human resources management.

The dominant functions also vary with stages. The raw material processor is dominated by geologists, petroleum engineers, and traders. The supply and distribution function which searches for the most economical end use is powerful. The manufacturers of commodities are dominated by engineers who come up through manufacturing. The downstream companies are dominated first by technologists in research and product development. Farther downstream, it is marketing and then merchandising that emerge as the power centers. The line of succession to the CEO usually runs through this dominant function.

In summary, the upstream and downstream companies are very different entities. The differences, a bit exaggerated here because of the dichotomy, lead to differences in organization structure, management processes, dominant functions, succession paths, management beliefs and values or, in short, the management way of life. Thus, companies can be in the same industry but be very different because they developed from a beginning at a particular stage of the industry. This beginning, and the initial successes, teaches management the lessons of that stage. The firm develops an integrated organization (structure, processes, rewards, and people) which is peculiar to that stage and forms the center of gravity.

Strategic Change

The first strategic change that an organization makes is to vertically integrate within its industry. At a certain size, the organization can move backward to prior stages to guarantee sources of supply and secure bargaining leverage on vendors. And/or it can move forward to guarantee markets and volume for capital investments and become a customer to feed back data for new products. This initial strategic move does not change the center of gravity because the prior and subsequent stages are usually operated for the benefit of the center-of-gravity stage.

The paper industry is used to illustrate the concepts of center of gravity and vertical integration. Figure 3 depicts five paper companies which operate from different centers of gravity. The first is Weyerhauser. Its center of gravity is at the land and timber stage of the industry. Weyerhauser seeks the highest return use for a log. They make pulp and paper rolls. They make containers and milk cartons. But they are a timber company. If the returns are better in lumber, the pulp mills get fed with sawdust and chips. International Paper (the name of the company tells it all), by contrast, is a primary manufacturer of paper. It also has timber lands, container plants, and works on new products around aseptic packaging. However, if the pulp mills ran out of logs, the manager of the woodlands used to be fired. The raw material stage is to supply the manufacturing stage, not seek the highest return for its timber. The Container Corporation (again, the name describes the company) is the example of the fabricator. It also has woodlands and pulp mills, but they are to supply the container making operations. The product producer is Appleton. It makes specialty paper

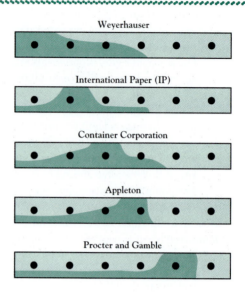

products. For example, Appleton produces a paper with globules of ink imbedded in it. The globules burst and form a letter or number when struck with an impact printer.

The last company is Procter & Gamble. P&G is a consumer products company. And, like the other companies, it operates pulp mills and owns timber lands. However, it is driven by the advertising or marketing function. If one wanted to be CEO of P&G, one would not run a pulp mill or the woodlands. The path to CEO is through the brand manager for Charmin or Pampers.

Thus, each of these companies is in the paper industry. Each operates at a number of stages in the industry. Yet each is a very different company because it has its center of gravity at a different stage. The center of gravity establishes a base from which subsequent strategic changes take place. That is, as a company's industry matures, the company feels a need to change its center of gravity in order to move to a place in the industry where better returns can be obtained, or move to a new industry but use its same center of gravity and skills in that industry, or make some combination of industry and center of gravity change. These options lead to different patterns of corporate developments.

BY-PRODUCTS DIVERSIFICATION

One of the first diversification moves that a vertically integrated company makes is to sell by-products from points along the industry chain. Figure 4 depicts this strategy. These companies appear to be diversified if one attributes revenue to the various industries in which the company operates. But the company has changed neither its industry nor its center of gravity. The company is behaving intelligently by seeking additional sources of revenue and profit. However, it is still psychologically committed to its center of gravity and to its industry. Alcoa is such a firm. Even though they operate in several industries, their output varies directly with the aluminum cycle. They have not reduced their dependence on a single industry, as one would with real diversification.

FIGURE 4
By-product
Diversification

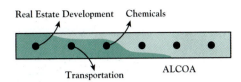

Real Estate Development   Chemicals

Transportation   ALCOA

RELATED DIVERSIFICATION

Another strategic change is the diversification into new industries but at the same center of gravity. This is called "related diversification." The firm diversifies into new businesses, but they are all related. The relationship revolves around the company's center of gravity. Figure 5 depicts the diversification moves of Procter & Gamble. After beginning in the soap industry, P&G vertically integrated back into doing its own chemical processing (fatty acids) and seed crushing. Then, in order to pursue new growth opportunities, it has been diversifying into paper, food, beverages, pharmaceuticals, coffee, and so on. But each move into a new industry is made at the company's center of gravity. The new businesses are all consumer products which are driven out of advertising by brand managers. The 3M Company also follows a related diversification strategy, but theirs is based on technology. They have 40,000 different products which are produced by some seventy divisions. However, 95% of the products are based on coating and bonding technologies. Its center of gravity is a product producer, and it adds value through R&D.

LINKED DIVERSIFICATION

A third type of diversification involves moving into new industries and operating at different centers of gravity in those new industries. However, there is a linkage of some type among various businesses. Figure 6 depicts Union Camp as following this pattern of corporate development. Union Camp is a primary producer of paper products. As such, it vertically integrated backwards to own woodlands. From there, it moved downstream within the wood products industry by running sawmills and fabricating plants. However, they recently purchased a retail lumber business.

They also moved into the chemical business by selling by-products from the pulping process. This business was successful and expanded. Recently, Union Camp was bidding for

FIGURE 5
Related
Diversification

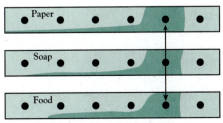

Paper

Soap

Food

PROCTER AND GAMBLE

FIGURE 6
Linked
Diversification

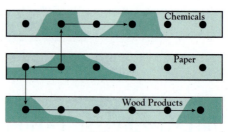

UNION CAMP

a flavors and fragrances (F&F) company. The F&F company is a product producer which adds value through creating flavors and fragrances for mostly consumer products companies.

Thus, Union Camp is an upstream company that is acquiring downstream companies. However, these new companies are in industries in which the company already diversified from its upstream center of gravity. But these new acquisitions are not operated for the benefit of the center of gravity but are stand-alone profit centers.

UNRELATED DIVERSIFICATION

The final type of strategic change is to diversify into unrelated businesses. Like the linked diversifiers, unrelated diversifiers move into new industries often at different centers of gravity. They almost always use acquisition, while related and linked companies will use some acquisitions but rely heavily on internal development. There is often very little relation between the industries into which the unrelated company diversifies. Textron and Teledyne have been the paradigm examples. They operate in industrial equipment, aerospace, consumer products, insurance, and so on. Others have spread into retailing, services, and entertainment. The purpose is to insulate the company's earnings from the uncertainties of any one industry, or from the business cycle.

CENTER OF GRAVITY CHANGE

Another possibility is for an organization to stay in the same industry but change its center of gravity in that industry. Recent articles describe the attempts of chemical companies to move downstream into higher margin, proprietary products. They went to move away from the overcapacity/undercapacity cycles of commodity businesses with their low margins and high capital intensity. In aerospace, some of the system integration houses are moving backward into making electronic components. For example, there are going to be fewer airplanes and more effort on the avionics, radars, weapons, and so on that go into airplanes. In either case, it means a shift in the center of gravity of the company.

In summary, several patterns of strategic change can occur in a company. These involve changes to the company's industry of origination, changes to the center of gravity of the company, or some combination of the two. For some of the strategic changes there are appropriate organizations and measures of their economic performance.

Strategy, Organization, and Performance

For a number of years now, studies have been made of strategy and structure of the *Fortune* 500. Most of these were conducted by the Harvard Business School. These studies were reviewed in previous work (Galbraith and Nathanson, 1978). The current view is illustrated in Table 1. If one samples the *Fortune* 500 and categorizes them by strategy and structure, the following relationships hold.

One can still find organizations staying in their same original business. Such a single business is Wrigley Chewing Gum. These organizations are run by centralized functional organizations. The next strategic type is the vertically integrated by-product seller. Again, these companies have some diversification but remain committed to their industry and center of gravity. The companies are also functional, but the sequential stages are often operated as profit and loss divisions. The companies are usually quite centralized and run by collegial management groups. The profit centers are not true ones in being independent to run their own businesses. These are almost all upstream companies.

The related businesses are those that move into new industries at their center of gravity. Usually these are downstream companies. They adopt the decentralized profit center divisions. However, the divisions are not completely decentralized. There are usually strong corporate staffs and some centralized marketing, manufacturing, and R&D. There may be several thousand people on the corporate payroll.

The clearest contrast to the related diversifier is the unrelated business company. These companies enter a variety of businesses at several centers of gravity. The organization they adopt is the very decentralized holding company. Their outstanding feature is the small corporate staff. Depending on their size, the numbers range between fifty and two hundred. Usually these are support staffs. All of the marketing, manufacturing, and R&D is decentralized to the divisions. Group executives have no staffs and are generally corporate oriented.

The linked companies are neither of these extremes. Often linked forms are transitory. The organizations that they utilize are usually mixed forms that are not easily classified. Some divisions are autonomous, while others are managed out of the corporate HQ. Still others have strong group executives with group staffs. Some work has been done on classifying these structures (Allen, 1978).

There has been virtually no work done on center of gravity changes and their changes in structure. Likewise, there has been nothing done on comparisons for economic performance. But for the other categories and structures, there is emerging some good data on relative economic performance.

The studies of economic performance have compared the various strategic patterns and the concept of fit between strategy and organization. Both sets of results have organization design implications. The economic studies use return on equity as the performance measure. If one compares the strategic categories listed in Table 1, there are distinct performance differences. The high performers are consistently the related diversifiers (Rumelt, 1974; Galbraith and Nathanson, 1978; Nathanson and Cassano, 1982; Bettis, 1981; Rumelt, 1982).

TABLE 1

STRATEGY	STRUCTURE
Single business	Functional
Vertical by-products	Functional with P&Ls
Related businesses	Divisional
Linked businesses	Mixed structures
Unrelated businesses	Holding company

There are several explanations for this performance difference. One explanation is that the related diversifiers are all downstream companies in businesses with high R&D and advertising expenditures. These businesses have higher margins and returns than other businesses. Thus, it may not be the strategy but the businesses the relateds happen to be in. However, if the unrelateds are good acquirers, why do they not enter the high-return businesses?

The other explanation is that the relateds learn a set of core skills and design an organization to perform at a particular center of gravity. Then, when they diversify, they take on the task of learning a new business, but at the same center of gravity. Therefore, they get a diversified portfolio of businesses but each with a system of management and an organization that is understood by everyone. The management understands the business and is not spread thin.

The unrelateds, however, have to learn new industries and also how to operate to a different center of gravity. This latter change is the most difficult to accomplish. One upstream company diversified via acquisition into downstream companies. It consistently encountered control troubles. It instituted a capital appropriation process for each investment of $50,000 or more. It still had problems, however. The retail division opened a couple of stores with leases for $40,000. It didn't use the capital process. The company got blindsided because the stores required $40 million in working capital for inventory and receivables. Thus, the management systems did not fit the new downstream business. It appears that organizational fit makes a difference. . . .

One additional piece of evidence results from the studies of economic performance. This result is that the poorest performer of the strategic categories is the vertically integrated by-product seller. Recall these companies are all upstream, raw material, and primary manufacturers. They make up a good portion of "Smokestack America." In some respects, these companies made their money early in the century, and their value added is shifting to lesser developed countries in the natural course of industrial development. However, what is significant here is their inability to change. It is no secret to anyone that they have been underperformers, yet they have continued to put money back into the same business.

My explanation revolves around the center of gravity. These previously successful companies put together an organization that fit their industry and stage. When the industry declined, they were unable to change as well as the downstream companies. The reason is that upstream companies were functional organizations with few general managers. Their resource allocation was within a single business, not across multiple products. The management skill is partly technological knowhow. This technology does not transfer across industries at the primary manufacturing center of gravity. The knowledge of paper making does not help very much in glass making. Yet both might be combined in a package company. Also, the capital intensity of these industries limits the diversification. Usually one industry must be chosen and capital invested to be the low-cost producer. So there are a number of reasons why these companies have been notoriously poor diversifiers.

In addition, it appears to be very difficult to change centers of gravity no matter where an organization is along the industry chain. The reason is that a center of gravity shift requires a dismantling of the current power structure, rejection of parts of the old culture, and establishing all new management systems. The related diversification works for exactly the opposite reasons. They can move into new businesses with minimal change to the power structure and accepted ways of doing things. Changes in the center of gravity usually occur by new start-ups at a new center of gravity rather than a shift in the center of established firms. . . .

There are some exceptions that prove the rule. Some organizations have shifted from upstream commodity producers to downstream product producers and consumer product firms. General Mills moved from a flour miller to a related diversified provider of products for the homemaker. Over a long period of time they shifted downstream into consumer food products from their cake mix product beginnings. From there, they diversified into related areas after selling off the milling operations, the old core of the company. . . . [In these cases], however, new management was brought in and acquisition and divestment used to make the transition. So, even though vestiges of the old name remain, these are substantially different companies. . . .

The vast majority of our research has examined one kind of strategic change—diversification. The far more difficult one, the change in center of gravity, has received far less [attention]. For the most part, the concept is difficult to measure and not publicly reported like the number of industries in which a company operates. Case studies will have to be used. But there is a need for more systematic knowledge around this kind of strategic change.

▼ READING 6.2   THE STRUCTURING OF ORGANIZATIONS*

by Henry Mintzberg

The "one best way" approach has dominated our thinking about organizational structure since the turn of the century. There is a right way and a wrong way to design an organization. A variety of failures, however, has made it clear that organizations differ, that, for example, long-range planning systems or organizational development programs are good for some but not others. And so recent management theory has moved away from the "one best way" approach, toward an "it all depends" approach, formally known as "contingency theory." Structure should reflect the organization's situation—for example, its age, size, type of production system, the extent to which its environment is complex and dynamic.

This reading argues that the "it all depends" approach does not go far enough, that structures are rightfully designed on the basis of a third approach, which might be called the "getting it all together" or "configuration" approach. Spans of control, types of formalization and decentralization, planning systems, and matrix structures should not be picked and chosen independently, the way a shopper picks vegetables at the market. Rather, these and other elements of organizational design should logically configure into internally consistent groupings.

When the enormous amount of research that has been done on organizational structure is looked at in the light of this conclusion, much of its confusion falls away, and a convergence is evident around several configurations, which are distinct in their structural designs, in the situations in which they are found, and even in the periods of history in which they first developed.

To understand these configurations, we must first understand each of the elements that make them up. Accordingly, the first four sections of this reading discuss the basic parts of organizations, the mechanisms by which organizations coordinate their activities, the parameters they use to design their structures, and their contingency, or situational, factors. The final section introduces the structural configurations, each of which will be discussed at length in Section III of this text.

Six Basic Parts of the Organization

At the base of any organization can be found its operators, those people who perform the basic work of producing the products and rendering the services. They form the *operating core*. All but the simplest organizations also require at least one full-time manager who

---

* Excerpted originally from *The Structuring of Organizations* (Prentice Hall, 1979), with added sections from *Power in and Around Organizations* (Prentice Hall, 1983). This chapter was rewritten for this edition of the text, based on two other excerpts: "A Typology of Organizational Structure," published as Chapter 3 in Danny Miller and Peter Friesen, *Organizations: A Quantum View*, (Prentice Hall, 1984) and "Deriving Configurations," Chapter 6 in *Mintzberg on Management: Inside Our Strange World of Organizations* (Free Press, 1989).

occupies what we shall call the *strategic apex,* where the whole system is overseen. And as the organization grows, more managers are needed—not only managers of operators but also managers of managers. A *middle line* is created, a hierarchy of authority between the operating core and the strategic apex.

As the organization becomes still more complex, it generally requires another group of people, whom we shall call the analysts. They, too, perform administrative duties—to plan and control formally the work of others—but of a different nature, often labeled "staff." These analysts form what we shall call the *technostructure,* outside the hierarchy of line authority. Most organizations also add staff units of a different kind, to provide various internal services, from a cafeteria or mailroom to a legal counsel or public relations office. We shall call these units and the part of the organization they form the *support staff.*

Finally, every active organization has a sixth part, which we call its *ideology* (by which is meant a strong "culture"). Ideology encompasses the traditions and beliefs of an organization that distinguish it from other organizations and infuse a certain life into the skeleton of its structure.

This gives us six basic parts of an organization. As shown in Figure 1, we have a small strategic apex connected by a flaring middle line to a large, flat operating core at the base. These three parts of the organization are drawn in one uninterrupted sequence to indicate that they are typically connected through a single chain of formal authority. The technostructure and the support staff are shown off to either side to indicate that they are separate from this main line of authority, influencing the operating core only indirectly. The ideology is shown as a kind of halo that surrounds the entire system.

These people, all of whom work inside the organization to make its decisions and take its actions—full-time employees or, in some cases, committed volunteers—may be thought of as *influencers* who form a kind of internal coalition. By this term, we mean a system within which people vie among themselves to determine the distribution of power.

In addition, various outside people also try to exert influence on the organization, seeking to affect the decisions and actions taken inside. These external influencers, who create a field of forces around the organization, can include owners, unions and other employee

FIGURE 1
The Six Basic Parts of the Organization

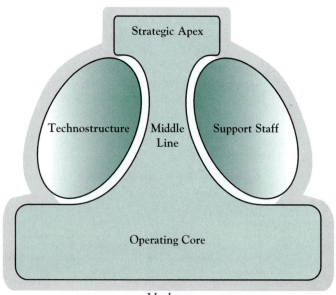

associations, suppliers, clients, partners, competitors, and all kinds of publics, in the form of governments, special interest groups, and so forth. Together they can all be thought to form an *external coalition*.

Sometimes the external coalition is relatively *passive* (as in the typical behavior of the shareholders of a widely held corporation or the members of a large union). Other times it is *dominated* by one active influencer or some group of them acting in concert (such as an outside owner of a business firm or a community intent on imposing a certain philosophy on its school system). And in still other cases, the external coalition may be *divided*, as different groups seek to impose contradictory pressures on the organization (as in a prison buffeted between two community groups, one favoring custody, the other rehabilitation).

Six Basic Coordinating Mechanisms

Every organized human activity—from the making of pottery to the placing of a man on the moon—gives rise to two fundamental and opposing requirements: the *division of labor* into various tasks to be performed and the *coordination* of those tasks to accomplish the activity. The structure of an organization can be defined simply as the total of the ways in which its labor is divided into distinct tasks and then its coordination achieved among those tasks.

1. *Mutual adjustment* achieves coordination of work by the simple process of informal communication. The people who do the work interact with one another to coordinate, much as two canoeists in the rapids adjust to one another's actions. Figure 2a shows mutual adjustment in terms of an arrow between two operators. Mutual adjustment is obviously used in the simplest of organizations—it is the most obvious way to coordinate. But, paradoxically, it is also used in the most complex, because it is the only means that can be relied upon under extremely difficult circumstances, such as trying to figure out how to put a man on the moon for the first time.

2. *Direct supervision* in which one person coordinates by giving orders to others, tends to come into play after a certain number of people must work together. Thus, fifteen people in a war canoe cannot coordinate by mutual adjustment; they need a leader who, by virtue of instructions, coordinates their work, much as a football team requires a quarterback to call the plays. Figure 2b shows the leader as a manager with the instructions as arrows to the operators.

Coordination can also be achieved by *standardization*—in effect, automatically, by virtue of standards that predetermine what people do and so ensure that their work is coordinated. We can consider four forms—the standardization of the work processes themselves, of the outputs of the work, of the knowledge and skills that serve as inputs to the work, or of the norms that more generally guide the work.

3. *Standardization of work processes* means the specification—that is, the programming—of the content of the work directly, the procedures to be followed, as in the case of the assembly instructions that come with many children's toys. As shown in Figure 2c, it is typically the job of the analysts to so program the work of different people in order to coordinate it tightly.

4. *Standardization of outputs* means the specification not of what is to be done but of its results. In that way, the interfaces between jobs is predetermined, as when a machinist is told to drill holes in a certain place on a fender so that they will fit the bolts being welded by someone else, or a division manager is told to achieve a sales growth of 10% so that the corporation can meet some overall sales target. Again, such standards generally emanate from the analysts, as shown in Figure 2d.

FIGURE 2
The Basic Mechanisms of Coordination

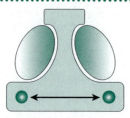

a) Mutual Adjustment

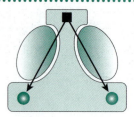

b) Direct Supervision

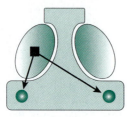

c) Standardization of Work

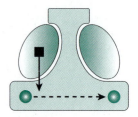

d) Standardization of Outputs

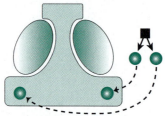

e) Standardization of Skills

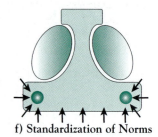

f) Standardization of Norms

5. *Standardization of skills*, as well as knowledge, is another, though looser way to achieve coordination. Here, it is the worker rather than the work or the outputs that is standardized. He or she is taught a body of knowledge and a set of skills which are subsequently applied to the work. Such standardization typically takes place outside the organization—for example in a professional school of a university before the worker takes his or her first job—indicated in Figure 2e. In effect, the standards do not come from the analyst; they are internalized by the operator as inputs to the job he or she takes. Coordination is then achieved by virtue of various operators' having learned what to expect of each other. When an anesthetist and a surgeon meet in the operating room to remove an appendix, they need hardly communicate (that is, use mutual adjustment, let alone direct supervision); each knows exactly what the other will do and can coordinate accordingly.

6. *Standardization of norms* means that the workers share a common set of beliefs and can achieve coordination based on it, as implied in Figure 2f. For example, if every member of a religious order shares a belief in the importance of attracting converts, then all will work together to achieve this aim.

These coordinating mechanisms can be considered the most basic elements of structure, the glue that holds organizations together. They seem to fall into a rough order: As organizational work becomes more complicated, the favored means of coordination seems to shift from mutual adjustment (the simplest mechanism) to direct supervision, then to standardization, preferably of work processes or norms, otherwise of outputs or of skills, finally reverting back to mutual adjustment. But no organization can rely on a single one of those mechanisms; all will typically be found in every reasonably developed organization.

Still, the important point for us here is that many organizations do favor one mechanism over the others, at least at certain stages of their lives. In fact, organizations that favor none seem most prone to becoming politicized, simply because of the conflicts that naturally arise when people have to vie for influence in a relative vacuum of power.

The Essential Parameters of Design

The essence of organizational design is the manipulation of a series of parameters that determine the division of labor and the achievement of coordination. Some of these concern the design of individual positions, others the design of the superstructure (the overall network of subunits, reflected in the organizational chart), some the design of lateral linkages to flesh out that superstructure, and a final group concerns the design of the decision-making system of the organization. Listed as follows are the main parameters of structural design, with links to the coordinating mechanisms.

▼ **Job specialization** refers to the number of tasks in a given job and the workers' control over these tasks. A job is *horizontally* specialized to the extent that it encompasses a few narrowly defined tasks, *vertically* specialized to the extent that the worker lacks control of the tasks performed. *Unskilled* jobs are typically highly specialized in both dimensions; skilled or *professional* jobs are typically specialized horizontally but not vertically. "Job enrichment" refers to the enlargement of jobs in both the vertical and horizontal dimension.

▼ **Behavior formalization** refers to the standardization of work processes by the imposition of operating instructions, job descriptions, rules, regulations, and the like. Structures that rely on any form of standardization for coordination may be defined as *bureaucratic*, those that do not as *organic*.

▼ **Training** refers to the use of formal instructional programs to establish and standardize in people the requisite skills and knowledge to do particular jobs in organizations. Training is a key design parameter in all work we call professional. Training and formalization are basically substitutes for achieving the standardization (in effect, the bureaucratization) of behavior. In one, the standards are learned as skills, in the other they are imposed on the job as rules.

▼ **Indoctrination** refers to programs and techniques by which the norms of the members of an organization are standardized, so that they become responsive to its ideological needs and can thereby be trusted to make its decisions and take its actions. Indoctrination too is a substitute for formalization, as well as for skill training, in this case the standards being internalized as deeply rooted beliefs.

▼ **Unit grouping** refers to the choice of the bases by which positions are grouped together into units, and those units into higher-order units (typically shown on the organization chart). Grouping encourages coordination by putting different jobs under common supervision, by requiring them to share common resources and achieve common measures of performance, and by using proximity to facilitate mutual adjustment among them. The various bases for grouping—by work process, product, client, place, and so on—can be reduced to two fundamental ones—the *function* performed and the *market* served. The former (illustrated in Fig. 3) refers to means, that is to a single link

FIGURE 3
Grouping by Function:
A Cultural Center

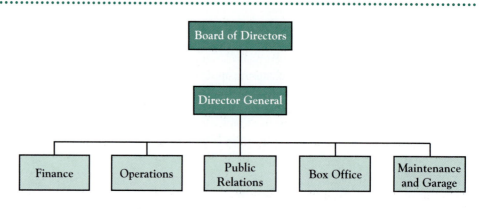

in the chain of processes by which products or services are produced; the latter (in Fig. 4) to ends, that is, the whole chain for specific end products, services, or markets. On what criteria should the choice of a basis for grouping be made? First, there is the consideration of workflow linkages, or "interdependencies." Obviously, the more tightly linked are positions or units in the workflow, the more desirable that they be grouped together to facilitate their coordination. Second is the consideration of process interdependencies—for example, across people doing the same kind of work but in different workflows (such as maintenance men working on different machines). It sometimes makes sense to group them together to facilitate their sharing of equipment or ideas, to encourage the improvement of their skills, and so on. Third is the question of scale interdependencies. For example, all maintenance people in a factory may have to be grouped together because no single department has enough maintenance work for one person. Finally, there are the social interdependencies, the need to group people together for social reasons, as in coal mines where mutual support under dangerous working conditions can be a factor in deciding how to group people. Clearly, grouping by function is favored by process and scale interdependencies. and to a lesser extent by social interdependencies (in the sense that people who do the same kind of job often tend to get along better). Grouping by function also encourages specialization, for example, by allowing specialists to come together under the supervision of one of their own kind. The problem with functional grouping, however, is that it narrows perspectives, encouraging a focus on means instead of ends—the way to do the job instead of the reason for doing the job in the first place. Thus grouping by market is used to favor coordination in the workflow at the expense of process and scale specialization. In general, market grouping reduces the ability to do specialized or repetitive tasks well and is more wasteful, being less able to take advantage of economies of scale and often requiring the duplication of resources. But it enables the organization to accomplish a wider variety of tasks and to change its tasks more easily to serve the organization's end markets. And so if the workflow interdependencies are the important ones and if the organization cannot easily handle them by standardization, then it will tend to favor the market bases for grouping in order to encourage mutual adjustment and direct supervision. But if the workflow is irregular (as in a "job shop"), if standardization can easily contain the important workflow interdependencies, or if the process or scale interdependencies are the important ones, then the organization will be inclined to seek the advantages of specialization and group on the basis of function instead. Of

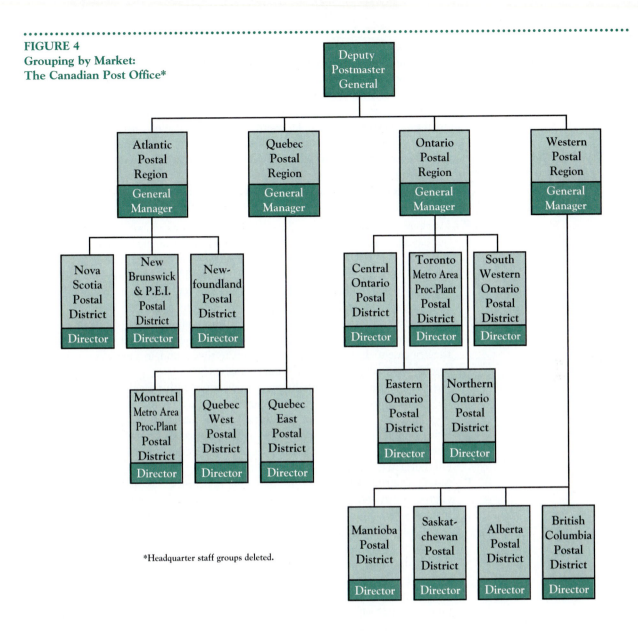

FIGURE 4
Grouping by Market:
The Canadian Post Office*

Deputy Postmaster General

Atlantic Postal Region — General Manager
Quebec Postal Region — General Manager
Ontario Postal Region — General Manager
Western Postal Region — General Manager

Nova Scotia Postal District — Director
New Brunswick & P.E.I. Postal District — Director
New-foundland Postal District — Director

Montreal Metro Area Proc.Plant Postal District — Director
Quebec West Postal District — Director
Quebec East Postal District — Director

Central Ontario Postal District — Director
Toronto Metro Area Proc.Plant Postal District — Director
South Western Ontario Postal District — Director

Eastern Ontario Postal District — Director
Northern Ontario Postal District — Director

Mantioba Postal District — Director
Saskatchewan Postal District — Director
Alberta Postal District — Director
British Columbia Postal District — Director

*Headquarter staff groups deleted.

course in all but the smallest organizations, the question is not so much *which* basis of grouping, but in what *order*. Much as fires are built by stacking logs first one way and then the other, so too are organizations built by varying the different bases for grouping to take care of various interdependencies.

▼ **Unit size** refers to the number of positions (or units) contained in a single unit. The equivalent term, *span of control*, is not used here, because sometimes units are kept small despite an absence of close supervisory control. For example, when experts coordinate extensively by mutual adjustment, as in an engineering team in a space agency, they will form into small units. In this case, unit size is small and span of control is low despite a relative absence of direct supervision. In contrast, when work is highly standardized (because of either formalization or training), unit size can be very large, because there is little need for direct supervision. One foreman can supervise dozens of assemblers, because they work according to very tight instructions.

▼ **Planning and control systems** are used to standardize outputs. They may be divided into two types: *action planning* systems, which specify the results of specific actions before they are taken (for example, that holes should be drilled with diameters of 3 centimeters); and *performance control* systems, which specify the desired results of whole ranges of actions after the fact (for example, that sales of a division should grow by 10% in a given year).

▼ **Liaison devices** refer to a whole series of mechanisms used to encourage mutual adjustment within and between units. Four are of particular importance:

   ▼ *Liaison positions* are jobs created to coordinate the work of two units directly, without having to pass through managerial channels, for example, the purchasing engineer who sits between purchasing and engineering or the sales liaison person who mediates between the sales force and the factory. These positions carry no formal authority per se; rather, those who serve in them must use their powers of persuasion, negotiation, and so on to bring the two sides together.

   ▼ *Task forces and standing committees* are institutionalized forms of meetings which bring members of a number of different units together on a more intensive basis, in the first case to deal with a temporary issue, in the second, in a more permanent and regular way to discuss issues of common interest.

   ▼ *Integrating managers*—essentially liaison personnel with formal authority—provide for stronger coordination. These "managers" are given authority not over the units they link, but over something important to those units, for example, their budgets. One example is the brand manager in a consumer goods firm who is responsible for a certain product but who must negotiate its production and marketing with different functional departments.

   ▼ *Matrix structure* carries liaison to its natural conclusion. No matter what the bases of grouping at one level in an organization, some interdependencies always remain. Figure 5 suggests various ways to deal with these "residual interdependencies": a different type of grouping can be used at the next level in the hierarchy; staff units can be formed next to line units to advise on the problems; or one of the liaison devices already discussed can be overlaid on the grouping. But in each case, one basis of grouping is favored over the others. The concept of matrix structure is balance between two (or more) bases of grouping, for example functional with market (or for that matter, one kind of market with another—say, regional with product). This is done by the creation of a dual authority structure—two (or more) managers, units, or individuals are made jointly and equally responsible for the same decisions. We can distinguish a *permanent* form of matrix structure, where the units and the people in them remain more or less in place, as shown in the example of a whimsical multinational firm in Figure 6, and a *shifting* form, suited to project work, where the units and the people in them move around frequently. Shifting matrix structures are common in high-technology industries, which group specialists in functional departments for housekeeping purposes (process interdependencies, etc.) but deploy them from various departments in project teams to do the work, as shown for NASA in Figure 7.

▼ **Decentralization** refers to the diffusion of decision-making power. When all the power rests at a single point in an organization, we call its structure centralized; to the extent that the power is dispersed among many individuals, we call it relatively decentralized. We can distinguish *vertical decentralization*—the delegation of formal power down the

FIGURE 5
Structures to Deal with
Residual Interdependencies

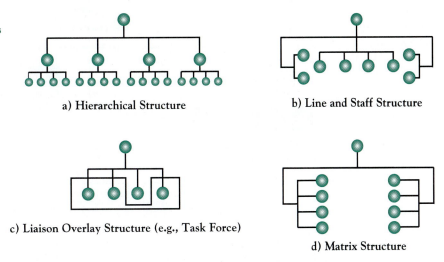

a) Hierarchical Structure

b) Line and Staff Structure

c) Liaison Overlay Structure (e.g., Task Force)

d) Matrix Structure

FIGURE 6
A Permanent Matrix
Structure in an
International Firm

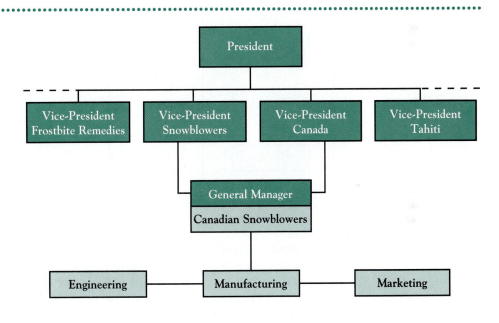

hierarchy to line managers—from *horizontal decentralization*—the extent to which formal or informal power is dispersed out of the line hierarchy to nonmanagers (operators, analysts, and support staffers). We can also distinguish *selective* decentralization—the dispersal of power over different decisions to different places in the organization—from *parallel* decentralization—where the power over various kinds of decisions is delegated to the same place. Six forms of decentralization may thus be described: (1) vertical and horizontal centralization, where all the power rests at the strategic apex; (2) limited horizontal decentralization (selective), where the strategic apex shares some power with the technostructure that standardizes everybody else's work; (3) limited vertical

FIGURE 7
Shifting Matrix Structure
in the NASA Weather
Satellite Program
Source: Modified from
Delbecq and Filley (1974:16).

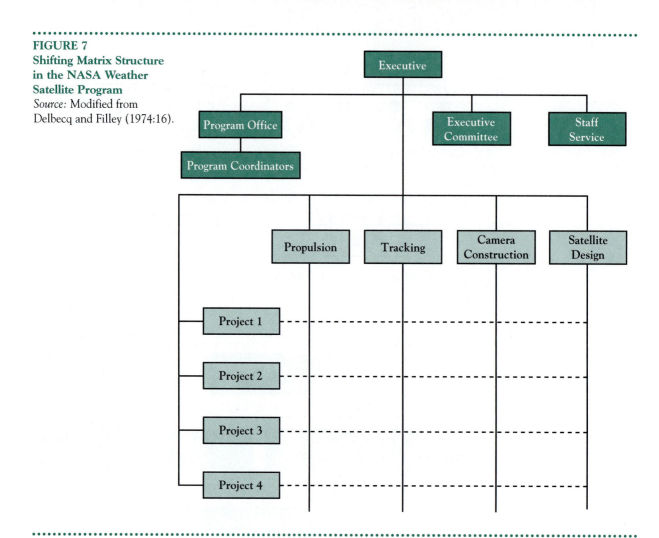

decentralization (parallel), where managers of market-based units are delegated the power to control most of the decisions concerning their line units; (4) vertical and horizontal decentralization, where most of the power rests in the operating core, at the bottom of the structure; (5) selective vertical and horizontal decentralization, where the power over different decisions is dispersed to various places in the organization, among managers, staff experts, and operators who work in teams at various levels in the hierarchy; and (6) pure decentralization, where power is shared more or less equally by all members of the organization.

The Situational Factors

A number of "contingency" or "situational" factors influence the choice of these design parameters, and vice versa. They include the age and size of the organization; its technical system of production; various characteristics of its environment, such as stability and complexity; and its power system, for example, whether or not it is tightly controlled by outside influencers. Some of the effects of these factors, as found in an extensive body of research literature, are summarized below as hypotheses.

AGE AND SIZE

▼ **The older an organization, the more formalized its behavior.** What we have here is the "we've-seen-it-all-before" syndrome. As organizations age, they tend to repeat their behaviors: as a result, these become more predictable and so more amenable to formalization.

▼ **The larger an organization, the more formalized its behavior.** Just as the older organization formalizes what it has seen before, so the larger organization formalizes what it sees often. ("Listen mister, I've heard that story at least five times today. Just fill in the form like it says.")

▼ **The larger an organization, the more elaborate its structure; that is, the more specialized its jobs and units and the more developed its administrative components.** As organizations grow in size, they are able to specialize their jobs more finely. (The big barbershop can afford a specialist to cut children's hair; the small one cannot.) As a result, they can also specialize—or "differentiate"—the work of their units more extensively. This requires more effort at coordination. And so the larger organization tends also to enlarge its hierarchy to effect direct supervision and to make greater use of its technostructure to achieve coordination by standardization, or else to encourage more coordination by mutual adjustment.

▼ **The larger the organization, the larger the size of its average unit.** This finding relates to the previous two, the size of units growing larger as organizations themselves grow larger because (1) as behavior becomes more formalized, and (2) as the work of each unit becomes more homogeneous, managers are able to supervise more employees.

▼ **Structure reflects the age of the industry from its founding.** This is a curious finding, but one that we shall see holds up remarkably well. An organization's structure seems to reflect the age of the industry in which it operates, no matter what its own age. Industries that predate the industrial revolution seem to favor one kind of structure, those of the age of the early railroads another, and so on. We should obviously expect different structures in different periods; the surprising thing is that these structures seem to carry through to new periods, old industries remaining relatively true to earlier structures.

TECHNICAL SYSTEM

Technical system refers to the instruments used in the operating core to produce the outputs. (This should be distinguished from "technology," which refers to the knowledge base of an organization.)

▼ **The more regulating the technical system—that is, the more it controls the work of the operators—the more formalized the operating work and the more bureaucratic the structure of the operating core.** Technical systems that regulate the work of the operators—for example, mass production assembly lines—render that work highly routine and predictable, and so encourage its specialization and formalization, which in turn create the conditions for bureaucracy in the operating core.

▼ **The more complex the technical system, the more elaborate and professional the support staff.** Essentially, if an organization is to use complex machinery, it must hire staff experts who can understand that machinery—who have the capability to design, select, and modify it. And then it must give them considerable power to make decisions concerning that machinery, and encourage them to use the liaison devices to ensure mutual adjustment among them.

▼ **The automation of the operating core forms a bureaucratic administrative structure into an organic one.** When unskilled work is coordinated by the standardization of work processes, we tend to get bureaucratic structure throughout the organization, because a control mentality pervades the whole system. But when the work of the operating core becomes automated, social relationships tend to change. Now it is machines, not people, that are regulated. So the obsession with control tends to disappear—machines do not need to be watched over—and with it go many of the managers and analysts who were needed to control the operators. In their place come the support specialists to look after the machinery, coordinating their own work by mutual adjustment. Thus, automation reduces line authority in favor of staff expertise and reduces the tendency to rely on standardization for coordination.

ENVIRONMENT

Environment refers to various characteristics of the organization's outside context, related to markets, political climate, economic conditions, and so on.

▼ **The more dynamic an organization's environment, the more organic its structure.** It stands to reason that in a stable environment—where nothing changes—an organization can predict its future conditions and so, all other things being equal, can easily rely on standardization for coordination. But when conditions become dynamic—when the need for product change is frequent, labor turnover is high, and political conditions are unstable—the organization cannot standardize but must instead remain flexible through the use of direct supervision or mutual adjustment for coordination, and so it must use a more organic structure. Thus, for example, armies, which tend to be highly bureaucratic institutions in peacetime, can become rather organic when engaged in highly dynamic, guerilla-type warfare.

▼ **The more complex an organization's environment, the more decentralized its structure.** The prime reason to decentralize a structure is that all the information needed to make decisions cannot be comprehended in one head. Thus, when the operations of an organization are based on a complex body of knowledge, there is usually a need to decentralize decision-making power. Note that a simple environment can be stable or dynamic (the manufacturer of dresses faces a simple environment yet cannot predict style from one season to another), as can a complex one (the specialist in perfected open heart surgery faces a complex task, yet knows what to expect).

▼ **The more diversified an organization's markets, the greater the propensity to split it into market-based units, or divisions, given favorable economies of scale.** When an organization can identify distinct markets—geographical regions, clients, but especially products and services—it will be predisposed to split itself into high level units on that basis, and to give each a good deal of control over its own operations (that is, to use what we called "limited vertical decentralization"). In simple terms, diversification breeds divisionalization. Each unit can be given all the functions associated with its own markets. But this assumes favorable economies of scale: If the operating core cannot be divided, as in the case of an aluminum smelter, also if some critical function must be centrally coordinated, as in purchasing in a retail chain, then full divisionalization may not be possible.

▼ **Extreme hostility in its environment drives any organization to centralize its structure temporarily.** When threatened by extreme hostility in its environment, the tendency for an organization is to centralize power, in other words, to fall back on its tightest coordinating mechanism, direct supervision. Here a single leader can ensure fast and tightly coordinated response to the threat (at least temporarily).

POWER

▼ **The greater the external control of an organization, the more centralized and formalized its structure.** This important hypothesis claims that to the extent that an organization is controlled externally, for example by a parent firm or a government that dominates its external coalition—it tends to centralize power at the strategic apex and to formalize its behavior. The reason is that the two most effective ways to control an organization from the outside are to hold its chief executive officer responsible for its actions and to impose clearly defined standards on it. Moreover, external control forces the organization to be especially careful about its actions.

▼ **A divided external coalition will tend to give rise to a politicized internal coalition, and vice versa.** In effect, conflict in one of the coalitions tends to spill over to the other, as one set of influencers seeks to enlist the support of the others.

▼ **Fashion favors the structure of the day (and of the culture), sometimes even when inappropriate.** Ideally, the design parameters are chosen according to the dictates of age, size, technical system, and environment. In fact, however, fashion seems to play a role too, encouraging many organizations to adopt currently popular design parameters that are inappropriate for themselves. Paris has its salons of haute couture; likewise New York has its offices of "haute structure," the consulting firms that sometimes tend to oversell the latest in structural fashion.

The Configurations

We have now introduced various attributes of organizations—parts, coordinating mechanisms, design parameters, situational factors, How do they all combine?

We proceed here on the assumption that a limited number of configurations can help explain much of what is observed in organizations. We have introduced in our discussion six basic parts of the organization, six basic mechanisms of coordination. as well as six basic types of decentralization. In fact, there seems to be a fundamental correspondence between all of these sixes, which can be explained by a set of pulls exerted on the organization by each of its six parts, as shown in Figure 8. When conditions favor one of these pulls, the associated part of the organization becomes key, the coordinating mechanism appropriate to itself becomes prime, and the form of decentralization that passes power to itself emerges. The organization is thus drawn to design itself as a particular configuration. We list here (see Table 1) and then introduce briefly the six resulting configurations, together with a seventh that tends to appear when no one pull or part dominates.

TABLE 1

CONFIGURATION	PRIME COORDINATING MECHANISM	KEY PART OF ORGANIZATION	TYPE OF DECEN-TRALIZATION
Entrepreneurial organization	Direct Supervision	Strategic apex	Vertical and horizontal centralization
Machine organization	Standardization of work processes	Technostructure	Limited horizontal decentralization
Professional organization	Standardization of skills	Operating core	Horizontal decentralization
Diversified organization	Standardization of outputs	Middle line	Limited vertical decentralization
Innovative organization	Mutual adjustment	Support staff	Selected decentralization
Missionary organization	Standardization of norms	Ideology	Decentralization
Political organization	None	None	Varies

FIGURE 8
Basic Pulls on the
Organization

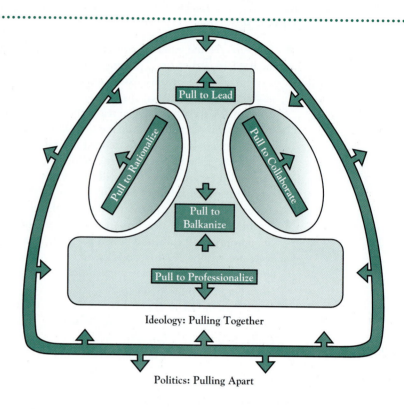

Ideology: Pulling Together

Politics: Pulling Apart

THE ENTREPRENEURIAL ORGANIZATION

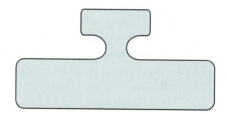

The name tells it all. And the figure above shows it all. The structure is simple, not much more than one large unit consisting of one or a few top managers, one of whom dominates by the pull to lead, and a group of operators who do the basic work. Little of the behavior in the organization is formalized and minimal use is made of planning, training, or the liaison devices. The absence of standardization means that the structure is organic and has little need for staff analysts. Likewise there are few middle line managers because so much of the coordination is handled at the top. Even the support staff is minimized, in order to keep the structure lean, the organization flexible.

The organization must be flexible because it operates in a dynamic environment, often by choice since that is the only place where it can outsmart the bureaucracies. But that environment must be simple, as must the production system, or else the chief executive could not for long hold on to the lion's share of the power. The organization is often young, in part because time drives it toward bureaucracy, in part because the vulnerability of its simple structure often causes it to fail. And many of these organizations are often small, since size too drives the structure toward bureaucracy. Not infrequently the chief executive purposely keeps the organization small in order to retain his or her personal control.

The classic case is of course the small entrepreneurial firm, controlled tightly and personally by its owner. Sometimes, however, under the control of a strong leader the organization can grow to large. Likewise, entrepreneurial organizations can be found in other sectors too, like government, where strong leaders personally control particular agencies, often ones they have founded. Sometimes under crisis conditions, large organizations also revert temporarily to the entrepreneurial form to allow forceful leaders to try to save them.

THE MACHINE ORGANIZATION

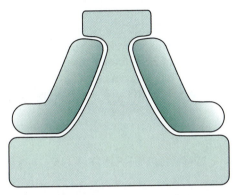

The machine organization is the offspring of the Industrial Revolution, when jobs became highly specialized and work became highly standardized. As can be seen in the figure above, in contrast to entrepreneurial organizations, the machine one elaborates its administration. First, it requires a large technostructure to design and maintain its systems of standardization, notably those that formalize its behaviors and plan its actions. And by virtue of the organization's dependence on these systems, the technostructure gains a good deal of informal power, resulting in a limited amount of horizontal decentralization reflecting the pull to rationalize. A large hierarchy of middle-line managers emerges to control the highly specialized work of the operating core. But the middle line hierarchy is usually structured on a functional basis all the way up to the top, where the real power of coordination lies. So the structure tends to be rather centralized in the vertical sense.

To enable the top managers to maintain centralized control, both the environment and the production system of the machine organization must be fairly simple, the latter regulating the work of the operators but not itself automated. In fact, machine organizations fit most naturally with mass production. Indeed it is interesting that this structure is most prevalent in industries that date back to the period from the Industrial Revolution to the early part of this century.

THE PROFESSIONAL ORGANIZATION

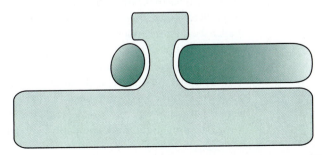

There is another bureaucratic configuration, but because this one relies on the standardization of skills rather than of work processes or outputs for its coordination, it emerges as dramatically different from the machine one. Here the pull to professionalize dominates. In having to rely on trained professionals—people highly specialized, but with considerable control over their work, as in hospitals or universities—to do its operating tasks, the organization surrenders a good deal of its power not only to the professionals themselves but also to the associations and institutions that select and train them in the first place. So the structure emerges as highly decentralized horizontally; power over many decisions, both operating and strategic, flows all the way down the hierarchy, to the professionals of the operating core.

Above the operating core we find a rather unique structure. There is little need for a technostructure, since the main standardization occurs as a result of training that takes place outside the organization. Because the professionals work so independently, the size of operating units can be very large, and few first line managers are needed. The support staff is typically very large too, in order to back up the high-priced professionals.

The professional organization is called for whenever an organization finds itself in an environment that is stable yet complex. Complexity requires decentralization to highly trained individuals, and stability enables them to apply standardized skills and so to work with a good deal of autonomy. To ensure that autonomy, the production system must be neither highly regulating, complex, nor automated.

THE DIVERSIFIED ORGANIZATION

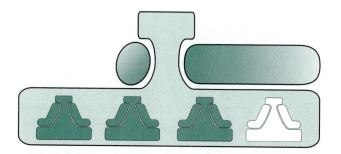

Like the professional organization, the diversified one is not so much an integrated organization as a set of rather independent entities coupled together by a loose administrative structure. But whereas those entities of the professional organization are individuals, in the diversified one they are units in the middle line, generally called "divisions," exerting a dominant pull to Balkanize. This configuration differs from the others in one major respect: it is not a complete structure, but a partial one superimposed on the others. Each division has its own structure.

An organization divisionalizes for one reason above all, because its product lines are diversified. And that tends to happen most often in the largest and most mature organizations, the ones that have run out of opportunities—or have become bored—in their traditional markets. Such diversification encourages the organization to replace functional by market-based units, one for each distinct product line (as shown in the diversified organization figure), and to grant considerable autonomy to each to run its own business. The result is a limited form of decentralization down the chain of command.

How does the central headquarters maintain a semblance of control over the divisions? Some direction supervision is used. But too much of that interferes with the necessary divisional autonomy. So the headquarters relies on performance control systems, in other words, the standardization of outputs. To design these control systems, headquarters creates a small technostructure. This is shown in the figure, across from the small central support staff that headquarters sets up to provide certain services common to the divisions such as legal counsel and public relations. And because headquarters' control constitutes external control, as discussed in the first hypothesis on power, the structure of the divisions tend to be drawn toward the machine form.

THE INNOVATIVE ORGANIZATION

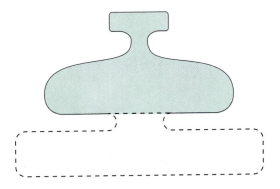

None of the structures so far discussed suits the industries of our age, industries such as aerospace, petrochemicals, think-tank consulting, and film making. These organizations need above all to innovate in very complex ways. The bureaucratic structures are too inflexible, and the entrepreneurial one too centralized. These industries require "project structures," ones that can fuse experts drawn from different specialties into smoothly functioning creative teams. That is the role of our fifth configuration, the innovative organization, which we shall also call "adhocracy," dominated by the experts' pull to collaborate.

Adhocracy is an organic structure that relies for coordination on mutual adjustment among its highly trained and highly specialized experts, which it encourages by the extensive use of the liaison devices—integrating managers, standing committees, and above all task forces and matrix structure. Typically the experts are grouped in functional units for housekeeping purposes but deployed in small market based project teams to do their work. To these teams, located all over the structure in accordance with the decisions to be made, is delegated power over different kinds of decisions. So the structure becomes decentralized selectively in the vertical and horizontal dimensions, that is, power is distributed unevenly, all over the structure, according to expertise and need.

All the distinctions of conventional structure disappear in the innovative organization, as can be seen in the figure above. With power based on expertise, the line-staff distinction evaporates. With power distributed throughout the structure, the distinction between the strategic apex and the rest of the structure blurs.

These organizations are found in environments that are both complex and dynamic, because those are the ones that require sophisticated innovation, the type that calls for the cooperative efforts of many different kinds of experts. One type of adhocracy is often associated with a production system that is very complex, sometimes automated, and so requires a highly skilled and influential support staff to design and maintain the technical system of the operating core. (The dashed lines of the figure designate the separation of the operating core from the adhocratic administrative structure.) Here the projects take place in the administration to bring new operating facilities on line (as when a new complex is designed in a petrochemicals firm). Another type of adhocracy produces its projects directly for its clients (as in a think tank consulting firm or manufacturer of engineering prototypes). Here, as a result, the operators also take part in the projects, bringing their expertise to bear on them; hence the operating core blends into the administrative structure (as indicated in the figure above the dashed line). This second type of adhocracy tends to be young on average, because with no standard products or services, many tend to fail while others escape their vulnerability by standardizing some products or services and so converting themselves to a form of bureaucracy.[1]

THE MISSIONARY ORGANIZATION

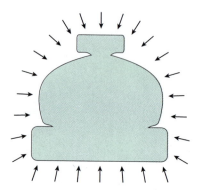

Our sixth configuration forms another rather distinct combination of the elements we have been discussing. When an organization is dominated by its ideology, its members are encouraged to pull together, and so there tends to be a loose division of labor, little job specialization, as well as a reduction of the various forms of differentiation found in the other configurations—of the strategic apex from the rest, of staff from line or administration from operations, between operators, between divisions, and so on.

What holds the missionary together—that is, provides for its coordination—is the standardization of norms, the sharing of values and beliefs among all its members. And the key to ensuring this is their socialization, effected through the design parameter of indoctrination. Once the new member has been indoctrinated into the organization—once he or she identifies strongly with the common beliefs—then he or she can be given considerable freedom to make decisions. Thus the result of effective indoctrination is the most complete form of decentralization. And because other forms of coordination need not be relied upon, the missionary organization formalizes little of its behavior as such and makes minimal use of planning and control systems. As a result, it has little technostructure. Likewise, external professional training is not relied upon, because that would force the organization to surrender a certain control to external agencies.

Hence, the missionary organization ends up as an amorphous mass of members, with little specialization as to job, differentiation as to part, division as to status.

Missionaries tend not to be very young organizations—it takes time for a set of beliefs to become institutionalized as an ideology. Many missionaries do not get a chance to grow very old either (with notable exceptions, such as certain long standing religious orders). Missionary organizations cannot grow very large per se—they rely on personal contacts among their members—although some tend to spin off other enclaves in the form of relatively independent units sharing the same ideology. Neither the environment nor the technical system of the missionary organization can be very complex, because that would require the use of highly skilled specialists, who would hold a certain power and status over others and thereby serve to differentiate the structure. Thus we would expect to find the simplest

[1] We shall clarify in a later reading these two basic types of adhocracies. Toffler employed the term adhocracy in his popular book *Future Shock*, but it can be found in print at least as far back as 1964.

technical systems in these organizations, usually hardly any at all, as in religious orders or in the primitive farm cooperatives.

THE POLITICAL ORGANIZATION

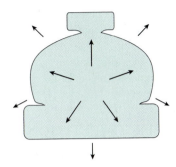

Finally, we come to a form of organization characterized, structurally at least, by what it lacks. When an organization has no dominate part, no dominant mechanism of coordination, and no stable form of centralization or decentralization, it may have difficulty tempering the conflicts within its midst, and a form of organization called the *political* may result. What characterizes its behavior is the pulling apart of its different parts, as shown in the figure above.

Political organizations can take on different forms. Some are temporary, reflecting difficult transitions in strategy or structure that evoke conflict. Others are more permanent, perhaps because the organization must face competing internal forces (say, between necessarily strong marketing and production departments), perhaps because a kind of political rot has set in but the organization is sufficiently entrenched to support it (being, for example, a monopoly or a protected government unit).

Together, all these configurations seem to encompass and integrate a good deal of what we know about organizations. It should be emphasized however, that as presented, each configuration is idealized—a simplification, really a caricature of reality. No real organization is ever exactly like any one of them, although some do come remarkably close, while others seem to reflect combinations of them, sometimes in transition from one to another.

The first five represent what seem to be the most common forms of organizations; thus these will form the basis for the "context" section of this book—labeled entrepreneurial, mature, diversified, innovation, and professional. There, a reading in each chapter will be devoted to each of these configurations, describing its structure, functioning, conditions, strategy-making process, and the issues that surround it. Other readings in these chapters will look at specific strategies in each of these contexts, industry conditions, strategy techniques, and so on.

The other two configurations—the missionary and the political—seem to be less common, represented more by the forces of culture and conflict that exist in all organizations than by distinct forms as such. Hence they will be discussed in the chapter that immediately follows this one, on "Dealing with Culture and Power." But because all these configurations themselves must not be taken as hard and fast, indeed because ideology and politics work within different configurations in all kinds of interesting ways, a final chapter in the context section, on managing change, will include a reading called "Beyond Configuration: Forces and Forms in Effective Organizations," that seeks to broaden this view of organizations.

by James Brian
Quinn, Philip
Anderson, and
Sydney Finkelstein

Many forces are combining to compel the end of static competitive advantage strategies. In today's hypercompetitive environments, firms face a continually shifting competitive landscape in which traditional sources of dominance—cost and quality, timing and know-how, the creation of competitive strongholds, and deep pockets—are constantly eroded. The key message of the hypercompetition concept is that the only enduring advantage results from the ability to generate new advantages: for example, while no cost or quality advantage is sustainable, the skill of generating new cost and quality advantages is sustainable. Furthermore, firms must keep pace with rivals in many different arenas; failure to keep up is not met with leniency (D'Aveni, 1994).

HYPERCOMPETITION AND ORGANIZATION FORMS

It is natural to conclude that organization forms designed for and adapted to a different era will not suffice in hypercompetitive environments. Indeed, it is quite widely accepted that new organization forms are emerging in response to such environmental trends as customization, globalization, rapid technological change, deregulation, and shifting work force demographics (Miles Snow, and Coleman, 1992). The dynamic driving the appearance of new forms appears to be a transformation from command and control to information-based organization (Drucker, 1988).

The term "network organization" has become a popular catch-all category, and is frequently used to describe any new organizational form that will supersede the multidivisional form as the dominant way of structuring a modern firm. Although the term "network organization" has been used in so many different ways that it is difficult to pin down the concept, a common theme of those describing networks as a new form of organization is de-bureaucratization. In the network organization, lateral relations are more important than vertical relations, and hierarchies are either very flat or disappear altogether. A central theme of this paper is that no one "network organizational form" will prevail as the dominant structure adapted to hypercompetitive environments.

We suggest these forms seldom occur in pure form across the entire entity, integrating all aspects of a major enterprise, and their evolution is not being driven by their emergence in totally new enterprises. Rather they are forms of organizing, not forms of organization, and they are typically embedded in larger organizational structures that are still at least partly bureaucratic. Because these forms are building blocks, with several typically co-existing inside larger organizations, a key challenge for top management is integrating these different forms of organizing into a coherent whole. The organization of the future will not be a hybrid, but will be polymorphic, containing within itself subunits whose fundamental ways of bringing intellect to bear upon problems are vastly different from one another

Five very different network configurations—adapted to different purposes and confronting managers with different challenges—will, however, be among the key building blocks. The fundamental difference between these forms is that they represent different models for deploying intellect, the key to hypercompetitive survival. Since the inception of administrative theory, organizational structure has been defined primarily by functional specialization, power relationships, and hierarchy. We suggest that today managers must focus instead upon how the enterprise develops and deploys intellect.

---

* Unpublished monograph, Amos Tuck School, Dartmouth College; used with the permission of the authors.

The Network Organization

At least since Burns and Stalker (1961), it has been widely agreed that organic organizational forms are better suited to turbulent environments than are mechanistic forms. However, hypercompetition is not simply turbulence. In hypercompetitive environments, firms cannot compete solely by emphasizing one advantage (e.g., cost, flexibility, or quality), and they cannot fall very far behind world-class standards on any key competitive dimension (D'Aveni, 1994). Firms must simultaneously be both efficient and flexible. In such environments, successful firms are unlikely to be purely organic—rather, they must combine both mechanistic and organic properties. This is precisely why network organizations are of such interest to scholars exploring what structures will thrive under hypercompetitive conditions. Networks seem able to achieve both efficiency and flexibility.

One group of scholars and practitioners conceives of network organizations as entities in which lateral ties are substituted for vertical ones. In this view, the formal structure will come to look more like the informal structure—employees at all levels will ignore boundaries, using information technology to locate and contact directly those individuals whose knowledge or cooperation they require. McKinsey & Co. popularized the use of the term "horizontal corporation" for such flat, boundary-less forms (Byrne, 1993), but scholars have been predicting for decades that future organizations will be much flatter than simple extrapolation from the past would suggest (e.g., Bennis and Slater, 1968).

In this view, what will replace the hierarchical department as the building block of organizations? There is no consensus answer, but many writers who conceive of the network organization in terms of lateral ties argue that cross-functional teams are emerging as the basic structural unit. . . . Another group of scholars takes a different view of network organization, stressing the replacement of command relationships by quasi-market mechanisms. . . . Both perspectives provide interesting insights. However, we contend that extremely flat designs are but one form of organization enabled by new information technologies, and we question whether cross-functional teams will serve as the universal building block of network organizations. Although quasi-market relationships lie at the core of one organizing form we analyze, we do not identify the "network organization" with a single control mechanism. We further contend that: (1) bureaucracy will not disappear; (2) hierarchy in the broadest sense—systems consisting of stably interrelated sub-assemblies—will continue to be the dominant mode of organizing; and (3) the core problem that network organization must address is the effective deployment of intellect. These contentions then lead us to an exploration of five emerging forms of network organizing that we suggest will serve as fundamental building blocks for organizations designed to cope with hypercompetition.

BUREAUCRACY

It is entirely likely that many, perhaps most, organizations will contain some highly bureaucratic subunits for the foreseeable future. The basic reason why bureaucracy will continue to prove indispensable is that under modern capitalism, goals of flexibility and efficiency must co-exist with demands for reliability, independence, or compliance. . . . Bureaucracy is an effective design for stable units whose paramount concern is consistency, accountability, and relative incrementalism. . . . We expect that organizations in hypercompetitive environments will often require some loosely coupled subunits whose bureaucratic design responds to such institutional needs.

HIERARCHY

It may well be that classic bureaucratic structure will be limited to those subunits whose principal mission is adapting the organization to institutional pressures. What then of the organizational core, charged with achieving simultaneous efficiency and flexibility? Will it consist of a flat web of teams with direct ties criss-crossing to all other teams in the organization? In hypercompetitive environments, organizations are likely to have to deal with more complex, not simpler events. Complex systems—those made up of a large number of parts that interact in a non-simple way (Simon, 1962)—are far more capable of adapting to environments which place multiple, simultaneous demands on the firm. As Simon notes, complexity very often takes the form of hierarchy, which he defines as a structure composed of interrelated subsystems that ultimately rest on a small number of fundamental building blocks. It is in this sense that we contend organizations in hypercompetitive environments will be hierarchical. Some hierarchy will clearly be necessary to resolve disputes and to allocate limited resources. Hierarchy will also survive because evolution and learning are accelerated by the existence of relatively stable organizational subassemblies containing high expertise (Simon, 1962). Learning is the fundamental challenge facing organizations under hypercompetition—the methodology for continually generating new advantages while old ones are eroded away.

NETWORKS, SPEED, AND INTELLECT

Generally, the emergence of network organization is attributed to contemporary pressures for speed and responsiveness without sacrificing efficiency. Network organizations, by combining the advantages of centralization with decentralization, are thought to overcome the classic mechanistic vs. organic dilemma. We contend that there is a more fundamental reason why some network forms of organizing hold the key to surviving in hypercompetitive environments. The basic challenge confronting the modern enterprise is the need to develop and deploy intellectual assets. The "intelligent enterprise" (Quinn, 1992) uses various network forms to bring its intellect to bear on critical problems. . . .

Driving the shift to network organizing forms is an epochal change in the nature of capitalism, from a mass-production system—where the principal source of value was capital and labor transforming materials into useful products—*toward* innovation-mediated production, where the principal component of value creation is knowledge and intellectual capabilities. Central to this transformation is the emergence of services as the critical links in a firm's value chain (Quinn, 1992). The creation and distribution of services and intangibles now accounts for over three-fourths of all economic activity, and much of this value added depends on capturing and distributing intellectual outputs to the point of their consumption or use. Even "manufacturing" firms find that service activities—like research, product design, logistics, marketing, or information management—account for most of the value added between raw materials and finished goods. . . . The shift toward services and innovation-mediated production means that firms must re-think what dominance is. Dominance is not simply a function of market share for a particular product class. In service-based enterprises, dominance means being able to bring more talent to bear on an activity critical to customers than any rival can. This occurs when (1) a company has the most effective presence in the specific service activities its segment of the market most desires, and (2) it can capture and defend some special experience or specialization benefits accruing to that activity share.

Different Organizations for Different Purposes

A complex organization often contains different units organized for different purposes with different sets of strengths and weaknesses. We suggest that "the network organization" (as that term has been used) is not a single form of organization, but embraces a complex variety of fundamentally different forms of organizing. Each represents a different model of how the firm brings intellect to bear on the challenges it faces. The firm "mixes and matches" these forms as necessary, depending on the problems with which it must cope.

TABLE 1
Outline of Five Forms of Organizing

	Infinitely Flat	Inverted	Spider's Web	Cluster	Starburst
Definition of node	Individual	Individual	Individual	Cluster	Business units
Locus of intellect	Center	Nodes	Nodes	Cluster	Center and nodes
Locus of novelty	Nodes	Nodes	Project	Project	Nodes
Mode of linkage	Center to nodes	None	Node to node	Cluster to project	Center to nodes
Source of leverage	Multiplicative	Distributive	Exponential	Additive	Synthetic
Management problems and challenges	• Lack of career path. • Need for pay based on individual performance. • Dependent on isolated professional management. • Need to maintain system flexibility.	• Loss of formal authority for line managers. • Need to simultaneously empower and control contact people at nodes.	• Need to foster communication without over-loading the system. • Managing competition across nodes.	• Individuals face dual pressures from clusters and cross-cluster teams. • Dependent on quality of leadership, breadth of training, and motivation of participants.	• Need to balance autonomy and control. • Need to generate significant resources.
Example	Brokerage firms	Hospitals	Internet	Corporate staff	Major movie studio

In the following section, we focus on five forms of organizing that have emerged from an intensive study of firms in service industries. We do not suggest that these five structures exhaust the range of possibilities. Rather, we hope to move the field beyond thinking of "the network organization" as a unitary structural form, perhaps the successor to the multi-divisional form as the dominant way of organizing an enterprise. In delineating these five forms, we first focus on what distinguishes one form from the others, what favors use of that particular form, and what the distinctive management problems are in each. Table 1 summarizes this analysis. Four intellectual dimensions most distinguish each form. These are:

▼ *Locus of intellect*, the principal domain(s) within the organization where deep knowledge of its fundamental disciplines reside(s).

▼ *Locus of novelty*, the principal location(s) at which intellect is converted to novel solutions.

▼ *Mode of linkage*, the direction of flow of information and how the locus of intellect and the locus of novelty are connected.

▼ *Source of leverage*, how the enterprise leverages its know-how base.

THE "INFINITELY" FLAT ORGANIZATION

In infinitely flat organizations—so called because there is no inherent limit to their span—the primary locus of intellect is the center of the organization. The central point of the network contains a highly specialized form of intellect; for example, the operations knowledge of a fast food franchising organization or the huge body of data and analysis possessed by a brokerage firm. Each node becomes the locus of novelty, the point at which the center's know-how is applied to customer problems. Know-how flows principally in a one-way direction, from the center to the nodes. Here, the source of leverage is multiplicative. There appears to be virtually no limit to the number of nodes that can be linked directly to a center, through which an organization can effectively make analyzed knowledge about the outside world useful and the *cumulative* experience curve of its many nodes available to each individual node. Single centers in such organizations have been observed to coordinate

FIGURE 1
The Infinitely Flat
Organization

20 ——→ 40 ——→ 100 ——→ 400 ——→ ∞

anywhere from 20 to 18,000 individual nodes. Common examples could include highly dispersed fast food, brokerage, airlines, shipping, or mail order operations.

In this organizing form, few orders for direct action are given by the line organization to those below. The nodes themselves rarely need to communicate with one another and can operate quite independently. Instead, the central authority usually becomes an information source, a communications coordinator, or a reference desk for unusual inquiries. Lower organizational levels generally connect into it to obtain information for the purpose of performing better, rather than for instructions or specific guidance. Rules are often programmed into the system and changed automatically by software, and many operations are monitored electronically.

For example, Merrill Lynch's more than 450 domestic brokerage offices each connect directly into their parents' central information offices for routine needs, yet can bypass the electronic system to gain personal access to individual experts in headquarters. Merrill Lynch has a PC-based workstation for each of its "financial consultants" (brokers) linked through local area networks and SNA connections to its central mainframe computers. Although regional marketing structures exist, business is conducted as if each of Merrill Lynch's 17,000-odd branch office contact people reported directly to headquarters, with their only personal oversight being at the local level. Computers extend Merrill Lynch's system capabilities to the level of individual customers, printing 400 million pages of output a year, largely customer reports captured directly from on-line transaction data. In effect, technology permits the company to compete in a coordinated fashion with the full power and scale economies of a major financial enterprise, yet local brokers can manage their own small units and accounts as independently as if they alone provided the total service on a local basis. From an operations viewpoint, the organization is absolutely flat; 17,000 brokers connect directly into headquarters for all their needs.

Infinitely flat organizations operate best when the activity at the node can be broken down and measured to the level of its minimum repeatable transaction elements; for example, cooking and operations procedures in fast food chains or the basic components of a financial transaction in a widely dispersed brokerage network. Response times can be nearly instantaneous, and within the programmed rules such organizations can accommodate high levels of empowerment and personalized sales behavior. Infinitely flat organizations can be established to support any degree of decentralized authority or responsibility desired. . . .

Infinitely flat organizations function well when each node is totally independent of other nodes. Managers residing at the center are often the most highly skilled professionals—e.g., investment analysts or logistics planners. The value they add stems from their ability to collect information from all internal and external sources, and to analyze and present relevant information to the nodes. Under proper circumstances, the electronic systems of infinitely flat organizations capture the experience curve of the organization, allowing less-trained people quickly to achieve levels of performance ordinarily associated with much more experienced personnel. Because quality and productivity can be monitored at the point of customer contact, well-designed systems simultaneously offer *both* highest responsiveness and maximum efficiencies. This allows firms to function in hypercompetitive environments, where firms configured to follow a single "generic" strategy (e.g., low cost or differentiation) would fail.

The infinitely flat organization presents certain inherent management problems. Perhaps the most severe is that in the absence of hierarchy, lower-level personnel wonder how to advance in a career path. In addition, under infinitely flat conditions traditional (e.g., "Hay point") systems of compensation break down, and new compensation systems based upon individual performance become extremely important. Reward systems may include a great variety of titles and intangible rewards, in addition to financial rewards for people at the nodes.

A second problem is that it is very difficult to train management coordinators in these systems. There is little opportunity to transfer personnel from the nodes to the center because the tasks are too different; indeed, the professionalism and analytical depth characteristic of the center may be incompatible with the more personalized service demands placed on people at the nodes.

Third, the information system must achieve a series of delicate balances. Measurement systems must capture both the quantitative and the intangible aspects of operations, or work at the nodes can become dehumanized. This usually means that electronic systems must be supplemented by customer sampling or personal observation systems. There is a tendency for systems to rigidify with time, if companies continue to use the same measurement and control systems over long periods. Consequently, internal systems must typically be bolstered by an external scanning system that forces the entire organization to adapt to environmental changes. In addition to the structured "hard information" linkages of the infinitely flat line organization, there frequently needs to be a team or cluster organization that conveys intangible information (e.g., values) from the center to the nodes, trains individuals in new tasks, and provides a level of professionalism the nodes lack when confronted with challenges such as public relations crises or the installation of new marketing concepts—as the specialized technology training or marketing teams of Merrill Lynch do.

THE INVERTED ORGANIZATION

In this form, the major locus of intellect is the nodes contacting customers, not the center. Hospitals or medical clinics, therapeutic care-giving units, or consulting engineering firms provide examples of such situations. The point of novelty creation is also at the node, typically because this is where a service is uniquely adapted and delivered to a customer. The nodes tend to be professional and self-sufficient. Accordingly, there is no direct linkage for routinely moving intellect from one point to another. The loci of intellect and novelty creation are the same points. When critical know-how diffuses, it usually does so informally from node to node—or formally from node to center—the opposite of the infinitely flat organization. The leverage of this form of organization is distributive. The role of the support structure is to provide logistics or specially requested support to the nodes and to relieve them of administrative detail. The center can also serve as a repository accessing new information from the outside and facilitating the acquisition of know-how from a limited number of other nodes through special interconnections, such as seminars or similar updating techniques.

In inverted organizations, the line hierarchy becomes a "support" structure instead of an "order-giving" structure. For example, the hospital CEO does not give orders to doctors, nor does the chief pilot give orders to airline pilots except in extreme emergencies. Hierarchy continues to exist because neither the CEO (in the hospital example) nor the chief pilot (in the airline example) can work for each individual contact person at the same time. The function of line managers becomes bottleneck breaking, culture development, communication of values, developing special studies and consulting upon request, expediting resource movements, and providing service economies of scale. Division of labor and hierarchy facilitate the ability of different managers to support contact personnel as needed—what was line management now performs essentially "staff" activities.

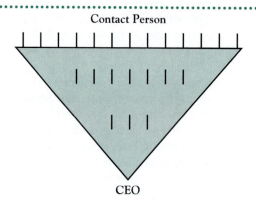

FIGURE 2
The Inverted
Organization

A well known example of the inverted organization is NovaCare, the largest provider of rehabilitation care in the U.S. and one of the fastest growing health care companies of the last decade. Its central resource—well trained physical, occupational, and speech therapists—are in short supply. NovaCare provides the business infrastructure for over 4,000 therapists, arranging contracts with nursing homes and chains, handling accounting and credit activities, providing training updates, and stabilizing and enhancing the therapists' earnings. The key to the business is the therapists and the quality of their service. The rest of the organization is consciously set up to support them and to solve problems for them. Executives, including the CEO, refer to therapists as "my bosses" and are judged on how well they respond to orders from the therapists, who—though well trained as caregivers— were not trained for and often disliked the business side of their activities. Electronic planning and monitoring systems allow the therapists to perform efficiently in very dispersed locations and accurately meet the constantly changing requirements of regulatory bodies, the profession, and payer groups.

The inverted organization works well when servicing the customer at the point of contact is the most important activity in the enterprise, *and* the person at the point of contact has more information about the individual customer's problem and its potential solutions than anyone else. Quite often this form is restricted to only certain units in direct contact with customers; however, in some intellectual aristocracies, such as law firms, medical clinics, or colleges, the inverted organization may pervade virtually all departments. Experience suggests that because they present unique problems, inverted organizations should be used sparingly, and not as "gimmicks" to improve empowerment. Their proper functioning depends on the genuinely superior knowledge of the contact people. Nevertheless, members of the line hierarchy retain substantive roles, particularly as analysts of special issues and arbiters of last resort. They also often enjoy greatly expanded opportunities to perform more influential long term activities (such as resource building or public policy participation) once freed of traditional routing burdens.

The inverted organization presents management with both people and systems challenges. The loss of formal authority can be very traumatic for line managers. Additionally, this form depends on continuous professional training for contact people, great attention to personnel selection, and reinforcement of consistent organizational values. Given acknowledged formal power, point people may tend to act ever more like specialists with strictly "professional" outlooks, and resist any set of organization rules or business norms. It is difficult for contact people—particularly those who must serve a diverse customer mix—to internalize or stay current with sufficient details concerning the firm's own complex internal systems. Empowerment of contact personnel without adequate control can be extremely dangerous (consider, for instance, the case of People Express). Therefore, very powerful information systems and constant reinforcement of operating norms are required to support inverted organizations.

THE "SPIDER'S WEB" ORGANIZATION

This form of organization is a true network; to avoid confusion with other "network-like" forms (particularly those which are more akin to matrix organizations), we use the term "spider's web" as its descriptor. Often there is no intervening hierarchy or order giving center between the nodes of these organizations. The locus of intellect is highly dispersed, residing largely at the contact nodes as in the inverted organization. However, the point of novelty is a project or a problem that requires nodes to interact intimately or to seek others who happen to have knowledge or special capabilities they need. The organization's know-how is essentially latent, until a project forces it to materialize through connections people make with each other. Information linkages are quite complex; know-how is moved from many nodes to many other nodes, which typically collaborate temporarily in delivering a service as part of a project. The source of leverage is exponential—as defined by interactive learning theory or network theory. With even a modest number of collaborating nodes (8 to 10), the number of connections through which knowledge may be created rapidly mounts into the hundreds or thousands.

Spider's web organizations emerge when highly dispersed nodes each contain a high level of specialized intellect, yet for client effectiveness must interact with each other directly and frequently. The nodes may have no hierarchical relationship to each other, and linkages are often activated solely on a voluntary basis. Individual nodes would operate independently if it were not essential to capture information economies of scale or scope. If there is a decision center, authority interactions tend to occur through ad hoc committees or task forces. Occasionally, individual nodes may need to operate in such a highly coordinated fashion that they delegate temporary authority to a project leader—as when widely dispersed researchers present a contract proposal or an investment banking consortium services a multinational client. The purest example of a spider's web organization is the Internet, the use of which is managed by no one. Using Internet, researchers may interact with other scientists around the world as collaborators working on particular segments of a problem, with little more than a goal, personal integrity, and professional discipline to provide cohesion. Other common examples include most open markets, security exchanges, library consortia, and political action groups.

Although spider's web networks have existed for centuries (among universities or scientists, and within trading groups), they enjoy selective advantages in hypercompetitive

FIGURE 3
The "Spider's Web"
Organization

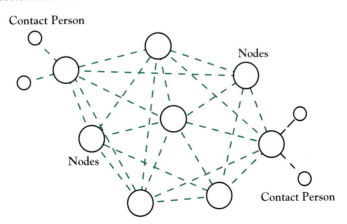

environments because they can simultaneously accommodate high specialization, multiple geographic locations, and a disciplined focus on a single problem or customer set. They are particularly useful in identifying or analyzing problems where customer sets are dispersed and highly diverse specialties need to be tapped. . . .Despite their many benefits, spider's webs present important challenges to managers. The dominant necessity is creating a culture for communication and willing sharing, since how one communicates and what one is willing to communicate are as important as the knowledge the nodes contain. Unfortunately, clearing these hurdles may bring on a host of other problems. Extreme overload can emerge as networks become jammed with trivia, but resist screening and sorting mechanisms. Dawdling is common, as nodes work on refining their specialist solutions instead of solving the complete problem together. Assigning credit for intellectual contributions is difficult, and cross-competition among nodes can inhibit the sharing upon which such networks depend. Appropriate incentives at both the network and local levels are essential.

THE CLUSTER ORGANIZATION

The cluster organization superficially resembles the spider's web, because the mode of know-how transport is once again from node to node. However, the locus of intellect lies in loosely formed clusters, which normally carry out some relatively permanent activity (such as staff analyses, long-term technical innovation, or customer relationships) requiring deep competence in specific disciplines (Mills, 1991). Within clusters people may form and reform into smaller teams to solve specific problems that are central to the cluster's own success. Members of clusters tend to be in close proximity most of the time, working on related problems. Occasionally, when the enterprise encounters tasks that call for a mix of skills, temporary teams are pulled together from the specialized clusters. The team is not a permanent unit; it is a temporary overlay on other organizing processes. However, the existence of cross-functional teams is not itself the defining characteristic of a cluster organization. Its essence lies in the fact that team members are cross-trained to help with enterprise-wide tasks, but spend most of their time in clusters of people who handle useful daily problems for the enterprise while they continue to build depth in their particular specialty.

In the spider's web network organization, projects generate knowledge via interaction. In the cluster organization, specialized units create knowledge; teams tend to assemble preexisting expertise into a larger package—e.g., to acquire a company or create an alliance of interest to the whole enterprise. The point of novelty occurs when a cross-cluster team must be formed to address a problem, and the mode of transport is from cluster to team. Unlike many spider's webs organizations, there is usually a clear decision making authority designated by the enterprise to head the task group. The source of leverage for clusters is additive; teams generally package together the sum of the clusters' know-how. When the packaging and delivery are complete, team members return to their primary tasks of building specialized know-how within a cluster and performing the routine tasks of that cluster, which also may involve some teaming of specialists within the cluster.

Clusters are effective when tasks that affect the whole enterprise (e.g., mergers, acquisitions, or new ventures) temporarily require deep knowledge beyond the bounds of any individual's or group's know-how. Specialization is required, but problems are so diverse that no one functional specialty can cope with them alone. Such organizations exploit scale economies when clusters are stably occupied with a base load of common activity; the effect is greater when skills for certain problem classes can be centralized geographically. Functional organization proves inadequate because the incidence of novel, cross-specialty problem solving is high both within and across clusters. Clusters do not function as well when activities are geographically dispersed or are routinized.

FIGURE 4
The Cluster Organization
(adapted from Mills, 1991)

NovaCare is a case in point. When NovaCare is acquiring or building a new hospital or therapeutic care system, it pulls together a task force of therapists, planners, software, accounting and finance, marketing, regional, facilities, and general management personnel who have worked together on similar projects in the past. When the project is over, team members return to their home base, where they both diffuse specific knowledge from the project and work on smaller teams developing some aspect of therapy management in depth.

The characteristic management problem of a cluster organization is that members perceive a tension between demands to build deep, cluster-specific competence to serve their normal clientele and pressures to contribute to cross-cluster teams. The effectiveness of these organizations is dependent on breadth of training and their ability to motivate team contributions external to the cluster. Assignment, not voluntarism, is common for cross-cluster teams—posing the usual problems of equity, identity, and reentry to the cluster. Commonly, employees take several years to become acculturated to the dual pressures cluster organizations create.

THE STARBURST ORGANIZATION

The four organizing forms described above tend to function well as long as they are not required to address standing, yet very diverse sets of external customer needs. Where markets are very diverse, one may observe a special kind of network organizing form, the starburst. The starburst organization is technically an inter-organizational network, but for special reasons the organizational units are under some shared ownership. Starburst organizations are usually creative organizations that constantly peel off more permanent, but separate, units from the core competencies of their parents, like shooting stars. Spin-off subsidiaries remain partially or wholly owned by the parent, usually can raise external resources independently, and are controlled primarily via market mechanisms. Examples of different forms of starburst organizations and their ownership relationships include movie studios, Raychem, Nypro, TechComm Group (TCG), Thermo Electron, Vanguard (mutual funds), and venture capitalists. Starburst forms are associated with strong internal corporate venturing strategies (Block and MacMillan, 1993).

In this form of organization, the locus of intellect is divided. Typically, the center retains deep knowledge of some common technology or knowledge base (e.g., specialized plastic molding technology for Nypro, managing no-load funds for Vanguard). The center is a core of intellectual competency, not simply a corporate bank as in the case of holding companies. The nodes—which are essentially separate business units, not individuals or temporary clusters—are the locus of specialized market and production knowledge. They are also the locus of novelty—as either the center or a developed node organization encounters a promising new domain, it establishes a subsidiary to apply that parent's core competencies to the new set of market opportunities. The movement of intellect is typically from the center outward toward the nodes—each node draws upon the core technical know-how of the more central units, but the center does not attempt to amalgamate the diverse market knowledge of its subsidiaries. The organization rarely transfers market

FIGURE 5
The Starburst Organization

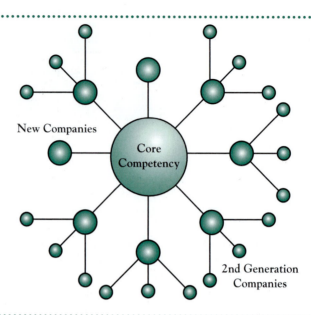

New Companies

Core Competency

2nd Generation Companies

knowledge from one node laterally to another, since each node faces such different market needs. The primary source of leverage is synthetic—the firm uses local application knowledge to amplify effects from its "core competency" knowledge base. In many cases, it further leverages through outside groups the special financial or expertise access the nodes can enjoy as independent bodies.

Starburst organizations differ from conglomerates because they maintain a cohesive intellectual competency center—usually some technological or high professional skills. The center is maintained, and recharged to develop new pulses, by charging the market units a fee. In return the nodes enjoy the economies of scale and new opportunities that a large, integrated knowledge base can provide. The corporate center primarily helps raise resources, invests in maintaining the core competency, manages the culture, and sets priorities by selecting people and letting them bid for resources.

Starburst organizations work well when the core is dominated by a few knowledgeable risk-takers who know they cannot micro-manage the diverse entities in the nodes. The appropriate environment for this sort of firm is one in which entrepreneurship, not merely flexible response, is critical. For example, venture capital firms and movie studios typically operate as starbursts because they need a continuing core of creative financial and management skills, supplemented by the capacity to attract and employ a combination of risk-taking and specialized talent for each venture. The starburst organization works well in very ambiguous environments where it is difficult to associate actions with outcomes in the absence of a market test.

The classic problem of this organizational form is that management often loses faith in free-standing "shooting stars" after some time and tries to consolidate functions in the name of efficiency—as Hewlett Packard did to its regret (but later solved by reversing its policies). However, the nodes are so different that even sophisticated computer systems cannot provide or coordinate all the information needed to run such firms from the center; rather than try, managers must either live with quasi-market control or spin off the subsidiary entirely. A second difficulty faced by starburst organizations is that when heavy investment is required to achieve mass production, the starburst may find it difficult to assemble the requisite resources without over-taxing its core or some of its units. For this reason, starburst organizations tend to work best for smaller scale, lower investment, opportunities.

Polymorphism

In emphasizing that these are forms of organizing instead of organizational forms, we suggest that organizations in the face of hypercompetition will typically be polymorphic. Like NovaCare, they will include as basic building blocks some very disparate ways of organizing networks. Additionally, at least some of their components are likely to be organized bureaucratically, in response to institutional pressures or a need to provide deeply knowledgeable centers of specialized professional skills. . . .

Although NovaCare has an inverted structure for delivering its physical, occupational, and speech therapies through its 4000 professional therapists nationwide, it supports these therapists through NovaNet, which keeps track of all therapists' activities in 15 minute "units" of detail. Detailed data from within those units are used for scheduling, compensation, billing, and follow up for all therapies. Through these data NovaCare can ensure that all its customers (patients, nursing homes, hospitals, hospital directors, doctors, nursing directors, payers, and regulating bodies) are properly served, charged, and compensated in appropriate fashion. Yet within the company there are centralized functional (accounting), cluster (acquisitions), geographical hierarchical (hospital), inverted (therapy), and spider's web (professional knowledge exchange) structures. . . .

Since polymorphic organizations are likely to include several of these new forms of organizing as subassemblies, a key challenge for top management will be integrating these disparate structures into an intelligent enterprise. Software systems predicated on traditional programming principles point toward some ways in which such integration is likely to be achieved, but only hint at the power that a new paradigm is bringing to the problem of deploying the firm's accumulated know-how. The increasing power of information technology does much more than flatten organizations. It also permits organizations to integrate polymorphic forms in ways that would not have been possible a few years ago. As environments become more hypercompetitive, we expect firms to move along a continuum whose endpoints range from no central coordination (spider's web) to total coordination through software (as automated order processing systems now do). A key supporting force in this evolution is the emergence of a new paradigm in software design, "object orientation." Since the concept of programming was invented by Von Neumann and his associates, the fundamental unit of a program has been a line of code. However, in the future the fundamental building blocks of programs will probably be "objects," integrated packets of data with built-in instructions for manipulating them.

The hallmark of the object approach is that it moves away from the notion that the organization's intellect consists of a body of data that are manipulated through various algorithms. Under the object-oriented approach, managers model real-world business processes in terms of pre-packaged data "objects" which can then be used ubiquitously in many specialized operating models. The impact of object-oriented programming techniques—and their rapidly developing companion, parallel processing—upon the intelligent enterprise is significant. First, more than ever an organization's intellect will be embodied in its information systems, particularly its software. Until recently, the organization's collective knowledge and experience constituted a pool of objects with their associated rules for manipulation and the interacting models governing each of its operations. The organization's data systems will contain the essence of its way of viewing the world and its competitive capabilities. Second, object-oriented systems will not only facilitate but render imperative the process of learning from highly decentralized experience. The essence of the new paradigm is flexible re-usability, continuously creating new programs from the basic building blocks of previous ones. Those firms which develop the most effective data collection systems and dynamic models about what they know will be able to outpace firms whose data and models are less robust and less representative of their experience.

CONCLUSION

We wish to close by emphasizing that our purpose is to stimulate debate, not to foreclose it. We do not contend that what we have presented are the only five forms of organizing that exist, or that we have captured all the richness of how these forms operate. Both managers and scholars will benefit from research that tells us more about the alternatives to traditional organizations that are emerging under hypercompetitive conditions.

▼ READING 6.4   COLLABORATING TO COMPETE*

by Joel Bleeke and David Ernst

For most global businesses, the days of flat-out, predatory competition are over. The traditional drive to pit one company against the rest of an industry, to pit supplier against supplier, distributor against distributor, on and on through every aspect of a business no longer guarantees the lowest cost, best products or services, or highest profits for winners of this Darwinian game. In businesses as diverse as pharmaceuticals, jet engines, banking, and computers, managers have learned that fighting long, head-to-head battles leaves their companies financially exhausted, intellectually depleted, and vulnerable to the next wave of competition and innovation.

In place of predation, many multinational companies are learning that they must collaborate to compete. Multinationals can create highest value for customers and stakeholders by selectively sharing and trading control, costs, capital, access to markets, information, and technology with competitors and suppliers alike. Competition does not vanish. The computer and commercial aircraft markets are still brutally competitive.

Instead of competing blindly, companies should increasingly compete only in those precise areas where they have a durable advantage or where participation is necessary to preserve industry power or capture value. In packaged goods, that power comes from controlling distribution; in pharmaceuticals, having blockbuster drugs and access to doctors. Managers are beginning to see that many necessary elements of a global business are so costly (like R&D in semiconductors), so generic (like assembly), or so impenetrable (like some of the Asian markets) that it makes no sense to have a traditional competitive stance. The best approach is to find partners that already have the cash, scale, skills, or access you seek.

When a company reaches across borders, its ability and willingness to collaborate is the best predictor of success. The more equal the partnership, the brighter its future. This means that both partners must be strong financially and in the product or function that they bring to the venture. Of 49 alliances that we examined in detail, two thirds of those between equally matched strong partners succeeded, while about 60% of those involving unequal partners failed. So, too, with ownership. Fifty-fifty partnerships had the highest rate of success of any deal structure that we have examined.

THREE THEMES

The need for better understanding of cross-border alliances and acquisitions is increasingly clear. Cross-border linkages are booming, driven by globalization, Europe 1992, the opening of Eastern European and Asian markets, and an increased need for foreign sales to cover the large fixed costs of playing in high-technology businesses. Go-it-alone strategies often take too long, cost too much, or fail to provide insider access to markets. Yet, large numbers of strategic alliances and cross-border acquisitions are failing. When we examined the cross-

---

* Excerpted from "Collaborating to Compete," *Directors and Boards* (Winter, 1994); used with the permission of McKinsey & Company.

border alliances and acquisitions of the largest 150 companies in the United States, Europe, and Japan, we found that only half of these linkages succeed. The average life expectancy for most alliances is approximately seven years. Common lessons from the wide experience of many companies in cross-border strategies are beginning to emerge.

In general, three themes emerge from our studies of alliances:

▼ First, as we have mentioned, companies are learning that they must collaborate to compete. This requires different measurements of "success" from those used for traditional competition.

▼ Second, alliances between companies that are potential competitors represent an arbitrage of skills, market access, and capital between the companies. Maintaining a fair balance in this arbitrage is essential for success.

▼ Third, it is important for managers to develop a vision of international strategy and to see cross-border acquisitions and alliances as a flexible sequence of actions—not one-off deals driven by temporary competitive or financial benefit. The remainder of this article discusses each of these three themes in more detail. . . .

Old measures such as financial hurdles and strategic goals only have meaning in the new context of collaboration. As markets become increasingly competitive, managers are beginning to measure success based on the scarcest resources, including skills and access, not only capital. In the global marketplace, maximizing the value of skills and access can often be achieved only if managers are willing to share ownership with and learn from companies much *different* from their own. Success increasingly comes in proportion to a company's willingness to accept differences.

Successful collaboration also requires flexibility. Most alliances that endure are redefined in terms of geographic or product scope. The success rate for alliances that have changed their scope over time is more than twice that of alliances where the scope has not evolved. Alliances with legal or financial structures that do not permit change are nearly certain to fail. (See Figure 1 which gives Kenichi Ohmae's Tips for Collaboration.)

ALLIANCES AS ARBITRAGE

If all markets were equally accessible, all management equally skilled, all information readily available, and all balance sheets equally solid, there would be little need for collaboration among competitors. But they are not, so companies increasingly benefit by trading these "chips" across borders.

The global arbitrage reflected in cross-border alliances and acquisitions takes place at a slower pace than in capital markets, but the mechanism is similar. Each player uses the quirks, irrational differences, and inefficiencies in the marketplace as well as each company's advantages to mutual benefit. This concept applies mostly to alliances, but cross-border acquisitions can also be viewed as an extreme example of arbitrage: all cash or shares from the buyer, for all the skills, products, and access of the other company. . . .

Successful alliance partners follow several patterns in handling the inherent tensions of arbitrating with potential competitors. To begin with, they approach the negotiation phase with a win-win situation. As one executive said, "Do not sit down to negotiate a deal—build links between the companies."

Successful partners also build in conflict-resolution mechanisms such as powerful boards of directors (for joint ventures) and frequent communication between top management of the parent companies and the alliance. The CEOs of the parent companies need to be absolutely clear on where cooperation is expected and where the "old rules" of competition will apply.

FIGURE 1
Kenichi Ohmae's Tips for Collaboration

1. Treat the collaboration as a personal commitment. It's people that make partnerships work.

2. Anticipate that it will take up management time. If you can't spare the time, don't start it.

3. Mutual respect and trust are essential. If you don't trust the people you are negotiating with, forget it.

4. Remember that both partners must get something out of it (money, eventually). Mutual benefit is vital. This will probably mean you've got to give something up. Recognize this from the outset.

5. Make sure you tie up a tight legal contract. Don't put off resolving unpleasant or contentious issues until "later." Once signed, however, the contract should be put away. If you refer to it, something is wrong with the relationship.

6. Recognize that during the course of a collaboration, circumstances and markets change. Recognize your partner's problems and be flexible.

7. Make sure that you and your partner have mutual expectations of the collaboration and its time scale. One happy and one unhappy partner is a formula for failure.

8. Get to know your opposite numbers at all levels socially. Friends take longer to fall out.

9. Appreciate that cultures — both geographic and corporate — are different. Don't expect a partner to act or respond identically to you. Find out the true reason for a particular response.

10. Recognize your partner's interests and independence.

11. Even if the arrangement is tactical in your eyes, make sure you have corporate approval. Your tactical activity may be a key piece in an overall strategic jigsaw puzzle. With corporate commitment to the partnership, you can act with the positive authority needed in these relationships.

12. Celebrate achievement together. It's a shared elation, and you'll have earned it!

Postscript

Two further things to bear in mind:

1. If you're negotiating a product original equipment manufacturer (OEM) deal, look for a quid pro quo. Remember that another product may offer more in return.

2. Joint development agreements must include joint marketing arrangements. You need the largest market possible to recover development costs and to get volume/margin benefits.

— Kenichi Ohmae

Kenichi Ohmae is Chairman of McKinsey & Co.'s offices in Japan.

In approaching alliances as arbitrage, managers should recognize that the value of "chips" is likely to change over time. The key is to maximize your bargaining power—that is, the value of your company's contribution to the alliance—while also being ready to renegotiate the alliance as necessary. Some of the best alliances have had built-in timetables for assessing partner contributions and clear rules for valuing the contributions going forward.

A SEQUENCE OF ACTIONS

Beyond the themes of collaboration and arbitrage involved in individual deals, cross-border alliances and acquisitions need to be viewed as a *sequence* of actions in the context of overall international strategy—not as one-off transactions. Companies that take a purely financial, deal-driven approach to cross-border alliances and acquisitions usually wind up in trouble.

Looking at cross-border M&A [mergers and acquisitions], the most successful companies make a series of acquisitions that build presence in core businesses over time in the target country. One consumer goods company, for example, made an "anchor" acquisition of a leading brand to establish a solid presence in an important European market, then used its enhanced distribution clout to ensure the acceptance of several brands that were subsequently acquired.

In our study of the cross-border acquisition programs of the largest Triad companies [Asia, Europe, North America], successful acquirers had nearly twice the average and median number of purchases as unsuccessful companies. Through initial acquisitions, the acquirer refines M&A skills and becomes more comfortable with, and proficient at, using M&A for international expansion. And by completing a sequence of transactions, particularly in the same geography, it is possible to gain economies through integrating operations and eliminating overlapping functions.

WILLINGNESS TO RETHINK

It is important to think about cross-border alliances, as well as acquisitions, as a part of a sequence of actions. Most alliances evolve over time, so the initial charter and contract often are not meaningful within a few years. Since trouble is the rule, not the exception, and since two thirds of all cross-border alliances run into management trouble during the first few years, alliances require a willingness by partners to rethink their situation on a constant basis—and renegotiate as necessary.

Alliances should usually be considered as an intermediate strategic device that needs other transactions surrounding it. Approximately half of all cross-border alliances terminate within seven years, so it is critical that managers have a point of view early on of "what's next?"

Most terminating alliances are purchased by one of the partners, and termination need not mean failure. But the high rate of termination suggests that both parties should think hard early on about likely roles as a buyer or seller—the probabilities are high that alliance partners eventually will be one or the other.

The companies that can bring the largest short-term synergies to an alliance are often those companies that will most likely be direct competitors in the long term. So, if the desired sequence of management action does not include selling the business, a different, more complementary partner may need to be found at the outset. Understanding the probable sequence of transactions is therefore important in selecting even early alliance of acquisition partners. As our colleagues in Japan remind us, nothing is worse in cross-border alliances or acquisitions than to have "partners in the same bed with different dreams."

POSTSCRIPT: A LOOK AHEAD

Global corporations of the future will be rather like amoebas. This single-celled aquatic animal is among the most ancient life-forms on earth. It gets all its nourishment directly from its environment through its permeable outer walls. These walls define the creature as distinct from its environment, but allow much of what is inside to flow out and much of what is outside to come in. The amoeba is always changing shape, taking and giving with the surroundings, yet it always retains its integrity and identity as a unique creature.

To be truly global and not merely "big," organizations of the future must hold this permeability as one of their highest values. When managers enter a new market, they should first ask these questions: "How is business here different? What do I need to learn?" They have to seek partners that can share costs and swap skills and access to markets. In the fluid global marketplace, it is no longer possible or desirable for single organizations to be entirely self-sufficient. Collaboration is the value of the future. Alliances are the structure of the future.

This has enormous impact on corporate strategy. It makes the world very complex, because there is no single valid rule book for all markets. As our studies have demonstrated, alliances are based on arbitrating the unique differences between markets and partners. And so it is impossible to standardize an approach to the topic. Managers at the corporate center must be able to tolerate and in fact encourage variation: 10 different markets, 10 different partners, 10 different organization charts, 10 reporting systems, and so on. Policies and procedures must be fluid. The word *schizophrenia* has negative connotations, but it captures this idea that truly global organization must entertain two seemingly contradictory aspects—a strong identity, along with an openness to different ways of doing business, to the values of different cultures and localities.

This duality is going to be very difficult for many of the "global" companies of today. Companies with a sales-based culture, where senior executives all come from a sales background, will have a particularly hard time adapting to this new collaborative world. Such companies see the world as "us and them." They reject ideas from the outside world, even if the concept is helpful. They find it hard to live without standardization. They find it hard to collaborate with partners. Deep down, they are trying to convert everyone to their own way of doing things.

This makes them inflexible and confrontational. They don't know how to communicate and work with the outside world on its own terms. They cannot be like the amoeba, with its permeable walls and changing shape, its openness to take from every environment. These companies may survive because they are large and powerful, but they will cease to be leaders.

DEALING WITH CULTURE AND POWER

Culture arrived on the management scene in the 1980s like a typhoon blowing from the Far East. It suddenly became fashionable in consulting circles to sell culture like some article of organizational clothing, much as "management by objectives" or "total information systems" were once sold. Power, in contrast, was always there, lurking in the background if not driving itself into the foreground. Yet the two represent different sides of the same coin in some respect—the centripetal forces that draw organizations together and the centrifugal force that can drive them apart. While power focuses on self-interest and the building of one's power base through individual initiative, culture concentrates on the collective interest and the building of a unified organization, through shared systems, beliefs, habits, and traditions. Hence, we combine culture and power in this chapter.

What gave culture its impetus was Peters and Waterman's book *In Search of Excellence* (1982). This depicted successful organizations as being rich in culture—permeated with strong and sustaining systems of beliefs. In our view—as in theirs—culture is not an article of fashion, but an intrinsic part of a deeper organizational "character." To draw on definitions introduced earlier, strategy is not just an arbitrarily chosen *position*, nor an analytically developed *plan*, but a deeply entrenched *perspective* which influences the way an organization develops new ideas, considers and weighs options, and responds to changes in its environment.

Culture thus permeates many critical aspects of strategy making. But perhaps the most crucial realm is the way people are chosen, developed, nurtured, interrelated, and rewarded in the organization. The kinds of people attracted to an organization and the way they can most effectively deal with problems and each other are largely a function of the culture a place builds—and the practices and systems which support it.

In some organizations, the culture may become so strong that it is best referred to as an "ideology" that dominates all else—as in the "missionary" configuration introduced in the Mintzberg reading on structure in Chapter 6. But culture is generally an influencing force in all organizations, and so it is appropriately considered in this book as an element of organization, alongside structure, systems, and power.

The first reading, drawn originally from two chapters of Mintzberg's book, *Power in and Around Organizations*, focuses on rich cultures—ideologies—and how these may promote "excellence" in certain situations. (Later we shall consider how culture and ideology can discourage excellence by making organizations resistant to strategic change.) It traces how ideologies evolve through three stages: their rooting in a sense of mission, their development through tradition and sagas, and their reinforcement through various forms of identifications. Mintzberg then briefly considers the missionary type organization and shows how other organizations, for example, regular business firms, sometimes overlay rich cultures on their more conventional ways of operating.

Our second reading, by Christopher Bartlett of the Harvard Business School and Sumantra Ghoshal of the London Business School, takes structure and considers it in a human sense—how to build it into the minds of managers. In that sense, the reading is really about culture—in their terms, about "building a shared vision" and developing people through recruitment and selection, training and development, and career-path management. These authors present a biological metaphor in which formal structure represents the organization's anatomy, while the interpersonal relationships and management processes are its physiology, and a shared vision together with a set of common norms and values are its psychology. They argue that to build organizational capability, large global firms must look beyond structure to vision, values, and processes.

In virtually all of the cases, culture is an important element of analysis. It provides support for some solutions, constraints for others. In some cases such as Genetech, Inc. (B), Intel Corporation, Microsoft Corporation (B), TCG, Ltd./Thermo Electron, The Hewlett Packard Company, Matsushita Electric Industrial Company 1994, Sony Corporation: Innovation System, Edward Marshall Boehm, Inc., NovaCare, Inc., or Anderson Consulting (Europe), culture is a critical strategic weapon and indeed determines the strategy to a large extent. Observations of such companies have led to the concept of "value-based strategies" which are extremely useful in many hypercompetitive, innovation-based, and professional/service environments.

Up to this point, the ideas and concepts we have presented in the book, for the most part, have a functionalist orientation in which organizations are viewed as rather rational and cooperative instruments. Strategies, whether formulated analytically or allowed to emerge in some kind of a learning process, nonetheless serve the good of the organization at large, as do the associated structures, systems, and cultures. True Quinn and Wrapp managers, for example, have consciously considered and dealt with potential resistance in creating and implanting their strategies. In doing so, they may have been forced to think in political terms. But the overt use of power and organized political action has largely been absent from our discussion.

An important group of thinkers in the field, however, have come to view the strategy process as an interplay of the forces of power, sometimes highly politicized. Rather than assuming that organizations are consistent, coherent, and cooperative systems, tightly integrated to pursue certain traditional ends (namely the delivery of their products and services in the pursuit of profit, at least in the private sector), these writers start with quite different premises. They believe that organizations' goals and directions are determined primarily by the power needs of those who populate them. Their analyses raise all kinds of interesting and unsettled questions, such as: For whom does the organization really exist? For what purposes? If the organization is truly a political entity, how does one manage effectively in it? And so on.

One work in the literature that sets this into perspective is the famous study of the United States' response to the Cuban Missile Crisis by Graham Allison (1971) of Harvard's Kennedy School of Government. Allison believed that our conception of how decision making proceeds in organizations can be considered from three perspectives: a "rational actor" model (which is the concept he believed the American leaders had of the Soviets), an "organizations process" model, and a "bureaucratic politics" model (both of which Allison thought could have been used as well to improve America's understanding of the Soviets' behavior). In the first model, power is embedded in a relatively rational and calculating center of strategy making as was described in Chapters 3 and 4. In the second, it is entrenched in various organizational departments, each using power to further its own particular purposes. In the third model, "politics" comes into full play as individuals and groups exercise their influence to determine outcomes for their own benefits.

Our third reading focuses especially on the third model, also incorporating aspects of the second. In parallel with Mintzberg's earlier reading in this chapter (and likewise based on two related chapters of his *Power In and Around Organizations* book), it considers first the general force of politics in organizations, what it is and what political "games" people play in organizations, and the various forms taken by organizations that are dominated by such politics, the extreme one labeled the "political arena." This reading concludes with a discussion of when and why politics sometimes plays a functional role in organizations.

The fourth reading of the chapter brings us back to strategy, but in a kind of political way. You may recall one of the definitions of strategy introduced in Chapter 1 that was not heard from since—that of ploy. In this fourth reading, ploy comes to life in the context of "competitive maneuvering," various means strategists use to outwit competitors. This reading is based on two short articles entitled "Brinkmanship in Business" and "The Nonlogical Strategy" by Bruce Henderson, drawn from his book, *Henderson on Corporate Strategy*, a collection of short, pithy, and rather opinionated views on management issues. Henderson founded the Boston Consulting Group and built it into a major international force in management consulting.

While the Mintzberg reading considers power and politics inside the organization in terms of the maneuverings of various actors to gain influence, the Henderson one looks at the maneuverings of organizations at large, vis-à-vis the competitors. This second theme is pursued in the last reading of this chapter, except that the context is extended beyond competitors to all of an organization's influencers (sometimes called "stakeholders," in contrast to only "shareholders"). To some observers, organizations are not merely instruments to produce goods and services but also political systems that seek to enhance their own power. We will refer to this as *macro* politics, in contrast to the *micro* politics that takes place within organizations.

This final reading of the chapter introduces another major theme about macro power. For whom does or should the large business corporation exist? Mintzberg proposes a whole portfolio of answers around a "conceptual horseshoe." In so doing, he perhaps helps to reconcile some of the basic differences between those who view organizations as agents of economic competition and those who consider them to be instruments of the public will, or else as political systems in their own right. This reading also discusses the concept of *social responsibility*, one of the traditional topics covered in policy or strategy courses. But here the subject is treated not in a philanthropic or ethical sense, but as a managerial or organizational one. This reading also reviews the issues of corporate democracy, of regulation and pressure campaigns, and of "free enterprise" as described by Milton Friedman.

While no case deals solely with issues of power, many involve aspects of the concepts developed in these readings. The IBM 360 Decision, Nintendo Co. Ltd., E & J Gallo Winery, The Pillsbury Company, Microsoft Corporation (A), MacArthur in the Philippines, The Transformation of AT&T, Andersen Consulting (Europe), Ford: Team Taurus, The New York Times Company, and the SAS and the European Airline Industry cases all suggest how different executives deal with the power perspectives and needs of those within and outside the organization. The Genentech, Inc. (B), Magnetic Levitation Train, Nintendo of America, NovaCare Inc., Argyle Diamonds, Exxon Corporation 1994, Ford: Team Taurus, Orbital Engine Company, and Mountbatten and India cases allow students to examine how social goods and controls interact with corporate and personal power perspectives. Many students and executives seem unaware of the extent to which national policies actually shape the nature of industries and the options of executives. These cases provide a basis for much broader perspectives on these topics.

by Henry Mintzberg

We all know that 2 + 2 = 4. But general systems theory, through the concept of synergy, suggests that it can also equal 5, that the parts of a system may produce more working together than they can apart. A flashlight and a battery add up to just so many pieces of hardware; together they form a working system. Likewise an organization is a working system that can entice from its members more than they would produce apart—more effort, more creativity, more output (or, of course, less). This may be "strategic"—deriving from the way components have been combined in the organization. Or it may be motivational: The group is said to develop a "mood," an "atmosphere," to have some kind of "chemistry." In organizations, we talk of a "style," a "culture," a "character." One senses something unique when one walks into the offices of IBM; the chemistry of Hewlett-Packard just doesn't feel the same as that of Texas Instruments, even though the two have operated in some similar businesses.

All these words are used to describe something—intangible yet very real, over and above the concrete components of an organization—that we refer to as its *ideology*. Specifically, an ideology is taken here to mean a rich system of values and beliefs about an organization, shared by its members, that distinguishes it from other organizations. For our purposes, the key feature of such an ideology is its unifying power: It ties the individual to the organization, generating an "esprit de corps," a "sense of mission," in effect, an integration of individual and organizational goals that can produce synergy.

The Development of an Organizational Ideology

The development of an ideology in an organization will be discussed here in three stages. The roots of the ideology are planted when a group of individuals band together around a leader and, through a sense of mission, found a vigorous organization, or invigorate an existing one. The ideology then develops over time through the establishment of traditions. Finally, the existing ideology is reinforced when new members enter the organization and identify with its system of beliefs.

STAGE 1: THE ROOTING OF IDEOLOGY IN A SENSE OF MISSION

Typically, an organization is founded when a single prime mover identifies a mission—some product to be produced, service to be rendered—and collects a group around him or her to accomplish it. Some organizations are, of course, founded by other means, as when a new agency is created by a government or a subsidiary by a corporation. But a prime mover often can still be identified behind the founding of the organization.

The individuals who come together don't do so at random, but coalesce because they share some values associated with the fledgling organization. At the very least they see something in it for themselves. But in some cases, in addition to the mission per se there is a "sense of mission," that is, a feeling that the group has banded together to create something unusual and exciting. This is common in new organizations for a number of reasons.

First, unconstrained by procedure and tradition, new organizations offer wide latitude for maneuver. Second, they tend to be small, enabling the members to establish personal relationships. Third, the founding members frequently share a set of strong basic beliefs, sometimes including a sense that they wish to work together. Fourth, the founders of new organizations are often "charismatic" individuals, and so energize the followers and knit them together. Charisma, as Weber (1969:12) used the term, means a sense of "personal

*Adapted from Henry Mintzberg *Power in and Around Organizations* (copyright © Prentice Hall 1983). Chaps. 11 and 21 used by permission of the publisher; based on a summary that appeared in *Mintzberg on Management: Inside Our Strange World of Organizations* (New York: Free Press, 1989).

devotion" to the leader for the sake of his or her personal qualities rather than formal position. People join and remain with the organization because of dedication to the leader and his or her mission. Thus the roots of strong ideologies tend to be planted in the founding of organizations.

Of course, such ideologies can also develop in existing organizations. But a review of the preceding points suggests why this should be much more difficult to accomplish. Existing organizations *are* constrained by procedures and traditions, many are *already* large and impersonal, and their *existing* beliefs tend to impede the establishment of new ones. Nonetheless, with the introduction of strong charismatic leadership reinforced by a strong new sense of mission, an existing organization can sometimes be invigorated by the creation of a new ideology.

A key to the development of an organizational ideology, in a new or existing organization, is a leadership with a genuine belief in mission and an honest dedication to the people who must carry it out. Mouthing the right words might create the veneer of an organizational ideology, but it is only an authentic feeling on the part of the leadership—which followers somehow sense—that sets the roots of the ideology deep enough to sustain it when other forces, such as impersonal administration (bureaucracy) or politics, challenge it.

STAGE 2: THE DEVELOPMENT OF IDEOLOGY THROUGH TRADITIONS AND SAGAS

As a new organization establishes itself or an existing one establishes a new set of beliefs, it makes decisions and takes actions that serve as commitments and establish precedents. Behaviors reinforce themselves over time, and actions become infused with value. When those forces are strong, ideology begins to emerge in its own right. That ideology is strengthened by stories—sometimes called "myths"—that develop around important events in the organization's past. Gradually the organization establishes its own unique sense of history. All of this—the precedents, habits, myths, history—form a common base of tradition, which the members of the organization share, thus solidifying the ideology. Gradually, in Selznick's (1957) terms, the organization is converted from an expendable "instrument" for the accomplishment of externally imposed goals into an "institution," a system with a life of its own. It "acquires a self, a distinctive identity."

Thus Clark described the "distinctive college," with reference particularly to Reed, Antioch, and Swarthmore (1972:178). Such institutions develop, in his words, an "organizational saga," "a collective understanding of a unique accomplishment based on historical exploits," which links the organization's present with its past and "turns a formal place into a beloved institution." The saga captures allegiance, committing people to the institution (Clark 1970:235).

STAGE 3: THE REINFORCEMENT OF IDEOLOGY THROUGH IDENTIFICATIONS

Our description to this point makes it clear that an individual entering an organization does not join a random collection of individuals, but rather a living system with its own culture. He or she may come with a certain set of values and beliefs, but there is little doubt that the culture of the organization can weigh heavily on the behavior he or she will exhibit once inside it. This is especially true when the culture is rich—when the organization has an emerging or fully developed ideology. Then the individual's *identification* with and *loyalty* to the organization can be especially strong. Such identification can develop in a number of ways:

▼ Most simply, identification occurs *naturally* because the new member is attracted to the organization's system of beliefs.

▼ Identification may also be *selected*. New members are chosen to "fit in" with the existing beliefs, and positions of authority are likewise filled from among the members exhibiting the strongest loyalty to those beliefs.

▼ Identification may also be *evoked*. When the need for loyalty is especially great, the organization may use informal processes of *socialization* and formal programs of *indoctrination* to reinforce natural or selected commitment to its system of beliefs.

▼ Finally, and most weakly, identification can be *calculated*. In effect, individuals conform to the beliefs not because they identify naturally with them nor because they even necessarily fit in with them, not because they have been socialized or indoctrinated into them, but skimpy because it pays them to identify with the beliefs. They may enjoy the work or the social group, may like the remuneration, may work to get ahead through promotion and the like. Of course, such identification is fragile. It disappears as soon as an opportunity calculated to be better appears.

Clearly, the higher up this list an organization's members identifications tend to be, the more likely it is to sustain a strong ideology, or even to have such an ideology in the first place. Thus, strong organizational belief systems can be recognized above all by the presence of much natural identification. Attention to selected identification indicates the presence of an ideology, since it reflects an organization's efforts to sustain its ideology, as do efforts at socialization and indoctrination. Some organizations require a good deal of the latter two, because of the need to instill in their new members a complex system of beliefs. When the informal processes of socialization tend to function naturally, perhaps reinforced by more formal programs of indoctrination, then the ideology would seem to be strong. But when an organization is forced to rely almost exclusively on indoctrination, or worse to fall back on forms of calculated identification, then its ideology would appear to be weakening, if not absent to begin with.

The Missionary Organization

While some degree of ideology can be found in virtually every organization, that degree can vary considerably. At one extreme are those organizations, such as religious orders or radical political movements, whose ideologies tend to be strong and whose identifications are primarily natural and selected. Edwards (1977) refers to organizations with strong ideologies as "stylistically rich," Selznick (1957) as "institutions." It is the presence of such an ideology that enables an organization to have "a life of its own," to emerge as "a living social institution" (Selznick 1949: 10). At the other extreme are those organizations with relatively weak ideologies, "stylistically barren," in some cases business organizations with strongly utilitarian reward systems. History and tradition have no special value in these organizations. In the absence of natural forms of identification on the part of their members, these organizations sometimes try to rely on the process of indoctrination to integrate individual and organizational goals. But usually they have to fall back on calculated identifications and especially formal controls.

We can refer to "stylistically rich" organizations as *missionaries*, because they are somewhat akin in their beliefs to the religious organizations by that name. Mission counts above all—to preserve it, extend it, or perfect it. That mission is typically (1) clear and focused, so that its members are easily able to identify with it; (2) inspiring, so that the members do, in fact, develop such identifications; and (3) distinctive, so that the organization and its members are deposited into a unique niche where the ideology can flourish. As a result of their attachment to its mission, the members of the organization resist strongly any attempt to change it, to interfere with tradition. The mission and the rest of the ideology must be preserved at all costs.

The missionary organization is a distinct configuration of the attributes of structure, internally highly integrated yet different from other configurations. What holds this organization together—that is, provides for its coordination—is the standardization of its norms, in other words, the sharing of values and beliefs among its members. As was noted, that can happen informally, either through natural selection or else the informal process of socialization. But from the perspective of structural design the key attribute is indoctrination, meaning formalized programs to develop or reinforce identification with the ideology. And once the new member has been selected, socialized, and indoctrinated, he or she is accepted into the system as an equal partner, able to participate in decision making alongside everyone else. Thus, at the limit, the missionary organization can achieve the purest form of decentralization: All who are accepted into the system share its power.

But that does not mean an absence of control. Quite the contrary. No matter how subtle, control tends to be very powerful in this organization. For here, the organization controls not just people's behavior but their very souls. The machine organization buys the "workers'" attention through imposed rules; the missionary organization captures the "members'" hearts through shared values. As Jay noted in his book *Management and Machiavelli* (1970), teaching new Jesuit recruits to "love God and do what you like" is not to do what they like at all but to act in strict conformance with the order's beliefs (1970:70).

Thus, the missionary organization tends to end up as an amorphous mass of members all pulling together within the common ideology, with minimum specialization as to job, differentiation as to part, division as to status. At the limit, managers, staffers, and operators, once selected, socialized, and indoctrinated, all seem rather alike and may, in fact, rotate into each other's positions.

The traditional Israeli kibbutz is a classic example of the missionary organization. In certain seasons, everyone pitches in and picks fruit in the fields by day and then attends the meetings to decide administrative issues by night. Managerial positions exist but are generally filled on a rotating basis so that no one emerges with the status of office for long. Likewise, staff support positions exist, but they too tend to be filled on a rotating basis from the same pool of members, as are the operating positions in the fields. (Kitchen duty is, for example, considered drudgery that everyone must do periodically.) Conversion to industry has, however, threatened that ideology. As suggested, it was relatively easy to sustain the egalitarian ideology when the work was agricultural. Industry, in contrast, generally called for greater levels of technology, specialization, and expertise, with a resulting increase in the need for administrative hierarchy and functional differentiation, all a threat to the missionary orientation. The kibbutzim continue to struggle with this problem.

A number of our points about the traditional kibbutz are summarized in a table developed by Rosner (1969), which contrasts the "principles of kibbutz organization"—classic missionary—with those of "bureaucratic organization," in our terms, the classic machine.

Principles of Bureaucratic Organization	Principles of Kibbutz Organization
1. Permanency of office.	Impermanency of office.
2. The office carries with it impersonal, fixed privileges and duties.	The definition of office is flexible—privileges and duties are not formally fixed and often depend on the personality of the official.
3. A hierarchy of functional authorities expressed in the authority of the officials.	A basic assumption of the equal value of all functions without a formal hierarchy of authority.

4. Nomination of officials is based on formal objective qualifications.	Officials are elected, not nominated. Objective qualifications are not decisive, personal qualities are more important in election.
5. The office is a full-time occupation.	The office is usually supplementary to the full-time occupation of the official.

We can distinguish several forms of the pure missionary organization. Some are *reformers* that set out to change the world directly—anything from overthrowing a government to ensuring that all domestic animals are "decently" clothed. Other missionaries can be called *converters*, their mission being to change the world indirectly, by attracting members and changing them. The difference between the first two types of missionaries is the difference between the Women's Christian Temperance Union and Alcoholics Anonymous. Their ends were similar, but their means differed, seeking to reduce alcoholism in one case by promoting a general ban on liquor sales, in the other by discouraging certain individuals, namely joined members, from drinking. Third are the *cloister* missionaries that seek not to change things so much as to allow their members to pursue a unique style of life. The monasteries that close themselves off from the outside world are good examples, as are groups that go off to found new isolated colonies.

Of course, no organization can completely seal itself off from the world. All missionary organizations, in fact, face the twin opposing pressures of isolation and assimilation. Together these make them vulnerable. On one side is the threat of *isolation*, of growing ever inward in order to protect the unique ideology from the pressures of the ordinary world until the organization eventually dies for lack of renewal. On the other side is the threat of *assimilation*, of reaching out so far to promote the ideology that it eventually gets compromised. When this happens, the organization may survive but the ideology dies, and so the configuration changes (typically to the machine form).

Ideology as an Overlay on Conventional Organizations

So far we have discussed what amounts to the extreme form of ideological organization, the missionary. But more organizations have strong ideologies than can afford to structure themselves in this way. The structure may work for an Israeli kibbutz in a remote corner of the Negev desert, but this is hardly a way to run a Hewlett-Packard or a McDonald's, let alone a kibbutz closer to the worldly pressures of Tel Aviv.

What such organizations tend to do is overlay ideological characteristics on a more conventional structure—perhaps machinelike in the case of McDonald's and that second kibbutz, innovative in the case of Hewlett-Packard. The mission may sometimes seem ordinary—serving hamburgers, producing instruments and computers—but it is carried out with a good dose of ideological fervor by employees firmly committed to it.

Best known for this are, of course, certain of the Japanese corporations, Toyota being a prime example. Ouchi and Jaeger (1978:308) contrast in the table reproduced below the typical large American corporation (Type A) with its Japanese counterpart (Type J):

Type A (for American)	*Type J (for Japanese)*
Short-term employment	Lifetime employment
Individual decision making	Consensual decision making
Individual responsibility	Collective responsibility
Rapid evaluation and promotion	Slow evaluation and promotion
Explicit, formalized control	Implicit, informal control

Specialized career path   Nonspecialized career path
Segmented concern   Holistic concern

Ouchi and Jaeger (1978) in fact make their point best with an example in which a classic Japanese ideological orientation confronts a conventional American bureaucratic one:

> [D]uring one of the author's visits to a Japanese bank in California, both the Japanese president and the American vice-presidents of the bank accused the other of being unable to formulate objectives. The Americans meant that the Japanese president could not or would not give them explicit, quantified targets to attain over the next three or six months, while the Japanese meant that the Americans could not see that once they understood the company's philosophy, they would be able to deduce for themselves the proper objective for any conceivable situation. (p. 309)

In another study, however, Ouchi together with Johnson (1978) discussed a native American corporation that does resemble the Type J firm (labeled "Type Z"; Ouchi (1981) later published a best seller about such organizations). In it, they found greater loyalty, a strong collective orientation, less specialization, and a greater reliance on informal controls. For example, "a new manager will be useless for at least four or five years. It takes that long for most people to decide whether the new person really fits in, whether they can really trust him." That was in sharp contrast to the "auction market" atmosphere of a typical American firm: It "is almost as if you could open up the doors each day with 100 executives and engineers who had been randomly selected from the country, and the organization would work just as well as it does now" (1978:302).

The trends in American business over several decades—"professional" management, emphasis on technique and rationalization, "bottom-line" mentality—have worked against the development of organizational ideologies. Certainly the missionary configuration has hardly been fashionable in the West, especially the United States. But ideology may have an important role to play there, given the enormous success many Japanese firms have had in head-on competition with American corporations organized in machine and diversified ways, with barren cultures. At the very least, we might expect more ideological overlays on the conventional forms of organizations in the West. But this, as we hope our discussion has made clear, may be both for better and for worse.

▼ READING 7.2   BUILDING STRUCTURE IN MANAGERS' MINDS*

by Christopher A. Bartlett and Sumantra Ghoshal

Top-level managers in many of today's leading corporations are losing control of their companies. The problem is not that they have misjudged the demands created by an increasingly complex environment and an accelerating rate of environmental change, nor even that they have failed to develop strategies appropriate to the new challenges. The problem is that their companies are organizationally incapable of carrying out the sophisticated strategies they have developed. Over the past 20 years, strategic thinking has far outdistanced organizational capabilities. . . .

In recent years, as more and more managers recognized oversimplification as a strategic trap, they began to accept the need to manage complexity rather than seek to minimize it. This realization, however, led many into an equally threatening organizational trap when they concluded that the best response to increasingly complex strategic requirements was increasingly complex organizational structures.

*Originally published as "Matrix Management: Not a Structure, a Frame of Mind," in the *Harvard Business Review*, (July-August 1990). Copyright © 1990 by the President and Fellows of Harvard College; all rights reserved. Reprinted with deletions by permission of the *Harvard Business Review*.

The obvious organizational solution to strategies that required multiple, simultaneous management capabilities was the matrix structure that became so fashionable in the late 1970s and the early 1980s. Its parallel reporting relationships acknowledged the diverse, conflicting needs of functional, product, and geographic management groups and provided a formal mechanism for resolving them. Its multiple information channels allowed the organization to capture and analyze external complexity. And its overlapping responsibilities were designed to combat parochialism and build flexibility into the company's response to change.

In practice, however, the matrix proved all but unmanageable—especially in an international context. Dual reporting led to conflict and confusion; the proliferation of channels created informational logjams as a proliferation of committees and reports bogged down the organization; and overlapping responsibilities produced turf battles and a loss of accountability. Separated by barriers of distance, language, time, and culture, managers found it virtually impossible to clarify the confusion and resolve the conflicts.

. . . For decades, we have seen the general manager as chief strategic guru and principal organizational architect. But as the competitive climate grows less stable and less predictable, it is harder for one person alone to succeed in that great visionary role. Similarly, as formal, hierarchical structure gives way to networks of personal relationships that work through informal, horizontal communication channels, the image of top management in an isolated corner office moving boxes and lines on an organization chart becomes increasingly anachronistic.

Paradoxically, as strategies and organizations become more complex and sophisticated, top-level general managers are beginning to replace their historical concentration on the grand issues of strategy and structure with a focus on the details of managing people and processes. The critical strategic requirement is not to devise the most ingenious and well coordinated plan but to build the most viable and flexible strategic process; the key organizational task is not to design the most elegant structure but to capture individual capabilities and motivate the entire organization to respond cooperatively to a complicated and dynamic environment.

BUILDING AN ORGANIZATION

While business thinkers have written a great deal about strategic innovation, they have paid far less attention to the accompanying organizational challenges. Yet many companies remain caught in the structural-complexity trap that paralyzes their ability to respond quickly or flexibly to the new strategic imperatives.

For those companies that adopted matrix structures, the problem was not in the way they defined the goal. They correctly recognized the need for multidimensional organization to respond to growing external complexity. The problem was that they defined their organizational objectives in purely structural terms. Yet formal structure describes only the organization's basic anatomy. Companies must also concern themselves with organizational physiology—the systems and relationships that allow the lifeblood of information to flow through the organization. And they need to develop a healthy organizational psychology— the shared norms, values, and beliefs that shape the way individual managers think and act.

The companies that fell into the organizational trap assumed that changing their formal structure (anatomy) would force changes in interpersonal relationships and decision processes (physiology), which in turn would reshape the individual attitudes and actions of managers (psychology).

But as many companies have discovered, reconfiguring the formal structure is a blunt and sometimes brutal instrument of change. A new structure creates new and presumably more useful managerial ties, but these can take months and often years to evolve into effective knowledge-generating and decision-making relationships. And since the new job requirements will frustrate, alienate, or simply overwhelm so many managers, changes in individual attitudes and behavior will likely take even longer.

As companies struggle to create organizational capabilities that reflect rather than diminish environmental complexity, good managers gradually stop searching for the ideal structural template to impose on the company from the top down. Instead, they focus on the challenge of building up an appropriate set of employee attitudes and skills and linking them together with carefully developed processes and relationships. In other words, they begin to focus on building the organization rather than simply on installing a new structure.

Indeed, the companies that are most successful at developing multidimensional organizations begin at the far end of the anatomy-physiology-psychology sequence. Their first objective is to alter the organizational psychology—the broad corporate beliefs and norms that shape managers' perceptions and actions. Then, by enriching and clarifying communication and decision processes, companies reinforce these psychological changes with improvements in organizational physiology. Only later do they consolidate and confirm their progress by realigning organizational anatomy through changes in the formal structure.

No company we know of has discovered a quick or easy way to change its organizational psychology to reshape the understanding, identification, and commitment of its employees. But we found three principal characteristics common to those that managed the task most effectively:

1. The development and communication of a clear and consistent corporate vision.
2. The effective management of human resource tools to broaden individual perspectives and develop identification with corporate goals.
3. The integration of individual thinking and activities into the broad corporate agenda by means of a process we call co-option.

BUILDING A SHARED VISION

Perhaps the main reason managers in large, complex companies cling to parochial attitudes is that their frame of reference is bounded by their specific responsibilities. The surest way to break down such insularity is to develop and communicate a clear sense of corporate purpose that extends into every corner of the company and gives context and meaning to each manager's particular roles and responsibilities. We are not talking about a slogan, however catchy and pointed. We are talking about a company vision, which must be crafted and articulated with clarity, continuity, and consistency: clarity of expression that makes company objectives understandable and meaningful; continuity of purpose that underscores their enduring importance; and consistency of application across business units and geographical boundaries that ensures uniformity throughout the organization.

CLARITY

There are three keys to clarity in a corporate vision: simplicity, relevance, and reinforcement. NEC's integration of computers and communications—C&C—is probably the best single example of how simplicity can make a vision more powerful. Top management has applied the C&C concept so effectively that it describes the company's business focus, defines its distinctive source of competitive advantage over large companies like IBM and AT&T, and summarizes its strategic and organizational imperatives.

The second key, relevance, means linking broad objectives to concrete agendas. When Wisse Dekker became CEO at Philips, his principal strategic concern was the problem of competing with Japan. He stated this challenge in martial terms—the U.S. had abandoned the battlefield; Philips was now Europe's last defense against insurgent Japanese electronics companies. . . .

The third key to clarity is top management's continual reinforcement, elaboration, and interpretation of the core vision to keep it from becoming obsolete or abstract. Founder

Konosuke Matsushita developed a grand, 250-year vision for his company, but he also managed to give it immediate relevance. He summed up its overall message in the "Seven Spirits of Matsushita," to which he referred constantly in his policy statements. Each January he wove the company's one-year operational objectives into his overarching concept to produce an annual theme that he then captured in a slogan. For all the loftiness of his concept of corporate purpose, he gave his managers immediate, concrete guidance in implementing Matsushita's goals.

CONTINUITY

Despite shifts in leadership and continual adjustments in short-term business priorities, companies must remain committed to the same core set of strategic objectives and organizational values. Without such continuity, unifying vision might as well be expressed in terms of quarterly goals.

It was General Electric's lack of this kind of continuity that led to the erosion of its once formidable position in electrical appliances in many countries. Over a period of 20 years and under successive CEOs, the company's international consumer-product strategy never stayed the same for long. . . . The Brazilian subsidiary, for example, built its TV business in the 1960s until it was told to stop; in the early 1970s, it emphasized large appliances until it was denied funding; then it focused on housewares until the parent company sold off that business. In two decades, GE utterly dissipated its dominant franchise in Brazil's electrical products markets.

Unilever, by contrast, made an enduring commitment to its Brazilian subsidiary, despite volatile swings in Brazil's business climate. Company chairman Floris Maljers emphasized the importance of looking past the latest political crisis or economic downturn to the long-term business potential. . . .

CONSISTENCY

The third task for top management in communicating strategic purpose is to ensure that everyone in the company shares the same vision. The cost of inconsistency can be horrendous. It always produces confusion and, in extreme cases, can lead to total chaos, with different units of the organization pursuing agendas that are mutually debilitating.

Philips is a good example of a company that, for a time, lost its consistency of corporate purpose. As a legacy of its wartime decision to give some overseas units legal autonomy, management had long experienced difficulty persuading North American Philips (NAP) to play a supportive role in the parent company's global strategies. The problem came to a head with the introduction of Philips's technologically first-rate videocassette recording system, the V2000. Despite considerable pressure from world headquarters in the Netherlands, NAP refused to launch the system, arguing that Sony's Beta system and Matsushita's VHS format were too well established and had cost, feature, and system-support advantages Philips couldn't match. Relying on its legal independence and managerial autonomy, NAP management decided instead to source products from its Japanese competitors and market them under its Magnavox brand name. As a result, Philips was unable to build the efficiency and credibility it needed to challenge Japanese dominance of the VCR business. . . .

But formulating and communicating a vision—no matter how clear, enduring, and consistent—cannot succeed unless individual employees understand and accept the company's stated goals and objectives. Problems at this level are more often related to receptivity than to communication. The development of individual understanding and acceptance is a challenge for a company's human resource practices.

DEVELOPING HUMAN RESOURCES

While top managers universally recognize their responsibility for developing and allocating a company's scarce assets and resources, their focus on finance and technology often overshadows the task of developing the scarcest resource of all—capable managers. But if there is one key to regaining control of companies that operate in fast-changing environments, it is the ability of top management to turn the perceptions, capabilities, and relationships of individual managers into the building blocks of the organization.

One pervasive problem in companies whose leaders lack this ability—or fail to exercise it—is getting managers to see how their specific responsibilities relate to the broad corporate vision. Growing external complexity and strategic sophistication have accelerated the growth of a cadre of specialists who are physically and organizationally isolated from each other, and the task of dealing with their consequent parochialism should not be delegated to the clerical staff that administers salary structures and benefit programs. Top managers inside and outside the human resource function must be leaders in the recruitment, development, and assignment of the company's vital human talent.

RECRUITMENT AND SELECTION

The first step in successfully managing complexity is to tap the full range of available talent. It is a serious mistake to permit historical imbalances in the nationality or functional background of the management group to constrain hiring or subsequent promotion. In today's global marketplace, domestically oriented recruiting limits a company's ability to capitalize on its worldwide pool of management skill and biases its decision-making processes.

Not only must companies enlarge the pool of people available for key positions, they must also develop new criteria for choosing those most likely to succeed. Because past success is no longer a sufficient qualification for increasingly subtle, sensitive, and unpredictable senior-level tasks, top management must become involved in a more discriminating selection process. At Matsushita, top management selects candidates for international assignment on the basis of a comprehensive set of personal characteristics, expressed for simplicity in the acronym SMILE: specialty (the needed skill, capability, or knowledge); management ability (particularly motivational ability); international flexibility (willingness to learn and ability to adapt); language facility; and endeavor (vitality, perseverance in the face of difficulty). These attributes are remarkably similar to those targeted by NEC and Philips, where top executives also are involved in the senior-level selection process.

TRAINING AND DEVELOPMENT

Once the appropriate top-level candidates have been identified, the next challenge is to develop their potential. The most successful development efforts have three aims that take them well beyond the skill-building objectives of classic training programs: to inculcate a common vision and shared values; to broaden management perspectives and capabilities; and to develop contacts and shape management relationships.

To build common vision and values, white-collar employees at Matsushita spend a good part of their first six months in what the company calls "cultural and spiritual training." They study the company credo, the "Seven Spirits of Matsushita," and the philosophy of Konosuke Matsushita. Then they learn how to translate these internalized lessons into daily behavior and even operational decisions. Culture-building exercises as intensive as Matsushita's are sometimes dismissed as the kind of Japanese mumbo jumbo that would not work in other societies, but in fact, Philips has a similar entry-level training practice (called "organization cohesion training"), as does Unilever (called, straightforwardly, "indoctrination").

The second objective—broadening management perspectives—is essentially a matter of teaching people how to manage complexity instead of merely to make room for it. To reverse a long and unwieldy tradition of running its operations with two- and three-headed management teams of separate technical, commercial, and sometimes administrative specialists, Philips asked its training and development group to de-specialize top management trainees. By supplementing its traditional menu of specialist courses and functional programs with more intensive general management training, Philips was able to begin replacing the ubiquitous teams with single business heads who also appreciated and respected specialist points of view.

The final aim—developing contacts and relationships—is much more than an incidental by-product of good management development, as the comments of a senior personnel manager at Unilever suggest: "By bringing managers from different countries and businesses together at Four Acres [Unilever's international management training college], we build contacts and create bonds that we could never achieve by other means. The company spends as much on training as it does on R&D not only because of the direct effect it has on upgrading skills and knowledge but also because it plays a central role in indoctrinating managers into a Unilever club where personal relationships and informal contacts are much more powerful than the formal systems and structures."

CAREER-PATH MANAGEMENT

Although recruitment and training are critically important, the most effective companies recognize that the best way to develop new perspectives and thwart parochialism in their managers is through personal experience. By moving selected managers across functions, businesses, and geographic units, a company encourages cross-fertilization of ideas as well as the flexibility and breadth of experience that enable managers to grapple with complexity and come out on top.

Unilever has long been committed to the development of its human resources as a means of attaining durable competitive advantage. As early as the 1930s, the company was recruiting and developing local employees to replace the parent-company managers who had been running most of its overseas subsidiaries. In a practice that came to be known as "-ization," the company committed itself to the Indianization of its Indian company, the Australization of its Australian company, and so on.

Although delighted with the new talent that began working its way up through the organization, management soon realized that by reducing the transfer of parent-company managers abroad, it had diluted the powerful glue that bound diverse organizational groups together and linked dispersed operations. The answer lay in formalizing a second phase of the -ization process. While continuing with Indianization, for example, Unilever added programs aimed at the Unileverization of its Indian managers.

In addition to bringing 300 to 400 managers to Four Acres each year, Unilever typically has 100 to 150 of its most promising overseas managers on short- and long-term job assignments at corporate headquarters. This policy not only brings fresh, close-to-the-market perspectives into corporate decision making but also gives the visiting managers a strong sense of Unilever's strategic vision and organizational values. In the words of one of the expatriates in the corporate offices, "The experience initiates you into the Unilever Club and the clear norms, values, and behaviors that distinguish our people—so much so that we really believe we can spot another Unilever manager anywhere in the world."

Furthermore, the company carefully transfers most of these high-potential individuals through a variety of different functional, product, and geographic positions, often rotating every two or three years. Most important, top management tracks about 1,000 of these people—some 5% of Unilever's total management group—who, as they move through the company, forge an informal network of contacts and relationships that is central to Unilever's decision-making and information-exchange processes.

Widening the perspectives and relationships of key managers as Unilever has done is a good way of developing identification with the broader corporate mission. But a broad sense of identity is not enough. To maintain control of its global strategies, Unilever must secure a strong and lasting individual commitment to corporate visions and objectives. In effect, it must co-opt individual energies and ambitions into the service of corporate goals.

CO-OPTING MANAGEMENT EFFORTS

As organizational complexity grows, managers and management groups tend to become so specialized and isolated and to focus so intently on their own immediate operating responsibilities that they are apt to respond parochially to intrusions on their organizational turf, even when the overall corporate interest is at stake. A classic example, described earlier, was the decision by North American's Philips's consumer electronics group to reject the parent company's VCR system.

At about the same time, Philips, like many other companies, began experimenting with ways to convert managers' intellectual understanding of the corporate vision—in Philips's case, an almost evangelical determination to defend Western electronics against the Japanese—into a binding personal commitment. Philips concluded that it could co-opt individuals and organizational groups into the broader vision by inviting them to contribute to the corporate agenda and then giving them direct responsibility for implementation.

In the face of intensifying Japanese competition, Philips knew it had to improve coordination in its consumer electronics among its fiercely independent national organizations. In strengthening the central product divisions, however, Philips did not want to deplete the enterprise or commitment of its capable national management teams.

The company met these conflicting needs with two cross-border initiatives. First, it created a top-level World Policy Council for its video business that included key managers from strategic markets—Germany, France, the United Kingdom, the United States, and Japan. Philips knew that its national companies' long history of independence made local managers reluctant to take orders from Dutch headquarters in Eindhoven—often for good reason, since much of the company's best market knowledge and technological expertise resided in its offshore units. Through the Council, Philips co-opted their support for company decisions about product policy and manufacturing location.

Second, and more powerful, Philips allocated global responsibilities to units that had previously been purely national in focus. Eindhoven gave NAP the leading role in the development of Philips's projection television and asked it to coordinate development and manufacture of all Philips television sets for North America and Asia. The change in the attitude of NAP managers was dramatic.

A senior manager in NAP's consumer electronics business summed up the feelings of U.S. managers: "At last, we are moving out of the dependency relationship with Eindhoven and that was so frustrating to us." Co-option had transformed the defensive, territorial attitude of NAP managers into a more collaborative mind-set. They were making important contributions to global corporate strategy instead of looking for ways to subvert it. . . .

THE MATRIX IN THE MANAGER'S MIND

Since the end of World War II, corporate strategy has survived several generations of painful transformation and has grown appropriately agile and athletic. Unfortunately, organizational development has not kept pace, and managerial attitudes lag even further behind. As a result, corporations now commonly design strategies that seem impossible to implement, for the simple reason that no one can effectively implement third-generation strategies through second-generation organizations run by first-generation managers.

Today the most successful companies are those where top executives recognize the need to manage the new environmental and competitive demands by focusing less on the quest for an ideal structure and more on developing the abilities, behavior, and performance of individual managers. . . .

▼ READING 7.3 POLITICS AND THE POLITICAL ORGANIZATION*

by Henry Mintzberg

How does conflict arise in an organization, why, and with what consequences? Years ago, the literature of organizations avoided such questions. But in the last decade or so, conflict and politics that go along with it have become not just acceptable topics but fashionable ones. Yet these topics, like most others in the field, have generally been discussed in fragments. Here we seek to consider them somewhat more comprehensively, first by themselves and then in the context of what will be called the political organization—the organization that comes to be dominated by politics and conflict.

Politics in Organizations

What do we mean by "politics" in organizations? An organization may be described as functioning on the basis of a number of systems of influence: authority, ideology, expertise, politics. The first three can be considered legitimate in some sense: Authority is based on legally sanctioned power, ideology on widely accepted beliefs, expertise on power that is officially certified. The system of politics, in contrast, reflects power that is technically illegitimate (or, perhaps more accurately, *a*legitimate), in the means it uses, and sometimes also in the ends it promotes. In other words, political power in the organization (unlike government) is not formally authorized, widely accepted, or officially certified. The result is that political activity is usually divisive and conflictive, pitting individuals or groups against the more legitimate systems of influence and, when those systems are weak, against each other.

Political Games in Organizations

Political activity in organizations is sometimes described in terms of various "games." The political scientist Graham Allison, for example, has described political games in organizations and government as "intricate and subtle, simultaneous, overlapping," but nevertheless guided by rules: "some rules are explicit, others implicit, some rules are quite clear, others fuzzy. Some are very stable; others are ever changing. But the collection of rules, in effect, defines the game" (1971:170). 1 have identified thirteen political games in particular, listed here together with their main players, the main reasons they seem to be played, and how they relate to the other systems of influence.

▼　*Insurgency game*: usually played to resist authority, although can be played to resist expertise or established ideology or even to effect change in the organization; ranges "from protest to rebellion" (Zaid and Berger, 1978:841), and is usually played by "lower participants" (Mechanic, 1962), those who feel the greatest weight of formal authority

*Adapted from Henry Mintzberg, *Power in and Around Organizations* (Copyright © Prentice-Hall, 1983), Chaps. 13 and 23, used by permission of the publisher; based on a summary that appeared in *Mintzberg on Management: Inside Our Strange World of Organizations* (Free Press 1989).

▼ *Counterinsurgency game*: played by those with legitimate power who fight back with political means, perhaps with legitimate means as well (e.g., excommunication in the church)

▼ *Sponsorship game*: played to build power base, in this case by using superiors; individual attaches self to someone with more status, professing loyalty in return for power

▼ *Alliance-building game*: played among peers—often line managers, sometimes experts—who negotiate implicit contracts of support for each other in order to build power base to advance selves in the organization

▼ *Empire-building game*: played by line managers, in particular, to build power bases, not cooperatively with peers but individually with subordinates

▼ *Budgeting game*: played overtly and with rather clearly defined rules to build power base; similar to last game, but less divisive, since prize is resources, not positions or units per se, at least not those of rivals

▼ *Expertise game.*: nonsanctioned use of expertise to build power base, either by flaunting it or by feigning it; true experts play by exploiting technical skills and knowledge, emphasizing the uniqueness, criticality, and irreplaceability of the expertise (Hickson et al., 1971), also by seeking to keep skills from being programmed, by keeping knowledge to selves; nonexperts play by attempting to have their work viewed as expert, ideally to have it declared professional so they alone can control it

▼ *Lording game*: played to build power base by "lording" legitimate power over those without it or with less of it (i.e., using legitimate power in illegitimate ways); manager can lord formal authority over subordinate or civil servant over a citizen; members of missionary configuration can lord its ideology over outsiders; experts can lord technical skills over the unskilled

▼ *Line versus staff game*: a game of sibling-type rivalry, played not just to enhance personal power but to defeat a rival; pits line managers with formal decision-making authority against staff advisers with specialized expertise; each side tends to exploit legitimate power in illegitimate ways

▼ *Rival camps game*: again played to defeat a rival; typically occurs when alliance or empire-building games result in two major power blocs, giving rise to two-person, zero-sum game in place of n-person game; can be most divisive game of all; conflict can be between units (e.g., between marketing and production in manufacturing firm), between rival personalities, or between two competing missions (as in prisons split between custody and rehabilitation orientations)

▼ *Strategic candidates game*: played to effect change in an organization; individuals or groups seek to promote through political means their own favored changes of a strategic nature; many play—analysts, operating personnel, lower-level managers, even senior managers and chief executives (especially in the professional configurations), who must promote own candidates politically before they can do so formally; often combines elements of other games—empire-building (as purpose of game), alliance-building (to win game), rival camps, line versus staff, expertise, and lording (evoked during game), insurgency (following game), and so on

▼ *Whistle-blowing game*: a typically brief and simple game, also played to effect organizational change; privileged information is used by an insider, usually a lower participant, to "blow the whistle" to an influential outsider on questionable or illegal behavior by the organization

▼ *Young Turks game*: played for highest stakes of all, not to effect simple change or to resist legitimate power per se, but to throw the latter into question, perhaps even to overthrow it, and institute major shift; small group of "young Turks," close to but not at center of power, seeks to reorient organization's basic strategy, displace a major body of its expertise, replace its ideology, or rid it of its leadership; Zald and Berger discuss a form of this game they call "organizational coup d'état," where the object is "to effect an unexpected succession"—to replace *holders* of authority while maintaining *system* of authority intact (1978:833).

Some of these games, such as sponsorship and lording, while themselves technically illegitimate, can nevertheless *coexist with* strong legitimate systems of influence, as found for example in the machine and missionary type organizations; indeed, they could not exist without these systems of influence. Other political games, such as insurgency and young Turks—usually highly divisive games—arise in the presence of legitimate power but are *antagonistic to it*, designed to destroy or at least weaken it. And still others, such as rival camps, often arise when legitimate power is weak and *substitute for* it, for example in the professional and innovative type organizations.

The implication of this is that politics and conflict may exist at two levels in an organization. They may be present but not dominant, existing as an overlay in a more conventional organization, perhaps a kind of fifth column acting on behalf of some challenging power. Or else politics may be the dominant system of influence, and conflict strong, having weakened the legitimate systems of influence or having arisen in their weakness. It is this second level that gives rise to the type of organization we call *political*.

Forms of Political Organizations

What characterizes the organization dominated by politics is a lack of any of the forms of order found in conventional organizations. In other words, the organization is best described in terms of power, not structure, and that power is exercised in ways not legitimate in conventional organizations. Thus, there is no preferred method of coordination, no single dominant part of the organization, no clear type of decentralization. Everything depends on the fluidity of informal power, marshaled to win individual issues.

How does such an organization come to be? There is little published research on the question. But some ideas can be advanced tentatively. First, conflict would seem to arise in a circumscribed way in an organization, say between two units (such as marketing and production) or between an influential outside group and a powerful insider (such as between a part owner and the CEO). That conflict may develop gradually or it may flare up suddenly. It may eventually be resolved, but when it becomes intense, it may tend to spread, as other influencers get drawn in on one side or the other. But since few organizations can sustain intense political activity for long, that kind of conflict must eventually moderate itself (unless it kills off the organization first). In moderated form, however, the conflict may endure, even when it pervades the whole system, so long as the organization can make up for its losses, perhaps by being in a privileged position (as in the case of a conflict-ridden regulatory agency that is sustained by a government budget, or a politicized corporation that operates in a secure cartel).

What we end up with are two dimensions of conflict, first moderate or intense and second confined or pervasive. A third dimension—enduring or brief—really combines with the first (intense conflict having to be typically brief, moderate conflict possibly enduring). Combining these dimensions, we end up with four forms of the political organization:

▼ *Confrontation*, characterized by conflict that is *intense, confined*, and *brief* (unstable)
▼ *Shaky alliance*, characterized by conflict that is *moderate, confined*, and possibly *enduring* (relatively stable)
▼ *Politicized organization*, characterized by conflict that is *moderate, pervasive*, and possibly *enduring* (relatively stable, so long as it is sustained by privileged position)

▼ *Complete political arena*, characterized by conflict that is *intense*, *pervasive*, and *brief* (unstable)*

One of these forms is called *complete* because its conflict is both intense and pervasive. In this form, the external influencers disagree among themselves, they try to form alliances with some insiders, while clashing with others. The internal activities are likewise conflictive, permeated by divisive political games. Authority, ideology, and expertise are all subordinated to the play of political power. An organization so politicized can pursue no goal with any consistency. At best, it attends to a number of goals inconsistently over time, at worst it consumes all its energy in disputes and never accomplishes anything. In essence, the complete political arena is less a coherent organization than a free-for-all of individuals. As such, it is probably the form of political organization least commonly found in practice, or, at least, the most unstable when it does appear.

In contrast, the other three forms of political organization manage to remain partial, one by moderating its conflict, a second by containing it, and the third by doing both. As a result, these forms are more stable than the complete form and so are probably more common, with two of them in particular appearing to be far more viable.

In the *confrontational* form, conflict may be intense, but it is also contained, focusing on two parties. Typical of this is the takeover situation, where, for example, an outside stockholder tries to seize control of a closed system corporation from its management. Another example is the situation, mentioned earlier, of two rival camps in and around a prison, one promoting the mission of custody, the other that of rehabilitation.

The *shaky alliance* commonly emerges when two or more major systems of influence or centers of power must coexist in roughly equal balance. The symphony orchestra, for example, must typically combine the strong personal authority of the conductor (entrepreneurial orientation) with the extensive expertise of the musicians (professional orientation). As Fellini demonstrated so well in his film *Orchestra Rehearsal*, this alliance, however uncomfortable (experts never being happy in the face of strong authority), is nevertheless a necessary one. Common today is the professional organization operating in the public sector, which must somehow sustain an alliance of experts and government officials, one group pushing upward for professional autonomy, the other downward for technocratic control.

Our final form, the *politicized organization*, is characterized by moderate conflict that pervades the entire system of power. This would appear to describe a number of today's largest organizations, especially ones in the public sector whose mandates are visible and controversial—many regulatory agencies, for example, and some public utilities. Here it is government protection, or monopoly power, that sustains organizations captured by conflict. This form seems to be increasingly common in the private sector too, among some of the largest corporations that are able to sustain the inefficiencies of conflict through their market power and sometimes by their ability to gain government support as well.

The Functional Role of Politics in Organizations

Little space need be devoted to the dysfunctional influence of politics in organizations. Politics is divisive and costly; it burns up energies that could instead go into the operations. It can also lead to all kinds of aberrations. Politics is often used to sustain outmoded systems of power, and sometimes to introduce new ones that are not justified. Politics can also paralyze an organization to the point where its effective functioning comes to a halt and nobody benefits. The purpose of an organization, after all, is to produce goods and services, not to provide an arena in which people can fight with one another.

---

* I do not consider conflict that is moderate, confined, and brief to merit inclusion under the label of political organization.

What does deserve space, however, because they are less widely appreciated, are those conditions in which politics and the political organization serve a functional role.

In general, the system of politics is necessary in an organization to correct certain deficiencies in its other, legitimate systems of influence—above all to provide for certain forms of flexibility discouraged by those other systems. The other systems of influence were labeled legitimate because their *means*—authority, ideology, or expertise—have some basis of legitimacy. But sometimes those means are used to pursue *ends* that are illegitimate (as in the example of the lording game, where legitimate power is flaunted unreasonably). In contrast, the system of politics, whose *means* are (by definition) illegitimate, can sometimes be used to pursue *ends* that are in fact legitimate (as in certain of the whistle-blowing and young Turks games, where political pressures are used against formal authority to correct irresponsible or ineffective behaviors). We can elaborate on this in terms of four specific points.

First, politics as a system of influence can act in a Darwinian way to ensure that the strongest members of an organization are brought into positions of leadership. Authority favors a single chain of command; weak leaders can suppress strong subordinates. Politics, on the other hand, can provide alternate channels of information and promotion, as when the sponsorship game enables someone to leap over a weak superior (McClelland, 1970). Moreover, since effective leaders have been shown to exhibit a need for power, the political games can serve as tests to demonstrate the potential for leadership. The second-string players may suffice for the scrimmages, but only the stars can be allowed to meet the competition. Political games not only suggest who those players are but also help to remove their weak rivals from contention.

Second, politics can also ensure that all sides of an issue are fully debated, whereas the other systems of influence may promote only one. The system of authority, by aggregating information up a central hierarchy, tends to advance only a single point of view, often the one already known to be favored above. So, too, does the system of ideology, since every issue is interpreted in terms of "the word," the prevailing set of beliefs. As for the system of expertise, people tend to defer to the expert on any particular issue. But experts are often closed to new ideas, ones that developed after they received their training. Politics, however, by obliging "responsible men ... to fight for what they are convinced is right" (Allison, 1971:145) encourages a variety of voices to be heard on any issue. And, because of attacks by its opponents, each voice is forced to justify its conclusions in terms of the broader good. That means it must marshal arguments and support proposals that can at least be justified in terms of the interests of the organization at large rather than the parochial needs of a particular group. As Bums has noted in an amusing footnote:

> It is impossible to avoid some reference from the observations made here to F. M. Cornford's well known "Guide for the Young Academic Politician." Jobs "fall into two classes, My Jobs and Your Jobs. My Jobs are public-spirited proposals, which happen (much to my regret) to involve the advancement of a personal friend, or (still more to my regret) of myself. Your Jobs are insidious intrigues for the advancement of yourself and your friends, spuriously disguised as public-spirited proposals." (1961-62:260)

Third, the system of politics is often required to stimulate necessary change that is blocked by the legitimate systems of influence. Internal change is generally threatening to the "vested interest" of an organization. The system of authority concentrates power up the hierarchy, often in the hands of those who were responsible for initiating the existing strategies in the first place. It also contains the established controls, which are designed to sustain the status quo. Similarly, the system of expertise concentrates power in the hands of senior and established experts, not junior ones who may possess newer, more necessary skills. Likewise, the system of ideology, because it is rooted in the past, in tradition, acts as a deterrent to change. In the face of these resistances, it is politics that is able to work as a kind of "invisible hand"—"invisible underhand" would be a better term—to promote necessary change, through such games as strategic candidates, whistle-blowing, and young Turks.

Fourth and finally, the system of politics can ease the path for the execution of decisions. Senior managers, for example, often use politics to gain acceptance for their decisions, playing the strategic candidates game early in promoting proposals to avoid having to play the more decisive and risky counterinsurgency game later in the face of resistance to them. They persuade, negotiate, and build alliances to smooth the path for the decisions they wish to make.

To conclude our discussion, while I am not personally enthusiastic about organizational politics and have no desire to live in a political organization, I do accept, and hope I have persuaded the reader to accept, that politics does have useful roles to play in a society of organizations. Organizational politics may irritate us, but it can also serve us.

▼ READING 7.4   COMPETITIVE MANEUVERING*

*by Bruce
Henderson*

Brinkmanship in Business

A businessman often convinces himself that he is completely logical in his behavior when in fact the critical factor is his emotional bias compared to the emotional bias of his opposition. Unfortunately, some businessmen and students perceive competition as some kind of impersonal, objective, colorless affair, with a company competing against the field as a golfer competes in medal play. A better case can be made that business competition is a major battle in which there are many contenders, each of whom must be dealt with individually. Victory, if achieved, is more often won in the mind of a competitor than in the economic arena.

I shall emphasize two points. The first is that the management of a company must persuade each competitor voluntarily to stop short of a maximum effort to acquire customers and profits. The second point is that persuasion depends on emotional and intuitive factors rather than on analysis or deduction.

The negotiator's skill lies in being as arbitrary as necessary to obtain the best possible compromise without actually destroying the basis for voluntary mutual cooperation of self-restraint. There are some commonsense rules for success in such an endeavor:

1. Be sure that your rival is fully aware of what he can gain if he cooperates and what it will cost him if he does not.
2. Avoid any action which will arouse your competitor's emotions, since it is essential that he behave in a logical, reasonable fashion.
3. Convince your opponent that you are emotionally dedicated to your position and are completely convinced that it is reasonable.

It is worth emphasizing that your competitor is under the maximum handicap if he acts in a completely rational, objective, and logical fashion. For then he will cooperate as long

---

* "Brinkmanship in Business" and "The Nonlogical Strategy," in *Henderson on Corporate Strategy* (Cambridge, MA, Abt Books, 1979), pp. 27-33, title selected for this book; section on "Rules for the Strategist" originally at the end of "Brinkmanship in Business" moved to the end of "The Nonlogical Strategy," reprinted by permission of publisher.

as he thinks he can benefit. In fact, if he is completely logical, he will not forgo the profit of cooperation as long as there is *any* net benefit.

FRIENDLY COMPETITORS

It may strike most businessmen as strange to talk about cooperation with competitors. But it is hard to visualize a situation in which it would be worthwhile to pursue competition to the utter destruction of a competitor. In every case there is a greater advantage to reducing the competition on the condition that the competitor does likewise. Such mutual restraint is cooperation, whether recognized as such or not.

Without cooperation on the part of competitors, there can be no stability. We see this most clearly in international relationships during times of peace. There are constant encroachments and aggressive acts. And the eventual consequence is always either voluntarily imposed self-restraint or mutual destruction. Thus, international diplomacy has only one purpose: to stabilize cooperation between independent nations on the most favorable basis possible. Diplomacy can be described as the art of being stubborn, arbitrary, and unreasonable without arousing emotional responses.

Businessmen should notice the similarity between economic competition and the peacetime behavior of nations. The object in both cases is to achieve a voluntary, cooperative restraint on the part of otherwise aggressive competitors. Complete elimination of competition is almost inconceivable. The goal of the hottest economic war is an agreement for coexistence, not annihilation. The competition and mutual encroachment do not stop; they go on forever. But they do so under some measure of mutual restraint.

"COLD WAR" TACTICS

A breakdown in negotiations is inevitable if both parties persist in arbitrary positions which are incompatible. Yet there are major areas in business where some degree of arbitrary behavior is essential for protecting a company's self-interest. In effect, a type of brinkmanship is necessary. The term was coined to describe cold war international diplomacy, but it describes a normal pattern in business, too.

In a confrontation between parties who are in part competitors and in part cooperators, deciding what to accept is essentially emotional or arbitrary. Deciding what is attainable requires an evaluation of the other party's degree of intransigence. The purpose is to convince him that you are arbitrary and emotionally committed while trying to discover what he would really accept in settlement. The competitor known to be coldly logical is at a great disadvantage. Logically, he can afford to compromise until there is no advantage left in cooperation. If, instead, he is emotional, irrational, and arbitrary, he has a great advantage.

CONSEQUENCE

The heart of business strategy for a company is to promote attitudes on the part of its competitors that will cause them either to restrain themselves or to act in a fashion which management deems advantageous. In diplomacy and military strategy the key to success is very much the same.

The most easily recognized way of enforcing cooperation is to exhibit obvious willingness to use irresistible or overwhelming force. This requires little strategic skill, but there is the problem of convincing the competing organization that the force will be used without actually resorting to it (which would be expensive and inconvenient).

In industry, however, the available force is usually not overwhelming, although one company may be able to inflict major punishment on another. In the classic case, each party can inflict such punishment on the other. If there were open conflict, then both parties would lose. If they cooperate, both parties are better off, but not necessarily equally so—particularly if one is trying to change the status quo.

When each party can punish the other, the prospects of agreement depend on three things:

1. Each party's willingness to accept the risk of punishment
2. Each party's belief that the other party is willing to accept the risk of punishment
3. The degree of rationality in the behavior of each party

If these conclusions are correct, what can we deduce about how advantages are gained and lost in business competition?

First, management's unwillingness to accept the risk of punishment is almost certain to produce either the punishment or progressively more onerous conditions for cooperation—provided the competition recognized the attitude.

Second, beliefs about a competitor's future behavior or response are all that determine competitive cooperation. In other words, it is the judgment not of actual capability but of probable use of capability that counts.

Third, the less rational or less predictable the behavior of a competitor appears to be, the greater the advantage he possesses in establishing a favorable competitive balance. This advantage is limited only by his need to avoid forcing his competitors into an untenable position or creating an emotional antagonism that will lead them to be unreasonable and irrational (as he is).

THE NONLOGICAL STRATEGY

The goal of strategy in business, diplomacy, and war is to produce a stable relationship favorable to you with the consent of your competitors. By definition, restraint by a competitor is cooperation. Such cooperation from a competitor must seem to be profitable to him. *Any competition which does not eventually eliminate a competitor requires his cooperation to stabilize the situation.* The agreement is usually that of tacit nonaggression; the alternative is death for all but one competitor. A stable competitive situation requires an agreement between competing parties to maintain self-restraint. Such agreement cannot be arrived at by logic. It must be achieved by an emotional balance of forces. This is why it is necessary to appear irrational to competitors. For the same reason, you must seem unreasonable and arbitrary in negotiations with customers and suppliers.

Competition and cooperation go hand in hand in all real-life situations. Otherwise, conflict could only end in extermination of the competitor. There is a point in all situations of conflict where both parties gain more or lose less from peace than they can hope to gain from any foreseeable victory. Beyond that point cooperation is more profitable than conflict. But how will the benefits be shared?

In negotiated conflict situations, the participant who is coldly logical is at a great disadvantage. Logically, he can afford to compromise until there is no advantage left in cooperation. The negotiator/competitor whose behavior is irrational or arbitrary has a great advantage if he can depend upon his opponent being logical and unemotional. The arbitrary or irrational competitor can demand far more than a reasonable share and yet his logical opponent can still gain by compromise rather than breaking off the cooperation.

Absence of monopoly in business requires voluntary restraint of competition. At some point there must be a tacit agreement not to compete. Unless this restraint of trade were acceptable to all competitors, the resulting aggression would inevitably eliminate the less efficient competitors leaving only one. Antitrust laws represent a formal attempt to limit competition. All antimonopoly and fair trade laws constitute restraint of competition.

Utter destruction of a competitor is almost never profitable unless the competitor is unwilling to accept peace. In our daily social contacts, in our international affairs, and in our business affairs, we have far more ability to damage those around us than we ever dare use. Others have the same power to damage us. The implied agreement to restrain our potential aggression is all that stands between us and eventual elimination of one by the other. Both war and diplomacy are mechanisms for establishing or maintaining this self-imposed restraint on all competitors. The conflict continues, but within the implied area of cooperative agreement.

There is a definite limit to the range within which competitors can expect to achieve an equilibrium or negotiate a shift in equilibrium even by implication. Arbitrary, uncooperative, or aggressive attitudes will produce equally emotional reactions. These emotional reactions are in turn the basis for nonlogical and arbitrary responses. Thus, nonlogical behavior is self-limiting.

This is why the art of diplomacy can be described as the ability to be unreasonable without arousing resentment. It is worth remembering that the objective of diplomacy is to induce cooperation on terms that are relatively more favorable to you than to your protagonist without actual force being used.

More business victories are won in the minds of competitors than in the laboratory, the factory or the marketplace. The competitor's conviction that you are emotional, dogmatic, or otherwise nonlogical in your business strategy can be a great asset. This conviction on his part can result in an acceptance of your actions without retaliation, which would otherwise be unthinkable. More important, the anticipation of nonlogical or unrestrained reactions on your part can inhibit his competitive aggression.

RULES FOR THE STRATEGIST

If I were asked to distill the conditions and forces described into advice for the business-strategist, I would suggest five rules:

1. You must know as accurately as possible just what your competition has at stake in his contact with you. It is not what you gain or lose, but what he gains or loses that sets the limit on his ability to compromise with you.
2. The less the competition knows about your stakes, the less advantage he has. Without a reference point, he does not even know whether you are being unreasonable.
3. It is absolutely essential to know the character, attitudes, motives, and habitual behavior of a competitor if you wish to have a negotiating advantage.
4. The more arbitrary your demands are, the better your relative competitive position—provided you do not arouse an emotional reaction.
5. The less arbitrary you seem, the more arbitrary you can in fact be.

These rules make up the art of business brinkmanship. They are guidelines for winning a strategic victory in the minds of competitors. Once this victory has been won, it can be converted into a competitive victory in terms of sales volume, costs, and profits.

by Henry Mintzberg

Who should control the corporation? How? And for the pursuit of what goals? Historically, the corporation was controlled by its owners—through direct control of the managers if not through direct management—for the pursuit of economic goals. But as shareholding became dispersed, owner control weakened; and as the corporation grew to very large size, its economic actions came to have increasing social consequences. The giant, widely held corporation came increasingly under the implicit control of its managers, and the concept of social responsibility—the voluntary consideration of public social goals alongside the private economic ones—arose to provide a basis of legitimacy for their actions.

To some, including those closest to the managers themselves, this was accepted as a satisfactory arrangement for the large corporation. "Trust it" to the goodwill of the managers was their credo; these people will be able to achieve an appropriate balance between social and economic goals.

But others viewed this basis of control as fundamentally illegitimate. The corporation was too large, too influential, its actions too pervasive to be left free of the direct and concerted influence of outsiders. At the extreme were those who believed that legitimacy could be achieved only by subjecting managerial authority to formal and direct external control. "Nationalize it," said those at one end of the political spectrum, to put ultimate control in the hands of the government so that it will pursue public social goals. No, said those at the other end, "restore it" to direct shareholder control, so that it will not waiver from the pursuit of private economic goals.

Other people took less extreme positions. "Democratize it" became the rallying cry for some, to open up the governance of the large, widely held corporation to a variety of affected groups—if not the workers, then the customers, or conservation interests, or minorities. "Regulate it" was also a popular position, with its implicit premise that only by sharing their control with government would the corporation's managers attend to certain social goals. Then there were those who accepted direct management control so long as it was tempered by other, less formal types of influence. "Pressure it," said a generation of social activists, to ensure that social goals are taken into consideration. But others argued that because the corporation is an economic instrument, you must "induce it" by providing economic incentives to encourage the resolution of social problems.

Finally, there were those who argued that this whole debate was unnecessary, that a kind of invisible hand ensures that the economic corporation acts in a socially responsible manner. "Ignore it" was their implicit conclusion.

This article is written to clarify what has become a major debate of our era, *the* major debate revolving around the private sector: Who should control the corporation, specifically the large, widely held corporation, how, and for the pursuit of what goals? The answers that are eventually accepted will determine what kind of society we and our children shall live in. . . .

As implied earlier, the various positions of who should control the corporation, and how, can be laid out along a political spectrum, from nationalization at one end to the restoration of shareholder power at the other. From the managerial perspective, however, those two extremes are not so far apart. Both call for direct control of the corporation's managers by specific outsiders, in one case the government to ensure the pursuit of social goals, in the other case the shareholders to ensure the pursuit of economic ones. It is the moderate positions—notably, trusting the corporation to the social responsibility of its managers—that are farthest from the extremes. Hence, we can fold our spectrum around so that it takes the shape of a horseshoe.

---

* Originally published in the *California Management Review* (Fall 1984), pp. 90-115, based on a section of Henry Mintzberg, *Power in and Around Organizations* (Prentice-Hall, 1983). Copyright © 1984 by The Regents of the University of California. Reprinted with deletions by permission of The Regents.

FIGURE 1
The Conceptual
Horseshoe

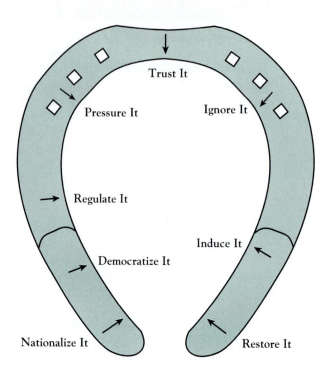

Figure 1 shows our "conceptual horseshoe," with "nationalize it" and "restore it" at the two ends. "Trust it" is at the center, because it postulates a natural balance of social and economic goals. "Democratize it," "regulate it," and "pressure it" are shown on the left side of the horseshoe, because all seek to temper economic goals with social ones. "Induce it" and "ignore it," both of which favor the exclusive pursuit of economic goals, are shown on the right side.

This conceptual horseshoe provides a basic framework to help clarify the issues in this important debate. We begin by discussing each of these positions in turn, circling the horseshoe from left to right. Finding that each (with one exception) has a logical context, we conclude—in keeping with our managerial perspective—that they should be thought of as forming a portfolio from which society can draw to deal with the issue of who should control the corporation and how.

"Nationalize It"

Nationalization of the corporation is a taboo subject in the United States—in general, but not in particular. Whenever a major corporation runs into serious difficulty (i.e., faces bankruptcy with possible loss of many jobs), mass government intervention, often including direct nationalization, inevitably comes up as an option. This option has been exercised: U.S. travelers now ride on Amtrak; Tennessee residents have for years been getting their power from a government utility; indeed, the Post Office was once a private enterprise. Other nations have, of course, been much more ambitious in this regard.

From a managerial and organizational perspective, the question is not whether nationalization is legitimate, but whether it works—at least in particular, limited circumstances.

As a response to concerns about the social responsibility of large corporations, the answer seems to be no. The evidence suggests that social difficulties arise more from the size of an organization and its degree of bureaucratization than from its form of ownership (Epstein, 1977; Jenkins, 1976). On the other hand, contrary to popular belief in the United States, nationalization does not necessarily harm economic efficiency. Over the years, Renault has been one of the most successful automobile companies outside Japan; it was nationalized by the French government shortly after World War II.... When people believe that government ownership leads to interference, politicization, and inefficiency, that may be exactly what happens. However, when they believe that nationalization *has* to work, then state-owned enterprises may be able to attract the very best talent in the country and thereby work well.

But economic efficiency is no reason to favor nationalization any more than is concern about social responsibility. Nationalization does, however, seem to make sense in at least two particular circumstances. The first is when a mission deemed necessary in a society will not be provided adequately by the private sector. That is presumably why America has its Amtrak [and why Third World nations often create state enterprises]. . . . The second is when the activities of an organization must be so intricately tied to government policy that it is best managed as a direct arm of the state. The Canadian government created Petrocan to act as a "window" and a source of expertise on the sensitive oil industry.

Thus, it is not rhetoric but requirement that should determine the role of this position as a solution to who should control the corporation. "Nationalize it" should certainly not be embraced as a panacea, but neither should it be rejected as totally inapplicable.

"Democratize It"

A less extreme position—at least in the context of the American debate—is one that calls for formal devices to broaden the governance of the corporation. The proponents of this position either accept the legal fiction of shareholder control and argue that the corporation's power base is too narrow, or else they respond to the emergent reality and question the legitimacy of managerial control. Why, they ask, do stockholders or self-selected managers have any greater right to control the profound decisions of these major institutions than do workers or customers or the neighbors downstream.

This stand is not to be confused with what is known as "participative management." The call to "democratize it" is a legal, rather than ethical one and is based on power, not generosity. Management is not asked to share its power voluntarily; rather, that power is to be reallocated constitutionally. That makes this position a fundamental and important one, *especially* in the United States with its strong tradition of pluralist control of its institutions.

The debate over democratization of the corporation has been confusing in part because many of the proposals have been so vague. We can bring some order to it by considering, in organizational terms, two basic means of democratization and two basic constituencies that can be involved. As shown in Figure 2, they suggest four possible forms of corporate democracy. One means is through the election of representatives to the board of directors, which we call *representative democracy*. The other is through formal but direct involvement in internal decision making processes, which we call *participatory democracy*. Either can focus on the *workers* . . . or else on a host of outside interest groups, the latter giving rise to a *pluralistic* form of democracy. These are basic forms of corporate democracy in theory. With one exception, they have hardly been approached—let alone achieved—in practice. But they suggest where the "democratize it" debate may be headed.

The European debate has focused on worker representative democracy. This has, in some sense, been achieved in Yugoslavia, where the workers of all but the smallest firms

FIGURE 2
Four Basic Forms of
Corporate Democracy

	GROUPS INVOLVED	
	Internal Employees	**External Interest Groups**
Board of Directors	Worker Representative Democracy (European style, e.g., "co-determination" or worker ownership)	Pluralistic Representative Democracy (American style, e.g., "public interest" directors)
Internal Decision-Making Process	Worker Participatory Democracy (e.g., works councils)	Pluralistic Participatory Democracy (e.g., outsiders on new product committees)

FOCUS OF ATTENTION

elect the members of what is the equivalent of the American board of directors. In Germany, under the so-called *Mitbestimmung* ("codetermination"), the workers and the shareholders each elect half of the directors.

The evidence on this form of corporate democracy has been consistent, and it supports neither its proponents nor its detractors. Workers' representation on the board seems to make relatively little difference one way or the other. The worker representatives concern themselves with wage and welfare issues but leave most other questions to management. Worker-controlled firms (not unlike the state-owned ones) appear to be no more socially responsible than private ones. . . .

On the other hand, worker representative democracy may have certain positive benefits. German Chancellor Helmut Schmidt is reported to have said that "the key to [his] country's postwar economic miracle was its sophisticated system of workers' participations" (in Garson, 1977:63). While no one can prove this statement, codetermination certainly does not seem to have done the German economy much harm. By providing an aura of legitimacy to the German corporation and by involving the workers (at least officially) in its governance, codetermination may perhaps have enhanced the spirit of enterprise in Germany (while having little real effect on how decisions are actually made). More significantly, codetermination may have fostered greater understanding and cooperation between the managers and the union members who fill most of the worker seats on the boards . . . .

. . . the embryonic debate over representative democracy in the United States has shown signs of moving in a different direction. Consistent with the tradition of pluralism in America's democratic institutions, there has been increasing pressure to elect outside directors who represent a wide variety of special interest groups—that is, consumers, minorities, environmentalists, and so on . . . .

Critics . . . have pointed out the problems of defining constituencies and finding the means to hold elections. "One-person, one-vote" may be easily applied to electing representatives of the workers, but no such simple rule can be found in the case of the consumer or environmental representatives, let alone ones of the public interest." Yet it is amazing how quickly things become workable in the United States when Americans decide to put their collective mind to it. Indeed, the one case of public directors that I came across is telling in this regard. According to a Conference Board report, the selection by the Chief Justice of the Supreme Court of New Jersey of 6 of the 24 members of the board of Prudential Insurance as public directors has been found by the company to be "quite workable" (Bacon and Brown, 1975:48). . . . [Note—see the associated box on "The Power of the Board."]

Despite its problems, representative democracy is crystal clear compared with participatory democracy. What the French call "autogestion" (as opposed to "cogestion," or code-termination) seems to describe a kind of bottom-up, grass-roots democracy in which the

---

THE POWER OF THE BOARD

Proposals for representative democracy, indeed those for nationalization and the restoration of shareholder control as well, rest on assumptions about the power of the board of directors. It may, therefore, be worth considering at this point the roles that boards of directors play in organizations and the board's resulting powers.

In law, traditionally, the business of a corporation was to be "managed" by its board. But of course, the board does no such thing. Managers manage, although some may happen to sit on the board. What, then, are the roles of the board, particularly of its "outside" directors?

The most tangible role of the board, and clearly provided for in law, is to name, and of course to dismiss as well, the chief executive officer, that person who in turn names the rest of the management. A second role may be to exercise direct control during periods of crisis, for example when the management has failed to provide leadership. And a third is to review the major decisions of the management as well as its overall performance.

These three constitute the board's roles of control, in principal at least because there is no shortage of evidence that boards have difficulty doing even these effectively, especially outside directors. Their job is, after all, part time, and in a brief meeting once in a while they face a complex organization led by a highly organized management that deals with it every day. The result is that board control tends to reduce to naming and replacing the chief executive, and that person's knowledge of that fact, nothing more. Indeed, even that power is circumscribed, because a management cannot be replaced very often. In a sense, the board is like a bee hovering near a person picking flowers. The person must proceed carefully, so as to not provoke the bee, but can proceed with the task. But if the bee does happen to be provoked, it only gets to sting once. Thus many boards try to know only enough to know when the management is not doing its job properly, so that they can replace it.

But if boards tend to be weaker than expected in exercising *control over* the organization, they also tend perhaps to be stronger than expected in providing *service to* the organization. Here board membership plays at least four other roles. First, it "co-opts" influential outsiders: The organization uses the status of a seat on its board to gain the support of people important to it (as in the case of the big donors who sit on university boards). Second, board membership may be used to establish contacts for the organization (as when retired military officers sit on the boards of weapons manufacturing firms). This may be done to help in such things as the securing of contracts and the raising of funds. Third, seats on the board can be used to enhance an organization's reputation (as when an astronaut or some other type of celebrity is given a seat). And fourth, the board can be used to provide advice for the organization (as in the case of many of the bankers and lawyers who sit on the boards of corporations).

How much do boards serve organizations, and how much do they control them? Some boards do, of course, exercise control, particularly when their members represent a well-defined constituency, such as the substantial owner of a corporation. But, as noted, this tends to be a loose control at best. And other boards hardly do even that, especially when their constituencies are widely dispersed.

To represent everyone is ultimately to represent no one, especially when faced with a highly organized management that knows exactly what it wants. (Or from the elector's point of view, having some distant representative sitting on a board somewhere hardly brings him or her closer to control over the things that impinge on daily life—the work performed, the products consumed, the rivers polluted.) In corporations, this has been shown to be true of the directors who represent many small shareholders no less than those who represent many workers or many customers, perhaps even those who represent government, since that can be just a confusing array of pressure groups. These boards become, at best, tools of the organization, providing it with the variety of the services discussed above, at worst mere façades of formal authority.

workers participate directly in decision making (instead of overseeing management's decisions from the board of directors) and also elect their own managers (who then become more administrators than bosses). Yet such proposals are inevitably vague, and I have heard of no large mass production or mass service firm—not even one owned by workers or a union—that comes close to this. . . .

What has impeded worker participatory democracy? In my opinion, something rather obvious has stood in its way; namely, the structure required by the very organizations in which the attempts have been made to apply it. Worker participatory democracy—and worker representative democracy too, for that matter—has been attempted primarily in organizations containing large numbers of workers who do highly routine, rather unskilled jobs that are typical of most mass production and service—what I have elsewhere called Machine Bureaucracies. The overriding requirement in Machine Bureaucracy is for tight coordination, the kind that can only be achieved by central administrators. For example, the myriad of decisions associated with producing an automobile at Volvo's Kalmar works in Sweden cannot be made by autonomous groups, each doing as it pleases. The whole car must fit together in a particular way at the end of the assembly process. These decisions require a highly sophisticated system of bureaucratic coordination. That is why automobile companies are structured into rigid hierarchies of authority. . . .

Participatory democracy *is* approached in other kinds of organizations . . . the autonomous professional institutions such as universities and hospitals, which have very different needs for central coordination. . . . But the proponents of democracy in organizations are not lobbying for changes in hospitals or universities. It is the giant, mass producers they are after, and unless the operating work in these corporations becomes largely skilled and professional in nature, nothing approaching participative democracy can be expected.

In principal, the pluralistic form of participatory democracy means that a variety of groups external to the corporation can somehow control its decision-making processes directly. In practice, of course, this concept is even more elusive than the worker form of participatory democracy. To fully open up the internal decision-making processes of the corporation to outsiders would mean chaos. Yet certain very limited forms of outside participation would seem to be not only feasible but perhaps even desirable. . . . Imagine telephone company executives resolving rate conflicts with consumer groups in quiet offices instead of having to face them in noisy public hearings.

To conclude, corporate democracy—whether representative or participatory in form—may be an elusive and difficult concept, but it cannot be dismissed. It is not just another social issue, like conservation or equal opportunity, but one that strikes at the most fundamental of values. Ours has become a society of organizations. Democracy will have decreasing meaning to most citizens if it cannot be extended beyond political and judicial processes to those institutions that impinge upon them in their daily lives—as workers, as consumers, as neighbors. This is why we shall be hearing a great deal more of "democratize it."

"Regulate It"

In theory, regulating the corporation is about as simple as democratizing it is complex. In practice, it is, of course, another matter. To the proponents of "regulate it," the corporation can be made responsive to social needs by having its actions subjected to the controls of a higher authority—typically government, in the form of a regulatory agency or legislation backed up by the courts. Under regulation, constraints are imposed externally on the corporation while its internal governance is left to its managers.

Regulation of business is at least as old as the Code of Hammurabi. In America, it has tended to come in waves. . . .

To some, regulation is a clumsy instrument that should never be relied upon; to others, it is a panacea for the problems of social responsibility. At best, regulation sets minimum and usually crude standards of acceptable behavior; when it works, it does not make any firm socially responsible so much as stop some from being grossly irresponsible. Because it is inflexible, regulation tends to be applied slowly and conservatively, usually lagging public sentiment. Regulation often does not work because of difficulties in enforcement. The problems of the regulatory agencies are legendary—limited resources and information compared with the industries they are supposed to regulate, the cooptation of the regulators by industries, and so on. When applied indiscriminately, regulation either fails dramatically or else succeeds and creates havoc.

Yet there are obvious places for regulation. A prime one is to control tangible "externalities"—costs incurred by corporations that are passed on to the public at large. When, for example, costly pollution or worker health problems can be attributed directly to a corporation, then there seems to be every reason to force it (and its customers) to incur these costs directly, or else to terminate the actions that generate them. Likewise, regulation may have a place where competition encourages the unscrupulous to pull all firms down to a base level of behavior, forcing even the well-intentioned manager to ignore the social consequences of his actions. Indeed, in such cases, the socially responsible behavior is to encourage sensible regulation. "Help us to help others," businessmen should be telling the government. . . .

Most discouraging, however, is Theodore Levitt's revelation some years ago that business has fought every piece of proposed regulatory or social legislation throughout this century, from the Child Labor Acts on up. In Levitt's opinion, much of that legislation has been good for business—dissolving the giant trusts, creating a more honest and effective stock market, and so on. Yet, "the computer is programmed to cry wolf" (Levitt, 1968:83). . . .

In summary, regulation is a clumsy instrument but not a useless one. Were the business community to take a more enlightened view of it, regulation could be applied more appropriately, and we would not need these periodic housecleanings to eliminate the excesses.

"Pressure It"

"Pressure it" is designed to do what "regulate it" fails to do: provoke corporations to act beyond some base level of behavior, usually in an area that regulation misses entirely. Here, activists bring ad hoc campaigns of pressure to bear on one or a group of corporations to keep them responsive to the activists' interpretation of social needs. . . .

"Pressure it" is a distinctively American position. While Europeans debate the theories of nationalization and corporate democracy in their cafes, Americans read about the exploits of Ralph Nader et al. in their morning newspapers. Note that "pressure it," unlike "regulate it," implicitly accepts management's right to make the final decisions. Perhaps this is one reason why it is favored in America.

While less radical than the other positions so far discussed, "pressure it" has nevertheless proved far more effective in eliciting behavior sensitive to social needs . . . [activist groups] have pressured for everything from the dismemberment of diversified corporations to the development of day care centers. Of special note is the class action suit, which has opened up a whole new realm of corporate social issues. But the effective use of the pressure campaign has not been restricted to the traditional activist. President Kennedy used it to roll back U.S. Steel price increases in the early 1960s, and business leaders in Pittsburgh used it in the late 1940s by threatening to take their freight-haulage business elsewhere if the Pennsylvania Railroad did not replace its coal burning locomotives to help clean up their city's air.

"Pressure it" as a means to change corporate behavior is informal, flexible, and focused; hence, it has been highly successful. Yet it is irregular and ad hoc, with different pressure campaigns sometimes making contradictory demands on management. Compared to the positions to its right on the horseshoe, "pressure it," like the other positions to its left, is based on confrontation rather than cooperation.

To a large and vocal contingent, which parades under the banner of "social responsibility," the corporation has no need to act irresponsibly, and therefore there is no reason for it to either be nationalized by the state, democratized by its different constituencies, regulated by the government, or pressured by activists. This contingent believes that the corporation's leaders can be trusted to attend to social goals for their own sake, simply because it is the noble thing to do. (Once this position was known as *nobelesse oblige*, literally "nobility obliges.")

We call this position "trust it," or, more exactly, "trust the corporation to the goodwill of its managers," although looking from the outside in, it might just as well be called "socialize it." We place it in the center of our conceptual horseshoe because it alone postulates a natural balance between social and economic goals—a balance which is to be attained in the heads (or perhaps the hearts) of responsible businessmen. And, as a not necessarily incidental consequence, power can be left in the hands of the managers; the corporation can be trusted to those who reconcile social and economic goals.

The attacks on social responsibility, from the right as well as the left, boil down to whether corporate managers should be trusted when they claim to pursue social goals; if so, whether they are capable of pursuing such goals; and finally, whether they have any right to pursue such goals.

The simplest attack is that social responsibility is all rhetoric, no action. E. F. Cheit refers to the "Gospel of Social Responsibility" as "designed to justify the power of managers over an ownerless system" (1964:172). . . .

Others argue that businessmen lack the personal capabilities required to pursue social goals. Levitt claims that the professional manager reaches the top of the hierarchy by dedication to his firm and his industry; as a result, his knowledge of social issues is highly restricted (Levitt, 1968:83). Others argue that an orientation to efficiency renders business leaders inadept at handling complex social problems (which require flexibility and political finesse, and sometimes involve solutions that are uneconomic). . . .

The most far reaching criticism is that businessmen have no right to pursue social goals. "Who authorized them to do that?" asks Braybrooke (1967:224), attacking from the left. What business have they—self-selected or at best appointed by shareholders—to impose *their* interpretation of the public good on society? Let the elected politicians, directly responsible to the population, look after the social goals.

But this attack comes from the right, too. Milton Friedman writes that social responsibility amounts to spending other people's money—if not that of shareholders, then of customers or employees. Drawing on all the pejorative terms of right-wing ideology, Friedman concludes that social responsibility is a "fundamentally subversive doctrine," representing "pure and unadulterated socialism," supported by businessmen who are "unwitting puppets of the intellectual forces that have been undermining the basis of a free society these past decades." To Friedman, "there is one and only one social responsibility of business—to use its resources and engage in activities designed to increase its profits so long as it stays within the rules of the game" (1970). Let businessmen, in other words, stick to their own business, which is business itself.

The empirical evidence on social responsibility is hardly more encouraging. Brenner and Molander, comparing their 1977 survey of *Harvard Business Review* readers with one conducted fifteen years earlier, concluded that the "respondents are somewhat more cynical about the ethical conduct of their peers" than they were previously (1977:59). Close to half the respondents agreed with the statement that "the American business executive tends not to apply the great ethical laws immediately to work. He is preoccupied chiefly with gain" (p. 62). Only 5% listed social responsibility as a factor "influencing ethical standards" whereas 31 % and 20% listed different factors related to pressure campaigns and 10% listed regulation. . . .

The modern corporation has been described as a rational, amoral institution—its professional managers "hired guns" who pursue "efficiently" any goals asked of them. The problem is that efficiency really means measurable efficiency, so that the guns load only with goals that can be quantified. Social goals, unlike economic ones, just don't lend themselves to quantification. As a result, the performance control systems—on which modern corporations so heavily depend—tend to drive out social goals in favor of economic ones (Ackerman, 1975). . . .

In the contemporary large corporation, professional amorality turns into economic morality. When the screws of the performance control systems are turned tight . . . economic morality can turn into social immorality. And it happens often: A *Fortune* writer found that "a surprising number of [big companies] have been involved in blatant illegalities" in the 1970s, at least 117 of 1,043 firms studied (Ross, 1980:57). . . .

How, then, is anyone to "trust it"?

The fact is that we have to trust it, for two reasons. First, the strategic decisions of large organizations inevitably involve social as well as economic consequences that are inextricably intertwined. The neat distinction between economic goals in the private sector and social goals in the public sector just doesn't hold up in practice. Every important decision of the large corporation—to introduce a new product line, to close an old plant, whatever—generates all kinds of social consequences. There is no such thing as purely economic decisions in big business. Only a conceptual ostrich, with his head deeply buried in the abstractions of economic theory, could possibly use the distinction between economic and social goals to dismiss social responsibility.

The second reason we have to "trust it" is that there is always some degree of discretion involved in corporate decision making, discretion to thwart social needs or to attend to them. Things could be a lot better in today's corporation, but they could also be an awful lot worse. It is primarily our ethics that keep us where we are. If the performance control systems favored by diversified corporations cut too deeply into our ethical standards, then our choice is clear; to reduce these standards or call into question the whole trend toward diversification.

To dismiss social responsibility is to allow corporate behavior to drop to the lowest level, propped up only by external controls such as regulation and pressure campaigns. Solzhenitsyn, who has experienced the natural conclusion of unrestrained bureaucratization, warns us (in sharp contrast to Friedman) that "a society with no other scale but the legal one is not quite worthy of man. . . . A society which is based on the letter of the law and never reaches any higher is scarcely taking advantage of the high level of human possibilities" (1978:B1).

This is not to suggest that we must trust it completely. We certainly cannot trust it unconditionally by accepting the claim popular in some quarters that only business can solve the social ills of society. Business has no business using its resources without constraint in the social sphere—whether to support political candidates or to dictate implicitly through donations how nonprofit institutions should allocate their efforts. But where business is inherently involved, where its decisions have social consequences, that is where social responsibility has a role to play: where business creates externalities that cannot be measured and attributed to it (in other words, where regulation is ineffective); where regulation would work if only business would cooperate with it; where the corporation can fool its customers, or suppliers, or government through superior knowledge; where useful products can be marketed instead of wasteful or destructive ones. In other words, we have to realize that in many spheres we must trust it, or at least socialize it (and perhaps change it) so that we can trust it. Without responsible and ethical people in important places, our society is not worth very much.

"Ignore It"

"Ignore it" differs from the other positions on the horseshoe in that explicitly or implicitly it calls for no change in corporate behavior. It assumes that social needs are met in the course of pursuing economic goals. We include this position in our horseshoe because it is held by many influential people and also because its validity would preempt support for the other positions. We must therefore, investigate it alongside the others.

It should be noted at the outset the "ignore it" is not the same position as "trust it." In the latter, to be good is the right thing to do, in the present case, "it pays to be good." The distinction is subtle but important, for now it is economics, not ethics, that elicits the desired behavior. One need not strive to be ethical; economic forces will ensure that social needs fall conveniently into place. Here we have moved one notch to the right on our horseshoe, into the realm where the economic goals dominate. . . .

"Ignore it" is sometimes referred to as "enlightened self-interest," although some of its proponents are more enlightened than others. Many a true believer in social responsibility has used the argument that it pays to be good to ward off the attacks from the right that corporations have no business pursuing social goals. Even Milton Friedman must admit that they have every right to do so if it pays them economically. The danger of such arguments, however—and a prime reason "ignore it" differs from "trust it"—is that they tend to support the status quo: corporations need not change their behavior because it already pays to be good.

Sometimes the case for "ignore it" is made in terms of corporations at large, that the whole business community will benefit from socially responsible behavior. Other times the case is made in terms of the individual corporation, that it will benefit directly from its own socially responsible actions. . . . Others make the case for "ignore it" in "social investment" terms, claiming that socially responsible behavior pays off in a better image for the firm, a more positive relationship with customers, and ultimately a healthier and more stable society in which to do business.

Then, there is what I like to call the "them" argument: "If we're not good, they will move in"—"they" being Ralph Nader, the government, whoever. In other words, "Be good or else." The trouble with this argument is that by reducing social responsibility to simply a political tool for sustaining managerial control of the corporation in the face of outside threats, it tends to encourage general pronouncements instead of concrete actions (unless of course, "they" actually deliver with pressure campaigns). . . .

The "ignore it" position rests on some shaky ground. It seems to encourage average behavior at best; and where the average does not seem to be good enough, it encourages the status quo. In fact, ironically, "ignore it" makes a strong case for "pressure it," since the whole argument collapses in the absence of pressure campaigns. Thus while many influential people take this position, we question whether in the realities of corporate behavior it can really stand alone.

"Induce It"

Continuing around to the right, our next position drops all concern with social responsibility per se and argues, simply, "pay it to be good," or, from the corporation's point of view, "be good only where it pays." Here, the corporation does not actively pursue social goals at all, whether as ends in themselves or as means to economic ends. Rather, it undertakes socially desirable programs only when induced economically to do so—usually through government incentives. If society wishes to clean up urban blight, then let its government provide subsidies for corporations that renovate buildings; if pollution is the problem, then let corporations be rewarded for reducing it.

"Induce it" faces "regulate it" on the opposite side of the horseshoe for good reason. While one penalizes the corporation for what it does do, the other rewards it for doing what it might not otherwise do. Hence these two positions can be direct substitutes: pollution can be alleviated by introducing penalties for the damage done or by offering incentives for the improvements rendered.

Logic would, however, dictate a specific role for each of these positions. Where a corporation is doing society a specific, attributable harm—as in the case of pollution—then paying it to stop hardly seems to make a lot of sense. If society does not wish to outlaw the harmful behavior altogether, then surely it must charge those responsible for it—the corporation and, ultimately, its customers. Offering financial incentives to stop causing harm would be to invite a kind of blackmail—for example, encouraging corporations to pollute so as to get paid to stop. And every citizen would be charged for the harm done by only a few.

On the other hand, where social problems exist which cannot be attributed to specific corporations, yet require the skills of certain corporations for solution, then financial incentives clearly make sense (so long, of course, as solutions can be clearly defined and tied to tangible economic rewards). Here, and not under "trust it," is where the "only business can do it" argument belongs. When it is true that only business can do it (and business has not done it to us in the first place), then business should be encouraged to do it. . . .

"Restore It"

Our last position on the horseshoe tends to be highly ideological, the first since "democratize it" to seek a fundamental change in the governance and the goals of the corporation. Like the proponents of "nationalize it," those of this position believe that managerial control is illegitimate and must be replaced by a more valid form of external control. The corporation should be restored to its former status, that is, returned to its "rightful" owners, the shareholders. The only way to ensure the relentless pursuit of economic goals—and that means the maximization of profit, free of the "subversive doctrine" of social responsibility—is to put control directly into the hands of those to whom profit means the most.

A few years ago this may have seemed to be an obsolete position. But thanks to its patron saint Milton Friedman . . . . it has recently come into prominence. Also, other forms of restoring it, including the "small is beautiful" theme, have also become popular in recent years.

Friedman has written,

> In a free-enterprise, private-property system, a corporate executive is an employee of the owners of the business. He has direct responsibility to his employers. That responsibility is to conduct the business in accordance with their desires, which generally will be to make as much money as possible while conforming to the basic rules of the society, both those embodied in law and those embodied in ethical custom. (1970:33)

Interestingly, what seems to drive Friedman is a belief that the shift over the course of this century from owner to manager control, with its concerns about social responsibility, represents an unstoppable skid around our horseshoe. In the opening chapter of his book *Capitalism and Freedom*, Friedman seems to accept only two possibilities—traditional capitalism and socialism as practiced in Eastern Europe. The absence of the former must inevitably lead to the latter:

> The preservation and expansion of freedom are today threatened from two directions. The one threat is obvious and clear. It is the external threat coming from the evil men in the Kremlin who promised to bury us. The other threat is far more subtle. It is the internal threat coming from men of good intentions and good will who wish to reform us. (1962:20)

The problem of who should control the corporation thus reduces to a war between two ideologies—in Friedman's terms, "subversive" socialism and "free" enterprise. In this world of black and white, there can be no middle ground, no moderate position between the black of "nationalize it" and the white of "restore it," none of the gray of "trust it." Either the owners will control the corporation of else the government will. Hence: " 'restore it' or else." Anchor the corporation on the right side of the horseshoe, Friedman seems to be telling us, the only place where "free" enterprise and "freedom" are safe.

All of this, in my view, rests on a series of assumptions—technical, economic, and political—which contain a number of fallacies. First is the fallacy of the technical assumption of shareholder control. Every trend in ownership during this century seems to refute the assumption that small shareholders are either willing or able to control the large, widely held corporation. The one place where free markets clearly still exist is in stock ownership, and that has served to detach ownership from control. When power is widely dispersed—among stockholders no less than workers or customers—those who share it tend to remain passive. It pays no one of them to invest the effort to exercise their power. Hence, even if serious shareholders did control the boards of widely held corporations (and one survey of all the directors of the *Fortune* 500 in 1977 found that only 1.6% of them represented significant shareholder interests, [Smith, 1978]), the question remains open as to whether they would actually try to control the management. (This is obviously not true of closely held corporations, but these—probably a decreasing minority of the *Fortune* 500— are "restored" in any event.)

The economic assumptions of free markets have been discussed at length in the literature. Whether there exists vibrant competition, unlimited entry, open information, consumer sovereignity, and labor mobility is debatable. Less debatable is the conclusion that the larger the corporation, the greater is its ability to interfere with these processes. The issues we are discussing center on the giant corporation. It is not Luigi's Body Shop that Ralph Nader is after, but General Motors, a corporation that employs more than half a million people and earns greater revenues than many national governments.

Those who laid the foundation for conventional economic theory—such as Adam Smith and Alfred Marshall—never dreamed of the massive amounts now spent for advertising campaigns, most of them designed as much for affect as for effect; of the waves of conglomeration that have combined all kinds of diverse businesses into single corporate entities; of chemical complexes that cost more than a billion dollars; and of the intimate relationships that now exist between giant corporations and government, as customer and partner not to mention subsidizer. The concept of arm's length relationships in such conditions is, at best, nostalgic. What happens to consumer sovereignty when Ford knows more about its gas tanks than do its customers? And what does labor mobility mean in the presence of an inflexible pension plan, or commitment to a special skill, or a one-factory town? It is an ironic twist of conventional economic theory that the worker is the one who typically stays put, thus rendering false the assumption of labor mobility, while the shareholder is the mobile one, thus spoiling the case for owner control.

The political assumptions are more ideological in nature, although usually implicit. These assumptions are that the corporation is essentially amoral, society's instrument for producing goods and services, and, more broadly, that a society is "free" and "democratic" so long as its governmental leaders are elected by universal suffrage and do not interfere with the legal activities of businessmen. But many people—a large majority of the general public, if polls are to be believed—seem to subscribe to one or more assumptions that contradict these "free enterprise" assumptions.

One assumption is that the large corporation is a social and political institution as much as an economic instrument. Economic activities, as noted previously, produce all kinds of social consequences. Jobs get created and rivers get polluted, cities get built and workers get injured. These social consequences cannot be factored out of corporate strategic decisions and assigned to government.

Another assumption is that society cannot achieve the necessary balance between social and economic needs so long as the private sector attends only to economic goals. Given the pervasiveness of business in society, the acceptance of Friedman's prescriptions would drive us toward a one-dimensional society—a society that is too utilitarian and too materialistic. Economic morality, as noted earlier, can amount to a social immorality.

Finally, the question is asked: Why the owners? In a democratic society, what justifies owner control of the corporation any more than worker control, or consumer control, or pluralistic control? Ours is not Adam Smith's society of small proprietors and shopkeepers. His butcher, brewer, and baker have become Iowa Beef Packers, Anheuser-Bush, and ITT Continental Baking. What was once a case for individual democracy now becomes a case for oligarchy. . . .

I see Friedman's form of "restore it" as a rather quaint position in a society of giant corporations, managed economies, and dispersed shareholders—a society in which the collective power of corporations is coming under increasing scrutiny and in which the distribution between economic and social goals is being readdressed.

Of course, there are other ways [than Friedman's] to "restore it." "Divest it" could return the corporation to the business or central theme it knows best, restoring the role of allocating funds between different businesses to capital markets instead of central headquarters. Also, boards could be restored to positions of influence by holding directors legally responsible for their actions and by making them more independent of managers (for example, by providing them with personal staffs and by precluding full-time managers from their ranks, especially the position of chairman). We might even wish to extend use of "reduce it" where possible, to decrease the size of those corporations that have grown excessively large on the basis of market or political power rather than economies of scale, and perhaps to eliminate certain forms of vertical integration. In many cases it may prove advantageous, economically as well as socially, to have the corporation trade with its suppliers and customers instead of being allowed to ingest them indiscriminately.*

I personally doubt that these proposals could be any more easily realized in today's society than those of Friedman, even though I believe them to be more desirable. "Restore it" is the nostalgic position on our horseshoe, a return to our fantasies of a glorious past. In this, society of giant organizations, it flies in the face of powerful economic and political forces.

Conclusion: If the Shoe Fits . . .

I believe that today's corporation cannot ride on any one position any more than a horse can ride on part of a shoe. In other words, we need to treat the conceptual horseshoe as a portfolio of positions from which we can draw, depending on circumstances. Exclusive

---

*A number of these proposals would be worthwhile to pursue in the public and parapublic sectors as well, to divide up overgrown hospitals, school systems, social agencies and all kinds of government departments.

reliance on one position will lead to a narrow and dogmatic society, with an excess concentration of power . . . the use of a variety of positions can encourage the pluralism I believe most of us feel is necessary to sustain democracy. If the shoe fits, then let the corporation wear it.

I do not mean to imply that the eight positions do not represent fundamentally different values and, in some cases, ideologies as well. Clearly they do. But I also believe that anyone who makes an honest assessment of the realities of power in and around today's large corporations must conclude that a variety of positions have to be relied upon [even if they themselves might tilt to the left, right or center of our horseshoe]. . . .

I tilt to the left of center, as has no doubt been obvious in my comments to this point. Let me summarize my own prescriptions as follows, and in the process provide some basis for evaluating the relevant roles of each of the eight positions.

First "trust it," or at least "socialize it." Despite my suspicions about much of the rhetoric that passes for social responsibility and the discouraging evidence about the behavior of large contemporary organizations (not only corporations), I remain firmly convinced that without honest and responsible people in important places, we are in deep trouble. We need to trust it because, no matter how much we rely on the other positions, managers will always retain a great deal of power. And that power necessarily has social no less than economic consequences. The positions on the right side of our horseshoe ignore these social consequences while some of those on the left fail to recognize the difficulties of influencing these consequences in large, hierarchical organizations. Sitting between these two sets of positions, managers can use their discretion to satisfy or to subvert the wishes of the public. Ultimately, what managers do is determined by their sense of responsibility as individual members of society.

Although we must "trust it," we cannot *only* "trust it." As I have argued, there is an appropriate and limited place for social responsibility—essentially to get the corporation's own house in order and to encourage it to act responsibly in its own sphere of operations. Beyond that, social responsibility needs to be tempered by other positions around our horseshoe.

Then "pressure it," ceaselessly. As we have seen, too many forces interfere with social responsibility. The best antidote to these forces is the ad hoc pressure campaign, designed to pinpoint unethical behavior and raise social consciousness about issues. The existence of the "pressure it" position is what most clearly distinguishes the western from the eastern "democracies." Give me one Ralph Nader to all those banks of government accountants.

In fact, "pressure it" underlies the success of most of the other positions. Pressure campaigns have brought about necessary new regulations and have highlighted the case for corporate democracy. As we have seen, the "ignore it" position collapses without "pressure it". . . .

After that, try to "democratize it." A somewhat distant third in my portfolio is "democratize it," a position I view as radical only in terms of the current U.S. debate, not in terms of fundamental American values. Democracy matters most where it affects us directly—in the water we drink, the jobs we perform, the products we consume. How can we call our society democratic when many of its most powerful institutions are closed to governance from the outside and are run as hierarchies of authority from within?

As noted earlier, I have no illusions about having found the means to achieve corporate democracy. But I do know that Americans can be very resourceful when they decide to resolve a problem—and this is a problem that badly needs resolving. Somehow, ways must be found to open the corporation up to the formal influence of the constituencies most affected by it—employees, customers, neighbors, and so on—without weakening it as an economic institution. At stake is nothing less than the maintenance of basic freedoms in our society.

Then, only where specifically appropriate, "regulate it" and "induce it." Facing each other on the horseshoe are two positions that have useful if limited roles to play. Regulation is neither a panacea nor a menace. It belongs where the corporation can abuse the power it has and can be penalized for that abuse—notably where externalities can be identified with specific corporations. Financial inducements belong, not where a corporation has created a problem, but where it has the capability to solve a problem created by someone else.

Occasionally, selectively, "nationalize it" and "restore it," but not in Friedman's way. The extreme positions should be reserved for extreme problems. If "pressure it" is a scalpel and "regulate it" a cleaver, then "nationalize it" and "restore it" are guillotines.

Both these positions are implicitly proposed as alternatives to "democratize it." One offers public control, the other "shareholder democracy." The trouble is that control by everyone often turns out to be control by no one, while control by the owners—even if attainable—would remove the corporation even further from the influence of those most influenced by it.

Yet, as noted earlier, nationalization sometimes makes sense—when private enterprise cannot provide a necessary mission, at least in a sufficient or appropriate way, and when the activities of a corporation must be intricately tied in to government policy.

As for "restore it," I believe Friedman's particular proposals will aggravate the problems of political control and social responsibility, strengthening oligarchical tendencies in society and further tilting what I see as the current imbalance between social and economic goals. In response to Friedman's choice between "subversive" socialism and "free" enterprise, I say "a pox on both your houses." Let us concentrate our efforts on the intermediate positions around the horseshoe. However, other forms of "restore it" are worth considering—to "divest it" where diversification has interfered with capital markets, competition, and economic efficiency; to "*dis*integrate it" vertically where a trading network is preferable to a managerial hierarchy; to strengthen its board so that directors can assess managers objectively; and to "reduce it" where size represents a power game rather than a means to provide better and more efficient service to the public. I stand with Friedman in wishing to see competitive markets strengthened; it is just that I believe his proposals lead in exactly the opposite direction.

Finally above all, don't "ignore it." I leave one position out of my portfolio altogether, because it contradicts the others. The one thing we must not do is ignore the large, widely held corporation. It is too influential a force in our lives. Our challenge is to find ways to distribute the power in and around our large organizations so that they will remain responsive, vital, and effective.

MANAGERIAL STYLES

This chapter on "managerial styles" is included in this book for the first time, partly to correct an earlier oversight and partly to reflect increasing attention to the importance of the "softer" aspect of style at the expense of the "harder" aspects of structure and systems. Three readings make up this chapter, each colorful in its own right.

The article by Pat Pitcher, of Montreal's École des Hautes Études Commerciales, summarizes her fascinating doctoral thesis, which focused on managerial style over the history of one large financial institution in particular. Pitcher contrasts artists, craftsmen, and technocrats—if you like, creative visionaries, sympathetic leaders, and systematic analysts. She is no friend of the technocrats, as you shall see, believing that artists and craftsmen have to take the lead in today's organizations.

The second article, by Peter Senge of the MIT Sloan School of Management and based on his highly successful book, *The Fifth Discipline*, characterizes the "leader's new work" as being to build the learning organization. Senge views the ability to learn as the primary source of a company's competitive advantage and argues that facilitating organizational learning is the principal task of the strategist. Like Hamel and Prahalad, Senge sees a long-term vision as the key source of tension in the organization and, therefore, of energy in the learning process. The manager must be the designer, the teacher, and the steward of the learning organization and to play these roles, he must develop a new set of skills, which Senge describes in the article. Above all, he promotes systems thinking. On balance, Senge's new leader may well be Pitcher's craftsman (see especially the quote he uses to end his discussion—hardly the technocrat or even the artist), in which case this reading fleshes out that style in an interesting way.

The third reading, by Leonard Sayles, who spent most of his career at the Columbia University business school, focuses on a much neglected but critical player in the organization, the middle manager. Sayles points out that if organizations want "to do things right," and not just "do the right things" (the concern of so much of the strategy literature), then they had better get smart about the role of middle managers, especially to hold things together and facilitate innovative and even strategic processes themselves. Sayles is perhaps most sympathetic to the craftsman style, too, but he also emphasizes the action level of management (as discussed in the Mintzberg reading of Chapter 2), in contrast to Pitcher and Senge, who put their attention more on the people level. Since most of you who use this book will be (or are) middle managers long before you may become senior managers, you would do well to give very careful attention to this reading. It is the superb statement of a man who has dedicated much of his career to the study of middle managers.

by Patricia Pitcher

. . .If you want to change corporate North America, you have to change its managers—not the culture, not the structure, but the people. All else is abstraction.

In my 20 years as an executive, a board member of multi-billion dollar corporations and, recently, an academic, one lesson stands out. Give a technocrat ultimate authority and he or she will drive out everything else: vision and its carriers—artists—will be replaced; experience and its carriers—craftsmen—will follow. Dissent will be driven from the board. The organization will ossify, turn inward and short-term. . . .

HOW TO IDENTIFY A TECHNOCRAT

Technocrats are never at a loss for words, charts, or graphs. They always have a plan of action in three parts. They rarely laugh out loud, except maybe at baseball games; never at work. When they explain to you why Jim or George had to be let go, they use expressions like, "He just wasn't tough, professional, modern, rigorous, serious, hard-working enough." If they go on to mention "too emotional," watch out! You have a technocrat on your hands. This person will be described by peers and colleagues as controlled, conservative, serious, analytical, no-nonsense, intense, determined, cerebral, methodical, and meticulous. Individually, any of these words might be a compliment; together, they represent a syndrome. Here is an example of how a technocrat thinks:

> Mirroring a world-wide trend . . . , we initiated in 1989 and continued in 1990 an extensive program under which operations were regrouped, assets sold, and activities rationalized. New chief executives have been appointed and our strategy is profitability.

In this one paragraph from an annual report, we notice three things. First, the technocrat loves conventional wisdom and thus the first phase, "Mirroring a world-wide trend"; if everyone else is doing it, it must be right. Second, we see the word "rationalized"; this is the watchword. Third, we are told that all the bad guys have been fired and replaced by serious folk. When things go wrong it is always the fault of someone else.

RECOGNIZING AN ARTIST

How do you recognize artists? Well, pretty much by the opposite. What is your strategic plan for the future? Answer: "to get big," "to hit $5 billion in sales," "to beat the pants off the competition," "to be a world leader by 2020." Artists may be a little short on the details, on the how. Board presentations are sometimes a little loose—unless they are done by the chief financial officer. The artist CEO might get overtly angry or euphoric at board meetings. How does the artist CEO talk? Listen to one.

> What is strategy anyway? Grand plan? No. You try to instill a vision you have and get people to buy in. The strategy comes from astrology; quirks, dreams, love affairs, science fiction, perception of society, some madness probably, ability to guess. It is clear but fluid. Action brings precision. Very vague, but becomes clear in the act of transformation. Creation is the storm.

When CEOs like this talk to their boards about "astrology; quirks, dreams," boards have a tendency to get a little uneasy. This person's peers and colleagues describe him or her as bold, daring, exciting, volatile, intuitive, entrepreneurial, inspiring, imaginative, unpredictable, and funny. Technocrats will apply labels like "star-trekky," or more simply, nuts. The artist makes both fast friends and abiding enemies. Very few have a neutral reac-

*Reprinted with deletions from the article originally titled "Balancing Personality Types at the Top" with permission of *Business Quarterly* (Winter 1993) published by the Western Business School, University of Western Ontario, London, Canada.

tion. The organization as a whole is an exciting place to be; confusing maybe, dizzying maybe, but exciting nonetheless.

AND NOW, THE CRAFTSMAN

Rosabeth Moss Kanter insists, and I think she is dead right, that people take the long view when they perceive their leaders as trustworthy, and that the sacrifices they are called upon to make are genuinely for the collective future and not to line someone else's pockets today. The organizational craftsmen embody these values. People trust them. They see the organization as an enduring institution, one that has a life of its own, a past and a future, one of which he or she is but a custodian. They tend to stay in one organization and are therefore intimately familiar with its past and infinitely careful about preserving its identity in the midst of change. The craftsman provides continuity and organizational glue, and stimulates loyalty and commitment.

Craft is fundamentally conservative, rooted in tradition. Samuel Johnson, the great British satirist, wrote, "You cannot with all the talk in the world, enable a man to make a shoe." Experience and practice are essential to judgment. What happens if you do not have experience in the firm, in the industry, in the organization? As one CEO once said, referring to a famous bright, young, professional, "He'll get hit by every blue-suede shoes man in the country." What he meant was that this brilliant young man would fall prey to idea salesmen peddling old ideas in new packages, and he would buy because he has no experience. He could not possibly know that the idea had been tried—and rejected—20 years ago. Craft demands submission to authority. Apprenticeship is long, frustrating and sometimes arduous. There are no short cuts. Polanyi argues:

> To learn by example is to submit to authority. You follow your master because you trust his manner of doing things even when you cannot analyze or account in detail for its effectiveness. A society which wants to preserve a kind of personal knowledge must submit to tradition.

Imagine the frustration of a brilliant young executive when his or her craftsman boss cannot answer the question, "Why?" Craft is inarticulate. The answer to the young manager's question is locked away in the tricks of the trade, in tacit knowledge. So, he or she thinks the boss a fool. If he or she is the boss, the employee is condemned as an old-fashioned fool and fired.

What does this tell us about craftsmen? First of all, craftsmen are patient, both with themselves and with others; they know that it took them a long time to acquire their skills and that it will be true for others. They regularly exhibit that much-sought-after commodity, judgement; judgment flows out of long experience. Young people rarely exhibit it. Their colleagues will describe them as wise, amiable, humane, honest, straightforward, responsible, trustworthy, reasonable, open-minded, and realistic. Here is a craftsman speaking about technocrats:

> Even if they had a vision, how would they get it done? There's no managerial continuity. At this year's planning meeting, there were four out of 14 people left over from two years ago. Every two years there's a new chief executive. There's no opportunity to fail, so there's no continuity. They focus directly on profit but they'll never get it because profit comes from the vision and the people and they won't invest in people. If you look after the people, the profit follows. You can't drive at it directly. Twelve and a half percent ROI is a joke; we'll be dead [in five years]. They refuse to see this. You can't correct a problem unless you see it exists. It's like me. I look in the mirror and I see a young fullback, not a balding, middle-aged man with his chest on his belly. You have to see reality to change it.

Craftsmen believe that technocrats do not have vision, and even if they did it would not do any good because they "won't invest in people." The craftsman speaking above objects to trend-line projections; "Twelve and a half percent ROI is a joke; we'll be dead [in five years]." His credo is, "If you look after the people, the profit follows.". . . (See Figure 1 for a summary of these three types of managerial stereotypes.)

TEAMWORK AND THE TYPES

When serious looks at funny what does it see? Red. It sees cavalier; it sees irresponsible; it sees childish. When analytical looks at intuitive, it sees dreamer, head-in-the-clouds. When wise stares at cerebral, it sees a head without a heart, it sees brilliance devoid of judgment. And so on down the list. In short, the three types of people cannot communicate. They live in different worlds, with different values and different goals. They frame different questions and different answers to all issues confronting the corporation. They believe that their conflicts center on ideas, whereas, in fact, they center on character.

For example, recently, a major international corporation experienced pronounced difficulty with its stock price. No matter what it did, its stock traded at a 50% discount from book value. Why? Listen in on the dialogue of the deaf that goes on between senior officers and the CEO inside that corporation. They are all talking about the same subject, but you would not know it.

An *artist*: "Of course the stock price is low! (He always talks with exclamation points.) We're not doing anything to create interest, magic! We haven't bought anything, launched anything, dreamt up anything in months! Nobody believes we have an exciting future ahead of us! The stock will go up when people believe in our dream!"

A *technocrat* (firmly): "It's all the so-called dreams which have turned into cost-nightmares. We haven't showed consistent quarterly earnings over the last three years. For two quarters, our earnings have reflected some marginal improvement. As soon as the street begins to have some faith in our capacity to control costs they'll turn into believers and start to recommend our stock."

A *craftsman*: "The people on the street are not stupid. They know that we've had so much managerial turnover that we have no continuity. They know we've fallen out of touch with our traditional markets. The guy brought in to run our main widgets division

---

FIGURE 1
Mangerial Sterotypes

THE ARTIST	THE CRAFTSMAN	THE TECHNOCRAT
Bold	Responsible	Conservative
Daring	Wise	Methodical
Exciting	Humane	No-nonsense
Volatile	Straightforward	Controlled
Intuitive	Open-minded	Cerebral
Entrepreneurial	Realistic	Analytical
Inspiring	Trustworthy	Determined
Imaginative	Reasonable	Meticulous
Unpredictable	Honest	Intense
Funny	Amiable	Serious

wouldn't know a widget if he fell over one. The whole sales force is disillusioned. What we need is to get back in touch with what we do best."

Sticking to your knitting is not some new theoretical concept to craftsmen; it is their life. They have always done it. It comes as naturally as breathing. The cost-cutting program inevitably proposed by the technocrat, strikes at the core of what the craftsman considers to be the answer to the problem. The technocrat wants to cut out the fat: inflated marketing budgets, sales training conferences, and staff development expenses. The craftsman sees the profitability problem as a symptom, a reflection of the demotivation of staff, as a diminished sense of loyalty and therefore of effort—a legacy of the last round of staff cuts and the replacement of leaders that they trusted. The technocrat is dangerous because, to the craftsman, he or she is too theoretical, "too distant from the coalface" to understand the real issues. . . .

In a major multinational I have studied for the last 10 years, the technocrats have truly triumphed. Figure 2 shows the ten-year evolution of the management team. Beginning with a healthy mix of artists, craftsmen and technocrats, by 1990 the structure had tilted irrevocably to the technocrat. The two remaining craftsmen were in the power structure only nominally; both were looking for jobs.

The result of this shift has been parallel changes in strategy and in structure. Under the aegis of the artist, the corporation had been outward-looking, increasingly internationally-oriented. Fueled both by internal growth and acquisitions, assets climbed. Subsidiaries were left pretty much on their own—the power structure was decentralized—and the atmosphere, prevailing ethic, or culture if you will, was of teamwork, growth and excitement. Out of insecurity or a simple error in judgment, the artist chose as his successor his opposite. Promoted into the number one spot, the technocrat began to install others and to rationalize, organize and control. The by-product of rationalization, systematization and control was centralization. The by-production of centralization was demoralization. The strategy became, in the words of the annual reports, profitability. Profitability was not and is not a strategy and it can certainly not inspire anyone as an ultimate goal: "What do you do for a living?" "I make profit." Losing the artists, the company lost vision. Losing the craftsmen, it lost its humanity. Although profitability became the watchword, profits did not go up. Nor did share prices. The group was eventually absorbed by a more ambitious rival.

THE TRIUMPH OF THE TECHNOCRAT

. . .Technocrats have a way of making us feel secure. With their ready answers, their charts and their graphs, they give us the feeling that everything will be all right if we just follow the rules: the rules of logic, the rules of good business practice, matrix management, participatory management, total quality management and the new rules of globalization and strategic alliances. They make everything sound so straightforward, so rational, so comforting, so reassuring—sort of like Betty Crocker.

. . .What does a manager look like, I ask my students. "He's calm, rational, well-balanced, measured, analytical, methodological, skilled, trained, serious," they say. It occurs to me that I am listening to a liturgy—a liturgy from the gospel of the technocratic school. The person they describe is one kind of manager, and he or she is now firmly anchored as the only kind. It has become definitional.

THE LEARNING ORGANIZATION

If we concede for a moment the narcissistic presumption that ours is an age of discontinuity, then the old ways of doing things no longer work. Organizations need to learn—rapidly and continuously. How does learning take place? At the turn of the century, American philosopher George Santayana wrote, "Man's progress has a poetic phase in which he imag-

FIGURE 2
The Technocratic
Transformation

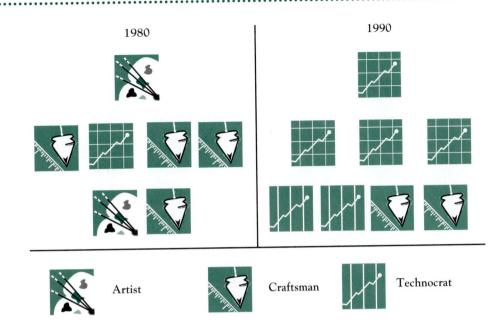

1980   1990

Artist   Craftsman   Technocrat

ines the world, then a scientific phase in which he sifts and tests what he has imagined." Culturally, we have always relied on our visionaries to point us toward the new way. In science, we call a visionary a genius; in letters, a poet; in politics, a statesman; in business, a leader; generically, an artist. What all these labels have in common is the idea of someone who breaks radically with conventional wisdom, someone who sees what others do not, someone who imagines a new order. This is discontinuous learning. We call it imaginative.

Then, there is continuous learning, daily learning. What is found in art comes into use and is transformed, concretized, shaped and sculpted by experience. A great idea, usually quite vague, is refined by practice over time. The bugs are worked out. Flesh is added to the skeleton. The slow accumulation of talent in its application is the domain of craft. We call its carrier, skilled.

Finally, there is a third form of learning. It comes from the codification of old knowledge; it comes from books and scientific papers. It comes from studying and diligence, and requires neither insight nor practice to make it our own. We call the person who possesses it knowledgeable, and if he or she possesses it to a very fine degree, brilliant.

With our religion we have eliminated both the poetic and the craft phase of learning, and tried to reduce everything to the scientific. (We are sons and daughters of the Enlightenment, after all.) We have come to believe that managers who have an MBA, can read a balance sheet and can talk knowledgeably about strategic alliances must make good CEOs. This is nonsense. If they have no imagination, they will only mimic the competition—strategy as paint-by-numbers art. If they have no skill, they will not understand their markets. If they have no wisdom, they will tear at the fabric of the organization.

VISION, CONTINUITY AND CONTROL

There are three ways of learning, each equally necessary. Leadership consists of knowing how to put the package together and make it work. It consists of integrating vision, continuity and control in the managerial team.

The first step is obviously diagnostic. What does my organization look like currently? How many artists, craftsmen and technocrats do I have, and how are they functionally distributed? What is the balance of power among them? What is the dominant ethic? Is there the freedom to fail, which is indispensable to the possibility to succeed? Is there sufficient pride of place given to emotion, to skill, to brilliance? This diagnosis is of course easier proposed than accomplished, and this for three main reasons:

1. Artists, craftsmen and technocrats rarely exist as such; they are archetypes. Real people come in more complex packages. We may see artists, for example, with an admixture of craft. We may see conservative, cerebral craftsmen and we may see emotionally hot technocrats, or highly analytical and determined artists. Rarely do we see someone who combines all three—although we all think we do.

2. The task is made more difficult by masquerades. Faced with an artistic type, we are rarely fooled. And, with their straightforwardness and frankness, craftsmen usually give themselves away. But the technocrat, particularly of the brilliant variety, is hard to see. Technocrats revere conventional wisdom—not wisdom of a traditional sort, but new wisdom. For example, I recently had the pleasure of listening to a discourse on total quality management and empowerment from an archetypal technocratic CEO. He had systematically eliminated all artists and craftsmen from his organization. Experimentation and loyalty were dead because one false step meant being fired. Now he wanted to graft onto this moribund organization new energies of empowerment. And, what is worse, he was sincere. He really could not know that these managerial recipes, conceived procedurally, will not work. The graft will not take. But, to his board and to other observers, this man was saying all the right things. He was masquerading as a craftsman. Others, again of the brilliant variety, will masquerade as artists; knowledgeable and well-read in a superficial sort of way, they will seem to know the future. Here, we can be radically mislead.

3. Finally, there is a third reason why the diagnosis is so fraught with uncertainty. It is us. What we see depends on where we sit. If I am a technocrat, I will have a tendency to see other, more brilliant technocrats as artists. I will think of them as visionary and entrepreneurial, far-sighted and bold. If I am a pure craftsman, I will have no use for any technocrats. As one craftsman CEO put it to me recently, "They make good consultants." To him, a brilliant technocrat is dangerous as a manager because he or she is intellectually disconnected from reality. And artists too, have their blind spots, not so much about people as about suitable objects of attention. Built into the diagnostic process, therefore, must be an element of collective judgment—judgment that does not rely too exclusively on the point of view of one or another of the archetypes. . . .

Growing frustration with formal managerial models coupled with increasing recognition of the difficulty of planning in a turbulent world, has led to the call for charismatic leadership, as though the presence of a charismatic leader could somehow take all the hard work out of managing a business. Certainly, the artists described here are charismatic and their presence is vital for success. But, they are not alone. You need artists, craftsmen and technocrats in the right dose and in the right places. You need someone with vision, but you also need someone who can develop the people, the structures and the systems to make the dream a reality. If you have the right people, they will do the job that comes naturally to them; you do not have to teach a fish how to swim. [The] key managerial task [of the CEO] is not to know everything but to build an executive team that can get the whole job done.

by Peter M. Senge

Human beings are designed for learning. No one has to teach an infant to walk, or talk, or master the spatial relationships needed to stack eight building blocks that don't topple. Children come fully equipped with an insatiable drive to explore and experiment. Unfortunately, the primary institutions of our society are oriented predominantly toward controlling rather than learning, rewarding individuals for performing for others rather than for cultivating their natural curiosity and impulse to learn. The young child entering school discovers quickly that the name of the game is getting the right answer and avoiding mistakes—a mandate no less compelling to the aspiring manager.

"Our prevailing system of management has destroyed our people," writes W. Edwards Deming, leader in the quality movement (Senge, 1990). "People are born with intrinsic motivation, self-esteem, dignity, curiosity to learn, joy in learning. The forces of destruction begin with toddlers—a prize for the best Halloween costume, grades in school, gold stars, and on up through the university. On the job, people, teams, divisions are ranked—reward for the one at the top, punishment at the bottom. MBO, quotas, incentive pay, business plans, put together separately, division by division, cause further loss, unknown and unknowable."

Ironically, by focusing on performing for someone else's approval, corporations create the very conditions that predestine them to mediocre performance. Over the long run, superior performance depends on superior learning. A Shell study showed. . . that "the key to the long term survival of the large industrial enterprise was the ability to run "experiments in the margin," to continually explore new business and organizational opportunities that create potential new sources of growth (deGues, 1988, pp. 70-74).

If anything, the need for understanding how organizations learn and accelerating that learning is greater today than ever before. The old days when a Henry Ford, Alfred Sloan, or Tom Watson *learned for the organization* are gone. In an increasingly dynamic, interdependent, and unpredictable world, it is simply no longer possible for anyone to "figure it all out at the top." The old model, "the top thinks and the local acts," must now give way to integrative thinking and acting at all levels. . . .

ADAPTIVE LEARNING AND GENERATIVE LEARNING

The prevailing view of learning organizations emphasizes increased adaptability. . . . But increasing adaptiveness is only the first stage in moving toward learning organizations. The impulse to learn in children goes deeper than desires to respond and adapt more effectively to environmental change. The impulse to learn, at its heart, is an impulse to be generative, to expand our capability. This is why leading corporations are focusing on *generative* learning, which is about creating, as well as *adaptive* learning, which is about coping. . . .

Generative learning, unlike adaptive learning, requires new ways of looking at the world, whether in understanding customers or in understanding how to better manage a business. For years, U.S. manufacturers sought competitive advantage in aggressive controls on inventories, incentives against overproduction, and rigid adherence to production forecasts. Despite these incentives, their performance was eventually eclipsed by Japanese firms who saw the challenges of manufacturing differently. They realized that eliminating delays in the production process was the key to reducing instability and improving cost, productivity, and service. They worked to build networks of relationships with trusted suppliers and to redesign physical production processes so as to reduce delays in materials procurement, production set up, and in-process inventory—a much higher-leverage approach to improving both cost and customer loyalty.

As Boston Consulting Group's George Stalk has observed, the Japanese saw the significance of delays because they saw the process of order entry, production scheduling, materials procurement, production, and distribution *as an integrated system.* "What distorts the system so badly is time," observed Stalk—the multiple delays between events and responses. "These distortions reverberate throughout the system, producing disruptions, waste, and inefficiency" (Stalk, 1988 pp. 41-51). Generative learning requires seeing the systems that control events. When we fail to grasp the systemic source of problems, we are left to "push on" symptoms rather than eliminate underlying causes. The best we can ever do is adaptive learning.

THE LEADER'S NEW WORK

. . . Our traditional view of leaders—as special people who set the direction, make the key decisions, and energize the troops—is deeply rooted in an individualistic and nonsystemic worldview. Especially in the West, leaders are *heroes*—great men (and occasionally women) who rise to the fore in times of crisis. So long as such myths prevail, they reinforce a focus on short-term events and charismatic heroes rather than on systemic forces and collective learning.

Leadership in learning organizations centers on subtler and ultimately more important work. In a learning organization, leaders' roles differ dramatically from that of the charismatic decision maker. Leaders are designers, teachers, and stewards. These roles require new skills: the ability to build shared vision, to bring to the surface and challenge prevailing mental models, and to foster more systemic patterns of thinking. In short, leaders in learning organizations are responsible for *building organizations* where people are continually expanding their capabilities to shape their future—that is, leaders are responsible for learning.

Creative Tension: The Integrating Principle

Leadership in a learning organization starts with the principle of creative tension (Fritz, 1989, 1990). Creative tension comes from seeing clearly where we want to be, our "vision," and telling the truth about where we are, our "current reality." The gap between the two generates a natural tension. . . .

Creative tension can be resolved in two basic ways: by raising current reality toward the vision, or by lowering the vision toward current reality. Individuals, groups, and organizations who learn how to work with creative tension learn how to use the energy it generates to move reality more reliably toward their visions. . . .

Without vision there is no creative tension. Creative tension cannot be generated from current reality alone. All the analysis in the world will never generate a vision. Many who are otherwise qualified to lead fail to do so because they try to substitute analysis for vision. They believe that, if only people understood current reality, they would surely feel the motivation to change. They are then disappointed to discover that people "resist" the personal and organizational changes that must be made to alter reality. What they never grasp is that the natural energy for changing reality comes from holding a picture of what might be that is more important to people than what is.

But creative tension cannot be generated from vision alone; it demands an accurate picture of current reality as well. Just as Martin Luther King had a dream, so too did he continually strive to "dramatize the shameful conditions" of racism and prejudice so that they could no longer be ignored. Vision without an understanding of current reality will more likely foster cynicism than creativity. The principle of creative tension teaches that *an accurate picture of current reality is just as important as a compelling picture of a desired future.*

Leading through creative tension is different than solving problems. In problem solving, the energy for change comes from attempting to get away from an aspect of current reality that is undesirable. With creative tension, the energy for change comes from the vision, from what we want to create, juxtaposed with current reality. While the distinction may seem small, the consequences are not. Many people and organizations find themselves motivated to change only when their problems are bad enough to cause them to change. This works for a while, but the change process runs out of steam as soon as the problems driving the change become less pressing. With problem solving, the motivation for change is extrinsic. With creative tension, the motivation is intrinsic. This distinction mirrors the distinction between adaptive and generative learning.

New Roles

The traditional authoritarian image of the leader as "the boss calling the shots" has been recognized as oversimplified and inadequate for some time. According to Edgar Schein (1985), "Leadership is intertwined with culture formation." Building an organization's culture and shaping its evolution is the "unique and essential function" of leadership. In a learning organization, the critical roles of leadership—designer, teacher, and steward—have antecedents in the ways leaders have contributed to building organizations in the past. But each role takes on new meaning in the learning organization and, as will be seen in the following sections, demands new skills and tools.

LEADER AS DESIGNER

Imagine that your organization is an ocean liner and that you are "the leader." What is your role?

I have asked this question of groups of managers many times. The most common answer, not surprisingly, is "the captain." Others say, "The navigator, setting the direction." Still others say, "The helmsman, actually controlling the direction," or "The engineer down there stoking the fire, providing energy," or "The social director, making sure everybody's enrolled, involved, and communicating." While these are legitimate leadership roles, there is another which, in many ways, eclipses them in all in importance. Yet rarely does anyone mention it.

The neglected leadership role is the *designer* of the ship. No one has a more sweeping influence than the designer. What good does it do for the captain to say, "Turn starboard 30 degrees," when the designer has build a rudder that will only turn to port, or which takes six hours to turn to starboard? It's fruitless to be the leader in an organization that is poorly designed.

The functions of design, or what some have called "social architecture," are rarely visible; they take place behind the scenes. The consequences that appear today are the result of work done long in the past, and work today will show its benefits far in the future. Those who aspire to lead out of a desire to control, or gain fame, or simply to be at the center of the action, will find little to attract them to the quiet design work of leadership.

But what, specifically, is involved in organizational design? "Organizational design is widely misconstrued as moving around boxes and lines," says Hanover Insurance Company's CEO William O'Brien. "The first task of organization design concerns designing the governing ideas of purpose, vision, and core values by which people will live." Few acts of leadership have a more enduring impact on an organization than building a foundation of purpose and core values. . . .

If governing ideas constitute the first design task of leadership, the second design task involves the policies, strategies, and structures that translate guiding ideas into business decisions. Leadership theorist Philip Selznick (1957) calls policy and structure the "institutional embodiment of purpose." "Policy making (the rules that guide decisions) ought to be separated from decision making," says Jay Forrester (1965 pp. 5-17). "Otherwise, short-term pressures will usurp time from policy creation."

Traditionally, writers like Selznick and Forrester have tended to see policy making and implementation as the work of a small number of senior managers. But that view is changing. Both the dynamic business environment and the mandate of the learning organization to engage people at all levels now make it clear that this second design task is more subtle. Henry Mintzberg has argued that strategy is less a rational plan arrived at in the abstract and implemented throughout the organization than an "emergent phenomenon." Successful organizations "craft strategy" according to Mintzberg, (1987 pp. 66-75) as they continually learn about shifting business conditions and balance what is desired and what is possible. The key is not getting the right strategy but fostering strategic thinking. "The choice of individual action is only part of . . . the policymaker's need," according to Mason and Mitroff (1981 p. 16). "More important is the need to achieve insight into the nature of the complexity and to formulate concepts and world views for coping with it."

Behind appropriate policies, strategies, and structures are effective learning processes: their creation is the third key design responsibility in learning organizations. This does not absolve senior managers of their strategic responsibilities. Actually, it deepens and extends those responsibilities. Now, they are not only responsible for ensuring that an organization have well-developed strategies and policies, but also for ensuring that processes exist whereby these are continually improved.

In the early 1970s, Shell was the weakest of the big seven oil companies. Today, Shell and Exxon are arguably the strongest, both in size and financial health. Shell's ascendance began with frustration. Around 1971 members of Shell's "Group Planning" in London began to foresee dramatic change and unpredictability in world oil markets. However, it proved impossible to persuade managers that the stable world of steady growth in oil demand and supply they had known for twenty years was about to change. Despite brilliant analysis and artful presentation, Shell's planners realized, in the words of Pierre Wack (1985 pp. 73-89), that they "had failed to change behavior in much of the Shell organization." Progress would probably have ended there, had the frustration not given way to a radically new view of corporate thinking.

As they pondered this failure, the planners' view of their basic task shifted: "We no longer saw our task as producing a documented view of the future business environment five or ten years ahead. Our real target was the microcosm (the 'mental model') of our decision makers." Only when the planners reconceptualized their basic task as fostering learning rather than devising plans did their insights begin to have impact. The initial tool used was "scenario analysis," through which planners encouraged operating managers to think through how they would manage in the future under different possible scenarios. It mattered not that the managers believed the planners' scenarios absolutely, only that they became engaged in ferreting out the implications. In this way, Shell's planners conditioned managers to be mentally prepared for a shift from low prices to high prices and from stability to instability. The results were significant. When OPEC became a reality, Shell quickly responded by increasing local operating company control (to enhance maneuverability in the new political environment), building buffer stocks, and accelerating development of non-OPEC sources—actions that its competitors took much more slowly or not at all.

Somewhat inadvertently, Shell planners had discovered the leverage of designing institutional learning processes, whereby, in the words of former planning director de Geus (1988), "Management teams change their shared mental models of their company, their markets, and their competitors." Since then, "planning as learning" has become a byword at Shell, and Group Planning has continually sought out new learning tools that can be integrated into the planning process. Some of these are described below.

LEADER AS TEACHER

"The first responsibility of a leader," writes retired Herman Miller CEO Max de Pree (1989 p. 9), "is to define reality." Much of the leverage leaders can actually exert lies in helping people achieve more accurate, more insightful, and more *empowering* views of reality.

Leader as teacher does *not* mean leader as authoritarian expert whose job it is to teach people the "correct" view of reality. Rather, it is about helping everyone in the organization, oneself included, to gain more insightful views of current reality. This is in line with a popular emerging view of leaders as coaches, guides, or facilitators. . . . In learning organizations, this teaching role is developed further by virtue of explicit attention to people's mental models and by the influence of the systems perspective.

The role of leader as teacher starts with bringing to the surface people's mental models of important issues. No one carries an organization, a market, or a state of technology in his or her head. What we carry in our heads are assumptions. These mental pictures of how the world works have a significant influence on how we perceive problems and opportunities, identify courses of action, and make choices.

One reason that mental models are so deeply entrenched is that they are largely tacit. Ian Mitroff, in his study of General Motors, argues that an assumption that prevailed for years was that, in the United States, "Cars are status symbols. Styling is therefore more important than quality" (Mitroff, 1988 pp. 66-67). The Detroit automakers didn't say, "We have a *mental model* that all people care about is styling." Few actual managers would even say publicly that all people care about is styling. So long as the view remained unexpressed, there was little possibility of challenging its validity or forming more accurate assumptions.

But working with mental models goes beyond revealing hidden assumptions. "Reality," as perceived by most people in most organizations, means pressures that must be borne, crises that must be reacted to, and limitations that must be accepted. Leaders as teachers help people *restructure their views of reality* to see beyond the superficial conditions and events into the underlying causes of problems—and therefore to see new possibilities for shaping the future.

Specifically, leaders can influence people to view reality at three distinct levels: events, patterns of behavior, and systemic structure.

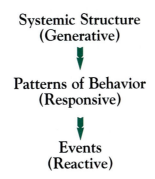

Systemic Structure
(Generative)

↓

Patterns of Behavior
(Responsive)

↓

Events
(Reactive)

The key question becomes *where do leaders predominantly focus their own and their organization's attention?*

Contemporary society focuses predominantly on events. The media reinforces this perspective, with almost exclusive attention to short-term, dramatic events. This focus leads naturally to explaining what happens in terms of those events: "The Dow Jones average went up sixteen points because high fourth-quarter profits were announced yesterday."

Pattern-of-behavior explanations are rarer, in contemporary culture, than event explanations, but they do occur. "Trend analysis" is an example of seeing patterns of behavior. A good editorial that interprets a set of current events in the context of long-term historical changes is another example. Systemic, structural explanations go even further by addressing the question, "What causes the patterns of behavior?"

In some sense, all three levels of explanation are equally true. But their usefulness is quite different. Event explanations—who did what to whom—doom their holders to a reactive stance toward change. Pattern-of-behavior explanations focus on identifying long-term trends and assessing their implications. They at least suggest how, over time, we can respond to shifting conditions. Structural explanations are the most powerful. Only they address the underlying causes of behavior at a level such that patterns of behavior can be changed.

By and large, leaders of our current institutions focus their attention on events and patterns of behavior, and, under their influence, their organizations do likewise. That is why contemporary organizations are predominantly reactive, or at best responsive—rarely generative. On the other hand, leaders in learning organizations pay attention to all three levels, but focus especially on systemic structure; largely by example, they teach people throughout the organization to do likewise.

LEADER AS STEWARD

This is the subtlest role of leadership. Unlike the roles of designer and teacher, it is almost solely a matter of attitude. It is an attitude critical to learning organizations.

While stewardship has long been recognized as an aspect of leadership, its source is still not widely understood. I believe Robert Greenleaf (1977) came closest to explaining real stewardship, in his seminal book *Servant Leadership*. There, Greenleaf argues that "The servant leader *is* servant first . . . . It begins with the natural feeling that one wants to serve, to serve *first*. This conscious choice brings one to aspire to lead. That person is sharply different from one who is leader first, perhaps because of the need to assuage an unusual power drive or to acquire material possessions."

Leaders' sense of stewardship operates on two levels: stewardship for the people they lead and stewardship for the larger purpose or mission that underlies the enterprise. The first type arises from a keen appreciation of the impact one's leadership can have on others. People can suffer economically, emotionally, and spiritually under inept leadership. If anything, people in a learning organization are more vulnerable because of their commitment and sense of shared ownership. Appreciating this naturally instills a sense of responsibility in leaders. The second type of stewardship arises from a leader's sense of personal purpose and commitment to the organization's larger mission. People's natural impulse to learn is unleashed when they are engaged in an endeavor they consider worthy of their fullest commitment. Or, as Lawrence Miller (1984) puts it, "Achieving return on equity does not, as a goal, mobilize the most noble forces of our soul."

Leaders engaged in building learning organizations naturally feel part of a larger purpose that goes beyond their organization. They are part of changing the way businesses operate, not from a vague philanthropic urge, but from a conviction that their efforts will produce more productive organizations, capable of achieving higher levels of organizational success and personal satisfaction than more traditional organizations. . . .

New Skills

New leadership roles require new leadership skills. These skills can only be developed, in my judgment, through a lifelong commitment. It is not enough for one or two individuals to develop these skills. They must be distributed widely throughout the organization. This is one reason that understanding the *disciplines* of a learning organization is so important. These disciplines embody the principles and practice that can widely foster leadership development.

Three critical areas of skills (disciplines) are building shared vision, surfacing and challenging mental models, and engaging in systems thinking.*

BUILDING SHARED VISION

How do individual visions come together to create shared visions? A useful metaphor is the hologram, the three-dimensional image created by interacting light sources.

If you cut a photograph in half, each half shows only part of the whole image. But if you divide a hologram, each part, no matter how small, shows the whole image intact. Likewise, when a group of people come to share a vision for an organization, each person sees an individual picture of the organization at its best. Each shares responsibility for the whole, not just for one piece. But the component pieces of the holograms are not identical. Each represents the whole image from a different point of view. It's something like poking holes in a window shade; each hole offers a unique angle for viewing the whole image. So, too, is each individual's vision unique.

When you add up the pieces of a hologram, something interesting happens. The image becomes more intense, more lifelike. When more people come to share a vision, the vision becomes more real in the sense of a mental reality that people can truly imagine achieving. They now have partners, co-creators; the vision no longer rests on their shoulders alone. Early on, when they are nurturing an individual vision, people may say it is "my vision." But, as the shared vision develops, it becomes both "my vision" and "our vision."

The skills involved in building shared vision include the following:

▼ *Encouraging Personal Vision*. Shared visions emerge from personal visions. It is not that people only care about their own self-interest—in fact, people's values usually include dimensions that concern family, organization, community, and even the world. Rather, it is that people's capacity for caring is *personal*.

▼ *Communicating and Asking for Support*. Leaders must be willing to continually share their own vision, rather than being the official representative of the corporate vision. They also must be prepared to ask, "Is this vision worthy of your commitment?" This can be difficult for a person used to setting goals and presuming compliance.

▼ *Visioning as an Ongoing Process*. Building shared vision is a never-ending process. At any one point there will be a particular image of the future that is predominant, but that image will evolve. Today, too many managers want to dispense with the "vision business" by going off and writing the Official Vision Statement. Such statements almost always lack the vitality, freshness, and excitement of a genuine vision that comes from people asking, "What do we really want to achieve?"

▼ *Blending Extrinsic and Intrinsic Visions*. Many energizing visions are extrinsic—that is, they focus on achieving something relative to an outsider, such as a competitor. But a goal that is limited to defeating an opponent can, once the vision is achieved, easily become a defensive posture. In contrast, intrinsic goals like creating a new type of product, taking an established product to a new level, or setting a new standard for customer satisfaction can call forth a new level of creativity and innovation. Intrinsic and extrinsic visions need to coexist; a vision solely predicated on defeating an adversary will eventually weaken an organization.

▼ *Distinguishing Positive from Negative Visions*. Many organizations only truly pull together when their survival is threatened. Similarly, most social movements aim at eliminating what people don't want: for example, anti-drugs, anti-smoking, or anti-nuclear arms movements. Negative visions carry a subtle message of powerlessness: people will only pull together when there is sufficient threat. Negative visions also tend to be short

---

* These points are condensed from the practices of the five disciplines examined in Senge (1990).

term. Two fundamental sources of energy can motivate organizations: fear and aspiration. Fear, the energy source behind negative visions, can produce extraordinary changes in shorter periods, but aspiration endures as a continuing source of learning and growth.

SURFACING AND TESTING MENTAL MODELS

Many of the best ideas in organizations never get put into practice. One reason is that new insights and initiatives often conflict with established mental models. The leadership task of challenging assumptions without invoking defensiveness requires reflection and inquiry skills possessed by few leaders in traditional controlling organizations.*

▼ *Seeing Leaps of Abstraction.* Our minds literally move at lightning speed. Ironically, this often slows our learning, because we leap to generalizations so quickly that we never think to test them. We then confuse our generalizations with the observable data upon which they are based, treating the generalizations *as if they were data.* . . .

▼ *Balancing Inquiry and Advocacy.* Most managers are skilled at articulating their views and presenting them persuasively. While important, advocacy skills can become counterproductive as managers rise in responsibility and confront increasingly complex issues that require collaborative learning among different, equally knowledgeable people. Leaders in learning organizations need to have both inquiry *and* advocacy skills. . . .

▼ *Distinguished Espoused Theory from Theory in Use.* We all like to think that we hold certain views, but often our actions reveal deeper views. For example, I may proclaim that people are trustworthy, but never lend friends money and jealously guard my possessions. Obviously, my deeper mental model (my theory in use), differs from my espoused theory. Recognizing gaps between espoused views and theories in use (which often requires the help of others) can be pivotal to deeper learning.

▼ *Recognizing and Defusing Defensive Routines.* As one CEO in our research program puts it, "Nobody ever talks about an issue at the 8:00 business meeting exactly the same way they talk about it at home that evening or over drinks at the end of the day." The reason is what Chris Argyris calls "defensive routines," entrenched habits used to protect ourselves from the embarrassment and threat that come with exposing our thinking. For most of us, such defenses began to build early in life in response to pressures to have the right answers in school or at home. Organizations add new levels of performance anxiety and thereby amplify and exacerbate this defensiveness. Ironically, this makes it even more difficult to expose hidden mental models, and thereby lessens learning.

The first challenge is to recognize defensive routines, then to inquire into their operation. Those who are best at revealing and defusing defensive routines operate with a high degree of self-disclosure regarding their own defensiveness (e.g., I notice that I am feeling uneasy about how this conversation is going. Perhaps I don't understand it or it is threatening to me in ways I don't yet see. Can you help me see this better?).

SYSTEMS THINKING

We all know that leaders should help people see the big picture. But the actual skills whereby leaders are supposed to achieve this are not well understood. In my experience, successful leaders often are "systems thinkers" to a considerable extent. They focus less on day-to-day events and more on underlying trends and forces of change. But they do this almost

---

*The ideas below are based to considerable extent on the work of Chris Argyris, Donald Schon, and their Action Science colleagues. C. Argyris and D. Schon, *Organizational Learning: A Theory-in-Action Perspective* (1978); C. Argyris, R. Putman, and D. Smith, *Action Science* (1985); C. Argyris, *Strategy, Change, and Defensive Routines* (1985); and C. Argyris, *Overcoming Organizational Defenses* (1990).

completely intuitively. The consequence is that they are often unable to explain their intuitions to others and feel frustrated that others cannot see the world the way they do.

One of the most significant developments in management science today is the gradual coalescence of managerial systems thinking as a field of study and practice. This field suggests some key skills for future leaders:

▼ *Seeing Interrelationships, Not Things, and Processes, Not Snapshots.* Most of us have been conditioned throughout our lives to focus on things and to see the world in static images. This leads us to linear explanations of systemic phenomenon. For instance, in an arms race each party is convinced that the other is *the cause* of problems. They react to each new move as an isolated event, not as part of a process. So long as they fail to see the interrelationships of these actions, they are trapped.

▼ *Moving Beyond Blame.* We tend to blame each other or outside circumstances for our problems. But it is poorly designed systems, not incompetent or unmotivated individuals, that cause most organizational problems. Systems thinking shows us that there is no outside—that you and the cause of your problems are part of a single system.

▼ *Distinguishing Detail Complexity from Dynamic Complexity.* Some types of complexity are more important strategically than others. Detail complexity arises when there are many variables. Dynamic complexity arises when cause and effect are distant in time and space, and when the consequences over time of interventions are subtle and not obvious to many participants in the system. The leverage in most management situations lies in understanding dynamic complexity, not detail complexity.

▼ *Focusing on Areas of High Leverage.* Some have called systems thinking the "new dismal science" because it teaches that most obvious solutions don't work—at best, they improve matters in the short run, only to make things worse in the long run. But there is another side to the story. Systems thinking also shows that small, well-focused actions can produce significant, enduring improvements, if they are in the right place. Systems thinkers refer to this idea as the principle of "leverage." Tackling a difficult problem is often a matter of seeing where the high leverage lies, where a change—with a minimum of effort—would lead to lasting, significant improvement.

▼ *Avoiding Symptomatic Solutions.* The pressures to intervene in management systems that are going awry can be overwhelming. Unfortunately, given the linear thinking that predominates in most organizations, interventions usually focus on symptomatic fixes, not underlying causes. This results in only temporary relief, and it tends to create still more pressures later on for further, low-leverage intervention. If leaders acquiesce to these pressures, they can be sucked into an endless spiral of increasing intervention. Sometimes the most difficult leadership acts are to refrain from intervening through popular quick fixes and to keep the pressure on everyone to identify more enduring solutions.

While leaders who can articulate systemic explanations are not rare, those who *can* will leave their stamp on an organization. . . . The consequence of leaders who lack systems thinking skills can be devastating. Many charismatic leaders manage almost exclusively at the level of events. They deal in visions and in crises, and little in between. Under their leadership, an organization hurtles from crisis to crisis. Eventually, the worldview of people in the organization becomes dominated by events and reactiveness. Many, especially those who are deeply committed, become burned out. Eventually, cynicism comes to pervade the organization. People have no control over their time, let alone their destiny.

Similar problems arise with the "visionary strategist," the leader with vision who sees both patterns of change and events. This leader is better prepared to manage change. He or she can explain strategies in terms of emerging trends, and thereby fosters a climate that is less reactive. But such leaders impart a responsive orientation rather than a generative one.

Many talented leaders have rich, highly systemic intuitions but cannot explain those intuitions to others. Ironically, they often end up being authoritarian leaders, even if they don't want to, because only they see the decisions that need to be made. They are unable to conceptualize their strategic insights so that these can become public knowledge, open to challenge and further improvement. . . .

I believe that [a] new sort of management development will focus on the roles, skills, and tools for leadership in learning organizations. Undoubtedly, the ideas offered above are only a rough approximation of this new territory. The sooner we begin seriously exploring the territory, the sooner the initial map can be improved—and the sooner we will realize an age-old vision of leadership:

> The wicked leader is he who the people despise.
>
> The good leader is he who the people revere.
>
> The great leader is he who the people say, "We did it ourselves."
>
> - Lao Tsu

▼ READING 8.3   MIDDLE MANAGERS TO "DO THINGS RIGHT"*

by Leonard R. Sayles

Recent strides by U.S. companies to become more competitive—by downsizing, restructuring, shedding extraneous businesses, or introducing new management techniques—fail to mask the fact that American industry allowed itself to become seriously weakened in the 70s and 80s. What went wrong? The talk in executive suites puts the blame on slothful workers, management hubris, corporate debt, leveraged buyouts, and deceptive financial readings caused by inflation, among other such culprits. But evidence suggests that the real problem was management's preoccupation with strategic issues, and its failure to concentrate on everyday performance.

Actually, it was only recently that managerial excellence was defined as the ability to make astute strategic decisions and handle hierarchical relationships effectively. But now, it seems, a fundamental and necessary shift in management priorities is taking place. A few years ago, popular wisdom told us, "The important thing is not whether you're doing something right, but whether you're doing the right thing." Now, astute managers are saying that what is really important is doing things right.

The following discussion is intended to reveal why this major shift in managerial focus is occurring, and what its implications are for middle-level managers. The conclusions are based on my own observation and interview studies, as well as on major field studies of day-to-day management issues in three multinational companies. . . .

THE SHIFT TO OPERATING CAPABILITIES

Amar Bhide, a consultant who works with large commercial banks, has observed that some companies do not have long-term strategic plans; instead, "they concentrate on operating details and doing things well." More recent studies of companies like Wal-Mart and Toyota come to the same conclusion: that operational capabilities are replacing strategic brilliance as the source of competitive advantage. Why? One clear reason is that it is easier for a competitor to copy a strategic decision (or product design or marketing campaign) than duplicate a finely tuned, highly effective day-to-day business operation.

* Originally published as "Doing Things Right: A New Imperative for Middle Managers," in *Organizational Dynamics* (Spring 1993), pp. 5-14; based on his book *The Working Leader* (Free Press, 1993); used with permission.

Closely related to the term "operational capabilities" is the relatively new, Japanese-developed management concept known as *core competencies*. Generally, core competencies can be defined as exquisitely developed operating capabilities. As a group, these capabilities form a body of accumulated organizational learning on how to integrate dispersed and diffuse technology and activities into a perfectly functioning work system.

To some, it may be surprising that companies are now turning their attention to these concepts. After all, isn't it true that nearly all modern companies already understand and can manage the everyday matters of getting things done? Industrial engineering and related fields matured decades ago, and production management is considered a strength that has propelled American companies into world prominence. Isn't "production" a core competency of almost every reasonably well-managed company? And aren't operations simply the dull routines that any good supervisor can maintain?

Not necessarily.

THE NEW MEANINGS OF "OPERATING" AND "PRODUCTION"

. . . In fact, many companies we studied had allowed themselves the luxury of higher production costs (and, presumably, lower profitability) until external pressures forced them to improve their operations. Ironically, external pressures to decrease pollution and increase quality often led to lower total operating costs, as managers were forced to improve their understanding and management of operations in order to accomplish these goals.

Clearly, operations is a difficult area for U.S. companies to master today. Why? Four major reasons stand out:

THERE ARE NO SIMPLE INTERFACES.

American industry became efficient, in part, by having jobs that interlocked easily. To oversimplify, if "A" made the screw the right size, it would fit perfectly in the hole that "B" drilled. But contemporary organizations have jobs with dozens or hundreds of elements—an "A" to "Z"—that need to "match," or be integrated with, those of other jobs. Without integration, performance will suffer. . . .

TASKS CANNOT BE PRECISELY PRESCRIBED.

Outside of mechanical assembly lines and other basic production and clerical operations, most functions defy simple prescription. There is simply a lot of "play," or leeway, when it comes to getting a job done. The technician or professional, for example, has no fixed template to match; therefore, his or her training, interests, and habits determine how work actually gets done. . . . What is useful or optimal for those who do a particular task may be incompatible with what others in the work flow need.

CHANGE IS ALMOST CONSTANT.

Again, unlike traditional production and white collar factories, where work might have remained fixed for years, most technologies we've observed are evolving constantly. Of course, many of the changes are small—a shortcut here, an elaboration there. But even small changes can have major repercussions in tightly interlocked systems. For example, in one company we studied, a programmer, in an effort to improve the software for making new credit cards, made one minor change in the program. However, this change in effect limited to 14 the number of spaces for customer names. Some weeks later, after many cards had been produced with contracted customer names, service management was deluged with complaints and canceled accounts.

ORGANIZATIONAL COHERENCE IS DIFFICULT TO ACHIEVE.

When management calls for change to provide better customer service, it is really asking for certain internal groups to be more adaptable and responsible to the outside world and to each other. Shorter product-development cycles require the same thing: more responsiveness on the part of one group to the work done at an earlier stage in the work flow. Higher efficiency, for the most part, means better coordination and integration, too—after all, what A does should fit neatly into B's work.

It is only through what Burlington Northern's CEO Gerald Grinstein calls "seamless service" that business can meet market requirements and implement its never-ending list of necessary technological changes and modifications. Even well-coordinated systems tend to degenerate over time, as the interdependent work groups initiate autonomous initiatives. Thus, contemporary organizations have the continuing challenge of coherence—of getting the parts to fit together and stay together.

THE PIVOTAL POSITION OF THE MIDDLE MANAGER

For many years, we were taught that "good" managers were "hands off" managers. They stood back, only rarely getting involved in work matters. The reasons managers behaved this way were compelling, or so they seemed:

1. Managers needed to focus on the future, on planning and bigger decisions. By practicing "management by exception," or attending only to those areas that were failing in one way or another, they could economize on their time.
2. By delegating and managing by results, managers could help motivate their workers, and provide them with a sense of responsibility.

Thus, middle managers have traditionally focused on developing a strategic vision and gaining the commitment and loyalty of subordinates. Managing operations has been the province of lower level supervisors and (in sophisticated companies) empowered, semiautonomous groups.

Ironically, however, senior executives have not perceived middle managers as occupying a critical strategic niche. When it came time to "trim the fat," many organizations made the middle ranks bear more than their share of the cuts. The implication seems to be that these individuals were "useless overhead."

To be sure, many organizations have been over-layered, and their middle-management levels needed to be trimmed. Historically, many middle managers have spent most of their time granting or withholding permission, and massaging data before sending it up the line. But excesses in these activities should not cause senior management to ignore the critical role that middle managers need to play.

What critical role is that? The middle manager should bear many of the burdens of building operating competencies. As mentioned above, the various parts of work systems are not programmed to fit together in a way that will ensure that the service department is responsive to customers, that work progresses "seamlessly," and that development projects are well coordinated. It is almost the rule, not the exception, that Department A, for good reason, will develop a way of doing things that makes Department B's work more difficult—or, in the case of a development project, even impossible.

Middle managers often become the players who can facilitate necessary trade-offs among the diverse parts of any work system. While project groups and teams and first-line supervisors can help, managerial intervention is often needed to resolve many of the contradictions and inconsistencies that exist in a large system. It is middle managers who must "massage" the parts and continuously "rejiggle" and reconfigure the interfaces. Without their initiatives, under conditions of modern technology, the real work of the organization will never be performed effectively.

To illustrate this point, we can look at some practical examples. Rebecca Henderson, a professor at M.I.T., conducted a meticulous research project of U.S. and Japanese firms in the photolithographic alignment equipment industry (machines used in semiconductor "chip" manufacturing). The study concluded, persuasively, that market leaders consistently lost their preeminent positions when a competitor introduced an improved product. Although the technology for the improvement was both obvious and available, other firms failed to integrate the improvement into their operations. Essentially the firms seeking to catch up simply "tacked" the improved feature onto their existing machine, but failed to introduce the resulting requisite changes into all the ancillary components. For the improvement to work properly, each ancillary component had to be reconfigured so that its interfaces with other components along the work flow would be effective.

My observation of this research leads to the conclusion that the "copy cat" companies had no middle managers available to renegotiate all the interfaces. Each company saw the improvement as a simple change in specifications. It is easier to make this kind of naive assumption than it is to delve into established routines, entrenched communications, and steady patterns.

On the other hand, in our own field work, we observed many energetic middle managers who recognized that nothing fit together easily. They took the initiative, painstakingly working through the necessary changes in both staff and line functions to produce an improved product or process.

For example, in one company we studied, a prestigious support group had established a standard for acquiring certain automation equipment. One division that intended to use the equipment, however, argued that the standard was unrealistic and dated. The middle manager of this division conducted an extended and risky series of negotiations, both with the management of the support group and with senior management. The effort paid off, and the support group granted an exception. . . .

WHY MIDDLE MANAGERS?

Many of the trade-offs that are necessary to make a work system effective involve tough decisions. These are not the benign "win-win" negotiations that are often emphasized in discussions of lateral relations. Rather, they are tough decisions requiring significant managerial intervention. The final choices will force well-entrenched staff groups to modify longstanding procedures, decision criteria, or routines. . . .

Of course, many problems require the input of senior management, which can approve a capital appropriation, a shift away from a previously approved technology, or some other shift in resources or jurisdiction. *But it takes a middle manager to get senior management's attention and make the case for change.*

Obviously, some fortunate general managers oversee truly decentralized operations and products. They pull all the strings and can function as entrepreneurs who run small businesses. They can make nearly all the necessary trade-offs—such as deciding what manufacturing must do to support a new marketing initiative—in their own heads. But for the foreseeable future, large organizations, consisting of some centralized and some decentralized activities, will remain critical contributors to our economic well-being. As long as some parts of the work system remain outside the span of control of a general manager, product manager, or service manager, substantial systems-leadership skills will be needed to maintain operational effectiveness.

WORKING LEADERS

We call effective middle managers "working leaders." They focus as much on operations—on getting things done effectively—as they do on maintaining the linkages between top management and supervisors. They act as hands-on, working managers. Instead of simply waiting for and evaluating results, they seek to intervene.

And the interventions they undertake require a more intimate knowledge of operations, and more involvement in the work, than those of traditional middle managers, who have historically relied more on delegation. Working leaders make real choices between the demands and apparent requirements of interdependent groups. They make persuasive arguments—supported by systematically presented, factual material—to convince senior managers to change established practices, appropriations, or jurisdictions. . . .

[One] middle manager we observed, Manager C, was responsible for a profitable product that needed continuous upgrading. That product was a component in a larger and potentially more profitable hardware system that the company was developing, which was controlled by Manager D. Since D needed to be sure that future generations of the profitable product would be compatible with her large, complex system, the software people responsible for the component also worked for her.

Thus, C and D were vendors (and customers) of one another, and since their needs were not compatible—at least not in the short run—they had numerous battles. Their mutual boss, a middle-level manager, needed an in-depth understanding of the technology to assure that the trade-offs between these two subordinate managers would support the overall financial and technological health of his department, and would properly balance short- and long-run interests.

THE WORK OF WORKING LEADERS

The work of the new breed of middle managers has at least four dimensions.

MAKING SURE THE TECHNOLOGY IS UNDERSTOOD

Middle managers today need to understand the key parameters that shape the performance of the systems for which they are responsible. It is easy to assume that this requirement is spelled out in company documents. In our research, however, we have often observed managers discovering new technical interrelationships even after they had been in their departments for several years. When managers are less-than-informed about their operations, serious problems can result. . . .

CONTINUOUS IMPROVEMENT

These same middle managers demanded that contradictions and flaws be reworked so that the frequency of problems would be reduced. And the excellent ones kept looking for additional ways of fine tuning their systems. At times, they had to be willing to take career risks by disagreeing openly with bosses and peers in order to "fix" the system. In short, they were proactive, high-initiative managers who were focused on work.

EVALUATING TRADE-OFFS

Today's middle managers also need to be close enough to actual operations to evaluate the technical quality of their subordinates' decisions. Weaker employees generally seek to maximize results by concentrating on the most obvious "target." (As one informant told us, "My people always want a clear stake in the ground that they can see and hit.") But a reality of modern business is that necessary trade-offs may, in the short run, result in inconsistent standards and requirements. . . .

PEOPLE MANAGEMENT

Finally, it is inaccurate to conclude that the middle manager's need for operational knowledge outweighs his or her need for people skills. Middle managers need finely developed interpersonal skills so they can obtain information and negotiate changes successfully. Highly involved middle managers cannot be "technocrats" or technicians who love to do things by themselves. They have to work closely with other people, most of whom have divergent interests and perspectives.

MAKING THE SYSTEM WORK

. . . The conventional view that good managers need to remove themselves from the details of work and, instead, manage by results may need revision. It worked well during that bygone era of long, fixed manufacturing runs and undifferentiated services, when customers, mesmerized by powerful advertising campaigns, took what was offered by comfortable dominant firms. It works less well in our world of constant product and market change.

We can now interpret the many observational studies of actual managerial behavior showing peripatetic managers engaging in never-ending lateral negotiations with more insight. Those managers are trying to make things work right. In our research, we observed middle managers who created core competencies and excellence in operations. They were indeed peripatetic: engaging in a never-ending series of negotiations to mediate the legitimate contradictions of supervisory-level subordinates; to encourage peers and staff to modify their demands and/or interfaces; and to persuade upper management to change policies or procedures that hampered the work flow. Most of all, they saw and appreciated larger system requirements, and while they were demanding of others, they were also able to make sacrifices in their own units to improve systems effectiveness.

Of course, we also observed traditional middle managers, who managed by results, massaged data, shifted blame and costs to adjacent departments when problems arose, and devoted their attention primarily to looking good and pleasing the boss. They had little understanding of their role as prime movers seeking to build self-maintaining work systems. Their focus was not on work, but on plans and results. They often appeared to meet their budgeted performance requirement, but their part of the organization never attained high effectiveness or achieved anything resembling core competencies.

Despite persistent rumors that he would soon step down as Publisher of *The New York Times* while remaining Chairman of the Board of The New York Times Company, in early 1990 Mr. Arthur Sulzberger, Sr. (nicknamed Punch) was still very much in control. Nonetheless, as Deputy Publisher, Arthur Sulzberger, Jr.'s name appeared with his father's on the masthead of the paper, and he was actively involved in all areas of the management of the newspaper itself. The Sulzbergers and their management team were considering how to position the company and the newspaper given the complex and rapid changes occurring in the publishing, broadcasting, and information worlds the company spanned.

A PRESTIGIOUS HISTORY

The New York Times newspaper had been published continuously since 1851. In 1896 it was purchased by Adolph Ochs and incorporated as The New York Times Company. From that time through 1990, a member of the Ochs family had headed *The Times*. Adolph Ochs was Publisher for 39 years. Arthur Hays Sulzberger, his son-in-law, succeeded him in 1935. And Sulzberger's son-in-law, Orville Dryfoos, became President and Publisher from 1961 until his untimely death shortly after a disastrous 1963 union strike against *The Times*. Punch Sulzberger, then only 37, took over the reins and accomplished some major restructurings at *The New York Times*. Throughout this extensive period, all Adolph Ochs' successors had subscribed to the classic statement of philosophy and objectives which he had penned.

Copyright © 1990 by James Brian Quinn. This case was written by Penny C. Paquette under the supervision of Professor Quinn. The generous cooperation of The New York Times Company is gratefully acknowledged.

It will be my earnest aim that *The New York Times* give the news, all the news, in concise and attractive form, in language that is permissible in good society, and give it as early, if not earlier, than it can be learned through any other medium. To give the news impartially, without fear or favor, regardless of party, section or interest involved; to make the columns of *The New York Times* a forum for the consideration of all questions of public importance, and to that end to invite intelligent discussion from all phases of opinion.[1]

More succinct—but not essentially different—is the motto on the masthead of the paper today: "All the news that's fit to print." Shortly before Punch Sulzberger took over at *The Times*, *Esquire* wrote an article which expounded *The Times* basic philosophies.

There is no need for ambiguity about what fashions *The Times*. It forms the paper's good qualities, explains its deficiencies, and charts it future course . . . in a deeper and more complete sense than any other journal that has ever existed, *The Times* is a record of events, a *news* paper.

If stressing the news is good business as well as good journalism, it also implies something much larger. It supposes, for one thing, that to make the truth known is to ensure its eventual triumph . . . it is a faith that enthrones goodwill, and accepts the rationality of humans and their ability to control the environment. For solid comfort and the views of the mighty, it maintains a healthy respect. . . . From such concepts as race, class, status, and the psyche, and from such weapons as wit and sarcasm, it shrinks as from the plague.

That is the creed that makes *The Times* good and grey, and it is in the paper every day. . . . Ochs had been so wary of seeming to color the news with bipartisanship that at one point he thought of doing away with editorials entirely. . . . A cartoon is no part of *The Times* editorial page precisely because of the slant. It can't, as Sulzberger once pointed out, say 'On the other hand.' This 'square' approach probably achieved its worst results in the handling of cultural affairs. All the fruitful critical attitudes from wry sophistication to zest for the news—appeared to be out of bounds for *Times* men. . . .

Still, if news emphasis has its limitations, it also harbors an agent of change. Never in one place, altering in focus, volume, substance, and meaning, now solemn, now hilarious, what happened yesterday presents to those who would report it a constant challenge.[2]

Despite its dynastic ownership (The New York Times Company shares had been publicly traded since 1968, but its Class B shares that could elect a majority of the directors were controlled by several Sulzberger family members), *The Times* had long allowed professionals to dominate its various news departments. To an extent not achieved by any other newspaper, *The New York Times* was "a reporter's paper." According to its Annual Reports the reportorial watchwords were "enterprise, completeness, objectivity, and clarity." Its tradition of leadership had included acting as "the newspaper of record," publishing entire state documents of major speeches of Presidents or key Administration figures, producing the entire text of such matters as the Warren Report on President Kennedy's Assassination, always reporting the entire new cabinet of a newly-formed country, and so on. But such thorough journalism had proved no bar to criticism. In a mid-1960s jibe—picked up and quoted by *Newsweek* and *Time*—one English journalist complained that *"The New York Times* shoveled every flake of information at its readers in the trust that they could be their own snowplows."

However, when Punch Sulzberger took over as Publisher, he began a series of steps to enliven the newspaper, to expand its coverage, to deal with the complex and unhappy union situation he had inherited, and to diversify The New York Times Company into other areas compatible with the interests of *The New York Times*. With many of these efforts reaching maturity in 1990, Mr. Sulzberger had to consider what other hallmarks he would like to leave as his legacy as he shaped The New York Times Company and *The New York Times* newspaper for a rapidly changing future.

A TIME OF CHANGE

Early on, Mr. Sulzberger had determined not to be held hostage by the labor unions of *The New York Times*. Motivated in large part by this objective, he embarked upon a diversification strategy making acquisitions outside of the New York area or in other businesses which were not dominated by the *The New York Times'* labor unions. In the succeeding 20 years, the company spent about a billion dollars on such acquisitions. It acquired 35 regional newspapers, numerous magazines, 5 TV stations, and a variety of other related businesses. (See Table 1.) But in 1987, 65% of its profits were from *The New York Times,* approximately what they had been in the early 1970s. Business in the New York area simply had grown as rapidly as the very extensive diversification program. As Mr. David Gorham, chief financial officer of The New York Times Company said, "We thought we'd move away from dependence on New York, but New York just ran away with us."

Overall, the company's acquisitions in small city newspapers and specialized magazines (like *Golf Digest, Tennis,* and *Family Circle*) had done very well. And in 1989, The New York Times Company had closed a more than $80 million acquisition of *McCall's* magazine to add to its "women's service" group of magazines. (See Table 2 for details.) In other fields, Mr. Gorham said the company had pulled out of the cable television business, feeling that "continued growth there was inhibited by the tremendous prices necessary to buy new cable networks." In 1990 The New York Times Company's five TV stations were not growing strongly because of the fragmentation created by VCRs, cable networks, and the drop-off in national TV advertising. And it only kept constant its equity position in two Canadian newsprint companies. These were held both as a vertical integration and for security of paper supplies.

By 1990, The New York Times' Regional Newspaper Group had 26 dailies (with average weekday circulations of a little more than 33,000) and 9 weeklies. In Florida it had five of the six fastest growing newspapers; and in other areas of the South, Southwest, and California, it had developed other strong freestanding operations. As Mr. Gorham said, "Many people try to buy a newspaper and pull a lot of cash out of it. Our primary concern is to build a permanent business. It costs you a lot of money to expand circulation at first, because there is a long lag between such increases and getting the advertising to go with it. Competing acquirers have often pulled back on circulation and upped their advertising rates to cover their acquisition costs. We've gone completely the opposite way—to build circulation first, then be in a position to charge more for advertising. For example, in Sarasota, Florida, we spent about $100 million for a paper with a circulation in the high 90,000s which was losing money in 1982. That paper now has a circulation of

TABLE 1

The New York Times Company

Acquisitions and Divestitures 1966–1989

NAME	TYPE OF BUSINESS	ACQUIRED	DIVESTED
Teaching Resources	Education	12/12/66	11/1/83
Microfilming Corporation of America	Microfilm	6/13/67	4/5/83
Arno Press (51%)	Books	3/5/68	6/30/82
Quadrangle Press	Books	2/25/69	11/30/84
Golf Digest	Magazine	2/28/69	
Malbaie (35%)	Newsprint	1/7/70	
Golf World (UK)	Magazine	2/19/70	
Educational Enrichment Materials	Filmstrips	6/30/70	1/17/83
Filmfax Productions	Filmstrips	7/10/70	1/17/83
Cowles:			
Cambridge	Books	4/30/71	8/29/80
Dental Survey	Magazine	4/30/71	1/11/77
Family Circle:			
United States	Magazine	4/30/71	
Great Britain	Magazine	4/30/71	7/11/72
Gainesville Sun (FL)	Newspaper	4/30/71	
Lakeland Ledger (FL)	Newspaper	4/30/71	
Lancet	Magazine	4/30/71	1/11/77
Modern Medicine:			
United States	Magazine	4/30/71	1/11/77
Australia	Magazine	4/30/71	4/10/81
Great Britain	Magazine	4/30/71	7/1/75
New Zealand	Magazine	4/30/71	4/10/81
Medimail	Magazine	4/30/71	1/11/77
Ocala Star Banner (FL)	Newspaper	4/30/71	
WREG-TV (Memphis)	Television	10/15/71	
Arno Press (49%)	Books	9/17/71	6/30/82
Leesburg Commercial (FL)	Newspaper	12/1/71	
Palatka Daily News (FL)	Newspaper	12/1/71	
Avon Park Sun (FL)	Newspaper	1/17/72	
Fernandina Beach Newsleader (FL)	Newspaper	1/17/72	
Lake City Reporter (FL)	Newspaper	1/17/72	
Sebring News (FL)	Newspaper	1/17/72	
Tennis	Magazine	10/30/72	
Marco Island Eagle (FL)	Newspaper	1/12/73	
Lexington Dispatch (NC)	Newspaper	11/1/73	
Hendersonville Times-News (NC)	Newspaper	5/31/74	
Metromedia Music Catalog	Music Publisher	12/28/74	2/7/77
Wilmington Star-News (NC)	Newspaper	1/17/75	
HFM Magazine	Magazine	4/14/75	11/1/77
Electronic Publishing Corp.	Education	6/28/78	5/16/79
Learning Concepts	Education	6/30/78	5/16/79
Zephyrhills News (FL)	Newspaper	12/15/78	1/31/84
KFSM (Ft. Smith, AR)	Television	10/1/79	
Madison Paper (40%)	Paper Mill	2/12/80	
US	Magazine	*	3/6/80
Anna Maria Islander (FL)	Newspaper	4/25/80	
WHNT-TV (Huntsville, AL)	Television	5/13/80	

*Start-ups

TABLE 1 (cont'd)

NAME	TYPE OF BUSINESS	ACQUIRED	DIVESTED
Houma Courier (LA)	Newspaper	12/1/80	
Thibodaux Daily Comet (LA)	Newspaper	12/l/80	
Cable Systems, Inc. (Cherry Hill, NJ)	Cable TV	3/2/81	8/15/89
Australia Family Circle	Magazine	*	4/10/81
Sarasota Herald Tribune (FL)	Newspaper	11/30/82	
Worrell Newspapers:			
Florence Times Daily (AL)	Newspaper	12/3/82	
Opelousas Daily World (LA)	Newspaper	12/3/82	
Corinth Daily Corinthian (MS)	Newspaper	12/3/82	
Lenoir News-Topic (NC)	Newspaper	12/3/82	
Harlan Daily Enterprise (KY)	Newspaper	12/3/82	
Middlesboro Daily News (KY)	Newspaper	12/3/82	
Dyersburg State Gazette (TN)	Newspaper	12/3/82	
Madisonville Messenger (KY)	Newspaper	12/3/82	
Booneville Banner-Independent (MS)	Newspaper	12/3/82	
Claiborne Progress (TN)	Newspaper	12/3/82	
York Cotinty Coast Star (ME)	Newspaper	12/3/82	
Information Bank License	Elec Archive	*	2/3/83
Cruising World	Magazine	7/6/84	
Carney Point (NJ) Cable	Cable TV	10/15/84	8/15/89
Public Welfare:			
Gadsden Times (AL)	Newspaper	4/18/85	
Spartanburg Herald-Journal (SC)	Newspaper	4/18/85	
Tuscaloosa News (AL)	Newspaper	4/18/85	
Santa Rosa Press-Democrat (CA)	Newspaper	4/30/85	
Santa Barbara News Press (CA)	Newspaper	6/21/85	
WQAD-TV (Moline, IL)	Television	10/3/85	
WNEP-TV (Scranton, PA)	Television	12/30/85	
Child	Magazine	5/15/87	
Gwinnett:			
Gwinnett Daily News (GA)	Newspaper	7/21/87	
Forsyth News (GA)	Newspaper	7/21/87	
Winder News (GA)	Newspaper	7/21/87	
Sailing World	Magazine	8/31/88	
Golf World	Magazine	12/29/88	
McCalls	Magazine	7/27/89	

*Start-ups

TABLE 2
The New York Times
Magazine Group:
Competitive Data

	AVERAGE PAID SUBSCRIPTION (000)		
	1980	**1985**	**1989**
Women's service magazines			
Family Circle	7,443	6,681	5,330
McCall's	6,237	6,272	5,120
Good Housekeeping	5,215	5,180	5,134
Redbook	4,294	4,149	3,904
Ladies Home Journal	5,502	5,138	5,078
Better Homes & Gardens	8,055	8,042	8,016
Woman's Day	7,667	6,367	4,543
First For Women	—	—	3,510
Parenting magazines			
Child	—	—	335
Parenting	—	—	489
Parents	1,503	1,718	1,753
Shelter magazines			
Decorating Remodeling	—	—	527
Home	—	699	925
Country	—	758	963
Metropolitan Home	825	718	709
1,001 Home Ideas	1,106	1,537	1,603
House Beautiful	900	840	940
Golf magazines			
Golf Digest	1,011	1,231	1,364
Golf World	—	86	112
Golf	732	804	1,019
Golf Illustrated	—	—	451
Tennis magazines			
Tennis	479	507	603
World Tennis	426	362	533
Ski magazines			
Snow Country	—	—	225
Ski	419	420	465
Skiing	434	440	447
Powder	—	—	147
Sailing magazines			
Cruising World	99	117	135
Sailing World	37	46	58
Sail	180	170	165
Yachting	142	143	133

Note: Publications in bold face type are part of The New York Times Magazine Group.

Sources: Corporate records; "Leading National Advertisers," Publishers Information Bureau, Inc.;
"1980 Magazine Service Supplement," Publishers Information Bureau and Leading National Advertisers, Inc.

ADVERTISING				
NO. OF PAGES		REVENUES ($MILLIONS)		
1980	1988	1980	1988	COMMENTS
1,592	1,856	90.4	134.4	Acquired in 1971; 3/4 single copy
1,228	1,035	64.0	62.6	Acquired in 1989; 85% subscription
2,006	1,621	90.2	129.3	Owned by Meredith Corp.
1,368	1,213	51.0	68.6	Owned by Meredith Corp.
1,220	1,366	52.7	83.8	Owned by Hearst
1,562	1,469	96.1	152.8	Owned by Hearst
1,614	1,686	96.6	115.6	
—	n/a	—	n/a	Owned by H. Bauer which also publishes Woman's World
—	n/a	—	n/a	Acquired in 1987; mainly subscription
n/a	n/a	n/a	n/a	
n/a	1,431	n/a	53.1	
—	n/a	—	n/a	Acquired in 1986; 50% subscription
n/a	729	n/a	16.3	
n/a	362	n/a	11.0	
n/a	1,061	n/a	28.9	
n/a	683	n/a	15.6	
n/a	856	n/a	26.1	
822	1,266	15.1	55.3	Acquired in 1969 with circulation of 350k, almost exclusively subscription
—	n/a	—	n/a	Acquired in 1989; subscription only
768	970	9.9	27.1	
n/a	394	n/a	2.7	
787	918	7.1	16.7	Acquired in 1972 with circulation of 70k, subscription
575	567	5.4	8.4	
n/a	n/a	n/a	n/a	Started up in 1988; 50% subscription
n/a	993	n/a	17.5	
n/a	868	n/a	17.7	
n/a	n/a	n/a	n/a	
n/a	n/a	n/a	n/a	Acquired in 1984; 2/3 subscription
n/a	n/a	n/a	n/a	Acquired in 1988; 2/3 subscription
n/a	n/a	n/a	n/a	
n/a	1,712	n/a	10.1	

over 180,000 and is making very good profits. We invested a lot of money in new plants, revised the paper's format, and built a genuine advertising strategy. In California, we're doing the same thing. However, to date we have allowed each of our operations to be run quite autonomously. We haven't forced similar distribution systems, editorial styles, formats, or anything else on the individual papers.

"We have also viewed ourselves primarily as a U.S. company. We have talked a lot about circulating *The Times* in Europe. We do, of course, have a 1/3 interest in the *International Herald Tribune* (*IHT*) which gives us a view into business in Europe. Although the *International Herald Tribune* is the only major profitable newspaper in Paris, there are many impediments for a newspaper company expanding in the international marketplace. For example, Canada has multiple laws against foreign press ownership, it's virtually impossible to do anything in Japan, and it is very difficult to enter most other areas. We currently print the *IHT* in Japan, Singapore, and Hong Kong as well as Europe and the U.S.[3] But many of the Asian markets are dominated by British newspapers like the *London Times* and *Financial Times*. In most foreign marketplaces, the newspapers make money on circulation, not advertising. This makes for a totally different business than the one we are used to." Investors and publishers indicated that while there is a global market for information, a newspaper is largely restricted by its place of origin.[4]

Although The New York Times Company had attempted a number of business ventures in related media areas, like videotext, an "information bank" (with extracts of *The New York Times* on line), and microfilming, it had sold off most of these ventures as money losers or unpromising. Nevertheless, as Mr. Gorham said, "We are still experimenting at various frontiers. seeing if we can find some way to expand beyond what we are now doing. We know there will be fascinating new opportunities out there for us. While we are trying to approach this creatively, there are certain inherent conflicts between our primary business of selling hard copy information to mass markets and making that information instantly available in an electronic format."

A TECHNOLOGY REVOLUTION

During Mr. Sulzberger's era, the technology of news collection and delivery had radically changed. Punch Sulzberger had championed many changes for *The New York Times*, which had aggressively applied available technology in the newspaper field. And, as one of the largest combined daily and Sunday newspaper publishers, *The New York Times* had often had to push the limits of scale and complexity of newspaper publishing technologies.

When Mr. Sulzberger assumed office, news was assembled by reporters in the field taking hand notes, telephoning these to the head office, or later transcribing their notes directly on typewriters. All editing was done on paper using pencils. International communications had to be accomplished by telegraph or often unreliable telephone lines. Changing copy or checking back with the field was extraordinarily costly and time consuming. Graphics were an underdeveloped resource, and a color reproduction—which did not exist at *The New York Times*—was very cumbersome and inaccurate. The type for newspapers was laboriously put in place by large typewriter-like (linotype) machines which selected individual letters and symbols in the form of brass molds from huge racks, spaced the letters mechanically, and then held the molds together to produce lines (slugs) cast from molten lead, columns of which became the masters for producing each page. At the end of each press run, these lead masters had to be melted down to form new lead slugs so the process could be repeated. The skills of the linotype operators were central to the production of a newspaper, and the typesetters union had become extraordinarily strong.

Computer and communication technologies were to change much of this. News could be assembled and typed on portable computers in the field, transmitted instantly by satellite to the central news room, editors could query field reporters directly for clarifications or corrections, layouts could be previewed on computer screens, and entire pages of text (in intended format) could be preset and communicated instantly to the press room by electronics. Perhaps the single most important technological change of recent decades was the shift from cold type to the computer. This became a burden on the news room in one sense, because reporters and editors suddenly became their own printers. It was a blessing in another sense; because it gave the news room much more control over all aspects of the final product. Yet, as one senior editor said, "As a writer myself I feel that writing on a computer is a liberating experience. It allows a more fluid and experimental style. It also allows more vigorous and experimental editing, because you can fix it, cancel it, and try it many other ways until you are happy. Many tasks have been simplified, like headline writing. The computer quickly tells us whether the headline will fit and how; in the past we used to sit there and actually count the widths of individual letters."

Perhaps the most important editorial movement was from what *The New York Times* referred to as "the front line," copy editing grammar, spelling, and forms of writing (etc.) to what it called the "back field." This was the appraisal group worrying about whether the story was right, was it fair, did it cover the subject the way *The Times* wanted to cover a story, was perhaps the real meaning of the story too far down in the copy, did the overall sequence need to be reorganized or reworked in light of developing space constraints. Increasingly, *The Times's* editors were doing these latter kinds of tasks. In part, this was because much of the news *The Times* covered was just more complicated. It was reporting on science and economics at a very high level, in a way that most reporters a generation ago could not have handled. Some editors felt that the more educated and complex the society and the story, the greater the demand for the kind of editorial appraisal and interpretation its audience expected of *The New York Times*.

But there were an increasing number of other important choices as well, such as when to use graphics instead of text or how to report stories with statistics in a much more vivid form than words allowed. In the past, it was rare if there were one or two graphs in the entire paper, and even then the Dow Jones stock market index was likely to be one of them. By the late 1980s virtually every other page had some kind of graphics element or artwork other than photographs. *The Times* was building up a large statistical department capable of presenting concepts in graphic form.

In addition, there was a whole new range of photographic technologies which allowed *The Times* a great deal more flexibility in the presentation of pictures. Once a photograph was reduced to digital components, it could be cropped, or enhanced, very quickly. But the technology had raised a host of new problems. It became easy to vary a background—say to put Gorbachev in China (when he really was in Thailand) and not only remove the spot on his head but to give him a head of hair, or anything else one desired. Photographs used to be documentation. Now a news group had to be very careful about each photo, its authenticity, and how to protect the integrity of the medium.

Each newspaper would have liked for all of its reporters and editors to be able to plug into each oth-

ers' computers throughout the system. But, as in many other companies, they had found that even close colleagues might not be quite as respectful of privacy in a computer system as they had generally been in the file drawers of the past. Under the time pressures of a rapidly developing story being edited in real time, some difficult problems could easily arise, and new rules and practices needed to evolve.

By 1990 new technologies provided newspapers with the ability to "close" certain sections of the paper nearer and nearer to the printing deadlines. Pagination systems made it possible to change and test format and copy until the final electronic transmission over to the presses. Such systems also changed the way the make-up department and art directors interacted with the editorial staff. Introducing color into the production process would add other complexities since one could not print color back to back on the same sheet and the presence of color on one page changed the way the reader reacted to the opposing black and white page. *The New York Times* was in the process of deciding how and where to introduce color and how to handle the resulting needs for compromises among the editorial, advertising, and production people in terms of how and where they could place color elements.

At the production level press speeds had increased remarkably and color registration could be as accurate as newsprint paper itself allowed. Although the company and various newspaper unions (especially in the printing area) had had difficult negotiations over each major technological advance, *The New York Times* had slowly been able to make significant modernization changes throughout the composing and press room areas. But in 1990 the full implementation of many technologies in these and other areas of *The New York Times* was still underway. The most important program, in sheer scale, was the building of a new $450 million automated plant in Edison, New Jersey. At the Edison plant, newsprint would come in on rail cars from the paper mills in Canada in which The New York Times Company held minority interests. The plant was so large (23 acres) that 12 rail cars could be under its roof at a single time. Large robots would pluck rolls of newsprint off the cars and place them in a computer controlled warehouse. When the presses indicated that they needed newsprint, a signal would tell another robot to pluck the roll off the shelf, bring it into position and put it on the correct press. The Edison plant would produce all sections of the newspaper which could be printed in advance of the publication day.

Instead of folding these and stacking them in "preprinted sections," the Edison plant would collect them on huge wheels (some 9-1/2 feet in diameter) which other robots would then put into storage.

When the time came to insert the section into a particular day's newspaper, a computer system would automatically fetch the right roll, position it for the inserting machines, run the newspaper in which that specialized section fit, cut and fold the section in the right places, insert it in the newspaper, stack the collated papers on pallets, wrap the pallets with plastic, and position the pallets for forklifts to put directly on designated trucks. The Edison plant would be by far the largest such automated printing facility in the world. The New York Times Company had tested this concept at its Santa Rosa, California facility before beginning construction of the Edison plant. If Edison proved successful, *The Times* might build another plant inside the New York metropolitan area to serve its New York readers. However, like all such major technology introductions, the plant posed significant risks, opportunities, and challenges to management.

Mr. Lance Primis, President of *The New York Times*, noted, "Some of the more interesting questions about the new technologies concern amortizing the $450 million Edison investment much of which is in the press rooms. Others involve the stages which follow the press operations. Automation has made our press rooms relatively smaller than in the past, but the individual presses are getting larger as we begin to run color. The presses themselves are much faster. But the flexibility of the product is limited by the capacity to capture and store different versions of the paper in the mailroom, get these on the right trucks, and get the trucks to their distribution points. The complexities of doing this with existing technology are so great that today I still hire from a 'shape up' most nights, just like at the docks. We hope that the new technology will help us stabilize the workforce.

"Today, it is hard to get the commitment to performance and productivity that you could get with a more stabilized workforce. The new equipment and associated mailroom systems also need substantially fewer people for the same size press run. We have been able to introduce substantial incentives in other areas of the business like marketing, circulation, and advertising. I would like to see us have similar structures in production. The only incentive plans we have today are based essentially on revenues of the company; we don't have many based on savings to the company.

Cost reduction is a big issue for us, not just in the production area, but across the entire company."

GATHERING AND REPORTING THE NEWS

Mr. Sulzberger often said, "The heart of *The New York Times* is its news department" and, as testimony to that fact, the corridors to the executive dining room were lined with photographs of 61 Pulitzer Prize winning reporters from *The New York Times*. In 1990, *The New York Times* with 425 domestic and 35 foreign reporters, photographers, and artists had more reporters in the field than any other single newspaper. It was also tied into most of the major wire services, although it competed with these services as a news gathering entity itself.

But technology had revolutionized the nature and processes of gathering and disseminating the news. Television news teams could be at any crisis spot in a very short time. Using remote transmission technique they could then present the news in real time, and even shape the way in which the news itself developed—as they often did in hostage situations. Sporting events and the visible elements of crises, like the 1989 San Francisco earthquake, could be in millions of homes instantaneously. Radio and cable-news services, along with business wire-news services, intensified the urgency and availability of the news and the information bases that supported it. Computer and videotape capabilities enabled homeowners to store such news (for as long as they wished) before consumption or to select and analyze it in entirely new ways.

Newspaper reporting had changed remarkably rapidly. As Warren Hoge, Assistant Managing Editor of *The New York Times*, noted, "When I was on the Foreign Desk less than three years ago, I had to place telephone calls five or six hours ahead of time to reach the Soviet Union or other remote spots. Now instantaneous hard copy communications through fax machines and electronics are possible virtually anywhere. The reporter's job has changed enormously and most reporting jobs are highly specialized. Now we don't just look for a good writer willing to do anything to track down a story. We look for a Washington communications and legal reporter, a science and health writer, a consumer affairs reporter, a stock market or management writer, an advertising copy writer, a food specialist, a consumer-travel reporter, or an aviation writer.

"The recruiting you have to do to fill those kinds of holes is very different than just going out and trying to find the ten best reporters and writers in the world. There are now many doctors, lawyers, architects, and engineers in news rooms. The study of journalism alone is not enough. You have to understand a specialty in depth. Managing such a group is a very different task from managing a group of journalists, who in the past shared very similar educational backgrounds and experiences." The whole organization was concerned with standards for news presentation and the tone of the language it used. *The Times'* philosophy was expressed by one of the senior editors this way: "We try to maintain a slow evolution in style, control it, but make it hospitable to change. There are stylistic themes we adhere to as noble tradition, and these are important to *The Times*. We have the well known *New York Times Style Book*, which details our approach, but this is only reprinted every 10–15 years. How we can best handle the evolving nature of acceptable style is a continuing dilemma. We wage a constant battle to keep out opinion while allowing legitimate interpretation to occur. Just how to do this is very tricky."

By far the largest part of the mechanisms and rules by which *The New York Times* operated were unwritten and inherited, not only concerning what was a fair story, but how a reporter could use or not use an anonymous quote, the right of an individual to reply to an attack in a news article, and so on. There were thousands of such rules which were almost taken for granted at *The Times*. It was doubtful that any single person could write them down cohesively. And while *The Times* had documented as many of its rules for style as possible, these tended to be fluid; the actual style of writing and editing had to be personal. As one respected senior editor said, "*The Times* standards for responsible and effective presentation of the news evolves case by case, day by day."

The reporting, editorial, and layout choices were further complicated by concerns like the following. How would the timing of a *Times* story relative to its electronic and print competitors affect how it reported a particular story? What could make one assault case deserve page 1 coverage while most were placed back in local news? How could the viewpoints of *The Times* very strong Washington bureau be blended appropriately with those of other knowledgeable reporters, looking at the same national issue from different vantage points? Given the capacity to cover a story with so many more data and interested viewpoints, how could one define the desired coverage for a particular story? Setting up mechanisms to constantly monitor, update, and com-municate about such choices within the organization had always been a central issue in the editorial control of the newspaper, but such efforts were made both simpler and more complex by new technologies. The phasing of "closing" times for the various sections of the paper and the sequencing of decisions required to make up an issue of any newspaper was extraordinarily complex, but that of *The New York Times* was even further complicated by the paper's size and its commitment to organize the news effectively for its readers. In the past, the newsroom had used a carefully negotiated and flexible schedule of closings for various aspects of the newspaper every few minutes from 5 P.M. to about 9 P.M. Efforts to use the instantaneous aspects of new technologies, including pagination and color, could necessitate far-reaching changes in the structure and processes of *The New York Times* news organization.

MEETING THE NEW COMPETITION

Along with all these changes came a number of important questions. If the reporter was to be the expert in the field, what would be the function of *The New York Times* editors? How could *The Times* obtain a consistent editorial philosophy among these many fragmented specialties? How could *The Times* position itself against the large number of specialist magazines, papers, and data bases which were appearing? No longer could *The New York Times* consider only the *Washington Post* or *Los Angeles Times* as its prime competitors. It had to position against many other high quality and specialized magazines (for example, in medicine, against *The New England Journal of Medicine*, *The Journal of the American Medical Association*, *Science Magazine*, and *Doctor's World*) which were the original sources of medical information as well as against the numerous public and private health magazines which had arisen to service specialized niches. As Mr. Hoge said, "A professional section like our law page obviously has to be sophisticated enough to appeal to well-educated lawyers, yet we must simultaneously try to make this field available and fascinating to people who are not lawyers. The university "law reviews" or Steven Brill's magazine, *The American Lawyer*, don't have to do that. You can imagine how difficult it is to define the role of our business sections against the *Wall Street Journal* and all the other excellent business publications there now are. We are trying to redefine our organizations and management structures now to do this." (See *The New York Times* news organization chart on page 445.)

Yet, while creating its own distinctiveness, *The Times* news department also had to learn to contain its costs. At one time, *The New York Times* had consciously put many more reporters on a major story than its competitors (especially in the New York area). With so many specialties to cover, this was no longer possible. As Mr. Hoge said, "In some respects, our reporting position is reversed. Out major competitors can often put in 2–3 times as much reporting time as we can on a particular specialty story. Trying to position our news and control its cost in this environment is a real problem."

CHANGING MARKETS

Positioning both The New York Times Company and *The New York Times* newspaper was made even more complex by the shifting nature of their markets. As Mr. Gordon Medenica, Vice President of Corporate Planning said, "We are basically in two different businesses: (1) gathering and packaging information, and (2) advertising. But every one of our information businesses is disproportionately dependent on advertising for its revenue. This is a major concern because of what's happening in the advertising field. For example,

in an advertiser's budget the traditional ratios between media and promotion have flipped from 60/40% ten years ago to 40/60% today, with many more dollars being put into promotion, rather than advertising. Advertisers are consistently looking for better efficiencies, better targeting, and a closer link between their advertising budgets and the actual selling of products.

"For example, direct mail has become a huge business. Also, some entire magazines are given away to their readers, financed solely by their advertising revenues. There is a company named Whittle Communications which has a product that has grown from launch to $80 million in no time at all, based on this concept. They do a series of "mini-magazines" called "special reports" targeted especially for particular doctors' offices, like OB-GYN. The magazines go into doctors' waiting rooms for those people who are captive there for a half hour. Whittle is also doing a special television broadcast format for high schools that contains 2 minutes of advertising in a 12 minute morning news show. There are a myriad of these specialist publications serving almost any need you can think of. While it is not clear if these products have long-term viability, they are certainly fragmenting advertising budgets today."

ADVERTISING COMPETITION

While *The New York Times* defined its major competition for newspaper advertising to be the very strong suburban newspapers around New York City, there were also 54 radio stations, a large number of TV signals off the air, over 50 cable stations, plus numerous demographic editions and regional editions of magazines available in the area. There were also videotext and home shopping experiments, but these had not yet affected *The New York Times* seriously in the advertising realm. In terms of readership, *The New York Times* enjoyed an enormous loyalty among influential, high income, intellectually curious people split roughly evenly between male and female readership. *The New York Times* readership profile was very attractive to advertisers. *The Times* considered anyone who met two out of three demographic criteria (income, professional status, and education) to be part of its target audience (see Table 3).

Mr. Primis commented, "Advertisers are asking us to do more for them within the local market. They are less interested in the potential expansion of this market than they are in penetration or coverage of the market. Penetration is the key word. Because of the density of our market, a lot of competitors are finding niched opportunities right underneath our coattails. We're too big to get small. Since it isn't easy for us to get smaller, the first challenge is how do we find ways of adding new readership inside this relatively mature market. Can we become important to people's lives nationally or regionally in ways which will attract new advertising revenues. I think the new technologies allow us some significant opportunities. An interesting question is whether our target audiences are really quite different in other markets than New York City. We need to think about this issue both as *The New York Times* newspaper and as The New York Times Company. There are some inherent conflicts of interest between *The New York Times* newspaper produced for the New York market, our regional and national editions, and the newspapers produced by our local newspaper subsidiaries."

Mr. Erich Linker, Executive Vice President of Advertising noted, "Of the top 20 newspapers in the country, approximately 5 of them are here in the New York market from a standpoint of advertising and lineage, including *Newsday*, *The Bergen Record*, *The Star Ledger*, and *Staten Island Advance* (see Table 4). We have very strong newspapers within the 27 county area in which we compete here. But in addition our strategy is keyed to building market share and advertising revenues in three different markets: Movie Show and Automotive National Advertising, the New York market, and the Northeast. National advertisers, like liquor producers, or technology companies are important categories. Local advertising comes largely from department stores, retail specialty stores, automotive dealers, help wanted, and real estate ads. Regional advertisers include financial institutions, retail chains, food chains, and some entertainment and large-scale retailer advertising." To capture special interests in depth, *The New York Times* published 70 complete magazines a year inside the newspaper alone—including its weekly Sunday magazine and 20 life style special interest magazines on Fashion, Entertaining, Health & Fitness, Travel, Home Design, and Business. Despite its regional and subject segmentation, two important trends were severely affecting *The New York Times'* advertising revenues. First, total advertising as a percentage of major companies' budgets was dropping. This had occurred largely because of the merger of multiple smaller companies into larger single corporations and the general shift from advertising to promotion. Second, while it continued to grow in absolute terms, newspaper advertising as a percentage of the total amount spent on advertising was declining steadily (see Table 5).

Mr. Primis continued, "What we have done is offer a number of choices for advertisers to be able to reach our audience selectively or en masse. Advertisers who find that their response comes from being in a certain location, or in a certain part of the paper are able to select those spots to the maximum extent possible. For example, in the business section there are opportunities for brokers and investment bankers in particular locations and for corporate advertisers in others. Similarly, we can offer special positions in the theme sections or specialized magazines we distribute with the newspaper from time to time. In addition, we have our regional (California) editions, and the developing national edition.

"In some areas, the advertising agencies can write and edit their copy right into our computers. In the film or amusement area, ADSAT provides a computerized hook-up which beams satellite copy to over 100 newspapers. All of these things give advertisers closer-to-closing-time opportunities to send in copy where fast-breaking product developments are important. Such immediacy is one of the strong viable products of a newspaper. But you can imagine the problems this can create for us in the make-up area. In fact, *The New York Times* newspaper may be the most complex single advertising institution in the world. Just our *New York*

Times Magazine does over 4000 pages of advertising a year. Coordinating the strategies among all our different audience and advertising targets is one of the most interesting management problems we have. We have in total some 74 business areas in which we work, and each requires a quantitative and qualitative strategy. With the new plant in Edison we are looking at the possibility of even more flexibility and segmentation.

"One of these is the possibility of freestanding inserts. This is an $800 million business that is growing rapidly. Our home delivery area—approximately 500,000 subscribers—gives us an opportunity to do some interesting demographic segmentation. Some of the strongest advertising trends are toward personalized marketing, sales promotion, point of purchase displays, sweepstakes, cross-tie promotions, and multiple media usage—where advertisements in one medium are linked and referenced to other media presentations that are in electronic or printed media. We see all of this offering us enormous new advertising markets, if we can develop the right types of flexibilities in our production, mail room, and distribution capabilities."

To meet its competition, *The New York Times* was available to advertisers in a variety of forms. Its primary product was a "full run" offering to the Northeast in four sections—with a "theme section" every day, in addition to a business section and two main news sections, one of which began with a "metropolitan format." The theme section on Monday was sports, Tuesday science, Wednesday living, Thursday home, and Friday weekend. Each had a highly targeted editorial product. Within those sections, *The New York Times* could offer zones for specific advertisers in New Jersey, Westchester County, Long Island, Connecticut, Brooklyn, or Manhattan. In addition, advertisers could select a national edition projected at over 200,000 circulation or a California edition with 60,000 circulation.

In addition to the above, *The New York Times* Sunday edition was a separate mammoth production in itself. Readers received three to ten pounds of material every Sunday. The Sunday edition also had numerous special sections and its own Sunday *Magazine* which featured longer articles by well-known authors. Certain sections or pages of the Sunday *Times* were so prestigious that there was a competition by individual advertisers for special positions within the Sunday *Times'* various news sections. Entire sections, like those on real estate, could have a dominantly advertising content. All this made the packaging, formatting, and

closing of the newspaper very complicated. One had to coordinate the unpredictability of late-breaking news, sudden changes in advertising copy for special sales or entertainment events, and the general unpredictability of classified and real estate advertising, which might vary enormously on any given day because of outside events, expected weather patterns, holidays, and so on.

Although national campaigns were planned long in advance, local advertisers liked to be able to place their ads as late as possible. Between 44–47% of the *Times* advertising revenue was from classified ads, many of which—oddly enough—were placed by some 1,000 advertising agencies. A major agency might place upward of 1,500 ads per week. On a peak weekend in the summer, there might be over 40 solid pages of help wanted ads. Although *The New York Times* had developed a number of rules and procedures for effectively allocating advertising and news space, it was constantly looking for new ways to make more effective use of the flexibilities new technologies offered.

NICHE COMPETITION

Within this complex structure, each of the sections had to compete against its own special subset of "niche players." For example, *The New York Times Book Review* section had its own very special marketplace, as did the sports section, the magazine section, the weekly news review section, the travel section, and so on. Within each of these, the advertising itself was becoming a major portion of the content information carried. But, as discussed above, *The New York Times* was fighting some strong negative trends in each area. For example, coupons, redemptions and point of sale promotions were growing at the expense of advertising. Such promotions were more efficiently distributed directly to households or retailers rather than through newspapers. In addition, cable TV, telemarketing, and other electronic techniques had created entirely new marketing modes. Using a home computer and a "900" number one could interactively obtain information on stocks, entertainment, rental cars, restaurants, etc.

Although there had been much discussion of potentially integrating its various media into a single corporate strategy, *The New York Times* had maintained its individual newspapers, magazines, and stations as independent businesses. In late 1989 the Time-Warner merger was much touted as creating a new form of "strongly integrated communications and media company." Rupert Murdoch had created a worldwide network of newspapers linked together by a "sky satellite" system and was moving into other media on a global basis. And others were looking at similar possibilities to exploit the new information and communications technologies.

WHAT NEXT FOR *THE NEW YORK TIMES?*

These various trends were expected to continue and to interact increasingly over the next decade, making it very difficult to position *The New York Times* for the future. Yet as Punch Sulzberger said, "We are in the process of building an enormous state-of-the-art production facility so, hopefully, there won't be too many new technology changes in the next five years. Right now, our task is to apply the technology that we have, not the technology that may be on the drawing boards. Besides printing and distribution technology, we must introduce news and advertising technology in the areas of pagination and the movement of copy. If we can accomplish this, I will be satisfied, for I do not see any other dramatic new devices or technologies that will impact too heavily over the next five years or so.

"Many people have predicted the demise of the American newspaper. I disagree. I do not see the news floating into the home each day in some mysterious way for a long time to come. Nevertheless, I think our business is going to change in many important ways. Of course, if you could tell me where the U.S. education system is going, I could make some better predictions. The decline in literacy, and reading skills in general, has me concerned as a citizen. But, as far as The New York Times Company is concerned, I believe the sophisticated, influential, upscale marketplace we serve will always contain plenty of readers. Our biggest problem will remain competition for their time. They are bombarded from so many different quarters that we must work to capture and maintain their interest. But we will not lower our sights to achieve this and are going to keep aiming for the top level of the marketplace."

Storage and Retrieval System at the Edison Plant. Advance sections of the Sunday paper are temporarily stored on large wheels which each hold up to 234,000 pages of material. The wheels are automatically placed in storage and later retrieved for distribution by one of five computer-controlled systems. There is room for up to more than 1,000 "wheels" of stored papers in the Edison facilitty.
Source: The New York Times Company

However, within *The New York Times* organization, technology was obliterating many functions and changing the tasks of the people who remained. Direct access to databases was eliminating many complex archival and research tasks within *The New York Times*. Direct layout of entire pages on computers was consolidating the tasks of copy, photography, and art editors. Direct electronic connections from newsroom computers to the press rooms had already eliminated many blue-collar jobs. But *The New York Times* still faced strong union organizations in its remaining blue- and white-collar tasks, and the company had to deal with 17 different unions across its operations. Even in the newsroom, approximately 800 of the 950 professionals were unionized.

MAJOR ISSUES FACING THE NEW YORK TIMES

The 1990s promised to be an exciting time at *The New York Times*. As Mr. Arthur Sulzberger, Jr., Deputy Publisher, said, "There are some fundamental issues facing us. The most obvious is the national edition question. The technology to go national in a variety of ways is available now, whereas it was not a few years ago. We have been experimenting with a three-part newspaper which we will roll out across the entire country. But we have to decide whether we want to own the presses we print the paper on in various places around the country. We are feeling a number of pressures both in our local markets and from large national competitors like *The Wall Street Journal*.

"Other newspapers expand the paper depending on how advertising is running. We refuse to do this; we take the burden of organizing things for the reader, producing a four-section paper every day. The reader knows on any given day what sections will be there. We could run the paper "straight" every day on the presses; using this method you get two copies of the same page on each revolution of the press cylinder. But by running "correct," as we do, you run the corresponding pages of different sections (say A1 and C1) on a single revolution. The upshot is that we can produce twice the number of individual pages, but half the number of copies, in a press run of a given length. This puts an enormous burden on the planning of the whole paper and coordinating of all pages and sections. As you can imagine, orchestrating this each day is a major management challenge; the two sections produced together must be the same length, and the closing of all the different news and advertising segments must be carefully coordinated.

"In addition to variations in *The New York Times* and our national edition, we have to consider what other opportunities our unique news gathering capabilities, technologies, and data banks may offer us. And we have to consider how we can redefine the news itself. In the past, food was not news, now it is. There will be other changes the marketplace dictates. Some things we do because our advertisers want them, or they make money. For example, we do 'Fashions of *The Times*' because it is profitable. On the other hand, *The New York Times Book Review* has not made money for years, but it provides a service beyond the call of profits. There are just some things that are so fundamental that they make *The New York Times* what it is. For example, there are tremendous forces pressing for cuts in news room staff. But that depth in staffing is what we are. And *The Book Review* is, in a way, our flag. It is our bonus. Without *The Review*, we would be much less of a newspaper. Other concepts are similarly fundamental to *The New York Times*, and we must preserve them."

In talking about the first of these issues, a national edition of *The New York Times*, *Fortune* had noted:

> The demographics of national circulation are much more attractive than they used to be. In 1962 (when *The New York Times* had tested its Western edition concept) *The Times* envisioned 100,000 potential readers there with college educations and comfortable incomes. . . . That number has soared in California and across the nation. To gauge the promise of this, *The Times*—with a weekday circulation of slightly over 1 million—need only look to the success story of *The Wall Street Journal* whose nearly 2 million subscribers make up the largest newspaper readership in the country. For almost 30 years *The Journal* has published four U.S. editions: Eastern, Midwestern, Southwestern, and Western.
>
> If any newspaper can go head-to-head—and coast-to-coast—with *The Wall Street Journal*, *The Times* is the most imposing candidate. With its longstanding and plausible claim to being the nation's most comprehensive and influential daily—and its editorial staff of over 900, the largest in the world—*The Times* has both the stature and resources for such combat. . . . [However, the sobering fact of life for *The Times* is that it has rarely earned a very fat profit margin. Last year's pre-tax earn-

ings came to around 10% of sales—a return high enough for *The Times* but far below that of many big-city dailies. For instance, one analyst estimated that the *Miami Herald* earned a 25% pre-tax margin and *The Washington Post* nearly a 20% margin.][5]

TECHNOLOGY IMPACTS

Through the 1980s *The Times* had been reluctant to be a technology leader, educating the market to new potentials. *The Times* was very large compared to most of its competitors, consequently its risk levels for any major moves were amplified. There was a tendency to say, "Don't send us a bread board, tell us when the technology is available and send us model #10". The goodwill and identity of *The Times* were clearly among its most important assets. Yet it constantly needed to innovate a new balance between the timing of its news, the accuracy and tone of its news versus its competitors, and the changing modes available for providing news to each of its many specialized audiences. Defining and maintaining this balance would be among the key strategic issues facing The New York Times Company and its prestigious newspaper in the 1990s.

All of this was occurring against a background in which mega-mergers like Time-Warner were occurring, and Wall Street was speculating about future deals. Would Coca-Cola sell Columbia Pictures to Telecommunications, Inc. (TCI), America's biggest cable operator—or perhaps to Japan's Sony which already owned CBS Records? Mr. Rupert Murdoch, the Australian newspaper entrepreneur, had bought Twentieth Century Fox, and the major book producers were merging madly. Large size was one way to absorb the risk of introducing new publications. People worldwide were reading much the same number of books and magazines, and watching the same amount of television and films each year in the industrialized countries.

However, the advantages of scale were beginning to show in this maturing industry. The big ten newspapers had moved from 37% to 43% of the U.S. market between 1980 and 1987, and the cost structure of the industry tended to favor larger newspapers. Papers with average circulations of 75,000 had variable costs of 26% while those with over 300,000 circulation had variable costs of 34%. However, broadcasting, newspapers, and other parts of the industry were surrounded by restrictions aimed to prevent huge companies from monopolizing the information content in particular industries or regions. The Federal Communication Commission's regulations covering multiple and cross ownership of various media, particularly within a single broadcast or circulation area, had been somewhat relaxed during the 1980s. For example, the number of television stations that could be owned by any single enterprise had increased from seven to twelve. However, as inter- and intra-media competition continued to increase, many expected the industry to be more seriously deregulated. "*The New York Times* is not a newspaper for everyone, but when I see two well dressed and apparently educated commuters on the railroad platform—one reading the paper and the other not—I wonder what we did wrong. For, there, without doubt, was a member of our target audience. My problem is compounded early each morning when I leave my apartment house and see the number of families that seem able to do without *The Times*. What is it that these potential readers want that we are not supplying?

"As I look to the future, the problem becomes more difficult. Will the printed word be further battered by the electronic signal? Will the introduction of fiber optics to the home bring entire new competitive pressures? Just as important, will those of us who wish to venture into this electronic world be competitively disadvantaged by the big players who own the wires and the "gateways" that control the flow of information through those wires?

"The future is getting closer. It will be exciting and will force all of us in the print media to reassess our corporate strategies."

1. What do you see as the most important issues facing The New York Times Company and newspapers' management in 1990? What should Punch Sulzberger attempt to do about these?

2. What should be the strategy of The New York Times Company? What should be the relationship between The New York Times Company and *The New York Times* newspaper? How should their respective management structures be aligned to reflect this?

3. How should *The New York Times* be positioned in its marketplace? How should *The Times* be related to the company's other publications in terms of positioning, operating synergies, portfolio considerations, and organizational structure? What specific policy issues and solutions are needed within its news operations, production-distribution activities, and advertising areas? Why?

4. What have been the most important implications of technology for management of the newspaper? What new competitive issues and potentials will technology pose in the future? What should *The Times* and The New York Times Company do about these? To what extent should The New York Times Company develop a common technology strategy for all its operations? What should this consist of? Why?

FIGURE 1
The New York Times
News Organization, 1990
Source: Corporate records

```
                          ┌─────────────────────┐      Magazine Editor
                          │  Executive Editor   │──────James Greenfield
                          │     Max Frankel     │
                          └─────────────────────┘
                                    │
                          ┌─────────────────────┐      Book Review Editor
                          │  Managing Editor    │──────Rebecca Sinkler
                          │   Joseph Lelyveld   │
                          └─────────────────────┘
```

Assistant Managing Ed. David Jones	Assistant Managing Ed. John Lee	Assistant Managing Ed. Warren Hoge	Assistant Managing Ed. Allan Siegal	Assistant Managing Ed. Carolyn Lee

Metropolitan Editor
John Darnton
National Editions Editor
Donna Laurie
Sports Editor
Joseph Vecchione
Real Estate Editor
Michael Sterne

Foreign Editor
Bernard Gwertzman
Senior Editor-Nights
William Borders
Senior Editor-Weekends
Mitchel Levitas
National Editor
Soma Golden
Week In Review Editor
Dan Lewis
Business/Finance Editor
Fred Andrews
Washington Editor
Howell Raines
Science/Health Editor
Philip Boffey
Media Editor
Martin Arnold

Culture Editor
Marvin Siegel
Arts & Leisure Editor
Constance Rosenblum
Style Editor
Claudia Payne
Travel Editor
Nancy Newhouse

Senior Editor-Production
Robert Sheridan
Design Director
Tom Bodkin
Picture Editor
Mark Bussell
Technology Editor
Judith Wilner
Information Services Director
Charles Robinson

Senior Editor-Recruitment
Paul Delaney
Senior Editor-Training/Devel.
William Connolly
Business Manager
Penny Abernathy

	Total U.S.	THE NEW YORK TIMES Weekday	THE NEW YORK TIMES Sunday	Total Northeast	THE NEW YORK TIMES Weekday	THE NEW YORK TIMES Sunday
Total adults	178,193	3,303	3,604	39,614	2,557	3,018
Males	85,056	1,954	2,073	19,012	1,483	1,683
Females	93,136	1,350	1,567	20,602	1,074	1,335
Age						
18-34	68,997	1,108	1,238	14,438	838	961
35-54	58,707	1,332	1,451	13,151	1,039	1,211
55-64	21,733	464	493	5,167	366	465
65+	28,756	399	459	6,858	324	382
Education						
College graduate	32,799	1,978	2,258	8,494	1,513	1,819
<College graduate	145,394	1,325	1,381	31,121	1,044	1,200
Occupation						
Top management	14,772	554	768	3,255	431	681
Professionals/managers	29,483	1,619	1,740	8,022	1,247	1,440
Technical/clerical/sales	36,012	623	658	8,191	400	524
All other employed	45,205	297	353	8,412	240	309
Not employed	67,492	764	889	14,989	669	746
Household income						
$75,000+	10,406	717	971	3,328	567	875
$50,000+	31,697	1,458	1,834	9,309	1,211	1,632
$35,000+	68,015	2,364	2,668	18,646	1,842	2,267
$25,000+	99,581	2,838	3,188	25,035	2,222	2,717
<$25,000	78,612	465	452	14,579	335	301

Source: Simmons Market Research Bureau, 1989; corporate records.

TABLE 3B
Readership Profile of the
New York ADI* and
Major New York
Newspapers, 1988
(in thousands of readers)

	TOTAL NY ADI	WEEKDAY NY Times	WEEKDAY Daily News	WEEKDAY NY Post	SUNDAY NY Times	SUNDAY Daily News
Total adults	14,162	2,310	3,901	1,506	3,024	4,080
Males	6,522	1,281	1,971	775	1,545	1,825
Females	7,640	1,029	1,930	731	1,479	2,255
Age						
18–49	8,792	1,447	2,306	969	1,929	2,335
35–49	3,847	724	1,012	472	966	1,023
25–54	7,999	1,385	2,145	928	1,871	2,138
Occupation						
Top management	0,817	261	188	109	338	158
Prof./managerial	3,215	1,014	734	361	1,293	700
Other empl.	5,554	621	1,562	594	805	1,534
Education						
College grad+	3,243	1,231	642	363	1,537	593
Any college	5,775	1,660	1,341	635	2,122	1,315
HS grad+	10,747	2,133	2,939	1,179	2,790	2,963
Household income						
$100,000+	952	308	208	106	403	187
$75,000+	1,918	558	454	216	773	416
$50,000+	4,118	986	997	443	1,283	947
$35,000+	7,316	1,529	1,897	829	2,031	1,&46
$25,000+	10,296	1,935	2,769	1,139	2,533	2,769
<$25,000	3,866	375	1,133	367	491	1,311
Place of residence						
NY City	5,685	1,226	2,518	0,982	1,541	2,775
Suburbs	8,478	1,084	1,384	0,524	1,483	1,305
Home ownership						
Own home	8,073	1,432	1,937	723	1,881	1,906
Value $300,000+	1,356	431	277	118	520	283
Value $250,000+	2,265	628	473	199	771	469
Value $200,000+	3,894	888	885	340	1,123	860

*ADI stands for Area of Dominant Influence as defined by the Arbitron rating service.

Source: 1988 *Scarborough Report*, corporate records.

TABLE 3C
Demographic and Readership Changes in the New York ADI*, 1980 to 1986
(in thousands of individuals)

	1980	1986
Population		
Manhattan	1,138	1,277
Rest of NYC	4,322	4,369
New Jersey	3,992	4,225
Long Island	1,928	1,995
Westchester/Rockland/Putnam	896	927
Rest of ADI	1,133	1,213
College graduates		
Manhattan	320	435
Rest of NYC	642	873
New Jersey	702	994
Nassau-Suffolk	383	463
Westchester/Rockland/Putnam	204	278
Rest of ADI	256	284
Professional/managerial		
Manhattan	263	396
Rest of NYC	659	851
New Jersey	765	1,118
Nassau-Suffolk	441	517
Westchester/Rockland/Putnam	203	350
Rest of ADI	239	350
Individuals with a household income of $35,000+		
Manhattan	136	375
Rest of NYC	548	1,503
New Jersey	789	2,169
Nassau-Suffolk	455	1,162
Westchester/Rockland/Putnam	224	512
Rest of ADI	234	607
Weekday *Times* Readership	2,278	2,443
Sunday *Times* Readership	3,107	3,142
Newspaper readership in the New York ADI**		
Adults		
Sunday	80%	76%
Daily	78	74
Men		
Sunday	80	77
Daily	81	79
Women		
Sunday	79	76
Daily	76	71
Employment in the New York ADI**		
Adults	58%	59%
Men	74	73
Women	44	48
Median household size		
ADI population	3.58	3.57
Sunday *Times*	3.53	3.21
Weekday *Times*	3.39	3.13

*ADI stands for Area of Dominant Influence as defined by the Arbitron rating service.

**Figures are for 1982 and 1986 rather than for 1980 and 1986.

Source: 1980, 1982, and 1986 *Scarborough Reports*; corporate records.

TABLE 3D
Demographic Trends in Readership, 1976 to 1986
(percentage of population or readers)

	TOTAL U.S.		WEEKDAY TIMES		SUNDAY TIMES	
	1976	1986	1976	1986	1976	1986
Male	48%	47%	65%	52%	49%	52%
Female	52	53	35	48	51	48
Median age	41	40	38	39	39	41
Race						
White			88	88	87	91
Non-white			12	12	13	9
Education						
College grad	13	17	36	60	40	61
Some college			23	20	23	18
H.S. grad			25	15	28	18
Marital status						
Single	17	21	31	36	27	31
Married	67	61	58	50	60	57
Div, sep, widowed	16	18	11	14	13	12
No. of children						
None	60	65	59	70	57	68
One	17	17	16	15	15	16
Two	15	15	14	11	14	13
Household size						
One	11	12	14	15	14	13
Two	31	31	28	34	29	35
Three/four	37	40	41	36	37	36
Five or more	21	17	17	15	21	17
Employed	59	61	71	75	68	73
Males employed			84	82	83	84
Females employed			45	69	53	65
Not employed			30	25	33	27
Prof/mgr'l	16	16	39	50	37	48
Own home	68	70	55	52	61	60
Place of residence						
Metro central city			50	42	43	38
Metro suburban			35	37	28	31
Median household Income (000)	$12.8	$25.4	$18.2	$42.7	$19.6	$45.5

Source: Simmons Market Research Bureau, 1976/77 and 1986; corporate records.

TABLE 3E
Times Reader Profile
(percent of readers)

	WEEKDAY		SUNDAY	
	1976	1986	1976	1986
Public activities (in past year)				
Voted	76%	48%	79%	52%
Written to editor	27	6	19	7
Written to elected official	25	13	26	16
Addressed a public meeting	27	9	27	9
Worked for a political party or candidate	14	5	15	5
Leisure activities etc. (in past year)				
Played golf	12	11	16	12
Played tennis	26	15	26	17
Indoor gardening	43	23	43	27
Boating	21	11	19	10
Bicycling	36	15	33	14
Cooked for fun	36	26	41	29
Bought a paperback book	50	45	54	50
Bought a hardback book	32	32	33	35
Own a still camera	38	63	38	68
Travel (in past year)				
Took a foreign trip	23	35	23	37
Took 1 domestic trip	13	16	14	17
Took 2 domestic trips	11	11	11	11
Took 3 or more domestic trips	39	31	43	31
Other				
Own an automobile	81	72	87	73
Own securities worth $50,000+	8	10	8	9
Own or use any credit card	63	68	69	72
Own a dog	25	17	34	17
Own a cat	15	11	16	10

TABLE 4
Competitor Profiles–
Circulation
(in thousands)

	DAILY		SUNDAY	
	1980	**1989**	**1980**	**1989**
New York Times	851	1,039	1,415	1,615
New York Daily News	1,619	1,282	2,273	1,623
New York Post	628	714	—	—
Newsday	506	633	554	681
Star Ledger (Newark)	408	465	569	676
Gannett (West/Rckl)	250	167	196	195
The Record (Bergen Co.)	151	157	213	228
Wall Street Journal	1,798	1,899	—	—
USA Today	—	1,329	—	—
Washingon Post	588	789	815	1,122

Source: ABC Audit Data, March 1980 and March 1989; corporate records.

TABLE 4 (cont'd)
20 Largest U.S. Daily
Newspapers: 1989
Circulation

CIRCULATION (IN THOUSANDS)	
The Wall Street Journal	1,836
USA Today	1,326
New York Daily News	1,194
Los Angeles Times	1,108
The New York Times	1,068
The Washington Post	773
Chicago Tribune	720
Newsday	700
The Detroit News	690
Detroit Free Press	626
San Francisco Chronicle	556
Chicago Sun-Times	536
The Boston Globe	516
New York Post	508
The Philadelphia Inquirer	505
The Newark Star-Ledger	460
Houston Chronicle	437
The Cleveland Plain Dealer	437
The Miami Herald	413
The Baltimore Sun	409

Source: *'90 Facts about Newspapers*, American Newspaper Publishers Association, Washington, D.C., April 1990.

	DAILY CIRCULATION	NUMBER OF DAILIES	SUNDAY CIRCULATION	NUMBER OF SUNDAY EDITONS
Gannett Co., Inc.	6,023	82	5,690	64
Knight-Ridder, Inc.	3,795	28	4,681	24
Newhouse Newspapers	2,998	26	3,785	21
Times Mirror Co.	2,627	8	3,144	7
Tribune Co.	2,698	9	3,429	7
Dow Jones & Co., Inc.	2,410	23	496	14
Thomson Newspapers, Inc.	2,127	122	1,682	70
The New York Times Co.	1,919	27	2,462	17
Scripps Howard	1,571	21	1,756	11
Cox Enterprises, Inc.	1,280	18	1,654	17

Source: '90 *Facts about Newspapers,* American Newspaper Publishers Association, Washington, D.C., April 1990.

TABLE 5
Trends in Annual U.S.
Advertising Expentitures
(in millions of dollars)

	1950	1960	1970	1975	1980	1985	1989
Newspapers, of which	2,070	3,681	5,704	8,234	14,794	25,170	32,510
National	518	778	891	1,109	1,963	3,352	3,700
Local	1,552	2,857	4,813	7,125	12,831	21,818	28,810
Magazines, of which	478	909	1,292	1,465	3,149	5,155	6,750
Weeklies	261	525	617	612	1,419	2,297	2,950
Women's	129	184	301	368	782	1,294	1,645
Monthlies	88	200	374	485	949	1,564	2,155
Television, of which	171	1,627	3,596	5,263	11,469	21,022	27,215
Three networks	85	820	1,658	2,306	5,130	8,060	9,260
Cable networks	—	—	—	—	45	594	1,225
Syndication (nat'l)	—	—	—	—	50	520	1,215
Spot (nat'l)	31	527	1,234	1,623	3,269	6,004	7,400
Spot (local)	55	280	704	1,334	2,967	5,714	7,775
Cable (non-network)	—	—	—	—	8	130	340
Radio, of which	605	693	1,308	1,980	3,702	6,490	8,385
Network	—	43	56	83	183	365	475
Spot (nat'l)	196	222	371	436	779	1,335	1,560
Spot (local)	273	428	881	1,461	2,740	4,790	6,350
Yellow Pages, of which	—	—	—	—	2,900	5,800	8,355
National					330	695	1,040
Local					2,570	5,105	7,315
Direct Mail	803	1,830	2,766	4,124	7,596	15,500	22,175
Business Pubs.	251	609	740	919	1,674	2,375	2,765
Total National	3,260	7,305	11,350	15,200	29,815	53,355	69,500
Total Local	2,440	4,655	8,200	12,700	23,735	41,395	55,340
GRAND TOTAL	5,700	11,960	19,550	27,900	53,550	94,750	124,840

Source: Corporate records; derived from McCann-Erickson, Inc., figures published in *Advertising Age* for various years.

TABLE 6
Financial Highlights:
The New York Times
Company, 1985 through
1989
(dollars in thousands
except per share data)

	YEAR ENDED DECEMBER 31				
	1989	1998	1987	1986	1985
Revenues and income					
Revenues	$1,768,893	$1,700,046	$1,642,424	$1,524,103	$1,357,699
Operating profit	169,044	251,065	283,656	266,373	209,645
Income from continuing operations before					
equity in operations of forest products group	84,097	132,033	138,274	110,165	93,223
Equity in operations of forest products group	(15,922)	28,928	17,990	19,560	21,387
Income from continuing operations	68,175	160,961	156,264	129,725	114,610
Gain on sale of cable television system and					
income from its operations, net of taxes	198,448	6,719	4,069	2,502	1,708
Net income	266,623	167,680	160,333	132,227	116,318
Cash flows from operations	**251,606**	**254,631**	**270,285**	**249,024**	**200,367**
Financial position					
Property, plant and equipment—net	972,474	814,739	644,253	483,988	437,712
Total assets	2,187,520	1,914,660	1,711,584	1,405,133	1,295,534
Long-term debt and capital lease obligations	337,417	377,527	390,630	216,515	273,611
Common stockholders' equity	1,064,446	872,937	823,093	704,744	585,575
Per share of common stock					
Continuing operations	.87	2.00	1.91	1.60	1.43
Discontinued operations	2.52	.08	.05	.03	.02
Net income	3.39	2.08	1.96	1.63	1.45
Dividends	.50	.46	.40	.33	.29
Common stockholders' equity (end of year)	13.63	11.02	10.04	8.59	7.24
Key ratios					
Operating profit to revenues	10%	15%	17%	17%	15%
Income from continuing operations before					
equity in operations of forest products					
group to revenues	5%	8%	8%	7%	7%
Return on average stockholders' equity	27%	20%	21%	20%	22%
Return on average total assets	13%	9%	10%	10%	11%
Long-term debt and capital lease obligations to					
total capitalization	24%	30%	32%	23%	32%
Current assets to current liabilities	.86	.70	1.03	.72	.77
Employees	10,600	10,700	10,500	10,000	10,350

Source: The New York Times Company, *Annual Report,* 1989.

TABLE 7
The New York Times
Company: Segment
Information, 1987
through 1989
(dollars in thousands)

	YEAR ENDED DECEMBER 31		
	1989	1988	1987
Revenues			
Newspapers[a]	$1,398,522	$1,380,080	$1,348,601
Magazines[b]	295,580	249,115	226,084
Broadcasting/information Services[c]	74,791	70,851	67,739
Total	1,768,893	$1,700,046	$1,642,424
Operating profit (loss)			
Newspapers	$ 182,878	$231,450	$266,075
Magazines	(12,241)	20,887	22,800
Broadcasting/Information Services	12,729	12,647	12,062
Unallocated corporate expenses	(14,322)	(13,919)	(17,281)
Total operating profit	169,044	251,065	283,656
Interest expense, net of interest income	20,680	27,202	22,911
Income taxes	64,267	91,830	122,471
Income from continuing operations before equity in operations of Forest Products Group	84,097	132,033	138,274
Equity in operations of Forest Products Group	(15,922)	28,928	17,990
Income from continuing operations	68,175	160,961	156,264
Income from discontinued operations	198,448	6,719	4,069
Net income	**$266,623**	**$167,680**	**$160,333**
Depreciation and amortization			
Newspapers	$64,041	$60,885	53,594
Magazines	19,820	3,934	3,529
Broadcasting/Information Services	14,199	12,203	11,597
Corporate	985	1,547	2,524
Discontinued operations	7,976	12,162	10,275
Total	$ 107,021	$90,731	$81,519
Capital expenditures			
Newspapers	$205,564	$260,416	$180,926
Magazines	3,088	3,187	10,955
Broadcasting/Information Services	7,911	13,353	10,904
Corporate	—	22	4,605
Discontinued operations	4,354	8,989	10,206
Total	$ 220,917	$285,967	$217,596
Identifiable assets at December 31			
Newspapers	$1,460,429	$1,317,414	$1,108,276
Magazines	292,730	173,828	141,604
Broadcasting/Information Services	135,952	136,360	126,721
Corporate	109,441	44,868	118,484
Investment in Forest Products Group[d]	188,968	179,635	145,212
Discontinued operations	—	62,555	71,287
Total	$2,187,520	$1,914,660	$1,711,584

[a]Newspapers: *The New York Times*, 35 regional newspapers and a one-third interest in the International Herald Tribune S.A.

[b]Magazines: Seventeen publications and related activities in the women's service and sports and leisure fields.

[c]Broadcast/Information Services: Five network-affiliated television stations, two radio stations, a news service, a features syndicate and licensing operations of *The New York Times* databases and microfilm.

[d]Forest Products Group: Equity interests in three newsprint companies and a partnership in a supercalendered paper mill that together supply the major portion of the Newspaper Group's annual paper requirements.

Source: The New York Times Company, *Annual Report*, 1989.

MATSUSHITA ELECTRIC INDUSTRIAL COMPANY 1994

Matsushita Electric Industrial Co. was often cited as one of the premier examples of the management practices and style that had made Japan into an industrial power, with a GNP second only to the United States. Matsushita's own brand names, Quasar, National, Panasonic, Victor (JVC), and Technic, were known around the world. Matsushita was Japan's largest producer of electric and electronic products and one of the world's largest firms in these fields. Why did its management practices work so well? To what extent were they applicable to other companies? Would they still enable the company to lead in the complex markets of the 1990s? Matsushita had transformed itself into a global manufacturing powerhouse and greatly increased its industrial sales, but it still had to contend with Sony's innovation machine and the rapid advance of digital technologies.

EARLY HISTORY

Matsushita (generally pronounced Mat *SOOSH* 'ta) was started in 1918 by Mr. Konosuke Matsushita, one of Japan's now legendary entrepreneurs. In 1911, Mr. Matsushita had joined the Osaka Electric Light Company (at age 15), convinced that electricity had a great future in Japan. Seven years later, then the

Case copyright © 1995 by James Brian Quinn. Research assistants—Penny C. Paquette and Allie J. Quinn.

Major historical sources for case were company interviews; company published records; and T. Kono, *Strategy and Structure of Japanese Enterprises* (Armonk, N.Y.: M.E. Sharpe, 1985); J. Cruikshank, "Matsushita," *Harvard Business School Bulletin*, February 1983; and R. Pascale and A. Athos, *The Art of Japanese Management* (N.Y.: Simon & Schuster, 1982). Footnotes (x,xx) indicate cited references and page numbers in these sources. The generous cooperation of Matsushita Electric is gratefully acknowledged.

youngest inspector on Osaka's payroll, he resigned to form his own company.

At that time the few wired Japanese homes typically had only one circuit, and that usually emerged inconveniently from the center of the ceiling in one room. To light another room or to use electricity meant using an awkward extension cord, dangling from the ceiling fixture. And the resident still had only one room lit. Mr. Matsushita, a tinkerer from his early days in his father's bicycle shop, conceived of a double-ended attachment for the outlet that permitted the main room to be lighted while a swivel socket allowed an extension cord to be guided elsewhere without tangling. When he offered his idea to Osaka Electric the company was not interested. Consequently, Mr. Matsushita took about $50 in savings and severance pay and—with his wife and brother-in law—began manufacturing his unique multiple socket in his own home. By using recycled light bulb bases, Matsushita was soon able to cut his already low costs (and prices) by some 30%, discouraging larger competitors from entering his market.

His next product was a bicycle lamp to replace the unreliable battery lamps (or in many cases small metal boxes with candles) then used by Japanese for cycling at night. Matsushita developed an improved battery, mounted his lamps in well-styled wooden casings, and left samples burning in Osaka's shop windows over weekends to prove that his lights would burn ten times longer than competitors'. From these humble beginnings began a great consumer electric products line. Matsushita became a public company in 1935. The National brand was registered in 1925; the first National radios were produced in 1930; washing machines, refrigerators, and televisions appeared in the post-World War II era; and a full range of high-fidelity electronics products starting in the 1960s. In the 1960s and 1970s Matsushita added industrial equipment, communications devices, and measuring systems. Its philosophy was to be a low cost, integrated manufacturer. Following Sony's example, in 1990 the company acquired MCA, Inc., whose assets include Universal Pictures (one of Hollywood's major film studios), an extensive film and music library, and the Universal Studios theme parks. At the time, Matsushita indicated that the acquisition would widen its business scope in the ever expanding audiovisual field. A breakdown of the company's major product groups in 1994 appears in Exhibit 1.

A 250-YEAR STRATEGY

In 1932 Konosuke Matsushita noticed a tramp drinking water from a water tap on the street. He later said, "I began to think about abundance. And I decided that the task of an industrialist was to make his products widely available at the lowest possible cost to bring a better living to the people of the world."[1] This became his exhortation to his employees on the company's 14th anniversary in 1932—and the cornerstone of the company's "250-year corporate strategy." Mr. Matsushita's 250-Year Plan to eliminate poverty is divided into ten 25-year segments. In the mid 1990s, Matsushita Company was in its third 25-Year Plan which was to include the "true internationalization of the Matsushita Electric Company."[1,75]

Several incidents exemplify the unique creative qualities Mr. Matsushita lent the company. In the early 1930s, a Japanese inventor/investor controlled many of the patents for radio circuitry, which was moving from the crystal set era toward the speaker radio. Mr. Matsushita approached this man—who intended to monopolize the new industry—and after lengthy negotiations bought out his patents for a huge price. Matsushita then opened the patents to the entire industry "so that everyone could manufacture in a more efficient way."

When General MacArthur's advisors decided to eliminate the *zaibatsu* (or "financial clique") which had controlled Japanese industry prior to World War II, they removed Mr. Matsushita as head of his company. Numerous delegations of workers approached the authorities, saying Matsushita represented the very entrepreneurial spirit which the Americans were professing. While tolerated by the *zaibatsu*, they said Matsushita was distinctly not a part of it. He had welcomed a union in the prewar era, reiterating his conviction that labor and management must work together for a greater good. But the American authorities refused to listen to these supplications, and for four years during Mr. Matsushita's enforced exile, his company shrank from 20,000 to 3,800 employees, with many divisions closing permanently. Only when he was reinstated in 1951 did the company begin to return to its former strength.

In the mid 1980s Mr. Matsushita noted in his book, *Japan at the Brink*, that "the Japanese miracle itself was on the verge of capsizing—politically, economically, and spiritually." He despised the bureaucracies that traditionally ran Japan's government. Among his many startling recommendations was the suggestion that Japan should abolish half of its universities. He felt much of the education was not worthwhile and that Japan's needs could be better provided by other institutions. Selling off the assets of Tokyo University (the nation's most prestigious university) alone would save the country some $500 million per year.

JAPAN'S INDUSTRY STRUCTURE

In the postwar era, Japan was a nation still emerging from feudalism and a military system gone berserk. Its industrial infrastructure had been destroyed, its youth decimated, and its illusions of military conquest dashed. The nation had no significant energy resources, few natural resources, a small land mass relative to its population, and a very poorly paid labor force. Many ordinary amenities had disappeared and its social system verged on breakdown or revolution. But for 300 years, its dominant feudal and religious (Confucian and Shinto) groups had emphasized devotion to one's family and organization. Personal courtesy had been ingrained in numerous rituals and was a necessity for a large population living on a small land mass. But respect for laborers had not been a widely held value, nor had wealth been widely distributed.

In the disillusioned and labor-short postwar era, more democratic values began to appear. There began a concerted national effort to improve the ordinary Japanese person's standard of living. Through its Ministry for International Trade and Industry (MITI) the government targeted certain industries for expansion and assisted them in developing their own technologies and in importing foreign technologies. To stabilize the society large Japanese companies began to emphasize lifetime employment (to age 55) and to take over many of the social roles other institutions provide in western countries. Companies often provided employee housing, recreation facilities, and a focal point for sports activities. Even today the Japanese government provides few unemployment or retirement benefits to workers. Instead, it attempts to stabilize price levels, manages the economy to maintain employment and offers supplementary employment opportunities only when necessary—through the national railroad system, public works, and public service (sanitary, groundskeeping, etc.) activities. Income and social security taxes are low. In most large companies employees are considered partners in the enterprise, not interchangeable parts of production; and in recession times employment is continued at the sacrifice of profits or dividends. Japanese executives often say that since maintaining sales and profit levels is management's responsibility—not that of factory workers—management (not workers) should take the brunt of any layoffs which are unavoidable.

Another unique feature of Japanese industry had been its financial structures. Large Japanese companies were heavy users of loan capital, with an equity ratio of only 20% (D/E=500%) being common. The largest equity shareholders, however, are also banks and insurance companies, which are forbidden individually to own more than 10% of a given company. They hold stock to secure a long-term relationship more than to reap current profits. Company shares were not widely held. Other shareholders tended to be important suppliers or buyers from the companies. Only some 30% of all stock is held by individuals. Some illustrative financial data appear in Table 1.

COMPANY PHILOSOPHY

Within this general framework, Matsushita Company has developed its own unique and extraordinarily powerful philosophy. Matsushita's stated mission is "to contribute to the well being of mankind by providing reasonably priced products and services in sufficient quantities to achieve peace, happiness, and prosperity for all." This is supported by "5 Principles": (1) Growth through mutual benefit between the company and the consumer, (2) Profit as a result of contributions to society, (3) Fair competition in the marketplace, (4) Mutual benefit between the company, its suppliers, dealers, and shareholders, (5) Participation by all employees.

"Seven Spirits" then provide the code of behavior for employees to follow in making decisions.[2] They are the:

> Spirit of Service Through Industry
> Spirit of Fairness and Faithfulness
> Spirit of Harmony and Cooperation
> Spirit of Struggle for Betterment
> Spirit of Courtesy and Humility
> Spirit of Adaptation and Assimilation
> Spirit of Gratitude

EXERCISES AND DISCUSSIONS

Every morning at Matsushita's plants in Japan (and in most areas throughout the world) every employee attends a "morning meeting" at which the Matsushita creed, principles, and/or spirits are recited

TABLE 1 Financial Ratios for Selected U.S. and Japanese Firms, Fiscal Year 1992		DEBT/EQUITY RATIO	PROFIT/ SALES	INVENTORY TURNOVER
	Apple computer	0.65	0.075	6.03
	Digital Equipment Corporation	1.01	-0.17	4.55
	General Electric Company	6.22	0.08	3.44
	International Business Machines	1.80	-0.11	3.16
	Hitachi	1.55	0.011	2.96
	Matsushita Electrical Industrial	1.21	0.01	4.17
	Mitsubishi Electric	2.99	0.01	3.74
	NEC	3.49	0.01	2.55
	Sanyo Electric	1.71	0.001	3.46
	Sony Corporation	1.84	0.01	3.06
	Toshiba Corporation	3.49	0.004	2.54

Source: Compustat Worldscope database.

aloud. Only a skeleton force of telephone operators, guards, process controllers, and so on is not present. In Japan the meeting begins with prearranged exercises learned in early grade school. Then in "relaxation exercises" each person massages and pounds the back of another person, and then both turn around to give or receive similar benefits. Following the Company Song and these recitations, a discussion leader—a task rotated daily—poses a question for the group to discuss and try to resolve. This can be an operating problem, a new opportunity, an important philosophical issue, etc., designed to promote interest. After 15 minutes or so, everyone goes off to work. At work stations the exercise routine is repeated for 5 minutes at the end of each hour and for 10–15 minutes at midmorning and afternoon. In other countries, the daily routine is adapted to accommodate local culture and customs; for instance, in Malaysia the company provides special prayer rooms at each plant and allow two prayer sessions per shift to reflect Muslim religious customs.[3]

In the company's early years, Mr. Matsushita used to interview all employees himself. As this became impossible, he and his wife annually hosted a gathering of newlywed employees. Now there are constant company messages in each employee's paycheck to personalize the company-individual relationship. Mr. Niwa, chairman of Matsushita Electric Works, said, "We try to develop the supportive idea that 'we are always with you' psychologically."[1,65] Within most plants is a "trophy area" where individual and plant awards for outstanding performance are displayed. Much emphasis is given to company awards and to the performance of company sports teams competing with those of other companies.

Mr. Kosaka, head of Matsushita's Overseas Training Center said, "We feel you must create a spirit in which everyone can share. . . . Once the philosophy is clear, it talks to every individual, and all communication in the company can be based on it."[1,63] In Matsushita's Japan operations virtually all employees wear company-provided blue uniforms with white tennis shoes. Overseas the company provides the uniforms, but the choice is up to individuals.

AN ORGANIZED MAVERICK

Despite what appears to be conformity and regimentation in its philosophy, Matsushita has consistently been a maverick in Japanese industry. From the first, Matsushita violated the usual rules used by Japanese and American companies of the era. Rather

than attempting to recoup investments as rapidly as possible, Matsushita has consistently cut its prices quickly and sought profits in the long run. While other companies used manufacturers' representatives to reach established retail channels, Matsushita set up its own distribution networks and went directly to retailers. Instead of an arm's length transaction with retailers, Matsushita offered innovative trade financing for them and pioneered the use of installment sales and point-of-purchase advertising in Japan. Rather than using the Matsushita name, the company promoted its National, Victor, and Panasonic brands.

A DECENTRALIZATION PIONEER

Although Matsushita is widely considered a "vertically integrated company," in the mid-1930s—paralleling Du Pont's pioneering efforts with a decentralized divisional structure—Matsushita and his talented controller, Takahashi, developed a similar concept with only 1,600 employees at the time. Matsushita was attracted not only to the organizational clarity and control the system offered, but to its motivational advantages as well. He wanted to keep things small, entrepreneurial, and market oriented in the rapidly emerging radio and small consumer appliance fields the company was in.

But, recognizing the inherent disadvantages of this system, Matsushita also centralized four key functions which remain so to the present. First, he created a cadre of controllers reporting directly to headquarters and a centralized accounting system across the company. Second, he institutionalized a company "bank" into which 60% of all divisional profits flowed and from which divisions have to seek funds for capital improvements. Divisions have no bank accounts except for day-to-day transactions. Divisions' "float" must be cleared monthly, and borrowings beyond this are charged out at prime plus 2%. Third, Matsushita centralized the personnel function; no employee is hired without a central prescreening, and all management promotions are reviewed and monitored by headquarters. Fourth, he centralized the company's training system with its heavy emphasis on the values described above. Each university level employee goes through an approximately eight month training cycle to inspire them with the company's goals and philosophies, as well as to provide them with essential technical skills.

During the '70s and '80s, unlike many large Japanese groups which used a Keiretsu form, Matsushita was closer to a divisionalized, vertically integrated company. Keiretsus typically had at their center a large bank (like Mitsubishi Bank) and an international trading company for the group. The bank held partial equity interests in the "first tier" central producing companies of the Keiretsu (e.g., Mitsubishi Heavy Industries). Japanese law limited any single bank's holding to 10% of a firm's equity. However, the central bank of the Keiretsu provided substantial loan funds to its "first tier" companies and their major suppliers. Within the Keiretsu, common interests (of supplier and customer), a shared identity, a shared international trading facility, and cross-linked boards—rather than equity interests—provided the major bases for common control. "Discussions" among members of the group were common. The central companies of the Keiretsu often held some equity interest in their "second tier" key suppliers, shared technologies, and coordinated plans closely with them. As a result, these suppliers were closely tied to the Keiretsu, highly stable, and enjoyed world class process and management support. This kind of "quasi-integration" did not apply to the smaller "third tier" suppliers who were independents competing, more or less as American suppliers would, for their customers' business. In the mid to late 1980s, these Keiretsu structures had often become slow moving and bureaucratic.

A PRODUCT GROUP MATRIX

Over the years, Matsushita's basic organization had oscillated back and forth with more (or less) autonomy given to the divisions depending on external economic or competitive conditions. In 1953 Matsushita introduced Product Groups with division heads reporting vertically to the president and horizontally to group vice presidents, who serve as specialists with detailed knowledge of a whole family of similar products.[4] This innovation was some ten years ahead of the widespread use of matrix organizations in the U.S. Matsushita tried not to take its formal organization charts too seriously and to "humanize" some of the inherent conflicts in the matrix structure. Controllers were called "coordinators" and housed directly in the factories they served.[4,35] To relieve some of the resistance to this matrix concept, Matsushita constantly reminded executives that everyone grew up with two bosses (a mother and a father), a situation that generally seemed quite tolerable. Even at the top level Matsushita established a three-person Executive Council to handle major decisions. He then slowly withdrew himself into a strategic role as chairman,

although in times of crisis he reserved the right to reemerge to assume direct control.

COMPETITION AND COOPERATION

Japanese corporations compete intensively with companies in the same line of business, but often cooperate extensively with other companies in a complementary relationship. For example, Matsushita has 120 "fully controlled" wholesalers selling only its products. It has 20% or more equity interest in all these distributors and serves them and other retailers through 100 sales offices which provide management assistance, showroom facilities, and other services to Matsushita's Japanese distribution network. Retailers include 25,000 National Shops, where Matsushita products account for 80% of sales and another 25,000 National Stores where its products exceed 50% of sales.

Matsushita does not hold shares in these retailers, but controls them by long term contracts and the special services it provides: management training, classes on new technologies, shared advertising and EDI systems, and some special rebates. Typically, products are sold at list in these channels, but they may have to meet the prices of the discount stores now becoming more common in Japan. Other separate channels exist for: (1) industrial and non-industrial construction products and (2) commercial, industrial, and government customers. Marketing for Matsushita was controlled from headquarters. Each product division could sell directly to its wholesalers or large customers like the government, but under rules established at headquarters. Until 1988, export sales are handled by an independent subsidiary, Matsushita Trading Co., which had worldwide sales branches for all products.

TECHNOLOGY AND MANUFACTURING

Matsushita is heavily integrated on the components side. It produces its own batteries, vacuum tubes, integrated circuits, circuit boards, condensers, transformers, speakers, tuners, magnetic heads, and so on. But it buys standard raw materials (wire, steel, aluminum sheet, etc.) outside. Purchases from subsidiaries have averaged about 80% of all purchased materials value. The company also sells components to outside groups. It only consumes about 50% of its component production, and is the largest single electronics component manufacturer in Japan. The manufacturing divisions are all profit centers, able to buy components outside if they so choose. These manufacturing divisions sell through the marketing channels described above. Products are sold by divisional salesmen, shipped directly to distributors or retailers, and transferred to Marketing at internal transfer prices. The Central Marketing group handles sales planning, marketing coordination, and promotional functions.

Although Matsushita started with two innovative products, it has rarely pioneered entirely new technologies.[4,30] Instead, it emphasizes quality and price. Its experience with video tape recorders (VTRs) is perhaps typical. Sony was generally acknowledged as the real pioneer of VTR technology with its Umatic and Betamax formats. While Matsushita had also done excellent early work on the technology, it took a license under Sony's early VHS-like format and turned its several divisions loose on improving the device for the marketplace. Discovering that customers wanted a 2–4 hour recording capacity (as opposed to Sony's 1-hour format), Matsushita designed this into a more compact VTR that was highly reliable and could be priced 10–15% below Sony. When Sony came up with its superior quality Beta format, Matsushita stayed with its well-developed VHS concept, got other major Japanese and U.S. firms to adopt its preferred format, and by the early 1980s manufactured two-thirds of all VTRs sold.

"Figure Out How to Do It Better"

Matsushita consistently invested some 4% of sales in R&D, much of which went into production engineering. The company had some 20 production engineering laboratories equipped with the latest available technology. Most of these were attached to individual product divisions. But Matsushita's Central Production Engineering Laboratory at corporate level was one of the world's outstanding units. The company also had a Central (basic) Research Laboratory, Wireless Research Laboratory, and Research Institute Tokyo (which operated on an independent basis and conducted research for both company and outside groups). In addition, there were a Corporate Product Development Division, Corporate Quality Assurance Division, and Corporate Patent and Legal Division under the Central Engineering structure.

The company's focus in R&D had been "to analyze competing products and figure out how to do the job better."[4,31] Its Engineering and Research Laboratories were backed up by one of the world's most awesome production line suggestion systems. Matsushita

processed some 460,000 employee generated suggestions or improvements per year. The company's motto was "Matsushita produces capable people before it produces products." Thus Matsushita's eight-month training for all university graduates involved: 3 weeks of headquarters training classes; 3 months in retail stores; one month in the factory; one month in cost accounting; and two months in marketing lectures and activities. Lesser time, but equal attention went into training rank and file workers. Job rotation was common throughout all ranks; 5% of all employees (comprised of 1/3 managers, 1/3 supervisors, and 1/3 workers) rotated from one division to another each year, and some 80% of all employees participated in quality circle activities. About 15% of all suggestions were accepted and formally implemented, others were simply implemented by informal agreement among supervisors and employees.[2,304] Of these about 35 "super suggestions" occurred each year. These won coveted awards. And sponsors of patentable suggestions could receive patents and monetary awards in their own names.[1,71]

"Manage from Goodwill"

Production plants tended to be spotlessly clean. Cleanliness standards were dictated from headquarters and were not subject to interpretation anywhere in the world. Work stations were typically separated by 8–10 feet, aisles were extremely wide (15–30 feet), noise levels were relatively low around work stations, and the production line itself moved more slowly than was typical in western plants. A substantial amount of small-scale automation was generally visible at individual work stations. Individual workers were directly responsible for quality results at their own stations, but heavily automated quality control and test facilities were in evidence all along electronics and consumer products lines. Employee turnover in Japan was of course extremely low, but even Matsushita's overseas plants tended to have 1/4 the turnover of comparable plants in their host countries—and often they rejected local unions.

Matsushita managers attributed this to the attempt to "manage from goodwill" and to "foster a homey, family atmosphere. We are first interested in nurturing a relationship of trust between management and labor. Once we achieve that goal, we can develop other things like suggestion systems, quality circles, and so on." North American employees responded, "You're not under a lot of pressure here; it's a comfortable place to work. Everyone understands we're all here to help each other, and to put out the best product we can."[1,86] In

1974 Matsushita Electric Company of America (MECA) had bought a 25-year-old Westinghouse heavy equipment plant near Toronto. During the 1980s, while most of the competitors left the market, MECA had the highest growth rate in its industry in Canada.

PLANNING AND CONTROL SYSTEMS

Matsushita had derived its planning system from Phillips (NV), the Dutch electronics giant. On New Year's Day some thousands of upper and middle managers assembled to hear the chairman and president declare the basic policy for the year. This contained some key dimensions and figures, but more broadly it presented the important elements to be emphasized in the company during the year. These strategic directions were later conveyed to all employees through the company magazine.

Every six months each division manager presented three plans. The first was a long-term (five-year) plan, updated as new technologies and environmental events occurred. Second was a two-year (midterm) plan which stated how the division would translate its long-term plan into such things as plant capacity or specific new products. Top line management did not review either extensively, but the product group side of the organization matrix did.[4,36]

The Six-Month Operating Plan received more attention. Here the division stated its monthly forecasts of sales, market share, profits, inventories, accounts receivable, capital expenditures, head count, quality targets, etc. When variances occurred the division manager and his controller had to be prepared to explain them. Market share, return on sales, asset turnover, and actual versus budgeted costs received particular attention, since these were considered to be under the division managers' control. Matsushita had rigorous standards for collections from its customers and payments to its suppliers—normally both less than 30 days—but the corporation could extend long-term credit to build sales channels, develop new markets, or meet special competitive needs.

Everyone understood that key variables would be tracked monthly and reviewed scrupulously. Figures were available within a few days after the end of each month and were widely shared in Matsushita's "open information system."[4,39] Three groups—corporate line officers, corporate staff, and a "peer review" by the heads of other divisions—provided performance reviews and rewards, based on actual vs. planned results. Matsushita expected every division to be completely self sustaining within five years and strongly resisted subsidizing losing divisions.

The 60% of each division's profits paid to headquarters covered Product Group Management, R&D, Production Engineering, and an equity return. The remaining 40% belonged to the divisions for facilities updating, production engineering, and new product development. However, corporate held the funds and paid the divisions interest for their use. Matsushita expected each division to make sure its current and future product lines were healthy and did not use "portfolio" concepts favored in U.S. companies.

PERFORMANCE REVIEWS

Corporate headquarters was deliberately lean, with only 1.5% of the company's total personnel there (excluding the Engineering Research Laboratories). However, each month the division manager spent several days at headquarters, going over each performance item and variance in detail with the Finance Office and with senior management. Key criteria were (1) the ability to stay on plan and (2) whether the division's management was "doing its best" and "as well as anyone in the market." If not, poor performers might be quickly transferred to other areas, "where their talents better fit circumstances."[4,37] In the "peer review" process (quarterly), summary operating results were shared before all divisions. Divisions were grouped A, B, C, or D; the A (outstanding) groups made their presentations first, Ds last. Though individuals or divisions were not singled out for embarrassment, each group's relative performance was clear to all.

Matsushita monitored its sales force and executives through exacting prospect lists and yield statistics, but backed its sales force with the largest advertising budget in Japan. Senior sales executives were expected to visit retail outlets regularly and to seek group-level help when they needed it. To support its strong sales channels, Matsushita also operated an elaborate network of "customer clubs" to keep informed about its users' needs and to solicit ideas for improvement of products or services. Even top executives, like Mr. Matsushita and Mr. Yamashita (then president), spent most of their time out of their offices and with customers. At various times both had gone into the field to solve specific crisis situations themselves. And in a 1970s' recession, even assembly line workers were shifted to door-to-door selling to cut inventories and to bring costs into line.

OVERSEAS OPERATIONS

Matsushita made its first move overseas in 1961, to Thailand. By early 1992, its global operations base included 69 manufacturing companies and 32 sales and finance companies in 32 countries. In 1988 Matsushita had merged Matsushita Electric with Matsushita Electric Trading Co., Ltd. in an effort to combine manufacturing and marketing expertise, and to unify domestic and international operations. In addition to marketing through its own affiliates, Matsushita also produced for private label distribution by OEMs abroad. It also had a series of licensing arrangements with foreign companies, most notably RCA (non exclusive) and Philips (exclusive) with the latter owning a minority position in Matsushita Electric Company. Matsushita had a variety of ownership arrangements in various host countries from full ownership to joint ventures, but never had less than a 50% board position.

A Japanese almost always headed an overseas unit, and many middle managers were Japanese. Almost all managerial people—whether Japanese or not—went through Matsushita's Overseas Training Center in Osaka, which offered specialized training in English, in overseas operations, in company policy, and in the company's value system. Because of scales of operation, tariff barriers, distances from Japan, etc., the specific organization of each subsidiary might be quite different. For example the Malaysian subsidiary had a small local market, was close to Japan, was heavily protected by tariffs, and had to deal with significant "local content" rules. The U.K. and Canada plants were bound by few such rules, but served huge domestic markets. Because of the company's size, its stock was traded on several of the world's stock markets (including the United States) and it often raised funds locally.

A PRAGMATIC APPROACH

Matsushita had a pragmatic approach to all problems. The heart of its style was "to get to the problem and fix it."[4.43] There was much latent conflict between its competing divisions, its matrix units, and its "Venture Capital Fund," administered from the corporation's 60% of profits. Divisions made proposals asking the Fund's managers to support new products or concepts which did not fit normal capital allocation processes well. Yet Matsushita executives expressed surprise when asked if there was much interdivisional fighting. They said, "We conflict without conflicting. Our underlying premise is that in life we make adjust-ments. . . . We presuppose that parties will fundamentally strive to pull together rather than push apart."[4.43]

Employees were not viewed as "participating in management," but their opinions were sought. The company's books were open to the union, and the union was consulted directly as each division prepared its long-term and six-month plans. Matsushita encouraged long-term managerial continuity in its divisions with five to seven years in key spots being common. But the Central Personnel group also tracked the top several performers in each division and consciously moved these people to openings as they occurred. Matsushita's maxim was "extraordinary results from ordinary people."[4.47] It did not make particular efforts to hire from the elite schools and was willing to jump younger people over dozens of their seniors if their performance warranted. Another maxim was, "If you make an honest mistake, the company will be very forgiving. Treat it as a training experience and learn from it. You will be severely criticized [a euphemism for dismissed] however if you deviate from the company's basic principles."[4.51]

For years, Matsushita's basic organization structure had changed little. But the early 1990s were a difficult time for the company. The yen experienced several years of sharp appreciation and Japan's domestic economy experienced a lengthy recession from which it was slowly recovering. (See Exhibits 2 and 3 for details of the company's financial situation and sales by segment.) In mid-1992, management acknowledged that the downturn foreshadowed a fundamental change rather than a temporary adjustment. It initiated a midterm strategic plan designed to ensure (1) solid profitability even during years when sales growth is minimal and (2) a focus on building sound foundations for future growth. In a joint effort with domestic retail outlets, Matsushita conducted direct surveys of 10 million households in Japan to help refocus its product development activities.

The company identified ten principal business areas that it would pursue worldwide: Audio/Video hardware, information and communications, home appliances, housing products, air-conditioning equipment, protection and health-care products, systems and networks, and AV software. Technological advances prompted the company to emphasize three of these areas—AV hardware, information and communications, and components and devices—for intensive, coordinated development by the entire corporation. In AV hardware digitization was driving high-definition TV, digital video, audio cassettes, and digital videodiscs.

Information processing and communications operations were also benefiting from digitization opportunities in cellular phones, digital broadcast transmission devices, and integrated information, communication, and display technologies for multimedia products.

In keeping with its new product focus and the growing need for integration across technologies, Matsushita was considering revamping its R&D structure in late 1993. Discussions included its corporate engineering divisions—formerly the heart of Matsushita's R&D structure—as well as more than 20 research centers and several development centers. Matsushita was painfully aware that product life cycles were growing ever shorter and that the distinction between consumer and commercial products was steadily decreasing. Despite investing 5.8% to 6% of sales in R&D, in the early 1990s, Matsushita was allowing its competitors to pioneer new products and then launching a huge invasion after the market took off. As product life cycles in camcorders approached 90 days, this became harder and harder to do. Yet in 1993 *The Economist* noted Matsushita had introduced no fundamentally new products in the last 3 years.

To coordinate its divisions Matsushita had installed a group or "sector system," under which each "sector" had jurisdiction over several operating divisions. This was also under review in 1994. There was much discussion of abolishing the sector system to "eliminate the roof on top of the roofs," and to streamline the corporate organization. One component of this was a reassessment of the international operations which accounted for 49% of all sales. In earlier times each foreign subsidiary had worked in one country and designed its sales and manufacturing efforts for that specific market, giving Matsushita's manufacturing techniques a "second life" in these markets. It often duplicated its processes "lock-stock-and-barrel" into these new markets. Sometimes Matsushita found these foreign units became more efficient than those in Japan. The continued appreciation of the yen, the emergence of new trading blocs, and increased competition had led to discussions about creating what Matsushita called "export centers" for certain of its commodity products—like TVs and air-conditioners that could be priced more

competitively if they were produced in smaller lots, with lower-cost labor and with parts sourced from outside Japan.[5] In the late 1990s, Matsushita expected significantly more than half of its total revenues to come from overseas operations and sales. But as an analyst had noted in 1994, "It doesn't matter how strong your overseas operations are if you can't keep your key people busy at home. The problem is, any product you make in Japan nowadays has to have enough value-added to justify the high costs of manufacturing. I don't know what those products are, and I'm not convinced Matsushita does either."[6]

While domestic sales were still lagging, overseas sales had been rising, in part due to vigorous sales of its color TVs, audio equipment, information processing, and industrial equipment in China, Southeast Asia, and the U.S. How Matsushita would position itself to maintain its Japanese dominance, compete in these emerging growth areas, and the markets of Eastern Europe—while maintaining its traditional core competencies and scale economies—was a major concern.

QUESTIONS

1. What was Japan's basic industrial strategy in the '50s and '70s? Why did it choose this strategy? How did it keep capital costs so low? What are the potential weaknesses in this strategy? How does this support Matsushita's strategy?

2. What has been Matsushita's basic strategy? What have been the most important policies involved in its implementation? Why were those chosen? What issues do they pose in the late 1990s? What changes are needed? How can they be implemented?

3. Based on the information in the case, draw an organization chart before and after the changes you propose. What issues do these pose? How would you measure performance for each major unit? How should overseas operations be organized? Coordinated? Why?

4. What functions has Matsushita's elaborately developed value system provided? What problems does it now pose? What should be done?

EXHIBIT 1
Matsushita's Major
Product Groups in 1994

Video Equipment   **20% of Total Sales**

Videocassette recorders, video camcorders and related equipment, color TVs, TV/VCR combination units, projection TVs, liquid crystal display TVs, videodisc players, satellite broadcast receivers, and satellite-communications-related equipment

Audio Equipment   **8% of Total Sales**

Radios, radio-cassette recorders, tape recorders, compact disc players, digital compact cassette players, stereo hi-fi and related equipment, car audio products, and electronic musical instruments

Home Appliances   **13% of Total Sales**

Refrigerators, room air conditioners, home laundry equipment, dishwashers, vacuum cleaners, electric irons, microwave ovens, rice cookers, electric fans, electric and kerosene heaters, infrared-ray warmers, electric blankets, and electrically heated rugs

Communication and Industrial Equipment   **25% of Total Sales**

Facsimile equipment, word processors, personal computers, copying machines, CRT displays, telephones, PBXs, CATV systems, measuring instruments, electronic-parts-mounting machines, industrial robots, welding machines, air-conditioning equipment, compressors, and vending machines

Electronic Components   **12% of Total Sales**

Integrated circuits, discrete devices, charge coupled devices, cathode-ray tubes, image pick-up tubes, tuners, capacitors, resistors, speakers, magnetic recording heads, electric motors, and electric lamps

Batteries and Kitchen-Related Products   **5% of Total Sales**

Dry batteries, storage batteries, solar batteries, solar energy equipment, gas hot-water supply systems, gas cooking appliances, kitchen sinks, kitchen fixture systems, and bath and sanitary equipment

Other   **8% of Total Sales**

Bicycles, cameras and flash units, electric pencil sharpeners, water purifiers, imported materials and products such as nonferrous metals, lumber, and paper and medical equipment

Entertainment   **9% of Total Sales**

Filmed entertainment, music entertainment, theme parks, book publishing, gift merchandise, pre-recorded video and audio tapes and discs

Source: Matsushita Electric Industrial Company, Ltd., *1994 Annual Report.*

EXHIBIT 2
**Matsushita Electric
Industrial Co., Ltd.,
Historical Financial
Summary**
(in millions of yen, except
per share amounts)

	1994	1990	1986	1982
Net sales				
Domestic	¥3,361,521	¥3,381,861	¥2,669,107	¥1,964,786
Overseas	3,262,065	2,620,925	2,141,667	1,684,785
Total	6,623,586	6,002,786	4,810,774	3,649,571
Net income	¥24,493	¥235,561	¥167,588	¥157,121
Net income per share	¥11.67	¥108.34	¥87.50	¥89.02
Dividends per share	13.50	10.00	9.52	9.09
Total assets	¥8,192,632	¥7,851,211	¥5,019,329	¥3,173,720
Stockholders' equity	¥3,288,945	¥3,200,903	¥2,188,093	¥1,453,313
Capital investment	¥266,522	¥354,757	¥204,609	¥161,045
Depreciation	317,747	237,749	207,377	115,507
R&D expenditures	381,747	345,679	257,958	151,164
Employees (thousands)	254,059	198,088	181,453	121,254

Source: Matsushita Electric Industrial Company, Ltd., various annual reports.

EXHIBIT 2 (cont'd)
Matsushita Electric Industrial Co., Ltd., Consolidated Income Statement—1994 versus 1983
(in millions of yen)

	1994	1983
Net sales	¥6,623,586	¥3,988,519
Cost of sales	4,573,964	2,571,006
Gross profit	2,049,622	1,417,513
SG&A	1,876,016	990,987
Operating profit	173,606	426,526
Other income (deductions)		
Interest and dividend income	79,832	92,405
Interest expenses	(99,790)	(50,257)
Other, net	(25,425)	12,294
Total net	(45,383)	71,548
Income before income taxes	128,223	498,074
Provision for income taxes		
Current	122,184	276,984
Deferred	(22,306)	(8,493)
Total/net	99,878	268,491
Minority interests	6,885	46,835
Equity in earnings of associated cos.	3,033	—
NET INCOME	**¥24,493**	**¥182,748**

Source: Matsushita Electric Industrial Company, Ltd., *1994 and 1983 Annual Reports.*

EXHIBIT 3
Matsushita's Sales by Segment

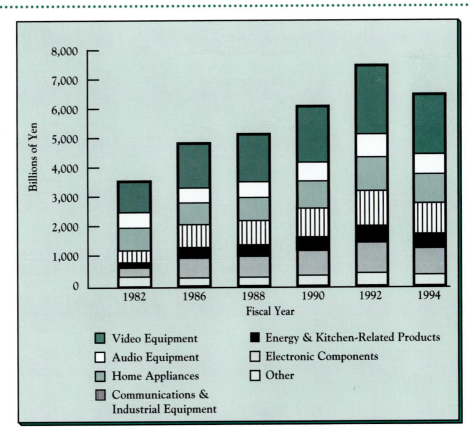

EXHIBIT 2 (cont'd)
Matsushita Electric
Industrial Co., Ltd.,
Consolidated Balance
Sheet—1994 versus
1983
(in millions of yen)

	1994	1983
Current Assets		
Cash and cash equivalents	¥1,392,991	¥553,998
Short-term investments	127,924	212,762
Net trade receivables	1,302,010	544,886
Inventories	924,411	528,529
Other current assets	326,361	179,179
Total current assets	4,073,697	2,019,344
Noncurrent receivables	341,244	—
Noncurrent inventories (film costs)	192,884	—
Investments and advances	1,248,921	831,277
Property, plant & equipment		
Land	272,973	73,584
Buildings	1,036,491	330,193
Machinery and equipment	2,422,315	642,789
Construction in progress	51,982	22,168
Total	3,782,761	1,068,734
less accumulated depreciation	2,388,307	603,709
Net property, plant & equipment	1,395,454	465,025
Other assets	940,432	134,947
TOTAL ASSETS	**¥8,192,632**	**¥3,450,593**
Current liabilities		
Short-term borrowings	¥900,756	¥196,211
Trade payables	585,144	362,547
Accrued income taxes	63,080	161,253
Accrued payroll	167,198	114,892
Other accrued expenses	450,494	198,375
Deposits and advances from customers	119,891	76,956
Employees' deposits	126,062	83,107
Other current liabilities	166,112	58,453
Total	2,578,737	1,251,794
Noncurrent liabilities		
Long-term debt	1,260,387	40,405
Retirement and severance benefits	347,226	179,247
Other liabilities	159,653	—
Total	1,767,266	219,652
Minority interests	557,684	377,073
Stockholders' equity	3,288,945	1,602,074
TOTAL LIABILITIES	**¥8,192,632**	**¥3,450,593**

Source: Matsushita Electric Industrial Company, Ltd., *1994* and *1983 Annual Reports.*

The Hewlett Packard Company (HP) had been a dynamic business built around innovation. It had traditionally been a fast-paced organization characterized by steady growth. From 1957 to 1984, sales increased from $28.1 million to $6 billion, and profits from $2.4 million to $665 million. In 1984 the company had close to 7,000 products on the market, and developed new products at a rate of 300 per year.

HP had become the world's leading manufacturer of electronic test and measurement equipment for engineers and scientists. Besides the electronics industry and scientific research programs, the principal markets for HP instruments included the telecommunications, aerospace, aircraft, and automotive industries. Its principal products were integrated instrument and computer systems, test and measurement instruments, computer systems and peripheral products, medical electronic equipment and systems, instrumentation and systems for chemical analysis, handheld calculators, and solid-state components. HP Laboratories, the company's common research facility, ranked as one of the world's leading electronics research centers.[1] HP was among the world's top ten companies in CAD/CAE/CAM sales. (See Table 1.)

TWO TALENTED COFOUNDERS

The two most influential people in HP's development had been its cofounders, William Hewlett and David Packard—in 1985 vice chairman and chairman of the board, respectively. Each was personally responsible for many of the company's most important products and diversification moves. Hewlett was an innovator with great technical expertise; he conceived of product lines and used parts of HP Labs for his own research. Packard was known for his sound business sense and outstanding managerial and administrative skills and was said to be the driving force behind such key decisions as HP's move into medical systems and its efforts to become a major factor in minicomputers.

DOING THINGS WELL

For HP, growth came from doing things well and was not an objective in itself. The company did not stipulate long-term targets for expected profit or market share growth, having explicitly made the decision not to become dependent on such growth. Its focus was on making quality products that commanded a premium price in the marketplace. If it did this job well, the company believed profits would follow. The company's attitude toward long-term formal planning was stated by Mr. Hewlett, "We operate on a very short lead time, and don't have a master plan. In terms of next year's detailed plan we try and wait until the last possible moment to get that in place."[2]

EARLY HISTORY

Hewlett and Packard started what was to become HP in 1938, in a garage behind the Packards' home in Palo Alto, California. The two founders were both graduates of Standard University's engineering program. The company began with an audio oscillator—a high-quality electronic instrument for use in developing and testing sound equipment. Among the early customers for their product was Walt Disney Studios. In 1938, Walt Disney asked them to develop eight oscillators having different frequency characteristics and different physical configurations. One result was the HP

TABLE 1 The Top Ten in CAD/CAE/CAM Worldwide Sales: Revenue by application ($million).	COMPANY	MECHANICAL ENGINEERING	ELECTRONIC/ ELECTRICAL ENGINEERING	ARCHITECTURAL/ ELECTRICAL/CIVIL ENGINEERING	MAPPING	SERVICES	TOTAL REVENUE
	Computervision	272	111	56	6	111	556
	IBM	391	13	16	—	109	529
	Intergraph	64	20	178	89	52	403
	Digital Equipment	107	103	22	32	37	301
	Calma Corp. (GE)	70	90	28	—	47	235
	McDonnell Douglas	94	—	24	—	16	134
	Applicon	62	25	1	—	13	101
	Hewlett Packard	45	36	6	—	10	97
	Control Data	54	7	9	—	23	93
	Prime Computer	53	3	14	—	20	90

Source: International Data Corp. in Paine Webber, Inc., *Hewlett Packard Company Report*, December 2, 1985.

Model 200A used in developing the soundtrack for the movie "Fantasia."

This large order provided a foundation for the company's early success. But growth was slow during World War II. Hewlett and Packard made a conscious decision not to pursue large military contracts because of their "boom or bust" possibilities. HP accepted only limited government work in microwave technologies and kept itself focused on instrumentation and microwave measurement.[3] HP operated as a partnership until 1947 when it incorporated.

AN EXPANDING PRODUCT LINE

After World War II the company began to expand its product line significantly and moved from being a focused instrument maker to a more diversified company. In 1957, when the organization reached 1,200 employees, this size was considered too large to manage by the informal methods HP had previously used.

For example, early in HP's history, two product development techniques had been prevalent. The first was known as the "next bench syndrome." A central strategy in the early years, this referred to listening to the problems of engineers on the next bench and finding ways to solve them. Since the company was working on the frontiers of its technologies, this approach helped the company identify new technical opportunities and needs; little market research was done, since the company could monitor most market needs internally.[4] A second approach was to design a machine specifically for one customer and then market it to others. This enabled the company to concentrate on products for a few customers, yet produce in volume and

charge high margins. Rather than compete on price, the intention was to develop products so advanced and adapted to customers' needs that the market would be willing to pay a premium for HP performance.

INSTITUTIONALIZING THE HP WAY

HP's "Corporate Objectives," embracing the company's basic values and philosophy, were put in writing in 1957 and became the "HP Way." (See Exhibit 1.) This same year the first personnel department was created. As Mr. Hewlett noted,

> Contrary to most companies at that time, we did not have a personnel department. We had strong convictions that one of a manager's most important jobs was to deal directly with his employees. We did not want to impose any artificial barriers to hinder direct communications.[5]

Mr. Hewlett later described the important organizational changes which were to occur in 1957 as follows:

> A real turning point for the company occurred in 1957, resulting in changes that would have a profound effect on the company in future years. Up to that time, HP was directed by the owner-founders operating in a single plant in Palo Alto, California. Most of the basic policies that directed the company were firmly in place, and we had a good team of people running the operation.
>
> But there were signs of strain appearing. I think the principal concern Dave and I had was that, as it increased in size, the company might lose the intimacy we felt was so important to the organization. Therefore, in January 1957, Dave and I took the top 10 or 12 people of the organization on a weekend retreat to discuss the future of the company, and to decide what action might be taken to insure its continued success.

Several conclusions were reached. First, we decided to divisionalize the company along product lines. We felt that by reducing the size of the operating units and decreasing the span of control, we would provide an opportunity to recapture the personal touch that everyone felt was so important. The managers of these divisions would assume direct responsibility for the health and welfare of their charge, but they would need some guidance. Second, it seemed that this guidance could best be achieved with a simple set of policy statements. In fact, these statements consisted of no more than a codification of past company policies. Coupled with this belief was the conviction that, with these guidelines, local managers could make better decisions than either Dave or me, because—if for no other reason—they would be closer to the problems.[3]

CORPORATE CULTURE AND ORGANIZATION

In order to appreciate the culture Hewlett and Packard attempted to foster, it is necessary to understand the founders' own backgrounds and beliefs. As Mr. Hewlett said,

> . . . it is important to remember that Dave and I were products of the Depression. We had observed its effects on all sides, and it could not help but influence our deci-

---

EXHIBIT 1
The HP Way

BUSINESS RELATED

1. Pay as you go—no long-term borrowing
   - Helps to maintain a stable financial environment during depressed business periods.
   - Serves as an excellent self-regulating mechanism for HP managers.
2. Market expansion and leadership based on *new* product contributions
   - Engineering excellence determines market recognition of our new products.
   - Novel new product ideas and implementations serve as the basis for expansion of existing markets or diversification into new markets.
3. Customer satisfaction second to none
   - We sell only what has been thoroughly designed, tested, and specified.
   - Our products have *lasting* value—they are highly reliable (quality) and our customers discover additional benefits while using them.
   - Best after-sales service and support in the industry.
4. *Honesty* and *integrity* in all matters
   - No tolerance for dishonest dealings with vendors or customers (e.g., bribes, kickbacks).
   - Open and honest communication with employees and stockholders alike; conservative financial reporting.

PEOPLE RELATED

1. *Belief* in our people
   - Confidence in, and respect for, our people as opposed to depending upon extensive rules, procedures, and so on.
   - Depend upon people to do their job right (individual freedom) without constant directives.
   - Opportunity for meaningful participation (job dignity).
2. Emphasis on working *together* and *sharing* awards (teamwork and partnership)
   - Share responsibilities; help each other, learn from each other, chance to make mistakes.
   - Recognition based on contribution to results—sense of achievement and self-esteem.
   - Profit sharing, stock purchase plan, retirement program, and so on; aimed at employees and company sharing in each other's successes.
   - Company financial management emphasis on protecting employee's job security.
3. A *superior* working environment which other companies seek but few achieve
   - Informality—open, honest communications; no artificial distinctions between employees (first-name basis); management by walking around; and open door communication policy.
   - Develop and promote from within—lifetime training, education, career counseling to help employees get maximum opportunity to grow and develop with the company.
   - Decentralization—emphasis on keeping work groups as small as possible for maximum employee identification with our businesses and customers.
   - Management by objectives (MBO)—provides a sound basis for measuring performance by employees as well as managers and is objective, not political.

Source: The Hewlett Packard Company.

sions on how a company should be run. Two thoughts were clear from the start. First, we did not want to run a hire and fire operation, but rather a company built on a loyal and dedicated work force. Further, we felt that this work force should be able to share to some extent in the progress of the company. Second, we wished to operate, as much as possible, on a pay-as-you-go basis, that our growth be financed by our earnings and not by debt.[3]

The new organization designed at the weekend retreat in 1957 was called the Product Division Structure. It separated the company into small divisions, which were to become HP's fundamental business units. Each product division became an integrated, self-sustaining organization with a great deal of independence, similar in some ways to a company. Each division had its own engineering, manufacturing, and marketing organization. The divisions had considerable latitude in developing individual products and product line strategies, but they were not permitted to go outside their assigned markets or to raise money outside the corporation.

Technological leadership was to be a major goal for each production division.[1] Operations were pragmatically specified around the division's technical focus. And what became known as HPs Originator/Producer strategy was introduced to move products to the marketplace. An idea's originator was expected to carry it through all stages of development and into the market if necessary. Bernard M. Oliver, vice president for R&D (in 1975) said,

> At the time we split R&D and product engineering. But we discovered that the only way to get things done in a timely fashion was to have the originator of an idea carry it through to the end. We've tried to remove the fences between research and production and make a chute that starts in the lab and ends at the shipping dock.[5] [To back up this concept] . . . [HP] Product Divisions are purposely kept small, seldom numbering more than 2000 people. This structure spurs entrepreneurship by allowing decisions to be made by the persons most responsible for putting them into action. Compact and action oriented, the HP division combines the flexibility of a small business with the resources of a large corporation.[1]

Key personnel worked together on projects without regard to their status in their own organizations. In developing new products, divisional project engineers organized technical development efforts, but product managers from Marketing joined the team early to provide inputs on design and price. For the most part, the early stage technical work done by the divisions was self-contained, requiring little communication across divi-

sions. And the company tried to keep each division's product-technical-market focus as discrete as possible.

MANAGEMENT BY OBJECTIVES AND INVOLVEMENT

Mr. Hewlett was later to say of the 1957 reorganization that:

> The recommendations of our 1957 meeting were quickly implemented by divisionalization and by wide distribution of the objectives. These objectives had an important role in training and guiding the new management teams. They served to reinforce the principles of cooperative management—the concept of leading, not directing. They stressed a management style that was informal, with give and take discussion, lack of private offices, casual dress and the universal use of first names.
>
> The informal structure of the company led to what was eventually known as its "open door" policy. In a sense this said that any employee who was unhappy could come in and talk with Dave or me or any other senior executive about his problems. Although such a technique could easily be abused, it never was, and it served as an excellent safety valve for the frustrations that occur in any organizations.[3]

To back up this philosophy, the organization developed two important policies. The first was Management by Objectives (MBO). Mr. Packard believed this was the most effective way for an innovative company like HP to operate:

> You establish some objectives with people, provide some incentives, and try not to direct the detailed way in which they do their work. We've found you're likely to get a much better performance that way than if you have a more military-type procedure where somebody gives orders and expects them to be followed in every detail.[6]

The second was Management by Walking Around (MBWA), a term later popularized by *In Search of Excellence*. This was an extra step HP took to make sure the open door policy was truly effective. It involved a friendly, unfocused and unscheduled series of interactions with any employee with whom a manager from any level happened to stop by to chat. The result was an implicit invitation to repay this visit and walk through that manager's open door at any time—management by involvement.[4]

EXPANSION AND DIVERSIFICATION

Also in 1957, HP's stock was first made available to the public. One year later the firm made its first acquisition, acquiring F. L. Moseley Co. of Pasadena, a producer of high-quality graphic recorders. By 1964, HP had acquired Sanborn Co. of Waltham, a pioneer in electrocardiography and a supplier of other recording instruments, and F. M. Scientific Corp., a manufacturer of chromatographic devices. Through these acquisitions HP entered medical electronics and analytic chemistry.

The first electronic calculator was designed at HP in 1966. An employee working for one of the calculator companies reportedly brought to HP a concept for an all electronic calculator. An HP team converted this concept into an electronic calculator to compete with the desk top mechanical calculators of that era. HP's calculator had a great deal of power, but was a large device measuring about one square foot.[4] HP successfully directed its early sales efforts toward educational, scientific, and engineering markets, where it was an established supplier of instruments.

Later, in 1972, HP introduced the first scientific handheld calculator, the HP-35. The original HP-35, championed and designed in part by Mr. Hewlett, went into production despite an outside market research study that scoffed at the idea. With no external marketing support, the company managed its own distribution. The HP-35 was introduced at a price of $395. It proved so popular that this price was maintained until mid-1973. The tremendous surge in calculator sales was accompanied by a 33% increase in employees as well as a rapid ballooning of inventories.

COMPLEXITY AND RESTRUCTURING

As product complexities grew, in 1970 HP established its first product group structure. Some sales organizations were created at the group level, separate from those of the product divisions.[7] In years to come, these posed a number of communication and integration issues across divisions, but only within the product group. There the units could be coordinated by a vice president or general manager. There was little or no mandated communication across product groups.

HP's first period of significant difficulty occurred in 1970, triggered by economic downturns in both the computer and aerospace industries. The company's sales decreased by nearly $40 million, the first decrease since HP went public. Mr. Hewlett stated how the company dealt with the situation:

> One of the most dramatic examples of working with our employees occurred during the recession in early 1970. It became evident that we had about 10 percent more employees than we needed for the production schedule.

Rather than lay off or furlough 10 percent of the work force, we simply decided that everyone in the company would take every other Friday off without pay. It worked very well. Employee after employee commented how much they appreciated the opportunity for continued employment, albeit at a reduced pay rate, when on all sides they saw people who were out of a job. After about six months, we were able to return to a full schedule. We helped our people and we preserved our work force, which was essential for continued development.[3]

Other policies characterized HP's approach to its people. Common coffee breaks were a ritual, and recreational facilities for all employees were available at every plant. Employees at all levels were entitled to use a cottage resort area on HP-owned land for vacations free of charge. HP still marks an employee's marriage with the gift of a silver bowl and the birth of a first child with a blanket,[8] and it has long done away with time clocks and rigid hours in favor of Flextime which it finds to be self-policing. Because HP believed that all employees contributed to the success of the organization and should be rewarded in good times, the company also had an attractive bonus plan for all employees. As of June 1985, the company had never had a union or an extensive layoff.

THE 1975 RESTRUCTURING

Mr. Packard began to perceive that HP had grown too fast in the boom years of 1972–1973. Business publications noted that inventories and accounts receivables were moving out of control, prices on new products were set too low to generate sufficient cash flows, and products often went into production before development was fully completed. Growth had been pursued vigorously without adequate concerns for profit. For the first time in the company's history, short-term borrowing had increased to the extent that long-term debt was considered.

Shaken by their need, in 1974, to become more personally involved in daily management, Hewlett and Packard wanted to develop an organization structure that could both respond better to growth and diversification needs and provide more effective management of day-to-day operations. Preparing the organization for an orderly management succession also became quite important; Mr. Packard would turn 65 in 1977 and Mr. Hewlett in 1978.

Accordingly, they restructured the organization in 1975. There were three main components to the change: (1) the basic product groups were expanded from four to six, (2) a new management level of top executives was added, and (3) an executive committee was established to oversee the day-to-day operations of the company.

SIX PRODUCT GROUPS

Prior to 1975, HPs four product groups had consisted of: Test and Measurement, Data Products, Medical Equipment, and Analytical Instrumentation. The six groups created by the reorganization were: Electronic Test and Measurement Instruments, Computer and Computer-Based Systems, Calculators, Solid-State Components, Medical Electronic Products, and Electronic Instrumentation for Chemical Analysis. (See Exhibit 2 for a diagram of the 1975 organization structure.)

Each of the product groups had both its own general manager and a sales service organization serving all the product divisions within that group. The product division marketing departments had as their responsibilities: order processing and shipping, sales engineering and contract administration, service engineering, technical writing, publications, and advertising and sales promotion. In addition, they provided sales forecasts and recommended and reviewed prices.

Nevertheless, because the actual selling and customer service activities were performed at the product group level, each division had to compete for the time of its group's field sales force. The objective of the more centralized sales organization was to increase cooperation and communication between divisional sales teams. Hewlett and Packard insisted that all customers receive similar treatment and be dealt with through consistent policies.[4]

The second element of the reorganization included the appointment of two executive vice presidents jointly responsible for operations—one was John Young who later became president—and a vice president for corporate administration. The new executive committee was made up of these three newly appointed executives and Mr. Hewlett and Mr. Packard. It was to meet weekly to coordinate all aspects of the company's operations.

LOSS OF CONTROL AND REGAINING DIRECTION

In early 1974, top management had made some basic strategy decisions. Long-term debt was to be avoided. Short-term debt would be decreased by controlling costs, managing assets and improving profit margins. Most importantly, top management began to realize that the company had somehow allowed market share to emerge as too strong an objective. To remedy this, Hewlett and Packard began a year-long campaign to reemphasize some principles they had developed when the partnership began. Packard was quoted as repeatedly telling company audiences:

> Somewhere we got into the idea that market share was an objective. I hope that is straightened out. Anyone can build market share; if you set your prices low enough, you can get the whole damn market. But I'll tell you it won't get you anywhere around here.[5]

Two further strategies were used to get the company back on track: all prices were increased by 10% and R&D by 20% from the previous year. The intent was to improve the company's profits, while controlling a rate of growth which had more than doubled sales in three years. By early 1975, profit improvements were dramatic. The reaction to the Hewlett and Packard tour of the divisions was quick: inventories were slashed, accounts receivable tightened, productivity improved, and hiring was dramatically decreased to a total of only 1000 new employees in 1974 down from 7000 in the previous year. From 1973 to 1974 sales increased by $215 million and profits by $33 million.

For a brief period, HP had been the leader in the business and scientific handheld calculator field. In 1974 this market had yielded some 30% of the company's profits. However, HP's lead soon fell to competition led by Texas Instruments. HP chose not to compete across the board in calculators. Instead it decided to remain in the specialized upper end of the market. It preferred to develop products so advanced they could command a premium price. HP executives commented publicly that this philosophy fit the company's style of operation. They also indicated that the company was not geared to compete solely on a price basis but wanted to maintain its reputation by adding something that was not already available in competitive products.

To maintain coherence and a sense of personal communication despite the growth that was taking place, HP started an activity in the late 1970s that became known as "communication luncheons." Mr. Hewlett defined the purpose and style of these luncheons as follows:

> You simply cannot run an operation and assume that everything is perfect. There are many ways to achieve this feedback. . . . One we have tried and which has been fairly successful, is a technique we call "communication luncheons." A senior executive will visit a division and ask to have lunch with a group of employees, 15 or 20 at most; no supervisors invited. Other employees know in

advance who will be attending and very often they pass on their own questions or complaints. . . .

This provides an opportunity to discuss company policy or company problems. . . . Sometimes you detect a pattern of problems—say, for example, inadequate supervisory training. Such problems can be dealt with on a broad company-wide basis. In any event you always learn more about how the company actually operates. Equally important, employees have a chance to hear first hand what is happening in the company and what management is trying to do.[3]

A New Era

In 1978 when Mr. Hewlett stepped down as CEO, John Young, who had been groomed since 1975 to replace him, was appointed president and CEO. He was to lead HP into the rapidly changing computer marketplace, a relatively new major thrust for the company. (See Exhibit 2.)

Mr. Young launched several major programs designed to improve HP's planning, to coordinate its marketing efforts, and to strengthen its presence in computer markets. Specific strategy changes supported these important endeavors:

▼ Mr. Young reorganized HP Laboratories after its R&D chief retired, replacing him with John Doyle, formerly HP's personnel executive. Young felt that the Labs needed management, not science, in its leadership. Doyle was particularly known for his ability to articulate HP's entrepreneurial culture.

▼ Doyle recruited 220 computer-oriented professionals and several key researchers from other successful computer companies.

▼ The firm substantially increased its R&D spending.

▼ For the first time, HP started forming research partnerships with universities.

▼ The firm worked to couple HP Laboratories more closely to the strategies of its company operating groups.

▼ HP acquired several small companies to obtain specific applications skills.

▼ HP set up its first applications marketing division and staffed this with specialists from other industries.

In addition, Mr. Young felt that a focus on quality was one of the best ways to control costs. He said,

A few years ago, the company did an internal study that had some surprising results. HP had always considered itself a quality leader in the industry—and indeed, it was. The company was therefore somewhat surprised when a study demonstrated that fully 25 percent of its manufacturing costs were involved in responding to bad quality.

A "stretch objective" was announced. Employees were asked to improve on product failure rates by a factor of ten during the decade of the 1980s. . . .

There has been a ripple effect of quality efforts throughout HP. The aggregate impact is large. In 1978, HP's inventory represented about 20.5 percent of sales. In 1983, it was down to 15.9 percent. Much of that reduction can be traced to better quality—less scrap, shorter cycles, and better flow.[9]

PROBLEMS WITH COMPUTERS

While these actions were having a positive impact, the effects of a decentralized organization were being adversely felt in its computer markets where HP's products—frequently overlapping and often incompatible in operation—were threatening the firm's fine quality and performance reputation.

HP faced conflicting demands, both within its organization and in the marketplace. In recent years HP had stressed profitability over market share. Of particular importance to HP had been creating unique products that commanded a premium price; HP had never been an organization to create "me-too" products. Said Mr. Young, "We are not in the clone business; we will differentiate our products." But according to *Fortune*, "Hewlett Packard's traditional approaches were all but useless in creating personal computers. In that business not being a clone—IBM compatible— was a good way to get clobbered in retail stores. . . ."[2]

Yet as one HP corporate executive was quoted by *Forbes*,

When it comes to the personal computer business, [HP has used] what I would describe as a very opportunistic approach to the marketplace. We have had several organizations in the company that were addressing the market. But none of them had it as their major focus. . . we had over $500 million sales in the personal computer market, which is not bad, but no significant focus on it.[10]

In addition, not many of HP's senior executives had specific experience in computer operations. In fact, most of HP's senior people had started with the organization on the instruments side, including those heading up the computer groups. Some believed this to be a problem, since the requirement of each business was rather distinct.

EXHIBIT 2
Simplified Organization
Chart, 1975

Board of Directors
Dave Packard, Chairman

Chief Executive Officer
Bill Hewlett, President

Special Assistant

Corporate Development

Research and Development

HP LABS
- Administration
- Electronics Research
- LSI
- Physical Electronics
- Physical Research
- Solid State
- Corporate Libraries

ADMINISTRATION

Vice-President Corp. Administration

Executive Vice-President

CORPORATE STAFF
- Corporate Engineering
- Corporate Services
- Finance
- Government Relations
- Legal
- Personnel
- Public Relations
- Secretary
- Marketing
- International

OPERATIONS

Executive Vice-President

PRODUCT GROUPS

Instruments	Computer Systems	Components	Medical	Calculators	Analytical
Boblingen (W. Ger.)	Automatic Measurments Boise	HPA Singapore	Andover	Advanced Products	Avondale
Civil Engineering	Data Systems Grenoble (Fr.)		Boblingen (W. Ger.)	Brazil	Grotzingen (W. Ger.)
Colorado Springs			Brazil	Singapore	Scientific Insruments
Delcon			McMinnville	Loveland Calculators	
Loveland Facility			Waltham		
Loveland Instruments					
Manufacturing (Loveland)					
Manufacturing (Palo Alto)					
New Jersey					
San Diego					
Santa Clara					
Santa Rosa					
Queensferry (U.K.)					
Stanford Park					
Instruments/Civil Engineering Sales/Service	Computer Systems Sales/Service	Components Sales/Service	Medical Sales/Service	Calculator Sales/Service	Analytical Sales/Service

U.S. and Canada Sales Administration
Eastern • Midwest • Southern • Western • Canada

International Sales and Subsidiary Administration
Europe: Northern Area • Germany • United Kingdom
Intercontinental: Asia/Africa • Australia • Brazil • Japan • Latin America • Southeast Asia

Source: Drawn from "Working Together: The HP Organization," *Measure*, April-May 1975, pp. 16-17. (*Measure* is an HP internal publication.)

PAST PRINCIPLES AND AN ORGANIZATION FOR THE FUTURE

Following is a 1983 description of the corporate objectives which encompassed HP's most important principles. Although there had been substantial change in the marketplace, few modifications had been made to the company's objectives since they were initially published in 1957.

1. *Profit:* to achieve sufficient profit to finance our company's growth and to provide resources we need to achieve our other corporate objectives.
2. *Customers:* to provide products and services of the highest quality and the greatest possible value to our customers, thereby gaining and holding their respect and loyalty.
3. *Fields of Interest:* to build on our strengths in the company's traditional fields of interest, and to enter new fields only when it is consistent with the basic purpose of our business and when we can assure ourselves of making a needed and profitable contribution to the field.
4. *Growth:* to let our growth be limited only by our profits and our ability to develop and produce innovative products that satisfy real customer needs.
5. *Our People:* to help HP people share in the company's success which they make possible: to provide job security based on their performance; to ensure them a safe and pleasant work environment; to recognize their individual achievements; and to help them gain a sense of satisfaction and accomplishment from their work.
6. *Management:* to foster initiative and creativity by allowing the individual greater freedom of action in attaining well-defined objectives.
7. *Citizenship:* to honor our obligations to society by being an economic, intellectual, and social asset to each nation and each community in which we operate.

HP's 1982 organization structure is outlined in Exhibit 3. In 1983 and again in 1984, the company restructured its organization in an attempt to deal with the issues posed by its move into computers. In Mr. Young's announcement of the organization changes of 1984, he spoke of this and previous fundamental reorganizations, ". . . each change has been a logical, evolutionary move that preserved the basic philosophy and integrity of the HP approach to business."[7] Mr. Young further added,

Becoming a computer company has had a dramatic effect on our company; the biggest challenge is to orchestrate the divisions and provide a strategic glue and direction for the computer effort, while keeping the work units small.

Having small divisions is not the only way to organize a company, but having organizations that people can run like a small business is highly motivational, especially for professionals. Keeping that spirit of entrepreneurship alive is very important to us.[11]

When asked to compare his management style with that of HP's founders, Young said, "Bill is a brilliant engineer and Dave is a great businessman. I stress organization, planning, and the process." He further replied to the question of what he most hoped to achieve, by saying, "To show that it is worth institutionalizing our founders' principles, hopefully by growing some and detracting nothing from the human elements that are so important."[8]

THE PROGRAM MANAGER CONCEPT

In response to these issues, a "program manager concept" had come into being at HP. Program managers had broad powers to tap various divisions for necessary support, components, or software. Previously, new products had always come from individual divisions, engineered typically in pursuit of the division's charter to "stay ahead of the game," or from HP Laboratories researchers who had "sold" their ideas and found a divisional sponsor.

The program manager concept was used for a special project called "Dawn." Under the direction of a program manager, half a dozen widely scattered HP divisions were coordinated on a $100 million project. On November 16, 1982, less than two years after "Dawn" began, the HP 9000, considered by many experts to be the ultimate in personal computers, was introduced. To succeed, the activities of the divisions had to be closely coordinated and the divisions' independence limited. As a target market for the HP 9000 (introduced in a remarkably short two years after a program manager was assigned), the company chose manufacturers, since these had been its primary customers for nearly ten years. It also selected four applications areas for focus: planning and control systems, factory automation, office systems, and engineering.

Traditionally, HP had marketed technologically sophisticated products and left applications details to its customers. That strategy worked well for many years because its customers were scientists who were often as

EXHIBIT 3
HP Organization Chart,
1982

ADMINISTRATION
Bob Boniface
Executive Vice President

OPERATIONS
Paul Ely
Executive Vice President

Corporate Controller
Jerry Carlson
Controller

Corporate Services
Bruce Wholey
Vice President

General Counsel &
Secretary
Jack Brigham
Vice President

International
Bill Doolittle
Senior Vice President

Government Affairs
Bob Kirkwood
Director

Patents & Licenses
Jean Chognard
Vice President

Personnel
Bill Craven
Director

Public Relations
Dave Kirby
Director

Marketing
Al Oliverio
Senior Vice President

Treasurer
Ed van Bronkhorst
Senior Vice President

EUROPE
Franco Mariotti
Vice President
Field Sales Regions
  France
  Germany
  Northern Europe
  South/East Europe
  United Kingdom
Manufacturing
  France
  Germany
  United Kingdom

INTERCONTINENTAL
Alan Bickell
Managing Director
Field Sales Regions
  Australasia
  Far East
  Japan
  Latin America
  South Africa
Manufacturing
  Brazil
  Japan
  Malaysia
  Mexico
  Puerto Rico
  Singapore

**U.S./CANADA
SALES**
Field Sales Regions
  Eastern
  Midwest
  Neely (Western)
  Southern
  Canada
Corporate
  Marketing Operations
  ● Parts Center

COMPUTERS

**TECHNICAL
COMPUTER GROUP**
Doug Chance
Vice President
■ Data Systems
■ Roseville
■ Desktop Computer
■ Engineering Systems
■ Böblingen Desktop
■ YHP Computer
■ Computer I.C.
  ● Cupertino I.C.
  ● Systems
    Technology

**COMPUTER
PERIPHERALS
GROUP**
Dick Hackborn
General Manager
■ Boise
■ Disc Memory
■ Greeley
  ● Singapore
■ Vancouver
  ● Bristol

**BUSINESS
COMPUTER GROUP**
Ed McCracken
General Manager
■ Computer Systems
  ● Roseville
■ Information Networks
  ● Office Systems
    Pinewood
  ● Office Systems
    Cupertino
  ● Grenoble Datacomm
■ Manufacturing Prod.
  ● Financial Systems
■ Böblingen
  General Systems
  ● Information
    Resources
  ● Guadalajara Computer

**COMPUTER
TERMINALS GROUP**
Cyril Yansouni
General Manager
■ Personal Office Computer
■ Roseville Terminals
■ Grenoble
  ● Puerto Rico

COMPUTER MARKETING GROUP
Jim Arthur, Vice President

■ Computer Support
■ Application Marketing
■ Personal Computer
  Marketing

● Systems Remarketing
● Computer Supplies

EXHIBIT 3 (cont'd)

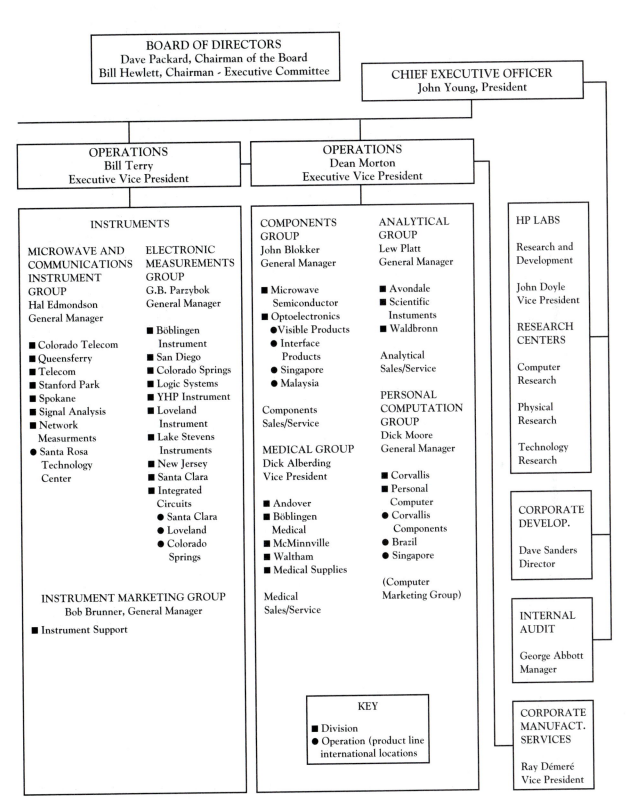

BOARD OF DIRECTORS
Dave Packard, Chairman of the Board
Bill Hewlett, Chairman - Executive Committee

CHIEF EXECUTIVE OFFICER
John Young, President

OPERATIONS
Bill Terry
Executive Vice President

OPERATIONS
Dean Morton
Executive Vice President

INSTRUMENTS

MICROWAVE AND COMMUNICATIONS INSTRUMENT GROUP
Hal Edmondson
General Manager

■ Colorado Telecom
■ Queensferry
■ Telecom
■ Stanford Park
■ Spokane
■ Signal Analysis
■ Network Measurments
● Santa Rosa Technology Center

ELECTRONIC MEASUREMENTS GROUP
G.B. Parzybok
General Manager

■ Böblingen Instrument
■ San Diego
■ Colorado Springs
■ Logic Systems
■ YHP Instrument
■ Loveland Instrument
■ Lake Stevens Instruments
■ New Jersey
■ Santa Clara
■ Integrated Circuits
  ● Santa Clara
  ● Loveland
  ● Colorado Springs

INSTRUMENT MARKETING GROUP
Bob Brunner, General Manager

■ Instrument Support

COMPONENTS GROUP
John Blokker
General Manager

■ Microwave Semiconductor
■ Optoelectronics
  ● Visible Products
  ● Interface Products
  ● Singapore
  ● Malaysia

Components
Sales/Service

MEDICAL GROUP
Dick Alberding
Vice President

■ Andover
■ Böblingen Medical
■ McMinnville
■ Waltham
■ Medical Supplies

Medical
Sales/Service

ANALYTICAL GROUP
Lew Platt
General Manager

■ Avondale
■ Scientific Instuments
■ Waldbronn

Analytical
Sales/Service

PERSONAL COMPUTATION GROUP
Dick Moore
General Manager

■ Corvallis
■ Personal Computer
● Corvallis Components
● Brazil
● Singapore

(Computer Marketing Group)

HP LABS

Research and Development

John Doyle
Vice President

RESEARCH CENTERS

Computer Research

Physical Research

Technology Research

CORPORATE DEVELOP.

Dave Sanders
Director

INTERNAL AUDIT

George Abbott
Manager

CORPORATE MANUFACT. SERVICES

Ray Démeré
Vice President

KEY

■ Division
● Operation (product line international locations

EXHIBIT 4
Hewlett Packard's
Manufacturing
Productivity Network
(MPN)

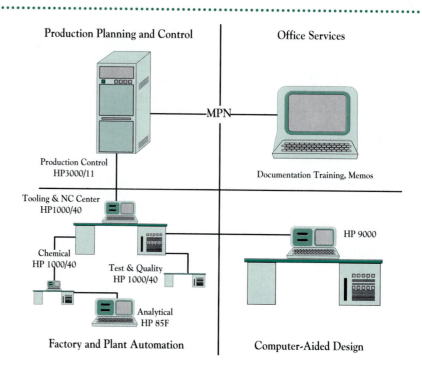

Production Planning and Control

Office Services

MPN

Production Control
HP3000/11

Documentation Training, Memos

Tooling & NC Center
HP1000/40

Chemical
HP 1000/40

Test & Quality
HP 1000/40

HP 9000

Analytical
HP 85F

Factory and Plant Automation

Computer-Aided Design

Source: Lehman Brothers Kuhn Loeb Research, *Hewlett Packard Co. Report,* July 26, 1983.

sophisticated about applications as HP was. Yet computer customers were no longer necessarily scientists or engineers. As one corporate executive said, "I keep telling my engineers that they now have five minutes to make a sale, not five hours like we used to. We have to focus on apparent user benefits."[2] This executive's own experience typified the problem. While talking to a potential customer he became a bit rhapsodic about the HP 150's ability to process 2.2 megahertz faster than the IBM PC. "What's a megahertz?" asked the prospect, a lawyer. "I have to get out documents—what can you do for me?"

But technology was rapidly revolutionizing the small computer markets in which HP competed. In 1980 the 64K memory chip had made the desktop *micro*computer into one of the fastest growing markets in the United States. By 1985 the 256K chip allowed production of desktop *mini*computers, powerful small lab computers, and engineering and production work stations of great complexity and power. By 1987 new megabit (one million bit) chips would permit mainframe powered computers to be produced in "micro" sizes. Pocket computers, electronic map navigators, and robots that could see and recognize some natural language commands were in the offing. By 1990 *micro*-

*super*computers based on 4 megabit chips were expected with powers dwarfing all but the largest laboratory models. Yet these remarkable creations were likely to be so inexpensive that they would quickly become "commodity" items. Managing this degree of complexity in a commodity marketplace would become a singular challenge.

One analyst had earlier commented that over the past two decades HP had transitioned from a test instrument firm into a major systems company. By 1986 HP was involved in an even more complex shift toward multisystem networks—complete link ups between computers, instruments and peripherals—for laboratory, factory, hospital, or office automation systems.[12] An example of such a multisystem network is outlined in Exhibit 4.

Finally HP had over 45 product divisions, of which at least 22 were directly related to computers. But in the burgeoning electronics markets of the mid-to-late 1980s increasing opportunities were appearing to link and relate what previously had been "stand alone" sensing, testing, measuring, processing, or controlling units. How HP could respond to these new needs, yet maintain its distinctive entrepreneurial style and culture was a critical issue for its management in the mid-1980s.

QUESTIONS

1. Why has HP been successful in the past? Why was its organization configured the way it was at each major transition point? Evaluate how well its structure and systems were adapted each time for their purposes.

2. What are the critical strategic issues facing HP in the mid 1980s? How should it respond to these?

Key financial and operations data appear in the attached exhibits.

3. How should HP organize to meet its future challenges? Why? What changes in management style, control systems, and incentives should accompany these changes?

EXHIBIT 5
Hewlett Packard
Company and
Subsidiaries: Financials,
1980–1984

CONSOLIDATED STATEMENT OF EARNINGS, 1982-1984

For the years ended October 31 (Millions except per share amounts)	1984	1983	1982
Net sales	$6,044	$4,710	$4,189
Costs and expenses:			
Cost of goods sold	2,865	2,195	1,967
Research and development	592	493	424
Marketing	1,066	771	631
Administrative and general	661	523	491
	5,184	3,982	3,513
Earnings before taxes	860	728	676
Provision for taxes	313	296	293
Reversal of DISC taxes*	(118)	—	—
	195	296	293
Net earnings	$665	$432	$383
Net earnings per share	$2.59	$1.69	$1.53

*Reversal of DISC taxes accrued prior to 1984 due to a change in U.S. tax law

SELECTED FINANCIAL DATA, 1980–1984

For the years ended October 31 (millions except per share amounts and employees)	1984	1983	1982	1981	1980
Domestic orders	$3,629	$2,901	$2,283	$1,918	$1,517
International orders	2,721	2,021	1,897	1,739	1,570
Total orders	$6,350	$4,922	$4,180	$3,657	$3,087
Net sales	$6,044	$4,710	$4,189	$3,528	$3,046
Earnings before taxes	860	728	676	567	513
Net earnings	665*	432	383	305	263
Per share					
Net earnings	$2.59*	$1.69	$1.53	$1.24	$1.09
Cash dividends	$ 0.19	$0.16	$0.12	$0.11	$0.10
At year-end					
Total assets	$5,153	$4,161	$3,470	$2,782	$2,350
Employees (thousands)	82	72	68	64	57

*Includes a one-time increase in net earnings of $118 million (46 cents per share) resulting from a tax law change.

Source: Hewlett Packard Company, *Annual Report,* 1984.

EXHIBIT 5 (cont'd)

CONSOLIDATED BALANCE SHEET, 1982–1984

October 31 (millions)	1984	1983	1982
Assets			
Current assets			
Cash and temporary cash investments	$938	$880	$684
Accounts and notes receivable	1,180	951	773
Inventories			
Finished goods	373	279	231
Purchased parts and fabricated assemblies	650	469	428
Other current assets	60	53	99
Total current assets	$3,201	$2,632	$2,215
Property, plant and equipment:			
Land	202	167	106
Buildings and leasehold improvements	1,416	1,102	940
Machinery and equipment	1,173	888	714
	2,791	2,157	1,760
Accumulated depreciation and amortization	923	726	589
	1,868	1,431	1,171
Other assets	84	98	84
	$5,153	$4,161	$3,470
Liabilities and shareholders' equity			
Current liabilities:			
Notes payable	$217	$148	$156
Accounts payable	281	203	139
Employee compensation and benefits	398	300	269
Other accrued liabilities	162	103	106
Accrued taxes on earnings	203	112	151
Other accrued taxes	61	54	42
Total current liabilities	$1,322	$920	$863
Long-term debt	81	71	39
Other liabilities	93	46	42
Deferred taxes on earnings	112	237	177
Shareholders' equity			
Common stock and capital in excess of $1 par value	775	733	587
Retained earnings	2,770	2,154	1,762
Total shareholders' equity	3,545	2,887	2,349
	$5,153	$4,161	$3,470

Source: Hewlett Packard Company, *Annual Report,* 1984.

EXHIBIT 5 (cont'd)

SEGMENT DATA, 1982–1984	1984	1983	1982
Business Segments* (millions)			
Gross sales			
Computer products	$3,269	$2,476	$2,161
Electronic test and measurement	2,289	1,779	1,595
Medical electronic equipment	378	355	323
Analytical instrumentation	229	184	176
	$6,165	$4,794	$4,255
Intersegment sales			
Computer products	73	56	44
Electronic test and measurement	47	26	21
Medical electronic equipment	1	2	1
	121	84	66
Total Net Sales	**$6,044**	**$4,710**	**$4,189**
Earnings before taxes			
Computer products	$ 439	$392	$ 370
Electronic test and measurement	514	381	339
Medical electronic equipment	41	61	60
Analytical instrumentation	37	23	28
Eliminations and corporate	(171)	(129)	(121)
	$860	$728	$676

Geographic Areas**	1984	1983	1982
Net sales			
United States	$3,527	$2,725	$2,270
Europe	1,620	1,392	1,318
Rest of world	897	593	601
	$6,044	$4,710	$4,189
Earnings before taxes			
United States	$768	$644	$ 554
Europe	138	148	157
Rest of world	110	59	95
Eliminations and corporate	(156)	(123)	(130)
	$ 860	$ 728	$ 676
Exports from			
United States	$1,420	$1,105	$1,081
Europe	145	100	61
Rest of world	277	160	164

*Sales between affiliates are made at market price, less an allowance for subsequent manufacturing and/or marketing.

**Net sales are based on the location of the customer. Earnings before taxes reflect the location of the company's facilities. Exports are primarily inter-area transfers to affiliates, which are made at market prices, less an allowance for subsequent manufacturing and/or marketing. Certain amounts have been reclassified to conform to the 1984 format.

Source: Hewlett Packard Company, *Annual Report*, 1984.

EXHIBIT 5 (cont'd)

BUSINESS SEGMENTS, 1982–1984	1984	1983	1982
Identifiable Assets (millions)			
Computer products	$2,182	$1,673	$1,358
Electronic test and measurement	1,379	1,022	903
Medical electronic equipment	268	224	191
Analytical instrumentation	154	133	104
Eliminations and corporate	1,170	1,109	914
	$5,153	$4,161	$3,470
Capital Expenditures (millions)			
Computer products	330	$248	$215
Electronic test and measurement	202	108	104
Medical electronic equipment	27	37	18
Analytical instrumentation	14	18	7
Corporate	88	55	18
	$ 661	$ 466	$ 362
Depreciation and Amortization (millions)			
Computer products	$ 128	105	$86
Electronic test and measurement	68	54	46
Medical electronic equipment	11	9	8
Analytical instrumentation	7	6	5
Corporate	23	17	13
	$ 237	$ 191	$ 158

*Direct and indirect sales to the U.S. Government amounted to approximately $550 million in 1984, $480 million in 1983 and $420 million in 1982. No other customer accounted for more than 5 percent of net sales.

Source: Hewlett Packard Company, *Annual Report*, 1984.

PRODUCTS AND BUSINESS SEGMENTS

The *Electronic Data Products* segment includes the following product groups: Business Computer, Technical Computer, Computer Peripherals, Computer Terminals, Computer Marketing and Personal Computation. Products include small to medium-scale computer systems for business, scientific and industrial applications; desktop, personal, and portable computers; personal scientific and business programmable calculators; computer peripherals; and a wide variety of software and support services.

The *Electronic Test and Measurement Products* segment includes the following product groups: Electronic Measurements, Microwave and Communication Instrument, Components, and Instrument Marketing. Products include instruments, systems and components for design, production and maintenance. Products used primarily in the communications, electronics manufacturing and aerospace industries.

Medical Electronic Equipment segment products perform a number of patient-monitoring, diagnostic, therapeutic, and medical and financial data-management functions for health care providers. Included are measurement and computation systems and a wide variety of software and support services.

Analytical Instrumentation segment products are used primarily to analyze chemical compounds. Products include gas and liquid chromatographs, mass spectrometers, spectrophotometers, laboratory automation systems, and integrators.

Source: Hewlett Packard Company, *Annual Report*, 1982.

EXHIBIT 5 (cont'd)

HEWLETT PACKARD COMPANY ESTIMATED SALES BREAKDOWN, 1982-1984

| | $ Million | | | The Market's |
	1982	1983E	1984E	5-Yr. Growth
Computers				
Graphics/CAD	$730	$ 900	$1,090	20%
HP 3000 (MPN)	635	635	750	15
Peripherals	500	600	750	25
Calculators	117	90	115	10
Microcomputers	100	170	215	25
Software	35	50	70	35
HP1000 (Factory)	0	12	35	65
HP9000 (CAE)	0	30	75	70
Total	2,117	2,487	3,100	
Instruments				
Microwave/Comm.	470	500	590	15
Elec. Test	835	925	1,130	20
Automatic Test	45	56	70	25
Components	224	250	285	10
Total	1,574	1,731	2,075	
Medical				
Patient Monitoring	195	180	205	15
Diagnostic Instr.	127	150	180	20
Hospital Mgmt.	0	19	26	30
Total	322	349	411	
Analytical				
Gas Chromatographs	45	35	45	15
Data Stations	105	127	150	20
UV/Visible Spec.	15	20	25	20
Liquid Chromatog.	10	12	15	30
Biotechnology	1	1	5	50
Total	176	195	240	
Company Total	$4,189	$4,762	$5,826	

Source: E. F. Hutton, Inc., Equity Research, *Hewlett Packard Company Action Report*, June 29, 1983.

EXHIBIT 6
Comparative Financials

ELECTRONIC BUSINESS 200 Rank			CALENDAR 1984			
1984	1983	Company	Electronics Sales ($ million)	Total Sales ($ million)	Net Income ($ million)	Return on Investment (%)
1	1	IBM	$45,937.0	$45,937.0	$6,582.0	21.8%
2	2	AT&T	17,406.7	33,187.5	1,369.9	5.9
3	3	General Electric	7,210.0	27,947.0	2,280.0	17.0
4	5	Xerox	6,981.0	8,791.6	375.6	6.0
5	4	ITT	6,589.0	12,701.0	302.5	3.4
6	8	Hewlett-Packard	6,297.0	6,297.0	564.0	18.2
7	9	Digital Equipment	6,229.6	6,229.6	486.9	7.4
8	6	Honeywell	6,073.6	6,073.6	334.8	10.9
9	10	Texas Instruments	5,741.6	5,741.6	316.0	16.4
10	12	Motorola	5,534.0	5,534.0	387.0	13.7
11	13	RCA	4,945.0	10,111.6	246.4	5.4
12	7	Hughes	4,925.0	4,925.0	300.0	NA
13	11	Burroughs	4,875.6	4,875.6	244.9	8.0
14	15	Sperry	4,648.0	5,370.0	262.2	5.6
15	16	Control Data	3,755.0	5,026.9	31.6	0.4
16	17	NCR	3,728.0	4,074.3	342.6	14.3
17	18	Raytheon	3,454.0	5,995.7	340.1	16.4
18	21	N. A. Philips	3,193.0	4,325.9	130.5	8.7
19	23	TRW	2,904.0	6,061.7	266.8	12.8
20	22	Tandy	2,771.1	2,771.1	234.9	21.1
27	29	Wang	2,421.1	2,421.1	231.0	12.9
31	49	Apple	1,897.9	1,897.9	104.3	13.8
34	38	Zenith	1,717.0	1,717.0	63.6	10.2
41	42	Tektronix	1,419.9	1,419.9	131.5	40.6
49	55	Perkin-Elmer*	1,169.0	1,255.5	79.2	10.2

*Leader in analytical instrumentation.

NA—Not available.

Source: *Electronic Business*, July 15, 1985.

LATEST FISCAL YEAR			5-YEAR GROWTH (Compounded Growth Rate)		Capital Outlays to Net Cash Flow After Dividends	Debt as % of Total Capital
Cost of Goods as % of Sales	R&D as % of Sales	Net Income per Employee ($ thousand)	Sales (% per year)	Net Income (% per year)		
33.6%	9.1%	$16.7	15.0%	16.9%	83.1%	12.4%
50.5	7.2	3.8	NA	NA	190.1	41.0
69.6	3.7	6.9	4.5	10.1	101.6	6.4
39.4	6.4	3.6	4.6	-7.8	146.4	27.1
76.4	7.7	1.2	-5.9	-4.5	150.0	31.3
45.6	9.8	8.1	20.7	26.8	77.5	3.0
56.0	11.3	3.8	25.4	13.0	77.8	10.0
61.6	6.9	3.6	7.6	6.9	67.7	22.5
68.5	6.4	3.7	12.2	12.8	102.1	19.9
57.9	7.4	3.9	15.3	20.2	128.6	19.1
71.5	2.4	2.3	6.3	-2.8	131.3	41.5
NA	NA	NA	NA	NA	NA	NA
54.9	5.7	3.8	11.5	-4.3	113.4	25.0
59.3	8.4	2.7	3.3	-2.3	103.1	21.0
51.1	6.0	0.6	17.5	-23.2	94.8	76.6
43.7	7.1	5.5	6.3	7.9	61.7	13.1
77.4	3.9	4.6	10.0	11.5	105.7	4.6
74.3	2.3	2.3	12.4	9.8	92.4	34.0
73.3	2.4	2.9	5.9	6.5	113.2	15.7
43.4	0.0	8.3	17.6	27.6	25.1	26.1
47.6	7.3	6.9	46.7	49.0	155.3	23.3
55.5	4.7	11.9	99.5	66.1	38.8	0.0
77.2	5.1	2.2	9.8	27.4	69.5	28.8
50.5	11.2	5.7	11.1	8.9	54.9	68.2
55.3	6.7	4.3	10.0	5.6	69.3	12.9

EXHIBIT 7
Representative Market
Share Data for HP
Products

A. WORLDWIDE 1985 SHARES (%) COMPUTERS

Small Systems ($12K-350K)		Microsystems (< $12K)	
IBM	20.0	IBM	27.7
DEC	12.7	Apple	9.0
Nixdorf	6.0	Commodore	4.2
HP	5.8	HP	4.2
Wang	4.3	NEC	3.6
NEC	3.1	AT&T	3.5
AT&T	2.4	Wang	2.7

Source: The Wall Street Journal, April 7, 1986, p. 26.

B. TEST & MEASUREMENT SHARES (%) 1984

Logic Analyzers		Universal Microprocessor Development Systems	
HP	30	HP	61
Tektronix	29	Tektronix	32
Gould	7	Kontron	4
Phillips NV	7	Millenium	3

Source: F. Eberstadt & Co., Inc., Test and Measurement Industry Report, May 20, 1985.

TCG, LTD./THERMO ELECTRON CORPORATION

TCG, TechComm Group (for Technical, Computer, and Graphics Group) was formed in 1971 by Peter Fritz and three other survivors of Scientific Computer Systems Limited (SCS)—a computer services company. SCS had failed in 1970 at the end of the Australian minerals boom, when its key customer went bankrupt. TCG began with a $5,000 overdraft secured on the founders' homes. Because of its entrepreneurial successes and its unique "honeycomb" organizational form, TCG became an entrepreneurial phenomenon in Australia. In 1984, Mr. Fritz received the BHP Award for Excellence in Commerce, Industry, and Management for the company's performance in the highly competitive computer and computer services market. In the early 1990s, TCG embraced several dozen companies with an annual turnover of $50 million, and in 1993 was taking several divisions public as TechComm Group, Ltd. (Financial information appears in Exhibits 1–2.) The company embodied many of the characteristics of the advanced, highly disaggregated, entrepreneurial firms espoused by theorists and managers alike.

Peter Fritz described his company's development as follows: "[There were] five separate phases in our development, [in which we] successfully grabbed the opportunities coming our way, expanding and forming our operation. The phases ranged from (1) a few disjointed projects by four individuals, through (2) a clearer division between data entry (punching), regular processing (services), to (3) some special [high tech development] projects, our first mini-computer project, and sundry other larger commer-

cial projects (including the first sale of a flatbed plotter). The fourth phase saw TCG expand further into hardware, and the fifth phase took us into a four company situation centering on (1) data entry, (2) regular processing, (3) mini-computers and professional software, and (4) engineering, graphics hardware, and consulting."[1]

THE 1993 SITUATION

By 1993, TCG enjoyed a strong customer base and a set of uniquely niched products. All TCG's products were recognized as advanced in design and of high quality manufacture.

Its *TechComm Control Simulation Group* manufactured, developed, and supplied simulators to the fossil-fueled power generation industry. TechComm Control Simulation's customers included major companies in Australia, Germany, U.K., Japan, and Zimbabwe. The systems were used to train personnel, control operations, and manage power stations.

TechComm Engineering Services Group provided maintenance and repair services on electronic equipment, mostly under contract. It was active in banking and finance (check proofing, EFT, POS, cash dispensing, and document processing); architectural and engineering (CAD systems, graphics peripherals, imaging); government (OCR document processing, scanning systems, graphics); retailing (point-of-sale, bar code, portable terminal, and price display); warehouse and distribution (RF equipment and portable terminals); commercial (PICK/UNIX, portable computer, and predictive dialing) and manufacturing (image processing, QA, plotting and cutting) systems.

TechComm Systems was primarily a marketing, distribution, and sales unit. It marketed mobile data capture equipment, RF systems, pen-based computers, notebook computers, electronic data interchange solu-

Case copyright © 1995 by James Brian Quinn. Research assistants Allie J. Quinn and Penny C. Paquette. The generous financial support of McKinsey and Co. and the Australian Graduate School of Management, University of New South Wales are gratefully acknowledged. Special appreciation is expressed for the helpful cooperation of Mr. Peter Fritz and TCG, Ltd.

EXHIBIT 1
TCG, Ltd., Statement of
Assets, Liabilities, and
Shareholder's Equity
(in thousands of Australian
dollars)

	30 JUNE 1993	PROFORMA
Current Assets		
Cash	61	2,081
Inventories	4,299	4,299
Receivables	1,801	1,801
Other	38	38
	6,199	8,219
Noncurrent Assets		
Plant and equipment	751	751
Intangible Assets*	12,606	12,606
Total Assets	19,556	21,576
Current Liabilities		
Creditors and borrowings	8,189	3,534
Provisions	298	298
	8,487	3,832
Noncurrent Liabilities		
Creditors and borrowings	21	21
Provisions	218	218
	239	239
Total Liabilities	8,726	4,071
Net Assets	**10,830**	**17,505**
Shareholders' Equity		
Capital	3,500	6,000
Reserves	7,000	11,175
Shareholders' equity attributable to the members of TechComm	10,500	17,175
Outside equity interest	330	330
Total Shareholders' Equity	**10,830**	**17,505**

* Intangible assets included in this total include: $1,963 for R&D, $1,000 for intellectual property, $500 for computer software, and $9,143 for goodwill.

Source: TCG's Prospectus for its 1993 Public Offering

tions, and several advanced mobile computer terminals. Each product was in a highly niched market. The FST (field service terminal), developed with Toshiba, was a durable, remote access, mobile computer terminal for field service applications. Its Gaming Terminal was a counter-top, scratch lottery, and lottery ticket verifier and communications terminal. TechComm owned a 70% interest in a unique electronic shelf-labeling system, which transmitted RF signals through the lighting system directly to LCD displays on the shelf. This allowed immediate remote price adjustments to be made throughout a retail store. The system incorporated an in-house pager and message receiving system to replace the public address systems within large retail stores. TechComm Systems was also developing advertising display panels able to feature changing "specials" within supermarkets, shopping centers, and other retail businesses.

A NETWORK SYSTEM COMPANY

In 1992, John Matthews described TCG as follows: "TCG is no ordinary company. In fact, it is not a company at all. Instead it has grown as a dynamic cluster of small firms, each specializing in certain operations, and each feeding work to the others. In 1993 it consisted of an operating core of twenty-four companies, organized as a cooperative network or cluster, but with a market coherence that gave the group profound advantages over its more conventional commercial rivals.

"How did TCG's network system operate? One of the TCG member firms, TCG Systems Automation Marketing (TCG-SAM) might gain a contract for perhaps 1,000 data terminals from a supermarket chain, with special features tailoring the products to the supermarket's business. TCG-SAM would take care of all aspects of delivery of the terminals—but it would sub-

EXHIBIT 2
TCG, Ltd., Income
Statements for Fiscal
1991–1993
(in thousands of Australian
dollars)

	30 JUNE 1991	30 JUNE 1992	30 JUNE 1993
Sales			
TechComm Control Simulation	3,203	2,917	4,030
TechComm Engineering Services	3,489	4,623	4,980
TechComm Systems	5,133	3,503	6,638
Ilid	187	279	213
Total sales	12,012	11,322	15,861
Operating Profit (Loss) Before Income Tax			
TechComm Control Simulation	975	864	1,257
TechComm Engineering Services	464	640	1,415
TechComm Systems	578	233	412
Ilid	(158)	(60)	128
Total operating profit before income tax	1,859	1,677	3,212
Income Taxes	666	429	845
Operating Profit After Tax	**1,193**	**1,248**	**2,367**

Research and Development

Research and Development costs have been capitalized during the year ended 30 June 1993 as follows:

	Amount capitalized during the year ended 30 June 1993	Balance at 30 June 1993
TechComm Control Simulation	309	309
TechComm Engineering Services	618	913
TechComm Systems	121	591
Ilid	274	274
	1,322	2,087
Less: accumulated depreciation		(124)
Research and development expenditure carried forward and acquired by TechComm		1,963

Source: TCG's Prospectus for its 1993 Public Offering

contract the details to other TCG firms. It would let a contract to TCG Systems Automation (TCG-SA) for the software engineering and maintenance; it would let a contract to TCG Manufacturing for the actual manufacture of the terminals to TCG-SAM's specifications. TCG Manufacturing would in turn let subcontracts for component supplies and assemblies to electronic firms around Sydney and (the world). If the terminals were to have communications facilities linking them to the supermarket's existing systems, then this work would be contracted by TCG-SAM to TCG-TEL. The original order from the supermarket [initiates] a sequence of activities regulated by strict commercial contract and performance relationships, and coordinated overall by the TCG company gaining the order. The customer deals only with one firm and gets maximum attention from that firm; ... quality and performance are strictly regulated by the demands of commercial contracts that the member firms negotiate with each other."[2]

THE TCG ORGANIZATION

By 1992, the twenty-four firms within TCG nestled together in what Peter Fritz liked to call a "beehive" structure, with each firm complementing the others in a network of interdependency that resembled a honeycomb. (See Figure 1.)

Management coordination was effected through TCG group members contracting with each other for services. There were no "coordinating divisions" or management superstructures to control operations. Financial coordination was through an original unit of

FIGURE 1
TCG, Ltd. Organization

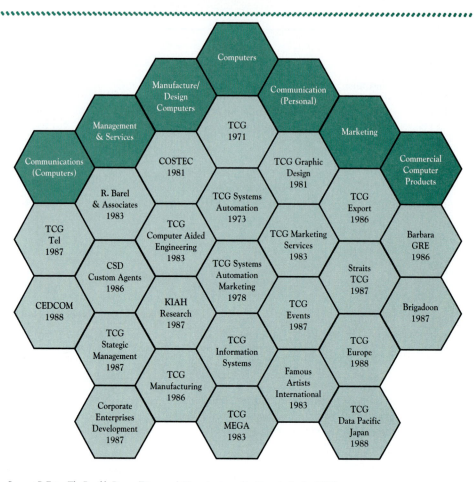

Source: P. Fritz, *The Possible Dream* (Ringwood, Victoria, Australia: Penguin Books, 1992).

TCG (Technical and Computer Graphics) which took on a modest amount of outside work, but mainly provided many routine accounting and other global support services to members of the TCG Group. Technical and Computer Graphics had installed the first minicomputer based order entry and stock control system in Australia. Its core business had remained software engineering. The unit provided the accounting and payroll functions for other members of the TCG Group. It also processed any order placed by a customer to any member of TCG and handled all invoices and payments TCG received for any service. It allocated receipts to each member company based upon the internal agreements made. Peter Fritz maintained financial and management control over this central unit, which also had an equity stake in each of the TCG member firms.

Mr. Fritz said, "I sit in a cell at the center of the honeycomb with a group of seven staff. Each of the surrounding cells of the honeycomb is a TCG company.

These companies operate independently and in different areas and markets, yet they cluster next to each other around our central administrative cell. I keep the books and conduct the administration for each of the companies: as company secretary and part-owner of each of the companies, I oversee and coordinate their activities, arrange finance, and resolve conflicts where necessary. Otherwise the companies run themselves. None is totally dependent upon or dominant over any of the others, yet all derive strength and security from their membership in the group.

"I was never a great technician. Even now, I don't get involved in the technical minutiae of ideas and product developments. My strong suit is not even new ideas. What I have developed is a capacity to recognize ideas for their own value, and to apply to them the management needed to transform them into commercial reality. That capacity is as much a commercial commodity as the idea itself."[3]

Overheads for the TCG group were extremely restricted. Most business functions were carried out by the individual member firms themselves. As noted, there were no staff positions to seed a bloated bureaucracy. Nonroutine accounting services for each member firm were available from one of the TCG companies, a specialist accountancy firm. R&D services were provided by another firm which made its own commercial way through ownership and licensing of intellectual property rights. There was no central board or committee allocating tasks and functions.

On the one hand, this internal network structure enabled the TCG companies to maintain their autonomy and flexibility—and to identify and seize market opportunities that would cost bigger firms much greater commitments of time and resources. On the other, TCG's internal and external connections protected its units from the vicissitudes that often disrupt and destroy independent ventures that are much larger. There had never been a bankruptcy in the TCG companies.

NEW PRODUCT DEVELOPMENT

TCG's product development technique was central to its activities. Rather than seeking to "go it alone," a TCG unit (or combination of units) first identified an opportunity. Then it actively sought out internal and external partners to share in the development, and financed the initial project through a major customer. After the product or concept was established, the TCG units involved would extend their networks outward into the global marketplace. Some examples were:

▼ TCG had expanded its remote data terminals, originally developed for the retail market, into the aviation fuel monitoring business. To do this, it developed a partnership with an existing manufacturer of (non-computerized) aviation fuel-metering systems and a major customer, Mobil Oil. The result was a new system, the Rapid Aviation Refueling Information System (RARIS) in which all three partners had a stake and had agreed to channels for commercial development.

▼ TCG had developed some electronic tags which could be applied to a wide array of products, from car engine numbers, to baggage tags, to consumer product serial markers, to identification cards, and even to animal markings. In the latter market, it formed a partnership with Trovan (a manufacturer) and entered the animal ear tags market through an

alliance with Leader, the world's largest supplier of non-electronic plastic ear tags.

▼ TCG's unique technique for supermarket shelf labeling was developed with the system's inventor as a partner and funded by the Coles-Myer retail chain, the largest in Australia. In 1993 TCG was developing a new field service terminal for use by maintenance crews—in partnership with a multinational computer firm and a major Australian utility.

TCG sought partners to complement its own strengths, through the formation of long-term collaborative arrangements governed by contracts. It sought a share of the development benefits—rather than the "100% or nothing" approach which other small and larger companies tended to follow.

THE TCG MODEL

Ten rules seemed to govern the TCG network. These included the following:

1. *Mutual independence*: The TCG network consisted of independent firms whose relations were governed by bilateral commercial contracts. There was no internal hierarchy, such as one of the firms being the "lead firm."

2. *Mutual preference*: Member firms gave preference to each other in the letting of contracts. This rule gave the group its identity; but tendering and contract letting was along strictly commercial lines. However, contracts were sometimes let outside the group, against a competitive bid from a member firm.

3. *Mutual non-competition*: Member firms did not compete head-to-head with each other. This rule established the necessary foundation for trust between members. It allowed them to discuss business opportunities with each other in ways which potential competition might impair.

4. *Mutual non-exploitation*: Member firms did not seek to make profits from transactions amongst themselves. The goal was to maximize profits from dealing with the outside world; internal transactions were a means toward this end.

5. *Flexibility and business autonomy*: Members did not need to seek group "approval" for entering any transaction or new line of business, provided the transaction did not breach other rules. This rule allowed for maximum flexibility, giving the network the appearance of a colony of organisms moving to wherever food was most plentiful.

6. *Network democracy*: There was no overall network owner, controller, or holding company. Nor was there any form of "central committee" or formal governance structure for the network as a whole. It cohered as a result of the commercial ties operating between member firms.

7. *Expulsion*: Member firms had natural incentives to cooperate with each other based on long-term interest maximization, rather than short-term spot transactions. These incentives were complemented by the sanction of expulsion, if any member willfully disobeyed the rules. (No firm had been expelled in twenty years.)

8. *Access to external work*: There were no "subcontractor only" firms within the TCG group; each member firm had access to the open market, and was free (and expected) to bring in work from the outside.

9. *Open entry*: New members were welcome, but were not to draw resources from the group as a whole. This rule meant that new members generally obtained capital through loans or bank overdrafts rather than from equity from other member firms. It was the group as a whole that generally provided the collateral for such loans.

10. *Free exit*: There were no impediments to a firm departing from TCG. On the other hand, there was no market for shares held in individual TCG member firms. Consequently, departure arrangements had to be negotiated in each case.[4]

Within these rules, firms operated more or less independently linked together in the "honeycomb" organization. Each firm tended to form and extend through a "triangular networking model." In essence, a TCG company formed a relationship with a complementary technology-based firm, with each unit bringing different strengths. The partner firm typically brought with it access to new markets or prospects of collaboration. The TCG company brought its own technologies and special skills, plus leveraged access to internal TCG members. But what really drove the arrangement was the major customer, who did not just place the first order but became a partner in the overall concept development. The customer offered the benefits of a first sales contract, and in return received certain rights such as preferential supply, best price, and sometimes further marketing rights in its particular spheres of competency.

These practices had sufficed for over twenty years. A brief history of TCG's formation follows. More details appear in Exhibit 3.

HISTORY OF TCG

TCG-SAM, *TCG Systems Automation Marketing P/L*, was formed in 1976 as a joint venture between Peter Fritz and Pat Gallagher. It has been run by Gallagher ever since. TCG-SAM pioneered Australia's entry into the portable data entry (PDE) market and in 1992 claimed a 60 percent share of that market—including retail order entry, meter reading, surveying, and stock taking. TCG-SAM was also an important supplier of cash registers and "smart" point-of-sale equipment. Recent products had established it as a major force in both the retailing, bank check, and stock coding markets. Mr. Gallagher was convinced that he would have been financially strapped on many occasions, had he not entered into the joint venture with TCG and had support of the group's resources to tide him through difficult periods.

TCG-SAM had itself formed joint arrangements internally that constituted a sub-cluster within the wider TCG Group. These included: TCG-POS P/L created with the acquisition of HUGIN-SWEDA Australia in 1984 for marketing point-of-sale and banking systems; and TCG-ILED P/L, established to develop the revolutionary in-store label updating system. TCG-SAM Joint Ventures had entered into a series of joint arrangements with one-person businesses, for example in developing the concept of the electronic ear tag with a local inventor, while partnering with large overseas firms for manufacturing or distribution.

Kiah Research P/L was set up in 1987 to undertake applied research on behalf of the TCG Group and its associated companies. It was set up specifically to solve problems associated with the MOX Point-of-Sale controller for TCG-SAM. It also undertook the development of the BOW Buffer Computer, whose marketing rights were held by TCG-SAM. In return for its investments, Kiah Research owned the intellectual property rights to its results, and could license or sell these to other TCG or outside groups.

TCG Manufacturing P/L (TCG-M) was established in 1988 to produce products and services for both Australian and export markets, rather than simply licensing TCG's technologies overseas. Most of its production went overseas. For example, Toshiba had commissioned TCG-M to produce interchangeable parts for its range of lap-top computers. TCG-M had also developed and manufactured interface products for use with cellular telephones in collaboration with Fujitsu Australia. Other products included a terminal for use by diabetics, a cash drawer interface for TCG-

EXHIBIT 3
Chronology of TCG
Group Formation

NAME	YEAR FORMED	STATUS
TCG	1971	Active
TCG Systems Automation	1973	Active
TCG Systems Automation Marketing	1976	Active
TCG Information Systems	1978	Active
COSTEC	1981	Active
TCG Mega	1983	Active
TCG Graphic Design	1983	Active
TCG Marketing Services	1983	Business name only
TCG Computer Aided Engineering	1983	Holding company
R. Barel and Associates	1983	Active
TCG Customs and Freight CSD	1986	Active
TCG Export	1986	Active
TCG Strategic Management	1987	Inactive
TCG TEL	1987	Active
Kiah Research	1987	Active
TCG Events	1987	Inactive
STRAITS TCG	1987	Active
CED	1987	Transferred out
CEDCOM	1988	Transferred out
CEI	1988	Inactive
TCG Manufacturing	1988	Active
Famous International Artists	1988	Inactive
TCG Europe	1988	Active
TCG Pacific Japan	1988	Active
Primary Production	1988	Active
Real Estate Development	1988	Closed
EDVIC	1989	Transferred out
CEDTAS	1989	Transferred out
Kiah Electronic	1989	Active
TCG Print Management	1989	Closed
SOFTEC	1989	Active
TCG Marketing Services UK	1989	Active
TCG Information Systems SWITZ	1989	Active
MARCEL	1989	Active

Source: TCG, Ltd.

POS; and a data logging device for Tomago Aluminum to use in rugged, hot environments. Rather than expanding its overheads and managing large numbers of production workers, TCG-M subcontracted virtually all its production operations to other electronics and computer firms. It maintained strategic alliances with these firms, controlling them through strictly drawn contract terms and outsourcing arrangements. Other major TCG companies (and their start dates) are shown in Exhibit 4.

INTERNAL MANAGEMENT TECHNIQUES

TCG companies are essentially autonomous entities, free to enter contracts and arrangements as their owner-managers saw fit, within the agreed-upon rules and overall financial constraints set up by TCG. Peter Fritz was a shareholder in each company and had access to the information flow among all the groups' constituents. There was no overall holding company for the TCG Group. Each firm dealt with the others on

EXHIBIT 4
Other Major
TCG Companies

TCG Information Systems (1978):	Mainframe computer consulting activities.
TCG-Tel P/L (1987):	EDI and telecommunications opportunities.
TCG Mega Systems P/L (1983):	Computer graphics systems specialists—supporting both PICK and UNIX multi-user operating systems.
TCG Graphic Design P/L (1983):	Graphics and publishing services for member companies and outsiders.
TCG Export P/L (1986):	Manager of overseas product launches, trade fairs, negotiations, etc., for TCG and external clients.
CSD P/L (1985):	Provides customs clearance arrangements and shipment monitoring mainly for TCG companies.
Ralph Barel and Associates:	Provides financial accounting services to TCG and external companies.

Source: TCG, Ltd.

a bilateral basis. At first, groups charged each other at cost plus 10 percent. Later they found this inflexible, particularly if one company in the group was working more for other members than outside customers. These groups later developed a "direct quotation" technique. Based upon its needs, one division would seek quotes for its requirements from both TCG member firms and external companies. Although there was an attempt to keep the business within the TCG Group, everyone understood that non-performing group divisions would not be carried by the rest of the group.

Divisions often used revenue sharing arrangements. For example, TCG Software might give another company within the TCG group a preferential quote (say a 30 percent discount from commercial rates) in return for a (2 percent) bonus on the total value of the product being sold. Such formula arrangements encouraged cooperation and sharing of risks and benefits. Guaranteed Minimum Returns were sometimes used. For example: Company A might agree to guarantee a minimum order to Company B, in return for receiving a preferential cost or hourly rate charge. This allowed Company B to plan its operations in advance and spread its risks. In such cases, Company A would have the right to review costs and timesheets in Company B. TCG companies might also use profit sharing arrangements on occasion. For example, Company A might agree to provide Company B with a service free of charge, on the understanding that spin-offs (such as a maintenance contract) would be given to Company A, plus one-third of any gross profits. These contractual arrangements helped solve the problem of cost allocations within the TCG Group. They also helped to bring partner companies together in mini-joint venture relationships.

TCG encouraged its groups to look at the advantages of having continuity of supply, understood trading arrangements, and rapid responses from internal partners as forms of insurance against risks. Initial capital for a new entity typically came from a bank overdraft rather than from resources drawn from other member firms. The new member then operated within the group enjoying all the advantages this offered, yet was free to secure as much business as possible from outside the group. Start-up firms which might otherwise have seemed poor risks to a bank could secure overdrafts readily simply because of their membership in TCG.

OPERATING PROBLEMS

Peter Fritz described the problems of operating in the network environment as follows: "In an environment where there are many owners, and in this network of companies every owner is a substantial owner, the difficulty is one of equals having to make a decision. Initially my role was primarily in finance and in external affairs, in getting the large relationships going. But at any point in time any of the partners in a particular company could in fact decide that he was going to manage the large relationships. When this occurred there could be territorial disputes. In general, I tried to act as a chairman rather than an operating president of the companies. . . . We tried to drive the business through customer demand. However, when partners came through with forecasts which were unrealistic or forecasts that were realistic but they did not meet, there could be problems. This was especially difficult since some of my partners were not financially literate; they were superb technical people or superb sales people. And they could not understand why, if they met the technical requirements of the contract this was not enough. They would set sales goals, but expense goals seemed to be less compelling."

Although it was understood that firms which evolved their own client base and internal capabilities might eventually "leave the nest" and strike out on their own, many members had chosen to stay on. TCG had not developed any specific rules or procedures to cover such departures. Hypercom (a telephone based communications company) had left because of personal differences between Mr. Fritz and Mr. Walner, the company's head. Hypercom's major customer, the Centel Telephone Company, had pulled out suddenly from the relationship. Trying to save Hypercom led to a $500,000 overdraft, which the major corporate shareholders felt was excessive. After working this down as much as possible, the shareholders agreed to a sell-out in which they lost about $100,000. Hypercom later steadily improved to the point where it became Australia's biggest exporter of telephonic communications equipment. The only formalized understanding in these exits was an agreement on the preemptive right of any shareholder to buy out another shareholder if the others initiated an attempted buyout themselves.[5]

"THE AUSTRALIAN INCUBATOR"

There was strong Australian interest in the TCG experiment. Small business is the largest sector in Australia in terms of economic value and employment. However, small business suffers from an astonishingly high 70 percent failure rate in the first five years of operation. The Australian Office of Small Business reports that of the 12,000 new enterprises which fail in Australia each year, 45 percent do so because of managerial incompetence. The report notes: "Small business failure has a greater impact on the economy than the loss suffered by the owner. Apart from the lost employment opportunities, the demise of the business affects government resources through loss of tax revenue and increased welfare payments, with a multiplier effect through other parties such as suppliers."

The concept of small business (incubators) had been given substantial publicity. "The incubator" is like a franchise where the business owner is never totally in control. In exchange for a certain amount of freedom, a fledgling business can be guided in its endeavor [inside the incubator] as a first step in making a break from working or an employer. Reports from the U.S. claim a survival rate of more than 85 percent for businesses in incubators, as against 15 percent of stand-alone small businesses. The same report cites British figures showing an 80–20 percent comparison.[6]

THE PUBLIC OFFERING

"Our public offering posed some interesting questions. Since we had financed heavily by overdrafts or debt, I had put up most of the equity in the enterprise. It was very tricky to explain to my partners why my portion of the business was worth 70+ percent and their combined worth was only 30 percent. Some were more concerned about proportions and percentages rather than the actual money they would be getting in the offering. It was a very tricky negotiation. We sought to raise $7.5 million. Structuring this to satisfy all parties was quite complicated. Among other things, we have several products in the new public company that will necessitate far more money than we could raise in the first public offering. In one instance, the market we are attacking is somewhere between $5–6 billion, and we have the best technology in the world. We don't want to lose this as a major opportunity, but there are two considerations: (1) should we put out a placement of the main company stock or (2) should we create a new company and sell part of that stock to the public? We may in time have other opportunities of this sort. What we obviously have are smaller opportunities already in development."

The TCG group had been very successful through 1993. By that time, three relatively large groupings of activity had emerged: TechComm Control Simulation, TechComm Systems, and TechComm Engineering Services. The activities of each group were described above. Looking to the future, Peter Fritz said, "The public float (featuring these divisions) will allow us to have a much broader vision. Our companies have a range of product and patent ownership which is very broad. We need to demonstrate that we can attack very large markets with our products. In Australia there are some very large companies like Coles, Australian Telecom, and BHP. These companies like to source interrelated products from a single vendor. We are unlocking these contacts and opportunities like the Australian Defense Department which could be a significant opportunity for us. The largest opportunity, of course, is to project our products more into international markets. All of this means that we must reassess our management strategies in light of our growth and public company situation.

"I feel that we are going to be a much bigger company. Although not making any promises, obviously, I would not be surprised to be capitalized within three years to about $100–120 million, with some similar multiple of our current turnover. We have always had a broad product and service offering. This gives us an advantage against very focused single-product companies. For example, if we are bidding for maintenance contracts in a bank, we can also handle their electronics for asset management, bartering, and handheld terminal operations. We have three offerings against one from each of our competitors. In all our operations we try to develop strong loyalties toward our customers, and vice versa. This requires a lot of "keeping your customers warm, communicating with them, telling them what's happening; it is basically what one wants oneself from a supplier. The issue of product quality is simply background. The product must perform to expectations, or you will not sell it, nor would you get repeat sales."

THE THERMO ELECTRON EXPERIENCE

As Peter Fritz thought about the company's future strategy, he was fascinated by the experience of Thermo Electron Corporation in the U.S. Thermo Electron received much attention due to its unique approach of spinning off and financing subsidiaries separately as a way of stimulating growth, spreading risks, increasing motivation, and rewarding entrepreneurial endeavor. It had generated stellar financial performance through 1994. Thermo Electron had grown revenues at an average rate of 20% over the last decade (from $202.4 million in 1983 to $1.25 billion in 1993). Operating income had grown at a compounded annual growth rate approaching 30%.

Through its ownership in nine public majority-owned, three non-public majority-owned, and seven wholly-owned subsidiaries and divisions, Thermo Electron had among the broadest, most diverse, and most advanced technology portfolios in the U.S. It had an interest in many emerging technologies, including: environmental monitoring, analytical instrumentation, paper recycling, energy co-generation, soil remediation, bomb detection, and a variety of biomedical technologies such as the company's left ventricular heart-assist device. A relatively large percentage of Thermo Electron's income had come from "non-operating gains" arising from gains on the stocks its partially-owned subsidiaries had issued. However, if these gains were ignored, Thermo Electron was selling for 26.7 x its adjusted net earnings. Exhibit 5 gives further details of Thermo Electron's financials in the early to mid 1990s.

A UNIQUE STARBURST OF COMPANIES

Dr. George Hatsopoulos had founded the company while he was still attending the Massachusetts Institute of Technology as a graduate student. He originally intended to exploit the potentials of thermionic energy converters. In these devices heat causes carefully selected and prepared materials to release their electrons, creating an electric current directly from heat. These systems could avoid the 50–70% energy losses inherent in steam-electrical generator cycles. When the high cost materials of thermionic converters proved to limit their use to highly specialized applications, Thermo Electron mutated into a research-driven company built around its strong core competencies in mechanical engineering, electron flows, and heat transfer capabilities. At first it existed on government and commercial contracts. Because of its strong technology orientation, it quickly began to attract top quality scientists and engineers in important related areas such as optoelectronics, materials engineering, and electrical engineering. Based on these skills, it soon began to sell specialized high technology devices and systems into a number of niched markets.

However, one of the company's most unique aspects was its capacity to constantly "split off" and finance these independent units like shooting stars peeled from the core competencies of the original parent and later its individual divisions. Spinning off minority interests in wholly owned subsidiaries became a trademark for Thermo Electron. During 1993 alone, it completed a total of eight financial offerings, raising aggregate net proceeds of over $500 million. These offerings typically used a creative mix of financial instruments including equity, rights, private placements, and convertible debentures. Through participation in these spinoffs, Thermo Electron provided its managers, scientists, and employees with a unique environment rewarding those who took risks in developing the new products and technologies. Those who stayed in wholly-owned divisions received stock options in Thermo Electron's own stock. Those who created new product lines or independent entities around a separately financible new technology might receive an equity position or options in the new enterprise they formed. Once Thermo Electron had developed a concept to the point where it could achieve free-standing annual growth of 40% and attract independent capital, Thermo tended to set up the endeavor as a separate division, take a majority position in that enterprise, and let it seek separate financing through instruments appropriate to its size, industry, and risk

EXHIBIT 5
Thermo Electron Corp.
Summary Financials

RATIOS (FY 12/31)	1992 A	1993 E	1994 E	1995 E
Earnings/Share	$ 1.48	$ 1.75	$ 2.05	$ 2.45
Cash Flow/Share	2.39	2.79	2.82	3.22
Book Value/Share	13.81	19.74	20.12	22.60
Price/Earnings	27.3x	24.7x	21.1x	17.6x
Price/Cash Flow	16.8x	15.5x	15.4x	13.4x
Price/Book Value	2.9x	2.2x	2.1x	1.9x
Return on Equity	10.8%	10.9%	10.6%	11.4%

MARKET DATA (March 1994)	
Common Shares (Millions)	47.5
Institutional Holdings (Millions)	32.6
Insider Holdings (Millions)	4.8
Market value ($ Millions)	$1,911.9

CAPITALIZATION (9/30/93)	$ Mil	% Cap
Long-Term Debt	$31.5	2.3%
Convertible Debentures	$495.7	36.4%
Common Equity	$834.0	61.3%
Total Capital	$1,361.2	100.0%

Source: C. Sassouni, "Thermo Electron Corporation Report," Raymond James and Associates, March 3, 1994, page 3

class. Although Thermo Electron's shareholders had benefited substantially by this strategy, by 1993 many were complaining that they would like the opportunity to take special "founder" positions in these separate spin-off enterprises as well.

CRITICAL SUCCESS FACTORS

One analyst cited several major contributors to Thermo Electron's success.

▼ "Entrepreneurial focus: One of Thermo Electron's greatest strengths may be its corporate culture which not only encourages risk taking in the cultivation of new ideas for new products but also allows room for failure as long as it serves as a learning experience. By rewarding employees with stock options, the interests of the managers are aligned with those of shareholders. . . .

▼ An operating committee which provides ongoing guidance to [Thermo Electron's] publicly-traded subsidiaries: . . . The [experienced and prestigious] operating committee acts as an advisory panel which oversees the activities of the company's various subsidiaries. It provides guidance to the subsidiaries' managers in areas such as short term and long range business strategy, selection and [integration] of acquisitions, management of the subsidiary's

growth and profitability, and assurance that the subsidiaries have adequate financial resources to meet their objectives.

▼ Financial sophistication leading to flexibility in raising capital: Thermo Electron has demonstrated a great deal of sophistication in the timing and selection of financial instruments when raising capital. The company is incredibly active in raising capital for itself and subsidiaries . . . "[7]

The same report cited management loyalty, a strong technology portfolio, and an enviable track record as other crucial elements in success. The report continued, "On the surface it is difficult to understand what ties the Thermo Electron businesses together. The common link involves the strategic vision of their founder and revered leader, Dr. George Hatsopoulos . . . [who earlier said], "If I were to design my life in an ideal fashion, I would like to study fundamental physics, understand the fundamental laws of physics, make a discovery there, use that discovery to come up with an invention, use that invention to start an enterprise, use that enterprise to build an organization, and by the end of my life have the largest technology-oriented corporation in the world. . . . As time goes on I am less preoccupied with what we are going to start next, than with those [people] we are going to attract who can start things. I have spent an enormous amount of time trying to create the framework in which these entrepreneurs can come in, have some guidance and training, and [start a particular enterprise]."

NOT A CONGLOMERATE

When in 1966 (after 10 years of contract research) the company had decided to go public and commercialize the products and innovations that it had been developing, its stock issue was a great success. This gave it critical funding for some selected product introductions and for more R&D. Then as its research group's innovations attained critical scale, the Hatsopoulos brothers (George and John, the CFO of Thermo Electron) began to spin off discrete groups with partial public financing. George Hatsopoulos noted, "The only way one can obtain equity at a reasonable price in this country is to focus on the gambling and entrepreneurial inclination of investors. These people aren't interested in a huge conglomerate because they can't get a feel for anything it does. We have repackaged the equity so that investors get a piece of one promising technology they can get excited about. We have gone much further in decentralizing than any company I know. In an effort to do that and create incentives for the employees, many of our divisions are set up as publicly owned organizations. Managers of each subsidiary know that what they do gets scrutinized not only by corporate management, but by their own shareholders. I really believe in small companies. But small companies have a big disadvantage. They don't have the support, financial, or management resources that big companies have. My answer is to have a bunch of small companies in a family, which gives them financial and management support as well as strategic direction. But at the same time they are acting as though they are independent companies with their own shareholders."[8]

The Hatsopouloses used two criteria for gauging when a subsidiary could be spun off: (1) it had to be able to grow at a compound rate of about 30% for a long period of time, (2) it must have a strong management team, since Thermo Electron would not bring in outside management to run it. By 1993, Thermo's spin-offs aggregated almost $1 billion in sales. These are summarized in Exhibit 6. Exhibit 7 summarizes their stock performance.

Each spin-off paid a management fee to the parent (Thermo Electron) of 1.25% of revenues. In exchange,

Thermo Electron provided subsidiaries with certain services: accounting, tax planning, treasury, legal, risk management, human resources, investor relations, and shareholder communications. Once a spin-off began developing its own internal technologies and market niches, it might in turn spin off a portion of itself for public financing. Thermo's management had stated publicly that, by the year 2000, it would like to have a total of 15–20 majority-owned public subsidiaries. One of Thermo's partially-owned groups, Thermo Trex, had been called by John Hatsopoulos, "the next Thermo Electron." It contained four or five different technologies that all had the potential to be spin-offs themselves, including: Medical Systems (mammography and medical imaging), Laser Communications (satellite packet transmission), Avionics (passive microwave cameras), Advanced Materials (composite ceramic parts), Thermo Lase (a combination skin cream and low-powered laser hair-removing system). The company's other groups also had potentials to spin out further enterprises for private and public financing. They included: Thermo Cardiosystems (left ventricular heart-assist devices acting as auxiliary pumps for weakened hearts); Thermo Energy Systems (power co-generation in the biomass burning niche market); Thermo Fibertek, Inc. (a leading manufacturer of paper recycling equipment, parts, and accessories for the paper making industry); Thermo Instrument Systems (environmental, health care, and industrial quality-assurance instrumentation); Environmental Services (global consulting services for environmental engineering, highway systems, water quality monitoring, ecological risk assessment, etc.); Thermedics (diverse technologies and products for the pharmaceutical, health care, detection, and other industries).

Thermo Electron's wholly-owned divisions offered longer term growth for the company. These included: International Technidyne ($25 million blood coagulation and precision blood sampling devices); Tecomet ($30 million precision machining for health care and aerospace applications); Metal Treating ($3 million specialty metal treatment, hardening, and annealing supplier); Napco ($15 million electroplating equipment supplier); Peter Brotherhood (£12 million steam turbine and gas compressor equipment manufacturer); Nicolet Biomedical ($50 million line of neurophysiological measurement and display equipment); and Thermo Technology ventures (evaluation and commercialization of new technologies from external sources like the National Laboratories).

EXHIBIT 6
Spin-Offs by Thermo
Electron

SUBSIDIARY OF THERMO ELECTRON	YEAR OF SPIN-OFF	1993 SALES	PERCENT OWNED BY THERMO ELECTRON	PRIMARY LINES OF BUSINESS
Thermedics	1983	$80.2 million	52%	Biomedical products, bomb detectors, drug sniffers
Thermo Cardiosystems	1989	$3.5 million	2.8%	Heart-assist device
Thermo Instrument Systems	1986	$585 million (E)	81%	Analytical instruments
Thermo Trex	1991	$54.3 million	55%	Medical imaging, avionics and contract R&D
Thermo Process Systems (March)	1986	$54 million (E)	72%	Heat-treating equipment and services
Thermo Voltek	1990	$18.1 million	13.9%	Electromagnetic compatibility testing
Thermo Power (Sept)	1987	$77 million	52%	Industrial refrigeration equipment and natural gas engines for vehicles and other applications
Thermo Remediation (March)	1993	$15 million (E)	0%	Soil decontamination equipment
Thermo Fibertek	1992	$137 million (E)	80%	Paper recycling equipment

(E) = Consensus estimates compiled from Zacks, IBES, and other sources. Thermo Instrument estimate from Raymond Jones.

Source: C. Sassouni, "Thermo Electron Corporation Report," Raymond James and Associates, March 3, 1994, page 3.

STRATEGIC ACQUISITIONS

Strategic acquisitions had been an integral part of the long term growth plan for Thermo Electron and its subsidiaries. The accounting handling of these acquisitions (pooling versus purchase, and later earnings consolidation) clearly affected the apparent growth and profitability of Thermo Electron, as did these subsidiary units' operating profitability and the success of their stock issuance transactions. Although as contributions to Thermo Electron's growth these non operating gains were at first trivial in impact, by 1992 some estimated that they comprised approximately $20.3 million or

53% of the company's operating income of $38.3 million. Some summary financials are shown below:

	1988	1989	1990	1991	1992	1993	1994E	1995E
Operating Inc.	$24M	$22M	$38M	$42M	$68M	$120M	$163M	$211M
Non Oper. Gains	6	17	20	27	30	35	30	30
Gains/Oper. Inc.	25%	75%	53%	65%	44%	29%	18%	14%

Because of its peculiar structure, one of the investment analyst groups said, "We believe there to be no

COMPANY	DATE OF IPO	SPLIT ADJ. IPO PRICE	3/3/94 PRICE	CAGR
Thermo Electron	10/12/67	$1.01	$40.25	15.23%
Thermedics	8/10/83	$2.51	$12.13	15.40%
Thermo Instrument	8/05/86	$3.56	$32.25	31.70%
Thermo Process	8/21/86	$1.83	$9.00	22.00%
Thermo Power	6/26/87	$8.50	$8.75	0.50%
Thermo Cardio	1/12/89	$2.27	$18.25	51.70%
Thermo Trex	7/24/91	$7.92	$15.50	25.10%
Thermo Fibertek	11/02/92	$8.00	$14.63	82.90%
Thermo Remediation	12/16/93	$12.50	$14.13	15.00%
Thermo Voltek	3/19/90	$2.56	$9.00	36.90%
Average				29.64%

Source: C. Sassouni, "Thermo Electron Corporation Report," Raymond James and Associates, March 3, 1994, page 3.

true comparable [to Thermo Electron]." As such, the company's shares should be valued in an "unconventional" manner. However, using a "spin-off valuation" technique—i.e., evaluating the market value of individual subsidiaries and divisions—the overall company historically traded at about a 30% discount to the sum of its parts. On a price-to-adjusted net earnings basis, the same source also estimated that Thermo Electron's shares, if fully evaluated, had "an upside potential of about 35%." Nevertheless, this source gave Thermo Electron its strongest "Buy 1" rating as a "core holding," noting the difficulty of estimating the corporate value of partial investments in individual divisions.

In December 1992, *Fortune* stated that Thermo Electron had prospered by "identifying emerging societal problems and developing technological solutions for them . . . [and that] Thermo Electron's structure allowed shareholders to diversify their risk by holding the parent's stock or to make pure plays in the technologies by investing in the individual divisions."[10] Some 50% of Thermo's employees owned shares in Thermo Electron enterprises. Thermo Electron's spectacular success and the clear potentials for shareholder and employee incentives had encouraged American Express, ARCO, Coca Cola, Disney, and IBM (among others) to spin off a number of their divisions in a similar fashion. Analysts raised three longer term questions: (1) How would the market see such enterprises as differing from classic conglomerates? (2) Why should the corporate center spin off its "golden eggs" rather than hatching and growing them on a 100% basis? (3) How would these enterprises fare as the complexity of their product lines, support technologies, and markets grew worldwide?

QUESTIONS

1. What are the major differences and similarities between TCG and Thermo Electron? Why has each prospered (suffered) to date? What should be changed in the future?

2. What would you see as the most challenging aspects of managing these radical new organization forms? Where are they most likely to find application? Why? What support (control, reward, performance measurement) systems do they call for?

3. What are the advantages and disadvantages of TCG's network organization? Where will it work well? What kind of problems would you anticipate? How could TCG deal with these?

4. How much financing could TCG support in its public offering? How would you structure this offering? How would you evaluate it as a potential professional investor?

5. What are the most important issues TCG faces for the future? How would you propose handling these? Draw up a specific strategy that will keep the main benefits of TCG's current organization, yet let it meet the challenges of the future.

6. What kind of management control system would have been appropriate for TCG in its earlier manifestation? What changes are essential for the future? How will these affect the style, innovativeness, and flexibility of the company for the future?

The Microsoft Corporation (A) case presents the strategic situation facing Microsoft in 1994. This case deals with its organization structure and management practices.

PAST MANAGEMENT STYLE

In the mid-1980s Microsoft's work environment for programmers had been described as "deliberately chaotic." There was little corporate hierarchy. Individual product development teams were small, usually no more than three people. Software creation was under the direct, day-to-day control of CEO-founder, Bill Gates. His philosophy was that with less structure people could be more creative and introduce more innovative products. Software tools that were supposed to work together were built by totally independent units, with little cross communication. Groups did not use each other's code or share information. Within Microsoft, people were promoted because of their technical prowess, and not for their management skills. To compound things, Gates' hands-on style often meant he jumped the chain of command and made major changes in direction or even programs without bothering to tell everyone involved. As one would expect, there was a constant conflict between each group's desire to make the product continuously better and the need to get the product out the door. Within Microsoft's very flat, unstructured organization the common crises of product development were often resolved by fierce confrontations and lots of yelling by all parties. Gates, actively in contact with the entire process and clearly in control of the company, dismissed these sessions simply as "high band width communications."[1] His clearly expressed goal of "being the lead-

ing producer of software for personal computers" overrode all else. Many observers said he displayed "competitive paranoia" that others might overtake, preempt, or destroy Microsoft and constantly sought not only to "win" but to destroy any such serious threats.

THE PC WORLD CHANGES

This style seemed to work well for early desktop operating and applications software, but became less effective as Microsoft developed major systems like Windows. However, Gates proved remarkably flexible in organizational matters. Between 1983 and 1994, recognizing his own limitations, Gates went through three COOs—with James Towne, Jon Shirley, and Michael Hallmann each contributing a new business discipline to the company—while reorganizing his own job. In a major step, in the middle of the $100 million Windows project, he also reorganized Microsoft into separate Systems Software and Business Applications divisions, each headed by a corporate vice president. The theory was that—with MS-DOS thus internally separated—external application programming groups designing around MS-DOS could communicate directly with the Systems group, without disclosing possible competitive information to Microsoft Applications groups. The upshot, ironically, was that Microsoft perhaps had even more knowledge of all its competitors' applications activities. Gates tried to counter outsiders' complaints by insisting on a "Chinese wall" between the two operations. But skeptics in the industry claimed this was probably more a sieve than a wall.[2]

THE BEST AND HARDEST WORKING PEOPLE

Microsoft's style had always been to hire the very best and hardest-working programmers from anywhere and then allow them wide discretion. Hundreds of peo-

Case copyright © 1995 by James Brian Quinn. The generous cooperation of Microsoft Corporation is gratefully acknowledged. Research associates on this case were Allie Quinn and Penny Paquette.

ple might be screened for a single hire. There was no headcount budget. Searchers were always free to hire that once-in-a-lifetime talent, once found. When hiring, Microsoft cared little about a candidate's formal education or experience. After all, neither founder, Bill Gates nor Paul Allen, had ever graduated from college. No matter how lofty the individual applicants' credentials might be, they were not hired until they had been thoroughly grilled on their programming knowledge and skills. The interview process was ferocious, lasting 1–2 hours with each of 4–6 programmers and managers. Interviewers would rip people to pieces, ask them very difficult technical questions, and suddenly hand them a piece of paper and pen and say, "Solve this problem." The emphasis was on how people thought and their capacity to perform under pressure.[3] Gates for a long time insisted on personally interviewing each programmer applicant. And in the 1990s Gates would still travel anywhere to land a special talent.

Among the most famous organizational features at Microsoft had been its "architects," the seven software samurai who had advised Gates, explored new technologies, and done much of the most important systems structuring. Below them each programmer was rated at one of six levels, from ten to fifteen. If a programmer made it to fifteen and became an architect, it was like being made a senior partner in a law firm. Huge stock options accrued. Development teams were consciously kept small even as projects became complex. For example, Microsoft had only 18 developers working on its entire spreadsheet business, while Lotus had about 120 in the early 1990s. Gates explained, "It takes a small team to do it right. When we started Excel, we had five people working on it, including myself. We have seven people working on it today."[4] The individual development groups writing new code operated in a Darwinian fashion—every six months developers were reviewed, and the bottom 5% were weeded out.

THE SOFTWARE DEVELOPMENT PROCESS

By 1994, the format for developing software at Microsoft had evolved into a somewhat less chaotic system. Mr. Robert Muglia, Director of Windows NT, said, "One of the things Microsoft has learned to do very well is to build products which meet the needs of customers, focus on what customers want, and at the same time do so in a way that is business savvy." Microsoft had created two basic roles: product managers and program managers. *Product managers* con-

trolled the overall relationship with specific sets of customers. They were responsible on a continuing basis for understanding their customers' needs at a descriptive level and for handling most customer presentations, sales issues, advertising, pricing, sales force building, channels management issues, etc. *Program managers* worked with product people to understand customer needs thoroughly at a technical level, then drove these into a set of detailed specifications for design purposes. Throughout the development process, program managers worked with development groups, test groups, and user education groups to make sure the product met defined needs.

Mr. Peter Neupert, Senior Director, International Product Development, noted:

> The original specs for program functionality—in terms of timing and the types of performance that are critical—are agreed to by Microsoft's top management. The second level of specification is programmatic interface specifications to make operating systems perform compatibly. The next level is application program interfaces or APIs. By this point there are a bunch of internal documents that describe the interactions between some of the components, memory management file systems, and things like that. Another critical interface is the programmatic interface in the hands of the end user. As we develop the product, we have to make sure that it is present or the programs will fail commercially. Keeping each person on a development team keyed to this during the programming process is a major challenge. These interfaces are so important that the small teams doing the program are often organized around them and the specific hand tools necessary to develop their subsystem, like a file system.

Mr. Muglia continued,

> Program managers own the specs and are responsible for ensuring that the product does what customers want at a very detailed level. They go to the level of saying precisely how the product should look to external customers. They do not go to the level of data structures that implement it. Instead, the development teams really own the code. This sets up a good relationship because most developers don't want to be the ones making the decisions about what to do, but they want to be in absolute control of the code and the algorithms.

THE SPECIFICATION PROCESS

> At the project team level, we sketch out issues and for the more important elements we use detailed specifications as to what the products need to do—but these tend to be verbal documents. We use whiteboards to discuss technical implementation [targets] which then some-

times get written into specs. Probably nine out of ten times, however they don't. We are not good about maintaining specifications on our products. There are so many things inside an 8 million line system like NT that to try to document all of them would probably double the size of our team and inhibit our ability to do things in the future. Generally our code becomes the specification. But the people who wrote it understand the detailed goals and the tradeoffs made. If we lost a whole division of people, we would have a great deal of trouble recreating the code and its reasoning. But we have people who have been working on "word processors" for example for eight years, and we are able to keep enough continuity there that a nucleus of people can maintain the needed knowledge levels. [We operate this way because] our technology changes so quickly.

Mr. Muglia continued,

We think of specs as a great starting point to document whatever agreement exists. Typically the development of the spec is a team process. Maybe only 10–20 percent of the time is spent actually writing the spec. But each key person is interacting with five or six others, developing agreement that this is what we should do. But by the time we have actually written down a spec, it is [usually] garbage anyway because we've learned fifty more things since we got the spec agreement. We don't then go and update our written specs. Instead, every quarter, we take all the "bug fixes" the customers have asked us to do and roll them into maintenance packs [which become the updated documentation for the program]. The same developers fix the code who originally wrote it.

COMPETITIVE TARGETS

Mr. Neupert said of this process,

We are incredibly focused on our competition. If there is a single figure of merit for a program, it is to beat the competition. In the networking business it is to be faster than Novell; in the spreadsheet business it was beat Lotus. From that point, you can start defining the dimensions needed for the purpose. These targets certainly aren't absolute, and they often are not totally quantifiable. We frequently need to make purely judgmental decisions. For example, one of the really tough calls in the OS business is what memory size do you want to fit in and what compatibilities do you need. These decisions get initiated on a very broad level between Bill (Gates) and Paul (Maritz). But the specifics get changed all the time as we find out what we can or cannot accomplish for one purpose and how it affects others. For example, in the first version of NT we wanted to make it work on eight megabytes. When that didn't work, the target became a twelve, and ultimately a sixteen megabyte system. These broad decisions seriously affect our market positioning. Another example is in our next version of Windows where we have to enable enough of the installed base of machines to make the program into a mass phenomenon. That means we set program criteria based on the hardware mix we think is important in the future. The point is that specs are a dynamic process. The primary focal points are where we think the competition will be and what we think the market expects.

PROJECT MANAGEMENT

Mr. Muglia continued,

Once a project is underway, we do project scheduling. One tool we absolutely use is Microsoft Project. The developers themselves set the schedule and they set the integration plans. They understand how all the pieces fit together at a real detailed level; they have a dependency tree and their project schedules to discipline sequences and dependencies. They hold at least monthly project reviews of everything. The development team goes off and presents exactly what each component group's status is and what functions they're working on. They all look ahead about a month for potential problems in functions or sequencing. As projects get into later stages, we increase the frequency of core team meetings to find and solve problems. People understand exactly what the bug count is, what needs to be fixed tomorrow, what the priorities are.

Paul Maritz, Vice President Operating Systems, amplified,

Some companies use a design and implement cycle. We don't. Unless you think of how you will implement the code at the time you design it, you will not implement it successfully. You must think in terms of cost issues as you design. Are the levels of abstraction too high? And so on. The first step is to lay out a taxonomy. Next we break this out into different functions and areas. Then we define the interfaces between these. We write these interface intentions down. Then we break the process into even smaller functions. The users of each of these smaller functions can critique them in terms of their goals and interfaces. Much of this is done informally with the teams interacting extensively. We try to lay out the criteria for each function and subfunction carefully at first. Everyone reads each other's code to have a common vocabulary. The whole process is inherently fraught with tradeoffs. Each group has a strong interest in its own functionalities, their purposes, and time sequences.

In this process Mr. Neupert noted,

We typically do not have teams purposely in competition with each other inside the company. You can certainly have strong dissenting opinions within a team as to what's the right approach or the right architecture. That is encouraged all the time. The challenge is to get the issue resolved one way or another. Even after an initial decision, you may have a loser go off and pursue his approach alone just to prove he's right. For example, there was a conflict between Windows and OS/2. It was widely believed internally that Windows couldn't really take advantage of the new Intel architectures, to exploit protect-mode memory and things like that. However, one guy kept on working on it despite the fact that ninety percent of our resources were bet on OS/2 at that stage. Nobody thought he could do it; but when he ultimately figured out a way to make Windows work, his solution had lots of better characteristics and seemed to fit the market better than OS/2. That's how we went from betting our future on OS/2 toward supporting Windows.

NO MAGIC FORMULA

Paul Maritz continued,

With 1500 people in Operating Systems, and typical programs that involve 2 million lines of code, the process is enormously complex. We don't have any magic in how we write our code. Our programs must run on multiple hardware platforms and be extendable as those platforms change. There is no single body of procedures we can follow. The basis of everything is smart people, but teams can surpass the experience and capability of individually smart people. The biggest problem is handling the spatial interactions between subsystems. Thousands of things are happening in parallel. This vastly exceeds the complexity of any CASE tools; consequently, we do not use such tools. Nor do we use "macro control" programs like Andersen's Method 1 or Method 2. Instead, people document the program as they go along.

Senior developers are responsible for the overall design. However, most of the problems occur in implementation. You can never afford to lose control over your code base. You have to get constant feedback from all the elements. At early stages in the development cycle, the practice is generally "to leave the gates relatively open" so that everyone can see everything going on. However, later, with over 200 developers on a program like NT, if you just let developers check stuff into the system, it wouldn't even boot. It would just break.

To maintain coordination, the Microsoft Operating Systems group used a technique called taking the program for a "build test drive." At least every week, but more often 2–3 times per week, each group would recompile its software so that the entire team could build a consistent, coherent product with all the new features and functions in place. Frequently, the attempt to assemble the entire program or subsystem would break down. However, the "builds" forced people to run down and fix what had gone wrong since the

last build. If errors were not fixed at this stage, interactions quickly became so vast that it would be impossible to fit them all together, even though each subsystem might operate effectively on its own.

Said Paul Maritz,

It is difficult to add performance later in any program. This means that in addition to the "builds," we break up the process into milestones, each of which is legitimate for a particular customer base. Although our "test designers" set up formal test suites to discipline each stage of this process, we can't possibly guess all the things that people can or will do with the program. Consequently, at the milestones we try to prepare the program to be used for a particular real-world purpose. Then we can get feedback from the people using it and work from there. We broaden the program for each succeeding step. At each one of the milestones, we take the bug backlog down to zero for that constituency and test suite.

For each subsystem, there is a team of one to ten people. You really can't have the teams any bigger. People must be able to grasp the entire complexity of their subsystem and its interfaces. They must know each other intimately and be able to trust and judge each other's needs and solutions. Consequently, we develop a series of rituals that force everyone to get together around the builds.

Mr. Peter Neupert noted, "Each of our applications groups used to have its own tools. Now we do have conventions and are building some tools, but these are not used consistently across groups. Rather than forcing tools or interactions, our general attitude is: 'When people need to know something, they should go find out about it.' But it's largely been on a personal basis. A person's length of time in the company is really useful in terms of knowing how to get around in the system, whom to ask, whom to talk to."

A PEOPLE DRIVEN BUSINESS

Mr. Neupert continued,

There's one thing no one is confused about from Bill on down. This is a people driven business. You can dream all you want, have all the vision you want, but you can't deliver on it without the right people beneath you. Although we think our people have done extraordinary things, we still argue that we have a lot of weaknesses. We've never been able to keep up with the number of people we need, because the challenges we take on always expand faster than the infrastructure. For example, the current cable TV programming and multimedia programming needs are growing very rapidly. We know the dimensions and capabilities that we need and have. We drive very hard to find and keep the excellent people we need. But, once here, it is awfully hard to get them to move between product groups. And the understanding of our people in one product group about the challenges in another is [very limited].

We don't have any formal mechanisms by which we move people through a progression of challenges in different groups. Because the demand for good people is so high, all the divisions want to hoard their good people. And despite our policies, we are not as good as we need to be at weeding out people at the bottom. Because our challenges continue to grow so fast, some groups just plateau people. There have been some who have stayed on the same level working on the same class of problem for ten years. That's okay, if they're competent and there are no more pressing problems, and their assignments still add value to the company. But this doesn't solve our real headcount shortages.

PERSONNEL DEVELOPMENT

Mr. Michael Murray, Vice President of Human Resources, described Microsoft's development practices.

Once recruited, people will be put directly on a small team with a set of deliverables where they are expected to write or test software code under very tight time schedules. This is not an apprenticeship. They are rubbing shoulders immediately with people who have been here one, two, five, or ten years and are very knowledgeable. We don't have a lot of seminars on how to work as teams on software development. A new developer or new employee in our product groups will only go through a couple of weeks of formalized indoctrination or introduction to the methodologies we use in development.

We have always emphasized three attributes: people who are smart, people who work hard, and people who know how to get things done. If you have those three things, you get a promotion first to a technical lead position on a small project, then to a group manager position managing several lead people. Wherever you are, the job is still very hands-on, action-oriented. It would be difficult to find a single executive (even at the VP level) who doesn't do some individual work on the actual content of programs.

We basically tell employees that the development of their career is their responsibility. We are only now developing our first formalized program where we may create a few development type positions—purposely moving somebody into a position for 6–8 months so they can gain varied experience in the company. We will certainly talk to people, and discuss different job opportunities. We also keep a database of our upcoming stars. We are beginning some formalized leadership programs to introduce these people to broader concepts of strategy, planning, and leadership. But at the lower level, we expect the normal informal, e-mail means of communications to take care of most opportunity identification.

In the past we'd say if the company grew, we could all grow together. Now we are still hiring the same overachievers as then, but we have moved from a 3,000–4,000 person company to a 17,000 person company, and the opportunities to move to or interact with the top aren't as great as they used to be. Now I emphasize that if a person wants to advance faster, they should look laterally. And if they move, they will probably find a very different company in some other areas. This thing we all think of as Microsoft is really many different cultures in different places. These different cultures have different ways of communicating, being rewarded, etc.

THE MICROSOFT CULTURE

Mr. Murray described the Microsoft culture as follows:

Part of our culture is questioning everything. In a presentation, the style is not to sit there and be impressed with the presentation. Instead the task is to figure out what's wrong with the presentation, where is the flaw, where did they fail to do good analytical thinking. Sometimes you walk out of a meeting feeling my gosh, this company is very cynical, bitter, or grumpy about everything. But I think it's simply a very cautious way to look at business. Another common aspect of our culture is a great intolerance: intolerance for imprecision or for inaccuracy in analysis, description of problems, or understanding of root issues. All this is driven by Bill Gates more than anyone else. It's a great learning tool to have him either take you apart or watch him take apart someone else's presentation. This can sometimes be very tough on a person who is less articulate, but nevertheless very bright.

Another part of our culture is our "60 hour week." I find this very similar to my experience at Apple. These companies were started by people who were young, enthusiastic, and incredibly passionate about what they were doing. Each time you came up with a new idea, you could see an additional three new possibilities. So there tended to be an infinite amount of work and only a finite amount of time. Everyone became incredibly impatient because things were always moving so fast. The people who founded and joined these companies were single, highly competitive, highly intelligent, and chose to define their lives by their work. Suddenly you found you'd created a high velocity work culture. It wasn't unconscious. The people themselves reinforced it: where you parked your car was the time you came in, whether your car was there last was an indicator of how long you'd worked. Even when you transfer into more administrative tasks, you find that this work ethic stays. None of us feels we can ever get our jobs really done.

All these cultural things took care of themselves when everybody rubbed elbows with everyone else. I'm not sure any of us yet realizes what having 17,000 employees means in terms of maintaining some of these cultural factors. You'll find that companies like Hewlett Packard or Intel spend a lot of time talking to their employees about the kind of company they are and want to be. I find that Bill Gates is quite passionate about what our corporate values are—or what we call our "success factors"—but he's not the kind of CEO who wants to talk frequently about them. He would rather talk about the new technology, the new product we're developing, the new business strategy we have.

Bill has a very well defined vision of where the company should be and great confidence in that vision. But it is a technical vision of where the company is going. Does he share the kind of company he wants us to be? I think not. That's not part of his script. But I think every employee would say, we are so glad Bill's our CEO. We love hearing him talk. We love hearing him talk about the future. We believe. We salute that flag. But this company doesn't tend to be introspective. Instead, we have a great big windshield that allows us to see this broad panorama in front of us, with a big fat gas pedal you can't miss on the floor, and a small but functional brake. But if you look around to see where you've been, that's not very interesting."

THE MOTIVATION SYSTEM

Microsoft employees earned relatively modest salaries compared to the rest of the industry. But successful employees received large bonuses in the form of stock options. Even Bill Gates—though an equity billionaire—had never earned more than $195,000 in salary per year. Nevertheless, employee turnover was well below the industry standard.

"What attracted people to Microsoft with its enormous personal demands and middling salaries? Paul Maritz, Vice President Operating Systems, said: "They come here because management understands software and is passionate about it. They have all been involved in software and like to interact with the project people. . . . Our people tend to motivate themselves through peer pressure. A basic motivation is the fact that 'it is done well.' We are driven by customers, competition, and success. We cannot overemphasize these facts. However, a major contributor has been the fact that we are a rapidly growing company; and this has given our stock option plans enormous leverage."

Bob Muglia amplified,

There has probably not been in modern times a company that has had the financial impact on as broad a set of people as Microsoft has. By being at Microsoft over time, people have been more successful financially than they perhaps could have been in starting their own businesses. A lot of the attractiveness comes from the reputation of the company's products, its position in the industry, and the fact that at Microsoft you meet a lot of smart folks. A lot of people who come directly out of college are not primarily motivated by finance and don't understand the real value of options. When they receive them, they kind of say, "oh great," but don't think about it. There are many horror stories where people sold their stock options after the stock went up $5 or so but could have made ten to twenty times that a year later. Over the years, people have often said Microsoft can not continue growing exponentially forever. This is undoubtably true, but where it will end no one can yet define.

A PERFORMANCE FOCUS

We don't do a lot of the cheerleading here that other companies may do. However, in certain ways things are pretty easy for programmers. You want to get a new computer with special features, okay you get what you want. People also enjoy knowing what the next generation operating systems will be and having a chance to play with them before anyone else does. But it's not all loose and unstructured. Every person has an annual performance review with mid-year "objectives checkups." The evaluation is pretty much by the objectives the people and their managers have set. Everybody has anywhere from five to ten objectives they are to accomplish within the next six months. Every six months each employee is given a blank review form. They take their previous six months' objectives and evaluate themselves against them. On an annual basis they also write what they think their strengths are, what their weaknesses are, and what they will do about them. Their managers then take that form and write their evaluations of the employee's results against the preceding six month objectives. They also write their opinions on the employee's strengths and weaknesses. Then together they set in concrete the employee's next six month objectives. It may be fun to work on other things, but these are the things you're supposed to get done.

Peter Neupert said,

We have tried to set up metrics for measuring productivity, experimenting on smaller projects. How much effect does it have on productivity to improve procedures on the front end of the design process or to define functionality and quality better? How many lines of code should an individual develop? How many bugs are tolerable per unit time? While we have some standards in our heads, it is hard to write these down or make them applicable across projects. It's also hard to watch people and tell what they're doing at the time. We purposely give our programmers private offices so they can have the time they need to work without interruption. We want them to unplug their phone and shut the door when they need to. But we also expect them to be team members and work all night when the team requires it.

The interesting thing is that these guys are obsessive perfectionists. The hardest thing to do is to get them to stop work and get the product out the door. They're upset when they think you are going to ship something less than perfection because they consider their name associated with the product and its performance. Another problem is that as you get further and further into a product, programming innovators come up and say, "Hey, we could do X. Isn't that a great idea," and regardless of what you say they may try to do it. They may not think about how X fouled up 3 other people who assumed that function was going to be Y. Programmers always think things are going to be easier than they really are. Generally, they are more difficult by a factor of 4. As you add complexity, what you think is going to take one week ends up taking six and might not look like your original target. The obsessive perfectionists say you've got to have all this other functionality, so they try to shove 2T performance into the original time T. And of course you never know how complex 2T is until a user actually works with it. The biggest problem is: the more subsystems are added, the more people you need, and the more specialized people must become. Obviously, coordination problems increase.

"But in the end," Bob Muglia says, "what people know is that they have to meet their objectives. We have a 5 point rating scale which has increments of .5. Practically, however, we only use the scale from about 2.5 to 4.5. Above 4s are super stars and 2.5s are people having some problems. Everyone also has a compensation level. The levels for professionals go from 10 to 15 which is the architects. Level increases are what real promotions are. Titles don't really mean much. When people are ready for the next level, we formally promote them, give them a big bonus, and also a raise associated with the promotion. However, we do not give special project performance bonuses. We have given division-wide recognition for people in the past. There has always been a real concern about taking ten or twenty people out of a thousand person pool and saying, 'you have done an extra special job.' There's a very fine line between the twentieth and twenty-first person on a project, and you may make fifty or hundred people feel worse by the selective bonus while only a few feel better."

Mr. Murray noted,

There is management feedback as well. Employees have the opportunity to write feedback on their managers and what they've done right or wrong. We also do a yearly employee survey, which is anonymous, to understand what general trends are, issues, what people like and don't like, and so forth. We try to learn from our experience by a process called a post mortem. After you finish something, you gather together all the key people, talk to customers and to whoever can give you some good feedback about what worked, what didn't work, what we should do better next time, what we learned from this. Then we try to write it up in a brief report. The question is, do the other groups read it? Do they care about it?

Another thing that jumps forward is the immense personal development power of a company that runs itself on e-mail. Knowledge gets shared so rapidly and so openly to so many that it becomes a constant schooling and educational process. A person like Nathan Myhrvold, Senior Vice President of Advanced Technology, often sends out a ten page e-mail message expounding upon his group's most current thoughts. A lot of us are included in that e-mail group. We may not do anything with the particular memo. But it plants ideas into our minds. Nathan may never even know the impact he has or on what person. But many people go home at night thinking about new ideas and the possibly of applying them in some novel way to a project they're working on. It all happens organically. There is simply no structure, no rules to all this. There is no way someone could try to create a controlled system around e-mail, trying to exploit its value as an educational tool. There are no specific rewards for joining in this e-mail sharing. It's all organic in the way we do the job.

LOOKING AT THE FUTURE

Microsoft's practices had clearly been very successful in the past and its organization had modified over time. (See Exhibit 1 for Microsoft's organization chart and other exhibits for market and trend data.) However, in 1994 there was great concern about how the company's increasing size, the changing nature of its marketplaces, and the vastly increased complexity and interactiveness of its programs would affect its management approaches. These factors had already caused Microsoft's product service and support groups, which handled calls from customers, to exceed 5% of revenues by 1994. Because Microsoft was so important to its large corporate customers, it had created Microsoft Consulting Services in 1990. Mike Hollmann, COO of Microsoft, noted, "We have not been well known for our customer support. By 1995 I want Microsoft to be as well known for its customer service and support as for its products. I want Microsoft to be the 'Maytag repairman' of software."[5] This placed increasing emphasis on the issue of controlling product quality before the product entered the marketplace, a problem Microsoft—because of its leadership—had often encountered. How to handle this in the highly decentralized style of Microsoft was a major issue. As

Microsoft's customers, complexity, and channels proliferated, there was a deep concern that the basic nature of the company would shift away from software development to marketing and service activities.

To anticipate the nature of these changes, Microsoft had launched a $200 million research program under Nathan Myhrvold, a physicist who had worked with Professor Stephen Hawking. Myhrvold was a very articulate, innovative, charismatic individual who enjoyed discussing imaginative and philosophical possibilities. He commented,

> We must learn to think of the information highway taking personal computing from a desktop phenomenon to one that is woven into the fabric of our lives—our living rooms, our dashboards, our pockets, our kitchens—wherever there are people and information tasks for computers and software. Up to now our primary market, personal computing, has been mostly local in nature. That's going away. And the same kinds of dramatic changes in price performance that microprocessors brought to the computer world are now coming from fiber optics, ATM (autosynchronous transfer mode) switching, and satellite communications.
>
> The really dramatic part of the computer and communications revolution will begin to occur in the next ten years. One reason Microsoft has been so successful in the past is that we have managed to maintain "cycle share." As computer capabilities have grown, we have maintained our share of the cycles-per-second consumed in the marketplace. Given the exponential growth of the market, we have been surfing on a wave. Basically our business has grown at the same rate that memory price-performance has grown. To keep this up, we will have to continue to expand exponentially. There are more personal computers than VCRs now and about the same number of personal computers as television sets in the world. But, while people don't replace their TV sets for twenty years, they change their PCs every few years. This will drive the replacement cycle of all software.
>
> Until now computing has been about making tools for people to analyze, to create documents, to design. In many areas computers have merely replaced pen, ink, physical models, and calculators. The next clear stage will be to read with them, obtain information with them, let the computer be our window on the world's information, and to communicate with them. E-mail will give way to true communications in short order. Once you get the fundamental capabilities of reading, interpreting, communicating, and distributing information, whole new worlds open. The technical challenge for us in the next five years is to really fill in all of what's necessary to make this effective. The present system is not going to gracefully allow you to do all the wonderful things you could postulate. And the software that supports those new communication networks is going to have to be figured out afresh.
>
> Many people have postulated that, as equipment gets ever cheaper, someone can come in and even obsolete the gigantic investments that all the RBOCs (Regional Bell Operating Companies) have. The value of the existing technologies are, almost by definition, evaporating at a rate of 50% per year. Just like the old mainframes, the switches and PBXs of the past will be under tremendous pressure. ATM may well be the new "microprocessor" of the communications world. It will certainly allow lots of new companies, concepts, and solutions to come in.
>
> When will the voice call system become essentially free? Already, much of the local and residential stuff is unmetered. Much of it costs only 5¢ a minute. What happens when you can move 60 megabytes per second over the installed systems that formerly handled only 10 kilobytes? The pricing of everything will change.
>
> We understand personal computers really well. And they are going to be one of the key nodes on the information highway—but by no means the only node. In the near future PCs will be the most available platform for doing almost anything. The installed base of PCs is impressive. And there were as many 486 Window's-based machines sold to American homes last year as there were Sega Genesis game machines. But nobody yet has a dominating or even deep expertise in the new systems that will emerge. Along the way there will be numerous mistakes and deaths in both the hardware and businesses. People say with all this competition it's only going to be a commodity business. I don't think so. Restructuring that whole communications world is going to spawn a bunch of billion dollar companies, just like the microprocessor did. One of the stupidest things I hear is that IBM made a huge error in not keeping its PC operating systems proprietary. But look at the cast of thousands that did try to keep it proprietary. From DEC and Xerox to HP and Wang, almost all are dead or suffering. Whereas IBM created a whole industry and is the largest player in it.
>
> The key question is how do you extract revenue from this rapidly changing software-oriented world. The key to that is managing these very bright people we have who create the software.

1. What are the most important organizational and structural reasons for Microsoft's success? What major problems do you see in their approach now? What issues do you see for the future?
2. What should the future macro structure of Microsoft look like? Why? How would you propose to resolve the specific issues and shortcomings you see in Microsoft's existing practices? How should it organize to exploit the emerging opportunities in software?

EXHIBIT 1
Microsoft Corporation's
Organization, 1994

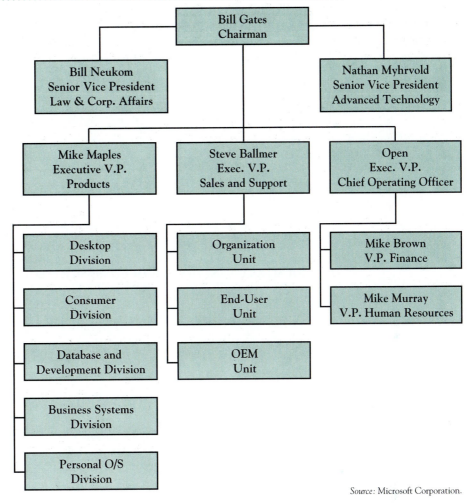

Source: Microsoft Corporation.

EXHIBIT 2
The Worldwide Software
Market 1991 and
Estimate for 1996

	1991	1996
Segments (billions of dollars)		
Service and maintenance	$ 9.7	$ 24.4
Applications	10.7	24.3
Development tools	6.7	16.4
Databases	4.1	10.4
Operating systems and utilities	13.9	26.0
Total software	45.1	101.5
Share of market by type (percentages)		
System vendors	54.7%	42.8%
Independent software vendors	45.3	57.2
Software Platforms (percentages)		
Timesharing	73.7%	55.6%
Client/Server	3.0	20.5
Filesharing	8.1	9.1
Standalone	15.2	14.8

Source: Forrester Research, Inc., Cambridge, MA, June 1992.

EXHIBIT 3
Digital/Electronic Media
(billions of dollars,
and percent)

U.S. MARKET VOLUMES FOR VARIOUS DIGITAL/ELECTRONIC MEDIA 1993

Telecom	$160
Computers	151
Publishing	89
Catalog shopping	52
TV/Radio advertising	35
Cable TV	26
Home video	12
Informational services	12
Records/CDs/tapes	10
Arcades	7
Movie theatres	6
Video games	6

Source: International Data Corporation/LINK Resources, Inc. and *U.S. Industrial Outlook, 1994.*

U.S. HOUSEHOLD PENETRATION OF CONSUMER ELECTRONICS PRODUCTS 1995

All television	98%
Home radios	98
Color TV	97
Corded phone	96
VCR decks	85
Telephone answering devices	54
Separate component systems	53
Cordless phone	52
Monochrome TV	47
Color TV with stereo	47
Video game software	44
Home CD players	44
Personal computers	33
Rack or compact audio system	30
Electronic car alarm	29
Cellular phone	24
Camcorder	20
Portable CD player	20
Home security	19
Multi-line phone	18
Car CD player	11
Projection TV	11
Modem or Fax/modem	10
All LCD TV	9
Home fax machines	6
Caller ID units	6
TV/VCR combinations	5
Laserdisc players	1

Source: EIA Market Research Department in *The U.S. Consumer Electronics Industry, 1995.*

EXHIBIT 4
The Networking Market

SHARES IN NETWORK OPERATING SYSTEM SALES

	1993	1997
Novell Netware	66.0%	62.0%
Microsoft	8.0	11.0
IBM	7.0	9.0
Banyan	6.5	7.0
Other	12.5	11.0

LAN APPLICATION GROWTH

	1993	1997
Mail/WorkGroup	325	1,041
Database Management systems	328	1,025
Communications	297	660

Source: International Data Corporation, *The Gray Sheet.*

1993 MARKET SHARES FOR ELECTRONIC MAIL SOFTWARE

Lotus cc:Mail	42.0%
Microsoft Mail	31.0
WordPerfect Office	15.0
Banyan Mail	6.0
CE QuickMail	4.0
Other	15.0

Source: PC Week, November 22, 1993, p. 115, from Dataquest, Inc.

PERCENTAGE USE OF DIFFERENT TYPES OF SOFTWARE FOR CUSTOMER SALES AND SERVICE

Word processing, miscellaneous	72.0%
Contact management	70.0
Electronic mail	69.0
Call history	60.0
Call reporting	58.0

Source: Software Magazine, September 1993, p. 72, from Sales Automation Service.

EXHIBIT 5
The Home Computer
and Multimedia Markets

HOMES COMPUTER USE BY ACTIVITY

	Adults	Children
Games	44%	84%
Schoolwork/household records	36	40
Learning to use	20	25
Word processing	62	25
Graphics	NA	12
Spreadsheet	21	NA

Source: Census and You, April 1991, p. 6 from *Computer Use in the United States, 1989.*

SHARES OF THE 1993 CD-ROM MARKET

Reference	40%
Games, entertainment	30
Home education	24
Other	6

Source: U.S. News & World Report, April 25, 1994, p. 70.

MARKET SHARES BY PUBLISHERS OF THE
$325 MILLION CONSUMER CD-ROM MARKET

Compton's New Media	18%
Software Toolworks	16
Interplay	9
Microsoft	8
Broderbund Software	6
Voyager	5
Sony Electronic Publishing	5
Knowledge Adventure	5
Other small companies	28

Source: The New York Times, July 27, 1994, p. C1, from Dataquest, Inc.

WORLDWIDE MULTIMEDIA MARKET, 1992–1996
(thousands of units shipped except as noted)

	1992	1993	Percent Change 1993–96
Total	4,815.4	10,315.1	26.9
Multimedia products	1,065.4	3,465.6	25.1
Authoring software	728.9	1,726.1	16.2
Multimedia PCs and workstations	325.0	1,690.5	31.2
Networks	11.6	49.0	72.2
Upgrade kits	675.0	1,109.5	-4.7
Peripherals	3,075.0	5,750.0	32.5
CD-ROM drives	825.0	1,720.0	27.6
Sound boards	1,800.0	3,200.0	28.6
Video boards	450.0	820.0	53.9

Source: Dataquest, Inc., in 1994 Electronic Market Data Book.

EXHIBIT 6
The Global Software
Market
(billions of dollars,
and percent)

1991 SALES AND MARKET SHARES BY COUNTRY

U.S.	$62.7	57.0%
Japan	14.3	13.0
France	8.8	8.0
Germany	7.7	7.0
Britain	6.6	6.0
Canada	3.3	3.0
Others	6.6	6.0

Source: Business Week, March 11, 1991, p. 98 from International Data Corporation.

GLOBAL DIFFERENCES IN MARKET TRENDS

Percent of Respondents	U.S.	Europe	Japan
Leasing CPU	29	26	68
Moving to Client/Servers	37	45	17
Open Systems	51	63	24
Unix-Oriented	34	40	17
% PCs on Local Area Networks	80	80	25
% PCs with Windows	70	70	12

Source: International Data Corporation, *The Gray Sheet.*

GLOBAL SOFTWARE SALES BY TYPE

	1993	1997
Applications	$29	$48
Application development tools	21	35
System-level software	22	32
Total	$72	$115

Source: International Data Corporation, *The Gray Sheet.*

EXHIBIT 7
Comparative Financial
Statisitics for
Software Firms
(thousands of dollars
except where noted)

	MICROSOFT CORP.	COMPUTER ASSOCIATES INT'L, INC.	NOVELL INC.	BORLAND INT'L, INC.	INTUIT INC.
1994					
Revenues	$4,649	$2,148	$1,998	$394	$194
Gross profit	386	2,146	1,531	286	125
Selling & administrative costs	1,550	1,102	724	263	87
Research & development expenses	610	211	347	66	174
Net income	1,146	401	207	-70	-176
Cash flow provided by operations	1,593	480	380	28	9
Net property, plant & equipment	930	564	395	162	24
Shareholders' equity	4,450	1,243	1,487	120	186
Net sales per employee	304	311	252	207	158
Net income to total assets (ratio)	0.21	0.16	0.11	-0.23	-0.72
Net sales to working capital (ratio)	1.37	4.77	2.02	-9.31	2.81
1993					
Revenues	$3,753	$1,841	$1,830	$464	$121
Gross profit	3,120	1,841	1,428	341	82
Selling & administrative costs	1,324	1,038	673	282	57
Research & development expenses	470	207	290	78	12
Net income	953	246	41	-49	8
Cash flow provided by operations	1,074	416	397	21	12
Net property, plant & equipment	867	715	404	144	7
Shareholders' equity	3,242	1,056	1,253	188	49
Net sales per employee	260	256	252	207	206
Net income to total assets (ratio)	0.25	0.10	0.02	-0.14	0.10
Net sales to working capital (ratio)	1.64	5.4	2.02	10.32	2.95
1992					
Revenues	$2,759	$1,509	$1,512	$483	$84
Gross profit	2,292	1,509	1,186	379	55
Selling & administrative costs	944	901	510	307	39
Research & development expenses	352	190	227	60	8
Net income	708	163	322	-110	5
Cash flow provided by operations	896	361	398	-36	7
Net property, plant & equipment	767	620	182	96	6
Shareholders' equity	2,193	988	938	228	17
Net sales per employee	239	204	411	231	173
Net income to total assets (ratio)	0.27	0.08	0.29	-0.30	0.18
Net sales to working capital (ratio)	2.09	4.85	2.11	3.61	8.07

Source: Worldscope database.

NovaCare was one of the largest and most rapidly growing national providers of contract rehabilitation services to health care institutions. Between 1988 and 1991, NovaCare had grown at 37.5% per year to $151 million in revenues. It provided speech-language, occupational, and physical therapy to patients with physical disabilities principally resulting from stroke, degenerative neurological disorders, or orthopedic problems. In 1991, NovaCare had over 3,000 contracts to provide rehabilitation services in approximately 1,800 facilities in over 32 states (see Figure 1). Despite its outstanding successes, NovaCare faced several important strategic issues.

Chief among these was how to position itself in the rapidly changing, problem-ridden health care industry of the early 1990s. Second was how to develop and organize its professional staff to provide the most efficient, highest-quality care in the rehabilitation field. Third was how best to develop the information, control, and incentive systems necessary to achieve these goals. An important portion of these efforts would be the development of NovaNet, an information system designed to accelerate the collection of field operations, administrative, and billing data. NovaCare had just completed pilot testing of NovaNet, but the system had not achieved anticipated productivity results. Chief Executive Officer John Foster wondered whether NovaNet should be released to the field, developed further, or designed for other purposes. NovaNet could be a key element in the company's future strategy.

Case Copyright © 1992 by James Brian Quinn.
Research assistants on this case were William Little and Patricia Higgins. The kind generosity and assistance of NovaCare, Inc., are gratefully acknowledged.

NOVACARE'S EARLY HISTORY

NovaCare began as a company named Inspeech, which coordinated a group of clinicians acting as entrepreneurs; each contracted independently and managed his or her own professional activities. Inspeech provided some common support services, financing, and professional management activities for which the clinicians were not specially trained. By 1985 Inspeech had become the largest speech rehabilitation practice in the country, with about 120 clinicians and $5 million in revenues. But Inspeech was operating in a crisis mode: the company had problems meeting its payroll, and its credit line was running out. Seeking further capital and management support, Inspeech sold out to Foster Management Company, a venture capital firm with about $130 million of capital under management. John Foster was the senior general partner of Foster Management Company (FMC).

After some initial excitement about the new ownership and the security its capital infusion gave, the clinicians' productivity suddenly plummeted. They began to question the motivation of the new management. They saw the FMC group as "businesspeople" concerned about profitability rather than as caregivers concerned about patient wellness. At this point, John Foster decided to take a more direct role as CEO, and his management team began emphasizing both patient care and the need for productivity. For 18 months, the new management team worked at rationalizing the business and made several complementary acquisitions with FMC funds. In November 1986, Inspeech made a public offering and raised about $40 million of equity.

Foster Management had recognized that there was a cluster of rehabilitation therapies in nursing homes which might be offered on a complementary basis. The most closely related of these were speech, physical, and

FIGURE 1
NovaCare Network

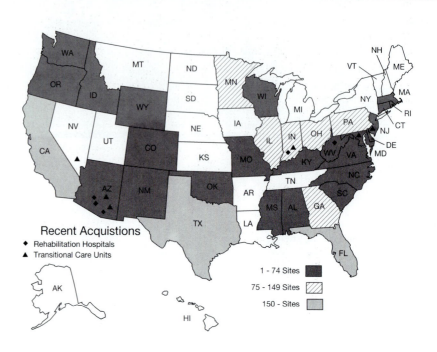

Recent Acquistions
♦ Rehabilitation Hospitals
▲ Transitional Care Units

1 - 74 Sites
75 - 149 Sites
150 - Sites

occupational therapy. In 1987, it diversified into the last two. Inspeech then grew quickly through market development and acquisition of other therapists' practices. Unfortunately, the company's rapid growth was accompanied by problems. John Foster said,

> We had very high levels of clinician turnover and a broad level of dissatisfaction throughout the company, partly reflecting indigestion from the 19 acquisitions we had made. Most health care professionals had never worked inside a large successful organization. They were, by tradition, sole practitioners. They were caregivers, and therefore highly sensitive, sensitized people. It was a very subtle thing to bring the concepts of business and productivity to a group of people who have been trained into a special mind-set, who have another language, and who were so sensitive to quality of care. Their view generally was that productivity and quality were mutually exclusive.

The company reached a low point in early 1988; customers were confused about how to interface with the company's multiple services. Its stock price was dropping. The clinician staff was quitting, and the company was missing its performance goals. Hal Price, Divisional Vice President, commented about this period,

> It was very confusing. . . . We had different sets of standards, different benefits. . . . It was all a result of trying to

bring different businesses into the company and not doing a smooth job of integrating them. Despite the fact that the financial results were not good, we knew that at a local facility level we were delivering good service.

In July 1988, the company reorganized into four geographic divisions each with a staff organization to support its business. Bud Locilento, Vice President of Human Resources, noted,

> We had been working from a highly centralized model of management. As we continued to grow very rapidly, we were losing our efficiency as an organization and made the decision to move to a more decentralized model. We would grow by penetrating new market areas and then densifying existing markets. We would modify our structure to reflect that approach.

A NEW VISION

In addition to decentralizing significantly, the company undertook a process that was widely referred to as a "healing event," following its many acquisitions and rapid growth. In 1989, the company's name was changed to NovaCare to reflect its broader spectrum of rehabilitation services. It also undertook to develop and document a complete new set of vision and culture statements. These consisted of a Vision Statement, a

Statement of Purpose, and a Statement of Beliefs. John Foster said, "These are integral to the culture of the company and the employee/manager relationship. These beliefs are an agreement between the corporation and the employee and create a report card that everyone can use to evaluate the performance of the company." NovaCare's Statement of Purpose begins with the words,

> We are fundamentally a clinical organization. All investment and organizational resources are intended to support the successful interaction of a clinician and the patient.
>
> The Direct Care Provider is the key person in our organization. All the corporate staff and resources exist to support the clinician in providing care to the patient. Line management supports the clinician in direct patient care. Technical experts, in turn, support line managers in providing the highest quality programs. This structure enables each Direct Care Provider to make the best clinical judgments.

The company's Vision Statement makes the following key points:

▼ "We apply our clinical expertise to benefit our patients through creative and progressive techniques.
▼ Our people are our most valuable asset. We are committed to the personal, professional, and career development of each individual employee. We are proud of what we do and dedicated to our company. We foster team work and create an environment conducive to productive communications among all disciplines.
▼ Our customers include national and local health care providers who share our goal of enhancing the patient's quality of life. In each community, our customers consider us a partner in providing the best possible care. Our reputation is based on our responsiveness, high standards, and effective systems of quality assurance. Our relationship is open and proactive.
▼ NovaCare is people committed to achieving excellence.
▼ Our ethical and performance standards require us to expend every effort to achieve the best possible results."

The company's Statement of Beliefs documented and detailed four major principles: (1) respect for the individual, (2) service to the customer, (3) pursuit of excellence, and (4) commitment to personal integrity. These were elaborated in a 16-page pamphlet that was widely distributed and constantly reinforced. John Foster said, "I have spent a great deal of time on the road and in the field articulating our purpose and our beliefs. In time, the soul of the company will come to be less a matter of 'it feels good to be here' and more a matter of an articulated set of values and highly precise purposes." Larry Lane, Vice President of Regulatory Affairs, echoed the statements and added, "The Purpose and Beliefs Statements provide very strong language about making a difference, empowering clinical behavior, service, advocacy, training, and commitment to professional skills. These concepts are central to our success and the way we operate on a day-to-day basis."

PROFESSIONAL STAFFING ISSUES

Demand for clinical professionals was significantly greater than supply. In late 1991, the company employed approximately 2,300 full-time equivalent (FTE) therapists in the provision of patient care. At that same date, the company had open positions for 800 additional full-time therapists who, if hired, could generate revenues immediately. The company employed 23 recruiters in eight regions, representing the largest recruiting function in the rehabilitation services industry. It differentiated its professional opportunities by offering a career ladder which was typically unavailable in other institutional settings. This allowed a trained professional to progress through clinician, team leader, district clinical coordinator, district manager, area manager, clinical consultant, and possibly divisional vice president. In addition, clinicians might choose to do administrative activities like recruiting, sales, or quality assurance.

The company performed sophisticated national salary surveys to ensure that its compensation programs were competitive. It provided excellent benefits and incentive bonuses for clinical productivity that exceeded industry averages. It awarded incentive stock options—commencing at the district manager level—on the basis of performance. It also invested significantly in clinical and management training programs for its professionals. It offered clinical training at company and independent university seminars, it had developed an interactive self-study video library for clinicians to use at home, and an expanding management training curriculum was mandatory for all district and area managers. As a result of these and other employee relations programs, NovaCare had increased its number of new hires by 130% from fiscal 1988 to fiscal 1990 and had reduced its therapist turnover from 55% in 1988 to 27% in 1991. Its number of FTEs (excluding therapists from acquired companies) had increased at a 33% compound annual growth rate.

Nevertheless, the shortage continued. John Foster estimated that each turnover cost the company $5,000 in recruiting costs and about $20,000 in lost revenue.

A THERAPISTS' COMPANY

A unique attribute of the company was that "NovaCare was a therapy company managed by therapists. It was a relatively young organization, hard charging, tending to be athletic, and 90% female," according to John Foster. He noted, "Clinicians tend to be high-caring, highly affiliative people. NovaCare employs many working mothers. This has important implications in terms of training, traveling, continuing education, and promotional opportunities." In 1991, the company was seeking clinicians in all of its fields, including:

▼ *Speech-language pathology*—the diagnosis and treatment of speech, language, swallowing, and hearing disorders usually arising from stroke, head injury, degenerative neurological disorders, or cancer. The speech-language pathologist is a licensed clinician with a baccalaureate degree and a clinically specific master's degree.

▼ *Occupational therapy*—improving muscular and neural responses to overcome patients' deficiencies for the basic activities of daily living. Occupational therapists were licensed professionals with a clinically specific baccalaureate degree; certified occupational therapy assistants (COTAS) could provide therapy under the supervision of an occupational therapist. Occupational therapy involved (1) restoring sensory functions, (2) teaching compensatory techniques to improve independence for daily living activities such as feeding, toileting, or bathing; and (3) designing, fabricating, and fitting assistive devices.

▼ *Physical therapy*—improves muscular and neural responses to enhance patients' physical strength and range of motion. The physical therapist was a licensed clinician with a clinically specific baccalaureate degree. Physical therapy comprised the application of stimuli like heat, cold, water, electricity, massage, or exercise.

NovaCare's revenue breakdown between the therapies is estimated in Table 1.

AN INVERTED ORGANIZATION

NovaCare refers to its organization as "inverted." The entire company exists to support the clinician in

TABLE 1
NovaCare Revenue Breakdown, 1987–1991

			1991		
	1987	1989	Year	2Q	3Q
Speech-language pathology	79%	51%	39%	39%	38%
Occupational therapy	16%	30%	39%	39%	40%
Physical therapy	5%	19%	22%	22%	22%

Source: Estimates by Alex Brown, Inc.

the delivery of service to the patient. John Foster considers himself "the lowest man in the inverted organization with everyone between me and the clinician in place solely to support the clinician. . . . This is a very important piece of understanding, not only for our clinical people to have in the field, but also for all of us as staff members to understand what role and relative importance we play in the organization." Vice President of Human Resources Bud Locilento says, "Our goal today is to get each clinician to have a high sense of empowerment, to make decisions for the patient, for the customer, and for their own well-being—instead of having them feel like they are swimming upstream against a pyramidical organization."

Running and maintaining an inverted organization required constant training, empowerment, and reinforcement. It was often confusing to hear executives referring to "my bosses," meaning those people closer to the field contact point, rather than the corporate center. Mr. Foster continued to try to find ways to get feedback or "instructions" from the field. He had established a Chairman's Council consisting of 15 to 20 people from around the entire country who met twice a year. These were representatives, clinical and managerial, from different divisions who represented a cross section of opinion and thought. Before each meeting, the representatives were to canvass their local groups to collect information and feedback for discussions. The company also had a bimonthly newsletter to keep clinicians informed, reinforce positive happenings in the company, pose issues for feedback, and reinforce the vision of the company. NovaCare clinicians, as sole practitioners operating in a remote nursing home or health facility, had to be independent decision makers. Yet in their formal training, they were not educated for this, nor were they prepared to make the compromises often required within a health care facility or nursing home environment.

A CLINICIAN FOCUS

Patient screening, or who goes on the caseload and when, is a critical issue for both NovaCare's and the health care facility's profits. Given the limited number of trained clinicians and the desire of all parties to show maximum patient benefit, it was often difficult to make choices among those who needed care, who would not benefit from care, and who could pay for care. Treatments eligible for repayment varied among different insuring groups. Unfortunately, when clinicians were trained, they were taught how to treat a particular condition, not how to identify from a pool of patients those whose conditions could be adequately and economically treated. Larry Lane, Vice President of Regulatory Affairs, said, "Our orientation has been to empower the clinicians to use professional judgment first and then fall back on to the other issues—are there constraints that will inhibit my professional judgment from being fully carried out?"

Within these limits, a clinician would assess and diagnose a patient and determine a strategy of treatment. The clinician had to establish long-term objectives for the treatment and define success on a case-by-case basis. From the fiscal intermediary's perspective, as long as the clinician had selected a legitimate therapy strategy for a disorder that fell under that payor's guidelines—and as long as the patient showed measurable progress—treatment might proceed. However, the clinician's time availability, specific skill capabilities, and psychic energy levels were also important. Certain forms of rehabilitation could be extremely taxing for the clinician. For example, the continuous physical and psychic drain of treating geriatric or seriously impaired individuals could rapidly "burn out" a clinician. Hence, it was essential to allow some significant variation in the types of patients, disorders, and locations that a clinician experienced. It was also important that the clinician not have to travel extensively between facilities. A number of subjective judgments were required to obtain the right balance.

THE SUPPORT ORGANIZATION

The organization supporting the field clinicians (also called direct care providers, or DCPs) was structured regionally. Each clinician belonged to a group called a district. Each district earned annual revenues of approximately $1 million and was home for an average of 15 FTE clinicians. Clinicians were coordinated by a district manager, district managers by an area manager, and area managers by a division vice president. An area had approximately $7–10 million in business. There were three to four area managers per division and four national divisions organized by geography. The four division vice presidents were coordinated by a vice president of field operations. In 1991, the business was managed on a weekly basis; clinicians scheduled their weekly activities in conjunction with their district manager. On Friday, clinicians telephoned their district managers to report their results—both clinical and administrative—for the week. The district manager consolidated these data and reported a summary to corporate headquarters on the following Monday.

An area manager described the weekly work activity as follows.

> Our whole company travels Tuesday through Thursday. On Friday, DCPs call the District Manager and report how many patients they've seen, how many evaluations they've done, how much time they've spent in preparation and documentation, and how many units of therapy service they've delivered. On Monday, I spent 9 hours on the telephone with each one of my District Managers going over each of the clinician reports. By 3:00 p.m. that afternoon I report to my Division Manager, who consolidates the information to be sent to the Corporate Operations Officer by 8:00 a.m. Tuesday morning. We are spending 20–25% of our time relaying information.

The district manager's job was to handle customer relations and develop good relations with each clinician. One of the division vice presidents, Hal Price, commented, "We've worked hard to reduce the number of facilities so the District Manager can spend as much time as possible with customers listening to their issues, addressing their problems, trying to constantly reassure them. You need to be constantly in front of the facility's management and staff. . . . Because employee retention is such a major concern for the company, the District Manager's role is critical to ensuring a happy work force." A key management challenge at the district level was the ratio of facilities covered to the number of clinicians. The converse of this question frequently got posed: "How many patients are going unserved in a given facility?"

Timothy Foster (no relation to John Foster), NovaCare's CFO, described the problem this way:

> Our central operations problem is that our service, as we charge it to the customer, is priced for the amount of time we spend with each patient, specific to that patient. So for every 15 minutes we spend treating a patient, we are reimbursed a given rate. Any individual therapist works in two or three facilities. That's the premise of our business—there isn't enough reimbursable activity to

employ a full-time therapist in any one facility. We are a consolidator of the practice in each facility and among several facilities.

Since the therapist is a fixed cost. we are motivated to optimize billable activity, or production, much as lawyers would be motivated to optimize their productivity/ billable time. On the other hand. a Director of Nursing in a facility is looking for many other behaviors that have nothing to do with billable time—team work, consulting or advising, in-servicing. and so on—that contribute to the long-term good of the facility and its caregiving capacity. But our therapist is not incented to do that by virtue of the way our incentive bonus program is oriented toward personal productivity, which may suggest that they get out of the facility quickly when there aren't any more patients to treat on a direct basis that day and go to the next facility.

COMPLEXITY OF THE CUSTOMER

NovaCare contracted with nursing home chains and independent operators for the provision of rehabilitation services to their patients. Contracts were written for one year, but could be canceled on 90 days' or less notice by either party. NovaCare was compensated on a fee-for-service basis from the nursing home, which in turn usually collected from a third-party payor, for example, an insurance company. NovaCare usually indemnified its customers against payment denials by third-party payors. For success, NovaCare had to serve many different constituencies. Each constituency had a different set of needs and expectations. Any group of people who had the ability to influence performance or contract termination directly at a customer facility was considered a constituency.

▼ *The patient* expects to get well by the treatment and expects a good personal relationship with the clinician. As the ultimate recipient of the service, although frequently not the direct payor, the patient could also influence third-party payors like insurance companies or local Medicare administrators. Their insurers—usually the ultimate payors for the service—would tell the nursing home they were unhappy, and the service would be canceled.

▼ *The director of nursing* has a strong caregiving orientation and is immediately attendant to the patient's needs. However, the director also has to coordinate the therapist's activities with all of the other patient support activities in the nursing area.

▼ *The nursing home administrator* is concerned with the quality of care and efficiency of operations as well as having a financial responsibility. The administrator's compensation is usually measured in financial

terms. Consequently, administrators look for optimal financial performance, with minimum risk, for the rehabilitation unit which NovaCare was contracting to serve or manage.

▼ *Owner-managers* were frequently removed from clinical issues, other than as they impacted regulatory compliance. Their primary responsibility was financial performance.

▼ *Third-party payors* were interested in maximizing therapeutic effects for lowest cost.

Each constituency had its own special array of needs and expectations from tender patient care and improved wellness, through smooth hassle-free service, to efficiency and optimal reimbursement, to defending the institution from any possible negative impacts like lawsuits or loss of reputation.

NovaCare served not just individual nursing facilities, but also many of the major nursing home chains on a national level. For these customers, NovaCare provided an additional level of services. Dr. Arnold Renschler, Chief Operating Officer, said,

> We provide our major customers, for example, a quarterly report that tells them what we're doing in terms of the generation of revenues for them on a therapy-by-therapy basis, and a location-by-location basis. That's a capability a smaller operator simply would not have. We have a full-time officer of the company who stays abreast of regulatory changes, changes in reimbursement, and the implications of potential future changes. He is seen as a resource to our major customers on all-regulatory issues.

The corporate staff of NovaCare numbered slightly over 100. The staff's size and functions were carefully tracked as a percentage of revenue, and this percentage had continued to shrink with time. Bud Locilento attributed this to "getting better people, increasing our reliance on technology and systems, and moving many of the staff functions into the field."

INCENTIVE SYSTEMS

An elaborate compensation system supported the highly decentralized, "inverted" organization of NovaCare. Starting in the days of Inspeech, the company had defined productivity in terms of 15-minute "units of billable time." The primary billable activity was direct patient care. But "units" included any time spent documenting what was done with the patient, consulting with other professionals, direct preparation time, patient care meetings, or anything done directly on behalf of the patient. In December 1984, the productivity standard was set at 100 units (or 25 hours) of billable time per week for each clinician. Above this, a bonus system came into effect. The remainder of the clinician's time was to allow them to do practice building, engage in marketing activities, and create a steadier flow of patients. The most productive therapists actively sought out opportunities to develop their practice and worked with doctors and other nursing home staff personnel to get patients needing care into their caseload.

NovaCare had developed state-of-the-art marketing programs to help make the facilities in which its clinicians worked real magnets for referrals from the community. NovaCare wanted potential referral sources (doctors, nurses, patients, nursing home directors, etc.) to recognize both the availability and quality of its service delivery. The therapist was the key link in converting the company's service concept into a reality. Each clinician was paid a bonus based on the number of units of patient care delivered each week over the agreed-upon standard. However, since speech and occupational therapy were the higher-margin services offered within a nursing home, the physical therapy bonus system was quite different.

NovaCare earned 100% of its revenues from service activities. These were dependent on the ability of its clinicians to form and cultivate one-to-one relationships with patients, facilities, and key personnel in those facilities. The company's revenues were constrained by the available time per clinician, available billable time per clinician, and the number of clinicians. NovaCare's management went to great lengths to educate its clinician work force that productivity and quality of care were in fact synonymous. It went even further, pointing out to the therapists that "In the process of being productive we are, in fact, enhancing our professions, enhancing the quality of care, and demonstrating the professional qualifications of our clinical staff."

QUALITY AND REVENUE CONTROL

Quality was an assumed ingredient in the delivery of health care services, although it was not precisely defined or measured by institutions, insurance companies, or other payors. NovaCare, through its systems and management practices, had attempted to "set the standard of care for its field" and to take the lead position within its industry. Hal Price said, "I don't think there is anyone in the country that comes close to doing what we do—delivering on a consistent basis, on a similar scale, the quality of care that we now deliver to our customers." NovaCare constantly sought areas

for minor improvements leading to perfection in the delivery of its therapies. Quality control was a basic responsibility of therapists.

District managers were measured on the revenue side of the business only. They were not accountable for managing costs. They were rewarded for (1) productivity, (2) gross unit production measured against budget, (3) retention of people, and (4) supplemental goals contained in personally agreed-upon management objectives. Productivity, production, and retention each accounted for 30% of the district manager's measured performance. Ten percent was allocated to the supplemental goals.

Area and division managers had incentives on three components: (1) gross operating profit, (2) retention, and (3) supplemental goals. Gross operating profit was 50%, retention 30%, and supplemental goals 20% of their performance measurement package. Operating profit incorporated both net revenue and margin performance targets.

NOVACARE'S STRATEGY AND FUTURE MARKETS

NovaCare's basic strategy had been to grow by consolidating practices of rehabilitation services through a program of disciplined internal growth and acquisitions. The strategy was designed to capitalize upon several external structural factors: (1) an unserved and growing demand for rehabilitation services, (2) an increasing concern with health care costs and the needs of the elderly, and (3) a highly fragmented competition made up of smaller regional firms and care centers. By 1991, the U.S. health care industry was in a state of crisis. The United States spent over $2,500 per person on health care and in the aggregate over $700 billion. Medicare alone cost roughly twice what Britain's entire national health service cost. It was estimated that at least 20% of all health care spending in the United States was on administration. Deep concerns had been expressed about the quality of health care in the United States. Yet the Congressional Budget Office projected that federal spending on health care programs would increase to almost 20% of its budget in 1996. There was an extensive national debate about (1) how to finance health care in the future, (2) access to the health care system for much of the population, and (3) the problems of delivering quality care to an increasing percentage of an aging or disabled population.

TABLE 2
Estimated Contract Therapy Market, 1988–1993
(in millions of dollars)

	SPEECH			OCCUPATIONAL		
	1988	1993E	CGR	1988	1993E	CGR
Nursing homes	$250	$365	8%	$250	$ 550	17%
Hospitals, other[a]	300	420	7	300	460	9
Home health	250	365	8	300	505	11
Therapy total	**$800**	**$1,150**	**8**	**$850**	**$1,515**	**12**

CGR—Compound growth rate.

[a]"Wholesale" pricing, that is, revenues generated by providers.

Source: Robertson, Stephens & Co. estimates.

TABLE 3
Product Mix Breakdown by Facility and Type of Contract, 1990–1991

CONTRACT TYPES	12-31-90	6-30-91	9-30-91	9-MONTH % CHANGE
Total Facilities	**1,813**	**1,724**	**1,804**	**-0.5**
Speech-language pathology contracts only	815	589	574	-29.6
Occupational therapy contracts only	45	49	59	31.1
Physical therapy contracts only	49	51	49	0.0
Speech-language pathology and occupational therapy contracts only	321	348	365	13.7
Speech-language pathology and physical therapy contracts only	44	23	22	-50.0
Occupational therapy and physical therapy contracts only	29	33	34	17.2
Speech-language pathology, occupational therapy, and physical therapy contracts	510	631	694	36.1
Total Contracts	**3,227**	**3,390**	**3,606**	**11.7**
Total speech-language pathology contracts	1,690	1,591	1,655	-2.1
Total occupational therapy contracts	905	1,061	1,152	27.3
Total physical therapy contracts	632	738	799	26.4

Source: Alex Brown, Inc., reports.

TABLE 4
NovaCare Financial Performance History, 1988–1991
(in thousands, except earnings per share)

	1991	1990	1989	1988
Net revenues	$151,532	$102,110	$69,975	$56,612
Gross profit	56,403	39,478	25,586	11,505
Gross profit margin	37%	39%	37%	36.5%
Operating profit	29,875	19,534	8,999	3,162
Operating profit margin	20%	19%	13%	5.6%
Loss on marketable securities	—	—	—	(2,468)
Net income (loss)	20,315	12,382	5,107	(1,045)
Net income per share	0.64	0.43	0.19	(0.04)
Working capital	66,721	41,680	33,294	31,515
Total assets	127,489	87,912	73,609	72,386
Total indebtedness	1,037	14,075	15,908	18,915
Total liabilities	13,975	25,107	23,831	27,781
Stockholders' equity	113,514	62,805	49,778	44,605
Return on average equity	23.0%	22.2%	10.9%	(2.4%)
Annual average FTEs	1,929	1,375	na	na
Revenues per FTE	79	74	na	na
Annual average therapist turnover rate	27.0%	32.0%	39.0%	na

Source: Rehabilitation Today, November–December 1991, and company reports.

	PHYSICAL			TOTALS		
1988	1993E	CGR		1988	1993E	CGR
$300	$420	7%		$800	$1,335	11%
1,000	1,470	8		1,600	2,350	8
550	900	10		1,100	1,770	10
$1,850	$2,790	9		$3,500	$5,455	9

TABLE 5
NovaCare Stock Market
Performance, 1989–1992E

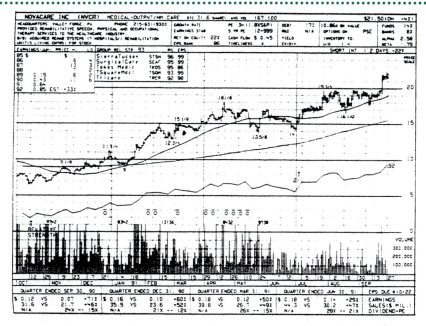

SHARE PRICE DATA

	1988	1989	1990	1991
High	7⅞	8¼	11⅟₁₆	29⅛
Low	1¹⁵⁄₁₆	2⅞₁₆	6½	12¼

EARNINGS PER SHARE

	1989		1990		1991		1992E	
		Y/Y		Y/Y		Y/Y		Y/Y
	Amount	% Change	Amount	% Change	Amount	% Change	Amount	% Change
1Q	$0.04	NM	$0.08	100.0%	$0.14	75.0%	$0.19	35.7%
2Q	0.04	NM	0.09	125.0	0.15	66.7	0.21	40.0
3Q	0.05	NM	0.12	140.0	0.17	41.7	0.23	33.1
4Q	0.07	NM	0.14	100.0	0.18	28.6	0.24	33.3
FY	$0.20	NM	$0.43	115.0	$0.64	48.8	$0.87	35.9

SOURCES OF PROFIT

	1991	1992
Therapy services	91%	87%
Rehabilitation centers	—	11
Interest income	9	2
Total	100%	100%

ANNUAL FINANCIAL DATA (IN MILLIONS OF DOLLARS)

	1989	1990	1991	1992E
Total revenues	$70.0	$102.0	$151.5	$281.8
Cash flow	6.0	13.3	21.2	34.5
Pretax margin	11.2%	18.6%	20.2%	17.0%
Return on average equity	12.8%	22.0%	23.0%	NE
Return on average assets	7.0%	15.3%	19.0%	NE

NE—No estimate. NM—Not meaningful. Y/Y—Year to year.
Source: Alex Brown & Sons, October 2, 1991.

An industry report on the rehabilitation market-place read:

> We expect the medical rehabilitation market, which had annual revenues of about $11 billion in 1990, to grow at an annual rate of 15–20% through the 1990s.
>
> Operating margins for well-managed, mature operations exceed 20%. We expect to see growth in this market for the following reasons:
>
> ▼ The number of people who experience activity limitations is increasing, as is the age and size of the population.
>
> ▼ The availability of rehabilitation is growing, as are consumers' and third-party payors' awareness of its benefits.
>
> ▼ Technological advances are expanding the pool of patients who can benefit from rehabilitation.
>
> ▼ The current focus on physical fitness, independence, and quality of life is expected to continue.
>
> ▼ The rehabilitation setting is cost effective relative to services in the acute care setting. Increasingly, insurers using a managed care approach are recognizing the economic benefits of rehabilitation. Studies have shown that for every dollar spent on rehab, anywhere from $11 to $38 is saved.[1]

Under the Medicare program, reimbursement for therapy services was cost based in all but the inpatient, acute care hospital setting. Coverage of rehabilitation therapies by Medicare had been expanded to include outpatient care for occupational therapy in 1987 and swallowing disorders in 1989. Regulators and third-party payors viewed rehabilitation services favorably because of the cost effectiveness of these services relative to acute care facilities. The principal settings for rehabilitation therapies were acute care hospitals, dedicated rehab hospitals, comprehensive outpatient rehab facilities, nursing homes, schools, outpatient clinics, psychiatric hospitals, and the patient's home. Among these providers, small (fewer than 350 bed) institutions frequently contracted with third-party suppliers to manage their rehabilitation requirements. The estimated contract therapy market is shown in Table 2.

According to industry data, in 1988 more than 71% of nursing homes outsourced their occupational therapy as did over 90% of those providing speech-language pathologies therapy. The same data indicated that rehab services compromised less than 1% of nursing home expenses. A greater number of homes provided physical therapy services, but 67% contracted for these as well. The Omnibus Budget Reconciliation Act of 1987 mandated that as of October 1, 1990, all nursing homes must be able to provide all three rehabilitation therapies. However, cost and other factors made this difficult to do internally. According to a professional association survey, only 14,400 of the 129,000 therapists certified in 1989 worked in a long-term care setting. There was a ratio of less than one speech-language pathologist for every ten facilities and one occupational therapist for every eight facilities. NovaCare's ratios were one speech-language pathologist for every three facilities it served and one occupational therapist for every two facilities. The changing mix of its services is shown in Table 3.

NovaCare's competition was made up of some regional companies, sole proprietors, and small-group practices within communities. The largest regional firms were approximately one-third to one-half NovaCare's size. Many of NovaCare's nursing home customers were national companies. In addition to an aggressive acquisition strategy, NovaCare focused its sales strategy on increasing the density of customers in existing markets to reduce the impact of travel on employee morale and productivity. By integrating its therapy programs, the company had realized significant growth through bringing to the attention of the caregiving institution the other therapies that NovaCare offered. As Table 4 indicates, NovaCare's growth had been extremely rapid and its stock market performance spectacular (see Table 5).

NOVANET: AN INFORMATION STRATEGY

In its 1990 IOK Report, the company described its new NovaNet initiative:

> The company has implemented, on a pilot basis, a laptop computer network enabling each clinician to record and transmit billing, payroll, productivity, and clinical documentation information daily. This innovation is designed to (1) eliminate much of the clinician's administrative burden, increasing time available for patient care; (2) reduce selling, general and administration expenses associated with information gathering and data processing; (3) accelerate the billing cycle thereby reducing days sales outstanding in receivables; and (4) improve the company's ability to capture and correlate clinical data in support of quality assurance standards. Management believes that this proprietary system will further distinguish the company as the employer of choice for therapists.

NovaNet was projected to be a $7–10 million information systems investment, the largest investment in systems NovaCare had ever made. The system would allow each clinician to report results daily. John Foster stated, "We believe NovaNet will have significant short-term, positive implications for clinician productivity. Over the long term, as we learn from the data that we collect, it will have a substantial impact on total productivity."

The NovaNet system had two components—an administrative and a clinical component. The administrative component was intended to eliminate duplicate forms, redundant or erroneous data entry, and administrative paperwork. Quality of documentation was important to NovaCare's customers to satisfy state and federal health care standards and to both NovaCare and the customer for reimbursement. Another objective was to free up time for clinicians so they could have more time to spend with patients. The system was intended to replace existing manual systems and telephone call reporting. Part of the design philosophy was to automate the front end of the manual process—the collection of data from the clinicians—without altering back-end processing systems. The latter included the billing system—which was provided by Shared Medical Systems—and a number of in-house management systems.

NovaNet was seen as providing several initial advantages. It provided accurate documentation for reports and billings, and it eased the administrative burdens of clinicians. Further, NovaNet would give clinicians a communication vehicle they currently did not have, allowing them to communicate electronically with their supervisors or other clinicians. One feature under consideration that excited many clinicians was potential use of the technology in the treatment of their patients. NovaCare management had initially targeted a 3% gain in productivity, that is, clinicians billing 103 units per week rather than 100 standard units. But much greater potentials were available. On average, clinicians spent 35% of their time in activities unrelated to direct patient care, that is, documentation, meetings, and traveling. Management also expected to be able to extend district managers' "spans of communication" beyond the current average of 15 clinicians, yet provide more time to improve the quality of relations with therapists and customer institutions.

NovaNet had been designed by a multifunctional team, including a project committee made up of the company's controller, vice president of MIS, vice president of professional services, and vice president of operations. Under this committee's supervision, a small design team had defined the parameters of the system and laid out its major design objectives. The team was made up of clinicians and staff people. The project's review and cost-benefit analysis had calculated a 1.7-year direct payback for the initial investment and a 33% return over a 5-year period. But various executives saw other less measurable quality, morale, flexibility, information exchange. and strategic applications as providing even greater long-term benefits. The question was how to implement the system best to achieve these longer-term potentials at the same time as NovaNet achieved desired short-term payback goals.

NovaCare only had a small systems group and made extensive use of outside service bureaus. It also had a strategy to outsource as much of the programming work as would be compatible with its goals. Given the breadth and scope of NovaNet, the company contracted with CompuServe to develop and deliver the system. CompuServe proposed to write the PC software, provide the telecommunications network, and staff an "800 number support desk" for questions. NovaCare's Board gave approval for the project, and system design began in January 1990.

IMPLEMENTATION AND QUESTIONS

Prior to the implementation of the NovaNet pilot, a time study had looked at how clinicians spent their time. This data was compared with similar data from groups participating in the NovaNet pilot after a period of use. It was found that productivity had not increased. Pat Larkins, Vice President of Professional Services, commented, "Our clinicians had to get used to the technology. I don't think you could get the desired increase in productivity by just teaching them how to input information, as opposed to also showing them how to use the information as a means of changing their established behaviors." Nevertheless, with the initial results at the clinician level less than promising, management began to look to other areas of productivity improvement to pay for the system in the short run, while it developed longer-term strategic uses.

Meanwhile, various government agencies were increasing their demands for information from all health care providers. The Health Care Finance Administration (HCFA), which managed the Medicare program, was attempting to define standards for basic data formats and electronic data submissions. The government and insurers had a vital interest in how effective their expenditures were in delivering better health care to patients. The Medicare program in particular was moving to a more outcomes-oriented approach in how it reimbursed for patient care. John Foster noted:

> As the largest service provider in our field, we should have some economies of scale in the collection and use of data that are not available to anyone else. In fact, if we devel-

op the system right, it might provide the ultimate barrier to entry for other competitors. Along with our other strategic initiatives to penetrate existing markets further and to acquire entry into new markets, NovaNet could be among our most important strategic investments.

Dr. Arnold Renschier said,

One of the issues being debated internally right now is: "Do we go ahead and roll out a successful administrative function (which is already available) before we have a successful clinical component for NovaNet?" Once we resolve that question, the administrative piece could be rolled out almost immediately. The big opportunity, though, in terms of improved productivity, consistency of treatment, and the potential to measure outcomes derives from the clinical piece. . . . If only the administrative piece is rolled out, the clinician will not feel the same degree of affirmation that they would experience if the clinical piece were working.

Yet if NovaCare did not go ahead, there could be significant public and employee relations problems for NovaCare. Internally, many clinicians had knowledge of the pilot and were eager to obtain the help it offered. Externally, NovaCare had announced its plans for NovaNet, and therefore many investment houses, customers, and shareholders might have anticipated benefits from the system.

NovaCare had to proceed cautiously. It operated within a highly regulated environment: 80–90% of its billings were dependent on Medicare reimbursement. Said Tim Foster, "The biggest strategic threat in any health care business is the regulatory environment and the questions of reimbursement from the public or private sector." Regulations or interpretations of existing laws could quickly change to stimulate, redirect, or curtail specific therapies or their reimbursement. Intermediaries also constantly used their ability to interpret or change reimbursement. These and the constant flow of new rehabilitation needs and therapeutic techniques were a continuing challenge.

Other threats included competition for rehabilitation patients from nursing homes themselves. Many nursing homes were trying to move out of the "hotel and beds" portion of the business and into higher-margin activities. Growing nursing homes might obtain a sufficient number of patients to justify employment of internal therapists. If consolidation occurred around these centers, NovaCare could be left primarily with the smaller facilities, with fewer patients, and highly dispersed from a travel standpoint. In addition, if the government undertook a massive program for training

therapists, the labor situation could change from a shortage to a surplus condition, seriously affecting NovaCare's margins. It was in this context that NovaCare's top management had to consider how best to position the total company, its organization, its controls and incentives, and its NovaNet information system for maximum future effectiveness. (See Exhibit 1 for brief profiles of NovaCare's competitors.)

Referring to the company's purposes and beliefs, John Foster noted,

As we make these decisions and we look around at successful leadership companies, we observe that those companies with the highest integrity also have the highest returns on capital and the highest profit margins on sales. Therefore, we are satisfied that if we are prepared to do whatever we do right, the yield should be outstanding financial performance. Quality, productivity, and integrity are the things that serve our shareholders best in the long run.

QUESTIONS

1. What is the basis for NovaCare's current competitive edge? How can it develop a permanent competitive edge against its many potential future rivals?
2. What should be the future directions of NovaCare's growth? What new fields should it enter? Why? In what sequence? What are the important timing parameters? What are the limiting factors on growth? How should these be handled?
3. What will be the effects of growth on NovaCare's organization structure? Management style? What are the critical factors for organizational success from NovaCare's viewpoint? The clinician's viewpoint? Clients' viewpoint? Patients' viewpoint? How should NovaCare deal with conflicts among these?
4. How should NovaCare position NovaNet for maximum future impact? Should it go ahead with the proposed rollout? What priorities in functions should NovaNet seek to achieve? How can NovaNet most contribute to the development of NovaCare's distinctive maintainable competitive edge? What will be the important questions to deal with in implementation of NovaNet? How can NovaNet be leveraged into other opportunities for NovaCare?

EXHIBIT 1
Competitor Situation:
Brief Profiles

In October–November 1991, *Rehab Management* ran an article profiling the rehab industry's largest providers. The following is summarized from that source.

Baxter Health Care Corp's Physical Therapy Division was purchased by $8 billion Baxter in 1984. Its history was in sports medicine. Baxter established the division as an entrepreneurial company within the parent. In 1991, the division had started a growth campaign to add as many as 150 centers in five years. Its stated intention was to focus on the outpatient market. The division handled roughly 100,000 patient visits a year and was establishing data bases on treatment, outcomes, and quality control.

MedRehab, Inc. had three primary business lines: contractual services in long-term care settings (350 nursing home sites); its own operation in 39 outpatient clinics; and 51 hospitals where it provided physical, occupational, speech, and respiratory therapy services. Founded in May 1987 as a start-up company, MedRehab had acquired a number of existing regional rehab companies. MedRehab saw the switch from inpatient to outpatient professionals at work and claimed to be maintaining a retention rate of better than 80% on an annualized basis. It had affiliations throughout the country with 75 universities which trained physical, occupational, and speech therapists.

HealthSouth Rehabilitation Corp. was an entrepreneurial company formed in 1984 and taken public in 1986. It had attempted to build outpatient rehab centers and hospitals that would be more cost effective than keeping patients in higher cost settings. It had built 40 facilities in its first five years and had continuing growth plans in similar directions. With 3,000 counties in the United States and only 175 comprehensive rehab facilities, HealthSouth saw no barriers to its development. Using careful financial controls, it had maintained a strong balance sheet and was able to move rapidly and price competitively.

Rehab Hospital Services Corp. was founded in 1979 and purchased by National Medical Enterprises in 1985. Since then, it had grown from six facilities to 33 facilities, 18 managed units, and two transitional living centers. It had one rehab outpatient facility of its own and was currently building three more. Its plans stated that it would seek to build five to ten freestanding hospital facilities per year. In 1991, it claimed to be the largest rehabilitation company in the country. It was aggressively managed and would consider all forms of expansion, both internal and through acquisitions. In public statements, it emphasized its "one to two referral marketing" program to generate new business. In each of its areas, it tried to develop "focused administrators," willing to take risks and aggressively pursue opportunities. It claimed its distinctive advantage was its human resources capability.

Continental Medical Systems was founded in 1986. It had a presence in 36 states, with 22 operating rehab hospitals in 11 states, 57 outpatient centers in 18 states, and four contract therapy companies which had a presence in 30 states. With over 7,500 employees, it had opened eight new hospitals in 1991 and was planning another eight in 1992. Its target was to be a billion-dollar company in the mid-1990s. It had purchased three of its 22 operating hospitals and all four of its contract service companies.

Healthfocus, Inc. was started in 1963 as a partnership. It was purchased by Hyatt in 1971 and then acquired by American Medical International (AMI) in 1980. It had started a rehab division in 1985 which officers and employees later purchased in a leverage buyout. Healthfocus had 55 freestanding clinics in 13 states and contracts with 85 hospitals in 31 states. In 1991 it was looking at work-health programs to augment its rehab and hospital activities.

There were also a number of other smaller regional players with specialized services, facilities, or capabilities. However, acquisition prices were increasing rapidly because of the success of these "Big 7" players and NovaCare.

Ralph Sarich, Chairman and Chief Executive of the Orbital Engine Company (OEC), smiled and said, "Now that you have seen the engine and the research labs, what do you think of our future?" The case writers were impressed and said so, and not only out of politeness. The research facilities and machine shops extended over three large buildings and enabled the company to do advanced research and testing in almost all aspects of combustion and related activities for internal combustion engines. "Yes, we are able to deliver an engine which is able to meet the most stringent emission standards in the world as well as having superior fuel efficiency. All of this comes from having the best team of automotive engineers you would find anywhere."

Sarich was 32 years old in 1970 when he decided to quit his job selling earthmoving equipment and introduce a new internal combustion engine into the automotive industry. The sheer audacity of the scheme did not deter him. Each year General Motors alone is offered 30,000 new inventions, and after preliminary sortings, it fully investigates only 2 or 3 of them. The chances of commercial success—even for an inventor with brilliant new technology—is extremely low. For an unknown engineer living in Perth, Western Australia, the chance of success bordered on zero.

In late 1972, Sarich gained national recognition in Australia when his revolutionary orbital engine won a special award on the Australian Broadcasting Commission's television program "The Inventors."

Case Copyright © by André Morkel, University of Western Australia, Perth, Australia. Reproduced by special permission. André Morkel and Kelvin Willoughby prepared the case in consultation with Orbital Engine Corporation. The support of the National Industry Extension Service (NIES) and the Technology and Industry Development Authority of Western Australia (TIDA) is gratefully acknowledged.

Superficially similar to a rotary engine, it involved a planetary motion rather than rotation as its key geometry.

Rotary engines had advantages of less vibration and reduced size over conventional reciprocating engines. However, they also suffered serious problems of sealing in the combustion chambers, resulting in gas leaks, loss of power, and emission pollution problems. The orbital engine had the potential of overcoming the sealing problems of rotary engines while retaining their advantages. It was hailed by experts as a major breakthrough in the automotive engine industry, and it attracted Australia's largest industrial company, The Broken Hill Proprietary Ltd. (BHP), as investor and major backer of the project.

THE ORBITAL TECHNOLOGIES

Sarich was developing his radical engine as early as 1969. Conceptually, it was quite complex and the result of his extraordinary talent for visualizing an end product. Working in proverbial "backyard inventor" conditions, he built and assembled a working prototype of the engine. There were several problems with the design, and soon afterward he and a small team of workers built a second and improved version of the orbital engine.

The second prototype created a flurry of publicity, including being featured on national television, and much attention from potential investors. This eventually led to participation by BHP in the project.

Sarich assembled a strong technical team and created a productive automotive research laboratory in Balcatta, a suburb of Perth. An orbital engine was successfully road tested in a Ford Cortina in 1974, with promising results. By 1982 a production version of the new engine, logging over 450 hours of performance trials, proved superior to equivalent piston engines of the day in fuel economy, emission levels, size, and weight.

Advantages over conventional engines included smaller size, fewer moving parts, less wear, reduced weight, and lower manufacturing cost. Despite its engine's demonstrated advantages, the company also faced a major problem. Although simpler in concept, mass production of the engine would require retooling of present manufacturing plants, which in turn would require huge capital expenditures, big market risks, and a complete reorientation of the giant and conservative automobile industry.

The Orbital Engine Company continued a program of research aimed at improving the engine's combustion efficiency. Along the way Sarich and his team invented a highly efficient, yet low-cost fuel injection system. Traditional fuel injectors spray fuel into cylinders under high pressure at the compression stage of the engine cycle. The new fuel injector worked at lower pressures and used air to propel the fuel into a fine mist with extremely small droplet size. Most of the droplets are below 6 microns in size compared to the 30- to 50-micron droplets of a diesel truck engine. This enabled dramatically improved fuel combustion with the potential for improved fuel efficiency and lower emission levels of unburned gases. The development became the basis of a completely new direction for the company.

The most successful application of the new fuel injection technology was in a 2-stroke engine with direct cylinder injection. The 2-stroke engine allowed the placement of the fuel injection system anywhere in the chamber of the cylinder. Considerable development work followed which led to a unique combustion system, the Orbital Combustion Process (OCP). The resulting 2-stroke, 3-cylinder (1.2-liter) OCP engine outperformed a conventional 4-stroke, 4-cylinder (1.6-liter) engine in all areas.

A 2-stroke engine can deliver the same power for less than half the size and weight of a comparable 4-stroke engine, because it fires at every second rather than every fourth piston stroke. In the past 2-stroke engines had major problems with fuel efficiency and polluting emissions. The Orbital Combustion Process was able to overcome these obstacles. The OCP engine also had about 200 fewer parts compared to the conventional 4-stroke engine and significantly lower manufacturing costs. The reduction in number of parts stems largely from eliminating inlet and outlet valves and associated assemblies such as the cam shaft and rocker arms.

Figure 1 shows a diagram of the OCP engine and its patents, while Table 1 shows a comparison with a

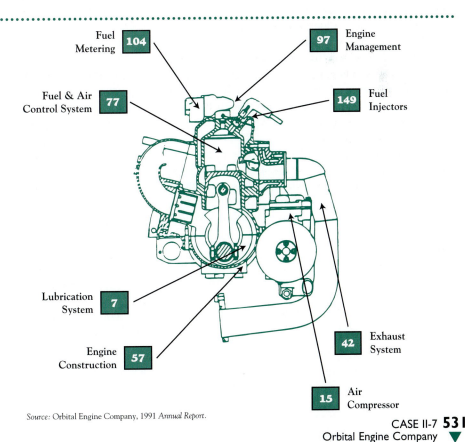

FIGURE 1
OCP Engine Design and Patents or Patent Applications

Fuel Metering **104**

Engine Management **97**

Fuel & Air Control System **77**

Fuel Injectors **149**

Lubrication System **7**

Engine Construction **57**

Exhaust System **42**

Air Compressor **15**

Source: Orbital Engine Company, 1991 Annual Report.

TABLE 1
Comparisons Between an
OCP and a Conventional
Engine

	OCP ENGINE	CONVENTIONAL ENGINE
Stroke	2 stroke	4 stroke
Displacement volume	1.2 liter	1.6 liter
Number of cylinders	3	4
Weight	53 kg	123 kg
Maximum torque	140 nm	125 nm
Maximum power	63 kw (84 HP)	64 kw (86 HP)

Source: Orbital Engine Company.

conventional engine. The OCP technology had been developed considerably beyond a few inventions and new ideas, into a sophisticated system of engine design, fuel metering and delivery, fuel-air mixing, cylinder gas flow dynamics, ignition technology, lubrication metering and delivery, gas scavenging, and emission controls.

The reduced packaging volume and weight of the OCP engine allowed car companies to explore designs for increased passenger space, additional safety features, and improved aerodynamic characteristics.

Late in 1983, the company decided to concentrate solely on the OCP engine and shelve the planetary orbital engine, at least for the time being.

The company continued to invest heavily in research and development and consistently improved the performance characteristics of its engines. By 1991, without the use of catalytic exhaust systems, OCP engines were able to meet the most stringent fuel consumption and gas emission standards, which the U.S. government through the Environmental Protection Agency (EPA) was proposing to introduce by the mid-1990s. The state of California had proposed even more demanding standards for an ultra low emissions vehicle

(ULEV), which were the most stringent emission requirements proposed anywhere in the world. The OCP engine was already able to meet these demanding standards as shown in Table 2. The U.S. government had also announced increased fuel economy levels, from the current (1991) levels of 27.5 miles per U.S. gallon to 40 miles per U.S. gallon by the year 2000, but U.S. manufacturers were resisting these strongly.

In October 1991, Orbital Engine arranged to have a Honda CRX HF fitted with the OCP engine and tested by the U.S. National Research Council Committee on Fuel Consumption, which had been retained by the U.S. Department of Transportation to determine what emission and performance levels were technologically achievable. The project vehicle, fitted with an OCP engine, exceeded 69 miles per U.S. gallon highway (83 miles per imperial gallon) and 62 miles per U.S. gallon metro (74 miles per imperial gallon). The car had a 4-second advantage in 0-60-mph acceleration time over the 4-stroke Honda. The company claimed that when the engine weight advantage and the acceleration advantage were properly accounted for, the fuel consumption advantage of the OCP engine over Honda's was around 20%.

TABLE 2
Exhaust Emission
Standards
(in grams per mile)

	US. 1994 CLEAN AIR ACT	1991 OCP PRODUCTION ENGINE AT 50,000 MILES	CALIFORNIA ULEV LIMITS BY END OF THE 1990s	OCP ULEV VEHICLE AT 2,000 MILES
Nonmethane hydrocarbons	0.25	0.21	0.04	0.03
Oxides of nitrogen	0.40	0.34	0.20	0.15
Carbon monoxide	3.40	1.17	1.70	0.15

Source: Orbital Engine Corporation, *Half Yearly Report to December 31, 1991.*

In March 1992, the company announced additional research programs of A$10 million to pursue goals of near-zero emissions, a further 5–10% fuel economy, and emissions durability. According to OEC Executive Director Kim Schlunke, "We've found that we are able to get tailpipe carbon monoxide and hydrocarbon levels below ambient levels in parts of California. In other words, we are cleaning up the environment," he said with a smile. Schlunke also revealed that the power output of the 1.2-liter engine had been boosted to 107 horsepower.

During August 1989, OEC announced a decision to establish a A$330 million manufacturing plant for the OCP engine at Tecumseh, about 50 kilometers southeast of Detroit. Initial capacity for 1993 was 100,000 engines a year, with a 250,000-per-year expansion planned soon after. The location decision was bolstered by an offer of an estimated A$80 million in incentives by the state of Michigan.

VALUE ADDING ACTIVITIES

The company had developed a range of new technological improvements and breakthroughs which were being exploited as opportunities in their own right. In some cases they were being developed in conjunction with established suppliers in their respective fields.

Motorola had entered into a joint development agreement with OEC to develop a production version of the electronic control unit for use on the OCP engine. This had resulted in a sophisticated and cost-effective design incorporating several innovative features such as engine-mounted ignition drivers, compact single-sided circuit boards, and highly efficient injector driver circuits. OEC and Motorola were investigating the use of these technologies for broader automotive applications.

The company was collaborating with Johnson-Matthey PLC, a major producer of catalysts, to produce a robust and cost-effective catalytic system for use on the OCP engine. The catalyst would be able to function adequately without the use of expensive rhodium and would use only modest amounts of platinum and other related metals compared to existing systems.

A range of fuel injection systems were being manufactured in the OEC subsidiary Orbital-Walbro Corporation of the United States and were already used on the numerous test engines produced by Orbital Engine, and after 1992 would be on production engines. Two-stroke engines were in wide use in smaller engines, where manufacturers were also testing the use of other fuels such as diesel fuel and methanol. Leading uses were outboard engines, lawn mowers, small generators, and lawn and gardening tools. Leading producers were Honda and Briggs and Stratton. Most 2-stroke engines were notorious for their pollution. The Japanese were developing much cleaner 4-stroke engines for these markets.

PROTECTING INTELLECTUAL PROPERTY

In addition to its core patents, the company also registered a range of related patents forming several layers of shielding patents around the core technology. This system, plus active monitoring, also served as an early warning system, alerting the company to would-be imitators and rivals seeking ways to bypass the OCP engine system. By June 30, 1991 the company had 548 patents and patent applications registered in 23 countries around the world, as shown in Table 3 and also in Figure 1.

Security on OEC technology was maintained both through patents and through routine in-house security. The annual cost to OEC of maintaining its patents and employing necessary legal counsel averaged about A$300,000 and had peaked at A$1 million.

NEGOTIATIONS AND RELATIONSHIPS WITH OTHER FIRMS

An important aspect of commercializing the technology had been the challenge of negotiating with the established, giant corporations in the engine and vehicle industries. Sarich's early experiences provided him with good schooling for dealing with large companies and a keen appreciation of the art of negotiating. After two years of negotiations with possible Australian manufacturers for his orbital engine, Sarich decided to concentrate on the real decision makers in the automotive industry. At that stage at least, the major players were in Detroit.

In addition to dealing with the carmakers, Sarich had to retain the backing of BHP, maintain the stock market's confidence in OEC, assuage government personnel and agencies, continually improve the Orbital technology in competition with improved conventional technology, nurture a high-class research and development team, deal with sometimes acrimonious criticisms and rumors circulated through the news media and elsewhere, and instill and maintain confidence from the big firms in his venture. OEC faced a familiar Australian problem, lack of credibility in the interna-

TABLE 3
Patent and Patent Applications for the OCP Engine

	NUMBER OF PATENT AND PATENT APPLICATIONS
Fuel metering	104
Fuel and air control systems	77
Lubrication systems	7
Engine construction	57
Engine management	97
Fuel injectors	149
Exhaust systems	42
Air compressor	15
Total OCP patents	548

Source: Orbital Engine Company, *1991 Annual Report.*

tional marketplace. Sarich had to take extra steps in demonstrating high performance to legitimize his invention. To satisfy demands imposed by General Motors (GM) and Ford, the company installed expensive testing facilities. Although the initial financial outlay was a burden, OEC's testing facilities proved critical to establishing OEC as a serious source of technology.

Before his international moves, Sarich had learned from early negotiations within Australia which promised much but did not deliver. These included hastily signed agreements with firms like James Kirby Products and Victa-Sunbeam to develop and manufacture his earlier inventions. All three firms spent much time researching and developing the technology further, duplicating much of his research, and departing too far from the original ideas. In the end, these efforts were not successful. Initially, Sarich approached specialized departments (e.g., research and development) within the large corporations but also with little success. Then Sarich, as chief negotiator for OEC, developed sophisticated methods for dealing with the giants of the automotive industry, leaving little to chance. The intentions of the EPA to lower acceptable emission levels in all areas worked in OEC's favor. However, there were limits to the extent OEC could be seen to lobby the U.S. government, and Sarich had to take into account the influence of the motor car companies in Washington and OEC's position as a foreign company.

OEC had to develop a pricing policy for its intellectual property at an early stage. Sarich calculated that the OCP engine would be about A\$200 to A\$300 cheaper to manufacture than conventional engines. Redesign of the car because of a lighter and smaller engine could save a further A\$200. He felt he needed to license his technology for between A\$30 to A\$40 per engine built. This, however, was more than 10 times as much as any royalty paid before in the industry and was considered outrageous by the carmakers. Consequently, Sarich developed a range of license options to allow companies to evaluate the technology before entering into final license agreements. Sarich was well aware that part of the evaluation process would be to do reverse R&D and to seek to circumvent his patents, that there would typically be a period of some years between a license option and a license agreement, and that there would be long delays before production.

DECISION POINT

What strategy should Mr. Sarich adopt relative to the large United States and European auto producers?

GM ultimately entered into a license agreement in June 1989 giving GM nonexclusive international rights to manufacture OCP engines. GM proceeded to conduct all test engine production and trials inhouse, remaining somewhat secretive about its intentions on manufacturing. At the Detroit Motor Show in January 1992, GM displayed, as the centerpiece of its exhibition, a fuel economy concept vehicle called the "Ultralite" fitted with a V6 OCP-type engine. The 635-kilogram four-seater Ultralite was capable of 2.4 liters/100 kilometer (100 miles/U.S. gallon) with an acceleration from 0–100 kilometers/hour (0–60 mph) in 7.8 seconds.

Ford converted an option for a license into a full license to manufacture OCP engines in June 1988. At the international motor show in Barcelona in May 1991, Ford displayed a futuristic compact, the Ghia Zag, powered by a 1.2-liter OCP engine. In contrast to GM, Ford adopted a more open approach to dealing with OEC, expressing a desire to buy early engines from OEC rather than produce them all inhouse. In March 1992, OEC shipped 25 OCP engines to Ford in Europe for fleet testing in Ford Fiesta cars in Germany, Sweden, and the United Kingdom. A further 35 engines would be sourced from OEC's Tecumseh plant, resulting in a total of 60 vehicles being exhaustively road tested by Ford. Bill Fike, President of Ford Europe, said that his company hoped to start low-volume production of 2-stroke engines in England in 1993.

Fiat Auto of Italy was the third major carmaker to sign a full license agreement in January 1991, and a year later in April 1992, a fourth large auto company was signed up. Confidentiality clauses prevented OEC from disclosing the identity of its latest client. The company also indicated that negotiations with yet another carmaker were at an advanced stage.

The big prize—volume production of the engine by the automotive manufacturers—still had not been won by early 1992. Ken Johnsen, Managing Director of OEC's U.S. operations at Tecumseh, Michigan, stated that the company had the capacity to proceed with manufacturing in its own right but that its preferred option was to generate income from royalty payments by the big carmakers.

WORK FORCE

Over the two decades following the first successful firing of the orbital engine, OEC had increased its number of full-time employees more than sevenfold. Ralph Sarich was very aware of the potential problems associated with rapid growth and of losing personal touch with employees. He attempted to minimize these by carefully selecting people to suit his organization, its purposes, and ways of operating. He provided employees with an opportunity to invest in OEC, encouraged employee participation in how the company operated, and kept in touch with enough key people to get a "feel" for issues at OEC.

His approach resulted in a loyal and committed work force. He recruited bright and talented young engineers fresh out of university, who were given considerable responsibility at an early stage while working together with more experienced personnel. But the company had some unique challenges. Sarich wanted his engineers to take on the large auto corporations of the world, but the experience and mind-set of most local firms were not conducive to the attitudes he wanted at Orbital Engine Company. Many Australian companies served undemanding local markets and were not internationally competitive. At the other end of the spectrum were many hi-tech start-up firms in Perth which exhibited plenty of bravado but lacked the professionalism and discipline to tackle large, world-class corporations.

Sarich preferred to home-grow the culture of his company. Employees were encouraged to contribute ideas and not be locked into the traditions of the automotive industry. There soon was active competition among graduate engineers to work at OEC, and the company was able to select top-quality employees. Sarich broke down barriers between academically trained engineers and technicians and between management and technical staff. An engineer could move between advanced development work and being part of a team to negotiate an intellectual property agreement and back again to development with ease. Sarich tried to make the atmosphere both supportive and demanding.

Ralph Sarich's personal influence was strong in the company, reinforced by his personal involvement with the development of key technologies, his skill in negotiating license agreements, and his unwavering faith in the ultimate success of OEC. His style of open and active discussion of problems, of listening and involving his development team, of listening to both trained and untrained staff, and of high professional demands made a strong impact on the work force. A visitor was struck by the respectful familiarity with which employees in the company referred to Ralph's views and leadership. This included attitudes which some may view as unusual, but which made sense within the company. For example, taking any form of alcohol during lunch or working hours was grounds for instant dismissal. Any rule the company had for its shop floor machinists applied right through the company, including Sarich. All the company's organization policies focused on obtaining flexibility, commitment, and absolute honesty from its people.

FINANCE

Getting enough money to finance his dream of being a successful inventor in the automotive field had been a major challenge for Sarich during the early start-up phase. He and his wife sold their newly acquired house to finance the venture. In the early stages, when the first prototype of the OCP engine was under development in his backyard workshop, Sarich did subcontracting work to earn further income, and he also ran a small business selling bolts, produced on a specialized lathe which he designed for this purpose.

The pioneering work on the orbital engine leading to the unsuccessful firing of the second prototype in 1972 had cost about A\$60,000. This was financed primarily by Sarich, although the government of Western Australia also assisted. This combined capital helped promote the orbital engine project to the stage where a prototype was presented on the earlier-mentioned television program "The Inventors." Dr. R. G. Ward (General Manager, Planning and Research) and Dr. H. W. Hosking (Executive Officer, Research) of BHP became intrigued by the invention. Under the joint venture, formed soon afterward, BHP agreed to provide capital for the development of the orbital engine, while Sarich was to supply technology and have autonomy in operating OEC. BHP also agreed to provide further capital (up to A\$50 million) for production if the new engine became viable.

The agreement was subject to ongoing evaluation, however, with OEC executives required to demonstrate the continuing viability of the project through letters of intent or commitment from interested firms. The continued financing of OEC was, therefore, dependent upon the capacity of Sarich and his colleagues to negotiate genuine commercial contracts. OEC claimed that it had the finest automotive testing equipment and facilities in Australia, having invested over A\$30 million in these assets. From the time of its founding up to June 1989 OEC had spent A\$55 million on its product development and operations (including the testing equipment and facilities). BHP's financing was crucial, particularly during the early years. Later, a public offering and further placements provided fully paid share capital of A\$143 million (in 1991).

Apart from these funds, the company was aided by financial contributions from both federal and state governments under a variety of programs and schemes, with a loan from the Western Australia government of A\$15 million outstanding in 1991. OEC also entered into protracted discussions with government officials regarding the establishment of a production facility for OCP engines. According to the company, it would cost about A\$30 million more to build a manufacturing plant in Australia than in the United States. However at this stage, the government's attitude toward support for new hi-tech ventures had waned considerably.

Overenthusiasm and some outright fraud in the government's 1980s programs had destroyed much of its earlier confidence. The delays in commercializing the OCP technology further undermined official enthusiasm for the project. In September 1988 the federal government offered OEC A\$15.2 million as a grant to start manufacturing the engine in Australia. Considerable negotiation and tension between disagreeing parties ensued over this issue, which left Sarich feeling bitter about the federal government. After the state of Michigan offered a considerably better package of incentives, the company decided to locate the manufacturing facility in Tecumseh and to raise additional funds for its construction with a stock issue in the United States. At the 1991 annual general meeting, Sarich called the federal government's inaction to his pleas for assistance an act of stupidity and said the government was embarrassed by the success of OEC. The government had also excluded OEC from its Export Facilitation Scheme under which Australian companies earn trade credits if they export. They could then import at a discount. However, it was ruled that only "service activity" was worthy of export credits, and regulations were drafted whereby patents and royalties were excluded. Sarich's view was, "They deliberately excluded us. OEC is the only significant licenser of world automotive industry technology in Australia and will probably have earned more than A\$100 million in export revenue from sales of intellectual property by the end of this financial year." He further warned that ownership of the company would eventually slip into U.S. hands because of the ignorance of the Australian government and the investment public toward technology development. Sarich paid tribute to the efforts of the West Australia state government to support the company and stated that without its support, the company would not have stayed in Perth.

OEC had already earned more than A\$67 million from its license option and license agreements up to 1991. As shown in Exhibit 1, the company earned A\$28.2 million in 1991 from licenses and related services. Share analysts had estimated that royalties from deals signed with Ford, GM, and Bajaj Auto could earn OEC A\$218 million before tax, over the six years to 1995.

When it was listed on the stock exchange in 1984, the balance sheet of OEC showed the company's net assets to be A\$4.2 million (see Exhibit 2). By 1992 the market value of OEC shares had reached more than A\$1 billion even though there were as yet no OCP engines in commercial use at that time. The rise in share price was not smooth, however, with fluctuations fueled by frequent rumors, claims, and counterclaims about the likely success or otherwise impending doom of deals for licensing and manufacturing.

BHP and the Sarich family had on occasion sold parcels of shares to increase the number of shares in active circulation and to harvest a portion of their investment in the company. BHP had about a 29% stake in OEC after selling sufficient shares to recoup its original investment. The Sarich family was reported to have sold more than A$50 million worth of shares while retaining a more than 20% shareholding in the company. A list of the top 20 OEC shareholders is shown in Exhibit 3.

On December 4, 1991 OEC began trading on the New York Stock Exchange, one of only six Australian companies to be listed in the United States. Under the more stringent U.S. listing requirements, the company was forced to wipe A$240 million from its intangible assets in its prospectus, slashing shareholders funds by 80% to A$54 million. At the time of listing, the company issued 23.12 million new ordinary shares to the U.S. market and successfully raised another A$110 million, further strengthening its balance sheet.

INNOVATION IN THE AUTOMOTIVE INDUSTRY

The U.S. automotive industry was very large and highly concentrated. In the late 1970s, the industry had employed over 1.5 million people. U.S. sales averaged over 10 million cars annually, with GM and Ford alone together accounting for over two-thirds of this market. The two firms were consistently among the five largest U.S. industrial companies.

The industry tended to be vertically integrated for the core components of a car, including engine, drive train, and body work, while outsourcing a large variety of original equipment manufacturers' (OEM) components and subassemblies. New entrants into car manufacture had to overcome extremely high entry barriers. More recently Japanese auto manufacturers had made significant inroads into the U.S. market, not only by exporting vehicles from Japan, but also by manufacturing and assembling both vehicles and components in the United States.

During 1988 there were approximately 45 million motor vehicles and about 100 million internal combustion engines built throughout the world. In 1991, there were an estimated 556 million motor cars in operation in the world. This provided a tremendous potential for any company which could successfully introduce cost saving technology across a broad base in the industry. It usually took around 4 to 5 years and hundreds of millions (to billions) of dollars to introduce a new model.

Adoption of radical engine developments had been practically nonexistent in the automotive industry. Since the 1920s, only one other engine type had reached even a modest level of commercialization—the German-invented Wankel rotary engine. The Wankel rotary engine is produced in the RX series Mazda sports cars. Some U.S. companies had experimented with diesel engines during the oil crisis years, but these had been abandoned for noncommercial vehicles.

In late 1991, Honda had introduced its Civic production car in the United States and European markets. This was fitted with Honda's new stratified combustion engine and novel piston head designs, and based on its advanced 4-stroke engine technology. The car displayed a major advance in fuel efficiency over existing cars, delivering 48 miles per U.S. gallon in town and 55 mpg on the highway. The lean-burn engine still faced obstacles. Current catalytic converters could not remove the oxides of nitrogen it emitted, and the engine was restricted to 1.5-liter capacity which inherently emitted less oxides of nitrogen. To meet California standards the air-fuel ratio had to be tuned to a less efficient (by 7%) 15:1 ratio rather than the 22:1 ratio used for maximum fuel efficiency.

Some other 2-stroke engine developers were seen by commentators to represent a potential threat to OEC technology. Chrysler, Toyota, and Fuji Heavy Industries, makers of Subaru cars, had all unveiled 2-stroke engines without acknowledging OCP know-how. Chrysler's engine sought to lower emissions by sucking exhaust gases from the cylinder with an external pump which worked like a turbocharger in reverse. Toyota had adapted existing overhead 4-stroke engines to a 2-stroke mode of operation. This design sacrificed much of the simplicity and compactness of the 2-stroke engine, but Toyota claimed it generated only one-fifth the vibration of conventional 4-stroke engines.

Improvements in battery technology and the pressure for zero emissions had stimulated a renewed interest in electric cars, and several concept cars had been displayed from time to time by carmakers and other inventors. However, costs and efficiencies would have to improve substantially before such cars could be considered seriously. In May 1990, GM exhibited a two-seater electric car, the "Impact." The limited production foreseen for the car would make it about twice as expensive as conventional cars, both to buy and to operate, and its range was limited by the capacity of its lead acid batteries to around 125 miles. Fiat was planning to introduce the Elettra, a US$20,000 version of its US$8,500 Panda economy car, which would get just 45 miles to a charge. Chrysler Corporation's experimental electric van used nickel-iron batteries which were lighter and lasted longer than the normal lead acid batteries. They were also more expensive and had to be constantly replenished with de-ionized water.

The ultimate in environmentally friendly cars, the solar-powered vehicle was as yet still in the novelty category with much publicity given to races for these vehicles in sunny parts of the world such as the interior of Australia. While improved solar cells to charge highly efficient batteries could eventually be developed, they were not serious contenders for the foreseeable future.

ORBITAL ENGINE COMPANY AND THE FUTURE

Though OEC was already successful by most measures, and seemed close to the realization of Sarich's personal vision, critical questions on the future of the Orbital Engine Company began to emerge by the end of the 1980s. What type of company did the directors want OEC to be? A fledgling automobile manufacturer? A producer of intellectual property? A technical consulting group? A specialized auto design company? A multipurpose engineering group? A holding company for advanced technology enterprises? Or was the company so tied to its range of engines that it had no other purpose for existence than their development and application?

In 1988 the directors of Sarich Technologies Trust presented the unit holders with the following ideas: "The success of OEC is due [to] the talents of the technical and management team put together by Ralph Sarich. That part of the OEC team which has been involved in the research and development of the technology to the stage of commercialization has almost finished that task. The Directors believe it is essential the OEC team should be kept together to pursue new opportunities."

The Australian stock market, even in its darkest days following the 1987 crash, had been giving the company a vote of confidence with price/earning ratios of between 40 and 60 times. However, until the first company used OCP technology in volume in its manufacture, the company was still in a development stage.

The ultimate success of the company would depend on its ability to convince the various car manufacturers to use its technology. Some companies had entered into license options and license agreements with OEC specifying that they should not be identified publicly. But Sarich felt it was almost impossible for a manufacturer to bring a modern, clean, two-stroke engine on the market without making use of some OEC technology.

QUESTIONS

1. What strategy should Ralph Sarich have followed in getting big automobile companies to adopt his technology? What should the critical elements of the license arrangements be? In particular how should he approach the U.S. market? (See the Ford: Team Taurus and Honda Motor Company 1994 cases for data about the marketplace.)

2. In 1992 what are the critical issues facing OEC? What positions do you think the company should take? Why? In particular, what should it do in the United States, Europe, Japan? How should it finance its next stage of growth?

3. What kinds of specific organizational policies should it follow? Will these be different in Australia and elsewhere? How can OEC differentiate itself. What should its distinctive competencies be for the future? Draw an organization chart for OEC.

EXHIBIT 1
Orbital Engine Company.
Extracts from Profit and
Loss Accounts,
June 30, 1990–1991
(in thousands of Australian
dollars)

	YEAR TO JUNE 30 1990	YEAR TO JUNE 3 1991
Revenue from trading operations	$26,498	$28,157
Interest income	1,302	2,695
Other income	727	828
Total revenue	$28,527	$31,680
Operating profit	23,485	25,381
Income tax	6,847	6,722
Profit after tax	$16,638	$18,659
Accumulated profit after taxes (beginning of year)	5,853	22,491
Accumulated profit after taxes (end of year)	22,491	41,150

Source: Orbital Engine Company, *1991 Annual Report.*

EXHIBIT 2
Orbital Engine Company.
Balance Sheet Extracts,
as of June 30, 1990–1991
(in thousands of Australian
dollars)

	AS OF JUNE 30, 1990	AS OF JUNE 30, 1991
Cash	$6,380	$32,089
Receivables	16,192	12,699
Inventories	385	879
Other	11	252
Total current assets	$22,968	$45,919
Receivables	7,473	10,856
Investments	1,402	1,402
Property, plant, and equipment	12,734	19,139
Intangibles	258,321	272,567
Other	8,952	12,072
Total non-current assets	$288,882	$316,036
Total assets	**$311,850**	**$361,955**
Creditors and borrowings	$1,422	$6,376
Provisions	917	1,427
Total current liabilties	$2,339	$7,803
Creditors and borrowings	15,000	15,000
Provisions	8,351	14,533
Total non-current liabilities	$23,351	$29,533
Total liabilities	**$25,690**	**$37,336**
Net assets	$286,160	$324,619
Share capital	$136,436	$143,755
Reserves	127,233	139,714
Accumulated profits	22,491	41,150
Total shareholders' equity	**$286,160**	**$324,619**
Shares issued and paid (50c)	272,871,618	287,509,100

Source: Orbital Engine Company, *1991 Annual Report.*

EXHIBIT 3

Orbital Engine Company.
Twenty Largest
Shareholders as of
August 14, 1991

	NUMBER SHARES HELD	% OF ISSUED SHARES
1. The Broken Hill Proprietary Company Ltd.	83,250,000	28.96%
2. Patricia Margaret Sarich	33,474,200	11.64
3. Ralph Tony Sarich	27,350,000	9.51
4. ANZ Nominees Ltd.	15,758,306	5.48
5. Chase AMP Nominees Ltd.	13,963,826	4.86
6. National Nominees Ltd.	12,034,346	4.19
7. Australian Mutual Provident Society	9,682,778	3.37
8. Henry Roy Young	5,346,095	1.86
9. Pasco Nominees Pty. Ltd.	5,110,420	1.78
10. State Treasurer of the State of Michigan	3,694,046	1.28
11. Australian Mutual Provident Society (A/C #I)	3,348,428	1.16
12. Australian Mutual Provident Society (A/C #3)	3,130,197	1.09
13. National Mutual Life Association of Australia	2,370,000	0.82
14. Barclays Australian Custodian Services Ltd.	1,982,958	0.69
15. Bank of New South Wales Nominees Ltd.	1,732,180	0.60
16. Saltbush Nominees Pty. Ltd.	1,362,393	0.47
17. AMP Custodian Services Ltd.	1,349,496	0.47
18. The State Government Insurance Commission	1,340,200	0.47
19. ISMG Nominees Pty. Ltd.	1,224,842	0.43
20. Asia Securities (Aust) Pty. Ltd.	1,180,650	0.41

Source: Orbital Engine Company, *1991 Annual Report.*

ANDERSEN CONSULTING (EUROPE): ENTERING THE BUSINESS OF BUSINESS INTEGRATION

A partner in Andersen Consulting defined its business as "helping clients manage complexity." As information systems technology had progressed over the decades, Andersen had emerged as the world's largest information systems consulting company through "analyzing and then systematizing business' current information requirements into commodity products and then quickly proceeding to the next tier of complexity." According to Terry Neill, head of services for the company's UK office:

> Andersen's greatest challenge is the constant commoditization of its products and services. Our success depends on our ability to stay ahead of the commoditization envelope.

In the 1940s, Andersen's expertise lay in designing the complex, manual accounting processes required to meet the increased reporting demanded by the Securities and Exchange Commission (SEC) in the United States. That business had become routine by the 1950s with many companies able to do the work as efficiently and cost-effectively as Andersen. By this time Andersen had moved on to the next emerging major system requirement, complex payroll systems. These too became commonplace by the 1960s, and the firm progressed to the development and integration of computerized accounting and payroll systems. The introduction of personal computers, networks, and the fast-paced change in 1970s and 1980s hardware and software capabilities offered another new stream of opportunities, as the company's clients struggled to exploit these technologies and to manage the increasing complexity of their businesses.

The business integration market—described by Andersen as the clients' need for an integrated business, information, and people strategy—was the company's target for the 1990s. Building from its unequaled strength in systems integration, Andersen sought to broaden its capabilities to help clients formulate and implement strategic thrusts encompassing all activities and functions on an integrated basis.

While there was a broad agreement among the senior partners on the need for pursuing the business integration market, there were considerable differences of opinion on how to implement the strategy. Differences in market structures in different countries called for a delicate balance between the need for a worldwide business integration strategy and the demand for implementation approaches adapted to each national operation. The new business integration market also required development of two new skill areas for Andersen—namely, "Strategy" and "Change Management"—and their seamless integration with the existing organizations supporting Andersen's unique systems integration and information technology strengths. However, to integrate clients' businesses successfully, Andersen needed first to integrate its own operations, this might prove the most difficult task the company had yet faced.

Copyright © 1992 INSEAD, Fontainebleau, France. Edited by Professor J. Brian Quinn and reproduced by special permission. This case was written by Mary Ackenhusen, Research Associate, under the supervision of Sumantra Ghoshal, Associate Professor at INSEAD. Financial support from the INSEAD Alumni Fund European Case Programme is gratefully acknowledged.

BRIEF HISTORY: ARTHUR ANDERSEN AND COMPANY

In 1913, Arthur Andersen, the son of Scandinavian immigrant parents, purchased a small audit firm in Chicago which later grew into the major accounting and consulting firm of Arthur Andersen and Company. Andersen's vision was to establish "a firm that will do more than routine auditing . . . a firm where we can measure our contribution more by the quality of the services rendered than by whether we are getting a good living out of it." For more than three quarters of a century, his philosophies continued to influence the firm's culture as well as the profession of accounting as a whole.

Extensive professional training, which became a well-known distinguishing feature of the company, had its roots in the 1920s. Training was strongly advocated by Andersen, beginning with mandatory lectures given by him and by other senior partners several times a week in the office and expanding to a rigorous course developed in the 1940s designed to teach common standards to all U.S. Andersen employees. From the beginning, these courses were taught by insiders, "because these people understand our methods and procedures." The culture built by Andersen was one of inscrutable professional honesty even at the cost of losing a client. He always said that if the staff "thought straight and talked straight," they would earn the respect of clients. Former CEO Duane Kullberg noted, "Those remain words we [still] live by—not simply a hand-me-down slogan."

The firm outpaced market growth in the 1950s and 1960s, expanding internationally and domestically through a mixture of a few high-quality acquisitions and the establishment of new offices. This period also saw the beginnings of Andersen's consulting arm which fueled growth in the 1970s and 1980s when the market for audits began to stagnate.

ANDERSEN CONSULTING

Andersen Consulting's origins lay in the industrial engineering function sponsored by the firm's founder, to ". . . show the strong or weak points in company position or management, and seek to correct such weak spots." This function received second priority to the audit business through the 1940s until, in 1951, Joe Glickauf, an influential partner, built a copy of an advanced design computer developed at the University of Pennsylvania. When he presented his vision of what the computer could mean for the future of business systems, the partners voted to give full support to the area's development. Andersen's implementation of an automated payroll system at GE was perhaps the first significant commercial application of a computer system.

Andersen's consulting business grew quickly with the advancement of information technology and its capabilities. The strong culture and training infrastructure established by Arthur Andersen for the accounting

practice became key strengths in this business also. Initially, most clients came from the audit business' customer base, but by 1990 that share was less than 20%. By 1990, Andersen Consulting was the largest player in information systems consulting and was, in fact, the largest consulting company in the world, with over 20,000 professionals, operating in more than 50 countries. Worldwide revenues of $1.9 billion represented a compounded annual growth rate of 30% between 1985 and 1990 (see Exhibit 1). The company designed and implemented large-scale information systems and provided all associated services including programming and training of client personnel. Andersen Consulting also developed and marketed its own proprietary software and was an increasingly active player in the business of facilities management (i.e., managing computer operations outsourced by its clients).

Andersen, the man, always stressed homogeneity within Andersen, the firm, with his maxim, "one firm, one voice." Continuous reinforcement of this principle—through standardized training and extensive formalization of work procedures—positioned the firm for consistent service and methods across all offices and countries. By the late 1980s, however, maintenance of the "one firm" concept had become increasingly difficult. Andersen began to branch off into two distinctly different businesses—"audit and tax" and "consulting"—with vastly different professional norms, market structures, business approaches, and compensation levels. The increasing demand of consulting partners for remuneration consistent with the significantly higher profitability and growth of the consulting practice led to the formal separation of the groups into two divisions in 1988. (See Exhibit 2.) While a 24-member board of partners provided oversight for the company as a whole, both strategic business units had significant strategic and operational autonomy.

ANDERSEN CONSULTING (EUROPE, MIDDLE EAST, AFRICA, AND INDIA)

Within this structure, Andersen Consulting in Europe, the Middle East, Africa, and India (EMEAI) had offices in 18 countries staffed with 6500 professionals who generated total 1990 billings of $695 million, the largest consultancy in Europe in terms of gross revenues. EMEAI had grown at a rate of 28% per year for the preceding five years.

The Andersen Consulting organization (see Exhibits 2 and 3) centered on geographically-based country practices. A matrix structure including industry functions, specialty skills, and functional skills overlaid this legally autonomous aggregation of national practices, creating an organization of considerable complexity. Each country or country group had a country managing partner who had as direct reports three industry sector heads and several heads of specialty skill or functional areas. The three industry sectors were Financial Services, Industrial and Consumer Products, and Government and Services. The number and types of specialty and functional heads depended on the size and expertise of the office and included Strategy and Change Management. Every professional in a country reported to either an industry, skill specialty, or functional head. Additionally, larger countries often had a number of industry subsector heads (e.g., oil and gas) and functional managers (e.g., logistics). These partners had no direct reports and reported into one of the industry sectors.

Each country was responsible for meeting annual (and multi-annual) fee and productivity targets. The country partners' most important job was managing their professionals to assure they were effectively utilized either within the country practice or in support of jobs outside the country. The office of the managing partner of EMEAI, Vernon Ellis, was in the UK. Each country managing partner reported to him as did the European heads of each of the three industry sectors and the heads of the specialty and functional skill areas. These regional, sector, or functional managers had responsibility for practice leadership—which included setting strategy and assisting in the staffing and execution of projects in their respective fields. They were linked to their counterparts in the country offices through "dotted line relationships."

BUILDING CAPABILITIES: DEVELOPING PEOPLE

While all professional service firms assert that people are their key asset, at Andersen Consulting this assertion translated into a set of institutionalized practices that lay at the core of what was known both within and outside the company as the "Andersen way." The company invested heavily in building the capabilities of its people and the systems which supported them. It then leveraged these capabilities through a well defined project team structure to provide value for clients.

Its training infrastructure was one of the distinguishing features of Andersen. Every new employee worldwide had to take a six week course, Computer Application Programming School (CAPS), taught in Andersen's luxurious St. Charles (Illinois) Education facility generally called "the university." This rigorous course taught the fundamentals of computer applications and programming through intensive work sessions designed to simulate project work at a client site. Eighty-hour weeks and the requirement of business attire throughout the program made the simulation realistic and emphasized that "At Andersen, training is serious business." The same methods were used to teach both liberal arts majors and engineers in the Andersen methodology of systems design and implementation. As one senior partner described:

> CAPS is a real shock at first . . . you wonder how you'll be able to keep up, it is very intense. . . but then you find that everyone is in this together and you begin working as a team helping each other to pull through. And since then, this group has been my main network within the company. The experience created a career-long bond with these cohorts.

Andersen Consulting educated all its professionals in a uniform approach to each aspect of a job whether it was systems design, programming, project management, or writing a proposal for new business. The tools were designed to eliminate any ambiguity in the nuts and bolts of a project. This common tool set—embodied in numerous, thick reference manuals—was used worldwide to assure consistency in firm performance and to enhance the ability of consultants from different countries and disciplines to work together. In combination, the uniform training program at St. Charles and the firm's sophisticated documentation tools provided the core of Andersen's success in management information consulting: the ability to hire new undergraduates and in six weeks turn them into productive, billable programmers. Box 1 describes some key elements of AA & Co.'s unique—and well recognized—approach to software management.

Training continued throughout a professional's career with a standardized system that required everyone to spend nearly 1000 hours over a five-year period in training, undertaking a pre-specified set of courses at pre-designated intervals (see Exhibit 4). All offices of the company around the world had to staff a fixed number of training hours, with each office allocating faculty roles among its partners and experienced staff. Although internal faculty members used standard materials for teaching their classes, they were encouraged to embellish sessions with examples from recent assignments. These new case stories then became a portion of the teaching materials provided the next faculty for the same sessions. Training costs were approximately £35,000 per new employee in their first five years, with an extraordinary 10% of Andersen's revenue overall going to professional training. Training was an important benefit of working for Andersen: "Your skills aren't just good news for the client. After training with Andersen Consulting, you could work for anyone, anywhere, or you could work for yourself."

Andersen had historically targeted a majority of its recruiting toward young undergraduates directly out of university. Each recruit had to undergo extensive interviewing. One objective was to seek out bright achievers who could best be "molded" into the Andersen pattern with the expectation of a long career in the firm. Recruiting was a major activity for all professionals at Andersen, including the partners. Likewise, the development and nurturing of new recruits was an important part of upper management's role. Andersen partners helped develop 20–30 subordinates through a formal counseling program. Each new employee received a "counseling partner" upon arrival and met with this partner every six months to discuss performance, career interests, and other pertinent topics.

The typical career path with Andersen Consulting began with 1–2 years as an "assistant consultant"—working mainly on large systems integration projects as a programmer, with regular formal and informal training in information technology and business skills. During the next 3–5 years, "senior consultants" broadened their technical and business skills in client engagements with more specialized training. In 5–8 years, a successful professional could expect to take on the role of project manager; and in 9–12 years, most recruits still with the firm would be considered for partnership.

A MERITOCRACY

Andersen followed the up or out principles of a meritocracy: each individual either performed well and moved up the ladder, or left the firm, opening up opportunities for others. The evaluation process was tough: only 50–60% of new professional recruits would make manager and perhaps 10% would become a partner. Project managers evaluated assistant and senior consultants' performance every three months. Both sides took the evaluations very seriously as tools for performance improvement. Theoretically, project partners evaluated project managers every six months, but these often turned into self-evaluations due to limited partner time. Consultant and manager compensation was strictly merit-based, though the pay differential between an

outstanding performer and a satisfactory performer was less than in other comparable firms. There was no bonus or profit sharing below the partner level.

To facilitate personal development and professional contacts, Andersen Consulting prided itself on its vast and varied methods of communication with the firm. Every industry, functional, and country group had at least one newsletter which helped its professionals stay on top of the new projects, successes, and issues in their areas of interest. Likewise, these groups often sponsored conferences and circulated files of interesting papers on current issues. For those consultants with wide areas of interest, oversaturation, not lack of communication, was the problem.

The ongoing training at St. Charles and the European Center in Eindhoven, Holland, provided professional and social stimulation. To help retain a small firm feeling, Andersen formed personnel groups of 100–200 people, solely for the purpose of regular social gatherings. Informal partner/manager dinners held on a regular basis also facilitated upward communication with partners. The end result was a strong cultural glue which helped Andersen employees to understand each others' objectives, methods, and motivations across offices and functions. As one manager remarked:

> It's hard for outsiders to work at Andersen. They just don't know our vocabulary, our systems. While those who grow up in Andersen can carry out a task based on one sentence directions, an outsider will be lost. Andersens can think alike.

Other firms in the industry expressed both their envy and their scorn for this strong internal homogeneity by applying the label "Andersen Androids," which became almost a source of pride within the company.

LEVERAGING CAPABILITIES: MANAGING PROJECT TEAMS

The project team was the main organizational unit used by Andersen to leverage its people's capabilities for client value. Each team contained at least one partner, one manager, and a number of junior level consultants, and had access to a worldwide network of experts who could participate on the team or advise. The ratio of partner time to consultant time on the project determined the economics of the project and its profitability to partners and the firm. At Andersen, the partner-to-consultant ratio was very low with, for example, only 180 partners out of 6500 professionals in EMEAI. This "leverage" resulted in relatively high potential compensation for the partners. (See Exhibit 5 for the economics of a typical professional service firm.) Somewhat off-setting the favorable economics of a high consultant to partner ratio, Andersen's target utilization rates were lower than the industry norm due to its emphasis on training and other forms of personnel development. Target rates for partner, manager, and consultant levels were 50%, 75%, and 80%, respectively.

The partner managing a client case chose a project manager based on the latter's skills, experience, and availability. With the partner's guidance, the project manager built the team and provided day-to-day management in the execution of the project. The project manager was responsible for meeting budget and time commitments and for the professional development of team members. The company had a worldwide database detailing each professional's skills and experience by industry and client, as well as their current assignments and availability. Partners complained, however, that it was too hard to codify all the important characteristics of a team player, and the database was typically used only as a last resort. Personal networks were often more important for selecting project managers and staffing teams.

Nevertheless, the scheduling database—which detailed who was available and when—was the most utilized formal database within Andersen. The Andersen culture would rarely allow someone to be pulled from a case before its completion: the client's needs came before the business'. Therefore, there was a relatively limited pool of available talent to be placed on a team, and there were considerable pressures to utilize anyone not currently on a team. Though Andersen professionals had some latitude in choosing projects which met their own career development needs, most conceded that the system did not and probably could not be expected to support this objective fully.

PROVIDING STEWARDSHIP: THE ROLE OF PARTNERS

Partners at Andersen spent 50% of their time on case work, 25% selling new projects, and 25% on development of subordinates. The partners were the entrepreneurs of the firm, traditionally developing their own portfolio of business based on their contacts and interests. Each partner owned a piece of the firm and participated in the management of the firm on a one-person, one-vote basis. According to one partner, "This is how we challenge sacred cows. Ownership is a great driver of arguments and strong opinions."

Partners shared costs on a worldwide basis. Partner income was determined by a distribution formula based on the number of his or her units. Unit allocations were set by a partner committee which evaluated each partner's business generated, business performed, development of personnel, team work, practice leadership, unique skills, and other performance dimensions. Practice management partners evaluated all partners working for them, although other partners could contribute to the review process as they felt appropriate. All management partners were evaluated by a comprehensive process of upward evaluation. This was set up to be non-attributable, though many partners chose to discuss their feedback with the management partners they were evaluating. All partners received a listing of the unit allocations of every other partner in the world. Though there was an appeal process, it was rarely used. In general, the partners approved of the fairness of the evaluation and compensation systems. As described by one, "It may not be perfect every year, but over a period of time everyone seems to get what they are due."

The partners saw themselves as the firm's stewards with an obligation to strengthen it for those who would follow. Sacrificing immediate personal income for the long-term benefit of the firm was a cherished norm. The first international expansion of the company in 1957 provided a good example. After the profits for the year had already been disbursed, a proposal to open new offices in Paris, London and Mexico was brought to the partners' meeting. Client needs required immediate opening of these offices, and the partners decided to pay back 40% of their income so that the firm could expand, even though many partners would not serve in the company long enough to reap the benefits. Likewise, year after year, the partners continued to approve the tremendous investment in training future generations of Andersens. Retiring partners took with them only their initial capital investment in the firm. No appreciation or goodwill accumulated over this period of partnership. One partner reflected, "The style of the organization is set by high quality people with high values which we pass on to the next generation. It's a strong cultural influence."

THE BUSINESS OF BUSINESS INTEGRATION

The information technology (IT) consulting business could be divided into two broad segments. The first segment—the larger and the more traditional of the two—was the IT professional services market that included custom software development, consulting, education and training, and systems operations. The second, more complex, segment was the systems integration market in which Andersen undertook the technical and administrative responsibility for tying together information networks involving multiple hardware and software vendors and multiple corporate functions. Systems integration projects usually ranged from $1 [million] to $10 million in the commercial sector, but could go as high as $100 million for large government projects.

In 1989, the IT professional service market for Europe had exceeded $15 billion and was growing at the rate of 20% per year. The forecast was for the market to approach $39 billion by 1994, with 68% coming from custom software development. By contrast, the systems integration market was only $1.9 billion in 1989, growing to about $6 billion in 1994 (over 30% per year), with over half the revenue coming from associated consulting services. The systems integration market in the United States was $8.8 billion in 1990, with growth to $20.5 billion expected by 1995. The decentralization of in-house information systems departments, fast-paced technological changes, increased outsourcing of formerly in-house corporate services, and the ongoing restructuring of major industrial markets were all driving these high growth rates.

European competition in these large, growing markets was stiff and attracting new entrants. In professional services, the market was quite fragmented with the key competitors being IBM (5.3%), Cap Gemini Sogeti, the French software multinational (4.7%), and Volmac, a Dutch software company which received 90% of its revenues from the Netherlands (2.0%). Andersen was number 13 with a 0.8% market share. The top three competitors in systems integration and their European market shares were IBM (12.5%), Cap Gemini Sogeti (11.8%) and Andersen Consulting (10.2%). (See Exhibit 6 for other competitors.) Many of these companies also competed in the related businesses of facilities management and packaged software. Facilities management was an important market because it often provided an entry into a systems integration project, and helped systems integration firms hone their own technical products. Packaged software was important because many clients demanded standardized solutions from a vendor before they would consider a later purchase of professional services. Andersen Consulting was active in both markets.

FROM SYSTEMS INTEGRATION TO BUSINESS INTEGRATION

The systems integration market had experienced some serious quality problems as projects fell short of client expectations in terms of functionality, cost, and completion deadlines. Many believed that a client could not realize the full potentials of IT until it had a clear business strategy to direct its proposed IT use *and* had made the necessary procedural and organizational changes for IT to properly support the business. Merely utilizing new IT capabilities to automate existing business practices rarely yielded its full potentials, or even expected, benefits for clients. Major payoffs lay in utilizing the new technology to support fundamental redirections of business strategy and new management processes. These were the driving forces behind "business integration consulting" as the next level of complexity beyond "systems integration."

According to preliminary market research, only a few European clients recognized the need to integrate their functional consulting and IT requirements through an integrated business strategy implemented by one firm. Nevertheless, Andersen felt confident the market was going that way. The traditional software and hardware companies such as Cap Gemini, IBM and DEC were likely to be strong competitors in the business integration market, with perhaps unequaled technical expertise but lacking in project management skills. Systems integrators like SD-Scicon and SEMA, two European based companies specializing in software services and integration, seemed technically very strong and further along in building needed project management skills. The large accounting firms were serious competitors in terms of project management skills, but with less perceived competence in technical areas. The general consulting firms—like McKinsey, PA Consulting, and others—had excellent reputations for developing and implementing corporate strategies, easy access to corporate board rooms, some experience in systems design, but minimal systems implementation experience.

Many of these companies had already begun to prepare for an expanded business integration market by broadening their skill bases or geographic scope through mergers, acquisitions, and alliances. IBM, for example, had taken minority positions in numerous companies with large European market shares. Andersen, for its part, had developed strategic alliances with companies such as DEC, IBM and Sun Microsystems. SEMA and SD-Scicon were both results of recent mergers.

ANDERSEN'S ENTRY INTO BUSINESS INTEGRATION

The need to link an IT project to the rest of the business was not a new concept to Andersen. By 1990, Andersen had adopted the formal concept of "business integration" with its associated four bubble graphic (see Exhibit 7). However, well before that it had begun to groom some specialists for the new area, described as:

> A seamless combination of skills from each of four areas: strategy, technology, operations, and people. In developing business solutions it [is] necessary to consider all four areas and select an appropriate balance, using different proportions in different situations. [This requires] people who are not narrowly based in a single discipline but who combine knowledge and understanding of each of these different areas.

In support of the four functions, Andersen formed four Centers of Excellence: Strategic Services, Change Management, Operations, and Information Technology. Strategic Services worked with clients to develop and implement successful strategies in all areas of corporate activity. Change Management worked with organizations to position their people, processes and technology to master change with maximum benefits. Operations helped clients develop effective day-to-day processes including implementation of JIT systems, plant re-layouts, quality assurance systems. Information Technology contained very specialized hardware and software experts to assist in implementing state-of-the-art customer solutions. For most country organizations, only Strategic Services and Change Management were distinct skill sets; Operations and Information Technology were still located within other functional or industry groups.

Each specialty area was to build up repeat and continuous experience of a world class nature. Many questioned whether the IT generalist background of a standard Andersen consultant was suitable to support these specialty areas sufficiently for competition in the business integration market. As described by Vernon Ellis:

> You could try to produce a complete Renaissance person but it is impossible these days. The business world is too complex. . . . We need both generalists and specialists. Some people will be in just one bubble, some in the middle of all the bubbles, and some at specific intersections.

These specialist groups were small compared to the rest of Andersen. In 1989/90, there were 170 strategy specialists and 290 change specialists within EMEAI. The majority of Andersen professionals were the IT generalists (the "engine room," as described by one consultant) in the middle of the graphic bubble chart—although the vast majority of these were also specialized in an industry or industry sector. IT generalists were the people who handled execution and possessed a "delivery mechanism" skill set. They were expected to have a good general business understanding of each specialist area as well as a thorough knowledge of IT, Andersen's traditional strength. The project manager's challenge was to glue the expertise of the specialists and the business understanding of the generalists together into a successful project team.

THE CHALLENGE OF MANAGING COMPLEXITY

By 1990, the strategy of business integration had been well-communicated and widely accepted within Andersen, though there were some different internal views on how the company was pursuing the market. At the core of these dichotomies lay the conflicting needs for building best-in-class capabilities in each of the skill areas supporting the business integration strategy and the demand for integrating these skills internally in a manner provided competitive advantage over the many other companies targeting the same opportunity. As described by Terry Neill:

> We are the best in the business systems piece. What goes with [the Strategy and Change Management practices] is that we have to be the best in each piece. In Strategy, there are established leaders like McKinsey and our challenge is to develop a reputation as good as theirs. The Change Management business is still fragmented, just like the IT marketplace in the 1960s and '70s, with small "guru" style firms and individuals. We are doing the same thing in Change Management that we did there.

Gerard Van Kemmel, Managing Partner of France agreed:

> I don't believe clients will buy a business integration project unless the supplier is the most skilled and best value in each area. Otherwise, a customer will hire the best firms and integrate themselves.

While the two perspectives were not necessarily contradictory, their operational implications were not easy to reconcile. As described by an external industry analyst,

> If you want to be the best in each piece, you have to grow each activity separately—specialize each group with the most challenging assignments dedicated to its particular area. If you want to really integrate, you need to develop

a different model of what strategy and change is all about, redefining them from the perspective of integrated delivery. Best-in-class specialization and effective integration require not just different structures and management processes, but even different definitions and visions of what each bubble represents.

Further, different views still existed on the right balance between letting individual partners and local practices develop their businesses entrepreneurially and pursuing a coherent worldwide business integration strategy. As described by Vernon Ellis:

> Historically, our partners have been entrepreneurs; that is why Andersen has been so successful. Partners built their own practices based on their skills, interests, and contacts. They managed the projects start to finish. Now we need a different approach. A worldwide strategy requires that the partner find the best person for each job, and often that person may not be [him or herself]. We need a change in partner mindset.

SOME NATIONAL DIFFERENCES

The corporate vision of "business integration" was also not always mirrored at the country operating level. For example, the UK and French offices implemented their business integration strategies differently due to the distinctive historical, competitive, and cultural differences in their practices and markets.

FRANCE

The French information technology market was the most developed in the world in terms of percentage of GNP spent on IT. It was also the largest such market in Europe. The French structure reflected a much clearer dichotomy between IT and business consulting. In the IT area, the market had several large world-class competitors such as Cap Gemini and SEMA who were able to compete successfully with Andersen on a cost basis. From this "IT only" view of the French market, Andersen was sometimes seen as a small player. In contrast, it was historically very strong in management consulting.

Culturally, in France, the corporate IT function enjoyed lesser stature than in the UK. In the UK, the top IT job was a key management position charged with helping the company integrate its business and information technology strategies. In France, the position of IT director was generally not a way to the top—top positions in corporations were reserved for the graduates of the elite "grandes écoles," a group of universities from which IT directors typically did not

come. French IT directors generally had little or no voice in corporate strategy and top management issues and ran relatively insular and controlled empires, without much top management interference. When they hired consultants they looked for firms who were cheap, had a flexible workforce, and most importantly, would allow them full control of the project. A successful consultant in France would never go around the IT director to top management.

To develop and maintain the French strength in management consulting, the French office had always tried to recruit from the "grandes écoles" educational system. When hired, these individuals were trained in the fundamentals of IT through the traditional Andersen process (CAPS, etc.) but were only required to work in IT for a very limited time period (6–12 months) after which they were assigned to the management consulting practice. However, the majority of Andersen employees in the French IT practice did not come from the "grandes écoles." They were on different pay scales—although these were significantly in excess of their French IT competitors. One career track within the organization did draw from the "grandes écoles" system; these were the employees who helped integrate the IT business with management consulting when needed and who were potential future partners of the IT business.

The French model maintained separate organizations for the information technology versus the management consulting businesses. Within the latter, there was a very successful stand-alone practice in Change Management. The Strategic Services function was not a separate area within the management consulting arm because the French management felt its professionals were well-schooled in strategy, making it unnecessary to develop this expertise in a separate group. Although the two organizations sometimes sold their services separately, more than 80% of their work was for common clients. While recognizing that the French model was very different from the corporate blueprint, the French management team strongly believed that its approach was better suited for the French market.

THE UNITED KINGDOM

By some measures, the UK was the third largest IT market in Europe and also very competitive. Andersen was very successful in the UK because the market was willing to pay relatively high rates due to the perception that a professional "integrator" could add extra value. Andersen could often command significantly higher rates in UK than in France for IT work. On the other hand, Andersen's UK competitors would often try to position Andersen as "IT consultants" to undermine the market perception of Andersen's strengths in business consulting.

Andersen UK had always been very strong in the IT business and had recruited carefully to develop and maintain this skill. Recruits came from the top British schools, were trained in the Andersen methodology, and were then required to work in systems design and programming for 3–5 years. The UK's organizational and implementation approaches to the "business integration strategy" differed substantially from the French. The UK implementation replicated the corporate vision as laid out by Mr. Ellis and integrated the four Centers of Excellence at the country level to present a "seamless combination of skills" for clients. The Strategy and Change Management areas were distinct organizations reporting into the Services Industry subsector. The professional development infrastructure was the same for all professionals in terms of training requirements, salary structure, and promotion opportunities.

The UK was organized around three main industry groups—Financial Markets, Products, and Services. A fourth division, Integration Services, housed specialist technology, software and systems management skills. The UK practice had three further centers of functional excellence—Strategy and Change Management, housed in Services, and Operations/Logistics, housed in Products. (See Exhibit 8.) The French version envisioned a Center of Excellence structure within each of the three industry groups (Financial Services, Products, and Services) as soon as each area had enough critical mass to justify the organization.

DEVELOPING NEW CAPABILITIES

Of the four Centers of Excellence, the newly formalized areas of Strategic Services and Change Management were still establishing themselves both internally and externally.

Change Management's organized roots were in providing training for clients in support of large complex systems being installed by Andersen. Since 1988, Change Management had expanded to reflect the cultural and organizational challenges major transformational changes posed for its customers. In the early 1990s, Change Management contained three practice areas: (1) Technology Assimilation which supported the training and education needed to ensure that the expected benefits of major IT investments were fully delivered; (2) Knowledge Transfer which covered training in all its aspects, including the use of advanced

training technologies; and (3) Organization Change which included the strategic and tactical aspects of process and organizational change. Much of Andersen's Change Management work during the period was still in training (Knowledge Transfer) but the balance was rapidly changing as partners recognized the key role of the people and change dimensions in executing Andersen's business integration strategy. Because the Change Management market was very fragmented with few large players, cost was an important element of competition.

Strategic Services marketed the following services in support of business integration: strategic management studies, competitive/industry analyses, market and sales planning, operational planning, information technology strategy, and organizational strategy and change management. In reality, most Strategic Services work seemed to have an operational bent. As one partner described the practice:

> Most of the strategy work [currently] is concerned with sorting out strategies to optimize a business, rather than [considering] what company one should go and acquire in the marketplace. In other words, it's what I would call internal strategic consulting, rather than external strategy consulting.

Some partners had expressed concerns about the potential overlaps between the Change Management and Strategic Services skill sets as Change Management moved into organizational change work. Others shared Terry Neill's view:

> Executing our business integration vision requires that we be able to mobilize project teams with a portfolio of skills in systems, strategy, process and change management. We need world class skills in each dimension and the ability to bring them together for a client without the client having to concern itself about divisions [within] the internal structures of Andersen Consulting. We now have a dozen large high quality UK clients where we are making business integration a working reality. These companies are seeing the value of our skills portfolio, and that will accelerate the removal of [our own] internal barriers. We are winning with those organizations who see the skills of strategy and execution as being inextricably intertwined.

CULTURAL DIFFERENCES

To fill its specialist needs, Andersen broke with its tradition of hiring recent graduates. Fifty percent of the Center of Excellence hires were experienced "outsiders" brought in at senior and manager levels, while the other 50% came from within the firm or MBA programs. In general, Strategic Services recruited MBAs from top business schools, and Change Management brought in experienced individuals from the fields of organization change, industrial psychology, and education. Though Andersen prided itself on growing organically and not through acquisition, it acquired a small UK manufacturing consulting firm in 1988 to enhance the skill base of its Operations specialty practice.

Absorbing a large number of outsiders was a significant challenge for a firm whose strong cultural roots were passed on from one generation of recruits to the next through the institutionalized mechanisms represented in the "Andersen way." Outsiders who came in at middle management levels with different ideals and methods naturally weakened the cultural glue that had traditionally bound a team of Andersen consultants. And some tensions were growing among various groups. The result of these difficulties was that the turnover in Strategic Services and Change Management was higher than for the firm in general.

The more experienced professionals hired from the "outside" often did not view the traditional Andersen training program at CAPS as an appropriate initiation for a senior employee. A recent MBA from a top institution recruited into Strategic Services was required to take the full 6 week CAPS course at St. Charles and then work for several months on a systems project—the typical progression for an undergraduate recruit. His view was that the requirement added no value, and he did not think it compared favorably to the first few months of strategy work that his counterparts at the strategy boutiques experienced. On-the-job-training was somewhat hindered because project opportunities for inexperienced newly trained specialists could only grow at the rate Andersen succeeded in taking its business integration strategy to the market.

There was also a concern within Strategic Services that Andersen's compensation and development philosophy might hamper its ability to recruit and retain top individuals. Andersen's base compensation was on a par with competition's, but in the boom times for strategy consulting in the eighties some partners felt that Andersen's unwillingness to have bonuses put the firm at a disadvantage in recruiting. On the other hand, Andersen grew by nearly 40% in the UK in 1991 while most of its competitors were laying off large numbers of people, many of whom applied to join Andersen partly because of its rapidly growing reputation in the strategy area.

INTEGRATING THE MULTINATIONAL NETWORK

Andersen saw one of its competitive advantages as its ability to serve a multinational client, or a client who would like to become multinational. Andersen's network of multinational offices could provide an integrated, pan-European, or even worldwide, solution. But supporting this capability required professionals who had a multinational perspective in terms of languages, culture, and business knowledge—and could be mobilized across national borders. As Andersen grew in size and organizational complexity it was becoming increasingly difficult to take advantage of its enormous people resources. As Terry Neill noted:

> A key impediment could become our ability to share knowledge quickly. In the past we have done it entirely by the personal network. . . now we're too big to do this. We need to improve our own IT network. But we also need to protect and improve our informal human network. Both are difficult, but both are challenges we must respond to urgently.

Any person identified as needed on a project team had first to be released by their country manager. Since the country manager was responsible for that locality's profits—and these specialists tended to be very effective on national cases—deployment of people to regional or worldwide teams was becoming a growing source of conflict. Although there were incentives within the partnership evaluation system to measure how well each partner supported multinational practice needs, in reality country interests generally came first. The conflict was expressed by Bill Barnard, the partner in charge of Market Development for Europe:

> In areas where we have very few specialists, we can't afford to have them only work in one country. We need to move them into different countries to work multinationally. This causes conflicts with the country managers. Some conflict is good, but we need to protect [our] people and to help them get repeat experience and develop their skill sets. Otherwise, their experience gets lost.

Andersen attacked this problem by trying to hire and develop people who liked multinational activity and by stressing in the education process that international relocation was part of the job. Nevertheless, Bill Barnard predicted that it would take until the end of the century before Andersen worked as a truly integrated European operation.

1. What are the main strategic issues Andersen must resolve? How should Andersen position itself in the European—and world—consulting markets? What should its distinctive competencies be? How should it support these to ensure Andersen Consulting is best-in-world at them?

2. What are the principal organizational options it has? Draw the organization chart for each. What performance measurement approaches would be needed to support each? How should the area specialization versus discipline specialization issue be resolved? How can Andersen Consulting encourage the use of its best resources on any multinational project?

3. What are the pros and cons of Andersen Consulting's approach to training? To software development? Compare the latter to that described in the Microsoft Corporation (B) case. What basic functions should Andersen's information and technology system provide? How can these best be developed? How can these be used to support its strategy in the marketplace?

4. How should Andersen Consulting relate to Arthur Andersen (tax, audit, accounting services)? How must the Andersen culture change? How would you bring about these changes, if you were Terry Neill? How should partners be compensated? How should they share in technology investment? Technology payoffs? Development of personnel? Sharing of personnel?

BOX 1

ANDERSEN SOFTWARE PROCESS

Andersen's process for designing software combined a highly decentralized process for writing each section of code with a rigorous centralized system to coordinate and control the overall system. At the center of this latter process have been two programs called METHOD/1 and DESIGN/1. METHOD/1 is a carefully designed step-by-step procedure for modularizing and controlling all the steps needed to design a major systems program. At the highest level are roughly "10 work units," each broken into approximately five "jobs." Below this are a similar number of "tasks" for each job and several "steps" for each task. Each component is numbered in hierarchical form and defines the exact elements the programmer needs to go through at that stage of the process. METHOD/1 has estimated times and costs built in for each step the programmer goes through. The project manager can explicitly override, substitute, or eliminate individual tasks or their time estimates as necessary for the specific project.

Supplementing this program is another program, DESIGN/1, which is a very elaborate computer-aided software engineering (CASE) tool. METHOD/1 and DESIGN/1 are each compiled programs of 20–30 diskettes in length, taking the place of a wall full of systems programming manuals Andersen formerly used to control programming. DESIGN/1 keeps track of all programming details as they develop and disciplines the programmer to define each element of the program carefully. It is structured to fit the METHOD/1 program so that each step in a work plan will be executed by those using DESIGN/1 and it allows customers to enter "pseudo" data or code so the customer can periodically test the "look and feel" of screen displays and data entry formats.

To attract and motivate good people, individual programmers are allowed to work alone on each small section of the code and must completely test all the metrics within their assigned section. A separate group does a systems or functional test for each type of business problem the code is to handle. Through METHOD/1 the project manager keeps track of progress on the entire project, checks that all steps are performed, estimates next stage needs, assigns programmers for these, and then updates progress and cost records for the system. It provides a number of internal checks to avoid over-assignments of personnel, to verify cost and sequence controls, and so on.

EXHIBIT 1
Andersen Consulting
Financial Summary

| | WORLDWIDE | | | EMEAI | | |
YEAR	NET REVENUES ($MM)	PARTNERS	PROFES-SIONALS	NET REVENUES ($MM)	PARTNERS	PROFES-SIONALS
1991	2,256	755	21,668	908	191	7,751
1990	1,850	692	18,188	663	172	6,263
1989	1,433	586	15,373	465	143	4,974
1988	1,106	529	12,009	360	123	3,743
1987	828	469	9,231	236	108	2,858

EXHIBIT 2
Worldwide Organization

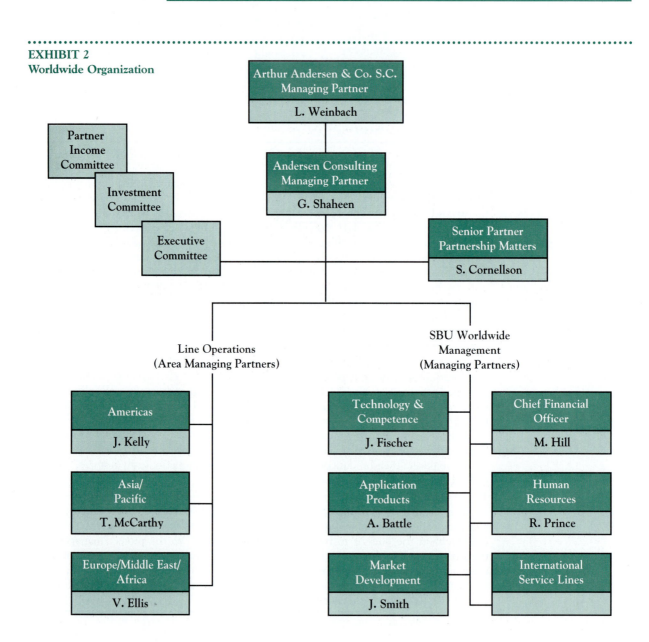

EXHIBIT 3
Andersen Consulting
EMEAI Organization

Managing Partner George Shaheen

EMEAI Vernon Ellis

Geographic Management

France

Spain/ Portugal

Italy

S. Arabia/ India/Greece/ Turkey

Germany/Austria Hungary/ Czechoslovakia

Scandinavia/ Benelux/ Switzerland/Africa

United Kingdom/ Ireland Country Manager

Administration

Products

Services

Financial Markets

Strategic and Change Management Services

Integration Services

Technical Systems Integration

Business and Operations Management

Business Development Management

Functional Management

Industry Leadership

Financial Services

Industrial/ Consumer Products

Government & Services

Speciality Areas

Strategic Services

Change Management

Technology and Software

Technology Competence

Systems Management

Market Development

Finance and Operation Support

EXHIBIT 4
Graduate to Manager
Training Sequence

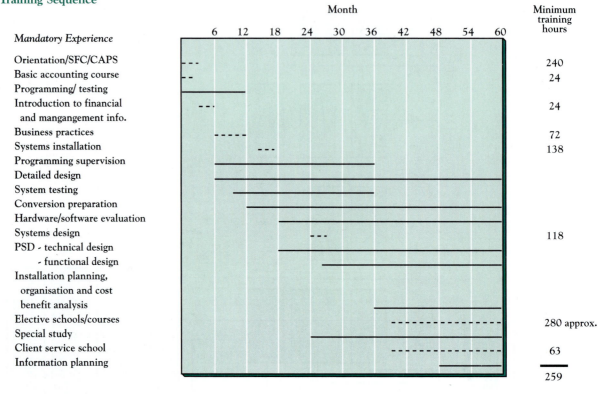

EXHIBIT 4
Graduate to Manager
Training Sequence

Month

	6	12	18	24	30	36	42	48	54	60	Minimum training hours

Mandatory Experience

Orientation/SFC/CAPS	240
Basic accounting course	24
Programming/ testing	
Introduction to financial and mangangement info.	24
Business practices	72
Systems installation	138
Programming supervision	
Detailed design	
System testing	
Conversion preparation	
Hardware/software evaluation	
Systems design	118
PSD - technical design	
- functional design	
Installation planning, organisation and cost benefit analysis	
Elective schools/courses	280 approx.
Special study	
Client service school	63
Information planning	
	259

Note: 1 Start and Finish points are the earliest and lastest respectively
2 Number of days is the minimum requirement
3 This sets out the quidelines for the *minimum* path to manager
4 Training programmes are set out in bold, others represent work experience

---

EXHIBIT 5
Economics for a Typical
Professional Service Firm

	RELATIVE NUMBER OF PROFESSIONALS BY LEVEL	RELATIVE NET BILLINGS PER HEAD BY LEVEL	RELATIVE COMPENSATION OF PROFESSIONALS BY LEVEL
Consultant	100	100	100
Manager	40	156	250
Partner	20	208	633

Key Assumptions:

(1) Target Utilization: Consultant (90%), Manager (75%), Partner (75%)

(2) Relative Net Billing per Head = Relative Billing Rate/Hours x Utilization Rate x Available Hours; Relative Billing Rate/Hours: Associate (100), Manager (187), Partner (250)

(3) Relative Compensation = salary + bonus

EXHIBIT 6
IT Professional Services
and Systems Integration
Europe—Key Competitors

COMPANY	1988 EUROPEAN PROF. SERVICES EST REVENUE ($MM)	1988 EUROPEAN PROF. SERVICES MARKETSHARE (%)	1988 EUROPEAN SYSTEMS INTEGR. EST. REVENUE ($MM)	1988 EUROPEAN SYSTEMS INTEGR. MARKET SHARE (%)	1989 WORLD REVENUE ($MM)	1989 WORLD PROFIT ($MM)	REVENUE CAGR (%) 1986–1989	PROFIT CAGR (%) 1986–1989
IBM	660	5.3	190	12.5	62710	3758	6.3	-7.8
Cap Gemini	590	4.7	180	11.8	1202	89.4	34	40
Volmac	245	2.0	[1]	[1]	283	53	12[2]	4.1[2]
Finsiel	225	1.8	[1]	[1]	625	N/A	N/A	N/A
Sema	220	1.8	80	5.3	478	18	55	44
Bull	220	1.8	35	2.3	5890	-48	23	N/A
Olivetti	200	1.6	45	2.9	7406	166	7.3	-29
Unysis	180	1.4	55	3.6	10097	-639	11	-145
Digital	140	1.1	1		12742	1073	19	20
SD-Scicon	140	1.1	85	5.6	462	5	66	3
Andersen	105	.8	155	10.2	1442	N/A	31	N/A
Logica	75	.6	65	4.3	280	20	29	42
Siemens	80	.6	65	4.3	32398	836	8	2
Others	9470	75	962	63	—	—	—	—
Total	12550	100	1520	100	—	—	—	—

[1]Market share is insignificant and included in "others"

[2]CAGR is 1987–1989

EXHIBIT 7
The Business of
Business Integration

- Strategic Planning
- Buyer Values/Customer Focus
- Product/Market Strategy
- Financial Strategy

- Business Process
  Improvement
- Logistics Optimization
- Facilities Planning

- Change Readiness
- Organization Design
- Knowledge Transfer
- Technology Assimilation

- Technology Assessment
- Information Technology Planning
- Systems Integration
- Computer Systems Management

....

EXHIBIT 8
Andersen Consulting
UK/Ireland

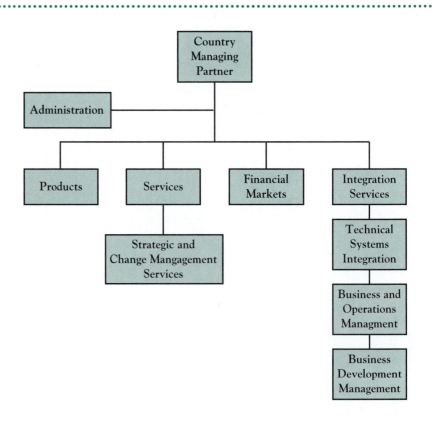

EXHIBIT 9
Andersen Consulting France

```
                              ┌─────────────┐
                              │   Country   │
                              │  Managing   │
                              │   Partner   │
                              └─────────────┘
         ┌──────────────┬───────────┴────────────┬──────────────┐
  ┌────────────┐ ┌──────────────┐  ┌──────────────┐  ┌──────────┐
  │  Produits  │ │  Stratégie and│  │  Ingénierie  │  │   Lyon   │
  │  Logiciels │ │  Management   │  │  Informatique│  │ Toulouse │
  └────────────┘ └──────────────┘  └──────────────┘  └──────────┘
```

Stratégie Produit/ Marché	Change Management Service	Entreprises Industrielles et Commerciales	Finance	Services

Polaroid started as an inventor's story on the classical model.[1] A superbly gifted inventor and scientist, Edwin Land, created Polaroid in 1937 and remained its chairman and director of research until 1982, when he stepped aside to pursue his research interests full time and be available as a consultant to Polaroid. Mr. William McCune, CEO since 1980 and a longtime colleague and friend of Dr. Land, had to reposition the company in light of some powerful new competitive forces.

EARLY HISTORY

Edwin Land never graduated from Harvard, preferring to form a company with one of his professors. His doctorate was honorary. But his attachment to research and invention was inseparable and ultimately led to his acquiring over 500 patents. Dr. Land's innovative mind caused one associate to claim, in reference to Land's original instant photography work: "100 Ph.D.'s would not have been able to duplicate Land's feat in ten years of uninterrupted work."[2] Yet Land developed the basic physical elements of this process within six months. Polaroid was actually founded on Land's invention of a light-polarizing sheet material, which filtered out all light except that vibrating in a single plane. Normally light waves vibrate in myriad planes as they emanate from a source. By crossing these planes two polarized sheets could eliminate light or glare as desired.

Land's early efforts concentrated on manufacturing easily marketed products like sunglasses and scientific products. And almost from the beginning, his company earned a profit. (2.154) In 1937 Land incorporated the

company, selling common stock to the Rothschilds and Baron Schroder under an unusual agreement that allowed him to maintain control. The agreement gave Land power over a trust that held the majority of the stock. (1,116) With this unusual beginning, Polaroid issued no long-term debt for years, financing itself internally and through stock issues. Among other innovations, Polaroid was one of the first public companies to consciously adopt a "low-dividend" policy, offering its stockholders the opportunity of taking almost all their profits as capital gains. The company grew rapidly through the World War II period when it was a government supplier of specialized optical products.

But Land hoped to design his product into automobile headlights and windshields to reduce night driving glare. (2,157) With windshields polarized in one direction and headlights in another, each driver would have a full view of the road ahead with no glare from oncoming lights. In 1947 although Detroit had successfully tested the headlight polarizing system, the automakers turned them down. (2.157) The industry saw no practical way to equip the 33 million cars then on the roads and was concerned that owners of those vehicles might be handicapped by the somewhat brighter headlights needed on filter equipped cars.

INSTANT PHOTOGRAPHY

The year 1947 started dismally, but all that changed in February when Land disclosed his now famous 60-second photographic process. Land's inspiration came one day during World War II as he was taking pictures of his daughter. She had asked impatiently why she could not see the finished picture right away. The question triggered Land's fertile imagination. And he soon conceptualized the basic idea for his revolutionary product. But he worked three long years before the process produced a sufficiently acceptable result. The secret lay in a self-developing film packet. Once he achieved initial success with this, Land moved quickly (in 1947) to design a camera to handle the film. William McCune, then a Polaroid engineer, and several associates contributed a series of important early inventions to support Land's work. (2,157) But this was only the beginning of a decades-long quest to develop improved films and cameras for instant photography.

The full requirements of the camera and film were beyond the financial capabilities of the young Polaroid Corporation, and it turned to outside contractors for much of its production. Protected by over 1000 patents, Polaroid ultimately had Bell & Howell and U.S. Time manufacture the camera, while Kodak supplied the negative film. Polaroid produced only the unique instant positive film and used its remaining manpower to market the camera.[3]

Sales grew from $1.5 million in 1947 to nearly $100 million by 1960. During this period Polaroid offered only black and white film—but vastly improved the quality of both its cameras and the film. It stayed strictly in the high (over $100) end of the camera market, while most of its potential competitors, including Kodak, scoffed at the idea of a large instant picture market. (2,125) In fact, Kodak worked with Polaroid, helping the growing fledgling introduce the world's first instant color film in 1963. This technological achievement spurred Polaroid's sales in the mid-1960s as Polaroid rode a burgeoning amateur photography market along with Kodak and its Instamatic line.

By 1963 Polaroid completely dominated the high-priced "instant" camera field and began to eye the much larger inexpensive segment controlled by Kodak. The Polaroid Swinger—a black and white camera selling under $20—introduced in the fall of 1965 was an immediate success.[4] Polaroid soon expanded its presence with the Big Swinger (in 1968) and Colorpak II in 1969. In each case, the new camera, priced within $5 of its predecessor, overwhelmed the former model, and large inventories of the older cameras were often sold below cost to discount houses.[4]

SX-70 AND SHOCKWAVES

Still, in this period Polaroid began to face some ominous problems. Its original patents for instant photography started to expire in 1965. While newer patents prevented immediate competition, other companies would be able to enter the instant picture market by 1970. And Polaroid's successful forays into the low price camera market had stimulated Kodak's interest in instant photography.[4]

In the early 1960s, Dr. Land began organizing a project team to revolutionize instant photography and leapfrog past his competition into another fortress of patents. As Land's project team pushed both film technology and the camera design art (Land called it forced evolution) Polaroid became involved in such seemingly unrelated fields as integrated circuits and batteries. Polaroid's new products had such demanding standards that they required significant design and manufacturing cooperation with suppliers. During this period, talented Polaroid engineers often "lived" with vendors to help them achieve new and rigorous design and production specifications. Virtually all of this project's work was performed without any market research except Polaroid's own confidence in knowing its customers' needs.[5]

Polaroid felt market research was only valid as a method of delineating an existing market, not for evaluating an entirely new concept. Land always held that Polaroid's product created the market, rather than the market dictating the product. This was in part why he could withstand the knee buckling skepticism and delays that accompanied the introduction of the revolutionary SX-70 line. He later scoffed at those who "couldn't see the potential of a $600 camera value marketed in the $100 range."[6]

In 1972, this project ("Aladdin") bore its professed creation, the SX-70. The camera offered startling improvements over previous models. Its color film literally developed before the customer's eyes. The distasteful refuse layers generated by the old "peel apart" process were eliminated. And the camera itself was a marvel of optical engineering. The SX-70's development costs had been staggering; some estimates were as high as $600 million (including buildings) over its full duration.

Polaroid initiated another important shift along with the introduction of the SX-70. Because of the camera's sophistication and Kodak's impending instant camera introduction, Polaroid decided to manufacture and assemble the major components of the camera "in house," as well as produce the negatives for its film. This decision not only required substantial investments in plant and equipment (over $200 million) between 1968 and 1972, but it strained the organization to adapt its highly unstructured management style to the routine operations of an assembly line.[7] The gamble also sent shockwaves down Wall Street, with many analysts doubting Polaroid's ability to maintain respectable earnings growth during this period. (3,125)

In fact, the SX-70's introduction was plagued with bad luck. The national introduction was delayed until late 1973, while engineers scrambled to solve its problems. Production difficulties caused product shortages in most locales. The 1974 recession cut deeply into the SX-70's potential sales, as its high price ($180) kept it from the volume markets. At the same time there were complaints about the quality of the SX-70's innovative self-developing pictures, and the sale of other Polaroid models fell off more than expected. Profits for 1974 dropped to $28.4 million, down $23.4 million from the previous year.

LAND CHANGES ROLES

In January 1975 Dr. Land stepped aside as president. Land wanted to get out of daily operations to concentrate on one of his favorite projects—instant movies—and he saw the need for a full-time operations manager. William McCune, who took over the presidency, was experienced in all phases of engineering and manufacturing and had spearheaded the project which removed Polaroid's color negative manufacturing from Kodak's benevolent control. "Bill" McCune had a warm, calm, and relaxed manner even in crisis situations. Slim and graying, McCune understood the unique Polaroid organization and Dr. Land's style well. He preferred to operate through consensus, but he was also demanding and wanted problems addressed. Said one executive at the time,

> "He has known for years that certain things needed to be done around here, and now that he's got the charter he's doing them. . . . We had been trying to get certain product decisions for as long as two years before Bill became president," the executive added. "The routine had been that one top guy thought this and another top guy thought that and the boss (Mr. Land) was waffling. So we'd go back and get more data and do it all over again. Now Bill just says, "Okay, do it.""[8]

McCune also removed some of the centralizing aura of Dr. Land's style from operating decisions.

> McCune's orders are usually clear, but if they aren't I can say, "Bill, what are you trying to tell me? Exactly what do you want me to do?" I would never dare ask Land that.[8]

A NEW ERA BEGINS

Polaroid faced its first direct competitor in 1975. Pint-sized Berkey Photo introduced an instant picture camera which used SX-70 film.[9] Polaroid's reaction was prompt and predictable; it immediately filed a patent infringement suit against Berkey. Despite this unexpected intruder into its domain, Polaroid rebounded to near record profits of $62.5 million in 1975. But the prospects of a much bloodier battle seemed in prospect when Kodak marketed its entry in April 1976. Instead, the entire instant photo market exploded. Even with Kodak initially grabbing 25% of the market, Polaroid's sales grew to $950 million with record profits of $79.7 million by the end of 1976.

But the threat from the Rochester giant was lethal; and Polaroid, armed with its vast patent portfolio, pursued an injunction against Kodak to cease and desist from further manufacture of instant cameras and film. Similar actions in Canada and the United Kingdom temporarily prevented Kodak from offering its product, but Kodak's lawyers soon found a way out from each injunction.[9] Still, counter-punching effectively with Kodak, Polaroid's sales and profits grew while Kodak's instant camera division operated in the red.[10] Then from the east, a third challenger, Fuji Photo of Japan, reared its head and began its tentative probing of what had been Polaroid's exclusive domain only two years before.

As a partial counter to these entries, in 1977 Polaroid introduced instant movies. Dr. Land had been determined to provide a moving picture complement to his instant still pictures. But the initial product entry, Polavision, was expensive ($699) and was positioned at the high end of a stagnant home movie market, representing only 10% of the total photography market. Unlike SX-70, the camera and hardware were manufactured outside Polaroid. With his characteristic optimism, Dr. Land entered the new field hoping to generate the same response that occurred 30 years before. (9,45) As he had so many times before, Dr. Land made the announcement of this new product dramatically at the 1976 stockholders meeting (April 1977), a year before the product was to be fully available in the marketplace.

Unfortunately, Polavision was a striking failure in both technology and marketing—the very areas in which the company had been so strong,[11] and it was financially costly with three years of "substantial" operating losses and a $68.5 million write off in 1979. But *Fortune* also noted,

> Polavision began in the late 1960s as part of Project Sesame, the code name the company used for experiments with film that is designed to be viewed by shining light through it (as opposed to film designed to produce printed pictures). One consolation for Polaroid is that Polavision is merely the first of the products that can be expected to grow out of Project Sesame . . . Polaroid may have discov-

ered a way to reduce the cost of manufacturing all instant color film . . . In any case, there is an obvious application of the Polavision technology—instant slides.[11]

NEW COMPETITIVE FORCES

Instant cameras reached a peak of 41% of the still photographic market in 1978, with Polaroid selling a record 9.4 million cameras worldwide. Confident of future growth, it launched an extensive capital expenditure program to increase production of SX-70 cameras and film worldwide.[12] In 1979, after a 4 year growth of 41%, the U.S. camera market dropped 3%.[13] Polaroid's unit sales plummeted more than 22% just as its capital expansion projects neared completion. The worldwide recession of the following several years hurt the whole photographic industry, but even more so the instant cameras and films which had always sold to lower income groups than those who bought conventional cameras.[14]

Polaroid fought to maintain and survive on its two-thirds share of the declining instant market. It introduced sonar automatic focusing, Time Zero Supercolor film, the Sun (light management system) cameras, and high-speed 600 ASA instant color film. Kodak's share dropped from 40% in 1978 to 30% in 1982. But by 1982 Polaroid's instant still sales had fallen to an estimated 4 million units annually.

Fuji Photo's instant system was doing well in its Japanese home market, and Eastman upgraded its somewhat deficient instant line in 1982. In addition Kodak's new disc system had proved an immediate novelty and consumer success. Nimslo International had introduced a three dimensional still process, but its market was generally considered a novelty.[15] Sony too had announced its all electronic Mavica camera and system, but in 1982 this required several cabinets of complex backup equipment to manipulate and display its images. Other important market trends are shown in Exhibits 2-7.

DIVERSIFICATION EFFORTS

Polaroid had for years marketed photographic products in non-consumer markets—such as instant cameras for use in hospitals and labs, microphotography cameras, panorama cameras, studio films, passport and drivers license photo equipment and special event cameras.[16] As the amateur market for instant photography declined, the company began to devote more of its energies toward expanding such markets and breaking into well-established (non-photography related) fields

with spinoffs from its instant photographic and optical technology (such as a wafer thin battery, a filter for video display terminal screens, a curing agent for polyurethene, an anticounterfelt labeling material, a sonar transducer, and precision optical devices).[16]

These diversification efforts were beginning to bear fruit by mid 1982. Sales of such products constituted a growing percentage of Polaroid's revenues, although not yet the 50% that represented the goal that *Business Week* had earlier reported.[17] Intensified development efforts in these areas were also paying off. The company's 1982 *Annual Report* stated,

> The new 35mm Autoprocess color and black and white rapid access slide film system adds a new dimension to 35mm photography and marks the first time Polaroid will be marketing products in a conventional film format for use in existing cameras and instruments. [Our prototype of a new low-cost business graphics system for use with the Apple II and IBM Personal Computers] consists of a menu-driven software program (supplied on a diskette) and a tri-color videoprinter which can produce 4 x 5 inch format color prints and 35mm rapid-access color and black and white slides. These new Polaroid tabletop imaging and processing systems make Polaroid instant photography a part of the flow of immediate information in the office and laboratory. In their design, these self-contained systems become logical extensions of their host electronic imaging systems, and in operation they expand and complement the functions of those systems.

The graphics hardcopy system was an offshoot of Polaroid's 23% stake in a small company, Image Resource Corp. But these endeavors did not remedy the decline of Polaroid's primary market and the failure of its Polavision product. Polaroid saw its EPS drop from a high of $3.60 in 1978 to $0.95 in 1981. In the same period, return on assets fell from 9.3% to 2.2% and pretax profits as a percent of sales went from 14.1% down to 4.4%.

MANAGEMENT AND ORGANIZATIONAL CHANGES

In April 1980, Bill McCune took over as CEO, and Land became chairman of the board and consulting director of Basic Research in Land Photography. Soon after he took office, Mr. McCune began to change Polaroid's unique organization. *Business Week* had summarized some of the key philosophies under Dr. Land as follows:

> Seldom, if ever, has a large American company so faithfully reflected the substance and style of one man as does

Other philosophies of Dr. Land were still important factors in Polaroid's 1982 culture. (See Appendix A.) Under Dr. Land, Polaroid's commitment to research and development had dominated the organization's structure and approach. By providing exceptional work flexibility, Dr. Land attempted to create an innovative atmosphere where the corporate structure did not interfere with employees' motivation. Major divisions were organized simply along functional lines (i.e., marketing, manufacturing). The heart of the corporation's creative capability was the research division headed by Dr. Land. The manufacturing and operating divisions were coordinated by Mr. McCune. A Management Executive Committee (M.E.C.), comprised of Land, McCune, Julius Silver (corporate attorney) and the heads of the major divisions, served as a forum to discuss key aspects of corporate policy and to exchange information about major operating decisions.

McCune had coordinated the functional operations of the company. However, not being a detail man, he preferred to delegate to his young, aggressive divisional managers, who in turn assumed firm control over their areas and promoted strong divisional loyalties and even some degree of proprietary control over divisional information. All the division and senior managers were long-time Polaroid employees. And, although McCune could act as an effective coordinator and buffer, all understood that Land's word had been final on crucial issues, especially those associated with product offerings. In fact, Land had held strategic direction strictly to himself, and often preempted decisions or overturned operating management's consensus on issues of particular interest to him. Although no official organization chart existed prior to 1980, published information and informed outside observers estimated key relationships to be as shown in Exhibit 10. Some details about each major activity and player follow.

MANUFACTURING DIVISION

Under the direction of I. M. "Mac" Booth, this division had responsibility for domestic camera and film pack production as well as all negative film coatings. Labor intensive operations such as the camera assembly were separated from the highly automated coating facilities for the negative and positive film production.

Polaroid had decided against consolidating all Boston area facilities into one giant Cambridge industrial complex, preferring to keep things in relatively smaller locations in Norwood, Needham, New Bedford, Freetown, and Waltham, Mass. It wanted to keep things more on a human and manageable scale, with workers having a greater opportunity to feel an integral part of what was happening. This dispersal also raised the company's profile in each community the way a single large Cambridge complex could not. (6,191)

In 1980 Booth (age 49) was a rising star at Polaroid. Tough, hard nosed, and inquiring, he often became the "devil's advocate" in top-level discussions. Booth had the difficult task of planning and operating the bulk of Polaroid's complex manufacturing facilities and coordinating them with the vagaries of the consumer marketplace and the magnificent spurts of inventiveness coming from Research. Booth believed in running a tight ship, was willing to experiment with new management techniques and prided himself on his capacities to select people. Booth had become the senior vice president of manufacturing after successfully developing and operating the company's new negative film manufacturing facilities. He had earlier served as an assistant to McCune and enjoyed excellent relationships with the president

MARKETING DIVISION

Since the company's early beginnings, its marketing division had always played an important role. Polaroid's innovative product line had required an aggressive and intelligent marketing program which Edwin Land personally supported. In 1980 the division was headed by youthfully graying, dapper, soft spoken, Peter Wensberg (age 52) who had become senior vice president in 1971. More philosophical than "Mac" Booth in many ways, Wensberg liked to talk about the long-term market positioning and management needs of Polaroid amid a collection of historical instruments and nautical devices that artistically decorated his office. Nevertheless, within his division Wensberg was known as a hard driver. Along with Richard Young, head of Polaroid's International Division. Wensberg had been considered one of the three likely successors to Land, before McCune was named to the position. (6,216) He had complete control over marketing and was a powerful force throughout the corporation. However, his nontechnical background limited the depth of his influence in the more technical divisions.

The marketing division was responsible for all domestic marketing including advertising, customer service, and marketing/sales. The marketing/sales department was divided into a consumer and an industrial product group with a separate sales force for each. Consumer products were distributed directly to large retail, department, and discount stores and through selected wholesalers to smaller retail outlets. Polaroid's sales force handled both cameras and film supplies within their regional territories. Industrial products—designed for commercial photographers and industrial, scientific, or medical applications—were sold through an industrial sales force or independent industrial agents. In addition, the marketing division also had its own market research, marketing planning, advertising, promotion, order processing, internal bookkeeping, (etc.) groups.

RESEARCH DIVISIONS

Since its inception Polaroid had been dominated by its research activities. And under Dr. Land's leadership research continued to be a major focal point of the corporation. No absolute delineation existed between applied and pure research; however, separate divisions had been set up to specialize in those two functions. The applied research division, referred to as the technology division, carried most new products or product improvements into production. It occasionally was responsible for manufacturing new products which either needed further design changes or whose market demand was not sufficient to justify transferring them to the huge manufacturing division. Dr. Sheldon Buckler (age 49), who had originally worked in pure research and had participated in a number of Land's entrepreneurial projects, had served as the division's manager since 1972. Dr. Land's great technical abilities and strong personality made this both a difficult and a highly rewarding role.

The research division worked primarily on more basic research projects and had fostered many major technological improvements in films and coatings. The division's close relations to Dr. Land gave it extremely high-level support in dealing with other divisions. In fact, some claimed that Research often had the controlling hand in such relationships. President McCune had also had a long association with research. When Land had come up with his early inventions McCune had been the one who followed up and built them. (6,216) In addition to McCune, research had served as an incubation ground for other senior managers, with three present members of the M.E.C.—Drs. Young, Buckler, and Bloom—each having at one time been Land's assistant director of research.

Land had philosophically conceptualized Polaroid as an extension of the scientific laboratory. He wanted to move the concept of scientific experimentation into the industrial sphere, with the same absence of guilt attached to business as to laboratory failures. In fact the company's success really came back to continual experiments and recombinations of technical work and business ventures that at many points in time had indeed been stopped or looked like failures. (6,184–5) Hence R&D teams were formed, dissolved and reformed with scientists and engineers fluidly following projects into development or production and then returning to the labs again.

Land believed in a strong relationship between the laboratory and the factory. In a manner reminiscent of Mao sending the intellectuals to the rice fields, he sometimes had research people "operating machines." He felt this exposure would give them a greater practical feel for their own theoretical work. In Land's vision, production was just a continuation of research and development, with McCune and Land participating (for example) in the design of machinery and components for SX-70. (6,190)

INTERNATIONAL DIVISION

Dr. Richard Young (age 54) had managed the International division with an independence and feistiness sometimes envied by the domestic managers. His entrepreneurial talents were put to work in the division when he was appointed its president in 1969 after a very successful career in the research division. By early 1980 international sales had grown to nearly 40% of total corporate revenues and the division controlled all manufacturing and marketing outside the United States. The manufacturing capabilities of the division included positive film coating operations, camera and film pack assembly, and sunglass production. It relied on the U.S. operation for batteries, negative film and other proprietary items but used local contractors for other components. International had three manufacturing facilities—in Scotland, in Ireland, and the Netherlands. The facilities in Scotland and the Netherlands were involved with most phases of production, whereas the plant in Ireland was strictly for film pack assembly. No research had been conducted by the division. Almost all of its products had been first introduced in the United States. And its product line had been essentially the same as the domestic unit's, with some local adaptations to accommodate metric measures, special market conditions, or local regulations.

In 1980 International marketed the full line of Polaroid products directly through wholly owned subsidiaries in some 20 countries.[19] It hired independent distributors in most other areas of the world. The sales force also had a line of sunglasses which was marketed along with its other products; otherwise the sales organization operated in a manner similar to the domestic group's.

International was reportedly the only profit center within Polaroid in 1980. With this distinction, it seemed to operate somewhat more independently and aggressively within the corporation. Financial controls for all divisions were maintained by McCune and the finance division. Financial allocations had generally been based largely on the presentations of each functional group as reviewed by the finance division and the M.E.C. With the exception of major new products there had been little attempt to interrelate capital programs between divisions. And there had been significant reluctance to develop integrated five-year plans among the divisions because of the entrepreneurial nature of the company and the uncertainty of the marketplace.

STAFF DIVISIONS

The remaining divisions represented specialized staff activities which supported the line manufacturing, research, and marketing divisions. The largest were the engineering, finance, and legal divisions—although there were also personnel, planning, systems analysis, and public relations specialists at the corporate level. The company's accounting and financial controls tended to follow functional lines, with each division handling the bulk of its own detailed bookkeeping, systems development, and data generation internally. Of course, the finance division specified the records and reports needed for corporate purposes and coordinated all contracts with outside capital sources.[20]

A SMORGASBORD OF TALENT

Dr. Land had used his flexible and creative organization as a "smorgasbord of talent." By selecting individuals with specific skills from any area in the corporation. Land could quickly assemble the highly diverse talents needed to handle desired tasks. For example, when he was confronted with an enormous project like "Aladdin" (SX-70), Land would reach into all his functional groups to gather the necessary people available within Polaroid. Then he would fill any gaps with outside specialists.

In such circumstances, Land reportedly maintained complete control over the project team's R&D activities, even to the information going to and from his team. Secrecy would often shroud his group's activities, and team members might purposely be kept isolated from nonessential contact with other groups in Polaroid. Land himself might be the only individual intimately aware of the entire project's work. (6,210) He would call for additional support work as necessary, and tried to make sure that each research task was the responsibility of a particular individual, rather than diffused as "an organizational responsibility."

As the project's concept crystalized into more definite shape, moved into development, or began scale-up, Dr. Land transferred his attention increasingly to marketing the evolving product. Individual technical team members usually followed their element of the project through full scale-up and debugging before returning to their former jobs. But occasionally, a team researcher or engineer ended up managing manufacturing for the developed component.

Under Land's care and feeding the Polaroid organization responded dynamically—and somewhat amorphously—to changing conditions. Teams formed and reformed around problems. (6,198) From the beginning Polaroid had encouraged employees to participate in decisions affecting their areas. In fact, innovation in organization and corporate human relations was a stated goal of the company. Employees were encouraged to take courses and advanced degrees at company expense. And many of Polaroid's more productive engineers were high school graduates or technicians who had never taken full time university training. Formal organizational constraints and authority relationships were kept to a minimum, and inconsistencies in managerial styles and even the corporation's functional setup were frequent. For example, digressions often arose when a development project moved into manufacturing or commercialization stages. At that point, the responsibility for the project's completion usually reverted to the team leader's division regardless of its function. Consequently, an applied research or engineering division might house manufacturing operations or a small commercial unit for some time. Eventually, however, the misplaced unit would be relocated to its proper functional area or occasionally operated as a small division more or less on its own.

Knowledgeable observers referred to the Polaroid organizations as a "moving target." The arrangement at any moment seemed to evolve naturally from the unstructured operational environment, and further adjustments might soon change any existing situation. The attached organizational charts indicate only those broad relationships which one could define from published data and external contacts with the company. And even these might change quickly with circumstances. There seemed to be substantial participation in decision making among affected parties *within* a division. But such participation *between* divisions was reportedly less common, and of course major interdivisional decisions had to be made at the very top level if substantial disagreements occurred.

THE 1980 REORGANIZATION

In October 1980, Mr. McCune began to restructure the top level activities of Polaroid, although many of its *operating* philosophies remained unchanged. He stated,

> Our goals are fourfold: to understand better our total potential, to encourage expanding fields such as our technical and industrial photographic businesses, to explore fields which are new for Polaroid such as batteries and the commercial chemical business; and to establish clear cut areas of responsibility for growth in both sales and profits.[21]

The office of the president was enlarged by the creation of four executive vice presidents. These were Drs. Buckler and Young, and Messrs. Booth and Wensberg. Major departments were consolidated on a worldwide basis to recognize global needs more fully in such areas as marketing, finance, manufacturing, and materials management[21] This was widely recognized as the beginning of several phased moves which would ensure Polaroid's competitiveness and continued innovativeness in the 1980s. Mr. McCune wanted to be ready to announce his final organization concept in 1982.

QUESTIONS

1. In light of its changing competitive situation, what should Polaroid's strategy have been in 1982? Why?
2. Design an organization suited to support this strategy. Draw an organization chart showing critical relationships down through the departmental level. Who should occupy each position at the division level or above? Why?
3. What control system is needed to make your strategy and organization effective? Define key measures at each level down to departments.
4. What other steps are necessary to implement your strategy?

APPENDIX A
Polaroid Corporation Philosophy and Culture

In May 1967, Dr. Land wrote down some key points of the Polaroid philosophy. These were still widely accepted in Polaroid in 1982:

> We have two basic products at Polaroid: (1) Products that are genuinely unique and useful, excellent in quality, made well and efficiently, so that they present an attractive profit to the Company; (2) A worthwhile working life for each member of the Company—a working life that calls out the member's best talents and skills—in which he or she shares the responsibilities and the rewards.
>
> These two products are inseparable. The Company prospers most, and its members find their jobs most worthwhile, when its members are contributing their full talents and efforts to creating, producing, and selling products of outstanding merit. (6,183)

In amplifying this Dr. Land was quoted as saying,

> What we're after in America is an industrial society where a person maintains at work the full dignity he has at home. I don't mean that they will all be happy. They'll be unhappy—but in new, exciting, and important ways. [At Polaroid, people] would work happy for that time. Polaroid eliminated the time clock, provided extensive educational opportunities inside and outside the company, and allowed employees to "try out" for other jobs if they thought they would be more satisfying. (6,188-9)

In a *Harvard Business Review* article Dr. Land further stated his philosophies;

> I think whether outside science or within science there is no such thing as *group* originality or *group* creativity or *group* perspicacity.
>
> I do believe wholeheartedly in the individual capacity for greatness, in one way or another in almost any healthy human being under the *right* circumstances; but being part of a group is, in my opinion, generally the *wrong* circumstance. Profundity and originality are attributes of single, if not singular, minds. Two minds may sometimes be better than one, provided that each of the two minds is working separately while the two are working together; yet three tend to become a crowd.[22]

EXHIBIT 1

Polaroid Corporation and Subsidiary Companies Ten-Year Financial Summary (Unaudited): Years Ended December 31, 1972–1981 (dollar amounts in millions, except per share data)

	1981	1980	1979
Consolidated Statement of Earnings			
Net sales:			
United States	$817.8	$791.8	$757.2
International	601.8	659.0	604.3
Total net sales	$1,419.6	$1,450.8	$1,361.5
Cost of goods sold	855.4	831.1	876.8
Marketing, research. engineering. and administrative expenses	520.8	483.9	449.4
Total costs	$1,376.2	$1,315.0	$1,326.2
Profit from operations	43.4	135.8	35.3
Other income	49.2	25.4	13.3
Interest expense	29.9	17.0	12.8
Earnings before income taxes	$ 62.7	$ 144.2	$35.8
Federal, state, and foreign income taxes (credit)	31.6	58.8	(0.3)
Net earnings	$ 31.1	$ 85.4	$ 36.1
Earnings per share	$0.95	$2.60	$1.10
Cash dividends per share	$1.00	$1.00	$1.00
Average number of shares (in millions)	32.9	32.9	32.9
Selected Balance Sheet Information			
Working capital*	$ 749.5	$ 721.9	$ 535.9
Net property, plant, and equipment	332.9	362.2	371.6
Total assets*	1,434.7	1,404.0	1,253.7
Long-term debt	124.2	124.1	—
Stockholders' equity*	958.2	960.0	907.5
Other Statistical Data			
Additions to property, plant, and equipment	$ 42.5	$ 68.1	$ 134.6
Depreciation	$ 69.2	$ 62.7	$ 51.7
Payroll and benefits	$ 550.5	$ 497.3	$ 464.1**
Number of employees, end of year	16,784	17,454	18,416
Return on equity* (two point average)	3.2%	0.1%	4.0

*Years 1972 through 1980 have been restated to reflect implementation of Financial Accounting Standards Board Statement No. 43 "Accounting for Compensated Absences."
**Restated.
Source: Polaroid Corporation. *Annual Report. 1981.*

APPENDIX A (cont'd)

Dr. Land believed in mutual trust and commitment between employees and management; and he expected his people to actively participate in this opportunity:

> I don't regard it as normal for a human being to have an eight-hour day, with two long coffee breaks, with a martini at lunch, with a sleepy period in the afternoon and a rush home to the next martini. I don't think that can be dignified by calling it working, and I don't think people should be paid for it.[23]

In 1977 Dr. Land reaffirmed his commitment to a high corporate ethic in Polaroid's Annual Report:

> A company has as many aspects to its character as a person has, seeking fulfillment and self expression, power, friendship, creativity, immediate recognition and ultimate significance. It has a conscience and high purpose and moral standards and vulnerability. It can sin, feel guilty and repent, it can love and it can hate, it can build and it can destroy. . . . Recognition of the analogs of human characteristics in corporate life will in my opinion rejuvenate the economy, regenerate national self-respect, initiate an intellectual renaissance, and reward us all with a vast family of blessings which in our blindness we hold stubbornly at arms length. (9,3)

1978	1977	1976	1975	1974	1973	1972
$ 817.4	$645.8	$586.7	$495.6	$ 487.3	$493.1	417.5
559.2	416.1	363.3	317.1	270.0	192.4	141.8
$1,376.6	$1,061.9	$950.0	$812.7	$757.3	$685.5	$559.3
778.3	575.7	511.8	467.9	485.2	358.0	260.1
418.2	337.3	294.9	237.0	239.3	251.6	236.7
$1,196.5	$913.0	$806.7	$704.9	$724.5	$609.6	$496.8
180.1	148.9	143.3	107.8	32.8	75.9	62.5
20.3	19.0	14.4	16.8	13.4	14.2	13.5
5.9	6.4	3.3	1.3	1.1	.3	.8
194.5	161.5	154.4	123.3	45.1	89.8	75.2
76.1	69.2	74.7	60.7	16.7	38.0	32.7
$118.4	$92.3	$79.7	$62.6	$28.4	$51.8	$42.5
$3.60	$2.81	$2.43	$1.91	$0.86	$1.58	$1.30
$0.90	$0.65	$0.41	$0.32	$0.32	$0.32	$0.32
32.9	32.9	32.9	32.9	32.9	32.9	32.8
$609.5	$589.6	$546.4	$475.1	$402.0	$380.1	$341.7
294.8	225.9	198.2	203.3	224.3	228.3	224.5
1,276.0	1,076.7	959.0	843.7	777.8	751.0	661.2.
—	—	—	—	—	—	—
904.3	815.5	744.6	678.4	626.3	608.4	566.2
$115.0	$68.7	$33.9	$21.8	$40.0	$40.3	$44.6
$43.0	$39.5	$38.3	$39.1	$39.6	$35.3	$32.0
$ 421.4**	$332.2**	$ 289.6**	$231.8**	$223.2	$191.3	$160.2
20,884	16,394	14,506	13,387	13,019	14,227	11,998
13.8%	11.8%	11.2%	9.6%	4.6%	8.8%	7.7%

EXHIBIT 2
Comparative Instant Camera and Film Data, 1982
(dollars in millions)

| | POLAROID 1982 | | | KODAK 1982 |
	TOTAL	NONAMATEUR	AMATEUR	ALL AMATEUR
Sales	$1,294	$390	$904	5425
Cost of goods	741	211	530	264
% of sales	57.3%	54.0%	58.6%	62.0%
S & A	473	128	345	162
% of sales	36.6%	32.8%	38.2%	38.2%
Operating profit	$80	$51	$29	$(1)
margins	6.2%	13.1%	3.2%	—

Source: Donaldson, Lufkin & Jenrette, *Research Bulletin*, September 28, 1983.

EXHIBIT 3
Manufacturers' Shipments of Photographic Equipment and Supplies, 1977–1982
($ millions)

	1977		1978	
	$	%	$	%
Sensitized film and paper	$3,874.1	39.0%	4,489.7	39.0%
Prepared photographic mchemicals	695.6	7.0	805.4	7.0
Micrographic equipment	298.1	3.0	345.2	3.0
Motion picture equipment	198.7	2.0	230.1	2.0
Still picture equipment	993.7	10.0	1,150.6	10.0
Reprographic equipment	3,876.8	39.0	4,485.0	39.0
Total	**$9,937.0**	**100%**	**$11,506.0**	**100%**
Yr. to yr. change			15.8%	

Source: Lehman Brothers Kuhn Loeb, *The Photographic Products Market*, August 4, 1983.

EXHIBIT 4
U.S. Imports and Exports of Photographic Equipment and Supplies:
Estimated Product Breakdown (1979–1982)
($ millions)

	1979			1980		
	EXPORTS	IMPORTS	NET	EXPORTS	IMPORTS	NET
Sensitized film and paper	$1,074.2	$390.7	$683.5	$1,349.9	$ 532.7	$817.2
Prepared photographic chemicals	133.9	6.7	127.2	137.8	9.1	128.7
Micrographic equipment	77.3	1.6	75.7	90.9	1.9	89.0
Motion picture equipment	82.7	68.3	14.4	99.1	69.4	29.7
Still picture equipment	420.5	731.7	(311.2)	450.3	644.5	(194.2)
Reprographic equipment	358.4	358.3	0.1	331.7	497.0	(165.3)
Total	**$2,147.0**	**$1,557.3**	**$589.7**	**$2,459.7**	**$754.6**	**$705.1**

Source: Lehman Brothers Kuhn Loeb, *The Photographic Products Market*, August 4, 1983.

Estimated Regional Breakdown (1979–1982)
($ millions)

	1979				1980			
	EXPORTS		IMPORTS		EXPORTS		IMPORTS	
	$	%	$	%	$	%	$	%
Europe	$ 972.6	45.3%	$294.3	18.9%	$1,167.7	45.4%	$ 352.7	20.1%
Canada	255.5	11.9	73.2	4.7	275.5	11.2	119.3	6.8
Latin America	188.9	8.8	1.6	0.1	206.6	8.4	1.8	0.1
Asia	298.5	13.9	1,175.7	75.5	332.1	13.5	11,272.1	72.5
Other	431.5	20.1	12.5	0.8	528.8	21.5	8.7	0.5
Total	**$2,147 .0**	**100.0%**	**$1,557.3**	**100.0%**	**$2,459.7**	**100.0%**	**$1,754.6**	**100.0%**

Source: Lehman Brothers Kuhn Loeb, *The Photographic Products Market*, August 4, 1983.

EXHIBIT 5
Estimated Breakdown of Still Pictures Taken by U.S. Consumers
(millions of Units)

	1977		1978	
	UNITS	CHG. %	UNITS	CHG. %
Color print negative	4,805	17.8%	6,010	25.1%
Slides (positive)	1,495	(4.4)	1,585	6.0
Instant	1,370	5.4	1,675	22.3
Black and white	660	(10.0)	600	(9.1)
Total	**8,330**	**8.5%**	**9,870**	**18.5%**

Source: Lehman Brothers Kuhn Loeb, *The Photographic Products Market*, August 4, 1983.

1979		1980		1981		1982	
$	%	$	%	$	%	$	%
$ 5,288.7	39.5%	$6,706.7	42.3%	$ 7,186.4	42.4%	$7,652.9	41.3%
937.2	7.0	1,030.6	6.5	1,033.9	6.1	1,080.4	5.8
401.7	3.0	539.1	3.4	793.2	3.5	948.5	4.0
267.8	2.0	269.5	1.7	220.3	1.3	298.3	1.6
1,405.9	10.5	1,442.8	9.1	1,271.2	7.5	1,466.5	7.9
5,087.7	38.0	5,866.3	37.0	6,644,0	39.2	7,310.4	39.4
$13,389.0	100%	$15,855.0	100%	$16,949.0	100%	$18,557.0	100%
16.4%		18.4%		6.9%		9.5%	

	1981			1982	
EXPORTS	IMPORTS	NET	EXPORTS	IMPORTS	NET
$1,346.1	$567.1	$779.0	$1,234.9	$607.7	$627.2
133.3	9.5	123.8	135.6	8.0	127.6
110.0	5.0	105.0	86.1	2.7	83.4
99.3	45.5	53.8	85.9	32.3	53.6
457.7	798.9	(341.2)	491.3	783.4	(292.1)
361.5	721.1	(359.6)	423.6	676.4	(252.8)
$2,507.9	$2,147.1	$360.8	$2,457.4	$2,110.5	$346.9

1981				1982			
EXPORTS		IMPORTS		EXPORTS		IMPORTS	
$	%	$	%	$	%	$	%
$ 969.4	38.7%	$ 329.7	15.3%	$1,069.7	43.5%	$ 373.2	17.7%
271.2	10.8	113.9	5.3	316.5	12.9	102.8	4.9
376.2	15.0	1.8	0.1	287.5	11.7	3.0	1
491.9	19.6	1,669.9	77.8	529.8	21.6	1,622.0	76.9
399.2	15.9	31.9	1.5	253.9	10.3	9.5	.4
$2,507.9	100.0%	$2,147.1	100.0%	$2,457.4	100.0%	$2,110.5	100.0%

1979		1980		1981		1982	
UNITS	CHG. %	UNITS	CHG. %	UNITS	CHG. %	UNITS	CHG.%
6,295	4.7%	6,645	5.6%	7,300	9.9%	7,950	8.9%
1,530	(3.5)	1,540	0.7	1,350	(12.3)	1,250	(7.4)
1,550	(7.5)	1,500	(3.3)	1,450	(3.3)	1,250	(13.8)
575	(4.2)	565	(1.7)	525	(7.1)	500	(4.8)
9,950	0.8%	10,250	3.0%	10,625	3.7%	10,950	3.1%

EXHIBIT 6

Estimated U.S. Consumer Purchases of Film, by Type, 1978–1982
(millions of units)

FILM TYPE	1978	1979	1980	1981	1982	CHANGE 1981–82
Instant B&W	18.8	12.8	7.9	5.8	4.4	(24.1)%
Instant color	119.6	124.1	124.2	126.0	110.9	(12.0)
35mm B&W	26.7	21.2	25.3	23.0	18.6	(19.1)
35mm color slide	61.3	56.2	55.3	57.0	52.0	(8.8)
35mm color print	84.8	98.5	119.9	137.0	146.8	7.2
110 cartridge B&W		18.4	14.0	10.0	13.9	39.0
110 cartridge color	16.1	170.7	182.3	193.0	196.5	1.8
126 cartridge B&W		14.3	9.2	8.0	9.0	12.5
126 cartridge color	221.6	104.2	103.1	105.0	90.0	(14.3)
Disc					21.0	
Other still B&W	20.0	8.2	6.9	6.7	6.5	(3.0)
Other still color	44.4	17.8	13.4	15.0	13.2	(12.0)
Movie	35.3	27.5	26.8	22.0	19.0	(13.6)
Total	**648.6**	**673.9**	**688.3**	**708.5**	**701.8**	**(0.9)%**

Source: Lehman Brothers Kuhn Loeb, *The Photographic Products Market*, August 4, 1983.

Estimated Breakdown of U.S. Consumer Camera Sales
(thousands of units)

	1974	1975	1976	1977	1978
Cartridge	8,590	8,630	9,050	9,250	10,200
35mm (all types)	825	708	980	1,560	2,300
Instant	3,300	3,900	4,500	6,600	8,200
8mm Movie	636	392	450	609	525
Other**	12	15	20	22	23
Total	**13,363**	**13,645**	**15,000**	**18,041**	**21,249**

	1979	1980	1981	1982	CHANGE 1981–1982
Cartridge*	8,800	7,500	7,000	2,800	(60)%
Disc	—	—	—	3,900	—
35mm (all types)	2,600	2,900	3,400	3,700	8.8
Instant	6,600	5,700	5,000	4,500	(10.0)
8mm movie	300	230	180	100	(44.4)
Other**	30	33	36	35	(2.8)
Total	**18,330**	**16,363**	**15,616**	**15,035**	**(3.7)%**

*110 and 126 combined.

**Roll and large format.

Source: Lehman Brothers Kuhn Loeb, *The Photographic Products Market*, August 4, 1983.

	1977	1978	1979	1980	1981	1982
Sales						
Worldwide ($)	1,061.9	1,376.6	1,361.5	1,450.8	1,419.6	1,293.9
United States	645.8	817.4	757.2	791.8	817.8	752.5
Europe	274.2	364.9	383.3	436.8	369.2	333.2
Rest of world including Asia	141.9	194.3	220.9	222.2	232.6	208.2
Worldwide (no. of units)						
Cameras	7.0+*	9.4	7.3	6.6	5.6	4.0
Film packs	N/A	200+	205**	198**	194**	N/A
Tech/Ind Photo as % of Total	N/A	N/A	N/A	25.30%	30%	33%
Financials ($)						
EPS	2.81	3.60	1.10	2.60	.95	.73
Dividends/share	.65	.90	1.00	1.00	1.00	1.00
R&D expense	88.9	86.5	109.6	114.0	121.4	118.4
Capital expense	68.9	115.0	134.7	68.1	42.5	31.5
Advertising expense	70.8	101.1	105.0	101.4	106.6	96.4
Return on assets	8.6%	9.3%	2.9%	6.1%	2.2%	1.8%
No. of employees	16,394	20,884	18,416	17,454	16,784	14,540

N/A—Not available.

*The Wall Street Journal, September 5, 1980.

**Merrill Lynch Securities Research Report, May 17,1982, p. 3.

Source: All data not otherwise noted drawn from Polaroid Corporation annual reports, 1978–1982.

EXHIBIT 8
Polaroid Executive
Officers 1981

NAME	OFFICE	AGE
Edwin H. Land	Chairman of the board	72
William J. McCune, Jr.	President and chief executive officer	66
I. M. Booth	Executive vice president	50
Sheldon A. Buckler	Executive vice president	50
Peter Wensberg	Executive vice president	53
Richard W. Young	Executive vice president	55
Milton S. Dietz	Senior vice president	50
Charles Mikulka	Senior vice president	68
Howard G. Rogers	Senior vice president and director of research	66
Harvey H. Thayer	Senior vice president, finance	54
Richard F. deLima	Vice president and secretary	51
Julius Silver	Vice president and chairman executive committee	81
Edward R. Bedrosian	Treasurer	49

Dr. Land, founder of the company, served as chairman of the board, chief executive officer and director of research from 1937 to 1980. In 1980, Dr. Land was reelected chairman of the board and assumed the new position of consulting director of basic research in Land photography. He is the inventor of synthetic sheet polarizer for light and of one-step photography. He is the holder of numerous honorary degrees and has been the recipient of many awards from various professional societies.

Mr. McCune joined the company in 1939 and has been a director since 1975. He was elected vice president, engineering in 1954; vice president, assistant general manager in 1963; executive vice president in 1969; president and chief operating officer in 1975; and to his present positions as president and chief executive officer in 1980.

Mr. Booth joined the company in 1958. He was elected assistant vice president and assistant to the president in 1975; vice president and assistant to the president in 1976; senior vice president in 1977; and to his present position as executive vice president in 1980.

Dr. Buckler joined the company in 1964. He was elected assistant vice president in 1969; vice president, research division in 1972; group vice president in 1975; senior vice president in 1977; and to his present position as executive vice president in 1980.

Mr. Wensberg joined the company in 1958. He was elected assistant vice president, advertising in 1966; vice president, advertising in 1968; senior vice president in 1971; and to his present position as executive vice president in 1980.

Dr. Young joined the company in 1962. He was elected vice president, assistant director of research in 1963; senior vice president in 1969; and to his present position as executive vice president in 1980.

Mr. Dietz joined the company in 1955. He was elected assistant vice president in 1975; vice president, engineering in 1977; and to his present position as senior vice president in 1980.

Mr. Mikulka joined the company in 1942. He was elected vice president, patents in 1960 and to his present position as senior vice president in 1975.

Mr. Rogers joined the company in 1937. He was elected vice president and senior research fellow in 1968; vice president, senior research fellow and associate director of research in 1975; senior vice president and associate director of research in 1979; and to his present positions as senior vice president and director of research in 1980.

Mr. Thayer joined the company in 1956. He was elected treasurer in 1970; vice president and treasurer in 1971; vice president, finance and treasurer in 1977; and to his present position as senior vice president, finance in 1980.

Mr. deLima joined the company as secretary in 1972. He was elected to his present positions as vice president and secretary in 1975.

Mr. Silver, a director and vice president since 1937 and chairman of the executive committee, is also a partner in the firm of Silver & Solomon, the company's general counsel.

Mr. Bedrosian joined the company in 1965. He was elected assistant treasurer in 1975 and to his present position as treasurer in 1980.

Source: Polaroid Corporation, *10K*, 1981.

EXHIBIT 9
Polaroid Corporation
Production Facilities as
of 1981

LOCATION	FUNCTION
Domestic	
Norwood, Mass.	Polarizer sheet production
Norwood, Mass.	Transparency film production
Norwood, Mass.	Camera assembly*
Waltham, Mass.	Battery assembly
Waltham, Mass.	Chemical production
Waltham, Mass.	Film pack production
Waltham, Mass.	Positive film production
Freetown, Mass.	Chemical production
Foreign	
Dumbarton, Scotland	Camera assembly, film pack assembly, positive film production, sunglass production
Enschede, Netherlands	Film pack assembly, positive film production, sunglass production
Newbridge, Ireland	Film pack assembly

*Highly labor intensive.
Source: Compiled from various annual reports.

EXHIBIT 10
Polaroid Corporation,
1980

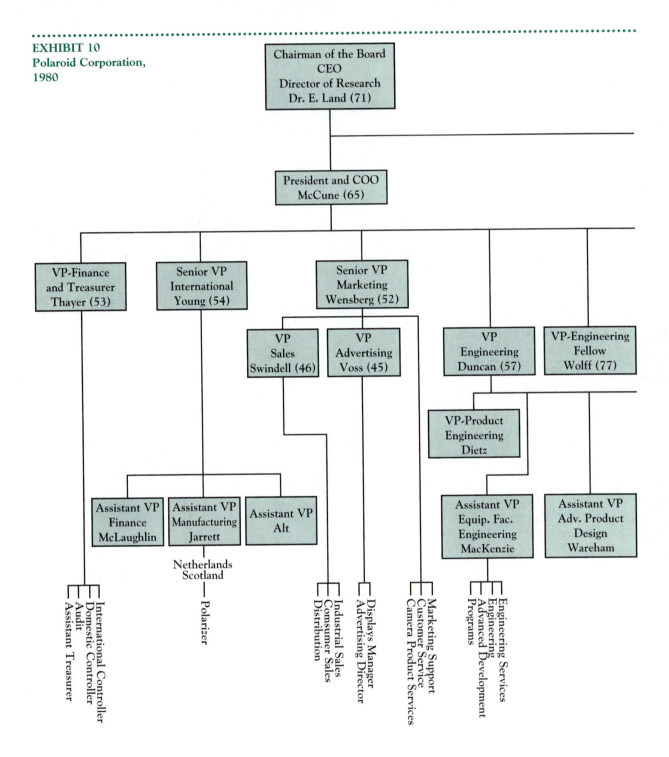

Note: Numbers in parentheses indicate the ages of the various executives.

Source: Approximate 1980, pre-reorganization, organizational chart drawn from various secondary sources. The company does not have an official organization chart.

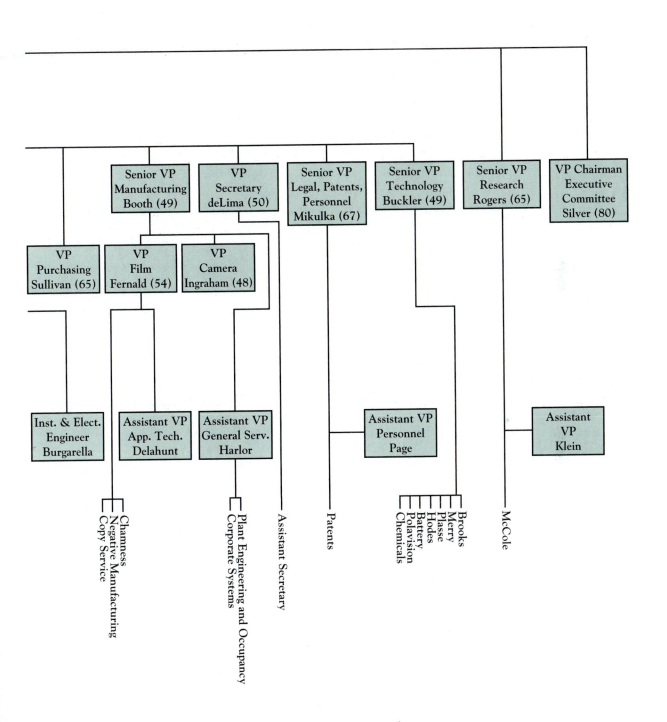

With total sales in 1993 of $111.2 billion, Exxon Corporation was one of the largest oil companies in the world. It held interests in a number of enterprises, mainly in the oil, gas, energy, minerals, and chemical industries. It also had an interest in electric power generation in Hong Kong. Exxon was a worldwide entity with exploration activities on all continents, large refineries in 16 different countries, and marketing activities in over 80 countries. In 1993, Exxon's holdings outside the U.S. comprised 60% of its $84.1 billion in assets and generated 70% of its earnings. It obtained 3 times more oil from its foreign than from U.S. sources, and its overseas affiliates refined and sold 3 times its U.S. volume. Its total proved resources had remained steady at almost 13.6 billion barrels for about 10 years, while producing on average about 1 billion barrels per year. (See Appendix A.) Exxon sold some 4.9 million barrels per day (B/D) of petroleum products or approximately 7.4% of the world's 66 million B/D demands. Its $10 billion chemicals business operated worldwide, and its 40 million metric tons of coal sales made it a major factor in that industry. The company's ownership was widely dispersed, with its 571 million shares held in many different countries throughout the world.

ORGANIZATION AND PHILOSOPHY

As a truly multinational company, Exxon attempted to decentralize operations as much as possible to its divisions and affiliates. These units were responsible for maintaining adequate returns on corporate investments in them. Since corporate policy was to staff each

subsidiary with nationals of its host countries, it was rare to find more than a few Americans in any non-U.S. subsidiary. Wherever possible, the boards, CEOs, and key executives of each unit were also nationals of the host country.

The corporation maintained some centralized units to help allocate overall corporate resources and to coordinate activities of operating groups where necessary. Whenever possible, raw materials, supplies, intermediate products, and services were transferred among divisions at market prices. When these could not be readily determined, negotiated transfer prices were generally used. The corporation's policy was to transfer materials and services "at arms length"—with divisions allowed to purchase outside the corporation if they so desired. Purchasing from and trading with other companies was common.

Certain major decisions were of course reserved to corporate headquarters. Operating heads were expected to clear major policy decisions having corporate-wide significance at the corporate level. No single listing of such decisions existed in the corporation.

Exxon also had its own $10 billion Exxon Chemicals operation, producing and supplying chemicals worldwide. Coordination between successive operations in both (petroleum and chemicals) groups was very important. Efficient plant sizes in either group were so large that their outputs could easily exceed the demands of smaller countries in which production occurred. Since petrochemicals and plastics were important inputs for many secondary and fabricating industries, it was common to find large chemical-industrial complexes growing up around refineries or petrochemical plants—located even in the most remote areas of individual countries.

Exxon's size and complexity inevitably exposed the company to a variety of different national policies, nationalistic pressures, and risks of retaliation or expropriation by host countries. As a mature and progressive company, Exxon's management had given considerable attention to the problem of host country relationships. Its expressed policy for years was: "To perform as a responsible and desirable corporate citizen in all host countries. . . (since) Exxon's interests are inextricably linked to the interests of our host countries throughout the world . . . ." The company had purposely not tried to refine this broad policy into rigid rules, binding on all its affiliates.

THREE SHOCKS

Three major shocks had unsettled the oil industry between 1973 and 1994. The first shock was in 1973. Crude oil prices had been steady at less than $2 per barrel through the 1960s, reflecting a general surplus supply balance. They had crept up very slowly to approximately $3 per barrel when in October 1973, Arab oil producing nations imposed a total ban on petroleum exports to Israel, the United States, and other "supporters" of Israel in the 1973 Arab-Israeli war. Posted prices leapt to $10 per barrel (bbl) during January–February 1974, with some oil auctioned in the spot markets for $17. Nevertheless, after the initial 1973–74 crisis subsided, oil prices increased only nominally until 1978, inflationary pressures actually forced the real price of oil to drop some 10–15% during this period.

The next major jolt came on October 31, 1978, when oil workers in Iran went on strike—cutting production from 5.3 million barrels per day (B/D) to 2 million B/D. The workers demanded higher wages and an end to martial law. In December, OPEC ended an 18-month price freeze on crude oil by announcing increases that boosted the price from $12.70/bbl to $14.54/bbl by October 1979. Iran announced price increases to $16.50/bbl. Saudi Arabia supported these prices by limiting its oil production in April to the ceiling of 8.5 B/D imposed before the Iranian Revolution. As production limits forced prices up, OPEC raised the posted price to $20.00/bbl in June 1979, approximately double the preceding year's prices. And a seeming "new era" in oil began.

In 1978, Exxon sales had been $63.9 billion with profits of $2.7 billion reported. Sales had been growing at 9.1% per year and profits at 3.8%. The company and its affiliates accounted for about 9% of the industry's crude runs. At that time, the company had deployed total assets of $41.5 billion against which it charged $1.7 billion in depreciation per year. Its announced crude reserves at that time were 23 billion barrels of crude, offering it an 11.9 year coverage in terms of 1978 refinery runs. Chase Econometrics and industry sources estimated that the industry would invest over $1.5 trillion worldwide in the next decade to replace existing facilities and to develop needed new resources.

Through the early 1980s, due to inertias in the energy system, there had been minimal shifts in overall oil use or in expected energy growth through the year 2000. Prices climbed rapidly to $36 per barrel, and most experts expected continued price rises through the end of the century. A price of $100 per barrel by the year 2000 was a common forecast. Despite extensive exploration by oil companies and ministries throughout the world, only a few large fields had been developed between 1974 and the early 1980s. Most publicized of these were the North Slope (Alaska-Canada), North Sea (Europe), and Mexican fields. The North Slope fields were thought to contain some 20–50 billion barrels of ultimately exploitable oil. Mexico's reserves at forecast prices were estimated at perhaps 200–300 barrels of petroleum liquids. Most writers projected long term shortages of crude even at much higher prices. Major forecasting and banking groups estimated that the industry would have to invest $2–3 trillion worldwide in the 1980s to meet forecast demands. Each country had its own special interests in the developing energy situation. The differing postures of some example countries are briefly described below.

DECISION POINT

Given this shortage scenario—which was widely accepted—what strategic posture should Exxon assume? What were the critical factors for survival during this period? What should have been Exxon's strategy vis-à-vis reserves? Markets? Financing? The U.S. government? Host country governments? Alternative energy sources?

What would be the implications for Exxon's overall organization? Structure? Policies? Portfolio? Measurement system? Public relations?

THE 1980S GLUT

In large part because of the policies of the "oil majors" like Exxon, oil prices collapsed in late 1981, plummeting back to $12–14/bbl, as a worldwide recession began. It was triggered largely by high U.S. interest rates, disastrous U.S. trade balances resulting from oil imports, and a credit crisis reflecting both wild deficit spending by the governments of oil producing countries throughout the world and the loss in asset value behind the loans previously made to these countries. Countries and companies which had seemed outrageously rich suddenly found their energy asset values and potential revenues reduced to commodity levels. The solidarity of OPEC, which had once seemed so firm, shattered as various oil producing countries tried to sell oil at any price in order to cover their debts and continue their lifestyles. Forecasts of worldwide economic growth suddenly became pessimistic with "zero to 1.7% growth rates" commonly projected. Stagflation, slow growth with continuous inflation, dominated most thinking. Now, with a presumed energy "glut" the oil companies faced another major change in strategy. Although total world reserves seemed plentiful (see Exhibit 1), the largest economies (North American, Japan, and Western Europe) were huge oil importers. During the "energy shortages" of the 1970s–early 1980s, most host countries with substantial holdings had expropriated the oil companies' crude reserves. For example, Exxon's own crude reserves of oil had dropped from some 45 billion barrels in 1972 to about 7 billion barrels in 1981, largely due to nationalizations. (See next section for information on key countries' positions.)

DECISION POINT

Given the long term anticipated energy glut, what strategy should Exxon follow in the mid-1980s? What are the critical factors for success? What are the implications for Exxon's portfolio? Marketing? Exploration? Production? Refining? Distribution? Policies?

How should Exxon shift its overall organization structure in response to these mid-1980s pressures? What changes should it make in its diversification, financial, resource, government relations, public relations, policies?

IMPORTANT NATIONAL INTERESTS

During all of these crisis periods, Exxon had to deal with a variety of host governments commanding widely different energy resources, market potentials, capital capabilities, political stabilities, and social philosophies. Exhibit 2 shows the net export-import balances of energy for a number of sample countries in 1978, 1983, and 1991. A brief summary of some key players' positions follows.

NORWAY

Until the discovery of oil in the North Sea in 1969, Norway had essentially no domestic oil industry. Hydroelectric sources had fulfilled most central power needs, while imported oil and gas had met transportation and other demands. Norway's highly dispersed population of 4.1 million did not represent a major— or concentrated—market for petroleum products. In fact, a large modern refinery would have a throughput vastly in excess of the sales any company could reasonably expect in Norway. However, Norway's recoverable oil and gas reserves were estimated to be "in the tens of billions" of barrels. By 1981, oil and gas accounted for 15% of Norway's GDP, more than all other manufactures combined. It had turned over exploitation of its holdings to a state run oil company, Stat Oil, although it continued to allow some concession rights for development by private oil companies, if they joined with Norwegian equity holders as "technical advisors."[1]

Because of a long history of occupation by other nations Norway feared loss of control over its key industries and dependency on other countries. The Norwegians were fiercely proud of their national identity, their beautiful natural surroundings, and their "unique quality of life." Norway was quite concerned about inflation, pollution, disruption, and loss of economic control if resources were exploited too rapidly. No slums existed in the major cities, and full employment had been a policy for decades. The government wished to shift exports away from the basic (wood products, mechanical products, electro metallurgical, ship building, and ship operating) industries which had dominated its past and into the high value added and "knowledge industries" of the future. At the time of the oil discoveries, there were no domestic companies with substantial oil and gas experience, and petrochemical research and curricula were either non-existent or quite underdeveloped in Norwegian universities. Norway's relationships with the USSR on its Northern border were delicate; no exploration was permitted North of the 62nd parallel.

BRITAIN

In contrast, Britain's initial interest was to get its North Sea oil explored and producing as soon as possible because of its weak balance of payments situation. At the time of the discovery, the Labor Party was in power and actively discussed nationalizing Britain's whole North Sea area. Instead, it both called for majority government interest in all concessions and formed the British National Oil Corporation (BNOC) to act as the vehicle for exercising the government's participation rights. Nevertheless, at one point in 1980 Britain "found itself in the strange position of charging $30/bbl for its oil while Saudi Arabia's was pegged at $24/bbl."[2] British motorists suffered a shortage of gasoline while 45% of all UK production was being exported to the U.S. and Western Europe. This was partly a function of Britain's need for exports and partly the fact that private oil companies controlled refining activities.[3]

The Conservative (Thatcher) government tried to "privatize" some of BNOC's activities in 1980 but was thwarted by other political interests which feared a massive oil boom in the 1980s followed by an abrupt re-entry to importation in the 1990s.[4] Britain had two world-class oil companies of its own, BP and Shell Oil. The government was anxious to develop its oil reserves in such a way as to "maximize" the government's and country's revenues from the UK North Sea. Britain was both a large potential producer and user of oil, although it was likely to remain a net importer of substantial significance.

JAPAN

Japan, with its powerful national economy, had very limited fossil fuel supplies. When the Iranian turmoil cut off 17% of this crucial supply in 1978, the government formed the Japan National Oil Company (JNOC), and MITI pressed for Japanese controlled oil sources to equal 30% of imports by mid-1980s. Seeking to limit imports, Nippon Oil, one of Japan's major refiners, boosted prices 15% immediately. Exxon only increased its prices by 1–2%, seeking to expand market share during this period. For its longer term needs, Japan started a joint venture with China to develop oil in the latter's Bohai Sea and stepped up its financial and technical aid to poorer oil exporting nations, notably Mexico and Indonesia.[5] Because of its tight pollution standards, Japan became the world's largest user of liquified natural gas (LNG)—for central power production and for propane in automobiles. It expanded its conservation and nuclear programs radically. However, because of its strong industrial base and high standard of living, Japan would remain a major

importer of fossil fuels, until significant low cost substitutes could be found.

CHINA

The size of the People's Republic of China's energy reserves was largely unknown, although the central government had force-fed the country's oil industry with funds and technical manpower for decades. Like many other aspects of China's industrial base, its energy industries were very inefficient. However, knowledgeable observers thought there could be several hundred billion barrels of potential oil in the China Sea and tens of billions more on shore. But there were severe financial, technological, and structural constraints on China developing these resources itself. China's huge population (1.3 billion people) and rapid economic growth rate (more than 10% per year), combined with its need to catch up on infrastructure investments meant that it would be a huge user of all energy forms. In the 1980s it had, like the USSR, used its energy reserves as sources of hard currency. Coal and water power had been its major domestic energy sources.

China, the world's sixth largest oil producer (ahead of Venezuela) became a net oil importer at the end of 1993. Energy consumption in China had increased twenty-two fold since 1952, despite a halving during the Great Leap Forward. If, as is expected, urbanization follows industrialization, by 2010 energy demand per person in China will grow by about 75%, and in India by 145%. If, by then, China's intensity of oil use is similar to that of Western Europe in the late 1950s, it will be consuming 40 million barrels of oil per day, more than all the OECD countries in 1993. Wherever possible, China will try to handle this demand by water power. If Chinese electrical demand were to grow no faster than its projected 7% economic growth, the country would need to open a medium-sized power station a week by 2000, and one every few days thereafter. Its planned development of the Yangtze Gorges (17,000 megawatts, equivalent to the electrical output of Austria) will be perhaps the largest single construction project in history, but such infrastructure investments alone will cost roughly 3% of China's GDP each year, creating a major capital drain. China and India together, with less than 10% of today's energy demand, plan to build what will amount to 1/4 of the world's new capacity. However, whether these projects will attract capital depends upon whether the countries continue to underprice energy in order to fuel economic growth (allowing only 0–8% returns on

RESER.	1973		1978	
	PROD.	RESER.	PROD.	RESER.
Western Hemisphere	**79.10**	**16.10**	**75.90**	**14.80**
United States	36.30	9.20	29.50	8.70
Canada	10.20	1.80	6.00	1.30
Mexico	2.80	0.50	14.00	1.20
Venezuela	13.70	3.40	18.20	2.10
Western Europe	**9.10**	**0.40**	**26.90**	**1.70**
United Kingdom	5.00	0.00	19.00	1.10
Norway	2.00	0.00	6.00	0.40
Eastern Europe & CIS	**101.50**	**8.90**	**78.30**	**11.90**
CIS	NA	8.40	75.00	11.40
Other	NA	0.50	3.30	0.50
Middle East	**355.30**	**21.10**	**365.80**	**21.10**
Saudi Arabia	138.00	7.60	150.00	8.10
Kuwait	64.90	3.00	67.00	1.90
Iran	65.00	5.90	62.00	5.20
Iraq	29.00	2.00	34.50	2.60
UAE	21.00	1.50	32.40	1.80
Africa	**106.40**	**5.90**	**59.20**	**6.00**
Algeria	47.00	1.10	6.60	1.10
Nigeria	15.00	2.00	18.70	1.90
Libya	30.40	2.20	25.00	2.00
Egypt	5.20	0.20	2.50	0.50
Asia-Pacific	**14.90**	**2.90**	**39.70**	**4.70**
Indonesia	10.00	1.30	10.00	1.60
India	0.80	0.20	3.00	0.20
Malaysia/Brunei	1.50	0.30	4.10	0.50
Australia	2.10	0.40	2.00	0.40
China	NA	0.70	20.00	1.90
OPEC Total	**463.70**	**30.80**	**439.90**	**29.70**
World Total	**666.40**	**55.30**	**645.70**	**60.30**

Source: *Energy Statistics Sourcebook*, Ninth Edition.

1983		1988		1993	
PROD.	RESER.	PROD.	RESER.	PROD.	RESER.
113.40	**16.10**	**148.40**	**16.00**	**153.80**	**15.80**
27.90	8.70	27.20	8.10	24.70	6.80
7.00	1.40	6.80	1.60	5.30	1.70
48.30	2.70	48.60	2.60	51.30	2.70
21.50	1.80	56.30	1.60	62.70	2.30
23.20	**3.30**	**22.50**	**3.90**	**15.80**	**4.80**
13.90	2.30	5.20	2.30	4.10	1.90
6.80	0.60	14.80	1.10	8.80	2.30
65.60	**12.80**	**60.80**	**12.90**	**59.20**	**8.10**
63.00	12.30	59.00	12.50	57.00	7.80
2.60	0.50	1.80	0.40	2.20	0.30
369.00	**11.50**	**564.70**	**14.40**	**661.80**	**18.40**
162.40	4.90	167.00	4.90	257.80	7.90
64.20	0.90	91.90	1.30	94.00	1.70
55.30	2.50	92.90	2.20	92.90	3.70
41.00	0.90	100.00	2.70	100.00	0.40
32.30	1.10	98.10	1.50	98.10	2.20
57.80	**4.30**	**55.30**	**5.00**	**61.90**	**6.20**
9.40	0.70	8.50	0.60	9.20	0.80
16.80	1.20	16.00	1.40	17.90	1.90
21.50	1.00	21.00	1.00	2.80	1.40
3.30	0.70	4.30	0.80	6.20	0.90
39.20	**4.90**	**37.80**	**5.90**	**44.60**	**6.50**
9.60	1.40	8.40	1.10	5.80	1.30
3.40	0.40	4.30	0.60	6.10	0.50
4.60	0.50	4.30	0.70	5.10	0.80
1.60	0.40	1.70	0.50	1.80	0.50
19.50	2.10	18.40	2.70	24.00	2.90
445.10	**17.40**	**670.70**	**19.60**	**770.60**	**25.00**
668.30	**53.00**	**889.30**	**58.00**	**997.00**	**59.70**

EXHIBIT 2

World Petroleum Supply and Disposition, 1978
(thousands of barrels per day)

	OIL PRODUCTION	CRUDE OIL IMPORTS	REFINED PRODUCTS IMPORTS	CRUDE OIL EXPORT	REFINED PRODUCTS EXPORTS	APPARENT CONSUMPTION
United States	10,270	6,360	2,010	160	200	18,850
Mexico	1,330	NM	30	370	NM	920
Venezuela	2,250	NM	NM	1,240	710	300
Brazil	170	930	20	NM	20	1,050
Germany	100	1,950	920	NM	130	3,050
France	50	2,360	190	NM	300	2,170
Italy	30	2,190	170	NM	370	2,180
United Kingdom	1,120	1,320	230	460	270	1,850
Norway	NA	NA	NA	NA	NA	NA
USSR	11,870	1,820	340	2,080	1,260	10,180
Middle East	21,510	520	150	19,130	1,050	-1,620
Algeria	1,260	NM	10	1,000	40	80
Libya	2,030	NM	20	1,850	50	90
Nigeria	1,900	NM	90	1,850	10	140
Japan	10	4,510	830	NM	20	5,140
China	2,080	NM	NM	10	10	1,810
India	NA	NA	NA	NA	NA	NA
World total	**63,270**	**32,660**	**7,880**	**31,510**	**8,380**	**62,840**

NM = Less than 500 barrels per day; NA = Not available.

Source: Energy Information Administration, U.S. Department of Energy, *International Energy Annual 1979.*

EXHIBIT 2 (cont'd)

World Petroleum Supply and Disposition, 1983
(thousands of barrels per day)

	OIL PRODUCTION	CRUDE OIL IMPORTS	REFINED PRODUCTS IMPORTS	CRUDE OIL EXPORT	REFINED PRODUCTS EXPORTS	APPARENT CONSUMPTION
United States	10,788	3,329	1,722	164	575	15,231
Mexico	2,954	0	17	1,537	84	1,301
Venezuela	1,871	0	NM	986	513	375
Brazil	438	731	37	1	96	975
Germany	81	1,326	924	0	157	2,291
France	55	1,447	445	0	221	1,913
Italy	46	1,550	310	5	262	1,732
United Kingdom	2,402	614	203	1,441	281	1,520
Norway	697	40	52	517	52	164
USSR	12,427	140	20	2,600	1,007	9,218
Middle East	12,171	526	195	8,997	1,392	2,360
Algeria	910	0	3	580	196	136
Libya	1,135	0	34	1,037	20	125
Nigeria	1,241	0	NM	1,087	10	233
Japan	10	3614	841	0	62	4,366
China	2,120	7	1	305	59	1,722
India	480	319	86	104	7	773
World total	**57,619**	**24,221**	**8,931**	**22,596**	**9,597**	**58,954**

NM = Less than 500 barrels per day; NA = Not available.

Source: Energy Information Administration, U.S. Department of Energy, *International Energy Annual 1984.*

EXHIBIT 2 (cont'd)
World Petroleum Supply
and Disposition, 1991
(thousands of barrels per day)

	OIL PRODUCTION	CRUDE OIL IMPORTS	REFINED PRODUCTS IMPORTS	CRUDE OIL EXPORT	REFINED PRODUCTS EXPORTS	APPARENT CONSUMPTION
United States	9,883	5,782	1,844	116	885	16,714
Mexico	3,165	0	137	1,369	105	1,795
Venezuela	2,509	0	16	1,381	736	405
Brazil	812	526	98	0	82	1,346
Germany	133	1,793	1,023	0	180	2,828
France	109	1,466	695	0	318	1,935
Italy	120	1,485	673	10	396	1,863
United Kingdom	1,993	936	448	1,073	484	1,801
Norway	1,987	30	57	1,729	188	184
USSR	10,412	2	31	1,205	879	8,350
Middle East	17,122	522	520	12,621	2,137	3,400
Algeria	1,371	0	9	704	457	208
Libya	1,523	0	4	1,220	141	166
Nigeria	1,897	0	34	1,610	42	277
Japan	48	4,180	1,396	0	188	5,284
China	2,835	121	90	453	104	2,499
India	629	480	185	0	103	1,190
World total	**66,623**	**28,406**	**12,710**	**28,165**	**13,052**	**68,707**

NM = Less than 500 barrels per day; NA = Not available.

Source: Energy Information Administration, U.S. Department of Energy, *International Energy Annual 1984.*

investment) or priced realistically to realize 15% or greater returns. Western countries and companies anticipated huge potential market growth in electricity worldwide, with more than $1 trillion being spent in electrical infrastructures alone during the 1990s.

INDONESIA

Indonesia had a population of some 188 million people, about half of OPEC's total. Despite increased oil revenues in recent years, Indonesia's per person annual income in the early 1990s ranked it as one of Asia's poorer countries. Its oil and economic history had been chaotic during the 1960s and 1970s when the Sukarno regime had created inflation rates of 650% per year in trying to accomplish its socialist goals. Petromina, the state oil company had, at that time, been badly mismanaged, but these situations were stabilized in the mid-1980s. However, because of too-rapid production from its fields, Indonesia's oil reserves had been significantly damaged, and it would take substantial investments to continue their development. Both governments and investors were haunted by memories of the debt crises of the 1980s, when monies lent to or invested in developing countries for energy

development were often re-directed to other "social projects." During the 1980s under-financed and technologically-limited national energy companies in these countries had struggled, along with their governments, to supply as much of their total energy demands as they could from domestic reserves. By the mid-1990s, international companies were being asked to join in the effort. Nevertheless, the demand in large oil-holding developing countries, like Indonesia, was so great that most were likely to become net oil importers by 2000 despite their substantial reserves.

VENEZUELA

Venezuela's oil had been originally developed by international oil companies. However, Venezuela nationalized substantially all of its very large oil resources in the mid-1970s. Its proved crude reserves of 62.7 billion barrels made it third in the Western hemisphere. But it was well known that Venezuela also had "trillions" of barrels of heavy oil in identified formations. Estimates of ultimately exploitable potentials varied from 2 to 3 trillion/bbl. This oil required an infusion of heat (or heat and chemicals) to make it flow through its sustaining formations. It also contained extraneous chemicals which had to be removed in a pre-processing stage before refining. New refining methods increasingly allowed heavy oils to be processed competitively with many crudes. In the early 1990s, Venezuela had the largest "steam flood" field in the world for processing heavy oil and was among the leaders in developing new crude processing technologies. At prices above $25 per barrel, many of these reserves became viable.

NIGERIA

Through the 1970s, Nigeria had become second only to Saudi Arabia in its export of oil to the United States. But Nigerian economic fortunes underwent a major reversal in 1978 and 1981 when world instabilities and dropping prices suddenly caused Nigeria's oil-based economy to crash. Oil payments had accounted for 85% of total government income, and there were serious problems of maladministration in the Nigerian National Petroleum Corp. (NNPC). Because of their location and quality, Nigeria's reserves were considered among the best in the world. Nigeria was often able to price its oil at premiums above other OPEC crudes. However, this had led to confrontations with various OPEC countries as prices crashed. In the mid-1990s, Nigeria was a serious independent supplier, with a strong willingness to allow international companies to develop its large unexplored reserves. However, like Indonesia and other developing countries, these reserves were often substantially more expensive than the ($0.30–$0.50 per barrel) finding and lifting costs encountered in some of the large Middle Eastern structures.

OPEC

Although the OPEC group's powers had faded during the 1980s, its cooperative structure still existed on paper. Among its members, the Middle East and Venezuela were the largest producers. However, in 1993 they produced only a third of the world's oil, despite the fact they possessed over 70% of its reserves. Low prices inevitably nudged market share back to the low cost Middle Eastern OPEC members. However low prices had already discouraged other nations' investments in oil during the 1980s and early 1990s. The World Petroleum Congress, an industry forum, said in 1991 that investment needed to be 50% higher in real terms in the 1990s than it had been in the 1980s. Another study found that the oil majors themselves were falling some 10% short of the investment needed merely to maintain their reserves, let alone to meet

new demands. Total investment by the international oil companies had fallen with the oil price. (See Exhibit 3.)

TOTAL RESERVES

The ultimately exploitable reserves of fossil fuels depended upon costs and prices. Proved reserves (currently identified and exploitable at existing real prices) were 1.5 trillion barrels, compared to mid-1990s use rates of 6 billion barrels per year. Some large undiscovered fields were expected in the South China Sea (more than 100/bbl), Northwest China (70/bbl), and Northern China (Karamay 70/bbl); limited amounts of other new oil might come from outside OPEC, with gains from countries like Mexico and Colombia perhaps offsetting expected declines in North America and the North Sea. Most other gains, if they occurred, were expected to come from the former Soviet Union and the Middle East. Russia's reserves were largely unknown, but substantial. Political chaos would probably limit their development in the next decade.

This left Venezuela and the Middle Eastern giants—Saudi Arabia, Iran, Iraq, Kuwait, and Abu Dhabi—as primary suppliers for the world's growing demands. In all these countries, oil is produced by the state, with state investment. And in four of the six countries, the state was desperately short of cash. Exhibit 1 shows the proven oil reserves of the world at the beginning of 1993. Under this scenario of "possibly foreseeable prices," North America's giant oil shale (3 trillion bbls) and tar sands (1–2 trillion bbls) become potential resources. In the mid-1990s, the OECD countries (Western Europe, North America, and Japan) were the major users of energy (see Exhibit 4). OECD used approximately half of the world's energy, while North America used approximately 25%. The use pattern, however, would change radically by 2020 with energy use in the developing world accounting for perhaps 60% of the world total, while OECD dropped to about 30%.

DEVELOPING COUNTRY GROWTH

The world's population would increase by 2.7 billion people to over 8 billion by 2020, with over 60% of the increase born in Asia and Latin America. As populations and economies grow in developing countries, energy use shifts from firewood, animal dung, and crop residues toward fossil fuels. During industrialization, energy intensity (energy use per person) increases enormously, only to decline later as infrastructures are completed and

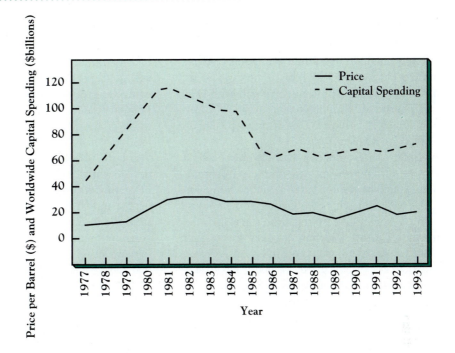

Source: *Annual EnergyReview 1993*, Energy Information Administration (prices): *Oil Industry Outlook*, Sixth Edition
(Capital Spending).

EXHIBIT 4
World Primary Energy
Consumption
(million tons of oil
equivalent)

COUNTRY	1970	1980	1985	1990	1993
United States	1,554	1,829	1,789	1,949	2,018
Japan	270	357	367	433	462
Germany	309	363	363	358	329
France	151	195	207	224	230
Canada	132	194	194	211	218
United Kingdom	213	204	205	214	216
Italy	117	143	140	157	163
Spain	40	70	74	92	99
Australia	53	71	75	89	99
Total	**4,785**	**6,596**	**7,051**	**7,919**	**7,998**

Source: Cambridge Energy Research Associates, *World Oil Trends 1994.*

economies shift toward a service base. The International Energy Agency (IEA) estimated that energy use in OECD would grow by 1.3% per year and Eastern Europe and the Soviet Union by 0.3% per year, compared with growth rates of 4.2% in developing countries. Even at its estimated oil price of $28 per barrel, IEA forecasts that oil demand in OECD will grow about 1% per year while coal demand grows by 1.3% per year.

In the near future, natural gas was expected to take over much of the expanding demand in developed countries. The combination of efficiency and clean burning offered by natural gas would drive this substitution. However, with 40% of the world's population, India and China would be major factors in the world's energy use. India's energy use was growing at 7–8%, while China's was growing at over 10% per year, even during its political disruptions. As these and other developing countries shifted toward an auto-based economy, oil supplies would be pressed even further. Royal Dutch Shell estimated that the number of cars worldwide could double to 1 billion in the early 2000s. The IEA saw oil demand growing to 94 million B/D by 2010, an increase of 28 million barrels over 1990's output, with almost 16 million B/D of the growth being in Latin America and Asia.

By 1990, serious concerns had developed about the effects of energy use on the environment. Emissions of carbon monoxide (CO) and carbon dioxide (CO_2) were thought to be causing a greenhouse effect which would increase the earth's average temperature by 1.4° C by 2020, with a similar increase for every further doubling of energy use. In addition, nitrous oxides (N_2O) emitted by combustion processes—as well as clorinated flourocarbons from the chemical industries—were attacking the ozone layer which protected the earth from the sun's damaging rays. Noxious gases and dust in city air were major health problems in all urban centers based upon fossil fuels. In the early 1990s the United Nations estimated that traffic jams in Bangkok cost $1 billion a year in medical and other side effect costs alone, plus another $1 billion wasted on the congestion itself. Once GDP surpassed $5,000 per person, people became more willing to spend for pollution control. Italy had placed serious controls on its Venetian industries to protect that historic city, and even India had shut down 212 factories to protect its Taj Mahal. In the 1990s some 6 million Indians died each year from acute respiratory infections caused by smoke from their fires and environmental pollution. New technologies could decrease the environmental impacts of various energy sources substantially, but at a substantial cost.

EXXON'S CURRENT OPERATIONS

In 1994 Exxon was among the largest industrial companies in the world. Its position depended upon how one ranked the large Japanese banking and holding companies. Key financial and operating data about Exxon are included as Appendix B. Its net income of $5.3 billion in 1993 was up 11%. More than 70% of its segment earnings were from outside the United States. Exxon led all major international oil companies in return on investment (12%) and return on shareholders' equity (15.4%) in 1993. Exxon's capital and exploration expenditures were $8.2 billion and exploration

discovery volumes reached their highest level in over a decade, adding 730 million oil equivalent barrels to Exxon's total resource base. Its drilling success in wells had risen from 3% in 1984 to 50% in 1993, with average yields per well growing from 5 million bbl of oil equivalent to 40 million. Exxon had strengthened its financial position in virtually all areas, despite declines in oil prices, which in late 1993 reached their lowest level in 5 years. Exxon's cash flows from operations had averaged $10–12 billion annually during the last decade while its cash uses had averaged $7.2 billion for plant property and equipment, $3.2 billion for dividends, and $1.6 billion for share repurchases. Its D/E ratio declined to 25% in 1993, the lowest level in five years. Its credit rating was AAA, despite the still-pending lawsuit for the *Exxon Valdez* accident in Alaska. It had reduced its workforce by approximately 10% to 91,000 over a three-year period. This was the lowest level since the early 1920s. The patterns of its investments over the past five years are shown in Appendix B, as are its functional earnings and average capital employed by business.

In addition to the above, Exxon managed perhaps the world's largest tanker fleet in 1993. Its own tankers were built to specifications in shipyards throughout the world, and it used an extensive group of contract carriers. It owned or shared in the ownership of extensive pipeline networks for crude, natural gas, chemical intermediates, and finished products. Because of the size and complexity of its worldwide operations, Exxon had been forced to develop extremely sophisticated techniques for long range planning, fleet operations and control, resource acquisition and trading, exploration and development, plant design, cost and management control, communications, data handling, and so on.

Exxon Research and Engineering (ER&E) was responsible for Exxon's long term technological activities worldwide. Its laboratories performed research, engineering, and technical service activities in close coordination with the operating companies and divisions they supported. Royalty income received was deducted from the total cost of ER&E's operations to obtain a "net cost" which was allocated to affiliates roughly in proportion to their sales at the point of manufacture. ER&E tried to allocate specific corporate R&D tasks to those laboratories in various countries which could most effectively perform on behalf of the total corporation. Whenever possible, ER&E tried to staff its research centers throughout the world with scientists and engineers representing many nationalities—not just those of the host country.

In 1993, oil prices were at their lowest "real cost" levels in decades. Host countries, with the exception of North America and Australia, had generally assumed ownership of "their" domestic energy resources. In 1993 Exxon produced 1.7 billion bbl of petroleum liquids from its own sources. It held 9.5 trillion cu. ft. of proved reserves of natural gas in the U.S. and 24 trillion cu. ft. in Europe, which provided 60% of its gas market in 1993. Most authorities agreed that, any fossil source could be converted—at a cost—for consumption in any particular use category—i.e., central power stations, automobiles, railroads, aircraft, remote power generation, industrial use, home use, plastics, etc. A BTU (British Thermal Unit) of energy was becoming an interchangeable commodity. Yet, with the enormous growing demands indicated above, there was likely to be both a fossil energy shortage and serious world pollution problems, unless there was substantial conversion to nuclear power, fusion power, renewable resources, or solar power. All of these demanded significant breakthroughs in either cost or perceived safety in order to be viable alternatives.

QUESTIONS

1. Why should any host country allow Exxon to participate in its markets or in the development of its resources? What are the most significant potential conflicts between Exxon's interests and those of the host countries? What should Exxon do about these tensions? In 1978? 1983? 1993?

2. What should be the principal strategic concerns of Exxon in 1993? What should its strategy be in response to these? Where can Exxon create unique value?

3. How should Exxon's strategy have changed at each of the crisis points indicated? 1978? 1983? And the post–Gulf War era? What organization changes should be undertaken at each point? Portfolio changes? Control system changes? In 1993 how should Exxon be organized for the future, given the uncertainty and complexity of the energy environment?

**Exxon Corporation
Petroleum Products Sales
by Geographic Area
and Use**
(thousands of barrels daily)

	1993	1991	1989
United States			
Aviation fuels	119	119	128
Motor gasoline, naphthas	616	645	582
Heating oils, kerosene, diesel oils	197	220	204
Heavy fuels	43	49	40
Lubes	31	28	31
Specialty petroleum products	146	148	162
Total market and net supply sales	1,152	1,209	1,147
Sales under purchase/sales agreements	—	1	—
Total market and supply sales	**1,152**	**1,210**	**1,147**
Canada			
Aviation fuels	25	27	39
Motor gasoline, naphthas	196	196	199
Heating oils, kerosene, diesel oils	124	139	157
Heavy fuels	39	46	54
Specialty petroleum products	65	61	78
Total market and net supply sales	449	469	527
Sales under purchase/sales agreements	68	58	98
Total market and supply sales	**517**	**527**	**625**
Latin America			
Aviation fuels	38	40	28
Motor gasoline, naphthas	165	151	149
Heating oils, kerosene, diesel oils	154	142	145
Heavy fuels	45	45	41
Specialty petroleum products	17	12	18
Total market and net supply sales	419	390	381
Sales under purchase/sales agreements	3	1	2
Total market and supply sales	**422**	**391**	**383**
Europe			
Aviation fuels	134	130	123
Motor gasoline, naphthas	457	475	422
Heating oils, kerosene, diesel oils	601	625	516
Heavy fuels	234	211	190
Specialty petroleum products	177	166	175
Total market and net supply sales	1,603	1,607	1,426
Sales under purchase/sales agreements	269	256	292
Total market and supply sales	**1,872**	**1,863**	**1,718**
Asia-Pacific and Other Eastern Hemisphere			
Aviation fuels	48	43	48
Motor gasoline, naphthas	212	197	201
Heating oils, kerosene, diesel oils	286	251	268
Heavy fuels	179	162	140
Specialty petroleum products	127	124	114
Total market and net supply sales	852	777	771
Sales under purchase/sales agreements	110	101	76
Total market and supply sales	**962**	**878**	**847**
Worldwide			
Aviation fuels	364	359	366
Motor gasoline, naphthas	1,646	1,664	1,553
Heating oils, kerosene, diesel oils	1,362	1,377	1,290
Heavy fuels	540	513	465
Specialty petroleum products	563	539	578
Total market and net supply sales	4,475	4,452	4,252
Sales under purchase/sales agreements	450	417	468
Total market and supply sales	**4,925**	**4,869**	**4,720**

Source: Exxon Corporation, *1993 Annual Report.*

	CONSOLIDATED SUBSIDIARIES				
	UNITED STATES	CANADA	EUROPE	AUSTRALIA AND FAR EAST	OTHER
Revenue (dollars per unit of sales)					
Crude oil and NGL	$13.19	$11.71	$16.68	$18.19	$16.04
Natural Gas	2.11	1.33	2.49	1.21	0.95
Other	—	—	—	—	—
Total revenue (dollars per barrel of net oil-equivalent production)	**13.28**	**10.95**	**16.18**	**15.50**	**15.82**
Less costs:					
Production costs excluding taxes	3.90	4.45	5.30	2.52	3.72
Exploration expenses	0.43	0.42	1.19	0.50	8.38
Depreciation and depletion	3.86	4.97	3.33	2.47	7.91
Taxes other than income	1.55	0.22	0.29	3.26	0.12
Related income tax	1.49	0.20	2.07	2.32	2.21
Results of producing activities	2.05	0.69	4.00	4.43	(6.52)

	Total Consolidated Subsidiaries	Non-consolidated Interests	Total	Worldwide (millions of dollars)
Revenue (dollars per unit of sales)				
Crude oil and NGL	$15.07	$16.07	$15.12	$8,955
Natural Gas	1.98	2.78	2.26	4,815
Other	—	—	—	87
Total revenue (dollars per barrel of net oil-equivalent production)	**14.27**	**16.57**	**14.64**	**13,857**
Less costs:				
Production costs excluding taxes	4.05	2.45	3.80	3,593
Exploration expenses	0.81	0.51	0.77	725
Depreciation and depletion	3.67	1.31	3.28	3,112
Taxes other than income	1.37	5.38	2.01	1,903
Related income tax	1.67	2.91	1.87	1,767
Results of producing activities	2.70	4.01	2.91	2,757
Other earnings	—	—	—	556
Total earnings				**3,313**

Source: Exxon Corporation, *1993 Annual Report.*

APPENDIX A (cont'd)
Exxon Corporation
Natural Gas Production
and Sales
(in millions of cubic
feet daily)

	1993	1991	1989
Production			
Net production available for sale			
United States	1,765	1,655	1,827
Canada	328	355	389
Europe	1,009	1,033	1,068
Australia and Far East	659	391	356
Other	6	66	59
Total consolidated subsidiaries	3,766	3,500	3,699
Proportional interests in production			
of non-consolidated interests	2,059	1,997	1,686
Total worldwide	**5,825**	**5,497**	**5,385**
Sales			
United States	2,041	1,934	1,986
Canada	521	583	620
Other Western Hemisphere	6	72	65
Europe			
Netherlands	3,169	3,074	2,657
Germany	1,198	1,191	1,143
United Kingdom	540	523	461
Other	187	283	352
Total Europe	5,094	5,071	4,613
Other Eastern Hemisphere			
Australia	329	326	364
Other	474	109	59
Total other eastern hemisphere	803	435	423
Worldwide	**8,465**	**8,095**	**7,707**

Source: Exxon Corporation, *1993 Annual Report.*

LIQUIDS (MILLIONS OF BARRELS AT YEAR-END)

	1993	1991	1989
Net Proved Developed and Undeveloped Reserves			
United States	2,324	2,448	2,487
Canada	1,135	1,323	1,580
Europe	1,400	1,455	1,425
Australia and Far East	808	861	942
Other	91	128	151
Total consolidated subsidiaries	5,758	6,215	6,585
Proportional interest in reserved of			
non-consolidated interests	492	498	566
Oil sands reserves—Canada	314	283	316
Total worldwide	**6,564**	**6,996**	**7,467**
Net Proved Developed Reserves Included Above			
United States	1,821	2,010	1,974
Canada	524	736	979
Europe	859	834	749
Australia and Far East	624	609	700
Other	81	94	114
Total consolidated subsidiaries	3,909	4,283	4,507
Proportional interest in reserved of			
non-consolidated interests	458	459	519
Oil sands reserves—Canada	314	283	316
Total worldwide	**4,681**	**5,025**	**5,342**

Source: Exxon Corporation, *1993 Annual Report.*

NATURAL GAS (BILLIONS OF CUBIC FEET AT YEAR-END)

	1993	1991	1989
Net Proved Developed and Undeveloped Reserves			
United States	9,530	10,155	9,365
Canada	2,505	3,396	4,258
Europe	7,349	6,455	7,247
Australia and Far East	6,320	5,345	5,032
Other	112	83	154
Total consolidated subsidiaries	25,816	25,434	26,056
Proportional interest in reserved of			
non-consolidated interests	16,435	17,365	15,779
Total worldwide	**42,251**	**42,799**	**41,835**
Net Proved Developed Reserves Included Above			
United States	7,935	7,816	7,903
Canada	2,022	2,959	3,798
Europe	4,098	4,018	4,287
Australia and Far East	4,009	2,895	3,062
Other	112	74	97
Total consolidated subsidiaries	18,176	17,762	19,147
Proportional interest in reserved			
of non-consolidated interests	8,067	8,779	14,199
Total worldwide	**26,243**	**26,541**	**33,346**

Source: Exxon Corporation, *1993 Annual Report.*

	1974	1979	1984	1989	1994
Revenues (billions of dollars)	45.82	84.81	97.29	96.29	113.9
Petroleum & Natural Gas	42.09	76.16	65.48	83.93	100.41
Chemicals	2.79	5.8	6.08	9.21	9.54
Other	0.15	1.59	3.59	2	2.18
Net income	3.14	4.3	5.53	3.51	5.1
R & D	0.17	0.38	0.74	0.59	0.56
Exploration expenses	0.36	1.05	1.34	0.87	0.67
Shareholders' equity	15.72	22.55	28.85	30.24	37.42
Total assets	31.33	49.49	63.28	83.22	87.86
Total debt	6.13	4.78	6.38	16.03	12.7
Net income per share ($)	14.04	9.75	6.77	2.74	4.07
Cash dividends per share ($)	5	3.9	3.35	2.3	2.91
Shares outstanding (millions)	223.77	440.84	816.17	1,264	1,242
Employees (thousands)	133	169	148	104	86
Net income to total revenue (%)	6.9	5.1	5.7	3.6	4.5
Current assets to liabilities (ratio)	1.56	1.29	1.13	0.75	0.94
Earnings to average shareholders' equity (%)	21.3	20.1	19	11.3	14.1
Fixed charge coverage (ratio)	n/a	n/a	9.7	3.9	7

Source: Exxon Corporation, *Annual Report*, various years.

APPENDIX B (cont'd)
Exxon Corporation
Earnings by Function
(in millions of dollars,
except per share amounts)

	1993	1991	1989
Petroleum and natural gas			
Exploration and production			
United States	$ 935	$ 628	$1,133
Non-U.S.	2,378	2,500	1,925
Total	3,313	3,128	3,058
Refining and marketing			
United States	465	514	370
Non-U.S.	1,550	2,041	728
Total	2,015	2,555	1,098
Total petroleum and natural gas	5,328	5,683	4,156
Chemicals			
United States	267	336	682
Non-U.S.	144	176	400
Total	411	512	1,082
Other operations	138	224	290
Corporate and financing	(597)	(817)	(873)
Valdez provision	—	—	(1,680)
Net Income	$5,280	$5,600	$3,510
Net income per common share	4.21	4.45	2.74

Source: Exxon Corporation, *1993 Annual Report.*

APPENDIX B (cont'd)
Exxon Corporation
Consolidated Statement
of Income
(in millions of dollars)

	1993	1991	1989
REVENUE			
Sales and other operating revenue			
Petroleum and natural gas			
Petroleum products, including excise taxes	$ 79,384	$ 84,717	$ 67,198
Crude oil	12,738	12,295	10,619
Natural Gas	3,579	3,592	3,109
Other	3,107	3,148	3,008
Total	98,808	103,752	83,934
Chemical products	8,641	9,171	9,210
Other	2,083	2,145	2,029
Total sales and operating revenue	109,532	115,068	95,173
Earnings from equity interests and other revenue	1,679	1,424	1,112
Total revenue	**$111,211**	**$116,492**	**$ 96,285**
COSTS AND OTHER DEDUCTIONS			
Crude oil and product purchases	$ 46,124	$ 46,847	$ 39,268
Operating expenses	12,111	13,487	10,535
Selling, general, and admin. expenses	7,009	7,881	6,398
Depreciation and depletion	4,884	4,824	5,002
Exploration expenses			
Dry holes	137	328	289
Other	511	586	583
Total	648	914	872
Interest expense	681	810	1,265
Valdez provision	—	—	2,545
Income, excise, and other taxes			
Income taxes, U.S. Federal	679	558	126
Income taxes, other	2,093	2,360	1,902
Total	2,772	2,918	2,208
Income applicable to minority and preferred interests	250	167	263
Total costs and other deductions	**$105,931**	**$110,892**	**$ 93,310**
NET INCOME	**$ 5,280**	**$ 5,600**	**$ 3,510**

Source: Exxon Corporation, *1993 Annual Report.*

Exxon Corporation Capital and Exploration Expenditures, 1989 and 1993
(millions of dollars)

	1993	1989
Total petroleum and natural gas		
United States	$1,894	$2,637
Non-U.S.	4,929	7,647
Total	6,823	10,284
Chemicals		
United States	411	416
Non-U.S.	169	350
Total	580	766
Coal		
United States	12	20
Non-U.S.	15	259
Total	27	279
Minerals		
United States	1	1
Non-U.S.	108	130
Total	109	131
Hong Kong power generation	477	93
Other operations and administrative	151	231
GRAND TOTAL	**$8,167**	**$11,784**
Of which:		
United States	2,395	3,147
Canada	410	4,630
Other Western Hemisphere	256	289
Europe	2,812	2,152
Other Eastern Hemisphere	2,294	1,566

Source: Exxon Corporation, *1993 Annual Report.*

Exxon Corporation Average Capital Employed and Return on Average Capital Employed by Business
(millions of dollars and percent)

	1993		1991		1989	
Petroleum and natural gas						
Exploration and production						
United States	$ 11,098	8.4	$ 11,735	5.4	$ 12,218	9.3
Non-U.S.	10,974	21.7	10,921	22.9	10,331	18.6
Total	22,072	15.0	22,656	13.8	22,549	13.6
Refining and marketing						
United States	3,322	14.0	3,423	15.0	3,207	11.5
Non-U.S.	11,075	14.0	11,805	17.3	9,464	7.7
Total	14,397	14.0	15,228	16.8	12,671	8.7
Total	$ 36,469	14.6	$ 37,884	15.0	$ 35,220	11.8
Chemicals						
United States	$ 2,926	9.1	$ 2,822	11.9	$ 2,235	30.5
Non-U.S.	3,520	4.1	3,442	5.1	2,602	15.4
Total	6,446	6.4	6,242	8.2	4,837	22.4
Other operations	4,778	2.9	4,599	4.9	4,324	6.7
Corporate and financing	(236)		(1,002)		(438)	
Corporate total	**$47,457**	**12.0**	**$47,745**	**12.8**	**$43,943**	**9.7**
Average capital employed applicable to equity cos. included above	$ 4,800		$ 4,774		$ 4,603	

Source: Exxon Corporation, *1993 Annual Report.*

Sony Corporation began in the rubble and chaos of Japan at the end of World War II. Its first quarters were a small corner room of a burned out department store in Tokyo's Ginza district. Masaru Ibuka (age 37) had brought along seven young engineers to start "some sort of electronics laboratory or enterprise." His earlier company, Japan Precision Instrument Co., had supplied vacuum tube voltmeters and other instruments to the now defunct war effort, and Mr. Ibuka felt an obligation to provide continued work for his people. "We realized we could not compete against companies already in existence and against products in which they specialized. We started with the basic concept that we had to do something that no other company had done before."

From these inauspicious beginnings sprang one of the world's most innovative companies with worldwide sales in fiscal 1990 (calendar 1989) of $18.3 billion. In a nation not previously known for product innovation, what had led to Sony's unique capabilities? Could its successful past policies survive the ferocious competitive atmosphere of the mid-1990s?

MEAGER BEGINNINGS

THE YOUNG TEAM

At first Ibuka's small group considered anything that would sell in the war ravaged economy: bean paste soup, slide rules, an electric rice cooker Ibuka invented. Ibuka

Case copyright © 1994 by James Brian Quinn. Research associate—Penny C. Paquette. The generous support of the Adolf H. Lundin Professorship at the International Management Institute, Geneva, Switzerland, is gratefully acknowledged. The generous cooperation of the International University of Japan and Sony Corporation is gratefully acknowledged.

slowly depleted his meager savings to keep his people employed during the first arduous years. Then Akio Morita joined the company. Though there was little money for a salary, Ibuka conveyed his missionary feelings about making electronics technology available to a peacetime civilian Japan, and convinced Morita to join him.

As a student at Waseda University, Ibuka had won patents and international awards for a system to transmit sound by modulating neon light. Morita had ghost written articles for his professors at Osaka Imperial University where he had specialized in electronics. But there the similarities ended. Ibuka was passionate about invention, a humanist, a dreamer in many ways. Morita was a realist who had been trained in business by his father since birth. Ibuka had little interest in accounting and the intricacies of marketing. Morita was an administrator, as well as an enthusiastic, outgoing man who could charm or spellbind an audience. The two became the closest of friends.

On May 7, 1946, the company was formally incorporated as Tokyo Telecommunications Engineering Co. (TTK being the Japanese acronym). Since companies capitalized at over 200,000 yen encountered more difficult incorporation regulations, TTK listed the company at 198,000 yen—$500–$600 in exchange value—which was not much of an exaggeration.

The Purposes of Incorporation were listed in the Prospectus along with the new company's "Management Policies." Both of these remarkable statements—little changed since then—are shown in Exhibit 1. In the 1980s Sony's Chairman Morita had restated some of these basic principles:

Young people who join our company next year will stay for 25 years. So that means for them the company should be prosperous for that period. All the top people feel responsible that the company live a long, long time, rather than

EXHIBIT 1
Sony Corporation

Purposes of Incorporation

- "The establishment of an ideal factory—free, dynamic, and pleasant—where technical personnel of sincere motivation can exercise their technological skills to the highest levels.
- Dynamic activities in technology and production for the reconstruction of Japan and the elevation of the nation's culture.
- Prompt application of the highly advanced technology developed during the war in various sections to the life of the general public.
- Making rapidly into commercial products the superior research results of universities and research institutes, which are worth applying to the daily lives of the public."

Management Policies

- We shall eliminate any untoward profit-seeking, shall constantly emphasize activities of real substance, and shall not seek expansion of size for the sake of size.
- Rather, we shall seek a compact size of operation through which the path of technology and business activities can advance in areas that large enterprises, because of their size, cannot enter.
- We shall be as selective as possible in our products and will even welcome technological difficulties. We shall focus on highly sophisticated technical products that have great usefulness in society, regardless of the quantity involved. Moreover, we shall avoid the formal demarcation between electricity and mechanics, and shall create our own unique products coordinating the two fields with a determination that other companies cannot overtake.
- Utilizing to the utmost the unique features of our firm, which shall be known and trusted among the acquaintances in the business and technical worlds, we shall open up through mutual cooperation our production and sales channels and our acquisition of supplies to an extent equal to those of large business organizations.
- We shall guide and foster subcontracting factories in directions that will help them become independently operable and shall strive to expand and strengthen the pattern of mutual help with such factories.
- Personnel shall be carefully selected, and the firm shall be comprised of as small a number as feasible. We shall avoid mere formal position levels and shall place our main emphasis on ability, performance, and personal character, so that each individual can show the best in ability and skills.

Source: Sony Corporation of America.

---

making a big current profit to make a very large bonus. That's why we don't pay bonuses to executives. We pay bonuses to employees because we like for the employees to feel and participate in the company's results.

Every year, when we receive our new graduate employees, I like to make a little speech to them. Now you have become a Sony employee. You will spend the most brilliant time of your life here. Nobody can live twice. This is the only life you can have, so I want you to become happy at Sony. If you don't feel happy, you better go out and change your job.*

---

* All quotations not footnoted are from personal interviews with Professor Quinn.

EXPANSION WITH UMBRELLAS

The American Occupation Forces (rebuilding Japan's destroyed communications systems to American standards) encountered some of TTK's equipment and were so impressed with its sophistication and quality that they began to order from the tiny company. TTK had slowly expanded through a series of Ibuka's inventions into some shacks in the Shinagawa district that were so dilapidated that executives had to use umbrellas during rainstorms. Nevertheless, Ibuka insisted on such rigorous design and quality standards that TTK—through clever use of a carefully developed supplier network—was soon performing almost all of Japan Broadcasting Network's (NHK's) revisions, converting its equipment to modern standards and building industrial and commercial electronic devices for other companies.

Ibuka had seriously considered a wire recorder, first introduced by the military in World War II. Japan's Dr. Kenzo Nagai held some key patents on the wire recorder, the device would be unique in consumer markets, and TTK had the proper skills to produce it. Ibuka was just about to commit his best resources to an onslaught on the wire recorder. Then one day as he was visiting the offices of NHK, a member of the Occupation Forces showed him a tape recorder from the United States, and history was made.

THE TAPE RECORDER

Tape recorders were unheard of in Japan—there wasn't even a word for them. There was little published information about either magnetic tapes or recorders. In Japan there was no plastic available to produce tape and no way to acquire any plastic through Japan's stringent import regulations. The TTK team tried cellophane; it stretched. They tried paper—Ibuka made tapes in his kitchen from rice paper and a paste of boiled rice—its edges caught and broke. Finally, Morita got a cousin in a paper manufacturing company to prepare a batch of specially calendered paper with a slick surface.

Ibuka's group had to develop special techniques to cut the paper, hold it, and coat it uniformly with magnetic powder. They had to compensate for the less controllable paper base by designing extra quality into the circuitry, recording head, feed systems, and amplifiers in the recorder. It was a great struggle. The accounting manager constantly warned they were spending too much; they could bankrupt the company. Morita kept saying, "Be a little more patient and we will make a fortune." Finally after many months they created not just a new concept in tapes, but a new recorder, a new testing technology, and their own complete tape coating machine. Sony became perhaps the first company in the world to make the entire range of products from tapes to recorders, skills involving nearly a dozen basic technologies. In late 1949 they made their first unit, the G-type recorder, weighing over 100 pounds and selling for $400.

After many months of effort the first unit sold to an *oden* shop—a kind of Japanese pub where people came to eat, sing, and talk noisily. Technically the expensive, cumbersome device performed well, but no one quite knew what to do with it. Ibuka's response was to take all his top engineers to an inn and work night and day to reduce the recorder's cost by 50% and to improve its size, weight, and portability. The result was a concept for a suitcase enclosed recorder at a reasonable price—and at less than one-half the G-type's weight.

As markets—at first to record NHK's English language programs for use in schools—opened, 3M began to sell its excellent magnetic tape to Japanese broadcasters and other large users. TTK tried to negotiate a license and reached a financially very attractive proposition. But in exchange for the license, 3M insisted that TTK drop its recorder manufacturing. After much consideration Morita and Ibuka said no, wanting no outside control over their product line. But this also meant TTK was now in competition with a much larger and very sophisticated world competitor, a very difficult situation for the young company.

TRANSISTOR RADIOS

In 1952 Ibuka went to the United States to explore possible markets for his tape recorder. While he was there, a U.S. friend told him that Western Electric was ready to license its transistor patent for the first time. Ibuka investigated, but when he heard the price was $25,000, he left the United States knowing the price was too much for TTK. Ibuka worried as he made the long trip home. He was convinced the transistor would revolutionize electronics, though no one then realized how. As he pondered what to do, another concern came into place. He had hired a number of young physicists. "Would tape recorders be challenge enough for them, motivate them to use their best abilities, or let them grow to their full potentials?" Ibuka was convinced they could not.

"A POCKETABLE RADIO"

By the time Mr. Ibuka reached Tokyo, his questions had crystallized into a strategy to keep his people and his company growing. A short time later he announced, "We're going to use the transistor to make radios small enough so that each individual can carry them for his own use, but with a receiving ability that will enable civilization to reach areas that have no electric power." At that time "portable radios" weighed 10–20 pounds, were briefcase sized, and had batteries that lasted only a few hours. Ibuka spoke of a "pocketable transistor radio." But no one had applied transistors to radios—or much of anything else. The thought of a quality radio the size of a cigarette pack seemed almost beyond belief.

Morita had negotiated a license agreement with Western Electric whereunder the $25,000 patent was credited against potential future royalties. But the Ministry of International Trade and Industry (MITI) had to approve the release of the $25,000 in foreign currency. MITI was furious. If the big Japanese companies weren't interested in transistors, why should MITI support TTK? They delayed approval for months until Ibuka's persuasiveness finally prevailed in early 1954.

Ibuka immediately left for the United States, where he found that no one had achieved satisfactory yields on the high-frequency transistors needed for radio. Even lower-frequency transistors for hearing aids sold for $150–$500. Ibuka and Kazuo Iwama, then a young physicist heading the team, visited all the U.S. laboratories and plants they could, sending detailed letters to Sony's task force each night. Months passed as the task force tried to reach the high frequencies needed for radio and the production yields required for commercial exploitation. Again the financial stability of the company was at risk as transistor program costs grew. Only an expanding tape recorder market kept it going.

A MARKET

In August 1955 TTK's team put their first radio on display. It was about 4" x 8" x 1 1/2". They set a goal of 10,000 transistor radios in the first year and achieved 8,000. "The success of Sony is," said Iwama later, "that we produced a little less than was required. When there is enough, the market is saturated." Still Ibuka wanted a "pocketable radio." Despite the skepticism of marketing experts who thought the product would be too small, squeaky, and unreliable, Ibuka pushed on. TTK's component suppliers refused to modify their standard product lines, which were largely copied from world designs. They too were doubtful of the product's success. Ibuka single-handedly persuaded them to go ahead by offering Sony's technical support and production guidance. It was a momentous change for Japan. Japanese manufacturers had to become truly independent of foreign technology for perhaps the first time. In March 1957 a "pocketable" Type 63 radio was introduced using almost exclusively Japanese know-how. Since the Type 63 was still slightly larger than a shirt pocket, Sony made special shirts into which they would fit. Over a million Type 63s were soon sold.

Once the principle was proved, the bigger companies moved in. TTK changed its name to Sony, derived from the Latin sonis (for sound). The name had been carefully chosen to be simple, recognizable, and pronounceable in many languages. The Sony name became almost generic for transistor radios. "Sunny"

and "Somy" trade names appeared and were fought off. Meanwhile, Sony had a two- to three-year technology lead and moved on to provide the world's first transistorized shortwave and FM receivers for consumers.

THE SONY SPIRIT

By now Sony was becoming known as a maverick among Japanese companies. It was not bound up in the traditions of older companies and relied as little as possible on the government or banks. Morita and Ibuka could make fast decisions, unhindered by the formalities of the *ringi* method of consensus building found in most larger companies. Over a single lunch Morita reached agreement with CBS for Sony to distribute CBS records in Japan. As the company grew at an amazing pace, it hired senior people away from other concerns—a practice frowned on by more traditional Japanese companies.

Some of the executives' backgrounds were unusual. Ibuka convinced Dr. Kikuchi, Sony's research head, to leave MITI after 26 years there. Shigeru Kobayashi was recruited from the printing industry, given charge of an ailing semiconductor plant, and told "do what you want." Norio Ohga—a music major destined to become a major opera baritone—was recruited upon his graduation from the university. He remained a consultant to Sony as he rose to operatic fame. When he returned from the stage—with no business training— he was made head of the tape recorder plant and rose to be a CEO of Sony. Morita and Ibuka always looked first for talent, not someone "to fill a job." Then with full trust they gave their selections a free hand. "I never knew what hidden abilities I had until I came to Sony," commented one of many so treated.

"DO SOMETHING CREATIVE"

Many of Sony's personnel policies derived from its original goal to "establish an ideal factory—free, dynamic, and pleasant." To Ibuka this meant "to have fixed production and budgetary requirements but within these limits to give Sony employees the freedom to do what they want. This way we draw on their deepest creative potentials."[1]

Many more specific policies flowed from the remarkable experiences of Shigeru Kobayashi who took over Sony's Atsugi plant after its brief—and only—strike in 1961. Ibuka told Kobayashi, who knew nothing about semiconductor technology, "You are free to do there whatever you like. Try to do something truly creative."

Kobayashi soon concluded the plant's problems derived from people feeling themselves insignificant there, what he called "a small pebble complex." He thought essential trust had been destroyed because management had tried to set up contrived Western methods for measuring output, increasing efficiency, and motivating people.

To eliminate cafeteria lines and to build trust Kobayashi removed all cashier attendants, letting people voluntarily place their meal coupons in appropriate boxes. He shut down the forbidding dormitories used by most Japanese companies then, built small prefabricated homes where a few employees could live together, and gave employees full autonomy over their premises. This had never been done in Japan. Next he eliminated time clocks, and created autonomy for Sony's recreation groups, moving away from the carefully controlled company teams so common in Japan.

CELLS AND TRUST

Then Kobayashi developed a series of vertical and horizontal interconnecting teams or "cells" in the plant. Each was a specialized unit that could take charge of its own work. In these small (2 to 20 person) cells, workers could more easily develop a team spirit and help each other. Each cell would respond to input from all other cells above, below, on its sides. The cell would determine what methods to follow and evaluate its own output. Orders did not flow from above. Management's job was to assist the cells, to help them solve problems, to set overall goals, and to praise superior performances, while the cells were to control specific tasks at the workplace and group levels. The specifics of Kobayashi's "cell" system are different in each plant now, but the spirit and values it conveys continue.

In most areas, all new employees—whether law graduates or finance specialists—must spend several months on the production line learning to appreciate the company's products, practices, and culture. All Japanese engineers and scientists hired still must work in sales for several weeks or months. Promising people are shifted every two to three years to new areas to expand their knowledge and to identify their abilities for promotion. Typically workers learn several processes and are switched among tasks to keep up their interest. Production lines may be purposely segmented so they can be restructured rapidly if product mixes change. Rewards flow not to individuals, but to groups.

Morita recently said, "The best way to train a person is to give him authority. . . . We tell our young people: don't be afraid to make a mistake, but don't make the same mistake twice. If you think it is good for the company, do it. If something is wrong, I'm the man who should be accused. As CEO it's my job to take on the critics from the outside. For example, this year our profits are down, I tell my management, don't you worry about that, just do your job right."

Unlike other Japanese companies where seniority determines responsibility, young Sony employees were loaded with work and responsibility. But there was a complex "godfather system" in which a high executive watched over and specifically trained younger talent. A new executive interacted almost daily with his corporate mentor and received sophisticated insights and a corporate perspective. Mr. Morita expressed the overall philosophy this way, "Sony motivates executives not with special compensation systems but by giving them joy in achievement, challenge, pride, and a sense of recognition."

MINIATURE AND OTHER TELEVISIONS

As its pocketable radio business boomed, Sony turned to all transistorized television. At first Sony's system could only drive small picture tubes, 5–8" across, but not the larger tubes then popular. When Ibuka proposed to introduce a "mini-TV," the market experts again said, "It will never sell. RCA tried it and failed. The market wants big screens." Undeterred, Ibuka introduced an 8" set in Japan (May 1960) and in the United States (June 1961). Again the road to the marketplace was complex and difficult, but Ibuka's "tummy television" sets became eminently successful.

During this rapid growth period Mr. Morita moved his family to New York so that Sony's top management would know the U.S. market, not through statistics, but through intuition. Although his wife and children could not speak English at first, he insisted that they meet and entertain Americans, enter American camps and schools. Their acculturation was rapid. Morita, himself, often helped sweep out the shabby rat-infested offices of Sony Corp. of America (Sonam), and worked 16-hour days and 7-day weeks. While joining in menial tasks, the distinguished Morita pushed Sonam to be the highest quality U.S. company. He insisted on "establishing proper servicing before distribution" and spent money to import more service engineers, rather than allowing Sonam to move into more acceptable sales headquarters in New York.

When offered a chance by a leading U.S. radio manufacturer to rebrand Sony transistor radios and have them introduced under the American company's well-accepted 50-year-old name, Morita refused. When asked how he could turn down the benefits of a fast start and 50 years' experience, Morita replied, "This is the first year of our 50 years' experience. If we do not do things ourselves, 50 years from now we will not be a great company like yours today."

"NO FUN IN COPYING"

By 1964 color television had begun to take over the U.S. market. After some diverse experimentation, virtually every color manufacturer operated under RCA's "shadow mask" system using a triangle of three electron guns and a grid of tiny color "dots" to create color. But Ibuka said, "I could see no fun in merely copying their excellent system." In 1961 Ibuka had seen the Chromatron tube invented by Dr. O. E. Lawrence (world famous physicist and developer of the first cyclotron). The tube used a series of phosphor "stripes" to generate color, was potentially much simpler to manufacture than the shadow mask, and produced about three times the brightness of the RCA system. Sony had introduced the Chromatron in Japan, but it was plagued with defects, service costs were crushing, and losses were mounting daily on the product. Sonam was stridently pressing for a color system to sell in the United States—using the shadow mask.

But Ibuka said, "We must produce a product of our own. There is nothing more pitiable than a man who can't or doesn't dream. Dreams give direction and purpose to life, without which life would be mere drudgery." During this difficult period, Morita himself feared for the financial viability of the company, yet he had to calm his dealers. "Business should be considered in ten-year cycles," he explained. "If we wait and develop a unique product, we may start several years later, but we will be stronger than all the others in 10 years."

Then toward the end of 1966, a young engineer, Miyaoka, made a mistake while experimenting. Using a single gun and three cathodes, he had produced a blurred picture. "But it was a picture"—and a new concept. Intuitively, Ibuka recognized the promise of this approach and said, "This is it. This is the system to go with."

Ibuka became the project manager himself. His team often worked all night, taking a few hours off to rest on the sofa. By February they thought they had a better picture than the RCA tube, but for months they had problems with electron acceleration and control. Repeatedly experiments failed, and the engineers despaired. Finally, on October 16, 1967, the new "Trinitron" system really worked for the first time. It was a totally unique concept—using phosphor stripes, a one gun, three-beam system, and a vertical stripe aperture grille—in a market dominated worldwide by the shadow mask system.

Within a year, the Trinitron dominated the small-screen market in Japan. After at first dismissing its added brightness as a function of its small 12" size—"a clever marketing ploy" said U.S. competitors—the U.S. market responded. The Trinitron earned the first Emmy in the United States ever given to a product innovation. Although named for the prize himself, Ibuka saw that his key engineers shared in it. Sony could not catch up with world demand for the fabulously successful Trinitron until the late 1970s.

VIDEO TAPE RECORDERS

A final example, the video tape recorder (VTR), offers other insights about Sony's management of innovation. The first practical VTR, the Quadruplex, was introduced by Ampex in 1956. It set the standard for commercial television broadcasting for almost 20 years. NHK, Japan's national television network, bought a Quadruplex and (along with MITI) encouraged electronics manufacturers' engineers to become familiar with it. The "Quad" cost about $60,000 and was a complex machine filling several closet-sized equipment racks. In 1958, 3 1/2 months after Mr. Ibuka first saw the Ampex machine, a team under Dr. Nobutshu Kihara and Mr. K. Iwama completed an operating prototype using similar principles.

Dr. Kihara, who headed Sony's VTR program, would later figure prominently in many of Sony's other famous innovations. When asked how Sony approached such radical innovations Dr. Kihara noted, "Mr. Ibuka would often come in with the 'seed or hint' of an idea and ask him to 'try it out.'" For example, shortly after Dr. Kihara had helped build the first VTR prototype (which would have to be priced at about 20 million yen or $55,000) Ibuka said, "We want to make commercial video recorders, can you develop one that will sell for 2 million yen ($5,500)?" After Kihara did that, Ibuka said, "Now can we make a color recorder for the home at 200,000 yen ($550). The complex sequence that ensued led to Sony's early preeminence in the home VTR market.

Sony's first commercial machine (in 1963) lacked Ampex's fidelity, but was one-twentieth of its size and sold for less than one-quarter of its $60,000 price. By 1965 Sony had the compact CV-2000 for $600, operating reel to reel in black and white to high commercial standards.

Its U-Matic machine, the first video cassette recorder, became quite successful in commercial color markets in 1972 at $1,100. But Sony's target was the home market; its product was to be the legendary Betamax.

Mr. Ibuka said "Ampex had invented a four-head machine. We invented the one-head machine. We developed our own system. I specifically ordered Sony engineers *not* to develop a broadcasting machine. Many engineers wanted to imitate the Ampex machine and make a good business in the broadcast field. I strongly ordered that we would make a $500 home machine."

The first all-transistorized VTR was the Sony PV100, a two-head 2" tape machine. The biggest customers were an American medical x-ray company and American Airlines—to monitor landings. In 1965 Sony introduced its first home use VTR, the CV-2000. No formal market research studies were made. "After our experience with the micro-TV, I didn't believe the marketing research people. Merchandising and marketing people cannot envision a market that doesn't exist."

Mr. Ibuka continued, "We decided that the video tape recorder must be a cassette type. Our experience in audio said that open reel types were not good in the home market. We succeeded with the U-Matic, which was the first video cassette recorder in the world. When we decided on the U-Matic (U format) standard, Japan Victor and Matsushita agreed on it. We supplied our technology to both companies. Shortly after, we were able to come up with the Beta form of recording which is a helical system using all the space on the tape. All the relevant technologies were invented by us. We asked Matsushita to join us in that standard. But they had a license to operate with our original patent. So they denied us."

Instead, Matsushita changed the size of their cassettes for their VHS format (which depended in part on Sony's patents) so they could record twice as long, two hours. Other Japanese companies went to potential Japanese and American manufacturers to get them to join in their (VHS) standard, not Beta. They even convinced MITI to ask Sony to make the VHS format the national standard. But Sony already had some 200,000 recorders and many tapes in the marketplace. As one of the many alternatives it had looked at, Sony had actually tried the VHS format and was convinced that its Beta—meaning "full coverage" in Japanese—format was much superior. Most other Japanese and American consumer electronic companies adopted VHS, although technical experts generally agree the Beta format offers superior quality.

THE DESIGN APPROACH

Dr. Kihara said, "My group started ten different major test options or approaches. Within these we developed two or three alternatives for each subsystem. . . . Much of the development process was trial and error. We did not have formal written plans. . . . For example, we developed a loading system with one reel and a leader, not two reels. We developed another where the wind up drum was inside the cassette. We developed the U-loading system, the M-loading system. We developed single heads, double heads, the skip system, and the asimuth system for reading and writing on the tapes. And so on. By taking the best of each option we ultimately developed Betamax."

A development team member said, "Kihara was in charge of what kind of developments would be pursued, what systems to use. At Sony development moves fast. We make quick—but not rash—decisions. Kihara makes the decisions himself." This was reiterated. "Kihara believes there are only a few people directly involved in a new technology who have adequate information or knowledge about that technology. With new products one must create a new market. Not many people know how these new markets will develop, what a product can do, how well it will function, how it could be used by customers." Says Dr. Kihara, "We have never been told by Morita or Ibuka 'this product's sales will be this big or must make this much money.'"

"In my engineering intuition, something interesting comes to mind. I look at the unique things I can do. . . . I don't want to be a copycat. I want to be first, number one. I don't worry about marketing figures. At other companies, top executives expect their top engineers to do managerial chores. Here they do not. They give me a lot of time for development work. . . . Most companies make profit the first priority. Sony's primary mission is to produce something new, unique, and innovative for the enhancement of people's lives. Technical people report right to the top of the organization. In the early development stages, there are typically only 5 or 6 people involved on a project team; for example in the Mavica camera there were 7 to 8. We work together until we have made a model. After we get the go ahead, the project may be expanded to perhaps 30 people."

In the 1980s there were no specific budgets for individual advanced development projects. Kihara reported to Morita once a year on his total budget. But most individual projects in Kihara's group were kept "beneath the surface," hidden in detail even from

Morita and Ibuka. Dr. Kihara met with his younger engineers in a prolonged session at least every two months. Said Kihara, "I try to transfer my technical knowhow and to cultivate an atmosphere of innovation." The Data Discman was developed in 1988 by a similar method. Like Kihara's group, a small team under Yoshitaka Ukita worked in a separate physical area and hid its project costs within conventional projects until a working prototype was ready to show top management. The result was a radical new portable electronic computer the size of a thick paperback, able to store and display 100,000 pages of text on 32,000 graphic images.

In Sony people from other areas may join a development team directly. They are trained on the spot by Research and Development people. Those most suited for production will go on with the project into production. This practice leaves a vacuum in development which can be filled by new people who infuse the department with fresh blood and ideas. Dr. Kikuchi, then director of research, said, "Everyone at the top has a strong interest in engineering and scientific problems and encourages people below to talk to them. And it is easy for us to talk to them. Even Sony's business people must talk technical languages, not just finance."

Sony thought the best technicians were those who were willing to move among product groups and try their hands at totally new experiences. It followed a policy of "self promotion," which allowed engineers to seek out projects anywhere in the company without notifying their supervisors. If they found something they were allowed to move. If they didn't, the boss never knew they were looking.

In 1990 the President and Chairman visited the R&D labs frequently as did (now honorary chairman) Ibuka. Mr. Morita frequently telephoned or brought in ideas from around the world on how to apply physics in new ways. For years Mr. Ibuka visited many places in Sony randomly. After playing golf near the research center, he would drop in at the laboratory. He wanted to see things, touch things. At 81 he said "The key to success in everything in business, science, and technology is never to follow the others. . . . I never had much use for specialists. They are inclined to argue why you can't do something, while our emphasis has always been on how to make something out of nothing."[2]

There were monthly meetings between the top board and the technical section heads. But there was little calculation of projected financial ratios or returns for particular projects. Dr. Kikuchi said, "We as management must define the problems, but only with sufficient specificity to leave many directions open for technical work. The goal must be clear. It may not be expressed numerically. At first there may not even be a date attached. But it must be clear and not change easily. We let the technical leaders choose the approaches."

Central Research coordinated efforts on more advanced technology projects. However, individual product groups were responsible for their own new product development efforts. The work of both groups was driven primarily by their own desire to excel. Nonetheless, there were formal incentives. Dr. Kikuchi said, "Periodically, I give a 'crystal award' for highly evaluated work. Even if a team has lost a competition within Sony, we will still give them a crystal award if their quality of work is especially good. . . . We also may give engineers a certain percentage of a new product's first year's sales if their ideas had particular merit. The amount of money is significant, but not huge."

THE WALKMAN AND MAVICA

Through 1990, Sony continued its innovative ways. It spent between 5.5% and 6% of sales on R&D supporting a force of over 8,000 scientists and engineers. It turned out an average of 1,000 new products per year, some 200 of which targeted whole new markets. In the late 1980s several new products offered interesting examples of Sony's innovation capabilities, the Walkman portable sound system, digital audio tapes (DAT), the MiniDisc portable CD player that could also record from digital sources, and the Mavica all-electronic still camera system.

As had happened so often before, the idea for Walkman (a compact cassette player with small earphones for highly portable listening) came from Ibuka and Morita. Mr. Morita, who purposely visited places where young people congregated, found that they wanted to listen to music on a very personal basis, especially if the sound was loud rock music. He also thought—as an avid golfer—that sportsmen would like a high-quality portable sound system. He gave the engineers a target of developing small high-quality earphones and a simple light tape player. When the marketing people heard of the project, they did not think such a system would sell well. They wanted to make the cassette record as well as play. Morita said, "No. Keep it small and simple." Despite marketing's skepticism, Mr. Morita was confident that there was a big market for the new concept. The Walkman sold out instantly upon introduction, and in 1990 was a major product line constantly being modified and updated for the special tastes of hundreds of countries and user segments. A new Walkman was released every two weeks on average.

Started in 1986, the MiniDisc—still in development in 1990—was stimulated by a contest initiated by Mr. Ohga, then president of Sony, to find a successor to the audio tape player. Five different teams competed on prototypes for evaluation. Mr. Ohga selected the 2.5 inch mini disc player because of its superior sound, 75 minute playback time (equivalent to standard 5" CDs), instant random access to sound tracks and capacity to operate without skipping when jostled. Like other Sony products, the prototype MiniDisc then went to the centralized Sony Design Center to be packaged with the distinctive Sony look and feel. When introduced, MiniDisc (MD) technology would compete directly against standard audio tape, DAT, and other digital formats which could read but not record digital signals (as MD could).

THE MAVICA STILL CAMERA

In the early 1980s, Sony had previewed its revolutionary Mavica all-electronic camera for shooting still pictures. Exhibit 2 describes the way the system operated. The camera used no film or chemical developing processes. Images were recorded on a small magnetic disk called Mavipak and could be viewed immediately on a home TV set through a specially designed playback unit. The system also had a color printer called the Mavigraph which could electronically produce hard copy prints from the video signals developed by the Mavica.

The key technical developments for the system formally announced in 1988 were (1) electronic recording using Sony's very-high-density magnetic disks, (2) the development of very high-quality charged couple devices (CCDs), which converted the optical image coming through the lens of the camera into a series of electrically charged spots on a semiconductor, and (3) the creation of high-density circuits small enough to operate the complex camera.

Information from the CCD could be transferred directly to a magnetic storage device (disk or semiconductor RAM) from which the original image could be later retrieved, electronically enhanced, or eliminated to make room for another image. The resolution of individual pictures was limited by the density of information the CCD could pick up. A color picture from a regular camera using regular instant film would contain about 100 million bits of information. In the mid 1980s CCDs could pick up about 400,000 bits of information for the same-sized black and white picture. But the density of information CCDs could pick up was dou-

bling every two to three years, and image processing software could improve the picture's appearance even more. Electronically enhanced pictures from a 600,000-bit source were difficult for the eye to discern from a regular film photograph.

The Mavica was no larger than a conventional 35mm single-lens reflex camera. Once its pictures were recorded on the Mavipak (or only on part of it), the disk could be removed from the camera and then inserted again with no fear of recording a new picture over a previous picture. Since the Mavipak could be erased, the memory disk could be used repeatedly with no deterioration of picture or color quality. Even small children could load a Mavipak into the camera. In the mid-1980s a Mavipak memory medium could record 100 still color pictures. But this technology was rapidly advancing in the mid-1980s when the product was first announced.

THE MAVICA MARKETPLACE

The Mavica camera would move into a marketplace that was yet to be defined. Projected prices in Japan were $650 for the camera, $220 for the playback unit, and $2.60 for each magnetic disk. No price was initially announced for the printer, but it was expected to cost approximately $800–$1,000. The Mavica could also be used as a video camera. By attaching it to a portable Sony video tape recorder, one could make video films. Images could also be transmitted electronically over telephone lines. In addition, the Mavigraph allowed one to make hard copies of the graphics created on the Sony computer system, other compatible computer systems, and certain imaging equipment like x-rays, CAT scanners, or commercial graphic arts devices. While the initial image on a standard U.S. television set would be limited to the 350 horizontal lines on the tube, Sony was demonstrating high-resolution screens of 1,500 lines for high density TV (HDTV) systems in 1988.

The investment community responded cautiously, but positively, concerning the product's impact. In its investment report, E. F. Hutton said, "In Hutton's view, the so-called photography industry is in the path of a tidal wave of digital electronic technology. The processing and display of scenes/images may become one of the most important uses of digital electronics yet seen. . . . The lion's share of the [photographic] industry's profits have been from the sale of consumables (photographic film, paper, and chemicals) as opposed to hardware. The consumables are chemical based, reasonably proprietary, highly profitable—with film and paper made by the mile and sold by the millimeter."[3]

EXHIBIT 2
Mavica System

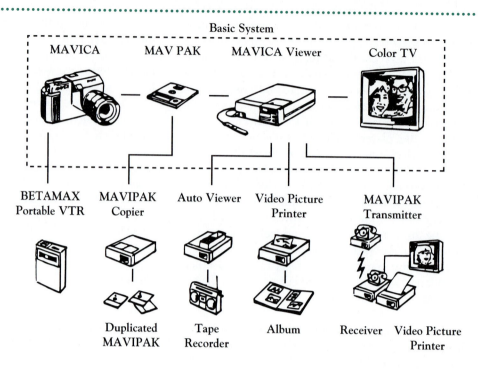

Source: Sony Corporation

In its report on the photographic and imaging industry, Smith Barney noted,

▼ Silver halide technology [which currently dominates consumer imaging] will continue to improve in film sensitivity and sharpness, and hardware will become more compact, reliable, and convenient.

▼ We expect electronic cameras and other hardware to be more expensive than their silver halide counterparts, but the electronic consumables or recording media will be less costly to use.

▼ We project a total market for consumer electronic imaging of about $4–5 billion in 1990, accounting for about 39% of total consumer imaging expenditures.[4]

Kodak quickly demonstrated a TV display device for displaying developed negatives from its disc cameras. This unit, informally dubbed the EkTViewer, used a 350,000-element CCD chip and provided a good-quality image on television. With a 2-1 zoom device, the unit allowed cropping into any quadrant of the original image with little loss of resolution. Kodak said the display unit would probably be priced around $300–$400. Others speculated that commercial extensions of the EkTViewer could allow zooming, cropping, focus adjustments, contrast changes, and shifts in color balance on the monitor. The commercial units were forecast to handle both disc and 35mm films, but would probably cost well over $1,000.

Polaroid had taken equity positions in a number of smaller companies in the high-density magnetic recording, fiber optics, ink jet printing, and continuous tone color film recording fields. Polaroid's Palette, which sold for about $1,500, was the most successful electronics-based color film recorder/printer introduced in the mid 1980s. This system allowed the user to output digital images from IBM, Apple, and DEC PCs and record them on either instant print or 135 film. Several Japanese competitors were also working on similar electronic camera and print systems. Sony's chairman Morita conceded that the initial Mavica posed little threat to conventional 35 millimeter cameras, but thought the Mavica could "open up new markets." Mavica might offer substantial cost advantages for the consumer. Estimated costs for the Mavica would be only 5–10 cents per picture against 80 cents for a Polaroid shot, or 42 cents for a pocket 110 shot on Kodak film. Exhibit 3 provides an overview of the photographic and reprographics market through 1990.

At the same time Sony announced the Mavica, it was also about to pioneer the first introduction of the

EXHIBIT 3
The Photographic
Equipment and Supplies
Market

	1980	1982	1984	1986	1988	1990
Equipment						
Sales of photo equipment and supplies ($ billions)	14.45	15.86	17.11	17.86	19.00	21.15
Hand-held still cameras (millions of units)	15.30	17.50	17.20	17.60	19.70	18.70
35mm reflex cameras (millions of units)	2.90	3.8	5.50	6.70	9.10	11.95
Photocopy equipment (millions of units)	0.45	0.68	0.96	1.12	1.27	1.41
Supplies (Still Picture Film)						
Black & white (millions of amateur photos)	550	500	450	390	420	420
Color (billions of amateur photos)	9.70	10.50	11.60	13.22	15.04	15.30

Source: Predicasts, Basebook 1991.

compact disc (CD) audio record player which could record 100 billion bits of information on its 5" disk, a small 8mm hand-held video camera (camcorder) which would threaten all existing amateur (Super 8) film systems, and a digital audio tape (DAT) system that promised tape audio performance equaling or (through enhancement) exceeding live performance quality. By 1988 Sony had also developed (along with other Japanese companies) a superb quality HDTV system. HDTV offered cinema-quality pictures and digital sound. The picture quality was so outstanding that one could walk up to Sony's full cinema-size HDTV projection screen in its Tokyo display center and see no granularity in the picture. This startling quality had implications for commercial, home, computer graphics reproductions. Each of these technologies was a radical departure within its field.

CD (compact laser disk) records and players allowed digital recording of the original disc and optical playback which eliminated the surface noise and distortions introduced by the recording process for other record and tape systems. However, it required that homeowners replace LP record players and tape players (as well as recordings) in which they had substantial investments. Sony had co-developed the CD with Phillips, a Netherlands company. Both parties were extremely enthusiastic about the quality of CD and its later potentials for distortion free recording of movies and video entertainment. The 8mm Camcorder could be made in formats comparable in size to 35mm film cameras. However, the high density metallic recording medium for 8mm would also fight against

a huge installed base of 1/2 inch VHS tape recorders in the marketplace. Observers agreed that Sony's 8mm picture was superior to 1/2 inch VHS reproduction from home video cameras at the time.

Digital audiotape could provide studio quality audio recordings of original performances and undistorted quality from any digital original. However, DAT still required an expensive recording and playback investment in 1990. Systems sold from a minimum of $3,500 to well over $12,000. Professionals said that DAT quality was in many respects superior to concert quality because of the capacity to capture all elements of a performance simultaneously from pick-up points near the sound source and to provide distortion free reproduction. However, record producers and distributors were very concerned about the inventory expense, customer confusion, and piracy possibilities offered by all these formats, and each would require $100s of millions to billions to introduce and support.

Some key statistics about potential markets for each of these devices are shown in Exhibit 4 and Exhibits 5–6 show summary financial statistics for Sony through 1990. The devices themselves proved that Sony's remarkable hardware innovation capabilities persisted into the 1990s. However, they also posed some significant new problems for management in positioning Sony for the future.

One of these was that shelf lives for new product models were becoming extremely short. It was common for models of Walkman or video cameras to have a shelf life of only a few months. Yet efficient innovation and production for key components required heavy investments over multiple years. (See Exhibit 7 "Laser Diode Production for CD Players.") Further, each country within Sony's worldwide marketplaces required some product modification, and individual markets for new products varied quite sharply among geographical areas. Production plants required large fixed investments for advanced componentry such as laser diodes or integrated circuits. These conflicting requirements called for new innovation, technology, and product coordination systems worldwide, and raised strong challenges for Sony's marvelously effective innovations system.

QUESTIONS

1. What are the most critical policies and practices which made Sony so innovative as a company?

Can tzey be transferred to other companies? What problems do they pose for Sony?

2. How does Sony compare and contrast with conventional views of "the Japanese management style?" How did it compare and contrast with the American approach to "entrepreneurship" when it was a young company?

3. What overall strategy should Sony follow in the early 1990s? Why? What major changes does it need in its portfolio? Organization? Policies?

4. How should Mavica fit into that strategy? What should be the specific strategy for introduction of Mavica? Why? What problems would you expect from the CD and DAT systems? What should Sony do?

EXHIBIT 4
U.S. Consumer
Electronics Markets

	1984		1986		1988		1990		1992 (EST.)	
	UNITS	$	UNITS	$	UNITS	$	UNITS	$	UNITS	$
VIDEO										
Color TV	16,083	5,377	18,204	5,858	20,216	6,277	20,384	6,247	29,500	6,650
Projection TV	195	385	304	530	302	529	351	6,256	400	715
VCR Decks	7,616	3,585	12,005	3,978	10,748	2,848	10,119	2,439	12,350	2,950
Camcorders	N/A	355	1,169	1,338	2,044	1,972	2,962	2,260	2,815	1,840
Laserdisc Players	N/A	N/A	N/A	N/A	N/A	N/A	168	72	200	80
AUDIO										
Compact & Track Systems	3,218	976	4,848	1,370	4,715	1,225	4,005	1,270	5,215	1,370
Portable Audio Equip.	N/A	N/A	N/A	N/A	36,436	1,547	39,154	1,645	42,250	2,100

Source: Electronic Market DataBook, 1993, Electronic Industries Association.

EXHIBIT 4 (cont'd)

	1984		1986		1988		1990		1992 (EST.)	
	UNITS	$	UNITS	$	UNITS	$	UNITS	$	UNITS	$
OTHER										
Cordless Phones	6,300	460	4,100	295	8,200	681	10,300	855	17,650	1,300
Telephone Answering Machines	3,000	230	6,450	464	11,100	755	13,800	842	15,475	1,000
Home Computers	5,100	2,250	3,800	2,890	4,500	3,150	5,500	3,795	7,125	4,525
Blank Video Tapes	133	771	296	1,235	297	936	338	948	360	875
Blank Audio Tapes	228	256	304	300	378	354	428	376	430	375

Source: Electronic Market DataBook, 1993, Electronic Industries Association.

EXHIBIT 5
Sony Corporation:
Summary Financials,
1974–1990
(millions of yen, except per share amounts)

	1974	1976	1978	1980	1982	1984	1986	1988	1990
Net sales									
Overseas	198,939	272,455	320,085	610,545	829,665	916,487	1,001,751	1,017,277	2,010,378
Domestic	198,112	191,073	214,832	282,218	284,157	345,059	450,339	537,942	869,478
Total	397,051	463,528	534,917	892,763	1,113,822	1,261,546	1,452,000	1,555,219	2,879,856
Operating income	53,880	61,974	30,766	117,245	109,584	131,769	42,144	60,664	295,191
Income before income taxes	46,414	64,388	52,378	116,748	85,542	140,376	84,128	71,836	227,429
Income taxes	23,693	35,625	29,387	53,026	45,871	77,165	48,802	41,465	126,976
Net income	22,518	30,926	25,874	68,643	45,820	77,431	41,244	37,236	102,808
Per depositary share	106.55	143.42	120.00	318.34	198.67	289.8	166.6	145.7	306.9
Depreciation	10,298	10,778	15,844	24,703	48,299	56,478	86,029	92,511	164,751
Net working capital	64,612	90,840	97,272	137,188	195,240	273,687	359,405	140,353	205,642
Capital investment (additions to fixed assets)	25,878	16,169	37,604	48,715	112,091	80,386	105,207	134,049	323,750
Shareholders' equity	160,115	201,034	251,024	325,523	474,592	542,180	600,059	646,076	1,430,058
Per depositary share	757.66	932.33	1,164.17	1,509.67	2,057.72	2,347.87	2,595.13	2,705.86	4,308.33
Total assets	416,681	509,859	618,854	877,413	1,240,355	1,309,659	1,532,919	1,945,447	4,370,085
Average number of shares (in thousands of shares)	211,328	215,625	215,625	215,625	230,639	230,923	231,223	249,600	337,682
Exchange rate ¥/$	282	301	232	248	241	225	179	127	153

Source: Sony Corporation, *Annual Reports*, various years.

EXHIBIT 6
Sony Corporation:
Segment Data
(percentage of
total revenues)

	1974	1978	1982	1986	1988	1990
Geographical Areas						
Japan	50	40	25	31.0	34.6	30.2
United States	26	28	29	30.0	27.9	29.8
Europe	13	16	24	21.7	22.6	24.8
Other	11	16	22	17.3	14.9	15.2
Product Groups						
Video Equipment	6	17	43	33.1	29.0	25.8
Audio Equipment	42	29	23	28.6	30.8	25.1
Televisions	37	31	23	22.8	20.3	15.5
Other Products	15	23	11	15.5	19.9	33.6

Source: Sony Corporation, *Annual Reports,* various years.

EXHIBIT 7
Decreasing Cost of
Laser Diodes

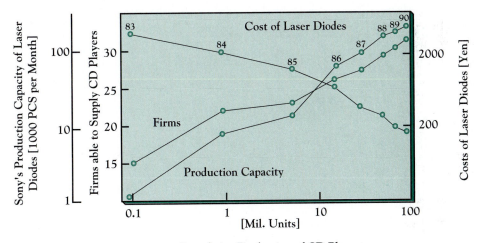

Cumulative Production of CD Players

Note: Decreasing the cost of the laser diode brings in new suppliers of CD players

Source: Takashi Shibuta, "Sony's Successful Strategy for Compact Discs," *Long Range Planning,* Vol. 26, No. 4, 1993, 16–21.

CONTEXTS

THE ENTREPRENEURIAL CONTEXT

The text of this book really divides into two basic parts, although there are three sections. The first, encompassing Chapters 1 through 8 and Sections I and II, introduces a variety of important *concepts* of organizations—strategy, the strategist, process, structure, systems, culture, power, style. The second, beginning here with Section III and Chapter 9, considers how these concepts combine to form major *contexts* of organizations. In effect, a context is a type of situation wherein can be found particular structures, power relationships, processes, competitive settings, and so on.

Traditionally, policy and strategy textbooks are divided into two very different parts—a first on the "formulation" of strategy, a second on its "implementation" (including discussion of structure, systems, culture, etc.). As some of the readings of Chapter 5 have already made clear, we believe this is often a false dichotomy: In many situations (that is, contexts), formulation and implementation can be so intertwined that it makes no sense to separate them. To build a textbook around a questionable dichotomy likewise makes no sense to us, and so we have instead proceeded by introducing all the concepts related to the strategy process first and then considering the various ways in which they might interact in specific situations.

There is no "one best way" to manage the strategy process. The notion that there are several possible "good ways" however—various contexts appropriate to strategic management—was first developed in the Mintzberg reading in Chapter 6. In fact, his *configurations* of structure serve as the basis for determining the set of contexts we include here. These are as follows:

We begin here in Chapter 9 with what seems to be the simplest context, certainly one that has had much good press in America since Horatio Alger first went into business—the *entrepreneurial* context. Here a single leader takes personal charge in a highly dynamic situation, as in a new firm or a small one operating in a growing market, or even sometimes in a large organization facing crisis.

We next consider in Chapter 10 a contrasting context that often dominates large business as well as big government. We label it the *mature* context, although it might equally be referred to as the stable context or the mass-production or mass-service context. Here, rather formal structures combine with strategy-making processes that are heavily planning and technique oriented.

Our third and fourth contexts are those of organizations largely dependent on specialists and experts. These contexts are called *professional* when the environment is stable, *innovation* when it is dynamic. Here responsibility for strategy making tends to diffuse throughout the organization, sometimes even lodging itself at the bottom of the hierarchy. The strategy process tends to become rather emergent in nature.

Fifth, we consider the context of the *diversified* organization, which has become increasingly important as waves of mergers have swept across various Western economies. Because product-market strategies are diversified, the structures tend to get divisionalized, and the focus of strategy shifts to two levels: the corporate or portfolio level and the divisional or business level. Following this, we consider the *international* context, really a form of diversification (i.e., geographical), but important enough in its own right to merit a separate chapter.

We complete our discussion of contexts with consideration of the problems of managing *change* from one of these contexts to another (often "cultural revolution") or from one major strategy and structure to another within a particular context.

In the chapter on each context, our intention is to include material that would describe all the basic concepts as they take shape in that context. We wish to describe the form of organizational structure and of strategic leadership found there, the nature of its strategy-making process, including its favored forms of strategy analysis and its most appropriate types of strategies (generic and otherwise), its natural power relationships and preferred culture, and the nature of its competition and industry structure as well as the social issues that surround it. Unfortunately, appropriate readings on all this are not available—in part we do not yet know all that we must about each context. But we believe that the readings that we have included in this section do cover a good deal of ground, enough to give a real sense of each different context.

Before beginning, we should warn you of one danger in focusing this discussion on contexts such as these: It may make the world of organizations appear to be more pat and ordered than it really is. Many organizations certainly seem to fit one context or another, as numerous examples will make clear. But none ever does so quite perfectly—the world is too nuanced for that. And then there are the many organizations that do not fit any single context at all. We believe, and have included arguments in a concluding chapter to this section, that in fact the set of contexts altogether form a framework by which to understand better all kinds of organizations. But until we get there, you should bear in mind that much of this material caricatures reality as much as it mirrors it. Of course, such caricaturing is a necessary part of formal learning and of acting. Managers, for example, would never get anything done if they could not use simplified frameworks to comprehend their experiences in order to act on them. As Miller and Mintzberg have argued in a paper called "The Case for Configuration," managers are attracted to a particular, well-defined context because that allows them to achieve a certain consistency and coherence in the design of their organization and so to facilitate its effective performance. Each context, as you will see, has its own logic—its own integrated way of dealing with its part of the world—that makes things more manageable.

This chapter of Section III discusses the entrepreneurial context. At least in its traditional form, this encompasses situations in which a single individual, typically with a clear and distinct vision of purpose, directs an organization that is structured to be as responsive as possible to his or her personal wishes. Strategy making thus revolves around a single brain, unconstrained by the forces of bureaucratic momentum.

Such entrepreneurship is typically found in young organizations, especially ones in new or emerging industries. Entrepreneurial vision tends to have a high potential payoff in these situations and may indeed be essential when there are long delays between the conception of an idea and its commercial success. In addition, in crisis situations a similar type of strong and visionary leadership may offer the only hope for successful turnaround. And it can thrive as well in highly fragmented industries, where small flexible organizations can move quickly into and out of specialized market niches, and so outmaneuver the big bureaucracies.

The word "entrepreneurship" has also been associated recently with change and innovation inside of larger, more bureaucratic organizations—sometimes under the label "intrapreneurship." In these situations, it is often not the boss, but someone in an odd corner of the organization—a "champion" for some technology or strategic issue—who takes on the entrepreneurial role. We believe, however, for reasons that will later become evident, that intrapreneurship better fits into our chapter on the innovation context.

To describe the structure that seems to be most logically associated with the traditional form of entrepreneurship, we open with material on the simple structure in Mintzberg's book *The Structuring of Organizations*. Combined with this is a discussion of strategy making in the entrepreneurial context, especially with regard to strategic vision, based on two sets of research projects carried out at McGill University. In one, strategies of visionary leadership were studied through biographies and autobiographies; in the other, the strategies of entrepreneurial firms were tracked across several decades of their histories.

Then, to investigate the external situation that seems to be most commonly (although not exclusively) associated with the entrepreneurial context, we present excerpts from a chapter on emerging industries from Michael Porter's book *Competitive Strategy*. The final reading of this chapter, by Amar Bhide of the Harvard Business School, tells how entrepreneurs go about crafting their strategies, based on his and his associates' research. Entrepreneurs select carefully but are also careful not to be too analytical (recall Pitcher's artists versus the technocrats of Chapter 8), and they maintain their ability to maneuver and to "hustle." Action must be integrated with analysis.

Many of the cases in this section, and elsewhere in the book, deal with entrepreneurship—both in smaller emerging companies and larger ones. The Genentech, Inc. (B), Orbital Engine Company, Argyle Diamonds, New Steel Corporation, Microsoft Corporation (A), Nintendo Co., Ltd., Apple Computer Company (A), Honda Motor Company 1994, and Sony Corporation: Innovation System cases deal with some of the most important start-ups of the modern era. These companies literally changed the entire profile of competition in their fields. All introduce the kinds of problems and potentials a highly centrist style poses in rapidly changing situations. The Hewlett Packard Company, TCG, Ltd. /Thermo Electron, The Vanguard Group, Inc., Microsoft Corporation (B), Sony Entertainment, and Polaroid Corporation cases suggest how entrepreneurial behavior can be encouraged on a systematic basis by structure or management practice. Entrepreneurial leadership provides much of the glamour of modern business. While we hope these cases and readings will make the entrepreneurial juices run strong, they also pose some most needed caveats for the unwary.

▼ READING 9.1   THE ENTREPRENEURIAL ORGANIZATION*

by Henry Mintzberg

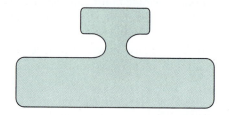

Consider an automobile dealership with a flamboyant owner, a brand-new government department, a corporation or even a nation run by an autocratic leader, or a school system

* Adapted from *The Structuring of Organizations* (Prentice Hall, 1979, Chap. 17 on "The Simple Structure"), *Power In and Around Organizations* (Prentice Hall, 1983, Chap. 20 on "The Autocracy"), and the material on strategy formation from "Visionary Leadership and Strategic Management," *Strategic Management Journal* (1989) coauthored with Frances Westley); see also, "Tracking Strategy in an Entrepreneurial Firm," *Academy of Management Journal* (1982), and "Researching the Formation of Strategies: The History of a Canadian Lady, 1939–1976," in R. B. Lamb, ed., *Competitive Strategic Management* (Prentice Hall, 1984), the last two coauthored with James A. Waters. A chapter similar to this appeared in *Mintzberg on Management: Inside Our Strange World of Organizations* (Free Press, 1989).

in a state of crisis. In many respects, those are vastly different organizations. But the evidence suggests that they share a number of basic characteristics. They form a configuration we shall call the *entrepreneurial organization*.

The Basic Structure

The structure of the entrepreneurial organization is often very simple, characterized above all by what it is not: elaborated. As shown in the opening figure, typically it has little or no staff, a loose division of labor, and a small managerial hierarchy. Little of its activity is formalized, and it makes minimal use of planning procedures or training routines. In a sense, it is nonstructure; in my "structuring" book, I called it *simple structure*.

Power tends to focus on the chief executive, who exercises a high personal profile. Formal controls are discouraged as a threat to the chief's flexibility. He or she drives the organization by sheer force of personality or by more direct interventions. Under the leader's watchful eye, politics cannot easily arise. Should outsiders, such as particular customers or suppliers, seek to exert influence, such leaders are as likely as not to take the organizations to a less exposed niche in the marketplace.

Thus, it is not uncommon in small entrepreneurial organizations for everyone to report to the chief. Even in ones not so small, communication flows informally, much of it between the chief executive and others. As one group of McGill MBA students commented in their study of a small manufacturer of pumps: "It is not unusual to see the president of the company engaged in casual conversation with a machine shop mechanic. [That way he is] informed of a machine breakdown even before the shop superintendent is advised."

Decision making is likewise flexible, with a highly centralized power system allowing for rapid response. The creation of strategy is, of course, the responsibility of the chief executive, the process tending to be highly intuitive, often oriented to the aggressive search for opportunities. It is not surprising, therefore, that the resulting strategy tends to reflect the chief executive's implicit vision of the world, often an extrapolation of his or her own personality.

Handling disturbances and innovating in an entrepreneurial way are perhaps the most important aspects of the chief executive's work. In contrast, the more formal aspects of managerial work—figurehead duties, for example, receive less attention, as does the need to disseminate information and allocate resources internally, since knowledge and power remain at the top.

Conditions of the Entrepreneurial Organization

A centrist entrepreneurial configuration is fostered by an external context that is both simple and dynamic. Simpler environments (say, retailing food as opposed to designing computer systems) enable one person at the top to retain so much influence, while it is a dynamic environment that requires flexible structure, which in turn enables the organization to outmaneuver the bureaucracies. Entrepreneurial leaders are naturally attracted to such conditions.

The classic case of this is, of course, the entrepreneurial firm, where the leader is the owner. Entrepreneurs often found their own firms to escape the procedures and control of the bureaucracies where they previously worked. At the helm of their own enterprises, they continue to loathe the ways of bureaucracy, and the staff analysts that accompany them, and so they keep their organizations lean and flexible. Figure 1 shows the organigram for Steinberg's, a supermarket chain we shall be discussing shortly, during its most classically entrepreneurial years. Notice the identification of people above positions, the simplicity of the structure (the firm's sales by this time were on the order of $27 million), and the focus on the chief executive (not to mention the obvious family connections).

FIGURE 1
Organization of Steinberg's, an Entrepreneurial Firm
(circa 1948)

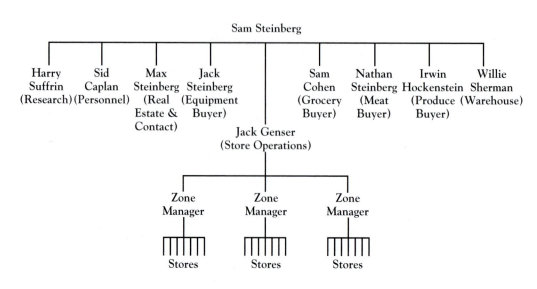

Entrepreneurial firms are often young and aggressive, continually searching for the risky markets that scare off the bigger bureaucracies. But they are also careful to avoid the complex markets, preferring to remain in niches that their leaders can comprehend. Their small size and focused strategies allow their structures to remain simple, so that the leaders can retain tight control and maneuver flexibly. Moreover, business entrepreneurs are often visionary, sometimes charismatic or autocratic as well (sometimes both, in sequence!). Of course, not all "entrepreneurs" are so aggressive or visionary; many settle down to pursue common strategies in small geographic niches. Labeled the *local producers*, these firms can include the corner restaurant, the town bakery, the regional supermarket chain.

But an organization need not be owned by an entrepreneur, indeed need not even operate in the profit sector, to adopt the configuration we call entrepreneurial. In fact, most new organizations seem to adopt this configuration, whatever their sector, because they generally have to rely on personalized leadership to get themselves going—to establish their basic direction, or *strategic vision*, to hire their first people and set up their initial procedures. Of course, strong leaders are likewise attracted to new organizations, where they can put their own stamp on things. Thus, we can conclude that most organizations in business, government, and not-for-profit areas pass through the entrepreneurial configuration in their formative years, during *start-up*.

Moreover, while new organizations that quickly grow large or that require specialized forms of expertise may make a relatively quick transition to another configuration, many others seem to remain in the entrepreneurial form, more or less, as long as their founding leaders remain in office. This reflects the fact that the structure has often been built around the personal needs and orientation of the leader and has been staffed with people loyal to him or her.

This last comment suggests that the personal power needs of a leader can also, by themselves, give rise to this configuration in an existing organization. When a chief executive hoards power and avoids or destroys the formalization of activity as an infringement on his or her right to rule by fiat, then an autocratic form of the entrepreneurial organization will tend to appear. This can been seen in the cult of personality of the leader, in business (the last days of Henry Ford) no less than in government (the leadership of Stalin in the Soviet Union). Charisma can have a similar effect, though different consequences, when the leader gains personal power not because he or she hoards it but because the followers lavish it on the leader.

The entrepreneurial configuration also tends to arise in any other type of organization that faces severe crisis. Backed up against a wall, with its survival at stake, an organization will typically turn to a strong leader for salvation. The structure thus becomes effectively (if not formally) simple, as the normal powers of existing groups—whether staff analysts, line managers, or professional operators, and so on, with their perhaps more standardized forms of control—are suspended to allow the chief to impose a new integrated vision through his or her personalized control. The leader may cut costs and expenses in an attempt to effect what is known in the strategic management literature as an *operating turnaround*, or else reconceive the basic product and service orientation, to achieve *strategic turnaround*. Of course, once the turnaround is realized, the organization may revert to its traditional operations, and, in the bargain, spew out its entrepreneurial leader, now viewed as an impediment to its smooth functioning.

Strategy Formation in the Entrepreneurial Organization

How does strategy develop in the entrepreneurial organization? And what role does that mysterious concept known as "strategic vision" play? We know something of the entrepreneurial mode of strategy making, but less of strategic vision itself, since it is locked in the head of the individual. But some studies we have done at McGill do shed some light on both these questions. Let us consider strategic vision first.

VISIONARY LEADERSHIP

In a paper she coauthored with me, my McGill colleague Frances Westley contrasted two views of visionary leadership. One she likened to a hypodermic needle, in which the active ingredient (vision) is loaded into a syringe (words) which is injected into the employees to stimulate all kinds of energy. There is surely some truth to this, but Frances prefers another image, that of drama. Drawing from a book on theater by Peter Brook (1968), the legendary director of the Royal Shakespeare Company, she conceives strategic vision, like drama, as becoming magical in that moment when fiction and life blend together. In drama, this moment is the result of endless "rehearsal," the "performance" itself, and the "attendance" of the audience. But Brook prefers the more dynamic equivalent words in French, all of which have English meanings—"repetition," "representation," and "assistance." Frances likewise applies these words to strategic vision.

"Repetition" suggests that success comes from deep knowledge of the subject at hand. Just as Sir Laurence Olivier would repeat his lines again and again until he had trained his tongue muscles to say them effortlessly (Brook, p. 154), so too Lee Iacocca "grew up" in the automobile business, going to Chrysler after Ford because cars were "in his blood" (Iacocca, 1984:141). The visionary's inspiration stems not from luck, although chance encounters can play a role, but from endless experience in a particular context.

"Representation" means not just to perform but to make the past live again, giving it immediacy, vitality. To the strategist, that is vision articulated, in words and actions. What distinguishes visionary leaders is their profound ability with language, often in symbolic form, as metaphor. It is not just that they "see" things from a new perspective but that they get others to so see them.

Edwin Land, who built a great company around the Polaroid camera he invented, has written of the duty of "the inventor to build a new gestalt for the old one in the framework of society" (1975:50). He himself described photography as helping "to focus some aspect of [your] life"; as you look through the viewfinder, "it's not merely the camera you are focusing: you are focusing yourself . . . when you touch the button, what is inside of you comes out. It's the most basic form of creativity. Part of you is now permanent" (*Time*, 1972:84). Lofty words for 50 tourists filing out of a bus to record some pat scene, but powerful imagery for someone trying to build an organization to promote a novel camera. Steve Jobs, visionary (for a time) in his promotion, if not invention, of the personal computer, placed a grand piano and a BMW in Apple's central foyer, with the claim that "I believe people get great ideas from seeing great products" (in Wise, 1984:146).

"Assistance" means that the audience for drama, whether in the theater or in the organization, empowers the actor no less than the actor empowers the audience. Leaders become visionary because they appeal powerfully to specific constituencies at specific periods of time. That is why leaders once perceived as visionary can fall so dramatically from grace—a Steve Jobs, a Winston Churchill. Or to take a more dramatic example, here is how Albert Speer, arriving skeptical, reacted to the first lecture he heard by his future leader: "Hitler no longer seemed to be speaking to convince; rather, he seemed to feel that he was experiencing what the audience, by now transformed into a single mass, expected of him" (1970:16).

Of course, management is not theater; the leader who becomes a stage actor, playing a part he or she does not live, is destined to fall from grace. It is integrity—a genuine feeling behind what the leader says and does—that makes leadership truly visionary, and that is what makes impossible the transition of such leadership into any formula.

This visionary leadership is style and strategy, coupled together. It is drama, but not playacting. The strategic visionary is born and made, the product of a historical moment. Brook closes his book with the following quotation:

> In everyday life, "if" is a fiction, in the theatre "if" is an experiment.
> In everyday life, "if" is an evasion, in the theatre "if" is the truth.
> When we are persuaded to believe in this truth, then the theatre and life are one.
> This is a high aim. It sounds like hard work.
> To play needs much work. But when we experience the work as play, then it is not work any more.
> A play is play. (p. 157)

In the entrepreneurial organization, at best, "theater," namely strategic vision, becomes one with "life," namely organization. That way leadership creates drama; it turns work into play.

Let us now consider the entrepreneurial approach to strategy formation in terms of two specific studies we have done, one of a supermarket chain, the other of a manufacturer of women's undergarments.

THE ENTREPRENEURIAL APPROACH TO STRATEGY FORMATION IN A SUPERMARKET CHAIN

Steinberg's is a Canadian retail chain that began with a tiny food store in Montreal in 1917 and grew to sales in the billion-dollar range during the almost 60-year reign of its leader. Most of that growth came from supermarket operations. In many ways, Steinberg's fits the entrepreneurial model rather well. Sam Steinberg, who joined his mother in the first store at the age of 11 and personally made a quick decision to expand it 2 years later, maintained complete formal control of the firm (including every single voting share) to the day of his death in 1978. He also exercised close managerial control over all its major decisions, at least until the firm began to diversify after 1960, primarily into other forms of retailing.

It has been popular to describe the "bold stroke" of the entrepreneur (Cole, 1959). In Steinberg's we saw only two major reorientations of strategy in the sixty years, moves into self-service in the 1930s and into the shopping center business in the 1950s. But the stroke was not bold so much as tested. The story of the move into self-service is indicative. In 1933 one of the company's eight stores "struck it bad," in the chief executive's words, incurring "unacceptable" losses ($125 a week). Sam Steinberg closed the store one Friday evening, converted it to self-service, changed its name from "Steinberg's Service Stores" to "Wholesale Groceteria," slashed its prices by 15–20%, printed handbills, stuffed them into neighborhood mailboxes, and reopened on Monday morning. That's strategic change! But only once these changes proved successful did he convert the other stores. Then, in his words, "We grew like Topsy."

This anecdote tells us something about the bold stroke of the entrepreneur—"controlled boldness" is a better expression. The ideas were bold, the execution careful. Sam Steinberg could have simply closed the one unprofitable store. Instead he used it to create a new vision, but he tested that vision, however ambitiously, before leaping into it. Notice the interplay here of problems and opportunities. Steinberg took what most businessmen would probably have perceived as a *problem* (how to cut the losses in one store) and by treating it as a *crisis* (what is wrong with our *general* operation that produces these losses) turned it into an *opportunity* (we can grow more effectively with a new concept of retailing). That was how he got energy behind actions and kept ahead of his competitors. He "oversolved" his problem and thereby remade his company, a characteristic of some of the most effective forms of entrepreneurship.

But absolutely central to this form of entrepreneurship is intimate, detailed knowledge of the business or of analogous business situations, the "repetition" discussed earlier. The leader as conventional strategic "planner"—the so-called architect of strategy—sits on a pedestal and is fed aggregate data that he or she uses to "formulate" strategies that are "implemented" by others. But the history of Steinberg's belies that image. It suggests that clear, imaginative, integrated strategic vision depends on an involvement with detail, an intimate knowledge of specifics. And by closely controlling "implementation" personally, the leader is able to reformulate en route, to adapt the evolving vision through his or her own process of learning. That is why Steinberg tried his new ideas in one store first. And that is why, in discussing his firm's competitive advantage, he told us: "Nobody knew the grocery business like we did. Everything has to do with your knowledge." He added: "I knew merchandise, I knew cost. I knew selling, I knew customers. I knew everything . . . and I passed on all my knowledge; I kept teaching my people. That's the advantage we had. They couldn't touch us."

Such knowledge can be incredibly effective when concentrated in one individual who is fully in charge (having no need to convince others, not subordinates below, not superiors at some distant headquarters, nor market analysts looking for superficial pronouncements) and who retains a strong, long-term commitment to the organization. So long as the business is simple and focused enough to be comprehended in one brain, the entrepreneurial approach is powerful, indeed unexcelled. Nothing else can provide so clear and complete a vision, yet also allow the flexibility to elaborate and rework that vision when necessary. The conception of a new strategy is an exercise in synthesis, which is typically best carried out in a single, informed brain. That is why the entrepreneurial approach is at the center of the most glorious corporate successes.

But in its strength lies entrepreneurship's weakness. Bear in mind that strategy for the entrepreneurial leader is not a formal, detailed plan on paper. It is a personal vision, a concept of the business, locked in a single brain. It may need to get "represented," in words and metaphors, but that must remain general if the leader is to maintain the richness and flexibility of his or her concept. But success breeds a large organization, public financing, and the need for formal planning. The vision must be articulated to drive others and gain their support, and that threatens the personal nature of the vision. At the limit, as we shall see later in the case of Steinberg's, the leader can get captured by his or her very success.

In Steinberg's, moreover, when success in the traditional business encouraged diversification into new ones (new regions, new forms of retailing, new industries), the organization moved beyond the realm of its leader's personal comprehension, and the entrepreneurial mode of strategy formation lost its viability. Strategy making became more decentralized, more analytic, in some ways more careful, but at the same time less visionary, less integrated, less flexible, and ironically, less deliberate.

CONCEIVING A NEW VISION IN A GARMENT FIRM

The genius of an entrepreneur like Sam Steinberg was his ability to pursue one vision (self-service and everything that entailed) faithfully for decades and then, based on a weak signal in the environment (the building of the first small shopping center in Montreal), to realize the need to shift that vision. The planning literature makes a big issue of forecasting such discontinuities, but as far as I know there are no formal techniques to do so effectively (claims about "scenario analysis" notwithstanding). The ability to perceive a sudden shift in an established pattern and then to conceive a new vision to deal with it appears to remain largely in the realm of informed intuition, generally the purview of the wise, experienced, and energetic leader. Again, the literature is largely silent on this. But another of our studies, also concerning entrepreneurship, did reveal some aspects of this process.

Canadelle produces women's undergarments, primarily brassieres. It too was a highly successful organization, although not on the same scale as Steinberg's. Things were going well for the company in the late 1960s, under the personal leadership of Larry Nadler, the son of its founder, when suddenly everything changed. A sexual revolution of sorts was accompanying broader social manifestations, with bra burning a symbol of its resistance. For a manufacturer of brassieres the threat was obvious. For many other women the miniskirt had come to dominate the fashion scene, obsoleting the girdle and giving rise to pantyhose. As the executives of Canadelle put it, "the bottom fell out of the girdle business." The whole environment—long so receptive to the company's strategies—seemed to turn on it all at once.

At the time, a French company had entered the Quebec market with a light, sexy, molded garment called "Huit," using the theme, "just like not wearing a bra." Their target market was 15–20-year-olds. Though the product was expensive when it landed in Quebec and did not fit well in Nadler's opinion, it sold well. Nadler flew to France in an attempt to license the product for manufacture in Canada. The French firm refused, but, in Nadler's words, what he learned in "that one hour in their offices made the trip worthwhile." He realized that what women wanted was a more natural look, not no bra but less bra. Another trip shortly afterward, to a sister American firm, convinced him of the importance of market segmentation by age and life-style. That led him to the realization that the firm had two markets, one for the more mature customer, for whom the brassiere was a cosmetic to look and feel more attractive, and another for the younger customer who wanted to look and feel more natural.

Those two events led to a major shift in strategic vision. The CEO described it as sudden, the confluence of different ideas to create a new mental set. In his words, "all of a sudden the idea forms." Canadelle reconfirmed its commitment to the brassiere business, seeking greater market share while its competitors were cutting back. It introduced a new line of more natural brassieres for the younger customers, for which the firm had to work out the molding technology as well as a new approach to promotion.

We can draw on Kurt Lewin's (1951) three-stage model of unfreezing, changing, and refreezing to explain such a gestalt shift in vision. The process of *unfreezing* is essentially one of overcoming the natural defense mechanisms, the established "mental set" of how an industry is supposed to operate, to realize that things have changed fundamentally. The old assumptions no longer hold. Effective managers, especially effective strategic managers, are supposed to scan their environments continually, looking for such changes. But doing so continuously, or worse, trying to use technique to do so, may have exactly the opposite effect. So much attention may be given to strategic monitoring when nothing important is happening that when something really does, it may not even be noticed. The trick, of course, is to pick out the discontinuities that matter, and as noted earlier that seems to have more to do with informed intuition than anything else.

A second step in unfreezing is the willingness to step into the void, so to speak, for the leader to shed his or her conventional notions of how a business is supposed to function. The leader must above all avoid premature closure—seizing on a new thrust before it has become clear what its signals really mean. That takes a special kind of management, one able to live with a good deal of uncertainty and discomfort. "There is a period of confusion," Nadler told us, "you sleep on it . . . start looking for patterns . . . become an information hound, searching for [explanations] everywhere."

Strategic *change* of this magnitude seems to require a shift in mind-set before a new strategy can be conceived. And the thinking is fundamentally conceptual and inductive, probably stimulated (as in this case) by just one or two key insights. Continuous bombardment of facts, opinions, problems, and so on may prepare the mind for the shift, but it is the sudden *insight* that is likely to drive the synthesis—to bring all the disparate elements together in one "eureka"-type flash.

Once the strategist's mind is set, assuming he or she has read the new situation correctly and has not closed prematurely, then the *refreezing* process begins. Here the object is not to read the situation, at least not in a global sense, but in effect to block it out. It is a time to work out the consequences of the new strategic vision.

It has been claimed that obsession is an ingredient in effective organizations (Peters, 1980). Only for the period of refreezing would we agree, when the organization must focus on the pursuit of the new orientation—the new mind-set—with full vigor. A management that was open and divergent in its thinking must now become closed and convergent. But that means that the uncomfortable period of uncertainty has passed, and people can now get down to the exciting task of accomplishing something new. Now the organization knows where it is going; the object of the exercise is to get there using all the skills at its command, many of them formal and analytic. Of course, not everyone accepts the new vision. For those steeped in old strategies, *this* is the period of discomfort, and they can put up considerable resistance, forcing the leader to make greater use of his or her formal powers and political skills. Thus, refreezing of the leader's mind-set often involves the unfreezing, changing, and refreezing of the organization itself! But when the structure is simple, as it is in the entrepreneurial organization, that problem is relatively minor.

LEADERSHIP TAKING PRECEDENCE IN THE ENTREPRENEURIAL CONFIGURATION

To conclude, entrepreneurship is very much tied up with the creation of strategic vision, often with the attainment of a new concept. Strategies can be characterized as largely deliberate, since they reside in the intentions of a single leader. But being largely personal as well, the details of those strategies can emerge as they develop. In fact, the vision can change too. The leader can adapt en route, can learn, which means new visions can emerge too, sometimes, as we have seen, rather quickly.

In the entrepreneurial organization, as shown in Figure 2, the focus of attention is on the leader. The organization is malleable and responsive to that person's initiatives, while the environment remains benign for the most part, the result of the leader's selecting (or "enacting") the correct niche for his or her organization. The environment can, of course,

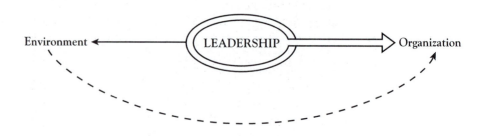

FIGURE 2
Leadership Taking Precedence in the Entrepreneurial Organization

flare up occasionally to challenge the organization, and then the leader must adapt, perhaps seeking out a new and more appropriate niche in which to operate.

Some Issues Associated with the Entrepreneurial Organization

We conclude briefly with some broad issues associated with the entrepreneurial organization. In this configuration, decisions concerning both strategy and operations tend to be centralized in the office of the chief executive. This centralization has the important advantage of rooting strategic response in deep knowledge of the operations. It also allows for flexibility and adaptability: Only one person need act. But this same executive can get so enmeshed in operating problems that he or she loses sight of strategy; alternatively, he or she may become so enthusiastic about strategic opportunities that the more routine operations can wither for lack of attention and eventually pull down the whole organization. Both are frequent occurrences in entrepreneurial organizations.

This is also the riskiest of organizations, hinging on the activities of one individual. One heart attack can literally wipe out the organization's prime means of coordination. Even a leader in place can be risky. When change becomes necessary, everything hinges on the chief's response to it. If he or she resists, as is not uncommon where that person developed the existing strategy in the first place, then the organization may have no means to adapt. Then the great strength of the entrepreneurial organization—the vision of its leader plus its capacity to respond quickly—becomes its chief liability.

Another great advantage of the entrepreneurial organization is its sense of mission. Many people enjoy working in a small, intimate organization where the leader—often charismatic—knows where he or she is taking it. As a result, the organization tends to grow rapidly, with great enthusiasm. Employees can develop a solid identification with such an organization.

But other people perceive this configuration as highly restrictive. Because one person calls all the shots, they feel not like the participants on an exciting journey, but like cattle being led to market for someone else's benefit. In fact, the broadening of democratic norms into the sphere of organizations has rendered the entrepreneurial organization unfashionable in some quarters of contemporary society. It has been described as paternalistic and sometimes autocratic, and accused of concentrating too much power at the top. Certainly, without countervailing powers in the organization the chief executive can easily abuse his or her authority.

Perhaps the entrepreneurial organization is an anachronism in societies that call themselves democratic. Yet there have always been such organizations, and there always will be. This was probably the only structure known to those who first discovered the benefits of coordinating their activities in some formal way. And it probably reached its heyday in the era of the great American trusts of the late nineteenth century, when powerful entrepreneurs personally controlled huge empires. Since then, at least in Western society, the entrepreneurial organization has been on the decline. Nonetheless, it remains a prevalent and important configuration, and will continue to be so as long as society faces the conditions that require it: the prizing of entrepreneurial initiative and the resultant encouragement of new organizations, the need for small and informal organizations in some spheres and of strong personalized leadership despite larger size in others, and the need periodically to turn around ailing organizations of all types.

▼ READING 9.2 COMPETITIVE STRATEGY IN EMERGING INDUSTRIES*

by Michael E. Porter

Emerging industries are newly formed or reformed industries that have been created by technological innovations, shifts in relative cost relationships, emergence of new consumer needs, or other economic and sociological changes that elevate a new product or service to the level of a potentially viable business opportunity. . . .

The essential characteristic of an emerging industry from the viewpoint of formulating strategy is that there are no rules of the game. The competitive problem in an emerging industry is that all the rules must be established such that the firm can cope with and prosper under them.

The Structural Environment

Although emerging industries can differ a great deal in their structures, there are some common structural factors that seem to characterize many industries in this stage of their development. Most of them relate either to the absence of established bases for competition or other rules of the game or to the initial small size and newness of the industry.

COMMON STRUCTURAL CHARACTERISTICS

TECHNOLOGICAL UNCERTAINTY
There is usually a great deal of uncertainty about the technology in an emerging industry: What product configuration will ultimately prove to be the best? Which production technology will prove to be the most efficient? . . .

STRATEGIC UNCERTAINTY
. . . No "right" strategy has been clearly identified, and different firms are groping with different approaches to product/market positioning, marketing, servicing, and so on, as well as betting on different product configurations or production technologies . . . . Closely related to this problem, firms often have poor information about competitors, characteristics of customers, and industry conditions in the emerging phase. No one knows who all the competitors are, and reliable industry sales and market share data are often simply unavailable, for example.

* Excerpted from *Competitive Strategy: Techniques for Analyzing Industries and Competitors*, by Michael E. Porter. Copyright © 1980 by The Free Press, a division of Macmillan, Inc. Reprinted by permission of the publisher.

High Initial Costs but Steep Cost Reduction

Small production volume and newness usually combine to produce high costs in the emerging industry relative to those the industry can potentially achieve. . . . Ideas come rapidly in terms of improved procedures, plant layout, and so on, and employees achieve major gains in productivity as job familiarity increases. Increasing sales make major additions to the scale and total accumulated volume of output produced by firms . . . .

Embryonic Companies and Spin-Offs

The emerging phase of the industry is usually accompanied by the presence of the greatest proportion of newly formed companies (to be contrasted with newly formed units of established firms) that the industry will ever experience. . . .

First-Time Buyers

Buyers of the emerging industry's product or service are inherently first-time buyers. The marketing task is thus one of inducing substitution, or getting the buyer to purchase the new product or service instead of something else. . . .

Short Time Horizon

In many emerging industries the pressure to develop customers or produce products to meet demand is so great that bottlenecks and problems are dealt with expediently rather than as a result of an analysis of future conditions. At the same time, industry conventions are often born out of pure chance. . . .

Subsidy

In many emerging industries, especially those with radical new technology or that address areas of societal concern, there may be subsidization of early entrants. Subsidy may come from a variety of government and nongovernment sources. . . . Subsidies often add a great degree of instability to an industry, which is made dependent on political decisions that can be quickly reversed or modified. . . .

EARLY MOBILITY BARRIERS

In an emerging industry, the configuration of mobility barriers is often predictably different from that which will characterize the industry later in its development. Common early barriers are the following:

▼ proprietary technology
▼ access to distribution channels
▼ access to raw materials and other inputs (skilled labor) of appropriate cost and quality
▼ cost advantages due to experience, made more significant by the technological and competitive uncertainties
▼ risk, which raises the effective opportunity cost of capital and thereby effective capital barriers

. . . The nature of the early barriers is a key reason why we observe newly created companies in emerging industries. The typical early barriers stem less from the need to command massive resources than from the ability to bear risk, be creative technologically, and make forward-looking decisions to garner input supplies and distribution channels. . . . There may be some advantages to late entry, however. . . .

STRATEGIC CHOICES

Formulation of strategy in emerging industries must cope with the uncertainty and risk of this period of an industry's development. The rules of the competitive game are largely undefined, the structure of the industry unsettled and probably changing, and competitors hard to diagnose. Yet all these factors have another side—the emerging phase of an industry's development is probably the period when the strategic degrees of freedom are the greatest and when the leverage from good strategic choices is the highest in determining performance.

SHAPING INDUSTRY STRUCTURE

The overriding strategic issue in emerging industries is the ability of the firm to shape industry structure. Through its choices, the firm can try to set the rules of the game in areas like product policy, marketing approach, and pricing strategy. . . .

EXTERNALITIES IN INDUSTRY DEVELOPMENT

In an emerging industry, a key strategic issue is the balance the firm strikes between industry advocacy and pursuing its own narrow self-interest. Because of potential problems with industry image, credibility, and confusion of buyers . . . in the emerging phase the firm is in part dependent on others in the industry for its own success. The overriding problem for the industry is inducing substitution and attracting first-time buyers, and it is usually in the firm's interest during this phase to help promote standardization, police substandard quality and fly-by-night producers, and present a consistent front to suppliers, customers, government, and the financial community. . . .

It is probably a valid generalization that the balance between industry outlook and firm outlook must shift in the direction of the firm as the industry begins to achieve significant penetration. Sometimes firms who have taken very high profiles as industry spokespersons, much to their and the industry's benefit, fail to recognize that they must shift their orientation. As a result, they can be left behind as the industry matures. . . .

CHANGING ROLE OF SUPPLIERS AND CHANNELS

Strategically, the firm in an emerging industry must be prepared for a possible shift in the orientation of its suppliers and distribution channels as the industry grows in size and proves itself. Suppliers may become increasingly willing (or can be forced) to respond to the industry's special needs in terms of varieties, service, and delivery. Similarly, distribution channels may become more receptive to investing in facilities, advertising, and so forth in partnership with the firms. Early exploitation of these changes in orientation can give the firm strategic leverage.

SHIFTING MOBILITY BARRIERS

As outlined earlier . . . the early mobility barriers may erode quickly in an emerging industry, often to be replaced by very different ones as the industry grows in size and as the technology matures. This factor has a number of implications. The most obvious is that the firm must be prepared to find new ways to defend its position and must not rely solely on things like proprietary technology and a unique product variety on which it has succeeded in the past. Responding to shifting mobility barriers may involve commitments of capital that far exceed those that have been necessary in the early phases.

Another implication is that the *nature of entrants* into the industry may shift to more established firms attracted to the larger and increasingly proven (less risky) industry, often competing on the basis of the newer forms of mobility barriers, like scale and marketing clout. . . .

TIMING ENTRY

A crucial strategic choice for competing in emerging industries is the appropriate timing of entry. Early entry (or pioneering) involves high risk but may involve otherwise low entry barriers and can offer a large return. Early entry is appropriate when the following general circumstances hold:

▼ Image and reputation of the firm are important to the buyer, and the firm can develop an enhanced reputation by being a pioneer.

▼ Early entry can initiate the learning process in a business in which the learning curve is important, experience is difficult to imitate, and it will not be nullified by successive technological generations.

▼ Customer loyalty will be great, so that benefits will accrue to the firm that sells to the customer first.

▼ Absolute cost advantages can be gained by early commitment to supplies of raw materials, distribution channels, and so on. . . .

TACTICAL MOVES

The problems limiting development of an emerging industry suggest some tactical moves that may improve the firm's strategic position:

▼ Early commitments to suppliers of raw materials will yield favorable priorities in times of shortages.

▼ Financing can be timed to take advantage of a Wall Street love affair with the industry if it happens, even if financing is ahead of actual needs. This step lowers the firm's cost of capital. . . .

The choice of which emerging industry to enter is dependent on the outcome of a predictive exercise such as the one described above. An emerging industry is attractive if its ultimate structure (not its *initial* structure) is one that is consistent with above-average returns and if the firm can create a defendable position in the industry in the long run. The latter will depend on its resources relative to the mobility barriers that will evolve.

Too often firms enter emerging industries because they are growing rapidly, because incumbents are currently very profitable, or because ultimate industry size promises to be large. These may be contributing reasons, but the decision to enter must ultimately depend on a structural analysis. . . .

▼ READING 9.3 HOW ENTREPRENEURS CRAFT STRATEGIES THAT WORK*

by Amar Bhide

However popular it may be in the corporate world, a comprehensive analytical approach to planning doesn't suit most start-ups. Entrepreneurs typically lack the time and money to interview a representative cross section of potential customers, let alone analyze substitutes, reconstruct competitors' cost structures, or project alternative technology scenarios. In fact, too much analysis can be harmful; by the time an opportunity is investigated fully, it may no longer exist. A city map and restaurant guide on a CD may be a winner in January but worthless if delayed until December.

Interviews with the founders of 100 companies on the 1989 Inc. "500" list of the fastest growing private companies in the United States and recent research on more than 100

* Originally published as "How Entrepreneurs Craft Strategies that Work," in the *Harvard Business Review*, March–April 1994, pp. 150–161. Copyright © 1994 by the President and Fellows of Harvard College; all rights reserved. Reprinted with deletions by permission of the *Harvard Business Review*.

other thriving ventures by my MBA students suggest that many successful entrepreneurs spend little time researching and analyzing. . . . And those who do often have to scrap their strategies and start over. Furthermore, a 1990 National Federation of Independent Business study of 2,994 start-ups showed that founders who spent a long time in study, reflection, and planning were no more likely to survive their first three years than people who seized opportunities without planning. In fact, many corporations that revere comprehensive analysis develop a refined incapacity for seizing opportunities. Analysis can delay entry until it's too late or kill ideas by identifying numerous problems.

Yet all ventures merit some analysis and planning. Appearances to the contrary, successful entrepreneurs don't take risks blindly. Rather, they use a quick, cheap approach that represents a middle ground between planning paralysis and no planning at all. They don't expect perfection—even the most astute entrepreneurs have their share of false starts. Compared to typical corporate practice, however, the entrepreneurial approach is more economical and timely.

What are the critical elements of winning entrepreneurial approaches? Our evidence suggests three general guidelines for aspiring founders:

1. Screen opportunities quickly to weed out unpromising ventures.
2. Analyze ideas parsimoniously. Focus on a few important ideas.
3. Integrate action and analysis. Don't wait for all the answers, and be ready to change course.

SCREENING OUT LOSERS

Individuals who seek entrepreneurial opportunities usually generate lots of ideas. Quickly discarding those that have low potential frees aspirants to concentrate on the few ideas that merit refinement and study.

Screening out unpromising ventures requires judgment and reflection, not new data. The entrepreneur should already be familiar with the facts needed to determine whether an idea has prima facie merit. Our evidence suggests that new ventures are usually started to solve problems the founders have grappled with personally as customers or employees. . . . Companies like Federal Express, which grew out of a paper its founder wrote in college, are rare.

Profitable survival requires an edge derived from some combination of a creative idea and a superior capacity for execution. . . . The entrepreneur's creativity may involve an innovative product or a process that changes the existing order. Or the entrepreneur may have a unique insight about the course or consequence of an external change: the California gold rush, for example, made paupers of the thousands caught in the frenzy, but Levi Strauss started a company—and a legend—by recognizing the opportunity to supply rugged canvas and later denim trousers to prospectors.

But entrepreneurs cannot rely on just inventing new products or anticipating a trend. They must also execute well, especially if their concepts can be copied easily. For example, if an innovation cannot be patented or kept secret, entrepreneurs must acquire and manage the resource needed to build a brand name or other barrier that will deter imitators. Superior execution can also compensate for a me-too concept in emerging or rapidly growing industries where doing it quickly and doing it right are more important than brilliant strategy.

Ventures that obviously lack a creative concept or any special capacity to execute—the ex-consultant's scheme to exploit grandmother's cookie recipe, for instance—can be discarded without much thought. In other cases, entrepreneurs must reflect on the adequacy of their ideas and their capacities to execute them.

Successful start-ups don't need an edge on every front. The creativity of successful entrepreneurs varies considerably. Some implement a radical idea, some modify, and some show no originality. Capacity for execution also varies among entrepreneurs. Selling an industrial niche product doesn't call for the charisma that's required to pitch trinkets through infomercials. Our evidence suggests that there is no ideal entrepreneurial profile either: successful founders can be gregarious or taciturn, analytical or intuitive, good or terrible with details, risk averse or thrill seeking. They can be delegators or control freaks, pillars of the community or outsiders. In assessing the viability of a potential venture, therefore, each aspiring entrepreneur should consider three interacting factors:

1. OBJECTIVES OF THE VENTURE

Is the entrepreneur's goal to build a large, enduring enterprise, carve out a niche, or merely turn a quick profit? Ambitious goals require great creativity. Building a large enterprise quickly, either by seizing a significant share of an existing market or by creating a large new market, usually calls for a revolutionary idea. . . .

Requirements for execution are also stiff. Big ideas often necessitate big money and strong organizations. Successful entrepreneurs, therefore, require an evangelical ability to attract, retain, and balance the interests of investors, customers, employees, and suppliers for a seemingly outlandish vision, as well as the organizational and leadership skills to build a large, complex company quickly. In addition, the entrepreneur may require considerable technical know-how in deal making, strategic planning, managing overhead, and other business skills. The revolutionary entrepreneur, in other words, would appear to require almost superhuman qualities: ordinary mortals need not apply.

Consider Federal Express founder Fred Smith. His creativity lay in recognizing that customers would pay a significant premium for reliable overnight delivery and in figuring out a way to provide the service for them. Smith ruled out using existing commercial flights, whose schedules were designed to serve passenger traffic. Instead, he had the audacious idea of acquiring a dedicated fleet of jets and shipping all packages through a central hub that was located in Memphis.

As with most big ideas, the concept was difficult to execute. Smith, 28 years old at the time, had to raise $91 million in venture funding. The jets, the hub, operations in 25 states, and several hundred trained employees had to be in place before the company could open for business. And Smith needed great fortitude and skill to prevent the fledgling enterprise from going under: Federal Express lost over $40 million in its first three years. Some investors tried to remove Smith, and creditors tried to seize assets. Yet Smith somehow preserved morale and mollified investors and lenders while the company expanded its operations and launched national advertising and direct-mail campaigns to build market share.

In contrast, ventures that seek to capture a market niche, not transform or create an industry, don't need extraordinary ideas. Some ingenuity is necessary to design a product that will draw customers away from mainstream offerings and overcome the cost penalty of serving a small market. But features that are too novel can be a hindrance; a niche market will rarely justify the investment required to educate customers and distributors about the benefits of a radically new product. Similarly, a niche venture cannot support too much production or distribution innovation; unlike Federal Express, the Cape Cod Potato Company, for example, must work within the limits of its distributors and truckers.

And since niche markets cannot support much investment or overhead, entrepreneurs do not need the revolutionary's ability to raise capital and build large organizations. Rather, the entrepreneur must be able to secure others' resources on favorable terms and make do with less, building brand awareness through guerrilla marketing and word of mouth instead of national advertising, for example.

Jay Boberg and Miles Copeland, who launched International Record Syndicate (IRS) in 1979, used a niche strategy, my students Elisabeth Bentel and Victoria Hackett found, to create one of the most successful new music labels in North America. Lacking the funds or a great innovation to compete against the major labels, Boberg and Miles promoted "alternative" music—undiscovered British groups like the buzzcocks and Skafish—which the major labels were ignoring because their potential sales were too small. And IRS used low-cost, alternative marketing methods to promote their alternative music. At the time, the major record labels had not yet realized that music videos on television could be used effectively to promote their products. Boberg, however, jumped at the opportunity to produce a rock show, "The Cutting Edge," for MTV. The show proved to be a hit with fans and an effective promotional tool for IRS. Before "The Cutting Edge," Boberg had to plead with radio stations to play his songs. Afterward, the MTV audience demanded that disc jockeys play the songs they had heard on the show.

2. LEVERAGE PROVIDED BY EXTERNAL CHANGE

Exploiting opportunities in a new or changing industry is generally easier than making waves in a mature industry. Enormous creativity, experience, and contacts are needed to take business away from competitors in a mature industry, where market forces have long shaken out weak technologies, strategies, and organizations.

But new markets are different. There start-ups often face rough-around-the-edges rivals, customers who tolerate inexperienced vendors and imperfect products, and opportunities to profit from shortages. Small insights and marginal innovations, a little skill or expertise (in the land of the blind, the one-eyed person is king), and the willingness to act quickly can go a long way. In fact, with great external uncertainty, customers and investors may be hesitant to back a radical product and technology until the environment settles down. Strategic choices in a new industry are often very limited; entrepreneurs have to adhere to the emerging standards for product features, components, or distribution channels.

The leverage provided by external change is illustrated by the success of numerous start-ups in hardware, software, training, retailing, and systems integration that emerged from the personal computer revolution of the 1980s. Installing or fixing a computer system is probably easier than repairing a car; but because people with the initiative or foresight to acquire the skill were scarce, entrepreneurs like Bohdan's Peter Zacharkiw built successful dealerships by providing what customers saw as exceptional service. . . . As one Midwestern dealer told me, "We have a joke slogan around here: We aren't as incompetent as our competitors!"

Bill Gates turned Microsoft into a multibillion-dollar company without a breakthrough product by showing up in the industry early and capitalizing on the opportunities that came his way. Gates, then 19, and his partner Paul Allen, 21, launched Microsoft in 1975 to sell software they had created. By 1979, Microsoft had grown to 25 employees and $2.5 million in sales. Then in November 1980, IBM chose Microsoft to provide an operating system for its personal computer. Microsoft thereupon bought an operating system from Seattle Computer Products, which it modified into the now ubiquitous MS-DOS. The IBM name and the huge success of the 1-2-3 spreadsheet, which only ran on DOS computers, soon helped make Microsoft the dominant supplier of operating systems.

3. BASIS OF COMPETITION: PROPRIETARY ASSETS VERSUS HUSTLE

In some industries, such as pharmaceuticals, luxury hotels, and consumer goods, a company's profitability depends significantly on the assets it owns or controls—patents, location, or brands, for example. Good management practices like listening to customers, maintaining quality, and paying attention to costs, which can improve the profits of a going business, cannot propel a start-up over such structural barriers. Here a creative new technology, product, or strategy is a must.

Companies in fragmented service industries, such as investment management, investment banking, head hunting, or consulting cannot establish proprietary advantages easily but can nonetheless enjoy high profits by providing exceptional service tailored to client demands. Start-ups in those fields rely mainly on their hustle (Bhide, 1986). Successful entrepreneurs depend on personal selling skills, contacts, their reputations for expertise, and their ability to convince clients of the value of the services rendered. They also have the capacity for institution building—skills such as recruiting and motivating stellar professionals and articulating and reinforcing company values. Where there are few natural economies of scale, an entrepreneur cannot create a going concern out of a one-man-band or ad hoc ensemble without a lot of expertise in organizational development. . . .

GAUGING ATTRACTIVENESS

Entrepreneurs should also screen potential ventures for their attractiveness—their risks and rewards—compared to other opportunities. Several factors should be considered. Capital requirements, for example, matter to the entrepreneur who lacks easy access to financial markets. An unexpected need for cash because, say, one large customer is unable to make a timely payment may shut down a venture or force a fire sale of the founder's equity. Therefore, entrepreneurs should favor ventures that aren't capital intensive and have the profit margins to sustain rapid growth with internally generated funds. In a similar fashion, entrepreneurs should look for a high margin for error, ventures with simple operations and low fixed costs that are less likely to face a cash crunch because of factors such as technical delays, cost overruns, and slow buildup of sales.

Other criteria reflect the typical entrepreneur's inability to undertake multiple projects: an attractive venture should provide a substantial enough reward to compensate the entrepreneur's exclusive commitment to it. Shut-down costs should be low: the payback should be quick, or failure soon recognized so that the venture can be terminated without a significant loss of time, money, or reputation. And the entrepreneur should have the option to cash in, for example, by selling all or part of the equity. An entrepreneur locked into an illiquid business cannot easily pursue other opportunities and risks fatigue and burnout. . . .

Ventures must also fit what the individual entrepreneur values and wants to do. Surviving the inevitable disappointments and near disasters one encounters on the rough road to success requires a passion for the chosen business. . . .

Surprisingly, small endeavors often hold more financial promise than large ones. Often the founders can keep a larger share of the profits because they don't dilute their equity interest through multiple rounds of financings. But entrepreneurs must be willing to prosper in a backwater; dominating a neglected market segment is sometimes more profitable than intellectually stimulating or glamorous. Niche enterprises can also enter the "land of the living dead" because their market is too small for the business to thrive but the entrepreneur has invested too much effort to be willing to quit. . . .

PARSIMONIOUS PLANNING AND ANALYSIS

To conserve time and money, successful entrepreneurs minimize the resources they devote to researching their ideas. Unlike the corporate world, where foil mastery and completed staff work can make a career, the entrepreneur only does as much planning and analysis as seems useful and makes subjective judgment calls when necessary. . . .

In setting their analytical priorities, entrepreneurs must recognize that some critical uncertainties cannot be resolved through more research. For example, focus groups and surveys often have little value in predicting demand for products that are truly novel. At first, consumers had dismissed the need for copiers, for instance, and told researchers they were satisfied with using carbon paper. With issues like this, entrepreneurs have to resist the temptation of endless investigation and trust their judgment. . . .

Revenues are notoriously difficult to predict. At best, entrepreneurs may satisfy themselves that their novel product or service delivers considerably greater value than current offerings do; how quickly the product catches on is a blind guess. Leverage may be obtained, however, from analyzing how customers might buy and use the product or service. Understanding the purchase process can help identify the right decision makers for the new offering. With Federal Express, for instance, it was important to go beyond the mailroom managers who traditionally bought delivery services. Understanding how products are used can also help by revealing obstacles that must be overcome before consumers can benefit from a new offering.

Visionary entrepreneurs must guard against making competitors rich from their work. Many concepts are difficult to prove but, once proven, easy to imitate. Unless the pioneer is protected by sustainable barriers to entry, the benefits of a hard-fought revolution can become a public good rather than a boon to the innovator. . . .

Entrepreneurs who hope to secure a niche face different problems: they often fail because the costs of serving a specialized segment exceed the benefits to customers. Entrepreneurs should therefore analyze carefully the incremental costs of serving a niche and take into account their lack of scale and the difficulty of marketing to a small, diffused segment. And especially if the cost disadvantage is significant, entrepreneurs should determine whether their offering provides a significant performance benefit. Whereas established companies can vie for share through line extensions or marginal tailoring of their products and services, the start-up must really wow its target customers. A marginally tastier cereal won't knock Kellogg's Cornflakes off supermarket shelves.

Inadequate payoffs also pose a risk for ventures that address small markets. For example, a niche venture that can't support a direct sales force may not generate enough commissions to attract an independent broker or manufacturers' rep. Entrepreneurs will eventually lose interest too if the rewards aren't commensurate with their efforts. Therefore, the entrepreneur should make sure that everyone who contributes can expect a high, quick, or sustainable return even if the venture's total profits are small.

Entrepreneurs who seek to leverage factors like changing technologies, customer preferences, or regulations should avoid extensive analysis. Research conducted under conditions of such turbulence isn't reliable, and the importance of a quick response precludes spending the time to make sure every detail is covered. . . .

Analyzing whether or not the rewards for winning are commensurate with the risks, however, can be a more feasible and worthwhile exercise. In some technology races, success is predictably short-lived. In the disk-drive industry, for example, companies that succeed with one generation of products are often leap-frogged when the next generation arrives. In engineering workstations, however, Sun enjoyed long-term gains from its early success because it established a durable architectural standard. If success is unlikely to be sustained, entrepreneurs should have a plan for making a good return while it lasts. . . .

INTEGRATING ACTION AND ANALYSIS

Standard operating procedure in large corporations usually makes a clear distinction between analysis and execution. In contemplating a new venture, managers in established companies face issues about its fit with ongoing activities: Does the proposed venture leverage corporate strengths? Will the resources and attention it requires reduce the company's ability to build customer loyalty and improve quality in core markets? These concerns dictate a deliberate, "trustee" approach: before they can launch a venture, managers must investigate an opportunity extensively, seek the counsel of people higher up, submit a formal plan, respond to criticisms by bosses and corporate staff, and secure a headcount and capital allocation.

Entrepreneurs who start with a clean slate, however, don't have to know all the answers before they act. In fact, they often can't easily separate action and analysis. The attractiveness of a new restaurant, for example, may depend on the terms of the lease; low rents can change the venture from a mediocre proposition into a money machine. But an entrepreneur's ability to negotiate a good lease cannot be easily determined from a general prior analysis; he or she must enter into a serious negotiation with a specific landlord for a specific property.

Acting before an opportunity is fully analyzed has many benefits. Doing something concrete builds confidence in oneself and in others. Key employees and investors will often follow the individual who has committed to action, for instance, by quitting a job, incorporating, or signing a lease. By taking a personal risk, the entrepreneur convinces other people that the venture *will* proceed, and they may believe that if they don't sign up, they could be left behind.

Early action can generate more robust, better informed strategies too. Extensive surveys and focus-group research about a concept can produce misleading evidence: slippage can arise between research and reality because the potential customers interviewed are not representative of the market, their enthusiasm for the concept wanes when they see the actual product, or they lack the authority to sign purchase orders. More robust strategies may be developed by first building a working prototype and asking customers to use it before conducting extensive market research.

The ability of individual entrepreneurs to execute quickly will naturally vary. Trial and error is less feasible with large-scale, capital-intensive ventures like Orbital Sciences, which had to raise over $50 million to build rockets for NASA, than with a consulting firm start-up. Nevertheless, some characteristics are common to an approach that integrates action and analysis:

HANDLING ANALYTICAL TASKS IN STAGES

Rather than resolve all issues at once, the entrepreneur does only enough research to justify the next action or investment. For example, an individual who has developed a new medical technology may first obtain crude estimates of market demand to determine whether it's worth seeing a patent lawyer. If the estimates and lawyer are encouraging, the individual may do more analysis to investigate the wisdom of spending money to obtain a patent. Several more iterations of analysis and action will follow before the entrepreneur prepares and circulates a formal business plan to venture capitalists.

PLUGGING HOLES QUICKLY

As soon as any problems or risks show up, the entrepreneur begins looking for solutions. For example, suppose that an entrepreneur sees it will be difficult to raise capital. Rather than kill the idea, he or she thinks creatively about solving the problem. Perhaps the investment can be reduced by modifying technology to use more standard equipment that can be rented instead of bought. Or under the right terms, a customer might underwrite the risk by providing a large initial order. Or expectations and goals for growth might be scaled down, and a niche market could be tackled first. Except with obviously unviable ideas that can be ruled out through elementary logic, the purpose of analysis is not to find fault with new ventures or find reasons for abandoning them. Analysis is an exercise in what to do next more than what not to do.

EVANGELICAL INVESTIGATION

Entrepreneurs often blur the line between research and selling. As one founder recalls, "My market research consisted of taking a prototype to a trade show and seeing if I could write orders." Software industry "beta sites" provide another example of simultaneous research and selling; customers actually pay to help vendors test early versions of their software and will often place larger orders if they are satisfied with the product.

From the beginning, entrepreneurs don't just seek opinions and information, they also look for commitment from other people. Entrepreneurs treat everyone whom they talk to as a potential customer, investor, employee, or supplier, or at least as a possible source of leads down the road. Even if they don't actually ask for an order, they take the time to build enough interest and rapport so they can come back later. This simultaneous listening and selling approach may not produce truly objective market research and statistically significant results. But the resource-constrained entrepreneur doesn't have much choice in the matter. Besides, in the initial stages, the deep knowledge and support of a few is often more valuable than broad, impersonal data.

SMART ARROGANCE

An entrepreneur's willingness to act on sketchy plans and inconclusive data is often sustained by an almost arrogant self-confidence. One successful high-tech entrepreneur likens his kind to "gamblers in a casino who know they are good at craps and are therefore likely to win. They believe: 'I'm smarter, more creative, and harder working than most people. With my unique and rare skills, I'm doing investors a favor by taking their money.'" Moreover, the entrepreneur's arrogance must stand the test of adversity. Entrepreneurs must have great confidence in their talent and ideas to persevere as customers stay away in droves, the product doesn't work, or the business runs out of cash.

But entrepreneurs who believe they are more capable or venturesome than others must also have the smarts to recognize their mistakes and to change their strategies as events unfold. Successful ventures don't always proceed in the direction on which they initially set out. A significant proportion develop entirely new markets, products, and sources of competitive advantage. Therefore, although perseverance and tenacity are valuable entrepreneurial traits, they must be complemented with flexibility and a willingness to learn. If prospects who were expected to place orders don't, the entrepreneur should consider reworking the concept. Similarly, the entrepreneur should also be prepared to exploit opportunities that didn't figure in the initial plan. . . .

The apparently sketchy planning and haphazard evolution of many successful ventures . . . doesn't mean that entrepreneurs should follow a ready-fire-aim approach. Despite appearances, astute entrepreneurs do analyze and strategize extensively. They realize, however, that businesses cannot be launched like space shuttles, with every detail of the mission planned in advance. Initial analyses only provide plausible hypotheses, which must be tested and modified. Entrepreneurs should play with and explore ideas, letting their strategies evolve through a seamless process of guesswork, analysis, and action.

THE MATURE CONTEXT

In this chapter, we focus on what has historically been one of the more common contexts for organizations. Whether we refer to this by its form of operations (usually mass production or the mass provision of services), by the form of structure adopted (machine-like bureaucracy), by the type of environment it prefers (a stable one in a mature industry), or by the specific generic strategy often found there (low cost), the context tends to give rise to certain relatively well-defined configurations. This context has received bad press of late, but don't think that it has gone away. Amidst all the talk of change, turbulence, and hypercompetition, this context remains common, indeed quite possibly still the most common of contexts an executive is likely to encounter. Bureaucracy has not left large organizations, private or public, we assure you!

The readings on what we shall refer to as the *mature* context cover these different aspects and examine some of the problems and opportunities of functioning in this realm. The first reading, on the machine organization, from Mintzberg's work, describes the structure for this context as well as the environment in which it tends to be found, and also investigates some of the social issues surrounding this particular form of organization. This reading also probes the nature of the strategy-making process in this context. Here we can see what happens when large organizations accustomed to stability suddenly have to change their strategies dramatically. The careful formal planning, on which they tend to rely so heavily in easier times, seems ill suited to dealing with changes that may require virtual revolutions in their functioning. A section of this reading thus considers what can be the role of planners when their formal procedures fail to come to grips with the needs of strategy making.

A particular technique designed for use with this strategy, and the mature context in general, is the subject of the second reading. Called "Cost Dynamics: Scale and Experience Effects" and written by Derek Abell and John Hammond for a marketing textbook, it probes the "experience curve." Developed by the Boston Consulting Group some years ago, this technique became quite popular in the 1970s. Although its limitations are now widely recognized, it still has certain applications to firms operating in the mature context.

Although low-cost strategies are common in the mature context, they rarely exist alone in modern competition. The cases suggest how in successful large enterprises they may coexist with other strategies such as product variety and quality (The Transformation of AT&T and Matsushita Electric Industrial Company 1994), large scale innovation (Sony Corporation: Innovation System and Ford: Team Taurus), value added (The Vanguard Group, Inc. or NovaCare, Inc.), differentiation (Honda Motor Company 1994 or SAS and the European Airline Industry), or alliances and disaggregation Apple Computer 1992 or Nintendo Co., Ltd.). All of these offer opportunities to challenge simpler strategic concepts in the mature setting.

by Henry Mintzberg

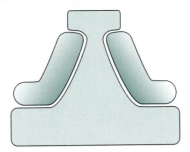

A national post office, a custodial prison, an airline, a giant automobile company, even a small security agency—all these organizations appear to have a number of characteristics in common. Above all, their operating work is routine, the greatest part of it rather simple and repetitive; as a result, their work processes are highly standardized. These characteristics give rise to the machine organizations of our society, structures fine-tuned to run as integrated, regulated, highly bureaucratic machines.

The Basic Structure

A clear configuration of the attributes has appeared consistently in the research: highly specialized, routine operating tasks; very formalized communication throughout the organization; large-size operating units; reliance on the functional basis for grouping tasks; relatively centralized power for decision making; and an elaborate administrative structure with a sharp distinction between line and staff.

THE OPERATING CORE AND ADMINISTRATION

The obvious starting point is the operating core, with its highly rationalized work flow. This means that the operating tasks are made simple and repetitive, generally requiring a minimum of skill and training, the latter often taking only hours, seldom more than a few weeks, and usually in-house. This in turn results in narrowly defined jobs and an emphasis on the standardization of work processes for coordination. with activities highly formalized. The workers are left with little discretion, as are their supervisors, who can therefore handle very large spans of control.

To achieve such high regulation of the operating work, the organization has need for an elaborate administrative structure—fully developed middle-line hierarchy and techno-structure—but the two clearly distinguished.

The managers of the middle line have three prime tasks. One is to handle the disturbances that arise in the operating core. The work is so standardized that when things fall through the cracks, conflict flares, because the problems cannot be worked out informally.

* Adapted from *The Structure of Organizations* (Prentice Hall, 1979), Chap. 18 on "The Machine Bureaucracy"; also *Power In and Around Organizations* (Prentice Hall, 1983), Chaps. 18 and 19 on "The Instrument" and "The Closed System"; the material on strategy formation from "Patterns in Strategy Formation," *Management Science* (1978); "Does Planning Impede Strategic Thinking? Tracking the Strategies of Air Canada, from 1937–1976" (coauthored with Pierre Brunet and Jim Waters), in R. B. Lamb and P. Shrivastava, eds., *Advances in Strategic Management*, Volume IV (JAI press, 1986); and "The Mind of the Strategist(s)" (coauthored with Jim Waters), in S. Srivastva, ed., *The Executive Mind* (Jossey-Bass, 1983); the section on the role of planning, plans, and planners is drawn from a book in process on strategic planning. A chapter similar to this appeared in *Mintzberg on Management: Inside Our Strange World of Organizations* (Free Press, 1989).

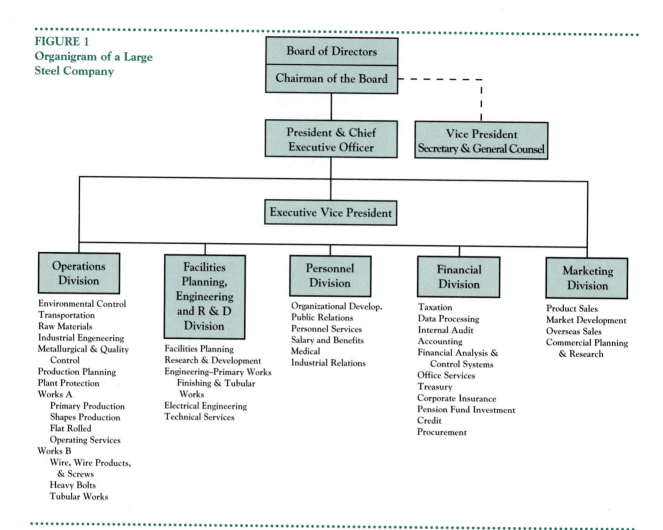

FIGURE 1
**Organigram of a Large
Steel Company**

Board of Directors

Chairman of the Board

**President & Chief
Executive Officer**

**Vice President
Secretary & General Counsel**

Executive Vice President

Operations Division	Facilities Planning, Engineering and R & D Division	Personnel Division	Financial Division	Marketing Division

Operations Division

Environmental Control
Transportation
Raw Materials
Industrial Engeneering
Metallurgical & Quality
   Control
Production Planning
Plant Protection
Works A
   Primary Production
   Shapes Production
   Flat Rolled
   Operating Services
Works B
   Wire, Wire Products,
     & Screws
   Heavy Bolts
   Tubular Works

Facilities Planning, Engineering and R & D Division

Facilities Planning
Research & Development
Engineering–Primary Works
   Finishing & Tubular
   Works
Electrical Engineering
Technical Services

Personnel Division

Organizational Develop.
Public Relations
Personnel Services
Salary and Benefits
Medical
Industrial Relations

Financial Division

Taxation
Data Processing
Internal Audit
Accounting
Financial Analysis &
   Control Systems
Office Services
Treasury
Corporate Insurance
Pension Fund Investment
Credit
Procurement

Marketing Division

Product Sales
Market Development
Overseas Sales
Commercial Planning
   & Research

So it falls to managers to resolve them by direct supervision. Indeed, many problems get bumped up successive steps in the hierarchy until they reach a level of common supervision where they can be resolved by authority (as with a dispute in a company between manufacturing and marketing that may have to be resolved by the chief executive). A second task of the middle-line managers is to work with the staff analysts to incorporate their standards down into the operating units. And a third task is to support the vertical flows in the organization—the elaboration of action plans flowing down the hierarchy and the communication of feedback information back up.

The technostructure must also be highly elaborated. In fact this structure was first identified with the rise of technocratic personnel in early-nineteenth-century industries such as textiles and banking. Because the machine organization depends primarily on the standardization of its operating work for coordination, the technostructure—which houses the staff analysts who do the standardizing—emerges as the key part of the structure. To the line managers may be delegated the formal authority for the operating units, but without the standardizers—the cadre of work-study analysts, schedulers, quality control engineers, planners, budgeters, accountants, operations researchers, and many more—these structures simply could not function. Hence, despite their lack of formal authority, considerable informal power rests with these staff analysts, who standardize everyone else's work. Rules and regulations permeate the entire system: The emphasis on standardization extends well beyond the operating core of the machine organization, and with it follows the analysts' influence.

A further reflection of this formalization of behavior are the sharp divisions of labor all over the machine organization. Job specialization in the operating core and the pronounced formal distinction between line and staff have already been mentioned. In addition, the administrative structure is clearly distinguished from the operating core; unlike the entrepreneurial organization, here managers seldom work alongside operators. And they themselves tend to be organized along functional lines, meaning that each runs a unit that performs a single function in the chain that produces the final outputs. Figure 1 shows this, for example, in the organigram of a large steel company, traditionally machinelike in structure.

All this suggests that the machine organization is a structure with an obsession—namely, control. A control mentality pervades it from top to bottom. At the bottom, consider how a Ford Assembly Division general foreman described his work:

> I refer to my watch all the time. I check different items. About every hour I tour my line. About six thirty, I'll tour labor relations to find out who is absent. At seven, I hit the end of the line. I'll check paint, check my scratches and damage. Around ten I'll start talking to all the foremen. I make sure they're all awake. We can't have no holes, no nothing.

And at the top, consider the words of a chief executive:

> When I was president of this big corporation, we lived in a small Ohio town, where the main plant was located. The corporation specified who you could socialize with, and on what level. (His wife interjects: "Who were the wives you could play bridge with.") In a small town they didn't have to keep check on you. Everybody knew. There are certain sets of rules. (Terkel, 1972:186, 406)

The obsession with control reflects two central facts about these organizations. First, attempts are made to eliminate all possible uncertainty, so that the bureaucratic machine can run smoothly, without interruption, the operating core perfectly sealed off from external influence. Second, these are structures ridden with conflict; the control systems are required to contain it. The problem in the machine organization is not to develop an open atmosphere where people can talk the conflicts out, but to enforce a closed, tightly controlled one where the work can get done despite them.

The obsession with control also helps to explain the frequent proliferation of support staff in these organizations. Many of the staff services could be purchased from outside suppliers. But that would expose the machine organization to the uncertainties of the open market. So it "makes" rather than "buys," that is, it envelops as many of the support services as it can within its own structure in order to control them, everything from the cafeteria in the factory to the law office at headquarters.

THE STRATEGIC APEX

The managers at the strategic apex of these organizations are concerned in large part with the fine-tuning of their bureaucratic machines. Theirs is a perpetual search for more efficient ways to produce the given outputs.

But not all is strictly improvement of performance. Just keeping the structure together in the face of its conflicts also consumes a good deal of the energy of top management. As noted, conflict is not resolved in the machine organization; rather it is bottled up so that the work can get done. And as in the case of a bottle, the cork is applied at the top: Ultimately, it is the top managers who must keep the lid on the conflicts through their role of handling disturbances. Moreover, the managers of the strategic apex must intervene frequently in the activities of the middle line to ensure that coordination is achieved there. The top managers are the only generalists in the structure, the only managers with a perspective broad enough to see all the functions.

All this leads us to the conclusion that considerable power in the machine organization rests with the managers of the strategic apex. These are, in other words, rather centralized structures: The formal power clearly rests at the top; hierarchy and chain of authority are paramount concepts. But so also does much of the informal power, since that resides in knowledge, and only at the top of the hierarchy does the formally segmented knowledge of the organization come together.

Thus, our introductory figure shows the machine organization with a fully elaborated administrative and support structure—both parts of the staff component being focused on the operating core—together with large units in the operating core but narrower ones in the middle line to reflect the tall hierarchy of authority.

Conditions of the Machine Organization

Work of a machine bureaucratic nature is found, above all, in environments that are simple and stable. The work associated with complex environments cannot be rationalized into simple tasks, and that associated with dynamic environments cannot be predicted, made repetitive, and so standardized.

In addition, the machine configuration is typically found in mature organizations, large enough to have the volume of operating work needed for repetition and standardization, and old enough to have been able to settle on the standards they wish to use. These are the organizations that have seen it all before and have established standard procedures to deal with it. Likewise, machine organizations tend to be identified with technical systems that regulate the operating work, so that it can easily be programmed. Such technical systems cannot be very sophisticated or automated (for reasons that will be discussed later).

Mass production firms are perhaps the best-known machine organizations. Their operating work flows through an integrated chain, open at one end to accept raw materials, and after that functioning as a sealed system that processes them through sequences of standardized operations. Thus, the environment may be stable because the organization has acted aggressively to stabilize it. Giant firms in such industries as transportation, tobacco, and metals are well known for their attempts to influence the forces of supply and demand by the use of advertising, the development of long-term supply contacts, sometimes the establishment of cartels. They also tend to adopt strategies of "vertical integration," that is, extend their production chains at both ends, becoming both their own suppliers and their own customers. In that way they can bring some of the forces of supply and demand within in their own planning processes.

Of course, the machine organization is not restricted to large, or manufacturing, or even private enterprise organizations. Small manufacturers—for example producers of discount furniture or paper products—may sometimes prefer this structure because their operating work is simple and repetitive. Many service firms use it for the same reason, such as banks or insurance companies in their retailing activities. Another condition often found with machine organizations is external control. Many government departments, such as post offices and tax collection agencies, are machine bureaucratic not only because their operating work is routine but also because they must be accountable to the public for their actions. Everything they do—treating clients, hiring employees, and so on—must be seen to be fair, and so they proliferate regulations.

Since control is the forte of the machine bureaucracy, it stands to reason that organizations in the business of control—regulatory agencies, custodial prisons, police forces—are drawn to this configuration, sometimes in spite of contradictory conditions. The same is true for the special need for safety. Organizations that fly airplanes or put out fires must minimize the risks they take. Hence they formalize their procedures extensively to ensure that they are carried out to the letter. A fire crew cannot arrive at a burning house and then turn to the chief for orders or discuss informally who will connect the hose and who will go up the ladder.

Machine Organizations as Instruments and Closed Systems

Control raises another issue about machine organizations. Being so pervasively regulated, they themselves can easily be controlled externally, as the *instruments* of outside influencers. In contrast, however, their obsession with control runs not only up the hierarchy but beyond, to control of their own environments, so that they can become *closed systems* immune to external influence. From the perspective of power, the instrument and the closed system constitute two main types of machine organizations.

In our terms, the instrument form of machine organization is dominated by one external influencer or by a group of them acting in concert. In the "closely held" corporation, the dominant influencer is the outside owner; in some prisons, it is a community concerned with the custody rather than the rehabilitation of prisoners.

Outside influencers render an organization their instrument by appointing the chief executive, charging that person with the pursuit of clear goals (ideally quantifiable, such as return on investment or prisoner escape measures), and then holding the chief responsible for performance. That way outsiders can control an organization without actually having to manage it. And such control, by virtue of the power put in the hands of the chief executive and the numerical nature of the goals, acts to centralize and bureaucratize the internal structure, in other words, to drive it to the machine form.

In contrast to this, Charles Perrow, the colorful and outspoken organizational sociologist, does not quite see the machine organization as anyone's instrument:

> Society is adaptive to organizations, to the large, powerful organizations controlled by a few, often overlapping, leaders. To see these organizations as adaptive to a "turbulent," dynamic, very changing environment is to indulge in fantasy. The environment of most powerful organizations is well controlled by them, quite stable, and made up of other organizations with similar interests, or ones they control. (1972:199)

Perrow is, of course, describing the closed system form of machine organization, the one that uses its bureaucratic procedures to seal itself off from external control and control others instead. It controls not only its own people but its environment as well: perhaps its suppliers, customers, competitors, even government and owners too.

Of course, autonomy can be achieved not only by controlling others (for example, buying up customers and suppliers in so-called vertical integration) but simply by avoiding the control of others. Thus, for example, closed system organizations sometimes form cartels with ostensible competitors or, less blatantly, diversify markets to avoid dependence on particular customers, finance internally to avoid dependence on particular financial groups, and even buy back their own shares to weaken the influence of their own owners. Key to being a closed system is to ensure wide dispersal, and therefore pacification, of all groups of potential external influence.

What goals does the closed system organization pursue? Remember that to sustain centralized bureaucracy the goals should be operational, ideally quantifiable. What operational goals enable an organization to serve itself, as a system closed to external influence? The most obvious answer is growth. Survival may be an indispensable goal and efficiency a necessary one, but beyond those what really matters here is making the system larger. Growth serves the system by providing greater rewards for its insiders—bigger empires for managers to run or fancier private jets to fly, greater programs for analysts to design, even more power for unions to wield by virtue of having more members. (The unions may be external influencers, but the management can keep them passive by allowing them more of the spoils of the closed system.) Thus the classic closed system machine organization, the large, widely held industrial corporation, has long been described as oriented far more to growth than to the maximization of profit per se (Galbraith, 1967).

Of course, the closed system form of machine organization can exist outside the private sector too, for example in the fundraising agency that, relatively free to external control, becomes increasingly charitable to itself (as indicated by the plushness of its managers' offices), the agricultural or retail cooperative that ignores those who collectively own it, even government that becomes more intent on serving itself than the citizens for which it supposedly exists.

The communist state, at least up until very recently, seemed to fit all the characteristics of the closed system bureaucracy. It had no dominant external influencer (at least in the case of the Soviet Union, if not the other East European states, which were its "instruments"). And the population to which it is ostensibly responsible had to respond to its own plethora of rules and regulations. Its election procedures, traditionally offering a choice of one, were similar to those for the directors of the "widely held" Western corporation. The government's own structure was heavily bureaucratic, with a single hierarchy of authority and a very elaborate technostructure, ranging from state planners to KGB agents. (As James Worthy [1959:77] noted, Frederick Taylor's "Scientific Management had its fullest flowering not in America but in Soviet Russia.") All significant resources were the property of the state—the collective system—not the individual. And, as in other closed systems, the administrators tend to take the lion's share of the benefits.

Some Issues Associated with the Machine Organization

No structure has evoked more heated debate than the machine organization. As Michel Crozier, one of its most eminent students, has noted,

> On the one hand, most authors consider the bureaucratic organization to be the embodiment of rationality in the modern world, and, as such, to be intrinsically superior to all other possible forms of organizations. On the other hand, many authors—often the same ones—consider it a sort of Leviathan, preparing the enslavement of the human race. (1964:176)

Max Weber, who first wrote about this form of organization, emphasized its rationality; in fact, the word *machine* comes directly from his writings (see Gerth and Mills, 1958). A machine is certainly precise; it is also reliable and easy to control; and it is efficient—at least when restricted to the job it has been designed to do. Those are the reasons many organizations are structured as machine bureaucracies. When an integrated set of simple, repetitive tasks must be performed precisely and consistently by human beings, this is the most efficient structure—indeed, the only conceivable one.

But in these same advantages of machinelike efficiency lie all the disadvantages of this configuration. Machines consist of mechanical parts; organizational structures also include human beings—and that is where the analogy breaks down.

HUMAN PROBLEMS IN THE OPERATING CORE

James Worthy, when he was an executive of Sears, wrote a penetrating and scathing criticism of the machine organization in his book *Big Business and Free Men*. Worthy traced the root of the human problems in these structures to the "scientific management" movement led by Frederick Taylor that swept America early in this century. Worthy acknowledged Taylor's contribution to efficiency, narrowly defined. Worker initiative did not, however, enter into his efficiency equation. Taylor's pleas to remove "all possible brain work" from the shop floor also removed all possible initiative from the people who worked there: the "machine has no will of its own. Its parts have no urge to independent action. Thinking, direction—even purpose—must be provided from outside or above." This had the "consequence of destroying the meaning of work itself," which has been "fantastically wasteful for industry and society," resulting in excessive absenteeism, high worker turnover, sloppy workmanship, costly strikes, and even outright sabotage (1959:67, 79, 70). Of course, there are people who like to work in highly structured situations. But increasing numbers do not, at least not *that* highly structured.

Taylor was fond of saying, "In the past the man has been first; in the future the system must be first" (in Worthy 1959:73). Prophetic words, indeed. Modern man seems to exist for his systems; many of the organizations he created to serve him have come to enslave him. The result is that several of what Victor Thompson (1961) has called "bureaupathologies"—dysfunctional behaviors of these structures—reinforce each other to form a vicious circle in the machine organization. The concentration on means at the expense of ends, the mistreatment of clients, the various manifestations of worker alienation—all lead to the tightening of controls on behavior. The implicit motto of the machine organization seems to be, "When in doubt, control." All problems have to be solved by the turning of the technocratic screws. But since that is what caused the bureaupathologies in the first place, increasing the controls serves only to magnify the problems, leading to the imposition of further controls, and so on.

COORDINATION PROBLEMS IN THE ADMINISTRATIVE CENTER

Since the operating core of the machine organization is not designed to handle conflict, many of the human problems that arise there spill up and over, into the administrative structure.

It is one of the ironies of the machine configuration that to achieve the control it requires, it must mirror the narrow specialization of its operating core in its administrative structure (for example, differentiating marketing managers from manufacturing managers, much as salesmen are differentiated from factory workers). This, in turn, means problems of communication and coordination. The fact is that the administrative structure of the machine organization is also ill suited to the resolution of problems through mutual adjustment. All the communication barriers in these structures—horizontal, vertical, status, line/staff—impede informal communication among managers and with staff people. "Each unit becomes jealous of its own prerogatives and finds ways to protect itself against the pressure or encroachments of others" (Worthy, 1950:176). Thus narrow functionalism not only impedes coordination; it also encourages the building of private empires, which tends to produce top-heavy organizations that can be more concerned with the political games to be won than with the clients to be served.

ADAPTATION PROBLEMS IN THE STRATEGIC APEX

But if mutual adjustment does not work in the administrative center—generating more political heat than cooperative light—how does the machine organization resolve its coordination problems? Instinctively, it tries standardization, for example, by tightening job descriptions or proliferating rules. But standardization is not suited to handling the nonroutine problems of the administrative center. Indeed, it only aggravates them, undermining the influence of the line managers and increasing the conflict. So to reconcile these coordination problems, the machine organization is left with only one coordinating mechanism, direct supervision from above. Specifically, nonroutine coordination problems between units are "bumped" up the line hierarchy until they reach a common level of supervision, often at the top of the structure. The result can be excessive centralization of power, which in turn produces a host of other problems. In effect, just as the human problems in the operating core become coordination problems in the administrative center, so too do the coordination problems in the administrative center become adaptation problems at the strategic apex. Let us take a closer look at these by concluding with a discussion of strategic change in the machine configuration.

Strategy Formation in the Machine Organization

Strategy in the machine organization is supposed to emanate from the top of the hierarchy, where the perspective is broadest and the power most focused. All the relevant information is to be sent up the hierarchy, in aggregated, MIS-type form, there to be formulated into integrated strategy (with the aid of the technostructure). Implementation then follows, with the intended strategies sent down the hierarchy to be turned into successively more elaborated programs and action plans. Notice the clear division of labor assumed between the formulators at the top and the implementors down below, based on the assumption of perfectly deliberate strategy produced through a process of planning.

That is the theory. The practice has been shown to be another matter. Drawing on our strategy research at McGill University, we shall consider first what planning really proved to be in one machinelike organization, how it may in fact have impeded strategic thinking in a second, and how a third really did change its strategy. From there we shall consider the problems of strategic change in machine organizations and their possible resolution.

PLANNING AS PROGRAMMING IN A SUPERMARKET CHAIN

What really is the role of formal planning? Does it produce original strategies? Let us return to the case of Steinberg's in the later years of its founder, as large size drove this retailing chain toward the machine form, and as is common in that form, toward a planning mode of management at the expense of entrepreneurship.

One event in particular encouraged the start of planning at Steinberg's: the company's entry into capital markets in 1953. Months before it floated its first bond issue (stock, always nonvoting, came later), Sam Steinberg boasted to a newspaper reporter that "not a cent of any money outside the family is invested in the company." And asked about future plans, he replied: "Who knows? We will try to go everywhere there seems to be a need for us." A few months later he announced a $5 million debt issue and with it a $15 million five-year expansion program, one new store every two months for a total of thirty, the doubling of sales, new stores to average double the size of existing ones.

What happened in those ensuing months was Sam Steinberg's realization, after the opening of Montreal's first shopping center, that he needed to enter the shopping center business himself to protect his supermarket chain and that he could not do so with the company's traditional methods of short-term and internal financing. And, of course, no company is allowed to go to capital markets without a plan. You can't just say: "I'm Sam Steinberg and I'm good," though that was really the issue. In a "rational" society, you have to plan (or at least appear to do so).

But what exactly was that planning? One thing for certain: It did not formulate a strategy. Sam Steinberg already had that. What planning did was justify, elaborate, and articulate the strategy that already existed in Sam Steinberg's mind. Planning operationalized his strategic vision, programmed it. It gave order to that vision, imposing form on it to comply with the needs of the organization and its environment. Thus, planning followed the strategy-making process, which had been essentially entrepreneurial.

But its effect on that process was not incidental. By specifying and articulating the vision, planning constrained it and rendered it less flexible. Sam Steinberg retained formal control of the company to the day of his death. But his control over strategy did not remain so absolute. The entrepreneur, by keeping his vision personal, is able to adapt it at will to a changing environment. But by being forced to program it, the leader loses that flexibility. The danger, ultimately, is that the planning mode forces out the entrepreneurial one; procedure replaces vision. As its structure became more machinelike, Steinberg's required planning in the form of strategic programming. But that planning also accelerated the firm's transition toward the machine form of organization.

Is there, then, such a thing as "strategic planning"? I suspect not. To be more explicit, I do not find that major new strategies are formulated through any formal procedure. Organizations that rely on formal planning procedures to formulate strategies seem to extrapolate existing strategies, perhaps with marginal changes in them, or else copy the strategies of other organizations. This came out most clearly in another of our McGill studies.

PLANNING AS AN IMPEDIMENT TO STRATEGIC THINKING IN AN AIRLINE

From about the mid-1950s, Air Canada engaged heavily in planning. Once the airline was established, particularly once it developed its basic route structure, a number of factors drove it strongly to the planning mode. Above all was the need for coordination, both of flight schedules with aircraft, crews, and maintenance, and of the purchase of expensive aircraft with the structure of the route system. (Imagine someone calling out in the hangar: "Hey, Fred, this guy says he has two 747s for us; do you know who ordered them?") Safety was another factor. The intense need for safety in the air breeds a mentality of being very careful about what the organization does on the ground, too. This is the airlines' obsession with control. Other factors included the lead times inherent in key decisions, such as ordering new airplanes or introducing new routes, the sheer cost of the capital equipment, and the size of the organization. You don't run an intricate system like an airline, necessarily very machinelike, without a great deal of formal planning.

But what we found to be the consequence of planning at Air Canada was the absence of a major reorientation of strategy during our study period (up to the mid-1970s). Aircraft certainly changed—they became larger and faster—but the basic route system did not, nor did markets. Air Canada gave only marginal attention, for example, to cargo, charter, and shuttle operations. Formal planning, in our view, impeded strategic thinking.

The problem is that planning, too, proceeds from the machine perspective, much as an assembly line or a conventional machine produces a product. It all depends on the decomposition of analysis: You split the process into a series of steps or component parts, specify each, and then by following the specifications in sequence you get the desired product. There is a fallacy in this, however. Assembly lines and conventional machines produce standardized products, while planning is supposed to produce a novel strategy. It is as if the machine is supposed to design the machine; the planning machine is expected to create the original blueprint—the strategy. To put this another way, planning is analysis oriented to decomposition, while strategy making depends on synthesis oriented to integration. That is why the term "strategic planning" has proved to be an oxymoron.

ROLES OF PLANNING, PLANS, PLANNERS

If planning does not create strategy, then what purpose does it serve? We have suggested a role above, which has to do with the programming of strategies already created in other ways. This is shown in Figure 2, coming out of a box labeled strategy formation—meant to represent what is to planning a mysterious "black box." But if planning is restricted to programming strategy, plans and planners nonetheless have other roles in play, shown in Figure 2 and discussed alongside that of planning itself.

FIGURE 2
Specific Roles of Planners

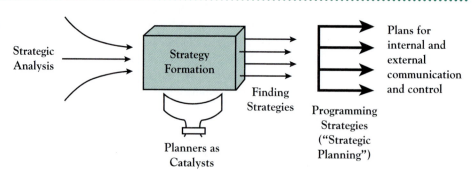

Strategic Analysis

Strategy Formation

Planners as Catalysts

Finding Strategies

Programming Strategies ("Strategic Planning")

Plans for internal and external communication and control

ROLE OF PLANNING

Why do organizations engage in formal planning? The answer seems to be: not to create strategies, but to program the strategies they already have, that is, to elaborate and operationalize the consequences of those strategies formally. We should really say that *effective* organizations so engage in planning, at least when they require the formalized implementation of their strategies. Thus strategy is not the *consequence* of planning but its starting point. Planning helps to translate the intended strategies into realized ones, taking the first step that leads ultimately to implementation.

This *strategic programming*, as it might properly be labeled, can be considered to involve a series of steps, namely the *codification* of given strategy, including its clarification and articulation, the *elaboration* of that strategy into substrategies, ad hoc action programs, and plans of various kinds, and the *translation* of those substrategies, programs, and plans into routine budgets and objectives. In these steps, we see planning as an analytical process that takes over after the synthesis of strategic formation is completed.

Thus formal planning properly belongs in the *implementation* of strategy, not in its formulation. But it should be emphasized that strategic programming makes sense when viable intended strategies are available, in other words when the world is expected to hold still while these strategies unfold, so that formulation can logically precede implementation, and when the organization that does the implementing in fact requires clearly codified and elaborated strategies. In other circumstances, strategic programming can do organizations harm by preempting the flexibility that managers and others may need to respond to changes in the environment, or to their own internal processes of learning.

ROLES OF PLANS

If planning is programming, then plans clearly serve two roles. They are a medium for communication and a device for control. Both roles draw on the analytical character of plans, namely, that they represent strategies in decomposed and articulated form, if not quantified then often at least quantifiable.

Why program strategy? Most obviously for coordination, to ensure that everyone in the organization pulls in the same direction, a direction that may have to be specified as precisely as possible. In Air Canada, to use our earlier example, that means linking the acquisition of new aircraft with the particular routes that are to be flown, and scheduling crews and planes to show up when the flights are to take off, and so on. Plans, as they emerge from strategic programming as programs, schedules, budgets, and so on, can be prime media to communicate not just strategic intention but also the role each individual must play to realize it.

Plans, as communication media, inform people of intended strategy and its consequences. But as control devices they can go further, specifying what role departments and individuals must play in helping to realize strategy and then comparing that with performance in order to feed control information back into the strategy-making process.

Plans can help to effect control in a number of ways. The most obvious is control of the strategy itself. Indeed what has long paraded under the label of "strategy planning" has probably had more to do with "strategic control" than many people may realize. Strategic control has to do with keeping organizations on their strategic tracks: to ensure the realization of intended strategy, its implementation as expected, with resources appropriately allocated. But there is more to strategic control than this. Another aspect includes the assessment of the realization of strategies in the first place, namely, whether the patterns realized corresponded to the intentions specified beforehand. In other words, strategic control must assess behavior as well as performance. Then the more routine and traditional form of control can come in to consider whether the strategies that were in fact realized proved effective.

ROLES OF PLANNERS

Planners, of course, play key roles in planning (namely, strategic programming), and in using the resulting plans for purposes of communication and control. But many of the most important things planners do have little to do with planning or even plans per se. Three roles seem key here.

First, planners can play a role in finding strategies. This may seem curious, but if strategies really do emerge in organizations, then planners can help to identify the patterns that are becoming strategies, so that consideration can be given to formalizing them, that is, making them deliberate. Of course, finding the strategies of competitors—for assessment and possible modified adoption—is also important here.

Second, planners play the roles of analysts, carrying out ad hoc studies to feed into the black box of strategy making. Indeed, one could argue that this is precisely what Michael Porter proposes with his emphasis on industry and competitive analysis. The ad hoc nature of such studies should, however, be emphasized because they feed into a strategy-making process that is itself irregular, proceeding on no schedule and following no standard sequence of steps. Indeed, regularity in the planning process can interfere with strategic thinking, which must be flexible, responsive, and creative.

The third role of the planner is as a catalyst. This refers not to the traditional role long promoted in the literature of selling formal planning as some kind of religion, but to encourage strategic *thinking* throughout the organization. Here the planner encourages *informal* strategy making, trying to get others to think about the future in a creative way. He or she does not enter the black box of strategy making so much as ensure that the box is occupied with active line managers.

A PLANNER FOR EACH SIDE OF THE BRAIN

We have discussed various roles for planning, plans, and planners, summarized around the black box of strategy formation in Figure 2. These roles suggest two different orientations for planners.

On one hand (so to speak), the planner must be a highly analytic, convergent type of thinker, dedicated to bringing order to the organization. Above all, this planner programs intended strategies and sees to it that they are communicated clearly and used for purposes of control. He or she also carries out studies to ensure that the managers concerned with strategy formation take into account the necessary hard data that they may be inclined to miss and that the strategies they formulate are carefully and systematically evaluated before they are implemented.

On the other hand, there is another type of planner, less conventional a creative, divergent thinker, rather intuitive, who seeks to open up the strategy-making process. As a "soft analyst," he or she tends to conduct "quick and dirty" studies, to find strategies in strange places, and to encourage others to think strategically. This planner is inclined toward the intuitive processes identified with the brain's right hemisphere. We might call him or her a *left-handed planner*. Some organizations need to emphasize one type of planner, others the other type. But most complex organizations probably need some of both.

STRATEGIC CHANGE IN AN AUTOMOBILE FIRM

Given planning itself is not strategic, how does the planning-oriented machine bureaucracy change its strategy when it has to? Volkswagenwerk was an organization that had to. We interpreted its history from 1934 to 1974 as one long cycle of a single strategic perspective. The original "people's car," the famous "Beetle," was conceived by Ferdinand Porsche: the factory to produce it was built just before the war but did not go into civilian automobile production until after. In 1948, a man named Heinrich Nordhoff was given control of the devastated plant and began the rebuilding of it, as well as of the organization and the strategy itself, rounding out Porsche's original conception. The firm's success was dramatic.

By the late 1950s, however, problems began to appear. Demand in Germany was moving away from the Beetle. The typically machine-bureaucratic response was not to rethink the basic strategy—"it's okay" was the reaction—but rather to graft another piece onto it. A new automobile model was added, larger than the Beetle but with a similar no-nonsense approach to motoring, again air-cooled with the engine in the back. Volkswagenwerk added position but did not change perspective.

But that did not solve the basic problem, and by the mid-1960s the company was in crisis. Nordhoff, who had resisted strategic change, died in office and was replaced by a lawyer from outside the business. The company then underwent a frantic search for new models, designing, developing, or acquiring a whole host of them with engines in the front, middle, and rear; air and water cooled; front- and rear-wheel drive. To paraphrase the humorist Stephen Leacock, Volkswagenwerk leaped onto its strategic horse and rode off in all directions. Only when another leader came in, a man steeped in the company and the automobile business, did the firm consolidate itself around a new strategic perspective, based on the stylish front-wheel drive, water-cooled designs of one of its acquired firms, and thereby turn its fortunes around.

What this story suggests, first of all, is the great force of bureaucratic momentum in the machine organization. Even leaving planning aside, the immense effort of producing and marketing a new line of automobiles locks a company into a certain posture. But here the momentum was psychological, too. Nordhoff, who had been the driving force behind the great success of the organization, became a major liability when the environment demanded change. Over the years, he too had been captured by bureaucratic momentum. Moreover, the uniqueness and tight integration of Volkswagenwerk's strategy—we labeled it *gestalt*—impeded strategic change. Change an element of a tightly integrated gestalt and it *dis*integrates. Thus does success eventually breed failure.

BOTTLENECK AT THE TOP

Why the great difficulty in changing strategy in the machine organization? Here we take up that question and show how changes generally have to be achieved in a different configuration, if at all.

As discussed earlier, unanticipated problems in the machine organization tend to get bumped up the hierarchy. When these are few, which mean conditions are relatively stable, things work smoothly enough. But in times of rapid change, just when new strategies are called for, the number of such problems magnifies, resulting in a bottleneck at the top, where senior managers get overloaded. And that tends either to impede strategic change or else to render it ill considered.

A major part of the problem is information. Senior managers face an organization decomposed into parts, like a machine itself. Marketing information comes up one channel, manufacturing information up another, and so on. Somehow it is the senior managers themselves who must integrate all that information. But the very machine bureaucratic premise of separating the administration of work from the doing of it means that the top managers often lack the intimate, detailed knowledge of issues necessary to effect such an integration. In essence, the necessary power is at the top of the structure, but the necessary knowledge is often at the bottom.

Of course, there is a machinelike solution to that problem too—not surprisingly in the form of a system. It is called a management information system, or MIS, and what it does is combine all the necessary information and package it neatly so that top managers can be informed about what is going on—the perfect solution for the overloaded executive. At least in theory.

Unfortunately, a number of real-world problems arise in the MIS. For one thing, in the tall administrative hierarchy of the machine organization, information must pass through many levels before it reaches the top. Losses take place at each one. Good news gets highlighted while bad news gets blocked on the way up. And "soft" information, so necessary for strategy information, cannot easily pass through, while much of the hard MIS-type information arrives only slowly. In a stable environment, the manager may be able to wait; in a rapidly changing one, he or she cannot. The president wants to be told right away that the firm's most important customer was seen playing golf yesterday with a main competitor, not to find out six months later in the form of a drop in a sales report. Gossip, hearsay, speculation—the softest kinds of information—warn the manager of impeding problems; the MIS all too often records for posterity ones that have already been felt. The manager who depends on an MIS in a changing environment generally finds himself or herself out of touch.

The obvious solution for top managers is to bypass the MIS and set up their own informal information systems, networks of contacts that bring them the rich, tangible, instant information they need. But that violates the machine organization's presuppositions of formality and respect for the chain of authority. Also, that takes the managers' time, the lack of which caused the bottleneck in the first place. So a fundamental dilemma faces the top managers of the machine organization as a result of its very own design: in times of change, when they most need the time to inform themselves, the system overburdens them with other pressures. They are thus reduced to acting superficially, with inadequate, abstract information.

THE FORMULATION/IMPLEMENTATION DICHOTOMY

The essential problem lies in one of the chief tenets of the machine organization, that strategy formation must be sharply separated from strategy implementation. One is thought out at the top, the other then acted out lower down. For this to work assume two conditions: first, that the formulator has full and sufficient information, and second, that the world will hold still, or at least change in predictable ways, during the implementation, so that there is no need for *re*formulation.

Now consider why the organization needs a new strategy in the first place. It is because its world has changed in an unpredictable way, indeed may continue to do so. We have just seen how the machine bureaucratic structure tends to violate the first condition—it misinforms the senior manager during such times of change. And when change continues in an unpredictable way (or at least the world unfolds in a way not yet predicted by an ill-informed management), then the second condition is violated too—it hardly makes sense to lock in by implementation a strategy that does not reflect changes in the world around it.

What all this amounts to is a need to collapse the formulation/implementation dichotomy precisely when the strategy of machine bureaucracy must be changed. This can be done in one of two ways.

In one case, the formulator implements. In other words, power is concentrated at the top, not only for creating the strategy but also for implementing it, step by step, in a personalized way. The strategist is put in close personal touch with the situation at hand (more commonly a strategist is appointed who has or can develop that touch) so that he or she can, on one hand, be properly informed and, on the other, control the implementation en route in order to reformulate when necessary. This, of course describes the entrepreneurial configuration, at least at the strategic apex.

In the other case, the implementers formulate. In other words, power is concentrated lower down, where the necessary information resides. As people who are naturally in touch with the specific situations at hand take individual actions—approach new customers, develop new products, et cetera—patterns form, in other words, strategies emerge. And this describes the innovative configuration, where strategic initiatives often originate in the grass roots of the organization, and then are championed by managers at middle levels who integrate them with one another or with existing strategies in order to gain their acceptance by senior management.

We conclude, therefore, that the machine configuration is ill suited to change its fundamental strategy, that the organization must in effect change configuration temporarily in order to change strategy. Either it reverts to the entrepreneurial form, to allow a single leader to develop vision (or proceed with one developed earlier), or else it overlays an innovative form on its conventional structure (for example, creates an informed network of lateral teams and task forces) so that the necessary strategies can emerge. The former can obviously function faster than the latter; that is why it tends to be used for drastic *turnaround*, while the latter tends to proceed by the slower process of *revitalization*. (Of course, quick turnaround may be necessary because there has been no slow revitalization.) In any event, both are characterized by a capacity to *learn*—that is the essence of the entrepreneurial and innovative configurations, in one case learning centralized for the simpler context, in the other, decentralized for the more complex one. The machine configuration is not so characterized.

This, however, should come as no surprise. After all, machines are specialized instruments, designed for productivity, not for adaptation. In Hunt's (1970) words, machine bureaucracies are performance systems, not problem-solving ones. Efficiency is their forte, not innovation. An organization cannot put blinders on its personnel and then expect peripheral vision. Managers here are rewarded for cutting costs and improving standards, not for taking risks and ignoring procedures. Change makes a mess of the operating systems: change one link in a carefully coupled system, and the whole chain must be reconceived. Why, then, should we be surprised when our bureaucratic machines fail to adapt?

Of course, it is fair to ask why we spend so much time trying to make them adapt. After all, when an ordinary machine becomes redundant, we simply scrap it, happy that it served us for as long and as well as it did. Converting it to another use generally proves more expensive than simply starting over. I suspect the same is often true for bureaucratic machines. But here, of course, the context is social and political. Mechanical parts don't protest, nor do displaced raw materials. Workers, suppliers, and customers do, however, protest the scrapping of organizations, for obvious reasons. But that the cost of this is awfully high in a society of giant machine organizations will be the subject of the final chapter of this book.

STRATEGIC REVOLUTIONS IN MACHINE ORGANIZATIONS

Machine organizations do sometimes change, however, at times effectively but more often it would seem at great cost and pain. The lucky ones are able to overlay an innovative structure for periodic revitalization, while many of the other survivors somehow manage to get turned around in entrepreneurial fashion.

Overall, the machine organizations seem to follow what my colleagues Danny Miller and Peter Friesen (1984) call a "quantum theory" of organization change. They pursue their

FIGURE 3
Organization Takes
Precedence

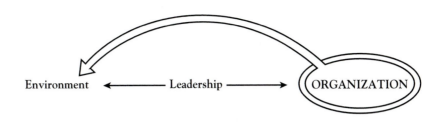

Environment ← Leadership → ORGANIZATION

set strategies through long periods of stability (naturally occurring or created by themselves as closed systems), using planning and other procedures to do so efficiently. Periodically these are interrupted by short bursts of change, which Miller and Friesen characterize as "strategic revolutions" (although another colleague, Mihaela Firsirotu [1985], perhaps better labels it "strategic turnaround as cultural revolution").

ORGANIZATION TAKING PRECEDENCE IN THE MACHINE ORGANIZATION

To conclude, as shown in Figure 3, it is organization—with its systems and procedures, its planning and its bureaucratic momentum—that takes precedence over leadership and environment in the machine configuration. Environment fits organization, either because the organization has slotted itself into a context that matches its procedures, or else because it has forced the environment to do so. And leadership generally falls into place too, supporting the organization, indeed often becoming part of its bureaucratic momentum.

This generally works effectively, though hardly nonproblematically, at least in times of stability. But in times of change, efficiency becomes ineffective and the organization will falter unless it can find a different way to organize for adaptation.

All of this is another way of saying that the machine organization is a configuration, a species, like the others, suited to its own context but ill suited to others. But unlike the others, it is the dominant configuration in our specialized societies. As long as we demand inexpensive and so necessarily standardized goods and services, and as long as people continue to be more efficient than real machines at providing them, and remain willing to do so, then the machine organization will remain with us—and so will all its problems.

▼ READING 10.2   COST DYNAMICS: SCALE AND EXPERIENCE EFFECTS*

by Derek F. Abell and John S. Hammond

Market share is one of the primary determinants of business profitability; other things being equal, businesses with a larger share of a market are more profitable than their smaller-share competitors. For instance, a study by the PIMS Program (Buzzell, Gale and Sultan, 1975) . . . found that, on average, a difference of 10 percentage points in market share is accompanied by a difference of about 5 points in pretax ROI ("pretax operating profits" divided by "long-term debt plus equity"). Additional evidence is that companies having large market shares in their primary product markets—such as General Motors, IBM, Gillette, Eastman Kodak, and Xerox—tend to be highly profitable.

* Originally published in *Strategic Market Planning: Problems and Analytical Approaches* (Prentice Hall, 1979), Chap. 3. Copyright © Prentice Hall, 1979; reprinted with deletions by permission of the publisher.

An important reason for the increase in profitability with market share is that large-share firms usually have *lower costs*. The lower costs are due in part to economies of scale; for instance, very large plants cost less per unit of production to build and are often more efficient than smaller plants. Lower costs are also due in part to the so-called *experience effect*, whereby the cost of many (if not most) products declines by 10–30 percent each time a company's experience at producing and selling them doubles. In this context *experience* has a precise meaning: it is the cumulative number of units produced to date. Since at any point in time, businesses with large market shares typically (but not always) have more experience than their smaller-share competitors, they would be expected to have lower cost. . . .

This [reading] considers how costs decline due to scale and to experience, practical problems in analyzing the experience effect, strategic implications of scale and experience, and limitations of strategies based on cost reduction. . . .

Scale Effect

As mentioned earlier, scale effect refers to the fact that large businesses have the potential to operate at lower unit costs than their smaller counterparts. The increased efficiency due to size is often referred to as "economy of scale"; it could equally be called "economy of size."

Most people think of economy of scale as a manufacturing phenomenon because large manufacturing facilities can be constructed at a lower cost per unit of capacity and can be operated more efficiently than smaller ones. . . .

Just as they cost less to build, large-scale plants have lower *operating* costs per unit of output. . . . While substantial in manufacturing, scale effect is also significant in other cost elements, such as marketing, sales, distribution, administration, R&D, and service. For instance, a chain with 30 supermarkets in a metropolitan area needs much less than three times as much advertising as a chain of 10 stores. . . . Economies of scale are also achieved with purchased items such as raw material and shipping. . . .

Although scale economies potentially exist in all cost elements of a business in both the short and long run, large size alone doesn't assure the benefits of scale. It is evident from the above illustrations that size provides an *opportunity* for scale economies; to achieve them requires strategies and actions consciously designed to seize the opportunity, especially with operating costs. . . .

Experience Effect

The experience effect, whereby costs fall with cumulative production, is measurable and predictable; it has been observed in a wide range of products including automobiles, semiconductors, petrochemicals, long-distance telephone calls, synthetic fibers, airline transportation, the cost of administering life insurance, and crushed limestone, to mention a few. Note that this list ranges from high technology to low technology products, service to manufacturing industries, consumer to industrial products, new to mature products. and process to assembly oriented products, indicating the wide range of applicability. . . .

. . . it is only comparatively recently that this phenomenon has been carefully measured and quantified; at first it was thought to apply only to the labor portion of *manufacturing* costs. . . . In the 1960s evidence mounted that the phenomenon was broader. Personnel from the Boston Consulting Group and others showed that each time cumulative volume of a product doubled, total value added costs—including administration, sales, marketing, distribution, and so on in addition to manufacturing—fell by a constant and predictable percentage. In addition, the costs of purchased items usually fell as suppliers reduced prices

FIGURE 1
A Typical Experience
Curve [85%]

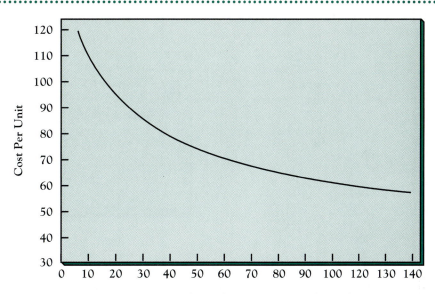

Experience (Cumulative Units of Production)

FIGURE 2
An 85% Experience
Curve Displayed on
Log-Log Scales

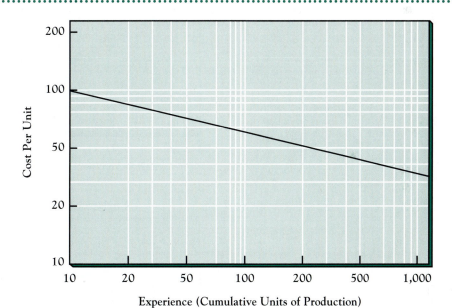

Experience (Cumulative Units of Production)

as their costs fell, due also to the experience effect. The relationship between costs and experience was called the *experience curve* (Boston Consulting Group, 1972).

An experience curve is plotted with the cumulative units produced on the horizontal axis, and cost per unit on the vertical axis. An "85%" experience curve is shown in Figure 1. The "85%" means that every time experience doubles, costs per unit drop to 85% of the original level. It is known as the *learning rate*. Stated differently, costs per unit decrease 15 percent for every doubling of cumulative production. For example, the cost of the 20th unit produced is about 85% of the cost of the 10th unit. . . .

An experience curve appears as a straight line when plotted on a double log paper (logarithmic scale for both the horizontal and vertical axes). Figure 2 shows the "85 percent"

FIGURE 3
Some Sample Experience
Curves

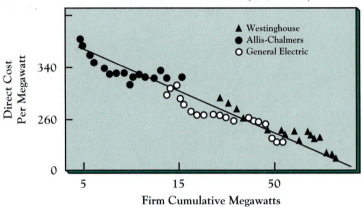

Steam Turbine Generators (1946-1963)

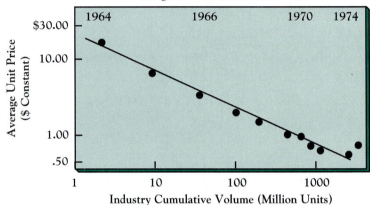

Integrated Circuits (1964-1974)

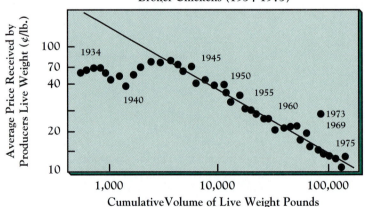

Broiler Chickens (1934-1975)

Note: Technically an experience curve shows the relationship between cost and experience. However, cost figures are seldom pubicly available; therefore most of the above experience curves show industry price (in constant dollars) vs. experience.

Source: The Boston Consulting Group.

experience curve from Figure 1 on the double logarithmic scale. . . . Figure 3 provides illustrations for [some specific] products.

Sources of the Experience Effect

Sources of the Experience Effect

The experience effect has a variety of sources; to capitalize on it requires knowledge of why it occurs. Sources of the experience effect are outlined as follows:

1. *Labor efficiency.* . . . As workers repeat a particular production task, they become more dextrous and learn improvements and shortcuts which increase their collective efficiency. The greater the number of worker-paced operations, the greater the amount of learning which can accrue with experience. . . .

2. *Work specialization and methods improvements.* Specialization increases worker proficiency at a given task. . . .

3. *New production processes.* Process innovations and improvements can be an important source of cost reductions, especially in capital-intensive industries. . . .

4. *Getting better performance from production equipment.* When first designed, a piece of production equipment may have a conservatively rated output. Experience may reveal innovative ways of increasing its output. . . .

5. *Changes in the resource mix.* As experience accumulates, a producer can often incorporate different or less expensive resources in the operation. . . .

6. *Product standardization.* Standardization allows the replication of tasks necessary for worker learning. Production of the Ford Model T, for example, followed a strategy of deliberate standardization; as a result, from 1909 to 1923 its price was repeatedly reduced, following an 85 percent experience curve (Abernathy and Wayne, 1974). . . .

7. *Product redesign.* As experience is gained with a product, both the manufacturer and customers gain a clearer understanding of its performance requirements. This understanding allows the product to be redesigned to conserve material, allows greater efficiency in manufacture, and substitutes less costly materials and resources, while at the same time improving performance on relevant dimensions. . . .

The foregoing list of sources dramatizes the observation that cost reductions due to experience don't occur by natural inclination; they are the result of substantial, concerted effort and pressure to lower costs. In fact, left unmanaged, costs rise. Thus, experience does not cause reductions but rather provides an opportunity that alert managements can exploit. . . .

The list of reasons for the experience effect raises perplexing questions on the difference between experience and scale effects. For instance, isn't it true that work specialization and project standardization, mentioned in the experience list, become possible because of the *size* of an operation? Therefore, aren't they each really scale effects? The answer is that they are probably both.

The confusion arises because growth in experience usually coincides with growth in size of an operation. We consider the experience effect to arise primarily due to ingenuity, cleverness, skill, and dexterity derived from experience as embodied in the adages "practice makes perfect" or "experience is the best teacher." On the other hand, scale effect comes from capitalizing on the size of an operation. . . .

Usually the overlap between the two effects is so great that it is difficult (and not too important) to separate them. This is the practice we will adopt from here on. . . .

Prices and Experience

In stable competitive markets, one would expect that as costs decrease due to experience, prices will decrease similarly. (The price-experience curves in Figure 3 are examples of prices falling with experience.) If profit margins remain at a constant percentage of price, average industry costs and prices should follow identically sloped experience curves (on double logarithmic scales). The constant gap separating them will equal the profit margin percentage; Figure 4 illustrates such an idealized situation.

In many cases, however, prices and costs exhibit a relationship similar to the one shown in Figure 5, where prices start briefly below cost, then cost reductions exceed price reductions until prices suddenly tumble. Ultimately the price and cost curves parallel, as they do in Figure 4. Specifically, in the development phase, new product prices are below average industry costs due to pricing based on anticipated costs. In the price umbrella phase, when demand exceeds supply, prices remain firm under a price umbrella supported by the market leader. This is unstable. At some point a shakeout phase starts; one producer will almost certainly reduce prices to gain share. If this does not precipitate a price decline, the high profit margins will attract enough new entrants to produce temporary overcapacity, causing prices to tumble faster than costs, and marginal producers to be forced out of the market. The stability phase starts when profit margins return to normal levels and prices begin to follow industry costs down the experience curve. . . .

Strategic Implications

In industries where a significant portion of total cost can be reduced due to scale or experience, important cost advantages can usually be achieved by pursuing a strategy geared to accumulating experience faster than competitors. (Such a strategy will ultimately require that the firm acquire the largest market share relative to competition.)

The dominant producer can greatly influence industry profitability. The rate of decline of competitors' costs must at least keep pace with the leader if they are to maintain profitability. If their costs decrease more slowly, either because they are pursuing cost reductions less aggressively or are growing more slowly than the leader, then their profits will eventually disappear, thus eliminating them from the market.

FIGURE 4
An Idealized Price-Cost Relationship When Profit Margin Is Constant

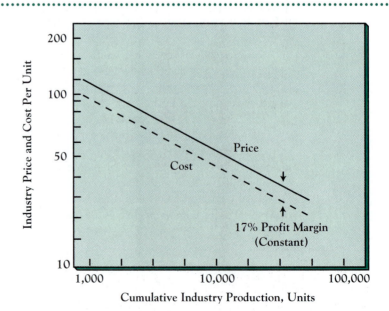

FIGURE 5
Typical Price-Cost
Relationship
Source: Adapted from
Perspectives on Experience
(Boston: The Boston
Consulting Group, 1972),
p. 21

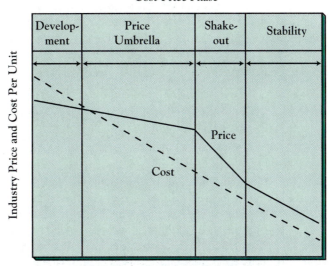

... the advantage of being the leader is obvious. Leadership is usually best seized at the start when experience doubles quickly (e.g., experience increases tenfold as you move from the 20th to the 2,000th unit, but only doubles as you move from the 2,000th to the 4,000th unit). Then a firm can build an unassailable cost advantage and at the same time gain price leadership. The best course of action for a product depends on a number of factors, one of the most important being the market growth rate. In fast-growing markets, experience can be gained by taking a disproportionate share of new sales, thereby avoiding taking sales away from competitors (which would be vigorously resisted). Therefore, with high rates of growth, aggressive action may be called for. But, share-gaining tactics are usually costly in the short run, due to reduced margins from lower prices, added advertising and marketing expense, new product development costs, and the like. This means that if it lacks the resources (product, financial, and other) for leadership and in particular if it is opposed by a very aggressive competitor, a firm may find it wise to abandon the market entirely or focus on a segment it can dominate. On the other hand, in no-growth or slowly growing markets it is hard to take share from competitors and the time it takes to acquire superior experience is usually too long and the cost too great to favor aggressive strategies.

In stable competitive markets, usually the firm with the largest share of market has the greatest experience and it is often the case that each firm's experience is roughly proportional to market share. A notable exception occurs when a late entrant to a market quickly obtains a commanding market share. It may have less experience than some early entrants. ...

Efficiency versus Effectiveness: Limitations to Strategies Based on Experience or Scale

The selection of a competitive strategy based on cost reduction due to experience or scale often involves a fundamental choice. It is the selection of cost-price *efficiency* over noncost-price marketing *effectiveness*. However, when the market is more concerned with product and service features and up-to-date technology, a firm pursuing efficiency can find itself offering a low-priced product that few customers want. Thus two basic questions arise: (1) when to use an efficiency strategy and (2) if used, how far to push it before running into dangers of losing effectiveness. . . .

Whether to pursue an efficiency strategy depends on answers to questions such as,

1. Does the industry offer significant cost advantages from experience or scale (as in semi-conductors or chemicals)?
2. Are there significant market segments that will reward competitors with low prices?
3. Is the firm well equipped (financially, managerially, technologically, etc.) for or already geared up for strategies relying heavily on having the lowest cost . . . ?

If the answer is "yes" to all these questions, then "efficiency" strategies should probably be pursued.

Once it decided to pursue an "efficiency" strategy a firm must guard against going so far that it loses effectiveness, primarily through inability to respond to changes. For instance, experience-based strategies frequently require a highly specialized work force, facilities and organization, making it difficult to respond to changes in consumer demand, to respond to competitors' innovations, or to initiate them. In addition, large-scale plants are vulnerable to changes in process technology, and the heavy cost of operation below capacity.

For example, Ford's Motel T automobile ultimately suffered the consequences of inflexibility due to overemphasizing "efficiency" (Abernathy and Wayne, 1974). Ford followed a classic experience-based strategy; over time it slashed its product line to a single model (the Model T), built modern plants, pushed division of labor, introduced the continuous assembly line, obtained economies in purchased parts through high volume, backward integrated, increased mechanization, and cut prices as costs fell. The lower prices increased Ford's share of a growing market to a high of 55.4% by 1921.

In the meantime, consumer demand began shifting to heavier, closed-body cars and to more comfort. Ford's chief rival, General Motors, had the flexibility to respond quickly with new designs. Ford responded by adding features to its existing standard design. While the features softened the inroads of GM, the basic Model T design, upon which Ford's "efficiency" strategy was based, inadequately met the market's new performance standards. To make matters worse, the turmoil in production due to constant design changes slowed experience-based efficiency gains. Finally Ford was forced, at enormous cost, to close for a whole year beginning May 1927 while it retooled to introduce its Model A. Hence experience or scale-based *efficiency* was carried too far and thus it ultimately limited *effectiveness* to meet consumer needs, to innovate, and to respond.

Thus the challenge is to decide when to emphasize efficiency and when to emphasize effectiveness, and further to design efficiency strategies that maintain effectiveness and vice versa. . . .

THE PROFESSIONAL CONTEXT

While most large organizations draw on a variety of experts to get their jobs done, there has been a growing interest in recent years in those organizations whose work, because it is highly complex, is organized primarily around experts. These range from hospitals, universities, and research centers to consulting firms, space agencies, and biomedical companies.

This context is a rather unusual one, at least when judged against the more traditional contexts discussed in previous chapters. Both its strategic processes and its structures tend to take on forms quite different from those presented earlier. Organizations of experts, in fact, seem to divide themselves into two somewhat different contexts. In one, the experts work in rapidly changing situations that demand a good deal of collaborative innovation (as in the biotechnology or semiconductor fields); in the other, experts work more or less alone in more stable situations involving slower-changing bodies of skill or knowledge (as in law, university teaching, and accounting). This chapter takes up the latter, under the label of the "professional" context; the next chapter discusses the former under the label of "innovation."

We open this chapter with a description of the type of organization that seems best suited to the context of the more stable application of expertise. Drawn from Mintzberg's work, primarily his original description of "professional bureaucracy," it looks at the structure of the professional organization, including its important characteristic of "pigeonholing" work, the management of professionals, the unusual nature of strategy in such organizations (drawing from a paper Mintzberg coauthored with Cynthia Hardy, Ann Langley, and Janet Rose), and some issues associated with these organizations.

The second reading in this chapter, written by David Maister and originally published in the *Sloan Management Review*, focuses on one particular instance of the professional context, but one that has become an increasingly important career option for management students: the professional service firm. Maister describes how companies in businesses like consulting, investment banking, accounting, architecture, and law manage the interactions between revenue generation, compensation, and staffing to ensure long-term balanced growth.

Overall, these two readings suggest that the traditional concepts of managing and organization simply do not work as we move away from conventional mass production—which has long served as the model for "one best way" concepts in management. Whether it be highly expert work in general or service work subjected to new technologies and skills in particular, our thinking has to be opened up to some very different needs. Peter Drucker has, in a widely discussed article ("The Coming of the New Organization," *Harvard Business Review*, January–February 1988), argued the case that work in general is becoming more skilled and so structures of organizations in general are moving toward what we would call the professional form. While we would not go that far—we maintain our "contingency" view of different needs for different contexts—we do believe this is becoming a much more important form of organization.

Because so many MBAs go into these kinds of organizations—and because of the expanding importance of managing professional intellect—we have expanded the number of cases with the theme. Students and executives will find the Andersen Consulting (Europe), PR&D, The New York Times Company, Orbital Engine Company, and NovaCare, Inc., cases offer challenging and exciting examples of these new concepts. Microsoft Corporation (B), Honda Motor Company 1994, Sony Entertainment, TCG, Ltd./Thermo Electron, and the Hewlett Packard Company cases illustrate some of the more profound issues managers face as they attempt to manage in multicultural settings where professionals must interface with more creative or innovative units.

▼ READING 11.1   THE PROFESSIONAL ORGANIZATION*

by Henry Mintzberg

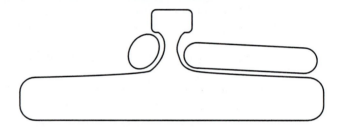

The Basic Structure

An organization can be bureaucratic without being centralized. This happens when its work is complex, requiring that it be carried out and controlled by professionals, yet at the same time remains stable, so that the skills of those professionals can be perfected through standardized operating programs. The structure takes on the form of professional bureaucracy, which is common in universities, general hospitals, public accounting firms, social work agencies, and firms doing fairly routine engineering or craft work. All rely on the skills and knowledge of their operating professionals to function; all produce standardized products or services.

THE WORK OF THE PROFESSIONAL OPERATORS

Here again we have a tightly knit configuration of the attributes of structure. Most important, the professional organization relies for coordination on the standardization of skills, which is achieved primarily through formal training. It hires duly trained specialists—professionals—for the operating core, then gives them considerable control over their own work.

Control over their work means that professionals work relatively independently of their colleagues but closely with the clients they serve—doctors treating their own patients and accountants who maintain personal contact with the companies whose books they audit. Most of the necessary coordination among the operating professionals is then han-

* Adapted from *The Structuring of Organizations* (Prentice Hall, 1979), Chap. 19 on "The Professional Bureaucracy"; also *Power In and Around Organizations* (Prentice Hall, 1983), Chap. 22 on "The Meritocracy"; the material on strategy formation from "Strategy Formation in the University Setting," coauthored with Cynthia Hardy, Ann Langley, and Janet Rose, in J. L. Bess (ed.) *College and University Organization* (New York University Press, 1984). A chapter similar to this one appeared in *Mintzberg on Management: Inside Our Strange World of Organizations* (Free Press, 1989).

dled automatically by their set skills and knowledge—in effect, by what they have learned to expect from each other. During an operation as long and as complex as open-heart surgery, "very little needs to be said [between the anesthesiologist and the surgeon] preceding chest opening and during the procedure on the heart itself . . . [most of the operation is] performed in absolute silence" (Gosselin, 1978). The point is perhaps best made in reverse by the cartoon that shows six surgeons standing around a patient on an operating table with one saying, "Who opens?"

Just how standardized the complex work of professionals can be is illustrated in a paper read by Spencer before a meeting of the International Cardiovascular Society. Spencer notes that an important feature of surgical training is "repetitive practice" to evoke "an automatic reflex." So automatic, in fact, that this doctor keeps a series of surgical "cookbooks" in which he lists, even for "complex" operations, the essential steps as chains of thirty to forty symbols on a single sheet, to "be reviewed mentally in sixty to 120 seconds at some time during the day preceding the operation" (1976:1179, 1182).

But no matter how standardized the knowledge and skills, their complexity ensures that considerable discretion remains in their application. No two professionals—no two surgeons or engineers or social workers—ever apply them in exactly the same way. Many judgments are required.

Training, reinforced by indoctrination, is a complicated affair in the professional organization. The initial training typically takes place over a period of years in a university or special institution, during which the skills and knowledge of the profession are formally programmed into the students. There typically follows a long period of on-the-job training, such as internship in medicine or articling in accounting, where the formal knowledge is applied and the practice of skills perfected. On-the-job training also completes the process of indoctrination, which began during the formal education. As new knowledge is generated and new skills develop, of course (so it is hoped) the professional upgrades his or her expertise.

All that training is geared to one goal, the internalization of the set procedures, which is what makes the structure technically bureaucratic (structure defined earlier as relying on standardization for coordination). But the professional bureaucracy differs markedly from the machine bureaucracy. Whereas the latter generates its own standards—through its technostructure, enforced by its line managers—many of the standards of the professional bureaucracy originate outside its own structure, in the self-governing associations its professionals belong to with their colleagues from other institutions. These associations set universal standards, which they ensure are taught by the universities and are used by all the organizations practicing the profession. So whereas the machine bureaucracy relies on authority of a hierarchical nature—the power of office—the professional bureaucracy emphasizes authority of a professional nature—the power of expertise.

Other forms of standardization are, in fact, difficult to rely on in the professional organization. The work processes themselves are too complex to be standardized directly by analysts. One need only try to imagine a work-study analyst following a cardiologist on rounds or timing the activities of a teacher in a classroom. Similarly, the outputs of professional work cannot easily be measured and so do not lend themselves to standardization. Imagine a planner trying to define a cure in psychiatry, the amount of learning that takes place in a classroom, or the quality of an accountant's audit. Likewise, direct supervision and mutual adjustment cannot be relied upon for coordination, for both impede professional autonomy.

THE PIGEONHOLING PROCESS

To understand how the professional organization functions at the operating level, it is helpful to think of it as a set of standard programs—in effect, the repertoire of skills the professionals stand ready to use—that are applied to known situations, called contingencies, also standardized. As Weick notes of one case in point, "schools are in the business of building and maintaining categories (1976:8). The process is sometimes known as *pigeonholing*. In this regard, the professional has two basic tasks: (1) to categorize, or "diagnose," the client's need in terms of one of the contingencies, which indicates which standard program to apply, and (2) to apply, or execute, that program. For example, the management consultant carries a bag of standard acronymic tricks: MBO, MIS, LRP, OD. The client with information needs gets MIS; the one with managerial conflicts, OD. Such pigeonholing, of course, simplifies matters enormously; it is also what enables each professional to work in a relatively autonomous manner.

It is in the pigeonholing process that the fundamental differences among the machine organization, the professional organization, and the innovative organization (to be discussed next) can best be seen. The machine organization is a single-purpose structure. Presented with a stimulus, it executes its one standard sequence of programs, just as we kick when tapped on the knee. No diagnosis is involved. In the professional organization, diagnosis is a fundamental task, but one highly circumscribed. The organization seeks to match a predetermined contingency to a standardized program. Fully open-ended diagnosis—that which seeks a creative solution to a unique problem—requires the innovative form of organization. No standard contingencies or programs can be relied upon there.

THE ADMINISTRATIVE STRUCTURE

Everything we have discussed so far suggests that the operating core is the key part of the professional organization. The only other part that is fully elaborated is the support staff, but that is focused very much on serving the activities of the operating core. Given the high cost of the professionals, it makes sense to back them up with as much support as possible. Thus, universities have printing facilities, faculty clubs, alma mater funds, publishing houses, archives, libraries, computer facilities, and many, many other support units.

The technostructure and middle-line management are not highly elaborated in the professional organization. They can do little to coordinate the professional work. Moreover, with so little need for direct supervision of, or mutual adjustment among, the professionals, the operating units can be very large. For example, the McGill Faculty of Management functions effectively with 50 professors under a single manager, its dean, and the rest of the university's academic hierarchy is likewise thin.

Thus, the diagram at the beginning of this chapter shows the professional organization, in terms of our logo, as a flat structure with a thin middle line, a tiny technostructure, but a fully elaborated support staff. All these characteristics are reflected in the organigram of a university hospital, shown in Figure 1.

Coordination within the administrative structure is another matter, however. Because these configurations are so decentralized, the professionals not only control their own work but they also gain much collective control over the administrative decisions that affect them—decisions, for example, to hire colleagues, to promote them, and to distribute resources. This they do partly by doing some of the administrative work themselves (most university professors, for example, sit on various administrative committees) and partly by ensuring that important administrative posts are staffed by professionals or at least sympathetic people appointed with the professionals' blessing. What emerges, therefore, is a rather democratic administrative structure. But because the administrative work requires mutual adjustment for coordination among the various people involved, task forces and especially standing committees abound at this level, as is in fact suggested in Figure 1.

Because of the power of their professional operators, these organizations are sometimes described as inverse pyramids, with the professional operators on top and the administrators down below to serve them—to ensure that the surgical facilities are kept clean and the

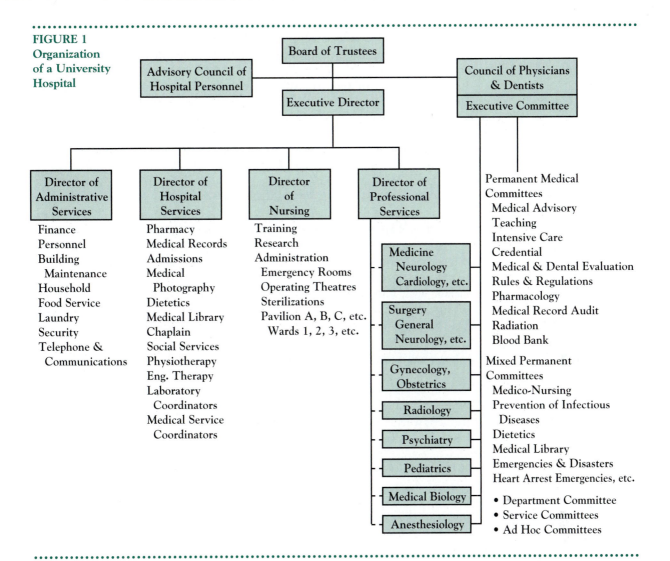

FIGURE 1
Organization of a University Hospital

Board of Trustees

Advisory Council of Hospital Personnel

Council of Physicians & Dentists

Executive Director

Executive Committee

Director of Administrative Services
Finance
Personnel
Building
  Maintenance
Household
Food Service
Laundry
Security
Telephone &
  Communications

Director of Hospital Services
Pharmacy
Medical Records
Admissions
Medical
  Photography
Dietetics
Medical Library
Chaplain
Social Services
Physiotherapy
Eng. Therapy
Laboratory
  Coordinators
Medical Service
  Coordinators

Director of Nursing
Training
Research
Administration
  Emergency Rooms
  Operating Theatres
  Sterilizations
  Pavilion A, B, C, etc.
  Wards 1, 2, 3, etc.

Director of Professional Services

Medicine
Neurology
Cardiology, etc.

Surgery
General
Neurology, etc.

Gynecology,
Obstetrics

Radiology

Psychiatry

Pediatrics

Medical Biology

Anesthesiology

Permanent Medical Committees
  Medical Advisory
  Teaching
  Intensive Care
  Credential
  Medical & Dental Evaluation
  Rules & Regulations
  Pharmacology
  Medical Record Audit
  Radiation
  Blood Bank

Mixed Permanent Committees
  Medico-Nursing
  Prevention of Infectious
    Diseases
  Dietetics
  Medical Library
  Emergencies & Disasters
  Heart Arrest Emergencies, etc.

• Department Committee
• Service Committees
• Ad Hoc Committees

classrooms well supplied with chalk. Such a description slights the power of the administrators of professional work, however, although it may be an accurate description of those who manage the support units. For the support staff—often more numerous than the professional staff, but generally less skilled—there is no democracy in the professional organization, only the oligarchy of the professionals. Such support units as housekeeping in the hospital or printing in the university are likely to be managed tightly from the top, in effect as machinelike enclaves within the professional configuration. Thus, what frequently emerges in the professional organization are parallel and separate administrative hierarchies, one democratic and bottom-up for the professionals, a second machinelike and top-down for the support staff.

THE ROLES OF THE ADMINISTRATORS OF PROFESSIONAL WORK

Where does all this leave the administrators of the professional hierarchy, the executive directors and chiefs of the hospitals and the presidents and deans of the universities? Are they powerless? Compared with their counterparts in the entrepreneurial and machine organizations, they certainly lack a good deal of power. But that is far from the whole story.

The administrator of professional work may not be able to control the professionals directly, but he or she does perform a series of roles that can provide considerable indirect power.

First, this administrator spends much time handling disturbances in the structure. The pigeonholing process is an imperfect one at best, leading to all kinds of jurisdictional disputes between the professionals. Who should perform mastectomies in the hospitals, surgeons who look after cutting or gynecologists who look after women? Seldom, however, can one administrator impose a solution on the professionals involved in a dispute. Rather, various administrators must often sit down together and negotiate a solution on behalf of their constituencies.

Second, the administrators of professional work—especially those at higher levels—serve in key roles at the boundary of the organization, between the professionals inside and the influencers outside: governments, client associations, benefactors, and so on. On the one hand, the administrators are expected to protect the professionals' autonomy, to "buffer" them from external pressures. On the other hand, they are expected to woo those outsiders to support the organization, both morally and financially. And that often leads the outsiders to expect these administrators, in turn, to control the professionals, in machine bureaucratic ways. Thus, the external roles of the manager—maintaining liaison contacts, acting as figurehead and spokesman in a public relations capacity, negotiating with outside agencies—emerge as primary ones in the administration of professional work.

Some view the roles these administrators are called upon to perform as signs of weakness. They see these people as the errand boys of the professionals, or else as pawns caught in various tugs of war—between one professional and another, between support staffer and professional, between outsider and professional. In fact, however, these roles are the very sources of administrators' power. Power is, after all, gained at the locus of uncertainty, and that is exactly where the administrators of professionals sit. The administrator who succeeds in raising extra funds for his or her organization gains a say in how they are distributed; the one who can reconcile conflicts in favor of his or her unit or who can effectively buffer the professionals from external influence becomes a valued, and therefore powerful, member of the organization.

We can conclude that power in these structures does flow to those professionals who care to devote effort to doing administrative instead of professional work, so long as they do it well. But that, it should be stressed, is not laissez-faire power; the professional administrator maintains power only as long as the professionals perceive him or her to be serving their interests effectively.

Conditions of the Professional Organization

The professional form of organization appears wherever the operating work of an organization is dominated by skilled workers who use procedures that are difficult to learn yet are well defined. This means a situation that is both complex and stable—complex enough to require procedures that can be learned only through extensive training yet stable enough so that their use can become standardized.

Note that an elaborate technical system can work against this configuration. If highly regulating or automated, the professionals' skills might be amenable to rationalization, in other words, to be divided into simple, highly programmed steps that would destroy the basis for professional autonomy and thereby drive the structure to the machine form. And if highly complicated, the technical system would reduce the professionals' autonomy by forcing them to work in multidisciplinary teams, thereby driving the organization toward the innovative form. Thus the surgeon uses a scalpel, and the accountant a pencil. Both must be sharp, but both are otherwise simple and commonplace instruments. Yet both allow their users to perform independently what can be exceedingly complex functions.

The prime example of the professional configuration is the personal-service organization, at least the one with complex, stable work not reliant on a fancy technical system. Schools and universities, consulting firms, law and accounting offices, and social work agencies all rely on this form of organization, more or less, so long as they concentrate not on innovating in the solution of new problems but on applying standard programs to well-defined ones. The same seems to be true of hospitals, at least to the extent that their technical systems are simple. (In those areas that call for more sophisticated equipment—apparently a growing number, especially in teaching institutions—the hospital is driven toward a hybrid structure, with characteristics of the innovative form. But this tendency is mitigated by the hospital's overriding concern with safety. Only the tried and true can be relied upon, which produces a natural aversion to the looser innovative configuration.)

So far, our examples have come from the service sector. But the professional form can be found in manufacturing too, where the above conditions hold up. Such is the case of the craft enterprise, for example, the factory using skilled workers to produce ceramic products. The very term *craftsman* implies a kind of professional who learns traditional skills through long apprentice training and then is allowed to practice them free of direct supervision. Craft enterprises seem typically to have few administrators, who tend to work, in any event, alongside the operating personnel. The same would seem to be true for engineering work oriented not to creative design so much as to modification of existing dominant designs.

Strategy Formation in the Professional Organization

It is commonly assumed that strategies are formulated before they are implemented, that planning is the central process of formulation, and that structures must be designed to implement these strategies. At least this is what one reads in the conventional literature of strategic management. In the professional organization, these imperatives stand almost totally at odds with what really happens, leading to the conclusion either that such organizations are confused about how to make strategy, or else that the strategy writers are confused about how professional organizations must function. I subscribe to the latter explanation.

Using the definition of strategy as pattern in action, strategy formation in the professional organization takes on a new meaning. Rather than simply throwing up our hands at its resistance to formal strategic planning, or, at the other extreme, dismissing professional organizations as "organized anarchies" with strategy-making processes as mere "garbage cans" (March and Olsen, 1976) we can focus on how decisions and actions in such organizations order themselves into patterns over time.

Taking strategy as pattern in action, the obvious question becomes, which actions? The key area of strategy making in most organizations concerns the elaboration of the basic mission (the products or services offered to the public); in professional organizations, we shall argue, this is significantly controlled by individual professionals. Other important areas of strategy here include the inputs to the system (notably the choice of professional staff, the determination of clients, and the raising of external funds), the means to perform the mission (the construction of buildings and facilities, the purchase of research equipment, and so on), the structure and forms of governance (design of the committee system, the hierarchies, and so on), and the various means to support the mission.

Were professional organizations to formulate strategies in the conventional ways, central administrators would develop detailed and integrated plans about these issues. This sometimes happens, but in a very limited number of cases. Many strategic issues come under the direct control of individual professionals, while others can be decided neither by individual professionals nor by central administrators, but instead require the participation of a variety of people in a complex collective process. As illustrated in Figure 2, we examine in turn the decisions controlled by individual professionals, by central administrators, and by the collectivity.

DECISIONS MADE BY PROFESSIONAL JUDGMENT

Professional organizations are distinguished by the fact that the determination of the basic mission—the specific services to be offered and to whom—is in good part left to the judgment of professionals as individuals. In the university, for example, each professor has a good deal of control over what is taught and how, as well as what is researched and how. Thus the overall product-market strategy of McGill University must be seen as the composite of the individual teaching and research postures of its 1,200 professors.

That, however, does not quite constitute full autonomy, because there is a subtle but not insignificant constraint on that power. Professionals are left to decide on their own only because years of training have ensured that they will decide in ways generally accepted in their professions. Thus professors choose course contents and adopt teaching methods highly regarded by their colleagues, sometimes even formally sanctioned by their disciplines; they research subjects that will be funded by the granting agencies (which usually come under professional controls); and they publish articles acceptable to the journals refereed by their peers. Pushed to the limit, then, individual freedom becomes professional control. It may be explicit freedom from administrators, even from peers in other disciplines, but it is not implicit freedom from colleagues in their own discipline. Thus we use the label "professional judgment" to imply that while judgment may be the mode of choice, it is informed judgment, mightily influenced by professional training and affiliation.

DECISIONS MADE BY ADMINISTRATIVE FIAT

Professional expertise and autonomy, reinforced by the pigeonholing process, sharply circumscribe the capacity of central administrators to manage the professionals in the ways of conventional bureaucracy—through direct supervision and the designation of internal standards (rules, job descriptions, policies). Even the designation of standards of output or

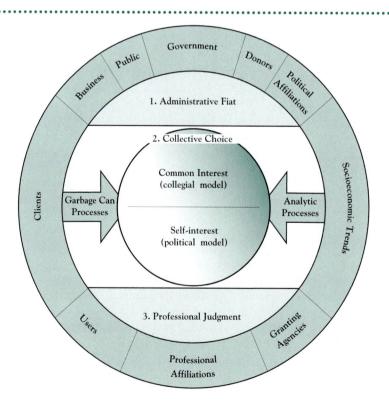

FIGURE 2
Three Levels of Decision Making in the Professional Organization

performance is discouraged by the intractable problem of operationalizing the goals of professional work.

Certain types of decisions, less related to the professional work per se, do however fall into the realm of what can be called administrative fiat, in other words, become the exclusive prerogative of the administrators. They include some financial decisions, for example, to buy and sell property and embark on fund-raising campaigns. Because many of the support services are organized in a conventional top-down hierarchy, they too tend to fall under the control of the central administration. Support services more critical to professional matters, however, such as libraries or computers in the universities, tend to fall into the realm of collective decision making, where the central administrators join the professionals in the making of choices.

Central administrators may also play a prominent role in determining the procedures by which the collective process functions: what committees exist, who gets nominated to them, and so on. It is the administrators, after all, who have the time to devote to administration. This role can give skillful administrators considerable influence, however indirect, over the decisions made by others. In addition, in times of crisis administrators may acquire more extensive powers, as the professionals become more inclined to defer to leadership to resolve the issues.

DECISIONS MADE BY COLLECTIVE CHOICE

Many decisions are, however, determined neither by administrators nor by individual professionals. Instead they are handled in interactive processes that combine professionals with administrators from a variety of levels and units. Among the most important of these decisions seem to be ones related to the definition, creation, design, and discontinuation of the pigeonholes, that is, the programs and departments of various kinds. Other important decisions here include the hiring and promotion of professionals and, in some cases, budgeting and the establishment and design of the interactive procedures themselves (if they do not fall under administrative fiat).

Decision making may be considered to involve the three phases of *identification* of the need for a decision, *development* of solutions, and *selection* of one of them. Identification seems to depend largely on individual initiative. Given the complexities of professional work and the rigidities of pigeonholing, change in this configuration is difficult to imagine without an initiating "sponsor" or "champion." Development may involve the same individual but often requires the efforts of collective task forces as well. And selection tends to be a fully interactive process, involving several layers of standing committees composed of professionals and administrators, and sometimes outsiders as well (such as government representatives). It is in this last phase that we find the full impact and complexity of mutual adjustment in the administration of professional organizations.

MODELS OF COLLECTIVE CHOICE

How do these interactive processes in fact work? Some writers have traditionally associated professional organizations with a *collegial* model, where decisions are made by a "community of individuals and groups, all of whom may have different roles and specialties, but who share common goals and objectives for the organization" (Taylor, 1983:18). *Common interest* is the guiding force, and decision making is therefore by consensus. Other writers instead propose a political model, in which the differences of interest groups are irreconcilable. Participants thus seek to serve their *self-interest,* and political factors become instrumental in determining outcomes.

Clearly, neither common interest nor self-interest will dominate decision processes all the time; some combination is naturally to be expected. Professionals may agree on goals yet conflict over how they should be achieved; alternatively, consensus can sometimes be achieved even where goals differ—Democrats do, after all, sometimes vote with Republicans in the U.S. Congress. In fact, we need to consider motivation, not just behavior, in order to distinguish collegiality from politics. Political success sometimes requires a collegial posture—one must cloak self-interest in the mantle of the common good. Likewise, collegial ends sometimes require political means. Thus, we should take as collegial any behavior that is *motivated* by a genuine concern for the good of the institution, and politics as any behavior driven fundamentally by self-interest (of the individual or his or her unit).

A third model that has been used to explain decision making in universities is the *garbage can*. Here decision making is characterized by "collections of choices looking for problems, issues and feelings looking for decision situations in which they may be aired, solutions looking for issues to which they might be an answer, and decision makers looking for work" (Cohen, March, and Olsen, 1972:1). Behavior is, in other words, nonpurposeful and often random, because goals are unclear and the means to achieve them problematic. Furthermore, participation is fluid because of the cost of time and energy. Thus, in place of the common interest of the collegial model and the self-interest of the political model, the garbage can model suggests a kind of *disinterest*.

The important question is not whether garbage can processes exist—we have all experienced them—but whether they matter. Do they apply to key issues or only to incidental ones? Of course, decisions that are not significant to anyone may well end up in the garbage can, so to speak. There is always someone with free time willing to challenge a proposal for the sake of so doing. But I have difficulty accepting that individuals to whom decisions are important do not invest the effort necessary to influence them. Thus, like common interest and self-interest, I conclude that disinterest neither dominates decision processes nor is absent from them.

Finally, *analysis* may be considered a fourth model of decision making. Here calculation is used, if not to select the best alternative, then at least to assess the acceptability of different ones. Such an approach seems consistent with the machine configuration, where a technostructure stands ready to calculate the costs and benefits of every proposal. But, in fact, analysis figures prominently in the professional configuration too, but here carried out mostly by professional operators themselves. Rational analysis structures arguments for communication and debate and enables champions and their opponents to support their respective positions. In fact, as each side seeks to pick holes in the position of the other, the real issues are more likely to emerge.

Thus, as indicated in Figure 2, the important collective decisions of the professional organization seem to be most influenced by collegial and political processes, with garbage can pressures encouraging a kind of haphazardness on one side (especially for less important decisions) and analytical interventions on the other side encouraging a certain rationality (serving as an invisible hand to keep the lid on the garbage can, so to speak!).

STRATEGIES IN THE PROFESSIONAL ORGANIZATION

Thus, we find here a very different process of strategy making, and very different resulting strategies, compared with conventional (especially machine) organizations. While it may seem difficult to create strategies in these organizations, due to the fragmentation of activity, the politics, and the garbage can phenomenon, in fact the professional organization is inundated with strategies (meaning patterning in its actions). The standardization of skills encourages patterning, as do the pigeonholing process and the professional affiliations. Collegiality promotes consistency of behavior; even politics works to resist changing existing patterns. As for the garbage can model, perhaps it just represents the unexplained variance in the system; that is, whatever is not understood looks to the outside observer like organized anarchy.

Many different people get involved in the strategy-making process here, including administrators and the various professionals, individually and collectively, so that the resulting strategies can be very fragmented (at the limit, each professional pursues his or her own product-market strategy). There are, of course, forces that encourage some overall cohesion in strategy too: the common forces of administrative fiat, the broad negotiations that take place in the collective process (for example, on new tenure regulations in a university), even the forces of habit and tradition, at the limit ideology, that can pervade a professional organization (such as hiring certain kinds of people or favoring certain styles of teaching or of surgery).

Overall, the strategies of the professional organization tend to exhibit a remarkable degree of stability. Major reorientations in strategy—"strategic revolutions"—are discouraged by the fragmentation of activity and the influence of the individual professionals and their outside associates. But at a narrower level, change is ubiquitous. Inside tiny pigeonholes, services are continually being altered, procedure redesigned, and clientele shifted, while in the collective process, pigeonholes are constantly being added and rearranged. Thus, the professional organization is, paradoxically, extremely stable at the broadest level and in a state of perpetual change at the narrowest one.

Some Issues Associated with the Professional Organization

The professional organization is unique among the different configurations in answering two of the paramount needs of contemporary men and women. It is democratic, disseminating its power directly to its workers (at least those lucky enough to be professional). And it provides them with extensive autonomy, freeing them even from the need to coordinate closely with their colleagues. Thus, the professional has the best of both worlds. He or she is attached to an organization yet is free to serve clients in his or her own way constrained only by the established standards of the profession.

The result is that professionals tend to emerge as highly motivated individuals, dedicated to their work and to the clients they serve. Unlike the machine organization, which places barriers between the operator and the client, this configuration removes them, allowing a personal relationship to develop. Moreover, autonomy enables the professionals to perfect their skills free of interference, as they repeat the same complex programs time after time.

But in these same characteristics, democracy and autonomy, lie the chief problems of the professional organization. For there is no evident way to control the work, outside of that exercised by the profession itself, no way, to correct deficiencies that the professionals choose to overlook. What they tend to overlook are the problems of coordination, of discretion, and of innovation that arise in these configurations.

PROBLEMS OF COORDINATION

The professional organization can coordinate effectively in its operating core only by relying on the standardization of skills. But that is a loose coordinating mechanism at best; it fails to cope with many of the needs that arise in these organizations. One need is to coordinate the work of professionals with that of support staffers. The professionals want to give the orders. But that can catch the support staffers between the vertical power of line authority and the horizontal power of professional expertise. Another need is to achieve overriding coordination among the professionals themselves. Professional organizations, at the limit, may be viewed as collections of independent individuals who come together only to draw on common resources and support services. Though the pigeonholing process facilitates this, some things inevitably fall through the cracks between the pigeonholes. But because the professional organization lacks any obvious coordinating mechanism to deal with these, they inevitably provoke a great deal of conflict. Much political blood is spilled in the continual reassessment of contingencies and programs that are either imperfectly conceived or artificially distinguished.

PROBLEMS OF DISCRETION

Pigeonholing raises another serious problem. It focuses most of the discretion in the hands of single professionals, whose complex skills, no matter how standardized, require the exercise of considerable judgment. Such discretion works fine when professionals are competent and conscientious. But it plays havoc when they are not. Inevitably, some professionals are simply lazy or incompetent. Others confuse the needs of their clients with the skills of their trade. They thus concentrate on a favored program to the exclusion of all others (like the psychiatrist who thinks that all patients, indeed all people, need psychoanalysis). Clients incorrectly sent their way get mistreated (in both senses of that word).

Various factors confound efforts to deal with this inversion of means and ends. One is that professionals are notoriously reluctant to act against their own, for example, to censure irresponsible behavior through their professional associations. Another (which perhaps helps to explain the first) is the intrinsic difficulty of measuring the outputs of professional work. When psychiatrists cannot even define the word *cure* or *healthy*, how are they to prove that psychoanalysis is better for schizophrenics than is chemical therapy?

Discretion allows professionals to ignore not only the needs of their clients but also those of the organization itself. Many professionals focus their loyalty on their profession, not on the place where they happen to practice it. But professional organizations have needs for loyalty too—to support their overall strategies, to staff their administrative committees, to see them through conflicts with the professional associations. Cooperation is crucial to the functioning of the administrative structure, yet many professionals resist it furiously.

PROBLEMS OF INNOVATION

In the professional organization, major innovation also depends on cooperation. Existing programs may be perfected by the single professional, but new ones usually cut across the established specialties—in essence, they require a rearrangement of the pigeonholes—and so call for collective action. As a result, the reluctance of the professionals to cooperate with each other and the complexity of the collective processes can produce resistance to innovation. These are, after all, professional *bureaucracies*, in essence, performance structures designed to perfect given programs in stable environments, not problem-solving structures to create new programs for unanticipated needs.

The problems of innovation in the professional organization find their roots in convergent thinking, in the deductive reasoning of the professional who sees the specific situation in terms of the general concept. That means new problems are forced into old pigeonholes, as is excellently illustrated in Spencer's comments: "All patients developing significant complications or death among our three hospitals . . . are reported to a central office with a narrative description of the sequence of events, with reports varying in length from a third to an entire page." And six to eight of these cases are discussed in the one-hour weekly "mortality-morbidity" conferences, including presentation of it by the surgeon and "questions and comments" by the audience (978:118). An "entire" page and ten minutes of discussion for a case with "significant complications"! Maybe that is enough to list the symptoms and slot them into pigeonholes. But it is hardly enough even to begin to think about creative solutions. As Lucy once told Charlie Brown, great art cannot be done in half an hour; it takes at least 45 minutes!

The fact is that great art and innovative problem solving require *inductive* reasoning—that is, the inference of the new general solution from the particular experience. And that kind of thinking is *divergent*; it breaks away from old routines or standards rather than perfecting existing ones. And that flies in the face of everything the professional organization is designed to do.

PUBLIC RESPONSES TO THESE PROBLEMS

What responses do the problems of coordination, discretion, and innovation evoke? Most commonly, those outside the profession see the problems as resulting from a lack of external control of the professional and the profession. So they do the obvious: try to control the work through other, more traditional means. One is direct supervision, which typically means imposing an intermediate level of supervision to watch over the professionals. But we already discussed why this cannot work for jobs that are complex. Another is to try to standardize the work or its outputs. But we also discussed why complex work cannot be formalized by rules, regulations, or measures of performance. All these types of controls really do, by transferring the responsibility for the service from the professional to the administrative structure, is destroy the effectiveness of the work. It is not the government that educates the student, not even the school system or the school itself; it is not the hospital that delivers the baby. These things are done by the individual professional. If that professional is incompetent, no plan or rule fashioned in the technostructure, no order from any administrator or government official, can ever make him or her competent. But such plans, rules, and orders can impede the competent professional from providing his or her service effectively.

Are there then no solutions for a society concerned about the performance of its professional organizations? Financial control of them and legislation against irresponsible professional behavior are obviously in order. But beyond that solutions must grow from a recognition of professional work for what it is. Change in the professional organization does not *sweep* in from new administrators taking office to announce wide reforms, or from government officials intent on bringing the professionals under technocratic control. Rather, change *seeps* in through the slow process of changing the professionals—changing who enters the profession in the first place, what they learn in its professional schools (norms as well as skills and knowledge), and thereafter how they upgrade their skills. Where desired changes are resisted, society may be best off to call on its professionals' sense of public responsibility or, failing that, to bring pressure on the professional associations rather than on the professional bureaucracies.

▼ READING 11.2 BALANCING THE PROFESSIONAL SERVICE FIRM*

by David H. Maister

The topic of managing professional service firms (PSF) (including law, consulting, investment banking, accountancy, architecture, engineering, and others) has been relatively neglected by management researchers. . . . Yet in recent years large (if not giant) PSFs have emerged in most of the professional service industries. . . .

The professional service firm is the ultimate embodiment of that familiar phrase "Our assets are our people." Frequently, a PSF tends to sell to its clients the services of particular

*Reprinted with deletions from the *Sloan Management Review* (Fall, 1982), pp. 15–29, by permission of publisher. Copyright 1982 by the Sloan Management Review Association, all rights reserved.

individuals (or a team of such individuals) more than the services of the firm. Professional services usually involve a high degree of interaction with the client, together with a high degree of customization. Both of these characteristics demand that the firm attract (and retain) highly skilled individuals. The PSF, therefore, competes in two markets simultaneously: the "output" market for its services and the "input" market for its productive resources —the professional work force. It is the need to balance the often conflicting demands and constraints imposed by these two markets that constitutes the special challenge for managers of the professional service firm.

This article explores the interaction of these forces inside the professional service firm, and examines some of the major variables that firm management can attempt to manipulate in order to bring these forces into balance. The framework employed for this examination is shown in Figure 1, which illustrates the proposition that balancing the demands of the two markets is accomplished through the firm's economic and organizational structures. All four of these elements—the two markets and the two structures—are tightly interrelated. By examining each in turn, we shall attempt to identify the major variables which form the links shown in Figure 1. First, the article will examine the typical organizational structure of the firm; second, it will explore the economic structure and its relation to other elements. It shall then consider the market for professional labor, and finally discuss the market for the firm's services. As we shall see, successful PSF management is a question of balance among the four elements of Figure 1.

THE ORGANIZATIONAL STRUCTURE OF THE PSF

The archetypal structure of the professional service firm is an organization containing three professional levels which serve as a normal or expected career path. In a consulting organization, these levels might be labeled junior consultant, manager, and vice-president. In a CPA firm they might be referred to as staff accountant, manager, and partner. Law firms

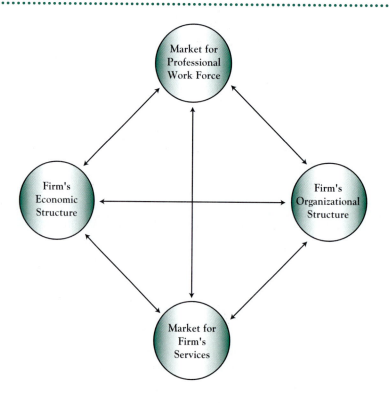

FIGURE 1
Framework for Analyzing the PSF

Market for Professional Work Force

Firm's Economic Structure

Firm's Organizational Structure

Market for Firm's Services

tend to have only two levels, associate and partner, although there is an increasing tendency in large law firms to formally recognize what has long been an informal distinction between junior and senior partners. Whatever the precise structure, nearly all PSFs have the pyramid form shown in Figure 2.

There is nothing magical about the common occurrence of three levels (a greater or lesser number may be found), but it is instructive to consider other organizations that have this pattern. One example is the university which has assistant professors, associate professors, and full professors. These ranks may be signs of status as well as function (reminding us of another three-level status structure: the common people, the peerage, and royalty). Another analogy is found in the organization of the medieval craftsman's shop which had apprentices, journeymen, and master craftsmen. Indeed, the early years of an individual's association with a PSF are usually viewed as an apprenticeship: the senior craftsmen repay the hard work and assistance of the juniors by teaching them their craft.

PROJECT TEAM STRUCTURE

What determines the shape or architecture of the organization—the relative mix of juniors, managers, and seniors that the organization requires? Fundamentally, this depends on the nature of the professional services that the firm provides, and how these services are delivered. Because of their customized nature, most professional activities are organized on a project basis: the professional service firms are the job shops of the service sector. The project nature of the work means that there are basically three major activities in the delivery of professional services: client relations, project management, and the performance of the detailed professional tasks.

In most PSFs, primary responsibility for these three tasks is allocated to the three levels of the organization: seniors (partners or vice-presidents) are responsible for client relations; managers, for the day-to-day supervision and coordination of projects; and juniors, for the many technical tasks necessary to complete the study. In the vernacular, the three levels are "the finders, the minders and the grinders" of the business.* Naturally, such an allocation of

FIGURE 2
The Professional Pyramid

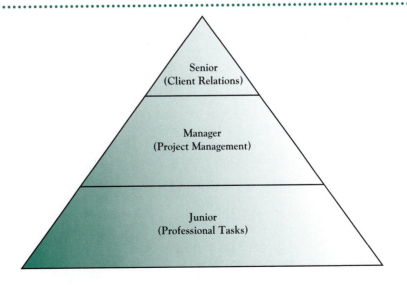

Senior
(Client Relations)

Manager
(Project Management)

Junior
(Professional Tasks)

---

* This characteristic is, of course, simplified. Additional "levels" or functions can be identified at both the top and the bottom of the pyramid. To the top we can add those individuals responsible for managing the *firm* (rather than managing projects). At the bottom of the pyramid lie both "nonprofessional" support staff and trainees.

tasks need not (indeed, should not) be as rigid as this suggests. In a well-run PSF, juniors are increasingly given "manager" tasks to perform (in order to test their competence and worthiness to be promoted to the manager level), and managers are gradually given tasks that enable them to develop client-relations skills to prepare for promotion to the senior level. Nevertheless, it is still meaningful to talk of "senior tasks," "manager tasks," and "junior tasks."

CAPACITY PLANNING

The required shape of the PSF is thus primarily influenced by the mix of client relations, project management, and professional tasks involved in the firm's projects. If the PSF is a job shop, then its professional staff members are its "machines" (productive resources). As with any job shop, a balance must be established between the types of work performed and the number of different types of "machines" (people) that are required. The PSF is a "factory," and the firm must plan its capacity. . . .

THE ECONOMICS OF THE PSF

Most professional service firms are partnerships; some are corporations. Regardless of the precise form, however, certain regularities in the economic structure are observable. For example, since most PSFs have few fixed assets, they only require capital to fund accounts receivable and other working capital items. Consequently, the vast majority of revenues are disbursed in the form of salaries, bonuses, and net partnership profits. A typical division of revenues might be 33 percent for professional salaries, 33 percent for support staff and overhead, and 33 percent for senior (or shareholder) salary compensation. However, in some PSFs, partnership salary and profits might rise to 50 percent or more, usually corresponding to lower support staff and overhead costs.

GENERATING REVENUES

If revenues are typically disbursed in this way, how are they generated? . . . The relevant variable is, of course, the billing rate—the hourly charge to clients for the services of individuals at different levels of the hierarchy. The ratio between the lowest and highest rates in some firms can exceed 3 or 4 to 1. The "rewards of partnership" come only in part from the high rates that top professionals can charge their clients. Partners' rewards are also derived, in large part, from the firm's ability, through its project team structure, to *leverage* the professional skills of the seniors with the efforts of juniors. As the managing senior of a top consulting firm observed, "How is it that a young MBA, straight from graduate school, can give advice to top corporate officers?" The answer lies in the synergy of the PSF's project team. Acting independently, the juniors could not "bill out" the results of their efforts at the rates that can be charged by the PSF. The firm can obtain higher rates for the juniors' efforts because they are combined with the expertise and guidance of the seniors. . . .

THE BILLING MULTIPLE

It is also instructive to compare the net weighted billing rate to compensation levels within the firm. This (conventional) calculation is known as the billing multiple, and is calculated (for either the firm or an individual) as the billing rate per hour divided by the total compensation per hour. . . . The average multiple for most firms is between 2.5 and 4.

The appropriate billing multiple that the firm can achieve will, of course, be influenced by the added value that the firm provides and by the relative supply and demand conditions for the firm's services. The market for the firm's services will determine the fees it can command for a given project. The firm's costs will be determined by its ability to deliver the service with a "profitable" mix of junior, manager, and senior time. If the firm . . . can find a way to deliver the service with a higher proportion of juniors to seniors, it will be able to achieve lower costs and hence a higher multiple. The project team structure of the firm is, therefore, an important component of firm profitability.

The billing multiple is intimately related to the breakeven economics of the firm. If total professional salaries are taken as an amount $Y, and support staff and overhead cost approximate, say, an equivalent amount $Y, then breakeven will be attained when the firm bills $2Y. This could be attained by charging clients a multiple of 2 for professional services, but only if all available time was billed out. If the firm wishes to break even at 50 percent target utilization (a common figure in many PSFs), then the required net billing multiple will be 4. . . .

THE PSF AND THE MARKET FOR PROFESSIONAL LABOR

One of the key characteristics of the PSF is that the three levels (junior, manager, senior) constitute a well-defined career path. Individuals joining the organization normally begin at the bottom, with strong expectations of progressing through the organization at some pace agreed to (explicitly or implicitly) in advance. While this pace may not be a rigid one ("up or out in the X years"), both the individual and the organization usually share strong expectations about what constitutes a reasonable period of time. Individuals that are not promoted within this period will seek greener pastures elsewhere, either by their own choice or career ambitions or at the strong suggestion of those who do not consider them promotable. Intermediate levels in the hierarchy are not considered by the individual or the organization as career positions. It is this characteristic, perhaps more than any other, that distinguishes the PSF from other types of organizations.

PROMOTION POLICY

While there are many considerations that attract young professionals to a particular firm, career opportunities within the firm usually play a large role. Two dimensions of this rate of progress are important: the normal amount of time spent at each level before being considered for promotion and the "odds of making it" (the proportion promoted). These promotion policy variables perform an important screening function. Not all young professionals are able to develop the managerial and client-relations skills required at the higher levels. While good recruiting procedures may reduce the degree of screening required through the promotion process, they can rarely eliminate the need for the promotion process to serve this important function. The "risk of not making it" also serves the firm by placing pressure on junior personnel to work hard and succeed. This pressure can be an important motivating tool in light of the discretion which many PSF professionals have over their working schedules. . . .

ACCOMMODATING RAPID GROWTH

. . . What adjustments can be made to allow faster growth? Basically, there are four strategies. First, the firm can devote more attention and resources to its hiring process so that a higher proportion of juniors can be routinely promoted to managers. (In effect, this shifts the quality-of-personnel screen from the promotion system to the hiring system, where it is often more difficult and speculative.) Second, the firm can attempt to hasten the "apprenticeship" process through more formal training and professional development programs, rather than the "learn by example" and mentoring relationships commonly found in smaller firms and those growing at a more leisurely pace. In fact, it is the rate of growth, rather than the size of the firm, which necessitates formal development programs. . . .*

---

* Speeding the development of individuals so that the firm can grow faster is, of course, not the only role for formal training programs. They can also be a device to allow the firm to hire less (initially) qualified and hence lower wage individuals, thereby reducing its cost for juniors.

The third mechanism that the firm can adopt to accelerate its target growth rate is to make use of "lateral hires": bringing in experienced professionals at other than the junior level. In most PSFs, this strategy is avoided because of its adverse effect upon the morale of junior personnel, who tend to view such actions as reducing their own chances for promotion. Even if these have been accelerated by the fast growth rate, juniors will still tend to feel that they have been less than fairly dealt with.

Modifying the project team structure is the final strategy for accommodating rapid growth without throwing out of balance the relationships between organizational structure, promotion incentives, and economic structure. In effect, the firm would alter the mix of senior, manager, and junior time devoted to a project. This strategy will be discussed in a later section.

TURNOVER

. . . In most PSF industries, one or more firms can be identified that have a high target rate of turnover (or alternatively, choose to grow at less than their optimal rate). Yet individuals routinely join these organizations knowing that the odds of "making it" are very low. Such "churning" strategies have some clear disadvantages *and* benefits for the PSF itself. One of the benefits is that the firm's partners (or shareholders) can routinely earn the surplus value of the juniors without having to repay them in the form of promotion. The high turnover rate also allows a significant degree of screening so that only the "best" stay in the organization. Not surprisingly, firms following this strategy tend to be among the most prestigious in their industry.

This last comment gives us a clue as to why such firms are able to maintain this strategy over time. For many recruits, the experience, training, and association with a prestigious firm compensate for poor promotion opportunities. Young professionals view a short period of time at such a firm as a form of "post-postgraduate" degree, and often leave for prime positions they could not have achieved (as quickly) by another route. Indeed, most of the prestigious PSFs following this strategy not only encourage this, but also provide active "outplacement" assistance. Apart from the beneficial effects that such activities provide in recruiting the next generation of juniors, such "alumni/ae" are often the source of future business for the PSF when they recommend that their corporate employers hire their old firm (which they know and understand) over other competitors. The ability to place ex-staff in prestigious positions is one of the prerequisites of a successful churning strategy. . . .

THE MARKET FOR THE FIRM'S SERVICES

The final element in our model is the market for the firm's services. We have already explored some of the ways in which this market is linked to the firm's economic structure (through the billing rates the firm charges) and to the organizational structure (through the project team structure and target growth rate).

We must add to our model one of the most basic linkages in the dynamics of the PSF: the direct link between the market for professional labor and the market for the firm's services. The key variable that links these two markets is the quality of professional labor that the firm requires and can attract. Earlier, when we considered the factors that attract professionals to a given PSF, we omitted a major variable that often enters into the decision process: the types of projects undertaken by the firm. Top professionals are likely to be attracted to the firm that engages in exciting or challenging projects, or that provides opportunities for professional fulfillment and development. In turn, firms engaged in such projects *need* to attract the best professionals. It is, therefore, necessary to consider different types of professional service activity.

PROJECT TYPES

While there are many dimensions which may distinguish one type of professional service activity from another, one in particular is crucial: the degree of customization required in the delivery of the service. To explore this, we will characterize professional service projects into three types: "Brains," "Grey Hair," and "Procedure."

In the first type (Brains), the client's problem is likely to be extremely complex, perhaps at the forefront of professional or technical knowledge. The PSF that targets this market will be attempting to sell its services on the basis of the high professional craft of its staff. In essence, this firm's appeal to its market is "hire us because we're smart." The key elements of this type of professional service are creativity, innovation, and the pioneering of new approaches, concepts, or techniques—in effect, new solutions to new problems. [See next chapter on the innovative context.]

Grey Hair projects may require highly customized "output," but they usually involve a lesser degree of innovation and creativity than a Brains' project. The general nature of the problem is familiar, and the activities necessary to complete the project may be similar to those performed on other projects. Clients with Grey Hair problems seek out PSFs with experience in their particular type of problem. The PSF sells its knowledge, its experience, and its judgment. In effect, it is saying: "Hire us because we have been through this before. We have practice in solving this type of problem."

The third type of project (Procedure) usually involves a well-recognized and familiar type of problem, at least within the professional community. While some customization is still required, the steps necessary to accomplish this are somewhat programmatic. Although clients may have the ability and resources to perform the work themselves, they may turn to the PSF because it can perform the service more efficiently; because it is an outsider; or because the clients' staff capabilities may be employed better elsewhere. In essence, the PSF is selling its procedures, its efficiency, and its availability: "Hire us because we know how to do this and can deliver it effectively."

PROJECT TEAM STRUCTURE

One of the most significant differences between the three types of projects is the project team structure required to deliver the firm's services. Brains projects are usually denoted by an extreme job-shop operation, involving highly skilled and highly paid professionals. Few procedures are routinizable: each project is a "one-off." Accordingly, the opportunities for leveraging the top professionals with juniors are relatively limited. Even though such projects may involve significant data collection and analysis (usually done by juniors), even these activities cannot be clearly specified in advance and require the involvement of at least middle-level (project management) professionals on a continuous basis. Consequently, the ratio of junior time to middle-level and senior time on Brains projects tends to be low. The project team structure of a firm with a high proportion of Brains projects will tend to have a relatively low emphasis on juniors, with a corresponding impact on the shape of the organization.

Since the problems to be addressed in Grey Hair projects are somewhat familiar, some of the tasks to be performed (particularly the early ones) are known in advance and can be specified and delegated. More juniors can be employed to accomplish these tasks, which are then assembled and jointly evaluated at some middle stage of the process. Unlike the "pure job-shop" nature of Brains projects, the appropriate process to create and deliver a Grey Hair project more closely resembles a disconnected assembly line.

Procedure projects usually involve the highest proportion of junior time relative to senior time, and hence imply a different organizational shape for firms that specialize in such projects. The problems to be addressed in such projects, and the steps necessary to complete the analysis, diagnosis, and conclusions, are usually sufficiently well established so that they can be easily delegated to junior staff (with supervision). Whereas in Grey Hair projects senior or middle-level staff must evaluate the results of one stage of the project before deciding how to proceed, in Procedure projects the range of possible outcomes for some steps may be so well known that the appropriate responses can be "programmed." The operating procedure takes on even more of the characteristics of an assembly line.

While the three categories described are only points along a spectrum of project types, it is a simple task in any PSF industry to identify types of problems that fit these categories. The choice that the firm makes in its mix of project types is one of the most important variables available to balance the firm. As we have shown, this choice determines the firm's project team structure, thereby influencing significantly the economic and organizational structures of the firm.

CONCLUSIONS: BALANCING THE PROFESSIONAL SERVICE FIRM

Figure 3 summarizes our review of the four major elements involved in balancing the PSF and the major variables linking these elements. What may we conclude from this review? Our discussion has shown that the four elements are, indeed, tightly linked. The firm cannot change one element without making corresponding changes in one or more of the other three. . . .

In performing these balance analyses, the firm must distinguish between the "levers" (variables that it controls) and the "rocks" (variables substantially constrained by the forces of the market). . . .

Perhaps the most significant management variable is the mix of projects undertaken and the implications this has for the project team structure. This variable is a significant force in influencing the economics of the firm, its organizational structure, and both markets. The project team structure as defined in this article (i.e., the *average* or typical pro-

FIGURE 3
Balancing the PSF

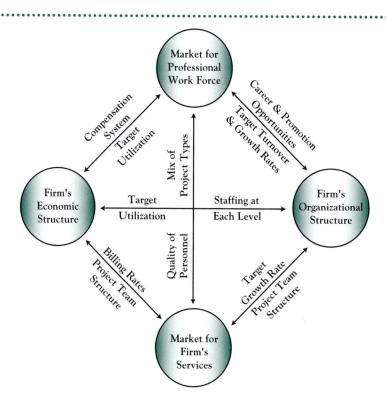

portion of time required from professionals at different levels) has not been a variable that is routinely monitored by PSF management. However, as we have shown, its role in balancing the firm is critical.

It is possible, and not uncommon, for the firm's project team structure to change over time. If it is possible to deliver the firm's services with a greater proportion of juniors, this will reduce the costs of the project. Competition in the market will, over time, require the firm to seek lower costs for projects, thus creating opportunities for more juniors to be used on projects that required a high proportion of senior time in the past. Projects that, in the past, had Brains or Grey Hair characteristics may be accomplished as Procedure projects in future years.*

When considering new projects to undertake, it is usually more profitable for the firm to engage in a project similar to one recently performed for a previous client. The knowledge, expertise, and basic approaches to the problem that were developed (often through significant personal and financial investment) can be capitalized upon by applying them to a similar or related problem. Frequently, the second project can be billed out to the client at a similar (or only slightly lower) rate, since the client perceives (and receives) something equally custom-tailored: the solution to his or her problem. However, the savings in PSF costs in delivering this customization are not all shared with the client (if, indeed, any are). The firm thus makes its most money by "leading the market": selling a service with reproducible, standardizable elements as a fully customized service at a fully customized price.

Unfortunately, even before the market catches up and refuses to bear the fully customized price, the firm may encounter an internal behavior problem. While it is in the best interest of the *firm* to undertake similar or repetitive engagements, often this does not coincide with the desires of the *individuals* involved. Apart from any reasons of status, financial rewards, or fulfillment derived from serving the clients' needs, most individuals join PSFs to experience the professional challenge and variety and to avoid routine repetition. While individuals may be content to undertake a similar project for the second or third time, they will not be for the fourth, sixth, or eighth. Yet it is in the interest of the firm (particularly if the market has not yet caught up) to take advantage of the experience and expertise that it has acquired. One solution, of course, is to convert the past experience and expertise of the individual into the expertise of the firm by accepting a similar project, but utilizing a greater proportion of juniors on it. Besides requiring a lesser commitment of time from the experienced seniors, this device serves to train the juniors.

For all these reasons, we might suspect that the proportion of juniors to seniors required by the firm *in a particular practice area* will tend to increase over time. If this is allowed to proceed without corresponding adjustments in the range of practice areas, the project team structure of the firms will be altered, causing significant impacts on the economics and organization of the firm. The dangers of failing to monitor the project team structure are thus clearly revealed. Examples of this failure abound in many PSF industries. One consulting firm that learned how to increasingly utilize junior professionals began to aggressively hire new junior staff. After a reasonable period of time for the promotion decision, the firm realized that, at its current growth rate, it could not promote its "normal" proportion of promotion candidates: it did not need as many partners and managers in relation to the number of juniors it now had. Morale and productivity in the junior ranks suffered. . . . Successful PSF management is a question of balance.

---

*This argument suggests that there is a "life-cycle" to professional "products" in the same way that such cycles exist for tangible products.

THE INNOVATION CONTEXT

Although often seen as a high-technology event involving inventor-entrepreneurs, innovation may, of course, occur in high- or low-technology, product or service, large or small organizational situations. Innovation may be thought of as the *first reduction to practice* of an idea in a culture. The more radical the idea, the more traumatic and profound its impact will tend to be. But there are no absolutes. Whatever is newest and most difficult to understand becomes the "high technology" of its age. As Jim Utterback of MIT is fond of pointing out, the delivery of ice was high technology at the turn of the century, later it was the production of automobiles. By the same token, fifty years from now, electronics may be considered mundane.

Our focus here, however, is not on innovation per se, but on the innovation *context*; that is, the situation in which steady or frequent innovation of a complex nature is an intrinsic part of the organization and the industry segment in which it chooses to operate. Such organizations depend, not just on a single entrepreneurial individual, but on teams of experts molded together.

The innovation context is one in which the organization often must deal with complex technologies or systems under conditions of dynamic change. Typically, major innovations require that a variety of experts work toward a common goal, often led by a single champion or a small group of committed individuals. Much has been learned from research in recent years on such organizations. While this knowledge may seem less structured than that of previous chapters, several dominant themes have emerged.

This chapter opens with a description of the fifth of Mintzberg's structures, here titled the innovative organization, but also referred to as "adhocracy." This is the structure that, as noted, achieves its effectiveness by being inefficient. This reading probes into the unusual ways in which strategies evolve in the context of work that is both highly complex and highly dynamic. Here we see the full flowering of the notion of emergent strategy, culminating in a description of a "grassroots" model of the process. We also see here a strategic leadership less concerned with formulating and then implementing strategies than with managing a process through which strategies almost seem to *form* by themselves.

The second reading of this chapter, James Brian Quinn's "Managing Innovation: Controlled Chaos" (another winner of a McKinsey prize for the best *Harvard Business Review* article), suggests how the spirit of adhocracy and strategy formation as a learning process can be integrated with some of the formal strategic processes of large organizations. To achieve innovativeness, other authors have advocated adhocracy with little or no reliance on planning. Quinn suggests that blending broad strategy planning with a consciously structured adhocracy gives better results. This reading also brings back the notion of "intrapreneurship," mentioned in the introduction to Chapter 9 on the entrepreneurial context.

When it is successful, intrapreneurship—implying the stimulation and diffusion of innovative capacity throughout a larger organization, with many champions of innovations—tends to follow most of Quinn's precepts. As such, it seems to belong more to this context than the entrepreneurial one, which focuses on organizations highly centralized around the initiatives of their single leaders, whether or not innovative.

Again many cases support the development of these key concepts. Indeed, the focus on innovation, entrepreneurship, and technology interactions is one of the unique features of this book. Since the changes they induce are central to all our lives as well as to strategic positioning in the modern world, all educated managers need to understand these processes better. The Genentech, Inc. (B), Apple Computer, Inc. (A), Microsoft Corporation (A) and (B), Intel Corporation, Nintendo Co. Ltd., Sony Corporation: Innovation System, Orbital Engine Company, and TCG, Ltd./Thermo Electron cases provide some classic small and mid-sized examples of this process. The Magnetic Levitation Train, Ford Team Taurus, The IBM 360 Decision, Honda Motor Company 1994, Matsushita Electric Industrial Company 1994, and The Hewlett Packard Company cases offer insights about larger scale innovation processes. Despite some executives' and authors' attempts to find a uniform formula or organization form that characterizes the innovative enterprise, these cases prove that no such simplistic structures exist. Many different innovation strategies are possible and each calls for a different management approach.

▼ READING 12.1   THE INNOVATIVE ORGANIZATION*

by Henry Mintzberg

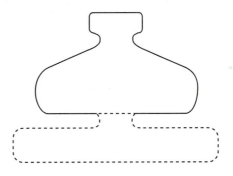

None of the organization forms so far discussed is capable of sophisticated innovation, the kind required of a high-technology research organization, an avant-garde film company, or a factory manufacturing complex prototypes. The entrepreneurial organization can certainly innovate, but only in relatively simple ways. The machine and professional organizations are performance, not problem-solving types, designed to perfect standardized programs, not to invent new ones. And although the diversified organization resolves some problem of strategic inflexibility found in the machine organization, as noted earlier it too is not a true innovator. A focus on control by standardizing outputs does not encourage innovation.

*Adapted from *The Structuring of Organizations* (Prentice Hall, 1979), Chap. 21 on the adhocracy; on strategy formation from "Strategy Formation in an Adhocracy," coauthored with Alexandra McHugh, *Administrative Science Quarterly* (1985: 160–197), and "Strategy of Design: A Study of Architects in Co-Partnership," coauthored with Suzanne Otis, Jamal Shamsie, and James A. Waters, in J. Grant (ed.), *Strategic Management Frontiers* (JAI Press, 1988). A chapter similar to this one appeared in *Mintzberg on Management: Inside Our Strange World of Organizations* (Free Press, 1989).

Sophisticated innovation requires a very different configuration, one that is able to fuse experts drawn from different disciplines into smoothly functioning ad hoc project teams. To borrow the word coined by Bennis and Slator in 1964 and later popularized in Alvin Toffler's *Future Shock* (1970), these are the *adhocracies* of our society.

The Basic Structure

Here again we have a distinct configuration of the attributes of design: highly organic structure, with little formalization of behavior; specialized jobs based on expert training; a tendency to group the specialists in functional units for housekeeping purposes but to deploy them in small project teams to do their work; a reliance on teams, on task forces, and on integrating managers of various sorts in order to encourage mutual adjustment, the key mechanism of coordination, within and between these teams; and considerable decentralization to and within these teams, which are located at various places in the organization and involve various mixtures of line managers and staff and operating experts.

To innovate means to break away from established patterns. Thus the innovative organization cannot rely on any form of standardization for coordination. In other words, it must avoid all the trappings of bureaucratic structure, notably sharp divisions of labor, extensive unit differentiation, highly formalized behaviors, and an emphasis on planning and control systems. Above all, it must remain flexible. A search for organigrams to illustrate this description elicited the following response from one corporation thought to have an adhocracy structure: "[We] would prefer not to supply an organization chart, since it would change too quickly to serve any useful purpose." Of all the configurations, this one shows the least reverence for the classical principles of management, especially unity of command. Information and decision processes flow flexibly and informally, wherever they must, to promote innovation. And that means overriding the chain of authority if need be.

The entrepreneurial configuration also retains a flexible, organic structure, and so is likewise able to innovate. But that innovation is restricted to simple situations, ones easily comprehended by a single leader. Innovation of the sophisticated variety requires another kind of flexible structure, one that can draw together different forms of expertise. Thus the adhocracy must hire and give power to experts, people whose knowledge and skills have been highly developed in training programs. But unlike the professional organization, the adhocracy cannot rely on the standardized skills of its experts to achieve coordination, because that would discourage innovation. Rather, it must treat existing knowledge and skills as bases on which to combine and build new ones. Thus the adhocracy must break through the boundaries of conventional specialization and differentiation, which it does by assigning problems not to individual experts in preestablished pigeonholes but to multidisciplinary teams that merge their efforts. Each team forms around one specific project.

Despite organizing around market-based projects, the organization must still support and encourage particular types of specialized expertise. And so the adhocracy tends to use a matrix structure: Its experts are grouped in functional units for specialized housekeeping purposes—hiring, training, professional communication, and the like—but are then deployed in the project teams to carry out the basic work of innovation.

As for coordination in and between these project teams, as noted earlier standardization is precluded as a significant coordinating mechanism. The efforts must be innovative, not routine. So, too, is direct supervision precluded because of the complexity of the work: Coordination must be accomplished by those with the knowledge, namely the experts themselves, not those with just authority. That leaves just one of our coordinating mechanisms, mutual adjustment, which we consider foremost in adhocracy. And, to encourage this, the organization makes use of a whole set of liaison devices, liaison personnel and integrating managers of all kinds, in addition to the various teams and task forces.

The result is that managers abound in the adhocracy: functional managers, integrating managers, project managers. The last-named are particularly numerous, since the project teams must be small to encourage mutual adjustment among their members, and each, of course, needs a designated manager. The consequence is that "spans of control" found in adhocracy tend to be small. But the implication of this is misleading, because the term is suited to the machine, not the innovative configuration: The managers of adhocracy seldom "manage" in the usual sense of giving orders; instead, they spend a good deal of time acting in a liaison capacity, to coordinate the work laterally among the various teams and units.

With its reliance on highly trained experts the adhocracy emerges as highly decentralized, in the "selective" sense. That means power over its decisions and actions is distributed to various places and at various levels according to the needs of the particular issue. In effect, power flows to wherever the relevant expertise happens to reside—among managers or specialists (or teams of those) in the line structure, the staff units, and the operating core.

To proceed with our discussion and to elaborate on how the innovative organization makes decisions and forms strategies, we need to distinguish two basic forms that it takes.

THE OPERATING ADHOCRACY

The *operating adhocracy* innovates and solves problems directly on behalf of its clients. Its multidisciplinary teams of experts often work under contract, as in the think-tank consulting firm, creative advertising agency, or manufacturer of engineering prototypes.

In fact, for every operating adhocracy, there is a corresponding professional bureaucracy, one that does similar work but with a narrower orientation. Faced with a client problem, the operating adhocracy engages in creative efforts to find a novel solution; the professional bureaucracy pigeonholes it into a known contingency to which it can apply a standard program. One engages in divergent thinking aimed at innovation, the other in convergent thinking aimed at perfection. Thus, one theater company might seek out new avant-garde plays to perform, while another might perfect its performance of Shakespeare year after year.

A key feature of the operating adhocracy is that its administrative and operating work tend to blend into a single effort. That is, in ad hoc project work it is difficult to separate the planning and design of the work from its execution. Both require the same specialized skills, on a project-by-project basis. Thus it can be difficult to distinguish the middle levels of the organization from its operating core, since line managers and staff specialists may take their place alongside operating specialists on the project teams.

Figure 1 shows the organigram of the National Film Board of Canada, a classic operating adhocracy (even though it does produce a chart—one that changes frequently it might be added). The Board is an agency of the Canadian federal government and produces mostly short films, many of them documentaries. At the time of this organigram, the characteristics of adhocracy were particularly in evidence: It shows a large number of support units as well as liaison positions (for example, research, technical, and production coordinators), with the operating core containing loose concurrent functional and market groupings, the latter by region as well as by type of film produced and, as can be seen, some not even connected to the line hierarchy!

THE ADMINISTRATIVE ADHOCRACY

The second type of adhocracy also functions with project teams, but toward a different end. Whereas the operating adhocracy undertakes projects to serve its clients, the *administrative adhocracy* undertakes projects to serve itself, to bring new facilities or activities on line, as in the administrative structure of a highly automated company. And in sharp contrast to the operating adhocracy, the administrative adhocracy makes a clear distinction between

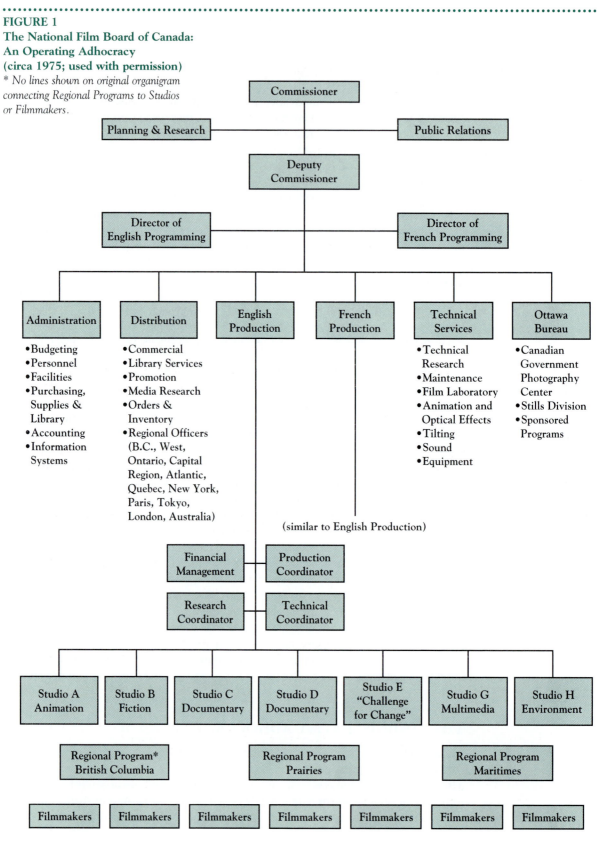

FIGURE 1
The National Film Board of Canada:
An Operating Adhocracy
(circa 1975; used with permission)
** No lines shown on original organigram
connecting Regional Programs to Studios
or Filmmakers.*

Commissioner

Planning & Research

Public Relations

Deputy Commissioner

Director of English Programming

Director of French Programming

Administration
- Budgeting
- Personnel
- Facilities
- Purchasing, Supplies & Library
- Accounting
- Information Systems

Distribution
- Commercial
- Library Services
- Promotion
- Media Research
- Orders & Inventory
- Regional Officers (B.C., West, Ontario, Capital Region, Atlantic, Quebec, New York, Paris, Tokyo, London, Australia)

English Production

French Production

Technical Services
- Technical Research
- Maintenance
- Film Laboratory
- Animation and Optical Effects
- Tilting
- Sound
- Equipment

Ottawa Bureau
- Canadian Government Photography Center
- Stills Division
- Sponsored Programs

(similar to English Production)

Financial Management

Production Coordinator

Research Coordinator

Technical Coordinator

Studio A Animation

Studio B Fiction

Studio C Documentary

Studio D Documentary

Studio E "Challenge for Change"

Studio G Multimedia

Studio H Environment

Regional Program* British Columbia

Regional Program Prairies

Regional Program Maritimes

Filmmakers | Filmmakers | Filmmakers | Filmmakers | Filmmakers | Filmmakers | Filmmakers its administrative component and its operating core. That core is *truncated*—cut right off from the rest of the organization—so that the administrative component that remains can be structured as an adhocracy.

This truncation may take place in a number of ways. First, when the operations have to be machinelike and so could impede innovation in the administration (because of the associated need for control), it may be established as an independent organization. Second, the operating core may be done away with altogether—in effect, contracted out to other organizations. That leaves the organization free to concentrate on the development work, as did NASA during the Apollo project. A third form of truncation arises when the operating core becomes automated. This enables it to run itself, largely independent of the need for direct controls from the administrative component, leaving the latter free to structure itself as an adhocracy to bring new facilities on line or to modify old ones.

Oil companies, because of the high degree of automation of their production process, are in part at least drawn toward administrative adhocracy. Figure 2 shows the organigram for one oil company, reproduced exactly as presented by the company (except for modifications to mask its identity, done at the company's request). Note the domination of "Administration and Services," shown at the bottom of the chart; the operating functions, particularly "Production," are lost by comparison. Note also the description of the strategic apex in terms of standing committees instead of individual executives.

THE ADMINISTRATIVE COMPONENT OF THE ADHOCRACIES

The important conclusion to be drawn from this discussion is that in both types of adhocracy the relation between the operating core and the administrative component is unlike that in any other configuration. In the administrative adhocracy, the operating core is truncated and becomes a relatively unimportant part of the organization; in the operating adhocracy, the two merge into a single entity. Either way, the need for traditional direct supervision is diminished, so managers derive their influence more from their expertise and interpersonal skills than from formal position. And that means the distinction between line and staff blurs. It no longer makes sense to distinguish those who have the formal power to decide from those who have only the informal right to advise. Power over decision making in the adhocracy flows to anyone with the required expertise, regardless of position.

In fact, the support staff plays a key role in adhocracy, because that is where many of the experts reside (especially in administrative adhocracy). As suggested, however, that staff is not sharply differentiated from the other parts of the organization, not off to one side, to speak only when spoken to, as in the bureaucratic configurations. The other type of staff, however, the technostructure, is less important here, because the adhocracy does not rely for coordination on standards that it develops. Technostructure analysts may, of course, be used for some action planning and other forms of analysis—marketing research and economic forecasting, for example—but these analysts are as likely to take their place alongside the other specialists on the project teams as to stand back and design systems to control them.

To summarize, the administrative component of the adhocracy emerges as an organic mass of line managers and staff experts, combined with operators in the operating adhocracy, working together in ever-shifting relationships on ad hoc projects. Our logo figure at the start of this chapter shows adhocracy with its parts mingled together in one amorphous mass in the middle. In the operating adhocracy, that mass includes the middle line, support staff, technostructure, and operating core. Of these, the administrative adhocracy excludes just the operating core, which is truncated, as shown by the dotted section below the central mass. The reader will also note that the strategic apex of the figure is shown partly merged into the central mass as well, for reasons we shall present in our discussion of strategy formation.

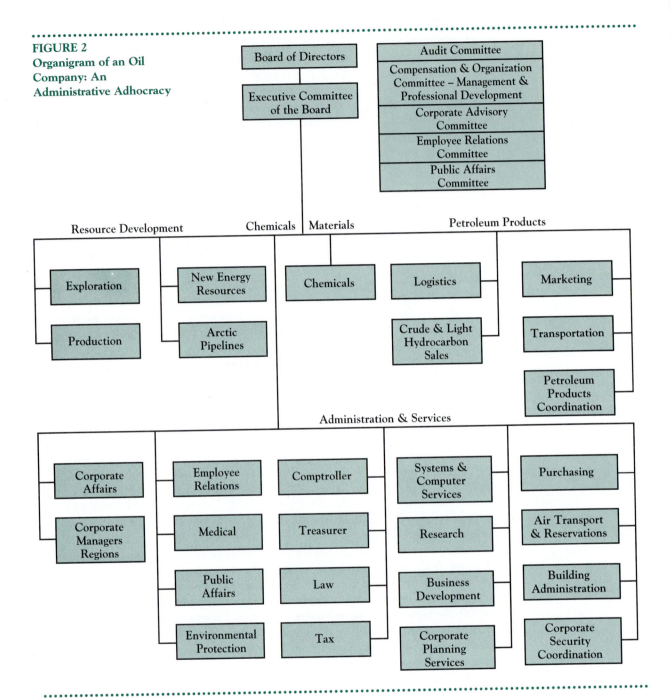

FIGURE 2
Organigram of an Oil Company: An Administrative Adhocracy

Board of Directors

Executive Committee of the Board

Audit Committee

Compensation & Organization Committee – Management & Professional Development

Corporate Advisory Committee

Employee Relations Committee

Public Affairs Committee

Resource Development

Exploration

Production

New Energy Resources

Arctic Pipelines

Chemicals | Materials

Chemicals

Logistics

Crude & Light Hydrocarbon Sales

Petroleum Products

Marketing

Transportation

Petroleum Products Coordination

Administration & Services

Corporate Affairs

Corporate Managers Regions

Employee Relations

Medical

Public Affairs

Environmental Protection

Comptroller

Treasurer

Law

Tax

Systems & Computer Services

Research

Business Development

Corporate Planning Services

Purchasing

Air Transport & Reservations

Building Administration

Corporate Security Coordination

THE ROLES OF THE STRATEGIC APEX

The top managers of the strategic apex of this configuration do not spend much time formulating explicit strategies (as we shall see). But they must spend a good deal of their time in the battles that ensue over strategic choices and in handling the many other disturbances that arise all over these fluid structures. The innovative configuration combines fluid working arrangements with power based on expertise, not authority. Together those breed aggressiveness and conflict. But the job of the managers here, at all levels, is not to bottle up that aggression and conflict so much as to channel them to productive ends. Thus, the managers of adhocracy must be masters of human relations, able to use persuasion, negotiation, coalition, reputation, and rapport to fuse the individualistic experts into smoothly functioning teams.

Top managers must also devote a good deal of time to monitoring the projects. Innovative project work is notoriously difficult to control. No MIS can be relied upon to provide complete, unambiguous results. So there must be careful personal monitoring of projects to ensure that they are completed according to specifications, on schedule and within budget (or, more likely, not excessively late and not too far in excess of cost estimates).

Perhaps the most important single role of the top management of this configuration (especially the operating adhocracy form) is liaison with the external environment. The other configurations tend to focus their attention on clearly defined markets and so are more or less assured of a steady flow of work. Not so the operating adhocracy, which lives from project to project and disappears when it can find no more. Since each project is different, the organization can never be sure where the next one will come from. So the top managers must devote a great deal of their time to ensuring a steady and balanced stream of incoming projects. That means developing liaison contacts with potential customers and negotiating contracts with them. Nowhere is this more clearly illustrated than in the consulting business, particularly where the approach is innovative. When a consultant becomes a partner in one of these firms, he or she normally hangs up the calculator and becomes virtually a full-time salesperson. It is a distinguishing characteristic of many an operating adhocracy that the selling function literally takes place at the strategic apex.

Project work poses related problems in the administrative adhocracy. Reeser asked a group of managers in three aerospace companies, "What are some of the human problems of project management?" Among the common answers: "[M]embers of the organization who are displaced because of the phasing out of [their] work . . . may have to wait a long time before they get another assignment at as high a level of responsibility" and "the temporary nature of the organization often necessitates 'make work' assignments for [these] displaced members." (1969:463) Thus senior managers must again concern themselves with a steady flow of projects, although in this case, internally generated.

Conditions of the Innovative Organization

This configuration is found in environments that are both dynamic and complex. A dynamic environment, being unpredictable, calls for organic structure; a complex one calls for decentralized structure. This configuration is the only type that provides both. Thus we tend to find the innovative organization wherever these conditions prevail, ranging from guerrilla warfare to space agencies. There appears to be no other way to fight a war in the jungle or to put the first man on the moon.

As we have noted for all the configurations, organizations that prefer particular structures also try to "choose" environments appropriate to them. This is especially clear in the case of the operating adhocracy. Advertising agencies and consulting firms that prefer to structure themselves as professional bureaucracies seek out stable environments; those that prefer the innovative form find environments that are dynamic, where the client needs are difficult and unpredictable.*

---

*I like to tell a story of the hospital patient with an appendix about to burst who presents himself to a hospital organized as an adhocracy: "Who wants to do another appendectomy? We're into livers now," as they go about exploring new procedures. But the patient returning from a trip to the jungle with a rare tropical disease had better beware of the hospital organized as a professional bureaucracy. A student came up to me after I once said this and explained how hospital doctors puzzled by her bloated stomach and not knowing what to do took out her appendix. Luckily, her problem resolved itself, some time later. Another time, a surgeon told me that his hospital no longer does appendectomies!

A number of organizations are drawn toward this configuration because of the dynamic conditions that result from very frequent product change. The extreme case is the unit producer, the manufacturing firm that custom-makes each of its products to order, as in the engineering company that produces prototypes or the fabricator of extremely expensive machinery. Because each customer order constitutes a new project, the organization is encouraged to structure itself as an operating adhocracy.

Some manufacturers of consumer goods operate in markets so competitive that they must be constantly changing their product offerings, even though each product may itself be mass produced. A company that records rock music would be a prime example, as would some cosmetic and pharmaceutical companies. Here again, dynamic conditions, when coupled with some complexity, drive the organization toward the innovative configuration, with the mass production operations truncated to allow for adhocracy in product development.

Youth is another condition often associated with this type of organization. That is because it is difficult to sustain any structure in a state of adhocracy for a long period—to keep behaviors from formalizing and thereby discouraging innovation. All kinds of forces drive the innovative configuration to bureaucratize itself as it ages. On the other hand, young organizations prefer naturally organic structures, since they must find their own ways and tend to be eager to innovate. Unless they are entrepreneurial, they tend to become intrapreneurial.

The operating adhocracy is particularly prone to a short life, since it faces a risky market which can quickly destroy it. The loss of one major contract can literally close it down overnight. But if some operating adhocracies have short lives because they fail, others have short lives because they succeed. Success over time encourages metamorphosis, driving the organization toward a more stable environment and a more bureaucratic structure. As it ages, the successful organization develops a reputation for what it does best. That encourages it to repeat certain activities, which may suit the employees who, themselves aging, may welcome more stability in their work. So operating adhocracy is driven over time toward professional bureaucracy to perfect the activities it does best, perhaps even toward the machine bureaucracy to exploit a single invention. The organization survives, but the configuration dies.

Administrative adhocracies typically live longer. They, too, feel the pressures to bureaucratize as they age, which can lead them to stop innovating or else to innovate in stereotyped ways and thereby to adopt bureaucratic structure. But this will not work if the organization functions in an industry that requires sophisticated innovation from all its participants. Since many of the industries where administrative adhocracies are found do, organizations that survive in them tend to retain this configuration for long periods.

In recognition of the tendency for organizations to bureaucratize as they age, a variant of the innovative configuration has emerged—"the organizational equivalent of paper dresses or throw-away tissues" (Toffler, 1970:133)—which might be called the "temporary adhocracy." It draws together specialists from various organizations to carry out a project, and then it disbands. Temporary adhocracies are becoming increasingly common in modern society: the production group that performs a single play, the election campaign committee that promotes a single candidate, the guerrilla group that overthrows a single government, the Olympic committee that plans a single game. Related is what can be called the "mammoth project adhocracy," a giant temporary adhocracy that draws on thousands of experts for a number of years to carry out a single major task, the Manhattan Project of World War II being one famous example.

Sophisticated and automated technical systems also tend to drive organizations toward the administrative adhocracy. When an organization's technical system is sophisticated, it requires an elaborate, highly trained support staff, working in teams, to design or purchase, modify, and maintain the equipment. In other words, complex machinery requires specialists who have the knowledge, power, and flexible working arrangements to cope with it, which generally requires the organization to structure itself as an adhocracy.

Automation of a technical system can evoke even stronger forces in the same direction. That is why a machine organization that succeeds in automating its operating core tends to undergo a dramatic metamorphosis. The problem of motivating bored workers disappears, and with it goes the control mentality that permeates the structure; the distinction between line and staff blurs (machines being indifferent to who turns their knobs), which leads to another important reduction in conflict; the technostructure loses its influence, since control is built into the machinery by its own designers rather than having to be imposed on workers by the standards of the analysts. Overall, then, the administrative structure becomes more decentralized and organic, emerging as an adhocracy. Of course, for automated organizations with simple technical systems (as in the production of hand creams), the entrepreneurial configuration may suffice instead of the innovative one.

Fashion is most decidedly another condition of the innovative configuration. Every one of its characteristics is very much in vogue today: emphasis on expertise, organic structure, project teams, task forces, decentralization of power, matrix structure, sophisticated technical systems, automation, and young organizations. Thus, if the entrepreneurial and machine forms were earlier configurations, and the professional and the diversified forms yesterday's, then the innovative is clearly today's. This is the configuration for a population growing ever better educated and more specialized, yet under constant encouragement to adopt the "systems" approach—to view the world as an integrated whole instead of a collection of loosely coupled parts. It is the configuration for environments that are becoming more complex and more insistent on innovation, and for technical systems that are growing more sophisticated and more highly automated. It is the only configuration among our types appropriate for those who believe organizations must become at the same time more democratic and less bureaucratic.

Yet despite our current infatuation with it, adhocracy is not the structure for all organizations. Like all the others, it too has its place. And that place, as our examples make clear, seems to be in the new industries of our age—aerospace, electronics, think-tank consulting, research, advertising, filmmaking, petrochemicals—virtually all of which experienced their greatest development since World War II. The innovative adhocracy appears to be the configuration for the industries of the last half of the twentieth century.

Strategy Formation in the Innovative Organization

The structure of the innovative organization may seem unconventional, but its strategy making is even more so, upsetting virtually everything we have been taught to believe about that process.

Because the innovative organization must respond continuously to a complex, unpredictable environment, it cannot rely on deliberate strategy. In other words, it cannot predetermine precise patterns in its activities and then impose them on its work through some kind of formal planning process. Rather, many of its actions must be decided upon individually, according to the needs of the moment. It proceeds incrementally; to use Charles Lindblom's words, it prefers "continual nibbling" to a "good bite" (1968:25).

Here, then, the process is best thought of as strategy *formation*, because strategy is not formulated consciously in one place so much as formed implicitly by the specific actions taken in many places. That is why action planning cannot be extensively relied upon in these organizations: Any process that separates thinking from action—planning from execution, formalization from implementation—would impede the flexibility of the organization to respond creatively to its dynamic environment.

STRATEGY FORMATION IN THE OPERATING ADHOCRACY

In the operating adhocracy, a project organization never quite sure what it will do next, the strategy never really stabilizes totally but is responsive to new projects, which themselves involve the activities of a whole host of people. Take the example of the National Film Board. Among its most important strategies are those related to the content of the hundred or so mostly short, documentary-type films that it makes each year. Were the Board structured as a machine bureaucracy, the word on what films to make would come down from on high. Instead, when we studied it some years ago, proposals for new films were submitted to a standing committee, which included elected filmmakers, marketing people, and the heads of production and programming—in other words, operators, line managers, and staff specialists. The chief executive had to approve the committee's choices, and usually did, but the vast majority of the proposals were initiated by the filmmakers and the executive producers lower down. Strategies formed as themes developed among these individual proposals. The operating adhocracy's strategy thus evolves continuously as all kinds of such decisions are made, each leaving its imprint on the strategy by creating a precedent or reinforcing an existing one.

STRATEGY FORMATION IN THE ADMINISTRATIVE ADHOCRACY

Similar things can be said about the administrative adhocracy, although the strategy-making process is slightly neater there. That is because the organization tends to concentrate its attention on fewer projects, which involve more people. NASA's Apollo project, for example, involved most of its personnel for almost ten years.

Administrative adhocracies also need to give more attention to action planning, but of a loose kind—to specify perhaps the ends to be reached while leaving flexibility to work out the means en route. Again, therefore, it is only through the making of specific decisions—namely, those that determine which projects are undertaken and how these projects unfold—that strategies can evolve.

STRATEGIES NONETHELESS

With their activities so disjointed, one might wonder whether adhocracies (of either type) can form strategies (that is, patterns) at all. In fact, they do, at least at certain times.

At the Film Board, despite the little direction from the management, the content of films did converge on certain clear themes periodically and then diverge, in remarkably regular cycles. In the early 1940s, there was a focus on films related to the war effort. After the war, having lost that raison d'être as well as its founding leader, the Board's films went off in all directions. They converged again in the mid-1950s around series of films for television, but by the late 1950s were again diverging widely. And in the mid-1960s and again in the early 1970s (with a brief period of divergence in between), the Board again showed a certain degree of convergence, this time on the themes of social commentary and experimentation.

This habit of cycling in and out of focus is quite unlike what takes place in the other configurations. In the machine organization especially, and somewhat in the entrepreneurial one, convergence proves much stronger and much longer (recall Volkswagenwerk's concentration on the Beetle for twenty years), while divergence tends to be very brief. The machine organization, in particular, cannot tolerate the ambiguity of change and so tries to leap from one strategic orientation to another. The innovative organization, in contrast, seems not only able to function at times without strategic focus, but positively to thrive on it. Perhaps that is the way it keeps itself innovative—by periodically cleansing itself of some of its existing strategic baggage.

THE VARIED STRATEGIES OF ADHOCRACY

Where do the strategies of adhocracy come from? While some may be imposed deliberately by the central management (as in staff cuts at the Film Board), most seem to emerge in a variety of other ways.

In some cases, a single ad hoc decision sets a precedent which evokes a pattern. That is how the National Film Board got into making series of films for television. While a debate raged over the issue, with management hesitant, one filmmaker slipped out and made one such series, and when many of his colleagues quickly followed suit, the organization suddenly found itself deeply, if unintentionally, committed to a major new strategy. It was, in effect, a strategy of spontaneous but implicit consensus on the part of its operating employees. In another case, even the initial precedent-setting decision wasn't deliberate. One film inadvertently ran longer than expected, it had to be distributed as a feature, the first for the organization, and as some other filmmakers took advantage of the precedent, a feature film strategy emerged.

Sometimes a strategy will be pursued in a pocket of an organization (perhaps in a clandestine manner, in a so-called "skunkworks"), which then later becomes more broadly organizational when the organization, in need of change and casting about for new strategies, seizes upon it. Some salesman has been pursuing a new market, or some engineer has developed a new product, and is ignored until the organization has need for some fresh strategic thinking. Then it finds it, not in the vision of its leaders or the procedures of its planners, not elsewhere in its industry, but hidden in the bowels of its own operations, developed through the learning of its workers.

What then becomes the role of the leadership of the innovative configuration in making strategy? If it cannot impose deliberate strategies, what does it do? The answer is that it manages patterns, seeking partial control over strategies but otherwise attempting to influence what happens to those strategies that do emerge lower down.

These are the organizations in which trying to manage strategy is a little like trying to drive an automobile without having your hands on the steering wheel. You can accelerate and brake but cannot determine direction. But there do remain important forms of control. First the leaders can manage the *process* of strategy-making if not the content of strategy. In other words, they can set up the structures to encourage certain kinds of activities and hire the people who themselves will carry out these activities. Second, they can provide general guidelines for strategy—what we have called *umbrella* strategies—seeking to define certain boundaries outside of which the specific patterns developed below should not stray. Then they can watch the patterns that do emerge and use the umbrella to decide which to encourage and which to discourage, remembering, however, that the umbrella can be shifted too.

A GRASS-ROOTS MODEL OF STRATEGY FORMATION

We can summarize this discussion in terms of a "grass-roots" model of strategy formation, comprising six points.

1. *Strategies grow initially like weeds in a garden, they are not cultivated like tomatoes in a hothouse.* In other words, the process of strategy formation can be overmanaged; sometimes it is more important to let patterns emerge than to force an artificial consistency upon an organization prematurely. The hothouse. if needed, can come later.

2. *These strategies can take root in all kinds of places, virtually anywhere people have the capacity to learn and the resources to support that capacity.* Sometimes an individual or unit in touch with a particular opportunity creates his, her, or its own pattern. This may happen inadvertently, when an initial action sets a precedent. Even senior managers can fall into strategies by experimenting with ideas until they converge on something that

works (though the final result may appear to the observer to have been deliberately designed). At other times, a variety of actions converge on a strategic theme through the mutual adjustment of various people, whether gradually or spontaneously. And then the external environment can impose a pattern on an unsuspecting organization. The point is that organizations cannot always plan where their strategies will emerge, let alone plan the strategies themselves.

3. *Such strategies become organizational when they become collective, that is, when the patterns proliferate to pervade the behavior of the organization at large.* Weeds can proliferate and encompass a whole garden; then the conventional plants may look out of place. Likewise, emergent strategies can sometimes displace the existing deliberate ones. But, of course, what is a weed but a plant that wasn't expected? With a change of perspective, the emergent strategy, like the weed, can become what is valued (just as Europeans enjoy salads of the leaves of America's most notorious weed, the dandelion!).

4. *The processes of proliferation may be conscious but need not be; likewise they may be managed but need not be.* The processes by which the initial patterns work their way through the organization need not be consciously intended, by formal leaders or even informal ones. Patterns may simply spread by collective action, much as plants proliferate themselves. Of course, once strategies are recognized as valuable, the processes by which they proliferate can be managed, just as plants can be selectively propagated.

5. *New strategies, which may be emerging continuously, tend to pervade the organization during periods of change, which punctuate periods of more integrated continuity.* Put more simply, organizations, like gardens, may accept the biblical maxim of a time to sow and a time to reap (even though they can sometimes reap what they did not mean to sow). Periods of convergence, during which the organization exploits its prevalent, established strategies, tend to be interrupted periodically by periods of divergence, during which the organization experiments with and subsequently accepts new strategic themes. The blurring of the separation between these two types of periods may have the same effect on an organization that the blurring of the separation between sowing and reaping has on a garden—the destruction of the system's productive capacity.

6. *To manage this process is not to preconceive strategies but to recognize their emergence and intervene when appropriate.* A destructive weed, once noticed, is best uprooted immediately. But one that seems capable of bearing fruit is worth watching, indeed sometimes even worth building a hothouse around. To manage in this context is to create the climate within which a wide variety of strategies can grow (to establish flexible structures, develop appropriate processes, encourage supporting ideologies, and define guiding "umbrella" strategies) and then to watch what does in fact come up. The strategic initiatives that do come "up" may in fact originate anywhere, although often low down in the organization, where the detailed knowledge of products and markets resides. (In fact, to be successful in some organizations, these initiatives must be recognized by middle-level managers and "championed" by combining them with each other or with existing strategies before promoting them to the senior management.) In effect, the management encourages those initiatives that appear to have potential, otherwise it discourages them. But it must not be too quick to cut off the unexpected: Sometimes it is better to pretend not to notice an emerging pattern to allow it more time to unfold. Likewise, there are times when it makes sense to shift or enlarge an umbrella to encompass a new pattern—in other words, to let the organization adapt to the initiative rather than vice versa. Moreover, a management must know when to resist change for the sake of internal efficiency and when to promote it for the sake of external adaptation. In other words, it must sense when to exploit an established crop of strategies and when to encourage new strains to displace them. It is the excesses of either—failure to focus (running blind) or failure to change (bureaucratic momentum)—that most harms organizations.

I call this a "grass-roots" model because the strategies grow up from the base of the organization, rooted in the solid earth of its operations rather than the ethereal abstractions of its administration. (Even the strategic initiatives of the senior management itself are in this model rooted in its tangible involvement with the operations.)

Of course, the model is overstated. But no more so than the more widely accepted deliberate one, which we might call the "hothouse" model of strategy formulation. Management theory must encompass both, perhaps more broadly labeled the *learning* model and the *planning* model, as well as a third, the *visionary* model.

I have discussed the learning model under the innovative configuration, the planning model under the machine configuration, and the visionary model under the entrepreneurial configuration. But in truth, all organizations need to mix these approaches in various ways at different times in their development. For example, our discussion of strategic change in the machine organization concluded, in effect, that they had to revert to the learning model for revitalization and the visionary model for turnaround. Of course, the visionary leader must learn, as must the learning organization evolve a kind of strategic vision, and both sometimes need planning to program the strategies they develop. And overall, no organization can function with strategies that are always and purely emergent; that would amount to a complete abdication of will and leadership, not to mention conscious thought. But none can function either with strategies that are always and purely deliberate; that would amount to an unwillingness to learn, a blindness to whatever is unexpected.

ENVIRONMENT TAKING PRECEDENCE IN THE INNOVATIVE ORGANIZATION

To conclude our discussion of strategy formation, as shown in Figure 3, in the innovative configuration it is the environment that takes precedence. It drives the organization, which responds continuously and eclectically, but does nevertheless achieve convergence during certain periods.* The formal leadership seeks somehow to influence both sides in this relationship, negotiating with the environment for support and attempting to impose some broad general (umbrella) guidelines on the organization.

If the strategist of the entrepreneurial organization is largely a concept attainer and that of the machine organization largely a planner, then the strategist of the innovative organization is largely a *pattern recognizer*, seeking to detect emerging patterns within and outside the strategic umbrella. Then strategies deemed unsuitable can be discouraged while those that seem appropriate can be encouraged, even if that means moving the umbrella. Here, then, we may find the curious situation of leadership changing its intentions to fit the realized behavior of its organization. But that is curious only in the perspective of traditional management theory.

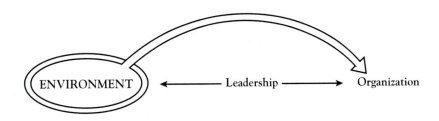

FIGURE 3
Environment Taking the
Lead in Adhocracy

---

*We might take this convergence as the expression of an "organization's mind"—the focusing on a strategic theme as a result of the mutual adjustments among its many actors.

Some Issues Associated with the Innovative Organization

Three issues associated with the innovative configuration merit attention here: its ambiguities and the reactions of people who must live with them, its inefficiencies, and its propensity to make inappropriate transitions to other configurations.

HUMAN REACTIONS TO AMBIGUITY

Many people, especially creative ones, dislike both structural rigidity and the concentration of power. That leaves them only one configuration, the innovative, which is both organic and decentralized. Thus they find it a great place to work. In essence, adhocracy is the only structure for people who believe in more democracy with less bureaucracy.

But not everyone shares those values (not even everyone who professes to). Many people need order, and so prefer the machine or professional type of organization. They see adhocracy as a nice place to visit but no place to spend a career. Even dedicated members of adhocracies periodically get frustrated with this structure's fluidity, confusion, and ambiguity. "In these situations, all managers some of the time and many managers all the time yearn for more definition and structure" (Bums and Stalker, 1966:122–123). The managers of innovative organizations report anxiety related to the eventual phaseout of projects; confusion as to who their boss is, whom to impress to get promoted; a lack of clarity in job definitions, authority relationships, and lines of communication; and intense competition for resources, recognition, and rewards (Reeser, 1969). This last point suggests another serious problem of ambiguity here, the politicization of these configurations. Combining its ambiguities with its interdependencies, the innovative form can emerge as a rather politicized and ruthless organization—supportive of the fit, as long as they remain fit, but destructive of the weak.

PROBLEMS OF EFFICIENCY

No configuration is better suited to solving complex, ill-structured problems than this one. None can match it for sophisticated innovation. Or, unfortunately, for the costs of that innovation. This is simply not an efficient way to function. Although it is ideally suited for the one-of-a-kind project, the innovative configuration is not competent at doing *ordinary* things. It is designed for the *extra*ordinary. The bureaucracies are all mass producers; they gain efficiency through standardization. The adhocracy is a custom producer, unable to standardize and so be efficient. It gains its effectiveness (innovation) at the price of efficiency.

One source of inefficiency lies in the unbalanced workload, mentioned earlier. It is almost impossible to keep the personnel of a project structure—high-priced specialists, it should be noted—busy on a steady basis. In January they may be working overtime with no hope of completing the new project on time; by May they may be playing cards for want of work.

But the real root of inefficiency is the high cost of communication. People talk a lot in these organizations; that is how they combine their knowledge to develop new ideas. But that takes time, a great deal of time. Faced with the need to make a decision in the machine organization, someone up above gives an order and that is that. Not so in the innovative one, where everyone must get into the act—managers of all kinds (functional, project, liaison), as well as all the specialists who believe their point of view should be represented. A meeting is called, probably to schedule another meeting, eventually to decide who should participate in the decision. The problem then gets defined and redefined, ideas for its solution get generated and debated, alliances build and fall around different solutions, until eventually everyone settles down to the hard bargaining over which one to adopt. Finally a decision emerges—that in itself is an accomplishment—although it is typically late and will probably be modified later.

THE DANGERS OF INAPPROPRIATE TRANSITION

Of course, one solution to the problems of ambiguity and inefficiency is to change the configuration. Employees no longer able to tolerate the ambiguity and customers fed up with the inefficiency may try to drive the organization to a more stable, bureaucratic form.

That is relatively easily done in the operating adhocracy, as noted earlier. The organization simply selects the set of standard programs it does best, reverting to the professional configuration, or else innovates one last time to find a lucrative market niche in which to mass produce, and then becomes a machine configuration. But those transitions, however easily effected, are not always appropriate. The organization came into being to solve problems imaginatively, not to apply standards indiscriminately, In many spheres, society has more mass producers than it needs; what it lacks are true problem solvers—the consulting firm that can handle a unique problem instead of applying a pat solution, the advertising agency that can come up with a novel campaign instead of the common imitation, the research laboratory that can make the really serious breakthrough instead of just modifying an existing design. The television networks seem to be classic examples of bureaucracies that provide largely standardized fare when the creativity of adhocracy is called for (except, perhaps, for the newsrooms and the specials, where an ad hoc orientation encourages more creativity).

The administrative adhocracy can run into more serious difficulties when it succumbs to the pressures to bureaucratize. It exists to innovate for itself, in its own industry. Unlike the operating adhocracy, it often cannot change orientation while remaining in the same industry. And so its conversion to the machine configuration (the natural transition for administrative adhocracy tired of perpetual change), by destroying the organization's ability to innovate, can eventually destroy the organization itself.

▼ READING 12.2 MANAGING INNOVATION: CONTROLLED CHAOS*

*by James Brian
Quinn*

Management observers frequently claim that small organizations are more innovative than large ones. But is this commonplace necessarily true? Some large enterprises are highly innovative. How do they do it? . . . This article [reports on a] 2½ year worldwide study . . . [of] both well-documented small ventures and large U.S., Japanese, and European companies and programs selected for their innovation records. . . . More striking than the cultural differences among these companies are the similarities between innovative small and large organizations and among innovative organizations in different countries. Effective management of innovation seems much the same, regardless of national boundaries or scale of operations.

There are . . . many reasons why small companies appear to produce a disproportionate number of innovations. First, innovation occurs in a probabilistic setting. A company never knows whether a particular technical result can be achieved and whether it will succeed in the marketplace. For every new solution that succeeds, tens to hundreds fail. The sheer number of attempts—most by small-scale entrepreneurs—means that some ventures will survive. The 90% to 99% that fail are distributed widely throughout society and receive little notice.

On the other hand, a big company that wishes to move a concept from invention to the marketplace must absorb all potential failure costs itself. This risk may be socially or managerially intolerable, jeopardizing the many other products, projects, jobs, and communities the company supports. Even if its innovation is successful, a big company may face

*Originally published in the *Harvard Business Review* (May–June, 1985); winner of the McKinsey prize for the best article in the *Review* in 1985. Copyright © 1985 by the President and Fellows of Harvard College; all rights reserved. Reprinted with deletions by permission of the *Harvard Business Review.*

costs that newcomers do not bear, like converting existing operations and customer bases to the new solution.

By contrast, a new enterprise does not risk losing an existing investment base or cannibalizing customer franchises built at great expense. It does not have to change an internal culture that has successfully supported doing things another way or that has developed intellectual depth and belief in the technologies that led to past successes. Organized groups like labor unions, consumer advocates, and government bureaucracies rarely monitor and resist a small company's moves as they might a big company's. Finally, new companies do not face the psychological pain and the economic costs of laying off employees, shutting down plants and even communities, and displacing supplier relationships built with years of mutual commitment and effort. Such barriers to change in large organizations are real, important, and legitimate.

The complex products and systems that society expects large companies to undertake further compound the risks. Only big companies can develop new ships or locomotives; telecommunication networks; or systems for space, defense, air traffic control, hospital care, mass foods delivery, or nationwide computer interactions. These large-scale projects always carry more risk than single-product introductions. A billion-dollar development aircraft, for example, can fail if one inexpensive part in its 100,000 components fails.

Clearly, a single enterprise cannot by itself develop or produce all the parts needed by such large new systems. And communications among the various groups making design and production decisions on components are always incomplete. The probability of error increases exponentially with complexity, while the system innovator's control over decisions decreases significantly—further escalating potential error costs and risks. Such forces inhibit innovation in large organizations. But proper management can lessen these effects.

Of Inventors and Entrepreneurs

A close look at innovative small enterprises reveals much about the successful management of innovation. Of course, not all innovations follow a single pattern. But my research—and other studies in combination—suggest that the following factors are crucial to the success of innovative small companies:

NEED ORIENTATION

Inventor-entrepreneurs tend to be "need or achievement oriented." They believe that if they "do the job better," rewards will follow. They may at first focus on their own view of market needs. But lacking resources, successful small entrepreneurs soon find that it pays to approach potential customers early, test their solutions in users' hands, learn from these interactions, and adapt designs rapidly. Many studies suggest that effective technological innovation develops hand-in-hand with customer demand (Von Hippel, 1982:117).

EXPERTS AND FANATICS

Company founders tend to be pioneers in their technologies and fanatics when it comes to solving problems. They are often described as "possessed" or "obsessed," working toward their objectives to the exclusion even of family or personal relationships. As both experts and fanatics, they perceive probabilities of success as higher than others do. And their commitment allows them to persevere despite the frustrations, ambiguities, and setbacks that always accompany major innovations.

LONG TIME HORIZONS

Their fanaticism may cause inventor-entrepreneurs to underestimate the obstacles and length of time to success. Time horizons for radical innovations make them essentially "irrational" from a present value viewpoint. In my sample, delays between invention and commercial production ranged from 3 to 25 years.* In the late 1930s, for example, industrial chemist Russell Marker was working on steroids called sapogenins when he discovered a technique that would degrade one of these, diosgenin, into the female sex hormone progesterone. By processing some ten tons of Mexican yams in rented and borrowed lab space, Marker finally extracted about four pounds of diosgenin and started a tiny business to produce steroids for the laboratory market. But it was not until 1962, over 23 years later, that Syntex, the company Marker founded, obtained FDA approval for its oral contraceptive.

For both psychological and practical reasons, inventor-entrepreneurs generally avoid early formal plans, proceed step-by-step, and sustain themselves by other income and the momentum of the small advances they achieve as they go along.

LOW EARLY COSTS

Innovators tend to work in homes, basements, warehouses, or low-rent facilities whenever possible. They incur few overhead costs; their limited resources go directly into their projects. They pour nights, weekends, and "sweat capital" into their endeavors. They borrow whatever they can. They invent cheap equipment and prototype processes, often improving on what is available in the marketplace. If one approach fails, few people know; little time or money is lost. All this decreases the costs and risks facing a small operation and improves the present value of its potential success.

MULTIPLE APPROACHES

Technology tends to advance through a series of random—often highly intuitive—insights frequently triggered by gratuitous interactions between the discoverer and the outside world. Only highly committed entrepreneurs can tolerate (and even enjoy) this chaos. They adopt solutions wherever they can be found, unencumbered by formal plans or PERT charts that would limit the range of their imaginations. When the odds of success are low, the participation and interaction of many motivated players increase the chance that one will succeed.

A recent study of initial public offerings made in 1962 shows that only 2 percent survived and still looked like worthwhile investments 20 years later (Business Economics Group, 1983). Small-scale entrepreneurship looks efficient in part because history only records the survivors.

FLEXIBILITY AND QUICKNESS

Undeterred by committees, board approvals, and other bureaucratic delays, the inventor-entrepreneur can experiment, test, recycle, and try again with little time lost. Because technological progress depends largely on the number of successful experiments accomplished per unit of time, fast-moving small entrepreneurs can gain both timing and performance advantages over clumsier competitors. This responsiveness is often crucial in finding early markets for radical innovations where neither innovators, market researchers, nor users can quite visualize a product's real potential. For example, Edison's lights first appeared on ships and in baseball parks; Astroturf was intended to convert the flat roofs and asphalt playgrounds of city schools into more humane environments; and graphite and boron compos-

---

*A study at Battelle found an average of 19.2 years between invention and commercial production. Battelle Memorial Laboratories, "Science, Technology, and Innovation," Report to the National Science Foundation, 1973; also Dean (1974:13).

ites designed for aerospace unexpectedly found their largest markets in sporting goods. Entrepreneurs quickly adjusted their entry strategies to market feedback.

INCENTIVES

Inventor-entrepreneurs can foresee tangible personal rewards if they are successful. Individuals often want to achieve a technical contribution, recognition, power, or sheer independence, as much as money. For the original, driven personalities who create significant innovations, few other paths offer such clear opportunities to fulfill all their economic, psychological, and career goals at once. Consequently, they do not panic or quit when others with solely monetary goals might.

AVAILABILITY OF CAPITAL

One of America's great competitive advantages is its rich variety of sources to finance small, low-probability ventures. If entrepreneurs are turned down by one source, other sources can be sought in myriads of creative combinations.

Professionals involved in such financings have developed a characteristic approach to deal with the chaos and uncertainty of innovation. First, they evaluate a proposal's conceptual validity: If the technical problems can be solved, is there a real business there for someone and does it have a large upside potential? Next, they concentrate on people: Is the team thoroughly committed and expert? Is it the best available? Only then do these financiers analyze specific financial estimates in depth. Even then, they recognize that actual outcomes generally depend on subjective factors, not numbers (Pence, 1982).

Timeliness, aggressiveness, commitment, quality of people, and the flexibility to attack opportunities not at first perceived are crucial. Downside risks are minimized, not by detailed controls, but by spreading risks among multiple projects, keeping early costs low, and gauging the tenacity, flexibility, and capability of the founders.

Large-Company Barriers to Innovation

Less innovative companies and, unfortunately, most large corporations operate in a very different fashion. The most notable and common constraints on innovation in larger companies include the following:

TOP MANAGEMENT ISOLATION

Many senior executives in big companies have little contact with conditions on the factory floor or with customers who might influence their thinking about technological innovation. Since risk perception is inversely related to familiarity and experience, financially oriented top managers are likely to perceive technological innovations as more problematic than acquisitions that may be just as risky but that will appear more familiar (Hayes and Garvin, 1982:70; Hayes and Abernathy, 1980:67).

INTOLERANCE OF FANATICS

Big companies often view entrepreneurial fanatics as embarrassments or troublemakers. Many major cities are now ringed by companies founded by these "nonteam" players—often to the regret of their former employers.

SHORT TIME HORIZONS

The perceived corporate need to report a continuous stream of quarterly profits conflicts with the long time spans that major innovations normally require. Such pressures often make publicly owned companies favor quick marketing fixes, cost cutting, and acquisition strategies over process, product, or quality innovations that would yield much more in the long run.

ACCOUNTING PRACTICES

By assessing all its direct, indirect, overhead, overtime, and service costs against a project, large corporations have much higher development expenses compared with entrepreneurs working in garages. A project in a big company can quickly become an exposed political target, its potential net present value may sink unacceptably, and an entry into small markets may not justify its sunk costs. An otherwise viable project may soon founder and disappear.

EXCESSIVE RATIONALISM

Managers in big companies often seek orderly advance through early market research studies or PERT planning. Rather than managing the inevitable chaos of innovation productively, these managers soon drive out the very things that lead to innovation in order to prove their announced plans.

EXCESSIVE BUREAUCRACY

In the name of efficiency, bureaucratic structures require many approvals and cause delays at every turn. Experiments that a small company can perform in hours may take days or weeks in large organizations. The interactive feedback that fosters innovation is lost, important time windows can be missed, and real costs and risks rise for the corporation.

INAPPROPRIATE INCENTIVES

Reward and control systems in most big companies are designed to minimize surprises. Yet innovation, by definition, is full of surprises. It often disrupts well-laid plans, accepted power patterns, and entrenched organizational behavior at high costs to many. Few large companies make millionaires of those who create such disruptions, however profitable the innovations may turn out to be. When control systems neither penalize opportunities missed nor reward risks taken, the results are predictable.

How Large Innovative Companies Do It

Yet some big companies are continuously innovative. Although each such enterprise is distinctive, the successful big innovators I studied have developed techniques that emulate or improve on their smaller counterparts' practices. What are the most important patterns?

ATMOSPHERE AND VISION

Continuous innovation occurs largely because top executives appreciate innovation and manage their company's value system and atmosphere to support it. For example, Sony's founder, Masaru Ibuka, stated in the company's "Purposes of Incorporation" the goal of a "free, dynamic, and pleasant factory . . . where sincerely motivated personnel can exercise their technological skills to the highest level." Ibuka and Sony's chairman, Akio Morita, inculcated the "Sony spirit" through a series of unusual policies: hiring brilliant people with nontraditional skills (like an opera singer) for high management positions, promoting young people over their elders, designing a new type of living accommodation for workers, and providing visible awards for outstanding technical achievements.

Because familiarity can foster understanding and psychological comfort, engineering and scientific leaders are often those who create atmospheres supportive of innovation, especially in a company's early life. Executive vision is more important than a particular management background—as IBM, Genentech, AT&T, Merck, Elf Aquitaine, Pilkington, and others in my sample illustrate. CEOs of these companies value technology and include technical experts in their highest decisions circles.

Innovative managements—whether technical or not—project clear long-term visions for their organizations that go beyond simple economic measures. . . . Genentech's original plan expresses [such a] vision: "We expect to be the first company to commercialize the [rDNA] technology, and we plan to build a major profitable corporation by manufacturing and marketing needed products that benefit mankind. The future uses of genetic engineering are far reaching and many. Any product produced by a living organism is eventually within the company's reach."

Such visions, vigorously supported, are not "management fluff," but have many practical implications.* They attract quality people to the company and give focus to their creative and entrepreneurial drives. When combined with sound internal operations, they help channel growth by concentrating attention on the actions that lead to profitability, rather than on profitability itself. Finally, these visions recognize a realistic time frame for innovation and attract the kind of investors who will support it.

ORIENTATION TO THE MARKET

Innovative companies tie their visions to the practical realities of the marketplace. Although each company uses techniques adapted to its own style and strategy, two elements are always present: a strong market orientation at the very top of the company and mechanisms to ensure interactions between technical and marketing people at lower levels. At Sony, for example, soon after technical people are hired, the company runs them through weeks of retail selling. Sony engineers become sensitive to the ways retail sales practices, product displays, and nonquantifiable customer preferences affect success. . . .

From top to bench levels in my sample's most innovative companies, managers focus primarily on seeking to anticipate and solve customers' emerging problems.

SMALL, FLAT ORGANIZATIONS

The most innovative large companies in my sample try to keep the total organization flat and project teams small. Development teams normally include only 6 or 7 key people. This number seems to constitute a critical mass of skills while fostering maximum communication and commitment among members. According to research done by my colleague, Victor McGee, the number of channels of communication increases as $n(2^{n-1}-1)$. Therefore:

For team size	=	1	2	3	4	5	6	7	8	9	10	11
Channels	=	1	2	9	28	75	186	441	1016	2295	5110	11253

Innovative companies also try to keep their operating divisions and total technical units small—below 400 people. Up to this number, only two layers of management are required to maintain a span of control over 7 people. In units much larger than 400, people quickly lose touch with the concept of their product or process, staffs and bureaucracies tend to grow, and

---

*Thomas J. Allen (1977) illustrates the enormous leverage provided such technology accessors (called "gatekeepers") in R&D organizations.

projects may go through too many formal screens to survive. Since it takes a chain of yesses and only one no to kill a project, jeopardy multiplies as management layers increase.

MULTIPLE APPROACHES

At first one cannot be sure which of several technical approaches will dominate a field. The history of technology is replete with accidents, mishaps, and chance meetings that allowed one approach or group to emerge rapidly over others. Leo Baekelund was looking for a synthetic shellac when he found Bakelite and started the modern plastics industry. At Syntex, researchers were not looking for an oral contraceptive when they created 19-norprogesterone, the precursor to the active ingredient in half of all contraceptive pills. And the microcomputer was born because Intel's Ted Hoff "happened" to work on a complex calculator just when Digital Equipment Corporation's PDP8 architecture was fresh in his mind.

Such "accidents" are involved in almost all major technological advances. When theory can predict everything, a company has moved to a new stage, from development to production. Murphy's law works because engineers design for what they can foresee: hence what fails is what theory could not predict. And it is rare that the interactions of components and subsystems can be predicted over the lifetime of operations. For example, despite careful theoretical design work, the first high performance jet engine literally tore itself to pieces on its test stand, while others failed in unanticipated operating conditions (like an Iranian sandstorm).

Recognizing the inadequacies of theory, innovative enterprises seem to move faster from paper studios to physical testing than do noninnovative enterprises. When possible, they encourage several prototype programs to proceed in parallel. . . . Such redundancy helps the company cope with uncertainties in development, motivates people through competition, and improves the amount and quality of information available for making final choices on scale-ups or introductions.

DEVELOPMENTAL SHOOT-OUTS

Many companies structure shoot-outs among competing approaches only after they reach the prototype stages. They find this practice provides more objective information for making decisions, decreases risk by making choices that best reflect marketplace needs, and helps ensure that the winning option will move ahead with a committed team behind it. Although many managers worry that competing approaches may be inefficient, greater effectiveness in choosing the right solution easily outweighs duplication costs when the market rewards higher performance or when large volumes justify increased sophistication. Under these conditions, parallel development may prove less costly because it both improves the probability of success and reduces development time.

Perhaps the most difficult problem in managing competing projects lies in reintegrating the members of the losing team. If the company is expanding rapidly or if the successful project creates a growth opportunity, losing team members can work on another interesting program or sign on with the winning team as the project moves toward the marketplace. For the shoot-out system to work continuously, however, executives must create a climate that honors high-quality performance whether a project wins or loses, reinvolves people quickly in their technical specialties or in other projects, and accepts and expects rotation among tasks and groups. . . .

SKUNKWORKS

Every highly innovative enterprise in my research sample emulated small company practices by using groups that functioned in a skunkworks style. Small teams of engineers, technicians, designers, and model makers were placed together with no intervening organizational or physical barriers to developing a new product from idea to commercial prototype stages. In innovative Japanese companies, top managers often worked hand in hand on projects with young engineers. Surprisingly, *ringi* decision making was not evident in these situations. Soichiro Honda was known for working directly on technical problems and emphasizing his technical points by shouting at his engineers or occasionally even hitting them with wrenches!

The skunkworks approach eliminates bureaucracies, allows fast, unfettered communications, permits rapid turnaround times for experiments, and instills a high level of group identity and loyalty. Interestingly, few successful groups in my research were structured in the classic "venture group" form, with a careful balancing of engineering, production, and marketing talents. Instead they acted on an old truism: introducing a new product or process to the world is like raising a healthy child—it needs a mother (champion) who loves it, a father (authority figure with resources) to support it, and pediatricians (specialists) to get it through difficult times. It may survive solely in the hands of specialists, but its chances of success are remote.

INTERACTIVE LEARNING

Skunkworks are as close as most big companies can come to emulating the highly interactive and motivating learning environment that characterizes successful small ventures. But the best big innovators have gone even farther. Recognizing that the random, chaotic nature of technological change cuts across organizational and even institutional lines, these companies tap into multiple outside sources of technology as well as their customers' capabilities. Enormous external leverages are possible. No company can spend more than a small share of the world's $200 billion devoted to R&D. But like small entrepreneurs, big companies can have much of that total effort cheaply if they try.

In industries such as electronics, customers provide much of the innovation on new products. In other industries, such as textiles, materials or equipment suppliers provide the innovation. In still others, such as biotechnology, universities are dominant, while foreign sources strongly supplement industries such as controlled fusion. Many R&D units have strategies to develop information for trading with outside groups and have teams to cultivate these sources. Large Japanese companies have been notably effective at this. So have U.S. companies as diverse as DuPont, AT&T, Apple Computer, and Genentech.

An increasing variety of creative relationships exist in which big companies participate-as joint venturers, consortium members, limited partners, guarantors of first markets, major academic funding sources, venture capitalists, spin-off equity holders, and so on. These rival the variety of inventive financing and networking structures that individual entrepreneurs have created.

Indeed, the innovative practices of small and large companies look ever more alike. This resemblance is especially striking in the interactions between companies and customers during development. Many experienced big companies are relying less on early market research and more on interactive development with lead customers. Hewlett-Packard, 3M, Sony, and Raychem frequently introduce radically new products through small teams that work closely with lead customers. These teams learn from their customers' needs and innovations, and rapidly modify designs and entry strategies based on this information.

Formal market analyses continue to be useful for extending product lines, but they are often misleading when applied to radical innovations. Market studies predicted that Haloid would never sell more than 5,000 xerographic machines, that Intel's microprocessor would never sell more than 10% as many units as there were minicomputers, and that Sony's transistor radios and miniature television sets would fail in the marketplace. At the same time, many eventual failures such as Ford's Edsel, IBM's FS system, and the supersonic transport were studied and planned exhaustively on paper, but lost contact with customers' real needs.

A Strategy for Innovation

The flexible management practices needed for major innovations often pose problems for established cultures in big companies. Yet there are reasonable steps managers in these companies can take. Innovation can be bred in a surprising variety of organizations, as many examples show. What are its key elements?

AN OPPORTUNITY ORIENTATION

In the 1981-1983 recession, many large companies cut back or closed plants as their "only available solution." Yet I repeatedly found that top managers in these companies took these actions without determining firsthand why their customers were buying from competitors, discerning what niches in their markets were growing, or tapping the innovations their own people had to solve problems. These managers foreclosed innumerable options by defining the issue as cost cutting rather than opportunity seeking. As one frustrated division manager in a manufacturing conglomerate put it: "If management doesn't actively seek or welcome technical opportunities, it sure won't hear about them."

By contrast, Intel met the challenge of the last recession with its "20% solution." The professional staff agreed to work one extra day a week to bring innovations to the marketplace earlier than planned. Despite the difficult times, Intel came out of the recession with several important new products ready to go—and it avoided layoffs.

Entrepreneurial companies recognize that they have almost unlimited access to capital and they structure their practices accordingly. They let it be known that if their people come up with good ideas, they can find the necessary capital—just as private venture capitalists or investment bankers find resources for small entrepreneurs.

STRUCTURING FOR INNOVATION

Managers need to think carefully about how innovation fits into their strategy and structure their technology, skills, resources, and organizational commitments accordingly. A few examples suggest the variety of strategies and alignments possible:

Hewlett-Packard and 3M develop product lines around a series of small, discrete, freestanding products. These companies form units that look like entrepreneurial start-ups. Each has a small team, led by a champion, in low-cost facilities. These companies allow many different proposals to come forward and test them as early as possible in the marketplace. They design control systems to spot significant losses on any single entry quickly. They look for high gains on a few winners and blend less successful, smaller entries into prosperous product lines.

Other companies (like AT&T or the oil majors) have had to make large system investments to last for decades. These companies tend to make longterm needs forecasts. They often start several programs in parallel to be sure of selecting the right technologies. They then extensively test new technologies in use before making systemwide commitments. Often they sacrifice speed of entry for long-term low cost and reliability.

Intel and Dewey & Almy, suppliers of highly technical specialties to EOMs, develop strong technical sales networks to discover and understand customer needs in depth. These companies try to have technical solutions designed into customers' products. Such companies have flexible applied technology groups working close to the marketplace. They also have quickly expandable plant facilities and a cutting edge technology (not necessarily basic research) group that allows rapid selection of currently available technologies.

Dominant producers like IBM or Matsushita are often not the first to introduce new technologies. They do not want to disturb their successful product lines any sooner than necessary. As market demands become clear, these companies establish precise price-performance windows and form overlapping project teams to come up with the best answer for the marketplace. To decrease market risks, they use product shoot-outs as close to the market as possible. They develop extreme depth in production technologies to keep unit costs low from the outset.

Finally, depending on the scale of the market entry, they have project teams report as close to the top as necessary to secure needed management attention and resources.

Merck and Hoffman-LaRoche, basic research companies, maintain laboratories with better facilities, higher pay, and more freedom than most universities can afford. These companies leverage their internal spending through research grants, clinical grants, and research relationships with universities throughout the world. Before they invest $20 million to $50 million to clear a new drug, they must have reasonable assurance that they will be first in the marketplace. They take elaborate precautions to ensure that the new entry is safe and effective, and that it cannot be easily duplicated by others. Their structures are designed to be on the cutting edge of science, but conservative in animal testing, clinical evaluation, and production control.

These examples suggest some ways of linking innovation to strategy. Many other examples, of course, exist. Within a single company, individual divisions may have different strategic needs and hence different structures and practices. No single approach works well for all situations.

COMPLEX PORTFOLIO PLANNING

Perhaps the most difficult task for top managers is to balance the needs of existing lines against the needs of potential lines. This problem requires a portfolio strategy much more complex than the popular four-box Boston Consulting Group matrix found in most strategy texts. To allocate resources for innovation strategically, managers need to define the broad, long-term actions within and across divisions necessary to achieve their visions. They should determine which positions to hold at all costs, where to fall back, and where to expand initially and in the more distant future.

A company's strategy may often require investing more resources in current lines. But sufficient resources should also be invested in patterns that ensure intermediate and long-term growth; provide defenses against possible government, labor, competitive, or activist challenges; and generate needed organizational, technical, and external relations flexibilities to handle unforeseen opportunities or threats. Sophisticated portfolio planning within and among divisions can protect both current returns and future prospects—the two critical bases for that most cherished goal, high price/earnings ratios.

An Incrementalist Approach

Such managerial techniques can provide a strategic focus for innovation and help solve many of the timing, coordination, and motivation problems that plague large, bureaucratic organizations. Even more detailed planning techniques may help in guiding the development of the many small innovations that characterize any successful business. My research reveals, however, that few, if any, major innovations result from highly structured planning systems. [Why?] . . .

The innovative process is inherently incremental. As Thomas Hughes says, "Technological systems evolve through relatively small steps marked by an occasional stubborn obstacle and by constant random breakthroughs interacting across laboratories and borders" (Hughes, 1984:83). A forgotten hypothesis of Einstein's became the laser in Charles Townes's mind as he contemplated azaleas in Franklin Square. The structure of DNA followed a circuitous route through research in biology, organic chemistry. x-ray crystallography. and mathematics toward its Nobel prize-winning conception as a spiral staircase of [base pairs]. Such rambling trails are characteristic of virtually all major technological advances.

At the outset of the attack on a technical problem, an innovator often does not know whether his problem is tractable, what approach will prove best, and what concrete characteristic the solution will have if achieved. The logical route, therefore, is to follow several paths—though perhaps with varying degrees of intensity—until more information becomes available. Not knowing precisely where the solution will occur, wise managers establish the widest feasible network for finding and assessing alternative solutions. They keep many options open until one of them seems sure to win. Then they back it heavily.

Managing innovation is like a stud poker game, where one can play several hands. A player has some idea of the likely size of the pot at the beginning, knows the general but not the sure route to winning, buys one card (a project) at a time to gain information about probabilities and the size of the pot, closes hands as they become discouraging, and risks more only late in the hand as knowledge increases. . . .

CHAOS WITHIN GUIDELINES

Effective managers of innovation channel and control its main directions. Like venture capitalists, they administer primarily by setting goals, selecting key people, and establishing a few critical limits and decision points for intervention rather than by implementing elaborate planning or control systems. As technology leads or market needs emerge, these managers set a few—most crucial—performance targets and limits. They allow their technical units to decide how to achieve these, subject to defined constraints and reviews at critical junctures.

Early bench-scale project managers may pursue various options, making little attempt at first to integrate each into a total program. Only after key variables are understood—and perhaps measured and demonstrated in lab models—can more precise planning be meaningful. Even then, many factors may remain unknown; chaos and competition can continue to thrive in the pursuit of the solution. At defined review points, however, only those options that can clear performance milestones may continue. . . .

Even after selecting the approaches to emphasize, innovative managers tend to continue a few others as smaller scale "side bets" or options. In a surprising number of cases, these alternatives prove winners when the planned option fails.

Recognizing the many demands entailed by successful programs, innovative companies find special ways to reward innovators. Sony gives "a small but significant" percentage of a new product's sales to its innovating teams. Pilkington, IBM, and 3M's top executives are often chosen from those who have headed successful new product entries. Intel lets its Magnetic Memory Group operate like a small company, with special performance rewards and simulated stock options. GE, Syntex, and United Technologies help internal innovators establish new companies and take equity positions in "nonrelated" product innovations.

Large companies do not have to make their innovators millionaires, but reward should be visible and significant. Fortunately, most engineers are happy with the incentives that Tracy Kidder (1981) calls "playing pinball"—giving widespread recognition to a job well done and the right to play in the next exciting game. Most innovative companies provide both. . . .

Match Management to the Process

. . . Executives need to understand and accept the tumultuous realities of innovation, learn from the experiences of other companies, and adapt the most relevant features of these others to their own management practices and cultures. Many features of small company innovators are also applicable in big companies. With top-level understanding, vision, a commitment to customers and solutions, a genuine portfolio strategy, a flexible entrepreneurial atmosphere, and proper incentives for innovative champions, many more large companies can innovate to meet the severe demands of global competition.

THE DIVERSIFIED CONTEXT

A good deal of evidence has accumulated on the relationship between diversification and divisionalization. Once organizations diversify their product or service lines, they tend to create distinct structural divisions to deal with each business. This relationship was perhaps first carefully documented in the classic historical study by Alfred D. Chandler, *Strategy and Structure: Chapters in the History of the Great American Enterprise.* Chandler traced the origins of diversification and divisionalization in Du Pont and General Motors in the 1920s, which were followed later by other major firms. A number of other studies elaborated on Chandler's conclusions; these are discussed in the readings of this chapter.

The first reading, drawn from Mintzberg's work on structuring, probes the structure of divisionalization—how it works, what brings it about, what intermediate variations of it exist, and what problems it poses for organizations that use it and for society at large. It concludes on a rather pessimistic note about conglomerate diversification and about the purer forms of divisionalization. A follow-up reading by Mintzberg describes the generic "corporate" strategies pursued by diversified organizations—that is, those of the group of businesses, as opposed to the "business" strategies pursued by individual divisions or self-standing businesses (as discussed in his reading in Chapter 4).

Across the world, diversified corporations take many different forms. That is why we have included the next reading, by Philippe Lasserre of INSEAD in France. Lasserre describes three forms that such organizations take in the West, which he labels industrial group, industrial holdings, and financial conglomerates. Then he describes three that are common in Asia, labeled entrepreneurial conglomerates, keiretsus, and national holdings. When he compares them, an interesting result emerges: While we in the West tend to control impersonally (or analytically), and yet in some ways more loosely (or less synergistically), the Asians favor softer and more personalized forms of control, yet often achieve tighter connections. (Harking back to Pitcher's three styles of Chapter 8, the technocrats are more common in the West apparently; the artists and craftsmen easier to find in the East.) Lasserre warns, however, that you cannot just adopt an approach because it looks good; beware of the limitations of your own culture!

Aspects of the diversified organization, particularly in its more conglomerate form, come in for some heavy criticism in this chapter, as in the next reading, too. But it quickly turns to the more constructive questions of how to use strategy to combine a cluster of different businesses into an effective corporate entity. This is Michael Porter's award-winning *Harvard Business Review* article "From Competitive Advantage to Corporate Strategy." Porter discusses in a most insightful way various types of overall corporate strategies, including portfolio management, restructuring, transferring skills, and sharing activities (the last two referred to in his 1985 book *Competitive Advantage* as "horizontal strategies"), the former dealing with "intangible," the latter "tangible" interrelationships among business units and conceived in terms of his value chain.

Again, a wide variety of cases support and challenge these concepts. The Hewlett Packard Company, Sony Innovation, Exxon Corporation 1994, The IBM 360 Decision, Sony Entertainment, Matsushita Electric Industrial Company 1994, and Polaroid Corporation cases deal with diversification through internal development and the traditional divisionalized structures that accompany such growth in many companies. TCG, Ltd./Thermo Electron, Honda Motor Company 1994, The Vanguard Group, Inc., Argyle Diamonds, Orbital Engine Company, and Microsoft Corporation (B) use newer honeycomb, paperweight, infinitely flat, spider's web, starburst, and alliance forms which challenge more conventional approaches and call for creative new management techniques not found in most texts. Finally The Pillsbury Company, The New York Times Company, Cadbury Schweppes, P.L.C., Sony Entertainment, Nintendo Co., Ltd., and The Battle for Paramount Communications, Inc. cases suggest the opportunities and problems of acquisition versus coalition strategies. All provide new insights on managing in today's more complex technological, information-intensive, and geographically dispersed markets. New times call for new techniques which you can help invent.

by Henry Mintzberg

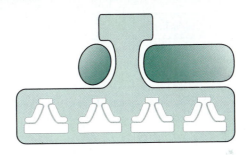

The Basic Divisionalized Structure

The diversified organization is not so much an integrated entity as a set of semiautonomous units coupled together by a central administrative structure. The units are generally called *divisions*, and the central administration, the *headquarters*. This is a widely used configuration in the private sector of the industrialized economy; the vast majority of the *Fortune* 500, America's largest corporations, use this structure or a variant of it. But, as we shall see, it is also found in other sectors as well.

In what is commonly called the "divisionalized" form of structure, units, called "divisions," are created to serve distinct markets and are given control over the operating functions necessary to do so, as shown in Figure 1. Each is therefore relatively free of direct control by headquarters or even of the need to coordinate activities with other divisions. Each, in other words, appears to be a self-standing business. Of course, none is. There *is* a headquarters, and it has a series of roles that distinguish this overall configuration from a collection of independent businesses providing the same set of products and services.

*Adapted from *The Structuring of Organizations* (Prentice Hall, 1979), Chap. 20 on "The Divisionalized Form." A chapter similar to this appeared in *Mintzberg on Management: Inside Our Strange World of Organizations* (Free Press, 1989).

FIGURE 1
**Typical Organigram for a
Divisionalized
Manufacturing Firm**

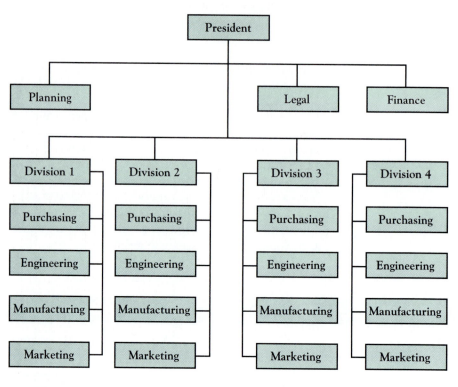

ROLES OF THE HEADQUARTERS

Above all, the headquarters exercises performance control. It sets standards of achievement, generally in quantitative terms (such as return on investment or growth in sales), and then monitors the results. Coordination between headquarters and the divisions thus reduces largely to the standardization of outputs. Of course, there is some direct supervision—headquarters' managers have to have personal contact with and knowledge of the divisions. But that is largely circumscribed by the key assumption in this configuration that if the division managers are to be responsible for the performance of their divisions, they must have considerable autonomy to manage them as they see fit. Hence there is extensive delegation of authority from headquarters to the level of division manager.

Certain important tasks do, however, remain for the headquarters. One is to develop the overall *corporate* strategy, meaning to establish the portfolio of businesses in which the organization will operate. The headquarters establishes, acquires, divests, and closes down divisions in order to change its portfolio. Popular in the 1970s in this regard was the Boston Consulting Group's "growth share matrix," where corporate managers were supposed to allocate funds to divisions on the basis of their falling into the categories of dogs, cash cows, wildcats, and stars. But enthusiasm for that technique waned, perhaps mindful of Pope's warning that a little learning can be a dangerous thing.

Second, the headquarters manages the movement of funds between the divisions, taking the excess profits of some to support the greater growth potential of others. Third, of course, the headquarters, through its own technostructure, designs and operates the performance control system. Fourth, it appoints and therefore retains the right to replace the division managers. For a headquarters that does not directly manage any division, its most tangible power when the performance of a division lags—short of riding out an industry downturn or divesting the division—is to replace its leader. Finally, the headquarters provides certain support services that are common to all the divisions—a corporate public relations office or legal counsel, for example.

STRUCTURE OF THE DIVISIONS

It has been common to label divisionalized organizations "decentralized." That is a reflection of how *certain* of them came to be, most notably Du Pont early in this century. When organizations that were structured functionally (for example, in departments of marketing, manufacturing, and engineering, etc.) diversified, they found that coordination of their different product lines across the functions became increasingly complicated. The central managers had to spend great amounts of time intervening to resolve disputes. But once these corporations switched to a divisionalized form of structure, where all the functions for a given business could be contained in a single unit dedicated to that business, management became much simpler. In effect, their structures became *more* decentralized, power over distinct businesses being delegated to the division managers.

But more decentralized does not mean *decentralized*. That word refers to the dispersal of decision-making power in an organization, and in many of the diversified corporations much of the power tended to remain with the few managers who ran the businesses. Indeed, the most famous case of divisionalization was one of relative *centralization*: Alfred P. Sloan introduced the divisionalized structure to General Motors in the 1920s to *reduce* the power of its autonomous business units, to impose systems of financial controls on what had been a largely unmanaged agglomeration of different automobile businesses.

In fact, I would argue that it is the *centralization* of power within the divisions that is most compatible with the divisionalized form of structure. In other words, the effect of having a headquarters over the divisions is to drive them toward the machine configuration, namely a structure of centralized bureaucracy. That is the structure most compatible with headquarters control, in my opinion. If true, this would seem to be an important point, because it means that the proliferation of the diversified configuration in many spheres—business, government, and the rest—has the effect of driving many suborganizations toward machine bureaucracy, even where that configuration may be inappropriate (school systems, for example, or government departments charged with innovative project work).

The explanation for this lies in the standardization of outputs, the key to the functioning of the divisionalized structure. Bear in mind the headquarters' dilemma: to respect divisional autonomy while exercising control over performance. This it seeks to resolve by after-the-fact monitoring of divisional results, based on clearly defined performance standards. But two main assumptions underlie such standards.

First, each division must be treated as a single integrated system with a single, consistent set of goals. In other words, although the divisions may be loosely coupled with each other, the assumption is that each is tightly coupled internally.*

Second, these goals must be operational ones, in other words, lend themselves to quantitative measurement. But in the less formal configurations—entrepreneurial and innovative—which are less stable, such performance standards are difficult to establish, while in the professional configuration, the complexity of the work makes it difficult to establish such standards. Moreover, while the entrepreneurial configuration may lend itself to being integrated around a single set of goals, the innovative and professional configurations do not. Thus, only the machine configuration of the major types fits comfortably into the conventional divisionalized structure, by virtue of its integration and its operational goals.

---

*Unless, of course, there is a second layer of divisionalization, which simply takes this conclusion down another level in the hierarchy.

In fact, when organizations with another configuration are drawn under the umbrella of a divisionalized structure, they tend to be forced toward the machine bureaucratic form, to make them conform with *its* needs. How often have we heard stories of entrepreneurial firms recently acquired by conglomerates being descended upon by hordes of headquarters technocrats bemoaning the loose controls, the absence of organigrams, the informality of the systems? In many cases, of course, the very purpose of the acquisition was to do just this, tighten up the organization so that its strategies can be pursued more pervasively and systematically. But other times, the effect is to destroy the organization's basic strengths, sometimes including its flexibility and responsiveness. Similarly, how many times have we heard tell of government administrators complaining about being unable to control public hospitals or universities through conventional (meaning machine bureaucratic) planning systems?

This conclusion is, in fact, a prime manifestation of the hypothesis [discussed in Chapter 6] that concentrated external control of an organization has the effect of formalizing and centralizing its structure, in other words, of driving it toward the machine configuration. Headquarters' control of divisions is, of course, concentrated; indeed, when the diversified organization is itself a *closed system*, as I shall argue later many tend to be, then it is a most concentrated form of control. And, the effect of that control is to render the divisions its *instruments*.

There is, in fact, an interesting irony in this, in that the less society controls the overall diversified organization, the more the organization itself controls its individual units. The result is increased autonomy for the largest organizations coupled with decreased autonomy for their many activities.

To conclude this discussion of the basic structure, the diversified configuration is represented in the opening figure, symbolically in terms of our logo, as follows. Headquarters has three parts: a small strategic apex of top managers, a small technostructure to the left concerned with the design and operation of the performance control system, and a slightly larger staff support group to the right to provide support services common to all the divisions. Each of the divisions is shown below the headquarters as a machine configuration.

Conditions of the Diversified Organization

While the diversified configuration may arise from the federation of different organizations, which come together under a common headquarters umbrella, more often it appears to be the structural response to a machine organization that has diversified its range of product or service offerings. In either case, it is the diversity of markets above all that drives an organization to use this configuration. An organization faced with a single integrated market simply cannot split itself into autonomous divisions; the one with distinct markets, however, has an incentive to create a unit to deal with each.

There are three main kinds of market diversity—product and service, client, and region. In theory, all three can lead to divisionalization. But when diversification is based on variations in clients or regions as opposed to products or services, divisionalization often turns out to be incomplete. With identical products or services in each region or for each group of clients, the headquarters is encouraged to maintain central control of certain critical functions, to ensure common operating standards for all the divisions. And that seriously reduces divisional autonomy, and so leads to a less than complete form of divisionalization.

Thus, one study found that insurance companies concentrate at headquarters the critical function of investment, and retailers concentrate that of purchasing, also controlling product range, pricing, and volume (Channon, 1975). One need only look at the individual outlets of a typical retail chain to recognize the absence of divisional autonomy: usually they all look alike. The same conclusion tends to hold for other businesses organized by regions, such as bakeries, breweries, cement producers, and soft drink bottlers: Their "divisions," distinguished only by geographical location, lack the autonomy normally associated with ones that produce distinct products or services.

What about the conditions of size? Although large size itself does not bring on divisionalization, surely it is not coincidental that most of America's largest corporations use some variant of this configuration. The fact is that as organizations grow large, they become inclined to diversify and then to divisionalize. One reason is protection: large organizations tend to be risk averse—they have too much to lose—and diversification spreads the risk. Another is that as firms grow large, they come to dominate their traditional market, and so must often find growth opportunities elsewhere, through diversification. Moreover, diversification feeds on itself. It creates a cadre of aggressive general managers, each running his or her own division, who push for further diversification and further growth. Thus, most of the giant corporations—with the exception of the "heavies," those with enormously high fixed-cost operating systems, such as the oil or aluminum producers—not only were able to reach their status by diversifying but also feel great pressures to continue to do so.

Age is another factor associated with this configuration, much like size. In larger organizations, the management runs out of places to expand in its traditional markets; in older ones, the managers sometimes get bored with the traditional markets and find diversion through diversification. Also, time brings new competitors into old markets, forcing the management to look elsewhere for growth opportunities.

As governments grow large, they too tend to adopt a kind of divisionalized structure. The central administrators, unable to control all the agencies and departments directly, settle for granting their managers considerable autonomy and then trying to control their results through planning and performance controls. Indeed the "accountability" buzzword so often heard in governments these days reflects just this trend—to move closer to a divisionalized structure.

One can, in fact, view the entire government as a giant diversified configuration (admittedly an oversimplification, since all kinds of links exist among the departments), with its three main coordinating agencies corresponding to the three main forms of control used by the headquarters of the large corporation. The budgetary agency, technocratic in nature, concerns itself with performance control of the departments; the public service commission, also partly technocratic, concerns itself with the recruiting and training of government managers; and the executive office, top management in nature, reviews the principal proposals and initiatives of the departments.

In the preceding chapter, the communist state was described as a closed-system machine bureaucracy. But it may also be characterized as the ultimate closed system diversified configuration, with the various state enterprises and agencies its instruments, machine bureaucracies tightly regulated by the planning and control systems of the central government.

Stages in the Transition to the Diversified Organization

There has been a good deal of research on the transition of the corporation from the functional to the diversified form. Figure 2 and the discussion that follows borrow from this research to describe four stages in that transition.

At the top of Figure 2 is the pure *functional* structure, used by the corporation whose operating activities form one integrated, unbroken chain from purchasing through production to marketing and sales. Only the final output is sold to the customers.* Autonomy cannot, therefore, be granted to the units, so the organization tends to take on the form of one overall machine configuration.

---

*It should be noted that this is in fact the definition of a functional structure: Each activity contributes just one step in a chain toward the creation of the final product. Thus, for example, engineering is a functionally organized unit in the firm that produces and markets its own designs, while it would be a market organized unit in a consulting firm that sells its design services, among other, directly to clients.

FIGURE 2
Stages in the Transition to
the Pure Diversified Form

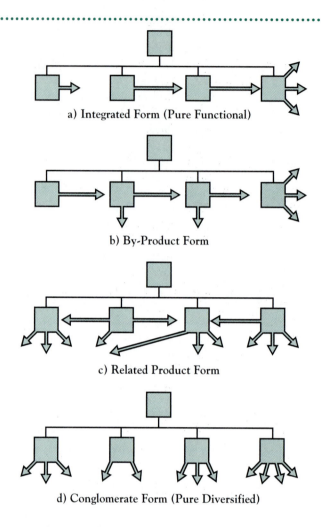

a) Integrated Form (Pure Functional)

b) By-Product Form

c) Related Product Form

d) Conglomerate Form (Pure Diversified)

As an integrated firm seeks wider markets, it may introduce a variety of new end products and so shift all the way to the pure diversified form. A less risky alternative, however, is to start by marketing its intermediate products on the open market. This introduces small breaks in its processing chain, which in turn calls for a measure of divisionalization in its structure, giving rise to the *by-product* form. But because the processing chain remains more or less intact, central coordination must largely remain. Organizations that fall into this category tend to be vertically integrated, basing their operations on a single raw material, such as wood, oil, or aluminum, which they process to a variety of consumable end products. The example of Alcoa is shown in Figure 3.

Some corporations further diversify their by-product markets, breaking down their processing chain until what the divisions sell on the open market becomes more important than what they supply to each other. The organization then moves to the *related-product* form. For example, a firm manufacturing washing machines may set up a division to produce the motors. When the motor division sells more motors to outside customers than to its own sister division, a more serious form of divisionalization is called for. What typically holds the divisions of these firms together is some common thread among their products, perhaps a core skill or technology, perhaps a central market theme, as in a corporation such as 3M that likes to describe itself as being in the coating and bonding business. A good deal

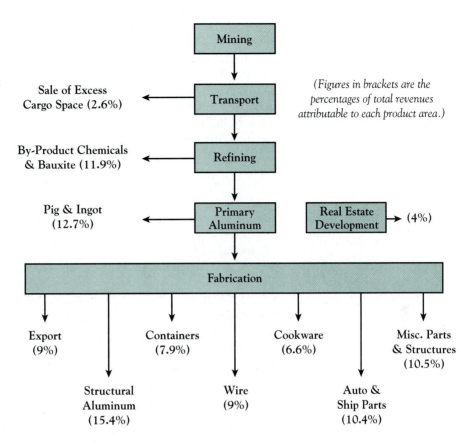

FIGURE 3
By-Product and End-Product Sales of Alcoa (from Rumelt, 1974:21)
Note: Percentages for 1969 prepared by Richard Rumelt from data in company's annual reports.

Mining

Transport

Sale of Excess Cargo Space (2.6%)

(Figures in brackets are the percentages of total revenues attributable to each product area.)

By-Product Chemicals & Bauxite (11.9%)

Refining

Pig & Ingot (12.7%)

Primary Aluminum

Real Estate Development → (4%)

Fabrication

Export (9%)

Structural Aluminum (15.4%)

Containers (7.9%)

Wire (9%)

Cookware (6.6%)

Auto & Ship Parts (10.4%)

Misc. Parts & Structures (10.5%)

of the control over the specific product-market strategies can now revert to the divisions, such as research and development.

As a related-product firm expands into new markets or acquires other firms with less regard to a central strategic theme, the organization moves to the *conglomerate* form and so adopts a pure diversified configuration, the one described at the beginning of this reading. Each division serves its own markets, producing products unrelated to those of the other divisions—chinaware in one, steam shovels in a second, and so on.* The result is that the headquarters planning and control system becomes simply a vehicle for regulating performance, and the headquarters staff can diminish to almost nothing—a few general and group managers supported by a few financial analysts with a minimum of support services.

Some Issues Associated with the Diversified Organization

THE ECONOMIC ADVANTAGES OF DIVERSIFICATION?

It has been argued that the diversified configuration offers four basic advantages over the functional structure with integrated operations, namely an overall machine configuration. First, it encourages the efficient allocation of capital. Headquarters can choose where to put

---

*I wrote this example here somewhat whimsically before I encountered a firm in Finland with divisions that actually produce, among other things, the world's largest icebreaker ships and fine pottery!

its money and so can concentrate on its strongest markets, milking the surpluses of some divisions to help others grow. Second, by opening up opportunities to run individual businesses, the diversified configuration helps to train general managers. Third, this configuration spreads its risk across different markets, whereas the focused machine bureaucracy has all its strategic eggs in one market basket, so to speak. Fourth, and perhaps most important, the diversified configuration is strategically responsive. The divisions can fine-tune their bureaucratic machines while the headquarters can concentrate on the strategic portfolio. It can acquire new businesses and divest itself of old, unproductive ones.

But is the single machine organization the correct basis of comparison? Is not the real alternative, at least from society's perspective, the taking of a further step along the same path, to the point of eliminating the headquarters altogether and allowing the divisions to function as independent organization? Beatrice Foods, described in a 1976 *Fortune* magazine article, had 397 different divisions (Martin, 1976). The issue is whether this arrangement was more efficient than 397 separate corporations.* In this regard, let us reconsider the four advantages discussed earlier.

In the diversified corporation, headquarters allocates the capital resources among the divisions. In the case of 397 independent corporations, the capital markets do that job instead. Which does it better? Studies suggest that the answer is not simple.

Some people, such as the economist Oliver Williamson (1975, 1985), have argued that the diversified organization may do a better job of allocating money because the capital markets are inefficient. Managers at headquarters who know their divisions can move the money around faster and more effectively. But others find that arrangement more costly and, in some ways, less flexible. Moyer (1970), for example, argued early on that conglomerates pay a premium above stock market prices to acquire businesses, whereas the independent investor need pay only small brokerage fees to diversify his or her own portfolio, and can do so easier and more flexibly. Moreover, that provides the investor with full information on all the businesses owned, whereas the diversified corporation provides only limited information to stockholders on the details inside its portfolio.

On the issue of management development, the question becomes whether the division managers receive better training and experience than they would as company presidents. The diversified organization is able to put on training courses and to rotate its managers to vary their experience; the independent firm is limited in those respects. But if, as the proponents of diversification claim, autonomy is the key to management development, then presumably the more autonomy the better. The division managers have a headquarters to lean on—and to be leaned on by. Company presidents, in contrast, are on their own to make their own mistakes and to learn from them.

On the third issue, risk, the argument from the diversified perspective is that the independent organization is vulnerable during periods of internal crisis or economic slump; conglomeration offers support to see individual businesses through such periods. The counterargument, however, is that diversification may conceal bankruptcies, that ailing divisions are sometimes supported longer than necessary, whereas the market bankrupts the independent firm and is done with it. Moreover, just as diversification spreads the risk, so too does it spread the consequences of that risk. A single division cannot go bankrupt; the whole organization is legally responsible for its debts. So a massive enough problem in one division can pull down the whole organization. Loose coupling may turn out to be riskier than no coupling!

Finally, there is the issue of strategic responsiveness. Loosely coupled divisions may be more responsive than tightly coupled functions. But how responsive do they really prove to

---

*The example of Beatrice was first written as presented here in the 1970s, when the company was the subject of a good deal of attention and praise in the business press. At the time of our first revision, in 1988, the company was being disassembled. It seemed appropriate to leave the example as first presented, among other reasons to question the tendency to favor fashion over investigation in the business press.

be? The answer appears to be negative: this configuration appears to inhibit, not encourage, the taking of strategic initiatives. The problem seems to lie, again, in its control system. It is designed to keep the carrot just the right distance in front of the divisional managers, encouraging them to strive for better and better financial performance. At the same time, however, it seems to dampen their inclination to innovate. It is that famous "bottom line" that creates the problem, encouraging short-term thinking and shortsightedness; attention is focused on the carrot just in front instead of the fields of vegetables beyond. As Bower has noted,

> [T]he risk to the division manager of a major innovation can be considerable if he is measured on short-run, year-to-year, earnings performance. The result is a tendency to avoid big risk bets, and the concomitant phenomenon that major new developments are, with few exceptions, made outside the major firms in the industry. Those exceptions tend to be single-product companies whose top managements are committed to true product leadership. . . . Instead the diversified companies give us a steady diet of small incremental change. (1970:194)

Innovation requires entrepreneurship, or intrapreneurship, and these, as we have already argued, do not thrive under the diversified configuration. The entrepreneur takes his or her own risks to earn his or her own rewards; the intrapreneur (as we shall see) functions best in the loose structure of the innovative adhocracy. Indeed, many diversified corporations depend on those configurations for their strategic responsiveness, since they diversify not by innovating themselves but by acquiring the innovative results of independent firms. Of course, that may be their role—to exploit rather than create those innovations—but we should not, as a result, justify diversification on the basis of its innovative capacity.

THE CONTRIBUTION OF HEADQUARTERS

To assess the effectiveness of conglomeration, it is necessary to assess what actual contribution the headquarters makes to the divisions. Since what the headquarters does in a diversified organization is otherwise performed by the various boards of directors of a set of independent firms, the question then becomes, what does a headquarters offer to the divisions that the independent board of directors of the autonomous organization does not?

One thing that neither can offer is the management of the individual business. Both are involved with it only on a part-time basis. The management is, therefore, logically left to the full-time managers, who have the required time and information. Among the functions a headquarters *does* perform, as noted earlier, are the establishment of objectives for the divisions, the monitoring of their performance in terms of these objectives, and the maintenance of limited personal contacts with division managers, for example to approve large capital expenditures. Interestingly, those are also the responsibilities of the directors of the individual firm, at least in theory.

In practice, however, many boards of directors—notably, those of widely held corporations—do those things rather ineffectively, leaving business managements carte blanche to do what they like. Here, then, we seem to have a major advantage to the diversified configuration. It exists as an administrative mechanism to overcome another prominent weakness of the free-market system, the ineffective board.

There is a catch in this argument, however, for diversification by enhancing an organization's size and expanding its number of markets, renders the corporation more difficult to understand and so to control by its board of part-time directors. Moreover, as Moyer has noted, one common effect of conglomerate acquisition is to increase the number of shareholders, and so to make the corporation more widely held, and therefore less amenable to director control. Thus, the diversified configuration in some sense resolves a problem of its own making—it offers the control that its own existence has rendered difficult. Had the corporation remained in one business, it might have been more narrowly held and easier to understand, and so its directors might have been able to perform their functions more effectively. Diversification thus helped to create the problem that divisionalization is said to solve. Indeed, it is ironic that many a diversified corporation that does such a vigorous job of monitoring the performance of its own divisions is itself so poorly monitored by its own board of directors!

All of this suggests that large diversified organizations tend to be classic closed systems, powerful enough to seal themselves off from much external influence while able to exercise a good deal of control over not only their own divisions, as instruments, but also their external environments. For example, one study of all 5,995 directors of the *Fortune* 500 found that only 1.6 percent of them represented major shareholder interests (Smith, 1978) while another survey of 855 corporations found that 84 percent of them did not even formally require their directors to hold any stock at all! (Bacon, 1973:40).

What does happen when problems arise in a division? What can a headquarters do that various boards of directors cannot? The chairman of one major conglomerate told a meeting of the New York Society of Security Analysts, in reference to the headquarters vice presidents who oversee the divisions, that "it is not too difficult to coordinate five companies that are well run" (in Wrigley, 1970:V78). True enough. But what about five that are badly run? What could the small staff of administrators at a corporation's headquarters really do to correct problems in that firm's thirty operating divisions or in Beatrice's 397? The natural tendency to tighten the control screws does not usually help once the problem has manifested itself, nor does exercising close surveillance. As noted earlier, the headquarters managers cannot manage the divisions. Essentially, that leaves them with two choices. They can either replace the division manager, or they can divest the corporation of the division. Of course, a board of directors can also replace the management. Indeed, that seems to be its only real prerogative; the management does everything else.

On balance, then, the economic case for one headquarters versus a set of separate boards of directors appears to be mixed. It should, therefore, come as no surprise that one important study found that corporations with "controlled diversity" had better profits than those with conglomerate diversity (Rumelt, 1974). Overall, the pure diversified configuration (the conglomerate) may offer some advantages over a weak system of separate boards of directors and inefficient capital markets, but most of those advantages would probably disappear if certain problems in capital markets and boards of directors were rectified. And there is reason to argue, from a social no less than an economic standpoint, that society would be better off trying to correct fundamental inefficiencies in its economic system rather than encourage private administrative arrangements to circumvent them, as we shall now see.

THE SOCIAL PERFORMANCE OF THE PERFORMANCE CONTROL SYSTEM

This configuration requires that headquarters control the divisions primarily by quantitative performance criteria, and that typically means financial ones—profit, sales growth, return on investment, and the like. The problem is that these performance measures often become virtual obsessions in the diversified organization, driving out goals that cannot be measured—product quality, pride in work, customers well served. In effect, the economic goals drive out the social ones. As the chief of a famous conglomerate once remarked, "We, in Textron, worship the god of Net Worth" (in Wrigley, 1970:V86).

That would pose no problem if the social and economic consequences of decisions could easily be separated. Governments would look after the former, corporations the latter. But the fact is that the two are intertwined; every strategic decision of every large corporation involves both, largely inseparable. As a result, its control systems, by focusing on economic measures, drive the diversified organization to act in ways that are, at best, socially unresponsive, at worst, socially irresponsible. Forced to concentrate on the economic consequences of decisions, the division manager is driven to ignore their social consequences. (Indeed, that manager is also driven to ignore the intangible economic consequences as well, such as product quality or research effort, another manifestation of the problem of the short-term, bottom-line thinking mentioned earlier.) Thus, Bower found that "the best records in the race relations area are those of single-product companies whose strong top managements are deeply involved in the business" (1970:193).

Robert Ackerman, in a study carried out at the Harvard Business School, investigated this point. He found that social benefits such as "a rosier public image . . . pride among managers . . . an attractive posture for recruiting on campus" could not easily be measured and so could not be plugged into the performance control system. The result was that

> . . . the financial reporting system may actually inhibit social responsiveness. By focusing on economic performance, even with appropriate safeguards to protect against sacrificing long-term benefits, such a system directs energy and resources to achieving results measured in financial terms. It is the only game in town, so to speak, at least the only one with an official scoreboard. (1975:55, 56)

Headquarters managers who are concerned about legal liabilities or the public relations effects of decisions, or even ones personally interested in broader social issues, may be tempted to intervene directly in the divisions' decision-making process to ensure proper attention to social matters. But they are discouraged from doing so by this configuration's strict division of labor: divisional autonomy requires no meddling by the headquarters in specific business decisions.

As long as the screws of the performance control system are not turned too tight, the division managers may retain enough discretion to consider the social consequences of their actions, if they so choose. But when those screws are turned tight, as they often are in the diversified corporation with a bottom-line orientation, then the division managers wishing to keep their jobs may have no choice but to act socially unresponsively, if not actually irresponsibly. As Bower has noted of the General Electric price-fixing scandal of the 1960s, "a very severely managed system of reward and punishment that demanded yearly improvements in earnings, return and market share, applied indiscriminately to all divisions, yielded a situation which was—at the very least—conducive to collusion in the oligopolistic and mature electric equipment markets" (1970:193).

THE DIVERSIFIED ORGANIZATION IN THE PUBLIC SPHERE

Ironically, for a government intent on dealing with these social problems, solutions are indicated in the very arguments used to support the diversified configuration. Or so it would appear.

For example, if the administrative arrangements are efficient while the capital markets are not, then why should a government hesitate to interfere with the capital markets? And why shouldn't it use those same administrative arrangements to deal with the problems? If Beatrice Foods really can control those 397 divisions, then what is to stop Washington from believing it can control 397 Beatrices? After all, the capital markets don't much matter. In his book on "countervailing power," John Kenneth Galbraith (1952) argued that bigness in one sector, such as business, promotes bigness in other sectors, such as unions and government. That has already happened. How long before government pursues the logical next step and exercises direct controls?

While such steps may prove irresistible to some governments, the fact is that they will not resolve the problems of power concentration and social irresponsibility but rather will aggravate them, but not just in the ways usually assumed in Western economics. All the existing problems would simply be bumped up to another level, and there increase. By making use of the diversified configuration, government would magnify the problems of size. Moreover, government, like the corporation, would be driven to favor measurable economic goals over intangible social ones, and that would add to the problems of social irresponsibility—a phenomenon of which we have already seen a good deal in the public sector.

In fact, these problems would be worse in government, because its sphere is social, and so its goals are largely ill suited to performance control systems. In other words, many of the goals most important for the public sector—and this applies to not-for-profit organizations in spheres such as health and education as well—simply do not lend themselves to measurement, no matter how long and how hard public officials continue to try. And without measurement, the conventional diversified configuration cannot work.

There are, of course, other problems with the application of this form of organization in the public sphere. For example, government cannot divest itself of subunits quite so easily as can corporations. And public service regulations on appointments and the like, as well as a host of other rules, preclude the degree of division manager autonomy available in the private sector. (It is, in fact, these central rules and regulations that make governments resemble integrated machine configurations as much as loosely coupled diversified ones, and that undermine their efforts at "accountability.")

Thus, we conclude that, appearances and even trends notwithstanding, the diversified configuration is generally not suited to the public and not-for-profit sectors of society. Governments and other public-type institutions that wish to divisionalize to avoid centralized machine bureaucracy may often find the imposition of performance standards an artificial exercise. They may thus be better off trying to exercise control of their units in a different way. For example, they can select unit managers who reflect their desired values, or indoctrinate them in those values, and then let them manage freely, the control in effect being normative rather than quantitative. But managing ideology, even creating it in the first place, is no simple matter, especially in a highly diversified organization.

IN CONCLUSION: A STRUCTURE ON THE EDGE OF A CLIFF

Our discussion has led to a "damned if you do, damned if you don't" conclusion. The pure (conglomerate) diversified configuration emerges as an organization perched symbolically on the edge of the cliff, at the end of a long path. Ahead, it is one step away from disintegration—breaking up into separate organizations on the rocks below. Behind it is the way back to a more stable integration, in the form of the machine configuration at the start of that path. And ever hovering above is the eagle, representing the broader social control of the state, attracted by the organization's position on the edge of the cliff and waiting for the chance to pull it up to a higher cliff, perhaps more dangerous still. The edge of the cliff is an uncomfortable place to be, perhaps even a temporary one that must inevitably lead to disintegration on the rocks below, a trip to that cliff above, or a return to a safer resting place somewhere on that path behind.

by Henry Mintzberg

In Chapter 3 we examined three sets of strategies—for locating, then distinguishing and elaborating the core business. These are appropriate for the business level. After locating the core business in a given industry, the strategist answers the business-level question of "How do we compete successfully in this industry?" by distinguishing and elaborating the core business.

Next comes the question of what strategies of a generic nature are available to extend and reconceive that core business. These are approaches designed to answer the corporate-level question, "What business should we be in?"

Extending the Core Business

Strategies designed to take organizations beyond their core business can be pursued in so-called vertical or horizontal ways, as well as combinations of the two. "Vertical" means backward or forward in the operating chain, the strategy being known formally as "vertical integration," although why this has been designated vertical is difficult to understand, especially since the flow of product and the chain itself are almost always drawn horizontally! Hence this will here be labeled chain integration. "Horizontal" diversification (its own geometry no more evident), which will be called here just plain diversification, refers to encompassing within the organization other, parallel businesses, not in the same chain of operations.

CHAIN INTEGRATION STRATEGIES

Organizations can extend their operating chains downstream or upstream, encompassing within their own operations the activities of their customers on the delivery end or their suppliers on the sourcing end. In effect, they choose to "make" rather than to "buy" or sell. *Impartation* (Barreyre, 1984; Barreyre and Carle, 1983) is a label that has been proposed to describe the opposite strategy, where the organization chooses to buy what it previously made (also called "outsourcing"), or sell what it previously transferred.

DIVERSIFICATION STRATEGIES

Diversification refers to the entry into some business not in the same chain of operation. It may be *related* to some distinctive competence or asset of the core business itself (also called *concentric* diversification); otherwise, it is referred to as *unrelated* or *conglomerate* diversification. In related diversification, there is evident potential synergy between the new business and the core one, based on a common facility, asset, channel, skill, even opportunity. Porter (1985: 323–4) makes the distinction here between "intangible" and "tangible" relatedness. The former is based on some functional or managerial skill considered common across the businesses, as in a Philip Morris using its marketing capabilities in Kraft. The latter refers to businesses that actually "share activities in the value chain" (p. 323), for example, different products sold by the same sales force. It should be emphasized here that no matter what its basis, every related diversification is also fundamentally an unrelated one, as many diversifying organizations have discovered to their regret. That is, no matter what is common between two different businesses, many other things are not.

---

*Abbreviated version, prepared for this book, of an article by Henry Mintzberg, "Generic Strategies: Toward a Comprehensive Framework," originally published in *Advances in Strategic Management*, Vol. 5 (Greenwich, CT: JAI Press, 1988), pp. 1–67.

STRATEGIES OF ENTRY AND CONTROL

Chain integration or diversification may be achieved by *internal development* or *acquisition*. In other words, an organization can enter a new business by developing it itself or by buying an organization already in business. Both internal development and acquisition involve complete ownership and formal control of the diversified business. But there are a host of other possible strategies, as follows:

STRATEGIES OF ENTRY AND CONTROL

Full ownership and control	• Internal development • Acquisition

Partial ownership and control	• Majority, minority
	• Partnership, including
	   –Joint venture
	   –Turnkey (temporary control)

Partial control without ownership	• Licensing • Franchising • Long-term contracting

---

COMBINED INTEGRATION-DIVERSIFICATION STRATEGIES

Among the most interesting are those strategies that combine chain integration with business diversification, sometimes leading organizations into whole networks of new businesses. *By-product diversification* involves selling off the by-products of the operating chain in separate markets, as when an airline offers its maintenance services to other carriers. The new activity amounts to a form of market development at some intermediate point in the operating chain. *Linked diversification* extends by-product diversification: one business simply leads to another, whether integrated "vertically" or diversified "horizontally." The organization pursues its operating chain upstream, downstream, sidestream; it exploits pre-products, end-products, and by-products of its core products as well as of each other, ending up with a network of businesses, as illustrated in the case of a supermarket chain in Figure 1. *Crystalline diversification* pushes the previous strategy to the limit, so that it becomes difficult and perhaps irrelevant to distinguish integration from diversification, core activities from peripheral activities, closely related businesses from distantly related ones. What were once clear links in a few chains now metamorphose into what looks like a form of crystalline growth, as business after business gets added literally right and left as well as up and down. Here businesses tend to be related, at least initially, through internal development of core competencies, as in the "coating and bonding technologies" that are common to so many of 3M's products.

WITHDRAWAL STRATEGIES

Finally there are strategies that reverse all those of diversification: organizations cut back on the businesses they are in. "Exit" has a been one popular label for this, withdrawal is another. Sometimes organizations *shrink* their activities, canceling long-term licenses, ceasing to sell by-products, reducing their crystalline networks. Other times they abandon or *liquidate* businesses (the opposite of internal development), or else they *divest* them (the opposite of acquisition).

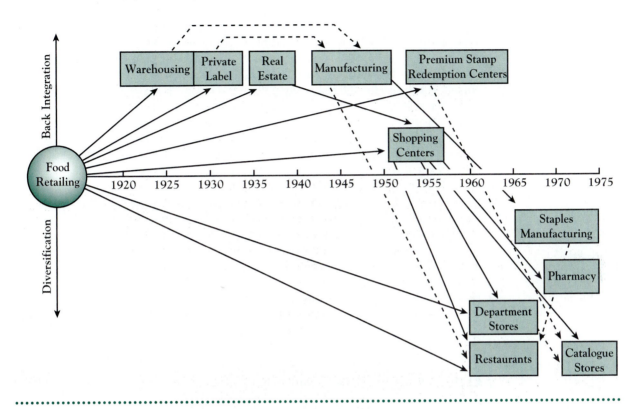

FIGURE 1
Linked Diversification on a Time Scale—
The Case of the Steinberg Chain
Source: From Mintzberg and Waters (1982: 490)

Reconceiving the Core Business(es)

It may seem strange to end a discussion of strategies of ever more elaborate development of a business with ones involving reconception of the business. But in one important sense, there is a logic to this: after a core business has been identified, distinguished, elaborated and extended, there often follows the need not just to consolidate it but also to redefine it and reconfigure it—in essence, to reconceive it. As they develop, through all the waves of expansion, integration, diversification, and so on, some organizations lose a sense of themselves. Then reconception becomes the ultimate form of consolidation: rationalizing not just excesses in product offerings or markets segments or even new businesses, but all of these things together and more—the essence of the entire strategy itself. We can identify three basic reconception strategies.

BUSINESS REDEFINITION STRATEGY

A business, as Abell (1980) has pointed out, may be defined in a variety of ways—by the function it performs, the market it serves, the product it produces. All businesses have popular conceptions. Some are narrow and tangible, such as the canoe business, others broader and vague, such as the financial services business. All such definitions, no matter how tangible, are ultimately concepts that exist in the minds of actors and observers. It therefore becomes possible, with a little effort and imagination, to *redefine* a particular business—

reconceive the "recipe" for how that business is conducted (Grinyer and Spender, 1979; Spender, 1989)—as Edwin Land did when he developed the Polaroid camera.*

BUSINESS RECOMBINATION STRATEGIES

As Porter notes, through the waves of diversification that swept American business in the 1960s and 1970s, "the concept of synergy has become widely regarded as passe"—a "nice idea" but "one that rarely occurred in practice" (1985: 317–18). Businesses were elements in a portfolio to be bought and sold, or, at best, grown and harvested. Deploring that conclusion, Porter devoted three chapters of his 1985 book to "horizontal strategy," which we shall refer to here (given our problems with the geometry of this field) as *business recombination strategies*—efforts to recombine different businesses in some way, at the limit to reconceive various businesses as one. Businesses can be recombined tangibly or only conceptually. The latter was encouraged by Levitt's "Marketing Myopia" (1960) article. By a stroke of the pen, railroads could be in the transportation business, ball-bearing manufacturers in the friction reduction business. Realizing some practical change in behavior often proved much more difficult, however. But when some substantial basis exists for combining different activities, a strategy of business recombination can be very effective. There may never have been a transportation business, but 3M was able to draw on common technological capabilities to create a coating and bonding business.** Business recombination can also be more tangible, based on shared activities in the value chain, as in a strategy of *bundling*, where complementary products are sold together for a single price (e.g., automobile service with the new car). Of course, *unbundling* can be an equally viable strategy, such as selling "term" insurance free of any investment obligation. Carried to their logical extreme, the more tangible recombination strategies lead to a "systems view" of the business, where all products and services are conceived to be tightly interrelated.

CORE RELOCATION STRATEGIES

Finally we come full circle by closing the discussion where we began, on the location of the core business. An organization, in addition to having one or more strategic positions in a marketplace, tends to have what Jay Galbraith (1983) calls a single "center of gravity," some conceptual place where is concentrated not only its core skills but also its cultural heart, as in a Procter & Gamble focusing its efforts on "branded consumer products," each "sold primarily by advertising to the homemaker and managed by a brand manager" (p. 13). But as changes in strategic position take place, shifts can also take place in this center of gravity, in various ways. First, the organization can move *along the operating chain*, upstream or downstream, as did General Mills "from a flour miller to a related diversified provider of products for the homemaker"; eventually the company sold off its flour milling operation altogether (p. 76). Second, there can be a shift *between dominant functions*, say from production to marketing. Third is the shift *to a new business*, whether or not at the same stage of the operating chain. Such shifts can be awfully demanding, simply because each industry is a culture with its own ways of thinking and acting. Finally, is the shift *to a new core theme*, as in the reorientation from a single function or product to a broader concept, for example, when Procter & Gamble changed from being a soap company to being in the personal care business.

This brings us to the end of our discussion of generic strategies—our loop from locating a business to distinguishing it, elaborating it, extending it and finally reconceiving it.

---

* MacMillan refers to the business redefinition strategy as "reshaping the industry infrastructure" (1983:18), while Porter calls it "reconfiguration" (1985:519–523), although his notion of product *substitution* (273–314) could sometimes also constitute a form of business redefinition.

** Our suspicion, we should note, is that such labels often emerge after the fact, as the organization seeks a way to rationalize the diversification that has already taken place. In effect, the strategy is emergent. (See Chapter 1 on "Five Ps for Strategy.")

We should close with a warning that while a framework of generic strategies may help to think about positioning an organization, use of it as a pat list may put that organization at a disadvantage against competitors that develop their strategies in more creative ways.

▼ READING 13.3 MANAGING LARGE GROUPS IN THE EAST AND WEST*

by Philippe Lasserre

. . . there is no one single best method for managing groups of businesses, and the globalization of markets and competition has revealed the emergence of organizational forms of business, particularly in the Asia Pacific region, which differs significantly from the one adopted in Europe and North America. The purpose of this article is to underline some of the salient differences between corporations in Asia and in Europe, to analyze the basis of those differences and finally to draw some recommendations.

In the first and second parts one will identify some prominent types of corporations in Europe and in Asia Pacific. In a third part, their organizational forms and their corporate control styles will be compared. Finally, some recommendations. . . will be proposed.

European Corporate Archtypes

European groups can be broadly classified into three major types: industrial groups, industrial holdings, and financial conglomerates.

A first type of corporation is characterized by a portfolio of business activities which share a common set of competences and in which a high degree of synergy is achieved by managing key interdependencies at corporate level. Andrew Campbell and Michael Goold at the Ashridge Strategic Management Center in the UK, in their study of British corporations, have named this type "Strategic Planning" groups (Campbell and Goold, 1987), because of the strong input from corporate headquarters in those groups into the strategy formulation of business units. Here, those groups are identified as *industrial groups*. Examples of industrial groups in Europe are British Petroleum or Glaxo in the UK, Daimler Benz or Henkel in Germany, Philips in the Netherlands, or l'Air Liquide and Michelin in France.

Industrial holdings are corporations in which the business units are clustered into subgroups or sectors. In this type of corporate grouping, synergies are strong within subgroups and weak between subgroups. In industrial holdings, the task of value creation through synergies is delegated to the subgroup level of management, while the corporate role is to impose management discipline through the implementation of planning and control systems, to manage acquisitions and leverage and allocate human and financial resources. Campbell and Goold call these groups "Strategic Control" groups, because of their intensive use of planning and control systems to regulate the relationships between business units and corporate headquarters. Examples of industrial holdings are: ICI or Courtaulds in the UK, BSN or Alsthom-Alcatel in France, Siemens or BASF in Germany.

Financial conglomerates are characterized by a constellation of business units which do not necessarily share any common source of synergies and whose corporate value is essentially created by the imposition of management discipline, financial leverage, and the management of acquisitions and restructuring. Heavy reliance on financial control systems as the major mechanisms of corporate governance have led Campbell and Goold to call these "Financial Control" groups. Hanson Trust or BTR in the UK are examples of financial con-

*Originally published as "The Management of Large Groups: Asia and Europe Compared," in *European Management Journal*, Vol. 10, No. 2, June 1992, 157–162. Reprinted with deletions with permission of the Journal, Elsciver Science Ltd., Pergamon Imprint, Oxford, England.

glomerates. A more recent and extreme version of financial conglomerates has appeared in the USA under the form of what Professor Michael Jensen at the Harvard Business School has identified as "LBO Partnerships," in which value is extracted through corporate restructuring and financial discipline imposed on business units under the form of heavy debts, as in the case of Kolberg, Kravis and Roberts (Jensen, 1989).

In Europe one can find examples of the three types of groups in a variety of corporate ownership arrangements, whether private or government-owned. In France one can find in the public sector industrial groups such as Renault, SNECMA, or Aerospatiale or, in the private sector, Peugeot, Dassault, or Michelin. Similarly Rhone Poulenc, a government-owned group, is managed as an industrial holding like BSN, which is a privately-owned group. . . .

Asian Corporate Archetypes

In the Asia Pacific region, where in the past three decades local corporations have emerged as strong competitors, one can possibly identify three major types: the entrepreneurial conglomerates, the Japanese Keiretsus, and the national holdings.

The *entrepreneurial conglomerate* is a prevailing form of corporate organization in South East Asia, Korea, Taiwan and Hong Kong. Entrepreneurial conglomerates are widely diversified into a large number of unrelated activities ranging from banking, trading, real estate, manufacturing, and services. These groups are usually under the leadership of a father figure who exercises control over the strategic decisions of business units and is the driving force behind any strategic move. Very little attempt is made in Asian entrepreneurial conglomerates to manage synergies. The major source of value in those groups emanates from the ability of the entrepreneur to leverage financial and human resources, to establish political connections, to conclude deals with governments and business partners, and to impose loyalty and discipline upon business units. One can distinguish three major types of entrepreneurial conglomerates in Asia: the large Korean groups or Chaebols such as Samsung, Daewoo, or Hyundai; the Overseas Chinese groups such as Liem Sioe Liong or Astra International in Indonesia, Formosa Plastics in Taiwan, Charoen Pokphand in Thailand or Li Ka Shing in Hong Kong; and the colonial "Hongs" such as Swire or Jardine Matheson in Hong Kong.

The *Keiretsus* are a unique feature of Japanese corporate organization. They constitute super groups, or clusters of groups in which businesses are either vertically integrated as in the case of Honda, NEC, Toyota, or Matsushita, or horizontally connected as in the case of Mitsubishi, Mitsui, or Sumitomo. Although some companies in the groups exercise greater "power" than others, Keiretsus are not hierarchically organized. They are like a club of organizations which share common interests. Linkages across companies are made through cross shareholdings, the regular meeting of a "Presidential council" in which chairmen of leading companies exchange views. Transfer of staff and, in some cases, long-term supplier-client relationships are also mechanisms used among the vertical Keiretsus. Value is added in Keiretsus through their ability to coordinate informally a certain number of key activities (R&D, export contracts), to transfer expertise through personnel rotation, and to build strong supplier-distributor chains.

The Asian *national holdings* groups have been formed more recently as an expression of industrial independence in order to capitalize on domestic markets and public endowment. Some of these are government-owned like Petronas in Malaysia, Singapore Airlines, Singapore Technology, Gresik in Indonesia, or private like Siam Cement in Thailand or San Miguel in the Philippines. Their business portfolios tend to be less diversified than the ones of the entrepreneurial conglomerates, and their value creation capabilities stem from their "nationality." . . .

Group Management: A Comparison

In order to proceed to a comparison of the ways groups organize themselves to control and coordinate their activities, one needs to define the key dimensions which capture the most significant differences. In the management literature, various parameters have been proposed to study organizational differences, and the objective of this article is not to review previous research, but to propose what seem to be the most salient measures of differences. Two dimensions are considered as the most important ones:

a. First, the way corporations organize the respective roles of headquarters, the "center," and business units, whether those are divisions or subsidiaries. This dimension is referred to as *Organizational Setting*.
b. Second, the way headquarters ensure that business units' performances and behavior are in line with corporate expectations. This is referred to as *Corporate Control*.

ORGANIZATIONAL SETTING

Corporations around the world appear to cluster themselves around four types of corporate organizational settings.

In the first type of organization, the center plays an important role in managing synergies. Strategic and operational integration and coordination of business units are considered to be the major sources of competitive advantage. Interdependencies are achieved through a variety of mechanisms, including centralized functions, top-down strategic plans, strong corporate identity and socialization of personnel. Given this high role assigned to the center of this form of organization, it can be qualified as a *federation*. This form prevails in the first type of European groups identified above: the industrial groups, and in certain of national holdings in the Asia Pacific region.

In a second type, the center functions as both resource allocator, guardian of the corporate identity, and source of strategic renewal. Business units enjoy a large degree of strategic autonomy provided that their strategies are "negotiated" and fit with the overall "corporate strategic framework" inspired by the center. Bottom-up planning, negotiated strategies, operational autonomy, and central mechanisms of financial and human resources allocation are key characteristics of this type of organizational setting. It differs from the federate organization by the more balanced power sharing between the center and the operating units; for that reason it is referred to, here, as a *confederation*. This form is most often characteristic of the European industrial holdings as well as Asian national holdings.

In a third category, one can find groups organized as a multitude of uncoordinated business units, each of them linked directly or indirectly to the center. The role of the center in those groups can be either "hands on," as in the case of Asian entrepreneurial conglomerates, or "hands off," as in the case of European financial conglomerates. What characterizes these groups is the fact that the relationships between business units and corporate headquarters are composed of a series of one to one "contractual" agreements. This form resembles a *constellation* and, as said earlier, is predominantly adopted by Asian and European conglomerates.

Finally, in a fourth type of organizational setting, one can find groups in which there is no center or, on the contrary, there are several centers. Some coordination mechanisms are loose, as in the case of informal meetings, while some are more tightly controlled, as in the case of long-term suppliers' contracts. Japanese Keiretsus are representative of this organizational type. Because it is structured as a network, it is called here the *connexion* type of organization.

CORPORATE CONTROL

Corporate control describes how groups ensure that business units' performances and behaviors are in line with corporate expectations. One can distinguish five major methods of exercising control: control by financial performance only, control by systems, control by strategy, direct subjective control of the persons, and control by ideology.

In groups which rely primarily on *financial controls*, headquarters assign financial goals based on financial standards (return on assets, shareholder value). Performances are monitored and evaluated according to achievement of these financial goals. Rewards and punishments of managers are based on those achievements and, for the group, the strategic value of businesses is assessed on their capacities to produce the "figures." This method of control prevails in European financial conglomerates.

The exercise of *control by systems* is based on the implementation of planning and control mechanisms such as interactive strategic planning sessions, investments decisions using capital budgeting techniques, control reviews, etc. Systems use financial as well as nonfinancial information (strategic, marketing). This mode of control predominates in the European industrial holdings and the European industrial groups.

In the *control by strategy* mode, the emphasis is neither on the financial measurement of performance nor on "systems," but on the appreciation of the strategic trajectory of business units and on their degree of fit with the whole corporation. This is done through task forces, corporate conferences, informal meetings, temporary assignments of key executives to business units, etc. European industrial groups and, to some extent, Japanese Keiretsus are practicing this form of control, whose purpose is not to measure or enforce, but to make sure that there is a coherent corporate strategic fit.

Personalized control is exercised through a direct interface between the group chairman and business units' key managers. Subjective, holistic forms of assessment are in use. Although some form of measurement and use of systems can be found in these groups, the main concern for unit managers is to behave according to the norms and beliefs of the chairman. Asian entrepreneurial conglomerates are practicing, nearly exclusively, this form of control.

Finally, with *ideological control* the focus is to make sure that managers have internalized the values of the group and are behaving accordingly. Systems, financial measurements, special relationships with the chairman, if used at all, do not play a dominant role here. What does matter is the development of strong beliefs, norms, values across the organization. Recruitments, socialization, training, rotation of staff are all kinds of process which build and maintain an ideology. This type of control prevails in the Asian national holdings in which strong national and corporate identities constitute the essential glue of group performance. Vertical Keiretsus are also well-known to use extensively this form of control.

Comparing European and Asian Groups

Those two dimensions combined give the opportunity to contrast the Asian groups with their European counterparts in the chart represented in Figure 1. As it appears in this figure, Asian and European large corporations live in a different organizational world. While they share some similarities in the way they control their operations, they differ in the way they design their organizational settings, and vice versa. What is interesting to observe in Figure 1 is that Asian corporations introduce, in any case, an interpersonal feature in their management system.

The Keiretsus are built around the ability of group members to connect to each other in one way or another through personal contacts. In the entrepreneurial conglomerate, the entrepreneur is in direct contact with business units and all relationships are personalized. In the case of national holdings, the personification of rapport is established through ideological means, sense of belonging, and nationalistic stand.

FIGURE 1
Asian and European
Groups

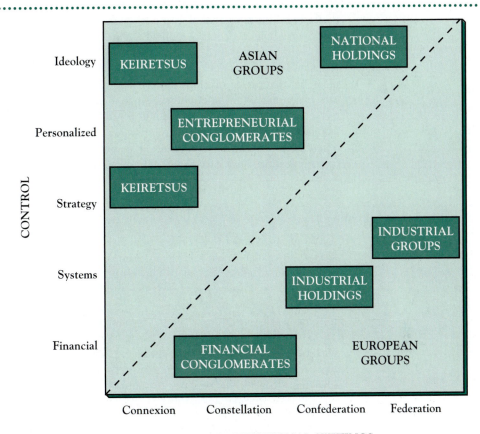

The European groups, by contrast, tend to prefer systematic or administrative features in their corporate management. Financial conglomerates are driven by "numbers," industrial holdings favor complex planning and control mechanisms, while industrial groups adopt structural and regulatory means of coordination. When confronted by a problem of change the typical reaction of a Western corporation will be to find a new "structure" or a new "system." . . .

Western corporate designers adopt an "engineering" approach to building and regulating organizational life. Although over the past 50 years behavioral sciences have brought an immense contribution to the art of management, this has been, most of the time, translated into practice with an instrumental perspective. Motivation theories have given birth to "management by objectives," experimental psychology using conditioning techniques has been used for the design of rewards and bonus systems, information theory is applied in the setting up of computer systems, etc. The rationale underlying this effort is probably the belief that human behavior can be influenced by the *manipulation* of organizational mechanisms. The main concern of Western managers confronted with a situation of strategic change is to install a new "organization" or a new "management system" which is supposed to align behavior with the new realities.

This instrumental engineering approach is challenged by Asian corporate architects who conceive enterprises as living entities where various individuals and groups obtain mutual benefit through cooperation. Organizations are not seen as independent of the people who compose them and, most of the time, enterprises are compared to "families." In 1984, Chairman Kim Woo Choong, founder of Daewoo, was participating in a session at the Harvard Business School with a group of US senior executives. He was asked by one participant how he could coordinate some 40 subsidiaries without controlling them. Chairman Kim answered that coordination was achieved through *"spiritual linkages"*! (Aguilar, 1984.) That does not mean that Asian firms do not use systems for their management, but that personification of interrelationships are given priorities over formal systems. One major underlying assumption of Asian managers is that organizational mechanisms are not set up to "manipulate" people but rather to give a structure to social interactions. In fact, most of the time, people are not rewarded for their performance, as measured in terms of results, but in terms of conformity to behavior. Organizations are not seen as machines (an engineering view) but as a set of "codified" relationships (a biological view).

Decoding Asian Firms

. . . When the competitive pressure from Asian firms becomes too intense, Western managers try to emulate them. One good example is provided by an article published in 1990 in the *Harvard Business Review* by Charles Ferguson (1990) in which the author proposes the creation of Western Keiretsus between US and European countries in the computer industry! This proposition reflects an engineering view of the organizational world: the machine "works" in Japan, why don't we import the machine? It is as if we asked US society to renounce individualism. What an ambition! Instead of trying to "import the machine," Western managers should be inspired to gain an understanding of the way the relationships function or don't function in these groups, what social roles do they play, in other terms to "decode" and not to "imitate" Asian organizations. This decoding ability requires three attitudes: (a) getting rid of *a priori* judgments, (b) making the necessary effort to study the social and cultural background of Asian societies, and (c) resisting the temptation of easy translations.

A. GET RID OF A PRIORI JUDGMENTS

More often than not, when presented with Asian cases, particularly successful ones, Western managers give ready-made explanations: Japan Inc. exploited manpower, "workaholism," nationalism, sacrificed generation, etc. Those views are meaningless because they are based on a simplistic engineering causality leading to defeatism or stubborn protectionism. Understanding the functionality of a social structure is the first necessary step in the analysis of organization, while the deciphering of causal links comes second. A rushed application of ready-made causal schemes based on superficial facts does not help to understand Asian partners and competitors.

B. INVEST IN THE STUDY OF CULTURES AND SOCIETIES

One of the dangers of "instrumental" thinking is that it bypasses what is not considered of immediate relevance. Cultural and social knowledge are all too frequently considered to be a waste of time or, at best, as subjects of "executive summaries." Organizations and business behavior are part of an historical and cultural heritage which, in the case of Asian societies, is very rich, complex, and heterogeneous. The manager who does not make the necessary efforts to enlighten him or herself with such knowledge is condemned to go from surprise to surprise if not from disillusion to disillusion.

C. RESIST THE TEMPTATION OF "EASY TRANSLATIONS"

Some managers fall into the trap of adopting, naively, a so-called "Asian" way of doing things. In the early 1980s, a European bank set up a regional office in Singapore, its first commitment in the region. The newly appointed general manager, a very enthusiastic person, decided that he would work "the Chinese way": handshakes, networking, personal trust, etc. He found himself trapped two years later with a portfolio of bad debts amounting to several million US$! Such horror stories can only fuel the resistance of corporate boards to commit resources for developing strategies in the Asia Pacific region. . . .

▼ READING 13.4 FROM COMPETITIVE ADVANTAGE TO CORPORATE STRATEGY*

by Michael E. Porter

Corporate strategy, the overall plan for a diversified company, is both the darling and the stepchild of contemporary management practice—the darling because CEOs have been obsessed with diversification since the early 1960s, the stepchild because almost no consensus exists about what corporate strategy is, much less about how a company should formulate it.

A diversified company has two levels of strategy: business unit (or competitive) strategy and corporate (or companywide) strategy. Competitive strategy concerns how to create competitive advantage in each of the businesses in which a company competes. Corporate strategy concerns two different questions: what businesses the corporation should be in and how the corporate office should manage the array of business units.

Corporate strategy is what makes the corporate whole add up to more than the sum of its business unit parts.

The track record of corporate strategies has been dismal. I studied the diversification records of 33 large, prestigious U.S. companies over the 1950–1986 period and found that most of them had divested many more acquisitions than they had kept. The corporate strategies of most companies have dissipated instead of created shareholder value.

The need to rethink corporate strategy could hardly be more urgent. By taking over companies and breaking them up, corporate raiders thrive on failed corporate strategy. Fueled by junk bond financing and growing acceptability, raiders can expose any company to takeover, no matter how large or blue chip. . . .

A Sober Picture

. . . My study of 33 companies, many of which have reputations for good management, is a unique look at the track record of major corporations. . . . Each company entered an average of 80 new industries and 27 new fields. Just over 70% of the new entries were acquisitions, 22% were start-ups, and 8% were joint ventures. IBM, Exxon, Du Pont, and 3M, for example, focused on startups, while ALCO Standard, Beatrice, and Sara Lee diversified almost solely through acquisitions. . . .

My data paint a sobering picture of the success ratio of these moves. . . . I found that on average corporations divested more than half their acquisitions in new industries and more than 60% of their acquisitions in entirely new fields. Fourteen companies left more than 70% of all the acquisitions they had made in new fields. The track record in unrelated acquisitions is even worse—the average divestment rate is startling 74%. Even a highly

*Originally published in the *Harvard Business Review* (May–June 1987) and winner of the McKinsey Prize for the best in the *Review* in 1987. Copyright ©1987 by the President and Fellows of Harvard College; all rights reserved. Reprinted with deletions by permission of the *Harvard Business Review*.

respected company like General Electric divested a very high percentage of its acquisitions, particularly those in new fields. . . . Some [companies] bear witness to the success of well-thought-out corporate strategies. Others, however, enjoy a lower rate simply because they have not faced up to their problem units and divested them. . . .

I would like to make one comment on the use of shareholder value to judge performance. Linking shareholder value quantitatively to diversification performance only works if you compare the shareholder value that is with the shareholder value that might have been without diversification. Because such a comparison is virtually impossible to make, my own measure of diversification success—the number of units retained by the company—seems to be as good an indicator as any of the contribution of diversification to corporate performance.

My data give a stark indication of the failure of corporate strategies.* Of the 33 companies, 6 had been taken over as my study was being completed. . . . Only the lawyers, investment bankers, and original sellers have prospered in most of these acquisitions, not the shareholders.

Premises of Corporate Strategy

Any successful corporate strategy builds on a number of premises. These are facts of life about diversification. They cannot be altered, and when ignored, they explain in part why so many corporate strategies fail.

COMPETITION OCCURS AT THE BUSINESS UNIT LEVEL

Diversified companies do not compete; only their business units do. Unless a corporate strategy places primary attention on nurturing the success of each unit, the strategy will fail, no matter how elegantly constructed. Successful corporate strategy must grow out of and reinforce competitive strategy.

DIVERSIFICATION INEVITABLY ADDS COSTS AND CONSTRAINTS TO BUSINESS UNITS

Obvious costs such as the corporate overhead allocated to a unit may not be as important or subtle as the hidden costs and constraints. A business unit must explain its decisions to top management, spend time complying with planning and other corporate systems, live with parent company guidelines and personnel policies, and forgo the opportunity to motivate employees with direct equity ownership. These costs and constraints can be reduced but not entirely eliminated.

SHAREHOLDERS CAN READILY DIVERSIFY THEMSELVES

Shareholders can diversify their own portfolios of stocks by selecting those that best match their preferences and risk profiles (Salter and Weinhold, 1979). Shareholders can often diversify more cheaply than a corporation because they can buy shares at the market price and avoid hefty acquisition premiums.

These premises mean that corporate strategy cannot succeed unless it truly adds value—to business units by providing tangible benefits that offset the inherent costs of lost independence and to shareholders by diversifying in a way they could not replicate.

---

* Some recent evidence also supports the conclusion that acquired companies often suffer eroding performance after acquisition. See Frederick M. Scherer, "Mergers, Sell-Offs and Managerial Behavior," in *The Economics of Strategic Planning*, ed. Lacy Glenn Thomas (Lexington, MA: Lexington Books, 1986), p. 143, and David A. Ravenscraft and Frederick M. Scherer, "Mergers and Managerial Performance," paper presented at the Conference on Takeovers and Contests for Corporate Control, Columbia Law School, 1985.

Passing the Essential Tests

To understand how to formulate corporate strategy, it is necessary to specify the conditions under which diversification will truly create shareholder value. These conditions can be summarized in three essential tests:

1. *The attractiveness test.* The industries chosen for diversification must be structurally attractive or capable of being made attractive.
2. *The cost-of-entry test.* The cost of entry must not capitalize all the future profits.
3. *The better-off test.* Either the new unit must gain competitive advantage from its link with the corporation or vice versa.

Of course, most companies will make certain that their proposed strategies pass some of these tests. But my study clearly shows that when companies ignored one or two of them, the strategic results were disastrous.

HOW ATTRACTIVE IS THE INDUSTRY?

In the long run, the rate of return available from competing in an industry is a function of its underlying structure [see Porter reading in Chapter 4]. An attractive industry with a high average return on investment will be difficult to enter because entry barriers are high, suppliers and buyers have only modest bargaining power, substitute products or services are few, and the rivalry among competitors is stable. An unattractive industry like steel will have structural flaws, including a plethora of substitute materials, powerful and price-sensitive buyers, and excessive rivalry caused by high fixed costs and a large group of competitors, many of whom are state supported.

Diversification cannot create shareholder value unless new industries have favorable structures that support returns exceeding the cost of capital. If the industry doesn't have such returns, the company must be able to restructure the industry or gain a sustainable competitive advantage that leads to returns well above the industry average. An industry need not be attractive before diversification. In fact, a company might benefit from entering before the industry shows its full potential. The diversification can then transform the industry's structure.

In my research, I often found companies had suspended the attractiveness test because they had a vague belief that the industry "fit" very closely with their own businesses. In the hope that the corporate "comfort" they felt would lead to a happy outcome, the companies ignored fundamentally poor industry structures. Unless the close fit allows substantial competitive advantage, however, such comfort will turn into pain when diversification results in poor returns. Royal Dutch Shell and other leading oil companies have had this unhappy experience in a number of chemicals businesses, where poor industry structures overcame the benefits of vertical integration and skills in process technology.

Another common reason for ignoring the attractiveness test is a low entry cost. Sometimes the buyer has an inside track or the owner is anxious to sell. Even if the price is actually low, however, a one-shot gain will not offset a perpetually poor business. Almost always, the company finds it must reinvest in the newly acquired unit, if only to replace fixed assets and fund working capital.

Diversifying companies are also prone to use rapid growth or other simple indicators as a proxy for a target industry's attractiveness. Many that rushed into fast-growing industries (personal computers, video games, and robotics, for example) were burned because they mistook early growth for long-term profit potential. Industries are profitable not because they are sexy or high tech; they are profitable only if their structures are attractive.

WHAT IS THE COST OF ENTRY?

Diversification cannot build shareholder value if the cost of entry into a new business eats up its expected returns. Strong market forces, however, are working to do just that. A company can enter new industries by acquisition or start-up. Acquisitions expose it to an increasingly efficient merger market. An acquirer beats the market if it pays a price not fully reflecting the prospects of the new unit. Yet multiple bidders are commonplace, information flows rapidly, and investment bankers and other intermediaries work aggressively to make the market as efficient as possible. In recent years, new financial instruments such as junk bonds have brought new buyers into the market and made even large companies vulnerable to takeover. Acquisition premiums are high and reflect the acquired company's future prospects—sometimes too well. Philip Morris paid more than four times book value for Seven-Up Company, for example. Simple arithmetic meant that profits had to more than quadruple to sustain the preacquisition ROI. Since there proved to be little Philip Morris could add in marketing prowess to the sophisticated marketing wars in the soft drink industry, the result was the unsatisfactory financial performance of Seven-Up and ultimately the decision to divest.

In a start-up, the company must overcome entry barriers. It's a real catch-22 situation, however, since attractive industries are attractive because their entry barriers are high. Bearing the full cost of the entry barriers might well dissipate any potential profits. Otherwise, other entrants to the industry would have already eroded its profitability.

In the excitement of finding an appealing new business, companies sometimes forget to apply the cost-of-entry test. The more attractive a new industry, the more expensive it is to get into.

WILL THE BUSINESS BE BETTER OFF?

A corporation must bring some significant competitive advantage to the new unit, or the new unit must offer potential for significant advantage to the corporation. Sometimes, the benefits to the new unit accrue only once, near the time of entry, when the parent instigates a major overhaul of its strategy or installs a first-rate management team. Other diversification yields ongoing competitive advantage if the new unit can market its product, through the well-developed distribution system of its sister units, for instance. This is one of the important underpinnings of the merger of Baxter Travenol and American Hospital Supply.

When the benefit to the new unit comes only once, the parent company has no rationale for holding the new unit in its portfolio over the long term. Once the results of the one-time improvement are clear, the diversified company no longer adds value to offset the inevitable costs imposed on the unit. It is best to sell the unit and free up corporate resources.

The better-off test does not imply that diversifying corporate risk creates shareholder value in and of itself. Doing something for shareholders that they can do themselves is not a basis for corporate strategy. (Only in the case of a privately held company, in which the company's and the shareholder's risk are the same, is diversification to reduce risk valuable for its own sake.) Diversification of risk should only be a by-product of corporate strategy, not a prime motivator.

Executives ignore the better-off test most of all or deal with it through arm waving or trumped-up logic rather than hard strategic analysis. One reason is that they confuse company size with shareholder value. In the drive to run a bigger company, they lose sight of their real job. They may justify the suspension of the better-off test by pointing to the way they manage diversity. By cutting corporate staff to the bone and giving business units nearly complete autonomy, they believe they avoid the pitfalls. Such thinking misses the whole point of diversification, which is to create shareholder value rather than to avoid destroying it.

Concepts of Corporate Strategy

The three tests for successful diversification set the standards that any corporate strategy must meet; meeting them is so difficult that most diversification fails. Many companies lack a clear concept of corporate strategy to guide their diversification or pursue a concept that does not address the tests. Others fail because they implement a strategy poorly.

My study has helped me identify four concepts of corporate strategy that have been put into practice—portfolio management, restructuring, transferring skills, and sharing activities. While the concepts are not always mutually exclusive, each rests on a different mechanism by which the corporation creates shareholder value and each requires the diversified company to manage and organize itself in a different way. The first two require no connections among business units; the second two depend on them. . . . While all four concepts of strategy have succeeded under the right circumstances, today some make more sense than others. Ignoring any of the concepts is perhaps the quickest road to failure.

PORTFOLIO MANAGEMENT

The concept of corporate strategy most in use is portfolio management, which is based primarily on diversification through acquisition. The corporation acquires sound, attractive companies with competent managers who agree to stay on. While acquired units do not have to be in the same industries as existing units, the best portfolio managers generally limit their range of businesses in some way, in part to limit the specific expertise needed by top management.

The acquired units are autonomous, and the teams that run them are compensated according to unit results. The corporation supplies capital and works with each to infuse it with professional management techniques. At the same time, top management provides objective and dispassionate review of business unit results. Portfolio managers categorize units by potential and regularly transfer resources from units that generate cash to those with high potential and cash needs. . . .

In most countries, the days when portfolio management was a valid concept of corporate strategy are past. In the face of increasingly well-developed capital markets, attractive companies with good managements show up on everyone's computer screen and attract top dollar in terms of acquisition premium. Simply contributing capital isn't contributing much. A sound strategy can easily be funded; small to medium-size companies don't need a munificent parent.

Other benefits have also eroded. Large companies no longer corner the market for professional management skills; in fact, more and more observers believe managers cannot necessarily run anything in the absence of industry-specific knowledge and experience. . . .

But it is the sheer complexity of the management task that has ultimately defeated even the best portfolio managers. As the size of the company grows, portfolio managers need to find more and more deals just to maintain growth. Supervising dozens or even hundreds of disparate units and under chain-letter pressures to add more, management begins to make mistakes. At the same time, the inevitable costs of being part of a diversified company take their toll and unit performance slides while the whole company's ROI turns downward. Eventually, a new management team is installed that initiates wholesale divestments and pares down the company to its core businesses. . . .

In developing countries, where large companies are few, capital markets are undeveloped, and professional management is scarce, portfolio management still works. But it is no longer a valid model for corporate strategy in advanced economies. . . . Portfolio management is no way to conduct corporate strategy.

RESTRUCTURING

Unlike its passive role as a portfolio manager, when it serves as banker and reviewer, a company that bases its strategy on restructuring becomes an active restructurer of business units. The new businesses are not necessarily related to existing units. All that is necessary is unrealized potential.

The restructuring strategy seeks out undeveloped, sick, or threatened organizations or industries on the threshold of significant change. The parent intervenes, frequently changing the unit management team, shifting strategy, or infusing the company with new technology. Then it may make follow-up acquisitions to build a critical mass and sell off unneeded or unconnected parts and thereby reduce the effective acquisition cost. The result is a strengthened company or a transformed industry. As a coda, the parent sells off the stronger unit once results are clear because the parent is no longer adding value, and top management decides that its attention should be directed elsewhere. . . .

When well implemented, the restructuring concept is sound, for it passes the three tests of successful diversification. The restructurer meets the cost-of-entry test through the types of company it acquires. It limits acquisition premiums by buying companies with problems and lackluster images or by buying into industries with as yet unforeseen potential. Intervention by the corporation clearly meets the better-off test. Provided that the target industries are structurally attractive, the restructuring model can create enormous shareholder value. . . . Ironically, many of today's restructurers are profiting from yesterday's portfolio management strategies.

To work, the restructuring strategy requires a corporate management team with the insight to spot undervalued companies or positions in industries ripe for transformation. The same insight is necessary to actually turn the units around even though they are in new and unfamiliar businesses. . . .

Perhaps the greatest pitfall . . . is that companies find it very hard to dispose of business units once they are restructured and performing well. . . .

TRANSFERRING SKILLS

The purpose of the first two concepts of corporate strategy is to create value through a company's relationship with each autonomous unit. The corporation's role is to be a selector, a banker, and an intervenor.

The last two concepts exploit the interrelationships between businesses. In articulating them, however, one comes face-to-face with the often ill-defined concept of synergy. If you believe the text of the countless corporate annual reports, just about anything is related to just about anything else! But imagined synergy is much more common than real synergy. GM's purchase of Hughes Aircraft simply because cars were going electronic and Hughes was an electronics concern demonstrates the folly of paper synergy. Such corporate relatedness is an ex post facto rationalization of a diversification undertaken for other reasons.

Even synergy that is clearly defined often fails to materialize. Instead of cooperating, business units often compete. A company that can define the synergies it is pursuing still faces significant organizational impediments in achieving them.

But the need to capture the benefits of relationships between businesses has never been more important. Technological and competitive developments already link many businesses and are creating new possibilities for competitive advantage. In such sectors as financial services, computing, office equipment, entertainment, and health care, interrelationships among previously distinct businesses are perhaps the central concern of strategy.

To understand the role of relatedness in corporate strategy, we must give new meaning to this often ill-defined idea. I have identified a good way to start—the value chain. [See

Readings 4–1 and 4–2.] Every business unit is a collection of discrete activities ranging from sales to accounting that allow it to compete. I call them value activities. It is at this level, not in the company as a whole, that the unit achieves competitive advantage.

I group these activities in nine categories. *Primary* activities create the product or service, deliver and market it, and provide after-sale support. The categories of primary activities are inbound logistics, operations, outbound logistics, marketing and sales, and service. *Support* activities provide the input and infrastructure that allow the primary activities to take place. The categories are company infrastructure, human resource management, technology development, and procurement.

The value chain defines the two types of interrelationships that may create synergy. The first is a company's ability to transfer skills or expertise among similar value chains. The second is the ability to share activities. Two business units, for example, can share the same sales force or logistics network.

The value chain helps expose the last two (and most important) concepts of corporate strategy. The transfer of skills among business units in the diversified company is the basis for one concept. While each business unit has a separate value chain, knowledge about how to perform activities is transferred among the units. For example, a toiletries business unit, expert in the marketing of convenience products, transmits ideas on new positioning concepts, promotional techniques, and packaging possibilities to a newly acquired unit that sells cough syrup. Newly entered industries can benefit from the expertise of existing units, and vice versa.

These opportunities arise when business units have similar buyers or channels, similar value activities like government relations or procurement, similarities in the broad configuration of the value chain (for example, managing a multisite service organization), or the same strategic concept (for example, low cost). Even though the units operate separately, such similarities allow the sharing of knowledge. . . .

Transferring skills leads to competitive advantage only if the similarities among businesses meet three conditions:

1. The activities involved in the businesses are similar enough that sharing expertise is meaningful. Broad similarities (marketing intensiveness, for example, or a common core process technology such as bending metal) are not a sufficient basis for diversification. The resulting ability to transfer skills is likely to have little impact on competitive advantage.
2. The transfer of skills involves activities important to competitive advantage. Transferring skills in peripheral activities such as government relations or real estate in consumer goods units may be beneficial but is not a basis for diversification.
3. The skills transferred represent a significant source of competitive advantage for the receiving unit. The expertise or skills to be transferred are both advanced and proprietary enough to be beyond the capabilities of competitors. . . .

Transferring skills meets the tests of diversification if the company truly mobilizes proprietary expertise across units. This makes certain the company can offset the acquisition premium or lower the cost of overcoming entry barriers.

The industries the company chooses for diversification must pass the attractiveness test. Even a close fit that reflects opportunities to transfer skills may not overcome poor industry structure. Opportunities to transfer skills, however, may help the company transform the structures of newly entered industries and send them in favorable directions.

The transfer of skills can be one time or ongoing. If the company exhausts opportunities to infuse new expertise into a unit after the initial post-acquisition period, the unit should ultimately be sold. . . .

By using both acquisitions and internal development, companies can build a transfer-of-skills strategy. The presence of a strong base of skills sometimes creates the possibility for internal entry instead of the acquisition of a going concern. Successful diversifiers that employ the concept of skills transfer may, however, often acquire a company in the target industry as a beachhead and then build on it with their internal expertise. By doing so, they can reduce some of the risks of internal entry and speed up the process. Two companies that have diversified using the transfer-of-skills concept are 3M and PepsiCo.

SHARING ACTIVITIES

The fourth concept of corporate strategy is based on sharing activities in the value chains among business units. Procter & Gamble, for example, employs a common physical distribution system and sales force in both paper towels and disposable diapers. McKesson, a leading distribution company, will handle such diverse lines as pharmaceuticals and liquor through superwarehouses.

The ability to share activities is a potent basis for corporate strategy because sharing often enhances competitive advantage by lowering cost or raising differentiation. . . .

Sharing activities inevitably involves costs that the benefits must outweigh. One cost is the greater coordination required to manage a shared activity. More important is the need to compromise the design or performance of an activity so that it can be shared. A salesperson handling the products of two business units, for example, must operate in a way that is usually not what either unit would choose were it independent. And if compromise greatly erodes the unit's effectiveness, then sharing may reduce rather than enhance competitive advantage. . . .

Despite . . . pitfalls, opportunities to gain advantage from sharing activities have proliferated because of momentous developments in technology, deregulation, and competition. The infusion of electronics and information systems into many industries creates new opportunities to link businesses. . . .

Following the shared-activities model requires an organizational context in which business unit collaboration is encouraged and reinforced. Highly autonomous business units are inimical to such collaboration. The company must put into place a variety of what I call horizontal mechanisms—a strong sense of corporate identity, a clear corporate mission statement that emphasizes the importance of integrating business unit strategies, an incentive system that rewards more than just business unit results, cross-business-unit task forces, and other methods of integrating.

A corporate strategy based on shared activities clearly meets the better-off test because business units gain ongoing tangible advantages from others within the corporation. It also meets the cost-of-entry test by reducing the expense of surmounting the barriers to internal entry. Other bids for acquisitions that do not share opportunities will have lower reservation prices. Even widespread opportunities for sharing activities do not allow a company to suspend the attractiveness test, however. Many diversifiers have made the critical mistake of equating the close fit of a target industry with attractive diversification. Target industries must pass the strict requirement test of having an attractive structure as well as a close fit in opportunities if diversification is to ultimately succeed.

Choosing a Corporate Strategy

. . . Both the strategic logic and the experience of the companies I studied over the last decade suggest that a company will create shareholder value through diversification to a greater and greater extent as its strategy moves from portfolio management toward sharing activities. . . .

Each concept of corporate strategy is not mutually exclusive of those that come before, a potent advantage of the third and fourth concepts. A company can employ a restructuring strategy at the same time it transfers skills or shares activities. A strategy based on shared activities becomes more powerful if business units can also exchange skills. . . .

My study supports the soundness of basing a corporate strategy on the transfer of skills or shared activities. The data on the sample companies' diversification programs illustrate some important characteristics of successful diversifiers. They have made a disproportionately low percentage of unrelated acquisitions, *unrelated* being defined as having no clear opportunity to transfer skills or share important activities. . . . Even successful diversifiers such as 3M, IBM, and TRW have terrible records when they strayed into unrelated acquisitions. Successful acquirers diversify into fields, each of which is related to many others. Procter & Gamble and IBM, for example, operate in 18 and 19 interrelated fields respectively and so enjoy numerous opportunities to transfer skills and share activities.

Companies with the best acquisition records tend to make heavier-than-average use of start-ups and joint ventures. Most companies shy away from modes of entry besides acquisition. My results cast doubt on the conventional wisdom regarding start-ups. . . . successful companies often have very good records with start-up units, as 3M, P&G, Johnson & Johnson, IBM, and United Technologies illustrate. When a company has the internal strength to start up a unit, it can be safer and less costly to launch a company than to rely solely on an acquisition and then have to deal with the problem of integration. Japanese diversification histories support the soundness of start-up as an entry alternative.

My data also illustrate that none of the concepts of corporate strategy works when industry structure is poor or implementation is bad, no matter how related the industries are. Xerox acquired companies in related industries, but the businesses had poor structures and its skills were insufficient to provide enough competitive advantage to offset implementation problems.

AN ACTION PROGRAM

. . . A company can choose a corporate strategy by:

1. Identifying the interrelationships among already existing business units. . . .
2. Selecting the core businesses that will be the foundation of the corporate strategy. . . .
3. Creating horizontal organizational mechanisms to facilitate interrelationships among the core businesses and lay the groundwork for future related diversification. . . .
4. Pursuing diversification opportunities that allow shared activities. . . .
5. Pursuing diversification through the transfer of skills if opportunities for sharing activities are limited or exhausted. . . .
6. Pursuing a strategy of restructuring if this fits the skills of management or no good opportunities exist for forging corporate interrelationships. . . .
7. Paying dividends so that the shareholders can be the portfolio managers. . . .

CREATING A CORPORATE THEME

Defining a corporate theme is a good way to ensure that the corporation will create shareholder value. Having the right theme helps unite the efforts of business units and reinforces the ways they interrelate as well as guides the choice of new businesses to enter. NEC Corporation, with its "C&C" theme, provides a good example. NEC integrates its computer, semiconductor, telecommunications, and consumer electronics businesses by merging computers and communication.

It is all too easy to create a shallow corporate theme. CBS wants to be an "entertainment company," for example, and built a group of businesses related to leisure time. It entered such industries as toys, crafts, musical instruments, sports teams, and hi-fi retailing. While this corporate theme sounded good, close listening revealed its hollow ring. None of these businesses had any significant opportunity to share activities or transfer skills among themselves or with CBS's traditional broadcasting and record businesses. They were all sold, often at significant losses, except for a few of CBS's publishing-related units. Saddled with the worst acquisition record in my study, CBS has eroded the shareholder value created through its strong performance in broadcasting and records.

Moving from competitive strategy to corporate strategy is the business equivalent of passing through the Bermuda Triangle. The failure of corporate strategy reflects the fact that most diversified companies have failed to think in terms of how they really add value. A corporate strategy that truly enhances the competitive advantage of each business unit is the best defense against the corporate raider. With a sharper focus on the tests of diversification and the explicit choice of a clear concept of corporate strategy, companies diversification track records from now on can look a lot different.

THE INTERNATIONAL CONTEXT

While the "international context" is hardly a situation like the others in this section of the book, there has been increasing attention to this dimension in recent years, most often under the label "global" (although few corporations in fact cover the globe, let alone significant parts of it). In a sense, the international context is diversified too, but in a particular respect—as to geography.

Operating in an international rather than a domestic arena presents managers with many new opportunities. Having worldwide operations not only gives a company access to new markets and specialized resources, it also opens up new sources of information to stimulate future product development. And it broadens the options of strategic moves and countermoves the company might make in competing with its domestic or more narrowly international rivals. However, with all these new opportunities comes the challenge of managing strategy, organization, and operations that are innately more complex, diverse, and uncertain. We include two readings on the international context.

The first, by George Yip, who teaches at the University of California in Los Angeles, focuses on the strategic aspects of managing in an international context. Yip's views on "global strategy" reflect the same orientation of industrial organization economics that influenced Porter's work: In deciding on markets to participate in, products and services to offer, and location of specific activities and tasks, managers must analyze the "globalization drivers" in their industries and find the right strategic fit.

In the second reading, Christopher Bartlett and Sumantra Ghoshal of the Harvard and London Business Schools, respectively, deal with the organizational aspects of managing in the international context. To operate effectively on a worldwide basis, Bartlett and Ghoshal suggest, companies must learn to differentiate how they manage different businesses, countries, and functions, create interdependence among units instead of either dependence or independence, and focus on coordination and co-option rather than control. The key to such organizational capability lies in the same elements of shared vision and values that they described in their article in Chapter 7, as essential for "building a matrix in managers' minds."

Since useful generalizations about the international context are so hard to come up with, we offer a wide variety of cases which allow students to probe these issues empirically. One group of companies—Sony Corporation, Matsushita Electric Industrial Company, Nintendo Co., Ltd., and Honda Motor Company—allow glimpses of different Japanese multinational styles. A second group—Andersen Consulting (Europe), Cadbury-Schweppes, P.L.C., The Transformation of AT&T, and SAS and the European Airlines Industry—focus on Europe. Orbital Engine Company, Argyle Diamonds, and TCG, Ltd./Thermo Electron provide the perspective of a small company looking outward. Finally, a number of U.S. multinationals—Ford Motor Company, IBM, Intel Corporation, Microsoft

Corporation, Exxon Corporation, New Steel Company, and PR&D among others—approach the international strategy problem from more of a U.S. viewpoint. The Nintendo of America and Sony Entertainment cases introduce some of the unique problems Americans working in foreign-owned firms often encounter. However, virtually every case in the book is set in an international context, and even companies operating solely in a domestic market are faced with global competitors and suppliers.

▼ READING 14.1   GLOBAL STRATEGY ... IN A WORLD OF NATIONS*

by George S. Yip

Whether to globalize, and how to globalize, have become two of the most burning strategy issues for managers around the world. Many forces are driving companies around the world to globalize by expanding their participation in foreign markets. Almost every product market in the major world economies—computers, fast food, nuts and bolts—has foreign competitors. Trade barriers are also falling; the recent United States/Canada trade agreement and the impending 1992 harmonization in the European Community are the two most dramatic examples. Japan is gradually opening up its long barricaded markets. Maturity in domestic markets is also driving companies to seek international expansion. This is particularly true of U.S. companies that, nourished by the huge domestic market, have typically lagged behind their European and Japanese rivals in internationalization.

Companies are also seeking to globalize by integrating their worldwide strategy. Such global integration contrasts with the multinational approach whereby companies set up country subsidiaries that design, produce, and market products or services tailored to local needs. This multinational model (also described as a "multidomestic strategy") is now in question (Hout et al., 1982). Several changes seem to increase the likelihood that, in some industries, a global strategy will be more successful than a multidomestic one. One of these changes, as argued forcefully and controversially by Levitt (1983) is the growing similarity of what citizens of different countries want to buy. Other changes include the reduction of tariff and nontariff barriers, technology investments that are becoming too expensive to amortize in one market only, and competitors that are globalizing the rules of the game.

Companies want to know how to globalize—in other words, expand market participation—and how to develop an integrated worldwide strategy. As depicted in Figure 1, three steps are essential in developing a total worldwide strategy:

▼ Developing the core strategy—the basis of sustainable competitive advantage. It is usually developed for the home country first.

▼ Internationalizing the core strategy through international expansion of activities and through adaptation.

▼ Globalizing the international strategy by integrating the strategy across countries.

Multinational companies know the first two steps well. They know the third step less well since globalization runs counter to the accepted wisdom of tailoring for national markets (Douglas and Wind, 1987).

This article makes a case for how a global strategy might work and directs managers toward opportunities to exploit globalization. It also presents the drawbacks and costs of globalization. Figure 2 lays out a framework for thinking through globalization issues.

---

*My framework, developed in this article, is based in part on M. E. Porter's (1986) pioneering work on global strategy. Bartlett and Ghoshal (1987) define a "transnational industry" that is somewhat similar to Porter's "global industry."

Originally published in the *Sloan Management Review* (Fall 1989). Copyright © *Sloan Management Review* Association 1989; all rights reserved; reprinted with deletions by permission of the publisher.

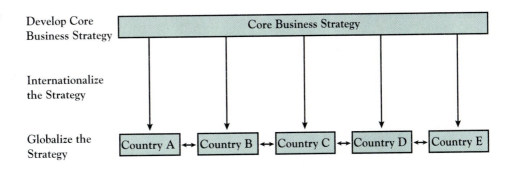

Industry globalization drivers (underlying market, cost, and other industry conditions) are externally determined, while global strategy levers are choices available to the world-wide business. Drivers create the potential for a multinational business to achieve the benefits of global strategy. To achieve these benefits, a multinational business needs to set its *global strategy levers* (e.g., use of product standardization) appropriately to industry drivers, and to the position and resources of the business and its parent company. The organization's ability to implement the strategy affects how well the benefits can be achieved.

What Is Global Strategy?

Setting strategy for a worldwide business requires making choices along a number of strategic dimensions. Table 1 lists five such dimensions or "global strategy levels" and their respective positions under a pure multidomestic strategy and a pure global strategy. Intermediate positions are, of course, feasible. For each dimension, a multidomestic strategy seeks to maximize worldwide performance by maximizing local competitive advantage, revenues, or profits; a global strategy seeks to maximize worldwide performance through sharing and integration.

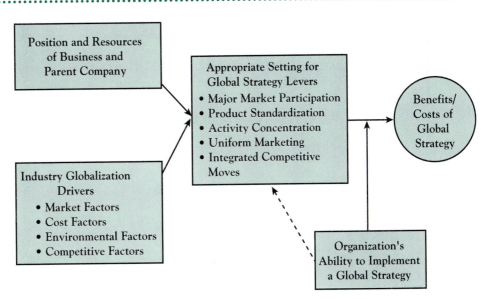

TABLE 1
Globalization Dimensions/
Global Strategy Levers

DIMENSION	SETTING FOR PURE MULTIDOMESTIC STRATEGY	SETTING FOR PURE GLOBAL STRATEGY
Market Participation	No particular pattern	Significant share in major markets
Product Offering	Fully customized in each country	Fully standardized worldwide
Location of Value-Added Activities	All activities in each country	Concentrated—one activity in each (different) country
Marketing Approach	Local	Uniform worldwide
Competitive Moves	Stand-alone by country	Integrated across countries

MARKET PARTICIPATION

In a multidomestic strategy, countries are selected on the basis of their stand-alone poten-tial for revenues and profits. In a global strategy, countries need to be selected for their potential contribution to globalization benefits. This may mean entering a market that is unattractive in its own right, but has global strategic significance, such as the home market of a global competitor. Or it may mean building share in a limited number of key markets rather than undertaking more widespread coverage. . . . The Electrolux Group, the Swedish appliance giant, is pursuing a strategy of building significant share in major world markets. The company aims to be the first global appliance maker. . . .

PRODUCT OFFERING

In a multidomestic strategy, the products offered in each country are tailored to local needs. In a global strategy, the ideal is a standardized core product that requires minimal local adaptation. Cost reduction is usually the most important benefit of product standardization. . . . Differing worldwide needs can be met by adapting a standardized core product. In the early 1970s, sales of the Boeing 737 began to level off. Boeing turned to developing coun-tries as an attractive new market, but found initially that its product did not fit the new environments. Because of the shortness of runways, their greater softness, and the lower technical expertise of their pilots, the planes tended to bounce a great deal. When the planes bounced on landing, the brakes failed. To fix this problem, Boeing modified the design by adding thrust to the engines, redesigning the wings and landing gear, and installing tires with lower pressure. These adaptations to a standardized core product enabled the 737 to become the best selling plane in history.

LOCATION OF VALUE ADDED ACTIVITIES

In a multidomestic strategy, all or most of the value chain is reproduced in every country. In another type of international strategy—exporting—most of the value chain is kept in one country. In a global strategy, costs are reduced by breaking up the value chain so each activity may be conducted in a different country. . . .

MARKETING APPROACH

In a multidomestic strategy, marketing is fully tailored for each country, being developed locally. In a global strategy, a uniform marketing approach is applied around the world, although not all elements of the marketing mix need be uniform. Unilever achieved great success with a fabric softener that used a globally common positioning, advertising theme, and symbol (a teddy bear), but a brand name that varied by country. Similarly, a product that serves a common need can be geographically expanded with a uniform marketing program, despite differences in marketing environments.

COMPETITIVE MOVES

In a multidomestic strategy, the managers in each country make competitive moves without regard for what happens in other countries. In a global strategy, competitive moves are integrated across countries at the same time or in a systematic sequence: a competitor is attacked in one country in order to drain its resources for another country, or a competitive attack in one country is countered in a different country. Perhaps the best example is the counterattack in a competitor's home market as a parry to an attack on one's own home market. Integration of competitive strategy is rarely practiced, except perhaps by some Japanese companies.

Bridgestone Corporation, the Japanese tire manufacturer, tried to integrate its competitive moves in response to global consolidation by its major competitors. . . . These competitive actions forced Bridgestone to establish a presence in the major U.S. market in order to maintain its position in the world tire market. To this end, Bridgestone formed a joint venture to own and manage Firestone Corporation's worldwide tire business. This joint venture also allowed Bridgestone to gain access to Firestone's European plants.

Benefits of a Global Strategy

Companies that use global strategy levers can achieve one or more of these benefits. . . .

▼ cost reductions
▼ improved quality of products and programs
▼ enhanced customer preference
▼ increased competitive leverage

COST REDUCTIONS

An integrated global strategy can reduce worldwide costs in several ways. A company can increase the benefits from economies of scale by *pooling production or other activities* for two or more countries. Understanding the potential benefit of these economies of scale, Sony Corporation has concentrated its compact disc production in Terre Haute, Indiana, and Salzburg, Austria.

A second way to cut costs is by *exploiting lower factor costs* by moving manufacturing or other activities to low-cost countries. This approach has, of course, motivated the recent surge of offshore manufacturing, particularly by U.S. firms. For example, the Mexican side of the U.S.-Mexico border is now crowded with "maquiladoras"—manufacturing plants set up and run by U.S. companies using Mexican labor.

Global strategy can also cut costs by *exploiting flexibility*. A company with manufacturing locations in several countries can move production from location to location on short notice to take advantage of the lowest costs at a given time. Dow Chemical takes this approach to minimize the cost of producing chemicals. Dow uses a linear programming model that takes account of international differences in exchange rates, tax rates, and transportation and labor costs. The model comes up with the best mix of production volume by location for each planning period.

An integrated global strategy can also reduce costs by *enhancing bargaining power*. A company whose strategy allows for switching production among different countries greatly increases its bargaining power with suppliers, workers, and host governments. . . .

IMPROVED QUALITY OF PRODUCTS AND PROGRAMS

Under a global strategy, companies focus on a smaller number of products and programs than under a multidomestic strategy. This concentration can improve both product and program quality. Global focus is one reason for Japanese success in automobiles. Toyota markets a far smaller number of models around the world than does General Motors, even allowing for its unit sales being half that of General Motors's. . . .

ENHANCED CUSTOMER PREFERENCE

Global availability, serviceability, and recognition can enhance customer preference through reinforcement. Soft drink and fast food companies are, of course, leading exponents of this strategy. Many suppliers of financial services, such as credit cards, must have a global presence because their service is travel related. . . .

INCREASED COMPETITIVE LEVERAGE

A global strategy provides more points from which to attack and counterattack competitors. In an effort to prevent the Japanese from becoming a competitive nuisance in disposable syringes, Becton Dickinson, a major U.S. medical products company, decided to enter three markets in Japan's backyard. Becton entered the Hong Kong, Singapore, and Philippine markets to prevent further Japanese expansion (Var, 1986).

Drawbacks of Global Strategy

Globalization can incur significant management costs through increased coordination, reporting requirements, and even added staff. It can also reduce the firm's effectiveness in individual countries if overcentralization hurts local motivation and morale. In addition, each global strategy lever has particular drawbacks.

A global strategy approach to *market participation* can incur an earlier or greater commitment to a market than is warranted on its own merits. Many American companies, such as Motorola, are struggling to penetrate Japanese markets, more in order to enhance their global competitive position than to make money in Japan for its own sake.

Product standardization can result in a product that does not entirely satisfy *any* customers. When companies first internationalize, they often offer their standard domestic product without adapting it for other countries, and suffer the consequences. . . .

A globally standardized product is designed for the global market but can seldom satisfy all needs in all countries. For instance, Canon, a Japanese company, sacrificed the ability to copy certain Japanese paper sizes when it first designed a photocopier for the global market.

Activity concentration distances customers and can result in lower responsiveness and flexibility. It also increases currency risk by incurring costs and revenues in different countries. Recently volatile exchange rates have required companies that concentrate their production to hedge their currency exposure.

Uniform marketing can reduce adaptation to local customer behavior. For example, the head office of British Airways mandated that every country use the "Manhattan Landing" television commercial developed by advertising agency Saatchi and Saatchi. While the commercial did win many awards, it has been criticized for using a visual image (New York City) that was not widely recognized in many countries.

Integrated competitive moves can mean sacrificing revenues, profits, or competitive position in individual countries, particularly when the subsidiary in one country is asked to attack a global competitor in order to send a signal or to divert that competitor's resources from another country.

Finding the Balance

The most successful worldwide strategies find a balance between overglobalizing and underglobalizing. The ideal strategy matches the level of strategy globalization to the globalization potential of the industry. . . .

Industry Globalization Drivers

To achieve the benefits of globalization, the managers of a worldwide business need to recognize when industry globalization drivers (industry conditions) provide the opportunity to use global strategy levers. These drivers can be grouped in four categories: market, cost, governmental, and competitive. Each industry globalization driver affects the potential use of global strategy levers. . . .

MARKET DRIVERS

Market globalization drivers depend on customer behavior and the structure of distribution channels. These drivers affect the use of all five global strategy levers.

HOMOGENEOUS CUSTOMER NEEDS

When customers in different countries want essentially the same type of product or service (or can be so persuaded), opportunities arise to market a standardized product. Understanding which aspects of the product can be standardized and which should be customized is key. In addition, homogeneous needs make participation in a large number of markets easier because fewer different product offerings need to be developed and supported.

GLOBAL CUSTOMERS

Global customers buy on a centralized or coordinated basis for decentralized use. The existence of global customers both allows and requires a uniform marketing program. There are two types of global customers: national and multinational. A national global customer searches the world for suppliers but uses the purchased product or service in one country. National defense agencies are a good example. A multinational global customer also searches the world for suppliers, but uses the purchased product or service in many countries. The World Health Organization's purchase of medical products is an example. Multinational global customers are particularly challenging to serve and often require a global account management program.. . . .

GLOBAL CHANNELS

Analogous to global customers, channels of distribution may buy on a global or at least a regional basis. Global channels or middlemen are also important in exploiting differences in prices by buying at a lower price in one country and selling at a higher price in another country. Their presence makes it more necessary for a business to rationalize its worldwide pricing. Global channels are rare, but regionwide channels are increasing in number, particularly in European grocery distribution and retailing.

TRANSFERABLE MARKETING

The buying decision may be such that marketing elements, such as brand names and advertising, require little local adaptation. Such transferability enables firms to use uniform marketing strategies and facilitates expanded participation in markets. A worldwide business can also adapt its brand names and advertising campaigns to make them more transferable, or, even better, design global ones to start with. Offsetting risks include the blandness of uniformly acceptable brand names or advertising, and the vulnerability of relying on a single brand franchise.

COST DRIVERS

Cost drivers depend on the economics of the business; they particularly affect activity concentration.

ECONOMIES OF SCALE AND SCOPE

A single-country market may not be large enough for the local business to achieve all possible economies of scale or scope. Scale at a given location can be increased through participation in multiple markets combined with product standardization or concentration of selected value activities. Corresponding risks include rigidity and vulnerability to disruption. . . .

LEARNING AND EXPERIENCE

Even if economies of scope and scale are exhausted, expanded market participation and activity concentration can accelerate the accumulation of learning and experience. The steeper the learning and experience curves, the greater the potential benefit will be. Managers should beware, though, of the usual danger in pursuing experience curve strategies—overaggressive pricing that destroyed not just the competition but the market as well. Prices get so low that profit is insufficient to sustain any competitor.

SOURCING EFFICIENCIES

Centralized purchasing of new materials can significantly lower costs. . . .

FAVORABLE LOGISTICS

A favorable ratio of sales value to transportation cost enhances the company's ability to concentrate production. Other logistical factors include nonperishability, the absence of time urgency, and little need for location close to customer facilities. . . .

DIFFERENCES IN COUNTRY COSTS AND SKILLS

Factor costs generally vary across countries; this is particularly true in certain industries. The availability of particular skills also varies. Concentration of activities in low-cost or high-skill countries can increase productivity and reduce costs, but managers need to anticipate the danger of training future offshore competitors. . . .

PRODUCT DEVELOPMENT COSTS

Product development costs can be reduced by developing a few global or regional products rather than many national products. The automobile industry is characterized by long product development periods and high product development costs. One reason for the high costs is duplication of effort across countries. The Ford Motor Company's "Centers of Excellence" program aims to reduce these duplicating efforts and to exploit the differing expertise of Ford specialists worldwide. As part of the concentrated effort, Ford of Europe is designing a common platform for all compacts, while Ford of North America is developing platforms for the replacement of the mid-sized Taurus and Sable. This concentration of design is estimated to save "hundreds of millions of dollars per model by eliminating duplicative efforts and saving on retooling factories" (*Business Week*, 1987).

GOVERNMENTAL DRIVERS

Government globalization drivers depend on the rules set by national governments and affect the use of all global strategy levers.

FAVORABLE TRADE POLICIES

Host governments affect globalization potential through import tariffs and quotas, nontariff barriers, export subsidies, local content requirements, currency and capital flow restrictions, and requirements on technology transfer. Host government policies can make it difficult to use the global levers of major market participation, product standardization, activity concentration, and uniform marketing; they also affect the integrated-competitive moves lever. . . .

COMPATIBLE TECHNICAL STANDARDS

Differences in technical standards, especially government-imposed standards, limit the extent to which products can be standardized. Often, standards are set with protectionism in mind. Motorola found that many of their electronics products were excluded from the Japanese market because these products operated at a higher frequency than was permitted in Japan.

COMMON MARKETING REGULATIONS

The marketing environment of individual countries affects the extent to which uniform global marketing approaches can be used. Certain types of media may be prohibited or restricted. For example, the United States is far more liberal than Europe about the kinds of advertising claims that can be made on television. The British authorities even veto the depiction of socially undesirable behavior. For example, British television authorities do not allow scenes of children pestering their parents to buy a product. . . .

COMPETITIVE DRIVERS

Market, cost, and governmental globalization drivers are essentially fixed for an industry at any given time. Competitors can play only a limited role in affecting these factors (although a sustained effort can bring about change, particularly in the case of consumer preferences). In contrast, competitive drivers are entirely in the realm of competitor choice. Competitors can raise the globalization potential of their industry and spur the need for a response on the global strategy levers.

INTERDEPENDENCE OF COUNTRIES

A competitor may create competitive interdependence among countries by pursuing a global strategy. The basic mechanism is through sharing of activities. When activities such as production are shared among countries, a competitor's market share in one country affects its scale and overall cost position in the shared activities. Changes in that scale and cost will affect its competitive position in all countries dependent on the shared activities. Less directly, customers may view market position in a lead country as an indicator of overall quality. Companies frequently promote a product as, for example. "the leading brand in the United States." Other competitors then need to respond via increased market participation, uniform marketing, or integrated competitive strategy to avoid a downward spiral of sequentially weakened positions in individual countries.

In the automobile industry, where economies of scale are significant and where sharing activities can lower costs, markets have significant competitive interdependence. As companies like Ford and Volkswagen concentrate production and become more cost competitive with the Japanese manufacturers, the Japanese are pressured to enter more markets so that increased production volume will lower costs. Whether conscious of this or not, Toyota has begun a concerted effort to penetrate the German market: between 1984 and 1987, Toyota doubled the number of cars produced for the German market.

GLOBALIZED COMPETITORS

More specifically, matching or preempting individual competitor moves may be necessary. These moves include expanding into or within major markets, being the first to introduce a standardized product, or being the first to use a uniform marketing program.

The need to preempt a global competitor can spur increased market participation. In 1986, Unilever, the European consumer products company, sought to increase its participation in the U.S. market by launching a hostile takeover bid for Richardson-Vicks Inc. Unilever's global archrival, Procter & Gamble, saw the threat to its home turf and outbid Unilever to capture Richardson-Vicks. With Richardson-Vicks's European system, P&G was able to greatly strengthen its European positioning. So Unilever's attempt to expand participation in a rival's home market backfired to allow the rival to expand participation in Unilever's home markets.

In summary, industry globalization drivers provide opportunities to use global strategy levers in many ways. Some industries, such as civil aircraft, can score high on most dimensions of globalization (Yoshino, 1986). Others, such as the cement industry, seem to be inherently local. But more and more industries are developing globalization potential. Even the food industry in Europe, renowned for its diversity of taste, is now a globalization target for major food multinationals.

CHANGES OVER TIME

Finally, industry evolution plays a role. As each of the industry globalization drivers changes over time, so too will the appropriate global strategy change. For example, in the European major appliance industry, globalization forces seem to have reversed. In the late 1960s and early 1970s, a regional standardization strategy was successful for some key competitors (Levitt, 1983). But in the 1980s the situation appears to have turned around, and the most successful strategies seem to be national (Badenfuller et al., 1987).

In some cases, the actions of individual competitors can affect the direction and pace of change; competitors positioned to take advantage of globalization forces will want to hasten them. . . .

More Than One Strategy Is Viable

Although they are powerful, industry globalization drivers do not dictate one formula for success. More than one type of international strategy can be viable in a given industry.

INDUSTRIES VARY ACROSS DRIVERS

No industry is high on every one of the many globalization drivers. A particular competitor may be in a strong position to exploit a driver that scores low on globalization. . . . The hotel industry provides examples both of successful global and successful local competitors.

GLOBAL EFFECTS ARE INCREMENTAL

Globalization drivers are not deterministic for a second reason: the appropriate use of strategy levers adds competitive advantage to existing sources. These other sources may allow individual competitors to thrive with international strategies that are mismatched with industry globalization drivers. For example, superior technology is a major source of competitive advantage in most industries, but can be quite independent of globalization drivers. A competitor with sufficiently superior technology can use it to offset globalization disadvantages.

BUSINESS AND PARENT COMPANY POSITION AND RESOURCES ARE CRUCIAL

The third reason that drivers are not deterministic is related to resources. A worldwide business may face industry drivers that strongly favor a global strategy. But global strategies are typically expensive to implement initially even though great cost savings and revenue gains should follow. High initial investments may be needed to expand within or into major markets, to develop standardized products, to relocate value activities, to create global brands, to create new organization units or coordination processes, and to implement other aspects of a global strategy. The strategic position of the business is also relevant. Even though a global strategy may improve the business's long-term strategic position, its immediate position may be so weak that resources should be devoted to short-term, country-by-country improvements. Despite the automobile industry's very strong globalization drivers, Chrysler Corporation had to deglobalize by selling off most of its international automotive businesses to avoid bankruptcy. Lastly, investing in nonglobal sources of competitive advantage, such as superior technology, may yield greater returns than global ones, such as centralized manufacturing.

ORGANIZATIONS HAVE LIMITATIONS

Finally, factors such as organization structure, management processes, people, and culture affect how well a desired global strategy can be implemented. Organizational differences among companies in the same industry can, or should, constrain the companies' pursuit of the same global strategy. . . .

by Christopher A. Bartlett and Sumantra Ghoshal

. . . Recent changes in the international operating environment have forced companies to optimize *efficiency*, *responsiveness*, and *learning* simultaneously in their worldwide operations (Bartlett and Ghoshal, 1987). To companies that previously concentrated on developing and managing one of these capabilities, this new challenge implies not only a total strategic reorientation but a major change in organizational capability, as well.

Implementing such a complex, three-pronged strategic objective would be difficult under any circumstances, but in a worldwide company the task is complicated even further. The very act of "going international" multiplies a company's organizational complexity. Typically, doing so requires adding a third dimension to the existing business- and function-oriented management structure. It is difficult enough balancing product divisions that bring efficiency and focus to domestic product-market strategies with corporate staffs whose functional expertise allows them to play an important counterbalance and control role. The thought of adding capable, geographically oriented management—and maintaining a three-way balance of organizational perspectives and capabilities among product, function, and area—is intimidating to most managers. The difficulty is increased because the resolution of tensions among product, function, and area managers must be accomplished in an organization whose operating units are often divided by distance and time and whose key members are separated by culture and language.

FROM UNIDIMENSIONAL TO MULTIDIMENSIONAL CAPABILITIES

Faced with the task of building multiple strategic capabilities in highly complex organizations, managers in almost every company we studied** made the simplifying assumption that they were faced with a series of dichotomous choices. They discussed the relative merits of pursuing a strategy of national responsiveness as opposed to one based on global integration; they considered whether key assets and resources should be centralized or decentralized; and they debated the need for strong central control versus greater subsidiary autonomy. How a company resolved these dilemmas typically reflected influences exerted and choices made during its historical development. In telecommunications, ITT's need to develop an organization responsive to national political demands and local specification differences was as important to its survival in the pre– and post–World War II era as was NEC's need to build its highly centralized technological manufacturing and marketing skills and resources in order to expand abroad in the same industry in the 1960s and 1970s.

When new competitive challenges emerged, however, such unidimensional biases became strategically limiting. As ITT demonstrated by its outstanding historic success and NEC showed by its more delayed international expansion, strong *geographic management* is essential for development of dispersed responsiveness. Geographic management allows worldwide companies to sense, analyze, and respond to the needs of different national markets.

Effective competitors also need to build strong *business management* with global product responsibilities if they are to achieve global efficiency and integration. These managers act as champions of manufacturing rationalization, product standardization, and low-cost

**The findings presented in this article are based on a three-year research project on the organization and management of multinational corporations. Extensive discussions were held with 250 managers in nine of the world's largest multinational companies, in the United States, Europe, and Japan. Complete findings are presented in *Managing across Borders: The Transnational Solution* (Boston: Harvard Business School Press, 1988).

global sourcing. (As the telecommunications switching industry globalized, NEC's organizational capability in this area gave it a major competitive advantage.) Unencumbered by either territorial or functional loyalties, central product groups remain sensitive to overall competitive issues and become agents to facilitate changes that, though painful, are necessary for competitive viability.

Finally, a strong, worldwide *functional management* allows an organization to build and transfer its core competencies—a capability vital to worldwide learning. Links between functional managers allow the company to accumulate specialized knowledge and skills and to apply them wherever they are required in the worldwide operations. Functional management acts as the repository of organizational learning and as the prime mover for its consolidation and circulation within the company. It was for want of a strongly linked research and technical function across subsidiaries that ITT failed in its attempt to coordinate the development and diffusion of its System 12 digital switch.

Thus, to respond to the needs for efficiency, responsiveness, and learning *simultaneously*, the company must develop a multidimensional organization in which the effectiveness of each management group is maintained *and* in which each group is prevented from dominating the others. As we saw in company after company, the most difficult challenge for managers trying to respond to broad, emerging strategic demands was to develop the new elements of multidimensional organization without eroding the effectiveness of their current unidimensional capability.

OVERCOMING SIMPLIFYING ASSUMPTIONS

For all nine companies at the core of our study, the challenge of breaking down biases and building a truly multidimensional organization proved difficult. Behind the pervasive either/or mentality that led to the development of unidimensional capabilities, we identified three simplifying assumptions that blocked the necessary organizational development. The need to reduce organizational and strategic complexity has made these assumptions almost universal in worldwide companies, regardless of industry, national origin, or management culture.

▼ There is a widespread, often implicit assumption that roles of different organizational units are uniform and symmetrical; different businesses should be managed in the same way, as should different functions and national operations.
▼ Most companies, some consciously, most unconsciously, create internal interunit relationships on clear patterns of dependence or independence, on the assumption that such relationships *should* be clear and unambiguous.
▼ Finally, there is the assumption that one of corporate management's principal tasks is to institutionalize clearly understood mechanisms for decision making and to implement simple means of exercising control.

Those companies most successful in developing truly multidimensional organizations were the ones that challenged these assumptions and replaced them with some very different attitudes and norms. Instead of treating different business functions, and subsidiaries similarly, they systematically *differentiated* tasks and responsibilities. Instead of seeking organizational clarity by basing relationships on dependence or independence, they built and managed *interdependence* among the different units of the companies. And instead of considering control their key task, corporate managers searched for complex mechanisms to *coordinate and coopt* the differentiated and interdependent organizational units into sharing a vision of the company's strategic tasks. These are the central organizational characteristics of what we described in an earlier article as transnational corporations—those most effective in managing across borders in today's environment of intense competition and rapid, often discontinuous change.

FROM SYMMETRY TO DIFFERENTIATION

. . . Just as they saw the need to change symmetrical structures and homogeneous processes imposed on different businesses and functions, most companies we observed eventually recognized the importance of differentiating the management of diverse geographic operations. Despite the fact that various national subsidiaries operated with very different external environments and internal constraints, they all traditionally reported through the same channels, operated under similar planning and control systems, and worked under a set of common generalized mandates.

Increasingly, however, managers recognized that such symmetrical treatment can constrain strategic capabilities. At Unilever, for example, it became clear that Europe's highly competitive markets and closely linked economies meant that its operating companies in that region required more coordination and control than those in, say, Latin America. Little by little, management increased the product-coordination groups' role in Europe until they had the direct line responsibility for all operating companies in their businesses. Elsewhere, however, national management maintained its historic line management role, and product coordinators acted only as advisers. Unilever has thus moved in sequence from a symmetrical organization to a much more differentiated one: differentiating by product, then by function, and finally by geography. . . .

But Unilever is far from unique. In all of the companies we studied, senior management was working to differentiate its organizational structure and processes in increasingly sophisticated ways. . . . For example, Procter & Gamble is differentiating the roles of its subsidiaries by giving some of them responsibilities as "lead countries" in product strategy development, then rotating that leadership role from product to product. . . . Thus, instead of deciding the overall roles of product, functional, and geographic management on the basis of simplistic dichotomies such as global versus domestic businesses or centralized versus decentralized organizations, many companies are creating different levels of influence for different groups as they perform different activities. Doing this allows the relatively underdeveloped management perspectives to be built in a gradual, complementary manner rather than in the sudden, adversarial environment often associated with either/or choices. Internal heterogeneity has made the change from unidimensional to multidimensional organization easier by breaking the problem up into many small, differentiated parts and by allowing for a step-by-step process of organizational change.

FROM DEPENDENCE OR INDEPENDENCE

. . . New strategic demands make organizational models of simple interunit dependence *or* independence inappropriate. The reality of today's worldwide competitive environment demands collaborative information sharing and problem solving, cooperative support and resource sharing, and collective action and implementation. Independent units risk being picked off one-by-one by competitors whose coordinated global approach gives them two important strategic advantages—the ability to integrate research, manufacturing, and other scale-efficient operations, and the opportunity to cross-subsidize the losses from battles in one market with funds generated by profitable operations in home markets or protected environments. . . .

On the other hand, foreign operations totally dependent on a central unit must deal with problems reaching beyond the loss of local market responsiveness. . . . They also risk being unable to respond effectively to strong national competitors or to sense potentially important local market or technical intelligence. This was the problem Procter & Gamble's

Japan subsidiary faced in an environment where local competitors began challenging P&G's previously secure position with successive, innovative product changes and novel market strategies, particularly in the disposable diapers business. After suffering major losses in market share, management recognized that a local operation focused primarily on implementing the company's classic marketing strategy was no longer sufficient; the Japanese subsidiary needed the freedom and incentive to be more innovative. Not only to ensure the viability of the Japanese subsidiary, but also to protect its global strategic position, P&G realized it had to expand the role of the local unit and change its relationship with the parent company to enhance two-way learning and mutual support.

But it is not easy to change relationships of dependence or independence that have been built up over a long history. Many companies have tried to address the increasing need for interunit collaboration by adding layer upon layer of administrative mechanisms to foster greater cooperation. Top managers have extolled the virtues of teamwork and have even created special departments to audit management response to this need. In most cases these efforts to obtain cooperation by fiat or by administrative mechanisms have been disappointing. The independent units have feigned compliance while fiercely protecting their independence. The dependent units have found that the new cooperative spirit implies little more than the right to agree with those on whom they depend.

Yet some companies have gradually developed the capability to achieve such cooperation and to build what Rosabeth Kanter (1983) calls an "integrative organization." Of the companies we studied, the most successful did so not by creating new units, but by changing the basis of the relationships among product, functional, and geographic management groups. From relations based on dependence or independence, they moved to relations based on formidable levels of explicit, genuine interdependence. In essence, they made integration and collaboration self-enforcing by making it necessary for each group to cooperate in order to achieve its own interests.

Procter & Gamble . . . in Europe, for example, has formed a number of Eurobrand teams for developing product-market strategies for different product lines.* Each team is headed by the general manager of a subsidiary that has a particularly well-developed competence in that business. It also includes the appropriate product and advertising managers from the other subsidiaries and relevant functional managers from the company's European headquarters. . . .

In observing many such examples of companies building and extending interdependence among units, we were able to identify three important flows that seem to be at the center of the emerging organizational relationships. Most fundamental was the product interdependence that most companies were building as they specialized and integrated their worldwide manufacturing operations to achieve greater efficiency, while retaining sourcing flexibility and sensitivity to host country interests. The resulting *flow of parts, components, and finished goods* increased the interdependence of the worldwide operations in an obvious and fundamental manner.

We also observed companies developing a resource interdependence that often contrasted sharply with earlier policies that had either encouraged local self-sufficiency or required the centralization of all surplus resources. . . .

Finally, the worldwide diffusion of technology, the development of international markets, and the globalization of competitive strategies have meant that vital strategic information now exists in many different locations worldwide. Furthermore, the growing dispersion of assets and delegation of responsibilities to foreign operations have resulted in the development of local knowledge and expertise that has implications for the broader orga-

---

*For a full description of the development of Eurobrand in P&G, see C.A. Bartlett, "Procter & Gamble Europe: Vizir Launch," Harvard Business School, Case Services #9-384-139.

nization. With these changes, the need to manage the *flow of intelligence, ideas, and knowledge* has become central to the learning process and has reinforced the growing interdependence of worldwide operations, as P&G's Eurobrand teams illustrate.

It is important to emphasize that the relationships we are highlighting are different from the interdependencies commonly observed in multiunit organizations. Traditionally, MNC managers have attempted to highlight what has been called "pooled interdependence" to make subunit managers responsive to global rather than local interests. (Before the Euroteam approach, for instance, P&G's European vice president often tried to convince independent-minded subsidiary managers to transfer surplus generated funds to other more needy subsidiaries, in the overall corporate interest, arguing that, "Someday when you're in need they might be able to fund a major product launch for you.")

As the example illustrates, pooled interdependence is often too broad and amorphous to affect day-to-day management behavior. The interdependencies we described earlier are more clearly reciprocal, and each unit's ability to achieve its goals is made conditional upon its willingness to help other units achieve their own goals. Such interdependencies more effectively promote the organization's ability to share the perspectives and link the resources of different components, and thereby to expand its organizational capabilities.*

FROM CONTROL TO COORDINATION AND COOPTION

The simplifying assumptions of organizational symmetry and dependence (or independence) had allowed the management processes in many companies to be dominated by simple controls—tight operational controls in subsidiaries dependent on the center, and a looser system of administrative or financial controls in decentralized units. When companies began to challenge the assumptions underlying organizational relationships, however, they found they also had to adapt their management processes. The growing interdependence of organizational units strained the simple control-dominated systems and underlined the need to supplement existing processes with more sophisticated ones. Furthermore, the differentiation of organizational tasks and roles amplified the diversity of management perspectives and capabilities and forced management to differentiate management processes.

As organizations became, at the same time, more diverse and more interdependent, there was an explosion in the number of issues that had to be linked, reconciled, or integrated. The rapidly increasing flows of goods, resources, and information among organizational units increased the need for *coordination* as a central management function. But the costs of coordination are high, both in financial and human terms, and coordinating capabilities are always limited. Most companies, though, tended to concentrate on a primary means of coordination and control—"the company's way of doing things." . . .

In a number of companies, we saw a . . . broadening of administrative processes as managers learned to operate with previously underutilized means of coordination. Unilever's heavy reliance on the socialization of managers to provide the coordination "glue" was supplemented by the growing role of the central product-coordination departments. In contrast, NEC reduced central management's coordination role by developing formal systems and social processes in a way that created a more robust and flexible coordinative capability.

Having developed diverse new means of coordination, management's main task is to carefully ration their usage and application. . . . It is important to distinguish where tasks can be formalized and managed through systems, where social linkages can be fostered to encourage informal agreements and cooperation, and where the coordination task is so vital or sensitive that it must use the scarce resource of central management arbitration. . . .

---

*The distinction among sequential, reciprocal, and pooled interdependencies has been made in J. D. Thompson, *Organizations in Action* (New York: McGraw-Hill, 1967).

We have described briefly how companies began to . . . differentiate roles and responsibilities within the organization. Depending on their internal capabilities and on the strategic importance of their external environments, organizational units might be asked to take on roles ranging from that of strategic leader with primary corporatewide responsibility for a particular business or function, to simple implementer responsible only for executing strategies and decisions developed elsewhere.

Clearly, these roles must be managed in quite different ways. The unit with strategic leadership responsibility must be given freedom to develop responsibility in an entrepreneurial fashion, yet must also be strongly supported by headquarters. For this unit, operating controls may be light and quite routine, but coordination of information and resource flows to and from the unit will probably require intensive involvement from senior management. In contrast, units with implementation responsibility might be managed through tight operating controls, with standardized systems used to handle much of the coordination—primarily of goods flows. Because the tasks are more routine, the use of scarce coordinating resources could be minimized.

Differentiating organizational roles and management processes can have a fragmenting and sometimes demotivating effect, however. Nowhere was this more clearly illustrated than in the many companies that unquestioningly assigned units the "dog" and "cash cow" roles defined by the Boston Consulting Group's growth-share matrix in the 1970s (see Haspeslagh, 1982). Their experience showed that there is another equally important corporate management task that complements and facilitates coordination effectiveness. We call this task *cooption*: the process of uniting the organization with a common understanding of, identification with, and commitment to the corporation's objectives, priorities, and values.

A clear example of the importance of cooption was provided by the contrast between ITT and NEC managers. At ITT, corporate objectives were communicated more in financial than in strategic terms, and the company's national entities identified almost exclusively with their local environment. When corporate management tried to superimpose a more unified and integrated global strategy, its local subsidiaries neither understood nor accepted the need to do so. For years they resisted giving up their autonomy, and management was unable to replace the interunit rivalry with a more cooperative and collaborative process.

In contrast, NEC developed an explicitly defined and clearly communicated global strategy enshrined in the company's "C&C" motto—a corporatewide dedication to building business and basing competitive strategy on the strong link between computers and communications. For over a decade, the C&C philosophy was constantly interpreted, refined, elaborated, and eventually institutionalized in organizational units dedicated to various C&C missions (e.g., the C&C Systems Research Laboratories, the C&C Corporate Planning Committee, and eventually the C&C Systems Division). Top management recognized that one of its major tasks was to inculcate the worldwide organization with an understanding of the C&C strategy and philosophy and to raise managers' consciousness about the global implications of competing in these converging businesses. By the mid-1980s, the company was confident that every NEC employee in every operating unit had a clear understanding of NEC's global strategy as well as of his or her role in it. Indeed, it was this homogeneity that allowed the company to begin the successful decentralization of its strategic tasks and the differentiation of its management processes.

Thus the management process that distinguished transnational organizations from simpler unidimensional forms was one in which control was made less dominant by the increased importance of interunit integration and collaboration. These new processes required corporate management to supplement its control role with the more subtle tasks of coordination and cooption, giving rise to a much more complex and sophisticated management process.

SUSTAINING A DYNAMIC BALANCE:
ROLE OF THE "MIND MATRIX"

Developing multidimensional perspectives and capabilities does not mean that product, functional, and geographic management must have the same level of influence on all key decisions. Quite the contrary. It means that the organization must possess a differentiated influence structure—one in which different groups have different roles for different activities. These roles cannot be fixed but must change continually to respond to new environmental demands and evolving industry characteristics. Not only is it necessary to prevent any one perspective from dominating the others, it is equally important not to be locked into a mode of operation that prevents reassignment of responsibilities, realignment of relationships, and rebalancing of power distribution. This ability to manage the multidimensional organization capability in a flexible manner is the hallmark of a transnational company.

In the change process we have described, managers were clearly employing some powerful organizational tools to create and control the desired flexible management process. They used the classic tool of formal structure to strengthen, weaken, or shift roles and responsibilities over time, and they employed management systems effectively to redirect corporate resources and to channel information in a way that shifted the balance of power. By controlling the ebb and flow of responsibilities, and by rebalancing power relationships, they were able to prevent any of the multidimensional perspectives from atrophying. Simultaneously, they prevented the establishment of entrenched power bases.

But the most successful companies had an additional element at the core of their management processes. We were always conscious that a substantial amount of senior management attention focused on the *individual* members of the organization. NEC's continual efforts to inculcate all corporate members with a common vision of goals and priorities; P&G's careful assignment of managers to teams and task forces to broaden their perspectives; Philips's frequent use of conferences and meetings as forums to reconcile differences; and Unilever's extensive use of training as a powerful socialization process and its well-planned career path management that provided diverse experience across businesses, functions, and geographic locations—all are examples of companies trying to develop multidimensional perspectives and flexible approaches at the level of the individual manager.

What is critical, then, is not just the structure, but also the mentality of those who constitute the structure. The common thread that holds together the diverse tasks we have described is a managerial mindset that understands the need for multiple strategic capabilities, that is able to view problems from both local and global perspectives, and that accepts the importance of a flexible approach. This pattern suggests that managers should resist the temptation to view their task in the traditional terms of building a formal global matrix structure—an organizational form that in practice has proven extraordinarily difficult to manage in the international environment. They might be better guided by the perspective of one top manager who described the challenge as "creating a matrix in the minds of managers."

Our study has led us to conclude that a company's ability to develop transnational organizational capability and management mentality will be the key factor that separates the winners from the mere survivors in the emerging international environment.

MANAGING CHANGE

Strategy is technically about continuity, not change: After all, it is concerned with imposing structured patterns of behavior on an organization, whether these take the form of intentions in advance that become deliberate strategies or actions after the fact that fall into the consistent patterns of emergent strategies. But today to manage strategy is frequently to manage change—to recognize when a shift of a strategic nature is possible, desirable, necessary, and then to act—possibly putting into place mechanisms for continuous change.

Managing major change is generally far more difficult than it may at first appear. The need for reorientation occurs rather infrequently, and when it does, it means moving from a familiar domain into a less well-defined future where many of the old rules no longer apply. People must often abandon the roots of their past successes and develop entirely new skills and attitudes. This is clearly a frightening situation—and often, therefore, the most difficult challenge facing a manager.

The causes of such change also vary, from an ignored steady decline in performance which ultimately demands a "turnaround" to a sudden radical shift in a base technology that requires a reconceptualization of everything the organization does; from the gradual shift into the next stage of an organization's "life cycle"; to the appearance of a new chief executive who wishes to put his or her particular stamp on the organization. The resulting strategic alignments may also take a variety of forms, from a shift of strategic position within the same industry to a whole new perspective in a new industry. Some changes require rapid transitions from one structural configuration to another, as in a machine organization that has diversified into new businesses and so must switch to a divisionalized form of structure. Other changes are accompanied by slower structural shifts, as when a small entrepreneurial firm grows steadily into a larger mature company. Each transition has its own management prerequisites and problems.

This chapter covers a number of these aspects of organizational change, presenting material on what evokes them in the first place, what forms they can take, and how they can and should be managed in differing situations. These readings appropriately cap the earlier chapters of this book: on strategy and its formation, structure and systems, power and culture, and the various contexts in which these come together. Major changes typically involve them all. Configuration, so carefully nurtured in earlier chapters, turns out to be a double-edged sword, promoting consistency on the one hand but sometimes discouraging change on the other.

The first reading seeks to bring some closure to our discussion of the different configurations of structure presented in Section III. Called "Beyond Configuration," it is, in a sense, Mintzberg's final chapter of his book on structure, except that it was written more recently and edited down to its essence for this edition of the text. The reading seeks to do just what its title says: make the point that while the different structural forms (configurations) of the last chapters can help us to make sense of and to manage in a complex world, there is also a need to go beyond configuration, to consider the nuanced linkages among these various forms. Mintzberg proposes that this be done by treating all the forms as a framework of forces that act on every organization and whose contradictions need to be reconciled. By so doing, we can begin to see the weaknesses in each form as well as the times when an organization is better off to design itself as a combination of two or more forms. Some organizations, to use a metaphor introduced in this reading, achieve greater effectiveness by playing "organizational LEGO"—creating their own form rather than letting themselves be put together like a jigsaw puzzle into a standard form. Finally, this reading discusses how the forces of ideology (representing cooperation—pulling together) and of politics (representing competition—pulling apart) work both to promote change and also to impede it, and how the contradictions among these two must also be reconciled if an organization is to remain effective in the long run.

Our second reading on managing the context of change considers the "unsteady pace of organizational evolution" in terms of distinct periods of "convergence" and "upheaval." Related to the literature on organizational life cycles, its three authors, Michael Tushman and William Newman of Columbia University's Graduate School of Business and Elaine Romanelli of the Georgetown business school, argue for what has also been referred to as a "quantum theory" of organizational change (Miller and Freisen, 1984). The essence of the argument is that organizations prefer to stay on course most of the time, accepting incremental changes to improve their strategies, processes, and structures. But periodically, they must submit to dramatic shifts in these—"strategic revolutions" of a sort—to realign their overall orientation.

This argument is obviously compatible with the earlier notion of configuration, which represents a form of alignment of strategy, structure, and processes that dictate a certain stability in an organization. But note that it differs from Quinn's concept of "logical incrementalism," introduced in Reading 5.1, which argues for more of a gradual shift in strategic thinking as a way to achieve major change in an organization. There appears to be merit in both approaches. But how can we reconcile them? Perhaps they are not as contradictory as they may seem. Consider three dimensions: (1) the specific aspects of the strategy change process that each considers, (2) the time frames of the two viewpoints, and (3) the types of organizations involved. Quinn's incrementalist view focuses on the processes going on in senior managers' minds as they help create new strategies. Because of the complexities involved, effective strategic thinking requires an incremental, interactive, learning process for all key players. The quantum approach, in contrast, focuses not on the strategists' intentions so much as on the strategies actually pursued by the organization (referred to in Reading 1.2 as the realized strategies of the organization). It is these that often seem to change in quantum fashion. It may be, therefore, that managers conceive and promote their intended strategies incrementally, but once that is accomplished they change their organizations in rapid, integrated leaps, quantum fashion.

But then again, each of these two approaches may also occur in their own situations. For example, quantum changes may more often take place in crisis situations, when top managements change, or when external environments compress time frames—often caused by technological or regulatory shifts. These were important drivers in the AT&T, Ford: Team Taurus, Exxon Corporation 1994, and SAS cases—as well as all the information technology cases including The New York Times Company. Nevertheless, even these companies generally proceeded to adjust their strategies incrementally. The MacArthur in the Philippines, NovaCare, Inc., The IBM 360 Decision, and Andersen Consulting (Europe) cases offer some details on the management of incrementalism in large basically healthy organizations. The Ford: Team Taurus, The Pillsbury Company,

SAS, and Mountbatten and India cases suggest how these processes occur under more stressful situations where crises compress time horizons. The Microsoft Corporation (A), Sony Corporation: Innovation System, The Hewlett Packard Company, Nintendo, Co., Ltd., and TCG, Ltd./Thermo Electron cases illustrate designs for continuous change. Please note that the styles of managers vary from quite analytical, to centrist, to political, to highly participative. We are not trying to sell any particular style, but rather to help students and executives understand the options available.

The last reading of this book, by Charles Baden-Fuller of the University of Bath and John Stopford of the London Business School, presents a specific model of how a company can rejuvenate itself. The key challenge, these authors believe, lies in rebuilding corporate entrepreneurship, and they describe a four-step process of renewal, which starts with galvanizing the top team to create a commitment to change. In the next phase, the company must simplify both its businesses and its organization so as to create the base for the third step of building new skills, knowledge, and resources. Then, in the final step, the company can restart the growth engine by leveraging the new sources of advantage it has created. Overall, this model of change builds directly on the concept of core competencies, and is quite consistent with Quinn's views on strategies for change with which we started on this journey of mapping the strategy process.

▼ READING 15.1　　　　　　　　　　　　BEYOND CONFIGURATION*

by Henry Mintzberg

"Lumpers" are people who categorize, who synthesize. "Splitters" are people who analyze, who see all the nuances. From the standpoint of organization, both are right and both are wrong. Without categories, it would be impossible to practice management. With only categories, it could not be practiced effectively.

The author was mostly a lumper until a colleague asked him if he wanted to play "jigsaw puzzle" or "LEGO" with his concepts. In other words, do all these concepts fit together in set ways and known images (puzzle), or were they to be used creatively to create new images? The remainder of this reading is presented in the spirit of playing "organizational LEGO." It tries to show how we can use splitting as well as lumping to understand what makes organizations effective as well as what causes many of their fundamental problems.

Forms and Forces

The configurations described in the chapters of this section of the book are *forms*, and they are laid out at the nodes of a pentagon in Figure 1. Many organizations seem to fit naturally into one of the original five, but some do not fit, to the lumpers' chagrin. To respond to this, five *forces* have been added, each associated with one of the original forms:

▼ *Direction* for the entrepreneurial form, for some sense of where the organization must go. This is often called "strategic vision." Without direction the various activities of an organization cannot easily work together to achieve common purpose.

▼ *Efficiency* for the machine form. This ensures a viable ratio of benefits gained to costs incurred. Lack of concern for efficiency would cause all but the most protected organization to fade.

---

*Adapted from a chapter of this title in *Mintzberg on Management: Inside Our Strange World of Organizations* (Free Press, 1989); an article similar to this chapter was published in the *Sloan Management Review*.

FIGURE 1
An Integrating Pentagon
of Forces and Forms

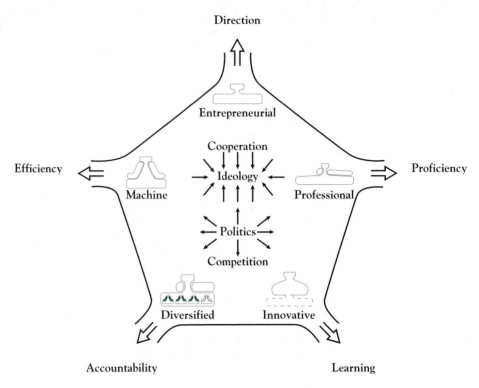

FIGURE 1
An Integrating Pentagon of Forces and Forms

▼ *Proficiency* for the professional form. Organizations need this to carry out tasks with high levels of knowledge and skill. The difficult work of organizations would otherwise simply not get done.

▼ *Accountability* for the diversified form. If individual units in an organization are not accountable for their efforts in particular markets, it becomes almost impossible to manage a diversified organization.

▼ *Learning* for the innovative or adhocracy form. Organizations need to be able to learn, to discover new things for their customers and themselves—to adapt and to innovate.

Two other forces exist that are not necessarily associated with a particular form:

▼ *Cooperation*, represented by ideology. This is the force for pulling together.
▼ *Competition*, represented by politics. This is the force for pulling apart.

For the lumpers we now have a *portfolio of forms*, and for the splitters we now have a *system of forces*. Both views are critical for the practice of management. One represents the most fundamental forces that act on organizations. All serious organizations experience all seven of them, at one time or another, if not all the time. The other represents the fundamental forms that organizations can take, which some of them do some of the time. Together, these forces and forms appear to constitute a powerful diagnostic framework by which to understand what goes on in organizations and to prescribe effective change in them.

When one force dominates an organization, it is drawn toward the associated *configuration*, but must deal with *contamination*. When no force dominates, the organization is a balanced *combination* of forces, including periods of *conversion* from one form to another. But then there is a problem of *cleavage*. Contamination and cleavage require the management of *contradiction*, which is where ideology and politics come in. We shall discuss each of these notions shortly.

Dominant forces drive an organization to one of the pure forms discussed earlier—entrepreneurial, machine, professional, diversified, innovative. These are not "real," but are abstract models designed to capture some reality. Some organizations *do* match the pure forms closely. If the form fits, the organization should wear it. Configuration has benefits: the organization achieves a sense of order, or integration. Configuration also helps outsiders understand an organization. The consistency of configuration keeps workers from being confused. For classification, for comprehension, for diagnosis, and for design, configuration seems to be effective. But only so long as everything holds still. Introduce the dynamics of evolutionary change and, sooner or later, configuration becomes ineffective.

CONTAMINATION BY CONFIGURATION

The harmony, consistency, and fit that is configuration's greatest strength is also its greatest weakness. The dominant force can become so strong that it drives out everything else. For example, control in machine organizations may contaminate the innovators in research. Machine organizations recognize this when they put their research and development facilities away from the head office, to avoid the contaminating effects of the central efficiency experts. The opposite case is also well known—the "looseness" in adhocracies may contaminate the efforts of the accountants concerned with efficiency. This contamination may be a small price to pay for being coherently organized, until things go out of control.

CONFIGURATION OUT OF CONTROL

When the need arises for change, the dominating forces may act to hold the organization in place. The other forces may have atrophied, and so the organization goes out of control. For instance, the machine organization in need of a new strategy may have no entrepreneurs and no innovators left to give it its new direction. Miller and Kets de Vries (1987) have developed five organizational "neuroses" that correspond roughly to what can happen in extreme cases of contamination in the five forms. Each is an example of a system that may once have been healthy but has run out of control.

▼ *Dramatic*: the entrepreneur, freed from other forces, may take the organization on an ego trip. This can even occur in large diversified organizations that are dominated by strong CEOs.
▼ *Compulsive*: this happens when there is completeness of control in machine organizations. This is the classic overbearing bureaucracy.
▼ *Paranoid*: paranoia is often a collective tendency in some professional organizations like universities and hospitals. Professors and doctors are always suspicious that their peers, or worse, the "administration," are planning to undermine their efforts.
▼ *Depressive*: this can be the result of an obsession with the bottom line in diversified organizations. Being a cash cow that is constantly being "milked" is very bad for morale.
▼ *Schizoid*: the need to innovate, and to get the commercial benefits from innovation, means that adhocracies can be in constant oscillation between divergent and convergent thinking.

In other words, behaviors that were once functional become dysfunctional when pursued to excess.

CONTAINMENT OF CONFIGURATION

Truly effective organizations thus do not exist in pure form. What keeps a configuration effective is not only the dominance of a single force but also the constraining effects of other forces. This is *containment*. To manage configuration effectively is to exploit one form but also to reconcile the different forces. Machine organizations must exploit their efficiency but must still allow for innovation. Innovative forms must exploit their power to create, but must find a way to remain somewhat efficient.

Combination

Configuration is nice if you can have it. But some organizations all of the time, and all organizations some of the time, are unable to have it. They must instead balance competing forces. Organizations like this can be called *combinations*; instead of being a node in the pentagon, they are somewhere within it.

KINDS OF COMBINATIONS

When only two of the five forces meet in rough balance, that is a *hybrid*. A symphony orchestra is an example, being a rough balance of entrepreneurial and professional forms. Some organizations experience *multiple combinations*. Apple Computer in Canada was once described as a combination of adhocracy (a legacy of its founder, Steve Jobs), machine (for efficiency in production and distribution), entrepreneurial (in the person of a dynamic sales manager), and professional (in marketing and training).

CLEAVAGE IN COMBINATIONS

If configuration encourages contamination, sometimes combination encourages *cleavage*. Instead of one force dominating, two or more confront each other to the point of paralyzing the organization. A common example from business organizations is the innovative drive of R&D against the machine-like drive of production.

Despite the problems created by having to balance forces, combination of one kind or another is probably necessary in most organizations. Effective organizations usually balance many forces. Configuration merely means a tilt toward one force; combination is more balanced.

Conversion

The preceding discussions of configuration and combination implied stability. But few organizations stay in one form or combination; they undergo *conversion* from one configuration or combination to another. Often these result from external changes. For example, an innovative organization decides to settle down as a machine to exploit an innovation. Or a suddenly unstable market makes a machine become more innovative. Conversions are often temporary, as in the machine organization that becomes an entrepreneurial organization during a crisis.

CYCLES OF CONVERSION

The forces that may destroy the organization may instead drive it to another, perhaps more viable, configuration. For example, the entrepreneurial form is inherently vulnerable, because of its reliance on a single leader. It may work well for the young organization, but with aging and growth a dominant need for direction may be displaced by that for efficiency. Then conversion to the machine form becomes necessary—the power of one leader must be replaced by that of administrators.

The implication is that organizations go through stages as they develop, sequenced into so-called life cycles. The most common life cycle is the one mentioned above. It begins with the entrepreneurial form and moves down along the left edge of the pentagon. Growth leads to the machine form, and even greater growth leads ultimately to the diversified form. Another life cycle, depicted along the right edge of the pentagon, occurs for firms dependent on expertise. They move from the entrepreneurial form to either the professional form (if they can standardize their services) or the innovative form (if their services are more creative). Another common conversion is when an innovative form decides to exploit and perfect the skills it has developed and settles into a professional form, a common conversion in consulting.

Ideology and politics play a role in conversion. Ideology is a more important form in young organizations. That is because cultures can develop more easily there, especially with charismatic leadership in the entrepreneurial stage. By comparison, it is extremely difficult to build a strong and lasting culture in a mature organization. Politics, by contrast, typically spreads as the energy of the young organization dissipates and its activities become more diffuse. As the organization becomes more formalized, its culture is blunted, and politics becomes a more important force.

CLEAVAGE IN CONVERSION

Some conversions are easy because they are so overdue. But most are more difficult and conflictual, requiring periods of transition, prolonged and agonizing. As the organization in transition sits between its old and new forms, it becomes a kind of combination. The forces that create the conversion also create the possibility of cleavage. How does the organization deal with these contradictions?

Contradiction

Organizations that have to reconcile contradictory forces, especially in dealing with change, often turn to the cooperative force of ideology or the competitive force of politics. Indeed, these two forces themselves represent a contradiction that must be managed if an organization is not to run out of control.

While it is true that each can dominate an organization, and so draw it toward a missionary or political form, more commonly they act differently, as *catalysts*. Ideology tends to draw behavior inwards toward a common core; politics drives behavior away from any central place. One force is centripetal, the other centrifugal. Both can act to promote change or also to prevent it. Either way, they sometimes render an organization more effective, sometimes less.

COOPERATION THROUGH IDEOLOGY

Ideology (or strong culture) represents the force for cooperation in an organization, for collegiality and consensus. It encourages members to look inward, to take their lead from the imperatives of the organization's own vision. One important implication is that infusion of ideology renders any particular configuration more effective. People get fired up to pursue efficiency or proficiency or whatever else drives the organization. When this happens to a machine organization—as in a McDonald's, very responsive to its customers and very sensitive to its employees—we have a "snappy bureaucracy." Bureaucratic machines are not supposed to be snappy, but ideology changes the nature of their quest for efficiency.

Another implication is that ideology helps an organization manage contradiction and so to deal with change. The innovative machine and the tightly controlled innovative organization are inherent contradictions. These organizations handle their contradictions by having strong cultures. Such organizations can more easily reconcile their opposing forces because what matters to their people ultimately is the organization itself, more than any of its particular parts, like efficient manufacturing or innovative R&D. This is how Toyota gets efficiency and high quality at the same time.

LIMITS TO COOPERATION

Ideologies sound wonderful, but they are difficult to build and sustain. And established ideologies can get in the way of organizational effectiveness. They may discourage change by forcing everyone to work within the same set of beliefs. This has implications for strategy. Change *within* strategic perspective, to a new position, is facilitated by a strong ideology. But change *of* perspective—fundamental change—is discouraged by it.

COMPETITION THROUGH POLITICS

Politics represents the force for competition in an organization, for conflict and confrontation. It too can infuse any of the configurations or combinations, in this case aggravating contamination and cleavage. In a configuration, the representative of the dominant force "lord it" over others. This could lead to contamination. In a combination, representatives of the various forces relish opportunities to do battle with each other, aggravating the cleavage.

One problem facing strategic managers is that politics may be a more "natural" force than ideology. Left to themselves, organizations seem to pull apart rather easily. Keeping them together requires considerable and constant effort.

BENEFITS OF COMPETITION

If the pulling together of culture discourages people from addressing fundamental change, then the pulling apart of politics may become the only way to ensure that happens. Change requires challenging the status quo. Politics may facilitate this; if there are no entrepreneurial or innovative forces stimulating strategic change, it may be the *only* available force for change.

Both politics and ideology can promote organizational effectiveness as well as undermine it. Ideology can be a force for revitalization, energizing the organization and making its people more responsive. But it can also hinder fundamental change. Likewise, politics often impedes necessary change and wastes valuable resources. But it can also promote important change that may be available in no other way. It can enable those who realize the need for change to challenge those who do not.

COMBINING COOPERATION AND COMPETITION

The last remaining contradiction is the one between ideology and politics themselves. Ideology and politics themselves have to be reconciled. Pulling together ideologically infuses life; splitting apart politically challenges the status quo. Only by encouraging both can an organization sustain its viability. Ideology helps secondary forces to contain a dominant one; politics encourages them to challenge it.

The balance between ideology and politics should be a dynamic equilibrium. Most of the time ideology should be pulling things together, contained by healthy internal competition. When fundamental change becomes necessary, however, politics should help pull the organization apart temporarily.

Competence

What makes an organization effective? The "Peterian" view (named after Tom Peters of *In Search of Excellence* fame) is that organizations should be "hands on, value driven." The

"Porterian" view (named after Michael Porter) says that organizations should use competitive analysis. To Porter, effectiveness resides in strategy, while to Peters it is the operations that count. One says do the right things, the other says do things right. But we need to understand what takes an organization to a viable strategy in the first place, what makes it excellent there, and how some organizations are able to sustain viability and excellence in the face of change.

Here are five views to guide us in our search for organizational effectiveness:

CONVERGENCE

First is the *convergence* hypothesis. Its motto is that there is "one best way" to design an organization. This is usually associated with the machine form. A good structure is one with a rigid hierarchy of authority, with spans of control no greater than six, with heavy use of strategic planning, MIS, and whatever else happens to be in the current fashion of the rationalizers. In *In Search of Excellence*, by contrast, Peters and Waterman argued that ideology was the key to an organization's success. We cannot dismiss this hypothesis—sometimes there *are* proper things to do in most, perhaps all, organizations. But we must take issue with its general thrust. Society has paid an enormous price for "one best way" thinking over the course of this century, on the part of all its organizations that have been drawn into using what is fashionable rather than functional. We need to look beyond the obvious, beyond the convergence hypothesis.

CONGRUENCE

Beyond convergence is the *congruence* or "it all depends" approach. Introduced into organization theory in the 1960s, it suggests that running an organization is like choosing dinner from a buffet table—a little bit of this, a little bit of that, all selected according to specific needs. Organizational effectiveness thus becomes a question of matching a given set of internal attributes, treated as a kind of portfolio, with various situational factors. The congruence hypothesis has certainly been an improvement, but like a dinner plate stacked with an old assortment of foods, it has not been good enough.

CONFIGURATION

The motto of the *configuration* hypothesis is "getting it all together." Design your organization as you would a jigsaw puzzle, fitting the organizational pieces together to create a coherent, harmonious picture. There is reason to believe that organizations succeed in good part because they are consistent in what they do; they are certainly easier to manage that way. But, as we have seen, configuration has its limits, too.

CONTRADICTION

While the lumpers may like the configuration hypothesis, splitters prefer the *contradiction* hypothesis. Their call is to manage the dynamic tension between contradictory forces. They point to the common occurrence of combinations and conversions, where organizations are forced to manage contradictory forces. This is an important hypothesis—together with that of configuration (which are in their own dynamic tension) it is an important clue to organizational effectiveness. But still it is not sufficient.

CREATION

The truly great organization transcends all of the foregoing while building on it to achieve something more. It respects the *creation* hypothesis. Creativity is its forte, "understand your inner nature" is its motto, LEGO its image. The most interesting organizations live at the edges, far from the logic of conventional organizations, where as Raphael (1976:5–6) has pointed out in biology (for example, between the sea and the land, or at the forest's edge), the richest, most varied, and most interesting forms of life can be found. This might be called the "Prahaladian" view (after C. K. Prahalad, and his ideas of "strategic intent" discussed in Chapter 2). Don't just do the right things right, but keep doing them! Such organizations keep inventing novel approaches that solve festering problems and so provide all of us with new ways to deal with our world of organizations.

▼ READING 15.2   CONVERGENCE AND UPHEAVAL: MANAGING THE UNSTEADY PACE OF ORGANIZATIONAL EVOLUTION*

by Michael L.
Tushman, William
H. Newman, and
Elaine Romanelli

A snug fit of external opportunity, company strategy, and internal structure is a hallmark of successful companies. The real test of executive leadership, however, is in maintaining this alignment in the race of changing competitive conditions.

Consider the Polaroid or Caterpillar corporations. Both firms virtually dominated their respective industries for decades, only to be caught off guard by major environmental changes. The same strategic and organizational factors which were so effective for decades became the seeds of complacency and organization decline.

Recent studies of companies over long periods show that the most successful firms maintain a workable equilibrium for several years (or decades), but are also able to initiate and carry out sharp, widespread changes (referred to here as reorientations) when their environments shift. Such upheaval may bring renewed vigor to the enterprise. Less successful firms, on the other hand, get stuck in a particular pattern. The leaders of these firms either do not see the need for reorientation or they are unable to carry through the necessary frame-breaking changes. While not all reorientations succeed, those organizations which do not initiate reorientations as environments shift underperform.

This reading focuses on reasons why for long periods most companies make only incremental changes, and why they then need to make painful, discontinuous, system-wide shifts. We are particularly concerned with the role of executive leadership in managing this pattern of convergence punctuated by upheaval. . . .

The task of managing incremental change, or convergence, differs sharply from managing frame-breaking change. Incremental change is compatible with the existing structure of a company and is reinforced over a period of years. In contrast, frame-breaking change is abrupt, painful to participants, and often resisted by the old guard. Forging these new strategy-structure-people-process consistencies and laying the basis for the next period of incremental change calls for distinctive skills.

Because the future health, and even survival, of a company or business unit is at stake, we need to take a closer look at the nature and consequences of convergent change and of differences imposed by frame-breaking change. We need to explore when and why these painful and risky revolutions interrupt previously successful patterns, and whether these discontinuities can be avoided and/or initiated prior to crisis. Finally, we need to examine what managers can and should do to guide their organizations through periods of convergence and upheaval over time. . . .

The following discussion is based on the history of companies in many different industries, different countries, both large and small organizations, and organizations in various stages of their product class's life-cycle. We are dealing with a widespread phenomenon—not just a few dramatic sequences. Our research strongly suggests that the convergence/upheaval

*Originally published in the *California Management Review* (Fall 1986). Copyright © 1986 by The Regents of the University of California. Reprinted with deletions by permission of the *Review*.

pattern occurs within departments at the business-unit level . . . and at the corporate level of analysis. . . . The problem of managing both convergent periods and upheaval is not just for the CEO, but necessarily involves general managers as well as functional managers.

Patterns in Organizational Evolution: Convergence and Upheaval

BUILDING ON STRENGTH: PERIODS OF CONVERGENCE

Successful companies wisely stick to what works well. . . .

. . . convergence starts out with an effective dovetailing of strategy, structure, people, and processes. . . . The formal system includes decisions about grouping and linking resources as well as planning and control systems, rewards and evaluation procedures, and human resource management systems. The informal system includes core values, beliefs, norms, communication patterns, and actual decision-making and conflict resolution patterns. It is the whole fabric of structure, systems, people, and processes which must be suited to company strategy (Nadler and Tuchman, 1986).

As the fit between strategy, structure, people, and processes is never perfect, convergence is an ongoing process characterized by incremental change. Over time, in all companies studied, two types of converging changes were common: fine-tuning and incremental adaptations.

▼ *Converging change: Fine-tuning*—Even with good strategy-structure-process fits, well-run companies seek even better ways of exploiting (and defending) their missions. Such effort typically deals with one or more of the following:
  ▼ *Refining* policies, methods, and procedures.
  ▼ Creating *specialized units and linking mechanisms* to permit increased volume and increased attention to unit quality and cost.
  ▼ *Developing personnel* especially suited to the present strategy—through improved selection and training, and tailoring reward systems to match strategic thrusts.
  ▼ Fostering individual and group *commitments* to the company mission and to the excellence of one's own department.
  ▼ Promoting *confidence* in the accepted norms, beliefs, and myths.
  ▼ *Clarifying* established roles, power, status, dependencies, and allocation mechanism.

The fine-tuning fills out and elaborates the consistencies between strategy, structure, people, and processes. These incremental changes lead to an ever more interconnected (and therefore more stable) social system. Convergent periods fit the happy, stick-with-a-winner situations romanticized by Peters and Waterman (1982).

▼ *Converging change: Incremental adjustments to environmental shifts*—In addition to fine-tuning changes, minor shifts in the environment will call for some organizational response. Even the most conservative of organizations expect, even welcome, small changes which do not make too many waves.

A popular expression is that almost any organization can tolerate a "ten percent change." At any one time, only a few changes are being made; but these changes are still compatible with the prevailing structures, systems, and processes. Examples of such adjustments are an expansion in sales territory, a shift in emphasis among products in the product line, or improved processing technology in production.

The usual process of making changes of this sort is well known: wide acceptance of the need for change, openness to possible alternatives, objective examination of the pros and cons of each plausible alternative, participation of those directly affected in the preceding analysis, a market test or pilot operation where feasible, time to learn the new activities, established role models, known rewards for positive success, evaluation, and refinement.

The role of executive leadership during convergent periods is to reemphasize mission and core values and to delegate incremental decisions to middle-level managers. Note that the uncertainty created for people affected by such changes is well within tolerable limits. Opportunity is provided to anticipate and learn what is new, while most features of the structure remain unchanged.

The overall system adapts, but it is not transformed.

CONVERGING CHANGE: SOME CONSEQUENCES

For those companies whose strategies fit environmental conditions, convergence brings about better and better effectiveness. Incremental change is relatively easy to implement and ever more optimizes the consistencies between strategy, structure, people, and process-es. At AT&T, for example, the period between 1913 and 1980 was one of ever more incremental change to further bolster the "Ma Bell" culture, systems, and structure all in service of developing the telephone network.

Convergent periods are, however, a double-edged sword. As organizations grow and become more successful, they develop internal forces for stability. Organizational structures and systems become so interlinked that they only allow compatible changes. Further, over time, employees develop habits, patterned behaviors begin to take on values (e.g., "service is good"), and employees develop a sense of competence in knowing how to get work done within the system. These self-reinforcing patterns of behavior, norms, and values contribute to increased organizational momentum and complacency and, over time, to a sense of organizational history. This organizational history—epitomized by common stories, heroes, and standards—specifies "how we work here" and "what we hold important here."

This organizational momentum is profoundly functional as long as the organization's strategy is appropriate. The Ma Bell . . . culture, structure, and systems—and associated internal momentum—were critical to [the] organization's success. However, if (and when) strategy must change, this momentum cuts the other way. Organizational history is a source of tradition, precedent, and pride which are, in turn, anchors to the past. A proud history often restricts vigilant problem solving and may be a source of resistance to change.

When faced with environmental threat, organizations with strong momentum

▼ may not register the threat due to organization complacency and/or stunted external vigilance (e.g., the automobile or steel industries), or

▼ if the threat is recognized, the response is frequently heightened conformity to the status quo and/or increased commitment to "what we do best."

For example, the response of dominant firms to technological threat is frequently increased commitment to the obsolete technology (e.g., telegraph/telephone; vacuum tube/transistor; core/semiconductor memory). A paradoxical result of long periods of success may be heightened organizational complacency, decreased organizational flexibility, and a stunted ability to learn.

Converging change is a double-edged sword. Those very social and technical consistencies which are key sources of success may also be the seeds of failure if environments change. The longer the convergent periods, the greater these internal forces for stability. This momentum seems to be particularly accentuated in those most successful firms in a product class . . . in historically regulated organizations . . . or in organizations that have been traditionally shielded from competition. . . .

ON FRAME-BREAKING CHANGE

FORCES LEADING TO FRAME-BREAKING CHANGE

What, then, leads to frame-breaking change? Why defy tradition? Simply stated, frame-breaking change occurs in response to or, better yet, in anticipation of major environmental changes—changes which require more than incremental adjustments. The need for discontinuous change springs from one or a combination of the following:

▼ *Industry discontinuities*—Sharp changes in legal, political, or technological conditions shift the basis of competition within industries. *Deregulation* has dramatically transformed the financial services and airlines industries. *Substitute product technologies* . . . or *substitute process technologies* . . . may transform the bases of competition within industries. Similarly, the emergence of industry standards, or *dominant designs* (such as the DC-3, IBM 360, or PDP-8) signal a shift in competition away from product innovation and towards increased process innovation. Finally, *major economic changes* (e.g., oil crises) and *legal shifts* (e.g., patent protection in biotechnology or trade/regulator barriers in pharmaceuticals or cigarettes) also directly affect bases of competition.

▼ *Product life-cycle shifts*—Over the course of a product class life cycle, different strategies are appropriate. In the emergence phase of a product class, competition is based on product innovation and performance, where in the maturity stage, competition centers on cost, volume, and efficiency. Shifts in patterns of demand alter key factors for success. For example, the demand and nature of competition for mini-computers, cellular telephones, wide-body aircraft, and bowling alley equipment was transformed as these products gained acceptance and their product classes evolved. Powerful international competition may compound these forces.

▼ *Internal company dynamics*—Entwined with these external forces are breaking points within the firm. Sheer size may require a basically new management design. For example, few inventor-entrepreneurs can tolerate the formality that is linked with large volume. . . . Key people die. Family investors may become more concerned with their inheritance taxes than with company development. Revised corporate portfolio strategy may sharply alter the role and resources assigned to business units or functional areas. Such pressures, especially when coupled with external changes, may trigger frame-breaking change.

SCOPE OF FRAME-BREAKING CHANGE

Frame-breaking change is driven by shifts in business strategy. As strategy shifts so too must structure, people, and organizational processes. Quite unlike convergent change, frame-breaking reforms involve discontinuous changes throughout the organization. These bursts of change do not reinforce the existing system and are implemented rapidly. . . . Frame-breaking changes are revolutionary changes *of* the system as opposed to incremental changes *in* the system.

The following features are usually involved in frame-breaking change:

▼ *Reformed mission and core values*—A strategy shift involves a new definition of company mission. Entering or withdrawing from an industry may be involved; at least the way the company expects to be outstanding is altered. . . .

▼ *Altered power and status*—Frame-breaking change always alters the distribution of power. Some groups lose in the shift while others gain. . . . These dramatically altered power distributions reflect shifts in bases of competition and resource allocation. A new strategy must be backed up with a shift in the balance of power and status.

▼ *Reorganization*—A new strategy requires a modification in structure, systems, and procedures. As strategic requirements shift, so too must the choice of organization form. A new direction calls for added activity in some areas and less in others. Changes in structure and systems are means to ensure that this reallocation of effort takes place. New structures and revised roles deliberately break business-as-usual behavior.

▼ *Revised interaction patterns*—The way people in the organization work together has to adapt during frame-breaking change. As strategy is different, new procedures, work flows, communication networks, and decision-making patterns must be established. With these changes in work flows and procedures must also come revised norms, informal decision-making/conflict-resolution procedures, and informal roles.

▼ *New executives*—Frame-breaking change also involves new executives, usually brought in from outside the organization (or business unit) and placed in key managerial positions. Commitment to the new mission, energy to overcome prevailing inertia, and freedom from prior obligations are all needed to refocus the organization. A few exceptional members of the old guard may attempt to make this shift, but habits and expectations of their associations are difficult to break. New executives are most likely to provide both the necessary drive and an enhanced set of skills more appropriate for the new strategy. While the overall number of executive changes is usually relatively small, these new executives have substantial symbolic and substantive effects on the organization. . . .

WHY ALL AT ONCE?

Frame-breaking change is revolutionary in that the shifts reshape the entire nature of the organization. Those more effective examples of frame-breaking change were implemented rapidly. . . . It appears that a piecemeal approach to frame-breaking changes gets bogged down in politics, individual resistance to change, and organizational inertia. . . . Frame-breaking change requires discontinuous shifts in strategy, structure, people, and processes concurrently—or at least in a short period of time. Reasons for rapid, simultaneous implementation include:

▼ *Synergy* within the new structure can be a powerful aid. New executives with a fresh mission, working in a redesigned organization with revised norms and values, backed up with power and status, provide strong reinforcement. The pieces of the revitalized organization pull together, as opposed to piecemeal change where one part of the new organization is out of synch with the old organization.

▼ *Pockets of resistance* have a chance to grow and develop when frame-breaking change is implemented slowly. The new mission, shifts in organization, and other frame-breaking changes upset the comfortable routines and precedent. Resistance to such fundamental change is natural. If frame-breaking change is implemented slowly, then individuals have a greater opportunity to undermine the changes and organizational inertia works to further stifle fundamental change.

▼ Typically, there is a *pent-up need for change*. During convergent periods, basic adjustments are postponed. Boat rocking is discouraged. Once constraints are relaxed, a variety of desirable improvements press for attention. The exhilaration and momentum of a fresh effort (and new team) make difficult moves more acceptable. Change is in fashion.

▼ Frame-breaking change is an inherently *risky and uncertain venture*. The longer the implementation period, the greater the period of uncertainty and instability. The most effective frame-breaking changes initiate the new strategy, structure, processes, and systems rapidly and begin the next period of stability and convergent change. The sooner fundamental uncertainty is removed, the better the chances of organizational survival and growth. While the pacing of change is important, the overall time to implement frame-breaking change will be contingent on the size and age of the organization.

PATTERNS IN ORGANIZATION EVOLUTION

This historical approach to organization evolution focuses on convergent periods punctuated by reorientation—discontinuous, organizationwide upheavals. The most effective firms take advantage of relatively long convergent periods. These periods of incremental change build on and take advantage of organization inertia. Frame-breaking change is quite dysfunctional if the organization is successful and the environment is stable. If, however, the organization is performing poorly and/or if the environment changes substantially, frame-breaking change is the only way to realign the organization with its competitive environment. Not all reorientations will be successful. . . . However, inaction in the face of performance crisis and/or environmental shifts is a certain recipe for failure.

Because reorientations are so disruptive and fraught with uncertainty, the more rapidly they are implemented, the more quickly the organization can reap the benefits of the following convergent period. High-performing firms initiate reorientations when environmental conditions shift and implement these reorientations rapidly. . . . Low-performing organizations either do not reorient or reorient all the time as they root around to find an effective alignment with environmental conditions. . . .

Executive Leadership and Organization Evolution

Executive leadership plays a key role in reinforcing systemwide momentum during convergent periods and in initiating and implementing bursts of change that characterize strategic reorientations. The nature of the leadership task differs sharply during these contrasting periods of organization evolution.

During convergent periods, the executive team focuses on *maintaining* congruence and fit within the organization. Because strategy, structure, processes, and systems are fundamentally sound, the myriad of incremental substantive decisions can be delegated to middle-level management, where direct expertise and information resides. The key role for executive leadership during convergent periods is to reemphasize strategy, mission, and core values and to keep a vigilant eye on external opportunities and/or threats.

Frame-breaking change, however, requires direct executive involvement in all aspects of the change. Given the enormity of the change and inherent internal forces for stability, executive leadership must be involved in the specification of strategy, structure, people, and organizational processes *and* in the development of implementation plans. . . .

The most effective executives in our studies foresaw the need for major change. They recognized the external threats and opportunities, and took bold steps to deal with them. . . . Indeed, by acting before being forced to do so, they had more time to plan their transitions.

Such visionary executive teams are the exceptions. Most frame-breaking change is postponed until a financial crisis forces drastic action. The momentum, and frequently the success, of convergent periods breeds reluctance to change. . . .

. . . most frame-breaking upheavals are managed by executives brought in from outside the company. The Columbia research program finds that externally recruited executives are more than three times more likely to initiate frame-breaking change than existing executive teams. Frame-breaking change was coupled with CEO succession in more than 80% of the cases. . . .

There are several reasons why a fresh set of executives are typically used in company transformations. The new executive team brings different skills and a fresh perspective. Often they arrive with a strong belief in the new mission. Moreover, they are unfettered by prior commitments linked to the status quo; instead, this new top team symbolizes the need for change. Excitement of a new challenge adds to the energy devoted to it.

We should note that many of the executives who could not, or would not, implement frame-breaking change went on to be quite successful in other organizations. . . . The stimulation of a fresh start and of jobs matched to personal competence applies to individuals as well as to organizations.

Although typical patterns for the when and who of frame-breaking change are clear—wait for a financial crisis and then bring in an outsider, along with a revised executive team, to revamp the company—this is clearly less than satisfactory for a particular organization. Clearly, some companies benefit from transforming themselves before a crisis forces them to do so, and a few exceptional executives have the vision and drive to reorient a business which they nurtured during its preceding period of convergence. The vital tasks are to manage incremental change during convergent periods; to have the vision to initiate and implement frame-breaking change prior to the competition; and to mobilize an executive team which can initiate and implement both kinds of change.

Conclusion

. . . Managers should anticipate that when environments change sharply:

▼ Frame-breaking change cannot be avoided. These discontinuous organizational changes will either be made proactively or initiated under crisis/turnaround conditions.
▼ Discontinuous changes need to be made in strategy, structure, people, and processes concurrently. Tentative change runs the risk of being smothered by individual, group, and organizational inertia.
▼ Frame-breaking change requires direct executive involvement in all aspects of the change, usually bolstered with new executives from outside the organization.
▼ There are no patterns in the sequence of frame-breaking changes, and not all strategies will be effective. Strategy and, in turn, structure, systems, and processes must meet industry-specific competitive issues.

Finally, our historical analysis of organizations highlights the following issues for executive leadership:

▼ Need to manage for balance, consistency, or fit during convergent period.
▼ Need to be vigilant for environmental shifts in order to anticipate the need for frame-breaking change.
▼ Need to manage effectively incremental as well as frame-breaking change.
▼ Need to build (or rebuild) a top team to help initiate and implement frame-breaking change.
▼ Need to develop core values which can be used as an anchor as organizations evolve through frame-breaking changes (e.g., IBM, Hewlett-Packard).
▼ Need to develop and use organizational history as a way to infuse pride in an organization's past and for its future.
▼ Need to bolster technical, social, and conceptual skills with visionary skills. Visionary skills add energy, direction, and excitement so critical during frame-breaking change. . . .

by Charles Baden-Fuller and John M. Stopford

Is rejuvenation really possible? How does a business paralyzed by years of turmoil and failure and constrained by limited resources create a vibrant organization committed to entrepreneurship? Unless the organization is frugal and produces some short-term results, it risks losing support from its many stakeholders. But short-term results alone are not enough; longer-term survival must be sought. A start must be made to initiate a form of entrepreneurial behavior that increases the chances of durable recovery. As one chairman said, "We have put in new controls and financial disciplines that have stanched the hemorrhaging, cut costs, and returned us, temporarily, to profit. That's the easy part. Getting some momentum going is much harder." . . .

The Crescendo Model

We regard building corporate entrepreneurship as the essential ingredient for lasting rejuvenation. . . . The task is difficult and often subtle. To ensure that all the attributes of entrepreneurship are diffused throughout an organization, the business must avoid the "quick fixes" so beloved by many. . . . Massive capital investment programs, aggressive but shallow attempts to force total quality management, or reengineering, or "cultural immersion" are usually ineffective if undertaken with insufficient attention to the issues we raised. The quick fix rarely delivers any long-term sustainable reward for, like the Tower of Babel, it falls if its foundations are insecure. The way forward must carry the whole organization to be self-sustaining.

Rebuilding a mature organization takes time; it cannot be done with a leap. It is, for example, seldom clear at the outset, because of information gaps, just where the business should be headed. Even when the direction has become clear, the details of the twists and turns in the road ahead can remain fogbound. Experimentation is necessary to test the feasibility of ideas. Too early commitment to a new direction can be unduly risky. A way has to be found to build consistently and to link newfound strengths before real and lasting transformation can be achieved.

While there are many routes mature businesses might take, the experience of firms can be distilled to identify one path that we feel is more sure than many others. It is a four-stage renewal process, an orchestrated crescendo. Crescendo is musical term meaning "a gradual increase in volume." Our renewal process is also gradual, requiring many steps over many years. The crescendo has to be managed and momentum for change established to allow businesses to reach for ever more challenging targets.

. . . We address the question of how businesses can get started and shrug off the stasis that has plagued so many mature firms. To place that start in context and show where we are headed, we begin with a brief summary of the overall model. . . .

BOX 1

FOUR STAGES FOR REJUVENATION

---

1. Galvanize: create a top team dedicated to renewal.
2. Simplify: cut unnecessary and confusing complexity.
3. Build: develop new capabilities.
4. Leverage: maintain momentum and stretch the advantages.

GALVANIZE

Although it seems obvious to begin by creating a top team dedicated to renewal, this vital stage is often overlooked. Rejuvenation is not the fixing up of a few activities or functions that have gone awry; it is the process of changing every part of an organization and the way its functions, territories, and various groups interact. No individual, not even the chief executive, can alone achieve this magnitude of change, but at the start it requires leadership from the top team. Such commitment carries important positive messages to the whole organization, for without that commitment those who labor in the firm become demoralized or frustrated.

To galvanize the top team, the agenda for action needs to be drawn up carefully. At the start, detailed plans of action are neither necessary nor wise. Instead there must be a broad understanding of the issues and a belief that progress will be achieved only by many small steps. There is serious danger in the early stages that top management will either try to buy its way out of difficulties with overgrandiose schemes, such as investing in expensive state-of-the-art technology that few in the organization understand, or spend too much time chasing culture change programs and not enough time initiating action.

SIMPLIFY

Simplifying the business helps change managers and workers' perceptions of what has been wrong and what new actions are required. Like clearing the rubbish from an overgrown garden, cutting some activities is a necessary precursor to building something new. Removing outdated control systems and incorrect data helps eliminate the causes of resistance to change. Simplifying the business concentrates scarce resources on a smaller agenda and so increases the chances of gaining positive results in the short to medium term. Simplification also signals to outside stakeholders—owners, suppliers, customers, bankers, and employers alike—that something positive is being attempted.

Actions to simplify the task and provide focus for the effort are no more than temporary measures. They must be regarded as work to provide a "beachhead" in complex industry structures that can be defended while work to build new strengths can proceed.

BUILD

In the third stage, which overlaps the second, the organization must set about building new advantages for later deployment as the business breaks out of the beachhead. It is at this stage that corporate rather than individual entrepreneurship must be developed. Beginning with raised aspirations to do better and resolve old problems, in the course of time new challenges need to be articulated, which will help all to work to a common purpose. That purpose, expressed in terms of visions and a direction for progress, is typically phrased in terms that all can understand. Making progress along the chosen path requires managers to experiment and to discover what can work and what fails.

Experiments, of necessity have to be small at the start: resources are limited, knowledge about possibilities uncertain, and the risks seem immense. As some experiments pay off, momentum should increase to the point where major investments in new technology for delivering the product or service may be required. Learning may also start slowly, though ordinarily some parts of the organization progress more quickly than others. Over time the organization must invest in deepening existing skills and acquiring new ones, developing new systems, data bases, and knowledge. Alongside these initiatives, teamwork must be developed, first on a small scale to deal with essential tasks but then growing across the whole organization and extending along the supply chain. The momentum created helps build the values that underpin the crucial ingredient of the will to win.

LEVERAGE

The final stage is leveraging advantages and maintaining momentum. As the organization grows in competitive strength, it can expand the sphere of its operations into new markets, new products, and new parts of the value chain. Leveraging capabilities can be by acquisition, alliances, or internal moves so that the business can extend its newfound advantages to a much wider sphere of activities. Pressures for expansion must be balanced against the danger of too much complexity slowing down the pace of innovation and forcing the organization to a standstill.

We label the rejuvenation process a *crescendo* to emphasize that the four stages are not discrete steps but rather activities which merge into each other as the magnitude of change increases over time. The reality of all organizations is messy, confusing, and complex. In the building of corporate entrepreneurship, activities in one department or at one level of the organization may proceed faster and more effectively than others. Moreover, organizations do not rejuvenate only once: they may need to do so repetitively. The challenges of one period may be resolved, but those of the next may again require organizational change.

The rejuvenation steps are summarized in Figure 1. The arrows are drawn as lines, though in practice progress is usually made in loops of learning. The dance to the crescendo of music is the samba. *One step back to take two steps forward* describes how organizations proceed—and it is exactly what happens with simplification and building. Let us use an analogy: renovators of old buildings know full well that the plaster has to come off the walls if a rotten structure is to be repaired. It is rarely possible to fix it without spoiling the decorations. . . .

We emphasize that in the early simplifying stage of renewal, cutting may have to be radical. The contraction can be tangible, for example, cutting out parts of the product range, geographic territory, or stages of the value chain; it can also be less tangible, for example, eliminating systems and procedures. Even profitable activities may have to be dropped if they distract attention and deflect resources from building the new "core."

In building, progress is best achieved by many small initiatives, because resources are limited. Small steps spread the risks and prevent the organization from betting everything on one initiative. As rejuvenation proceeds, the risks become better understood and progress more secure, allowing the steps to get bigger. Small steps also allow the organization to encourage initiatives from below and help build an entrepreneurial culture. Whereas

FIGURE 1
Critical Path for
Corporate Renewal

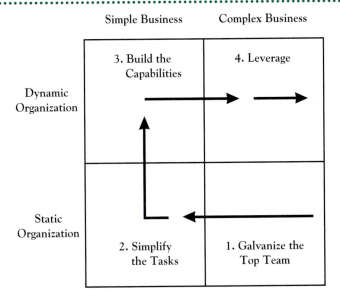

instructions for surgery are imposed from the top, it is the bottom-up flow of ideas and actions that accelerates the convalescence and return to fighting fitness.

We stress that organizations need a long time to rejuvenate. It takes years to build a truly entrepreneurial company. Like builders of houses, who spend almost two-thirds of the cost and time below ground digging foundations and preparing the site, effective organizations that aim to become entrepreneurial also have to sink deep foundations; rushing for the quick-fix solution is unlikely to result in long-term rewards. . . .

Galvanizing the Top Team

Rejuvenating a mature organization is impossible without commitment from the top. As we pointed out, . . . many mature organizations show signs of life with innovative actions being taken in parts, and include many able individuals who are committed to change. Entrepreneurial individuals generally labor in isolated groups. They are unable to make the connections essential to altering the path of the organization, for that requires linkages across functions and territories, which cannot be achieved without the backing of top management.

Initial moves are often made by a new chief executive, and in all the firms we studied, the CEO played a vital and decisive role. The effective ones, however, did not act alone; they all realized the importance of teams. . . .

Building a top team dedicated to change provides continuity and reduces the risks that the process will falter if one person leaves. In several of our organizations the chief executive changed without loss of momentum. . . .

Effective top teams span all the key functions. Rejuvenation involves changing the way in which the functions work and the way in which they relate. An effective top team must have a real understanding of the functions so that it understands what is technically possible, what is required by customers, suppliers, the work force, and other stakeholders. Without shared knowledge within the team, there can be no intuition, which is vital for the business.

The need to involve the key functions also ensures the involvement of the vital power brokers of the organization. Functional or territorial heads carry weight in getting things done. They can influence the perceptions and actions of their group, perhaps because of their position but often because of their background and skills. Unless they are involved in the early stages, the power brokers may sabotage or slow down the process through misunderstanding and lack of appreciation.

For rejuvenation, all members of the top team must share an understanding of the problem. An effective top team avoids vacillation, does not seek outsiders to resolve its problems (although they may help), does not look for a quick fix or shirk dealing with immediate issues. In short, many rocks and whirlpools have to be avoided. To sidestep these hazards, the team must believe that there is a crisis, that action has to be taken, and that the action must extend throughout the organization. Only where there is real common acceptance of these three priorities does the top team feel empowered to start the process of rejuvenation. Achieving consensus is not easy, so we examine the issues. (See Table 1.)

SENSING THE NEED TO START

What triggers actions that can lead to rejuvenation? Why is correct sensing so critical to generating a sense of urgency? Earlier we discussed the difficulty of recognizing crises in a form that can lead to action and the even more serious problem of using the recognition of an opportunity as a way of focusing energies to change behavior. It is one thing to bring together a top team, quite another to have it share, collectively, a sense that change is imperative.

TABLE 1 Galvanizing the Top Team	LIMITING PERCEPTIONS	GALVANIZING PERCEPTIONS
	The problem we face is temporary.	There is a crisis and the issues are major and fundamental.
	We must move slowly to avoid upsetting the existing order.	There is a sense of urgency. Change must must be set into motion even if we do not know exactly where we are going.
	It is someone else's fault that we are in trouble.	We must understand why we are in the mess, so that we, the top team, can lead the way forward.
	The problems lie in specific areas of the organization; they are not widespread.	Firmwide change is needed across functions, territories, and hierarchy.
	The financial figures tell us what is wrong.	We have to look behind the figures to find out where the markets are going and the needed capabilities.

We use the word sense advisedly, because at the earliest stages only rarely does hard data indicate a clear direction; information by itself seldom "proves" or "disproves" any action.

Consider what can happen when managers sense the signals for change. They may seem so vague that they are effectively ignored. They may point to solutions that are beyond current capabilities, they can provoke responses of general concern, but the actions are little more than tinkering with the symptoms. More precise signals can also be ignored, even when the solutions are within capabilities, because the team has yet to share a common will to respond. The issue of the urgency is also embodied in the message. Managers may feel that they have plenty of time and allow other agendas to preoccupy them. Alternatively, an urgent message may seem to be so complex that appropriate responses are hard to calculate.

We found that all the top teams of rejuvenating firms had experienced many of these difficulties before they could commit themselves to collective internal action. Often, we found top teams working to exhaust all the "obvious" actions before they could perceive the need to consider more radical approaches to transform the business as a whole. Rational calculations of partial response to complex challenges can be used, perhaps unwittingly, to perpetuate the inertia of maturity. The problem is exacerbated when the agenda is so complex that team members cannot agree on priorities. . . .

It is important to appreciate that the data in signals for change need to be interpreted for others, particularly when they are weak. Consider the assessment of competitors, so commonly undertaken by top management. Measures of competition may cover profitability, productivity, reliability, or customer acceptance. Generally, a few competitors are doing better on some if not all the measures, but many may be similar to a given organization and some may be doing worse. Should this fact be seen as a trigger for action or a signal for complacency? Unless someone has high aspirations and a sense of danger, complacency prevails. . . . There are always those who believe that poor performance, be it in profits or some other measure, can be excused: "It is not our fault." Worse yet, competitor benchmarking studies can be used to justify the status quo. One mature firm that later went out of business went so far as to reject a study that indicated the need for a fundamental change of approach. In the words of one director, it was "obviously fallacious. If this was possible, we would be doing it already."

There are many other reasons why managers may fail to react to changing circumstance. Mature organizations can become trapped in an illusion bred of undue focus on accounting profits. Of necessity, accounting figures can register only what has happened, not what is about to happen; when confronted by "satisfactory" profits, many top groups ignored other signals indicating declining competitiveness. . . .

Only a few of our rejuvenators did the obvious thing at the start, that is, establish measures that heighten the sense of urgency to deal with emergent problems before they become serious. Wise and successful organizations broaden their measures of performance to include specific indicators of relative achievement of financial and nonfinancial goals. A broader and more balanced scorecard helps top teams in general, and chief executives in particular, to anticipate where trouble might strike. It amplifies the weak signals that forewarn of danger and diminishes those signals which encourage complacency. If the top team does not anticipate it, the organization may be submerged and unable to retrieve itself when the real crisis arrives.

TRIGGERS FOR ACTION

Sensing impending doom is not always sufficient to induce action. Although it comes late in the day, falling profitability seems to be the most common trigger for inducing a sufficient enough sense of urgency and crisis that actions to cure the roots of the problem can be instituted. . . .

Must firms wait for a financial crisis before top managers do more than tinker with some of the parts? Though harder to do, it is possible for individuals to anticipate a looming crisis and initiate corrective action before it is too late or too expensive to try. It is relatively easier for that to happen when an individual has the power to act. The awareness may come first to shareholders, who appoint a new chief executive to carry the message, or the chief executive may be prescient. It is more difficult when the messages come from outside and are heard by individual managers without power. Dealings with suppliers, customers, bankers, and innumerable others can highlight the problem and stir up action within isolated groups. But when that happens, action to change business fundamentally usually has to wait until. . . there is a chief executive who listens and buys into the possibilities.

. . . It is possible to anticipate a real crisis. Those who have done so have been able to take positive action at less cost than would have been incurred had they procrastinated. In such instances, hindsight seems to show repetitively that the actions taken were less risky than a policy of standing still. But before the event, the risks may have appeared large.

EMPOWERING MANAGEMENT

Bringing together a top team and making its members realize that there is a crisis is not enough to start rejuvenation: the team must believe that it has the power and the responsibility to do something. It is necessary that certain aspects of the problem are appreciated by the top team: that the problem is not limited to a single part of the organization, that the quick fix does not work. The top team must also appreciate that it does not have to know all the answers before it can act. Its job is to chart the direction ahead and enlist the aid of others in finding durable solutions. It is tempting to suggest that the realization comes quickly, but the truth is that appreciation comes gradually.

. . . Managers of mature organizations are often keen to fasten blame on others. Sometimes they blame the environment, poor demand, overfussy customers, adverse exchange rates, even the weather. Sometimes they blame the decisions of previous top management and sometimes the failure of current middle management to implement decisions made by the top team. While an element of blame may rightly be attached to these groups, in all cases top management showed insufficient appreciation of the issues at stake. Progress can take place only when team members appreciate the extent of a problem and realize that they, and only they, are ultimately responsible for [their] organization's failures. More important, only the top team can lead the organization out of its mess.

It is also common for senior managers to perceive that the problems (and hence the solutions) lie in a single function or part of their organization. Blaming particular functions, territories, or groups is often unhelpful, as the crisis reflects failures of the whole organization. For example, when high-cost products are also poor quality, the production department is usually blamed. Such finger-pointing is naive, for rarely is production alone to blame for poor quality. It may be that production, not being told by the service department which failures occur most frequently, is trying to improve the wrong elements. Distribution may be at fault, damaging goods in transit. Purchasing may be paying insufficient attention to ensuring that suppliers provide quality components, and marketing may insist on designs that are difficult and expensive to produce. Quality at low cost can be achieved only when all functions work closely together. . . .

The dawning realization that the problems are serious and that the causes extend beyond a single function to all parts of the organization is one step on the road toward taking necessary corrective actions. But before effective action can be initiated, hard choices among many alternatives must be made. Here the chief executive has the central role of holding the ring as people test their intuition against always imperfect data. Lacking hard evidence, a top team always has members with competing senses of priority. And lacking anything more than a common will to be positive, the debates can all too readily become unproductive without firm leadership.

Choosing Effective Action

Some top teams choose to manage their way forward by exhaustive analysis of the alternatives they can perceive at the time of crisis. Others feel their way by trying solutions and discovering what does and does not work. Still others examine the experience of other organizations. And often all these approaches are combined. However choices are made, there are many false paths and blind alleys, which can seduce and lull management into thinking that it is effectively dealing with the issues at hand.

The steps that we suggest mark out the most effective path of action are in stark contrast to other actions we observed. Simplification involves cutting to conserve resources, revealing a new core, and pointing the way forward. The subsequent building, later described in detail, lays new foundations for the entrepreneurial organization and requires an extended time perspective. These measured steps contrast with the following alternatives, which many have taken and which fail to address key issues effectively: scrapping everything and starting afresh—rather than saving what is of value, looking to outsiders to alleviate a problem—as a substitute for internal action; vacillation among extreme directives issued by top management—paralyzed uncomprehending top management; large-scale investments in state-of-the-art technology and systems at the initial stages—quick fix or big hit; and culture change programs without parallel actions—denying that there is an immediate crisis. These issues. . . are discussed more fully below.

SCRAP EVERYTHING AND START AFRESH

Consider first the problem of those Cassandras who argue that it is hopeless to try to rejuvenate—better to give up without a struggle and go elsewhere. Their pessimistic views can be justified if *all* the alternatives are more costly and more risky. Only if all else fails must an organization be extinguished.

One U.S. company considered seeking the rejuvenation of an existing operation a waste of time. Instead of tackling the deep-seated problems in its Midwest plants, it moved the whole operation to the South, leaving its past behind. In so doing, the company abandoned many skilled and loyal workers who might have been capable of adapting to new working methods faster than it took to train a brand new workforce and at less cost. The Japanese experience of buying U.S. facilities and doubling or trebling productivity within less than a year illustrates that the possibility of rejuvenation often exists. Their experience also confirms that faster returns may come from renewal rather than greenfield initiatives, a point often overlooked by those in a hurry to "get something going."*

Sometimes, to be sure, troubled organizations do not have the option of a clean start elsewhere. Even though they might wish to walk away, the owners may not be able to afford the exit costs. They may also face severe union opposition and the resistance of politicians and local government officials. In such cases, management is obliged to try to find a middle way, regardless of how many Cassandras argue that the effort will be in vain.

SEEKING OUTSIDE SUPPORT

For years, many major European chemical companies, particularly the Italian giants, the French and Belgians, and even the British ICI, perceived the problems of their industry as being caused by government's failure to manage demand in the economy and allowing the Middle Eastern countries power over oil prices. In these firms, top management consistently lobbied governments for support to resolve their problems and failed to take internal initiatives. ICI, one of the bigger culprits, was also one of the first to break out of the vicious circle and realize that internal action was necessary. A galvanized top management led the way, and ten years later, in better shape than many of its European counterparts, it is still trying to pull its organization around. . . .

Lest we be accused of ignoring politics and reality, we fully recognize that all organizations have a role to lobby and put their case to government, and all need to watch and influence events. However, we draw a distinction between this approach and those failing organizations which do nothing for themselves while waiting to be rescued by the white knight of outside support. The first puts the role of public policy in perspective, while the second fails in the duties of management.

TOP-DOWN DIRECTIVES THAT ADDRESS SYMPTOMS, NOT CAUSES

Many top managers seem to believe that issuing orders from the top and expecting immediate responses is the best way to start things going. . . . This is unlikely to instill corporate entrepreneurship. As a sense of crisis looms, if statements from the top become hysterical, they can be met by inaction or lack of results from below. Vacillation is usually another sign that top management is not really in control and does not understand either the causes of a problem or how to respond effectively. Seldom can top-down directives do more than preserve yesterday's "formula.". . .

GOING FOR THE BIG HIT

The recognition that an organization is far behind in its capabilities can drive top management to seek a quick fix. At the beginning of the renewal process there is a temptation to spend money on modern capital by buying state-of-the-art factories, service delivery systems, or other forms of technology. Typically, consultants or other outsiders have suggested

---

*The West German approach to rebuilding East Germany also has the appearance of trying to start afresh: old factories are demolished, workers dismissed, and the new owners act as if they are setting up greenfield sites. For an academic view of when it is best to start afresh, see M. T. Hannan and J. Freeman, "Structural Inertia and Organizational Change," in K. S. Cameron, R. I. Sutton, and D. A Whetten, eds., *Readings in Organizational Decline* (Cambridge, Mass.: Ballinger, 1988).

that such investments permit a firm to catch up with its industry leaders. Usually the investments are large, take several years to build, and commit the organization to a single unchangeable route for the future. There is often an absence of understanding in the organization of how the new technology works, and certainly a lack of appreciation for all the issues it involves. At the early stages of rejuvenation, big programs are dangerous, not least because most of the organization's resources are bet on a single course.

For the mature organization in crisis, the arrival of massive amounts of new capital, new computers, or new systems without a corresponding building of a skill base risks disasters. All our rejuvenators discovered, if they did not already know, that skills have to be built in tandem with investment in hardware. Without the proper skills and awareness throughout the whole organization, the investments are misused or underused. Little progress is made in delivering either financial results or building a competitive edge. Worse, the spirit of entrepreneurial enthusiasm with its characteristics of learning and experimentation may be repressed.

We should make it clear that large investment programs can pay off handsomely when undertaken by firms that have gained entrepreneurial capabilities. When organizations have built their internal skills and processes, they can leverage new investments effectively.

CULTURE CHANGE PROGRAMS WITHOUT CORRESPONDING ACTION

If the big hit is dangerous because it squanders resources, takes unnecessary risks, and does not build a new organization, the culture change program goes to the opposite extreme. It is certainly true that mature organizations need to change their culture if they are to become entrepreneurial, but many mistakenly believe that the culture has to be changed before actions for improvement can be taken, or that culture change is sufficient in itself. A culture change program without action is very risky because it denies the existence of a crisis and takes the organization's attention away from the necessity for immediate action. Moreover, it fails to appreciate the most obvious fact that organizations change only through actions because actions reflect and alter beliefs.

Our finding echoes the observations of Tom Peters and Robert Waterman, [1982], who noted that effective organizations had a bias for action. Their point was that unless action is taken, progress cannot be made. Their message is highly appropriate for rejuvenating organizations. We found a surprising number of firms investing heavily in changing the culture of their organizations without ensuring that deliberate progress was made in the specification of the actual tasks. . . .

Rejuvenating a business does require a culture change, but change must be linked to action. Our research suggests that effective culture change requires managers to deal with tasks. Thus, abolishing the executive dining room at one firm did help, but only because it reinforced other important initiatives dealing with productivity and quality. In many organizations, quality circles and the like are introduced, and it seems that those which work well are those which have short-term tangible goals as well as long-term ones. Grand schemes for change without action seldom work. . . .

THE QUICK FIX: TQM OR PROCESS REENGINEERING

All our rejuvenators subscribed in one way or another to aspects of total quality management (TQM) and all have reengineered their processes, occasionally several times over. But what they did. . . bore little relation to those peddlers of snake oil who claim instant results.

A few less careful proponents of TQM or process engineering (or the equivalent) portray complex philosophies as quick-fix solutions. They understate the investment in the time, energy, and effort required to yield results. In their desire for speed, they fail to stress the need to teach the organization the skills to ensure that the process can be continued and typically do not build a proper foundation for lasting success. Not surprisingly, recent surveys of organizations that took up the TQM fad in the 1980s show that many have been disappointed and stopped earlier initiatives.* To be sure, there have been successes, but we suggest that they have probably been organizations which were either far down the rejuvenation road or, like our mature firms, patient and persistent ones. We forecast the same for process reengineering.

Claims by consultants that process reengineering can deliver a ten-fold improvement come as no surprise. . . . But boasts that such progress is achieved quickly do not ring true. Long before the recent fad, we observed mature firms attempting such rapid engineering without preparation and failing. . . .

The Way Forward

To go forward, the mature firm aspiring to rejuvenate must galvanize and build a top team committed to action. Crucial choices need to be made about the scope of the firm and how and where it will compete. In addition, action must be taken to start the building of entrepreneurship, which we assert is necessary for renewal and any higher aspirations. Some businesses have found that outside stakeholders can play a role. One such group is the top team of a business that is part of a holding company or parent organization. . . .

There may be a gap in cultural perceptions on these matters about what is and is not effective. Where many U.S. managers espouse the value of directives from the very top and point to the benefits of the resulting focus and speed of change, many we spoke to across Europe adopted a different perspective. Those whose job it was to look after a whole portfolio often preferred to work on encouraging managers to embrace the values of creativity, innovation, and challenge to conventions without specifying the actions or processes. Many set challenging targets, but some who regarded their approach as slower and harder to control, bet that the end results would be much more durable.

There is no way we know to resolve the issue of which is the superior approach. Both have good and bad points and both are dependent on the climate of attitudes into which such initiatives are introduced. The difference of opinion, however, serves to reinforce the point we made at the start: . . . real transformation of a business cannot begin in earnest without the recognition by its top managers that a new direction must be found.

---

*See, for instance, the studies by Arthur D. Little in the United States and A. T. Kearney in the United Kingdom as reported in *The Economist*, April 18, 1992.

SONY ENTERTAINMENT

In a highly publicized series of moves, Sony Corporation acquired CBS Records for approximately $2 billion in 1988 and Columbia Pictures Entertainment in 1989 for $3.4 billion. One initial controversy—a hue and cry over Japanese purchase of U.S. "cultural assets"—quickly subsided. Several others remained in 1994. Had Sony paid too much ($7 billion including backup costs) for its acquisitions? Could it successfully manage its more artistically based enterprises in the highly volatile entertainment industry? Could it integrate its magnificently creative hardware operations with its U.S. "software" operations to achieve synergies no one had accomplished in the past? How would Sony position itself against Time Warner, Viacom-Paramount and the other information and entertainment giants attempting to exploit the "information superhighway" of the mid 1990s?

ACQUISITION HISTORY

Sony had long enjoyed a (50% Sony–50% CBS) distribution relationship with CBS Records in Japan. In a friendly 1985 takeover, Laurence Tisch of Loews Corporation had bought control of CBS, Inc. 1986 turned into a record year for CBS Records. But Tisch was still worried about the seeming uncontrollability of CBS Records' costs and the wild cyclicality of its earnings ($112 million in '78, $22 million in '82, and $162 million in '86). In October 1986, Tisch announced a $1.25 billion price for CBS Records to which Sony

responded. However, CBS's board rejected Sony's offer. In September 1987 Sony increased its offer to $2 billion. After the stock market crashed in October 1987, CBS agreed to the sale; and Sony acquired CBS Records with its subsidiaries, as well as the remaining half of CBS/Sony. CBS Records' reported sales, assets, and profits at the time appear in Table 1 (page 782). CBS Records' sales and profits crashed in the late 1980s; but, stimulated by several new recording groups brought in by CBS Records' head, Walter Yetnikoff, its worldwide sales exploded to $2.9 billion in fiscal 1990.

In September 1989, Sony made a tender offer for 100 percent of the shares of Columbia Pictures Entertainment at a price of $3.4 billion. (Columbia Pictures Entertainment had been formed in late 1987. It was a combination of TriStar Pictures and various entertainment businesses of Coca-Cola including Columbia Pictures.) After closing the merger transaction in November, Sony announced the hiring of producers Peter Guber and Jon Peters, whose recent successes had included "Batman," "Rainman," and "The Color Purple." Sony bought out their production company at a price of $200 million (reportedly well above market value) and reportedly offered them each five-year contracts with guaranteed salaries of $2.75 million and a share of a $50 million bonus pool after five years. Unfortunately, the Sony contract led to a lawsuit by Warner Brothers for breach of its contract with Peters and Guber. In an out-of-court settlement, reports speculated that Warner received "several hundred million dollars" in assets from Columbia and CBS Records. It was also reported that there was a further contingent bonus in which the executives would split 8% of any appreciation in Columbia's assessed value during those 5 years. Columbia Pictures' financials just before the merger listed assets, revenues, and earnings as shown in Table 2 and segment data as shown in Table 3.

TABLE 1
CBS Records Group Financials, 1982–1987 ($ millions)

	1982	1983	1984	1985	1986	1987
Revenues	1,067	1,159	1,265	1,230	1,489	1,548
Amortization	1.0	1.3	1.3	0.9	0.6	n/a
Net Income from Operations	22	109	124	90	192	132
Identifiable Assets	734	836	782	843	937	n/a

Source: CBS, Inc., *Annual Reports*, various years.

In describing the purposes of the acquisition, Mr. Ohga, CEO, Sony Corporation, said, "In buying Columbia, I did not necessarily seek the venture only on the basis of return on investment. That would not be the purpose of our having a movie company. Its prime purpose was to support our hardware with software. You would certainly have to invest that much money if you were to create a whole library of software. The value of the vast library we have of over 3,000 movies plus TV programs, plus all the know-how and power that has been produced through all the years of Columbia's experience, is priceless."[1]

EARLY PROBLEMS AND SUCCESSES

In the early 1990s, a series of articles seriously questioned the validity of Sony's acquisitions.[2] Columbia Pictures, once a major Hollywood name, had run down in the 1980s, after its purchase by Coca Cola. Sony's first few big production pictures (including $50 million "Hudson Hawk," $25 million "Ishtar," and Stephen Spielberg's $70 million "Hook") were initially box office bombs, but several of them later became more successful. After the expensive deal to move Guber and Peters, Sony quickly lost Peters who left to start his own production company. Reporters said Sony had to invest another $100 million to consolidate and upgrade aging

Columbia Pictures facilities. But hidden in Sony's purchase was Columbia Pictures' television division, formerly called Screen Gems. Although the television division had produced many successful series including *Bewitched*, *Police Woman*, *Wheel of Fortune*, *Jeopardy*, *Facts of Life*, and *Who's the Boss?*, its line-up was distinctly dated at the time of the acquisition. In the 1988–89 season, not one of its three new series was renewed. Only after numerous unsuccessful attempts, did it finally hit paydirt with *Designing Women*, *Married With Children*, which along with *Jeopardy* and *Wheel of Fortune*, were still operating in 1994.

In the record business, Sony had faced expensive renewals of its contracts with stars like Barbra Streisand, Michael Jackson, Bruce Springsteen, and New Kids on the Block. Then suddenly Walter Yetnikoff—CBS Records' brilliant but frequently uncontrollable music mogul who had brought many of these talents aboard—departed. Reportedly through the end of 1991, Sony's entertainment groups had absorbed some $7 billion in capital and reportedly were a cash flow drain of about $150 million per year for Sony Corporation.[3] For its fiscal year ending March 1993, Sony found its net profits 71% lower than in 1992, with Sony's entertainment companies major contributors to its problems.

Fortunately when Sony took over CBS Records, it also inherited a vast collection of old master disks from

TABLE 2
Columbia Pictures Entertainment, Inc. Financials, 1985–1989 (millions)

	1985	1986	1987[a]	1988[b]	1989
Revenues	$1,076	$1,355	$1,066	$217	$1,616
Profits	109	102	51	(105)	22
Cash Flow	n/a	97	(315)	(171)	(187)
Assets	2,686	2,771	3,457	3,423	3,565
Stock Price Range	7⅛–11½	8½–16⅛	7¼–16⅛	n/a	7–16¼
No. of Shares Outstanding	n/a	75.2	75.2	109.8	112.8

(a) Fiscal year January 1-December 17, 1987.
(b) Fiscal year December 18, 1987-February 28, 1988.
Source: Columbia Pictures Entertainment, Inc., *Annual Reports*, various years.

TABLE 3
Columbia Pictures Entertainment, Inc. Segment Data

	1986	1987[a]	1988[b]	1989
Revenues				
Theatrical	551	430	95	756
Television	759	594	90	620
Exhibition (Loews)	—	—	27	235
Other	44	42	5	4
Operating Income				
Theatrical	27	27	(23)	26
Television	240	154	5	156
Exhibition (Loews)	—	—	5	33
Other	(8)	(7)	7	3
Identifiable Assets				
Theatrical	585	1,278	1,000	1,147
Television	1,046	1,289	1,174	1,096
Exhibition (Loews)	—	341	335	670
Other	97	83	74	—
Depreciation				
Theatrical	1.9	3.1	0.9	2.8
Television	1.8	2.1	0.4	2.3
Exhibition (Loews)	—	—	2.7	20
Other	0.6	0.6	0.1	—
Capital Expenditures				
Theatrical	3.8	3.8	0.3	6.1
Television	0.7	2.5	0.4	1.1
Exhibition (Loews)	—	—	2.6	34.4
Other	0.5	0.9	0.1	—

(a) Fiscal year from January 1-December 17, 1987.
(b) Fiscal year from December 18, 1987-February 29, 1988.
Source: Columbia Pictures Entertainment, Inc., *Annual Report 1989.*

which record platters are pressed. Among these were the classic "Columbia Masterworks Series" of symphonic and opera recordings as well as original pressings of Frank Sinatra, Louis Armstrong, and blues legend Robert Johnson. It also controlled masters of classical musicals like *South Pacific* and *West Side Story.* By 1993, with a changed movie strategy and some outstanding movie successes—like "A Few Good Men," "A League of Their Own," "Basic Instinct," "Howards End," "Indochine," "Sleepless in Seattle," "Prince of Tides"— Sony pictures as a whole had moved into strong #1 position ahead of Time Warner and Disney. Nevertheless, in early 1994, Morgan Stanley began to report "Performance in the [Sony] Pictures Division has been worse than expected. That division will likely show a substantial operating loss on a consolidated basis in fiscal 1993. . . . Movie profits collapsed due to poor box office receipts in the U.S. and Sony's writing off of production costs for all its loss-making moving pictures.

Sony produced and distributed 25–30 movies a year, and when there were no big hits, the amortization costs (accounted for as cost of sales) soared and threw movie operations into a loss position."[4] Sony Corporation's profits had also continued to oscillate (see Table 4).

THEN WHY THE ACQUISITIONS?

In explaining the reasons for the acquisitions Mr. Norio Ohga, CEO, Sony Corporation, said, "In our previous way of doing business in the entertainment field, everything was based on hardware. I still think that hardware is the center of our entertainment business. We already have a lot of equipment sold to homes. But hardware doesn't mean anything unless you have good software; it's only a box of components. As you know, Time Warner has a vision for 500 or more TV channels. So there will be a need for programs to fill those channels; to satisfy customers you will need a great deal of software.

TABLE 4
Sony Income and
Cash Flows
(billions of yen)

	SALES	NET INCOME	DEPREC./ AMORTIZ.	CAP. INVEST.	DIVS. PAID	NET CASH FLOW[1]	LT DEBT	NET PAYMENTS, ACQUISITIONS
1981	1,051	66.9	32.4	98.1	8.1	-6.8	20.5	
1982	1,114	45.8	48.2	112.1	10.1	-28.2	56.8	
1983	1,111	29.8	55.3	56.6	10.2	+18.3	97.6	
1984	1,261	71.4	56.5	80.4	10.2	+37.4	89.2	
1985	1,421	73.0	72.0	130.4	10.2	+4.5	134.4	
1986	1,452	41.2	86.0	105.2	10.2	+11.9	143.9	
1987[2]	609	13.3	37.3	58.2	4.3	-11.9	143.4	
1988	1,555	37.2	92.5	134.0	10.6	-14.9	201.1	221.7
1989	2,145	72.5	125.8	215.6	12.4	-29.8	220.8	
1990	2,880	102.8	164.8	323.8	16.5	-72.7	646.0	550.7
1991	3,616	116.9	214.1	411.7	16.9	-97.5	694.5	
1992	3,821	120.1	265.2	453.1	17.8	-85.6	885.3	38.1
1993	3,879	36.3	274.5	251.1	18.6	41.1	880.4	

All figures are in billions of yen.[1] Net cash flow = Net Income + Depreciation/Amortization - Capital Investment - Dividends paid.[2] 1987 numbers are for five months ended March 31 of that year. Through 1986, Sony's fiscal year ended on October 31; as of 1987 it ended on March 31.

Source: Sony Corporation, *Annual Reports*, various years.

"Software also makes hardware meaningful; hardware does not exist without software. They must be developed mutually. Tape recorder manufacturers often say that it is the manufacture of the tapes and tape recorder [itself] that creates value; but what is it you use a tape recorder for? It is for the software, the music or video; that is what makes the tape recorder valuable. Further, the value of the software is protected by copyrights. I think that as we go into the 21st Century, the value of software will become even more important. In the 1980s, when we purchased the software for the audio and video businesses, I had the vision that a hardware company without software would probably not exist in the future. I envision Sony being approximately 50–50 hardware and software in the year 2000. [By that] I do not necessarily mean the volume of sales—but the emphasis or relative importance to the company."

Mr. Michael (Mickey) Schulhof, President Sony Entertainment and Software, amplified further: "It is important to understand what the two epiphanies were that changed management's viewpoint. The first was Betamax, a product introduced with a technological lead in 1975 and by all rights even today technically superior to the VHS format. Nevertheless, as JVC and Matsushita aggressively promoted the VHS format in the marketplace, they generated a feedback mecha-

nism driven by the availability of pre-recorded software. Once there was a threshold of hardware available, it became the driving force in determining the purchasers' choice of format. Had it not been for software, the two formats (VHS and Beta) could easily have coexisted. What really tilted the marketplace was that VHS had passed a threshold of penetration, and the retailers did not want to carry double inventories of motion picture software. That ultimately drove people's purchasing decisions, and had a very profound impact on Sony's thinking.

"The second incident was the introduction of the CD. This technology required pre-recorded software, unlike the Betamax [VTR] which was able to function with off-the-air recording. Compact disc players simply could not function without the availability of [pre-recorded] music and, therefore, needed the support of the recording industry—a support which was virtually withheld by every record company throughout the world with the exception of two. One of those was PolyGram, a company controlled by Phillips, and the second was Sony's Japanese venture, managed by Sony, although owned 50–50 with CBS Records. CD could easily have been stillborn had it not been for the influence of those two record companies and [the fact that] subsequently the consumer and the artist community liked the product.

"There were two other things happening simultaneously in the middle 1980s that made our future strategy even more receptive to the concept of entering the software business. One was the accelerating digitalization of electronics which—although it enhanced product quality, product features, and consumer benefit—also made it less and less likely that the technology of any hardware company could give it clear superiority over competitors. Software, on the other hand, has clear product differentiation [potentials] because of the talent. People don't go into the store and ask to see the latest Sony or Warner record releases. They are driven in their purchasing decision by the talent and the performance—which are differentiable. If you want Barbra Streisand you do not go out and buy Whitney Houston because she's close. You go after the performance or talent of interest to you; and you are not concerned about what company it comes from. The same holds true in the motion picture business and in every other software creative enterprise. Talent is more important than corporate identity.

"Our greatest asset is talent. In the last five years there has been a fundamental shift in talent managed corporations. The record industry became a truly big business only in the last decade. All told we did close to $4 billion worldwide in pre-recorded music [last year]. But ten years ago that number was probably closer to $800 million. At that time the style was very entrepreneurial, very unstructured. The size of all those businesses was considerably smaller. Now the small, independent, little companies have found they are no longer able to compete when bidding for major talent."

ENTERTAINMENT CONGLOMERATES

"Another thing that was becoming obvious in the mid-1980s was that electronics was going to be the facilitator of new business enterprises, but was not likely to be the profit generator for new enterprises. Sony is in the business of facilitating new industries. CD was a new industry. High definition is going to be a new industry. Digital video disks will become a new industry. Yet the aggregate profitability created within those industries will clearly come more from the software [than the hardware] side. . . . A year after buying CBS Records, we began to think about completing the visual side of the entertainment business and spent about a year studying the motion picture industry and ultimately wound up purchasing Columbia Pictures. [Along with Columbia Pictures came TriStar Pictures and the Loews theater group.]"

Soon other companies began to move into the entertainment software businesses from various vantage points. Matsushita made a $6.1 billion purchase of MCA, owner of Universal Studios in late 1990. Telecoms groups like Viacom and magazine publishers like Time, Inc., began to merge with other studios (Paramount and Warner Brothers). The term "information-entertainment conglomerates" began to be widely used. However, in 1993, the integration and financial viability of these conglomerates was yet to be proved. *The Economist* noted. . . "When Matsushita bought MCA, outsiders and insiders alike assumed the Japanese would soon let America's show-business elite know who was the boss. . . . Far from taking over, the Japanese are [currently] being mugged. This is [also] happening to an array of smaller Japanese investors, dabbling in film finance chiefly for tax reasons. . . . Nobody in Hollywood thinks the Japanese firms will ever get value for that money. . . . Although the Japanese can learn about the entertainment business, they cannot take it over unless American culture ceases to dominate the world music and film markets. The vital ingredient, in other words, is in America. In both music and film, much of the profit goes to those who add the value—the stars and the producers—regardless of who owns the firms."[5]

HOW TO ORGANIZE?

Mr. Schulhof noted in 1990, "We have now created a new definition for the word *entertainment*. It is no longer just programming or delivery. It's now a system drawing on our ability to treat software and hardware as a combined system." Sony Chairman Akio Morita's long articulated philosophy of "global localization" would be severely strained by the challenge such integration posed.

Sony's traditional approach had been to use loose organizational structures and to depend on dedicated and motivated people. These systems had worked well when the company was largely Japanese based and most personnel had grown up within its culture. However, by the early 1990s, the interaction between various elements of the company had become quite complex. Figure 1 sets forth the overall Sony structure. Within this structure Sony U.S.A. had sales of $8.3 billion (28% of Sony's global sales) in 1993. Sony of North America (SONAM) had started as a marketing organization. But manufacturing of Sony Trinitron tubes began in 1972 in San Diego. By 1993, Sony was exporting more than $500 million from thirteen manufacturing facilities in the U.S. and performed research, development, and engineering in fifteen different areas in the U.S., including San Jose (CA), Boulder (CO), Dothan (AL) and San Diego (CA). By 1993, Sony had approximately 20,000 employees in the United States.

In 1990, Sony USA (SUSA) had been reorganized into three basic groups. (1) SUSA itself was a central operation to handle tax, finance, administration, real estate, and acquisitions. Executives described it as "an extension of the corporate activities at headquarters"—rather than as a coordinator among divisions in the U.S. This latter function took place in Japan, which coordinated major issues on a global basis. SUSA was then overseen by Mr. Ohga as Chairman, Masaaki Morita as Deputy Chairman, and Mickey Schulhof as President. Schulhof was also appointed to Sony's board of directors in 1989, the first American elevated to that post. (2) SONAM continued to handle the U.S. marketing activities which had been its province since its inception. (3) SEMA (Sony Engineering and Manufacturing of America) was formed to include the manufacturing and engineering facilities of the U.S.

SEMA was responsible for the U.S. manufacture of products as diverse as consumer and industrial display products, professional audio and video products, audio speakers, computer peripherals, and factory automation equipment. However, its scope did not include magnetic products, which were produced in a separate division. SEMA's job was to provide assistance, not direct the U.S. plants. Each plant operated as a part of a worldwide production network within each of Sony's worldwide, product-oriented business groups. Ultimate control rested with these business groups. SEMA's responsibility included extending the company's manufacturing culture into its U.S. plants, recruiting and training future managers, transferring technical know-how, meeting local content objectives, and so on. Each production plant reported back to its respective center in Japan. Most televisions, tapes, and speakers sold in the U.S. were made domestically, while VCRs, CD players, and Walkmans were produced mainly in Japan.

Sony Magnetic Products Group America (SMPGA) was a part of Sony's worldwide Recording Media Product Group (RMPG). This included audio and videotapes, floppy disks, magneto optical disks, and data storage cartridges. Sony's Terre Haute, Indiana, plant for CDs and CD-ROMs in 1994 was the world's largest with about half the world's output. RMPG operated plants in many countries. Its operations were broken into three zones: the United States (SMPGA), Europe (SMPE), and Japan. SMPGA was a separate business division responsible for all magnetic products plants. These units represented a concerted effort by Sony Corporation to establish regional groupings that could better understand the issues in their local marketplaces and could respond more rapidly to changing opportunities in each area. Yet at the same time, Sony wished to maintain a corporate capability to coordinate product emphasis, capital investment, corporate learning, and technology transfer. There was a strong philosophical preference in Sony for having a relatively flat organization operating in smaller units, whenever possible.[6]

SONY'S ENTERTAINMENT AND SOFTWARE BUSINESSES

After their acquisition, CBS Records and Columbia Pictures initially both reported directly to Mr. Ohga. Below this, an executive committee consisting of Messrs. Guber, Peters, Morita, Ohga, and Schulhof, oversaw Columbia Pictures. The primary communication linkage between hardware and software operations was provided by SUSA under the leadership of Mr. Schulhof. Mr. Schulhof was trained as a physicist and had enjoyed extensive management experience in Sony's hardware operations before taking over responsibilities for the U.S. Entertainment and Software Group. In 1994, the question of how to organize Sony Entertainment and Software was still unresolved.

At first, no one from Sony was allowed to visit either of the U.S. entertainment businesses without the permission of either Mr. Ohga or Mr. Schulhof. By the early 1990s, almost all key positions in the U.S. were held by Americans. Although Sony had a long established policy of rotating talented young people around at lower operations levels, it also needed to decide on the proper top-level linkages to achieve desired coordination. Mr. Morita had said "[Our concept] is to move the communication link as high in the organization as possible, letting local top executives run their businesses locally and communicate directly to Tokyo. This will not only help our headquarters better understand the real situation (locally) but will also help our [decentralized groups do their] jobs more effectively." Unlike most of its Japanese competitors, SUSA operated as a "U.S. company with a Japanese parent" while other Japanese companies managed their U.S. units as "branches" or "subsidiaries."[7]

FIGURE 1
Sony Corporate and Hardware Organization, September 1, 1993

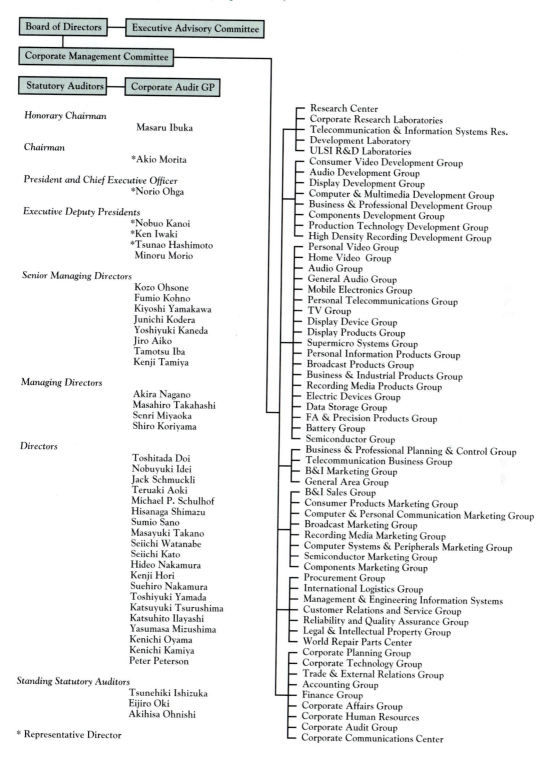

Source: *Sony Corporation: Globalization,* Harvard Business School, Case 9-391-071 (Revised February 14, 1991).

Mr. Schulhof noted, "There is one policy I have adopted that is fairly unique to Sony. That is: the structure at any one time within each of our operating units is a function of the person who runs the unit, not a function of something intrinsic to the unit itself. Our style is not one of having an organizational chart, and when a person moves finding the most suitable replacement to fit that chart. On the other hand, I frequently will say, 'I'm going to give you this job but you have to do the following three things'. . . . Among these may be a grouping of which people are needed to complement [the new executive's] strengths, weaknesses, character, personality, and so on."

Mr. Schulhof also commented, "[In the early phases of our development here] we refused to allow very much cross-communication between the various companies. We did not want people to either feel intimidated by their outside colleagues or to have the larger, more mature electronics units feel an air of superiority. . . . Now everybody knows that all three of the businesses within the U.S. are on a totally equal footing. There is an open atmosphere to encourage new business development across company lines that might not otherwise happen. For example, we have created an electronic publishing company which simply could not exist if it did not have strong ties into the hardware company, the music company, the motion picture company. . . . I've had, on occasion, to knock a few heads to get cooperation. However, the launch of MiniDisc (which we are still in the middle of) has been a totally collaborative effort between Sony Music and Sony Electronics. . . . The shift over to digital technology in all segments will encourage this kind of integration. I don't think there's a new electronic platform that Sony will ever introduce again that won't require strong interaction with the software group.[8]

The first real test of such integration was MiniDisc, first heavily marketed in 1992. MiniDisc (MD) offered the superb quality of standard digital CD recordings in playback, but could itself record from any digital source. Its 2 1/2" disks and clever engineering to avoid skips when jostled made the format extremely attractive, convenient, and portable. However, in 1992 Matsushita and Phillips also introduced a digital compact cassette (DCC) which used high density tape to record and play back digital sound. Its price of $550 was comparable to MiniDisc, but higher than a $200 high end Sony Walkman. DCC could play old analog tapes, but not with digital quality. MD and DCC could both record digital sound and were somewhat comparable in size and weight. MD was 3.3" x 4.4" and 10.2

oz., while DCC was 1.4" x 4.7" x 6" and 16.2 oz. In 1992 about 3.1 billion audiotapes (blank and prerecorded) were produced annually, while MD was backed only by a library of 1200 prerecordings in place, but billions of 5" CDs in consumer hands.

THE ENTERTAINMENT BUSINESS

Sony's entertainment businesses exemplified the company's "loose organization" concept. Both the music and movie groups reported directly to Mr. Schulhof. Mr. Mamora Sakuma, General Manager—Entertainment Planning and Control, in Sony's Tokyo office said, "There is no specific written strategy for the Sony entertainment businesses worldwide. Their main focus, however, is clear: to become the number one entertainment company in the world. That includes profitability, market share, creativity, management—not only in software but hardware activities. We have a mid-range plan and a long-range plan, and of course there are some numbers in those reports. In addition, of course, there is a constant conversation between Mr. Ohga, Mr. Schulhof, and the Tokyo offices. But to be the number one entertainment company in the world; that is our goal."

When Mr. Ohga was asked how the corporation attempted to integrate the business and people from the software units with those from hardware, he responded: "We have never attempted to force synergy to happen. The intention is to have the [Sony Entertainment] Enterprises be the most powerful in the industry. And the key to that is to generate the most creative software. If we can develop such software, that will be a central force for the next generation of hardware. For example with high definition TV, the hardware is only a box. It won't be worth much until you have [adequate] software. Now there is only a broadcast signal for eight hours a day on NHK, and much of the programs there are not as interesting. Whether you have one or eight hours is not very meaningful. Unless you have something attractive you will not be able to generate audiences. Even then, when you are giving away the software for free, you are wasting your time if the programs are not attractive."

Mr. Ohga continued, "In hardware, quality is important, but in software it is the only thing. We make about 20–30 new movies per year, but if those 30 movies are poor quality, it means nothing. Nothing whatsoever. The most important thing is to produce movies that can be revitalized as software over and over again. The value of hardware can be counted in so many units. But in software, no matter what number you have in inventory, if they are bad movies, they are worth less than a dollar. If you have only three hits, they will be worth more in value than a thousand junk movies. But it may be impossible, not just difficult, to produce all good movies."

MOVIE ECONOMICS

The Economist summarized this reasoning—and the economics of moviemaking—as follows: "There are probably only three basic rules: the sunk cost rule, the hit rule, and the nobody knows anything rule.

"The sunk cost rule dictates that nearly all the cost of making entertainment software is fixed and up front. An average American film takes around two years to complete from script to opening night. Its production cost is around $20 million, with a further $7 million to market in America and $3 million of studio overheads. That $30 million cost is sunk—it will barely change whether the movie makes $10 million, $100 million, or $1 billion. The typical film will eventually bring in a bit more than $30 million, but painfully slowly. First comes the American theater release. Only 20% of movies earn their cash back at the box office in America. The "typical" film brings in just over $30 million there. The exhibitor keeps just over half, leaving the studio with $13 million. It earns $6 million (net of marketing expenses) at foreign box offices, so that at the end of its theatrical release, it is still $11 million dollars short of covering its costs.

"The gap is filled by what Hollywood calls the 'ancillaries.' The film earns $9 million from video and a further $2 million from cable. So the film is still in the red until it eventually receives $3 million from the American networks for the free TV rights, nearly three years after theatrical release, and nearly 5 years after the project was approved. Thereafter, the cash will continue to trickle in—perhaps $250,000–$500,000 a year—from continuing television and video sales.

"What about television programs? Most American television shows are deficit-financed. That means that the program's first sale (usually to a television network) is for less than its cost—roughly $300,000 less than for a $1.2 million hour-long, prime-time feature. Some of the deficit can be made up in the foreign TV market, but typically the owner has to wait for the syndication market—when the show can be resold to independent TV stations before he is in profit. Records and books do not have deficit-financing (though some books make money only when they are in paperback). The sums of money

are much smaller. However, the cost of keeping a hostile-unfriendly rock band together is a form of fixed cost. As one record executive puts it there can be 'protracted and expensive periods of silence before the muse arrives.'

"The hit rule is that most of the profit comes from a tiny part of the output. Just three percent of the films released [last year] accounted for close to a third of box office receipts. Because most of the cost is fixed, any revenue above that line is profit. McKinsey has calculated that, assuming costs do not change, a 10% increase in an entertainment company's revenues pushes profits up around 50%. Only 4 out of 10 films are ever profitable, but they pay for a string of flops. "Batman" cost Warner $75 million; by the time all the merchandising rights, video, records, and T-shirts are added in, the film will bring in around $1 billion. On a smaller scale, "Sex, Lies, and Videotape" cost $1 million to make; it has earned $24 million at the American box office.

"Other entertainment businesses are similar. American television stations recently paid Viacom $500 million for the first 3 1/2 years of reruns of "The Cosby Show." Madonna has indirectly financed a lot of bad rap bands. Dick Francis and Frederick Forsythe may lack literary class, but their workman-like efforts pay for a lot of unreadable biographies of Bloomsbury figures. . . .

"Nobody knows anything [is the final rule]. Popular taste and creative talent being as fickle as they are, there is no sure-fire formula for making a hit. An instinctive reaction is that any fool could have predicted that "Batman" was going to be a hit. But in a jokey poll of 1500 entertainment experts to guess the winner at America's box office [in its first summer after release], only 25% picked "Batman." Mr. Christopher Dickson at Kidder Peabody, an investment bank, points out that the calculation about hit or miss is even harder to make before production has begun. Imagine that you were a mogul and you were offered a script for an expensive comedy/action picture, to be produced by George Lucas or Stephen Spielberg and to feature a lovable animal and a lot of expensive gimmickry. The result: either Mr. Spielberg's hit, "Who Framed Roger Rabbit?," or Mr. Lucas' flop, "Howard the Duck."

"From these three rules it follows that two things will always rule the entertainment industry: talent and capital. The first goes almost without saying. In an industry where nobody knows anything, an established pop star, a director, or even a mogul with a good "hunch record" will always be in demand. But an entertainment company also needs financial muscle to produce enough software to give itself a decent chance of bringing in a hit, and the marketing muscle to make the most of that hit when it happens. . . . The big studios produced fewer than a third of the films [last year] yet they accounted for 80% of the box office take. In the record industry, the Big 5 companies are just as dominant."[9]

But the industry was rapidly changing. In 1990 Hollywood made 75% of its revenues in the U.S.; in the mid-to-late 1990s international film revenues were expected to exceed those domestically. In music, Sony was already fully integrated in the major local markets with 50% of revenues coming from locally produced artists in Germany, France and Latin America. Mr. Schulhof foresaw further huge leveraging through new electronic equipment—"when one can telephone-order *any* videotaped film from huge central libraries to be played in the home on a single rental basis. The movie theater [itself] will be like an electronic theme park with enhanced electronic experiences available in many forms: you'll see it, feel it, ride it. HDTV will make home entertainment equivalent in quality to the best film. Digital radio will make its quality equal to the best recordings and expand bandwidths indefinitely. Interactive movies will add change of outcomes to the experience. 'Narrow casting' will devote channels to specific demographics and tastes. CDs could eventually take over the tape markets for both audio and video entertainment, and standard movies could merge with games in interactive variations of both."[10]

MEDIA MERGERS

Perhaps such visions fanned the media mergers of the 1988–94 era. In the U.S. alone, the entertainment industry brought in over $350 billion in 1994 sales and was increasing at 10–15% per year. In the U.S., affluent "Baby Boomer" children jumped onto every new fad. See Table 5 for a breakdown of the 1993 U.S. entertainment industry. Demographics, technology, and globalization contributed to its attractions. In all advanced countries, increasingly large proportions of the population in their retirement years looked for less active recreation. And lowering costs of hardware made entertainment ever more available to rapidly growing developing countries. Popular singing, athletic, or movie stars were folk heroes in all countries. Many songs and movies merely needed translation to cross borders. Hit tunes from movies became golden records in the music business. Popular books became hit movies, and vice versa. And some hit movies like *Jurassic Park* became theme parks and videogames. Many speculated that there would be enormous opportunities when "multi-media" devices allowed tapes, CDs, interactive games, network games, databases, computer graphics, and home editing of any digital source to be available everywhere.

On the hardware side, Goldman Sachs commented on the coming *Communacopia*. "The marrying of the cable converter box with the computer, the digitizing and compression of audio and video programming, the widespread use of film-optic technology, as well as head end and PC software development could, in our view, ultimately allow immediate access to and manipulation of a bounty of informational products, transaction services, educational and instructional services, databases, and the like . . . [In movies alone] between 1980 and 1992 direct spending for U.S. theatrical products increased to about $22 billion from $3 billion, more than an 18% compounded rate."[11] Of this consumers

TABLE 5 U.S. Consumer Spending on Entertainment, 1993	U.S. CONSUMER SPENDING ON ENTERTAINMENT, 1993	
	Toys and Sporting Equipment	$65B
	VCRs, TVs, Consumer Electronics, Recorded Music, and Videotapes	58
	Books, Magazines, Newspapers	47
	Gambling	28
	Cable TV	19
	Amusement & Theme Parks	14
	Movie Admissions, Video Rentals	13
	Home Computers	8
	Live (Non Sports) Entertainment	6
	Other Entertainment	83
	Total	$341B

Source: Commerce Department per *Business Week*, March 14, 1994.

spent about $12 billion in the videocassette market, $9 billion in rentals and $3 billion in sellthroughs.

This expansion was largely driven by new technologies and modes of distribution. During the 1980s revenues increased 400% in foreign markets vs. 250% in the U.S. Appendix A at the end of the case shows the shifting nature of this marketplace. Pay TV (with 40.9 million subscribers) was dominated by HBO (17.4 million), Showtime (7.6 million), Disney (7.1 million), and Cinemax (6.3 million). HBO and Cinemax belonged to Time Warner.

To exploit these possibilities, in addition to the early Matsushita and Sony acquisitions, Australian publishing mogul Rupert Murdock (News Corporation) had gobbled up Twentieth Century Fox, and Time Inc. had merged with Warner Communications. Paramount Communications then merged with Viacom, a cable television (Showtime and The Movie Channel) and telecommunications giant which later sought a merger with Blockbuster Video, the largest distributor of videotapes. (Viacom and QVC—an electronic shopping channel—had both proposed purchase prices of about $10 billion for Paramount which had 1992 profits of $270 million and operating cash flows of $218 million. Over $80 billion was committed to such mergers in 1988–89 alone.) Tables 6 and 7 show the revenues and structure of these major competitors in 1994.

At the distribution level, in the early 1990s Blockbuster Entertainment purchased several major mini-distribution chains. Recordhouse, a distribution giant, bought up many small record producers. And Alliance (wholesalers) bought out four of the main one-stop (video and record outlet) chains to control over 1/3 of that business. Musicland, the country's largest music retailer, aligned itself with Prodigy—a computer network with more than 2 million subscribers. Musicland offered 1000s of titles in an electronic catalog. Other chains allowed consumers to sample records through a modem. Several telephone and cable networks had begun to distribute video and music "on-demand," as well as to provide two-way interactivity to the home. As Asynchronous Transfer Mode (ATM) standards were adopted, interactive services would become available first to any cable-connected home and later to virtually all telephone homes which had the proper equipment to use them. This would make possible the purchase or use in the home of any digitized (unidirectional or interactive) form of entertainment without physically going out to a store to obtain a copy. In 1994 Sony's new "mini discs" could already record and play back digitized entertainment and compact disks could hold 650 megabytes of recorded music, video, or data.[12]

TABLE 6 Entertainment/Media Conglomerates, 1993 Revenues ($ billions)	1993 REVENUES ($ BILLIONS)	
	General Electric	$60.56
	Matsushita	58.30
	Sony	34.42
	Philips NV	27.40
	Time Warner	14.53
	Matra Hachette	11.11
	Bertlesmann	11.01
	Disney	8.53
	News Corporation, Ltd.	7.48
	Capital Cities/ABC	5.67
	Paramount Communications	4.27
	Tele-Communications, Inc.	3.57
	CBS, Inc.	3.51
	Thorn/EMI	2.96
	Blockbuster Entertainment	2.91
	Viacom	2.01
	Turner Broadcasting	1.92
	Reed International	1.86
	QVC	1.22

* There are also several privately held media giants including Fininvest and Fujikankei.

Source: Compiled from various corporations' records and directories.

TABLE 7
Major Entertainment/Media Firms and Segments

COMPANY	FILM & TV PRODUCTION	MUSIC PRODUCTION	NETWORK/ CABLE BROAD- CASTING	DISTRIBUTION (OWN/OPERATE THEATERS, TV, CABLE, RADIO STATIONS)	RETAILING OF AUDIO/ VIDEO PRODUCTS	PUBLISHING (BOOKS, NEWSPAPERS & MAGAZINES)	ENTERTAINMENT CENTERS (THEME PARKS, GAME PARKS)
General Electric	●		●	●			
Matsushita	●	●			●	●	●
Sony	●	●		●		●	
Philips NV	●	●					
Time Warner	●	●	●	●	●	●	●
Matra Hachette	●	●		●		●	
Bertlesmann	●	●	●	●		●	
Disney	●	●	●	●	●	●	●
News Corporation	●		●	●		●	
Capital Cities/ABC	●		●	●		●	
Paramount Comm.	●		●	●		●	●
Tele-Comm., Inc.	●		●	●			
CBS	●		●	●			
Thorn/EMI		●					
Blockbuster Entertainment	●			●	●		
Viacom	●		●	●	●		●
Turner Broadcasting			●				●
Reed International						●	
QVC	●						

Source: Annual Reports of cited companies.

In a sense, the centralization of the entertainment industry seemed to move counter to the disaggregation and decentralization trends in other fields. Contrary to most successful consolidations, the merging industries were very people—not capital—intensive. As Walter Yetnikoff, former President of CBS Records, said, "The only business more people intensive than this one is prostitution."[13] And the industry's flamboyant, egotistical, and highly paid talent created many unique problems. Stars are a highly mobile commodity, and often work for different studios as they are cast in varying pictures. Whenever film or recording profits rise, actors, authors, and pop stars quickly move to claim a higher share of the take. The fickle consumer adds another constant element of surprise. People rarely buy entertainment on a rational basis, like they do other products. Instead, they look for what they like "when they are in the mood to be entertained." They will flip channels or scan movie listings to suit their mood at a particular moment. Books and records are more rational purchases, but even these generally flash on the scene and disappear. Many questioned whether stable corporations dominated by blue-suited executives could thrive in these environments.

MANAGING CREATIVE ARTISTS

A major issue was the difference between managing a hardware product's development versus that of a new software product. Mr. Robert Sherwood, Vice President—Sound Technology Marketing at Sony, described it this way:

"The development of a hardware product has a timeline; it tends not to waiver that much. [Developers] can start from the very beginning and project a long way out exactly what they're going to do, and how they're going to do it. They are capable of thinking in terms of some pretty dramatic shifts as the market or the product changes, but they're looking at a firm, orderly structure of creating the product and then putting it in the consumer's hands with a reasonably [predictable] shelf life, replacement pattern, and so on. The music business where I come from tends to offer extremely short shelf life, a very narrow window of opportunity, and it's driven by an intricately creative artist, whose feelings and mind are changing all the time. [As a manager] you have to make an extraordinary number of instant decisions based on what is sometimes not full information. Music production demands a quick turnaround; attention spans can be short on these projects, but not so on the longer term marketing aspects.

"[Even the production side has some long-term dimensions.] Giving the artist who creates the product an ideal environment in which to create is very important. Every company wants to do that because it pays off in the long run. At Sony we have a big studio operation here in New York. We are attempting to make this a special creative environment. The idea is to have a sound stage, recording rooms, video capability, rehearsal halls, all of the lights and effects to make tapes, and so forth for both big artists like Billy Joel or "baby acts" who are brand new artists. [Artists] can have all the tools they need to do a live show better and to make the best possible video. It's also much easier to create an artist's image if you're working with them every step of the way, instead of having the video done here, the music there, and something elsewhere. The company is very careful to lead their artists to write, but to let their creative spirits drive them. There are certain artists who won't use certain recording studios. For example, there's a story about a big name artist who went out to record at a place called Caribou Ranch in Colorado. This is Nirvana for most people, horseback riding, snow, mountains, just a beautiful place. This artist couldn't perform there. His group wanted trash in the studio, things being thrown around, because he's a New York street kid and needs the sense, the feel, the tension of New York to be able to create, to be able to write and record.

"Every company tries to get these things under control in some way or another. But there will be a hit you didn't expect that goes to the moon, and because it is by an artist with a lower royalty, you make a zillion dollars—until the attorneys come in and re-do the deal. Like film, it is a spikey kind of business; the successes are huge and the failures can be extremely costly. If you put accountant mentalities in that environment, they can't control it because they can't make Springsteen go in and make a record. They can't make Pink Floyd do anything, no matter what the contract says. It's driven by the artist, and artists do not live under the same schedule that most human beings do. Frankly, I think this is one reason Tisch allowed CBS Records to go away—it drove him absolutely guppy, and he could not truly project numbers no matter how hard the experts tried.

Mr. Schulhof noted: "[As we've grown in size], we've developed our own style of segregating financial controls from creative controls. From the start, we wanted to make sure that the people driving the creative decisions were not being run by accountants, but knew the financial consequences of all their decisions.

TABLE 8
Estimated Worldwide Music Business Revenues, 1991–1993 (in millions of U.S. dollars)

	1991	1992E	1993E	% CHG.
United States	7,834.0	8,663	9,489	9.5%
United Kingdom	2,311.7	2,331	2,104	9.7%
France	1,632.4	1,760	1,820	3.4%
Germany	2,574.1	2,727	2,964	8.7%
Japan	3,435.6	3,981	4,410	2.5%
Rest of World	8,025.9	8,269	8,474	2.5%
TOTAL	25,813.7	27,731	29,283	5.6%

Source: R. Simon and M. Fineman, "Music Industry Update 1993," Goldman Sachs Investment Research, January 18, 1993.

TABLE 9
U.S. Music Industry Dollar Sales (millions)

DOLLAR VALUE	1981	1982	1983	1984	1985
Vinyl Singles	$ 256.4	$ 283.0	$ 269.3	$ 298.7	$ 281.0
LPs	2,341.7	1,925.1	1,689.0	1,548.8	1,280.5
CDs	0.0	0.0	17.2	103.3	389.5
Cassettes	1,062.8	1,384.5	1,810.9	1,383.9	2,411.5
CD Singles	0.0	0.0	0.0	0.0	0.0
Cassette Singles	0.0	0.0	0.0	0.0	0.0
Music Videos	0.0	0.0	0.0	0.0	0.0
TOTAL	**$3,969.9**	**$3641.6**	**$3,814.3**	**$4,370.4**	**$4,387.8**

1986	1987	1988	1989	1990	1991
$ 228.1	$ 203.3	$ 180.4	$ 116.4	$ 94.4	$ 63.9
983.0	793.1	532.3	220.3	86.5	29.4
930.1	1,593.6	2,089.9	2,587.7	3,451.6	4,337.7
2,499.5	2,959.7	3,385.1	3,345.8	3,472.4	3,019.6
0.0	0.0	9.8	(0.7)	6.0	35.1
0.0	14.3	57.3	194.6	257.9	230.4
0.0	0.0	0.0	115.4	172.3	118.1
$4,651.1	**$5,567.5**	**$6,254.8**	**$6,579.5**	**$7,541.1**	**$7,834.2**

Compound Annual Growth

	1981–91	1986–91
Vinyl Singles	(13.0)	(22.5)
LPs	(35.5)	(50.4)
Cassettes	11.0	3.9
CD Singles	NM	NM
Cassette Singles	NM	NM
TOTAL	7.0	11.0

Source: RIAA.

We have very strong, tight, financial controls—and a clear order that prohibits the financial people from influencing the creative decision. . . . But neither Mr. Ohga nor I interferes with the creative judgments related to the marketplace. We want to participate in whom the company hires and keeps, but once we've made a decision to bring people on-board, we really step back."

Mr. Sherwood continued, "Sometimes with an artist, they run out of creativity. They get writer's block. They don't want to tour anymore. Some of them develop problems with too much cough medicine. There are marriages that suddenly blow up, band members leave without explanation, and it turns out that the sum of the parts is greater than the individuals. You will never have control over those things. You can do your best to make the environment work but it's out of your hands. Sometimes a brilliant concert performer like Springsteen will just want to do an artistic record like "Nebraska." You don't think it will work. But it's important to him and you've got to let him get it out of his system. Springsteen does not allow people to come in and help him with his music. That's what he does himself. If you want to change that, he goes away.

"[On the other hand] each year, artists may want to change their specific style, presentation, or image; and each time it's a bit of a risk. You may be counting on a certain amount of billings for that artist and have to re-think it. The cost of selling the tour and the record that goes with it may take new radio promotion, advertising, sales and marketing. The whole presentation can be different, and there is a cost attached to that. Artists may not be ready for the tour at the time you need them. They may be appealing to different parts of the market than you planned. You have to have enough going on all the time to fill the gaps, to handle the peaks, but you have to have the same amount of marketing infrastructure to keep quality people together. You've got to feed the monster on a regular basis, so you need some control. And that control has to come in the form of things you can control, but things that don't have a particular shelf life or a specialized demographic dimension. When you are a big company, you have to manage all this variability yet try to optimize your factories for [totally unpredictable] production runs.

"Generally with a creative piece, you don't even know what it's going to be until very near the actual release. You have to buy advertising time and space well ahead, but you don't know what the art work will be until the last minute. It sometimes takes longer to get the art work done than the music. The artist may come in with finished goods and say, 'here is my video.' Of course, you have been talking to the artist, but until that music actually arrives and you see and hear it, you don't know what you have. Sometimes, the artist is all ready with the music, but you don't have visual images to go with it. Yet the videotape and the record must come out together. These are real challenges."

A HUGE AND GROWING BUSINESS

Despite its uncertainties, the music business was huge and growing. 1993 music sales worldwide were approximately $29 billion, with revenues distributed as shown in Table 8. Unit volumes had been essentially flat in 1993, while sales revenues grew at about 5 1/2%. In 1992 the digital compact cassette (DCC) and minidisc (MD) were introduced, but as yet had little impact on industry performance. The U.S. was the largest marketplace with about 30% of sales. Japan was second with about 13%. But market shares for media were rapidly changing. (See Table 9.) Four major companies—Time Warner, Sony, PolyGram, and Thorn-EMI accounted for 75–80% of world sales, while BMG and Matsushita accounted for 9% and 5% respectively.

The music industry was clearly global in scope, but much of it had a huge problem with piracy. Countries like Poland, Thailand, and the United Arab Emirates had more than 90% pirated sales; Italy had 50%, Mexico 46%, Saudia Arabia 47% and India 40%.[14] No one could foresee the impact that digitization and interconnection of a "globalized information superhighway" would have in the future.

FUTURE VISION

In this tumultuous, but rapidly growing marketplace, Mr. Schulhof described his vision for the future of Sony Entertainment. "We must become a seamless entertainment company—seamless in the sense that the word "entertainment" is an umbrella capturing entertainment in its broadest sense—electronics, movies, music, and multimedia—embracing both the content and the vehicles that deliver that content to a user. They are together the entertainment experience. Motion pictures are meaningless celluloid without a theater to project them or without a television screen to show them in the living room. Music is a meaningless master tape without a delivery system to bring it into the home either through packaged media, by compact disk, or by electronic media. The crossover in terms of what drives the electronics we manufacture in the future has to be influenced more and more by people who are making creative decisions to bring entertainment products into the home, and vice versa. This requires much more direct communication than we've ever had between the entertainment side and the electronic side of business. Those are areas where I spend a lot of my time. . . . I would like us to be either the #1 or #2 motion picture company, television production company, music company, electronic software company, in terms of games or educational multi-media, and #1 or #2 in the delivery systems for that same content. I do not think that we have a role in the ownership of any distribution system that our content uses."

In late 1993, *Forbes* stated, "Sony has skillfully positioned itself as a leader—perhaps the leader—in blending under one roof both the machines that carry information/entertainment into homes and the entertainment/information itself. There are bigger companies than Sony on the hardware side, and there are bigger companies on the software side, but none has gone so far in integrating the medium and the message. . . . With its Columbia and TriStar Movie Studios, Loews movie houses, video games, Columbia and Epic Records, Sony today has as much of its U.S. assets in entertainment as it does in manufacturing electronic gear."[15] Nevertheless, actually getting the synergy or extra value-added from these different businesses remained a major challenge for Sony Corporation and Sony Entertainment Enterprises.

1994 AND FORWARD

Despite its continuing innovation successes in hardware and current successes in software, Sony revenues for fiscal 1994 fell about 7% and margins slid to 7.4% from 1990's level of 13.7%. Return on equity fell precipitously to 2.4% from 8.8% during the same period. These weakened earnings were more alarming in view of the debt burden Sony had undertaken to become a major factor in the entertainment business. And Sony's stock price (in U.S. financial markets) had suffered as well, dropping from a high of 59 3/4 in calendar 1989 to a high of 38 in 1992. Sony's segment financial profile is contained in Table 10.

Nevertheless, looking forward, Chairman Norio Ohga said: "The vision and destiny of management determines the destiny of a company. I believe this is even more important in a movie company than in hardware companies. I do not make it a practice to give advice to my executives as to whether they should make violent or non-violent movies. I do not give any instructions about creative activities. But every time I have a chance to meet with Peter Guber or Mickey Schulhof we exchange ideas—you know—what dreams we have. When Mr. Morita or I are in Los Angeles, we make a point of meeting with Peter Guber, not for the sake of the meeting, but for the sake of sharing ideas. We do not ever put out a memo or make a formal direction; discussion is a more natural and more casual way of sharing ideas together.

TABLE 10 **Sony Corporation Segment Data** (billions of yen)	1991	1992	1993	(EST) 1994
Revenues				
Electronics	¥2,974	¥3,159	¥3,173	¥2,952
Entertainment	738	783	835	794
Operating Income				
Electronics	263	127	80	91
Entertainment	49	66	60	25
Identifiable Assets				
Electronics	2,667	2,940	2,674	2,639
Entertainment	1,569	1,635	1,540	1,380
Depreciation & Amortization				
Electronics	168	219	228	193
Entertainment	44	44	45	43
Capital Expenditures				
Electronics	374	398	194	155
Entertainment	34	45	52	35

Source: Sony Corporation, *Annual Report*, various years.

"Clearly, one key to the future is how we can maintain the competitiveness of Sony as a hardware company. Even though we have a strong software company, I have no intention of changing the hardware company for that reason. The main pullers of the hardware side are audio, video, and TV; and we have begun to restructure the [software and hardware sides] to work together to fill in gaps between their structures. Everyone talks about multimedia. Everyone is carried away by the illusion of multimedia. Personally, I do not know what multimedia means. But if multimedia is successful, it will have to come out with a new way of blending the capabilities of software, hardware, and the different distribution media."

QUESTIONS

1. Evaluate Sony's strategy (a) in acquiring and (b) in implementing its entertainment, music, and software operations. Using the various models available, what strategic criteria should be applied to this evaluation? How should one evaluate the price paid for these operations?

2. How can Sony Corporation best manage these units? What should it do about the inherent cultural differences involved? What strategic controls should Sony Corporation maintain if it decentralizes these operations to the U.S.?

3. Assuming Sony continues in the entertainment, music, and software businesses, what should its strategy be? In the U.S.? Globally? How should it organize its production endeavors? Creative endeavors? How does such a strategy differ from other types of strategy?

APPENDIX A
Entertainment—Industry Growth, Spending, 1986–1991
(dollars in millions)

INDUSTRY SEGMENT	1986 GROSS EXPENDITURES	1986-91 COMPOUND ANNUAL GROWTH	1991 GROSS EXPENDITURES	1991-96 COMPOUND ANNUAL GROWTH	1996 GROSS EXPENDITURES
Television Broadcasting	**$21,427**	**2.4%**	**$24,110**	**6.3%**	**$32,800**
TV Networks	8,342	2.5	9,435	6.2	12,750
TV Stations	13,085	2.3	14,675	6.4	20,050
Radio Broadcasting	**$6,949**	**4.0%**	**$8,450**	**6.4%**	**$11,500**
Radio Networks	423	3.2	495	5.8	655
Radio Stations	6,526	4.0	7,955	6.4	10,845
Cable Television	**$9,405**	**13.6%**	**$17,780**	**8.6%**	**$26,920**
Advertising	855	18.3	1,985	12.1	3,510
Subscriptions	8,550	13.1	15,795	8.2	23,410
Filmed Entertainment	**$15,483**	**9.9%**	**$24,773**	**7.5%**	**$35,580**
Box Office	3,778	4.9	4,803	6.9	6,720
Home Video	5,015	17.0	10,995	8.1	16,230
Television Programs	6,090	4.8	7,700	6.7	10,650
Barter Syndication	600	16.3	1,275	9.2	1,980
Recorded Music	**$4,651**	**11.0%**	**$7,834**	**6.3%**	**$10,620**
GDP	$4,268,600	5.8%	$5,674,400	7.3%	$8,070,000

Note: 1992–96 are estimated figures.

Source: The Hollywood Reporter, June 26, 1992 and Veronis, Suhler & Associates Communications.

**APPENDIX A (cont'd)
Entertainment—Real
Personal Consumption
Expenditures (PCE),
1980–1992**
(dollars in billions)

	Total PCE	TOTAL RECREATION[a]		RECREATION SERVICES	
		Amount	As a Pct. of Total PCE	Amount	As a Pct. of Total PCE
1980	$2,447.10	$90.96	3.72%	$59.32	2.42%
1981	2,476.90	96.26	3.89	63.79	2.58
1982	2,503.70	100.09	4.00	67.46	2.69
1983	2,619.40	109.72	4.19	72.78	2.78
1984	2,746.10	117.82	4.29	76.72	2.79
1985	2,865.80	127.39	4.45	82.63	2.88
1986	2,969.10	136.45	4.60	85.81	2.89
1987	3,052.20	146.04	4.78	90.51	2.97
1988	3,162.40	159.23	5.03	96.26	3.04
1989	3,223.30	167.95	5.21	100.60	3.12
1990	3,260.40	173.43	5.32	101.76	3.12
1991	3,240.80	177.33	5.47	102.78	3.17
1992	3,314.00	186.33	5.82	105.08	3.17

[a]Total Recreation includes Recreation Services; Radio, TV, Records and Musical Instruments; Books and Maps; and Motion Picture Admission.

Sources: U.S. Department of Commerce and Salomon Brothers Inc. estimates.

**APPENDIX A (cont'd)
Filmed Entertainment—
MPAA Average
Production Costs Versus
Box Office Revenue,
1980–1992**
(dollars in thousands)

YEAR	AVERAGE PRODUCTION COST PER FEATURE	PERCENTAGE CHANGE OVER PRIOR YEAR	1992 VERSUS	NUMBER OF FILMS	BOX OFFICE PER PICTURE	AVERAGE GROSS PROFIT/LOSS
1980	$9,382.5	5.3%	207.6%	233	$11,796	$2,414
1981	11,335.6	20.8	154.6	239	12,408	1,072
1982	11,849.5	4.5	143.5	428	8,067	(3,783)
1983	11,884.8	0.3	142.8	495	7,608	(4,277)
1984	14,412.6	21.3	100.2	536	7,519	(6,894)
1985	16,779.2	16.4	72.0	470	7,977	(8,802)
1986	17,454.6	4.0	65.3	451	8,376	(9,079)
1987	20,050.5	14.9	43.9	507	8,388	(11,663)
1988	18,061.3	(9.9)	59.8	491	9,080	(8,981)
1989	23,453.5	29.9	23.0	492	10,230	(13,224)
1990	26,783.2	14.2	7.7	410	12,248	(14,535)
1991	26,135.5	(2.4)	10.4	448	10,721	(15,414)
1992	28,858.3	10.4	—	484	10,064	(18,794)

Source: Motion Picture Association of America, Inc.

RADIO, TV, RECORDS & MUSICAL INSTRUMENTS		BOOKS AND MAPS		MOTION PICTURE ADMISSION	
Amount	As a Pct. of Total PCE	Amount	As a Pct. of Total PCE	Amount	As a Pct. of Total PCE
$17.57	0.72%	$10.25	0.42%	$3.83	0.16%
18.12	0.73	10.50	0.42	3.85	0.16
18.17	0.73	10.28	0.41	4.18	0.17
22.25	0.85	10.69	0.41	3.99	0.15
25.52	0.93	11.56	0.42	4.02	0.15
29.75	1.04	11.38	0.40	3.63	0.13
35.36	1.19	11.69	0.39	3.59	0.12
39.02	1.28	12.99	0.43	3.52	0.12
45.46	1.44	14.08	0.45	3.43	0.11
49.24	1.53	14.69	0.46	3.42	0.11
53.25	1.63	15.24	0.47	3.19	0.10
56.20	1.73	15.43	0.48	2.93	0.09
61.84	1.87	16.39	0.49	3.01	0.09

APPENDIX A (cont'd) Filmed Entertainment—Percentage of Ticket Admission for Films Made in the U.S., the Home Country or Elsewhere, 1981, 1986 and 1991

	U.S. SHARE			INDIGENOUS SHARE			OTHER		
	1981	1986	1991	1981	1986	1991	1981	1986	1991
France	30.8%	43.3%	58.7%	49.6%	43.7%	30.1%	19.6%	13.0%	11.2%
Germany	52.9	62.6	77.0	18.7	22.1	13.0	28.4	15.3	10.0
Italy	32.6	51.3	68.0	44.1	32.0	24.0	23.3	16.7	8.0
Spain	50.0	64.1	68.7	21.4	12.4	10.9	28.6	23.5	20.4
U.K.	85.0	86.0	89.0	13.0	12.0	5.5	2.0	2.0	5.5
Sweden	6.1	9.3	10.4	—	—	80.3	93.9	90.7	9.3
Japan	NA	30.0	49.7	54.5	50.2	41.9	NA	19.8	8.4
India	NA	NA	3.5	NA	NA	95.0	NA	NA	1.5
United States	99.9	99.0	99.0	99.0	99.0	99.9	1.0	1.0	1.0

Sources: *Screen Digest* and *The Wall Street Journal*, March 26, 1993.

APPENDIX A (cont'd) Market Share by Studio of the Top 15 Rental Films of 1992	RENTALS	RANK	MARKET SHARE	TOTAL MKT. SHARE FOR THE STUDIO	% OF STUDIO'S TOTAL MARKET SHARE
Buena Vista					
Sister Act	62,420,000	4	2.5%		
Aladdin	60,000,000	5	2.4%		
The Hand that Rocks the Cradle	39,334,000	12	1.6%		
Total	161,754,000		6.5%	19%	34.1%
Sony					
A League of Their Own	53,100,000	7	2.1%		
Basic Instinct	53,000,000	8	2.1%		
A Few Good Men	52,000,000	10	2.1%		
Bram Stoker's Dracula	47,200,000	11	1.9%		
Total	205,300,000		8.2%	19%	43.2%
Fox					
Home Alone 2: Lost in New York	102,000,000	1	4.1%	14%	29.1%
Paramount					
Wayne's World	54,000,000	6	2.2%		
Patriot Games	37,500,000	13	1.5%		
Total	91,500,000		3.7%	10%	36.6%
Universal					
Fried Green Tomatoes	37,402,287	14	1.5%	12%	12.5%
Warner Brothers					
Batman Returns	100,100,000	2	4.0%		
Lethal Weapon 3	80,000,000	3	3.2%		
The Bodyguard	52,900,000	9	2.1%		
Unforgiven	36,000,000	15	1.4%		
Total	269,000,000		10.8%	20%	53.8%
TOTAL			**34.7%**	**94.0%**	**36.9%**

Source: Variety.

APPENDIX A (cont'd) Filmed Entertainment— Domestic Box Office Market Shares, 1993 Through May 23

RANK	STUDIO/DISTRIBUTOR	# OF PICTURES	SHARE
1	Buena Vista (Disney)	16	18.1%
2	Warner Brothers	14	17.6
3	Columbia (Sony)	10	12.3
4	Universal (Matsushita)	10	11.7
5	Paramount	5	9.1
6	Fox (News Corp.)	11	8.1
7	New Line (Turner)	16	6.5
8	Miramax (Disney)	12	6.3
9	MGM	5	3.7
10	TriStar (Sony)	3	1.9

Source: Daily Variety.

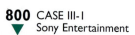

	SONY*	FOX	MGM/UA	PARA	UNIV	WB	BV	ORI	TOTAL MAJORS
1992	19%	14%	1%	10%	12%	20%	19%	0%	96%
1991	20	12	2	12	11	14	14	9	93
1990	14	13	3	15	13	13	16	6	93
1989	16	7	6	14	17	17	14	4	95
1988	10	12	10	15	10	11	19	7	94
1987	9	9	4	20	8	13	14	10	87
1986	16	8	4	22	9	12	10	7	88
1985	20	11	9	10	16	18	3	5	92
1984	21	10	7	21	8	19	4	5	95
1983	14	21	10	14	13	17	3	4	96
1982	10	14	11	14	30	10	4	3	96
1981	13	13	9	15	14	18	3	1	86
1980	14	16	7	16	20	14	4	2	93

*TriStar included since 1984.

Source: *Variety.*

	1980	1981	1982	1983	1984	1985	1986
Box Office Rentals							
Domestic	1235	1335	1555	1700	1800	1635	1650
Foreign	650	675	775	910	900	795	850
TOTAL	1885	2010	2330	2610	2700	2430	2500
Pay TV							
Domestic	120	225	350	550	600	625	600
Foreign	0	0	0	0	0	0	35
TOTAL	120	225	350	550	600	625	635
Home Video							
Domestic	10	50	150	400	950	1335	1630
Foreign	15	100	200	350	450	625	885
TOTAL	25	150	350	750	1400	1960	2515
Television							
Domestic	350	370	390	410	410	450	450
Foreign	75	95	105	125	135	145	175
TOTAL	425	465	495	535	545	595	625
Video Disks							
Domestic	0	0	25	50	10	1	2
Foreign	0	0	0	0	0	0	0
TOTAL	0	0	25	50	10	1	2
Other							
Domestic	30	35	45	50	50	55	60
Foreign	10	10	10	15	15	15	20
TOTAL	40	45	55	65	65	70	80
TOTAL							
Domestic	1745	2015	2515	3160	3820	4101	4392
Foreign	750	880	1090	1400	1500	1580	1965
TOTAL	2495	2895	3605	4560	5320	5681	6357

Source: Goldman Sachs Estimates.

							COMPOUND ANNUAL GROWTH				
1987	1988	1989	1990	1991	1992	1993E	80–85	80–92	87–92	91–92	92–93
1830	1920	2165	2260	2160	2100	2163	5.8	4.5	2.8	(2.8)	3.0
940	1100	1225	1380	1510	1715	1820	4.1	8.4	12.8	13.6	6.1
2770	3020	3390	3640	3670	3815	3983	5.2	6.1	4.0	4.4	
575	630	670	725	750	770	790	39.1	16.8	6.0	2.7	2.6
70	110	225	300	350	370	395	NM	NM	39.5	5.7	6.8
645	740	895	1025	1100	1140	1185	39.1	20.6	12.1	3.6	3.9
1915	2460	2760	3220	3760	4230	4525	NM	NM	17.2	12.5	7.0
1135	1460	1690	1945	2120	2345	2605	110.8	NM	15.6	10.6	11.1
3050	3920	4450	5165	5880	6575	7130	139.3	NM	16.6	11.8	8.4
425	425	525	600	650	675	700	5.2	5.6	9.7	3.8	3.7
250	550	575	700	750	800	850	14.1	21.8	26.2	6.7	6.2
675	975	1100	1300	1400	1475	1550	7.0	10.9	16.9	5.4	5.1
5	30	40	85	150	295	340	NM	NM	126.0	96.7	15.3
5	40	50	90	150	225	275	NM	NM	114.1	50.	22.2
10	70	90	175	300	520	615	NM	NM	120.4	73.3	18.3
60	60	65	65	70	75	80	12.9	7.9	4.6	7.1	6.7
20	20	20	22	25	25	25	8.4	7.9	4.6	0.0	0.0
80	80	85	87	95	100	105	11.8	7.9	4.6	5.3	5.0
4810	5525	6225	6955	7540	8145	8598	18.6	13.7	11.1	8.0	5.6
2420	3280	3785	4437	4905	5480	5970	16.1	18.0	17.8	11.7	8.9
7230	8805	10010	11392	12445	13625	14568	17.9	15.2	13.5	9.5	6.9

THE VANGUARD GROUP, INC. (A)

Vanguard has emerged as the leader of the mutual fund industry. And this is only as is should be, given not only our history, but our heritage. For each warship in the Royal Navy has a special badge—a distinctive mark that identifies its crew. For HMS Vanguard, the badge depicts in gold a pugnacious lion holding a spear, topped with a crow of sails with "Vanguard" printed atop a field of cerulean blue. In addition to their crests, many of these warships also had their own mottos. HMS Vanguard had a motto. The motto echoes the naval battles of yore, but also foreshadows this modern era of competitive business battles. It is: "We lead."[1]

John C. Bogle
Chairman and CEO

In the Spring of 1992, The Vanguard Group, Inc. was a unique force in the U.S. investment community. In its 18 years of operation, it had consistently served as an innovator in the mutual fund industry. In doing so, Vanguard had fashioned a no-nonsense, value-oriented, corporate culture under the command of 62 year old Chairman and CEO Jack Bogle. Vanguard's fierce sense of purpose clearly had an impact on those who worked with and for the company, and Vanguard management believed that Vanguard was the organization against which other mutual fund companies had to measure themselves.

Vanguard's low-cost strategy of no-load funds, small expense ratios, candid client communication, high-quality service, and predictable performance had won itself a considerable niche in the mutual fund industry, behind only Fidelity and Merril Lynch in market share in 1991 (see Exhibit 1). Bogle and Vanguard had long since decided that providing savings on the expense side of mutual funds would deliver more net return to cur-rent fund holders, with more certainty, than expensive but uncertain attempts to improve investment performance or enlarge the fund shareholder base.

The walls of offices in Vanguard's headquarters in Valley Forge, Pennsylvania (and often Vanguard Fund annual reports) were adorned with paintings of Lord Horatio Nelson's HMS Vanguard, the namesake Bogle chose for the operation. In Nelson's greatest battle, he led an undermanned fleet of ships against Napoleon's French armada. Nelson won, through an exercise of cunning and daring leadership. Because he had chosen to send a crucial detachment of ships through previously unnavigated waters, Nelson took the bigger and bulkier French fleet by surprise. Bogle would often draw comparisons between Nelson's HMS Vanguard and his own:

That battle—and that flagship—were the inspiration for choosing the name of our enterprise. This modern-day Vanguard—the ship on which we all sail together—has also had its share of daring maneuvers.[2]

VANGUARD HISTORY

Even the pre-origins of Vanguard had unconventional, if not daring, roots. In 1928, Walter L. Morgan founded the forerunner of the Wellington Management Company, based in Philadelphia, with investment banker A. Moyer Kulp. Morgan and Kulp made their "Wellington Fund" an open-end fund, one of a handful in the country at the time. With amazing prescience, or fortuitous luck, the pair also decided to make their fund unleveraged, and discouraged risk taking and specula-tive strategies. A third feature of the company fund was that it was not a common stock fund, but a "balanced" fund, reducing its dependence on equities, with 30% of the portfolio composed of bonds. When the stock mar-ket crashed in 1929, Morgan's fund, although it lost value, outperformed most of its peers thanks to the conservative nature of its investment strategy. The fund grew through the 1930s, reaching $1 million in size in 1935 and $4 million by 1938.

The Wellington Fund continued to grow through the war years and into the 1950s, selling its shares through stock brokers across the nation. But as the stock market soared through the 1950s, the Wellington Fund's conservative strategy became out of vogue, and Wellington Management only belatedly responded to the market by bringing out its first stock fund, "Windsor," in 1958. Windsor, a "growth and income" fund, didn't completely fulfill investors' needs either, which were increasingly for "performance" funds during the 1960s. Although by 1966 Wellington Fund was $1.8 billion strong and was still the third largest fund in the United States, Wellington Management leadership believed something would need to be done to retain WMC's position in the U.S. mutual fund market.

WELLINGTON ACTS

In 1966, Wellington Management's executive vice president, John C. Bogle, was confronted with Wellington's strategic problem. Bogle had been hired in 1951 by Morgan himself after Morgan read Bogle's Princeton senior thesis on the mutual fund industry. And by 1966, Jack Bogle was Morgan's heir apparent. A tall, lean, bright 38 year old with a crew-cut, Bogle was often referred to as a "whiz kid" by the media. Bogle, whose work ethic helped lead to a heart attack at age 31, approached the problem in a typically aggressive way. He decided Wellington should attempt to take three major steps:

1. Acquire an aggressive growth fund with an outstanding record.
2. Enter the (newly burgeoning) investment counseling business.
3. Attract some capable portfolio managers.

Bogle moved to solve all three problems at once, by merging Wellington Management with Thorndike, Doran, Paine & Lewis, Inc. (TDP&L) a Boston-based investment counseling firm which also ran the Ivest Fund, a small growth fund with an impressive recent performance record. The merger solved problems for both firms. Wellington Management added a hot fund, Ivest, in a fraction of the time it would have taken to start and develop its own growth fund. It also got the services of the principals of TDP&L, four men—all 35 or younger—who were experienced in investment counseling and in fund management. For TDP&L, the merger would give them a first class sales operation for the Ivest Fund, which, although a good performer, hadn't been selling well.

With the Ivest Fund and several small funds introduced after the Ivest acquisition, Wellington had 12 funds by 1970. The Wellington Fun was still the dominant fund in the group, with nearly 60% of assets, but it accounted for less that 5% of WMC fund sales, and over half of WCM redemptions.[3]

CRACKS IN THE FACADE

After the TDP&L merger and the subsequent retirement of Walter Morgan, Jack Bogle became the President and CEO at Wellington Management. Two TDP&L principals, Robert Doran and Nick Thorndike, served as Executive Vice Presidents for Investment/Marketing and Administrative Divisions, respectively. Both men remained in Boston, and Doran supervised the head of mutual fund management, Walter Cabot, who was also based in Boston. Reporting to Cabot were the portfolio managers for each of the funds. Of these, only one, John Neff, who ran the Windsor fund, was based in Philadelphia. Bogle served as chairman of each of the funds. By federal law, each mutual fund had its own board of directors, a majority of whom were required to be independent of the management company. Wellington Management had its own board of directors as well, of which Jack Bogle also was chairman.

As time went on, it became increasingly clear that the merger was not working out as well as the parties had hoped. Ivest Fund performance slumped, Wellington Fund sales failed to improve, and tensions arose between Bogle and the TDP&L group. Under the terms of the merger, the board of directors of Wellington Management had become controlled by the Boston-based TDP&L group, and in January 1974, the board fired Jack Bogle. Hurt by the exile from "his" company, Bogle did not wallow in self pity. He went to the board of the mutual funds, and persuaded them to retain him as chairman of the funds, arguing that it made little sense for a huge fund enterprise to be run by a management company. Why not, asked Bogle, have the funds have their own structure, and operate purely for the benefit of fund shareholders? The funds' board was composed of just enough non-Wellington directors to allow for an independent decision, and the directors opted for Bogle's plan.

Since Wellington Management wanted to keep its name, the family of funds would need a new collective identifier. Thus, in September, 1974, The

Vanguard Group was created. The initial role of the Vanguard management was to administer the funds: portfolio accounting, shareholder record keeping and communications, and monitoring compliance with laws regarding mutual funds. These were, of course, thought to be relatively mundane and uninspiring tasks. Wellington Management still acted as the investment advisor and managed the wholesaling organization that distributed the funds, presumably the two most important functions.

VANGUARD—A NEW ENTERPRISE

The relationship between Wellington and the new and curious Vanguard Group was bound to change. First, though, the slump in fund sales which helped speed Bogle's ouster continued for Vanguard and for the entire mutual fund industry after the 1974 upheaval. Throughout the mid- and late-1970s, the industry as a whole experienced redemptions greater than their sales.

INDEX FUND. In 1976, Vanguard introduced the industry's first index investment fund, Vanguard Index Trust 500, a fund which attempted to mirror the performance of the S&P 500. Initially, the index fund did not sell well, with only $14 million by the first year's end. The reaction from the rest of the Wall Street community to Vanguard's implicit assumption—that the fund could perform as well as a portfolio managed actively by an advisor—was certainly a contributor to the chilly reception the fund received. Vanguard and Bogle were widely criticized for accepting mediocrity and the index fund was described as "un-American." It was neither the first nor the last time Bogle would be harshly derided.

THE MOVE TO NO-LOAD. Although the index fund was a big step, Bogle had had something else in his sights from the moment of Vanguard's inception. In a later speech, Bogle remembered his goal at the time:

> Proper administration is the sine qua non of a mutual fund's affairs, essential to its very essence. However challenging it is to perform these tasks with something akin to perfection, I was not sure doing so played to my strengths. Rather, for me the fun and challenge lay in the exhilarating competition for investor acceptance in the mutual fund marketplace, and in the demanding competition for investment returns in the securities markets. So, the newly formed Vanguard quickly set itself to the challenge of gathering in the responsibility for marketing and portfolio management.[4]

In February of 1977, after a marathon board meeting concluding at 1:30 a.m., the board of The Vanguard Group voted 7–4 to commit to a "no-load" strategy for all of its funds, which eliminated broker commissions, and required that Vanguard take charge of its own distribution.*

Bogle laid out the reasoning behind the decision to go no-load:

> First, to recognize the obvious fact that in a maturing industry, with growing public recognition; in an expanding economy, with larger personal wealth; and in a better-educated marketplace, with the self-evident logic of lower costs; the elements of change were firmly in place. Second, to postulate not only that these elements of change would not abate, but that they would accelerate. Third, to carefully calculate the interim risks of near-zero sales volume and soaring redemptions, and then to guess how long it would be before the tide would turn. Fourth, having made these reasoned judgments, to have the courage—and to persuade other to have the courage—to do the deed.[5]

While the vision for handling its own direct distribution was clearly evident at Vanguard, getting SEC approval was another story altogether. Ironically, the SEC conducted perhaps the longest hearing in history of the Investment Act of 1940, and ultimately rejected Vanguard's application. Vanguard, however, was able to amend its application, which was approved on the second try. The delay of approval, which came in 1981, surely would have stranded Vanguard with no means of selling shares in its funds, had the SEC not allowed Vanguard to assume distribution responsibilities while the application and re-application were pending.

As The Vanguard Group began to develop its skills in marketing and distributing directly to the public, it also began to increase the number of fund offerings, picking up where Wellington Management Company had left off before 1974, offering eight new funds from 1977–1980.

FIXED INCOME GOES IN HOUSE

In 1981, Vanguard took another important step toward fulfilling Bogle's vision when he and Wellington

---

*By eliminating the "load" on their funds, Vanguard took away any commission that retail brokers could receive from the sale of Vanguard funds. The intended result of the removal of the load was that Vanguard would assume responsibility for the direct sales and distribution of its funds to the investing public, rather than relying upon the wholesaling distribution of the Wellington organization which had managed this function through retail brokers.

Management began to part ways. Believing that the secret to high net returns to the investor in at least some fixed income funds was simply low cost (and not high-priced advice), Vanguard internalized the investment advisory functions for its six money market and municipal bond portfolios. In this new structure, Vanguard would itself provide the advisory function to the funds, at cost, and these costs would be carefully controlled.

Like other large mutual fund complexes, Vanguard spent the 1980s busily adding funds, tripling its offerings through the creation of specialty equity funds, specialty fixed income funds, tax free funds (including four state-specific tax free funds), and a smattering of other funds. (See Exhibit 2 for Vanguard Family of Funds, June 1992). Most of the funds were designed to provide steady and predictable rates of return.

For some of these funds, including most of the fixed income funds, The Vanguard Group provided a low cost investment advisory function in-house, at cost. For other funds, Vanguard continued to retain the Wellington Management organization, its historical advisor. But for some of the newer, more specialized equity funds, Vanguard chose new and different advisors, organizations with which Vanguard had not had an earlier relationship. By 1992, Vanguard employed 13 such external investment advisors, and had clearly progressed relatively far toward becoming a "manager of managers" for its equity funds.

When it considered the offering of a new fund, Vanguard applied a simple test: could the fund be run without employing a large and/or expensive investment research function? If so, and if the fund was relatively generic in nature, Vanguard would manage the fund itself. For the other funds, Vanguard would hire external advisors to handle the fund's portfolio, but bargain hard for low advisory fees.

THE ORGANIZATION AND ITS CULTURE

The creation of The Vanguard Group in 1974 was unique in the U.S. mutual fund industry. For the first time, a major mutual fund complex was operated "at cost" solely for the benefit of the shareholders of the funds. Specifically, the Vanguard Group was owned by its constituent funds. Any "profits" of Vanguard were thus remitted back to the funds themselves, as opposed to the owners of the management company. This fact had ramifications throughout the organization. Whereas most mutual fund companies sought to reap profits, Vanguard defined its mission as keeping costs down, in order to benefit shareholders.

The emphasis on containing costs was reinforced through the employee incentive plan. Employees were paid an annual bonus based upon the aggregate cost savings that Vanguard produced for its fund shareholders, as measured by the actual funds' expenses relative to what these expenses would have been if the funds' expense ratio were equal to the average of the industry. Thus, the lower the costs of the actual Vanguard funds, the higher the employee bonuses.

Bogle's zealous pursuit to provide the best possible result for shareholders led to other important cultural phenomena at Vanguard. First and foremost was Bogle's insistence on full and candid disclosure to shareholders. John Brennan, Vanguard's 38 year old President, stated it simply, "We consider ourselves the conscience of the industry." For example, Bogle's reports to shareholders would candidly describe any underperformance in one of its funds, and analyze why it had occurred. Conversely, if a fund had recently done well just because a particular market sector had done well, Bogle's reports would pointedly caution the fund holders that such performance would probably not continue. In general, Vanguard's reports attempted to make fund holders conscious of and knowledgeable about a fund's possible risks. Also, callers to Vanguard who inquired about a particular Vanguard fund would be politely reminded over the phone if the fund had a redemption fee, even though such information was clearly and plainly stated in the materials that would be sent to the callers. (Only the specialized equity funds carried a redemption fee of 1%.)

In 1991, during a boom period for health care industry stocks, Bogle sent an extraordinary letter to shareholders of Vanguard's Health Care industry fund, cautioning them about the risks associated with sector funds and reminding them that the stock market would not always favor health care stocks as it was at the time:

> In recent months, the Health Care Portfolio has attracted a good deal of publicity about its excellent *past* performance. Almost simultaneously, the Portfolio has had substantial cash inflows (totaling $76 million in the past three months) from thousands of new and existing shareholders. As press attention has focused almost exclusively on the strong performance of the Health Care Portfolio, and other mutual funds specializing in this field, we wanted to write this note to ensure that our shareholders and prospective investors have a balanced understanding of the risks and the potential rewards of investing in the Portfolio.
> **Past Performance Does Not Predict Future Results.** The returns of the Health Care Portfolio have been very strong. Through February 28, 1991, the Portfolio's annualized returns for the past one-, three-, and five-year peri-

ods were +39.7%, +24.5%, and +20.4%, respectively (compared to +14.7%, +15.1%, and +13.9% for the unmanaged Standard & Poor's 500 Stock Price Index over the same periods). However, it is highly unlikely that such absolute returns—or even the Portfolio's relative performance advantage—will be matched in the future. The Portfolio's performance resulted from particularly favorable returns of health care companies as a group. Experience has shown that such periods of superior performance by an industry group do not continue indefinitely. Indeed, periods of outperformance are often followed by periods of underperformance.

Bogle continued on in the letter to remind shareholders that concentration in one industry brings risk associated with lack of diversification, that health care stocks were not particularly cheap by historical standards, and that the Health Care Portfolio should be viewed as a long term investment vehicle, not as a short term industry play.

Bogle firmly believed that clear and plain-spoken client communication was not merely an ethical principle; it was good business. In a 1991 speech, Bogle commented:

> There is no mystery about the benefits of candor. Making investors aware of risk is not only ethically essential, but represents wise shareholder relations, and good public relations. In short, miracle of miracles, candor has proved to be a sensational business strategy, and Vanguard is, I think without challenge, its greatest proponent within the mutual fund industry. We have turned candor into an art form, and we distinguish ourselves by being straightforward rather than strident, understating rather than overstating, using litotes rather than hyperbole.[6]

Bogle believed that too many mutual funds hid costs from shareholders through complex and obfuscatory prospectuses, and by deceiving fee structures. Often, for example, a mutual fund would initially waive fees when building up fund assets; but, once the fund was established, it would begin charging fees up to some pre-disclosed maximum level, in the hope that clients would not then switch.

Bogle had similar distaste for so-called 12b-1 charges. These fees, named after the SEC regulation which authorized them, allowed mutual funds to charge an additional fee to the fund, the proceeds of which would go for advertising (or other sales-related expenses) for new shareholders, under the assumption that more shareholders would create economies of scale for mutual fund companies, thus benefitting existing shareholders. Bogle believed 12b-1 expenses did not, in fact, benefit existing shareholders, but rather just increased the profit to the management company as a fund grew. Vanguard thus never used a 12b-1 charge, just as it never charged a front-end load.

Vanguard took seriously its self-anointed position in the U.S. as a candid distributor, as a leader in shareholder service, and as a model for other investment companies. In a December 1987 speech, Bogle reminded the employees of Vanguard's role:

> We work in a marvelously competitive industry. To the regret of many investors, however, competition has worked perversely in recent years, producing a discreditable picture of rising prices, debased products, and disillusioning performance—destructive competition. During the coming year, I hope we can work together to help restore productive competition in the mutual fund field, with a focus on providing value to investors, as befits the long tradition of this industry.[7]

Because The Vanguard Group was a corporation operated solely for the benefit of the shareholders of its member funds, and provided all of its services on an "at cost" (i.e., non-profit making) basis, its goals were more difficult to define than a traditional investment management firm, which could use profit, dividends, stock price, or some other financial measure as a benchmark for success. Bogle commented on Vanguard's purpose:

> What the objective of our firm is is very hard to say. Certainly we don't have financial objectives in the customary sense, where someone would say we've got to get a 12% return on capital or an 18% return on capital. But I guess I'd say it is to be an enterprise that gives the customers, clients as we call them, a fair shake. And that means high quality funds, with objectives that at least have the hope of being achieved, low costs, and a high service component. It sounds a little bit like motherhood, but we have an opportunity to do that that really other people don't . . . If you shove me into a corner and say "What is your mission?" I guess as much as anything, I'd love to be known as the one who brought price competition to the mutual fund business.

Bogle told visitors that higher market share was not a Vanguard goal or strategy: servicing his clients was. But Vanguard often celebrated when it reached milestones in asset size, and Bogle himself would occasionally publicly muse about how various competitors regarded the taste of the figurative dust in which Vanguard left them as Vanguard's asset size and market share grew. (See Exhibit 3 for Direct Marketers market share.)

ROLES AT VANGUARD

The Vanguard Group of Funds was headed by a board of directors, who also served as directors of each of the funds which comprised The Vanguard Group, as was customary with mutual funds.

One of the most fiercely maintained aspects of Vanguard culture was the ethic of the relationship between its employees, customers, and products. Bogle believed quite strongly, however, that each of those terms was not useful as it applied to Vanguard:

> We do not have "employees"—people who work here with the understanding that if they do exactly as they are told they will be paid a fixed wage in return. Rather, at least in the ideal, we have a "crew," working together in partnership from the highest job to the humblest, sharing in its "earnings," and doing our best to assure that HMS Vanguard, as our crew's proud symbol, sails purposefully and on course through calm and rough waters alike.
>
> We do not have "products"—something manufactured for consumers, aggressively advertised, impulsively purchased, and finally used up. Rather we have "investment companies" in which the fiduciary duty of trusteeship is our watchword.
>
> We do not have "customers"—those whose never-ending cycle is purchase and consume, purchase and consume, purchase and consume, and whose loyalty is based more on transitory "special sales," or glamorous packaging, or the fads and fashions of the day, than on valuable and durable service. Rather, we have "clients," intelligent investors who have chosen to enter in what we expect will be a long-term professional relationship with us.[8]

THE STRATEGY

In the nearly two decades since its inception, Vanguard strove to offer ever lower cost money market funds and mutual funds. A thrifty corporate environment, in which the offices were well appointed but not plush, and in which no one—not even Bogle or Brennan—flew first class, helped reinforce the idea of cost containment, Vanguard's chief competitive advantage over other funds.

Vanguard's efforts at cost containment were reflected in its expense ratios, which, in 1992, were by far the lowest in the industry (see Exhibit 4). The turning point for Vanguard's low costs came in 1977, when they decided to make their funds "no-load." But the expense ratios continued to decline in subsequent years, as Vanguard strove to reduce its operating costs, moved toward low cost internal management, and negotiated to reduce the advisory fees it paid to

Wellington and its other external investment advisors. At Vanguard, it was a nearly-annual ritual for Bogle to come to the bargaining table and attempt to negotiate advisory fee scale reductions as assets grew (to reflect the reality that advisory costs are relatively fixed).

In keeping with its low cost philosophy, Vanguard did not spend much on advertising, approximately $5 million in 1991 (compared to an estimated $70 million for Fidelity).* Bogle occasionally wondered aloud about whether Vanguard should spend any money at all on advertising; his belief was that word of mouth and the financial press were the most effective advertisements Vanguard had. Additionally, Bogle railed against rivals' advertisements which he felt were often deceptive. Fund advertisements tended to highlight certain accomplishments for very carefully chosen periods of time, which would show the funds only in the best possible light:

> In one recent publication I counted 15 ads for funds that claimed to be the #1 this or that. That kind of stuff is really misleading. Some of these fund companies act like they were making soap.[9]

The theory behind the Vanguard low-cost line of funds, that better net returns to shareholders could be generated through controlling the cost end, not the performance end of the business, meant that Vanguard would generally offer funds whose portfolios were relatively controlled and whose performance results were therefore relatively predictable relative to some market standard, be it a market index or segment of the market. Because higher relative *gross* returns weren't necessary, portfolio managers could hold quite diversified and representative portfolios of high quality securities, which would result in Vanguard funds providing a more predictable performance than other funds.

CLIENT SERVICE. Vanguard had 1,900 employees who worked in client service, handling the needs of the company's 2.2 million shareholders and their (often several each) accounts. 500 phone representatives answered the daily deluge of calls. If callers were kept waiting for 20 seconds, an array of lower, middle, and senior managers would rush to the phone lines to take calls.[10] Vanguard sent out monthly statements, as well as a statement each time a purchase in a fund was made. Together, the mailings came to 35 million pieces a year. Vanguard's computer system wasn't yet to the point where it could integrate all shareholder funds

---

*Like other mutual fund families, the advertising Vanguard did do was primarily in the form of print ads in publications like *The New York Times* or *The Wall Street Journal.*

into an "integrated client system" instead of a "shareholder account system." In this respect, they trailed several other important fund complexes. In general, Bogle had decided not to attempt to be the technology leader in the industry, because of the higher costs that such a strategy would entail. Thus, Vanguard clients who bought into more than one Vanguard fund would receive multiple copies of Vanguard's annual report, for instance. Jack Bogle noted that even this minor expense rubbed some clients the wrong way:

> Vanguard shareholders cannot tolerate the idea of waste. So when they get seven newsletters from us or if they own six of the different portfolios in Vanguard fixed income fund and receive six glossy annual reports, they don't like it; and when they don't like it, they write the boss.

THE PENSION MARKET

Three quarters of Vanguard's business came from individuals, and one quarter came from institutional sources, mainly self-directed retirement plans, including defined contribution plans and 401(k) and 403(b) plans. 401(k) plans, which were legally authorized in the late 1970s but caught on in the early 1980s, allowed individuals to set up supplemental retirement plans by choosing from a short menu of mutual funds or other investment opportunities proffered by the employer who established the plan. Vanguard originally entered into the pension business with an eye toward defined benefit plans; as time passed, however, it became apparent to Vanguard leadership that its real advantage was in the self-directed area. And while Vanguard continued to serve defined benefit plans, its growth—like that of the industry—was in defined contribution plans, as well as the related supplemental 401(k) and 403(b) plans.* Vanguard officials believed it had several advantages in serving this market, including their excellent shareholder communications record, their ability to provide daily (if necessary) exchanges for the funds, and their low cost, high quality operation, which tended to appeal to company offi-

---

*In a defined benefit plan, the employer promises to provide specified benefits in specified retirement years for recipients. In a defined contribution plan, the employer merely sets aside a specified dollar amount each year for each employee, and the employees themselves determine how the money is to be invested, and later receive retirement benefits based upon the success of their investment choices. Employees in the defined contribution system generally had a set of investment options from which to choose, often from one or more mutual fund companies. Thus, defined contribution plans changed the nature of retirement planning to make it more participant oriented, and transferred the investment risk to the participants. Defined contribution pensions became increasingly popular during the 1980s.

cials who were charged with selecting a mutual fund family or other provider of investment alternatives.

In order to increase their share of the pension market, Vanguard built up an administrative unit in the mid 1980s, which handled the tasks associated with those self-directed plans. By 1992 Vanguard had 500 employees assigned to administer this business, and also employed a team of 12 professionals as a sales force.

MANAGEMENT OF THE FUNDS

THE FIXED INCOME GROUP

All of Vanguard's money market portfolios and most of their fixed income funds were managed in house. Ian MacKinnon, Senior Vice President, oversaw Vanguard's Fixed Income Group, which employed eight portfolio managers and eight analysts, in addition to support staff. The Fixed Income Group had an annual budget of $3 million, with which it managed approximately $39 billion in assets, for an advisory expense ratio of 8/10 of a basis point (or .008%).

The eight portfolio managers managed 26 separate fixed income funds: one managed the three taxable money market funds, one managed the four taxable short-term and intermediate-term funds, one managed the long-term U.S. Treasury and Bond market Portfolios and was a quantitative specialist active in the futures markets, two managed the many tax-exempt money market funds (including the state specific ones), one managed the short-term and intermediate-term tax-exempt funds, one managed the long-term tax-exempt funds, and one managed the high yield tax-exempt fund and was responsible for the tax-exempt group as a whole.

The eight analysts in the Fixed Income Group were primarily engaged in credit analysis and credit forecasting. The goal of the analysts was to predict changes in credit rating before they occurred, thereby reaping the price advantages which came with good analysis. The analysts were paid incentives if they were able to correctly anticipate rating changes.

The fixed income portfolios were actively managed, but tended to avoid big interest rate bets. Specifically, the funds each had an average duration (maturity) benchmark, and their actual duration (maturity) was rigorously controlled within ±10% of this benchmark. The entire group, led by Ian MacKinnon, would have a specific "top-down" fundamentally based forecast of interest rates at any given time, so that all of their portfolios as a group would tend to be a little longer than their respective benchmarks, or shorter, or the same. Once this relative duration strategy was established across the group, each portfolio manager individually managed his or her own portfolios. They made substantial use of the credit analysis supplied by their analysts, and always attempted to stay within the higher quality spectrum relative to other competitors' funds. They made substantial use of quantitative models to assess the relative values of various put features, call features, sinking funds, or other unique features of various instruments. They were very active in the various fixed income derivative markets, including the municipal futures contracts. Indeed, at times in the past four years, Vanguard had accounted for an astonishing 30–50% of the open interest in the municipal futures contract. In various ways, the Fixed Income Group attempted to arbitrage the differentials between the taxable and tax-exempt markets in the short, intermediate, and long maturity ranges so as to add incremental value over time to their many portfolios. All of these tools for management were used particularly actively in the tax-exempt markets, which Ian MacKinnon thought were not particularly efficiently-priced. In general, MacKinnon believed that Vanguard's group was on the leading edge of innovation and active fixed-income management.

In 1992, Wellington Management Company still served as advisor to four Vanguard taxable income funds, including the GNMA, Investment Grade, and High Yield Bond portfolios, as well as the Wellesley Income Fund. MacKinnon explained that Wellington's costs were close enough to Vanguard's to justify retaining Wellington:

> Fees on the Wellington-managed bond funds have been negotiated down to a level where there is not that much difference between what they charge and what my expenses are. So there's only nominal cost savings. On top of that, the Wellington fund managers have done a great job of running the money. Their funds, as our funds, have been consistently among the best in returns. So there's neither a cost advantage nor a performance problem to justify internalizing them.

THE QUANTITATIVE EQUITY GROUP

The only other internal money management group within Vanguard itself was the quantitative equity or indexing group. This group of five professionals was managed by George U. Sauter, a young expert in quantitative investment methods. It included two other researchers whose principal focus was analyzing

and reducing the tracking errors that arose in the process of building different index portfolios. It also included two traders who were responsible for the day-to-day operations and trading of the index portfolios.

The group managed the five different domestic index funds of Vanguard, which totaled over $7 billion: the Index Trust 500 (the S&P 500), the Extended Market Index Trust (the remaining 4500 stocks of the Wilshire 5000), the Total Stock Market Index Trust (a capitalization-weighted composite of the first two index trusts), the Institutional Index Trust (the S&P 500 for large institutional accounts), and the Small Capitalization Stock Fund (an index fund of small companies). They also managed two newer international index funds begun in 1990, one for European stocks and one for Pacific Basin stocks, which totaled about $350 million. They made active use of stock lending and financial derivative, particularly various equity index futures, in managing these portfolios in an effort to add a very small but predictable performance increment to the indexed returns.

In addition, this group had been studying various ways of building highly structured and passive (that is, non-trading) portfolios to track various market sectors. Their goal was to develop low-cost methods for producing portfolios which could follow the returns of a market sector with great relative predictability, and yet add some value through disciplined stock selection algorithms. They had already begun to manage one small segment of the Windsor II fund in the manner, hoping to produce the same value-oriented performance results of their outside managers, but at lower cost. Clearly, there might be considerable opportunity to launch other such in-house quantitatively-controlled experiments within the Vanguard equity funds, as supplements to Vanguard's stable of outside managers, an increasing number of whom were well-respected quantitative investment management firms.

THE RESULTS

Vanguard enjoyed a substantial increase in assets throughout the 1980s, moving from $5 billion in 1982 to over $85 billion in mid-1992. Vanguard's mutual fund market share also more than tripled during that period of time. The financial press often trumpeted Vanguard's achievements, and Vanguard was also bolstered by reports, like the 1990, 1991, and 1992 *Financial World* magazine surveys of customer service, which put it at the top of the mutual fund industry.

Vanguard's success in growth of market share during the 1980s did not go unnoticed by competitors and commentators in the mutual fund industry. One industry report compared Vanguard's strategy in mutual funds to that of Wal-Mart in retailing:

> The similarity between their market share progressions is striking. Both organizations seek to exploit good service and brand-name products using a structurally lower expense base. The share gains these companies have achieved have bred continued and greater cost advantages.[11]

There was another related way of measuring results, the aggregate cost "savings" to Vanguard shareholders. Exhibit 5 shows the average Vanguard expense ratios, those of a competitive group, and the dollar savings represented by this difference applied to the aggregate Vanguard assets. Bogle believed that this was perhaps the best measure of the success of the Vanguard strategy, as seen by its clients, the fund shareholders.

SOME COMPETITORS RESPOND

While Vanguard continued its growth, a number of important competitors began to respond. For example, from 1990 through 1992, Fidelity Investments developed a line of "Spartan Funds," which were low-cost, high minimum investment (typically $10,000 or greater) funds targeted directly at relatively affluent shareholders in Vanguard's market niche. Typically these funds were initially marketed not only as no-loads but also with very low or no annual management fees, making them initially not only competitive with, but sometimes an even lower cost alternative than, Vanguard. Fidelity retained the right to later increase the annual fees to some higher level, though, where the funds would still be low-cost but not nearly so low-cost as the typical Vanguard fund. In general, they seemed to be targeted at a long-term expense (or price) point mid-way between Vanguard's expense ratios and those of Fidelity's other non-Spartan funds. Almost all of these Spartan funds were in the money market and fixed-income fund areas. Indeed, many of them were just a repackaging of existing Fidelity products into a lower cost higher minimum investment format. Fidelity advertised these Spartan funds widely and intensively throughout the financial press. The market response was truly impressive, as billions of dollars flowed into these funds, across the full product line.

This was an interesting development in the mutual fund business. For many years, while the front-end loads of load funds had been decreasing, the annual expense ratios of many funds had been increasing, making them more costly to investors but more profitable to the fund management companies. The obvious exception to this general trend toward higher annual fees, including 12b-1 fees, had been Vanguard's rather lonely and iconoclastic strategy. Now, however, with the Spartan challenge from Fidelity, this general trend was much in doubt.

THE MONEY MARKET WARS

Nowhere was the competitive interaction more challenging than in the money market arenas, where Fidelity had introduced a flotilla of Spartan funds: U.S. Treasury, U.S. Government, general taxable, general tax-exempt, state-specific tax-exempt funds for the largest states, etc. Dreyfus, long one of the leaders in the money market fund arena, had little choice but to respond; and it did so with its own line of new funds which initially waived all management fees. After the waiver period, however, fees would return to their usual levels, above Vanguard's. All of this led to what was generally called the "Money Market Wars." Dreyfus was gaining some market share with its new funds, albeit presumably at a substantial and costly loss in profitability. Vanguard stood pat with its low cost structure, and continued to gain share. Fidelity and most other competitors continued to lose. The pricing strategies of competitors and the competitive structure of the market were in considerable dynamic flux.

THE BOND FUND ARENA

The competitive dynamics might also be changing in bond funds, which was the second largest segment of the industry ($429 billion, versus $592 billion in money market funds, and $400 billion in equity funds). Bond funds, with their relatively predictable and stable nature, were ideally suited for Vanguard's low-cost strategy. Indeed, in relative terms, Vanguard's market share was largest in this segment (see Exhibit 6). And their recent gains in market share were also largest there (see Exhibit 7).

But, very recently, Fidelity had targeted a number of its Spartan Funds directly at this market, and they were gathering considerable assets. Other competitors, including Dreyfus, were in the process of doing the same. There was some reason to believe that the price competition which had recently characterized money market funds might be spilling over into this bond fund segment too.

EQUITY FUND ARENA

In the equity fund arena, however, competition generally took a different turn. More and more new equity funds continued to be introduced by the principal competitors, to the point where it was sometimes difficult to distinguish many of the funds, even within a family, from each other. Product proliferation appeared to be the dominant strategy, coupled with aggressive promotion and distribution of successful performance records. Fidelity, for example, had introduced a number of actively managed smaller company funds, and an entire menu of 33 different "select funds," each specializing in a different industry such as airlines, or chemicals, or biotechnology stocks. Also, Fidelity was expanding its international offerings, with a variety of actively managed foreign, global, European, and Pacific funds. Other competitors were doing the same.

Jack Bogle was concerned with some elements of this proliferation, at least as a possible strategy for Vanguard. Small growth funds could be very unpredictable and very disappointing for investors, something he wanted to minimize. International funds might be useful for some diversification, he grudgingly admitted to his younger Vanguard colleagues, but only in limited numbers and formats. In general, he thought product proliferation could go too far, at least from the perspective of helping fund holders make reasoned and appropriate investment choices.

Of course, the equity fund arena was not totally without some signs of price competition. Fidelity and Dreyfus, for example, had both introduced index funds in late 1990, designed to track the S&P 500. The expense ratios on these funds were kept low; in Fidelity's case at 35 basis points per year. This was higher than Vanguard's Index Trust 500 expense ratio of 20 basis points, but still substantially lower than all of Fidelity's other equity funds. The Fidelity index fund was not widely advertised or promoted, and it had grown to only about $200 million by mid-1992, as compared with about $5 billion in Vanguard's Index Trust 500. It was not clear how these new index funds would eventually fit into Fidelity's and Dreyfus' evolving strategies. What was clear was that the index fund segment was important to Vanguard, for it rather consistently accounted for about 40% of their equity fund sales.

THE FUTURE

In June of 1992, Bogle believed that Vanguard was in good shape. Fidelity, Dreyfus, and other mutual fund groups were beginning to offer cut-rate funds, but Bogle was only encouraged by that sign. Competing on low fees was competing on Vanguard's turf, and Bogle was comfortable playing by those rules.

And while the mutual fund industry was becoming more and more saturated with more and more funds, Bogle really didn't worry. Vanguard's market share was unimportant, he felt; servicing Vanguard shareholders was what really mattered. In fact, one of his biggest concerns was with handling the growth that Vanguard was going through. New money was flowing into Vanguard bond and equity funds, and into those of most mutual fund groups, at unprecedented rates in 1992. Most parts of his organization were growing very rapidly, with increasing demands and he didn't know exactly how that might affect Vanguard's performance and culture.

To make matters more confusing, the SEC had just released a slate of proposed regulatory changes for the mutual fund industry. If enacted, these would be the first significant change in the industry's regulation in 50 years. One proposed change would make it easier for customers to buy an advertised fund by just clipping a coupon from an advertisement and ordering the fund, without first having to see the fund's prospectus. (Bogle, for his part, announced that even if the change was enacted, Vanguard would still insist that clients read the prospectus before ordering a fund.) Another change would make it possible to broadly offer private unregistered funds to qualified wealthy investors, without the inhibiting SEC regulations which precluded the use of leverage, short-selling, and various derivative instruments, among other things, in traditional mutual fund portfolios. Another proposed change would, for the first time, unfix the front-end loads charged by load funds, ushering in competition on a price basis within the differing channels of distribution for these funds. Most observers thought this would create a general pressure for lower loads, more competitive pricing, and the gradual disappearance of any sharp differences between load and no-load funds. Whatever the future effects of these specific regulatory proposals and many others, it was clear in general that some segments of the mutual fund industry would be encountering a faster pace of change in its distribution practices over the next decade than ever before.*

---

*For his part, Bogle was quite disappointed with the proposed SEC changes, for he felt they did not address the more pressing issues in the mutual fund industry. Bogle believed that SEC regulations should focus instead on "trusteeship," placing more emphasis on directors' responsibility, including a new statutory standard of fiduciary duty that would require fund directors to give more careful attention to fees, complete and candid shareholder reports, and accuracy in advertising.

The mutual fund industry was in a period of flux, as it had been for the past 15 years. Some of the flux was attributable to Vanguard's pricing, but most elements were clearly motivated by other problems or opportunities. New methods of distributing mutual funds would test Vanguard's "word of mouth" advertising. Several of the large competitors, including Fidelity, were briskly diversifying into brokerage, insurance, credit cards, and a whole spectrum of other financial service businesses. The ultimate goal appeared to be "one-stop shopping centers," outlets where clients could take care of all of their financial services at once. Other channels were opening up as new distribution outlets: banks, even automatic teller machines. And Vanguard, with its pure no-load low-cost culture, would be unable to pay commissions of 12b-1 fees to facilitate the sale of its funds through any of these new channels.

Jack Bogle needed to consider all of this, and make sure that he steered the HMS Vanguard on an appropriate course through some relatively murky and uncharted waters. His greatest fear was that as Vanguard grew larger and more successful, it would become complacent and lose the innovative and daring spirit that had characterized its early years. And yet, it was not clear what the next innovative stage of Vanguard's development should or could be.

QUESTIONS

1. Evaluate Vanguard's past strategy. Do not merely describe it. Using criteria provided in various articles evaluate why the strategy has worked. What are Vanguard's critical current strengths and vulnerabilities?
2. How should other competitors in the financial community—such as Fidelity, Dreyfus, or Charles Schwab—respond? What countermoves should Vanguard undertake? What new directions is the mutual fund business likely to take? How should Vanguard respond to these?
3. How is Vanguard organized now? What are its core competencies, unique leverage points? Should Mr. Bogle develop more in-house asset management capabilities? How? What will be the impact?
4. What major changes should Mr. Bogle undertake now? What are his biggest risks? Biggest opportunities?

EXHIBIT 1
Mutual Fund Industry Market Shares—Year End 1991
Note: Groups with open-end amounts of at least $20 billion on December 31, 1991

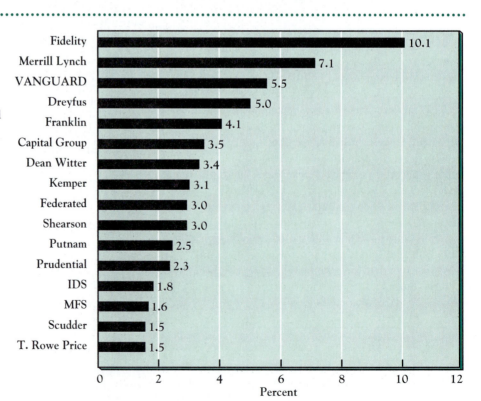

	Percent
Fidelity	10.1
Merrill Lynch	7.1
VANGUARD	5.5
Dreyfus	5.0
Franklin	4.1
Capital Group	3.5
Dean Witter	3.4
Kemper	3.1
Federated	3.0
Shearson	3.0
Putnam	2.5
Prudential	2.3
IDS	1.8
MFS	1.6
Scudder	1.5
T. Rowe Price	1.5

Note: Groups with open-end assets of at least $20 billion on December 31, 1991.

EXHIBIT 2
The Vanguard Group, Inc.
Family of Funds,
June 1992*

FUND NAME	YEAR OF INCEPTION	ADVISOR	ASSETS ($ MILLIONS)	EXPENSE RATIO (%)
Vanguard Money Market Reserves				
Prime Portfolio	1975	Vanguard Group	13004.2	.30
Federal Portfolio	1981	Vanguard Group	1965.2	.30
U.S. Treasury Portfolio	1983	Vanguard Group	2071.3	.30
Institutional Money Market Portfolio	1989	Vanguard Group	229.2	.15
Tax-Free Income Funds (Municipal Bond Funds)				
Money Market Portfolio	1980	Vanguard Group	2793.0	.25
Short-Term Portfolio	1977	Vanguard Group	874.2	.25
Limited-Term Portfolio	1987	Vanguard Group	547.0	.25
Intermediate-Term Portfolio	1977	Vanguard Group	2489.1	.25
Insured Long-Term Portfolio	1984	Vanguard Group	1701.6	.25
Long-Term Portfolio	1977	Vanguard Group	837.8	.25
High-Yield Portfolio	1978	Vanguard Group	1341.8	.25
State Tax-Free Income Funds				
California Money Market	1987	Vanguard Group	753.8	.24
New Jersey Money Market	1988	Vanguard Group	549.0	.24
Ohio Money Market	1990	Vanguard Group	79.0	.26
Pennsylvania Money Market	1988	Vanguard Group	817.1	.24
California Insured Long-Term	1986	Vanguard Group	645.9	.25
New Jersey Insured Long-Term	1988	Vanguard Group	452.9	.24
Ohio Insured Long-Term	1990	Vanguard Group	62.1	.27
Pennsylvania Insured Long-Term	1985	Vanguard Group	872.5	.25
New York Insured Long-Term	1985	Vanguard Group	431.1	.27
Taxable Income Funds				
Bond Market Fund (Index)	1985	Vanguard Group	848.9	.21
Fixed Income Securities Fund				
Short-Term U.S. Treasury	1991	Vanguard Group	39.3	.26
Short-Term Federal	1987	Vanguard Group	1179.5	.28
Short-Term Bond	1982	Vanguard Group	1866.4	.27
Intermediate-Term U.S. Treasury**	1991	Vanguard Group	133.7	.26
GNMA	1980	WMC Mgmt.	5297.5	.30
Long-Term U.S. Treasury	1985	Vanguard Group	592.5	.28
Investment Grade Bond	1973	WMC Mgmt.	2005.6	.33
High Yield Corporate	1978	WMC Mgmt.	1452.4	.45
Wellesley Income Fund	1970	WMC Mgmt.	1934.1	.45
Balanced Funds				
Vanguard Asset Allocation Fund (sampling of equity bond money market Portfolios)	1988	Mellon Capital Mgmt. Corp.	341.2	.44
Vanguard STAR Fund (sampling of 7 Vanguard funds)	1985	(managers of funds in portfolio)	1547.0	.00
Wellington Fund	1929	WMC Mgmt.	3818.4	.35
Convertible Securities Fund	1986	Desai Capital Mgmt.	50.4	.81
Gemini II (closed and dual fund)				

*Fund assets and expense ratios taken from December, 1991.

**Assets and expense ratios reflect less than one year from inception of fund.

EXHIBIT 2 (cont'd)

FUND NAME	YEAR OF INCEPTION	ADVISOR	ASSETS ($ MILLIONS)	EXPENSE RATIO (%)
DOMESTIC EQUITY FUNDS				
Growth Biased				
World Fund, U.S. Growth	1981	Lincoln Capital	755.2	.74
PRIMECAP Fund	1984	PRIMECAP Mgmt.	437.4	.75
Vanguard/Morgan Growth Fund	1968	WMC Mgmt. Franklin Portfolio Roll & Ross	876.8	.55
Explorer Fund	1957	WMC Mgmt. Granahan Invest.	366.7	.64
Value Biased				
Equity Income Fund	1988	Newell Associates	518.0	.53
Trustee Comingled, U.S. Portfolio	1980	Geewax, Terker	105.9	.47
Windsor (closed fund)	1958	WMC Mgmt.	7800.1	.37
Windsor II	1985	Barrow, Hanley, Mewhinney & Strauss Tuckman Vanguard	3213.4	.52
Index				
Index Trust 500	1976	Vanguard	3640.9	.19
Index Trust, Extended Market	1987	Vanguard	302.9	.21
Index Trust, Total Stock Market	1992	Vanguard	149.4	.22
Institutional Index	1990	Vanguard	878.5	.09
Small Capitalization Stock	1989	Vanguard	111.5	.23
FOREIGN EQUITY FUNDS				
Growth Biased				
World Fund, Int'l Growth	1981	Schroder Capital	875.9	.68
Value Biased				
Trustees' Commingled	1983	Batterymarch	911.5	.43
Index				
Int'l Equity, European	1990	Vanguard	163.5	.33
Int'l Equity, Pacific	1990	Vanguard	84.1	.32
OTHER				
Quantitative Portfolios	1985	Franklin Portfolio	305.8	.48
Specialized—Energy	1984	WMC	123.4	.35
Specialized—Gold & Precious Metals	1984	M&G Investment	172.3	.42
Specialized—Health Care	1984	WMC	428.6	.36
Specialized—Service Economy	1984	WMC	20.8	.59
Specialized—Technology	1984	WMC	21.1	.48
Specialized—Utilities	1992	Vanguard	N/A	N/A
Preferred Stock	1975	WMC	99.1	.53
Vanguard Real Estate Funds I & II (Real Estate Investment Trusts)		AEW		

*Fund assets and expense ratios taken from December 1991.

Source: The Vanguard Group, Inc.

EXHIBIT 3
Year-End Assets Direct
Marketing Share

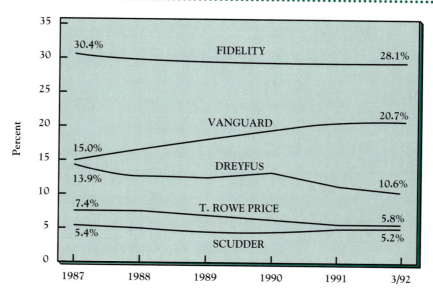

Market share of other direct marketers: 27.9% in 1987 and 29.6% in March, 1992

Source: Compiled by authors.

EXHIBIT 4
The Vanguard Cost
Advantage—1990

	ANNUAL COSTS*				VANGUARD VS. AVERAGE
	HIGHEST 10%	AVERAGE	LOWEST 10%	VANGUARD	
Equity Funds	3.19%	1.99%	0.91%	0.45%	-77%
Bond Funds	2.93	1.85	0.76	0.36	-81
Municipal Bond Funds	2.52	1.60	0.61	0.25	-84
Money Market Funds	1.22	0.75	0.51	0.28	-63
Total	2.72%	1.70%	0.77%	0.35%	-79%

*The cost figures were prepared by Lipper Analytical Services, Inc. They reflect annual expense ratios, plus any front-end and deferred sales charges, amortized over five years. The Vanguard Funds, of course, are "pure no-load" and thus reflect only their expense ratios.

Source: Compiled by authors.

EXHIBIT 5
"Savings" to Vanguard Shareholders

	EXPENSE RATIOS			VANGUARD ASSETS (MILLIONS)	"SAVINGS"[b] (000)
	VANGUARD	**COMPETITORS**[a]	**DIFFERENCE**		
1980	.58%	.62%	.04%	$3,026	$1,210
1981	.58	.65	.07	4,109	2,876
1982	.61	.68	.07	5,617	3,932
1983	.60	.68	.08	7,258	5,806
1984	.54	.70	.16	9,925	15,880
1985	.52	.72	.20	16,511	33,022
1986	.46	.76	.26	24,961	64,899
1987	.40	.81	.41	27,157	111,344
1988	.40	.86	.46	34,206	157,348
1989	.35	.86	.51	47,576	242,638
1990	.35	.85	.50	55,817	279,085
1991	.32	.86	.54	77,023	415,924

[a]Sixteen of the largest mutual fund complexes
[b]Expense ratior advantage times Vanguard average assets
Note: Data excludes all sales charges

Source: The Vanguard Group, Inc.

EXHIBIT 6
Vanguard's Share of Direct Marketing Assets 1987–1992

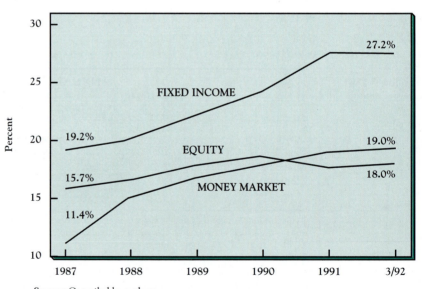

Source: Compiled by authors.

EXHIBIT 7
Direct Marketing Market Share Changes— December 1987–March 1992

	ALL FUNDS	EQUITY	BOND	MONEY MARKET
Vanguard	+5.7%	+2.3%	+8.0%	+7.6%
Fidelity	-2.3	-1.9	-1.1	-3.4
Dreyfus	-3.4	-2.5	-8.3	+0.7
Scudder	-0.2	-0.3	+0.4	-1.2
T. Rowe Price	-1.7	-0.5	-1.9	-3.1
Other	+1.9%	+2.9%	+2.9%	-0.6%

Source: Compiled by authors.

THE BATTLE FOR PARAMOUNT COMMUNICATIONS, INC.

We have put together the No. 1 software company in the world, a monster entertainment company. We've succeeded in changing the faces of our own companies and in changing the face of the media business. We will be the most powerful software-driven company in the world, and that is not an understatement. We are indeed staggered by what we have wrought.

Sumner Redstone, September 12–13, 1993

I believed that the future would go to those who were involved in the architecture of interactivity at the convergence of the telephone, computer and television set. Those that have visited QVC's headquarters saw the power of the infrastructure that had been built and believed with me that QVC's strategy to lay down interactive distribution tracks in retailing information and education services was a sound one. . . . And that is exactly the underlying argument for why QVC and Paramount should be combined.

Barry Diller, October 20, 1993

Sumner Redstone, CEO and Chairman of Viacom, Inc. and Barry Diller, CEO of QVC Network, Inc., were embroiled in an extraordinarily well-publicized takeover battle for Paramount Communications Inc. As the rapidly changing entertainment and communications industry evolved, it was becoming clearer to both strong-willed executives that assets such as those of Paramount would only become more valuable over time. As they sat in their respective offices on January 31, 1994, they considered the chain of events that had transpired over the past five months and wondered what their next steps should be. (See timeline Exibit 1.)

Case copyright © 1994 Sydney Finkelstein. This case was developed and written by Todd D. Clark (T'95) under the supervision of Professor Sydney Finkelstein as a basis for classroom discussion.

PARAMOUNT COMMUNICATIONS, INC.

Paramount Communications, Inc. was a diversified multimedia company with assets in television and movie production studios, publishing, sports teams, theme parks, cable stations, local television stations and theaters. The present company was formed through the acquisitions (and some divestitures) of Gulf & Western Corporation founder Charles Bluhdorn and a series of restructuring moves by present Chairman and CEO Martin Davis.

As Gulf & Western Industries, Inc., the company acquired businesses from "auto parts to zinc" in the 1960s, including Paramount Pictures Corporation in 1966. By 1971 the conglomerate was divided into twelve business segments: financial services, auto replacement parts, industrial products, metals forming, precision engineering, leisure time, consumer products, natural resources, forest & paper products, food products and international. In the mid-'70s Gulf & Western acquired the venerable publisher Simon & Schuster, Inc. through a stock swap. As a result of rising interest rates, the sharp early '80s recession and Wall Street's anti-conglomerate sentiment, Bluhdorn began a process of consolidating the business segments to a total of seven.

Martin Davis, a lifelong employee of Paramount, took over as CEO following the death of Bluhdorn in 1983. Immediately, Davis began a campaign to streamline the firm by concentrating in three business segments: entertainment and communications, financial services, and consumer & industrial products. In 1983 and 1984, Gulf & Western Industries sold a wide range of assets including Consolidated Cigar Corporation, natural resource operations, foreign automotive operations, industrial operations, building products operations, the Food Products Segment, and the company's investment portfolio (Table A). By 1985, Davis was ready to divest the Consumer & Industrial Products Group, selling the apparel & hosiery, manufacturing, bedding & home furnishings, and automotive parts & distribution operation to Wickes Companies for $1 billion. In 1986, Gulf & Western Industries became Gulf + Western, Inc.

The 1989 sale of Associates First Capital Corp., a consumer and commercial lending unit, capped the streamlining project. The company received proceeds of roughly $2.6 billion on the sale. Newly named Paramount Communications, Inc. would concentrate on entertainment and publishing. Up to this point, Davis had used his cash conservatively investing approximately $2 billion in small, focused acquisitions of publishing companies, movie theaters, and broadcasting properties. The largest of these was the 1984 acquisition for $710 million of Prentice-Hall, Inc., a publisher of books, business information and educational materials.

In June 1989, Davis changed his tactics and launched a $10.7 billion hostile bid for Time, Inc. when that corporation was in the process of negotiating a merger agreement with Warner Communications. Since the Paramount bid represented a significant premium over the Time deal, Davis became a vocal advocate of delivering value to shareholders. Eventually however, Time merged with Warner following a ruling by the Delaware Supreme Court. The court ruled that the business judgment rule applied to the Time board of directors, thereby allowing them to turn down the higher value Paramount offer in favor of the better strategic fit of Warner.*

---

*The business judgment rule is a legal precedent providing managers protection from shareholder intervention in corporate decision making.

Between 1989 and 1993, Davis continued his search for a strategic partner. Talks were rumored with network powers such as Capital Cities/ABC and GE's NBC unit, cable provider Tele-Communications, Inc., cable network owner Turner Broadcasting, record producers Geffen Records and Thorn EMI, and foreign media firms such as Bertelsmann AG (Germany) and Phillips Electronics (Holland).

In 1993, Paramount maintained two main operating segments: Entertainment and Publishing. (See Exhibits 2, 5, and 7 for financial and stock data.)

ENTERTAINMENT

Entertainment consisted of Motion Pictures and Television, and Theaters, Sports and Other Entertainment.

MOTION PICTURES AND TELEVISION (50% OF REVENUES). Motion Pictures and Television included Paramount Pictures, Paramount Television, and Paramount Stations Group.

▼ Paramount Pictures produced and distributed motion pictures, constantly adding to an already considerable movie library and creating opportunities for such sequel franchises as the Star Trek and Beverly Hills Cop movies. In 1992, Paramount's estimated market share in motion picture production and distribution was 15%, trailing only Disney and Columbia/TriStar.

▼ Paramount Television produced network television (Cheers, Wings) and syndicated television

---

TABLE A
Selected Transactions of Martin Davis

YEAR	UNIT	PRICE ($M)
Divestitures		
1984	Food Products Segment	$ 201
1985	Consumer & Industrial Products Group	1,000
1989	Associates First Capital Corp.	2,600
Acquisions		
1984	Prentice-Hall, Inc.	$ 710
1985	Ginn & Company	110
1986	Silver Burdett Company	125
1986	Mann Theatres Corp.	220
1989-91	TVX Broadcast Group Inc.	180
1991	Macmillan Computer Publishing	158
1992	Kings Entertainment Company and Kings Island Company	400
1993	WKBD-TV, Detroit	105

Source: Compiled by the authors.

(Star Trek: The Next Generation, Entertainment Tonight) programming.

▼ Paramount Stations Group owned and operated three Fox affiliates and three independent UHF stations which collectively reached 4.9% of U.S. households. This unit also owned 50 percent of the advertiser-supported cable networks, USA Network, and Sci-Fi Channel. USA ranked fourth among advertiser-supported cable networks in terms of 1992 revenues (market share = 12.2%).

THEATERS, SPORTS AND OTHER ENTERTAINMENT (12% OF REVENUES).

Theaters, Sports and Other Entertainment included Famous Music, Madison Square Garden, Paramount Parks, and motion picture theater operations.

▼ Famous Music administered and licensed approximately 100,000 music copyrights and marketed arrangements for recordings, printed editions, films, television, and advertising.

▼ Madison Square Garden operated a 20,000 seat arena, the New York Rangers NHL hockey club, the New York Knickerbockers NBA basketball team, and Madison Square Garden Network—a local cable network broadcasting, among other things, Rangers and Knicks games.

▼ Paramount Parks was comprised of three wholly-owned theme parks in the U.S. and a 20 percent interest in a park in Canada.

▼ Motion picture theater operations owned, or owned through partnership, theater circuits in 12 countries including Cinamerica (382 screens in U.S.) and Famous Players (474 screens in Canada).

PUBLISHING

The Paramount Publishing business segment developed out of a series of acquisitions of independent publishing companies such as Simon & Schuster, Inc. (1975), Esquire, Inc. (1984), Prentice-Hall, Inc. (1984), Ginn & Company (1985), and Silver Burdett Company (1986). The Simon & Schuster unit itself represented the largest book publishing company in the U.S. Education, consumer, business, technical and professional, and international markets were served by the publishing arm.

EDUCATION (18% OF REVENUES). The education segment published textbooks for elementary, secondary and higher education schools, as well as technology-based learning products for all levels.

CONSUMER (9% OF REVENUES). Consumer publishing encompassed hardcover, trade paperback, mass market paperback, travel information (American Express, Frommner's), general reference (J.K. Lasser, Webster's New World Dictionaries) and audiocassettes.

BUSINESS, TECHNICAL AND PROFESSIONAL (7.5% OF REVENUES). This segment offered computer and technical books, and marketed computer software, multimedia training programs, medical textbooks and health care-related material, and on-line legal and accounting information.

INTERNATIONAL (4% OF REVENUES). Paramount published books in the United Kingdom, Australia, and New Zealand and had publishing subsidiaries and partnerships in 24 other countries.

In addition to the current publishing operations, Richard Snyder, the head of publishing operations, was

TABLE B Paramount Communications Operating Cash Flow, 1987–1992 (in millions)	FYE	NET INCOME	DEPRECIATION AND AMORTIZATION	ADJUSTMENTS	OPERATING CASH FLOWS
	10/31/92	$270	$1,038	($1,090)	$218
	10/31/91	122	1,132	(1,169)	84
	10/31/90	259	983	(1,055)	187
	10/31/89	12	685	(635)	62
	10/31/88	385	629	(730)	284
	10/31/87	356	588	(427)	517

Source: Paramount Communications, Inc., *Annual Reports.*

expected to make a bid for Macmillan Publishing Company. Macmillan had been in bankruptcy proceedings following the death of Chairman Robert Maxwell in 1991. The company would be expected to supplement college textbook publishing and increase Paramount's currently low profile in children's books.

In the larger picture of the multimedia industry, Paramount had a significant presence in the software aspect of the business with its production and publishing activities. As the world moved toward the interactive programming era, the question remained as to how important it would be for Paramount to expand distribution segments such as cable channels and local television stations and add hardware segments such as cable systems and telecommunications technology.

VIACOM, INC.

Viacom International, Inc. was established in 1971 from a subsidiary of Columbia Broadcasting System, Inc. ("CBS") after CBS was forced to spin-off its rerun and cable television businesses.* The resulting company syndicated first run shows (What's My Line) from independent producers as well as popular series reruns (Dick Van Dyke, Wild Wild West). In addition, the company operated community antenna television ("CATV") systems in Northern California, Oregon, and Washington.

Viacom built the company initially through the acquisition of cable systems such as Telerama, Inc. and Petra Cablevision Corp. In 1976 Viacom established the Showtime pay-cable network to compete with Home Box Office ("HBO"). Subsequently, it purchased production and broadcast assets such as local television and radio stations.

In 1987, corporate raider Carl Icahn made a hostile takeover bid for Viacom that prompted CEO Terrence Elkes and other top managers to pay $30 million in greenmail and make an LBO attempt of their own. Sumner Redstone's National Amusements, Inc. outbid the management-led LBO team to gain control of Viacom for a price of $3.4 billion, acquiring $2.2 billion of bank debt in the process.

After gaining control of Viacom in 1987, Redstone hired Frank Biondi, Jr. as CEO. Biondi, 48, formerly ran Home Box Office, a pay cable channel. Prior to that, he oversaw Coca-Cola's TV operations

before they were sold to Sony. During his tenure at Viacom, he was known for instituting fiscal controls and methodically paying down debt.

Redstone, 70, owned 76.3 percent of Viacom valued at $6.03 billion as of September 10, 1993. He had maintained a reputation as a shrewd entertainment investor, credited with building a family-owned chain of drive-ins into an 800-screen chain of theaters, National Amusements, Inc.

Another aspect of Redstone's reputation was his tendency to resort to legal proceedings in business dealings. In fact, as recently as late 1989, Viacom and Paramount Pictures were engaged in a legal battle over movie rights.** Two days prior to this lawsuit, Mr. Redstone had sued Time-Warner, Inc. over alleged monopolistic practices which hurt Viacom's Showtime pay-cable network.

Viacom pursued four main lines of business: cable networks, cable systems, entertainment and broadcasting. (See Exhibits 3, 5, and 7 for financial and stock data.)

CABLE NETWORKS

Cable networks comprised 61% of 1993 revenues. MTV: Music Television, Nickelodeon, and VH-1: Video Hits One were wholly-owned, advertising supported, U.S. basic cable services. Viacom also owned interests in Comedy Central and Lifetime networks. Showtime, The Movie Channel and Flix served the premium subscription market. MTV Networks Group, the fastest growing cable television network included 100% ownership of MTV Europe and a revenue-sharing interest in MTV Asia.

CABLE SYSTEMS

Cable television system operations, 21% of 1993 revenues, served 1.1 million subscribers in California, Oregon, Washington, Ohio, and Tennessee that represented approximately 3 percent of the U.S. market. All subscribers received primary service for which they paid a monthly fee. Systems also offered premium cable services that provided customers with access to pay-cable channels such as HBO and Showtime.

ENTERTAINMENT

The entertainment unit, 10% of 1992 revenues, produced and distributed network and syndicated pro-

---

*The U.S. government restricted television networks such as CBS from operating program syndication and cable system businesses simultaneously.

**Paramount Pictures actually sued Viacom over financial obligations owed by Viacom to Paramount for the distribution of movies to the Showtime unit under exclusive distribution agreements.

gramming including such hits as The Cosby Show, A Different World, and Roseanne.

BROADCASTING

Broadcasting, contributing 9% to gross revenues, consisted of five local television stations and 14 radio stations. The radio station group was the fifth largest in the U.S., reaching 22 percent of the population.

Viacom's presence in cable networks was quite significant with combined market share for MTV and Nickelodeon at 14.3 percent in terms of revenue and Showtime holding a 4.4% share of the cable audience. The current trend toward integrated entertainment corporations was not lost on Viacom, which was interested in developing or acquiring valuable assets in two major areas. First, on the software end of the product chain, Viacom invested $100 million per year in production activities (by comparison, Paramount spent $800 million a year on production activities). Second, with the impending advent of interactive television, cable system operators such as Viacom were considering forming alliances with local telephone companies to obtain needed technology. Both of these strategies were expected to play an important role in the proposed 500-channel, interactive video age to come.

QVC NETWORK, INC.

QVC Network, Inc. was a satellite-carried television station specializing in programs that market consumer products. The primary channel reached approximately 41.8 million cable subscribers, about 75% of all cable television homes in the U.S., 94% of whom received programming 24-hours-per-day, seven-days-per-week. A secondary channel reached 6 million cable homes.

The company began part-time programming in late 1986 prior to the 24-hour-per-day, seven-day-per-week schedule initiated on January 1, 1987. From 1988 to 1991, sales grew seven-fold to $776 million.

The company's founder, Joseph Segel, had previously started Franklin Mint Corp., a mail-order marketer of commemorative coins. Ralph Roberts, chairman of Comcast Corporation, a cable system operator, provided some of the seed capital and persuaded other cable operators to carry the QVC programming.

The initials QVC stood for quality, value, and convenience.

▼ Quality, the corporate credo, applied to the program, presentations, products (all come with a 30-day, money-back guarantee) and personnel.
▼ Value resulted from the smaller cost per minute in comparison to traditional commercials and less intensive capital investments than traditional retailers.
▼ Convenience stemmed from pre-scheduled programming and the toll-free number for ordering by telephone.

Two agreements had propelled QVC to become the largest home shopping network. First, the company acquired CVN Companies, Inc. for $464 million in 1989, replacing CVN programming with the QVC Network for the 23 million former CVN subscribers. Second, a 1991 renewable agreement with JC Penney Television Shopping Channel ("JCPTV") provided another 5.9 million cable homes in return for a percentage of net sales from these subscribers.

The programming, produced at the company's West Chester, PA headquarters, consisted of one-hour and multi-hour "program segments." The program segments divided the merchandise offered, jewelry (42% of sales), housewares (12%), apparel (18%), electron-

TABLE C Viacom Operating Cash Flows, 1987–1993 (in millions)	FYE	OPERATING CASH FLOWS
	12/31/93	$148
	12/31/92	102
	12/31/91	55
	12/31/90	99
	12/31/89	132
	12/31/88	111
	12/31/87	214

Source: Viacom, Inc., *Annual Reports.*

ics (9%), collectibles, toys and cosmetics into categories based on products or lifestyles. Each program segment had one or more hosts who described the use, quality, features, and price of products. Viewers used toll-free numbers to order merchandise by major credit card (or private-label credit card offered by the company). In return for carrying its programming, QVC offered local cable operators affiliation agreements that paid out 5% of net sales within their service area.

QVC owned portions of two international ventures, QVC-The Shopping Channel in UK and CVC Telemercado Alameda in Mexico. The former was a joint venture with BSkyB serving UK, Ireland and Europe, while the latter concentrated on Mexico with plans to branch out into other Spanish and Portuguese-speaking markets. Analysts expected these ventures to suffer losses through 1997 and 1995 respectively.

In 1992, Barry Diller made a $25 million investment in QVC concurrently agreeing to become the company's Chairman and CEO. He was recruited by Brian Roberts, President of Comcast (which owns 12.5% of QVC), and son of Ralph Roberts. Liberty Media Corporation, spun off to shareholders of Telecommunications, Inc. ("TCI") in 1991, owns 22% of QVC. The triumvirate of Diller, Comcast and Liberty agreed as of May 1993 to vote their shares as a group, controlling a 47% plurality of the voting shares.

Barry Diller had led a successful career in the entertainment industry. He spent his early career as an ABC programming executive where he is credited with playing a major part in developing such innovations as the "ABC Movie of the Week" and the television miniseries. After leaving ABC, Diller headed the Paramount Pictures unit at Gulf & Western beginning in 1974 and led the studio to some of its most successful years. Diller, in fact, supported Martin Davis for the top spot following the death of Bluhdorn in 1983. Soon thereafter, however, their relationship soured. Apparently, the two held differing opinions as to the party responsible for the success of the studio. Diller was also interested in utilizing the Paramount studio more fully by launching a fourth broadcast network, a venture that Davis considered too risky. In 1984, Diller left Paramount to head News Corp.'s Fox studio where he successfully masterminded the Fox Network.

The idea-driven and creative Diller ended a 10-month, post-Fox job search by taking Roberts' offer to head QVC. He set his sights on taking the $922 million per year home-shopping channel to new heights of programming by positioning the company as a leader in interactivity and possibly entering into the network television market. In his 1992 letter to the shareholders, Diller described his vision,

> When I left Fox a year ago, I knew the world of communications and media was beginning a process of fundamental change. I felt that the television set, the computer, and a conduit thick enough to carry huge loads of pictures and data were going to converge. At that point a true and radical revolution of basic habits would be certain to follow. When I came upon QVC and saw how offer and response, simple and direct interactivity, were already being conducted with sophisticated systems even before the promised tomorrow of these technological breakthroughs, I knew this Company could be at the axis of all that would come, playing a central role in its architecture and development.

Since his arrival, Diller had followed his vision on three fronts. First, in early 1994, he planned to scrap the company's Fashion Channel programming on the secondary channel replacing it with two new offerings: Q2, which targets busy active people by broadcasting on weekends, and On Q, which would target 18 to 35-year-olds during the week. Second, Diller had been discussing a $1.4 billion merger with Home Shopping Network, Inc. ("HSN"). This deal would have not only strengthened the QVC grip on home shopping, but the 12 local network affiliates owned by HSN could have provided a platform from which to launch a fifth network. Lastly, Diller coveted a major production studio such as Paramount from which he could launch interactive movies and programming. He had made no secret of his interest in Paramount especially during his now famous lunch with Martin Davis on July 21, 1993.* (See Exhibits 4 and 7 for financial and stock data.)

MULTIMEDIA INDUSTRY AND COMPETITION

The current spate of entertainment industry merger and acquisition activity was the result of rapidly advancing technology in computer software and hardware, consumer electronics, cable, and telecommunications. The vision in the industry was a future of interactive multimedia that broke down the barriers between content, distribution, and hardware. (See Exhibit 6 for a breakdown of the multimedia assets of players in the Paramount bid.)

---

*Davis invited Diller to lunch that day in the private dining room overlooking Central Park in the 43rd floor executive suite of the Paramount headquarters. Davis informed Diller that Paramount was not for sale and intimated that he was aware of Diller's plans when he said, "I know you're coming after me."

TABLE D	FYE	OPERATING CASH FLOWS
QVC Operating Cash Flows, 1988–1994 (in millions)	01/31/94	$ 73
	01/31/93	101
	01/31/92	137
	01/31/91	21
	01/31/90	40
	01/31/89	7
	01/31/88	(7)

Source: QVC Network, Inc., *Annual Reports.*

Traditionally, content consisted of film production, television production, and writing. The distribution functions included film exhibitors (theaters), broadcast television networks, cable television stations, video/audio recordings and magazine, newspaper and book publishers. Hardware was maintained by cable system operators, electronic manufacturers, telecommunications companies, and local television affiliates.

CONTENT

Film and television producers maintained production studios, chose the scripts and stories to produce, hired actors, actresses, directors, and other staff, and marketed the product. Given the differentiation in this segment of the entertainment industry, these entities had long maintained the power in relationships with distribution and hardware providers.

DISTRIBUTION

Broadcast networks currently included CBS, ABC, NBC, and FOX. Through a network of affiliates, they distributed content "over the air" to licensed affiliates, a reference to the preferred mode of transmission prior to the cable revolution. To the affiliates, networks offered access to content and a national advertising base. The affiliates provided local access and local advertising to the network.

Cable network was actually a misnomer; cable stations would have been a better representation of the situation. Cable stations provided signal to a satellite transponder and, for a fee, licensed local cable operators to transmit the programming to consumers. Cable stations were generically divided into basic stations which were provided to customers at no extra fee with cable service, and pay stations for which cable operators charged a monthly fee. Pay-per-view programs were often distributed by cable stations to viewers who paid a

fee for a one-time viewing. Lastly, traditional movie theaters and video outlets provided distribution services.

HARDWARE

Cable system operators owned plant and equipment consisting of cable, poles, and satellite receivers to physically transmit programming to cable homes. They had to purchase the right to transmit each signal from the individual "over the air" networks, cable stations, pay stations and pay-per-view distributors.

Telecommunications companies had been prohibited from transmitting video to their telephone customers until BellAtlantic challenged that issue in federal court and won the right to do so in their home region. Telecommunications firms were divided into two classes: local telephone carriers and long-distance carriers. Local telephone service, dominated by the seven Baby Bells created out of the break-up of the AT&T monopoly, provided local calling and long-distance service within the service region. Long distance, dominated by AT&T, Sprint, and MCI, provided inter-region and international long-distance service. In recent years, competition had arisen in both markets, leading former Bell companies to branch into other areas such as cellular phone service, computer and network technology, and consulting.

Finally, electronics companies such as Sony and Matsushita researched, developed, and manufactured products to receive video and audio signals from transmitting and recorded technology.

TRENDS

As the 500-channel interactive future loomed, the question of the power distribution between content, distribution, and hardware remained unknown. One thing was certain: video on demand, interactive shopping, and video games played between viewers in dif-

TABLE E
Major Recent Media Transactions
(in millions)

YEAR	BUYER	UNIT SOLD	PRICE (TM)
1993	U.S. West	Time Warner Entertainment (25.5%)	$52,500.0
1990	Matsushita Electric Industrial Co.	MCA, Inc. (Universal Studios)	6,588.8
1989	Time, Inc.	Warner Communications, Inc.	11,650.3
1989	Sony Corporation	Columbia Pictures Entertainment, Inc.	2,989.9
1988	News Corp., Ltd.	Triangle Publications, Inc.	3,000.0
1988	Maxwell Cornmunications	Macmillan, Inc.	2,334.6
1988	Sony Corporation	CBS Records	2,000.0
1986	Capital Cities Communications	ABC	3,517.0
1986	General Electric Company	RCA Corp. (NBC)	6,460.0
1985	News Corp., Ltd.	20th Century Fox Film Corp.	575.0

Source: Compiled by authors.

ferent locations would require additional development and combinations of technology.

As such, telecommunications companies and cable operators rushed to form alliances to merge high speed switching technology with cable systems capable of carrying video signals. Production studios allied with electronics companies, theaters, broadcast affiliates, and cable stations. Cable operators increasingly owned cable stations. The whole industry seemed to be driven by an urge to combine the entire product chain from production to distribution to hardware to consumer as a hedge against future developments. (See Table E for a summary of recent major multimedia transactions.)

THE VIACOM-PARAMOUNT MERGER

On September 12, 1993, Viacom announced that it would acquire Paramount for $8.2 billion. The bid provided $9.10 in cash, 0.1 shares of Viacom Class A common stock (which closed on October 10 at a price of $66 per share), and 0.9 shares of Viacom Class B common stock ($59 3/8 per share) for each of the 118.5 million shares of Paramount. Viacom intended to finance the deal using $1.5 billion worth of bank debt. (See Exhibit 1 for a timeline of events.)

The deal culminated four years of merger discussions for Martin Davis following his failure to break up the Time-Warner merger in 1989. For Redstone and Viacom, it represented access to the programming assets of the last independent Hollywood studio other than Disney. The two CEOs had met numerous times in the past to discuss merging their companies but talks had always broken down over Davis' two sticking points: control and value. Negotiations in the past summer placed Davis in a position to become the CEO of the merged company, but he had refused to accept an offer of less than $70/share for Paramount common stock.

The agreement valued Paramount at $69.14/share. Davis and Redstone tried to discourage other bids by installing a lock-up agreement to supplement the current poison pill provision already in place at Paramount.

The so-called lock-up agreement had two main features. The first, triggered by any rival bid, allowed Viacom to purchase 24 million newly-issued Paramount shares at $69.14. The second, resulting from a successful hostile bid, required Paramount to pay a cash settlement of $100 million to Viacom.

Mario Gabelli, the owner of Gabelli Funds, a major institutional shareholder of both companies, said of the deal, "It's a logical deal with terrific synergies, and one plus one equals two and a half with Viacom and Paramount." The merger seemed to offer the two companies ample opportunity to combine their assets and create lines of business such as a broadcast network, new cable channels, cross fertilizing themes for movie production, and maybe even interactive television.

DILLER'S HOSTILE OFFER

Eight days later, on September 20, Barry Diller confirmed Wall Street's expectations that another bidder would emerge. QVC's bid of $80 per share consisted of considerably more cash (at $30 per share) than the Viacom offer. The rest of the proposal provided 0.893 shares of QVC common stock that currently traded at $56/share on NASDAQ. The total package reached $9.5 billion, or $80/share, topping Viacom by almost $17/share and $2 billion in total. (See Exhibits

8 and 9 for a graphic of share prices and estimated bid values over time.)

Industry insiders and Wall Street analysts speculated that Diller's bid was an attempt to wrest control from his rival Davis. Mr. Diller's reaction: "Our proposal had no emotional aspect, other than the fondness I have for the 10 years I spent at Paramount."

Diller lined up investments of $500 million apiece from Comcast and Liberty Media. Each agreed to purchase $500 million worth of QVC convertible preferred stock at $65.45 which would pay an initial dividend of 6.5% and later switch to 7.5%. The security is convertible to QVC common stock when that stock reaches $100/share.

The following day, September 21, in trading on the American Stock Exchange ("AMEX"), Viacom's Class A shares fell 4.22% on news that another bidder had entered the battle. In NASDAQ trading, QVC's stock showed a modest increase of 12.5¢. Over the previous three trading days, however, QVC had shown a 10.76 percent decline in price.

Paramount's shares, meanwhile, surged by more than 10% rising $7.25 to $77 in trading on the NYSE. At this point, it is worth noting that if Redstone decided to exit the bidding process, he could realize a profit of approximately $366 million. That sum would be the result of exercising the lock-up agreement between Viacom and Paramount which would pay Viacom $100 million in cash and purchasing 24.5 million shares of Paramount at $69.14 which Redstone could then sell to QVC for $80/share.

Whatever the interpretation of the equity markets, Redstone vowed not to change his offer for Paramount based on the principle that Viacom offered the greater synergies and therefore long-term value to Paramount shareholders.

Rather, Redstone and Davis responded in two other ways. First, they denigrated the value of QVC as a strategic partner for Paramount and questioned whether QVC had financing.* Another provision of the Viacom-Paramount merger agreement restricted Paramount from holding merger discussions with a party that had "material contingencies related to financing."

Second, Viacom filed an antitrust lawsuit against QVC, Liberty Media and TCI on September 23. The suit alleged the following:

---

*Redstone was quoted as saying, "In our meetings we talk about the obvious strategic advantages of putting Paramount together with a global media company like Viacom against the advantage of QVC, which is essentially a shopping channel."

The QVC bid. . . "would be but the latest step in a systematic and broad-ranging conspiracy to monopolize the American cable industry. In the American cable industry, one man has . . . seized monopoly power. Using bully-boy tactics and strong-arming of competitors, suppliers and customers, that man has inflicted antitrust injury on . . . virtually every American consumer of cable services and technologies. That man is John C. Malone."

The suit further alleged that without the subscribers to the TCI cable systems, programmers cannot gain "critical mass." Lastly, the complaint explained that TCI has refused to renegotiate with Viacom's Showtime and Movie Channel units programming agreements that had lapsed earlier in the year. This allegedly was a tactic by TCI to force Showtime to merge with Liberty Media's Encore pay cable station.

JOHN C. MALONE AND TCI

The lawsuit placed much more emphasis on Mr. Malone's participation in the cable industry than it did on Mr. Diller. The CEO of TCI and Chairman of Liberty Media has been called the "king of cable" for his strong arm tactics with competitors and suppliers. These practices even led Vice President Al Gore during his days as a Tennessee Senator to refer to Malone as "the ringleader of the cable Cosa Nostra."

As CEO, Malone was known for three things:

▼ His ability to convince the financial community, including commercial and investment bankers, that the negative earnings and high leverage of cable companies [were] not as important as healthy cash flows.

▼ Consummating intricate, innovative transactions such as the series of transactions between TCI and related companies that concentrated super-voting shares of TCI in the hands of Malone and Bob Magness, Chairman of TCI.

▼ A reputation for anticompetitive behavior with regulators, competitors, and customers. Foremost among these controversies, from the standpoint of Viacom, was the 1990 purchase of Financial News Network by 49% TCI-owned Discovery Channel after another bidder, Viacom's Learning Channel, was forced to abandon its bid when TCI removed Learning Channel from its cable systems. Regulators have clashed with him over rates, TCI's entry into the satellite business, and TCI's ownership of cable television stations.

TCI is the largest multi-system cable operator ("MSO") in the U.S. reaching more than 10 million of the nation's 60 million cable homes and producing a cash flow of $1.1 billion in 1993 from sales of $4 billion.

The company owns 23% of Turner Broadcasting System, Inc., making TCI the second largest shareholder after Ted Turner's 51%. The interest resulted from TCI's role in the bailout of CNN, TNT, and TBS. TCI also holds a controlling interest in Home Shopping Network and shares ownership of Asia Business News (Singapore) and Pte. Ltd.

In 1991, the company spun-off Liberty Media Corporation to shareholders to defuse criticism in Washington. Malone maintained the lion's share of his personal wealth in controlling over 50% of Liberty's shares valued at almost $700 million and served as the Chairman of the Board. Liberty held stakes in many cable channels including Discovery Channel, Turner Broadcasting, Black Entertainment Network, Family Channel, and American Movie Classics. In addition, Liberty owned 90% of Encore which was launched in 1991 by TCI. Liberty also served as one of the three controlling partners of QVC. (See Exhibit 10.)

Observers believed Viacom and Paramount had ample reason to target Malone in the lawsuit. In 1989, Malone and TCI offered $70/share to acquire Paramount. In addition, earlier in September 1993, TCI announced plans to launch a hybrid music-video and home shopping channel with Bertelsmann Music Group which would compete with Viacom's MTV and VH-1. Malone, however, continually denied playing a large role in the Paramount merger, characterizing Liberty as a passive investor in QVC.

QVC Delivers Financing

Paramount refused to discuss the QVC offer without evidence of financing and downplayed the strategic fit between the two firms. Davis said, "Consistent with our legal obligations we will consider the QVC bid if and when we have satisfactory evidence of financing . . . if we ever get into QVC discussions, we will have other big concerns that go beyond the issues of financing."

The next day, September 29, Chemical Bank agreed to supply $800 million to $1 billion in financing for QVC and obtain the remainder of the $3 billion financing effort from other lenders. On October 6, Herbert Allen of Allen & Co., the QVC investment bank, presented Felix Rohatyn of Lazard Freres & Co. with the bank commitments. However, although the

Paramount directors authorized "informational discussions" with QVC on October 11, formal negotiations were not offered.

Institutional holders of Paramount viewed things differently. Many felt that Davis had put Paramount "in play" by agreeing to be acquired by Viacom. Guy Wyser-Pratte, whose firm owns over 100,000 Paramount shares said, "Once they had the financing delivered by QVC, I believe Paramount had a responsibility to declare themselves in an auction mode. I can assure you we will assemble a posse if they continue to forestall putting themselves up for sale."

Viacom Adds Partners

Although Sumner Redstone continued to deny any intention to sweeten his offer for Paramount, he lined up investments from Blockbuster Entertainment Corporation and NYNEX.

On September 29, Chairman H. Wayne Huizenga of Blockbuster agreed to purchase for $70/share preferred stock convertible to Viacom Class B common shares. The total investment of $600 million will pay a dividend of 5% and would be redeemable in 5 years.

Blockbuster was interested in reducing its dependence on home video retailing and rental, the very business which mergers like Viacom-Paramount could jeopardize by offering interactive home video featuring video-on-demand services. Home video provides 85% of Blockbuster's operating profits. Recently, they had navigated a course to diversify the firm's entertainment holdings. The company owned 70% of Spelling Entertainment, a production studio which purchased Republic Pictures for $100 million earlier in September. Blockbuster also owned Sound Warehouse and Music Plus music chains.

Blockbuster, which had been negotiating with QVC prior to the agreement with Viacom, would be entitled to a seat on the Viacom board.

The following Monday, October 4, NYNEX Corporation also agreed to purchase convertible preferred Viacom stock for $70/share. The NYNEX investment of $1.2 billion did not include a management role for the firm. Viacom would, however, provide NYNEX with a 24-month period during which it would not deal with any other local telephone companies and NYNEX would work to provide an interactive video/voice network to Viacom customers.

New York City and Boston, the two major service areas of NYNEX, had large customer bases providing rival, non-Baby Bell local telephone providers with a fertile ground for competing with NYNEX. The alliance with Viacom gave them the opportunity to diversify by "learning" entertainment and having access to content such as Viacom programming. As William Ferguson, the Chairman, said, "Our intent is to have a multimedia broadband interactive network. . . . It is important that we have a relationship with a content provider that helps to fill out the strategic portfolio."

Redstone, however, stuck to his guns by touting both deals as long-term strategic alliances with no relation to financing the Paramount bid: "This press conference isn't about Paramount-Viacom. What you see today and in connection with Blockbuster isn't about money. This is about picking the right strategic partner." The deal with Blockbuster, however, contained a provision allowing either party to cut in half the Blockbuster investment if the Viacom-Paramount merger had not been completed by August 1994. The investments, totaling $1.8 billion, would allow Viacom to increase the cash portion of the bid by more than $15 per Paramount share if they wished.

MALONE DROPS TWO BOMBS

As QVC and Viacom worked on financing, TCI announced two major transactions within one week. The first had TCI reacquiring Liberty Media and the second involved BellAtlantic acquiring TCI.

The October 7 news that TCI would acquire Liberty Media in a $3.8 billion stock swap came in response to more lenient than expected FCC regulations limiting vertical integration. Publicly Malone touted that the deal was necessary for TCI to remain a powerful player amid the media consolidations. However, analysts noted that the $100 million preliminary loss still expected from the Encore unit would be buried in the financial statements of the combined firm.

Three business days later, Malone announced a stock swap with BellAtlantic valuing TCI at $35/share or $16 billion. Malone and Raymond Smith, Chairman of BellAtlantic, said they planned to pursue the interactive video future as co-chairmen of the $33 billion combined company on which TCI would hold five of the 15 board seats.

Barry Diller expressed surprise when informed about the BellAtlantic-TCI deal. Malone, for his part, emphasized that the QVC bid for Paramount was "peripheral to" the BellAtlantic-TCI pact. He stated that the outcome of the Paramount situation was not "central to or a core part of the BellAtlantic or TCI strategy."

DILLER'S TENDER OFFER

During the week of October 17, Diller showed that QVC was firmly in command of its own offer by lining up additional equity financing by Monday, delivering a proposed acquisition agreement to Paramount on Wednesday, and changing his bid to a tender offer on Thursday.

The additional financing came from two privately held companies, Cox Enterprises, Inc. and Advance Publications, Inc. Cox, based in Atlanta, owned newspaper and cable system assets. Advance also ran newspaper and cable systems in addition to Random House book publishing and the Conde Nast magazine company.

The terms of the prior agreements with Liberty Media and Comcast were modified such that all four $500 million investments were identical. Each would purchase $250 million of QVC common stock at $60/share and $250 million of convertible exchangeable preferred stock with a 6% dividend to be paid in cash or QVC common stock. The preferred stock was convertible at $65.45 per common share. If the QVC-Paramount deal did not go through, Cox and Advance had the option to invest $100 million in QVC common at $60/share.

Diller spent time with analysts touting his plans for Paramount, where he was openly critical of their current management. He suggested he might manage Paramount's assets by:

▼ Selling Paramount's TV stations and theme-park business.
▼ Increasing the number of films produced by the studio while lowering the costs of production. He was critical of the number of big budget films produced in recent years.
▼ Forming a new TV broadcast network without using the current affiliates owned by Paramount.
▼ Developing interactive programming like Betty Crocker cookbooks, Frommer travel books, and J. K. Lasser Tax guides.

Diller delivered the acquisition proposal to Paramount on Wednesday. It was nearly identical to that of Viacom, excluding the breakup fee and the lock-up provision. However, traders complained that QVC took too long to deliver the documents to Paramount and that Viacom would soon win government approval to purchase Paramount shares. That same day, QVC also had a board meeting at which they considered their options: (1) litigation against Paramount and Viacom and (2) a cash tender offer.

The board chose to do both. First, it launched a tender offer the next day, accelerating government approval of certain aspects of the deal and boosting shareholder pressure on Paramount's board. Second, QVC filed a lawsuit in a Delaware court to invalidate the lock-up agreement in the Viacom-Paramount deal. This was important because the Paramount board was still unwilling to consider QVC's offer, and in addition, until the poison pill provision was dropped, QVC could not purchase any Paramount stock.

The $9.5 billion tender offer was essentially the same as QVC's earlier bid, topping Viacom's bid by almost $2 billion. It involved a two-tier offer under which QVC would tender $80/share for the first 51% of the Paramount shares and pay for the remaining portion with QVC stock valued at $80.71/share. Observers noted the irony in Martin Lipton, an attorney from the Wall Street firm of Wachtell, Lipton, Rosen & Katz, providing legal advice for QVC in light of his 1980s condemnations of tender offers as coercive to shareholders. Diller implied that he had no choice, "What underlies our decision to commence a tender offer and what has been obscured over the last few weeks is the significant differential between the total value and cash portions of the QVC and Viacom offers."

It appears that QVC's tender offer occurred just in time as the Justice Department gave antitrust clearance to the Viacom-Paramount agreement the same day.

REDSTONE'S COUNTER TENDER OFFER

On October 22, Sumner Redstone's hand was forced by Diller's tender offer. He finally raised the total value of his bid and changed the structure to match that of QVC.* Viacom management was confident that matching QVC's bid resulted in a superior offer not only because of the perceived better strategic fit, but also because of the promise of a quicker payoff for shareholders given that Viacom had already successfully cleared several regulatory and antitrust hurdles.

In addition, the QVC offer had dropped to an average value of $79.30 per share thanks to a $1.50/share drop in the price of QVC common stock. Thus, the $80/share two-step offer of Viacom actually exceeded the total value of the QVC bid.**

Martin Davis issued a statement regarding the bids, "We believe that the revised merger with Viacom represents superior long-term value to our stockholders." As a result, it appeared that Diller would get no respite from the Paramount board. In addition, the Viacom offer was scheduled to expire on November 22,

before QVC's November 24 deadline. It now seemed that Diller's options were to once again raise his bid or to pursue further litigation.

On October 29, Diller chose to step up the legal pressure on Paramount by revising the QVC lawsuit against Paramount. The changes were intended to block Viacom's bid until QVC received regulatory approval for a merger with Paramount. In addition, the new allegations took issue with Paramount's poison-pill defense and the board's consideration of an amended Viacom offer while refusing to negotiate with QVC. The court date was set for November 16.

VIACOM SWEETENS BID

After receiving bank commitments for $4.5 billion in financing on November 3, Viacom increased its bid by $5 per share to $85/share in cash for 51% of the Paramount shares. The increased financing protected Viacom with a $1 billion bridge loan should regulatory matters delay the NYNEX investment. Viacom's offer would expire on November 22.

QVC SWEETENS BID

As the week before the court date came to a close, the QVC camp added a major investor, lost a major investor, and increased its offer for Paramount.

BellSouth agreed on Thursday, November 11 to invest $1.5 billion in QVC through a combination of common and preferred stock. The investment involved first purchasing $1 billion in newly issued common stock and then replacing the $500 million investment of Liberty Media (Table F).

The result is that Liberty would completely divest its 14% stake by selling the shares on the open market. This would have the added benefit of circumventing the antitrust issues that had been dogging the Liberty-QVC camp for the past two months. The BellSouth deal was contingent upon a QVC-Paramount merger: the agreement called for Liberty to maintain its stake

---

*The details of the bid include $80/share in cash for 51% of the Paramount shares followed by a package of securities for the remaining 49%. For each Paramount share, the package contains 0.204 Class A shares, 1.083 non-voting Class B shares, and 0.204 convertible exchangeable preferred shares.

**The announced value was also inflated because Paramount chose to include unexercised Paramount stock options in the valuation of Viacom's offer. The additional 6 million outstanding Paramount options raised the total number of shares to 124.5 million. Applying this method to both offers resulted in a total value of approximately $10 billion.

TABLE F
Allies in the Bidding Contest

ALLY	PRIMARY BUSINESS	INVESTMENT
VIACOM		
Blockbuster Entertainment	Home video retailing	$600 million
NYNEX	Telecommunications	$1.2 billion
QVC NETWORK		
Comcast	Cable system operator	$500 million
Cox Enterprises	Cable system operator	$500 million
Advance Publications	Publisher	$500 million
BellSouth	Telecommunications	$1.5 billion

Source: Compiled by the authors.

and for BellSouth to pare its investment to $500 million if the Paramount deal fell through.

After QVC restructured its financial backing, on November 12 it revised its tender offer by adding $1.2 billion in cash. The new offer not only increased the cash portion by $10 to $90/share, but changed the composition of the back-end to a combination of common and preferred QVC stock valued at $76.92 per Paramount share for the final 49% of the shares. The bid was valued at $10.5 billion, and was set to expire on November 26.

The following day the Paramount directors again rejected the QVC bid saying that it was too conditional due to legal and financial contingencies. The real test of the QVC bid, however, was not to be decided at present by the Paramount board of directors but by the Delaware Chancery Court and Chancellor Jack Jacobs.

RULING AGAINST PARAMOUNT

On November 16, the battle between Paramount attorney Barry Ostrager and QVC attorney Herbert Wachtell began. Two previous rulings set the legal precedents in this case. The first is a ruling made by the Delaware Supreme Court in 1986 in relation to a hostile bid by Ronald Perleman to acquire Revlon, Inc. The "Revlon rule" states that once a company puts itself up for sale, it is obligated to open up the bidding process to the highest price. The second ruling, "the business judgment rule" was also made in a Delaware court of law, and stems from the Time-Warner litigation that allowed Time's board to reject a more generous bid from Paramount in favor of a strategic merger with Warner Brothers Communications.

Ostrager and an attorney for Viacom defined .the transaction between Viacom and Paramount as a strategic merger that would maximize long-term share-

holder value. Therefore, the directors were not obligated to auction Paramount. This argument is notable in that it is the polar opposite of the Paramount argument in the Time-Warner case that shareholders deserve to receive the highest-priced offer. In addition, the Paramount group argued that the lock up provisions provided incentive for Viacom to enter into the agreement.

Wachtell defined the transaction as a sale, but concentrated on Davis' motive for making the agreement when he did. He pointed to the years of merger negotiations between Viacom and Paramount that broke down because of Davis' dissatisfaction with the value placed on Paramount and the management of the merged entity. He used deposition testimony by Davis describing the July lunch with Diller at the Paramount headquarters where the Paramount chairman told Diller, "I know you're coming after me." Wachtell argued that a merger was finally agreed upon and the lock-up provisions were added to prevent Diller and other rivals from making a bid.

Given the current four day timing advantage of Viacom, the unknown status of the court's decision, and the November 22 deadline for the Viacom tender offer, QVC made an effort to influence the Paramount board and shareholders. This came as a Saturday, November 20, announcement that QVC had obtained bank financing for its revised tender offer.

Over the weekend, the Paramount board postponed considering the QVC offer until a 9:30 a.m. conference call with Judge Jacobs on Monday. Paramount still pointed to contingencies in the QVC bid, but a frustrated Diller identified the only contingencies as the lock-up agreement of which Paramount had full control. During the conference call, Jacobs asked both parties to extend their offers by two business days until he made his ruling.

The results of the conference call satisfied the QVC camp that Paramount shareholders would not tender their shares to Viacom without knowing the ruling of the Chancery Court. Most shareholders seemed to prefer the lower Viacom offer due to the uncertainty surrounding the QVC bid which may or may not have been caused by the statements of the Paramount directors.

Thanksgiving week brought many changes to Paramount. On the same day that the judge delayed his ruling, Paramount stock was removed from the Standard & Poor's 500 stock index. As a result, because index funds were expected to sell, traders hoped to purchase Paramount at a depressed price near the end of the trading day. Too many traders had the same idea sending the stock soaring to a $79 price at the close of NYSE trading. On Tuesday, the FCC approved both the Viacom and QVC bids allowing either to purchase the shares tendered to them. The shares had to be placed in a voting trust, however, until the FCC completed a longer formal review. To date, Viacom had received 12.7 million shares compared to less than 250,000 for QVC.

Wednesday, November 24, the day before Thanksgiving, Vice Chancellor Jacobs ruled that Paramount's board had acted improperly in rejecting the QVC bid. The ruling termed the Viacom-Paramount transaction as a sale rather than a strategic merger. The key factor in this judgment was that majority ownership of Paramount would pass to one individual, Sumner Redstone. Therefore, this transaction represented the only opportunity for shareholders to receive a takeover premium for their shares based on voting privileges.* This also constituted a broader definition of sale, and restricted the board's use of the business judgment rule to determine superior long-term shareholder value. Using the Revlon precedent for a sale, the directors were obliged to follow the "Revlon rule" and put the company up for auction to any bidder.

The decision interpreted the lock-up agreement as a breach of the Paramount directors' fiduciary duty because it discouraged other bidders. However, the $100 million break-up fee was upheld because of its relatively small size in relation to the entire transaction.

The judge also criticized Martin Davis, the Paramount directors, and the Wall Street law firm representing Paramount, Simpson Thatcher & Bartlett. Davis used "skillful advocacy" to convince the board not to explore the QVC offer. He felt that the board did not completely evaluate options in the shareholders' best interest. He also criticized a legal opinion of Simpson Thatcher & Bartlett concluding that the Viacom-Paramount merger barred Paramount from negotiating with QVC. (See Exhibit 11 for a list of the Paramount board of directors.)

On Friday, both Viacom and QVC agreed to freeze their bids until the Delaware Supreme Court ruled on Viacom's appeal of the Chancery Court decision.

SUPREME COURT RATIFICATION: PARAMOUNT FOR SALE

On December 9, the Delaware Supreme Court upheld the decision of the Chancery Court. Judge Veasey concurred with the lower court's condemnation of the Paramount directors, the no-shop clause, and the lock-up option while stating that he would have invalidated the $100 million break-up fee if QVC had challenged it.

The following Tuesday (December 14), the Paramount directors presented the procedure they would follow for the auction of Paramount. First, the company agreed to drop the poison-pill antitakeover device for the first bidder to draw 51 % of the shares. Second, in an effort to eliminate the coercive nature of a two-step tender offer, the directors required that the winning bidder leave its offer open for 10 days after acquiring the majority of the shares. In this way, shareholders would have the opportunity to withdraw shares tendered to the losing bidder and resubmit to the winner. Third, the board would not necessarily choose the bid with the highest current market value, concentrating also on the growth prospects of the combined entity and on any stock price protection offered by the bidder. Fourth, Davis convinced the board not to form a special committee of outside directors to consider the bid. And finally, even though the court did not specifically throw out the $100 million break-up fee, Paramount agreed not to make the payment should Viacom cease bidding. Bids were due on Monday, December 20, and the bidding process would proceed until February 1, if necessary.

On the same day, Paramount announced a 5.5% drop in second-quarter fiscal earnings. While publishing posted record profits, entertainment earnings sagged almost 19% from the previous year.

THE DECEMBER 20 DEADLINE

On December 20 QVC presented a revised proposal to Paramount that increased the cash portion of the two-step offer to $92/share for 51% of the shares.

---

*Typically, in takeover situations, investors receive a premium for their shares.

The back-end consisted of 1.43 QVC common shares, regular preferred stock with a dividend of 6% compared to the previous offer of convertible preferred stock paying a dividend of 5%, and warrants for the right to buy QVC shares at $70.34. QVC insiders considered the $2/share increase in cash roughly equal to the funds previously budgeted for the $100 million breakup fee.

In response, Viacom asked for more time as Redstone negotiated further investments in his corporation. Diller's response was to gain assurance from the Paramount board that QVC would be permitted to make another sweetened offer should Viacom raise its own at some later date.

On Wednesday, December 22, the Paramount directors agreed to be acquired by QVC advising shareholders to tender shares to QVC over Viacom. Under the rules, the QVC offer must remain open for 10 business days, or until January 7. The announcement set off a flurry of activity on Wall Street as QVC shares fell $1.75 on NASDAQ before trading was halted. Viacom Class B shares initially jumped $4 on AMEX on rumors that the battle was over. The drop in the value of QVC shares underscored a five-day period of trading over the winter holidays where Paramount shares slid 5% and QVC plummeted by 12.9% causing the value of its offer to fall to within $200 million of the Viacom offer.

VIACOM AND BLOCKBUSTER

Finally, on Wednesday of the final week of the year, there was news that Viacom might be making a move. The newspapers reported that Blockbuster had filed with the SEC to triple its credit line under the agreement to $1 billion, signaling the possibility of an enhanced investment in Viacom.

On the deadline for Diller's tender offer, January 7, Viacom agreed to acquire Blockbuster for $8.4 billion, or $31/share in Viacom securities. Blockbuster also agreed to purchase 23 million shares of Viacom Class B stock for $55/share. This turn of events could presumably allow Viacom to obtain financing from the balance sheet of Blockbuster, which contains $1.25 billion in cash, to increase the Paramount bid.

Viacom followed up the Blockbuster deal with a new bid for Paramount that increased the per-share cash price to $105 from $85 while decreasing the percentage of shares to 50.1% from 51%. The new back-end decreased in value by almost $18/share, however, as Viacom removed Class A shares from the package and decreased the number of Class B shares. The result was that the new offer was valued at only $78.36/share

or $9.4 billion. Buoyed by a 5% increase in QVC common stock, Diller's deal now had a total value of $82.49/share, or $9.9 billion. Despite this, most of the 28% of Paramount shares already tendered to QVC by this point were withdrawn on the news that Viacom was still participating in the bidding.

The other new feature of Viacom's first postlitigation bid was the absence of Martin Davis in the management plans for the combined entity. Redstone and Viacom planned to hand the CEO reins to Frank Biondi following the transaction.

QVC immediately claimed that Viacom had violated the rules of the auction by revising its offer without increasing the value. On January 12, the Paramount directors rejected the Viacom offer but stopped short of specifically addressing Viacom's compliance with the rules of the bidding process.

The following day, however, Paramount issued a statement clarifying the rules and indicated that February 1 was the deadline for the "highest and final bids" including both tiers of the proposals.

VIACOM ADDS A COLLAR

On January 18, Viacom used a new weapon to increase the desirability of its offer. The "collar," which provides downside protection if Viacom Class B shares traded below $48/share one year after the acquisition, came in the form of a contingent value right, or CVR. The CVR was a derivative security incorporating two partially offsetting put options on Viacom B shares.

The new proposal also provided $2/share more in cash, resulting in $107/share for 50.1% of the shares. The complete back-end contained 0.93065 shares of Class B stock, Viacom preferred stock, a three-year warrant to purchase Viacom stock at $60/share, and the CVR.

Although the bid was valued at only $9.7 billion compared to the current market value of $10.1 for the QVC offer, evidence quickly mounted that current market value was not the only way to judge the offer. While QVC dismissed the lower offer, many Wall Street traders indicated that under the current situation, they would tender their shares to Viacom due to the downside protection. The stock market seemed to reflect this as Viacom Class A shares fell 4% on January 18. Paramount directors also endorsed the Viacom offer stating that it provided "marginally superior" value to shareholders.

Diller's response was threefold. First, he extended his current offer through January 31 to match the most recent Viacom offer. Second, he visited analysts to drum up support for his offer (and was told to reduce the dependence of his offer on the whims of the stock market). Third, he scheduled a board meeting for January 31 to discuss QVC's final offer, an action that persuaded a majority of shareholders, now mostly takeover arbitrageurs, not to tender to Viacom in anticipation of final-day bid increases.

THE FINAL DEADLINE

As Barry Diller convened the QVC board, he knew that the takeover battle was at a critical juncture. The next day, February 1, was the deadline for final bids. Looking out his own office window, Sumner Redstone also knew the next 24 hours were crucial. As the deadline approached, Diller and Redstone faced many issues.

Among those facing Diller:

▼ Should he place some sort of collar on the back-end of his offer?

▼ Should he raise the cash in his offer?

▼ Did he need additional partners? Would this require giving up too much power?

▼ Was there really a strategic fit between his loosely-knit alliance of cable, publishing, telecommunications, and programming interests, his own expertise as a media executive, and Paramount? How would he be able to integrate the new entity?

▼ What other tactics might influence investors to tender shares to QVC?

▼ Was Paramount worth the cash? Would the fixed income payments be too much to handle?

Redstone faced similar issues:

▼ Was Paramount worth the cash? Would the fixed income payments be too much for Viacom to handle?

▼ How would he turn around the performance of the Paramount studio?

▼ Who should be the CEO of the merged company? What to do with Martin Davis?

▼ What tactics can he use to influence investors to tender to Viacom?

In addition, there were more general issues:

▼ Is either offer a good deal? For Paramount? For the bidders?

▼ What is the definition of a good deal?

▼ Who are the winners? Who are the losers?

EXHIBIT 1
Major Events in the
Paramount Deal

TIMELINE

9/12/93 Viacom agrees to acquire Paramount for $8.2B. The $69.14/share bid includes $9.10/share in cash.

9/20/93 QVC offers $9.5B for Paramount in a hostile bid. The $80/share includes $30 in cash and 0.893 shares of QVC common stock currently trading at $56/share. Comcast and Liberty each agree to invest $500M in QVC convertible preferred stock.

9/23/93 Viacom files an antitrust lawsuit against QVC, Liberty and TCI that singles out John Malone as causing injury to Viacom and consumers of cable services.

9/29/93 Blockbuster agrees to buy Viacom convertible preferred stock for a total investment of $600M. The agreement allows either party to cut the investment in half if the Paramount-Viacom deal does not go through by August 1994.

10/04/93 NYNEX agrees to invest $1.2B in Viacom by purchasing convertible preferred stock.

10/17/93 Cox Enterprises, Inc. and Advance Publications, Inc. agree to invest in QVC on the same terms as Comcast and Liberty Media.

10/21/93 QVC announces a tender offer consisting of $80 cash for 51% of Paramount shares and QVC stock for the remainder.

10/22/93 Viacom announces a tender offer of $80 cash for 51% and a package of securities for the remainder.

11/06/93 Viacom increases its bid by $5 per share to $85/share for 51%.

11/10/93 Paramount wins the bankruptcy auction for Macmillan with a bid of $552.8 million.

11/11/93 BellSouth agrees to invest $1.5B in QVC. The Baby Bell pays $1B for new common stock and replaces the $500M investment of Liberty for a 14% stake and Liberty's place in the three-way partnership that controls QVC. Liberty agrees to divest its stake.

11/12/93 QVC increases offer to $90/share for 51% and a package of securities for the remainder.

11/24/93 Delaware Chancery Court judge Jack Jacobs rules that the deal with Viacom amounts to a sale of Paramount. In addition, he throws out the lock-up option and barred Paramount from dropping the poison pill for Viacom and not QVC.

12/09/93 The Delaware Supreme Court upholds the decision of the Chancery Court.

12/14/93 Paramount puts itself up for auction to "all present and prospective bidders" with bids due on December 20.

12/20/93 QVC increases its bid to $92 cash for 51% of Paramount shares.

12/21/93 Viacom requests time to submit a higher offer.

12/22/93 Paramount agrees to be acquired by QVC.

1/07/94 Viacom increases the cash offer for Paramount to $105/share for 50.1% but decreases the back-end from $69.40/share to $51.66/share. Viacom agrees to acquire Blockbuster for $8.4B.

1/12/94 Paramount directors reject the revised Viacom offer stating that QVC's offer "represents the best value available to Paramount shareholders."

1/18/94 Viacom revises its offer to $107/share for 50.1% of the shares and a combination of four securities for the remaining 49.9%. The deal includes a "collar" provision protecting Paramount shareholders.

1/23/94 Paramount directors endorse the Viacom bid as marginally superior to the QVC bid.

1/31/94 QVC's offer is scheduled to expire.

Source: Compiled by authors.

EXHIBIT 2
Financial Statements of
Paramount
Communications Inc.

BALANCE SHEET	6 MONTHS 04/30/93	FISCAL YEAR ENDING: 10/31/92	10/31/91
ASSETS (000$)			
Cash	$372,600	$324,300	$555,300
Marketable securities	569,700	912,000	1,020,700
Receivables	829,600	972,900	904,100
Inventories	617,300	580,200	590,400
Other current assets	531,900	482,400	523,300
Total current assets	2,921,100	3,271,800	3,593,800
Property, plant & equipment	1,409,100	1,374,800	1,026,300
Accumulated depreciation	336,100	315,500	268,200
Net property & equipment	1,073,000	1,059,300	758,100
Investment in affiliates	243,900	228,900	204,400
Other current assets	689,800	604,700	483,000
Deferred charges	429,500	364,200	376,100
Intangibles	1,517,500	1,528,100	1,239,300
Total assets	**$6,874,800**	**$7,057,000**	**$6,654,700**
LIABILITIES (000$)			
Accounts payable	$194,700	$143,700	$119,800
Current long-term debt	109,800	10,000	198,300
Accrued expenses	1,128,400	1,114,100	1,002,500
Income taxes payable	26,600	139,200	131,400
Total current liabilities	1,459,500	1,407,000	1,452,000
Deferred charges	805,900	822,400	828,000
Long-term debt	707,300	812,100	519,900
Total liabilities	2,972,700	3,041,500	2,799,900
Common stock, net	118,200	117,500	117,800
Capital surplus	712,800	665,700	629,500
Retained earnings	3,082,500	3,228,600	3,096,400
Other equities	(11,400)	3,700	11,100
Shareholder equity	3,902,100	4,015,500	3,854,800
Total liabilities & net worth	**$6,874,800**	**$7,057,000**	**$6,654,700**
INCOME STATEMENT(000$)			
Net sales	$1,898,100	$4,264,898	$3,895,400
Cost of goods sold	1,286,800	2,739,800	2,638,700
SG&A expense	621,400	1,129,000	1,098,900
Operating income	(10,100)	396,098	157,800
Other income (expense)	41,200	120,000	145,100
Interest expense	47,900	118,800	123,200
Income before tax	(16,800)	397,298	179,700
Provision for income taxes	(7,700)	127,100	57,500
Net income before ext. items	(9,100)	270,198	122,200
Extraordinary items & disc. ops.	(66,900)	(8,800)	0
Net income	**($76,000)**	**$261,398**	**$122,200**
Outstanding shares	118,199	119,000	117,460

Source: Paramount Communications, Inc., *Annual Reports.*

	FISCAL YEAR ENDING:			
10/31/90	10/31/89	10/31/88	10/31/87	10/31/86
$1,112,800	$2,520,400	$615,800	$365,000	$61,500
553,600	576,800	0	0	0
808,700	783,500	667,700	642,600	540,300
577,900	467,100	416,400	324,600	277,600
478,700	496,100	447,100	405,100	390,800
3,531,700	4,843,900	2,147,000	1,737,300	1,270,200
871,200	671,000	578,700	520,300	514,100
225,800	192,300	164,800	142,200	121,500
645,400	478,700	413,900	378,100	392,600
197,000	165,800	1,376,800	1,463,200	1,016,000
600,300	387,000	318,200	286,200	369,500
425,900	253,600	236,800	200,400	155,900
1,138,900	936,200	885,400	863,700	1,039,200
$6,539,200	$7,065,200	$5,378,100	$4,928,900	$4,243,400
$143,700	$114,100	$142,900	$122,900	$95,400
21,700	20,600	117,200	64,900	29,800
1,010,100	1,034,200	776,900	741,000	643,100
161,200	791,600	43,600	32,200	9,900
1,336,700	1,960,500	1,080,600	961,000	778,200
661,200	663,400	641,000	526,400	302,300
712,100	723,800	1,390,300	1,334,900	1,260,800
2,710,000	3,347,700	3,111,900	2,822,300	2,341,300
117,400	120,000	116,200	60,100	61,700
575,900	539,000	467,700	505,800	508,100
3,120,400	3,054,700	1,673,800	1,548,000	1,363,700
15,500	3,800	8,500	(7,300)	(31,400)
3,129,200	3,717,500	2,266,200	2,106,600	1,902,100
$6,539,200	$7,065,200	$5,378,100	$4,928,900	$4,243,400
$3,869,000	$3,391,600	$3,055,900	$2,903,600	$2,093,800
2,542,600	2,202,800	1,848,100	1,753,500	1,215,800
1,022,200	995,900	832,300	751,800	671,300
304,200	192,900	375,500	398,300	206,700
215,900	21,100	434,100	364,400	340,700
139,100	194,900	168,500	154,000	161,100
381,000	19,100	641,100	608,700	386,300
121,900	7,600	256,400	252,600	157,600
259,100	11,500	384,700	356,100	228,700
0	1,453,900	0	0	38,700
$259,100	$1,465,400	$384,700	$356,100	$267,400
117,363	119,994	119,500	61,700	62,300

EXHIBIT 3
Financial Statements of
Viacom, Inc.
(in thousands of dollars)

BALANCE SHEET	FISCAL YEAR ENDING:		
	12/31/93	12/31/92	12/31/91
ASSETS (000$)			
Cash	$1,882,381	$48,428	$28,722
Receivables	351,765	319,804	322,682
Other current assets	452,247	390,256	366,773
Total current assets	2,686,393	758,488	718,177
Property, plant & equipment	901,445	763,613	628,807
Accumulated depreciation	347,243	306,548	248,973
Net property & equipment	554,202	457,065	379,834
Investment in affiliates	0	0	44,145
Other current assets	263,281	228,784	257,515
Intangibles	2,706,818	2,658,058	2,637,401
Deposits & other assets	206,174	214,699	151,306
Total assets	**$6,416,868**	**$4,317,094**	**$4,188,378**
LIABILITIES (000$)			
Accounts payable	$96,579	$71,199	$70,932
Current long-term debt	55,004	0	48
Accrued expenses	285,605	329,166	240,607
Income taxes payable	140,453	96,529	110,299
Other current liabilities	-387,977	414,602	434,012
Total current liabilities	965,618	911,496	875,898
Deferred charges	0	0	0
Long-term debt	2,378,286	2,397,014	2,320,919
Other long-term liabilities	354,850	252,073	292,068
Total liabilities	3,698,754	3,560,583	3,488,885
Preferred stock	1,800,000	0	0
Common stock, net	1,208	1,205	1,202
Capital surplus	920,864	917,466	909,416
Retained earnings	-(3,958)	(162,160)	(211,125)
Shareholder equity	2,718,114	756,511	699,493
Total liabilities & net worth	**$6,416,868**	**$4,317,094**	**$4,188,378**
INCOME STATEMENT(000$)			
Net sales	$2,004,949	$1,864,683	$1,711.562
Cost of goods sold	877,609	853,977	790,816
SG&A expense	589,288	517,977	475,648
Operating income	538,052	492,729	445,098
Depreciation & amortization	153,057	144,802	132,864
Non-operating income	61,774	1,756	(6,536)
Interest expense	144,953	194,104	297,451
Income before tax	301,816	155,579	8,247
Provision for income taxes	129,815	84,848	42,600
Other income	(2,520)	(4,646)	(12,743)
Net income before ext. items	169,481	66,085	(46,556)
Extraordinary items & disc. ops.	1,471	(17,120)	(3,101)
Net income	**$170,952**	**$48,965**	**($49,657)**
Outstanding shares	120,796	120,450	120,227

Source: Viacom, Inc., *Annual Reports.*

12/31/90	12/31/89	FISCAL YEAR ENDING: 12/3L/88	12/3L/87
$43,061	$12,443	$16,418	$19,297
260,753	244,334	235,767	188,373
350,263	334,094	301,179	239,145
654,077	590,871	553,364	446,815
585,602	536,846	555,699	511,113
193,804	156,548	105,149	36,735
391,798	380,298	450,550	474,378
25,663	16,959	13,618	42,258
283,570	301,350	257,800	257,819
2,578,795	2,400,191	2,602,493	2,607,905
94,024	63,293	102,230	107,702
$4,027,927	$3,752,962	$3,980,055	$3,936,877
$84,527	$80,066	$44,410	$53,010
61	56	157,051	200,049
221,815	239,676	223,136	159,467
99,425	79,269	62,696	49,332
392,787	314,012	299,393	202,315
798,615	713,079	786,686	664,173
0	0	1,797	0
2,537,263	2,283,118	2,185,855	2,174,981
325,886	300,821	219,112	188,162
3,661,764	3,297,018	3,193,450	3,027,316
0	0	444,304	378,543
1,068	534	534	533
526,563	527,097	544,534	610,136
(161,468)	(71,687)	(202,767)	(79,651)
366,163	455,944	786,605	909,561
$4,027,927	$3,752,962	$3,980.055	$3,936,877
$1,599,625	$1,436,220	$1,258,501	$583,586
778,188	712,767	599,876	272,755
460,192	443,786	359,632	156,572
361,245	279,667	298,993	154,259
137,414	134,951	139,323	77,309
(483)	312,363	13,656	1,626
293,711	312,166	289,284	159,909
(70,363)	144,913	(115,958)	(81,333)
20,367	19,178	10,402	(1,682)
949	5,345	3,244	0
(89,781)	131,080	(123,116)	(79,651)
0	0	0	0
($89,781)	$131,080	($123,116)	($79,651)
106,732	106,732	53,365	53,362

EXHIBIT 4
Financial Statements of
QVC Network Inc.

BALANCE SHEET

	FISCAL YEAR ENDING:		
	01/31/94	01/31/93	01/31/92
ASSETS (000$)			
Cash	$15,873	$4,279	$36,804
Receivables	183,162	97,008	67,979
Inventories	148,209	118,712	108,929
Other current assets	65,285	14,396	3,266
Total current assets	412,528	234,395	216,977
Net property & equipment	80,579	72,863	68,949
Intangibles	351,389	383,409	414,598
Deposits & other assets	33,664	9,028	14,015
Total assets	**$878,160**	**$699,695**	**$714,539**
LIABILITIES (000$)			
Accounts payable	$81,594	$51,622	$40,310
Current long-term debt	3,114	24,073	49,698
Accrued expenses	225,989	151,358	146,284
Total current liabilities	310,697	227,053	236,292
Long-term debt	7,044	7,586	152,461
Other long-term liabilities	0	0	0
Total liabilities	317,741	234,639	388,753
Preferred stock	56	93	114
Common stock. net	399	357	250
Capital surplus	446,027	409,970	325,948
Retained earntngs	113,937	54,636	(456)
Treasury stock	0	0	70
Shareholder equity	560,419	465,056	325,786
Total liabilities & net worth	**$878,160**	**$699,695**	**$714,539**
INCOME STATEMENT(000$)			
Net sales	$1,222,104	$1,070,587	$921,804
Cost of goods sold	723,175	621,840	534,650
SG&A expense	303,985	284,024	256,095
Operating income	194,944	164,723	131,059
Depreciation & amortization	16,682	17,105	16,679
Non-operating income	(61,386)	(20,886)	(22,503)
Interest expense	1,590	18,364	38,979
Income before tax	115,286	108,669	52,898
Provision for income taxes	59,975	52,080	31,165
Net income before ext. items	55,311	56,588	21,733
Extraordinary iterm & disc. ops.	3,990	1,496	(2,108)
Net income	**$59,301**	**$55,092**	**$19,625**
Outstanding shares	39,895	35,734	25,013

01/31/91	01/31/90	FISCAL YEAR ENDING: 01/31/89	01/31/88	01/31/87
$23,090	$26,580	$1,251	$1,733	$6,215
61,973	67,681	3,088	3,046	409
100,500	79,890	30,584	14,643	2,909
2,534	29,462	927	419	417
188,097	203,613	35,850	19,841	9,950
83,460	86,576	26,685	19,851	12,498
446,119	453,268	5,973	4,820	0
22,507	24,764	0	0	3,024
$740,183	$768,221	$68,508	$44,512	$25,472
$33,065	$72,940	$14,823	$8,576	$3,160
33,166	13,801	821	128	0
98,484	74,041	6,443	3,699	1,660
164,715	160,782	22,787	14,747	4,927
366,688	396,233	12,552	6,604	0
0	4,075	0	0	0
531,403	561,090	35,339	21,351	4,927
125	105	52	48	0
176	172	101	101	101
228,628	210,018	38,650	37,657	28,910
(20,081)	(3,096)	(5,627)	(14,638)	(8,466)
68	68	7	7	0
208,780	207,131	33,169	23,161	20,545
$740,183	$768,221	$68,508	$44,512	$25,472
$776,029	$453,325	$193,150	$112,302	$2,189
479,899	282,840	120,118	73,128	1,893
220,432	131,919	58,228	40,490	8,552
75,699	38,566	14,804	(1,316)	(8,256)
16,229	8,972	3,692	2,164	550
(27,327)	(7,595)	(908)	(697)	340
49,127	12,902	1,193	638	0
(16,985)	9,097	9,011	(4,815)	(8,466)
0	2,750	0	0	0
(16,985)	6,347	9,011	(4,815)	(8,466)
0	0	0	(1,341)	0
($16,985)	$6,347	$9,011	($6.156)	($8,466)
17,481	17,130	10,080	10,080	10,117

EXHIBIT 5
Line of Business
Financial Data for
Paramount and Viacom

PARAMOUNT COMMUNICATIONS (FORMERLY GULF + WESTERN)

FISCAL YEAR ENDING:

	10/31/93 EST.	10/31/92	10/31/91	10/31/90	10/31/89	10/31/88	10/31/87
Entertainment revenues ($M)							
Motion pictures $ television							
Features	N/A	1,259.4	1,190.3	1,329.6	—	—	—
Television	N/A	655.0	578.5	617.3	—	—	—
Station & network	N/A	201.4	185.1	107.0	—	—	—
Motion pictures	N/A	—	—	—	541.5	484.3	N/A
Television & home video	N/A	—	—	—	1,170.1	1,069.7	N/A
Administrative & other	N/A	21.4	18.5	14.4	13.0	12.5	N/A
Theatres, sports & other	N/A	520.2	407.8	378.4	347.2	295.7	N/A
Entertainment financial data ($M)							
Revenues	2,820.6	2,657.4	2,380.2	2,446.7	2071.8	1,862.2	1,849.5
Operating Income	175.6	279.6	66.2	212.5	252.2	251.8	297.3
Depreciation	62.7	49.0	38.1	28.0	21.6	18.7	17.8
Capital expenditures	110.9	94.3	146.6	174.7	69.2	46.9	37.2
Identifiable assets	3,585.4	3,221.9	2,493.7	2,223.0	1,635.8	1,235.3	1,360.9
Publishing revenues ($M)							
Education							
School	N/A	315.9	363.1	339.4	307.3	249.3	N/A
Higher education	N/A	298.8	280.9	256.1	227.2	218.2	N/A
Supplementary education	NA	84.8	86.4	117.5	103.6	91.7	N/A
Educational technology	N/A	61.1	49.4	—	—	—	N/A
Consumer	N/A	387.2	364.1	343.4	306.1	286.4	N/A
Business & professional	N/A	320.1	247.4	246.8	234.2	187.4	N/A
International	N/A	154.9	138.7	125.9	111.9	102.8	N/A
Other	N/A	(15.3)	(14.8)	(6.8)	29.5	57.9	NIA
Publishing financial data ($M)							
Revenues	1,495.8	1,607.5	1,515.2	1,422.3	1,319.8	1,193.7	1,074.0
Operating Income	172.2	182.0	156.2	155.5	1.6	180.0	161.5
Depreciation	23.2	20.9	19.1	15.8	13.2	11.2	9.3
Capital expenditures	23.2	24.6	25.8	12.6	24.4	17.1	16.6
Identifiable assets	2,603.9	2,403.6	2,227.3	2,192.5	2,009.2	1,908.0	1,706.4

Note: Originally, 1990 entertainment segment revenue data reported the line items *Motion pictures* ($542.3) and *Television & home video* ($1,511.6) rather than *Features, Television,* and *Station & network.*

Source: Paramount Communications, Inc., *Annual Reports.*

VIACOM, INC.

	FISCAL YEAR ENDING:					
	12/31/93	12/31/92	12/31/91	12/31/90	12/31/89	12/31/88
Revenues ($M)						
Networks	1,221.2	1,058.8	922.2	843.0	752.0	642.6
Entertainment	209.1	248.3	273.5	282.2	254.5	161.1
Cable television	416.0	411.1	378.0	330.5	300.6	330.0
Broadcasting	181.8	168.8	159.2	164.0	146.1	141.2
Other					3.8	5.0
Intercompany elimination	(23.1)	(22.4)	(21.3)	(20.0)	(20.8	(21.4)
	2,005.0	1,864.6	1,711.6	1,599.7	1,436.2	1,258.5
Earnings from operations ($M)						
Networks	272.1	205.6	172.3	90.2	77.0	46.1
Entertainment	32.5	59.7	73.2	76.4	71.9	61.3
Cable television	110.2	122.0	104.0	76.5	60.9	58.1
Broadcasting	42.3	32.0	27.7	38.3	35.2	35.5
Other					3.8	5.0
Corporate	(72.0)	(71.3)	(65.0)	(57.5)	(104.2)	(46.4)
	385.1	348.0	312.2	223.9	144.6	159.6
Depreciation & amortization ($M)						
Networks	44.8	41.8	30.1	30.6	29.6	28.8
Entertainment	9.5	6.8	7.2	7.2	7.2	6.7
Cable television	71.5	68.5	66.6	66.8	71.5	78.8
Broadcasting	23.5	24.5	27.1	26.8	23.9	23.9
Corporate	3.8	3.2	1.9	6.1	2.8	1.1
	153.1	144.8	132.9	137.5	135.0	139.3

Source: Viacom, Inc., *Annual Reports.*

EXHIBIT 6
Multimedia Assets of
Players in Paramount
Bid

	PRODUCTION STUDIOS	CABLE & WIRELESS SYSTEMS	BROADCAST STATIONS	CABLE NETWORKS
Paramount	Paramount Pictures Paramount Television		3 Fox affiliates; 3 ind UHF	USA Network (50% Sci-Fi Channel (50%) MSG Network
Viacom	TV studios	1.1M cable subscribers	2 CBS 3 NBC	Ad supported: MTV, Nickelodeon, VH1, Comedy Central (%), Lifetime (%) Pay: Showtime, Movie Channel, Flix
QVC	TV studio			QVC Network Q2 and On Q Grupo Televisa S.A. de C.V. JV with BSkyB
TCI/ Liberty Media		10.5M cable subscribers		Discovery Channel Black Entertainment Network, Family Channel, American Movie Classics, Home Shopping Network, Asia Business News Pay TV: Encore
Blockbuster	Spelling (70%); Republic Pictures			
Advance Publications		Yes		
Cox Enterprises Comcast		Yes 3M cable subs.; UK cable systems; 7.4M cellular phone phone subs.		Interest: QVC, Turner Broadcasting. E!Entertainment, Music Choice, Viewers' Choice

Source: Compiled by authors.

SPORTS TEAMS	PUBLISHING	THEATERS/ PARKS	VIDEO LIBRARY	VIDEO RETAILING	MUSIC
New York Knicks New York Rangers	Simon & Schuster Prentice-Hall Macmillan	Madison Square Garden; Paramount Parks Theater circuits	Motion Pictures; Syndicated programming; Sequel Franchises		Famous Music
		National Amusements	Television reruns		
Florida Marlins Miami Dolphins (Huizenga-owned)				Blockbuster Video	Sound Warehouse; Music Plus
	Conde Nast (magazines); Newspaper; Random House				
	Newspaper				

EXHIBIT 7
Historical Stock Prices

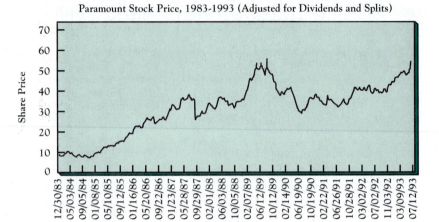

Paramount Stock Price, 1983-1993 (Adjusted for Dividends and Splits)

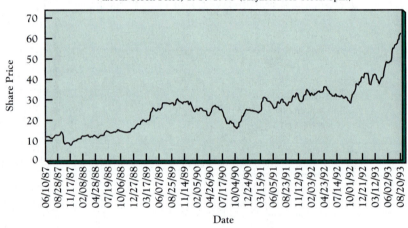

Viacom Stock Price, 1987-1993 (Adjusted for Stock Split)

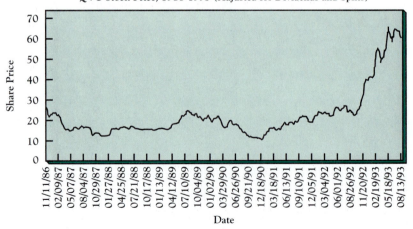

QVC Stock Price, 1986-1993 (Adjusted for Dividends and Splits)

EXHIBIT 8
Share Prices During the
Bidding Process

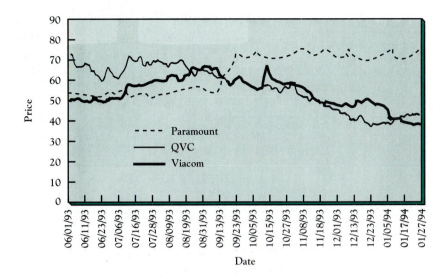

EXHIBIT 9
Estimated Market Value
of Alternative Bids
Over Time

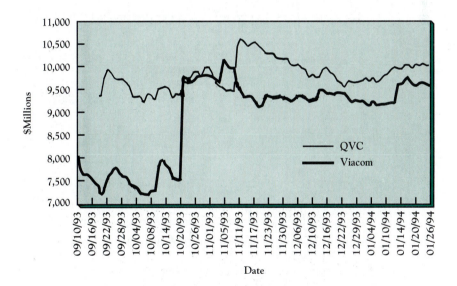

EXHIBIT 10
Leadership in the QVC Camp

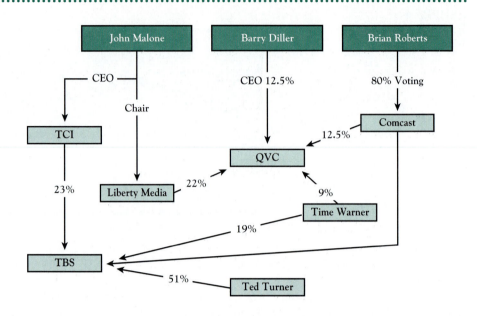

EXHIBIT 11
Paramount's Board of Directors

DIRECTOR	POSITION	COMMENTS
Martin S. Davis	Chairman & CEO, Paramount	
Grace J. Flippinger	Former Treasurer, NYNEX	NYNEX allied with Viacom.
Irving R. Fischer	Chairman & CEO, HRH Construction Corp.	Does charity work with Davis.
Benjamin L. Hooks	Senior V.P., Chapman Co. Former Exec. Director, NAACP	
Stanley R. Jaffe	President & COO, Paramount	Davis might pick him as successor.
J. Hugh Liedtke	Chairman, Penzoil	Saw QVC as another Texaco
Franz J. Lutolf	Former General Manager, Swiss Bank Corp.	
Ronald L. Nelson	CFO, Paramount	Added to board by Davis in 1992.
Donald Oresman	General Counsel & CAO, Paramount	Davis' Number 2.
James A. Pattison	Chairman & CEO, Jim Pattison Group	
Lester Pollack	General Partner of Lazard Freres	Lazard acting as Paramount adviser.
Irwin Schloss	President of Marcus Schloss & Co.	
Samuezl J. Silberman	Former Chairman, Consolidated Cigar	Cons. Cigar divested by G + W in 1983.
Lawrence M. Small	President & COO, Fannie Mae	
George Weissman	Former Chairman, Phillip Morris	Knew Davis at Samuel Goldwyn.

Source: Compiled by authors from Paramount reports and published articles.

HONDA MOTOR COMPANY
1994

Starting from scratch in industries dominated by giants, Honda Motor Company, Ltd., had been a major force in revolutionizing the motorcycle and small car industries of the world. What were the keys to success for this unique Japanese company? After moving into third position in Japan's auto industry and developing the largest single selling auto in the U.S., the Accord, in the early 1990s, where could Honda look for future successes?

A JAPANESE ENTREPRENEUR

Mr. Soichiro Honda began his career at Arto Shokai, an auto repair shop in Tokyo. At age 16, during the Great Kanto earthquake of 1923, the young apprentice who had never driven a car leapt to the wheel of a customer's vehicle and in a bit of daring-do maneuvered it to safety. Soon the owner-"master" set up Mr. Honda as head of a branch of Arto Shokai in Hamamatsu, Honda's home town. There Honda patented cast-metal spokes to replace the wooden ones—like those that burned out, almost wrecking his car, during the earthquake episode—and gathered the first of over 100 personal patents in his lifetime. The Japanese trading companies soon began exporting his spokes all over the Far East.

By age 25, Honda was one of the youngest Japanese entrepreneurs around. He became *the* Hamamatsu playboy, not only plying from one geisha house to the next, but piling geishas into his own car for wild drives and drunken revels around the town. In one such escapade his car full of geishas went off a bridge, but landed safely in the mud—no injuries. In another, he tossed a geisha from a second story window. She landed on some electric wires below—from which a suddenly sobered Honda carefully extracted her—again fortunately no injuries. These are only some of the many colorful stories about the young Mr. Honda.

Honda also loved motors and engines. When the head of Arto Shokai suggested Honda might build a racer (on his own time), Honda spent months of midnight hours to build a car from spare parts and war surplus aircraft engines. He soon began to drive his products himself, to win races, to make basic changes in racing car designs, and soon to set new speed records. But in the All Japan Speed Rally of 1936, traveling at 120 kph—a record not exceeded for years—another car jumped in front of Honda, demolishing Honda's car and leaving him with lifetime injuries, which redirected his energies from racing toward engineering. Seeing more opportunities in manufacturing than repairs, Honda formed Tokai Heavy Industries in 1937 to make piston rings for cars.

PISTON RINGS AND WAR

But Honda knew nothing about the complex casting processes involved. For months he and his assistant lived in their factory, day-and-night. Honda became a working hermit, complete with uncut hair and bristling chin. His limited savings wasted away. He sold his wife's jewelry to keep on, but he persisted, knowing his family would starve if he failed. After many frustrating failures, Honda sought the specialized technical knowledge he lacked because he had dropped out of school. After painfully gaining entry to the Hamamatsu High

Case Copyright © 1995 by James Brian Quinn. Research associates: Allie J. Quinn and Penny C. Paquette. Primary references include: T. Sakiya, *Honda Motor: The Men, The Management, The Machines,* Kodansha International, Ltd. Tokyo, 1982; S. Sanders, *Honda: The Man and His Machines,* Little Brown, Boston, 1975; R. Guest, "The Quality of Work Life in Japan. . .," *Hokudai Economic Papers,* Tokyo, Vol. XII, 1982–83; R. Shook, *Honda: An American Success Story,* Prentice Hall, 1988. Numbers in parentheses indicate the reference and page number for material from a previously footnoted source.

School of Technology—ten years older than his class-mates, an unprecedented act in age-and-class-conscious Japan—Honda promptly upset the authorities by only attending classes of interest to him, listening carefully to what mattered to him, and not even taking notes on the rest. He refused to take examinations, saying that a diploma was worth less than a movie ticket; at least the ticket guaranteed you got into the theater.[1]

As Honda began to understand the technicalities of his product, he sold rings to the low end of the market, but soon developed special automated equipment that let him meet the major manufacturers' quality standards for rings and later for aircraft propellers. During the war American bombings and an earthquake destroyed much of his operation. Honda sold off the rest of his assets as the war ended. With the proceeds he bought a huge drum of medical alcohol, made his own sake, and spent an inebriated year visiting with friends and trying to decide what to do next.

HONDA MOTORS BEGINS

The postwar era was terrible. Japan's cities were destroyed. City dwellers had to sortie into the country to buy their daily food. Trains were overcrowded and gasoline was in short supply. Honda later said, "I happened on the idea of fitting an engine to a bicycle simply because I didn't want to ride the incredibly crowded trains and buses myself, and it became impossible for me to drive my car because of the gasoline shortage."[2] Using small, war-surplus gasoline powered motors which had provided electricity for military radios, Honda made motor bikes that were an instant hit.

Honda realized that his simple motorbikes would not last long once Japan began its postwar recovery. In 1949 he raised some $3,800 from friends and designed a longer range two stroke, 3 hp (98cc) machine—the Type D with a superior stamped metal frame, christened the "Dream." Soon Honda was selling 1,000 bikes and motorcycles a month to black marketeers and small bicycle shops. But Honda's bill collectors often found their customers had disappeared or gone bankrupt before they paid the company. Honda was more interested in the product and its engineering than in profits. Production and sales were doing well, but the company was facing imminent bankruptcy. Honda welcomed the recommendation of an acquaintance that he take on Takeo Fujisawa as his head of finance and marketing. Fujisawa's heavy and ponderous style contrasted sharply with Honda's waspish, impatient, even rude directness, but the two became friends for life.

They moved the company from sleepy, gossipy, Hamamatsu—where the neighbors objected to Honda's flamboyant, noisy, sake-filled 3 a.m. returns on his motorcycle—to Tokyo and promptly applied for government support to produce 300 motorcycles per month. MITI—Japan's coordinating agency for industrial, technology, and trade affairs—thought no one could sell that many motorcycles, and denied its support. Ignoring MITI's skepticism, Fujisawa wrote an impassioned letter to all of the 18,000 bicycle shops in Japan, presenting Honda's product as their wave of the future and promising to train them in its sale and repair. While Japan's largest producers typically had only regional distribution, Honda soon had a national network of 5,000 dedicated dealers.

Next, instead of emulating the 4 stroke, side-valve machine competitors had, Honda created a 146cc 4 stroke, overhead valve (OHV) engine which doubled the available horsepower with no added weight, and became the basis for Honda's appeal to the high performance marketplace. Honda integrated the production of the key components, engines, frames, chains, and drives essential to top performance. But it outsourced non-critical parts as much as possible, and purchased a relatively small old sewing machine plant for assembly operations. Lacking large scale production facilities, Honda and his people designed special small scale assembly equipment—and simply stayed at work each day as long as it took to meet orders.

"MR. THUNDER"

While other manufacturers milked a single winning design in the domestic marketplace, Honda thought Type E did not hit a wide enough market. "I concluded I must make a motorcycle that would substitute for the bicycle."[2] Honda developed a new 50cc engine from the ground up, and coupled this with a small friendly looking frame for informal users. Sensing an untapped market niche for local delivery vehicles for small businesses, he designed in a step-through frame, an automatic transmission, and one hand controls that allowed riders to carry a package in the other hand. The market for the "Cub" boomed, and Honda moved into large volume manufacturing for the first time.

In 1951, top officials of the larger Japanese manufacturers invited Honda and Fujisawa to attend a private meeting to determine incentive policies for Japanese exporters. Honda refused to attend, thus beginning a long pattern of nonparticipation with the central political and business forces directing Japan's economic recovery. He felt that high quality goods needed no such supports and knew no national boundaries.

Honda was talkative, energetic, gregarious—always excited by the technology and his products, never (according to Mr. Fujisawa) "by the profits we would make next year." But Honda earned the nickname Kaminari-san—"Mr. Thunder"—because of his instantaneous temper and sometimes erratic behavior. He spent most of his time in the factory or development shop working side-by-side with his workers. Employees from his early years remember his shouting at engineers or pounding himself on the head when they made a mistake. On one occasion, after finding some bolts improperly tightened, he grabbed a wrench from a technician, did the job right, and then popped the technician with the wrench while shouting, "You damned fool. This is how you are supposed to tighten bolts."[1,72] People later avoided close contact when Honda was carrying a wrench.

EXPANDING INVESTMENTS

Honda's financial problems were solved in a unique way. Once they saw the Honda Cub, dealers were so impressed that they came to the company to buy whatever inventory they could. This was in sharp contrast to their usual practice of selling whatever models the big manufacturers had been able to force on them. Fujisawa cleverly used this demand to his advantage. He allocated production to those who could pay in advance and began weeding out slow paying distributors and dealers. Soon Honda had not only the widest, but the strongest, motorcycle dealer network in Japan. Unable and unwilling to obtain government financing and lacking access to Japan's closely controlled equity markets Mr. Fujisawa used creative—high risk—trade financings to see the company through its major plant and distribution expansions.

EXPANSION TO WORLD MARKETS

About this time Honda decided that motorcycle racing could assert to the world his company's true expertise in motorcycle design. After some disappointing initial entries in international races, Honda realized that the key to success was lighter, more efficient engines, getting more power from more thorough combustion. Honda engineers ultimately designed an engine with the cam shaft at the top—the then unique overhead cam (OHC) engine—and made crucial discoveries about mixing gases in the combustion chamber that led to the CVCC engines of its later automobiles.

Honda's motorcycles won the Manufacturer's Team Prize for the company in 1959 and the first five places (in both 125 and 250cc sizes) at the Isle of Man races in 1961. These were considered the "Olympics of racing" at the time.

TIME FOR STRATEGY

While Mr. Honda was mesmerized by the sheer technological questions of these "racing years," Mr. Fujisawa was concerned with the company's longer term strategy. He thought there was a large untapped market for smaller, safer "bikes," geared to customers who resisted larger motorcycles as expensive, dangerous, and associated with the black leather jacket crowd. He wanted a small 50cc bike for novices, youthful executives, or young couples. At first Mr. Honda ignored his colleague's unusual vision. Then around 1958, Honda designed and built a full-sized example of a "scooter" that would do the trick. Fujisawa was immediately excited by the product and soon predicted sales of 30,000 units per month—a bit ambitious in a Japanese market that then constituted only 20,000 per month for all two-wheelers.

Now considered to be the Model T of two-wheeled vehicles and probably Honda's masterpiece, the new motorbike was called the Super Cub. Revolutionary in design, the Super Cub had a light, carefree image, a step-through configuration which made it easier for women to ride, and a graceful, stylish appearance. The company's best selling earlier model had sold only 3,000 units per month. Yet Honda invested 10 billion yen in a single factory to build 30,000 Super Cubs a month, with no guarantee of maintaining that level of sales. Fujisawa intuitively pushed ahead. He described the Super Cub to retailers as "more like a bicycle than a motorcycle," and began to sell the vehicles directly to retailers, mostly bicycle shops. By 1959 Honda was the largest motorcycle producer in the world.

AMERICAN HONDA

Honda and Fujisawa thought the time now had come to pursue the world market actively. Honda executives regarded Europe and Southeast Asia as the best markets to target, since Americans were so tied to the automobile and held an unattractive image of motorcycles and their riders. After several unsuccessful years of trying to pry open the underdeveloped country markets of Asia, Mr. Fujisawa—thinking that American preferences might set the trends for the rest of the

FIGURE 1
The First Super-Cub
("Step-Through")
Inaugurated in 1958

Source: Honda Motor Corporation

world—targeted the U.S. as crucial. Despite onerous exchange restrictions by the Japanese government, American Honda Motor Co. was formed in June 1959 with a Los Angeles headquarters, and its own executive vice president. Mr. Kihachiro Kawashima.

The company had gone to MITI for a currency allocation, but was rebuffed. MITI reasoned that if the giant Toyota had earlier failed at the same venture, how could Honda succeed? Its meager $110,000 currency allocation meant Honda had to start its U.S. operations with only $250,000 of paid in capital. Initially, Honda's cycles did not sell well in the U.S. But Kawashima and his two associates dug in, shared an apartment for $80 a month, rented a warehouse in a run-down area of Los Angeles, and personally stacked motorcycle crates, swept the floors, and built and maintained the parts bin. Early 1960 became disastrous when customers reported Honda's larger motorcycles frequently leaked oil or experienced serious clutch failures on the longer, harder, and faster roads and tracks of the U.S. In a move that presaged later policies, Kawashima air-freighted the motorcycles to Japan where engineering teams, working night and day, found a way to fix the problem in one short month.

Then events took a surprising turn. Up to this point, executives of America Honda had promoted sales of the larger, more luxurious motorcycles because they seemed more suited to the U.S. market. Although they had not attempted to sell the 50cc Super Cubs—priced at $250 vs. $1500 for bigger European and American bikes—through U.S. dealers, the executives rode them around Los Angeles themselves and noticed the bikes attracted considerable attention. With the larger bikes facing engineering problems, American Honda decided to increase emphasis on its 50cc line, just to generate cash flows.

American Honda was extremely concerned that it not lose the "black leather jacket" customers which comprised the high margin portion of the business. But Honda's retailers continually reported that Super Cub customers were normal everyday Americans. Because of Japanese government restrictions, however, American Honda had to operate on a cash basis, building its inventory, advertising, and distribution systems without using Japanese generated yen. The Pascale article (Reading 5-3) details Honda's unique entry strategy to the U.S. By 1962-63 Honda's export earnings (from motorcycles) surpassed those of Nissan or Toyota. And by 1965, Honda America's motorcycle sales had jumped to $77 million and a whopping 63% market share.

FOUR WHEELS FOR HONDA

In the 1950s Japan had intensified its now famous programs for coordinating the development of selected high priority industries. MITI announced in 1960 that it planned to divide the existing passenger car manufacturers into three groups (a mass-production car group, a mini-car group, and a special-purpose vehicle group) and that no other manufacturers would be permitted to enter. The government reasoned that the move would reduce destructive domestic competition and allow the industry to achieve scale economies for world penetration. But Honda, which would have been foreclosed from the market, was outraged. Fortunately, the proposal was never officially enacted. But it did stimulate Mr. Honda, who had dreamed since childhood of building automobiles, to move rapidly.

RACERS AND NEW TECHNOLOGY

Although MITI actively opposed Honda's entry into automobiles, at the 1962 Tokyo Motor Show, Honda revealed a light-duty (T-360) truck and a (S-500) sports car prototype. The T-360 performed like a sports car and was the first truck of its class to permit high speeds. Soon Honda introduced the N-360 mini car, with an air-cooled, two-cylinder engine, and a front wheel drive (FWD) system unprecedented in automobile design. The N-360 was an instant success and captured 31.2% of Japan's total sales in its class, a mere two months after its 1967 introduction.

As he moved to automobile engines, Mr. Honda adapted the technology he had created for his previous motorcycle designs. Honda's basic approach had always been to develop a special engine to solve each specific problem. Since he was strapped for cash, he had designed efficient small engines which were compact but powerful. Replicating their motorcycle strategy, Honda engineers by 1964 had developed a Formula I racer. The company's 1965 Formula I entry won Honda's first Grand Prix victory in Mexico City. In 1966 Britisher Jack Brabham drove to eleven straight victories in a Honda Formula II equipped with a 4 cylinder 1,000cc (160 HP) water-cooled engine. But within a few years Honda withdrew his cars (and later his motorcycles) from racing, saying the company had gained all the technology and publicity it could from that source.

THE CVCC

In 1970 the U.S. Congress amended the Clean Air Act, requiring a 90 percent reduction in the emission of hydrocarbons, carbon monoxide, and nitrogen oxides by 1976. From the beginning Honda engineers had sought an engine that Mr. Honda demanded offer both the highest internal efficiency and greatest "external merit" in terms of its cleanliness and safety. Recognizing that any system which used an after-treatment device inherently wasted the potential energy of fuel, the company had developed its surprisingly effective CVCC (compound vortex controlled combustion) engine.

Each cylinder ignited a much richer fuel mixture (about 4.5:1) in an auxiliary chamber and let the explosion expand into a main chamber, which had the desired lean (18:1 or 20:1) mixture to keep operating temperatures low within the engine, while minimizing exhausts. Detroit executives vociferously maintained that such "stratified charge" engines could only be put on small cars. But Honda proved its principle by modifying two 8-cylinder Chevy Impala engines to its design and improving their engine efficiency, gasoline mileage, and emission characteristics sufficiently to meet promulgated 1975 air quality standards. At that time, the CVCC was the only engine in the world which, operating in its normal mode, could meet the proposed U.S. Air Quality Standards. Despite Detroit's continued opposition, Honda used the CVCC and its superbly engineered small cars in three basic models (red, white, and brown) to invade the U.S. marketplace. Lacking distribution, Hondas were at first sold as "second cars" through established U.S. dealerships.

HONDA IN THE 1980S

By the late 1980s Honda had become the fourth largest maker of American cars. Honda had decided in 1979 to build a 150,000 unit U.S. auto assembly plant alongside its Marysville, Ohio motorcycle plant. Accords began rolling off in December, 1982. When that plant's capacity became seriously strained in 1985, Honda moved quickly to double it. The new space was used to produce Honda's popular Civic, the smallest and least expensive car Honda sold in the U.S. Honda's investments in plant were substantially below competitors'. The $250 million Honda had invested in its Marysville plant compared favorably with the $660 million Nissan had spent for a similar capacity plant in the U.S.[3] or the $500 million Toyota was preparing to spend on its new 200,000 unit Camry facility.[4] About 1/2 the value of a Honda's parts was imported from Japan. Some were made to order by the parent company (especially for the Accord) but others were cheaper than U.S. parts or of higher quality. Honda said it had planned to use a higher proportion of U.S. made parts, "but the attitude of some suppliers was that their job was only to give us the parts, and that we must check the quality ourselves. . . . We told them that wasn't enough, we expected 100% good parts." Some suppliers responded, others did not. Honda could build a fully equipped 1985 Accord for about $8,000, some $1,000–$1,500 less than it cost General Motors to build a comparably equipped version of its Buick or Olds line. And by 1988 it could ship the cars to Japan from the U.S. at a profit.

Honda aggressively built its image in the U.S. through a quietly sophisticated advertising program. According to professional analysts, American consumers perceived the Honda name as being synonymous with quality, just as they perceived the Sony brand. Engineering and automotive magazine ratings of the world's best cars almost always included the Honda Accord. In the mid-1980s, testers for Road and Track had paired the Mercedes-Benz 190E with the Accord SE-i; the Mercedes at $23,000 scored 166 points, the Accord at $13,000 scored 163.[5]

In 1983 Honda eased past Mazda to take over the number three sales position with 8% of the Japanese market, following Toyota's 41% share and Nissan's 26%. Honda's partly plastic bodied, CRX two-seater car won the Car of the Year Award in Japan, leading all contenders by a big margin. And in America, EPA gave the CRX its highest rating for fuel economy—51 miles per gallon.

THE TECHNOLOGY ORGANIZATION

Honda Motor Company had long operated under an "expert system" which Mr. Fujisawa initiated, where creative people—experts—could fully utilize their skills and be rewarded appropriately. Fujisawa sought a flat or "paperweight" organization in which a promising person was not dependent upon or restrained by his immediate superior. He envisioned the organization as a kind of web "with engineers lined up sideways instead of top to bottom." According to Dr. Kowomoto of Honda R&D, any number of people could have top engineering positions based solely on their technical "expert" qualifications, even with no one reporting to them.

Fujisawa's organization recognized that fundamental research was unique. It needed to concentrate on scientific understanding, faced many non-commercializable failures, and rarely worked well in a structured environment. By contrast production/development had to be carefully controlled, financially driven, and make no mistakes. Honda's researchers could define their own research themes and pursue their projects to conclusion. However, research was focused on product-oriented activities in small teams, typically 2 to 10 people. Engineering was independent of Research and concentrated on process development.

INTEGRATED DESIGNS

Once development began, projects were managed across research, design, product engineering, and early production stages. Each person in a project group both maintained his own specialty and worked directly with other team members. Dr. Kowomoto emphasized that few risks were taken once a product or process was prototyped. Using its special coordination techniques, Honda operated on a 2-3 year cycle from development to production, as compared to a worldwide average of over 4 years for the auto industry.

Honda's development process centered on its SED (Sales, Production Engineering, and Development) system. Through constant reviews and their own training, engineers were encouraged to "think like customers." Each group on a team advanced its arguments based on its own analysis of the potentials, requirements, constraints, it saw for the new product. Interactions among the groups was based on a principle that the company characterized as "mutual aggression." Each was strongly encouraged to pursue its individual position all the way until a final decision was reached. Within R&D different subgroups pursued competing technical solutions until the most appropriate one was selected by the team. The R&D organization developing new products had "no pyramidal or hierarchical organization, just engineers and chief engineers." On a project team, titles did not influence decisions; even the newest engineers—in a manner antithetical to most Japanese companies—were to "argue frankly" with senior people, including vice presidents who might be on or visit their team. One person—like a metallurgy specialist—might be on many different teams simultaneously, developing completely different new products in parallel for each.

A very specific schedule was set for each project early on, and no deviations from the schedule were allowed despite problems which might develop. People were expected to work as hard as necessary to maintain planned progress, which was reviewed every 3 months by an SED oversight group, where each function presented its views as vigorously as possible. Development people argued for the best technological solution, Engineering for the best quality-cost solution, and Sales to see that the design fitted market trends. Since Honda first introduced its cars in Japan, they had to be successful in the Japanese market. But the same car—modified only for local safety, right hand driving, or environmental standards—had to meet other countries' market demands as well. Although Honda, as a smaller manufacturer, outsourced many of its raw materials, sheet metal, and fabricated parts (other than key engine parts), it had been reluctant to share its design information with outside suppliers until final specifications were set.

Because its cars had often featured new technology Honda noted that its process was often one of "trial and error." For example, in 1970 Honda's 1300cc model introduced with considerable confidence by Marketing had suffered a terrible market failure. In contrast, the Civic had an unstylish look which many feared would not sell well. Instead it became a popular product and Honda's staple-volume production model with a potential for long product life. The first marketed model of the Honda Prelude had so little power that it was sometimes the "Quaalude." But the company quickly restyled it, increased the power of its engine, gave it a much more "macho" appeal, and made it a success.

A unique aspect of Honda's design process was the fact that workers could suggest and implement process changes themselves right on the production line. A visitor would see small areas (20' x 20') out on the factory floor where workers were building their own new prototype processes. When asked if they were supervised by engineers, the answer would be, "No! If they need engineers they will find them." Changes were not limited to single work stations. Workers had automated whole body-panel and body-assembly sections this way. Each year Honda sponsored an "idea contest" and gave awards for its employees' most ingenious ideas, both for company use and for sheer inventiveness. One winner was a three-wheeled "all terrain" powered bike that became a major product line.

PRODUCTION ORGANIZATION

Honda also enjoyed some unique policies in the production area. In its foreign operations, it encouraged employees to wear uniforms, like its Japanese employees. Most did. Each individual was called an "associate," a term which described how each person related to other members of the organization and conveyed a feeling of respect for the individual. Overseas, Honda preferred to develop its own people in order to reduce the chances of employees bringing bad work habits with them. Newly hired associates were often rotated to other tasks and dispatched to Honda plants in Japan where they learned Honda's methodologies of producing to exact specifications.

Once trained, Honda promoted the best qualified person to do a job. Unlike other companies in Japan,

seniority never had a high priority in determining advancement. Even in its U.S. operations, where other companies stressed seniority, young Honda managers often occupied high positions that would take 5 to 10 years more to achieve in other companies.

Everyone was treated as an equal. Even the ubiquitous, identical uniforms of Honda employees emphasized equality, rather than rank. Everyone ate in the same cafeteria. No one had a private office. Managers and engineers routinely handled parts and equipment on the shop floor. Soichiro Honda believed that good leaders should perform even the most undesirable jobs willingly, and at least once. Accordingly, he was known to sweep factory floors, empty ash trays, and pick up paper towels from restroom floors wherever he went.

Dr. Robert Guest, a world authority on automotive organizations, described Honda's organization practices this way. "Almost all members of Honda's operating management started in the shop itself, as did 65% of its Japanese sales personnel. Mr. Honda by skill and temperament was a 'shop man' who was always concerned about the product, production details, and more importantly about the role played by people on the shop floor and their creative potentials. There is frequent movement of workers laterally and through promotions. Everyone understands that automation will be targeted first at the most onerous tasks. Much of the machinery at Honda is built by a Honda engineering subsidiary, which was set up because of the many new ideas that were originated by the workforce themselves.

"No one fears problems of technological unemployment, as growth continues. Work standards are written up by the employees themselves, in conjunction with their foremen. Honda threw out American style scientific management systems when they found that their workers slowed down while being timed and objected to the process."[6]

ORGANIZATION STRUCTURE

True to their stated policy of "proceed always with ambition and youthfulness," Soichiro Honda (68) and Takeo Fujisawa (62) retired from active management of the company on its 25th anniversary in 1973, becoming "advisers" to the firm. During the 1980s, the top management group was assembled on the 3rd floor of Honda's Tokyo headquarters office—using an open-plan executive suite where 32 directors worked together in a single open room. Just as in Honda's factories, senior executives including Honda's president occupied desks in an open office with chairs scattered around. While decisions at this level were widely discussed in the room, Honda's president Tadashi Kume, an engineer who had earlier opposed and defeated Honda in a showdown over the development of air-cooled engines, was clearly the first among equals. He was "a passionate man in the Honda tradition, a man who, like the founder, sometimes shouted to make himself heard. . . . He listed as his hobby drinking sake, but cars, and more particularly the engines in them were still his passion."

Through the 1980s the company's unique management structure had three levels. At the top was a board of directors, consisting of 24 company officers, including its 2 "supreme advisors." Within the board was a senior managing director's group, a decision making body consisting of the president, two executive vice presidents, and 4 senior management directors. The president's expertise was in technology; one vice president's was in sales; and the other, responsible for the company's financial policies, was an engineer by training and a generalist by experience at Honda.

At the corporate level, this group controlled three specialist groups, each made up of managing directors and ordinary directors and joined as needed by the heads of semi-independent affiliated companies. The three specialist groups were responsible for matters relating to "people, things, and money." The individual sections and divisions responsible for day to day operations and for specific areas of profit-making reported to the "president's office." They were under the general oversight of the specialist groups, which did not represent any specific section with daily responsibilities for profit. Among other things, these specialist groups were responsible for overseeing major new projects of the company. Examples were the task forces to select production sites for Honda's U.S. motorcycle (and later, automobile) assembly operations.

At the operational level, Honda had utilized basically a worldwide functional organization for its line activities. For example, a North American Sales Division reported directly to the headquarters Sales group; overseas Production divisions to the headquarters Manufacturing group; and small overseas R&D units to corporate R&D. However, engine R&D, engine manufacture, and manufacture of some key subassemblies were kept in Japan. Some products were designed and built in Japan directly for export; some were built in Japan and modified for export; others were built entirely in overseas operations.

THE EUROPEAN MARKET

In contrast to its U.S. strategy, Honda had been reluctant in the 1980s to invest heavily in Europe, apart from its motorcycle plants. It had undertaken a joint production arrangement with British Leland for a new 2 liter car, bigger than any Honda had ever built. Total Japanese penetration of European markets was also not nearly as great as in the U.S. Quotas had long restricted imports of Japanese cars into individual European countries. But Spain and some of the "Mediterranean countries" with lower labor costs were pressing to break these quotas in 1992. Building sales in Europe would be difficult against the well-known, high quality, and accepted European brands. However, many European producers had not updated their plants as dramatically as either the Japanese or the Americans, and some of the great European brands had not won a "Car of the Year" award in over a decade.

The European market had been highly fragmented by national boundaries, language differences, and special taste preferences. The Common Market in 1992 was supposed to mitigate this. However, like the Japanese and American markets, over-capacity (of about 20%) plagued the European marketplace in the late 1980s. This was largely offset by exports of the upper-line European cars, like BMW, Daimler-Benz, Jaguar, Saab, and Volvo, mostly to the U.S. Few of the "lower-end" European cars enjoyed a substantial export market. But because of such considerations, France, Italy, and Spain (which together accounted for about 40% of total European sales) had been virtually closed to Japanese producers, and other countries had applied ceilings to Japanese imports.

Cost structures in the automobile industry began changing rapidly in the late 1980s. Components and materials comprised about 50%-60% and labor about 20% of an auto's factory cost. Plants for sophisticated components like engines, gear trains, or trans-axles might cost $500–$800 million, while assembly plants were decreasing in size, but increasing in the complexity of their flexible automation. About 30% of the pre-tax price of a car was accounted for by marketing and distribution. While U.S.-owned companies had a strong presence in Europe, Japanese companies had been much later to enter. Japanese car companies' investment problems were compounded by rapidly increasing price cutting and retail competition in Japan. Toyota and Nissan seemed strong enough to withstand any onslaught, but both Mitsubishi and

Mazda were plagued with scale and distribution problems, despite some fine individual products.

MID-1990S ISSUES

Although still drawing heavy fire from politicians and the American press, the Japanese auto presence in North America had shifted significantly. Many more Japanese cars were being produced in the U.S.—736,000 cars in 1987 and 1,687,000 in 1992. At the same time Japanese motor vehicle exports to the U.S. had dropped from 3.4 million to 1.7 million cars per year. Japanese automakers had invested over $9.6 billion in U.S. plants through 1992. Honda led the field, with total investments of $2.6 billion and production capacity for 458,000 units in the U.S. The comparative investments, employment, and units for other Japanese companies are shown in Exhibit 1. Japanese automakers purchased $13.6 billion worth of U.S.-made parts and materials annually and 158,000 cars built in Japanese-owned or joint-ownership plants were exported from the U.S. to other countries. In 1992, their exports of 114,600 cars exceeded the big three automakers' exports of 105,600. Honda was the second largest exporter of passenger cars (after General Motors) with 55,850 cars exported to countries other than Canada. American companies enjoyed numerous alliances with Japanese companies as shown in Exhibit 2. Honda had major facilities in Marysville, Ohio; Torrance, California; Denver, Colorado; and Mojave Desert, California.

A MAJOR REORGANIZATION

In 1990, when Mr. Nobuhiko Kawamoto became CEO of Honda he radically reorganized the company. He took line responsibility for the company's global automobile operations and for Honda R&D. He then reorganized the business into three product lines—automobiles, motorcycles, and power equipment. A year later, in a second stage of this reorganization, he divided the automobile operation into four regional components: (1) the Americas, (2) Europe, the Middle East, and Africa, (3) Asia and Oceania, and (4) Japan. Chief operating officers in each region then had the authority for development, production and sales, and marketing. The executive committee at world headquarters, of which Mr. Kawamoto was a member, was free of line responsibilities, focusing on long-term global strategies. A group of coordinating staff operations remained at headquarters. There were four support groups responsible for motorcycles, automobiles, power products, and service parts, respectively. Mr. Kawamoto noted, "This new blueprint will give Honda greater agility."

Some keys to Mr. Kawamoto's strategy for the Americas were: increasing automobile capacity in the U.S. and Canada to 720,000 units by 1997 and starting up auto production in Mexico in 1995; expanding Honda's U.S. engine plant from 500,000 to 750,000 engines per year in 1998, including production of Honda's first U.S. made V-6 engines in 1996. All of this would expand Honda's total North American investment to more than $3.8 billion. The company's stated goal was "to establish in the United States a self-

EXHIBIT 1 Japanese Automakers' Investments in the U.S., 1992		TOTAL INVESTMENT (millions of dollars)	MODELS	UNITS PRODUCED	EMPLOYEES
	Honda	$2,600	Accord, Civic	458,251	10,200
	Nissan	$1,300	Altima, Sentra	300,328	5,860
	Mazda	$ 550	Mazda MX-6 and 626 Ford Probe	169,566	3,700
	Mitsubishi	$1,400	Mitsubishi Eclipse Chrysler Laser and Talon	140,156	3,100
	Toyota	$1,150	Toyota Corolla Geo Prism	256,799	4,200
	Subaru-Isuzu	$ 620	Fuji Legacy Isuzu Pickup and Rodeo	124,020	1,900

Source: "How Japanese Automakers Contribute to the U.S. Economy," Japan Automobile Manufacturers Association, Inc., 1993.

EXHIBIT 2
Partnerships between
Japanese and U.S.
Automakers, 1992

	JAPANESE	U.S.	RELATIONSHIP
Capital Ties			
	Isuzu Motors	GM	GM owns 37.5% of Isuzu
	Suzuki	GM	GM owns 3.5% of Suzuki
	Mazda	Ford	Ford owns 24.5% of Mazda
	Mitsubishi Motors	Chrysler	Chrysler owns 5.9% of Mitsubishi
Joint Production			
	Toyota Motor	GM	NUMMI
	Nissan Motor	Ford	Joint production of minivans
	Mazda	Ford	AutoAlliance International, Inc.
	Suzuki	GM	CAMI (Canada)
Joint Development			
	Nissan Motor	Ford	Joint development of minivans
Supply of Vehicles			
	Mazda	Ford	Mutual supply of completed cars
	Mitsubishi Motors	Chrysler	Supply of completed cars to U.S.
	Isuzu Motors	GM	Supply of completed cars to U.S.
	Suzuki	GM	Supply of completed cars to U.S.
Supply of Parts			
	Toyota Motor	GM	Supply of parts to Japan
	Toyota Motor	Chrysler	Supply of parts to Japan
	Nissan Motor	GM	Supply of parts to Japan
	Mazda	Ford	Mutual supply of parts
	Mitsubishi Motors	Chrysler	Mutual supply of parts
	Isuzu Motors	GM	Supply of parts to U.S.
	Suzuki	GM	Supply of parts to U.S.
Sales in Japan			
	Honda Motor	Chrysler	Sales of Chrysler cars in Japan
	Mazda	Ford	Sales of Ford cars in Japan
	Isuzu Motors	GM	Sales of GM European cars in Japan

Source: "How Japanese Automakers Contribute to the U.S. Economy," Japan Automobile Manufacturers Association, Inc.

reliant motor vehicle company, which will be an important part of Honda's international operation with the resources to compete in the world market."

Mr. Kawamoto noted, "We have been able to raise the local content of our U.S.-made automobiles to over 80%. . . . More than 60% of the cars we sell in America are made there. Several models have been developed in America as well. . . . We are expanding engine production in the U.S. and auto production in the U.S. and Canada—without building new plants. We are doubling our North American R&D capabilities, lowering the cost of development and manufacturing, increasing our use of local parts and materials. We will begin auto production in Mexico with the support of our U.S. manu-

facturing operations. . . . By the end of the decade we will double exports of automobiles and component sets from the U.S. and Canada."

Mr. Kawamoto also looked elsewhere, "Honda's unique experience in marketing and manufacturing motorcycles [in the Asia/Oceania] will be invaluable as the Asian automobile market grows. Through our own factories and joint ventures, we produce almost 3 million motorcycles in Asia outside of Japan. . . . In the future we believe the auto industry will experience modest growth in mature markets. But the potential for growing demand in emerging markets could have a major impact. Such growth will place new demands on the world's energy supply. It will also increase CO_2 levels, raising environmental concerns."

NEW CAR: NEW CULTURE

To support these changes Mr. Kawamoto launched the most wrenching cultural realignment in Honda's history. After he took office in June 1990, the Japanese auto market began a three year slide. By December 1992 Ford's Taurus had broken Accord's run as the top selling car in America, and early 1993 Accord sales plunged as Honda removed the dealer rebates it had introduced to battle Ford. Profits slumped 62% in the first quarter of 1993. To offset this, Kawamoto pushed development of replacements for its great—but 1980s styled—Accords and Civics. Fortunately, design of the new Accord (for entry in 1994) had started in 1989. But Mr. Kawamoto thought that Honda's earlier design practices had "lacked discipline"—a 10% cost overrun on the just completed 1990 Accord. He was determined to change that culture, although he was a product of it and a protégé of Soichiro Honda.

Despite the great market success of the 1990 Accord, Kawamoto's design team set new objectives for the '94 design: (1) hold total spending level with the 1990 Accord, (2) cut new investment in half, (3) carry-over 50% of the parts from the 1990 Accord, and (4) anchor the price at the 1990 Accord's level. Although he let four "studios" compete actively on styling the '94 Honda for its markets, Kawamoto sought strongly to avoid the production glitches which occurred when the 1990 "Japanese-designed" Accord was produced internationally. As a portion of the new car's technical design, its engineers borrowed the Variable Valve Timing and Lift System from Honda's $60,000 NSX sports car. Research for the engine had begun in 1984 and was introduced as the VTEC in Japan's Civic in 1991. This lean-burn engine got 55–60 miles to the gallon on the highway. Honda then managed the startling feat of introducing manufacture of the new Civic with a new engine on two continents simultaneously. It also began experimentation with Orbital Engine's advanced two stroke engines (see Case II-7), which offered over 75 mpg, but had been spurned by U.S. companies.

CURING "BIG COMPANY DISEASE"

Before introducing these changes, Mr. Kawamoto had personally toured the facilities employing 70% of Honda workers and interviewed suppliers and dealers to see what they thought of Honda. He concluded that in its rapid growth, Honda had contracted "big company disease" and had lost touch with its customers. Its policy had been not to sell cars on price, but to consis-tently promote them on value. This view, and the complexity of Honda's organization, convinced him that there were "too many walls within our organization." To remedy this, he changed the open-space, sharing style in Honda's central office to a new style where each person had a specific responsibility. Decisions would be made by that executive alone. Once a plan was approved, each member of the board assumed responsibility for implementation in his area.

In its largest international operation, Honda began gradually transferring management from Japanese to Americans. Overall, one-third of its employees were foreign. Honda's American operations were becoming larger than those in Japan, and there was much press discussion of Honda possibly moving its headquarters to the U.S. Through 1993, however, Honda had not sold its shares on international markets or consciously tried to diversify its ownership base. The issue of local control was compounded by questions of whether Honda cars made in the U.S. were considered "Japanese imports" in the EEC or whether Canadian-produced Hondas or parts sent to the U.S. were "Japanese" or covered under NAFTA. In 1991, 38% of a Honda's value was in parts imported by Honda—26% from U.S.-based Japanese suppliers and 16% from U.S. suppliers—while 20% of costs were in depreciation and overhead. For the Honda's engine, 58% of its value was in parts imported by Honda. U.S.-based Japanese suppliers provided another 37%, and U.S. suppliers produced only 5% (or $58) of its value. With auto vehicles and parts making up approximately $30 billion of the U.S.-Japanese trade deficit of $35 billion in 1991, these statistics presented tender political issues.

WINNERS AGAIN

Capping off these changes, in 1992 the Honda Civic won the Japanese Car of the Year Award and the 1994 Accord won *Motor Trend's* Import Car of the Year Award. Since the U.S. accounted for over three-quarters of total Accord volume, a majority of the development effort for the new fifth generation model went into devising a package with maximum appeal to U.S. customers. After Ford's Taurus-Sable slipped past the Accord for top sales honors in 1992, Honda had vowed to retake the number one position. Consequently, despite its improved features, Honda held the '94 Accord DX prices to 1993 levels. The new Accord was specially designed to make a stronger visual statement than its predecessors, yet maintain its family appeal. Styling for the new car was locked in by December

1990, twelve months earlier in the design process than for preceding cars. To ensure its transition to the U.S., 57 production engineers and their families from Honda America were transported to Japan.

Improving customer satisfaction beyond the legendary Accords of the late 1980s was difficult. However, features like 38% more torsional rigidity and 25% increased bending stiffness along with strengthening the central tunnel, firewall, and pillar constructions—as well as redesigned crumple zones to provide a quantum increase in occupant protection—vastly improved functional quality. Along with this came a world class passenger environment with many of Honda's uniquely engineered "extras" for passenger comfort and convenience. Despite featuring an 8.1 second 0–60 MPH capability, the new Honda VTEC (Variable Valve Timing and Lift Electronic Control) engine gave substantially improved mileage. All these features boomed export sales of the new Accords as well as redesigned Civics. Data on Honda's U.S. sales are shown in Exhibits 3 and 4.

By 1993 the Japanese market for automobiles was quite mature and competitive. The nation's economy was undergoing a serious stagnation with auto production forecast to drop 5–6% in 1994 and 1995. Honda's 1993 passenger car sales in Japan stayed about one-fourth of Toyota's and 40% of Nissan's in Japan. (See Exhibit 5.) Its imports of Accords and Civics made Honda the leading automobile importer in Japan. In keeping with this trend, Honda was reducing its capacity in Japan from 1.22 million units to 1 million units in the mid-1990s. In North America, on the other hand, its U.S. plants produced 417,000 automobiles, and Honda Canada added another 102,000 units. Honda's Acura maintained its leadership among all luxury import plates in North America, while its motorcycles accounted for nearly 30% of all U.S. motorcycle sales. In Europe, Honda produced approximately 35,000 Accords in its Swindon (U.K.) facility. Trends in the European marketplace are indicated in Exhibits 6, 7. Company and comparative financial data for Honda in the early 1990s appear in Exhibits 8, 10.

1993 AND BEYOND

Given the massive capital requirements of the automobile industry, few would have thought a new entrant like Honda could have survived, much less prospered, in the capital intensive world of automobiles. (See Exhibits 11 and 12 for data on world auto demand by region and the largest automakers.) But as *Fortune* concluded, "A few years ago when Japanese cars flooded the American market, Detroit appeared frozen in indecision. The established Japanese companies, by comparison, seemed invincible. Now relative newcomer Honda is making all the other Japanese car makers look ponderous and timid . . . against a company willing to take risks and move fast."[3] While the markets of the mid-1990s posed formidable new challenges for Japan's number 3 auto producer, Mr. Kawamoto was determined to position his company for continued growth in its complex markets.

QUESTIONS

1. What important patterns have guided Honda's strategy in the past? How do these affect its future strategy? What do you think of its 1980s' organization structure and practices? What lessons can be learned from Honda during this period?

2. What were the critical factors for Honda's success during its early entrepreneurial development? Compare and contrast this pattern with that of other entrepreneurial Japanese and U.S. companies. What are the most important similarities and differences?

3. Draw your version of Mr. Kawamoto's new organization chart. What are its advantages? Potential problems? How should Honda further position itself in the early 1990s? Why? How should Detroit respond to this positioning? What should Honda's response be to that?

4. What implications does Honda's past history have for the future of the auto industry?

EXHIBIT 3
U.S. Market Shares by
Manufacturer, 1984–1993

SHARE OF TOTAL CAR MARKET

	1981	1983	1985	1987	1989	1991	1993
General Motors	44.6	44.3	42.7	36.6	35.2	35.6	34.1
Ford	16.6	17.2	18.9	20.2	22.3	20.0	22.0
Chrysler	9.9	10.4	11.3	10.8	10.4	8.6	9.8
Honda	4.4	4.4	5.0	7.2	8.0	9.8	8.4
Toyota	6.7	5.9	5.3	6.0	6.9	9.1	8.7
Nissan	5.5	5.7	5.2	5.2	5.2	5.1	5.7
Mazda	2.0	1.9	1.9	2.0	2.3	2.7	3.1
Mitsubishi	NA	NA	0.5	0.6	1.1	2.0	2.0
Others	10.4	10.2	9.1	11.4	8.5	7.2	6.2

SHARE OF SALES OF DOMESTIC CARS

	1987	1989	1991	1993
General Motors	50.2	46.3	45.4	42.3
Ford	28.5	29.3	25.6	27.3
Chrysler	13.6	14.1	10.4	11.4
Honda	4.5	5.0	7.9	6.2
Toyota	0.6	1.0	5.4	5.5
Nissan	1.7	1.4	1.8	3.7
Mazda	0.0	0.4	1.3	1.5

Source: Ward's *Automotive Yearbook*, various years.

EXHIBIT 4
Honda's Position in U.S.
Car Market—1994

	TOTAL UNITS SOLD IN SEGMENT	PERCENTAGE OF TOTAL UNITS SOLD	AMERICAN SHARE	JAPANESE SHARE	OTHER SHARE	HONDA SHARE
Budget	779,468	8.7%	51.7%	40.0%	8.3%	0.0%
Small	1,740,847	19.4	60.7	35.6	3.7	15.3
Lower mid-range	1,196,142	13.3	74.2	19.7	6.1	5.6
Mid-range	2,602,198	28.9	64.4	34.7	0.9	14.1
Upper mid-range	870,833	9.7	83.2	16.7	0.1	0.0
Near Luxury	431,200	4.8	39.2	24.6	36.2	2.0
Luxury	655,401	7.3	62.7	18.2	19.1	5.5
Sporty	642,280	7.1	69.7	29.4	0.9	0.0
Specialty	72,148	0.8	44.1	38.3	17.6	0.7
Total	8,990,517	100.0				

Note: The five top-selling cars in each segment are shown below:

Budget	Nissan Sentra, Dodge Neon, Toyota Tercel, Plymouth Neon, Chevrolet/Geo Metro
Small	Ford Escort, Saturn, Honda Civic, Toyota Corolla, Chevrolet Cavalier
Lower mid-range	Pontiac Grand Am, Chevrolet Corsica-Beretta, Nissan Altima, Ford Tempo, Acura Integra
Mid-range	Ford Taurus, Honda Accord, Toyota Camry, Oldsmobile Ciera, Buick Century
Upper mid-range	Buick LeSabre, Nissan Maxima, Ford Crown Victoria, Chevrolet Caprice, Mercury Grand Marquis
Near luxury	Chrysler New Yorker, Buick Park Avenue, Volvo 800 Series, BMW 3 Series, Lexus ES300
Luxury	Cadillac DeVille, Lincoln Town Car, Cadillac Seville, Acura Legend, Lincoln Continental
Sporty	Ford Mustang, Chevrolet Camaro, Ford Probe, Mitsubishi Eclipse, Pontiac Firebird
Specialty	Chevrolet Corvette, Mitsubishi 3000GT, Dodge Stealth, Nissan 300ZX, Mercedes-Benz SL

Source: "1995 Market Data Book," *Automotive News.*

EXHIBIT 5
Domestic Sales of Vehicles by Japanese Automakers, 1992–1993
(thousands of units)

	1992			1993		
	FULL SIZE CARS	MINIS	TRUCKS & BUSES	FULL SIZE CARS	MINIS	TRUCKS & BUSES
Toyota	1,574	—	655	1,465	—	593
Nissan	886	—	314	821	—	277
Honda	402	65	129	340	81	131
Mazda	275	49	159	228	44	133
Mitsubishi	222	113	409	228	129	360
Fuji	78	94	136	97	92	122
Suzuki	26	227	283	24	225	280
Daihatsu	20	225	189	23	202	173
Isuzu	17	—	148	5	—	124
Total	3,498	774	2,505	3,232	772	2,268

Source: 1994 Ward's *Automotive Yearbook.*

EXHIBIT 6
European New Car Registrations by Manufacturer
(thousands of units)

	1985		1988		1992		1993	
	UNITS	PERCENT	UNITS	PERCENT	UNITS	PERCENT	UNITS	PERCENT
VW Group	1,529	14.4	1,930	14.9	2,358	17.5	1,879	16.45
GM Total[b]	1,212	11.4	1,375	10.6	1,679	12.4	1,480	12.96
Peugeot Group	1,226	11.5	1,672	12.9	1,645	12.2	1,401	12.27
Fiat Group	1,304	12.3	1,916	14.8	1,604	11.9	1,271	11.12
Ford Total[a]	1,268	11.9	1,466	11.3	1,521	11.3	1,311	11.48
Renault	1,139	10.7	1,326	10.2	1,433	10.6	1,196	10.47
BMW	290	2.7	355	2.7	441	3.3	369	3.23
Nissan	307	2.9	378	2.9	438	3.2	402	3.52
Mercedes	394	3.7	445	3.4	410	3.0	355	3.11
Austin Rover	420	3.9	448	3.5	331	2.5	363	3.18
Toyota	248	2.6	349	2.7	338	2.5	314	2.75
Mazda	203	1.9	245	1.9	269	2.0	193	1.69
Volvo	255	2.4	265	2.0	201	1.5	172	1.51
Honda	n/a	n/a	140	1.1	175	1.3	162	1.42
Mitsubishi	116	1.1	156	1.2	161	1.2	138	1.21

(a) of which more than 99% is sold by Ford Europe
(b) of which more than 98% is sold by Opel/Vauxhall
Source: 1989, 1993, and 1994, Ward's *Automotive Yearbook.*

EXHIBIT 7
European Car Markets

	PERCENTAGE OF EUROPEAN MARKET	NEW CAR REGISTRATIONS (000)			JAPANESE IMPORT PENETRATION (%)		
		1988	1991	1993	1988	1991	1993
France	15.0	2,217	2,031	1,721	2.9	4.3	4.5
Germany	30.8	2,808	4,159	3,194	14.8	14.7	13.7
Italy	17.3	2,184	2,341	1,890	0.0	2.9	4.6
Spain	6.6	1,046	887	742	0.7	3.2	4.6
UK	11.8	2,216	1,593	1,778	11.4	11.6	12.7
Total Europe	100.0	12,978	13,504	11,424	11.3	13.4	12.4

EUROPEAN MARKET SHARES FOR JAPANESE AUTOMAKERS

	MARKET SHARE (%)		
	1988	1991	1993
Nissan	2.9	3.2	3.5
Toyota	2.7	2.7	2.8
Mazda	1.9	2.1	1.7
Mitsubishi	1.2	1.4	1.2
Honda	1.1	1.2	1.4

Source: Ward's *Automotive Yearbook*, various years.

EXHIBIT 8
Honda Motor Co., Ltd.,
Segment Data

	1990	1992	1993	1994
Motorcycle Business				
Net sales (billions of yen)				
Japan	134	164	167	154
North America	34	57	55	59
Europe	81	123	138	107
Other	99	175	210	227
Total	348	519	570	547
Unit sales (thousands)				
Japan	802	804	733	671
North America	98	124	102	114
Europe	343	316	347	292
Other	1,744	2,370	2,769	3,092
Total	2,987	3,614	3.951	4,169
Operating income (loss)	na	21	45	49
Automobile Business				
Net sales (billions of yen)				
Japan	856	1,185	1,118	1,034
North America	1,627	1,875	1,542	1,465
Europe	237	373	378	298
Other	114	177	242	236
Total	2,838	3,610	3,280	3,033
Unit sales (thousands)				
Japan	679	669	616	566
North America	946	953	794	828
Europe	191	196	181	156
Other	120	143	202	203
Total	1,936	1,961	1793	1,753
Operating income (loss)	na	128	49	4
Power Products/Other Businesses				
Net sales (billions of yen)				
Japan	na	97	95	94
North America	na	109	124	126
Europe	na	37	39	34
Other	na	21	25	28
Total	115	263	283	282
Unit sales (thousands)				
Japan	106	99	89	92
North America	537	436	531	607
Europe	437	382	399	425
Other	441	499	515	590
Total	1,521	1,416	1,534	1,714
Operating income (loss)	na	4	14	26

EXHIBIT 9
Honda Motor Co., Ltd.,
Financial and Operating
Statistics
(billions of yen;
thousands of units)

	1986	1989	1990	1992	1994
Net sales and other operating revenue	¥3,009	¥3,489	¥3,853	¥4,392	¥3,863
Cost of sales	1,917	2,544	2,764	3,199	2,820
Selling, general, and administrative	555	584	702	847	775
Operating income	319	177	201	153	78
Net income	147	97	82	60	24
Cash dividends paid	11	11	13	14	14
Research and development	136	184	186	192	189
Interest paid	33	25	36	43	35
Total assets	1,817	2,284	2,842	3,154	2,921
Stockholders' equity	761	901	1,085	1,098	967
Depreciation	110	131	165	191	143
Capital expenditures	281	279	333	238	122
Unit sales					
Motorcycles	3,093	3,032	2,987	3,614	4,169
Automobiles	1,365	1,903	1,936	1,961	1,753
Power products	1,816	1,543	1,521	1,416	1,714
Number of employees	59,000	71,200	79,200	90,500	91,300
Average exchange rate (yen amounts per U.S. dollar)	239	128	143	133	108

Source: Honda Motor Company, Ltd., *Annual Report*, various years.

EXHIBIT 10
Comparative Financials—
FY 1992
(millions of dollars)

	HONDA[1]	NISSAN[2]	MAZDA[3]	TOYOTA[4]
Sales	33,059	48,255	20,470	81,307
Other Income	118	576	6	330
Total Revenues	33,177	48,831	20,476	81,637
Cost of Sales	24,083	37,764	17,870	70,172
S, G & A Expense	6,373	9,331	2,272	9,387
Interest Expense	321	1,227	323	395
Other Expenses	80	—	—	—
Income Before Taxes	984	1,251	136	3,423
Income Taxes	505	510	75	1,700
Other Special Items*	—	—	—	—
Net Income	488	762	70	1,903
Cash Dividends	102	264	61	538
Inventories	3,600	5,762	1,080	3,375
Total Assets	23,757	53,177	12,129	76,662
Long-Term Debt and Other Oblig.	4,541	13,795	2,451	12,603
Shareholders' Equity	8,301	13,645	3,151	37,751

*   Honda—Equity Earnings; Nissan—Minority Interests and Extraord. Items; Mazda—Net of Equity in Net Income of Unconsolid. & Affil. Cos. and Minority Interest; Toyota—Special Items; Ford—Minority Interest (Equity in Net Income of Unconsolid. subs. is included under Other Income).

(1) Honda Motor Co., Ltd. manufactures and sells motorcycles, autos, pumps, lawn mowers, power tillers, etc.

(2) Nissan Motor Co., Ltd. manufactures and sells autos, rockets, forklifts, textile machinery, boats, etc.

(3) Mazda Motor Corp. manufactures passenger cars, trucks, buses, machine tools, etc.

(4) Toyota Motor Co., Ltd. manufactures passenger cars, commerical vehicles, prefabricated housing units, etc. Merged with Toyota Motor Sales Co., Ltd. July 1982.

Source: Compiled from Moody's *Industrial Manual* and Moody's *International*, 1989 edition.

EXHIBIT 11
World Vehicle Production
(in thousands)

COMPANY	1987 CARS	1987 TOTAL	1991 CARS UNITS	1991 CARS OVERSEAS %	1991 TOTAL UNITS	1991 TOTAL OVERSEAS %
1. General Motors (USA)	5,605	7,497	4,969	49.8	6,635	43.9
2. Ford (USA)	4,000	5,892	3,452	66.1	5,138	52.7
3. Toyota (Japan)	2,796	3,730	3,597	11.6	4,511	9.4
4. VW Group (Germ.)	2,338	2,475	2,921	49.9	3,088	49.0
5. Nissan (Japan)	2,017	2,658	2,333	16.6	3,026	23.0
6. Peugeot Group (France)	2,301	2,512	2,257	50.1	2,467	51.5
7. Renault (France)	1,742	2,053	1,706	20.8	2,004	18.7
8. Honda (Japan)	1,362	1,581	1,765	31.2	1,909	28.9
9. Fiat Group (Italy)	1,675	1,880	1,637	27.7	1,899	37.3
10. Chrysler (USA)	1,186	2,188	660	22.7	1,674	35.8
11. Mitsubishi (Japan)	595	1,231	1,104	17.2	1,595	11.9
12. Mazda (Japan)	858	1,202	1,251	13.3	1,551	10.6
13. Suzuki (Japan)	297	868	542	2.0	913	6.0
14. Daimler-Benz (Germ.)	596	823	576	0.0	861	12.5
15. Hyundai (Korea)	545	607	670	4.3	795	3.5
16. VAZ (USSR)	725	1,605	675	0.0	687	0.0
17. Daihatsu (Japan)	142	598	420	0.0	670	0.0
18. Fuji-Subaru (Japan)	267	605	388	15.0	644	18.1
19. BMW (Germ.)			536	0.0	536	0.0
20. Isuzu (Japan)	204	542	130	0.0	471	0.0
21. Kia (Korea)			260	0.0	425	0.0
22. Rover Group (UK)	472	537	396	0.0	420	0.0
23. Volvo (Sweden)			281	32.7	343	32.4
Top 40 Manufacturers	**32,727**	**44,609**	**33,957**		**44,335**	
Japanese Cos.	8,536	13,080	11,531		15,381	
North American Cos.	10,792	15,663	9,081		13,517	
Western European Cos.	10,371	11,759	10,565		11,912	
Eastern European Cos.	2,086	2,975	1,502		1,730	
Korean Cos.	790	966	1,121		1,424	
Total World Production	**33,007**	**45,914**	**34,656**		**46,496**	

Source: Compiled by the Motor Vehicle Manufacturers Association of the U.S., Inc. from reports of various overseas motor vehicle associations. Published in *Facts and Figures, 1989* and *1993.*

EXHIBIT 12
Free World Passenger Car
Demand by Region
(millions of units)

	1985	1987	1992	1997
U.S.	11.0	10.3	10.5	11.1
Canada	1.1	1.1	1.1	1.2
Europe	10.6	12.4	12.9	13.7
Latin America	1.2	1.1	1.6	2.0
Mid-East	0.4	0.3	0.6	0.7
Africa	0.3	0.3	0.5	0.7
Asia-Pacific	4.2	4.4	5.3	6.1
Total	28.8	29.9	32.5	35.5

Source: 1989 Ward's *Automotive Yearbook*, page 77.

THE PILLSBURY COMPANY

"We laughed at Pillsbury ten years ago," said a General Mills executive as the 1980s began. "But now for better or for worse, Pillsbury seems to be getting all the action."[1] With fine performances by both companies over the preceding decade, this was rare praise in one of the strongest crosstown rivalries in the whole business world. What caused the spectacular turnaround at Pillsbury? What could be learned from these events? In May 1985, Mr. William Spoor, the man most associated with the changes at Pillsbury would step down as CEO and turn this authority over to his president, Jack Stafford. What actions should Stafford take to ensure the company's continuing success? And what should Pillsbury's strategies be for the late 1980s and early 1990s?

EARLY HISTORY AND BACKGROUND

Both companies had grown up in the burgeoning grain and flour markets of the mid-1800s. Both had headquarters in Minneapolis. And both began to diversify away from their stagnating flour milling activities in the early 1950s. In contrast to General Mills which moved into electronics, chemicals, and appliances, Pillsbury concentrated on flour, grains, baking mixes, and dough products through the 1950s. And it remained primarily a U.S.-based company.

Under President Paul S. Gerot, Pillsbury expanded in the 1960s into powdered drink mixes, calcium cyclamate, and poultry.[2] And it made some small related acquisitions in Canada and Latin America.[3] But earnings remained unstable; and when 1966 earnings

Case copyright © 1985 by James Brian Quinn. Material is partly adapted from an earlier case written by James Brian Quinn and Marianne Jelinek. Research associates—Penny C. Paquette and Allie J. Quinn. The generous cooperation of the Pillsbury Company is gratefully acknowledged.

dropped 3% despite a 9% sales growth, a new management team was named.

Robert J. Keith—who had engineered the company's 1940s entry into consumer baking mixes and 1950s expansion into refrigerated dough products moved from president of the Consumer Division to chief executive officer. And Terrance Hanold, a lawyer with computer expertise, became president. Messrs. Keith and Hanold diversified Pillsbury further. In 1967, Call-A-Computer, a computer time sharing subsidiary, was formed; but more importantly, Burger King, a $12 million Miami restaurant chain, was acquired. Burger King expanded rapidly, growing by 150 restaurants in 1969 alone, to a total of 850 in 1972, when with less than one-sixth of Pillsbury's sales it began to provide more than one-fourth of total earnings.[4] In 1969, Pillsbury acquired majority interest in Poppin' Fresh Pie Shops. In 1970, J-M Poultry Packing was acquired, as were Pemton, Inc. (a residential and community developer of experimental housing),[5] Bon Appetit, (a gourmet foods magazine), and Bon Voyage (travel services). In 1971, Bachman's European Flower Markets (retail outlets for cut flowers, plants, and accessories) were added. In 1972, the company acquired Mallory Restaurants; Souverain Cellars, a California vintner; and Moline, Inc.

Messrs. Keith and Hanold also decentralized Pillsbury's organization, establishing Consumer Products, Agri-Products, Pillsbury Farms (poultry operations), Burger King, Food Service (commercial foods), and International as "freestanding businesses." But companywide profit margins hovered between 4.7% and 5.8% from 1967 to 1972 while rival General Mills achieved 7.8% to 11.4%. Consumer food sales stagnated at $267–$272 million for three years. And Pillsbury was a slow third behind General Mills' (Betty Crocker) and P&G's (Duncan Hines) brands in the crucial cake mix field.[6]

The Pillsbury Dream

About this time (early 1972) CEO Robert Keith named an executive team to consider new goals and strategies for Pillsbury. As William Spoor, then vice president and general manager of international operations, recalls,

> The process kind of evolved in a natural way. I was talking to Bob Keith. I said, "You know, Bob, this is the fifth year of my stock options and they're all under water." He responded, "Bill, if you're dissatisfied with the results of the company, why don't you develop an alternate strategy?" I said, "Are you serious?" And he said, "Yes! You're free to use anyone you want in the company." So I got the general managers together and we agreed to meet 2–3 times a month to put together a preliminary plan.

A NEW MANAGEMENT TEAM

But Mr. Keith did not live to see the results of these deliberations. At the age of 59, he developed cancer, resigned in December 1972, and died only a few months later. In a move surprising to most outsiders, Mr. Hanold "stepped aside for youth." Bill Spoor (age 49), a tough numbers-oriented executive with acquisitions and overseas experience, was named chairman and CEO. James R. Peterson (age 45), a fast-rising grocery products and marketing executive, became president. Both had been hand-selected by Mr. Keith as potential contenders for the top job.

Mr. Spoor's strategy group had met over an eight-month period in 1972, before the seriousness of Mr. Keith's illness was known. In November, when Mr. Keith's condition worsened, Spoor and Peterson were asked to prepare a strategy presentation for the Board. They were given 30 days. Mr. Peterson, on vacation, reportedly added a few comments to the draft Mr. Spoor worked up with the help of inside and outside experts. The presentation was a distillation of the general managers' strategy deliberations, what the new team would do with the company, Mr. Spoor's philosophy, and a bit about proposed management style:

> One executive who saw this document noted, "It talked about the kind of teamwork they were going to develop, the kind of company they would try to build, the kind of people they would try to acquire. It was on a high plane. It didn't say we were going to be 1/3 restaurants, 1/3 consumer, 1/3 agri. It talked about the approach to the business, the strengthening of our staff, attracting stronger people through aggressive compensation, and good business planning . . . about the use of the executive committee as kind of the conscience and central nervous system of the company. It was seen on an informal basis—pieces of it—by senior management inside the company . . . [in addition to the Board's nominating committee]."

As a portion of drawing up the statement, Mr. Spoor asked each outside board member to identify the company's strengths and weaknesses and why each thought the company's performance had been so lackluster. He also asked 12 outside analysts both these questions and why Pillsbury wasn't more attractive to the investing public. Said Spoor,

> If you put them all together they said basically the same thing: inconsistent performance in earnings per share growth, poor profit record, a shotgun approach to our portfolio without the necessary resources to support all our businesses, the failure to make acquisitions in support of our basic businesses, which were then Agri-Products and Consumer Products. And last was a simple observation that we had some businesses making money, but too many that were losing money. With this in mind we sat down and laid out a plan that we knew would have the support of the general managers because, after all, they helped create it.

SETTING GOALS FOR A NEW ERA

A portion of the process was the examination of other companies in the food business. Each member of the general managers' strategy group took three or four companies in the foods business and analyzed why they were successful. How they got there? What their performance measures were? Why they were great? Why the investors and analysts liked them? And so on. The general managers next extracted a composite of concepts they thought made attractive goals for Pillsbury and some things they were convinced the company really could do. Then, Mr. Spoor said,

> We laid out the key objectives of what we called "the Pillsbury dream." We said we wanted a five-year-record of consistent growth in sales and earnings per share. We wanted more than anything else, credibility, not only with our Board and ourselves, but with the investing public. We needed quality earnings: consistent, repetitive, growing. We wanted an average 10% growth per year in sales, minimum 10% growth in EPS, an ROE of 16%, an ROI on total capital employed of 20%, and a P/E ratio in the upper 1/3 of the leading food companies. We felt if we had a record of performance [like that] the stock price would follow. We said that recruiting, development, and

motivation of people was key. We wanted to be a quality company, first class in all respects—in our people, our products, our facilities, and our business conduct.

After almost a year of discussion there was a strong consensus. Of the goals, Mr. Spoor said, "There was no issue at all. The big issue became how do we know we're going to do it? What are our plans?" The next steps were unique. "We decided to really put ourselves on the spot. I suggested to the Board that we go public with our objectives, really lay the company out. . . . They said, 'Why? Why don't you just wait?' So we waited until the May Board meeting; then we laid out [for the Board] the presentation we wanted to take to the New York security analysts." Two months later (on July 19, 1973) Spoor, Peterson, and Arthur Rosewall (CEO of Burger King) publicly announced certain key strategies and objectives at a meeting of the New York Society of Security Analysts. Highlights are included in Exhibit 1. Mr. Spoor said, "I think people understood this was a different group [of managers] with different aspirations. But they still had doubts we could achieve what we said."

THE CHANGEOVER

Certain actions were already under way. Organizationally, most of the operations now reported directly to Spoor: Wallin in Agriproducts, Elston (whom Spoor brought in from McKinsey) in International, Rosewall in Burger King, and most corporate staff units. Although Peterson had the title of president, he was not chief operating officer. His role was more that of group vice president over the consumer business. Spoor quickly started "Monday morning staff meetings" attended by these top line people and ultimately a few staff people. He made it clear that the style of Pillsbury had changed. He was going to be involved. He would call the shots. He would listen to people, but he was going to make the decisions. As one executive said, "Peterson didn't get to make many decisions—very aggravating to Jimmy," a man who had been considered a genuine candidate for the top spot.

According to some, "Pillsbury had become a bit inbred at this time." There was an inside Board with many Minneapolis people on it. The tenor of the company was described as "hold things the way they were." Sales growth had been largely through inflation. Relationships at the top level had been "very gentlemanly." In this milieu Spoor's style created a new driving force. His style was described as follows:

He's a challenger. He really takes nothing at face value, even after you've worked with him for a long time. I'm as liable as ever to go up to his office and be really grilled. He's not doing it to grill me, but to really penetrate, to see how carefully an idea has been thought through, how ready it is to be hatched—and how strongly I believe it. He may oppose me and disguise his reason for opposition, just to see how deeply I feel about a thing. He's a challenger, a questioner. He's an options open kind of guy. . . But he has very strong opinions on things. To change an opinion you just have to tackle him and break his shoulder.

He's also very much a scorecard guy. He says, "I keep a scorecard, good and bad." Each time the Board meets, he says this is what I said I was going to do. This is what we've done. This is what we haven't done. This is what we're going to do the next period. And this is how I'll come to you to measure my and the corporation's performance. He has said, "I'm on this stage for awhile; then somebody else is going to have it. Some people have stayed here too long. I'm not going to. . . . I expect to be taken care of if I do a good job here, but don't keep me here a month longer than I am really contributing." He means it.

He's not a gentle, caring, warm, human being. He's fun. He likes to have a drink, to tell a good story, to laugh. But he's an intensive, inward guy—very performance oriented. Unfortunately, there's a lot of fear of Bill Spoor too. Sometimes it costs him in terms of some people's willingness to really say where they are on issues. He seeks a lot of input, listens to people he respects and trusts, thinks. He doesn't make a decision until he has to. I don't mean that he procrastinates. He keeps every option open, whether it's who he'll have lunch with, who he'll name to the Board, or what organizational form he'll use. He doesn't commit his mind to a course of action until he has everything he can learn about it. He's a very bright guy, and a very clear thinker, especially on paper. Yet he's very low on self ego, very unselfish in his management style.

THE CHICKEN IS THE EGG

The first real test of the new management team was in stabilizing earnings. A key element in this had to be Pillsbury Farms' chicken business. Two years before Mr. Spoor's accession, *Financial World* had pointed out,

[In 1971] Pillsbury's first half sales rose 4% from those in the corresponding period of fiscal 1969–70, but common share earnings fell from $2.34 to $1.30. This sharp drop would be startling enough even in a company dependent mainly on the badly depressed broiler market; but Pillsbury Farms, the chicken division, brought in only

16% of the sales in the fiscal 1969–70, so it's obvious that the chicken impact is really staggering.[7]

THE BIGGEST QUESTION

According to Mr. G. M. Donhowe, vice president and treasurer at the time,

Bill knew before he took the job that the biggest question he'd have to face was to stay in or get out of chickens. Within a few months after taking over he asked a number of people who he knew were protagonists on one side or the other for whatever memoranda or position papers they had in their files on the subject. Then he invited any member of senior management who wanted to present a position paper to do so. He got papers from Terry Hanold, who was a strong advocate of the chicken business; Dean McNeal, who was on the Board and had formerly run our Agricultural Products group which included chickens; and Mike Harper, who had run the operation trying to sell branded chickens (fresh and frozen) and frozen processed chickens . . . I was a chief protagonist for getting rid of it. I was joined in that position substantially by Paul Kelsey, the controller. Just about everyone else was sitting in the wings. . . .

Spoor had purposely commissioned two papers on each side of the issue: Hanold and McNeal for retention, Harper and Donhowe for divestiture. But the decision was not easy. As Mr. Spoor said later, "Poultry was some $140 million of our [roughly] $700 million in sales, and in that particular year it was on an up cycle. In the last full year of our ownership, poultry made $6 million." Management was split on the issue. And to complicate matters, Mr. Hanold, the past president who had been largely responsible for the chicken business concept, was still on the Board and was chairman of the Executive Committee.

DEBATE AND DECISION

With the position papers as background, management debated the issue for 12 months "very hotly and under difficult circumstances." Spoor and Donhowe visited Ralston Purina which had recently made a similar divestiture. They invited consultants to look at the issue. And they asked Lehman Brothers what Pillsbury Farms' real value was. Lehman responded that they could sell it to a potential European buyer at a price higher "by some healthy margin" than the present value of the division's then projected five-year cash flows. Finally this information, the position papers, and management's own recommendation to divest went to the Board. The Board continued the debate for some

months. When the issue finally came to a vote, only Mr. Hanold voted against divestiture. According to some, this signaled Mr. Hanold's "break with management." And shortly afterward at his own request Hanold "went onto special assignment." Mr. Spoor later commented very sympathetically, "A very brilliant man! A shame, but that's just the way it went."

Following the Board's vote on March 6, 1974, Pillsbury Farms was sold to Imperial Group, Ltd., for over $20 million. Mr. Spoor later noted: "This really taught everyone a lesson—that anything that wasn't performing, that didn't have good long-range plans and prospects, was in trouble." But in his public announcement of the decision, he emphasized that,

Pillsbury Farms is a good business directed by sound management. Our decision to sell is based on strategic fit and price—not inadequate performance. . . . To remain with Farms would call for a significant reinvestment program. . . . We do not believe that selection of broiler chickens for growth investments meets the corporate objectives we outlined to you in our meeting with the New York Society last July.[8]

The divested division had made $3 million net in fiscal 1974 before its sale.[9] In the next year, it reportedly lost money for its new owner, and in the words of one executive, "Spoor became an overnight hero. He gained a lot of ground with the Board."

A FOODS COMPANY

"By then, after a year," said Mr. Spoor, "we had decided that we wanted to be a foods company. As we looked back, that was the only thing that we'd really made money on. Once we'd agreed on that . . . we got rid of all the sideshows. We dumped housing, timesharing, the gourmet magazine, wines, and fresh flowers—all after careful study. But you have to give people a rationale—a truthful rationale—as to why you do these things. So we said, we want to be a foods company. We've agreed to that. This or that division or business doesn't fit, besides which it is losing money."

For example, housing had lost a lot of money. And, according to one major participant, "top management really didn't even know the vocabulary of the business." Time-sharing had been created because the company had excess computer capacity and the former president—who was interested in computer applications[10]—had pushed the opportunity. This business clearly did not fit well into the "foods" concept. On the other hand, Spoor later said, "We should have been able to make *Gourmet* magazine go, but I couldn't find anyone who would take the challenge. That was an easy sale because the business could have been made profitable."

OUT OF WINE

Souverain Cellars was much more complicated because it involved big losses. In 1972 Pillsbury had bought Souverain in California's Napa Valley and had pumped in some $8 million to boost production from 12,000 cases toward 1978 goals of 570,000 cases. But the total industry overexpanded to an extent that it outran both consumer demand and its own storage facilities. By mid-1975 Souverain had lost money for two consecutive years, and its near term future looked just as bleak.[11]

Pillsbury tried several management teams in an attempt to turn the company around, but with little success. Finally Mr. Spoor asked the president of Souverain, "How much money could we make if every case was sold for margin." The president responded, "$2 million before taxes." At that time Pillsbury had already lost $6 million on Souverain. Shortly thereafter Souverain's president came back to Spoor and recommended, himself, that Pillsbury leave the wine business.

Several rationales presented themselves for this action in 1975. First, Souverain was a losing operation. Second, certain states prohibited alcoholic beverage producers from selling alcohol in their own restaurants. This would have prevented Burger King from ever selling beer. And it would have precluded an attractive potential acquisition, Steak and Ale, which suddenly appeared. But executives noted the divestiture decision was really underway much earlier. "We had a 1 1/2% market share and no real ability—without just mammoth investments—to become major. . . . Also, remember, Bill Spoor wants to be big and recognizable in anything he does, whether it's hitting a tennis ball or business. Steak and Ale just accelerated the decision. We had enormous earnings in 1975 so we could afford to take the bath then."

Of this early period, Mr. Spoor said,

I used to do quiet things at night. I was convinced if we could just turn off these loss divisions, we could really make some money. We were draining the company for no purpose at all. I've always got hedges in the back of my mind. I'm never overcommitted to a business unless I know there's something back there. I get surprised sometimes. But I knew if we got rid of all these, we'd have a better income later. Maybe that could give us 3–4% of our 10% target profit growth.

Mr. Spoor also noted that in this divestiture period,

In several cases the people who were directly involved in the management of troubled divisions—for example the president of Souverain—came in with recommendations that theirs were businesses we ought to get out of. In Souverain's case it was a major problem area. We had proven we couldn't manage it. We had made lots of fundamental managerial mistakes in terms of how we ran it.

But essentially the same thing occurred in the European Flower Markets. In its final year as a part of Pillsbury, that reported to me; I'd told the general manager that I'd like to have his recommendation for the future of the business. . . . And his recommendation was to get out of it. He has a very important role elsewhere in Pillsbury now.

REINVESTMENT AND DIVERSIFICATION

With the cash freed up by divestitures, Pillsbury began to reinvest in growth opportunities. Primary among these, at the time, was Burger King. As Spoor said, "With cake mix you could only grow two ways—by a new product expanding the total market or by increasing your market share. But with Burger King we could grow these two ways, or we could grow geographically. Burger King was the throttle on our growth. [With care we could open it up a little or close it down] to control our growth rate and credibility." Another advantage of restaurants was that they could, in part, finance themselves without impairing the capital access of the rest of the company. All debt and lease obligations of the restaurant subsidiaries were obtained on the basis of their own credits and not guaranteed by the parent company. Eventually the company carried some 65% of its combined restaurant capitalization as debt or debt equivalent."[12]

In 1975 Pillsbury began another important entry into the restaurant field. As Mr. Spoor recalls,

I got a call from an outside director, John Whitehead, on Steak and Ale Restaurants of America. They were being courted and were almost at the point of being acquired by Ralston Purina . . . We were not looking [at Steak and Ale] at all. John Whitehead had just picked up signals about it informally . . . So I called Norm Brinker, who was a cofounder of Steak and Ale, and he and I talked very quietly. We hit it off. We talked the same way, we were trying to do the same things in life, and we had a similar upbringing . . . We just clicked. Finally, during later negotiations, Brinker said, "Bill, if we can put this thing together, I'll go with Pillsbury. But I have one condition, I will only report to you."

It seems another top Pillsbury executive, after spending days looking at Steak and Ale Restaurants, had given up around 10:30 one night while Spoor had hung on for as long as Brinker wanted. Spoor said, "He was a nondrinker, so it was pretty dry at times. . . . But a sensitive guy like that is selling his life's blood. He wants to know he's loved, accepted, part of the organization. . . . Little things like that make a big difference."

Mr. Walter Scott, chief financial officer of Pillsbury, later noted,

> At that stage we were not particularly out looking for new acquisitions in the restaurant business. We were concentrating our efforts on consumer products companies. Nevertheless through our acquisitions department we looked at the particular sector in which Steak and Ale was operating to determine whether (on a long-term basis) it looked like an interesting aspect of the restaurant business and what it would do for Pillsbury—positive and negative. We commissioned some outside studies to try to help us in developing a conviction as to whether we were on the right track. All this was orchestrated by the acquisition department with lots of plug-ins from other parts of the company.

By the end of 1976 the company had begun to assume a new shape. Pillsbury had pared off all its non-food-related lines and some of its smaller food lines overseas. In addition to Pillsbury Farms, *Bon Appetit*, Pemton, Standard Computer, Souverain, and European Flower Markets, Pillsbury had divested McLaren's (Canadian—pickles and olives), Lara (Mexican—cookies), Calgary Mills (Canadian—flour), and Gringoire-Brossard (French-bakery products). Spoor began to say publicly: "I'm only interested in businesses that fall into three categories . . . consumer foods, foods-away-from-home, and agri-products."[13]

THE CONSUMER GROUP

Of these, Pillsbury's consumer foods activities posed special problems for Mr. Spoor. *Fortune* described some of the key issues this way:

> In picking Pillsbury's new chief, Spoor's predecessor sidestepped his own protege, James R. Peterson, whose management skills were much admired by many Pillsbury executives despite the lackluster performance of the consumer group he headed. When Spoor was appointed CEO, Peterson was named President with continuing responsibility for consumer products.
>
> It soon became apparent that neither man was too comfortable working with the other. Spoor gradually began to limit Peterson's role. Peterson sensed erosion in the high level support he was used to in previous jobs—and subordinates found him more difficult to work for. Ultimately, Peterson was forced out by pressures from

above and below. In December, 1975, one of his ranking subordinates, George Masko, resigned. Using this resignation along with statements of dissatisfaction from another veteran consumer products executive, Raymond V. Kimrey, Spoor argued to the Board that Peterson's subordinates were up in arms. Confronted with an unappealing choice—the departure of the President or his two top lieutenants—the directors opted to get rid of Peterson.[14*]

When Mr. Peterson left in April 1976 (as executive vice president and director of R. J. Reynolds) Pillsbury's Consumer Group, which provided some 36% of fiscal 1976 profits, included Grocery Products, Refrigerated Products (largely dough), Frozen Foods (principally pizza), Wilton Enterprises (cake and party decorations), and Pillsbury's international consumer activities. According to *Fortune* the group "had seldom developed exciting new products or provided consistent marketing support for the winners it had."[14] To wake up the operation Spoor went after a new top man and recruited Raymond F. Good, who as its president had restored Heinz' domestic foods operations to profitability.

Each of the Consumer Group's divisions had its own problems. The Grocery Division was mired in cake mixes, flour, potatoes, etc. with declining markets in which it held only a number two or three position. It had to accept price levels set by the leaders, but lacked their modern facilities and scale. The refrigerated dough business, where Pillsbury's market share was high, also appeared to be in a long-term declining industry. The only bright spot in Consumer was frozen foods; Totino's[15] pizza brand—acquired in 1975—was on its way to a strong second-place market share. Although frozen foods in general were declining, frozen pizzas were booming. Said *The Wall Street Journal*,

> Totino's is the market leader almost everywhere it competes. The frozen pizza market is growing rapidly and is already larger than the cake mix or refrigerated dough markets, previously Pillsbury's major consumer food areas.[16]

Good had a choice of two overall strategies: (1) put up the long-term massive advertising necessary to gain first-place penetration for more of his products or (2) manage the declining products for cash and build future businesses in other growth markets. Wishing to avoid the negative profit impact of the former course, Good chose the latter. He commissioned a McKinsey & Company study, which suggested positive consumer trends toward convenience foods, natural foods, more

---

*W. Kiechel, "Now for the Greening of Pillsbury," *Fortune*, November 5, 1979. Copyright © 1979 by Time, Inc. All rights reserved.

nutritious foods, snacks, and "foods-to-match-changing-lifestyles" where the sitdown family meal was becoming the exception rather than the rule. At Spoor's request Good presented the complete plan for Consumer's redevelopment to the Board. "You could have heard a pin drop . . . It was so good," said Spoor soon afterward.

Good brought in Edgar Mertz, a former Heinz executive vice president, as his number two man and pressed hard on cost cutting programs to yield savings of 2–3% of sales. Then he plowed the margins into Totino's and selected acquisitions like Speas Farm (apple juice and vinegar) and American Beauty (macaroni). For a while these things seemed to work. By late 1978, however, company veterans were complaining about the new Consumer team's management style, and Good's relations with Spoor seemed to deteriorate. According to *Fortune* Spoor became progressively more insistent that Good clean up "the mess in grocery," show some dramatic financial improvements, and deal with Mertz's abrasive style which was becoming a "time bomb" about to explode the consumer operation.[14] When Spoor needed money to make up shortfalls elsewhere, Good grudgingly cut back on Consumer's advertising and promotional activities and slashed marketing budgets to meet short-term profit goals. On the other hand, while Spoor wanted more profits from Consumer, he was reportedly reluctant to back away from its traditional baking products. So the division in 1979 began to press hard to increase its market share on those lines—with all that implied.[14]

AGRI-PRODUCTS

Agri-Products had provided the remaining quarter of Pillsbury's sales and earnings. Agri—which included mainly Industrial Foods (flour milling, baking mix, hydro-processing), Commodity Merchandising (of grain and feed ingredients), Food Service (volume feeding to institutions), and Export—had been the foundation of Pillsbury's original foods business. But by the late 1970s these activities were declining in relative importance to Pillsbury. In boom years Agri fared well as its grain merchandising and flour milling activities responded to industry cycles. But even as the largest flour producer, Pillsbury found it hard to maintain acceptable margins in bad years.

Nevertheless, Agri was one of the world's largest grain merchandising operations, and enjoyed gross sales of over $3 billion in 1983. Only gross margins from these operations appeared in consolidated sales. The industries on which Agri was based (especially grain production and feed ingredients) were huge and growing at some 3% per year. In summary, in 1983 Agri-Products was (1) the nation's largest flour miller, (2) its eighth largest rice miller, (3) its largest feed ingredient merchandiser, (4) its largest flour exporter, (5) among the top five in grain and oilseed origination, and (6) a major producer of bakery mixes.

PHASE TWO

In 1976-77 Pillsbury entered phase two of its overall plan. Most of its divestitures were complete, and a new management team was coming into place. About this time Spoor started to talk about becoming "a truly great corporation." How was this to be measured? "We have 12 foods companies we measure ourselves against—like General Mills, General Foods, Kraft, Ralston Purina. We want our P/E ratio to be in the upper one-third of these food companies," said Spoor. But he also wanted to have "the best management" of these companies and "to be number one or number two in every product category we compete in." Spoor continued, "I also want to leave the next management with the same kind of growth vehicle we inherited."[17]

The latter idea became known throughout the company as Spoor's "superbox." Anticipating that in a decade or so the fast-food market would be saturated, Spoor was planting the seeds for a totally new opportunity farther down the road. "It can be almost anything—food, non-food, or food related." This was the first official break with the "foods" concentration that had emerged from the divestiture period. In 1976-77 Spoor allocated some $350,000 to an open ended search for "superbox." The concept was not clearly specified—only that it was to be a large move and one that would provide the basis for growth in the late 1980s. Said Spoor at the time,

> "I deal in dreams. You can't deal just in the hard facts in this kind of job. Somebody's got to dream. And then you get some smart people to put meat on the dreams . . . ."[17] He observed: "We broke the initial Pillsbury Dream into sub-missions. We started out with the spirit of '76. We said by 1976, the 200th anniversary of our company, we can break $1 billion in sales and have a $5 EPS. We had things to talk about, magic things, because people need handles. We talked about the 'spirit of '76' first, which was a dream. And we hit that about a year in advance. That then let us push forward the financial dream. We wanted to split the shares, call the converts, clean up the balance sheet, and really get a powerful balance sheet for the first time—all of which we did . . . zap! The next dream is superbox."

ORGANIZATION CHANGES

Mr. Spoor later said, "In terms of everything that's happened at Pillsbury, it's the people that make the big difference." The people changes began shortly after Spoor took office, and seven years later they were still a dramatic portion of Pillsbury's activities. Along with the early divestitures outlined above, Mr. Spoor quickly began to modify the company's overall organizational structure. He said,

> We inherited the "free standing business" concept which I felt was hurting the company more than anything we could have done organizationally. We took great strengths and fragmented them. So one of the early ideas was to pull the company back together. The idea of what specifically to do wasn't too far advanced at that time. . . . I couldn't just go to a lower-level unit and get anything (coordinated] done. I'd have to talk to Grocery or Refrigerated and so forth first. . . . Among other things the former management had delegated acquisitions to each of the businesses, but no one had made an acquisition. . . . And so on. The company was very split up; a "this is mine, that's yours idea" prevailed. We were really going to have to change the culture to get needed coordination.

CONSOLIDATION AND ACQUISITION

Spoor immediately had most operations report directly to him: Rosewall of Burger King, Wallin in Agri-Products, Elston (whom Spoor brought in from McKinsey) in International, and Peterson in Consumer Products. In addition, the various corporate staff units reported to Spoor. Most important among these were Personnel and Finance where Spoor recruited two high-powered heads from outside the company—Walter D. Scott and Edwin H. Wingate. Both were top candidates from extensive head hunts. Like many others recruited later, both were reportedly extremely well paid and offered "the opportunity to fulfill their career objectives" with Pillsbury. In short order Spoor also brought in Philip D. Aines from Procter & Gamble to head up research and Jerry W. Levin to handle mergers and acquisitions. Most agree that these were all outstanding people, extremely talented. Commentary like that used about Mr. Scott would apply to many of these executives:

> Wally Scott was a gifted man—not just good—he was gifted. He had given up two years of his life at about one tenth of his industrial income to make his government better. He was then at OMB. He liked the Pillsbury Dream we had started by then and saw the challenge. At the time he was interviewed the head hunters said "These final two men are great men, but we think you'll find Mr. Scott head and shoulders above."

After Mr. Wingate had been aboard a short time, Spoor asked him to "Think about the kinds of businesses we are in, how we ought to be structured." With substantial impact from Mr. Willys H. Monroe, a Board member, the three began to discuss how to organizationally restructure Pillsbury. From the first, it was abundantly clear that we were in three businesses. Win Wallin had the agribusiness, Jimmy Peterson had the consumer business, and Arthur Rosewall had the restaurants (which was really Burger King at that time). The key questions then were: "How do we take best advantage of these businesses, use the people we've got, and develop succession management?" In response to these questions Wingate and Monroe wrote up "white papers" for Spoor. Finally the three men, working largely from the Monroe document, designed the basic outlines of the new organization. Mr. Wingate noted,

> These papers weren't done in a vacuum. They were reviewed with Spoor often, and we'd test different thoughts. It's hard to say which day it really happened. . . . There was talk even a year earlier in the consumer companies that some day it would be possible to take advantage of synergies that undoubtedly existed in production, sales, marketing, and research—to restructure activities so that this body of knowledge could be focused against the whole retail market.

Distron—which was part of Burger King and was the second largest food distribution system in the United States—could service 2–5 restaurant chains. Davmor, a manufacturer of kitchen equipment and furniture for restaurants, could also apply staff across the board. Real Estate could work across the various businesses. There was a lot of construction in the groups. And so on. Mr. Wingate later said,

> In developing the final format there were many discussions with corporate level people before the new organization could be officially put on paper. . . . There were extensive interchanges and seminar activities on "how this or that would work?" before anything was done. . . . There evolved a consensus understanding—if not a consensus agreement—on where we were heading. . . . Individuals might not even recall who articulated the concept to them or when. People simply gained an appreciation and were able to internalize the fact that some organization changes were going to take place. They knew what was being considered and could project how they would be affected.

In the area of what became the new senior management committee, there was serious opposition from the heads of the "free standing businesses" and staff people who would not be on that committee any more. The new group was line, just seven people: Spoor, Scott, Powell, and the four line executive vice presidents—instead of the 15 general managers who had previously funneled into the executive office. Most of these now reported to the executive VPs as staff heads or heads of individual product or activity centers. Support activities for each unit were consolidated at the group level whenever possible. Some of the very senior people reportedly found this quite hard to swallow. Nevertheless, by mid-1976 the new structure was largely in place. But it kept evolving over the next several years as pieces of Peterson's former activities were split between Spoor and Scott.

CHANGES AT THE TOP

Meanwhile Spoor kept up his search for first-rate talent to run his line operations. As was noted, Ray Good had taken over Consumer Products. In 1977 Spoor hired Donald N. Smith (then 36 and McDonalds' third-ranking executive) as CEO of Burger King, and the talented newcomer began to bring that diverse enterprise under more effective operating control. But Burger King had an uphill profitability fight against McDonalds' larger distribution system and outlet size ($200,000 per year greater sales than the average Burger King unit).

Then unfortunately, after a glowing few years, Ray Good's relationship with Spoor began to deteriorate seriously as Consumer profit performance lagged and it developed internal management problems. When Spoor suddenly picked the much liked head of Agri-Products, Winston R. Wallin, to be president, both Good and "Wally" Scott were deeply unsettled. In the process of selection the Board's nominating committee reviewed all the top line and staff people. Mr. Spoor later described events this way,

> I went to the Board in March (1978) and said, "We need a president of this company." They were absolutely aghast. They said, "But things are going so well. Why rush into naming a president now and risk losing all those top candidates you brought in? The reason they're good is they're scrambling for the open slot." I answered, "Because the company could be run more effectively." They replied, "Let us think about it." And basically they turned me down.
>
> In May I went back and I was irate . . . I said, "I want to set up the time this company can be managed more

effectively; and frankly it can be. There's something called the concentration of power—in me. Everybody listens too carefully to what I say—and I'm not that good—it becomes 'Spoor said this, and Spoor said that.' I know what I can do and what I can't do within reason. . . . If you want to put this company at risk, just let me go on like this for another couple of years." . . . Zap! The situation changed in two seconds. We announced Wallin as president in June.

A few years before, Spoor and Wallin had participated in an encounter group at the National Training Laboratories. There they had spent a lot of time together and had gotten to know each other quite well. Spoor said, "Win has a marvelous sense of humor. He is very slow on the draw and will let people speak their piece. But when he comes out, he has a point of view that is absolutely spectacular. I have built up extreme confidence in Win."

THE GREEN GIANT ARRIVES

Then in late 1978 Spoor began negotiations with Green Giant Company, a large well-established foods company headed by Thomas H. Wyman, formerly second in command at Polaroid. Before the merger, Spoor reportedly told visitors, "No one at Pillsbury can run Green Giant." And Wyman—who was considered one of the rising stars of the U.S. executive world—was assured like other talented managers that his "career expectations could be fulfilled at Pillsbury."[14]

On completion of the merger, Wyman personally received a windfall of almost $1 million in salary, bonuses, and benefits. The question then became where to put Wyman in the Pillsbury structure. The solution was an executive office—with Wallin as president, Wyman as vice chairman, and Scott as executive vice president. Explained Spoor, "I had to offer Wyman the top job to keep him and to make the merger work."[18] Discouraged by these events, Good left the company in July 1979 and became president of Munsingwear in October of that year. When asked why he was willing to sacrifice Good, Spoor replied bluntly, "Tom's better."[19]

By March 1980 Spoor could report to analysts that Pillsbury had "the finest management team in the foods industry." Then began a series of high level defections that staggered the company. In early May, Wally Scott resigned to head Investors Diversified Services, Inc. Then shortly thereafter Don Smith left for the top spot at PepsiCo, Inc. *Business Week* noted however that: "Spoor had created an atmosphere of intense competition among the top officers, luring each initially with the promise of succession." But perhaps the biggest jolt came on May 23 when Tom Wyman agreed to become president and chief executive of CBS. While upset by the turmoil, Spoor responded philosophically, "There were solid reasons behind each of the moves. Tom Wyman couldn't turn down the offer CBS made him . . . [reportedly a $1 million bonus and $800,000 per year guaranteed salary]. . . . And we would have destroyed our pay structures trying to meet the offers."[20]

One consolation for Spoor was that along with Wyman, Pillsbury got Jack Stafford, Green Giant's chief operating officer. Stafford's background seemed ideal for Pillsbury. In addition to his success at Green Giant, he had spent 12 years in consumer advertising at Leo Burnett and had risen to senior vice president–marketing at Kentucky Fried Chicken Corporation. Stafford was named an executive vice president at Pillsbury in 1979, became head of Consumer Foods in 1981, and joined the board of directors in 1983.

CONTINUED PERFORMANCE

Despite the turmoil, Pillsbury's financial performance continued to be exceptionally strong. (See Exhibits 2–4.) And the departed executives had all left their own positive imprints. Before leaving, Don Smith had brought a new discipline to Burger King. He had expanded menus and increased sales in real terms during a period when McDonald's and Wendy's real sales declined. Green Giant's Stafford had moved into the top slot at Consumer, and Spoor claimed "the company could now market in the league with Kraft and General Mills."

The company also continued both to acquire and divest operations in keeping with its extraordinary goals.

The company had changed in important qualitative dimensions as well. At the time the Pillsbury Dream was first drawn up, the management group had decided it wanted to share its proposed successes with all important constituencies, including stockholders, the board of directors, employees, customers, suppliers, and especially the communities where the company operated. The management group set general goals in each area and resolved to monitor progress against these. As profits grew, the company multiplied its contributions to community causes to $3.5 million in 1983. Pillsbury occasionally bought out the remaining tickets to the Minnesota Vikings games and gave them to United Way so local people could see games which would have been blacked out on TV. During the Vietnam refugee crisis, company officers went to Washington to see what Pillsbury could do to help and gave every person in the company who would "adopt" a Vietnamese family $1,000—or a year's supply of food for the family.

In addition, top management engaged Survey Research, Inc., to do a series of employee attitude surveys to see how people at all levels regarded Pillsbury in terms of compensation, supervisory practices, planning, communications, and so on. The company changed a number of employee practices: better explaining each individual's compensation and role in the total enterprise, posting and allowing bidding for all internal openings, improving the house medium *The Pillsbury Reporter* to explain where the company was going, the progress it was making, and the reasons things were being done. Top executives noted,

TABLE 1 Acquisitions and Divestments Fiscal 1974–1983	DIVESTMENTS	ACQUISITIONS
	Pillsbury Farms (poultry)	Wilton Enterprises (cake decorating)
	Pemton (housing development)	Totino's Finer Foods (frozen pizza)
	Standard Computer (time-sharing)	Steak & Ale Restaurants of America
	Lara (Mexican cookie manufacturer)	American Beauty Macaroni Company
	Bon Appetit (gourmet magazine)	Fox Deluxe Pizza
	Souverain Wine	Green Giant
	European Flower Markets	Wickes Agricultural
	Calgary Flour Mill	Pioneer Rice
	Wilson Enterprises	B & B Mushrooms
	Poppin Fresh Pie Shops	Jokish
	McLaren's (pickles and olives)	Hoffman Menüu
	Gringoire-Brossard (bakery products)	Hammonds
		Häagen-Dazs

"Recruiting is a lot easier than it was. We have people coming to us now—good people—saying they hear what's happening here and want to be a part of it."

1985 AND BEYOND

In 1984–85 Mr. Spoor announced a new set of goals for Pillsbury. These were: annual growth rates of 12–15% for EPS, 25% for ROI, and 18% for ROE. How this should be accomplished was an open question. Mr. Spoor had told analysts and public audiences that Pillsbury wished to remain dominantly a foods company. But to achieve its goals it would consider: making tactical acquisitions, joining in major mergers where Pillsbury was the surviving entity, and entering non-foods fields where Pillsbury could add significant value through use of its skills and resources. In keeping with this Pillsbury had recently acquired Häagen Dazs (a quality ice cream producer and distributor), Sedutto Ice Creams (for the full service market), Azteca Corn Products (refrigerated tortillas), Apollo Foods (high-quality ethnic foods), and Van de Kamps (frozen foods).

In June 1983, it had attempted to acquire Stokley-Van Camp, Inc., for a $62 per share tender offer. When the target company's management fought the offer and Quaker Oats put in a "friendly" tender of $77 per share, Pillsbury withdrew with a pretax gain of over $6 million.[21] A similar scenario occurred when Pillsbury made a bid for the Joan of Arc Co., a closely-held producer of specialty canned goods.[22]

Summary financial data for Pillsbury's major divisions are included in Exhibit 2. Burger King continued to be the most significant contributor to 1984 gains in sales (20%) and operating profit (60%). Its systemwide sales rose to $3.43 billion. Over the preceding two years, operating profit had increased 74% while return on invested capital had increased from 18% to nearly 26%. By year end Burger King had 3,827 restaurants worldwide, with 14% operating as company owned units. While experiencing losses during fiscal 1984, Burger King's international operations improved substantially over the preceding year, and it was making substantial progress with its institutional franchise program. By the end of fiscal 1984, Häagen Dazs had a total of 316 units located in 32 states. Steak & Ale Restaurants numbered 32, with average restaurant sales increasing to $1.5 million. Bennigan's, the popular fern bar, continued its growth with average unit sales of $2.3 million and instituted a number of programs to offer non-alcoholic drinks and to discourage intoxicated individuals from driving. By year end it had 148

units. J. J. Muggs, a gourmet hamburger restaurant concept that began in fiscal 1983, showed strong consumer acceptance and had been expanded to 5 units.

Pillsbury's Foods Group included Consumer Foods and Agri-Products. Overall sales increased 10% to $2.4 billion and operating profits rose 16% to $181 million. Agri-Products, aided by a large sale of flour to Egypt and the movement of grain as part of the government's Payment-in-Kind program to support farm prices, showed an increase of 111% over the preceding year's depressed profit levels. However, profits for fiscal 1984 remained below acceptable levels in barge transportation, grain exporting, rice milling, and edible beans.[23]

Consumer Foods 1984 performance was led by strong profit gains from Refrigerated Foods and Häagen Dazs with important volume growth in Frozen Foods. Partially due to the attention given to EDB, the Dry Grocery business experienced a marginal year with profits and volume somewhat below fiscal 1983. Häagen Dazs sales increased 22% during 1984, and Refrigerated Foods set new records for profits and sales. Within the Foods Group, all of International's wholly owned businesses finished fiscal 1984 ahead of the preceding year in their local currencies. However, the strength of the U.S. dollar resulted in operating profits below fiscal 1983.

Pillsbury's capital spending increased dramatically during fiscal 1984 to $282 million, a 16% increase over 1983. Restaurant expansion was the primary focus of investment, with other major capital projects supporting Häagen Dazs's major new production facilities and some tactical acquisitions domestically and abroad.

In his last two years as CEO, Mr. Spoor had emphasized both internal development of Pillsbury's three basic businesses (see Exhibit 4) and an aggressive acquisition program. He had formed a venture capital unit within Pillsbury to help it investigate and take positions in promising new areas and had commissioned studies by Stanford Research Institute (SRI) and Hudson Institute to define promising areas for future growth.

In early 1984 when Pillsbury announced that Jack Stafford (age 46) was moving up to president, replacing Win Wallin who became vice chairman, the press suggested that Spoor had identified his successor.[24] At that time Stafford took over responsibility for all foods operations while Wallin managed the restaurant businesses. Agri-Products was broken up into Commodities Marketing under Mr. Coonrod and Industrial Foods overseen by Kent Larson, who was responsible for the Dry Grocery portion of Consumer Foods.

As Mr. Stafford assumed the role of CEO, he faced a strong and much different Pillsbury than that of the early 1970s. Analysts, both within and outside the company, were wondering what he would make the hallmarks of his era. Mr. Spoor had worked hard to create a "superbox" for his successor, but what it should be and how Pillsbury should change its overall structure and portfolio to meet the opportunities and challenges of the late 1980s and 1990s were still unclear.

QUESTIONS

1. Evaluate Mr. Spoor's handling of the early stages in his strategy changes at Pillsbury. Why were these steps taken in this sequence? What could have been improved? How?
2. What do you think of the way Pillsbury's acquisition-expansion program was planned? Implemented? What changes would you have made? Why?
3. What should Mr. Stafford's strategy be for the late 1980s? Why? What should he do to implement it? What should Pillsbury's "superbox" be? How would you identify it? Implement it?

EXHIBIT 1
Highlights of a Presentation by the Pillsbury Company to the New York Society of Security Analysts July 19, 1973

Strategic Posture (Mr. Spoor)

I believe I can best outline our strategic posture by simply stating a group of propositions about the kind of company we intend to be:

- We are and will continue to be a market- and marketing-oriented company.
- We will be international in scope.
- We will be diversified beyond our food base.
- We will be dominated by our brand-oriented businesses serving rapidly growing consumer needs.
- There remains an important place for the basic commodity oriented enterprises in Pillsbury, provided earnings can be demonstrated to meet corporate standards for volatility.

We selected this kind of company over other alternates for two reasons.

First, this posture represents a natural extension of what we are and what we know how to do best. Secondly, we believe there are an ample number of investment opportunities available within this definition to satisfy our objectives. . . .

Corporate Objectives

In the general category

- We know that we must have a consistent record of growth in sales and earnings.
- We are hopeful of a price/earnings ratio in the upper one-third of a selected sample of food-based companies.
- We intend to continue our dividend policy.

If we can manage ourselves like that, in fiscal 1976 our sales would exceed $1 billion and earnings per share $5.00.

Applied against the base of fiscal 1973 results, this means we will have to grow at a compounded annual rate of 10% in both sales and earnings per share.

We recognize that these are demanding objectives, particularly for a company that historically has not operated at these levels. . . .

Agri-Products

The oldest business function of Pillsbury is our Agri-Products group, led by flour milling. Producing flour and selling it to the baker is a thoroughly mature business. We happen to be number one in this industry, and I think in more ways than capacity. Nonetheless we have in the past and will continue to employ a very disciplined allocation of capital for reinvestment in this business. Our objective is to sustain the most satisfactory earnings stream from flour milling on a constant or modestly declining capital base. . .

International

Our International operations finished a fine year. Jim Peterson will comment on the momentum in our consumer businesses in Europe, all of which are healthy and growing. Economic nationalism in Latin America, however, points to some difficult times ahead. We do not intend to walk away from these investment areas which have been very good to us. However, the desire for local government participation in several of our businesses and the recent adoption of Andean Pact legislation in Venezuela suggest a reduction rather than expansion of our developing country investments. . . .

EXHIBIT 1 (cont'd)

Pillsbury Farms

Finally, I want to report to you on Pillsbury Farms, our broiler poultry business. First, you should understand that after the pruning and re-direction of the business, which was begun two years ago, and included our recent withdrawal from further processed and microwave operations, Farms has become a healthy business. Aided by a strong price level, Farms turned in a record performance last year, delivering in excess of $5 million profit before tax. There is no doubt in my mind that this is an extremely well-run business with a management team second to none.

The question that we have been wrestling with is whether or not this well-run and profitable business fits the strategy we have laid out for Pillsbury. This is not an easy question to answer because one does not, with haste, decide to dispose of a major source of earnings per share where the likelihood for replacement is through internal development. . . .

So, at this point we are not prepared to make a definite statement as to what the answer to the question on Farms will be other than to say that all options remain open. . . .

Consumer Strategies (Mr. Peterson)

1. The importance of our consumer business in size, as well as in quality of earnings, identifies the fundamental need for accelerated growth here first if we are to move the total company.
2. The retail food industry with sales of over $100 billion in 1972 represents a broad array of opportunities for the mass marketing of branded consumer food products and an increasing opportunity in the 1970s for the mass marketing of non-food products.
3. We are keenly aware that to be a leader in our industry and to maintain the leverage that will ensure premium profitability, we must be both a leader in the markets in which we participate or plan to enter and that we must generate a growing share of retail grocery sales.
4. One's ability to grow in today's highly competitive food business and the rapidly emerging non-food areas of the supermarket depends on one's understanding of the consumer environment with its ever more rapidly increasing levels of personal income (both here and abroad), resulting in demands for ever-increasing levels of quality and convenience in both products and services.

We finally stated that we felt our plans for the future of our consumer businesses were soundly based on these principles, that they represented a balanced program and a continuing opportunity for premium growth.

Our four point strategy was stated as follows:

1. We are committed to a larger share of market in our current business areas. We will continue to place the investment of resources behind our fundamental consumer businesses to continue their share growth.
2. We believe that internal growth from new products can continue to be a source of increased earnings even in our mature areas.
3. The third part of our strategy involves the internal development of new business in areas that we are not in currently.
4. We will increase our acquisition activities and this will be a primary accountability of the executive office.

In February, I emphasized the importance of the development of brand franchises through the application of our marketing skills. We are giving great priority to the acceleration of this process. . . .

Consumer Orientation

As I stated earlier, we have based our consumer products efforts on the belief that the consumer is demanding rapidly increasing levels of quality and convenience and that this rate of change, fueled by increasing levels of personal income, provides an excellent opportunity for premium growth for those food companies that have the insight to identify the desired changes and are organized to commercialize them. We have reorganized our new products' teams to do both.

In each of the consumer business areas that I have discussed, branded products of high quality and convenience, keyed to contemporary life styles and value systems, clearly dominate our strategy. How we apply this philosophy to increase our share of market in our basic businesses, to accelerate our new product program, to develop products for new areas, and to acquire new consumer businesses will, in our view, determine our record in the months ahead. . . .

Burger King Restaurants (Mr. Rosewall)

Looking ahead for fiscal 1974 through fiscal 1977, our present planning horizon:

1. The fast-food industry is expected to grow at a compound rate of 11% per year, increasing from present annual sales of $5.9 billion to $9.9 billion.
2. The number of Burger King restaurants is expected to increase at a rate of 18% per year.
3. Total Burger King restaurant sales are expected to increase at a rate of 27% per year.

EXHIBIT 1 (cont'd)

Attainment of these objectives would result in the number of restaurants increasing from the 982 in operation at the end of fiscal 1973 to 1,930. Company operated units would increase from 278 to 670, or to about 35% of the total.

Total restaurant sales would increase from last year's $338 million to $891 million, with average sales per store, for comparable stores, moving from fiscal 1973's $376,000 to $492,000.

We want to continue to be Pillsbury's major investment opportunity.

Social Responsibility (Mr. Spoor)

This discussion of our business performance would not be complete without reporting on that broad and important topic "social responsibility." We are convinced that excellence in performance in these areas is a requirement our customers, employees and stockholders expect if we intend to compete successfully in the marketplace. This is not an extracurricular activity, but rather an integral part of the practice of management.

Source: Company records.

EXHIBIT 2
Sales, 1975–1984
(billions)

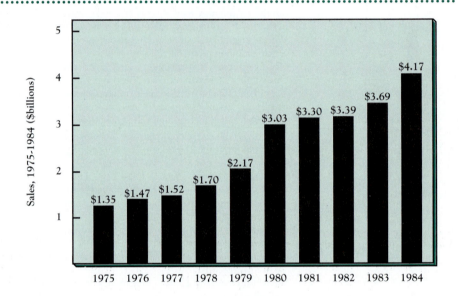

Source: The Pillsbury Company, *Annual Report,* 1975-1984.

EXHIBIT 2 (cont'd)
Net Earnings, 1975–1984
(millions)

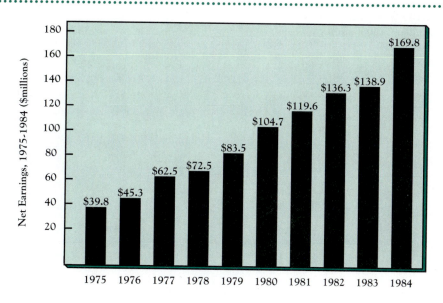

Source: The Pillsbury Company, *Annual Report,* 1975-1984.

EXHIBIT 2 (cont'd)
Cash Dividends, 1975–1984
(per share)

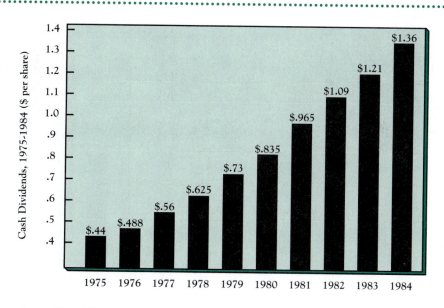

Source: The Pillsbury Company, *Annual Report,* 1975-1984.

EXHIBIT 2 (cont'd)
Charitable Contributions,
1973 vs. 1983–1984
(millions)

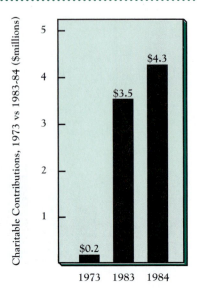

Source: The Pillsbury Company, *Annual Report*, 1973, 1983, 1984.

EXHIBIT 2 (cont'd)
Consumer Foods
Operating Profits
1979–1984
(millions)

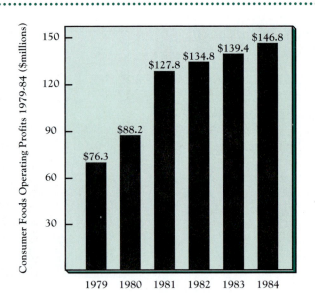

Source: The Pillsbury Company, *Annual Report*, 1979-1984.

EXHIBIT 2 (cont'd)
Restaurant Operating
Profit, 1979–1984
(millions)

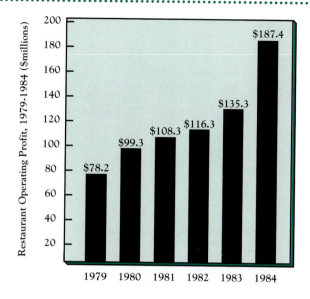

Source: The Pillsbury Company, *Annual Report*, 1979-1984.

EXHIBIT 2 (cont'd)
Agri Products Operating
Profit, 1979–1984
(millions)

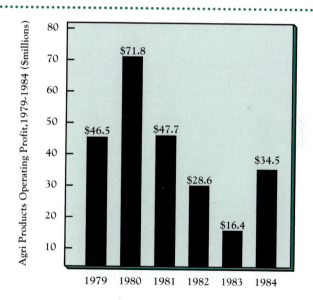

Source: The Pillsbury Company, *Annual Report*, 1979-1984.

EXHIBIT 3
The Pillsbury Company
and Subsidiaries
Consolidated Balance
Sheets, 1983–1984
(in millions of dollars)

ASSETS

	May 31 1984	May 31 1983
Current assets		
Cash and equivalents	$142.5	$129.6
Receivables, less allowance for doubtful accounts of $11.5 million and $12.9 million, respectively	355.8	350.6
Inventories		
Grain	75.5	52.9
Finished products	214.1	204.1
Raw materials, containers, and supplies	150.6	133.7
	440.2	390.7
Advances on purchases	107.7	128.4
Prepaid expenses	25.6	22.3
Total current assets	1,071.8	1,021.6
Property, plant, and equipment*		
Land and improvements	199.2	179.3
Buildings and improvements	885.1	788.2
Machinery and equipment	692.5	600.3
	1,776.8	1,567.8
Less: Accumulated depreciation	583.8	514.6
	1,193.0	1,053.2
Net investment in direct financing leases	184.0	178.7
Intangibles	83.2	21.6
Investments and other assets	76.3	91.5
	$2,608.3	**$2,366.6**

LIABILITIES AND STOCKHOLDERS' EQUITY

	May 31 1984	May 31 1983
Current liabilities		
Notes payable	17.3	$10.5
Current portion of long-term debt	94.3	32.8
Trade accounts payable	369.2	279.6
Advances on sales	136.0	136.7
Employee compensation	83.8	72.4
Taxes on income	16.5	20.8
Other liabilities	169.3	152.1
Total current liabilities	986.4	704.9
Long-term debt, noncurrent portion	503.1	572.4
Deferred taxes on income	149.3	108.5
Other deferrals	22.3	24.4
Stockholders' equity		
Preferred stock, without par value, authorized 500,000 shares, no shares issued		
Common stock, without par value, authorized 80,000,000 shares, issued 43,516,019 shares and 43,462,156 shares, respectively	306.2	284.1
Common stock in treasury at cost, 322,785 shares and 180,318 shares, respectively	(11.7)	(4.6)
Accumulated earnings retained and used in the business	792.4	704.9
Accumulated foreign currency translation	(40.7)	(28.0)
Total stockholders' equity	1,046.2	956.4
	$2,608.3	**$2,366.6**

*See Summary of Significant Accounting Policies and Notes to Consolidated Financial Statements provided in company's annual report.

Source: The Pillsbury Company, *Annual Report,* 1984.

EXHIBIT 4
Summary by Industry
Segment; The Pillsbury
Company and
Subsidiaries, 1982–1984
(in millions of dollars)

	YEAR ENDED MAY 31		
	1984	1983	1982
Net Sales			
Consumer Foods	$1,793.9	$1,652.1	$1,635.7
Restaurants	1,768.7	1,494.6	1,279.3
Agri-Products	694.8	627.5	568.6
Less Agri-Products intersegment sales	(85.1)	(88.3)	(98.5)
Total	4,127.3	3,685.9	3,385.1
Operating profit			
Consumer Foods	146.8	139.4	134.8
Restaurants	187.4	135.3	116.3
Agri-Products	34.5	16.4	28.6
Total	368.7	291.1	279.7
General corporate expense, net	(20.8)	(21.5)	(12.4)
Interest expense, net	(44.2)	(39.4)	(39.3)
Earnings before taxes on income	303.7	230.2	228.0
Identifiable assets			
Consumer Foods	836.3	725.4	747.9
Restaurants	1,191.2	1,025.7	993.3
Agri-Products	498.2	486.1	536.6
Corporate	82.6	129.4	150.5
Total	2,608.3	2,366.6	2,428.3
Capital expenditures			
Consumer Foods	59.4	48.7	50.0
Restaurants	197.4	164.0	126.8
Agri-Products	13.8	20.9	15.8
Corporate	11.8	10.3	15.9
Total	282.4	243.9	208.5
Depreciation expense			
Consumer Foods	36.1	33.0	30.3
Restaurants	59.5	54.7	48.6
Agri-Products	14.2	13.6	11.5
Corporate	4.8	4.2	2.4
Total	114.6	105.5	92.8
Foreign operations included in the above categories are as follows			
Net sales	355.5	360.1	357.9
Operating profit	16.2	18.0	22.8
Identifiable assets	241.8	212.8	241.8
Capital expenditures	20.4	16.3	22.6
Depreciation expense	9.7	10.3	8.8

Pillsbury is a diversified international food company operating in three major segments of the food industry. Net sales by segment include both sales to unaffiliated customers, as reported in the consolidated statements of earnings, and intersegment sales made on the same basis as sales to unaffiliated customers. Operating profit of reportable segments is net sales less operating expenses. In computing operating profit, none of the following items has been included: Interest income and expense, general corporate income and expenses, equity in net earnings (losses) of unconsolidated affiliates, and income taxes.

Source: The Pillsbury Company, *Annual Report*, 1984.

EXHIBIT 5
10-Year Comparisons in
Foods Industry,
1973–1983

COMPANY NAME	ANNUAL GROWTH EPS	ANNUAL GROWTH NET SALES	10 YEAR CHANGE IN ROE	10 YEAR CHANGE IN ROIC*
Pillsbury Co.	17.7%	17.0%	115.4%	76.8%
Heinz (J. J.) Co.	15.5	15.1	69.8	85.4
General Mills, Inc.	14.7	15.8	31.9	48.7
Kellogg Co.	13.5	13.3	25.2	5.4
Carnation Co.	12.8	11.9	10.4	6.0
CPC International, Inc.	12.5	11.6	35.3	41.0
Quaker Oats Co.	12.4	14.4	20.7	21.9
Ralston Purina Co.	11.6	11.6	9.1	22.8
Beatrice Foods Co.	10.2	17.0	(7.6)	(2.5)
General Foods Corp.	8.0	11.2	5.8	7.2

*Return on invested capital (pretax).

Source: *Prepared Foods*, September 1983.

All large (food) companies have broken out of their product boundaries. They are no longer the bread, beer, meat, milk or confectionery companies they were a relatively short time ago—they are food and drink companies.

Sir Adrian Cadbury, Chairman (retired),
Cadbury Schweppes, P.L.C.[1]

In the early 1990s, Cadbury Schweppes, P.L.C., seemed an archetypical modern food conglomerate. With extensive international operations in confectionery products and soft drinks, the company maintained a diversified global presence. Although Cadbury had enjoyed a relatively stable competitive environment through much of its history, recent developments in the international arena presented Cadbury's management with many new and critical challenges.

HISTORY OF CADBURY

The company began in 1831 when John Cadbury began processing cocoa and chocolate in the United Kingdom to be used in beverages. In 1847, the company became Cadbury Brothers. In 1866, it enjoyed its first major technical achievement when the second generation of Cadburys found a better way to process cocoa. By using an imported cocoa press to remove unpalatable cocoa butter from its hot cocoa drink mix instead of adding large quantities of sweeteners, Cadbury capitalized on a new, but growing, public concern about adulterated food.

Later, the company prospered even more when it found that cocoa butter could be used in recipes for edible chocolates. In 1905, Cadbury introduced Cadbury Dairy Milk (CDM) as a challenge to Swiss firms' virtual monopoly in British milk chocolate sales. A year

later, the firm scored another major success with the introduction of a new hot chocolate drink mix, Bournville Cocoa. These two brands provided much of the impetus for Cadbury's early prosperity.[2]

Cadbury faced rather benign competition throughout many of its early years. In fact, at one point, Cadbury provided inputs for the U.K. operations of the American firm, Mars, Inc.[3] Cadbury also formed trade associations with its U.K. counterparts (J. S. Fry and Rowntree & Co.) for the purpose of, among other things, reducing uncertainty in cocoa prices. The company later merged financial interests with J. S. Fry, but spurned offers to consolidate with Rowntree in 1921 and 1930.[4]

Facing growing protectionist threats in overseas markets following World War I, Cadbury began manufacturing outside the United Kingdom, primarily in Commonwealth countries: Australia (1921), New Zealand (1930), Ireland (1933), and South Africa (1937). Its international growth was also prompted by increasing world and domestic competition. By 1932 Cadbury management considered the Swiss company, Nestlé, as its primary competitor in the international arena.

In 1969, Cadbury merged with Schweppes, a worldwide producer of soft drinks and mixers. The merger offered both companies an array of advantages, both defensive and offensive. First, both companies were facing potential takeover threats from larger firms. The merger placed the new company in a better defensive posture to ward off unwanted suitors. Second, the marriage allowed the new company to compete better on a worldwide scale.

Since Cadbury had invested primarily in Commonwealth countries and Schweppes had branched out into Europe and North America, the new company enjoyed greater geographic dispersion. Its increased international presence also allowed the company to obtain some scale economies, notably, in defraying product development costs over a wider geographic base. The new company also enjoyed much greater bargaining power over suppliers; for example, following the merger, Cadbury Schweppes became the largest U.K. purchaser of sugar.[5]

The British confectionery companies historically pursued a different strategy from that of their American counterparts. While U.S. companies—such as Mars, Inc.—manufactured narrow product lines and employed centralized production, Cadbury supported 237 confectionery products in the marketplace until World War II forced it to scale back to 29. While there was a lack of intense competition, Cadbury's brand proliferation strategy was maintainable. But as rivalry heated up in the mid-1970s, Cadbury's share of the U.K. chocolate market fell from 31% in 1975 to 26.2% in 1977. Its management then began to shift over to a lower-cost, American-style strategy—with rationalized product lines and centralized production—as a more viable means of competition.[6]

Cadbury had long been famous for its unique management style. "Cadburyism" was strongly influenced by the founders' Quaker heritage of supporting worker welfare and harmonious community relations. Following Cadbury's reorientation around fewer core products and more rationalized production, the company's old management style also underwent a transformation. Confectionery manufacturing personnel decreased from 8,565 to 4,508 between 1978 and 1985.[7] In the process, management's traditionally close relationship with its workers, which had been built through years of maintaining employment stability, began to erode as work force reduction became an explicit goal of Cadbury executives.

THE ENVIRONMENT

As is the case with many other products in the food industry, many of Cadbury's product lines enjoyed very long product life cycles. (See Table 1.) Most food and beverage companies derived substantial benefits

---

TABLE 1

Brand Names Developed by Cadbury Schweppes and Its Confectionery Competition

Cadbury Schweppes

Cadbury Dairy Milk (CDM)	Roses
Milk Tray	Whole Nut
Crunchie	Fruit and Nut
Whispa	Trebor

Nestlé

Nestlé Crunch Bar	Polo
Kit Kat	Quality Street
Smarties	Yorkie
After Eight	Aero
Rolo	Black Magic
Dairy Box	Fruit Pastilles
Butterfinger	Baby Ruth

M&M/Mars, Inc.

Mars Bar	Galaxy
Twix	Maltesers
Bounty	Milky Way
M&Ms	Snickers

Hershey

Hershey Bar	Reese's Peanut Butter Cup
Hershey Kisses	Reese's Pieces
Mounds	Almond Joy
Bar None	

Phillip Morris

Milka
Tobler One
E. J. Brachs candy

Source: Compiled by authors.

from their long-established products—such as Cadbury's CDM bar—and their new product introductions frequently required little in the way of sophisticated technological investment. Food companies competed primarily by seeking cost reductions through process improvements and automation, by finding alternative new materials to replace more expensive ones, by enhancing flavor, and by introducing creative packaging and marketing.[8]

Successful new product introductions were sporadic; many of the most successful confectionery products—such as Mars Bar and Kit Kat—had been around since the 1930s.[9] Unsatisfied demands and new opportunities still existed, however, as Rowntree's successful 1976 launch of its Yorkie bar, Mars' profitable introduction of Twix a few years later, Cadbury's notable 1984 U.K. launch of its Whispa bar, and Hershey's 1988 introduction of Bar None proved.[10]

Nevertheless, new brand introductions required immense (tens to hundreds of millions of dollars) investments in development and marketing with only limited probabilities of success. Various research reports suggested that approximately 60 percent of all new food product introductions had been withdrawn inside of five years—and this figure might be an underestimate.[11] Established brands with customer loyalty represented crucial assets for food and beverage companies.

MODERN CADBURY SCHWEPPES

International expansion was key to Cadbury's plans. Chief Executive Officer Dominic Cadbury commented, "if you're not operating in terms of world market share, you're unlikely to have the investment needed to support your brands."[12] In 1986, Cadbury shared third place in the world with Rowntree and Hershey, each having approximately 5% of the market. Nestlé held second place with about 7.5%, while Mars dominated internationally with approximately 13%."[13]

To generate its desired worldwide expansion, Cadbury saw two primary markets in which it could gain position. Enjoying a dominant share in its home market, the company realized that the remaining countries of the European Economic Community and the United States provided critical opportunities for an expanded worldwide presence. According to Terry Organ, director of international confectionery, "Rightly or wrongly . . . we decided to tackle the U.S. first."[14] in 1978, Cadbury acquired Peter Paul in order to compete more vigorously in the United States. By 1980, however, the company still controlled only about 3.5% of the U.S. confectionery market, far eclipsed by its bigger rivals, Hershey and Mars.

Cadbury did not have sufficient size to employ a sales force comparable to those of its competitors. The company, therefore, had to rely on food brokers to push products to wholesalers, which meant the firm was farther removed from its consumers. Furthermore, its two larger rivals could easily outspend the company in advertising and promotion.[15]

To compound its problems, the company also committed two major blunders in the U.S. market. First, when Cadbury introduced Whispa—the company's marketing success of the decade in the United Kingdom—its management did not recognize that its distribution channels in the United States were much longer than those in the United Kingdom. Consequently, its candy bars had aged seven to nine months by the time they reached test markets in New England, and consumers reacted accordingly.

The company's second mistake occurred following an effort to standardize its candy bar size across countries. When Cadbury first introduced its CDM bar in the United States, the bar commanded a higher price than its U.S. rivals. Since CDM was also larger than U.S. competitors' regular bars, consumers were willing to pay a little extra. When Cadbury reduced the bar's size, it soon discovered that given the choice between CDM and American confectionery products of equal size and price, U.S. consumers usually chose the more familiar American products.[16] In a rather colorful commentary, one former Cadbury executive said, "What happened in the United States was a gigantic, gargantuan cock-up, and the fact that London (Cadbury headquarters) did not know what was happening is a sheer disgrace."[17]

Not all the news from the western side of the Atlantic was bad, however. Although Peter Paul-Cadbury controlled only a small piece of the market, some products—like its Coconut Mounds and York Peppermint Patties—dominated their segments. Cadbury's Creme Eggs also enjoyed a large (Easter) seasonal success. Moreover, the company's acquisition of Canada Dry from R. J. Reynolds provided Cadbury Schweppes with a strong position in the carbonated mixers market in the United States and in many other countries. (See Table 2 for U.S. market shares.) Although Cadbury Schweppes commanded only about a 3% total market share in the $43 billion U.S. soft drink industry, the company sold Canada Dry (the number one ginger ale and club soda in the United States) and Schweppes (the leading tonic water in the

TABLE 2
Top Five Soft Drink
Companies in the United
States, 1986–1990
(percentage of total market)

	1986	1987	1988	1989	1990
Coca-Cola, Co.	39.8%	39.9%	39.8%	40.0%	40.4%
Classic	19.1	19.8	19.9	19.5	19.4
Diet Coke	7.2	7.7	8.1	8.8	9.1
Sprite	3.6	3.6	3.6	3.6	3.6
PepsiCo	30.6	30.8	31.3	31.7	31.8
Pepsi-Cola	18.6	18.6	18.4	17.8	17.3
Diet Pepsi	4.4	4.8	5.2	5.7	6.2
Mountain Dew	3.0	3.3	3.4	3.6	3.8
Dr Pepper	4.8	5.0	5.3	5.6	5.8
Dr Pepper	3.9	4.0	4.3	4.6	4.8
Diet Dr Pepper	0.4	0.4	0.4	0.4	0.4
Seven-Up	5.0	5.1	4.7	4.3	4.0
7-Up	3.5	3.4	3.1	3.0	2.9
Diet 7-Up	1.4	1.0	1.0	0.9	0.9
Cadbury Schweppes	4.2	3.7	3.5	3.1	3.2
Canada Dry	1.4	1.4	1.4	1.3	1.2
Sunkist	0.9	0.7	0.7	0.7	0.7
Schweppes products	0.5	0.5	0.5	0.6	0.6
Crush	1.4	1.0	0.8	0.6	0.6
Total market share of top five	84.5	84.5	84.5	84.6	85.2

Source: Standard & Poor's Industry Surveys, 1991.

American market).[18] The cola giants, Coca-Cola and PepsiCo, did not (as yet) vigorously market products in segments dominated by Cadbury Schweppes. Overall, though, the company faced an uphill struggle in many segments of the U.S. market.

In an effort to remedy some of its problems in the U.S. confectionery market, Cadbury decided to sell its U.S. manufacturing assets to Hershey in 1988, catapulting the Pennsylvania company into the dominant position in the U.S. market. (See Table 3.) Cadbury also granted Hershey licenses to manufacture and sell its Peter Paul products, including Mounds, Almond Joy, and York Peppermint Patties. Under this arrangement, Cadbury gained the benefit of Hershey's marketing muscle behind the Peter Paul products.[19]

Cadbury faced additional challenges in building its market share in the European Economic Community (EEC). Schweppes beverages enjoyed success on the continent, but Europe's confectionery industry had proved difficult to break into. The market remained dominated by family-owned firms and suffered from overcapacity.[20] Successful expansion in the EEC, however, seemed crucial to Cadbury's remaining a dominant player in the worldwide food and beverage industries.

CONTEMPORARY CHALLENGES

The 1990s brought about radical shifts in the industries in which Cadbury Schweppes competed. First, corporate leaders (and stock markets) had discovered that food and beverage enterprises with established brand names were not mundane investments offering only lackluster financial returns. Purchasing popular brands—or taking over companies that had portfolios full of well-known products—often provided a safer and more economical avenue for growth than attempting to develop entirely new products. In 1985, for instance, Philip Morris acquired General Foods for $5.75 billion, approximately three times book value, while R. J. Reynolds laid out $4.9 billion for Nabisco Brands.

Some of these attempts to acquire popular brands were dictated by the dramatic industrywide changes which were altering the nature of competition faced by international food and beverage enterprises. First, the push by the 12 countries of the European Economic Community to remove trade barriers among the member nations by 1992 sparked a buying frenzy of European food companies with established brand names. (See Table 4 for a comparison of the North

TABLE 3
Top Five Companies in the $8 Billion U.S. Confectionery Market, 1980 versus 1988
(percentage of total market)

1980		1988	
COMPANY	MARKET SHARE	COMPANY	MARKET SHARE
Mars	17.0%	Hershey	20.5%
Hershey	15.3	Mars	18.5
Nabisco	7.1	Jacob Suchard	6.7
E. J. Brachs	6.4	Nestlé	6.7
Peter Paul-Cadbury	3.5	Leaf	5.6

Source: J. Weber, "Why Hershey Is Smacking Its Lips," *Business Week*, October 30, 1989.

American and EEC markets and Table 5 for European food sales by company.) Many non-European companies feared that the EEC would eventually increase tariff barriers for products from outside the Community, which could effectively close foreign companies out of the European market. Anticipation of a "Fortress Europe" mentality sent companies without EEC operations scurrying to acquire European enterprises.

Second, the common perception that only the largest companies in most industries would survive in Europe—as well as internationally—contributed to the takeover hysteria. To become big quickly, companies began aggressively acquiring rival food companies. For example, Nestlé scored a major victory in July 1988 when it outbid its Swiss counterpart, Jacob Suchard, to acquire Cadbury's longtime U.K. competitor, Rowntree. In the process, Nestlé moved from a minor status in the EEC confectionery market into a first place duel with Mars. In the U.K. market, Nestlé's acquisition put the company in a second place battle with Mars and within striking distance of first place Cadbury.[21] In January 1992, Nestlé attempted to continue its acquisitions by launching a hostile takeover bid for the French mineral water company, Source Perrier.

Other major food conglomerates, such as Phillip Morris (U.S.) and Unilever Group (U.K./Netherlands), were also rumored to be on the prowl for acquisitions in Europe.[22] These heavyweights not only presented medium-sized food and beverage companies like Cadbury with increased competition in the marketplace, they also represented potential bidders in any acquisitions attempted by Cadbury. This increased competition threatened to drive up acquisition prices for popular brand names. In fact, as the takeover battles became more heated, stock market analysts speculated that Cadbury and other medium-sized companies could themselves become targets of acquisition attempts.[23]

The European food and beverage industries were undergoing other changes along with their acquisition restructurings. At the end of the food and beverage distribution pipeline, for example, many European supermarkets were also consolidating. In April 1990, eight EEC grocery chains formed an alliance to combine their buying power and promote their house brands. Their increased power threatened future profits of food and beverage companies in several ways. For example, since supermarkets normally carried only the top two or three brands for each product type, food and beverage companies faced the risk of losing shelf space in stores.[24]

TABLE 4
1987 Comparisons of the United States and the European Economic Community[a]

	UNITED STATES	EEC
Population	243.8 million	323.6 million
Gross national product (in 1987 $US)	$4.436 trillion	$3.782 trillion
Per capita GNP	$18,200	$11,690
Inflation	3.7%	3.1%
Unemployment	6.1%	11.0%

[a]EEC members include the United Kingdom (England, Scotland, Wales, Northern Ireland), Ireland, Denmark, Germany, France, Belgium, the Netherlands, Luxembourg, Portugal, Spain, Italy, and Greece.

Source: "The '90s & Beyond," *The Wall Street Journal*, January 23, 1989, p. A8.

TABLE 5
Food Sales—Europe
(Including the United
Kingdom)

IN BILLIONS	
Nestlé	$15.1
Unilever	12.2
Phillip Morris[a]	8.0
BSN	7.8
Mars	4.1
Cadbury Schweppes	3.1

[a]Includes Jacob Suchard.

Source: J. Templeman and R. A. Melcher, "Supermarket Darwinism: The Survival of the Fattest," *Business Week*, July 9, 1990.

In response to these massive changes in the industry, Cadbury began acquiring name-brand products and searching for strategic alliances. In 1986, for example, the company decided to end its bottling agreement with Pepsi and formed a joint venture with Coke in the United Kingdom.[25] In 1990, Cadbury purchased the European soft drink operations of Source Perrier, and in 1991, it formed a joint venture with Appolinarus Brunnen AG, a German bottler of sparkling water. (See Table 6 for Cadbury Schweppes worldwide sales figures.)

With the competitive environment heating up, Cadbury's management faced a number of critical questions. Could the company continue to compete independently against the food and beverage megacorporations that were then forming, or should Cadbury merge with another company before being faced with a hostile takeover attempt? Did Cadbury have the resources to acquire more brand names, or should its management continue to investigate the joint venture route? Should the company reduce its emphasis on Europe and perhaps attempt to exploit new opportunities in the underdeveloped Asian market? Whatever Cadbury Schweppes' managers decided to do, they had to move quickly. Time was of the essence.

QUESTIONS

1. How should Cadbury Schweppes position itself in the new marketplace? What are its major threats? How should it deal with these? What is or should be its maintainable competitive edge? Why? Does it need to internationalize further?

2. What priorities should it place geographically? In terms of products? In terms of timing? Why? How should it organize for the purpose? Why?

3. What role should joint ventures play? Why? What should Cadbury Schweppes offer in these ventures? Look for? Why? What should its acquisition strategy be? What criteria should it use to evaluate any acquisition? Why? What other steps should it take to undertake a successful acquisition strategy?

REGION	TOTAL SALES	CONFECTIONERY	BEVERAGES
United Kingdom	1,476.0	715.4	760.6
Continental Europe	638.0	195.6	442.4
Americas	403.7	18.3	373.5
Pacific Rim	495.5[b]	N/A	N/A
Africa and other	132.9	91.2	38.8

N/A - Not available.

[a]1 £ = $1.93.

[b]Sales primarily in Australia/New Zealand.

Note: Total sales will not always equal confectionery plus beverages. In the United States (Americas region), for example, Cadbury Schweppes also generated sales from its Mott's subsidiary.

Source: Compact Disclosure (Information Database), Disclosure, Inc.

EXHIBIT 1
Cadbury Schweppes
Financial Data,
December 31,
1988–1990

BALANCE SHEET	1990	1989	1988
Assets			
Cash	$62,600	$57,400	$41,300
Marketable securities	118,000	33,300	200,700
Receivables	554,100	548,200	434,500
Inventories	328,200	334,800	253,400
Total current assets	$1,062,900	$973,700	$929,900
Net property, plant and equipment	978,800	822,500	602,200
Other long-term assets	320,700	332,600	20,700
Total assets	**$2,362,400**	**$2,128,800**	**1,552,800**
Liabilities			
Notes payable	$60,100	$57,400	$92,200
Accounts payable	272,100	263,900	409,500
Current capital leases	76,200	76,300	21,900
Accrued expenses	320,900	305,900	52,100
Income taxes	78,200	95,800	81,800
Other current liabilities	154,700	143,600	118,800
Total current liabilities	962,200	$942,900	$776,300
Long-term debt	407,900	381,400	124,700
Other long-term liabilities	108,401	124,000	74,600
Total liabilities	$1,478,500	$1,448,300	$975,600
Preferred stock	300	N/A	3,300
Net common stock	174,400	173,600	150,400
Capital surplus	95,800	36,700	33,000
Retained earnings	115,800	167,600	88,800
Miscellaneous	381,600	217,400	210,500
Total shareholders' equity	$767,900	$595,300	$486,000
Minority interest	116,000	85,200	91,200
Total liabilities and net worth	**$2,362,400**	**$2,128,800**	**$1,552,800**
1£ =	$1.93	$1.61	$1.81

INCOME STATEMENT	1990	1989	1988
Net sales	$3,146,100	$2,766,700	$2,381,600
Cost of goods sold	1,738,400	1,596,900	1,365,000
Gross profit	$1,407,700	$1,179,800	$1,016,600
Selling, general, and administrative expenses	1,074,700	907,500	787,800
Income before interest and taxes	$333,000	$272,300	$228,800
Nonoperating income	3,800	3,100	4,400
Interest expense	57,200	31,100	17,500
Income before taxes	$279,600	$244,300	$215,700
Taxes and miscellaneous expenses	100,200	85,500	75,200
Income before extraordinary items	$179,400	$157,800	$140,500
Extraordinary items	—	15,200	28,400
Net income	**$179,400**	**$173,000**	**$168,900**
1£ =	$1.93	$1.61	$1.81

N/A—Not available.

Source: Compact Disclosure (Information Database), Disclosure, Inc.

CASE

III-7

SCANDINAVIAN AIRLINES
SYSTEM AND THE
EUROPEAN AIRLINE
INDUSTRY

SAS IN 1988

When the SAS Group's financial results for the fiscal year 1986–87 were released, it marked the tri-national transport group's sixth straight profitable year, and its best year ever, with a net operating income of SEK 1.6 billion on revenues of SEK 23.9 billion. This was a huge improvement over the situation in 1981, when losses were mounting and the airline was rapidly losing market share. A summary of the company's recent financial results, along with relevant exchange rates, is shown in Exhibit 1.

Much of the credit for the company's dramatic turnaround was ascribed to Jan Carlzon who succeeded Carl-Olov Munkberg as president and CEO in 1981 and quickly initiated a number of major changes in the airline and its associated companies. He reoriented SAS toward the business travel market and gave top priority to customer service. This involved a complete reorganization of the company and a major decentralization of responsibility. As a result, SAS had become the leading carrier of full-fare traffic in Europe. Carlzon had joined SAS as executive vice president in 1980, after serving as president of Linjeflyg, the Swedish domestic airline. Previously, he had been managing director of the SAS tour subsidiary Vingresor.

Despite these successes, dramatic as they were, the company still faced considerable threats, and many analysts questioned if it could survive as a viable competitor in the increasingly global and competitive airline industry. Its population base of only 17 million spread out over a large area was too small by itself to support a comprehensive international traffic system. In addition, its geographic location at the periphery of Europe was a disadvantage when compared to Western Europe's densely populated areas,

The most pressing problem was the airline's operating costs, which were among the highest in the industry (see summary in Exhibit 2). It was estimated that labor charges accounted for 35% of SAS's total costs, compared with only 25% for the major U.S. carriers since deregulation and 18% for the large Asian airlines. The evolution of the U.S. "megacarriers" was a major concern as they eyed Europe as an area for continued expansion.

Senior managers of the company were fully aware of these challenges. In discussing future developments in the airline industry, and SAS's role in particular, Helge Lindberg, Group Executive Vice President, noted:

> I doubt very much that SAS can survive alone as a major intercontinental airline. We need to expand our traffic system in order to compete with major European carriers having much larger population bases, as well as with the major American and Asian carriers who maintain considerably lower operating costs. We need to develop with other partners a global traffic system with daily connections to the important overseas destinations. The nature of our industry is such that if you are not present in the market the day the customers wish to travel, the business is lost. Another priority is to reduce our costs. Our social structure in Scandinavia leaves us with one of the highest personnel costs in the industry, coupled with the fact that increased emphasis on service caused us to lose our traditional budget consciousness over the past few years. A third major issue is to develop a competitive distribution system, a problem we are about to solve in partnership with Air France, Iberia, and Lufthansa, with the so-called Amadeus system.

Case Copyright © 1998 INSEAD, Fontainebleau, France. Reprinted with the permission of INSEAD.

This industry note is intended to accompany the SAS case, and both were written by Ronald Berger Lefebure, Johnny Jorgensen, and David Staniforth, research assistants under the supervision of Sumantra Ghoshal, Associate Professor at INSEAD.

THE TURNAROUND

Sweden, Denmark, and Norway had always shared a common interest in creating an ambitious air service, both to link their scattered communities and to ensure a role for Scandinavia among the world's international airlines. They first considered a joint airline in the 1930s when all three countries wanted to establish a route to America. No firm agreement was reached until 1940, however, when they decided to operate a joint service between New York and Bergen, on Norway's west coast. This plan was unfortunately scuttled by the German invasion three days later.

The Bermuda conference on international air travel in 1946 put an end to any hopes of true freedom of the air and served to underline the importance of developing a common airline in order to establish a stronger world presence. The three countries agreed upon an ownership structure, and in the summer of 1946 a DC-4 lifted off from Stockholm bound for Oslo and New York bearing the Scandinavian Airlines System name. Sweden controlled three-sevenths of the new airline and Norway and Denmark two-sevenths each, with ownership split 50/50 between the respective governments and private interests.

EARLY POSTWAR HISTORY

SAS gained a strong foothold in the European market—at the expense of the Germans who were forbidden from establishing their own airline—and quickly developed a worldwide route network. The airline established numerous firsts in the early years of worldwide air travel, beginning with the Swedish parent company ABA in 1945, who was the first to reestablish trans-Atlantic service after the war. SAS pioneered the Arctic route in 1954 with a flight from Copenhagen to Los Angeles via Greenland, and in 1957 inaugurated transpolar service to Tokyo, cutting travel time by half. The Scandinavians were the first to operate the French Caravelle, introducing twin-engine jet travel within Europe, and worked with Douglas Aircraft to develop the ultralong-range DC-8-62, capable of flying nonstop to the U.S. west coast and Southeast Asia. A list of the airline's major milestones is shown in Exhibit 3. SAS had often looked for overseas partners and purchased 30% of Thai Airways International in 1959. This stake was bought back by the Thai government in 1977, but the two airlines had since entered into a cooperative service agreement.

The 1960s and early 1970s were the golden years for the airline. Apart from 1972 when profits shrank to US$8 million due to currency fluctuations, average annual net profits from 1969 to 1975 were between US$15 million and US$20 million. In the late 1970s, the second oil shock had a severe effect on profits, and the airline sustained considerable losses in 1979–80 and 1980–81.

SAS had developed close relationships with Swissair and KLM. An agreement between the three airlines (KSSU agreement) was signed in 1969 with the objectives of strengthening technical cooperation and of jointly assessing any new aircraft entering the market. For example, it was agreed that SAS would be responsible for overhauling the Boeing 747 engines of all three airlines, while the other partners performed other joint maintenance activities.

Although the tri-national airline had generally functioned smoothly, there had been some problems among the constituent groups, particularly when Denmark joined the EEC in 1973. This underlying rivalry was reflected in Norway by the statement, "SAS is an airline run by the Swedes for the benefit of the Danes," in reference to the airline's head office in Stockholm and its main traffic hub at Kastrup airport in Copenhagen. Nonetheless, the larger traffic base and increased bargaining power afforded by the union had helped to make SAS a major world airline.

PROBLEMS FACING SAS IN 1981

When Jan Carlzon assumed the presidency of SAS in August 1981, he realized that major changes would have to be made to restore the airline and associated companies to profitability and to meet the growing challenges of an increasingly competitive industry. After 17 profitable years, the SAS group had posted operating losses of SEK 63.1 million and SEK 51.3 million in fiscal years 1979–80 and 1980–81, respectively. This dramatic decline had given rise to rumors that the three constituent countries were considering disbanding SAS and running their own separate airlines.

In addition to the problems that beset the industry—the international recession, higher interest rates and fuel costs, overcapacity, and less regulated competition—specific problems had plagued SAS in recent years. The airline had been losing market share, even in its home territory; its fleet mix and route network did not meet market needs; and its reputation for service and punctuality had deteriorated. For example, on-time performance (defined as percentage of arrivals within 15 minutes of schedule) had slipped from over 90% to 85%, a major drop by airline standards.

In addition, many regular travelers from Norway and Sweden were increasingly avoiding transitting through Copenhagen's troublesome Kastrup airport—SAS's major hub—in favor of more attractive and efficient terminals at Amsterdam, Frankfurt, or Zurich. Under the umbrella of regulation, bad habits had developed within the company's management ranks. Carlzon felt that SAS, like most airlines, had allowed itself to become too enamored with technology—new aircrafts, new engines—often at the cost of meeting the customer's needs. They had become a product-driven airline instead of being a service-driven one. A typical example was the acquisition of the state-of-the-art Airbus A300 aircraft in the late 1970s. These larger planes required high load factors to be profitable, and this necessitated lower flight frequencies—not in the best interests of customers who needed frequent and flexible flight schedules. In the past, customers had been willing to plan their trips according to a particular airline's schedule and had even been willing to sacrifice some time to do so, since air travel was still something of a novelty. The market had since changed, and experienced travelers now chose flights to suit their travel plans, not vice versa. "In the past, we were operating as booking agents and aircraft brokers," said Carlzon. "Now we know, if we want the business we must fight for it like the 'street fighters' of the rough-and-tumble American domestic market."

A NEW STRATEGY FOR SAS

Faced with the situation of a stagnant market, general overcapacity in the industry, and continuing loss of market share to competitors, Carlzon recognized that a new strategy was necessary to turn SAS around. In a similar situation when he was the president of Linjeflyg, Carlzon had decided to increase flight frequency and cut fares dramatically in order to improve aircraft utilization and boost load factors. These actions had proven to be very successful, and profitability had improved substantially. However, the market SAS operated in was quite different from that of Linjeflyg, and it was not clear that a similar strategy could be applied successfully. Another possible option was to initiate a major cost-reduction program aimed at obtaining a better margin from a declining revenue base. This strategy would have required significant staff cuts, fleet reduction, and an overall lower level of flight frequency and service.

In the airline industry, the most stable market segment was the full-fare-paying business traveler who provided the vast majority of revenues. First class travel within Europe was declining, mainly because businesses could not justify the extra expense, especially during a recession. All the major, scheduled airlines were after the business traveler, and some had created a separate "business" class priced at a 10–20% premium over economy, which offered many of the amenities of first class.

"THE BUSINESSMAN'S AIRLINE"

SAS chose the strategy of focusing on the business traveler. As described by Helge Lindberg, then Executive Vice President-Commercial, "although other options were considered, we quickly decided there was no alternative but to go after the business traveler segment with a new product which offered significant advantages over the competition." In the words of Jan Carlzon: "We decided to go after a bigger share of the full-fare-paying pie."

There were a number of risks involved in this strategy. Increasing investment to provide an improved level of service at a time of mounting losses could bankrupt the airline if revenues did not improve sufficiently. On the other hand, if investment was the way to go, perhaps it could be better spent on more efficient aircraft so as to reduce costs. Another concern was that differentiating the product could alienate the tourist class passengers, especially among Scandinavian customers, who might resent any increase in passenger "segregation." In spite of these considerable risks, management increased expenditures and staked the future of the airline on their ability to woo the European business traveler away from the competition.

As a result, first class was dropped and "EuroClass" was introduced, offering more amenities than competing airlines' business classes, but at the old economy fare. (A similar service, First Business Class, was introduced on intercontinental routes, where first class was retained.) Thus any passenger paying full fare would be entitled to this new service, which included separate check-in, roomier seating, advance seat selection, free drinks, and a better in-flight meal. The other European airlines reacted strongly. Air France saw EuroClass as a serious threat to its own "Classe Affaires," which cost 20% more than economy, and at one point refused to book any EuroClass fares on its reservation system. Other airlines protested to their local government authorities, but to no avail, and the new fare structures were allowed to remain. SAS backed up the new service with the largest media advertising campaign ever launched by the airline (see Exhibit 4).

In conjunction with the new EuroClass services, a drive was launched to improve flight schedules and punctuality. The aircraft fleet mix was modified in order to meet the demands of increased flight frequency. The recently acquired, high-capacity Airbus aircraft were withdrawn from service and leased to SAS's Scanair charter subsidiary since they were not suitable for the frequent, nonstop flights which the new schedule demanded. For the same reason some Boeing 747s were replaced by McDonnell Douglas DC-10s, and the older DC-9s were refurbished instead of being replaced since they were of the right size for the new service levels.

On certain short-distance routes such as Copenhagen-Hamburg, a new "EuroLink" concept was introduced. This involved substituting 40 passenger Fokker F-27s for 110 passenger DC-9s and doubling flight frequencies to provide a more attractive schedule. In short, the previous high-fixed-cost, high-capacity fleet was changing into a lower-fixed-cost, high-frequency one. This evolution of the SAS fleet is shown in Exhibit 5.

EXAMINE ALL TASKS AND FUNCTIONS

Every effort was made to differentiate the business traveler product as much as possible from the lower-priced fares. In this respect, "Scanorama" lounges were introduced at many of the airports served by SAS in an effort to improve service further. These lounges were for the exclusive use of the full-fare-paying passenger and offered telephones and telex machines and a more relaxing environment to the business traveler. A joint agreement with the Danish Civil Aviation Authority was reached to invest in refurbishing Kastrup airport to bring it up to competitive standards. The objective was to make Kastrup Europe's best airport by the end of the decade.

The introduction of these new products and related services represented a change in the overall philosophy of SAS. All tasks and functions within the organization were examined. If the business traveler benefited from a particular service or function, it was maintained or enhanced; otherwise, it was cut back or dropped altogether. Managers were urged to look upon expenses as resources, to cut those that didn't contribute to revenue, but not to hesitate in raising those that did. Administrative costs were slashed 25%, but at the same time an extra SEK 120 million was invested on new services, facilities, aircraft interiors, and other

projects that affected the passengers directly. As a result, annual operating costs were increased by SEK 55 million at a time of deep deficits and continuing losses. Furthermore, these additional investments for improved service delayed the acquisition of new, more efficient aircraft to replace the aging DC-9 fleet.

The results of this new strategy were dramatic. Full-fare-paying passenger traffic rose over 8% in the first year, and profits rose to SEK 448 million for the 1981-82 fiscal year. In punctuality, SAS improved on-time performance to 93%, a record in Europe. The share of full-fare-paying passengers rose consistently, and by 1986, it had risen to 60%, giving SAS the highest proportion of any airline in Europe. Accompanying this change in passenger mix were impressive profit gains. In 1986, SAS turned in the third best profit performance among the world's major airlines with a net operating profit of SEK 1.5 billion. (A comparison of financial and operating results of major world airlines is shown in Exhibit 6.)

A CORPORATE CULTURAL REVOLUTION

Due in part to the protected, stable growth environment, the SAS organization was not ready to meet new competitive challenges without a major restructuring. Previously, the reference point had been fixed assets and technology, with emphasis on return on investment, centralized control, and orders from top management. Across-the-board cost-cutting was the usual approach to improve profits and to adapt to changing market conditions. The customer interface had been neglected. As described by a senior manager of the company,

> In those days, many employees felt that passengers were a disturbing element they had to contend with, rather than the ones who were in fact paying their salary. Taking control of a situation, and bypassing the regulations in order to please a customer were not the things to do in SAS.

Thus personal initiative was discouraged, and adherence to the company policy manuals was the norm. A large corporate staff was needed to run this bureaucracy, with layers of middle management to follow up directives from the top. Throughout the organization the morale of employees was low, and the level of cooperation among them, such as between ground staff and air crews, was not always the best. "There was a feeling of helplessness, and a fear for the future of the company," remarked an SAS pilot when asked to comment on the situation prevailing prior to 1981.

"FROM BUREAUCRATS TO BUSINESSMEN"

A transformation "from bureaucrats to businessmen" was essential, and an emphasis on the customer was needed. A major reorientation had been contemplated by Carlzon's predecessor, Carl-Olov Munkberg, but it was felt that implementation of a new organization would be more effective under a new CEO. "New brooms sweep clean," remarked Carlzon in relating his decision to replace or relocate 13 of the 14 executives in the management team of SAS. Helge Lindberg, the sole survivor in the top management team, was put in charge of the day-to-day running of the airline. Lindberg's extensive knowledge and experience was valued by Carlzon, who saw him as a "bridge between old and new" and a valuable asset now that the time for change had arrived.

In the past, SAS had focused on instructions, thereby limiting potential contributions from the employees. A key element of the cultural revolution under Carlzon was a new emphasis on information instead of instructions. The practical implications of this were that any employee in the "front line" (i.e., in the SAS/customer interface) should have the decision-making power necessary to do, within reasonable limits, whatever that person felt appropriate to please the customer. Each "moment of truth," when the customer encountered the service staff, would be used to its full potential so as to encourage repeat business. "Throw out the manuals and use your heads instead!" was the message from Lindberg. The underlying assumptions, made explicit throughout the organization, were that an individual with information could not avoid assuming responsibility and that hidden resources were released when an individual was free to assume responsibility instead of being restricted by instructions.

"CARLZON'S LITTLE RED BOOKS"

Some of the tools used by Carlzon in the reorganization were personal letters and several red booklets ("Carlzon's little red books") distributed to all employees. In these booklets the company's situation and its goals were presented in very simple language, using cartoonlike drawings to emphasize their importance (see examples in Exhibit 7). Some employees found this form of communication too simple, but overall, the response was very positive. In his first year Carlzon spent approximately half of his time traveling, meeting with SAS employees all over the world. This made it very clear to everyone that management was deeply committed to turning things around and helped to implement the changes quickly.

Education was considered necessary to reap the full benefits of the new organization, and both managers and front-line staff were sent to seminars. The courses for the front-line personnel were referred to by many as the "learn-to-smile seminars," but the real benefits probably resulted more from the participants' perception that the company cared about its employees than from the actual content of the courses.

Certain problems were encountered in the process of change. Confusion and frustration were typical reactions of many middle managers when they suddenly found themselves bypassed by the "front-line," on the one hand, and by the top management, on the other. "You can't please everyone, and some people will have to be sacrificed," said an SAS manager when asked to comment on this problem. Cross-training of employees to perform several tasks was attempted, but met with resistance from the unions. An example was the "turnaround" check—a visual check of the aircraft performed between each flight. This could very well be done by the pilots, but the mechanics' union insisted upon this task being done by their people, resulting in higher operating costs.

MAINTAINING MOMENTUM

Another problem was that the first reorientation had short-term goals, and when these were achieved, the early momentum diminished. By 1984 SAS had received the "Airline of the Year" award from *Air Transport World* magazine, and its financial situation had improved dramatically. These factors led to a feeling of contentment, and people started to fall back into old habits. Demands for salary increases were again raised. Some people thought that SAS was now out of danger and wanted to harvest the fruits of hard work. Small "pyramids" started to crop up in the organization, and it became evident that the problems in the middle management were not solved. "The new culture was taking roots, but we had problems keeping up the motivation," noted Lindberg.

Consequently, a "second wave" of change was launched, and new goals with a much longer time horizon were outlined. Management wanted to prepare the company for the coming liberalization in the airline industry and ensure a level of profitability sufficient to meet upcoming fleet replacement needs. The ultimate goal was for SAS to be the most efficient airline in Europe by 1990.

THE SECOND WAVE

SAS wanted to integrate the various elements of the travel package offered to the business traveler: to develop a full-service product for the full-fare-paying passenger. In the words of Lindberg, "We wanted to be a full-service, door-to-door travel service company. We aimed to offer a unique product which we could control from A to Z." To meet this objective, the SAS service chain concept was established by creating a distribution system and network of services that met the needs of the business travelers, from the time they ordered their tickets to the time they got back home. This meant that the development of a hotel network, reservation system, and credit card operation were decisive for the company's future.

SAS INTERNATIONAL HOTELS (SIH)

In 1983, SIH became a separate division within the SAS Group. A new concept, the SAS Destination Service—"ticket, transport, and hotel package"—was introduced in September 1985. SAS market research indicated that ground transportation and hotel reservations ranked high among the needs of business travelers. Indeed, surveys also indicated that more than 50% of the Scandinavian business travelers had no prior knowledge of the hotels where they had been booked and thus would appreciate the standards and facilities guaranteed by the SAS Destination Service. The hotels where guaranteed reservations could be made under this scheme totaled 80, and the chain, already one of the biggest in the world, was marketed as SAS Business Hotels. With this new service, passengers were able to order airline tickets, arrange for ground transportation, and confirm hotel reservations with one telephone call.

At each SAS destination where public transport from the airport to the city center was time consuming or complicated, a door-to-door limousine service was made available at reasonable prices to full-fare-paying passengers. A helicopter shuttle service was introduced for travelers transferring between New York's Kennedy and LaGuardia airports. Many of the hotels featured SAS Airline Check-in. This meant that passengers could check their luggage and obtain boarding passes before leaving the hotel in the morning and then go directly to the gate at the airport for afternoon or evening departures. With the creation of the SAS Destination Service, a complete door-to-door transport service was offered, and it reflected SAS's conviction that, to a large extent, the battle for full-fare-paying passengers would be won on the ground. The total product had to be seen as an integrated chain of services for the business travel market, including reservations, airport limousines, EuroClass, hotels, car rentals, airline check-in at the hotel, hotel check-in at the airport, airport lounges, and the SAS 24-hour telephone hot line.

SAS RESERVATION SYSTEM

SAS was facing a rising number of reservation transactions: 1 million in 1980 and 2 million in 1983. This demand created the need for an integrated information system and a network able to accept higher access without increasing the response time. To respond to this need, the company introduced a new reservation system in 1984. Developed at a cost of over SEK 250 million, the new system had more than 13,000 terminals around the world which were connected with SAS's centralized computing center. The company believed that innovative and aggressive applications of computerized information and communication technology would decide which airlines would survive. The strategy was to ensure that SAS products found the shortest and least expensive access to the market, either directly or via travel agencies. Management believed that the company had to retain independence from credit card companies and the huge distribution systems of the major U.S. airlines. By creating its own information and communication system to assure continued direct access to markets, SAS would have control of the complete purchase process.

Controversy over ticket distribution had increased in Europe, and European carriers maneuvered to protect their national markets. The threat of competition from the U.S. systems and the danger of losing control of the distribution process forced Europe's major airlines to improve and update their computer reservation systems. A summary of the major American systems can be found in Exhibit 8. In 1987, SAS joined a CRS study group formed by Air France, Lufthansa, and Iberia. Later that year, the group announced its intention to develop one of the world's largest and most complete reservation and distribution systems. Known as Amadeus, the system was expected to provide travel agencies with product and service information, reservation facilities for a worldwide array of airlines, hotels, car rentals, trains, ferries, and ticketing and fare quoting systems. Representing a total investment of US$270 million, the system was scheduled to be operational in mid-1989 and was expected to handle 150 million annual booking transactions. Finnair (Finland), Braathens S.A.F.E. (Norway), Air Inter, and UTA (France) had joined the AMADEUS group by the end of 1987. A competing system, known as GALILEO, was also announced in 1987 grouping, among others, British Airways, KLM, Swissair, Alitalia, and Austrian Airlines.

CREDIT CARDS AND SERVICE PARTNERS

In 1986, through the acquisition of Diners Club Nordic, SAS took over franchise rights in the Nordic countries for the Diners Club card, which had 150,000 cardholders in Scandinavia, Finland, and Iceland. The annual sale of hotels and transport services was a multi-

billion Kronor business in Scandinavia. SAS alone sold SEK 11 billion worth of airline tickets in Scandinavia during its 1984–85 fiscal year. Credit card purchases accounted for 13% of these sales, and the share was steadily rising. The credit card acquisition was seen as an important element in SAS's distribution strategy, being a practical tool for the business traveler.

SSP, an SAS subsidiary in the catering business, was expanded from 12 international airline flight kitchens to an enterprise with more than 7,000 employees in over 100 locations. The subsidiary operated in 13 countries from the United States to Japan, delivering 18 million airline meals a year. SSP was made up of a group of independent companies in airline catering and the international restaurant business. In 1984, SSP catered to more than 100 airlines, operated flight

EXHIBIT 1

SAS Group Financial and Operating Results, Fiscal 1977–1986
(in millions of SEK, except operating statistics)

Financial Summary—Group	77/78	78/79	79/80	80/81
Operating revenue	7,050	8,066	9,220	10,172
Operating expenses	(6,437)	(7,551)	(8,920)	(9,664)
Depreciation	(347)	(360)	(391)	(430)
Financial and extra items	(140)	(7)	28	(129)
Net operating income	126	148	(63)	51
Exchange Rate (SEK $US)	4.60	4.15	4.17	5.61
Revenue by Business Area				
SAS Airline Consortium				
SAS International Hotels				
SAS Service Partner				
SAS Leisure (Vingresor)				
Other				
Group eliminations				
Total				
Income by Business Area				
SAS Airline Consortium				
SAS International Hotels				
SAS Service Partner				
SAS Leisure (Vingresor)				
Other				
Group eliminations				
Extraordinary items				
Total				
Operating Statistics—SAS Airline				
Cities served	98	102	103	105
Kilometers flown (millions)	123	124	120	113
Passengers (thousands)	7,886	8,669	8,393	8,413
Cabin load factor (%)	56.4%	59.9%	59.4%	60.9%
Employees	16,010	16,755	17,069	16,425

N/A — Not available.

Source: Company annual reports.

kitchens for several others, and ran airport restaurants in all three Scandinavian countries as well as in England and Ireland. It had a separate unit for its Saudi Arabian business, which was expected to have possibilities for growth in the Middle and Far East. In the early 1980s, Chicago had been chosen as the entry point in a planned expansion among U.S. airports. Despite the cyclical nature of the airline business, the subsidiary had remained consistently profitable. SAS believed that more and more airlines would concentrate on operating aircraft and leave service industry tasks like catering to specialist companies. British Airways was an example, having handed over its short- and medium-haul catering at London's Heathrow airport to SSP.

OTHER RELATED ACTIVITIES

SAS had also begun to offer a dedicated service to U.S. magazine publishers wishing to distribute their products in Europe. The airline offered a fast freight and delivery service at a reasonable price through a single distribution system, and management believed this to be a growing market. This new activity allowed otherwise unused cargo capacity to be put to productive use.

The role of Vingresor, an SAS subsidiary since 1971, and Sweden's largest tour operator, was also expanded considerably. All-inclusive tours on charter flights from Sweden and Norway remained the basic service offered. Additional service products such as Vingresor's resorts with hotels in Europe and Africa

81/82	82/83(%)	83/84(%)	84/85(%)	85/86(%)	86/87(%)
12,807	15,972	18,005	19,790	21,586	23,870
(11,895)	(14,696)	(16,415)	(18,256)	(19,369)	(21,524)
(474)	(483)	(545)	(574)	(863)	(1,126)
10	(192)	(77)	57	162	443
448	601	968	1,017	1,515	1,663
6.28	7.83	8.70	7.40	6.91	6.40
	12,600 (79)	14,151 (79)	15,434 (78)	16,495 (76)	17,510 (73)
	732 (5)	843 (5)	948 (5)	1,083 (5)	1,230 (5)
	1,681 (11)	2,049 (11)	2,393 (12)	2,712 (13)	3,223 (14)
	1,311 (8)	1,474 (8)	1,537 (8)	1,897 (9)	2,379 (10)
	456 (3)	460 (3)	390 (2)	415 (2)	730 (3)
	(808)(-5)	(972)(-5)	(912)(-5)	(1,017)(-5)	(1,202)(-5)
	15,972 (100)	18.005 (100)	19,790 (100)	21,585 (100)	23,870 (100)
	461 (77)	729 (75)	811 (80)	1,207 (80)	1,453 (87)
	14 (2)	21 (2)	67 (7)	72 (5)	73 (4)
	75 (12)	15 (2)	81 (8)	123 (8)	180 (11)
	41 (7)	43 (4)	81 (6)	133 (9)	141 (8)
	17 (3)	5 (1)	(15)(-1)	(31) (-2)	(99)(-6)
	(25)(-4)	(21)(-2)	(7)(-1)	(22)(-1)	(85)(-5)
	18 (3)	176 (18)	-1 (0)	34 (2)	0 (0)
	601 (100)	968 (100)	1,017 (100)	1,516 (100)	1,663 (100)
99	93	91	88	89	85
113	120	124	125	136	N/A
8,861	9,222	10,066	10,735	11,708	N/A
63.6%	65.5%	67.2%	67.2%	66.2%	68.9%
16,376	17,101	17,710	18,845	19,773	N/A

had been developed, as well as a travel program including the Vingresor family concept.

NEW GROUP STRUCTURE

In March 1986, SAS was reorganized into five independent business units: the airline, SAS Service Partner, SAS International Hotels, SAS Leisure (Vingresor), and SAS Distribution (see Exhibit 9). The rationale was that each of these businesses faced very different strategic demands, and therefore, each was required to have its own management team to allow for more aggressive business development in an increasingly competitive climate. The same philosophy was pushed further down the line: for example, the new organization restructured the airline's route sectors into separate business units functioning as independent profit centers. The SAS Group management, consisting of the chief executive officer, three executive officers, and three executive vice presidents representing Denmark, Norway, and Sweden, was expected to focus primarily on overall development of the SAS Group's business areas.

It had been planned to introduce the new organization as early as 1984, but Carlzon had felt that the time was not ripe because the airline was involved in a public debate on air safety and there were problems with various trade union groups. "Now, I fear we might have waited too long. It has become clear that the two jobs cannot be combined. The burdens of the day-to-day operation of the airline and work on the future development of it and other business units are simply too heavy," he commented in 1986.

1988: FACING THE FUTURE

Looking ahead to the turn of the century, management of SAS was concerned about the future of the company. The globalization trend in the airline industry was gaining momentum, exemplified by the actions of giants like British Airways and American Airlines. BA had made it clear that it did not intend to stop growing after its acquisition of British Caledonian and the so-called "marketing merger" with United Airlines, in which the two carriers agreed to coordinate flight schedules and marketing programs, offer joint fares, and share terminals in four U.S. cities. American Airlines was moving into Europe, having recently closed a leasing deal covering 40 new wide-body aircrafts. "Globalization is inevitable," commented Carlzon. "Nobody will fly European unless we have a shake-out and become more efficient." This underlined the threat of being relegated to a regional carrier, and SAS's need to unite with other airlines to create a "pan-European" system.

Aircraft replacement was another threat to SAS. The average age of its 60 strong DC-9 fleet (exclusive of the newer MD-80s) was 25 years, and an upcoming EEC directive on noise levels could, if put into effect in 1992, ground 30 aircraft. The required investment in new aircraft was estimated at SEK 40 billion over the next decade, which translated into one new plane per month from 1988 until the year 2000. This process of replacement had started, with the purchase of 9 Boeing 767s for trans-Atlantic traffic. To be able to finance these projects, the airline had to attain a gross profit level of 13% (before depreciation), compared to 11%

EXHIBIT 2

Comparison of Airline Operating Costs

Estimated Airline Operating Costs, 1982–1986 (in U.S. cents per available ton-kilometer)

AIRLINE	1982	1983	1984	1985	1986
Singapore Airlines	36	36	33	32	30
British Caledonian	37	37	29	35	38
United Airlines	39	39	38	44	40
KLM	35	29	26	35	44
Pan American	34	36	38	36	N/A
British Airways	40	38	31	37	44
Delta	42	43	43	45	44
Lufthansa	51	44	40	53	57
Swissair	54	47	41	53	58
Sabena	53	43	44	56	63
SAS	53	53	50	65	76

N/A — not available.

Source: Company annual reports.

EXHIBIT 3
SAS Milestones,
1946–1977

1946—July 31—August 1
DDL, DNL, and SILA found SAS for the operation of intercontinental services to North and South America.

1946—September 17
Route to New York opened.

1946—November 30
Route to South America opened.

1948—April 18
ABA, DDL, and DNL form ESAS to coordinate European operations.

1948—July 1
SILA and ABA amalgamated.

1949—October 26
Route to Bangkok opened.

1950—October 1
ABA, DDL, and DNL transfer all operations to SAS in accordance with a new consortium agreement dated February 8, 1951, with retroactive effect.

1951—April 18
The Bangkok route is extended to Tokyo.

1951—April 19
Route to Nairobi is inaugurated.

1952—November 19
First transarctic flight by commercial airliner.

1953—January 8
The Nairobi route is extended to Johannesburg.

1954—November 15
Polar route to Los Angeles inaugurated.

1956—May 9
Prewar route to Moscow reopened.

1957—February 24
Inauguration of North Pole short cut to Tokyo.

1957—April 2
SAS participates in formation of Linjeflyg.

1957—April 4
Route opened to Warsaw.

1957—April 16
First flight to Prague.

1958—October 6
Agreement of cooperation signed by SAS and Swissair.

1959—August 24
SAS and Thai Airways Co. establish THAI International.

1960—July 2
Monrovia added to South Atlantic network.

1961—October 1
SAS Catering established as subsidiary.

1962—May 15
Inauguration of all-cargo service to New York.

1963—May 4
Route opened across top of North Norway to Kirkenes.

1963—November 2
First service to Montreal.

1964—April 2
Route to Chicago inaugurated.

1965—April 5
Nonstop service New York–Bergen begun.

1966—September 2
Inauguration of service to Seattle via polar route.

1967—November 4
Opening of Trans-Asian Express via Tashkent to Bangkok and Singapore.

1968—March 31
Dar-Es-Salaam added to East African network.

1969—November 1
Route opened to Barbados and Port-of-Spain in West Indies.

1970—February 18
KSSU agreement ratified.

1971—April 3
Trans-Siberian Express to Tokyo inaugurated.

1971—November 1
SAS participates in formation of Danair.

1972—April 5
Route to East Berlin opened.

1972—May 24
New York-Stavanger route opened.

1973—November 4
All-cargo express route opened to Bangkok and Singapore.

1973—November 6
Delhi added to Trans-Orient route.

1975—September 2
Inauguration of Svalbard route, world's northernmost scheduled service.

1976—April 21
Route opened to Lagos.

1977—April 7
Kuwait added to Tran-Orient route.

1977—November 2
Opening of Gothenburg-New York route.

Source: "The SAS Saga," Anders Buraas, Oslo, 1979.

EXHIBIT 4
Example of EuroClass
Advertisement, 1981

SAS Advertisement:
Of the eight major airlines competing in Sweden for European traffic, five do not give you separate check-in and seating, separate cabin, or free drinks. Of the three remaining airlines, two do not give you extra room and larger seats. Only one airline in Europe has EuroClass which gives you more service and comfort for the economy fare.

Lufthansa Advertisement:
You can still fly first class in Europe!

Source: Advertising Age, 1981.

EXHIBIT 5
Evolution of SAS's Fleet,
Fiscal 1977–1986

AIRCRAFT TYPE[a]		SEAT CAPACITY	77/78	78/79	79/80	80/81	81/82	82/83	83/84	84/85	85/86	86/87
Boeing 747		405	3	4	4	5	5	3	5	5	2	0
Airbus Industries	A300	242	0	0	2	4	1	1	0	0	0	0
McDonnell-Douglas	DC-10-30	230	5	5	5	5	5	5	6	8	9	11
McDonnell-Douglas	DC-8-62	N/A	5	5	2	3	3	3	3	3	3	0
	DC 8-63	170	5	3	4	2	2	2	2	2	2	0
McDonnell-Douglas	DC-9-21	75	9	9	9	9	9	9	9	9	9	9
	DC-9-33	(freight)	2	2	2	2	2	2	2	2	2	2
	DC-9-41	110/122	45	49	49	49	49	49	49	49	49	49
	DC-9-81	133	0	0	0	0	0	0	0	0	6	8
	DC-9-82	156	0	0	0	0	0	0	0	0	6	8
	DC-9-83	133	0	0	0	0	0	0	0	0	0	4
Fokker F-27		40	0	0	0	0	0	0	4	6	9	9
Total			**74**	**77**	**77**	**79**	**76**	**74**	**80**	**84**	**97**	**100**

[a]Aircraft owned or leased by SAS that were leased to other operators are not included in this table.

Source: Company annual reports.

---

in 1986. This increase was difficult to achieve in an increasingly competitive environment and one in which SAS had a cost disadvantage with respect to other airlines.

WHAT IS NEEDED FOR THE FUTURE

Partnerships or mergers with other airlines were clearly attractive options, but the company had been frustrated in its attempts to develop such relationships. In the spring of 1987, SAS entered into negotiations with Sabena of Belgium with the goal of merging the operations of the two companies. Sabena was 52% state owned, and the Belgian government had expressed an interest in selling part of its holdings to the private sector. With US$3.3 billion in sales, the merged carrier would have been Europe's fourth largest. Sabena Chairman Carlos Van Rafelghem had stated that any accord with SAS would involve combining medium- and long-distance networks in a system based on hubs in Copenhagen and Brussels. The negotiations failed, however, mainly on the issue of the degree of integration. SAS wanted to include all of Sabena's operations, including hotels and catering, while the Belgian carrier was interested only in merging the airline systems.

In the fall of that same year, SAS launched a bid to acquire a major shareholding in British Caledonian Airways (BCal). SAS was eager to expand its traffic base and gain access to BCal's American, African, and Middle East destinations and to the carrier's Gatwick Airport hub outside London. A battle for control with British Airways ensued, with BA emerging the winner, having paid £250 million, more than double the original bid. A major issue during the takeover battle was the implication of SAS gaining control of a British airline. The question of national control was important because

EXHIBIT 6

Comparison of Major
World Airlines' Statistics
1986 World Airline
Operating and Financial
Statistics

Passengers	(000s)	Revenues Per Kilometer	(000,000s)
1. Aeroflot	115,727	1. Aeroflot	188,056
2. United	50,690	2. United	95,569
3. American	45,983	3. American	78,499
4. Eastern	42,546	4. Eastern	56,164
5. Delta	41,062	5. Delta	50,480
6. TWA	24,636	6. TWA	48,100
7. All Nippon	24,503	7. Northwest	46,346
8. Piedmont	22,800	8. British Airways	41,405
9. USAir	21,725	9. Japan Air Lines	38,903
10. Continental	20,409	10. Pan American	34,844
22. SAS	11,700	30. (est) SAS	12,471

Fleet Size	(No. Aircraft)	Employees	
1. Aeroflot	2,682	1. Aeroflot	500,000
2. United	368	2. American	51,661
3. American	338	3. United	49,800
4. Northwest	311	4. Eastern	43,685
5. Eastern	289	5. Federal Express	43,300
6. Delta	253	6. Delta	38,901
7. Continental	246	7. British Airways	37,810
8. CAAC (China)	241	8. Air France	35,269
9. TWA	167	9. Lufthansa	34,905
10. Republic	165	10. Northwest	33,250
18. SAS	106	22. SAS	19,773

Operating Revenues	(US $000,000s)	Operating Profit	(US $000,000s)
1. United	6,688	1. American	392
2. American	5,857	2. Federal Express*	365
3. Air France	4,747	3. SAS	260
4. Japan Air lines	4,578	4. Delta	225
5. Eastern	4,522	5. Cathay Pacific	206
6. Delta	4,496	6. Swissair	200
7. Northwest	3,598	7. Northwest	167
8. TWA	3,181	8. USAir	164
9. Federal Exprese	2,940	9. Continental	143
10. Pan American	2,580	10. KLM	131
11. SAS	2,387		

*Freight only.

Source: "1986 World Airline Operating and Financial Statistics," *Air Transport World,* June 1987.

of bilateral agreements. If BCal were deemed to be non-British, the foreign partner in an agreement might revoke the airline's licenses on routes to that country.

By the middle of 1988, it was clear to the corporate management of SAS that while past actions had led to a sound base for the future, they were not sufficient by themselves to ensure long-term viability of the company. Within the rapidly changing environment, a new thrust was necessary, and it had to be found without much delay.

THE EUROPEAN AIRLINE INDUSTRY

MARKET ENVIRONMENT

Most industry forecasts projected the European air transport market to grow steadily between 5% and 6% per year to 1990, and about 4% annually to 2000, somewhat better than the 2–4% recorded during the early 1980s. Although some 60–70% of scheduled air traffic in Europe was for business travel, this market

EXHIBIT 7
**Examples from "Carlzon's
Little Red Books"**

Hopeless odds.
When we looked around a year ago, our hopes of "getting our nose up" were sinking. Demand had stopped increasing. We could no longer regard ourselves rich; i.e., there was less hope for continued growth and thus automatically increased revenues. The competition got harder. How could we survive?

Certain competitors "throw in the towel."
At the time when SAS achieves its best results ever, the majority in the airline industry are doing poorly. The IATA companies are this year losing around US$2 billion! But they should be making a profit of US$3 billion (7.5% of turnover) to have a chance of meeting their future aircraft investments. From this we can draw two conclusions:

SAS is not like the other IATA companies. Our result is nothing less than a world sensation.

The IATA companies will probably fight for their lives in the future—just as we started to do a year and a half ago. They will probably use all their force to beat us in the coming rounds.

Note: Translation from Swedish by casewriters.

Source: SAS

EXHIBIT 8
Selected Operating Data
for U.S. CRS Systems,
1986–1987

	SABRE (AMERICAN)	APOLLO (UNITED)	SYSTEM ONE (TEXAS AIR)	PARS (TWA/NWA)	DATAS II (DELTA)
Terminals:					
United States	54,800	40,688	21,450	17,907	9,600
Abroad	316	330	100	352	300
Subscriber locations	13,018	8,944	6,350	4,816	3,100
% total agency sales processed January-June 1986[a]	43	30.1	8.5	8.5	4.1
% U.S. RPMs of airlines January-May 1987	14.136	17.124	19.212	17.766	12.317
1986 revenues[b] (in millions)	$336	$318	N/A	N/A	N/A
1986 profits (in millions)	$412	N/A	N/A	N/A	N/A
Airline booking fees					
—Basic	$1.75	$1.85	$1.75	$1.75	$1.50
—Direct access	$2.00	$1.85	$1.75	$1.75	$1.50
Direct access airlines as of July 1987	13	30	20	13	5
Current strengths	Size; greatest depth of data	Size; depth of data	Aggressiveness	International pricing; large number installed in corporations; flexibility	

N/A — not available.

[a]USA only, Sabre estimate.

[b]American is the only airline reporting publicly; Apollo estimate as published previously by the author and not disputed by the company.

Sources: Compiled from CRS vendors; *Travel Weekly, Aviation Daily*; author's estimates, by *Travel and Tourism Analyst.*

segment was expected to remain stagnant over the next ten years, with the majority of the growth coming from the leisure travel market. Part of this future growth was expected to come from greater freedom to compete as the market was progressively deregulated. This anticipated effect of deregulation was confirmed by the 13% increase in traffic between Great Britain and the Netherlands in the year following the signing of their liberalized bilateral agreement, compared with an 8% increase for all intra-European traffic. See Exhibit 10 for data on size, growth, and share of some of the major international airlines.

COMPETITION

Traditionally, competition in the highly regulated European market had focused on route negotiations and access to other nations' airports. The largest

European carriers were British Airways, Air France, Lufthansa, Iberia, Swissair, Alitalia, and SAS, with the first three controlling 40% of the available passenger-kilometers on scheduled intra-European flights. A table comparing the international route network of SAS with those of some of its competitors can be found in Exhibit 11. A large country with a strong national carrier had a lot of leverage in route negotiations and could often choose the most profitable time slots for arrivals and departures. The product offered did not vary much among competing airlines, and fares were usually fixed in bilateral agreements that were strictly adhered to. These fixed fares allowed airlines with higher operating costs to remain competitive due to the presence of an artificial price umbrella.

For SAS there was not one major competitor, but rather one in each market it served, for example, British

EXHIBIT 9
SAS Group Structure

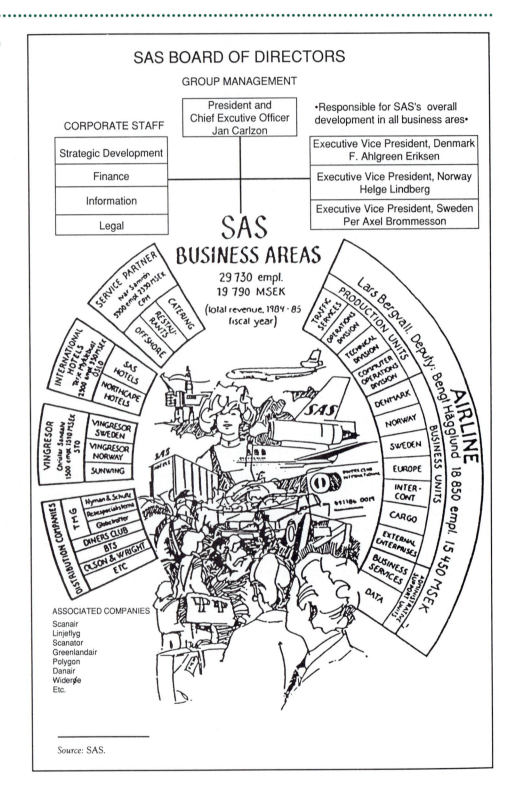

SAS BOARD OF DIRECTORS

GROUP MANAGEMENT

President and Chief Excutive Officer
Jan Carlzon

• Responsible for SAS's overall development in all business ares •

Executive Vice President, Denmark
F. Ahlgreen Eriksen

Executive Vice President, Norway
Helge Lindberg

Executive Vice President, Sweden
Per Axel Brommesson

CORPORATE STAFF

- Strategic Development
- Finance
- Information
- Legal

SAS BUSINESS AREAS

29 730 empl.
19 790 MSEK

(total revenue, 1984 - 85 fiscal year)

SERVICE PARTNER — Nur Samén 5900 empl 2350 MSEK CPH
- CATERING
- RESTAURANTS
- OFFSHORE

INTERNATIONAL HOTELS — Park Myrbakal 2300 empl 930 MSEK OSLO
- SAS HOTELS
- NORTHCAPE HOTELS

VINGRESOR — Christer Sandan 1500 empl 1510 MSEK STO
- VINGRESOR SWEDEN
- VINGRESOR NORWAY
- SUNWING

DISTRIBUTION COMPANIES — TMG
- Hyman & Schulz
- Reisespecialisterna
- Globe trotter
- DINERS CLUB
- BTS
- OLSON & WRIGHT
- ETC.

AIRLINE — Lars Bergvall, Deputy: Bengt Hägglund 18 850 empl. 15 450 MSEK

PRODUCTION UNITS
- TRAFFIC SERVICES
- OPERATIONS DIVISION
- TECHNICAL DIVISION
- COMPUTER OPERATIONS DIVISION

BUSINESS UNITS
- DENMARK
- NORWAY
- SWEDEN
- EUROPE
- INTER-CONT
- CARGO
- EXTERNAL ENTERPRISES
- BUSINESS SERVICES
- DATA
- ADMINISTRATIVE SUPPORT UNITS

ASSOCIATED COMPANIES

Scanair
Linjeflyg
Scanator
Greenlandair
Polygon
Danair
Widerøe
Etc.

Source: SAS.

Airways in the U.K. sector and Bräthens S.A.F.E. on domestic routes in Norway. In the late 1970s, the impact of the second oil shock led to poor financial results for most airlines, and the competition for passengers increased (see Exhibit 12). The airlines tried to differentiate their products, and to improve in-flight service by offering free drinks and better meals and introducing a separate class for business travelers. However, new service elements introduced by one airline were quickly copied by others, making it difficult to sustain a competitive advantage.

In addition to the obvious threat from the major national carriers, increased competition came from the regional feeder and charter airlines (regional in this context includes international flights and is defined as flights with aircraft capacity of 70 passengers or fewer). The former category had a fairly small share of the market at less than 5%, but had exhibited high growth. In the period from 1978 to 1986, the number of regional airlines, aircraft, and seat capacity in Europe doubled. This trend was expected to continue, or accelerate, as regulations were relaxed and as regional carriers were allowed into major traffic hubs. However, the major airlines had not passively watched their markets erode, but had countered by "expropriating" developed regional routes or by expanding their own regional traffic. This had been achieved either by operating a separate commuter division or by partial acquisition of, or a joint venture with, a regional carrier. According to Association of European Airlines (AEA) data, in 1986 SAS offered the highest number of "regional" seats on international departures in Europe, while in 1978 it was not even among the top 10. Although around 10% of total scheduled international departures within Europe were with regional aircraft, this amounted to only 3% in terms of passengers and only 1.5% of passenger kilometers.

In 1985, charter traffic in Europe accounted for 57% of the world's nonscheduled revenue-passenger-kilometers (RPK) versus only 38% in the mid-1970s. In 1986, around half of the intra-European air traffic was non-scheduled. European charter traffic had grown at an average annual rate of around 5–6% from 1975 to 1985, compared to only 1.7% for the world charter market. Scheduled carriers usually operated charters, or a charter subsidiary, to improve aircraft utilization on weekends and during low-demand periods. SAS was no exception, having a charter subsidiary Scanair, which operated eight McDonnell-Douglas DC-8s on long-term lease from the parent company. In addition, Scanair leased extra capacity from SAS during weekends and holiday periods. Although charter traffic accounts for only 1–3% of the major airlines' RPKs, this market segment could be quite important for the smaller and medium-sized carriers (for the Irish flag carrier Aer Lingus, it represented 18% of revenues in 1986). The major players in the charter market were the independents. The United Kingdom's Britannia Airways, Europe's largest charter operator, carried as many passengers a year as KLM. The trend in the charter market was toward larger aircraft and increased capacity so as to reduce operating costs.

The "seat-only" concept (when a charter airline offered only basic transport) was a growing threat to the scheduled airlines. On certain routes, seat-only accounted for up to 25% of passengers carried by ACE airlines (Association des Compagnies Aeriennes de la Communauté Européenne, which represented charter airlines in Europe). The demand for seat-only services was expected to grow significantly. Diversification into scheduled services by charter airlines was another trend seen in the mid-1980s, although in 1987 it represented only about 3% of total RPKs for these airlines. In the future, this proportion was expected to increase, not only to meet the growing demand for seat-only, but also to counter the scheduled carriers' increased presence in the cut-price holiday segment.

The air charter industry had traditionally been much less regulated than the scheduled carriers. An early International Air Transport Association (IATA) provision (stating that a package holiday should not be priced lower than the lowest scheduled fare) kept prices high, but by the mid-1970s several governments had abolished most price and capacity controls. However, in many countries the charter industry remained under quite strict control.

EFFECTS OF REGULATION/DEREGULATION

The European airline industry was entering a period of liberalization as a result of increasing competitive pressures. European consumers were urging their national governments toward deregulation in an effort to bring travel costs down. Some individual countries, notably, Great Britain and the Netherlands, had modified their bilateral agreements with other nations to allow more competition on capacity and fares. However, a number of factors made the situation in Europe quite different from that experienced in the United States following deregulation of the airline industry in that country.

The cartel within the IATA had given member airlines a protected market. In addition, bilateral treaties between European nations allowed their airlines to share the market through pooling arrangements. According to a study by the European Civil Aviation Conference (ECAC), 75–85% of the ton-kilometers on European scheduled flights were subject to these pooling agreements. These could take several forms, such as agreements to share revenues and capacity (although not always equally), agreements to limit the number of flights between two cities, and agreements by one carrier to pay another not to fly certain routes. A final important feature of these agreements was a commitment to price setting. The bilateral treaties usually declared that the airlines should, subject to government approval, reach agreement on their air fares, and it was often stated that the price-setting machinery of IATA would be used whenever possible.

Through these pooling agreements, capacity had been divided up on a 50/50 basis between the respective countries. If, for example, KLM offered 150 seats from Stockholm to Amsterdam, SAS was entitled to offer 150 seats on the same route. A number of proposals had been put forward to modify this procedure. One proposal supported by the European Parliament was to increase the maximum capacity that could be offered by airlines of one country from the present 50–75% of the total capacity on the route without the consent of the other country. The AEA/IATA proposal limited this to 55%, and this latter modification had been adopted in some of the new agreements, such as the one between Britain and France. The agreement signed between the United Kingdom and the Netherlands in 1984 was the most competitive in Europe, with no limits on route entry or capacity. As a result, a total of seven carriers were flying the London-Amsterdam route. The average fare had not decreased significantly although the range of fares and services had expanded considerably. This is illustrated in Exhibit 13, which compares fares on this route in 1983 and 1985.

The European market was too fragmented to enable a surge of new competitors with significant fare reductions on major routes as happened in the United States in the late 1970s. The size of the U.S. market and the presence of only one regulatory authority allowed rapid deregulation to take place. This led to the entry of new competitors in virtually all markets, and low-cost carriers, such as People Express, were formed. These carriers typically employed nonunion personnel and operated used aircraft. Consequently, they had lower operating costs compared to the estab-

lished major carriers, and they used this advantage to undercut the majors on price. They were helped further by falling fuel prices since their older aircraft were not as fuel efficient as those of the established carriers. These lower prices could be profitable in the long term only if traffic bases were increased. The resulting scramble for volume led to a shake-out, and seven major carriers came to dominate the U.S. market after a series of takeovers and mergers: American Airlines, Texas Air Corp. (having acquired Continental, Eastern and People Express), United Airlines (having acquired Pan Am's Pacific routes), Northwest (having acquired Republic), Delta (having acquired Western), TWA (having acquired Ozark), and USAir (having acquired Piedmont and Pacific Southwest). These airlines had also forged links with regional carriers to feed more traffic into their respective systems.

Although the EEC commission was urging its members toward greater liberalization, it represented only about half of the countries that made up the more conservative ECAC. There were also significant differences within the EEC countries themselves. Great Britain and the Netherlands were the most liberal, followed by Luxembourg, West Germany, and Belgium. They were still outnumbered by the seven other members who remained more conservative.

Deregulation was progressing on a piecemeal basis, with new bilateral agreements being negotiated with individual countries, instead of on a Europe-wide basis, which would be necessary to provide the level of free competition which existed in the United States. The EEC was pressing for a more unified European stance to enable negotiations with the United States on a multilateral, rather than bilateral basis. A problem with the piecemeal approach was that single routes themselves did not provide a viable network for new entrants. This factor limited the possibility of a new carrier gaining a major foothold in a more competitive European market in the manner that People Express did in the United States. Although it was widely believed that deregulation would result in lower overall fares for European travelers, studies of the U.S. experience do not necessarily confirm this view. In a 1983 study, Britain's Civil Aviation Authority (CAA) concluded that normal fares on U.S. routes with limited competition were only 10–15% below U.K.–Europe equivalents, although where additional competitors had entered, fares were as much as 33% lower. Much of these differences could be attributed to higher labor, fuel, and associated costs of operating in Europe compared with those in the United States. Some U.K.–Europe routes were found to offer promotional fares which were actually lower than any fare on an equivalent U.S. route. The Dutch aviation authorities undertook a similar study of deregulation's effect on fares. Applying the results of these studies to European scheduled routes in general suggested possible fare reductions of approximately 10% if service levels were maintained, and up to 20% if service levels were reduced. Actual realization of such reductions, however, depended on the pace of new entry, for which the opportunities, as noted earlier, were not as great in Europe as they had been in the United States.

NEW DEVELOPMENTS

Confronted with these environmental changes, many of the major airlines were expanding their range of services by integrating into related aspects of the travel sector, such as hotels, travel agencies, car rental, and financial services. Among the European carriers, seven companies had built substantial interests in hotels: Aer Lingus, Air France, British Caledonian, KLM, Lufthansa, SAS, and Swissair. Airlines were also considering expanding into the field of credit cards to increase the range of services offered to customers and to provide management of corporate travel expenses for business related travel.

In February 1987, United Airlines had joined together with Westin and Hilton International Hotels and Hertz car rental under the Allegis corporate name, becoming the world's most vertically integrated travel service company. However, only five months later, Allegis's board rejected the travel supermarket concept. Both the car rental and hotel chains were put up for sale. In spite of the Allegis experience, the trend toward travel service integration was expected to continue as the industry became more global and competitive.

New areas of cooperation for mutual cost savings and benefits were developing among European carriers. For example, most airlines were under pressure to provide automated ticket and boarding pass facilities to improve customer service. Prototype machines were purchased jointly by AEA member airlines, and testing began in 1987. Worldwide interest in the concept had increased, and discussions had been held to develop a common design to supply most of the IATA carriers.

Computer Reservations Systems (CRS) and their implications for the airlines' sales distribution networks had become increasingly important, particularly in light of worldwide developments. These networks were expected to become the primary link between the airlines and the marketplace. The major U.S. airlines had launched a drive to place their CRS systems in travel agencies outside the United States and were focusing on Europe. The retailing of airline tickets in the United States prior to deregulation was relatively straightforward, since distribution was via a cartel system. Deregulation meant that the airlines had to build marketing relationships with individual travel agencies, and the CRS system was a key element in this strategy. The massive investments required to develop these systems made this area a critical strategic issue.

QUESTIONS

1. Between 1981 and 1986, SAS went through one of the most dramatic and visible processes of strategic change. How was this turnaround achieved? Why did it succeed? What can we learn from the process?

2. Why was the "second wave" necessary? How do you feel about the direction SAS is following? Will this second round of change work? What might Carlzon do to make it work?

3. How do you evaluate the role played by Carlzon since taking over the presidency of the company in 1981? What has he done well? With the benefit of hindsight, what might he have done differently? What lessons do you draw about the roles and tasks of general managers in large world-wide companies?

4. In light of the changes occurring in the European airline industry, what strategic changes should SAS undertake? Why? What are the most likely alignments among existing companies? With whom should SAS align? What should it do about developments in Eastern Europe?

EXHIBIT 10
Air Traffic Market Data;
Transatlantic and Europe

TRANSATLANTIC SCHEDULED AND CHARTER PASSENGERS, SELECTED AIRLINES, 1975–1985

	1975		1980		1985	
	Amount (thousands)	% of Total	Amount (thousands)	% of Total	Amount (thousands)	% of Total
TWA	$ 1,736	14%	$ 2,352	13%	$ 3,757	16%
Pan American	1,643	9	2,230	12	2,631	11
British Airways	1,217	10	2,201	12	2,136	9
Lufthansa	673	5	1,052	6	1,182	5
KLM	593	5	818	4	1,079	5
Air France	613	5	736	4	843	4
Swissair	346	3	536	3	649	3
SAS	401	3	525	3	537	2
British Caledonian	—		149	1	430	2
Sabena	243	2	291	2	356	2
Delta	—		252	1	374	2
American	—		—		367	2
Others	4,953	—	8,158	—	8,894	—
Total	**$12,418**	**100%**	**$18,775**	**100%**	**$23,235**	**100%**

Source: Travel and Tourism Analyst, May 1986.

INTRA-EUROPEAN SCHEDULED PASSENGER-KILOMETERS FOR SELECTED EUROPEAN CARRIERS, 1980 VERSUS 1984

	1980		1994	
	Miles (millions)	% of Total	Miles (millions)	% of Total
British Airways	8,066	16%	7,698	14%
Lufthansa	5,732	11	6,302	12
KLM	2,236	4	2,541	5
Air France	7,397	15	7,794	14
Swissair	3,736	7	4,092	6
SAS	3,250	7	3,623	7
Sabena	1,209	>2	1,202	2
British Caledonian	321	<1	396	<1
Others	18,053	—	20,860[a]	—
Total	**54,504**	**100%**	**50,000**[a]	**100%**

[a]Estimate.

Source: Travel and Tourism Analyst, March 1986.

EXHIBIT 11
Comparison of
Competing Airlines'
Route Structures
World Airline Route
Structures, 1987–1988
(approximate number of
major[a] international
destinations served)

AIRLINE	NORTH AMERICA	SOUTH AMERICA	EUROPE	AFRICA	AUSTRALIA-ASIA
SAS	5	1	40[b]	0	6
Air France	12	16	75	25	33
British Airways	19	7	65	9	33
British Caledonian	5	0	13	13	7
KLM	11	16	55	18	26
Lufthansa	18	10	74	17	28
Pan American	35	13	40	1	5
Sabena	8	0	N/A	26	10
Singapore Airlines	3	0	12	1	32
Swissair	7	4	52	18	21
United Airlines	55+	0	N/A	0	13

[a]The distinction is somewhat arbitrary, and the numbers are intended as an indicator only.

[b]This number does not include smaller Scandinavian destinations.

Source: Company annual reports and route maps.

EXHIBIT 12
**Air Traffic versus
Economic Trends**
Economic Activity and
Air Traffic, 1971–1985

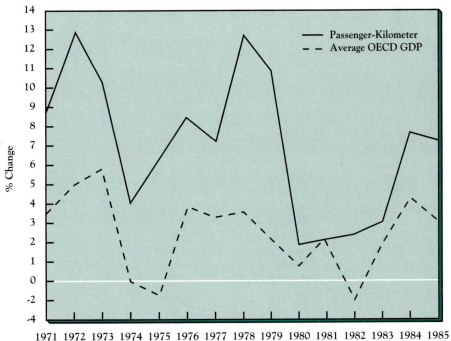

**EXHIBIT 12 (cont'd)
% Change in Real Oil
Prices, 1971–1986**

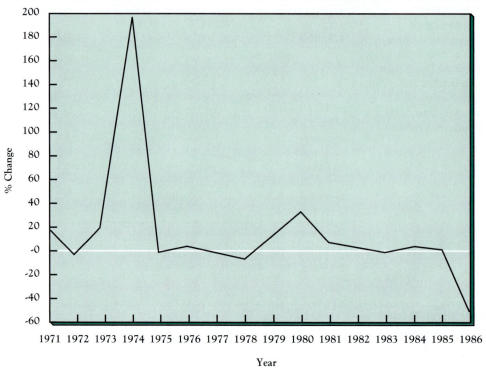

Source: AEA/OECD/*Travel and Tourism Analyst.*

**EXHIBIT 13
Example of Fare
Structure: London-
Amsterdam Fares, 1983
versus 1985**

(nominal pounds sterling)

	1983	1985
British Airways & KLM		
Economy fare	148	162
Eurobudget (any flight)	126	138
Eurobudget (designated flights)	105	115
PEX (stay over one Saturday)	99	109
SuperPEX (more restrictive than PEX)	88	91
Late Saver (very restrictive)	—	55
British Caledonian		
Peak fare	148	109
Shoulder fare	—	89
Off-peak fare	98	69
Average	116	104

Source: *Travel and Tourism Analyst,* March 1986.

The accounting profession, which had long been very stable and predictable, began changing dramatically during the 1970s and 1980s. First, the merger boom of the 1970s cut the ranks of publicly owned corporations normally served by the Big Eight accounting firms. The audit fee from a merged firm was usually about 65% of the combined fees the two firms had paid independently. While this saved the client companies substantial amounts, it cut dramatically into the fees of the accounting firms.

Then in the late 1970s the Federal Trade Commission (FTC), seeking to increase competition in the accounting profession, forced the profession to eliminate its self-imposed strictures against advertising and the solicitation of other firms' clients. Client corporations quickly learned they could radically reduce audit fees by replacing their auditors every few years. Reputation and long-standing client ties were no longer enough to attract or hold clients, or to shield accounting firms from price competition. As firms began actively courting competitors' clients, they also aggressively sought ways to cut their internal costs and to provide new client services. This led to substantial investments in computer and other technologies designed to reduce—or gain higher yields from—the high-priced labor involved in an audit. It also promoted further diversification into management consulting, tax counseling, systems design, and other services.

INDUSTRY STRUCTURE

Despite such efforts, *The Public Accounting Report* stated that revenues at the eight largest firms grew a total of only 22% from 1982–1985, down from 40%

Case copyright © 1989, James Brian Quinn. This case was developed by Penny Paquette under the guidance of Professor Quinn.
*Disguised name of a real firm. Internal figures of PRA&D have been adjusted by constants in each exhibit.

over the preceding two-year span. But accounting revenues rose only 14%; the biggest gains in the early 1980s came from consulting fees, up 33%. Simultaneously, net income per partner was being depressed by diminishing ratios of professional staff to partners (caused by the decreased demand in the audit area for ordinary "number crunchers"), by lower utilization rates (because more professional hours had to be spent on non-chargeable activities such as marketing or practice development as it was called in the industry), and by the increasing cost of recruiting and retaining the higher-quality professional staff firms now needed. So intense were the pressures on revenues that one of the larger firms took the unprecedented step of pushing out or retiring 10% of its partners.

Smaller and medium-sized firms either developed specialized niches or merged to broaden their services, gain expertise, or gain necessary economies of scale. In the mid-1980s some of the larger firms had even merged to gain the worldwide sales and expertise demanded by their large multinational clients. As such mergers increasingly divided the remaining members of the Big Eight from the smaller firms, their greater scale and potentials began raising antitrust issues.

The 1982 *Census of Service Industries* reported some 49,000 U.S. accounting firms, with revenues totaling $14.6 billion. The Big Eight among these firms (then Arthur Andersen; Peat Marwick; Ernst & Whinney; Coopers & Lybrand; Price Waterhouse; Arthur Young; Touche Ross; and Deloitte, Haskins, & Sells) earned more than 28% of all industry revenues, while the 12 largest firms received 32% of the total. Less than 3% of all firms had revenues of more than $1 million in 1982, and less than 1% had revenues exceeding $2.5 million. The Big Eight firms had an estimated $3.8 billion in non-U.S. billings in 1984, and foreign billings accounted for at least 25% of total

TABLE 1
1982 Revenues by Type for Accounting Firms

TYPE OF SERVICE	U.S. ACCOUNTING PROFESSION AVERAGE	TYPICAL BIG EIGHT FIRM
Accounting/auditing	50.8%	50–75%
Tax preparation and consulting	26.8	15–25
Bookkeeping	11.9	
Management advisory	8.2	10–30
Other	2.4	

Source: Office of Technology Assessment, *Trade in Services*, OTA-ITE-316, September 1988, p. 48.

billings for each of the Big Eight. (See Appendix A for a profile of the largest accounting firms.) Their international operations, originally established primarily to serve U.S.-based multinationals, tended to be organized abroad as loose collections of largely autonomous partnerships. Smaller accounting firms conducted considerably less international business. Table 1 breaks out revenues by type of service for the U.S. accounting profession as a whole and for a typical Big Eight firm in 1982. The size, number, ranking, and names of the largest accounting concerns actually shifted substantially as the 1980s emerged.

A study by the Congressional Research Service found that in 1980 clients of the then Big Eight accounted for 94% of all sales, 94% of all profits, 90% of all income taxes paid, 94% of all people employed, and 94% of all assets owned by New York Stock Exchange members. The eight to ten largest CPA firms tended to handle the preponderance of all *Fortune* 500 companies' business, but smaller companies and numerous not-for-profits and governmental organizations were also among their clients. Larger clients purchased tax and consulting services well in excess of what they spent on audits. But in the mid-1980s only about a fifth of the Big Eight's revenues were from nonaudit services.

TRENDS IN THE PROFESSION

The main focus of the profession's diversification efforts had been into management advisory or consulting services which in the United States yielded profit margins of about 20%, almost three times that on standard audits. While consulting competitors complained about unfair competition from auditing firms, the firms themselves felt that the experience they gained as

auditors made them better consultants for their clients and that consulting improved the quality of their audits by helping them know more about their clients. The profession maintained that it had erected a careful "Chinese wall" between their auditing and consulting functions and cited the fact that only 10–40% of their audit clients ended up as consulting clients. But criticism was mounting against CPA firms for moving into specific areas of consulting some thought bordered on "conflicts of interest" with the objectivity needed in the auditing side of the business. For example, Peat Marwick had bought a major share in a public relations firm; Arthur Andersen had become a major factor in the asset-appraisal business; and Deloitte, Haskins, & Sells and Touche Ross were putting increased emphasis on consulting for investment bankers in corporate mergers, reorganizations, and bankruptcies. Others wondered openly whether an audit unit could really offer an unbiased appraisal of a system, major project, or decision its consulting group had recommended.

Aggravating matters was the fact that consultants in most firms were paid a bit more than auditors, and the disparate nature of the two activities often led to a culture clash. Public accountants had taken rigorous professional training and examinations to be certified as public accountants. They had to be not only knowledgeable about and adhere to the regulations of government bodies affecting financial and reporting matters but to the rules of the profession as interpreted by Generally Accepted Accounting Principles (GAAP) and the SEC in its Financial Accounting Standards Board (FASB) rulings. They had their own professional journals and looked to their professional colleagues for support and movement elsewhere in the industry.

The conflicts of this professionalism with the more freewheeling style of the consultants was further exacerbated by the partnership form that CPA firms followed. Accountants from the firms' earlier history usually dominated the partnership numerically. Consultants, who typically were not CPAs, could only be quasi-partners in that portion of the firm certifying audits. And disproportions between audit and consulting fees affected one group's willingness to share incomes and investments with the other. How these conflicts—and the power relationships they involved—could be resolved was an open question in the late 1980s.

Even so, the FTC was pushing for further sweeping changes in the professional codes which governed the accounting profession. The FTC was proposing that accountants would soon be free to draw contingent fees from sums recovered for clients as a result of audit work done in lawsuits, to accept commissions from the sellers of financial products the accountants had reviewed or recommended to customers, and to form private or even publicly held companies to process regular bookkeeping and accounting transactions for clients. The traditional partnership form the profession had adopted had made partners "fully and personally responsible" for their firm's CPA certifications and opinions. Many accountants were concerned that such moves would convert public accounting from its previous status as a "profession" with responsibilities beyond mere commercial concerns into "just another business." While the industry was fighting the FTC's efforts to promote harmful competition and to protect its image as a profession, legal actions against auditing firms had mounted, and most of the Big Eight had faced at least one potentially devastating lawsuit. Firms were hard pressed to get enough malpractice insurance to cover possible losses.

PRA&D POSITION

In the mid-1980s Peet, Russ, Anderson, & Detroit (PRA&D) sought to adjust its strategic position to respond to these changes in its industry and to the new global business environment it faced. PRA&D was among the largest and most prestigious of the public accounting firms. It was heavily represented among both manufacturing and service clients in the United States and in international markets. Well respected and conservative, PRA&D had so far moved cautiously in terms of diversification and marketing aggressiveness, but had developed strong consulting, tax, and systems units. PRA&D's headquarters were in a major Atlantic seaboard city, but it had branches or affiliates in most large U.S., European, Asian, Latin American, and Pacific Rim cities as well. Its past organization had given extensive autonomy to its partners in each local branch. But its central office had exerted strong policy controls in most functional areas, particularly those dealing with audit, tax, and ethical standards. Despite the presence of a Management Committee—elected by the partnership and usually containing the top functional and branch heads of the firm—PRA&D's Managing Partner, Henry Johnson, exercised very significant influence throughout the firm because of his personality and highly respected professional skills.

In 1989, concerned about the developing fragmentation resulting from its many specialized activities, its continued growth, and PRA&D's necessarily localized presence in so many different geographical areas, Mr. Johnson began to worry about how to reorganize and reposition his firm in light of the new competitive pressures. He wanted to establish a more focused organization and operating philosophy to deal with the complexities the firm then faced.

A considerable amount of self-analysis over the last two years had convinced the Management Committee that the 1980s' rapid rates of change, intense competition, new technology development, and needs for specialized skills would increase rather than decline. PRA&D felt it was well positioned in some market segments (notably with large traditional multinational manufacturers) and not as well in others (particularly smaller and mid-sized services companies). As a mid-sized member of the then Big Eight, PRA&D did not have the resources to develop a dominating presence in all areas. The gap in size between PRA&D and its largest competitors was already significant, and if past growth rates continued, the gap would increase in the future.

PRA&D's commitment to providing high-quality professional services through autonomous professional partners was fundamental to its culture. The firm had enjoyed well-deserved strengths in terms of its name recognition and its reputation for quality, integrity, and service—especially to its large clients. The latter were rather widely distributed both geographically and by industry classification.

However, PRA&D felt it lacked partner presence in many business segments and in some geographical areas which were likely to be important to its future. Over the last several years, growth pressures had been so great that the Management Committee was beginning to doubt whether there were an adequate number of partners to pursue its former highly decentralized strategy in the future. PRA&D's resources seemed spread among many smaller practice units, making it difficult to concentrate resources on a single client's needs, and indeed to provide the full array of services it wished in many markets.

Because of its highly decentralized partnership structure, PRA&D had often placed more emphasis on current profitability than on long-term investments in many of the growing areas of accounting and consulting. Although its client listings in the *Fortune* 500 were high relative to its competitors, there was some concern whether the firm was growing with the new clients who would become the next generation of *Fortune* 500 companies. Because of its highly decentralized structure and management philosophy, PRA&D found it difficult to develop the levels of specialization some of its stronger competitors had. As a consequence, PRA&D was suffering from lower billing rates and profitability in some key growth areas, especially in specialized industries like health care, financial services, and high-technology manufacturing. In the past, PRA&D had grown primarily by developing new business at its local geographic offices and by attempting to give each office the capability to deliver PRA&D's full range to all types of clients in its area.

While this strategy was extremely successful into the late 1970s, fragmentation and lack of coordination had become serious problems by the late 1980s. Only a few offices had the resources to carry out a full-service strategy across the full range of businesses in their areas. Because PRA&D was smaller than some of its major competitors, it had fewer partners, and its partnership skills were being badly stretched to meet the increasingly wide array of customer needs. Most of PRA&D's geographical offices and professional services were still very highly regarded in the industry, especially among its existing clients. However, it was becoming ever more difficult for its partners to find the time to generate new business or to focus on new emerging markets in any coordinated way across the United States—much less PRA&D's many international markets.

A Market-Driven Strategy

Intuitively, Mr. Johnson and the Management Committee strongly preferred a "market-driven strategy," focusing PRA&D's efforts on the services, delivery needs, and specialized capabilities key growth markets would demand in the future. However, they were concerned that PRA&D did not have enough partners or associates in its development pipeline (1) to maintain its existing customer base with the kind of quality for which PRA&D was known and (2) to simultaneously develop new "key growth markets." Although they had generally risen through PRA&D's auditing ranks, most members of its Management Committee recognized that the increasing complexities of the CPA market place required greater specialization on many professional disciplines in their practice (like taxes, mergers, international regulations, and computer systems) as well as on the needs of specific types of clients (like not-for-profit, government, consortia, financial services, etc. groups). They also recognized that many organizational and incentive changes would be essential to shift PRA&D from its traditional stance into a market-driven enterprise.

Organization And Incentive Issues

In the past, PRA&D's partners had been primarily rewarded based upon the profitability and growth their particular geographical office generated. No special incentives existed to develop specific new markets or to cooperate with other offices on a large *Fortune* 500 client's audit which might need staffing support in their geographic area, yet be coordinated by a Practice Partner in another area. The local practice office and the disciplines (like audit, tax, or systems) within the office were the central organizational units in PRA&D. Regional, industry specialist, and other "specialized practice units" were generally subordinate to the practice offices. However, there had been much discussion about the desirability of centralizing some of the disciplines more or developing Regional Partners who would work with all the other partners in a designated geographical area. As envisioned, the Regional Partners would have primary responsibility (rather than simply a coordinating role) for regionwide strategy, planning, market development, and emphasis, and the allocation of many personnel and financial resources. The Regional Partners (reporting to the Management Committee) would be responsible for balancing the goals and needs of all "practice units" and geographical areas within their region into a consolidated strategy. Together, they would be responsible for drawing up a firmwide strategy and operating plan extending at least three years into the future. Although the development of such Regional Partners had been considered for some time, the concept had not been implemented.

The basic problem of organizing PRA&D—as with other major accounting firms—revolved around some very complex coordination and incentive issues.

Within PRA&D there were at least seven levels of organization which needed to interact: (1) *Specialized Practice Units* focused on special issues, like government contracting, acquisitions and mergers, bankruptcies, or employee benefits and pensions; (2) *Industry Specialist Units* focused on particular industries like health care, law, retailing, minerals, or energy development; (3) *Practice Offices* having coordinative responsibilities for all local audit, law, systems, and specialized services activities; (4) *Regional Offices* which—if implemented—would be under a Regional Partner responsible for coordination, supervision, and operating performance of the overall practice within a large geographical area; (5) *Activity Partners* at both the national and major city offices, responsible for tax, systems, or management consulting services; (6) *Audit or Practice Partners* who coordinated large audits or consulting projects nationwide (or globally) and often had continuing responsibilities for client relationships with that customer, (7) the *Managing Partner* (and *Management Committee*) elected by all full partners.

COMMUNICATION AND COORDINATION AMONG GROUPS

Within PRA&D, as in other major accounting firms, the Management Consulting activity had grown rapidly. Although not as large as its biggest competitors in management consulting, PRA&D had developed a fine reputation for professional consulting. However, it had been unable to obtain substantial synergies between its Accounting and Management Consulting groups. At first, PRA&D had hoped that each group would be able to build the other's business by recognizing particular skills in its sister organization and recommending to clients that they enquire about PRA&D's capabilities in those areas. For example, an auditor might see a genuine inventory control problem developing in a client firm and suggest PRA&D Consulting's excellent inventory control group to work on it. Similarly, PRA&D's Consulting Group might develop an acquisition strategy for a client and recommend some of PRA&D Accounting's very sophisticated services at key junctures for the client. For a variety of reasons, this type of relationship had not developed well.

However, it had proved to be equally difficult for PRA&D to transfer specialized knowledge even within its Accounting Group or its Management Consulting Group. For example, the Accounting Group might develop an extremely sophisticated solution to a complex problem in Seattle, but other PRA&D offices might never hear about the solution. The Chicago Accounting Office might identify interesting new growth areas among high-technology or services companies in its area or develop a superb sales methodology for generating new clients. But such information was rarely effectively transmitted to or exploited by other offices,. The Management Committee was deeply concerned that the firm was losing substantial profits by not utilizing its full capabilities and solutions to problems which existed inside PRA&D. The firm's highly decentralized, partner-centered, operating philosophy had dictated that all plans—for goals, client service activities, office or departmental operations—be generated "bottom up." The Management Committee was concerned that these plans were not properly coordinated across the entire firm, and that they did not serve well as the basis for PRA&D's most important strategic decisions: partner evaluation, business development, and partner deployment.

The Management Committee was also concerned that its current methodology of awarding partnership shares exacerbated local offices' independence, and hindered their coordination with others' activities. It also encouraged development of specialization at local levels, where it was difficult to find enough clients to justify the critical mass of people necessary to develop a specialty in real depth. Finally, it was extremely difficult to move a highly qualified specialist—or a partner with strongly developed client contacts—from one local office to another, either temporarily or permanently. Such people often had very strong personal preferences for a particular job location. In addition, they tended to be major contributors to local profitability. Consequently, practice offices were reluctant to transfer such people to other locations, or to lend them for any substantial period of time. And individuals hesitated to move to another location where they would lose income or partnership shares while they rebuilt their contacts and billing capabilities in the new area.

The reverse problem often occurred when another office asked a local practice office for support on a large client audit or consulting project which had a division or activity in its area. The local office might have its resources entirely deployed against its own high-priority client base, and be reluctant to take top-rated people from those clients to support another office's project. There were also great difficulties in stimulating local partners to invest substantial amounts of time or money in developing new skill sets or specialties which might not bring profits to their local office for many years. And, finally, many partners tended to resist investment in technologies (especially those they could not directly control) which were not immediately or solely related to their own particular practice's development and profitability. These were common problems for many CPA firms. But PRA&D, which had very sophisticated systems people and techniques for serving clients, had been slower than others to develop the coordinated computer, management information, incentives, and networking systems needed for its own operations.

The Management Committee was deeply aware of these problems and perplexed by them. Many of the specialist, practice, and local partners also shared these concerns, although many others were less worried. Because enough partners had been making very high incomes and were quite comfortable with existing practices, it had been extraordinarily difficult to develop an integrated strategy which could focus PRA&D's enormous potentials on selected markets either in the United States or worldwide.

QUESTIONS

1. What major strategic options exist for PRA&D? How can PRA&D evaluate those options effectively given the diverse interests of its various internal constituencies? What strategy would you recommend and why?
2. How does strategy in this professional environment differ from that in other fields? How does the interaction of Management Consulting, Accounting, and other specialist groups affect the decision?
3. What problems would you foresee in implementing your strategy? Specifically, how should PRA&D deal with these?

APPENDIX A—PROFILE OF THE MAJOR ACCOUNTING FIRMS

GROWTH AND SOURCE OF INTERNATIONAL VERSUS U.S. REVENUES, 1977 AND 1986

FIRM	U.S. Versus Total Revenues		Comp. Annual Growth Rate 1977-1986		Trend in Geographic Emphasis
	1977	1986	Worldwide	US.	
Peat Marwick Main	71%	52%	20%	16%	Overseas
Arthur Andersen	75	76	16	16	Balanced
Coopers & Lybrand	52	56	14	15	Domestic
Price Waterhouse	51	53	12	13	Domestic
PRA&D	50	52	10	14	Overseas
Ernst & Whinney	74	68	15	14	Overseas
Arthur Young & Co.	54	47	15	13	Overseas
Touche Ross & Co.	53	53	14	14	Balanced
Deloitte, Haskins	54	55	12	12	Balanced

Source: 1977 figures from P. Bernstein, "Competition Comes to Accounting," *Fortune,* July 17, 1978; and 1986 figures from *Public Accounting Report,* as cited in "Peat Marwick and KMG Main Agree to Merge," *The Wall Street Journal,* September 4, 1986.

1986 RELATIVE MARKET POSITIONS INTERNATIONAL VERSUS U.S.

FIRM	WORLDWIDE		UNITED STATES	
	Revenues ($ millions)	Relative Position	Revenues ($ millions)	Relative Position
Peat Marwick Main	$2,700	1.5	$1,400	1.0
Arthur Andersen	1,800	1.2	1,360	1.5
Coopers & Lybrand	1,550	1.1	865	1.2
PRA&D	1,450	1.0	790	1.1
Price Waterhouse	1,400	1.0	742	1.2
Ernst & Whinney	1,360	1.0	930	1.1
Arthur Young & Co.	1,330	1.2	625	1.0
Touche Ross & Co.	1,120	1.0	590	2.4
Deloitte, Haskins & Sells	1,100	2.6	610	1.0

Note: Relative market positions are calculated by dividing a firm's revenues by those of the next largest competitor.

Source: 1976 revenues from *Public Accounting Report*, as cited in "Peat Marwick and KMG Main Agree to Merge," *The Wall Street Journal*, September 4, 1986.

CONSULTING PRACTICES OF MAJOR CPA FIRMS

FIRM	1987 WORLDWIDE CONSULTING REVENUES ($ Millions)	% OF TOTAL REVENUES WORLDWIDE	NUMBER OF CONSULTANTS
Arthur Andersen	$838	36%	9,639
Peat Marwick Main	438	13	4,700
PRA&D	390	20	3,750
Coopers & Lybrand	381	18	4,712
Ernst & Whinney	374	21	3,255
Price Waterhouse	345	20	4,300
Touche Ross & Co.	248	17	2,142
Deloitte, Haskins & Sells	209	14	2,271
Arthur Young & Co.	204	12	2,443

Source: *Consultants News* and *Bowman's Accounting Report*, in "Cutting the Pie," *The Wall Street Journal*, July 26, 1988.

Entering 1994, Nintendo Co., Ltd. was clearly the world leader in video games. Although pundits repeatedly forecast saturation, the market and Nintendo continued to grow despite a worldwide recession and a 30% stronger yen. Nintendo had released a variety of new game concepts including its *Mario Kart*, a unique action-racing game; *Mario Paint*, allowing users to draw pictures and compose music with a "mouse"; and *Star Fox*, the first game using Nintendo's proprietary FX (16 bit) chip which generated very realistic 3D animation pictures at faster speeds than competitive machines. This supported Nintendo's new "Super NES" export version of its Super Famicom player in Europe and America.[1] Unfortunately, games for the original NES [See Nintendo Co., Ltd., Case I-12] did not work on the new machine.

Both technologies and markets continued to explode worldwide. An astonishing 34% of Nintendo users were adults, courted with addictive puzzle-like games such as *Jeopardy* and *Tetris*, developed surprisingly in Russia. Nintendo's 100% owned Nintendo of America (NOA) accounted for over 50% of its sales and profits on a $100 million investment base, while its $40 million (investment) Nintendo of Europe was poised for expansion. In 1993 alone NOA and its direct licensees sold 28 million game cartridges. Signaling potential future moves into educational markets, Nintendo had invested $3 million in MIT studies on how children learn.[2] Given Nintendo's huge installed base of 40 million systems in the U.S., Apple Computer's president Michael Spindler, when asked which company Apple feared most, answered "Nintendo."[3]

Case Copyright © James Brian Quinn 1995. All rights reserved. The generous cooperation of Nintendo Co., Ltd. and Nintendo of America are gratefully acknowledged. Research Associates for this case were Nobuo Okochi and Penny Paquette.
D. Scheff, *Game Over*, Random House, New York, 1993 provides an excellent history and insights into the game industry and Nintendo Company, Ltd. References to this work are noted (1, __) in the text.

Largely because of Nintendo's success, a number of other competitors had entered the games market. Japanese giants Matsushita, Sony, and NEC were poised to bring truly formidable scale, brand names, and distribution power to bear for the first time in Nintendo's markets. NEC had partnered with Hudson, largest of Hokkaido's rapidly growing software industry, to develop a 16 bit micro processor, called PC Engine, to replace the jerky movements of on-screen characters by using a new "compression chip."[4] However, its system cost $199 as opposed to Nintendo's $70. Sony was developing its own system, while Matsushita's Panasonic Division was providing the hardware for 3DO's revolutionary 32 bit entry many thought might soon be followed by a 64 bit system. The technologies supporting PCs and advanced games were rapidly converging, and 19% of PC users cited "games" as a significant use.

All of this posed some interesting problems for Nintendo and NOA. No one doubted Nintendo's marketing and distribution potentials. But Nintendo had traditionally kept its advertising to about 2% of sales, compared to the 17–18% of most "toy" companies.[1,188] Instead, it developed a formidable array of methods to reach and get feedback from its young audience. Its *Nintendo Power* magazine enjoyed the largest paid subscription circulation of any magazine to kids and teens. NOA also had 400 people answering about 150,000 calls a week, responding to questions about how to solve game problems, when and where games would be available, and so on. In 1990 this "800-line" service had become so expensive that Nintendo converted it over to a regular toll system. Even then the service was so popular that— to avoid annoying parents—counselors were told to terminate a child's call after seven minutes. In the early 1990s NOA accounted for a massive 20% of most U.S. toy stores' sales and even more of their profits. And despite competition, Nintendo's international sales had been growing rapidly. Suddenly, however, market changes posed some interesting problems for both Nintendo Co., Ltd. (NCL) and NOA in both creating and distributing games.

NCL'S SOFTWARE ORGANIZATION

Mr. Yamauchi, Nintendo's entrepreneurial CEO, had centralized all internal software development in Japan. Early on, he saw that the real key to success in the games business was not hardware, with its limited market, but software which was unlimited. At that time Yamauchi decided Nintendo should become a haven for video game artists. "An ordinary man cannot develop good games no matter how hard he tries. A handful of people in this world can develop games that everyone wants. Those are the people we want at Nintendo," he said.(1,38) He wanted Nintendo to be the place where the "hottest game designers" most wanted to be. Yet there had been a problem. In Japan, most employees stayed with one company for their entire career. Nintendo could not hope to pirate talent from competitors or other software companies. Consequently, by 1994 it had developed 377 third party game sources in Japan, plus 190 worldwide.

Yamauchi's style seemed ill-suited for attracting and nurturing software geniuses. He had a reputation for aloofness, self-assuredness, and authoritarianism that had grown along with Nintendo. There were legends about his squashing people or companies that crossed him. He had no engineering background. Nevertheless, Yamauchi made himself head of all R&D, "the heart of this company." Yamauchi had never played a video game in his life, yet he alone was the judge and jury when it came to deciding which games Nintendo would release. He had hand-picked his three subordinates—Yokoi, Uemura, and Takeda— to be heads of R&D 1, 2, and 3. Within each R&D group were many teams pitted against each other. Miyamoto—the games genius who had created *Donkey Kong*, *Legend of Zelda*, and the *Mario Bros.*—operated a separate small group on his own, using his own unique style of laying games out on huge paper spreadsheets across several tables in a chaotic setting.

THE YAMAUCHI STYLE

Hiroshi Yamauchi was the highest paid ($6.3 million income) CEO in Japan, yet that was a mere fraction of salaries of top U.S. CEOs. Yamauchi was soft spoken, but very intense, opinionated, and unpre-

dictable. Although he was often criticized for being ruthless in his employee and business practices, no one questioned Yamauchi's genius at choosing successful games. Yamauchi insisted that R&D was sacrosanct. No one told his creative people what to create. The marketing department saw games only when they were completed. Yamauchi thought marketing people could only pick what was popular now, not what would be new and fresh in the future. In his judgments, he was very final. "Months of work could be disposed of with a single scowl," said one engineer. His style created much frustration and anger at times. Some left; others exhausted or disappointed were sent on sabbatical and told, "Spend the time, relax. Come back fresh."[1,40] Then, however, they seemed to come back for more, determined to have their game chosen the next time.

Unlike other Japanese companies, what Nintendo did not seem to seek was harmony in its operations. Yamauchi seemed to carefully parcel out his praise. If any one team had too much success, it could be slapped down. As a result each team came to excel in different areas and at different moments. Yamauchi divided the R&D work among his three teams. Yokoi, the oldest and most traditional engineer, headed R&D1, a software game design group. His team of 30 engineers operated as a small, dedicated "band of samurai" cranking out major successes like *Game Boy* and *Meteoroid*. Uemura's team, R&D2, developed the hardware itself. This included peripherals like the communications adapter. Takeda, said to be "the sharpest designer" of all, ran R&D3. Takeda's 20 person staff consisted of computer hackers and nerds. Takeda said, "There are no limitations, no boundaries; since we are on our own there is nothing we cannot do; when you start with nothing you can do everything. . . . We have to have more talented people because we are given unthinkable tasks. . . . Becoming maniacs is the idea."[1,44]

Although it also designed successful games, R&D3 often came up with the technologies that allowed the other games to run, for example, the Nintendo Read Only Memory (NROM) chips onto which a game program was reproduced. The amount of information in a game was limited only by the size of the NROM. Takeda's group expanded this enormously by creating a special cartridge called UNROM, a RAM (random access memory) which stored information until it was needed: for example until the lead character entered a new room whose features and creatures the UNROM provided only while the hero was in that "room." The group created Memory Map Controllers (MMCs) that, through information compression and storage tricks, gave cartridges 32 times their original capacity and extended the life of Nintendo's early systems substantially.

While the rest of Nintendo (reflecting Mr. Yamauchi's preferences) was Spartan in the extreme, the R&D groups worked in spacious, private laboratories with significantly more staff and resources than many other laboratories allowed. In keeping with Japanese practice, software developers were paid a salary with a year-end bonus based on the company's performance. Despite Yamauchi's focus on software, 90% of Nintendo's games were produced by outside suppliers in 1994. Yamauchi's goal for each internally produced program was preeminence. Given the cost of each game, he believed that it was far better to put resources into the production of one or two hit games per year rather than several minor successes. When a game went into full production, it typically required a million dollars of engineering and development backup, plus several millions more for marketing introduction.

THE NOA STYLE

In striking contrast to Nintendo's tough, disciplined Japanese image, NOA under its founder, Minora Arakawa, allowed much informality and practical joking. There was a "no suits on Friday" dress code. "Managers were conspicuously young . . . and everything and everybody was closely connected."[1,199] Arakawa took out all the walls between managers and workers, and had weekly meetings with key elements of his staff to keep communications open. Offices were decorated with baseballs, windup toys, stuffed animals, basketball hoops, and other toys. Yet a Spartan Japanese atmosphere still existed. There were no corporate jets, all offices were a 10' x 10' square, and there were no executive suites. Employees often worked late, past midnight. Although NOA followed the Japanese model of controlling executive compensation relative to other workers, employees could earn up to a 50% bonus on their salary if the company's earnings and their individual performance warranted. Top managers spent a full weekend twice a year going through all employees' performance and salaries in detail and awarding bonuses based on evaluations made by their groups.

Arakawa was determined to avoid the elaborate, expensive bureaucracies and perquisites he thought had destroyed Atari and other game companies in the volatile and cut-throat toy business. [See Nintendo Co., Ltd. case.] Through 1993 Arakawa or his then COO, Howard Lincoln, had to approve any hiring.

Lower level executives could only approve expenditures up to $5,000. Anything above $50,000 had to have Arakawa's approval—an anomaly in a business where it cost millions to develop and manufacture a new product for introduction and tens of millions to go to full production and marketing.

THE NOA MARKETING CONCEPT

NOA is operated as a wholly owned subsidiary of Nintendo Co., Ltd. (NCL). (See Exhibit 1 for details on NCL's subsidiaries.) Mr. George Harrison, Director of Marketing and Corporate Communications, said,

> In the last few years we have moved from being an export-driven Japanese company in which NOA was essentially a sales office just receiving products from Japan. We are now a more international company where it is recognized that other large markets (the U.S. being one) have special needs, interests in other types of software and products, and special cultural characteristics. For example, the sports category of video games was not really very big at all in Japan, but it has grown to be very, very important in the U.S. and was the strategic wedge that some competitors used very successfully in the last few years. Recently, we've been able to direct some product acquisitions from the U.S. and we've sent people who are familiar with football, basketball and baseball to find products that were appropriate here.
>
> Even today we don't develop any products here in the U.S. We have a group of people who go out and scan contract developers to see what interesting products they may have available to acquire. To some extent this places us in competition with our own licensees as we seek to buy products we could publish ourselves. Now, suppliers want to publish the same product on a variety of systems so the same title can come out simultaneously on all. We've always taken great care to make sure that Nintendo's product is the best quality. That's the only thing that ultimately distinguishes our systems. Most licensees have extremely limited resources to spread their games over all available systems. Traditionally, developers had been paid on almost a flat fee basis as a contract group to produce something. Publishers [like us] then marketed the games and made the large variable revenues that go with that. Developers enjoyed relatively low risk under this system, but seeing the profits going elsewhere they are now attempting to market their own products. This is changing the structure of the industry enormously.
>
> With marketing and introduction costing as much as ten times what development does, all parties are seeking ways to decrease their risks. Unfortunately, like the movie industry, a few really large hits are where you make your money. To gain better control, many firms are trying to

vertically integrate; and in response we are trying to leverage our own unique position in the market. In the design area, you will find that our games have distinctive looks, for example if you put our Mario character games up against SEGA's Sonic games. Ultimately, we can only be as good as our creative product. The industry has been littered with people who have introduced interesting game titles, new techniques, or tricks, but many lacked originality in their characters or stories. That's where our Mr. Miyamoto's great strengths have been.

There are licensees who have introduced Barbie games and others they thought were specifically targeted for particular demographic audiences. To date we haven't gone out and asked a specific demographic group through market research, "What would you like?" and then tried to develop it. We tend to let our nose be our guide in the marketplace. Decreasing your risks [in this marketplace is very difficult. One means is] locking up the best creative talents in the world with some form of exclusive development arrangement. However, this very act may also increase your costs and risks in other ways. As the technology has become more sophisticated, the cost of development has gone up to a point where [front end investments are very high, and] a video game developer can't really be some guy working in a garage anymore.

TECHNOLOGY OR CONTENT?

A phenomenon like SEGA was probably inevitable, given our market share and strong Japanese base. However, when you've been so successful for so long you can't change your practices just because someone in the last sixty days has taken a major piece out of the business. Last year consumers seemed to be just fascinated by technology, jumping on CD players and 16 bit machines just because they were "more advanced products." SEGA has kept up a steady strategy of talking about things like virtual reality goggles, the SEGA Channel, and claims that they were the wave of the future. The strategic question is, do you try to meet this currently or hunker down, conserve your resources, then wait until you have a truly superior system to push back with? We have always held that it is more important to have an important entertainment piece to go with the new technology that really makes someone want to buy that technology.

Today there is a lot of hoopla about CD-ROMs and the fact that millions of people have them installed in PCs. But the percentage who use them for games in computers is small and those who go on to buy additional CD programs is extremely small. Our focus on staying with cartridges has not been a popular stance, but we feel that the electricity piercing through a micro chip is always going to be faster than a spinning disk that's being read by an optical reader. CDs are fine for some purposes [like recalling major stored programs] but not for others. On the other hand, CDs enjoy some advantages in terms of manufacturing and distribution costs.

Distribution is another key element. As the number of platforms and titles expand, the retailer has a large challenge on how to manage inventories so as not to get burned. As program costs increase, customers want to pretest a program either through in-store testings or rentals. These problems, and the capabilities of the information highway, will be changing channels enormously. How we participate will be a critical strategy. About a year ago NCL made an investment in a Japanese satellite company called St. Giga and after the first of the year will begin broadcasting five channels of entertainment by direct broadcast satellite. These channels will include language education, radio TV guide listings, other services, and video games. The small 18" satellite dishes are especially important in Japan because little cable TV exists there. This opens whole new market opportunities. When researchers ask consumers which of all the "information highway services" they would most want, entertainment always comes to the top. It is the Trojan Horse to get the other services into the home.

To expand markets, we have to deliver sustained success, not just exploit fads or passing phenomena. Customer service has always been a key strength of ours. Our goal is to have people most satisfied with our products. This has been the function of our Call Center, our correspondence group, and our *Nintendo Power* magazine. We now have to push these concepts further using the capacities of the new technologies available. Another form of customer service is to respond to our retail customers quickly. We have built a very sophisticated warehouse outside of Seattle that allows us to ship product to arrive at the store level within three days, bypassing storage warehouses and distribution centers. Logistics may not sound like a sexy part of the business, but in a hit-driven business it is very important."

THE NOA ORGANIZATION

Nintendo of America had a very flat organization and a series of policies to maintain informality. NOA had two subsidiaries, NES Merchandising, Inc. and Nintendo of Canada, Ltd. in Vancouver. Its basic organization form was functional (see Exhibit 2 for details), but within that structure it employed a large number of part-time and inexperienced people. About 400 were in its Consumer Service unit and 150 in Merchandising, NOA's largest units. The Consumer Service force was very important. It answered calls about games day in and day out. Inquiries typically focused on the availability of specific games in different areas and the details of how to get a game character through a particular problem. Answers had to be extremely polite, friendly, and knowledgeable. Operating from small carrels in the same floor area, telephone answerers typically handled 50–100 calls a day. The pressures caused serious problems with burn-out and major challenges in creating opportunities for personal growth. In addition to 150,000 telephone inquiries per week, Consumer Service also handled about 5,000–10,000 letters. Although detailed technical questions about games dominated the inquiries, telephone answerers also had to field broad policy questions about Nintendo's position on violence in video games, what was happening currently in lawsuits, etc.

Maintaining quality in all these contacts was a serious concern for NOA's management. Although each job in the Nintendo operations area carried a job description and job rating, employees were encouraged to feel that they were not confined by that description and were encouraged to initiate ideas and better work methods. Ms. Beverly Mitchell, Director of Personnel, said:

> We have a bonus program which is very unique. All employees participate in the same program and the bonuses, although discretionary—meaning the company may or may not pay any bonuses—range between 0-40% of compensation based on employee performance. All employees from officers to hourly workers are on the same program. In evaluating performance for bonus purposes, one of the things employees are rewarded for are ideas they brought forward which have been implemented. In addition to this method of encouraging improved work methods and ideas, we have a very strong open door policy. It's not just a vehicle for airing complaints. It's the way we get things done. Everyone feels free to go to the source. We feel this is imperative because our fast-paced environment demands that we get things done now.

CORPORATE CONTROLS

Like many Japanese companies, Nintendo's corporate control systems varied from those common in the U.S. As Bruce Holdren, Director of Finance, said:

> The primary thing that NCL looks at is how the company is doing vis-a-vis competitors, in terms of serving customers with a reasonable financial return. Headquarters recognizes the value of sacrificing short-term profits to preserve good relationships with retailers or to deal with an inventory situation; they deal with those decisions without a great deal of hand-wringing. To the best of my knowledge, there is no written strategic plan. NOA's officers do provide input to NCL in terms of the worldwide strategy: which products to develop, and so forth. But the final decisions are basically at NCL; NOA then does its best to adapt those products and marketing strategies to

be successful in North America. In this very dynamic entertainment type business we have to be very flexible. The idea of a written five-year or three-year plan, I think, would just be laughed at here. Key people on the technology and marketing sides in Japan, I am sure, are thinking three years out. We tend to consider more what's going to happen next year, what products we will have to sell, and how we can best do that job of selling. To the best of my knowledge there are no ROI, ROR, or ROE targets given us by Japan.

NO BUDGETS

One of our unique features is that we don't have budgets. That goes right to Mr. Arakawa's belief that this is a very dynamic, fast-paced business and we could get too tied up in managing budgets. There are two basic risks: (1) we might not be responsive to the market either on the upside or the downside and (2) we could go ahead and spend money despite the fact that conditions have changed. He's afraid that a budget is a bit of a self-fulfilling prophecy, that people will manage to a set of plans that are several months old rather than managing to what's happening today in the marketplace. However, we do provide cost center reports to all the department managers and their supervisors, and those have details on what has been spent year to date and versus last year.

[An interesting set of tools we use is] a process called action memos and an authority chart. The authority chart is about a twenty-page document with basically one page for each major function or department. It says that "the following decisions require approval by (person's name)." For each level the chart defines what we consider to be discretionary expenses. Basically up to $5,000 a director can authorize discretionary expenses with no further approval. From $5,000 to $50,000 the director needs to prepare an action memo and submit it to an NOA corporate officer. That gets circulated, but that's the final sign off. Above $50,000 Mr. Arakawa and Mr. Lincoln are required to sign off. Below these limits, the corporate officer just signs and doesn't request approvals. Payroll and routine, recurring costs such as utilities are considered non-discretionary and not subject to approval, but hiring additional people, position changes, marketing costs, etc., do need approval. A new building or piece of capital investment is discussed in a fair amount of detail concerning its location, strategy fit, etc. But, in general, there are no hurdle rates imposed by NCL.

ACTION MEMOS

In addition, there are certain non-financial decisions that are important enough to require approvals in the authority chart. Examples might be the change in a CPA firm, a change in advertising agency, the sign-off on a six-month merchandising department plan, and so forth. Messrs. Lincoln and Arakawa thought very carefully about what the key success and expense factors are in this business and said that "these are the things—whether there's a direct dollar impact or not—we want the opportunity to sign off on." So the action memos were initiated: to provide the full context for such decisions. We all look at them primarily as a communications tool. We are not just trying to control things; we're trying to ensure that the officers and Mr. Lincoln and Mr. Arakawa, in particular, are aware of what's going on. Some people who come here don't understand why they can approve only up to $5,000, when at the same rank elsewhere they could have approved $1 million. The answer is, our system is designed to ensure that the officers know what's going on. For example, an action memo is written for the marketing launch expenditure for each new title. That way senior management can say, okay, this launch will cost $3 million, but that sum is not warranted for this title. On the other hand, we have some titles that we'll spend $10 million launching because they are really strategic or we have huge sales expectations. The officers have a full financial breakdown as well as a verbal rationale for these projects.

There is very close, frequent contact among the officers. There are regularly scheduled staff meetings for each division in which all the directors assemble and receive a report on what's going on in a particular area. The areas reporting are scheduled and rotated to ensure that each group reports at least once a month. In specific areas like the customer service group, we keep lots of statistics on the types of questions, comments, complaints, and inquiries they get as well as the efficiency with which they answer these. This activity is monitored thoroughly for quality because it is an absolutely key communication with our customers. In the credit area, we have policies where we step back and ask whether certain controls are necessary for individual customers, what the cost of these controls is versus the probable credit or goodwill losses, etc. We try to eliminate those controls that are unnecessary. The old 80–20 rule is very important for us.

Servicing that last 20% of customer desires can be very expensive. Essentially, the VP of Operations sets a total target cost, has that approved, and says, "I'm going to hold to this total cost and will achieve this level of service." At the retail level, we have a department (now three people) whose sole purpose is to monitor what is selling at retail, analyze that, and translate it into information executives can use for decisions. We now basically meet with all major customers and get that data via EDI, following not just what is shipped to Toys 'R Us, but what specific titles are selling where. This data is crucial for all aspects of our operations including the potentials of new product launches, where it helps calibrate the "gut feel" of our officers concerning how well a product should do and is performing.

PRODUCT DEVELOPMENT

Mr. Donald W. James, Director of Product Analysis and Development, said:

All final decisions on product direction are made by NCL in Japan. But in the last 2–3 years, we've been expanding the product development areas of NOA because we are now a global company. Focus is given to the industrial design side, like the plastic housings, controllers, colors, graphics, human factor, and design elements for the American market. We look for new game concepts or ways to deliver entertainment. We also search for various technologies and are approached by non-Japanese companies from all over the world with new concepts or technologies we can possibly utilize.

We do not develop software internally at Nintendo of America. We may use third party developers in the U.S. or Western Europe to produce Nintendo published titles. But most often, we help other publishers develop their concepts for Nintendo hardware platforms. They take all the development and marketing risk, but we suggest ways to help make a better product, hardware concept, or game. This obviously helps Nintendo overall. One of the key differences between movie and interactive entertainment is that in an interactive environment, you have lots of intangibles that can only be evaluated through testing. In an interactive environment, you must keep going back and re-doing things so that it becomes more and more fun. You have to take into account all of the things a kid can think of while playing the game and what they can do to make the software fail.

Nintendo, though, will continue to work on a game for as long as necessary until it is as fun as it can be. You can't really put a hard time schedule on this. The important thing is to get it right. Unfortunately, the public in any retail environment can be very fickle. Fighting games, which are hot now, may not be so next year. Yet it often takes 20 months or more to make a really interesting new game. Every program is different and requires a certain expertise. If you're doing a baseball game, you need people to spend a lot of time researching baseball, doing stats, getting the situations right and so forth. Although most concepts that do well in Japan also do well here, there are notable exceptions due to the cultural differences. In making a game, you have a designer-creator who develops the concepts, characters, and entertainment features. But he generally isn't a programmer. You have someone also to design and direct the visuals and graphics. Artists create the backgrounds and character movements, and there is someone else who directs the music. Pulling this together worldwide is quite a challenge.

THE NATURE OF BUSINESS

The 1994 video game business was peculiar. Big product hits came and went with the whims of millions of children. Both the market and the distribution system were dominated by a few large chains like Toys 'R Us which alone controlled over 20% of all toy sales in the U.S. About 60% of all toys had been sold during the month before Christmas in North America. Toy manufacturers normally had to carry credit for their retailers until Christmas season sales cleared. This was a risk Arakawa was determined to avoid. The question was how.

Sales of hardware depended on the adequacy of the software available. Although virtually all Nintendo's product development and most cartridge production were still in Japan, foreign markets were difficult to gauge. Mr. Yamauchi said,

> It is impossible for us to judge or investigate whether or not a game we will introduce two years later will successfully sell in any market by utilizing polls or available questionnaire techniques. Only experienced engineers or designers can tell whether games should be financed and whether games will attract large audiences. We do have several groups inside the company who do the evaluation of the finished product. They are composed of some software science people and hardware engineers, and some people doing the administrative work here (in Kyoto). Adding to that, we hire some students who do moonlighting for Nintendo and are so-called "game bugs." They love to play games, so they play our games extensively and say anything freely to us as to whether they like it or don't like this or that feature. Games are given scores. But the fact that a game got an 80 to 90 score doesn't necessarily mean this game will sell extensively. We cannot tell unless we see the actual result in the market place. But when a game is marked only 50 to 60, we are quite sure it will not sell.
>
> If there are 100 games introduced to the market a week, the market will regard only about 10% as interesting or fun. We continuously make about 100 games a year, but we concentrate on that 10% of interesting games. If others cannot produce very good software which will be appreciated by Japanese audiences, there is no way for them to be successful in this market."

An American with a Nintendo system averaged 7 game cartridges. A Japanese averaged 12. Average cartridge prices had been about $40.00. Unfortunately, software was relatively easy to duplicate for most systems. Consequently, counterfeiting was a major problem. Another was a glut of games with inferior quality.

To deal with these issues Nintendo of America had instituted the "lock and key" system (between game software and NES hardware) to prevent use of unauthorized software and had insisted on an exclusivity clause which (1) limited its licensees to producing only 5 Nintendo games per year and (2) prevented their release for other video game systems. NOA-approved games could not be sold outside the United States and Canada. Anyone who attempted to abuse its strict license terms was dealt with stringently by Nintendo, which also enforced its copyright and intellectual property with vigor throughout the world. In the early 1980s, Arakawa and his then legal counsel, Howard Lincoln, had masterminded several landmark cases—against MCA and Atari among others—defending Nintendo's positions. Many licensees complained about Nintendo's restrictions, but none had been able to have them set aside by the courts. Approved games obtained the Nintendo quality seal, an important item on retail shelves. NCL either self-manufactured or controlled the production of all cartridges at selected vendors. Licensees would mark-up the cartridge prices by 50–100%, and retailers would double it again. Licensees could show their wares in the Nintendo booth at important industry trade shows, distribute their products through Nintendo's channels, and have access to Nintendo's game counseling system. Despite the licenses' restrictions, Nintendo's marketing power enabled licensees to sell a startling average of 75,000—and sometimes millions of—copies of every game approved by Nintendo.

THE NEW COMPETITION

However the new competition was impressive. In 1994 the most potent competition was SEGA. SEGA's new 16-bit "Genesis System" had accompanied its introduction of its popular *Sonic The Hedgehog* game. True to its strategy, SEGA cut its systems price quickly from $190 to $150 and began to offer *Sonic The Hedgehog* as a promotion for new sales. Despite increasing its market share, SEGA's profits hovered around half those of Nintendo.

Nintendo's and SEGA's successes also stimulated a whole new software industry. In the U.S., companies like Acclaim, which had developed popular programs such as *Aliens 3, Terminator 2*, and *WWF Super Wrestle–Mania Challenge* found their stocks quadrupling in one year and trading at 27–30 times earnings.[5] In Japan, software companies like Capcom had broken sharply from Japanese business practices. In these software houses, a new style prevailed. Individuality was prized, head-hunting was rife, compensation systems no longer depended on seniority, and entrepreneurship was praised. Traditional firms like Matsushita's JVC and giant NEC had formed alliances with young American software suppliers like Electronic Arts, while independent firms like Japan's Enix—developer of *Dragon Quest*—became financial phenomena, selling 3–10 million copies of games at $80 each, almost overnight, through alliances or licensing.[6]

FROM DISNEY TO 3DO

Disney had entered the marketplace with its game version of *Aladdin*. New combination games-and-films companies introduced "adult-oriented interactive movies" like *Voyeur* allowing players to solve sexy mysteries by seeking clues in different rooms viewed through a telescopic lens. Alliances with AT&T, Time-Warner, and Tele–Communications Inc.—and the Paramount–Viacom (MTV) combination, one of the largest mergers in history—were changing the structure of the entire entertainment industry. A new company, 3DO, was introducing a 32-bit processor which promised high definition television (HDTV) quality pictures, hi-fi sound quality, fast response times, and much more flexibility in game design. Headed by Trip Hawkins, 3DO became one of the hottest initial public offerings of 1993. It sought to combine the visual power of a Hollywood movie with the interactivity of a video game. [See Nintendo Co., Ltd. case.]

Time-Warner and Tele–Communications had agreed to create a special SEGA Channel for their cable TV systems, giving subscribers access to 50 games each month. ImagiNation Network allowed people to compete with each other in a "virtual amusement park" covering many western communities in the U.S. Increasing numbers of video games based on best-selling movies like *Cliff Hanger*, *Last Action Hero*, or *Jurassic Park* began to emerge. Virtually every major Hollywood studio either had a video game division or had bought a video game company. In Sony's Entertainment Division, its Sony Interactive Group screened every movie script for its game potentials, and could send a team out to videotape sequences simultaneously with the making of the movie. The creative potentials of many other possible combinations were still untested.

However, as kids became addicted to games (Americans averaged nearly 1.5 hours per day), parents became extremely concerned about the degree of violence in various games. Unlike the gentle whimsy of the *Super Mario Bros.*, other games featured graphic decapitations, monsters (and heroes) tearing the hearts

out of victims, and vampires creating bloody havoc. In the U.S. these led to Congressional hearings, a major media outcry, and threats of protective legislation.[7]

THE NINTENDO POSITION

In this complicated marketplace, both NOA and NCL had to review their strategic positions. Nintendo's Super NES System was the leading (15 million unit) 16-bit central processor, although it had only 128K of workable RAM. Through its advanced "mode 7" graphics capability, it offered spectacular 360° game play for titles like *Super Mario Kart*, *NCAA Basketball*, and *NHL Stanley Cup*. It could display 256 colors from a palette of 32,768 colors—compared to 16–64 colors displayed and a palette of only 512 on most competing systems. Through the technological magic of R&D3, Super NES offered very high resolution, full digital stereo sound, and a game library of over 200 titles as compared to the more limited offerings of other individual competitors. Nintendo's compact *Game Boy* led the market in portable game systems, while its "Gateway" system offered interactive multimedia access in airplanes, hotels, and other venues. Its initial target was 20 million travelers. *Game Boy* contained the same computing power as the NES, yet fit in the palm of a person's hand. A *Super Game Boy* adapter allowed full color play on a home screen. In advanced technology terms, Nintendo was looking beyond 3DO to a "Nintendo Ultra 64" (64 bit) system for planned introduction in late 1995 (planned price around $250). In game software, *Super Mario Bros. 3* was the undisputed single game leader of the current era with more than 9.6 million copies sold in 1993 alone. And Super NES enjoyed a library of 600 titles. In terms of market penetration, in early 1994 Nintendo compared to other home systems in the U.S. as shown in Table 1. (For other market and trend data see Appendix A.)

Player demographics for Nintendo showed some interesting patterns as indicated in Table 2. Nintendo's U.S. sales broke down as shown in Tables 1, 2 and 3.

THE UNEXPECTED HAPPENS

In late 1993 the previously unimaginable happened. After over a decade of rapid, continuous growth, Nintendo announced in the fourth quarter that its worldwide profits had declined 24%. Nintendo blamed the suddenly high exchange rates for the yen, which clearly affected its international profits. But SEGA, its most important competitor, reported a prof-

TABLE 1
U.S. Household Penetration of Various Electronic Systems

SYSTEM	PENETRATION
Color television	97%
VCRs	80%
CD players	42%
Nintendo systems	40%
Personal computers	35%

Source: Nintendo Co., Ltd., *1993 Annual Report.*

TABLE 2
Demographic Characteristics of Nintendo Players in the U.S.

AGE	SUPER NES	GAME BOY	NES
Under 6	3%	4%	4%
6–14	50%	43%	54%
15–17	10%	9%	7%
18–24	13%	11%	10%
25–45	19%	28%	21%
45+	5%	5%	4%
Total 18+	37%	44%	35%

Source: Nintendo Co., Ltd., *1993 Annual Report.*

TABLE 3
Nintendo's U.S. Sales

SYSTEM	MILLIONS OF UNITS FISCAL 1993	MILLIONS OF UNITS FISCAL 1994	CUMULATIVE UNITS THROUGH FISCAL 1994
Hardware			
Super NES	6.6	8.5	23.8
Game Boy	4.0	4.5	20.7
NES	2.7	2.0	39.2
Software			
Super NES	23.0	40.0	91.5
Game Boy	25.0	27.0	106.0
NES	28.0	20.0	279.0
Total Retail Dollars	$4,285	$5,174	

Note: Fiscal 1994 figures are Nintendo projections, not actual.
Source: Nintendo Co., Ltd., *1993 Annual Report.*

it increase to ¥57 billion on sales of ¥380 billion. Nintendo's 16-bit games began to decline in demand as Atari launched its 32-bit "Jaguar System," Sony set up a joint venture to market its new 32-bit system, and SEGA joined with Hitachi to develop a 32-bit successor for its new "Game Gear" series. And 3DO announced its even more impressive 32-bit, movie-quality advanced game machine, which (with anticipated 64-bit quality) could ultimately provide highly articulated 3 dimensional movements. 3DO was also designed to accommodate voice activation, which was rapidly becoming a reality for computer systems.[8] [See the Nintendo Co., Ltd. case for details about 3DO.]

In the U.S. Nintendo's total retail revenues grew by 22% during 1993. Nintendo still had a market share of 80% both in the U.S. and worldwide. The cumulative growth rate of Nintendo had been 438% in the U.S. for 5 years as compared to the total video game industry's growth of 380%. No other system came close to the 60 million installed base of Nintendo worldwide, where its total sales had also increased by 13% during fiscal 1993. However, the industry was expecting to sell 40 million more games over the next five years as new, more powerful chips poured out of Silicon Graphics, Matsushita, and NEC. Chip speeds were doubling every 3 years toward 400–500 mhz levels by 2000. Storage capacity per chip was reliably predicted to go from 1993's 16 megabits to between 500–1000 megabits by 2000. Totally new entertainment concepts seemed sure to develop as those capacities merged with the desires of a teenage population growing at 15% per year, from a base of over 75 million in America alone in 1994.

THE SONIC BOOMS

SEGA, Nintendo's most successful competitor, had been started in Japan by two Americans and became an American company in 1984 when Gulf and Western acquired it. SEGA had been unable to entice Japanese software producers to abandon Nintendo, but had been very successful in lining up some U.S. producers, notably Electronic Arts, which had helped create its "Genesis System." SEGA's *Sonic the Hedgehog* was one of the most successful concepts to challenge Nintendo's *Super Mario Brothers* in the early 1990s; and SEGA's 16-bit Genesis machine (using the chip that powered Apple's Macintosh) had beaten Nintendo to that market. It had also beaten Nintendo to the market with CD-ROM capabilities in its 1992 machines. It had used preemptive pricing to forestall Nintendo's responses. And to support its low price strategy, SEGA—unlike Nintendo—moved half its production to Southeast Asia.

In the three years from 1990 to 1993 SEGA increased its sales five times and profits six times. But in a bloody price war, SEGA's 1993 profits had plunged by 2/3 to $100 million. (See the Nintendo Co., Ltd. case for SEGA's and Nintendo's financials.) SEGA was concentrating on its next generation "Saturn System" operating on CD, while Nintendo stayed with its cartridge system. SEGA also began to plug money into virtual reality theme parks, electronic toys, and interactive systems for the electronic superhighway. It had worked out collaborations with Time-Warner and TCI, which had agreed to download SEGA games over their pay-channel systems. AT&T had developed a special modem to enable interactive games over a "SEGA Network" using its phone lines. SEGA was also working on virtual reality "rides" which would give the effects of roller coasters and spin rides while sitting in an enclosed room on a mobile chair.[9]

By 1994 Panasonic's REAL multiplayer had been used to introduce 3DO's 32-bit CD-ROM system. Based on the almost photographically realistic graphics of Amiga computers, 3DO's upgradable system (if successful) would allow much faster responses, higher quality graphics, and a lower royalty payout (only $3 vs. $20 for Nintendo) to game designers than did competing systems. 3DO did no manufacturing. Its CD-ROM systems and disks would be produced by others. Many saw 3DO's system as the most promising bridge to realistic imaging for virtual reality, multimedia, and many new arcade concepts as well as for corporate training systems.[10]

LOOKING FORWARD

Commenting on the late 1993 situation, Mr. Hiroshi Yamauchi had said,

In Japan we occupy more than 90% of the video game entertainment market. However, in Europe and the U.S. there are a substantial number of people competing with Nintendo. Some types of games, called action games, are loved by people around the world. Other types of games like "role-playing games" are very popular in Japan but don't do well in the United States or Europe. A second difference is how people approach cost, or the retail prices of these games. In Europe and America people make much of retail prices, and our competitors try to bundle several different software packages or to cut prices to make them attractive. In the case of Japan it is very different. As long as the game software is not interesting, people will not buy, however cheap it is. I think this cost consciousness is the main reason why competitors like SEGA are becoming important against Nintendo in European and American markets. It's interesting that in Japan Nintendo's prices are 50 to 60% higher than SEGA's, but in Japan SEGA is not selling at all. As 3DO, Atari, and others try to enter these markets, those are the conditions they will have to meet.

Nintendo's continuing success remains based on our unique ability to create the thrill of great game play experiences and appealing characters to share them with.... Nintendo's characters come to life because players can relate to them, experience adventures and excitement with characters you'd be proud to storm a castle with.... No one creates interaction better than Nintendo.... Nintendo will be in the forefront of (both hardware and software) developments. We will develop these in a way appropriate to our players, by making them both affordable and fun. We remain committed to pursuing record financial performance in the coming years, while delivering ever-more exciting and unique entertainment to people all around the world.

1. Evaluate Nintendo's approach to software development. How does this correspond to your view of "the Japanese management style"? Why has Nintendo been as successful as it has in the past? What problems would you expect in the future? Why does Nintendo make so much money?

2. What are the main opportunities and threats NCL and NOA must respond to? How should NCL and NOA position themselves strategically in the new environment? How should they be organized for the future? What should be the relationship between NCL and NOA? What does this mean for their organizational, control, and reward systems?

3. Why does NOA use the kind of control system it does? How would you propose to evaluate the performance of software people, telephone answerers, and other key elements of NOA's operation? What types of motivation systems might be more appropriate in NOA? NCL?

EXHIBIT 1
1994 Organization Chart

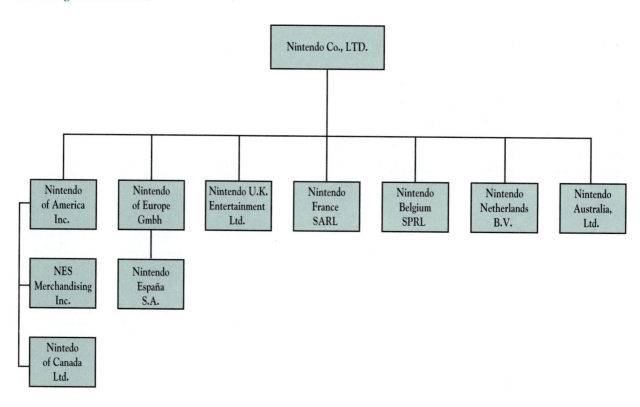

Source: Nintendo Co., Ltd.

EXHIBIT 2
Nintendo of America's
1994 Organization

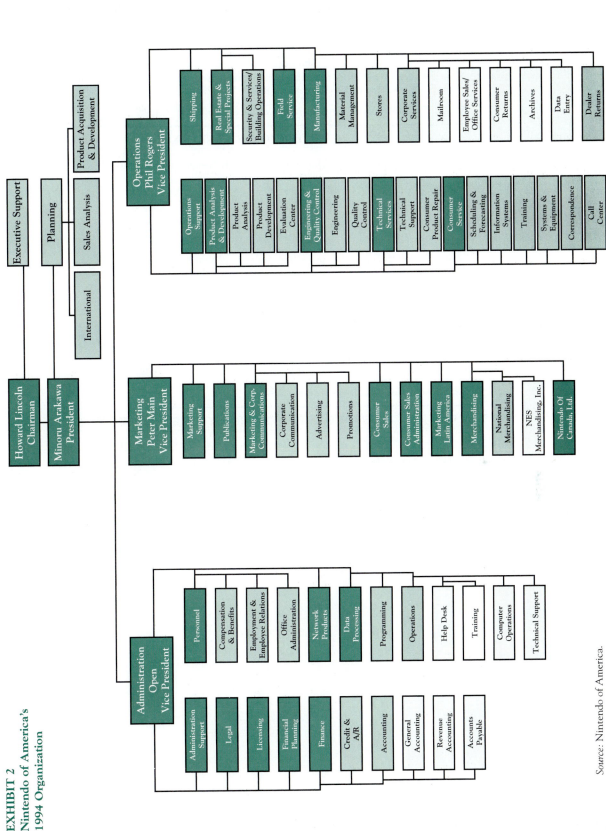

Source: Nintendo of America.

GEOGRAPHIC SHARES IN THE GLOBAL VIDEO GAME MARKET

U.S.	50%
Japan	30%
Europe	15%

Note: Forbes estimated that the video game industry is worth $7 billion worldwide in 1992. ("That Is Where the Money Is," *Forbes*, January 18, 1993.)

Source: "Dream Machines," *Far Eastern Economic Review*, December 24, 1992.

NINTENDO U.S. PENETRATION

(% of U.S. households with Nintendo game units)

1986	1.2
1987	4.6
1988	11.8
1989	21.2
1990	28.6

Source: Technology Futures, Inc. in *The Wall Street Journal*, October 21, 1991. p. R15.

NINTENDO'S U.S. MARKET SHARE

1988	$2.3	75%
1989	$3.4	80%
1990	$4.0	85%
1991	$4.4	79%
1993	$5.3	80%

Source: Nintendo Co., Ltd., *Annual Report*, 1993.

SALES OF GAME SOFTWARE BY TYPE IN JAPAN, 1992

	Number of titles	Percent of total sales
Fighting and action games	60	34.3%
Simulations	27	15.4%
Role-playing games	25	14.3%
Sports games	24	13.7%
Shooting games	12	6.9%
Others	27	15.4%

Source: Nihon Keizai Shimbun in *Japan Economic Almanac* 1994.

MOUNTBATTEN AND INDIA

Louis Francis Albert Victor Nicholas Mountbatten, Viscount of Burma, was, at forty-six, one of the most famous men in England. He was a big man, over six feet tall, but not a trace of flab hung from his zealously exercised waistline. . . . Mountbatten knew perfectly well why he had been summoned to London. Since his return from his post as Supreme Allied Commander Southeast Asia, he had been a frequent visitor to Downing Street as a consultant on the affairs of the Asian nations that had fallen under S.E.A.C.'s command. On his last visit, however, the Prime Minister's questions had quickly focused on India, a nation that had not been a part of [Mountbatten's] theater of operations. The young admiral had suddenly had "a very nasty, very uneasy feeling." His premonition had been justified. Attlee intended to name him Viceroy of India. The viceroy's was the most important post in the Empire, the office from which a long succession of Englishmen had held domain over the destinies of a fifth of mankind. Mountbatten's task, however, would not be to rule India from that office. His assignment would be one of the most painful an Englishman could be asked to undertake—to give it up.

A HISTORIC TRAP

Mountbatten wanted no part of the job. He entirely endorsed the idea that the time had come for Britain to leave India, but his heart rebelled at the thought that he would be called on to sever the ancient links

binding England and the bulwark of her empire. To discourage Attlee, he had produced a whole series of demands, major and minor, from the number of secretaries he must be allowed to take with him, to the make of the aircraft, the York MW-102 which had carried him around the world as Supreme Commander Southeast Asia, which would be placed at his disposal. The admiral still hoped somehow to resist Attlee's efforts to force the Indian assignment on him. . . .

There was much more to Mountbatten than his [impeccable] public image reflected; the decorations on his naval uniform were proof of that. The public might consider him a pillar of the Establishment, but the Establishment's members themselves tended to regard Mountbatten and his wife as dangerous radicals. His command in Southeast Asia had given him a vast knowledge of Asian nationalist movements, and there were few Englishmen who could match it. He had dealt with the supporters of Ho Chi Minh in Indochina, Sukharno in Indonesia, Aung San in Burma, Chinese Communists in Malaya, unruly trade unionists in Singapore. Realizing that they represented Asia's future, he had sought accommodations with them rather than try to suppress them as his staff and the Allies had urged. The nationalist movement with which he would have to deal if he went to India was the oldest and most unusual of them all. In a quarter of a century of inspired agitation and protest, its leadership had forced history's greatest empire to the decision that Attlee's party had taken to quit India in good time rather than to be driven out by forces of history and rebellion.

THE SUBLIME PARADOX

The Indian situation, the Prime Minister began, was deteriorating with every passing day, and the time for an urgent decision was at hand. It was one of the sublime paradoxes of history that at this critical juncture, when Britain was at last ready to give India her freedom—she could not find a way to do so. What should have been Britain's finest hour in India seemed destined to become a nightmare of unsurpassed horror. She had conquered and ruled India with what was, by the colonial standard, relatively little bloodshed. Her leaving threatened to produce an explosion of violence that would dwarf in scale and magnitude anything she had experienced in three and a half centuries there.

The root of the Indian problem was the age-old antagonism between India's 300 million Hindus and 100 million Moslems. Sustained by tradition, by antipathetic religions, by economic differences subtly exacerbated through the years by Britain's own policy of divide and rule, their conflict had reached a boiling point. The leaders of India's 100 million Moslems now demanded that Britain destroy the unity she had so painstakingly created and give them an Islamic state of their own. The cost of denying them their state, they warned, would be the bloodiest civil war in Asian history. Just as determined to resist their demands were the leaders of the Congress Party, representing most of India's 300 million Hindus. To them, the division of the subcontinent would be a mutilation of their historic homeland, an act almost sacrilegious in its nature.

Britain was trapped between those two apparently irreconcilable demands. Time and again British efforts to resolve the problem had failed. So desperate had the situation become that the present viceroy, an honest, forthright soldier, Field Marshal Sir Archibald Wavell, had just submitted to the Attlee government a final, and drastic, recommendation [called Operation Madhouse]. Should all else fail, he proposed, the British should "withdraw from India in our own method and in our own time and with due regard to our own interests; we will regard any attempt to interfere with our program as an act of war which we will meet with all the resources at our command. . . ."

Each morning brought a batch of cables to the India Office announcing an outburst of wanton savagery in some new comer of the subcontinent. It was, Attlee indicated, Mountbatten's solemn duty to take the post he had been offered. . . . Wavell had all the right ideas, Mountbatten thought. "If he couldn't do it, what's the point of my trying to take it on?" Yet he was beginning to understand that there was no escape. He was going to be forced to accept a job in which the risk of failure was enormous and in which he would easily shatter the brilliant reputation he'd brought out of the war.

POLITICAL CONDITIONS

If Attlee was going to drive him into a corner, Mountbatten was determined to impose on the Prime Minister the political conditions that would give him some hope of success. His talks with Wavell had given him an idea what they must be. He would not accept, he told the Prime Minister, unless the government agreed to make an unequivocal public announcement of a precise date on which British rule in India would terminate. Only that, Mountbatten felt, would convince India's skeptical intelligentsia that Britain was really leaving and infuse her leaders with the sense of urgency needed to get them into realistic negotiations.

Second, he demanded something no other viceroy had ever dreamed of asking: full powers to carry out his assignment without reference to London, and above all, without constant interference from London. The Attlee government could give the young admiral his final destination, but he alone was going to set his course and run the ship along the way.

"Surely," Attlee said, "you're not asking for plenipotentiary powers above His Majesty's Government, are you?"

"I am afraid, sir," answered Mountbatten, "that that is exactly what I am asking. How can I possibly negotiate with the Cabinet constantly breathing down my neck?"

A stunned silence followed his words. Mountbatten watched with satisfaction as the nature of his breathtaking demand registered on the Prime Minister's face, and he hoped that it would prompt Attlee to withdraw his offer. Instead, the Prime Minister indicated with a sigh his willingness to accept even that. . . . As he got back into his Austin Princess, a strange thought struck Mountbatten. It was exactly seventy years to the day, almost to the hour, from the moment when his own great-grandmother had been proclaimed Empress of India on a plain outside Delhi. [16–20]

LAST TATTOO FOR A DYING RAJ

George VI [Lord Mountbatten's cousin] comprehended perfectly well that the great imperial dream had faded and that the grandiose structure fashioned by his great-grandmother's ministers was condemned. But if the empire had to disappear, how sad it would be if some of its achievements and glories could not survive, if what it had represented could not find an expression in some new form more compatible with a modern age. "It would be a pity," he observed, "if an independent India were to turn its back on the Commonwealth."

The Commonwealth could indeed provide a framework in which George VI's hopes might be realized. It could become a multiracial assembly of independent nations, with Britain *prima inter pares* at its core. Bound by common traditions, a common past, by common symbolic ties to his crown, the Commonwealth could exercise great influence in world affairs. If that ideal was to be it was essential that India remain within the Commonwealth when she got her independence. If India refused to join, the Afro-Asian nations, which in their turn would accede to independence in the years to come, would almost certainly follow her example. That would condemn the Commonwealth to becoming just a grouping of the Empire's white dominions instead of the body the King longed to see emerge from the remains of his empire. . . .

Sitting there in their Buckingham Palace sitting room, Victoria's two great-grandsons reached a private decision that January day. Louis Mountbatten would become the agent of their common aspiration for the Commonwealth's future. In a few days Mountbatten would insist that Attlee include in his terms of reference a specific injunction to maintain an independent India, united or divided, inside the Commonwealth if at all possible. In the weeks ahead, there could be no task to which India's new viceroy would devote more thought, more persuasiveness, more cunning than the one conceived that afternoon in George VI's sitting room, that of maintaining a link between India and his cousin's crown. [45-46]

THE CORONATION

The closing chapter in a great story was about to begin. In a few minutes, on this morning of March 24, 1947, the last Englishman to govern India would mount his gold-and-crimson viceregal throne. Installed upon that throne, Louis Mountbatten would become the twentieth and final representative of a prestigious dynasty, his the last hands to clasp the scepter that had passed from Hastings to Wellesley, to Cornwallis and Curzon. The site of his official consecration was the ceremonial Durbar Hall of a palace whose awesome dimensions were rivaled only by those of Versailles and of the Peterhof of the Tsars. . . .

In Poona, Peshawar and Simla—wherever there was a military garrison in India—troops on parade presented arms as the first gun exploded in Delhi. Frontier Force Rifles, the Guides Cavalry, Hodsons and Skinners Horse, Sikhs and Dogras, Jats and Pathans, Gurkhas and Madrassis poised while the cannon thundered out their last tattoo for the British raj. As the sound of the last report faded through the dome of Durbar Hall, the new viceroy stepped to the microphone. The situation he faced was so serious that, against the advice of his staff, Mountbatten had decided to break with tradition by addressing the gathering before him.

"I am under no illusion about the difficulty of my task," he said. "I shall need the greatest good will of the greatest possible number, and I am asking India today for that good will." As he finished, the guards threw open the massive Assam teak doors of the Hall. Before Mountbatten was the breathtaking vista of Kingsway and its glistening pools, plunging down the heart of New Delhi. Overhead the trumpets sent out another strident call. . . . That brief ceremony, he realized, had turned him into one of the most powerful men on earth. He now held in his hand an almost life-and-death power over four hundred million people, one-fifth of mankind. [90–91]

OPERATION SEDUCTION

India's last viceroy might, as he had glumly predicted at Northolt Airport, come home with a bullet in his back, but he would be a viceroy unlike any other that India had seen. Mountbatten firmly believed "it was impossible to be viceroy without putting up a great, brilliant show." He had been sent to New Delhi to get the British out of India, but he was determined that they would go in a shimmer of scarlet and gold, all the old glories of the raj honed to the highest pitch one last time.

He ordered all the ceremonial trappings that had been suppressed during the war restored—A.D.C.s in dazzling full dress, guard-mounting ceremonies, bands playing, sabers flashing—"the lot." . . . He intended to replace Wavell's "Operation Madhouse" with a kind of "Operation Seduction" of his own, a minirevolution in style directed as much toward India's masses as toward their leaders, with whom he would have to negotiate. It would be a shrewd blend of contrasting values, of patrician pomp and a common touch, of the old spectacles of the dying raj and new initiatives prefiguring the India of tomorrow.

Strangely, Mountbatten began his revolution with the stroke of a paint brush. To his aides' horror, he ordered the gloomy wooden panels of the viceregal study, in which so many negotiations had failed, covered with a light, cheerful coat of paint more apt to relax the Indian leaders with whom he would be dealing. He shook Viceroy's House out of the leisurely routine it had developed, turning it into a humming, quasi-military headquarters. He instituted staff meetings, soon known as "morning prayers," as the first official activity of each day.

Mountbatten astonished his new I.C.S. subordinates with the agility of his mind, his capacity to get at the root of a problem and, above all, his almost obsessive capacity for work. He put an end to the parade of *chaprassis*, who traditionally bore the viceroy his papers for his private contemplation in green leather dispatch boxes. He preferred taut, verbal briefings.

"When you wrote 'May I speak?' on a paper he was to read," one of his staff recalled, "you could be sure you'd speak, and you'd better be ready to say what was on your mind at any time, because the call to speak could come at two o'clock in the morning."

But it was, above all, the public image Mountbatten was trying to create for himself and his office that represented a radical change. For over a century, the viceroy of India, locked in the ceremonial splendors of his office, had rivaled the Dalai Lama as the most remote god in Asia's pantheon of ruling gods. Two unsuccessful assassination attempts had left him enrobed in a kind of security cocoon isolating him from all contact with the brown masses that he ruled. . . . Hundreds of bodyguards, police, and security men followed each of his moves. If he played golf, the fairways of his course were cleared and police were posted along them behind almost every tree. If he went riding, a squadron of the viceroy's bodyguard and security police jogged along after him.

Mountbatten's first announcement, that he and his wife or daughter would take their morning horseback rides unescorted, sent a shock wave of horror through the house. It took him some time to get his way, but suddenly the Indian villagers along the route of their morning rides began to witness a spectacle so wholly unbelievable as to seem a mirage: the Viceroy and Vicereine of India trotting past them, waving graciously, alone and unprotected.

Then he and his wife made an even more revolutionary gesture. He did something that no viceroy had deigned to do in two hundred years; he visited the home of an Indian who was not one of a handful of privileged princes. To the astonishment of all India, the viceregal couple walked into a garden party at the simple New Delhi residence of Jawaharlal Nehru. While Nehru's aides looked on dumb with disbelief, Mountbatten took Nehru by the elbow and strolled off among the guests casually chatting and shaking hands. The gesture had a stunning impact. "Thank God," an awed Nehru told his sister that evening, "we've finally got a human being for a viceroy and not a stuffed shirt."

Anxious to demonstrate that a new esteem for the Indian people now reigned in Viceroy's House, Mountbatten accorded the Indian military, two million of whom had served under him in Southeast Asia, a long-overdue honor. He had three Indian officers attached to his staff as A.D.C.s. Next, he ordered the doors of Viceroy's House opened to Indians. Only a handful of Indians had been invited into its precincts before his arrival. He instructed his staff that there were to be no dinner parties in the Viceroy's House without Indian guests. And not just a few token Indians. Henceforth, he ordered, at least half the faces around his table were to be Indian. . . .

Not long after their arrival, *The New York Times* noted that "no viceroy in history has so completely won the confidence, respect and liking of the Indian people." Indeed, within a few weeks, the success of "Operation Seduction" would be so remarkable that Nehru himself would tell the new viceroy only half-jokingly that he was becoming a very difficult man to negotiate with, because he was "drawing larger crowds then anybody in India." [93–95]

STRAIGHT FOR CIVIL WAR

[But time was short. George Abell, whose reputation for brilliance and understanding of India was unsurpassed] told Mountbatten with stark simplicity that India was heading straight for a civil war. Only by finding the quickest of resolutions to her problems was he going to save her. The great administrative machine governing India was collapsing. The shortage of British officers, which was caused by the decision to stop recruiting during the war, and the rising antagonism between its Hindu and Moslem members meant that the rule of that vaunted institution, the Indian Civil Service, could not survive the year. The time for discussion and debate was past. Speed, not deliberation, was needed to avoid a catastrophe.

Coming from a man of Abell's stature, those words gave the new viceroy a dismal shock. Yet, they were only the first in a stream of reports and actions which engulfed him during his first fortnight in India. He received an equally grim analysis from the man he had handpicked to come with him as his chief of staff, General Lord Ismay, Winston Churchill's chief of staff from 1940 to 1945. A veteran of years on the subcontinent as an officer in the Indian Army and military secretary to an earlier viceroy, Ismay had concluded that "India was a ship on fire in mid-ocean with ammunition in her hold." The question, he told Mountbatten, was could they get the fire out before it reached the ammunition?

The first report that Mountbatten received from the British governor of the Punjab warned him that "there is a civil-war atmosphere throughout the province." It mentioned [in passing] a recent tragedy in a rural district near Rawalpindi. A Moslem's water buffalo had wandered onto the property of his Sikh neighbor. When its owner sought to reclaim it, a fight, then a riot erupted. Two hours later, a hundred human beings lay in the surrounding fields, hacked to death with scythes and knives because of the vagrant humors of a water buffalo. Five days after the new viceroy's arrival, incidents between Hindus and Moslems took ninety-nine lives in Calcutta. Two days later, a similar conflict broke out in Bombay, leaving forty-one mutilated bodies on its pavements.

Confronted by those outbursts of violence, Mountbatten called India's senior police officer to his study and asked if the police were capable of maintaining law and order in India. "No, Your Excellency," was the reply, "we cannot.". . .

Mountbatten quickly discovered that the government with which he was supposed to govern India, a coalition of the Congress Party and the Moslem League put together with enormous effort by his predecessor, was in fact an assembly of enemies so bitterly divided that its members barely spoke to one another. It was clearly going to fall apart, and when it did, Mountbatten would have to assume the appalling responsibility of exercising direct rule over one-fifth of humanity himself, with the administrative machine required for the task collapsing underneath him.

Confronted by that grim prospect, assailed on every side by reports of violence and the warnings of his most seasoned advisers, Mountbatten reached what was perhaps the most important decision he would make in India in his first ten days in the country; it was to condition every other decision of his viceroyalty. The date of June 1948 established in London for the transfer of power, the date that he himself had urged on Attlee, had been wildly optimistic. Whatever solution he was to reach for India's future, he was going to have to reach it in weeks, not months.

"The scene here," he wrote in his first report to the Attlee government on April 2, 1947, "is one of unrelieved gloom. . . . I can see little ground on which to build any agreed solution for the future of India." After describing the country's unsettled state, the young admiral issued an anguished warning to the man who had sent him to India. "The only conclusion I have been able to come to," he wrote, "is that unless I act quickly, I will find the beginnings of a civil war on my hands." [95–96]

THE FOUR INDIANS

Because of the urgency of the situation facing him, Mountbatten had decided to employ a revolutionary tactic in his negotiation with India's leaders. For the first time in its modern history, India's destiny was not being decided around a conference table, but in the intimacy of private conversations. . . . Five men would participate in them: Louis Mountbatten and four Indian leaders. The four Indians had spent the better part of their lives agitating against the British and arguing with one another. All were past middle age. All were lawyers who had learned their forensic skills in London's Inns of Court. . . .

In Mountbatten's mind, there was no question what the outcome of that debate should be. Like many Englishmen, he looked on India's unity as the greatest legacy Britain could leave behind. He had a deep, almost evangelical desire to maintain it. To respond to the Moslem appeal to divide the country was, he believed, to sow the seeds of tragedy. Every effort to persuade India's leaders to agree on a solution to their country's problems in a formal meeting had led to a deadlock. [But here in the privacy of his study] he was going to try to achieve in weeks what his predecessors had been unable to achieve in years—get India's leaders to agree on some form of unity. . . .

THE KASHMIRI BRAHMAN

Nehru was the only Indian leader whom Mountbatten already knew. [At the end of World War II] to the horror of his staff Mountbatten rode through Singapore's streets in his open car with Nehru at his side. His action, his advisers had warned, would only dignify an anti-British rebel. "Dignify him?" Mountbatten had retorted, "It is he who will dignify *me*. Some day this man will be Prime Minister of India." [97-98]

There was a great deal to bind the scion of a three-thousand-year-old line of Kashmiri Brahmans and the man who claimed descent from the oldest ruling family in Protestantism. They both loved to talk, and they expanded in each other's company. Nehru, the abstract thinker, admired Mountbatten's practical dynamism, the capacity for decisive action that wartime command had given him. Mountbatten was stimulated by the subtlety of Nehru's thought. He quickly understood that the only Indian politician who would share and understand his desire to maintain a link between Britain and a new India was Jawaharlal Nehru.

With his usual candor, the Viceroy told Nehru that he had been given an appalling responsibility and he intended to approach the Indian problem in a mood of stark realism. As they talked, the two men rapidly agreed on two major points: a quick decision was essential to avoid a bloodbath and the division of India would be a tragedy. Then Nehru turned to the actions of the next Indian leader who would enter Mountbatten's study, the penitent Mohandas Gandhi marching his lonely path through Noakhali and Bihar. The man to whom he had been so long devoted was, Nehru said, "going around with ointment trying to heal one sore spot after another on the body of India instead of diagnosing the cause of the eruption of the sores and participating in the treatment of the body as a whole."

In offering a glimpse into the growing gulf separating the Liberator of India and his closest companions, Nehru's words provided Mountbatten with a vital insight into the form that his actions in Delhi should take. If he could not persuade India's leaders to keep their country united, he was going to have to persuade them to divide it. Gandhi's unremitting hostility to partition could place an insurmountable barrier in his path and confront him with a catastrophe. His only hope, then, would be to divorce the leaders of Congress from their aging leader. Nehru would be the key if that happened. He was the only ally Mountbatten must have; only he might have the authority to stand up against the Mahatma.

Now that words had revealed the discord between Gandhi and his party chief, Mountbatten might be forced to widen and exploit that gap to succeed. He needed Nehru, and he spared no effort to win his support. On none of India's leaders would Operation Seduction have more impact than on the realistic Kashmiri Brahman. . . . Taking Nehru to the door, Mountbatten told him, "Mr. Nehru, I want you to regard me not as the last British viceroy winding up the raj, but as the first to lead the way to a new India." Nehru turned and looked at the man he had wanted to see on the viceregal throne. "Ah," he said, a faint smile creasing his face, "now I know what they mean when they speak of your charm as being so dangerous." [101–102]

THE MOST FAMOUS ASIAN ALIVE

[The next man to see Mountbatten was unique, a saint in his own time. He was Mohandas Gandhi—called Mahatma, meaning "Great Soul."] At every village, his routine was the same. As soon as be arrived, the most famous Asian alive would go up to a hut,

preferably a Moslem's hut, and beg for shelter. If he was turned away, and sometimes he was, Gandhi would go to another door. "If there is no one to receive me," he had said, "I shall be happy to rest under the hospitable shade of a tree." Once installed, he lived on whatever food his hosts would offer mangoes, vegetables, goat's curds, green coconut milk. Every hour of his day in each village was rigorously programmed. Time was one of Gandhi's obsessions. Each minute, he held, was a gift of God to be used in the service of man. . . . He got up at two o'clock in the morning to read his Gita and say his morning prayers. From then until dawn he squatted in his hut, patiently answering his correspondence himself with a pencil, in longhand. He used each pencil right down to an ungrippable stub, because he held that it represented the work of a fellow human being and to waste it would indicate indifference to his labors. . . .

The aging leader did not stop with words. Gandhi had a tenacious belief in the value of one concrete act. To the despair of many of his followers who thought a different set of priorities should order his time, Gandhi would devote the same meticulous care and attention to making a mudpack for a leper as preparing for an interview with a viceroy. So, in each village he would go with its inhabitants to their wells. Frequently he would help them find a better location for them. He would inspect their communal latrines, or if, as was most often the case, they didn't have any, he would teach them how to build one, often joining in the digging himself. [52]

Determined to convert [the Congress Party] into a mass movement attuned to his nonviolent creed, Gandhi presented the party a plan of action in Calcutta in 1920. It was adopted by an overwhelming majority. From that moment until his death, whether he held rank in the party or not, Gandhi was Congress's conscience and its guide, the unquestioned leader of the independence struggle. . . . Gandhi's tactic was electrifyingly simple, a one-word program for political revolution: noncooperation. Indians, he decreed, would boycott whatever was British; students would boycott British schools; lawyers, British courts; employees, British jobs; soldiers, British honors. . . .

Above all, his aim was to weaken the edifice of British power in India by attacking the economic pillar upon which it reposed. Britain purchased raw Indian cotton for derisory prices, shipped it to the mills of Lancashire to be woven into textiles, then shipped the finished products back to India to be sold at a substantial profit in a market that virtually excluded non-British textiles. It was the classic cycle of imperialist exploitation, and the arm with which Gandhi proposed to fight it was the very antithesis of the great mills of the Industrial Revolution that had sired that exploitation. It was a primitive wooden spinning wheel. For the next quarter of a century Gandhi struggled with tenacious energy to force all India to forsake foreign textiles for the rough cotton khadi cloth spun by millions of spinning wheels. Convinced that the misery of India's half million villages was due above all to the decline in village crafts, he saw in a renaissance of cottage industry, heralded by the spinning wheel, the key to the revival of India's impoverished countryside. For the urban masses, spinning would be a kind of spiritual redemption by manual labor, a constant, daily reminder of their link to the real India, the India of half a million villages. [61–62]

"The British want us to put the struggle on the plane of machine guns where they have the weapons and we do not," he warned. "Our only assurance of beating them is putting the struggle on a plane where we have the weapons and they have not." Thousands of Indians followed his call, and thousands more went off to jail. The beleaguered governor of Bombay called it "the most colossal experiment in world history and one which came within an inch of succeeding."

It failed because of an outburst of bloody violence in a little village northeast of Delhi. Against the wishes of almost his entire Congress hierarchy, Gandhi called off the movement because he felt that his followers did not yet fully understand nonviolence. Sensing that his change of attitude had rendered him less dangerous, the British arrested him. Gandhi pleaded guilty to the charge of sedition, and in a moving appeal to his judge, asked for the maximum penalty. He was sentenced to six years in Yeravda prison near Poona. He had no regrets. "Freedom," he wrote, "is often to be found inside a prison's walls, even on a gallows; never in council chambers, courts and classrooms." [64]

"A leader," Gandhi replied, "is only a reflection of the people he leads." The people had first to be led to make peace among themselves. Then, he said, "their desire to live together in peaceful neighborliness will be reflected by their leaders." [53]

[Once Winston Churchill had called Mohandas Gandhi "a half-naked fakir."] Now that half-naked fakir was sitting in the viceregal study, "to negotiate and parley on equal terms with the representative of the King-Emperor." He's rather like a little bird, Louis Mountbatten thought, as he contemplated that famous figure at his side, a kind of "sweet, sad sparrow perched on my armchair." . . .

So important had Mountbatten considered this first meeting with Gandhi, that he had written the Mahatma inviting him to Delhi before the ceremony enthroning him as viceroy. Gandhi had drafted his reply immediately, then, with a chuckle, told an aide, "Wait a couple of days before putting it in the mail. I don't want that young man to think I'm dying for his invitation." That "young man" had accompanied his invitation with one of those gestures for which he was becoming noted and which sometimes infuriated his fellow Englishmen. He had offered to send his personal aircraft to Bihar to fly Gandhi to Delhi. Gandhi had declined the offer. He had insisted on traveling, as he always did, in a third-class railway car.

To give their meeting a special cordiality, Mountbatten had asked his wife to be present. Now, with the famous figure opposite them, worry and concern swept over the viceregal couple. The Mahatma, they both immediately sensed, was profoundly unhappy, trapped in the grip of some mysterious remorse. Had they done something wrong? Neglected some arcane law of protocol? . . .

[Finally] a slow, sorrowful sigh escaped the Indian leader. "You know," he replied, "all my life, since I was in South Africa, I've renounced physical possessions." He owned virtually nothing, he explained—his Gita, the tin utensils from which he ate, mementos of his stay in Yeravda prison, his three "gurus." And his watch, the old eight-shilling Ingersoll that he hung from a string around his waist because, if he was going to devote every minute of his day to God's work, he had to know what time it was.

"Do you know what?" he asked sadly. "They stole it. Someone in my railway compartment coming down to Delhi stole the watch." As the frail figure lost in his armchair spoke those words, Mountbatten saw tears shining in Gandhi's eyes. It was not an eight-shilling watch an unknown hand had plucked from him in that congested railway car, but a particle of his faith. After a long silence, Gandhi began to talk of India's current dilemma. Mountbatten interrupted with a friendly wave of his hand.

"Mr. Gandhi," he said, "first, I want to know who you are." He was determined to get to know these Indian leaders before allowing them to begin assailing him with their minimum demands and final conditions. By putting them at ease, by getting them to confide in him, he hoped to create an atmosphere of mutual confidence and sympathy in which his own dynamic personality could have greater impact. The Mahatma was delighted. He loved to talk about himself, and in the Mountbattens he had found a charming pair of people genuinely interested in what he had to say. He rambled on about South Africa, his days as a stretcherbearer in the Boer War, civil disobedience, the Salt March. Once, he said, the West had received its inspiration from the East in the messages of Zoroaster, Buddha, Moses, Jesus, Mohammed, Rama. For centuries, however, the East had been conquered culturally by the West. Now the West, haunted by specters like the atomic bomb, had need to look eastward once again. There, he hoped, it might find the message of love and fraternal understanding that he sought to preach. [103-104] [Much later] India's new viceroy moved into a serious exchange with Gandhi with trepidation. He was not persuaded that the little figure "chirping like a sparrow" at his side could help him elaborate a solution to the Indian crisis, but he knew that he could defeat all efforts to find one. The hopes of many another English mediator had foundered on the turns of his unpredictable personality. It was Gandhi who had sent Cripps back to London empty-handed in 1942. His refusal to budge on a principle had helped thwart Wevell's efforts to untie the Indian knot. His tactics had done much to frustrate the most recent British attempt to solve the problem of liberation. Only the evening before, Gandhi had reiterated to his prayer meeting that India would be divided "over my dead body. So long as I am alive, I will never agree to the partition of India." . . .

It had always been British policy not to yield to force, he told Gandhi, by way of opening their talks on the right note, but his nonviolent crusade had won, and come what may, Britain was going to leave India. Only one thing mattered in that coming departure, Gandhi replied. "Don't partition India," be begged. "Don't divide India," the prophet of nonviolence pleaded, "even if refusing to do so means shedding rivers of blood."

Dividing India, a shocked Mountbatten assured Gandhi, was the last solution he wished to adopt. But what alternatives were open to him? Gandhi had one. So desperate was he to avoid partition that he was prepared to give the Moslems the baby instead of cutting it in half. Place three hundred million Hindus under Moslem rule, he told Mountbatten, by asking his rival Jinnah and his Moslem League to form a government. Then hand over power to that government. Give Jinnah all of India instead of just the part he wants, was his nonviolent proposal.

"Whatever makes you think your own Congress Party will accept?" Mountbatten asked.

"Congress," Gandhi replied, "wants above all else to avoid partition. They will do anything to prevent it."

"What," Mountbatten asked, "would Jinnah's reaction be?"

"If you tell him I am its author his reply will be, 'Wily Gandhi,'" The Mahatma said, laughing. [106–109]

THE BULLY

Why, this man is trying to bully me, an unbelieving Louis Mountbatten thought. His Operation Seduction had come to a sudden, wholly unexpected halt at the rocklike figure planted in the chair opposite his. With his Khadi dhoti flung about his shoulders like a toga, his bald head glowing, his scowling demeanor, his visitor looked to the Viceroy more like a Roman senator than an Indian politician.

Patel was Indian from the uppermost lump of his bald head to the calluses on the soles of his feet. His Delhi home was filled with books, but every one of them was written by an Indian author about India. He was the only Indian leader who sprang from the soil of India. Emotion, one of his associates once observed, formed no part of Patel's character. The remark was not wholly exact. Patel was an emotional man, but he never let those emotions break through the composed facade he turned to the world. If he gave off one salient impression, it was that of a man wholly in control of himself. In a land in which men talked constantly, threw their words around like sailors flinging away their money after three months at sea, Patel hoarded his phrases the way a miser hoarded coins. His daughter, who had been his constant companion since his wife's death, rarely exchanged ten sentences with him a day. When Patel did talk, however, people listened.

Vallabhbhai Patel was India's quintessential politician. He was an Oriental Tammany Hall boss who ran the machinery of the Congress Party with a firm and ruthless hand. He should have been the easiest member of the Indian quartet for Mountbatten to deal with. Like the Viceroy, he was a practical pragmatic man, a hard but realistic bargainer. Yet the tension between them was so real, so palpable, that it seemed to Mountbatten he could reach out and touch it. Its cause was in no way related to the great issues facing India. It was a slip of paper, a routine government minute issued by Patel's Home Ministry dealing with an appointment. But Mountbatten had read it as a calculated challenge to his authority.

Patel had a well-earned reputation for toughness. He had an almost instinctive need to take the measure of a new interlocutor, to see how far he could push him. The piece of paper on his desk, Mountbatten was convinced, was a test, a little examination that he had to go through with Patel before he could get down to serious matters. The Viceroy looked at the note which had offended him, then passed it across his desk to Patel. Quietly he asked him to withdraw it. Patel brusquely refused. Mountbatten studied the Indian leader. He was going to need the support of this man and the machinery he represented. But he was sure he would never get it if he did not face him down now.

"Very well," said Mountbatten. "I'll tell you what I'm going to do. I'm going to order my plane."

"Oh," said Patel, "why?"

"Because I'm leaving," Mountbatten replied. "I didn't want this job in the first place. I've just been looking for someone like you to give me an excuse to throw it up and get out of an impossible situation."

"You don't mean it," exclaimed Patel.

"Mean it?" replied Mountbatten. "You don't think I am going to stay here and be bullied around by a chap like you, do you? If you think you can be rude to me and push me around, you're wrong. You'll either withdraw that minute, or one of us is going to resign. And let me tell you that if I go, I shall first explain to your prime minister, to Mr. Jinnah, to His Majesty's Government, why I am leaving. The breakdown in India which will follow, the blood that will be shed, will be on your shoulders and no one else's." Patel stared at Mountbatten in disbelief. A long silence followed. "You know," Patel finally sighed, "the awful part is I think you mean it." "You're damned right I do," answered Mountbatten. Patel reached out, took the offending minute off Mountbatten's desk and slowly tore it up. [109-111]

THE FATHER OF PAKISTAN

The man who would ultimately hold the key to the subcontinent's dilemma in his hands was the last of the Indian leaders to enter the Viceroy's study. A quarter of a century later, an echo of his distant anguish still haunting his voice, Louis Mountbatten would recall, "I did not realize how utterly impossible my task in India was going to be until I met Mohammed Ali Jinnah for the first time."

Inside the study, Jinnah began by informing Mountbatten that he had come to tell him exactly what he was prepared to accept. As he had done with Gandhi, Mountbatten interrupted with a wave of his hand. "Mr. Jinnah," he said, "I am not prepared to dis-

cuss conditions at this stage. First, let's make each other's acquaintance." Then with his legendary charm and verve, Mountbatten turned the focus of Operation Seduction on the Moslem leader. Jinnah froze. To that aloof and reserved man who never unbent, even with his closest associates, the very idea of revealing the details of his life and personality to a perfect stranger must have seemed appalling. Gamely Mountbatten struggled on, summoning up all the reserves of his gregarious, engaging personality. For what seemed to him like hours, his only reward was a series of monosyllabic grunts from the man beside him.

The man who would one day be hailed as the Father of Pakistan had first been exposed to the idea at a black-tie dinner at London's Waldorf Hotel in the spring of 1933. His host was Rahmat Ali, the graduate student who had set the idea to paper. Rahmat Ali had arranged the banquet with its oysters on the half shell and un-Islamic Chablis at his own expense, hoping to persuade Jinnah, India's leading Moslem politician, to take over his movement. He received a chilly rebuff. Pakistan, Jinnah told him, was "an impossible dream." The man whom the unfortunate graduate student had sought to lead a Moslem separatist movement had, in fact, begun his political career by preaching Hindu-Moslem unity. . . [115]

Like Gandhi, Jinnah had gone to London to dine in the Inns of Court and had been called to the bar. Unlike Gandhi, however, he had come back from London an Englishman. He wore a monocle, superbly cut linen suits, which he changed three or four times a day to remain cool and unruffled in the soggy Bombay climate. He loved oysters and caviar, champagne, brandy and good Bordeaux. A man of unassailable personal honesty and financial integrity, his canons were sound law and sound procedure. He was, according to one intimate, "the last of the Victorians, a parliamentarian in the mode of Gladstone or Disraeli."

A more improbable leader of India's Moslem masses could hardly be imagined. The only thing Moslem about Mohammed Ali Jinnah was the fact his parents happened to be Moslem. He drank, ate pork, religiously shaved his beard each morning, and just as religiously avoided the mosque each Friday. God and the Koran had no place in Jinnah's vision of the world. His political foe Gandhi knew more verses of the Moslem holy book then he did. He had been able to achieve the remarkable feat of securing the allegiance of the vast majority of India's ninety million Moslems without being able to articulate more than a few sentences in their traditional tongue, Urdu.

Jinnah despised India's masses. He detested the dirt, the heat, the crowds of India. Gandhi traveled India in filthy third-class railway cars to be with the people. Jinnah rode first-class to avoid them. Jinnah had only scorn for his Hindu rivals. He labeled Nehru "a Peter Pan"; a "literary figure" who "should have been an English professor, not a politician"; "an arrogant Brahman who covers his Hindu trickiness under a veneer of Western education." Gandhi, to Jinnah, was "a cunning fox," "a Hindu revivalist." The sight of Mahatma, during an interval in a conversation in Jinnah's mansion, stretched out on one of his priceless Persian carpets, his mudpack on his belly, was something Jinnah had never forgotten or forgiven. . . .

His disenchantment with the Congress Party dated from Gandhi's ascension to power. It was not the impeccably dressed Jinnah who was going to be bundled off to some squalid British jail half naked in a dhoti and wearing a silly little white cap. Civil disobedience, he told Gandhi, was for "the ignorant and the illiterate." The turning point in Jinnah's career came after the 1937 elections, when the Congress Party refused to share with him and his Moslem League the spoils of office in those Indian provinces where there was a substantial Moslem minority. Jinnah, a man of towering vanity, took Congress's action as a personal insult. It convinced him that he and the Moslem League would never get a fair deal from a Congress-run India. The former apostle of Hindu-Moslem unity became the unyielding advocate of Pakistan, the project that he had labeled an "impossible dream" barely four years earlier. [116–117]

Mountbatten and Jinnah held six critical meetings during the first fortnight of April 1947. They were the vital conversations—not quite ten hours in length—that ultimately determined the resolution of the Indian dilemma. Mountbatten went into them armed with "the most enormous conceit in my ability to persuade people to do the right thing, not because I am persuasive so much as because I have the knack of being able to present the facts in their most favorable light." As he would later recall, he "tried every trick I could play, used every appeal I could imagine," to shake Jinnah's determination to have partition. Nothing would. There was no trick, no argument that could move him from his consuming determination to realize the impossible dream of Pakistan. . . . He had made himself the absolute dictator of the Moslem League. There were men below who might have been willing to negotiate a compromise, but as long as Mohammed Ali Jinnah was alive, they would hold their silence. . . .

Mountbatten and Jinnah did agree on one point at the outset—the need for speed. India, Jinnah declared, had gone beyond the stage at which a compromise solution was possible. There was only one solution, a speedy "surgical operation" on India. Otherwise, he warned, India would perish. When Mountbatten expressed concern that partition might produce bloodshed and violence, Jinnah reassured him. Once his "surgical operation" had taken place, all troubles would cease and India's two halves would live in harmony and happiness. It was, Jinnah told Mountbatten, like a court case that he had handled, a dispute between two brothers embittered by the shares assigned them by their father's will. Yet two years after the court had adjudicated their dispute, they were the greatest friends. That, he promised the Viceroy, would be the case in India. . . .

. . . "India has never been a true nation," Jinnah asserted. "It only looks that way on the map. . . . The cows I want to eat, the Hindu stops me from killing. Every time a Hindu shakes hands with me he has to go wash his hands. The only thing the Moslem has in common with the Hindu is his slavery to the British." . . . [118]

For Jinnah, the division that he proposed was the natural course. However, it would have to produce a viable state, which meant that two of India's great provinces, the Punjab and Bengal, would have to be included in Pakistan, despite the fact that each contained enormous Hindu populations. Mountbatten could not agree. The very basis of Jinnah's argument for Pakistan was that India's Moslem minority should not be ruled by its Hindu majority. How then to justify taking the Hindu minorities of Bengal and the Punjab into a Moslem state? If Jinnah insisted on dividing India to get his Islamic state, then the very logic he had used to get it would compel Mountbatten to divide the Punjab and Bengal.

Jinnah protested—that would give him an economically unviable, "motheaten Pakistan." Mountbatten, who didn't want to give him any Pakistan at all, told the Moslem leader that if he felt the nation he was to receive was as "motheaten" as all that, he would do well to abandon his plan.

"Ah," Jinnah would counter, "Your Excellency doesn't understand. A man is a Punjabi or a Bengali before he is Hindu or Moslem. They share a common history, language, culture and economy. You must not divide them. You will cause endless bloodshed and trouble." "Mr. Jinnah I entirely agree." "You do?" "Of course," Mountbatten would continue. "A man is not only a Punjabi or Bengali before he is a Hindu or a

Moslem, he is an Indian before all else. You have presented the unanswerable argument for Indian unity." "But you don't understand at all," Jinnah countered—and the discussion would start again.

Mountbatten was stunned by the rigidity of Jinnah's position. "I never would have believed," he later recalled, "that an intelligent man, well educated, trained in the Inns of Court, was capable of simply closing his mind as Jinnah did. It wasn't that he didn't see the point. He did, but a kind of shutter came down. He was the evil genius in the whole thing. The others could be persuaded, but not Jinnah. While he was alive nothing could be done." [191]

If Louis Mountbatten, Jawaharlal Nehru, or Mahatma Gandhi had been aware in April 1947 of one extraordinary secret, the division threatening India might have been avoided. That secret was sealed onto the gray surface of a piece of film, a film that could have upset the Indian political equation and would almost certainly have changed the course of Asian history. Yet so precious was the secret which the film harbored that even the British C.I.D., one of the most effective investigating agencies in the world, was ignorant of its existence. The heart of the film was two dark circles no bigger than a pair of Ping-Pong balls. Each was surrounded by an irregular white border like the corona of the sun eclipsed by the moon. Above them, a galaxy of little white spots stretched up the film's gray surface toward the top of the thoracic cage. That film was an x-ray, the x-ray of a pair of human lungs.

The damage was so extensive that the man whose lungs were on that film had barely two or three years to live. . . . The lungs depicted on them belonged to the rigid and inflexible man who had frustrated Louis Mountbatten's efforts to preserve India's unity. Mohammed Ali Jinnah, the one unmovable obstacle between the Viceroy and Indian unity, was living under a sentence of death. . . . [124]

Meditating alone in his study after Jinnah's departure, Mountbatten realized that he was probably going to have to give him Pakistan. His first obligation in New Delhi was to the nation that had sent him there, England. He longed to preserve India's unity, but not at the expense of his country's becoming hopelessly entrapped in an India collapsing in chaos and violence. . . .

Military command had given Mountbatten a penchant for rapid, decisive actions, such as the one he now took. In future years, his critics would assail him for having reached it too quickly, for acting like an impetuous sailor and not a statesman, but Mountbatten was not going to waste any more time on what he was certain would be futile arguments with Jinnah. . . . Neither logic nor Mountbatten's power to charm and persuade had made any impact on him. The partition of India seemed the only solution. It now remained to Mountbatten to get Nehru and Patel to accept the principle and to find for it a plan that could get their support.

THE INDIAN RAJAHS

Yadavindra Singh presided over the most remarkable body in the world, an assembly unlike any other that man had ever devised. He was the Chancellor of the Chamber of Indian Princes (the fabled Rajahs). His state of Patiala in the Punjab was one of the richest in India. He had an army the size of an infantry division, equipped with Centurion tanks to defend it if necessary.

The princes' anachronistic situation dated to Britain's haphazard conquest of India, when rulers who received the English with open arms or proved worthy foes on the battlefield were allowed to remain on their thrones provided that they acknowledged Britain as the paramount power in India. The system was formalized in a series of treaties between the individual rulers and the British Crown. The Princes had recognized the "Paramountcy" of the King-Emperor as represented in New Delhi by the viceroy, and they ceded to him control of their foreign affairs and defense. They received in return Britain's guarantee of their continuing autonomy inside their states. [See map page 955.] . . .

Certain princes like the Nizam of Hyderabad or the Maharaja of Kashmir ruled over states which rivaled in size or population the nations of Western Europe. Others like those in the Kathiawar peninsula near Bombay lived in stables and governed domains no larger than New York City's Central Park. Their fraternity embraced the richest man in the world and princes so poor that their entire kingdom was a cow pasture. Over four hundred princes ruled states smaller than twenty square miles. A good number of them offered their subjects an administration far better than that the British provided. A few were petty despots more concerned with squandering their states' revenues to slake their own extravagant desires than with improving the lot of their peoples. Whatever their political proclivities, however, the future of India's 565 ruling princes, with their average of eleven titles, 5.8 wives, 12.6 children, 9.2 elephants, 2.8 private railway cars, 3.4 Roll-Royces, and 22.9 tigers killed, posed a grave problem in the spring of 1947. No solution to the Indian equation would work if it failed to deal with their peculiar situation. [165,166]

A SUBTLE MOSAIC

Inevitably, Mountbatten's decision would lead to one of the great dramas of modern history. Whatever the manner in which it was executed, it was bound to end in the mutilation of a great nation. . . . To satisfy the exigent demands of Mohammed Ali Jinnah, two of India's most distinctive entities, the Punjab and Bengal, would have to be carved up. The result would make Pakistan a geographic aberration, a nation of two heads separated by 1,500 kilometers (900 miles) of Himalayan mountain peaks, all purely Indian territory. Twenty days, more time than was required to sail from Karachi to Marseilles, would be needed to make the sea trip around the subcontinent from one half of Pakistan to the other. [120] . . .

The Punjab was a blend as subtle and complex as the mosaics decorating the monuments of its glorious Royal past. To divide it was unthinkable. Fifteen million Hindus, sixteen million Moslems, and five million Sikhs shared the neighborhoods and alleyways of its 17,932 towns and villages. Although divided by religion, they shared a common language, joint traditions, and a great pride in this distinctive Punjabi personality. Wherever the boundary line went, the result was certain to be nightmare for millions of human beings. Only an interchange of populations on a scale never effected before in history could sort out the havoc that it would create. From the Indus to the bridges of Delhi, for over 500 miles, there was not a single town, not a single village, cotton grove or wheat field that would not somehow be threatened if the partition plan were to be carried out.

The division of Bengal at the other end of the subcontinent held out the possibilities of another tragedy. Haboring more people than Great Britain and Ireland combined, Bengal contained thirty-five million Moslems and thirty million Hindus spread over an expanse of land running from the jungles at the foot of the Himalayas to the steaming marshes through which the thousand tributaries of the Ganges and Brahmaputra rivers drained into the Bay of Bengal. Despite its division into two religious communities, Bengal, even more than the Punjab, was a distinct entity of its own. Whether Hindu or Moslem, Bengalis sprang from the same racial stock, spoke the same language, shared the same culture. They sat on the floor in a certain Bengali manner, ordered the sentences they spoke in a peculiar Bengali cadence, each rising to a final crescendo, celebrated their own Bengali New Year

on April 15. Their poets like Tabore were regarded with pride by all Bengalis. [122]

A land seared by droughts that alternated with frightening typhoon-whipped floods, Bengal was an immense, steaming swamp, in whose humid atmosphere flourished the two crops to which it owed a precarious prosperity, rice and jute. The cultivation of those two crops followed the province's religious frontier rice to the Hindu west, jute to the Moslem east. But the key to Bengal's existence did not lie in its crops. It was a city, the city that had been the springboard for Britain's conquest of India, the second city, after London, of the Empire, and the first port of Asia—Calcutta, site of the terrible Hindu-Moslem killings of August 1946.

Everything in Bengal—roads, railroads, communications, industry—funneled into Calcutta. If Bengal was split into its eastern and western halves, Calcutta, because of its physical location, seemed certain to be in the Hindu west, thus condemning the Moslem east to a slow but inexorable asphyxiation. If almost all of the world's jute grew in eastern Bengal, all the factories that transformed it into rope, sacks and cloth were clustered around Calcutta, in western Bengal. The Moslem east, which produced the jute, grew almost no food at all, and its millions survived on the rice grown in the Hindu west. . . .

Yet, no aspect of partition was more illogical than the fact that Jinnah's Pakistan would deliver barely half of India's Moslems from the alleged inequities of Hindu majority rule which had justified the state in the first place. The remaining Moslems were scattered throughout the rest of India so widely that it was impossible to separate them. Islands in a Hindu sea, even after the amputation, India would still harbor almost fifty million Moslems, a figure that would make her the third-largest Moslem nation in the world, after Indonesia and the new state drawn from her own womb. [123]

THE GOVERNORS

The eleven men seated around the oval table in the conference chamber solemnly waited for Lord Mountbatten to begin the proceedings. They were, in a sense, the descendants of the twenty-four founding fathers of the East India Company, the men whose mercantile appetites had sent Britain along the sea lanes to India three and a half centuries earlier. . . . Their meeting was an awkward confrontation for Mountbatten. At forty-six, he was the youngest man at the table. . . . He was a comparative stranger in the

India to which most of the eleven governors had devoted an entire career, mastering its complex history, learning its dialects, becoming, as some of them had, world-renowned experts on the phases of its existence. They were proud men, certain to be skeptical of any plan put before them by the neophyte in their midst. . . . [126]

Mountbatten began by asking each governor to describe the situation in his province. Eight of them painted a picture of dangerous, troubled areas, but provinces in which the situation still remained under control. It was the portrait offered by the governors of the three critical provinces, the Punjab, Bengal, and the Northwest Frontier Province, that sobered the gathering.

His features drawn, his eyes heavy with fatigue, Sir Olaf Caroe spoke first. He had been kept awake all night by a stream of cables detailing fresh outbursts of trouble in his Northwest Frontier Province. The labyrinth grottoes of his mountainous province sheltered scores of secret arms factories, from which flowed a profusion of ornate and deadly weapons to arm Mahsuds, Afridis, Wazirs, the legendary warrior tribes of the Pathans. The situation in the N.W.F.P. was close to disintegrating, he warned, and if that happened, the old British nightmare of invading hordes from the northwest forcing the gates of the Empire might be realized. The Pathan tribes of Afghanistan were poised to come pouring down the Khyber Pass to Peshawar and the banks of the Indus in pursuit of land they had claimed as theirs for a century. "If we're not jolly careful." he said "we are going to have an international crisis on our hands."

The portrait drawn by Sir Evan Jenkins, the taciturn governor of the Punjab, was even grimmer than Caroe's. . . . Whatever solution was chosen for India's problems, he declared, it was certain to bring violence to the Punjab. At least four divisions would be needed to keep order if partition was decided upon. Even if it was not, they would still face a demand by the Sikhs for an area of their own. "It's absurd to predict the Punjab will go up in flames if it's partitioned," he said; "its already in flames." [127]

The third governor, Sir Frederick Burrows of Bengal, was ill in Calcutta, but the briefing of the province's situation as offered by his deputy was every bit as disquieting as the reports from the N.W.F.P. and the Punjab. When those reporters were finally finished, Mountbatten's staff passed out a set of papers to each governor. They carried the details, Mountbatten announced, "of one of the possible plans under examination." It was called, "for easy reference," Plan

Balkan, and it was the first draft of a partition plan that Mountbatten had ordered his chief of staff, Lord Ismay, to prepare a week earlier. . . . The plan, aptly named for the Balkanization of the states of Central Europe after World War I, would allow each of India's eleven provinces to choose whether it wished to join Pakistan or remain in India; or, if a majority of both its Hindus and Moslems agreed, become independent. Mountbatten told his assembled governors that he was not going to "lightly abandon hope for a united India." He wanted the world to know that the British had made every effort possible to keep India united. If Britain failed it was of the utmost importance that the world know it was "Indian opinion rather than a British decision that had made partition the choice." He himself thought a future Pakistan was so inherently unviable that it should "be given a chance to fail on its own demerits," so that later "the Moslem League could revert to a unified India with honor."

Those eleven men who represented the collective wisdom of the service that had run India for a century displayed no enthusiasm for the idea that partition might have to be the answer to India's dilemma. Nor did they have any other solution to propose. [128]

VISIT TO PESHAWAR

Louis Mountbatten had decided to suspend temporarily the conversations in his air-conditioned office while he, personally, took the political temperature of his two most troubled provinces, the Punjab and the N.W.F.P. The news that he was coming had swept over the Frontier. For twenty-four hours, summoned by the leaders of Jinnah's Moslem League, tens of thousands of men from every corner of the province had been converging on Peshawar. Overflowing their trucks, in buses, in cars, on special trains, chanting and waving their arms, they had spilled into the capital for the greatest popular demonstration in its history.

Now those tall, pale-skinned Pathans prepared to offer the Viceroy a welcome of an unexpected sort to Peshawar. . . . The police had confined them in an enormous low-walled enclosure running between a railroad embankment and the sloping walls of Peshawar's old Mogul fortress. Irritated and unruly, they threatened to drown the conciliatory tones of Operation Seduction with the discordant rattle of gunfire.

They were there because of the anomalous political situation of a province whose population was 93 percent Moslem, but was governed by allies of the Congress Party. . . . Stiffed by Jinnah's agents, the population had turned against the Congress leader Ghaffar Khan who supported Gandhi and the government that he had installed in Peshawar. The huge, howling crowd greeting Mountbatten, his wife and seventeen-year-old daughter Pamela was meant to give final proof that it was the Moslem League and not the "Frontier Gandhi" that now commanded the province's support. [129] The crowd, growing more unruly by the hour, threatened to burst out of the area in which the police had herded them and start a headlong rush on the governor's residence. If they did, the vastly outnumbered military guarding the house would have no choice but to open fire. The resulting slaughter would be appalling. It would destroy Mountbatten, his hopes of finding a solution, and his viceroyalty in a sickening blood bath.

There was one way out, an idea condemned by the police and army commander as sheer madness. Mountbatten might present himself to the crowds, hoping that somehow a glimpse of him would mollify them. Mountbatten pondered a few moments. "All right, I'll take a chance and see them." To the despair of Caroe and his security officers, Edwina, his wife, insisted on coming with him. . . . A few minutes later, a jeep deposited the viceregal couple and the governor at the foot of the railway embankment. On the other side of that precarious dike, 100,000 hot, dirty, angry people were shouting their frustration in an indecipherable din. Mountbatten took his wife by the hand and clambered up the embankment. As they reached the top, they discovered themselves only fifteen feet away from the surging waves of the sea of turbans. The ground under their feet shook with the impact of the gigantic crowd stampeding forward in front of them. That terrifying ocean of human beings incarnated in their shrieks and gesticulations the enormity and the passions of the masses of India. Whirling spirals of dust stirred by thousands of rushing feet clotted the air. The noise of the crowd was an almost tangible layer of air crushing down on them. It was a decisive instant in Operation Seduction, an instant when anything was possible. . . . In that crowd were twenty, thirty, forty thousand rifles. Any madman, any bloodthirsty fool could shoot the Mountbattens "like ducks on a pond."

For the first few seconds Mountbatten did not know what to do. He couldn't articulate a syllable of Pushtu, the crowd's language. As he pondered, a totally unexpected phenomenon began to still the mob, stopping perhaps with its strange vibrations an assassin's hand. For this entirely unplanned meeting with the Empire's most renowned warriors, Mountbatten happened to be wearing the short-sleeved, loose-fitting bush jacket that he had worn as Supreme Allied Commander in Burma. Its color, green, galvanized the crowd. Green was the color of Islam, the blessed green of the hadjis, the holy men who had made the pilgrimage to Mecca. Instinctively, those tens of thousands of men read in that green uniform a gesture of solidarity with them, a subtle compliment to their great religion.

His hand still clutching hers, but his eyes straight ahead, Mountbatten whispered to his wife, "Wave to them." Slowly, graciously, the frail Edwina raised her arm with his to the crowd. India's fate seemed for an instant suspended in those hands climbing above the crowd's head. A questioning silence had drifted briefly over the unruly crowd. Suddenly, Edwina's pale arm began to stroke the sky; a cry, then a roaring ocean of noise burst from the crowd. From tens of thousands of throats came an interminable, constantly repeated shout, a triumphant litany marking the successful passing of the most dangerous seconds of Operation Seduction.

"Mountbatten Zindabad!" those embittered Pathan warriors screamed, "Mountbatten Zindabad!" ("Long live Mountbatten!") [130-131]

SLAUGHTER AT KAHUTA

[Soon, however,] a shocked Mountbatten was to get his first direct contact with the horrors sweeping India in the cruel springtime of 1947. The naval officer who had seen most of his shipmates die in the wreck of his destroyer off Crete, the leader who had led millions through the savage jungle war in Burma, was overwhelmed by the spectacle he discovered in that village of 3,500 people, which had once been typical of India's half million villages.

For centuries, Kahuta's dirt alleys had been shared in peace by 2,000 Hindus and Sikhs and 1,500 Moslems. That day, side by side in the village center, the stone minaret of its mosque and the rounded dome of the Sikhs' gurudwara were the only identifiable remnants of Kahuta left on the skyline of the Punjab. Just before Mountbatten's visit, a patrol of the British Norfolk Regiment on a routine reconnaissance mission passed through the village. Kahuta's citizens, as they had been doing for generations, were sleeping side by side in mutual confidence and tranquility. By dawn, Kahuta had for all practical purposes ceased to exist, and its Sikhs and Hindus were all dead or had fled in terror into the night

A Moslem horde had descended on Kahuta like a wolf pack, setting fire to the houses in its Sikh and

Hindu quarters with buckets of gasoline. In minutes, the area was engulfed in fire and entire families, screaming pitifully for help, were consumed by the flames. Those who escaped were caught, tied together, soaked with gasoline and burned alive like torches. Totally out of control, the fire swept into the Moslem quarter and completed the destruction of Kahuta. A few Hindu women, yanked from their beds to be raped and converted to Islam, survived; others had broken away from their captors and hurled themselves back into the fire to perish with their families.

"Until I went to Kahuta," Mountbatten reported back to London, "I had not appreciated the magnitude of the horrors that were going on." This confrontation with the crowd in Peshawar and the atrocious spectacle of one devastated Punjabi village was the last proof Mountbatten needed. Speed was the one absolute, overwhelming imperative if India was to be saved. . . . And if speed was essential, then there was only one way out of the impasse, the solution from which he personally recoiled, but which India's political situation dictated—partition. [131–132]

THE SHATTERED DREAM

The last, painful phase in the lifelong pilgrimage of Mahatma Gandhi began on the evening of May 1, 1947, in the same spare hut in New Delhi's sweepers' colony in which a fortnight before he had unsuccessfully urged his colleagues to accept his plan to hold India together. Crosslegged on the floor, a water-soaked towel plastered once again to his bald head, Gandhi followed with sorrow the debate of the men around him, the high command of the Congress Party. The final parting of the ways between Gandhi and those men, foreshadowed in their earlier meeting, had been reached. All Gandhi's long years in jail, his painful fasts, his hartals and his boycotts had been paving stones on the road to this meeting. He had changed the face of India and enunciated one of the original philosophies of his century to bring his countrymen to independence through nonviolence; and now his sublime triumph threatened to become a terrible personal tragedy. His followers, their tempers worn, their patience exhausted, were ready to accept the division of India as the last, inescapable step to independence. . . .

Gandhi's tragedy was that he had that evening no real alternative to propose beyond his instincts, the instincts those men had so often followed before. This night, however, he was no longer a prophet. "They call me a Mahatma," he bitterly told a friend later, "but I tell you I am not even treated by them as a sweeper." Jinnah, he told his followers, will never get Pakistan unless the British give it to him. The British would never do that in the face of the Congress majority's unyielding opposition. They had a veto over any action Mountbatten proposed. Tell the British to go, he begged, no matter what the consequences of their departure might be. Tell them to leave India "to God, to chaos, to anarchy if you wish, but leave.". . .

Nehru was a torn and anguished man, caught between his deep love for Gandhi and his new admiration and friendship for the Mountbattens. Gandhi spoke to his heart, Mountbatten to his mind. Instinctively, Nehru detested partition; yet his rationalist spirit told him it was the only answer. Since reaching his own conclusion that there was no other choice, Mountbatten and his wife had been employing all the charm and persuasiveness of Operation Seduction to bring Nehru to their viewpoint. One argument was vital. With Jinnah gone, Hindu India could have the strong central government that Nehru would need if he was going to build the socialist state of his dreams. Ultimately, he too stood out against the man he had followed so long. With his and Patel's voices in favor, the rest of the high command quickly fell in line. Nehru was authorized to inform the Viceroy that while Congress remained "passionately attached to the idea of a united India," it would accept partition, provided that the two great provinces of Punjab and Bengal were divided. The man who had led them to their triumph was alone with his tarnished victory and his broken dream. [132–134]

"SHEER MADNESS"

All Mountbatten's hopes had foundered, finally, on the rock of Jinnah's determined, intransigent person. . . . For the rest of his life, Mountbatten would look back on that failure to move Jinnah as the single greatest disappointment of his career. His personal anguish at the prospect of going down in history as the man who had divided India could be measured by a document flown back to London with Ismay in Mountbatten's viceregal York, his fifth personal report to the Attlee government.

Partition, Mountbatten wrote, "is sheer madness," and "no one would ever induce me to agree to it were it not for this fantastic communal madness that has seized everybody and leaves no other course open. . . . The responsibility for this mad decision," he wrote, must be placed "squarely on Indian shoulders in the eyes of the world, for one day they will bitterly regret the decision they are about to make." [134]

More serious, however, was the real concern which underlay his growing apprehension. If the implications in the plan that he had sent to London were fully realized, the great Indian subcontinent would be divided into three independent nations, not two. Mountbatten had inserted in his plan a clause that would allow the sixty-five million Hindus and Moslems of Bengal to join into one viable country, with the great seaport of Calcutta as their capital.

Contrasted to Jinnah's aberrant, two-headed state, that seemed an entity likely to endure, and Mountbatten had quietly encouraged Bengal's politicians, Hindu and Moslem alike, to support it. He had even discovered that Jinnah would not oppose the idea. He had not, however, exposed it to Nehru and Patel, and it was this oversight that disturbed him now. Would they accept a plan that might cost them the great port of Calcutta with its belt of textile mills owned by the Indian industrialists who were their party's principal financial support? If they didn't, Mountbatten, after all the assurances he had given London, was going to look a bloody fool in the eyes of India, Britain, and the world.

A sudden inspiration struck Mountbatten. He would reassure himself privately, informally, with the Indian leader, whom, to the distress of his staff, he had invited to vacation with him in Simla, [Jawaharlal Nehru]. [159] To show the plan to Nehru without exposing it to Jinnah would be a complete breach of faith with the Moslem leader, they pointed out. If he discovered it, Mountbatten's whole position would be destroyed. For a long time, Mountbatten sat silently drumming the tabletop with his fingertips.

"I am sorry," he finally announced, "your arguments are absolutely sound. But I have a hunch that I must show it to Nehru, and I'm going to follow my hunch." That night, Mountbatten invited Nehru to his study for a glass of port. Casually, he passed the Congress leader a copy of the plan as it had been amended by London, asking him to take it to his bedroom and read it. Then perhaps he might let him know informally what reception it was likely to get from Congress. Flattered and happy, Nehru agreed.

[After a few hours], Nehru began to scrutinize the text designed to chart his country's future. He was horrified by what he read. The vision of the India that emerged from the plan's pages was a nightmare . . . an India divided, not into two parts but fragmented into a dozen pieces. Bengal would become, Nehru foresaw, a

wound through which the best blood of India would pour. He saw India deprived of the port of Calcutta along with its mills, factories, steelworks; Kashmir, his beloved Kashmir, an independent state ruled by a despot he despised; Hyderabad become an enormous, indigestible Moslem body planted in the belly of India, half a dozen other princely states clamoring to go off on their own. The plan, he believed, would exacerbate all India's fissiparous tendencies of dialect, culture, and race to the point at which the subcontinent would risk exploding into a mosaic of weak, hostile states. White-faced, shaking with rage, Nehru stalked into the bedroom of his confidant V. P. Menon, who had accompanied him to Simla. With a furious gesture, he hurled the plan onto his bed. "It's all over!" he shouted. . . .

Mountbatten got his first intimation of his friend's violent reaction in a letter early the following morning. For the confident Viceroy, it was "a bombshell." As he read it, the whole structure he had so carefully erected during the past six weeks came tumbling down like a house of cards. The impression that his plan left, Nehru wrote, was one of "fragmentation and conflict and disorder." It frightened him and was certain to be "resented and bitterly disliked by the Congress Party." Reading Nehru's words, the poised, self-assured Viceroy, who had proudly announced to England that he was going to present a solution to India's dilemma in ten days' time, suddenly realized that he had no solution at all. The plan that the British Cabinet was discussing that very day, the plan that he had just assured Attlee would win Indian acceptance, would never get past the one element in India that had to accept it, the Congress Party.

Mountbatten's critics might accuse him of overconfidence, but he was not a man to brood at setbacks. Instead of descending into a fit of despondency at Nehru's reaction, Mountbatten congratulated himself on his hunch in showing him the plan, and set out to repair the damage. [161] To redraft his plan, Mountbatten called into his study the highest-ranking Indian in his viceregal establishment. It was a supreme irony that at that critical juncture the Indian to whom Mountbatten turned had not even entered that vaunted administrative elite, the Indian Civil Service. No degree from Oxford or Cambridge graced his office walls. No family ties had hastened his rise. V. P. Menon was an incongruous oddity in the rarefied air of Viceroy's House, a self-made man.

Mountbatten informed Menon that before nightfall he would have to redraft the charter that would give India her independence. Its essential element, partition, had to remain, and it must continue to place the burden of choice on the Indians themselves. Menon finished his task in accordance with Mountbatten's instructions by sunset. Between lunch and dinner, he had performed a tour de force. The man who had begun his career as a two-finger typist had culminated it by redrafting, in barely six hours on an office porch looking out on the Himalayas, a plan that was going to encompass the future of one-fifth of humanity, reorder the subcontinent, and alter the map of the world. [162–163]

A DAY CURSED BY THE STARS

[When the day came to approve this plan] the lusterless eyes of Robert Clive gazed down from the great oil painting upon the wall at the seven Indian leaders filing into the Viceroy's study. Representatives of India's 400 million human beings, those millions whom Gandhi called "miserable specimens of humanity with lusterless eyes," they entered Mountbatten's study on this morning of June 2, 1947, to inspect the deeds that would return to their peoples the continent whose conquest the British general had opened two centuries before. The papers, formally approved by the British Cabinet, had been brought from London by the Viceroy just forty-eight hours before. . . .

For the first time since he had arrived in Delhi, Mountbatten was now being forced to abandon his head-to-head diplomacy for a round-table conference. He had decided, however, that he would do the talking. He was not going to run the risk of throwing the meeting open for a general discussion that might degenerate into an acrimonious shouting match that could destroy his elaborately wrought plan. Aware of the poignancy and historic nature of their gathering, he began by noting that during the past five years he had taken part in a number of momentous meetings at which the decisions that had determined the fate of the war had been taken. He could remember no meeting, however, at which decisions had been taken whose impact upon history had been as profound as would be the impact of the decision before them.

Briefly, Mountbatten reviewed his conversations since arriving in Delhi, stressing the terrible sense of urgency they had impressed on him. Then, for the record and for history, he formally asked Jinnah one last time if he was prepared to accept Indian unity as envisaged by the Cabinet Mission Plan. With equal formality, Jinnah replied that he was not, and Mountbatten moved on to the matter at hand. Briefly, he reviewed the details of his plan. The dominion-status clause that had ultimately won Winston Churchill's support was not, he stressed, a reflection of a British desire to keep a foot in the door beyond her time, but to assure that British assistance would not be summarily withdrawn if it was still needed. He dwelt on Calcutta, on the coming agony of the Sikhs.

He would not, he said, ask them to give their full agreement to a plan, parts of which went against their principles. He asked only that they accept it in a peaceful spirit and vow to make it work without bloodshed. His intention, he said, was to meet with them again the following morning. He hoped that before that, before midnight, all three parties, the Moslem League, Congress, and the Sikhs, would have indicated their willingness to accept the plan as a basis for a final Indian settlement. If this was the case, then he proposed that he, Nehru, Jinnah, and Baldev Singh announce their agreement jointly to the world the following evening on All India Radio. Clement Attlee would make a confirming announcement from London.

"Gentlemen," he concluded, "I should like your reaction to the plan by midnight." [191–192]

A NOD OF THE HEAD

[That night] in Louis Mountbatten's study the lights still burned, illuminating the last meeting of his harrowing day. He stared at his visitor with uncomprehending disbelief. Congress had indicated in time their willingness to accept his plan. So, too, had the Sikhs. Now the man it was designed to satisfy, the man whose obdurate, unyielding will had forced partition on India, was temporizing. Everything Jinnah had been striving for for years was there, waiting only his acknowledgment. For some mysterious reason, Jinnah simply could not bring himself this night to utter the word that he had made a career refusing to pronounce—"yes."

Inhaling deeply one of the Craven A's that he chain-smoked in his jade holder Jinnah kept insisting that he could not give an indication of the Moslem League's reaction to Mountbatten's plan until he had put it before the League's Council, and he needed at least a week to bring its members to Delhi. All the frustrations generated by his dealings with Jinnah welled up in Mountbatten. Jinnah had gotten his damn Pakistan. Even the Sikhs had swallowed the plan. Everything he had been working for he had finally gotten, and here, at the absolute eleventh hour, Jinnah was preparing to destroy it all, to bring the whole thing crashing down with his unfathomable inability to articulate just one word, "yes."

Mountbatten simply had to have his agreement. Attlee was standing by in London waiting to make his historic announcement to the Commons in less than twenty-four hours. He had gone on the line personally to Attlee, to his government with firm assurances that this plan would work; that there would be no more abrupt twists like that prompted by Nehru in Simla; that this time, they could be certain they had approved a plan that the Indian leaders would all accept. He had, with enormous difficulty, coaxed a reluctant Congress up to this point, and, finally, they were prepared to accept partition. Even Gandhi, temporarily at least, had allowed himself to be bypassed. A final hesitation, just the faintest hint that Jinnah was maneuvering to secure one last concession, and the whole carefully wrought package would blow apart.

"Mr. Jinnah," Mountbatten said, "if you think I can hold this position for a week while you summon your followers to Delhi, you must be crazy. You know this has been drawn up to the boiling point . . . . The Congress has made their acceptance dependent on your agreement. If they suspect you're holding out on them, they will immediately withdraw their agreement and we will be in the most terrible mess."

No, No, Jinnah protested, everything had to be done in the legally constituted way, "I am not the Moslem League," he said. . . .

"Now, now, come on, Mr. Jinnah," said Mountbatten, icy calm, "don't try to tell me that. You can try to tell the world that. But don't kid yourself that I don't know what's what in the Moslem League. . . . Mr. Jinnah, I'm going to tell you something. I don't intend to let you wreck your own plan. I can't allow you to throw away the solution you've worked so hard to get. I propose to accept on your behalf.

"Tomorrow at the meeting," Mountbatten continued, "I shall say I have received the reply of the Congress, with a few reservations that I am sure I can satisfy, and they have accepted. The Sikhs have accepted. . . . Then I shall say that I had a very long, very friendly conversation with Mr. Jinnah last night, that we went through the plan in detail, and Mr. Jinnah has given me his personal assurance that he is in agreement with this plan.

"Now at that point, Mr. Jinnah," Mountbatten continued, "I shall turn to you. I don't want you to speak. I don't want Congress to force you into the open. I want you to do only one thing. I want you to nod your head to show that you are in agreement with me. . . . If you don't nod your head, Mr. Jinnah," Mountbatten concluded, "then you're through, and there'll be nothing more I can do for you. Everything will collapse. This is not a threat. It's a prophecy. If you don't nod your head at that moment, my usefulness here will be ended, you will have lost your Pakistan, and as far as I am concerned, you can go to hell." [196]

The meeting that would formally record the Indian leaders' acceptance of the Mountbatten plan to divide India began exactly as Mountbatten had said it would. Once again, on the morning of June 3, the Viceroy condemned the leaders to an unfamiliar silence by dominating the conversation himself. As he had expected, he said, all three parties had had grave reservations about his plan and he was grateful that they had aired them to him. Nonetheless Congress had signified its acceptance. So, too, had the Sikhs. He had had, he said, a long and friendly conversation the previous evening with Mr. Jinnah, who had assured him the plan was acceptable.

As he spoke those words, Mountbatten turned to Jinnah, seated at his right. At that instant Mountbatten had absolutely no idea what the Moslem leader was going to do. The captain of the *Kelly*, the supreme commander who had had an entire army corps encircled and cut off by the Japanese on the Imphal Plain, would always look back on that instant as "the most hair-raising moment of my entire life." For an endless second, he stared into Jinnah's impassive, expressionless face. Then slowly, reluctance crying from every pore, Jinnah indicated his agreement with the faintest, most begrudging nod he could make. His chin moved barely half an inch downward, the shortest distance it could have traveled consonant with accepting Mountbatten's plan. With that brief, almost imperceptible gesture, a nation of forty-five million human beings had received its final sanction.

A SHARP CRACK

However abortive its form, however difficult the circumstances that would attend its birth, the "impossible dream" of Pakistan would at last be realized. Mountbatten had enough agreement to go ahead. Before any of the seven men could have a chance to formulate a last reservation or doubt, he announced that his plan would henceforth constitute the basis for an Indian settlement.

While the enormity of the decision they had just taken began to penetrate, Mountbatten had a thirty-four-page, single-spaced document set before each man. Clasping the last copy himself with both hands, the Viceroy lifted it over his head and whipped it back down onto the table. At the sharp crack that followed the slap of paper on wood, Mountbatten read out the imposing title on his equally imposing document—"The Administrative Consequences of Partition."

It was a carefully elaborated christening present from Mountbatten and his staff to the Indian leaders, a guide to the awesome task that now lay before them. Page after page, it summarized in its dull bureaucratic jargon the appalling implications of their decision. None of the seven was in even the remotest way prepared for the shock they encountered as they began to turn the pages of the document. Ahead of them lay a problem of a scope and on a scale no people had ever encountered before, a problem vast enough to beggar the most vivid imagination. They were now going to be called upon to settle the contested estate of 400 million human beings, to unravel the possessions left behind by thirty centuries of common inhabitation of the subcontinent, to pick apart the fruits of three centuries of technology. The cash in the banks, stamps in the post office, books in the libraries, debts, assets, the world's third-largest railway, jails, prisoners, inkpots, brooms, research centers, hospitals, universities, institutions and articles staggering in number and variety would be theirs to divide.

A stunned silence filled the study as the seven men measured for the first time what lay ahead of them. Mountbatten . . . had forced these seven men to come to grips with a problem so imposing that it would leave them neither the time nor the energy for recrimination in the few weeks of coexistence left to them.

"NO JOY IN MY HEART"

Shortly after seven o'clock on that evening of June 3, 1947, in the New Delhi studio of All India Radio, the four key leaders formally announced their agreement to divide the subcontinent into two separate sovereign nations. As befitting his office, Mountbatten spoke first. His words were confident, his speech brief, his tones understated. Nehru followed, speaking in Hindi. Sadness grasped the Indian leader's face as he told his listeners that "the great destiny of India" was taking shape, "with travail and suffering." Baring his own emotions, he urged acceptance of the plan that had caused him such deep personal anguish, by concluding that "it is with no joy in my heart that I commend these proposals to you."

Jinnah was next. Nothing would ever be more illustrative of the enormous, yet wholly incongruous nature of his achievement than that speech. Mohammed Ali Jinnah was incapable of announcing to his followers the news that he had won them a state

in a language that they could understand. He had to tell India's ninety million Moslems of the "momentous decision" to create an Islamic state on the subcontinent in English. An announcer then read his words in Urdu. . . . [197–199]

Gandhi walked into Mountbatten's study at 6 p.m. His prayer meeting was at seven. That left Mountbatten less than an hour in which to ward off a potential disaster. His first glance at the Mahatma told Mountbatten how deeply upset he was. Crumpled up in his armchair "like a bird with a broken wing," Gandhi kept raising and dropping one hand lamenting in an almost inaudible voice: "It's so awful, it's so awful."

In that state Gandhi, Mountbatten knew, was capable of anything. A public denunciation of his plan would be disastrous. Nehru, Patel, and the other leaders the Viceroy had so patiently coaxed into accepting it would be forced to break publicly with Gandhi or break their agreement with him. Vowing to use every argument his fertile imagination could produce, Mountbatten began by telling Gandhi how he understood and shared his feelings at seeing the united India he had worked for all his life destroyed by this plan. Suddenly as he spoke, a burst of inspiration struck him. The newspapers had christened the plan the "Mountbatten Plan," he said, but they should have called it the "Gandhi Plan." It was Gandhi, Mountbatten declared, who had suggested to him all its major ingredients. The Mahatma looked at him perplexed.

Yes, Mountbatten continued, Gandhi had told him to leave the choice to the Indian people, and this plan did. It was the provincial, popularly elected assemblies which would decide India's future. Each province's assembly would vote on whether it wished to join India or Pakistan. Gandhi had urged the British to quit India as soon as possible, and that was what they were going to do. "If by some miracle the assemblies vote for unity," Mountbatten told Gandhi, "you have what you want. If they don't agree, I'm sure you don't want us to oppose their decision by force of arms."

Approaching seventy-eight, Gandhi was, for the first time in thirty years, uncertain of his grip on India's masses, at odds with the leaders of his party. In his despair and uncertainty, he was still searching in his soul for an answer, still waiting for an illuminating whisper of the inner voice that had guided him in so many of the grave crises of his career. That June evening, however, the voice was silent, and Gandhi was assailed by doubt. Should he remain faithful to his instincts, denounce partition, even (as he had earlier urged) at the price of plunging India into violence and chaos? Or should he listen to the Viceroy's desperate plea for reason? . . .

Less than an hour later, cross-legged on a raised platform in a dirt square in the midst of his Untouchables colony, Gandhi delivered his verdict. Many in the crowd before him had come, not to pray, but to hear from the lips of the prophet of nonviolence a call to arms, a fiery assault on Mountbatten's plan. No such cry would come this evening from the mouth of the man who had so often promised to offer his own body for vivisection, rather than accept his country's division. It was no use blaming the Viceroy for partition, he said. Look to yourselves and in your own hearts for an explanation of what has happened, he challenged. Louis Mountbatten's persuasiveness had won the ultimate and most difficult triumph of his viceroyalty.

As for Gandhi, many an Indian would never forgive him his silence, and the frail old man whose heart still ached for India's coming division would one day pay the price of their rancor. [200]

THE ANNOUNCED DATE

For Mountbatten the public announcement was the apotheosis, the consecration of a remarkable *tour de force*. In barely two months, virtually a one-man band, he had achieved the impossible, established a dialogue with India's leaders, set the basis of an agreement, persuaded his Indian interlocutors to accept it, extracted the whole hearted support of both the government and the opposition in London. He had skirted with dexterity and a little luck the pitfalls marring his route. And as his final gesture he had entered the cage of the old lion himself, convinced Churchill to draw in his claws and left him too, murmuring his approbation.

[As] Mountbatten concluded his talk to the assembled world press [there was] a burst of applause. He opened the floor to questions. He had no apprehension in doing so. "I had been there," he would recall later. "I was the only one who had been through it all, who'd lived every moment of it. For the first time the press were meeting the one and only man who had the whole thing at his fingertips." Suddenly, when the long barrage of questions began to trickle out, the anonymous voice of an Indian newsman cut across the chamber. His final question was the last square left to Mountbatten to fill in the puzzle he had been assigned six months before.

"Sir," the voice said, "If all agree that there is most urgent need for speed between today and the transfer of power, surely you should have a date in mind?"

"Yes, indeed," replied Mountbatten.

"And if you have chosen a date, sir, what is that date?" the questioner asked.

A number of rapid calculations went whirring through the Viceroy's mind as he listened to those questions. He had not, in fact, selected a date. But he was convinced it had to be very soon.

"I had to force the pace," he recalled later. "I knew I had to force Parliament to get the bill through before their summer recess to hold the thing together. We were sitting on the edge of a volcano, on a fused bomb and we didn't know when the bomb would go off." Like the blurred images of a horror film, the charred corpses of Kahuta flashed across Louis Mountbatten's mind. If an outburst of similar tragedies was not to drag all India into an apocalypse, he had to move fast. After three thousand years of history and two hundred years of *Pax Britannica*, only a few weeks remained, the Viceroy believed, between India and chaos. He stared at the packed assembly hall. Every face in the room was turned to his. A hushed, expectant silence broken only by the whir of the wooden blades of the fans revolving overhead stilled the room. "I was determined to show I was the master of the whole event," he would remember.

"Yes," he said, "I have selected a date for the transfer of power."

As he was uttering those words, the possible dates were still spinning through his mind like the numbers on a revolving roulette wheel. Early September? Middle of September, middle of August? Suddenly the wheel stopped with a jar and the little ball popped into a slot so overwhelmingly appropriate that Mountbatten's decision was instantaneous. It was a date linked in his memory to the most triumphant hours of his own existence, the day in which his long crusade through the jungles of Burma had ended with the unconditional surrender of the Japanese empire. A period in Asian history had ended with the collapse of that feudal Asia of the Samurai. What more appropriate date for the birth of the new democratic Asia arising to take its place than the second anniversary of Japan's surrender? His voice constricted with sudden emotion; the victor of the jungles of Burma, about to become the liberator of India, announced:

"The final transfer of power to Indian hands will take place on August 15, 1947." [201–202]

As soon as the radio announced Mountbatten's date, astrologers all over India began to consult their charts. Those in the holy city of Benares and several others in the South immediately proclaimed August 15 a date so inauspicious that India "would be better advised to tolerate the British one day longer rather than risk eternal damnation.". . .

"What have they done? What have they done?" one famous astrologer shouted to the heavens whose machinations he interpreted for man. Despite the discipline of his physical and spiritual forces acquired in years of yoga, meditation, and tantric studies in a temple in the hills of Assam, the astrologer lost control of himself. Seizing a piece of paper he sat down and wrote an urgent appeal to the man inadvertently responsible for this celestial catastrophe. "For the love of God," he wrote to Mountbatten, "do not give India her independence on August 15. If floods, drought, famine and massacres follow, it will be because free India was born on a day cursed by the stars."

QUESTIONS

1. What were the main forces that Mountbatten had to consider in his handling of the Indian situation?
2. Evaluate the way he handled each critical opponent and situation.
3. Evaluate the overall British strategy in leaving India.
4. What can one conclude about handling negotiation strategies from this case?

FIGURE 1
India Under the British Raj

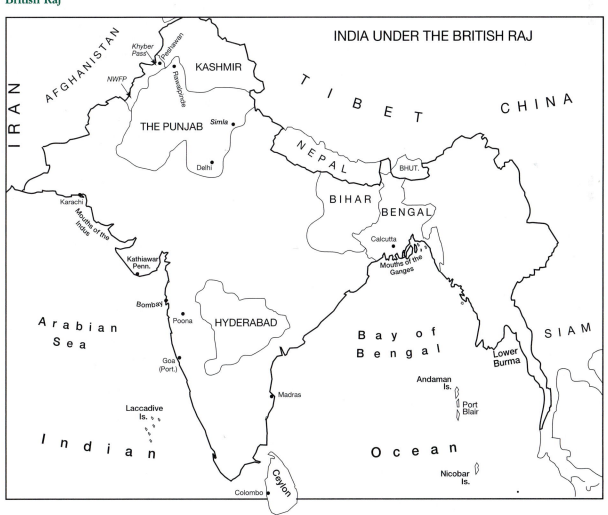

INDIA UNDER THE BRITISH RAJ

CASE I-3
MacArthur in the Philippines

1. Frazier Hunt, *The Untold Story of Douglas MacArthur*. New York: Devin-Adair Co., 1954, p. 318.

2. Charles A. Willoughby and John Chamberlain, *MacArthur, 1941–1951*. New York: McGraw-Hill, 1954; Charles A. Rawlings, "They Paved Their Way with Japs," *Saturday Evening Post*, October 7, 1944.

3. Hunt, *Untold*, p. 318; Douglas MacArthur, *Reminiscences*. New York: McGraw-Hill, 1964, pp. 166–167; Alfred Steinberg, *Douglas MacArthur*. New York: Putnam, 1961, p. 113; Willoughby and Chamberlain, *MacArthur*, p. 206.

4. Richard H. Rovere and Arthur M. Schlesinger, Jr., *The General and the President, and the Future of American Foreign Policy*. New York: Farrar, Straus and Young, 1951, pp. 65–66; Willoughby and Chamberlain, *MacArthur*, p. 206.

5. Jay Luvaas, ed., *Dear Miss Em: General Eichelberger's War in the Pacific, 1942–1945*. Westport, Conn.: Greenwood Press, 1972, p. 75.

6. Gavin M. Long, *MacArthur as Military Commander*. London: 1969, p. 219; Earl Blaik, *The Red Blaik Story*. New York: Arlington House, 1974, p. 501; James M. Burns, *Roosevelt: The Soldier of Freedom, 1940–45*. New York: Harcourt Brace Jovanovich, 1970, p. 488.

7. Daniel E. Barbey, *MacArthur's Amphibious Navy: Seventh Amphibious Force Operations, 1943–1945*. Annapolis: U.S. Naval Institute, 1969, p. 219; Blaik, *Red Blaik Story*, p. 501; Burns, *Roosevelt*, p. 488.

8. Author's interviews with Roger Egeberg, October 18, 1976; MacArthur, *Reminiscences*, p. 199; Dorris Clayton James, *The Years of MacArthur, 1941–1945, Vol. II*. Boston: Houghton Mifflin, 1975, p. 530; Luvaas, *Miss Em*, p. 155; William D. Leahy, *I Was There*. New York: Whittlesey House, 1950, p. 250; Stanley L. Falk, *Decision at Leyte*. New York: W. W. Norton, 1966, p. 28.

9. Leahy, *I Was There*, p. 251; James, *Vol. II*, p. 530; MacArthur, *Reminiscences*, p. 197.

10. David J. Steinberg, *Philippine Collaboration in World War II*. Ann Arbor: University of Michigan Press, 1967, p. 101; George C. Kenney, *The MacArthur I Know*. New York: Duell, Sloan and Pearce, 1951, pp. 155–156; Willoughby and Chamberlain, *MacArthur*, p. 233.

11. MacArthur, *Reminiscences*, p. 198; Leahy, *I Was There*, pp. 250–251.

12. Robert R. Smith, *Triumph in the Philippines*. Washington, D.C.: Office of the Chief of Military History, Department of the Army, 1963, p. 11.

13. John Toland, *The Rising Sun*. New York: Random House, 1970, pp. 533–534; Barbey, *Amphibious*, p. 227; Robert J. Bulkley, *At Close Quarters: PT Boats in the United States Navy*. Washington, D.C.: Naval History Division, 1962, p. 376; William F. Halsey and Joseph Bryan III, *Admiral Halsey's Story*. New York: Whittlesey House, 1947, p. 199.

14. Halsey and Bryan, *Admiral Halsey's Story*, pp. 198–201; Henry H. Arnold, *Global Mission*. New York: Harper, 1949, pp. 527–528; James, *Vol. II*, pp. 537–539; Toland, *Sun*, p. 534; George C. Kenney, *General Kenney Reports: A Personal History of the Pacific War*, Washington, D.C.: Office of Air Force History, U.S. Air Force, 1987, p. 434.

15. Manuel Quezon, *The Good Fight*. New York and London: D. Appleton-Century Co., 1946, p. 295; Robert I. Eichelberger, with Milton McKaye, *Our Jungle Road to Tokyo*. New York: Viking Press, 1950, p. 181; J. Griggin, "Philippines," *Holiday*, July 1967.

16. Carlos P. Romulo, *I Saw the Fall of the Philippines*. Garden City, N.Y.: Doubleday & Co., 1942, p. 54; David Steinberg, *Collaboration*, pp. 104–105.

17. James, *Vol. II*, pp. 542–543.

18. Carlos P. Romulo, *I See the Philippines Rise*. Garden City, N.Y.: Doubleday & Co., 1946, p. 190; Toland, *Sun*, p. 537; David Steinberg, *Collaboration*, p. 101.

19. MacArthur, *Reminiscences*, p. 172; Hunt, *Untold*, p. 314.

20. Toland, *Sun*, p. 534; "Promise Fulfilled," *Time*, October 30, 1944.

21. MacArthur, *Reminiscences*, p. 212; Kenney, *Know*, p. 156; Alfred Steinberg, *Douglas MacArthur*, p. 127.

22. Falk, *Leyte*, p. 29; Hunt, *Untold*, p. 342.

23. Author's interviews with Egeberg, October 18, 1976; MacArthur, *Reminiscences*, p. 216; James, *Vol. II*, pp. 554–555; "MacArthur Returns and Returns," *Life*, February 18, 1972; Kenney, *General*, p. 448; Charles A. Lockwood and Hans C. Adamson, *Battle of the Philippine Sea*. New York: 1967, pp. 157–158; "Battle for the Philippines," *Fortune*, June 1945.

24. Author's interviews with Romulo, October 18, 1976; Romulo, *Rise*, pp. 3, 94–95; Falk, *Leyte*, p. 111.

25. Records of General Headquarters, United States Army Forces, Pacific (USAF-PAC), 1942–1945; Carlos P. Romulo, *I Walked with Heroes*. New York: Holt, Rinehart and Winston, 1961, pp. 235–236; James, *Vol. II*, pp. 557–558; MacArthur, *Reminiscences*, pp. 216–217; Long, *Commander*, p. 152; Falk, *Leyte*, p. 103; David Steinberg, *Collaboration*, p. 105; Vorin E. Whan, ed., *A Soldier Speaks: Public Papers and Speeches of General of the Army Douglas MacArthur*. New York: Praeger, 1965, pp. 132–133.

26. Kenney, *General*, p. 452.

27. Romulo, *Rise*, p. 165.

28. Falk, *Leyte*, p. 220.

29. Falk, pp. 71, 273; James, *Vol. II*, p. 580; Toland, *Sun*, pp. 576–577.

30. James, *Vol. II*, p. 585, Eichelberger, *Jungle*, p. 174; Falk, *Leyte*, p. 293.

31. James, *Vol. II*, p. 584; Kenney, *General*, pp. 64–65; author's interviews with Egeberg, October 18, 1976.

32. Edward M. Flanagan, Jr., *The Angels: A History of the 11th Airborne Division, 1943–1946*. Washington, D.C.: Infantry Journal Press, 1948, p. 621.

33. MacArthur, *Reminiscences*, p. 241; James, *Vol. II*, p. 621.

34. *The New York Times*, January 11, 1945; MacArthur, *Reminiscences*, p. 242.

35. Hunt, *Untold*, p. 364; Bertram C. Wright, comp., *The 1st Cavalry Division in World War II*, Tokyo: Toppan Print Co., 1947, pp. 125–128; author's interviews with Romulo, October 18, 1976; Flanagan, *Angels*, pp. 77–80; author's interviews with Egeberg, October 18, 1976; James, *Vol. II*, p. 641; Romulo, *Rise*, p. 191.

36. MacArthur, *Reminiscences*, pp. 245–246; Luvaas, *Miss Em*, p. 225.

37. Luvaas, *Miss Em*, p. 203; Eichelberger, *Jungle*, p. 187; MacArthur, *Reminiscences*, p. 260.

38. Luvaas, *Miss Em*, p. 203.

39. "In Remembrance of MacArthur," *Life*, April 17, 1964; Luvaas, *Miss Em*, p. 260; Willoughby and Chamberlain, *MacArthur*, p. 267.

40. Luvaas, *Miss Em*, pp. 278–279; Kenney, *General*, pp. 552–553; Kenney, *Know*, pp. 132–133.

41. Hanson W. Baldwin, *Great Mistakes of the War*. New York: Harper, 1949, p. 97.

42. Records of General Headquarters, United States Army Forces, Pacific (USAF-PAC), 1942-45; James, *Vol. II*, pp. 765–766; Leahy, *I Was There*, p. 385; Leslie R. Groves, *Now It Can Be Told*. New York: Harper, 1962, pp. 263–264.

43. Hunt, *Untold*, p. 402.

44. James, *Vol. II*, p. 785; Norman Richards, *Douglas MacArthur*. Chicago: Children's Press, 1967, p. 76; Jules Archer, *Front-Line General: Douglas MacArthur*. New York: Messner, 1963, pp. 143–144; John Gunther, *The Riddle of MacArthur: Japan, Korea, and the Far East*. New York: Harper, 1951, p. 2.

45. Courtney Whitney, *MacArthur, His Rendezvous with History*. New York: Alfred A. Knopf, 1955, p. 216; MacArthur, *Reminiscences*, p. 271; "On the Record," *Time*, March 31, 1947; James, *Vol. II*, pp. 786–787.

46. Collection of Messages (radiograms), 1945–1951; Whitney, *Rendezvous*, pp. 216–217; James, *Vol. II*, pp. 787–788; MacArthur, *Reminiscences*, pp. 271–272; William Craig, *The Fall of Japan*. New York: Dial Press, 1967, pp. 297–298.

47. Toshikazu Kase, *Journey to the Missouri*. New Haven: Yale University Press, 1950, p. 13; MacArthur, *Reminiscences*, pp. 276–277.

CASE I-5 INTEL CORPORATION

1. "The Five Best Managed Companies," *Dun's Review*, December 1980.

2. Gene Bylinsky, quoted from *The Innovation Millionaires*. Copyright © 1976, 1974, 1973, 1967 by Gene Bylinsky. Reprinted with the permission of Charles Scribner's Sons.

3. *Electronic News*, December 27, 1974.

4. "Meet Bob Noyce," *Computer Decisions*, June 1974.

5. *The Wall Street Journal*, October 4, 1969.

6. "Special Report: Where the Action Is in Electronics," *Business Week*, October 4, 1969.

7. *Electronic News*, August 26, 1968.

8. *Electronics*, March 31, 1969.

9. "Intel Gambles for Continued Rapid Growth," *International Management*, November 1981.

10. "Creativity by the Numbers," *Harvard Business Review*, May–June 1980.

11. "American Industry and What Ails It," *The Atlantic*, May 1980.

12. George Gilder, *Microcosm*. New York: Simon & Schuster, 1989, p. 152. (These figures do not include U.S. captive suppliers—IBM and AT&T. If captive suppliers are included, Japan's share of the U.S. market falls to 65%.)

13. *The Wall Street Journal*, June 21, 1989, p. B5, and *San Francisco Chronicle*, June 22, 1989, p. C1. (Some companies, notably Apple and Sun Microsystems, were reluctant to invest in U.S. Memories, due to relationships with existing DRAM manufacturers, according to the *San Francisco Chronicle*, September 26, 1989.)

14. *Business Week*, November 26, 1990, p. 122.

15. Goldman Sachs, *The Future of Microprocessors*, April 23, 1990.

16. *The Wall Street Journal*, February 28, 1989, p. A1.

CASE I-8 MICROSOFT CORPORATION (A)

1. J. Wallace and J. Erickson, *Hard Drive*. New York: Harper Business, 1993. Personal incidents in the above section drawn largely from this source.

2. *Ibid.*, p. 61.

3. *Ibid.*, p. 107.

4. *Ibid.*, p. 117.

5. The following four major sections are drawn from G. Danforth, R. McGrath, and G. Castrogiovanni, "Microsoft Corporation" (case), Louisiana State University, 1992.

6. J. Henry, "The Silicon Muscleman," *Business Month*, November 1990; "Microsoft's Web of Fear," *The Economist*, January 9, 1993, p. 58.

7. "Bill Gates' Vision," *Business Week*, June 27, 1994, p. 57.

8. "Microsoft's Web of Fear."

9. "Microsoft Hits the Gas," *Business Week*, March 21, 1994, p. 34.

10. "Novell, End of an Era," *Business Week*, November 22, 1993, p. 95.

11. "The Battle of the Network Stars Boots Up," *Business Week*, April 25, 1994, p. 128.

12. "Microsoft Is Like an Elephant Rolling Around Squashing Ants," *Business Week*, October 30, 1989.

13. K. Wiegner and J. Pitta, "Can Anyone Stop Bill Gates?" *Forbes*, April 1, 1991, p. 108.

14. "Bill Gates' Vision," p. 62.

15. "Microsoft's Antitrust Blues," *Fortune*, April 18, 1994, p. 12.

16. "Home Computers," *Business Week*, November 28, 1994.

17. Wallace and Erickson, *Hard Drive*, pp. 255–256.

18. *Ibid.*, p. 369.

CASE I-10 THE IBM 360 DECISION

1. K. D. Fishman, *The Computer Establishment.* New York: Harper & Row, 1981.

2. "IBM's Battle to Look Superhuman Again," *Fortune*, May 19, 1980.

3. "The Lean, Mean New IBM," *Fortune*, June 13, 1983; and "The Colossus That Works," *Time*, July 11, 1983.

CASE I-12 NINTENDO CO., LTD.

1. D. Scheff, *Game Over.* Random House: New York, 1993. (1,xx) indicates the page reference.

2. All quotes by Mr. Yamauchi are from interviews by Professor James Brian Quinn and Mr. Nobuo Okochi, September 1993.

3. This section is paraphrased with special permission from P. Anderson, "New Technologies Group," Case, Amos Tuck School, Hanover N.H., 1994. All rights reserved to the original author.

4. "Dream Machines," *Far Eastern Economic Review*, December 24–31, 1992.

CASE I-13
MAGNETIC LEVITATION TRAIN

GENERAL SOURCES

1. "Advanced Rail Technology," Report by Subcommittee on Transportation, Aviation and Materials, Committee on Science and Technology, U.S. House of Representatives, September 1982.

2. Y. Ishigami, "Hitachi Cable Supplies Superconducting Products to Researchers," *Business Japan*, July 1990.

3. "Magnetic Levitation Trains; Coming Home," *The Economist*, October 13, 1990.

4. H. Tanaka, "JR Group Probes Maglev Frontiers," *Railway Gazette International*, July 1990.

5. "U.S. Passenger Rail Technologies," U.S. Congress, Office of Technology Assessment, OTA-STI-222, Washington D.C., December 1983.

6. J. Vranich, "The Puzzling Politics of High Speed Rail," *Railway Age*, October 1992.

CASE FOOTNOTES

1. *Kyodo News International*, September 17, 1991.

2. "RTRI: Creating a New Generation of Railway," Railway Technical Research Institute, Tokyo, Japan, 1992.

3. J. Fujie, "The Current Status and Future Outlook for Development of a Super Conducting Maglev System in Japan," *Science & Technology in Japan*, March 1992.

4. "Riding on Air," *Scientific American*, February 1992.

5. G. Stix, "Air Trains," *Scientific American*, August 1992.

6. P. Moynihan, "How to Lose: The Story of Maglev," *Scientific American*, November 1989.

7. "Riding on Air."

8. R. Thornton, "Why the U.S. Needs a Maglev System," *Technology Review*, April 1991.

9. Stix, "Air Trains."

10. *Ibid.*

11. *Ibid.*

12. *Ibid.*

13. Fujie, "Current Status."

14. Stix, "Air Trains."

15. R. Jenner, "Japan's New Whiz Kids," *Management Today*, January 1989.

16. H. Tanaka, "Advanced Materials for Magnetically Levitated Train," *Quarterly Report, Railway Technical Research Institute*, Vol. 33, no. 3 (1992).

17. H. Tanaka, "Application of Superconductivity to Transportation: Magnetically Levitated Train," Monograph, 1991.

CASE I-14 FORD: TEAM TAURUS

1. James W. Botkin, Dan Dimancescu, and Ray Stata, *The Innovators.* New York: Harper & Row, 1984, p. 29.

2. "A Ford Man Tunes Up Nissan," *Fortune*, November 24, 1986, pp. 140–144.

3. "Ford's Lewis Veraldi: Man of the Year," *Automotive Industries*, February 27, 1987, pp. 65–68.

4. "In the Fast Lane," *Business Week*, February 11, 1985, pp. 48–52.

5. "A 'Hot Dog' Tries to Cut the Mustard at Ford," *Industry Week*, August 18, 1980, pp. 76–82.

6. "What's Creating an Industrial Miracle at Ford?" *Business Week*, July 30, 1984, pp. 80–84.

7. "Ford's Drive for Quality," *Fortune*, April 18, 1983, pp. 62–70.

8. "Ford Team Taurus Concept Is Blueprint for Future Cars," *Automotive News*, May 6, 1985, p. 2.

9. "Detroit Comes Through," *Business Week*, June 30, 1986, p. 69.

10. "Team Taurus," *Ward's Auto World*, February 1985, pp. 26–31.

11. "Ford's Mr. Turnaround: 'We Have More to Do,'" *Fortune*, March 4, 1985, pp. 83–89.

12. "Hot 'Lanta! Taurus Takes Off," *Automotive Industries*, November 1985, p. 46.

13. "Ford Motor Delays Introduction Date of Taurus Sable," *The Wall Street Journal*, September 20, 1985, p. 15.

14. "Can Ford Stay on Top?" *Business Week*, September 28, 1987, pp. 78–81.

15. "What's Ahead in the World Auto War?" *Fortune*, November 9, 1987, p. 74.

16. "Ford Puts $100M on Table to Power Taurus and Sable," *Advertising Age*, November 18, 1985, p. 1.

17. "Ford to Introduce Taurus, Sable Today with High Hopes Despite Short Supply," *The Wall Street Journal*, December 26, 1985, p. 2.

18. "The Road Warriors," *Marketing and Media Decisions*, March 1987, pp. 60–69.

19. "Now It's Simultaneous Car Design—," *Industry Week*, April 1, 1985, pp. 17–26.

20. Various articles in *The Wall Street Journal*.

21. A. Taylor, "U.S. Cars Come Back," *Fortune*, November 16, 1992.

22. *Ibid.*

23. "Detroit's Big Chance," *Business Week*, June 29, 1992, p. 90.

24. *Business Week*, January 18, 1993.

25. "Shaking Up Jaguar," *Fortune*, September 6, 1993.

26. "The Endless Road: A Survey of the Car Industry," *The Economist*, October 17, 1992.

CASE I-15 ARGYLE DIAMONDS

1. "Argyle Diamonds Sparkle for Investors," *W. A. Review*, March 1990, pp. 13–15.

2. N. Bushnell and J. McIlwraith, "Argyle Gets Down to Marketing Nitty Gritty," *Australian Business*, June 6, 1990, p. 19.

3. "Major Upgrade for Argyle Diamond Mine," *Australia's Mining Monthly*, December 1989–January 1990, p. 19.

4. "Argyle Diamonds Sparkle for Investors," p. 15.

5. CRA, *Limited Report to Shareholders*, 1990, p. 33.

6. "Diamond Production Hits Target," *Australia's Mining Monthly*, July 1986, p. 15.

7. "The Western Australian Diamond Industry," Western Australian Department of Resources, Prospect No. 1, 1988, p. 4.

8. "Major Upgrade for Argyle Diamond Mine," p. 31.

9. "Diamond Production Hits Target."

10. "Major Upgrade for Argyle Diamond Mine," p. 32.

11. *Ibid.*

12. *Ibid.*, p. 27.

13. "Record Profits for DeBeers," *Mining Journal*, London, March 18, 1988, p. 231.

14. *Register of Australian Mining*. London: Ross Louthean, 1981, p. 215.

15. "A Good Year for Diamonds," *Mining Journal*, London, February 5, 1988, p. 98.

16. "Soviets Sign $66 Million Diamonds Agreement," *The Australian*, July 27, 1990, p. 1.

17. *Ibid.*

18. D. E. Koskoff, *The Diamond World*. New York: Harper & Row, 1981, p. 273.

19. *Ibid.*, pp. 274–275.

20. *Ibid.*, pp. 302–314.

21. *Inflation Shelters, 1993: Diamonds, Gold, Silver, Platinum*, Economist Intelligence Unit, Special Report No. 136, Spencer House, London.

22. Koskoff, *The Diamond World*, p. 100.

23. "Diamonds Could Be High Tech's Best Friend," *Business Week*, February 12, 1990, pp. 58–59.

24. Employment figures are based on P. Temple, "The Investors Best Friend," *Accountancy*, September 1989, pp. 60–61.

25. Koskoff, *The Diamond World*, p. 247.

26. *Ibid.*, p. 281.

27. *Ibid.*, p. 283.

28. *Ibid.*, pp. 290–291.

29. *Inflation Shelters, 1993*, p. 7.

30. *Ibid.*

31. *Ibid.*, p. 27.

32. Bushnell and McIlwraith, "Argyle Gets Down to Marketing Nitty Gritty," p. 18.

33. "The Western Australian Diamond Industry."

CASE II-1
THE NEW YORK TIMES COMPANY

1. E. Davis, *History of The New York Times*. New York: The New York Times, 1921, p. 194.

2. J. Draft, "The Future of *The New York Times*," *Esquire*, April 1961, p. 121.

3. C. David Rambo, "Lee Huebner: IHT Publisher's Talents Match Global Challenges," *presstime*, February 1990, p. 34.

4. Mary A. Anderson, "Global Buying Spree Skips U.S. Dailies," *presstime*, February 1990, p. 8.

5. "The New York Times?" *Fortune*, July 28, 1980, pp. 84–85.

CASE II-2 MATSUSHITA ELECTRIC INDUSTRIAL COMPANY 1994

1. J. Cruikshank, "Matsushita," *Harvard Business School Bulletin*, February 1983, page 63.

2. T. Kono, *Strategy and Structure of Japanese Enterprises*. Armonk, N.Y.: M. E. Sharpe, 1985, p. 50.

3. B. Schlender, "Matsushita Shows How to Go Global," *Fortune*, July 11, 1994.

4. R. Pascale and A. Athos, *The Art of Japanese Management*. New York: Simon & Schuster, 1981, p. 33.

5. Schlender, "Matsushita Shows How to Go Global."

6. *Ibid.*

CASE II-3 THE HEWLETT PACKARD COMPANY

1. *Hewlett Packard in Brief*, Hewlett Packard Company.

2. "Hewlett Packard Discovers Marketing," *Fortune*, October 1, 1984.

3. William R. Hewlett, "The Human Side of Management," Eugene B. Clark Executive Lecture, March 25, 1982.

4. Thomas L. Wheelen and J. David Hunger, *Strategic Management and Business Policy*. Reading, Mass.: Addison-Wesley, 1983.

5. "Hewlett Packard: Where Slower Growth Is Smarter Management," *Business Week*, June 9, 1975.

6. "Hewlett Packard's Calculated Rise," *Management Today*, August 1977.

7. John Young, *HP White Paper on Organization Changes*, Hewlett Packard Company, July 19, 1985.

8. Bro Uttla, "Mettle-Test Time for John Young," *Fortune*, April 29, 1985.

9. John Young, "The Quality Focus at Hewlett Packard," *Journal of Business Strategy*, Winter 1985.

10. "Back into the Race," *Forbes*, October 10, 1983.

11. "Can John Young Redesign Hewlett Packard?" *Business Week*, December 6, 1982.

12. E. F. Hutton, *Hewlett Packard Company Action Report*, June 28, 1983.

CASE II-4 TCG, LTD./THERMO ELECTRON

1. P. V. Martin, "The ATG Case, A Case Study in Enterprise Management," University of New South Wales, 1992.

2. John Matthews, "TCG: Sustainable Economic Organization Through Networking," Industrial Relations Research Center, the University of New South Wales, Sydney, Australia, 1992 is the major source of information for this section of the case. Sections quoted by special permission.

3. All interview quotes are from interviews by Professor Quinn (December 1993) and approved by their sources.

4. Matthews, "TCG: Sustainable," pp. 25–27.

5. P. Fritz, *The Possible Dream*. New York: Penguin Books, 1988, pp. 153–159.

6. *Ibid.*, p. 181.

7. C. Sassouni, Raymond James, and Associates, *Thermo Electron Corporation Report*, March 4, 1994, p. 3.

8. *Ibid.*, p. 6.

9. *Ibid.*, p. 8.

10. "How to Grow Big by Staying Small," *Fortune*, December 28, 1992, p. 50.

CASE II-5 MICROSOFT CORPORATION (B)

1. J. Wallace and J. Erickson, *Hard Drive*. New York: Harper Business, 1993, p. 303.

2. "Microsoft Is Like An Elephant . . . ," *Business Week*, October 30, 1989.

3. *Ibid.*; Wallace and Erickson, *Hard Drive*, p. 261.

4. "Microsoft Is Like An Elephant"; Wallace and Erickson, *Hard Drive*, p. 125.

5. "Bill Gates and the Management of Microsoft," Harvard Business School, Case 9-392-019.

CASE II-6 NOVACARE, INC.

1. Donaldson, Lufkin & Jenrette, *Health Care Services and Hospital Management—Industry Report*, February 1, 1991.

CASE II-7 ORBITAL ENGINE COMPANY

1. "Big Bets on a Little Engine," *Business Week*, January 15, 1990, pp. 53–54.

2. P. Davis, *Sarich: The Man and His Engines*, Hurstville, New South Wales: Marque, 1989, Chapters 2, 7, and 8.

3. "55 Miles per Gallon: How Honda Did It," *Business Week*, September 23, 199, pp. 40–41.

4. "GM Drives the Electric Car Closer to Reality," *Business Week*, May 14, 1990, pp. 30–31.

5. J. Holmes, "Technical Change and the Restructuring of the North American Automobile Industry." In K. Chapman and G. Humphrys, eds., *Technical Change and Industrial Policy*. Oxford: Basil Blackwell, 1987.

6. "Lawnmower Limousines," *The Economist*, November 25, 1989, p. 109.

7. A. Mair, R. Florida, and M. Kenney, "The New Geography of Automobile Production: Japanese Transplants in North America," *Economic Geography*, Vol. 64, no. 4 (October 1988), 352–353.

8. National Mutual Life Nominees Limited (Trustee) and ST Management Limited (Manager), *Scheme for Reorganization of the Affairs of Sarich Technologies Trust*, Perth, October 1988.

9. Sarich Technologies Limited, *Notice of Meeting, Explanatory Statement, Independent Expert's Report*, Perth, 1989.

10. "Sarich vs. the Skeptics," *Australian Business Monthly*, January 1992, pp. 62–65.

11. Kim Schlunke, "The Orbital Combustion Process Engine—Fuel Economy Potential," *Report to the National Research Council, Committee on the Fuel Economy of Automobiles and Trucks*, July 8–12, 1991.

12. Kim Schlunke, R. Ahern, R. Leighton, and M. R. Kitson, "Fuel Consumption and Emissions Reduction in Small Displacement Two Stroke Cycle Engines," undated paper, Orbital Engine Company.

13. L. J. White, "The Motor Vehicles Industry." In R. R. Nelson, ed., *Government and Technical Progress: A Cross-Industry Analysis*. New York: Pergamon Press, 1982, pp. 414–415.

CASE II-9 POLAROID CORPORATION

1. "In Light of Polaroid," *Fortune*, September 1938, p. 76.

2. Francis Bello, "The Magic That Made Polaroid," *Fortune*, April 1957, p. 158.

3. Richard Karp, "The Clouded Picture at Polaroid," *Dun's Review*, November 1973, p. 61.

4. Phillip Siekman, "Kodak and Polaroid: An End to Peaceful Coexistence," *Fortune*, November 1970, p. 86.

5. Donald Silverman, "Cash in a Flash?" *Systems Engineering Today*, February 1974, p. 31.

6. Mark Olshaker, *The Instant Image*. New York: Stein and Day, 1978, pp. 206–207.

7. "Dr. Land Redesigns His Camera Company," *Business Week*, April 15, 1972, p. 71.

8. Richard Martin, "The Team Builder: Polaroid's New President Faces Problems of Earning Woes and Kodak Competition," *The Wall Street Journal*, April 25, 1975, p. 17.

9. Polaroid Corporation, *Annual Report*, 1977, p. 42.

10. "Polaroid's One Step Is Stopping Kodak Cold," *Fortune*, February 13, 1978, p. 78.

11. Bernstein, "Polaroid Struggles to Get Back in Focus," *Fortune*, April 7, 1980.

12. H. Weil, "Polaroid and Kodak—Instant Winners," *Financial World*, February 15, 1979.

13. Lehman Brothers, *Polaroid Corporation Research Report*, August 1983.

14. Donaldson, Lufkin & Jenrette, *Polaroid Corporation Research Report*, December 20, 1982.

15. Dean Witter Reynolds, Inc., *Technology Group Research Note*, August 16, 1982.

16. P. Maher, "Polaroid Seeks Business Focus," *Industrial Marketing*, October 1981.

17. "We Must Broaden Our Base, CEO McCune Declares," *Business Week*, March 2, 1981.

18. "Informal, Personal, and Paternalistic, "*Business Week*, May 4, 1974, p. 44.

19. Polaroid Corporation, *Annual Report*, 1977.

20. See Exhibit 8 for a description of the roles and backgrounds of Polaroid staff members as derived from SEC data and *Who's Who in America*.

21. Polaroid Corporation, *Annual Report*, 1980.

22. Edwin Land, "Thinking Ahead," *Harvard Business Review*, September–October 1959, p. 8.

23. Subrata Chakravarty, "An Interview with Dr. Edwin Land," *Forbes*, June 1, 1975, p. 49.

CASE II-10 EXXON CORPORATION 1994

1. "Norway: Still Just Crumbs for Foreign Oil Companies," *World Oil*, October 1981.

2. "Problems of a European Oil Sheik," *The Economist*, January 12, 1980.

3. "Why North Sea Oil Gushes, but the Pumps Run Dry," *The Economist*, June 16, 1979.

4. "U.K. Government Revenues from North Sea Oil," *The Banker*, July 1980.

5. "Japanese Adjust to Oil Supply Changes," *Oil & Gas Journal*, January 26, 1981.

CASE II-11 SONY CORPORATION: INNOVATION SYSTEM

1. Akio Morita, "International Marketing of Sony Corporation," Monograph, Tokyo, July 14, 1969.

2. B. Schlender, "How Sony Keeps the Magic Going," *Fortune*, February 24, 1992.

3. R. D. Schwartz, E. F. Hutton Group, Inc., *Imaging Technology—Industry Report*, June 13, 1985.

4. P. J. Enderlin, Smith Barney, Harris Upham & Co., Inc., *Electronic Imaging—Impact on Consumer Photography*, December 20, 1984.

CASE III-1 SONY ENTERTAINMENT

1. All interview quotes from personal interviews with James Brian Quinn, October 1993 and Spring 1994. All quotes cleared by their sources.

2. N. Perry, "Will Sony Make It in Hollywood?" *Fortune*, September 9, 1991; "Living Off Its Past," *Forbes*, April 18, 1992; and "Hooked by Hollywood," *The Economist*, September 21, 1991.

3. Perry, "Will Sony Make It in Hollywood?"

4. Morgan Stanley, *Investment Research: Japan and Asia Pacific*, February 22, 1994.

5. *The Economist*, September 21, 1992.

6. This section paraphrased from *Sony Corporation: Globalization* (case) Harvard Business School, February 14, 1991.

7. N. Cope, "Walkman's Global Stride," *Fortune*, March 1990.

8. S. Lubove and N. Weinberg, "Creating a Seamless Company," *Forbes*, December 30, 1993.

9. "The Entertainment Industry: Special Survey," *The Economist*, December 23, 1989.

10. M. Schulhof, "Globalization and Technologies, The Future of Entertainment," World Affairs Council, February 23, 1990.

11. R. P. Simon, *Movie Industry Update—1993*, Goldman Sachs, New York, April 7, 1993.

12. M. Schulhof, "Record Retailing in the Electronic World," Sony Corporation, New York, March 20, 1994.

13. "The Entertainment Economy," *Business Week*, March 14, 1994, pp. 58–64.

14. R. Simon and M. Fineman, *Music Industry Update—1993*, Goldman Sachs, New York, January 18, 1993.

15. Lubove and Weinberg, "Creating a Seamless Company."

CASE III-2
THE VANGUARD GROUP, INC. (A)

1. John C. Bogle, "We Lead," 15th Anniversary Celebration Remarks, The Vanguard Group, June 23, 1990.

2. John C. Bogle, "Daring and Caring," Remarks to the Crew, The Vanguard Group, December 11, 1991.

3. Hugo Uyterhoeven, Robert Ackerman, and John Rosenbloom, *Strategy and Organization: Text and Cases in General Management*. Homewood, Ill.: Richard D. Irwin, 1973, p. 397.

4. John C. Bogle, "Vanguard—The First Century," An address to the Newcomen Society, The Vanguard Group, January 15, 1992.

5. John C. Bogle, "Creative Destruction," Remarks, The Vanguard Group, June 17, 1991.

6. Bogle, "Daring and Caring."

7. John C. Bogle, "Like a Rock," Remarks, The Vanguard Group, December 6, 1987.

8. John C. Bogle, "If You Build It, They Will Come," Remarks, The Vanguard Group.

9. Andrew E. Serwer, "Vanguard: A Fund Family for the 1990s," *Fortune*, December 30, 1991, p. 82.

10. *Ibid.*, p. 88.

11. Michael L. Golstein and Lili Lynton, *The Future of the Money Management Industry*, Sanford C. Bernstein & Co., Inc., p. 44.

CASE III-4
HONDA MOTOR COMPANY 1994

1. T. Sakiya, *Honda Motor: The Men, The Management, The Machines*. Tokyo: Kodansha International, Ltd. 1982.

2. S. Sanders, *Honda: The Man and His Machines*. Boston: Little Brown, 1975.

3. "Honda the Market Guzzler," *Fortune*, February 20, 1984.

4. "Toyota's Fast Lane," *Business Week*, November 4, 1985.

5. "A Car is Born," *Business Week*, September 13, 1993.

6. R. Guest, "The Quality of Work Life in Japan. . . ," *Hokudai Economic Papers*, Tokyo, Vol. XII (1982–1983).

CASE III-5 THE PILLSBURY COMPANY

1. *The Wall Street Journal*, September 10, 1979, p. 8.

2. *Industrial Manual*, Moody's, 1970.

3. "The Name of the Games Is Still General Mills," *Forbes*, April 1, 1970.

4. "An Unforeseen Succession at the Biggest Miller," *Fortune*, February 1973, p. 18.

5. "Pillsbury Mills Its Future," *Financial World*, February 3, 1971, p. 12.

6. "Pillsbury Turnaround . . . ," *Advertising Age*, January 12, 1974.

7. "Pillsbury Mills Its Future."

8. "Consumer Analysts' Meeting," *The Wall Street Transcript*, March 19, 1974.

9. "Recipe at Pillsbury Calls for Quick Results," *Barron's*, July 29, 1974, p. 25.

10. T. Hanold, "An Executive View of MIS," *Datamation*, November 1972.

11. "Pillsbury's Winery," *Business Week*, September 8, 1975, p. 32.

12. W. Scott, Comments before the Dain, Kalman & Quail Food Conference, March 1977.

13. "The One Man Show at Pillsbury," *Business Week*, January 19, 1976.

14. W. Kiechel, "Now for the Greening of Pillsbury," *Fortune*, November 5, 1979.

15. Acquired in November 1975 for 516,175 shares of Pillsbury with about $25 million; Moody's *Industrial Manual*, 1976.

16. *The Wall Street Journal*, December 6, 1976, p. 24.

17. "William H. Spoor, Pillsbury Company," *Financial World*, April 1, 1977, p. 20.

18. "Can Pillsbury Rise Above the Defections," *Business Week*, June 9, 1980.

19. "CBS Chooses Wyman . . . ," *The Wall Street Journal*, November 12, 1984.

20. "Friendly Whopper . . . ," *Barron's*, September 10, 1984.

21. "Rising to the Top at Pillsbury," *Business Week*, March 12, 1984.

CASE III-8 CADBURY SCHWEPPES, P.L.C.

1. C. Smith, J. Child, and M. Rowlinson, *Reshaping Work: The Cadbury Experience*. Cambridge: Cambridge University Press, 1990.

2. G. Jones, "The Chocolate Multinationals: Cadbury, Fry, and Rowntree, 1918–1939." In G. Jones, ed., *British Multinationals: Origins, Management and Performance*. Brookfield, Vt.: Gower, 1986, pp. 96–118.

3. Smith, Child, and Rowlinson, *Reshaping Work*.

4. Jones, "The Chocolate Multinationals."

5. Smith, Child, and Rowlinson, *Reshaping Work*.

6. Ibid.

7. Ibid.

8. J. Child and C. Smith, "The Context and Process of Organizational Transformation—Cadbury Limited in Its Sector," *Journal of Management Studies*, Vol. 24 (1987), 565–593.

9. P. Tisdall, "Chocolate Soldiers Clash," *Marketing*, July 19, 1982, pp. 30–34.

10. J. Weber, "Why Hershey Is Smacking Its Lips," *Business Week*, October 30, 1989, p. 140.

11. Smith, Child, and Rowlinson, *Reshaping Work*.

12. A. Borrus, J. Sassen, and M. A. Harris, "Why Cadbury Schweppes Looks Sweet to the Raiders," *Business Week*, January 13, 1986, pp. 132–133.

13. A. van de Vliet, "Bittersweet at Cadbury," *Management Today*, March 1986, pp. 42–49.

14. Ibid.

15. Ibid.

16. Ibid.

17. K. Gofton, "Has Cadbury Got His Finger on the Button?" *Marketing*, July 31, 1986, pp. 20–25.

18. P. Winters, "Cadbury Schweppes' Plan: Skirt Cola Giants," *Advertising Age*, August 13, 1990, pp. 22-23.

19. R. L. Swarns and B. Toran, "Hershey to Buy U.S. Business from Cadbury," *The Wall Street Journal*, July 25, 1988, p. 30.

20. van de Vliet, "Bittersweet at Cadbury."

21. "The Nestle-Rowntree Deal: Bitter Battle, Sweet Result," *Mergers and Acquisitions*, September–October 1989, pp. 66–67.

22. E. S. Browning and M. Studer, "Nestle and Indosuez Launch Hostile Bid for Perrier in Contest with Agnellis," *The Wall Street Journal*, January 21, 1992, p. A3.

23. Ibid.

24. J. Templeman and R. A. Mecher, "Supermarket Darwinism: The Survival of the Fattest," *Business Week*, July 9, 1990, p. 42.

25. Gofton, "Has Cadbury Got His Finger on the Button?"

CASE III-9 NINTENDO OF AMERICA

1. D. Scheff, *Game Over*. New York: Random House, 1993.

2. J. Palmer, "Joy Toy—Nintendo's Future Not All Fun and Games," *Barron's*, June 26, 1989.

3. S. Moffat, "Can Nintendo Keep on Winning?" *Fortune*, November 5, 1990.

4. "Software Valley," *Far Eastern Economic Review*, October 8, 1992.

5. *Forbes*, December 15, 1993.

6. G. Eisenstadt, "That Is Where the Money Is," *Forbes*, January 18, 1993.

7. "The Amazing Video Game Boom," *Time*, September 27, 1993.

8. "Nintendo: Game Over?" *The Economist*, November 20, 1993.

9. "Sega!" *Business Week*, February 21, 1994.

10. R. Tetzeli, "Videogames: Serious Fun," *Fortune*, December 27, 1993.

▼ BIBLIOGRAPHY FOR READINGS

ABELL, D. F., *Defining The Business: The Starting Point of Strategic Planning.* Englewood Cliffs, N.J.: Prentice Hall, 1980.

ABERNATHY, W. J., & K. WAYNE, "Limits On the Learning Curve," *Harvard Business Review,* September–October 1974: 109–119.

ACKERMAN, R. W., *The Social Challenge to Business.* Cambridge, Mass.: Harvard University Press, 1975.

ADVISORY COMMITTEE ON INDUSTRIAL INNOVATION: FINAL REPORT. Washington, D.C.: U.S. Government Printing Office, 1979.

AGUILAR, F. J., *Scanning the Business Environment.* New York: Macmillan, 1967.

———, Interview With Kim Woo Chong, Harvard Business School, 1984.

ALLEN, M. P., "The Structure of Interorganizational Elite Cooptation: Interlocking Corporate Directorates," *American Sociological Review,* 1974: 393–406.

ALLEN, S. A., "Organizational Choices and General Management Influence Networks In Divisionalized Companies," *Academy Of Management Journal,* 1978: 341–365.

ALLISON, G. T., *Essence of Decision: Explaining the Cuban Missile Crisis.* Boston: Little, Brown, 1971.

ANSOFF, H. I., *Corporate Strategy: An Analytic Approach to Business Policy for Growth and Expansion.* New York: McGraw-Hill, 1965.

ARGYRIS, C., "Double Loop Learning In Organizations," *Harvard Business Review,* September–October 1977: 115–125.

———, & D. A. SCHON, *Organizational Learning: A Theory of Action Perspective.* Reading, Mass.: Addison-Wesley, 1978.

ASHBY, W. R., *Design for a Brain.* London: Chapman & Hall, 1954.

ASTLEY G., & C. J. FOMBRUN, "Collective Strategy: Social Ecology of Organizational Environments," *Academy of Management Review,* 1983: 576–587.

BACON, J., *Corporate Directorship Practices: Membership and Committees of The Board.* Conference Board and American Society Of Corporate Secretaries. Inc., 1973.

———, & J. K. BROWN, *Corporate Directorship Practices: Role, Selection and Legal Status of The Board.* New York: The Conference Board, 1975.

BADEN FULLER, C., ET AL., "National Or Global? The Study of Company Strategies and the European Market for Major Appliances," London Business School Centre for Business Strategy, Working Paper Series No. 28 (June 1987).

BARNARD, C. I., *The Functions of the Executive.* Cambridge, Mass.: Harvard University Press, 1938.

BARREYRE, P. Y., "The Concept of 'Impartition' Policy In High Speed Strategic Management." Working Paper, Institut d'Administration Des Entreprises, Grenoble, 1984.

———, "The Concept of Impartition Policies: A Different Approach to Vertical Integrating Strategies," *Strategic Management Journal,* 1988(9): 507–520.

———, & M. CARLE, "Impartition Policies: Growing Importance in Corporate Strategies and Applications to Production Sharing in Some World-Wide Industries." Paper Presented at Strategic Management Society Conference, Paris, 1983.

BARRIER, M., "Walton's Mountain," *Nation's Business,* April 1988: 18–26.

BARTLETT, C. A., "Proctor & Gamble Europe: Vizir Launch." Boston: Harvard Business School, Case Services #9-384-139.

———, & S. GHOSHAL, "Managing Across Borders: New Strategic Requirements," *Sloan Management Review,* Summer 1987: 7–17.

BATY, G. B., W. M. EVAN, & T. W. ROTHERMEL, "Personnel Flows As Interorganizational Relations," *Administrative Science Quarterly,* 1971: 430–443.

BAUER, R. A., 1. POOL, & L. A. DEXTER, *American Business and Public Policy.* New York: Atherton Press, 1968.

BAUMBACK, C., & J. MANCUSO, *Entrepreneurship and Venture Management.* Englewood Cliffs, N.J.: Prentice Hall, 1975.

BECKER, G., *Human Capital.* New York: National Bureau of Economic Research, 1964.

BEER, S., *Designing Freedom.* Toronto: CBC Publications, 1974.

BENNIS, W. G., & P. L. SLATER, *The Temporary Society.* New York: Harper & Row, 1968.

BERLEW, D. E. & D. T. HALL, "The Management of Tension in Organization: Some Preliminary Findings," *Industrial Management Review,* Fall 1964: 31–40.

BERNSTEIN, L., "Joint Ventures In the Light of Recent Antitrust Developments," *The Antitrust Bulletin,* 1965: 25–29.

BETTIS, R. A., "Performance Differences In Related and Unrelated Diversified Firms," *Strategic Management Journal,* 1981: 379–394.

BHIDE, A. "Hustle As Strategy," *Harvard Business Review,* September–October 1986.

BLOCK, Z, & I. C. MACMILLAN, *Corporate Venturing: Creating New Businesses Within the Firm.* Boston, Mass.: Harvard Business School Press, 1993.

BOSTON CONSULTING GROUP, *Perspective on Experience.* Boston, 1972.

———, *Strategy Alternatives for the British Motorcycle Industry.* London: Her Majesty's Stationery Office, 1975.

BOULDING, K. E., "The Ethics of Rational Decision," *Management Science*, 1966: 161–169.

BOWER, J. L., "Planning Within the Firm," *The American Economic Review*, 1970: 186–194.

BOWMAN, E. H., "Epistemology, Corporate Strategy, and Academe," *Sloan Management Review*, Winter 1974: 35–50.

BRAYBROOKE, D., "Skepticism of Wants, and Certain Subversive Effects of Corporations on American Values," in S. Hook, Ed., *Human Values and Economic Policy*. New York: New York University Press, 1967.

————, & C. E. LINDBLOM, *A Strategy of Decision: Policy Evaluation as a Social Process*. New York: Free Press, 1963.

BRENNER, S. N., & E. A. MOLANDER, "Is the Ethic of Business Changing?" *Harvard Business Review*, January–February 1977: 57–71.

BROOK, P., *The Empty Space*. Harmondsworth, Middlesex: Penguin Books, 1968.

BROOM, H. N., J. G. LONGNECKER & C. W. MOORE, *Small Business Management*. Cincinnati, Ohio: Southwest, 1983.

BRUNSSON, N., "The Irrationality of Action and Action Rationality: Decisions, Ideologies, and Organizational Actions," *Journal Of Management Studies*, 1982(1): 29–44.

BUCHELE, R. B., *Business Policy In Growing Firms*. San Francisco, Calif.: Chandler, 1967.

BURNS, T., "Micropolitics: Mechanisms of Institutional Change," *Administrative Science Quarterly*. December 1961: 257–281.

————, & G. M. STALKER, *The Management of Innovation*, 2d Ed. London: Tavistock, 1966.

BUSINESS ECONOMICS GROUP, W. R. Grace & Co., 1983.

BUSINESS WEEK, "Japan's Strategy for the '80s," December 14, 1981: 39–120.

————, "The Hollow Corporation," March 3, 1986: Supplement.

BUZZELL, R. D., B. T. GALE, & R. G. M. SULTAN, "Market Share—A Key to Profitability," *Harvard Business Review*, January–February 1975: 97–106.

BYRNE, J. A. "The Horizontal Corporation," Business Week, December 20, 1993: 76–81.

CAMPBELL, A. & M. GOOLD, *Strategy and Style: The Role of the Centre in Managing Diversified Corporations*. Oxford: Basil Blackwell, 1987.

CARLZON, J., *Moments of Truth*. New York: Ballinger Press, 1987.

CHANDLER, A. D., *Strategy and Structure: Chapters in the History of the Industrial Enterprise*. Cambridge, Mass.: M.I.T. Press, 1962.

CHANNON, D. F., "The Strategy, Structure and Financial Performance of the Service Industries," Working Paper, Manchester Business School, 1975.

CHEIT, E. F., "The New Place of Business: Why Managers Cultivate Social Responsibility," in E. F. Cheit, Ed., *The Business Establishment*. New York: John Wiley, 1964.

CHRISTENSON, C. R., K. R. ANDREWS, & J. L. BOWER, *Business Policy: Text and Cases*. Homewood, Ill.: Richard D. Irwin, 1978.

CLARK, B. R., *The Distinctive College: Antioch, Reed and Swarthmore*. Chicago: Aldine, 1970.

————, "The Organizational Saga In Higher Education,"*Administrative Science Quarterly*, 1972: 178–184.

CLARK, R. C., *The Japanese Company*. New Haven: Yale University Press, 1979.

COHEN, K. J, & R. M. CYERT, "Strategy: Formulation, Implementation and Monitoring," *The Journal of Business*, 1973: 349–367.

————, & J. P. OLSEN, "A Garbage Can Model of Organizational Choice," *Administrative Science Quarterly*, 1972: 1–25.

COHN, T., & R. A. LINDBERG, *How Management Is Different in Small Companies*. New York: American Management Association, 1972.

COLE, A. H., *Business Enterprise in Its Social Setting*. Cambridge, Mass.: Harvard University Press, 1959.

COLE, R. E., *Japanese Blue Collar: The Changing Tradition*. Berkeley: University of California Press, 1971.

————, *Work, Mobility and Participation*. Berkeley: University of California Press, 1979.

COPEMAN, G. H., *The Role of the Managing Director*. London: Business Publications, 1963.

COYNE, K. P., "Sustainable Competitive Advantage," *Business Horizons*, January–February 1986: 54–61.

CROZIER, M., *The Bureaucratic Phenomenon*. Chicago: University of Chicago Press, 1964.

CVAR, M. R., "Case Studies in Global Competition," in M. E. Porter, Ed., *Competition in Global Industries*. Boston: Harvard Business School Press, 1986.

CYERT, R. M., W. R. DILL, & J. G. MARCH, "The Role of Expectations In Business Decision Making." *Administrative Science Quarterly*, 1958: 307–340.

CYERT, R. M., & J. G. MARCH, *A Behavioral Theory of the Firm*. Englewood Cliffs, N.J.: Prentice Hall, 1963.

D'AVENI, R. A., *Hypercompetition*. New York: Free Press, 1994.

————, & A. ILLINICH, "Complex Patterns of Vertical Integration in the Forest Products Industry," *Academy of Management Journal*, 1992(35): 596–625.

D'AVENI, R. A., & D. RAVENSCRAFT, "Economics of Integration vs. Bureaucracy Costs: Does Vertical Integration Improve Performance?" *Academy of Management Journal*, 1994 (37): 1167–1206.

DAVIS, R.T., *Performance and Development of Field Sales Managers*. Boston: Harvard Business School, 1957.

DE GEUS, A. P., "Planning as Learning," *Harvard Business Review,* March–April 1988: 70–74.

DE PREE, M., *Leadership Is an Art.* New York: Doubleday, 1989.

DELBECQ, A. & A. C. FILLEY, *Program and Project Management in a Matrix Organization: A Case Study.* Madison, Wis.: University of Wisconsin, 1974.

DOERINGER, P., & M. PIORE, *Internal Labor Market and Manpower Analysis.* Lexington, Mass.: Lexington Books, 1971.

DOUGLAS, S. P., & Y. WIND, "The Myth of Globalization," *Columbia Journal of World Business,* Winter 1987: 19–29.

DRUCKER, P. F., *The Practice of Management.* New York: Harper & Row, 1954.

———, *Management: Tasks, Responsibilities, Practices.* New York: Harper & Row, 1974.

———, "Clouds Forming Across the Japanese Sun," *The Wall Street Journal,* July 13, 1982.

———, "The Coming of the New Organization," *Harvard Business Review,* Vol. 66, No. 1: 1988: 45–53.

EDWARDS, J. P., "Strategy Formulation as a Stylistic Process," *International Studies of Management and Organization,* Summer 1977: 13–27.

ELECTRONIC BUSINESS, "Services Get the Job Done," September 15, 1988: 87–90.

EPSTEIN, E. M., *The Corporation in American Politics.* Englewood Cliffs, N.J.: Prentice Hall, 1969.

———, "The Social Role of Business Enterprise in Britain: An American Perspective; Part II," *The Journal of Management Studies,* 1977: 281–316.

ESSAME, H., *Patton: A Study in Command.* New York: Charles Scribner's Sons, 1974.

EVERED, R., *So What Is Strategy?* Working Paper, Naval Postgraduate School, Monterey, 1980.

FARAGO, L., *Patton: Ordeal and Triumph.* New York: I. Obolensky, 1964.

FERGUSON, C., "Computers and the Coming of US Keiretsus," *Harvard Business Review,* July–August 1990.

FIRSIROTU, M. Y. S., "Strategic Turnaround as Cultural Revolution: The Case of Canadian National Express," Doctoral Dissertation, Faculty of Management, 1985.

FLEISHMANN, E. A., E. F. HARRIS, & H. E. BURT, *Leadership and Supervision in Industry: An Evaluation of Supervisory Training Program.* Columbus, Ohio: The Ohio State University, 1955.

FOCH, F., *Principles of War,* Translated By J. Demorinni. New York: AMS Press, 1970. First Published London: Chapman & Hall, 1918.

FORRESTER, J. W., "A New Corporate Design," *Sloan Management Review,* Fall 1965: 5–17.

———, "Counterintuitive Behavior of Social Systems," *Technology Review,* January 1971: 52–68.

FRANKLIN, B., *Poor Richard's Almanac.* New York: Ballantine Books, 1977. First Published, Century Company,1898.

FRIEDMAN, M., *Capitalism and Freedom.* Chicago: University of Chicago Press, 1962.

———, "A Friedman Doctrine: The Social Responsibility of Business Is to Increase Its Profits," *The New York Times Magazine,* September 13, 1970.

FRITZ, R., *The Path of Least Resistance.* New York: Ballantine, 1989.

———, *Creating.* New York: Ballantine, 1990.

GALBRAITH, J. K., *American Capitalism: The Concept of Countervailing Power.* Boston: Houghton Mifflin, 1952.

———, *The New Industrial State.* Boston: Houghton Mifflin, 1967.

GALBRAITH, J. R., *Organization Design.* Reading, Mass.: Addison-Wesley, 1977.

———, "Strategy and Organization Planning," *Human Resource Management,* 1983: 63–77.

———, & D. NATHANSON, *Strategy Implementation.* St. Paul, Minn.: West Publishing, 1978.

GARDNER, J. W., "The Anti-Leadership Vaccine," In *Carnegie Corporation of New York Annual Report,* 1965.

GARSON, G. D., "The Codetermination Model of Worker's Participation: Where Is It Leading?" *Sloan Management Review,* Spring 1977: 63–78.

GERTH, H. H., & C. WRIGHT MILLS, eds. *From Max Webber: Essays in Sociology.* New York: Oxford University Press, 1958.

GHISELLI, E. E., "Managerial Talent," In D. Wolfe, Ed., *The Discovery of Talent.* Cambridge, Mass.: Harvard University Press, 1969.

GILDER, G., *Wealth and Poverty.* New York: Basic Books, 1981.

GILMORE, F. F., "Overcoming the Perils of Advocacy in Corporate Planning," *California Management Review,* Spring 1973: 127–137.

GLUECK, W. F., *Business Policy and Strategic Management.* New York: McGraw Hill, 1980.

GOSSELIN, R., *A Study of the Interdependence of Medical Specialists in Quebec Teaching Hospitals.* Ph.D. thesis, McGill University, 1978.

GREEN, P., *Alexander the Great.* New York: Frederick A. Praeger, 1970.

GREENLEAF, R. K., *Servant Leadership: A Journey Into the Nature of Legitimate Power and Greatness.* New York: Paulist Press, 1977.

GREINER, L. E., "Evolution and Revolution As Organizations Grow," *Harvard Business Review,* July–August 1972: 37–46.

———, "Senior Executives As Strategic Actors," *New Management,* vol. 1, no. 2, Summer 1983.

GRINYER, P. H., & J. C. SPENDER, *Turnaround—Management Recipes For Strategic Success*. New York: Associated Business Press, 1979.

GROSS, W., "Coping with Radical Competition," in A. Gross & W. Gross, Eds., *Business Policy: Selected Readings and Editorial Commentaries*. New York: Ronald Press, 1967.

GROVE, A., *High Output Management*. New York: Random House, 1983.

GUEST, R. H., "Of Time and the Foreman," *Personnel*, May 1956: 478–486.

HAITANI, K., "Changing Characteristics of the Japanese Employment System," *Asian Survey*, 1978: 1029–1045.

HAMERMESH, R. G., M. J. ANDERSON, JR. & J. E. HARRIS, "Strategies for Low Market Share Business," *Harvard Business Review*, May–June 1978: 95–102.

HART, B. H. L., *Strategy*. New York: Frederick A. Praeger, 1954.

HASPESLAGH, P., "Portfolio Planning: Uses and Limits," *Harvard Business Review*, January–February 1982: 58–73.

HATTORI, I., "A Proposition on Efficient Decision-Making in Japanese Corporation," *Management Japan*, Autumn 1977: 14–20.

HAYES, R. H. & W. J. ABERNATHY, "Managing Our Way to Economic Decline," *Harvard Business Review*, July–August 1980: 67–77.

———, & D. A. GARVIN, "Managing As If Tomorrow Mattered," *Harvard Business Review*, May–June 1982: 70–79.

HAZAMA, H., "Characteristics of Japanese-Style Management," *Japanese Economic Studies*, Spring–Summer 1978: 110–173.

HEDBERG, B. L. T., "How Organizations Learn and Unlearn," in P. C. Nystrom and W. H. Starbuck, Eds., *Handbook of Organizational Design*, Volume 1. New York: Oxford University Press, 1981.

———, & S.A. JÖNSSON, "Designing Semi-Confusing Information Systems for Organizations in Changing Environments," *Accounting Organizations and Society*, 1978: 47–64.

———, P. C. NYSTROM, & W. H. STARBUCK, "Camping on Seesaws: Prescriptions for a Self-Designing Organization," *Administrative Science Quarterly*, 1976: 41–65.

HICKSON, D. J., C. A. LEE, R. E. SCHNECK & J. M. PENNINGS, "A Strategic Contingencies' Theory of Intraorganizational Power," *Administrative Science Quarterly*, 1971: 216–229.

HIRSCH, P. M., "Organizational Effectiveness and the Institutional Environment," *Administrative Science Quarterly*, 1975: 327–344.

HOFER, C. W., & D. SCHENDEL, *Strategy Formulation: Analytical Concepts*. St. Paul, Minn.: West Publishing, 1978.

HOSMER, A., "Small Manufacturing Enterprises," *Harvard Business Review*, November–December 1957: 111–122.

HOUSE OF REPRESENTATIVES, Staff Report to the Antitrust Subcommittee of the Committee on the Judiciary, *Interlocks In Corporate Management*. Washington, D.C.: U.S. Government Printing Office, 1965.

HOUT, T., M. E. PORTER, & E. RUDDEN, "How Global Companies Win Out," *Harvard Business Review*, September–October 1982: 98–108.

HUGHES, T., "The Inventive Continuum," *Science 84*, November 1984.

HUNT, R. G., "Technology and Organization," *Academy of Management Journal*, 1970: 235–252.

IACOCCA, L., WITH W. NOVAK, *Iacocca: An Autobiography*. New York: Bantam Books, 1984.

IMAI, K., I. NONAKA, & H. TAKEUCHI, "Managing the New Product Development Process: How Japanese Companies Learn and Unlearn," In K. B. Clark, R. H. Hayes, and C. Lorenz, Eds., *The Uneasy Alliance*. Boston: Harvard Business School Press, 1985.

IRVING, D., *The Trail of the Fox*. New York: E. P. Dutton, 1977.

JACOBS, D., "Dependency and Vulnerability: An Exchange Approach to the Control of Organizations," *Administrative Science Quarterly*, 1974: 45–59.

JAMES, D. C., *The Years of MacArthur, 1941–1945*. Boston: Houghton Mifflin, 1970.

JANIS, I., *Victims of Group Think*. Boston: Houghton Mifflin, 1972.

JAY, A., *Management and Machiavelli*. New York: Penguin Books, 1970.

JENKINS, C., *Power at the Top*. Westport, Conn.: Greenwood Press, 1976.

JENNINGS, E. E., *The Mobile Manager*. Ann Arbor: University Of Michigan, 1967.

Jensen, M., "The Eclipse of the Public Corporation," *Harvard Business Review*, September–October 1989.

JOHNSON, S. C., & C. JONES, "How to Organize for New Products," *Harvard Business Review*, May–June 1957:49–62.

JOMINI, A. H., *Art of War*, Translated by G. H. Mendell and W. P. Craighill. Westport, Conn.: Greenwood Press, 1971. Original Philadelphia: J. B. Lippincott, 1862.

JÖNSSON, S. A. & R. A. LUNDIN, "Myths and Wishful Thinking as Management Tools," in P. C. Nystrom and W. H. Starbuck Eds., *Prescriptive Models of Organizations*. Amsterdam: North-Holland, 1977.

JORDAN, W. A., "Producer Protection Prior Market Structure and the Effects of Government Regulation," *Journal of Law and Economics*, 1972.

KAGONO, T., I. NONAKA, K. SAKAKIBARA, & A. OKUMURA, *Strategic vs. Evolutionary Management: A U.S.-Japan Comparison of Strategy and Organization*. Amsterdam: North-Holland, 1985.

KAHN, R. L., D. M. WOLFE, R. P. QUINN, J. D. SNOEK, & R. A. ROSENTHAL, *Organizational Stress.* New York: John Wiley, 1964.

KAMI, M. J. & J. E. ROSS, *Corporate Management In Crisis: Why the Mighty Fall.* Englewood Cliffs, N.J.: Prentice Hall, 1973.

KANO, T., "Comparative Study of Strategy, Structure and Long-Range Planning in Japan and in the United States," *Management Japan,* 1980(1): 20–34.

KANTER, R. M. *The Change Masters.* New York: Simon & Schuster, 1983.

KATZ, R. L., *Cases and Concepts in Corporate Strategy.* Englewood Cliffs, N.J.: Prentice Hall, 1970.

——, "Time and Work: Towards an Integrative Perspective," in B. M. Staw and L. L. Cummings, Eds., *Research In Organizational Behavior,* Vol. 1. Greenwich, Conn.: JAI Press, 1980.

KIDDER, T., *The Soul of a New Machine.* Boston: Little, Brown, 1981.

KIECHEL, W., III, "Sniping At Strategic Planning (interview with himself)," *Planning Review,* May 1984: 8–11.

KONO, T., "Comparative Study of Strategy, Structure and Long-Range Planning in Japan and in the United States," *Management Japan,* Spring 1980: 20–34.

KOTLER, P., & R. SINGH, "Marketing Warfare in the 1980s," *Journal of Business Strategy,* Winter 1981: 30–41.

KOTTER, J. P., & L. A. SCHLESINGER, "Choosing Strategies for Change," *Harvard Business Review,* March–April 1979: 106–114.

KUHN, T., *The Structure of Scientific Revolutions.* Chicago: University of Chicago Press, 1970.

LAND, E., "People Should Want More From Life . . ." *Forbes,* June 1, 1975.

LAPIERRE, L., "Le Changement Stratégique: Un Rêve En Quête De Réel." Ph.D. Management Policy Course Paper, McGill University, Canada, 1980.

LEARNED, E. P., C. R. CHRISTIANSEN, K. R. ANDREWS & W. D. GUTH, *Business Policy: Text and Cases.* Homewood, Ill.: Richard D. Irwin, 1965.

——, D. N. ULRICH, & D. R. BOOZ, *Executive Action.* Boston: Harvard Business School, 1951.

LENIN, V. I., *Collected Works of V.I. Lenin,* Edited and Annotated. New York: International Publishers, 1927.

LEVINSON, H., "On Becoming a Middle-Aged Manager," *Harvard Business Review,* July–August 1969: 51–60.

——, *Executive Stress.* New York: Harper & Row, 1970.

LEVITT, T., "Marketing Myopia," *Harvard Business Review,* July–August 1960: 45–56.

——, "Why Business Always Loses," *Harvard Business Review,* March–April 1968: 81–89.

——, "Industrialization of Service," *Harvard Business Review,* September–October 1976: 63–74.

——, "Marketing Success Through Differentiation—Of Anything," *Harvard Business Review,* January–February 1980: 83–91.

——, "The Globalization of Markets," *Harvard Business Review,* May–June 1983: 92–102.

——, *The Marketing Imagination.* New York: Free Press, 1983.

LEWIN, K., *Field Theory In Social Science.* New York: Harper & Row, 1951.

LIKERT, R., *New Patterns of Management.* New York: McGraw-Hill, 1969.

LINDBLOM, C. E., "The Science of 'Muddling Through,'" *Public Administration Review,* 1959: 79–88.

——, *The Policy-Making Process.* Englewood Cliffs, N.J.: Prentice Hall, 1968.

LITTLE, A. D., INC., "*Transportation Planning In the District of Columbia, 1955–65: A Review and Critique,*" Report to the Policy Advisory Committee to the District Commissioners. Washington, D.C.: U.S. Government Printing Office, 1966.

LODGE, G. C., *The New American Ideology.* New York: Alfred A. Knopf, 1975.

LOHR, S., "Japan Struggling with Itself," *The New York Times,* June 13, 1982.

MACAVOY, P. W., *The Economic Effects of Regulation.* Cambridge, Mass.: M.I.T. Press, 1965.

MACMILLAN, I.C., "Seizing Competitive Initiative," *Journal of Business Strategy,* Spring 1982: 43–57.

——, "Preemptive Strategies," *Journal of Business Strategy,* Fall 1983: 16–26.

——, & P. E. JONES, "Designing Organizations to Compete," *Journal of Business Strategy,* Spring 1984: 11–26.

——, M. McCAFFERY & G. VAN WIJK, "Competitors' Responses to Easily Imitated New Products—Exploring Commercial Banking Product Introductions," *Strategic Management Journal,* 1985: 75–86.

MACE, M. L. & G. G. MONTGOMERY, *Management Problems of Corporate Acquisitions.* Boston: Harvard Business School, 1962.

MACHIAVELLI, N., *The Prince, and the Discourses.* New York: Modern Library, 1950.

MACKWORTH, N. H., "Originality," in D. Wolfe, ed., *The Discovery of Talent.* Cambridge, Mass.: Harvard University Press, 1969.

MAETERLINCK, M., *The Life of the Bee.* New York: Dodd, Mead, 1918.

MAGEE, J. F., "Decision Trees for Decision Making," *Harvard Business Review,* July–August, 1964: 126–138.

——, *Desirable Characteristics of Models in Planning,* a paper delivered at the Symposium on the Role of Economic Models in Policy Formulation, sponsored by the Department Of Housing and Urban Development, Office of Emergency Planning, National Resource Evaluation Center, Washington, D.C., October, 1966.

MAJONE, G., "The Use of Policy Analysis," in *The Future and the Past: Essays on Programs,* Russell Sage Foundation Annual Report, 1976–1977.

MALINEY, G. J., "The Choice of Organizational Form . . ." *Strategic Management Journal,* 1992(13): 559–584.

MAO TSE-TUNG, *Selected Military Writings, 1928–1949.* San Francisco: China Books, 1967.

MARCH, J. G., & J. P. OLSEN, *Ambiguity and Choice in Organizations.* Bergen, Norway: Universitetsforlaget, 1976.

———, & H. A. SIMON, *Organizations.* New York: John Wiley, 1958.

MARSHALL, G. L., *Predicting Executive Achievement.* Ph.D. thesis, Harvard Business School, 1964.

MARTIN, L. C. "How Beatrice Foods Sneaked Up on $5 Billion," *Fortune,* April 1976: 119–129.

MASON, R. & I. MITROFF, *Challenging Strategic Planning Assumptions.* New York: John Wiley, 1981.

MATLOFF, M. & E. M. SNELL, *Strategic Planning for Coalition Warfare (1941–42).* Washington, D. C.: Office of Chief of Military History, Department of the Army, 1953.

MAYO, E., *The Social Problems of an Industrial Civilization.* Boston: Harvard Business School, 1945.

McCLELLAND, D.C., "The Two Faces of Power," *Journal of International Affairs,* 1970: 29–47.

McDONALD, J., *Strategy in Poker, Business and War.* New York: W.W. Norton, 1950.

McINTYRE, S. H., "Obstacles to Corporate Innovation," *Business Horizons,* January–February 1982: 23–28.

MECHANIC, D., "Sources of Power of Lower Participants In Complex Organizations," *Administrative Science Quarterly,* 1962: 349–364.

MILES, R. & C. SNOW, "Organizations, New Concepts and New Forms," *California Management Review,* Spring 1986: 62–73.

———, & H. J. COLEMAN, JR., "Managing 21st Century Network Organizations," *Organization Dynamics,* 1992.

MILLER, D., & P. H. FRIESEN, "Archetypes of Strategy Formulation," *Management Science,* May 1978: 921–933.

———, *Organizations: A Quantum View.* Englewood Cliffs, N.J.: Prentice Hall, 1984.

———, & M. KETS DE VRIES, *The Neurotic Organization.* San Francisco: Jossey-Bass, 1984.

———, *Unstable at the Top.* New York: New American Library, 1987.

———, & H. MINTZBERG, *Strategy Formulation in Context: Some Tentative Models.* Working Paper, McGill University, 1974.

MILLER, L., *American Spirit: Visions of a New Corporate Culture.* New York: William Morrow, 1984.

MILLS, D. Q., *Rebirth of the Corporation.* New York: John Wiley, 1991.

MINTZBERG, H., "Research on Strategy-Making," *Academy of Management Proceedings,* 1972: 90–94.

———, *The Nature of Managerial Work.* New York: Harper & Row, 1973.

———, "Strategy Making in Three Modes," *California Management Review,* Winter 1973b: 44–53.

———, "The Manager's Job: Folklore and Fact," *Harvard Business Review,* July–August 1975: 49–61.

———, "Generic Strategies: Toward a Comprehensive Framework," *Advances in Strategic Management,* Vol. 5, pp. 1–67. Greenwich, Conn.: JAI Press, 1988.

———, "Crafting Strategy," *Harvard Business Review,* July–August 1987: 66–75.

———, D. RAÌSINGNANÌ, & A. THÉORÉT, "The Structure of 'Unstructured' Decision Processes," *Administrative Science Quarterly,* 1976: 246–275.

———, & J. A. WATERS, "Tracking Strategy in an Entrepreneurial Firm," *Academy of Management Journal,* 1982: 465–499.

———, "Of Strategies, Deliberate and Emergent," *Strategic Management Journal,* 1985: 257–272.

MITROFF, I., *Break-Away Thinking.* New York: John Wiley, 1988.

MONTGOMERY, B. L., *The Memoirs of Field-Marshal The Viscount Montgomery of Alamein.* Cleveland: World Publishing, 1958.

MORITANI, M., *Japanese Technology: Getting the Best for the Least.* Tokyo: Simul Press, 1981.

MOYER, R. C., "Berle and Means Revisited: The Conglomerate Merger," *Business and Society,* Spring 1970: 20–29.

NADLER, D. A. & E. E. LAWLER, III, "Motivation—A Diagnostic Approach," in J. R. Hackman, E. E. Lawler, III, & L. W. Porter, Eds., *Perspective on Behavior in Organizations.* New York: McGraw-Hill. 1977.

NADLER, D., & M. L. TUSHMAN, *Strategic Organization Design.* Homewood, Ill.: Scott Foresman, 1986.

NAISBITT, J., *Megatrends.* New York: Warner Books, 1982.

NAPOLEON, I., "Maximes de Guerre," in T. R. Phillips, Ed., *Roots of Strategy.* Harrisburg, Pa.: Military Service Publishing, 1940.

NATHANSON, D., & J. CASSANO, "Organization Diversity and Performance," *The Wharton Magazine,* Summer 1982: 18–26.

NEUSTADT, R. E., *Presidential Power: The Politics of Leadership.* New York: John Wiley, 1960.

NOËL, A., "Strategic Cores and Magnificent Obsessions: Discovering Strategy Formation through Daily Activities of CEOs," *Strategic Management Journal* 1989(10): 33–49.

NONAKA, I., "Creating Organizational Order Out of Chaos: Self-Renewal in Japanese Firms," *California Management Review*, Spring 1988: 57–73.

NORMANN, R., *Management for Growth*, translated by N. Adler. New York: John Wiley, 1977.

NYSTROM, P. C., B. L. T. HEDBERG, & W. H. STARBUCK, "Interacting Processes as Organization Designs," in R. H. Kiltmann, L. R. Pondy, & D. P. Slevin, eds., *The Management of Organization Design*, Vol. 1. New York: Elsevier North-Holland, 1976.

OGILVY, D., *Ogilvy on Advertising*. New York: Crown, 1983.

OHMAE, K., *The Mind of the Strategist*. New York: McGraw-Hill, 1982.

ONO, H., "Nihonteki Keiei Shisutemu to Jinji Kettei Shisutemu" ("Japanese Management System and Personnel Decisions"), *Soshiki Kagaku*, 1976: 22–32.

OUCHI, W. G., "Market, Bureaucracies and Clans," *Administrative Science Quarterly*, 1980: 129–140.

————, *Theory Z*. Reading, Mass.: Addison-Wesley, 1981.

————, & A. M. JAEGER, "Type Z Organization: Stability in the Midst of Mobility," *Academy of Management Review*, 1978: 305–314.

————, & B. JOHNSON, "Types of Organizational Control and Their Relationship to Emotional Well Being," *Administrative Science Quarterly*, 1978: 293–317.

PARSONS, T., *Structure and Process in Modern Societies*. Glencoe, Ill.: Free Press, 1960.

PASCALE, R. T., "Perspectives on Strategy: The Real Story Behind Honda's Success," *California Management Review*, Spring 1984: 47–72.

PAUL, N. L., "The Use of Empathy in the Resolution of Grief," in *Perspective in Biology and Medicine*. Chicago: University of Chicago Press, 1967.

PENCE, C. C., *How Venture Capitalists Make Venture Decisions*. Ann Arbor, Mich.: UMI Research Press, 1982.

PERROW, C., "The Analysis of Goals in Complex Organizations," *American Sociological Review*, 1961: 854–866.

————, *Organizational Analysis: A Sociological Review*. Belmont, Calif.: Wadsworth, 1970.

————, *Complex Organizations: A Critical Essay*, New York: Scott, Foresman, 1972.

PETERS, T. J., "A Style for All Seasons," *Executive*, Summer 1980: 12–16.

————, & R. H. WATERMAN, *In Search of Excellence: Lessons from America's Best Run Companies*. New York: Harper & Row, 1982.

PFEFFER, J., "Size and Composition of Corporate Boards of Directors: The Organization and Its Environment," *Administrative Science Quarterly*, 1972a: 218–228.

————, "Merger as a Response to Organizational Interdependence," *Administrative Science Quarterly*, 1972b: 382–394.

————, "Size, Composition and Function of Hospital Boards of Directors: A Study of Organization-Environment Linkage," *Administrative Science Quarterly*, 1973: 349–364.

————, "Administrative Regulation and Licensing: Social Problem or Solution?" *Social Problems*, 1974: 468–479.

————, *Management as Symbolic Action: The Creation and Maintenance of Organizational Paradigms*. Working Paper, Stanford University, 1979.

————, & H. LEBLEBICI, "Executive Recruitment and the Development of Interfirm Organizations," *Administrative Science Quarterly*, 1973: 449–461.

————, & P. NOWAK, "Patterns of Joint Venture Activity: Implication for Antitrust Policy," *The Antitrust Bulletin*, 1976: 315–339.

————, "Joint Ventures and Interorganizational Interdependence," *Administrative Science Quarterly*, 1976b: 398–418.

————, *Organizational Context and Interorganizational Linkages Among Corporations*. Working Paper, University of California at Berkeley, no date.

————, & H. LEBLEBICI, "The Effect of Uncertainty on the Use of Social Influence in Organizational Decision-Making," *Administrative Science Quarterly*, 1976: 227–245.

PFIFFNER, J. M., "Administrative Rationality," *Public Administration Review*, 1960: 125–132.

PHILLIPS, T. R. ed., *Roots of Strategy*. Harrisburg, Pa.: Military Service Publishing, 1940.

PORTER, M. E., *Competitive Strategy: Techniques for Analyzing Industries and Competitors*. New York: Free Press, 1980.

————, *Competitive Advantage: Creating and Sustaining Superior Performance*. New York: Free Press, 1985.

————, "Generic Competitive Strategies," in M. E. Porter, *Competitive Advantage*, pp. 34–46. New York: Free Press, 1985.

————, "Competition in Global Industries: A Conceptual Framework," in M. E. Porter, ed., *Competition in Global Industries*. Boston: Harvard Business School Press, 1986.

————, "From Competitive Advantage to Corporate Strategy," *Harvard Business Review*, May–June 1987: 43–59.

POSNER, B., & B. BURLINGHAM, "The Hottest Entrepreneur in America," *Inc.*, January 1988, 44–58.

POSNER, R. A., "Theories of Economic Regulation," *Bell Journal of Economics and Management Science*, 1974: 335–358.

PRAHALAD, C., & G. HAMEL, "The Core Competence of the Corporation," *Harvard Business Review*, May–June 1990: 79–91.

PRICE, J. L., "The Impact of Governing Boards on Organizational Effectiveness and Morale," *Administrative Science Quarterly*, 1963: 361–378.

PUCIK, V., "Getting Ahead In Japan," *The Japanese Economic Journal*, 1981: 970–971.

————, "Promotions and Intra-Organizational Status Differentiation among Japanese Managers," *The Academy of Management Proceedings*, 1981: 59–63.

PURKAYASTHA, D., "*Note on the Motorcycle Industry 1975.*" Copyrighted Case, Harvard Business School, 1981.

QUINN, J. B., "Strategic Goals: Process and Politics," *Sloan Management Review*, Fall 1977: 21–37.

————, *Strategies for Change: Logical Incrementalism.* Homewood, Ill.: Richard D. Irwin, 1980.

————, *Intelligent Enterprise.* New York: Free Press, 1992.

————, "Leveraging Knowledge and Service Based Strategies Through Strategic Outsourcing," In *Intelligent Enterprise.* New York: Free Press. 1992.

————, T. DOORLEY, & P. C. PAQUETTE, "Technology In Services: Rethinking Strategic Focus," *Sloan Management Review*, January 1990.

RAPHAEL, R., *Edges.* New York: Alfred A. Knopf, 1976.

REESER, C., "Some Potential Human Problems in the Project Form of Organization," *Academy of Management Journal*, 1969: 459–467.

REID, S. R., *Mergers, Managers, and the Economy.* New York: McGraw-Hill, 1968.

RHENMAN, E., *Organization Theory for Long-Range Planning.* New York: John Wiley, 1973.

ROHLEN, T. P., *For Harmony and Strength: Japanese White-Collar Organization in Anthropological Perspective.* Berkeley: University Of California Press, 1974.

ROSNER, M., *Principle Types and Problems of Direct Democracy in the Kibbutz.* Working Paper, Social Research Center on the Kibbutz, Givat Haviva, Israel, 1969.

ROSS, I., "How Lawless Are the Big Companies?" *Fortune*, December 1, 1980: 56–64.

ROSSOTTI, C. O., *Two Concepts of Long-Range Planning.* Boston: The Management Consulting Group, The Boston Safe Deposit & Trust Company, no date.

RUMELT, R. P., *Strategy, Structure and Economic Performance.* Boston: Harvard Business School Press, 1974.

————, "A Teaching Plan for Strategy Alternatives for the British Motorcycle Industry," in *Japanese Business: Business Policy.* New York: The Japan Society, 1980.

————, "Diversification Strategy and Profitability," *Strategic Management Journal*, 1982: 359–370.

————, Strategic Management Society Conference, Montreal, October 1982.

SAHLMAN, W. A., & H. H. STEVENSON, "Capital Market Myopia," *Journal of Business Venturing*, Winter 1985: 7–30.

SAKIYA, T., "The Story of Honda's Founders," *Asahi Evening News*, June–August, 1979.

————, *Honda Motor: The Men, The Management, The Machines.* Tokyo, Japan: Kadonsha International, 1982.

SALTER, M. S., & W. A. WEINHOLD, *Diversification Through Acquisition.* New York: Free Press, 1979.

SAYLES, L. R., *Managerial Behavior: Administration In Complex Organizations.* New York: McGraw-Hill, 1964.

————, "How Graduates Scare Bosses," *Careers Today*, January 1969.

————, *The Working Leader*, New York: Free Press, 1993.

SCHEIN, E., *Organizational Culture and Leadership.* San Francisco: Jossey-Bass, 1985.

SCHELLING, T. C., *The Strategy of Conflict*, 2d ed. Cambridge, Mass.: Harvard University Press, 1980.

SCHENDEL, D. G., R. PATTON, & J. RIGGS, "Corporate Turnaround Strategies: A Study of Profit Decline and Recovery," *Journal of General Management*, Spring 1976: 3–11.

SCOTT, W. E., "Activation Theory and Task Design," *Organizational Behavior and Human Performance.* September 1966: 3–30.

SELZNICK, P., *TVA and the Grass Roots.* Berkeley: University Of California Press, 1949.

————, *Leadership in Administration: A Sociological Interpretation.* New York: Harper & Row, 1957

SENGE, P. *The Fifth Discipline: The Art and Practice of the Learning Organization.* New York: Doubleday/Currency, 1990.

SHUBIK, M., *Games for Society, Business, and War: Towards a Theory of Gaming.* New York: Elsevier, 1975.

SIMON, H. A., "The Architecture of Complexity," *Proceedings of the American Philosophical Society*, 1962(106): 122–137.

SIMON, M. A., "On the Concept of Organizational Goals," *Administrative Science Quarterly*, 1964–1965: 1–22.

SIMONS, R., "The Role of Management Control Systems in Creating Competitive Advantage: New Perspectives," *Accounting, Organizations and Society*, 1990(15): 127–143.

————, "Strategic Orientation and Top Management Attention to Control Systems," *Strategic Management Journal*, 1991(12): 49–62.

SMITH, L., "The Boardroom Is Becoming a Different Scene," *Fortune*, May 8, 1978: 150–88.

SMITH, W. R., "Product Differentiation and Market Segmentation as Alternative Marketing Strategies," *Journal of Marketing*, July 1956: 3–8.

SOLZHENITSYN, A., "Why the West Has Succumbed to Cowardice," *The Montreal Star: News and Review*, June 10, 1978.

SPEER, A., *Inside the Third Reich.* New York: Macmillan, 1970.

SPENCER, F. C., "Deductive Reasoning in the Lifelong Continuing Education of a Cardiovascular Surgeon," *Archives of Surgery*, 1976: 1177–1183.

SPENDER, J. C., *Industry Recipes: The Nature and Sources of Managerial Judgement*. London: Basil Blackwell, 1989.

STALK, G., JR., "Time: The Next Source of Competitive Advantage," *Harvard Business Review*, July–August 1988: 41–51.

STARBUCK, W. H., "Organizations and Their Environments," in M. D. Dunnette, ed., *Handbook of Industrial and Organizational Psychology*. Chicago: Rand McNally, 1976.

STARBUCK, W. H. & B. L. T. HEDBERG, "Saving an Organization from a Stagnating Environment," in H. B. Thorelli, ed., *Strategy + Structure = Performance*. Bloomington: Indiana University Press, 1977.

THE STATE OF SMALL BUSINESS, A REPORT TO THE PRESIDENT. Washington, D.C.: U.S. Government Printing Office, 1984.

STERN, L. W., B. STERNTHAL, & C. S. CRAIG, "Managing Conflict in Distribution Channels: A Laboratory Study," *Journal of Marketing Research*, 1973: 169–179.

STEVENSON, "Defining Corporate Strengths and Weaknesses," *Sloan Management Review*, Spring 1976: 51–68.

STEVENSON, W., *A Man Called Intrepid: The Secret War*. New York: Harcourt Brace Jovanovich, 1976.

STEWART, R., *Managers and Their Jobs*. London: Macmillan, 1967.

STIGLER, C. J., "The Theory of Economic Regulation," *Bell Journal of Economics and Management Science*, 1971: 3–21.

SUN TZU, *The Art of War*, translated by S. B. Griffith. New York: Oxford University Press, 1963. Original 500 B.C.

TAKEUCHI, H., & I. NONAKA, "The New New Product Development Game," *Harvard Business Review*, January–February 1986: 137–146.

TAYLOR, W. H., "The Nature of Policy Making In Universities," *The Canadian Journal of Higher Education*, 1983: 17–32.

TECHNOLOGICAL INNOVATION: ITS ENVIRONMENT AND MANAGEMENT. Washington, D.C.: U.S. Government Printing Office, 1967.

THOMPSON, J. D., *Organizations in Action*. New York: McGraw-Hill, 1967.

THOMPSON, V. A., *Modern Organizations*. New York: Alfred A. Knopf, 1961.

TILLES, S., "How to Evaluate Corporate Strategy," *Harvard Business Review*, July–August 1963: 111–121.

TIME, "The Most Basic Form of Creativity," June 26, 1972.

TOFFLER, A., *Future Shock*. New York: Bantam Books, 1970.

TREGOE, B., & I. ZIMMERMAN, *Top Management Strategy*. New York: Simon & Schuster, 1980.

TSUJI, K., "Decision-Making in the Japanese Government: A Study of Ringisei," in R. E. Wards, ed., *Political Development in Modern Japan*, Princeton: Princeton University Press, 1968.

TSURUMI, Y., *Multinational Management: Business Strategy and Government Policy*. Cambridge, Mass.: Ballinger, 1977.

TUCHMAN, B. W., *The Guns of August*. New York: Macmillan, 1962.

TURNER, D., & M. CRAWFORD, "Managing Current and Future Competitive Performance: The Role of Competence." Kensington, Australia, University of New South Wales, Australian Graduate School of Management, Center for Corporate Change, 1992.

URBAN, G. L., R. CARTER, S. GASKIN, & Z. MUCHA, "Market Share Rewards to Pioneering Brands," *Management Science*, June 1986(6): 645–659.

VANCIL, R. F., "Strategy Formulation in Complex Organizations," *Sloan Management Review*, Winter 1976: 1–18.

———, & P. LORANGE, "Strategic Planning in Diversified Companies," *Harvard Business Review*, January–February 1975: 81–90.

VAN DOREN, M., *Liberal Education*, Boston: Beacon Press, 1967.

VARNER, V. J. & J. I. ALGER, eds., *History of the Military Art: Notes for the Course*. West Point, N.Y.: U.S. Military Academy, 1978.

VICKERS, G., "Is Adaptability Enough?" *Behavioral Science*, 1959: 219–234.

VOGEL, E., *Japan As Number One*. Cambridge, Mass.: Harvard University Press, 1979.

VON BÜLOW, D. F., *The Spirit of the Modern System of War*, translated by C. M. DeMartemont. London: C. Mercier, 1806.

VON CLAUSEWITZ, C., *On War*, translated by M. Howard and P. Paret. Princeton, N.J.: Princeton University Press, 1976.

VON HIPPEL, E., "Get New Products from Customers," *Harvard Business Review*, March–April 1982: 117–122.

VON NEUMANN, J. & O. MORGENSTERN, *Theory of Games and Economic Behavior*. Princeton, N.J.: Princeton University Press, 1944.

WACK, P. "Scenarios: Uncharted Waters Ahead," *Harvard Business Review*, September–October 1985: 73–89.

WARD, L. B., *Analysis of 1969 Alumni Questionnaire Returns*. Unpublished Report, Harvard Business School, 1970.

WATERMAN, R. H., JR., T. J. PETERS & J. R. PHILLIPS, "Structure Is Not Organization," *Business Horizons*, June 1980: 14–26.

WEBER, M., "The Three Types of Legitimate Rule," translated by H. Gerth, in A. Etzioni, ed., *A Sociological Reader on Complex Organizations*. New York: Holt, Rinehart and Winston, 1969.

WEICK, K. E., "Educational Organizations As Loosely Coupled Systems," *Administrative Science Quarterly*, 1976: 1–19.

————, *The Social Psychology of Organizing*. Reading, Mass: Addison-Wesley, 1979.

WESTLEY, F., & H. MINTZBERG, "Visionary Leadership and Strategic Management," *Strategic Management Journal*, 1989: 11–32.

WHEELWRIGHT, S. C., "Japan—Where Operations Really Are Strategic," *Harvard Business Review*, July–August 1981: 67–74.

WHITE, T. H., *In Search of History: A Personal Adventure*. New York: Warner Books, 1978.

WHITEHEAD, A. N., *Aims of Education and Other Essays*. New York: Macmillan, 1929.

WHYTE, W. F., *Street Corner Society*. Chicago: University of Chicago Press, 1955.

WILLIAMSON, O. E., *Markets and Hierarchies: Analysis and Antitrust Implications*. New York: Free Press, 1975.

————, *The Economic Institutions of Capitalism*. New York: Free Press, 1985.

WISE, D., "Apple's New Crusade," *Business Week*, November 26, 1984.

WITTE, E., "Field Research on Complex Decision-Making Processes—The Phase Theorem," *International Studies of Management and Organization*, Summer 1972: 156–182.

WODARSKI, J. S., R. L. HAMBLIN, D. R. BUCKHOLDT, & D. E. FERRITOR, "Individual Consequences versus Different Shared Consequences Contingent on the Performance of Low-Achieving Group Members," *Journal of Applied Social Psychology*, 1973: 276–290.

WOO, C., & A. COOPER, "Strategies of Effective Low Share Businesses," *Strategic Management Journal*, 1981: 301–318.

WORTHY, J. C., "Organizational Structure and Employee Morale," *American Sociological Review*, 1950: 169–179.

————, *Big Business and Free Men*. New York: Harper & Row, 1959.

WRAPP, H. E., "Good Managers Don't Make Policy Decisions," *Harvard Business Review*, September–October 1967: 91–99.

WRIGLEY, L., "Diversification and Divisional Autonomy," DBA dissertation, Graduate School of Business Administration, Harvard University, 1970.

YOSHINO, M., *Japan's Managerial System*. Cambridge, Mass.: M.I.T. Press, 1968.

YOSHINO, M. Y., "Global Competition in a Salient Industry: The Case of Civil Aircraft," in M. E. Porter, ed., *Competition in Global Industries*. Boston: Harvard Business School Press, 1986.

YOUNG, D., *Rommel: The Desert Fox*. New York: Harper & Row, 1974.

ZALD, M. N., "Urban Differentiation, Characteristics of Boards of Directors and Organizational Effectiveness," *American Journal of Sociology*, 1967: 261–272.

————, & M. A. BERGER, "Social Movements in Organizations: Coup D'etat, Insurgency, and Mass Movements," *American Journal of Sociology*, 1978.

ZALEZNIK, A., "Power and Politics in Organizational Life," *Harvard Business Review*, May–June 1970: 47–60

Abbott, George, 479
Abell, D.F., 634, 719
Abell, George, 938
Abernathy, Penny, 447
Abernathy, W.J., 111, 653, 656, 696
Acheson, Dean, 139
Ackenhusen, Mary, 239
Ackerman, R.W., 402, 715
Aguilar, F.J., 20, 726
Aiko, Jiro, 787
Aines, Philip D., 874-75
Alberding, Dick, 479
Alexander of Macedonia, 2, 5-7
Alger, J.I., 5
Ali, Rahmat, 943
Allen, Bob, 193-94, 195, 201, 239-40, 241-42, 244, 245, 246-47, 248
Allen, Paul, 503, 629
Allen, S.A., 333
Allen, T.J., 698
Allison, G.T., 372, 386, 390
Alt, 574
Amdahl, Gene, 225
Andersen, Arthur, 541-42
Anderson, 325
Anderson, P., 254
Andrews, Fred, 447
Andrews, K.R., 9
Andrews, Ken, 46, 74
Ansoff, H.I., 46, 74, 83, 91, 92
Aoki, Teruaki, 787
Arakawa, Minora, 257-58, 924, 926, 927, 928
Argyris, C., 62, 424
Armstrong, Louis, 783
Arnold, Hap, 128-29, 130
Arnold, Martin, 447
Arthur, Jim, 478
Ashby, W.R., 62
Astley, G., 14
Athos, A., 457
Attlee, Clement, 935, 936, 937, 950, 951, 952

Bacon, J., 398, 714
Baden-Fuller, Charles, 746, 757
Baekelund, Leo, 698
Ballmer, Steve, 511
Barnard, Bill, 550
Barrett, Craig, 156, 158-59
Barreyre, P.Y., 717
Bartlett, C.A., 372, 737, 738, 748, 751
Batteyri, P.Y., 65
Battle, A., 552
Bedrosian, Edward R., 572
Bennis, W.G., 19, 33, 355, 366, 680
Bentel, Elisabeth, 628
Benton, Philip, 294
Berger, M.A., 387
Berndt, John, 247

Bernstein, P., 920
Bettis, R.A., 334
Bewley, Stuart, 210
Bhide, A., 426, 614
Bickell, Alan, 478
Biondi, Frank, Jr., 822, 833
Blaauw, Gerrit, 225
Blamey, Thomas, 127
Bleeke, Joel, 325
Bloch, Erich, 227
Block, Z., 363, 366
Blokker, John, 479
Bloom, 565
Bluhdorn, Charles, 819, 824
Boberg, Jay, 628-29
Bodkin, Tom, 447
Boehm, Edward Marshall, 119-20
Boffey, Philip, 447
Bogle, John C., 804, 805, 806, 807, 808, 809, 810, 813, 814
Boniface, Bob, 478
Booth, I.M. "Mac," 562, 565, 572, 575
Borders, William, 447
Bosco, Henry, 247
Boulding, K.E., 36
Bower, J.L., 9, 713, 715
Bowman, E.H., 14
Boxer, Grant, 309
Boyer, Herbert, 68, 121
Brabham, Jack, 853
Braybrooke, D., 8, 402
Brennan, John, 807, 809
Brenner, S.N., 402
Bricklin, Daniel, 169
Brigham, Jack, 478
Bronfamn, Edgar, Jr., 211
Brook, P., 617
Brooks, Fred, 223, 224, 225, 226, 227
Brown, J.K., 398
Brown, Mike, 511
Brunner, Bob, 479
Brunsson, N., 15
Buckler, Sheldon A., 563, 565, 572, 575
Bunker, Laurence E., 135
Buraas, A., 903
Burgarella, 575
Burnett, Leo, 876
Burns, T., 21, 355, 366, 390, 691
Burrows, Frederick, 947
Bush, George, 278
Bushnell, Nolan, 168
Bussell, Mark, 447
Buzzell, R.D., 649
Byrne, J.A., 355, 366

Cabot, Walter, 805
Cadbury, Adrian, 887
Cadbury, Dominic, 889
Cadbury, John, 887
Caldwell, Philip, 290, 292, 294, 299, 304

Campbell, A., 721
Capian, Sid, 616
Carle, M., 717
Carlson, Jan, 894, 895, 896, 898, 902
Carlson, Jerry, 478
Caroe, Olaf, 947
Carsten, Jack, 159
Carter, R., 60
Cary, Frank, 232, 233
Cassano, J., 334
Castrogiovanni, G., 887
Chamberlin, Stephen J., 127
Chance, Doug, 478
Chandler, A.D., 326, 327, 704
Channon, D.F., 708
Cheit, E.F., 402
Chew, W.B., 303
Chiang Kai-shek, 130
Chognard, Jean, 478
Choran, 21
Christenson, C.R., 9
Churchill, Winston, 140, 618, 938, 941, 951
Clark, B.R., 375
Clark, K.B., 300, 303
Clark, T.D., 819
Cleid, Dr., 122
Clive, Robert, 951
Cohen, K.J., 666
Cohen, Sam, 616
Cohen, Stanley, 121
Cole, A.H., 618
Coleman, H.J.Jr., 354, 366
Coleman, James, 214
Combs, J., 887
Connolly, William, 447
Coonrod, 877
Copeland, Miles, 628
Copeman, G.H., 21
Cornellson, S., 552
Cornford, F.M., 390
Craven, Bill, 478
Crawford, M., 68
Crea, Dr., 122
Crozier, M., 640
Cruikshank, J., 457

Darnton, John, 447
D'Aveni, R.A., 65, 70, 325, 354, 355, 366
Davis, Martin S., 819, 820, 824, 826, 827, 828, 830, 831, 832, 833, 848
Davis, R.T., 21
De Geus, 417, 420
Dekker, Wisse, 381
Delahunt, 575
Delaney, Paul, 447
DeLima, Richard, 572, 575
Dell, Michael, 177
Démeré, Ray, 479
Deming, W. Edwards, 293
De Pree, 421

Dickson, Christopher, 789
Dietz, Milton S., 572, 574
Diller, Barry, 819, 824, 826-27, 829, 830, 831, 833, 834
Doi, Toshitada, 787
Donhowe, G.M., 870
Doolittle, Bill, 478
Doorley, T., 63
Doran, Robert, 805
Douglas, S.P., 738
Doyle, John, 475, 479
Drucker, P.F., 14, 354, 366, 657
Dryfoos, Orville, 432
Duncan, 574
Dunwell, Stephen, 231

Edmondson, Hal, 479
Edwards, J.P., 376
Egeberg, Dr., 135
Eichelberger, 128, 137, 138, 140
Eilers, Dan, 174
Eisenhower, Dwight D., 22
Ellis, Vernon, 543, 547, 548, 549, 552, 553
Elston, 869
Ephlin, Don, 292
Epstein, E.M., 396
Ernst, David, 325
Essame, H., 8
Evans, Bob, 220, 224, 225, 226, 233
Evered, R., 2, 11

Faggin, Federico, 152, 153
Fairclough, John, 224, 225, 228, 230
Farago, L., 8
Fardon, David, 316
Farrell, Joanne, 311
Fayol, Henri, 19
Fellers, Bonner, 140
Ferguson, C., 726
Ferguson, William, 829
Fike, Bill, 535
Finkelstein, 325
Firsirotu, M., 649
Fischer, Irving R., 848
Fischer, J., 552
Flippinger, Grace J., 848
Foch, F., 5
Fombrun, C.J., 14
Ford, Henry, 11, 12, 289
Ford, Henry, II, 289, 290
Forrester, J.W., 8, 420
Forsythe, Frederick, 789
Foster, John, 517, 518-19, 520, 527-28
Foster, Timothy, 521-22, 528
Francis, Dick, 789
Frankel, Max, 447
Franklin, B., 12
Frankston, Robert, 169

Frederick the Great, 7
Friedman, M., 373, 402, 403, 404, 405, 407, 409
Friesen, P.H., 106, 107, 649, 756
Fritz, Peter, 489, 491-98
Fritz, R., 418
Fujimoto, T., 303
Fujisawa, Takeo, 113-14, 115, 117, 850, 851-52, 854, 855

Gabelli, Mario, 826
Galbraith, J.K., 640, 715
Galbraith, J.R., 85, 324, 326, 327, 333, 334, 720
Gale, B.T., 649
Gallagher, Pat, 494
Gallo, David, 214
Gallo, Ernest, 209-11, 212-13, 214
Gallo, Joseph, 209, 212, 214
Gallo, Julio, 209-11, 212-13
Gallo, Philip, 212
Gallo, Robert, 214
Gandhi, Mohandas K., 940-42, 944, 945, 948, 949, 952, 953-54
Garson, G.D., 397
Garvin, D.A., 111, 696
Gaskin, S., 60
Gates, Bill, 193-94, 195, 197, 198, 199, 201-2, 503, 511, 629
Genser, Jack, 616
George VI, King of England, 936-37
Gerot, Paul S., 867
Gerth, H.H., 640
Ghoshal, S., 239, 372, 737, 738, 748
Gibson, 229, 231
Gilbert, 87
Glickauf, Joe, 542
Glueck, W.F., 11, 55
Goddard, Robert, 278
Goeddel, Dr., 122
Golden, Soma, 447
Good, Raymond F., 872-73, 875
Goold, M., 721
Gore, Al, 827
Gorham, David, 433, 438
Gosselin, R., 659
Grant, Ulysses S., 14
Graziano, Joe, 181
Green, P., 5
Greenleaf, R.K., 422
Grinstein, Gerald, 428
Grinyer, P.H., 719
Grove, A., 34, 151, 152, 153, 154, 161-62
Guber, Peter, 782, 786, 797
Guest, R.H., 20, 855
Gunther, John, 140
Guthrie, A.L., 294
Gwertzman, Bernard, 447

Haanstra, John, 226, 229, 230
Hackborn, Dick, 478
Hackett, Victoria, 628
Hallmann, Michael, 503
Halsey, William Frederick, 127, 130, 132, 133, 134-35, 136
Hamel, G., 19, 65, 410
Hammond, John, 634
Hanold, Terry, 867, 870
Hardy, Cynthia, 657, 658
Harlor, 575
Harper, Mike, 870
Harrison, George, 924
Hart, B.H.L., 5, 7, 259-62, 264-65
Hashimoto, Tsunao, 787
Haspeslagh, P., 753
Hatsopoulos, George, 498, 499, 500
Hatsopoulos, John, 500
Hawkins, Bob, 510
Hawkins, Trip, 263-65, 929
Hayes, R.H., 111, 696
Henderson, Bruce, 373
Henderson, Rebecca, 429
Hewlett, William, 469-71, 472, 473, 474-75, 476, 479
Hickson, D.J., 387
Higgins, Patricia, 517
Hill, M., 552
Hilmer, F.G., 47
Hirohito, Emperor, 139-40
Hockenstein, Irwin, 616
Hofer, C.W., 14
Hoff, M.E. "Ted," 152, 153, 699
Hogan, W.T., 146
Hoge, Warren, 440, 441, 447
Holder, Bob, 246
Holdren, Bruce, 926
Honda, Soichiro, 113-16, 117, 699, 849, 850-52, 853, 855, 859
Hooks, Benjamin L., 848
Hopkins, 139
Hori, Kenji, 787
Hosking, H.W., 536
Houston, Whitney, 785
Hout, T.M., 738
Huff, 127
Hughes, T., 702
Huizenga, H. Wayne, 828
Hume, David, 12
Humphrey, Watts, 227
Hunt, R.G., 648

Iacocca, Lee, 617
Iba, Tamotsu, 787
Ibuka, Masaru, 595, 597, 598, 599, 600, 601, 697, 787
Icahn, Carl, 822
Idei, Nobuyuki, 787
Ilayashi, Katsuhito, 787
Illinich, A., 65
Imanishi, Hiroshi, 254
Irving, D., 8
Ishizuka, Tsunehiki, 787

Ismay, General Lord, 938
Itakura, Dr., 122
Iwabuchi, Sanji, 138
Iwaki, Ken, 787
Iwama, Kazuo, 598

Jackson, Michael, 782
Jacobs, Jack, 831, 832, 846
Jaeger, A.M., 378, 379
Jaffe, Stanley R., 848
James, D.C., 8
James, Donald W., 927
Jarrett, 574
Jay, A., 377
Jenkins, C., 396
Jenkins, Evan, 947
Jensen, 721
Jinnah, Mohammed Ali, 943-45, 946, 949, 951, 952, 953
Jobs, Steve, 68, 168, 169, 173, 618, 759
Joel, Billy, 793
Johnsen, Ken, 535
Johnson, B., 379
Johnson, Henry, 917, 918
Johnson, Robert, 783
Johnson, S.C., 92
Johnson, Samuel, 412
Jomini, A.H., 7
Jones, C., 92
Jones, David, 447
Jones, Gilbert, 229
Jorgensen, J., 894
Juio, Matsuichi, 128

Kamiya, Kenichi, 787
Kaneda, Yoshiyuki, 787
Kanoi, Nobuo, 787
Kanter, R.M., 412, 751
Karpin, David, 311
Kato, Seiichi, 787
Kawamoto, Nobuhiko, 857, 858, 859
Kawashima, Kihachiro, 115, 852
Keith, Robert J., 861, 868
Kelleher, Diana, 214
Kelly, J., 552
Kelsey, Paul, 870
Kennedy, John F., 401
Kenney, 127, 133, 134, 136, 138, 139
Kets De Vries, M., 758-59
Kidder, T., 703
Kiechel, W., 872
Kierkegaard, S., 109-10
Kihara, 601-2
Kikuchi, 598, 602
Kim Woo Choong, 725-26
King, Admiral, 128
King, W.L. Mackenzie, 130
Kinkaid, Tom, 132, 134-35
Kirby, Dave, 478
Kirkwood, Bob, 478
Klein, 575

Knaplund, Paul, 231
Kobayashi, Shigeru, 598-99
Kodera, Junichi, 787
Kohn, Les, 160-61
Kohno, Fumio, 787
Koiso, 132
Konev, 137
Kono, T., 457
Koriyama, Shiro, 787
Kosaka, 460
Kowomoto, Dr., 854
Krueger, 127, 137
Kullberg, Duane, 542
Kulp, A., Moyer, 804
Kume, Tadashi, 856
Kurita, Takeo, 134, 135

Land, Edwin H., 90, 182, 558-59, 560, 561, 562, 563, 564, 572, 574, 617-18
Lane, Larry, 519, 521
Langley, Ann, 657, 658
Lao Tsu, 426
Lapierre, L., 15
Lapworth, Bill, 222
Larkins, Pat, 527
Larson, Kent, 878
Lasserre, Philippe, 704
Laurie, Donna, 447
Lawrence, O.E., 600
Leacock, Stephen, 646
Leahy, William D., 129
Learson, T. Vincent, 98, 222, 223, 224, 225, 226, 227, 230, 231, 232
Lee, C.A., 387, 447
Lee, John, 447
Lefebure, R.B., 894
Lelyveld, Joseph, 447
Lenin, V.I., 5
Levin, Jerry W., 874-75
Levitas, Mitchel, 447
Levitt, T., 89, 401, 402, 720, 738, 746
Lewin, K., 620
Lewis, Dan, 447
Liedtke, J. Hugh, 848
Light, J.O., 804
Lincoln, Howard, 258, 924, 926, 927, 928
Lindberg, Helge, 894, 896, 898, 899
Lindblom, C.E., 8, 687
Linker, Erich, 442
Lipton, Martin, 830
Locilento, Bud, 518, 520, 522
Lodge, G.C., 51
Lohrke, F.T., 887
Lorange, P., 8
Lucas, George, 789
Lutolf, Franz J., 848

MacArthur, Douglas, 7-8, 19
McCarthy, T., 552

McClelland, D.C., 390
McCracken, Ed, 478
McCune, William J., Jr., 558, 559, 560, 561-62, 563, 564, 565, 572, 574
McDonald, J., 4
McGee, Victor, 698
Machiavelli, N., 5
McHugh, Alexandra, 679
MacKenzie, 574
MacKinnon, Ian, 810-11
McKinsey, 789
McLaren, Norman, 105
McLaughlin, 574
MacLeish, Archibald, 139
MacMillan, I.C., 363, 366
McNeal, Dean, 870
McNealy, Scott, 160
Madonna, 789
Maeterlinck, M., 29
Magness, Bob, 827
Maister, David, 657
Majone, G., 12
Makino, Shiro, 135
Maljers, Floris, 382
Malone, John C., 199, 827-28, 829, 846
Maloney, G.J., 65
Manoogian, 299
Mao Tse-Tung, 5
Maples, Mike, 511
March, J.G., 663
Mariotti, Franco, 478
Maritz, Paul, 505, 506
Marker, Russell, 694
Markkula, A.C., "Mike," 168-69
Marshall, Alfred, 406
Marshall, Dick, 130, 136
Marshall, George, 128, 132, 137
Martin, L.C., 712
Mason, R., 420
Matloff, M., 7
Matsushita, Konosuke, 381-82, 383, 457, 458, 460, 463
Matthews, John, 490
Maxwell, Robert, 821-22
Mayo, John, 244
Mazor, 153
Mechanic, D., 386
Medenica, Gordon, 441-42
Melcher, R.A., 892
Menon, V.P., 950-51
Mertz, Edgar, 873
Mical, R.J., 261
Mikulka, Charles, 572, 575
Miles, R., 65, 354, 366
Miller, D., 106, 107, 422, 613, 649, 756, 758-59
Mills, C.W., 640
Mills, D.Q., 362, 363, 366
Mintzberg, H., 3, 5, 11, 13, 20, 86, 94, 324, 371, 373, 386, 420, 466, 612, 613, 614, 634, 635, 657, 678, 704, 705, 717, 719, 755, 756
Mitchell, Beverly, 926
Mitchell, Mike, 309, 315
Mitroff, I., 420, 421

Miyamoto, Sigeru, 256, 258, 261, 262, 923, 925
Miyaoka, Senri, 600, 787
Mizushima, Yasumasa, 787
Molander, E.A., 402
Monroe, Willys H., 874-75
Montgomery, B.L., 5
Moore, Dick, 479
Moore, Gordon E., 149-50, 151, 152, 153
Morgan, Walter, L., 804, 805
Morgenstern, O., 4, 10
Morio, Minoru, 787
Morita, Akio, 595-96, 597-98, 599-600, 601, 602, 604, 697, 785, 787, 797
Morita, Masaaki, 786
Morket, A., 309, 530
Morse, David, 259-62, 264-65
Morton, Dean, 479
Mountbatten, Louis Francis Albert Victor Nicholas, 935-55
Moyer, Don, 247
Moyer, R.C., 712
Moynihan, Patrick, 277, 278, 279
Mucha, Z., 60
Muggs, J.J., 877
Muglia, Robert, 504-5, 508, 509
Mulroney, Helen, 311
Munkberg, Carl-Olov, 898
Murdoch, Rupert, 444, 446, 791
Murray, Michael, 507-8, 509
Murray, Mike, 511
Myers, S., 277
Myhrvold, Nathan, 510, 511

Nader, Ralph, 401, 404, 406
Nadler, D., 765
Nadler, Larry, 620
Nagai, Kenzo, 597
Nagano, Akira, 787
Nakamura, Hidio, 787
Nakamura, Suehiro, 787
Napoleon, I., 5
Nathanson, D., 327, 333, 334
Needle, Dave, 261
Neff, John, 805
Nehru, Jawaharlal, 938, 939-40, 945, 949, 950, 951, 952, 953
Neill, Terry, 541, 547, 549, 550
Nelson, Horatio, 804
Nelson, Ronald L., 848
Neukom, Bill, 511
Neupert, Peter, 504, 505-7, 508-9
Newhouse, Nancy, 447
Newman, Bill, 46, 74
Newman, William, 756
Nimitz, Chester William, 128, 129, 130, 132
Nishimura, Teji, 134-35
Niwa, 460
Noël, A., 23, 24
Nordhoff, Heinrich, 646
Noyce, Robert N., 149-50, 151, 152, 153, 154, 155

O'Brien, William, 419
Ochs, Adolph, 432
Ohga, Norio, 598, 603, 782, 783, 786, 788, 795, 796-97
Ohmae, K., 368
Ohnishi, Akihisa, 787
Ohsone, Kozo, 787
Oki, Bijiro, 787
Okochi, N., 922
Oldendorf, Jesse, 134-35
Oliver, Bernard M., 472
Oliver, Laurence, 617
Oliverio, Al, 478
Olsen, J.P., 663, 666
Olson, Jim, 239-40
Oppenheimer, Anthony, 309
Oppenheimer, Ernest, 311
Oppenheimer, H.F., 311
Oresman, Donald, 848
Organ, Terry, 889
Osmena, Sergio, 134
Ostrager, Barry, 831
Otis, Suzanne, 679
Ouchi, W.G., 378, 379
Oyana, Kenichi, 787
Ozawa, Jisaburo, 134-35

Packard, David, 469-70, 471, 472, 473, 474, 476, 479
Page, 575
Paquette, P.C., 63, 457, 922
Parker, Gerry, 157
Parzybok, G.B., 479
Pascale, R., 94, 457
Patel, Vallabhbhai, 942-43, 953
Patterson, Tim, 195
Pattison, James A., 848
Patton, George S., 8
Payne, Claudia, 447
Pelson, Vic, 248
Pence, C.C., 696
Pennings, J.M., 387
Perleman, Ronald, 831
Perrow, C., 15, 639
Pestillo, Pete, 292
Peters, John, 782, 786
Peters, T.J., 326, 371, 621, 762, 765, 779
Peters, Tom, 19, 24, 33, 762
Petersen, Donald E., 290-92, 299, 300
Peterson, James R., 868, 869, 872, 874-75, 878, 879
Peterson, Peter, 787
Philip of Macedonia, 2, 5-7
Phillips, J.R., 326
Phillips, T.R., 7
Picasso, Pablo, 11
Piore, Emanuel, 229, 231
Pitcher, Pat, 410
Platt, Lew, 479
Polanyi, 412
Poling, Harold A. "Red," 292, 294, 299, 300
Pollack, Lester, 848
Porsche, Ferdinand, 646

O'Brien, William, 419
Ochs, Adolph, 432
Porter, M.E., 11, 33, 60, 74, 76, 83, 85-86, 87, 88, 614, 623, 645, 704, 717, 720, 737, 738, 762
Powell, 875
Prahalad, C.K., 19, 65, 410, 764
Price, Hal, 518, 521, 523
Primis, Lance, 439-40, 442-43
Prince, R., 552
Puette, Bob, 180
Purkayastha, D., 112
Putman, R., 424

Quezon, Manuel, 134
Quinn, Allie J., 457
Quinn, J.B., 2, 11, 47, 63, 64, 93, 94, 119, 121, 127, 142, 193, 220, 239, 254, 272, 325, 356, 366, 457, 489, 517, 541, 558, 576, 595, 596, 678-79, 781, 849, 867, 915, 922, 935

Rafelghem, Carlos Van, 904
Raines, Howell, 447
Ravencraft, D., 70, 728
Redstone, Sumner, 19, 820, 826, 827, 828, 829, 830, 832, 833, 834
Reed, Bob, 159
Reeser, C., 584-85, 692
Renschier, Arnold, 522, 528
Richardson, Robert C., 129
Riggs, Arthur D., 68
Riggs, Dr., 122
Riney, Hal, 213
Risk, John, 294
Roberts, Brian, 824
Roberts, Ed, 193-94
Roberts, Ralph, 823
Robinson, Charles, 447
Rock, Arthur, 150
Rogers, Howard G., 572, 575
Rohatyn, Felix, 828
Romanelli, Elaine, 756
Rommel, Erwin, 8
Romulo, Carlos P., 134
Roosevelt, Franklin D., 22, 128, 129-30, 133
Rose, Janet, 657, 658
Rosenblum, Constance, 447
Rosewall, Arthur, 869, 874-75, 879-80
Rosner, M., 377-78
Ross, I., 402
Ross, Lewis, 304
Rudden, E., 738
Rumelt, R.P., 13, 14, 46, 65, 112-13, 334, 711, 714
Rutman, Bernard, 211

Sailer, J.E., 804
Sakiya, T., 112, 113, 114, 849

Sakuma, Mamora, 788
Salter, M.S., 728
Sanders, Dave, 479
Sanders, S., 849
Sano, Sumio, 787
Santayana, George, 414
Sarich, Ralph, 530-31, 533-34, 535-36, 538
Sarich family, 537
Sassouni, C., 502
Sauter, George U., 811
Sayles, L.R., 31, 410
Scharnhorst, 7
Scheff, D., 922
Schein, E., 419
Schelling, T.C., 11, 62
Schendel, D., 14
Scherer, F.M., 728
Schipper, L., 277
Schloss, Irwin, 848
Schlunke, Kim, 533
Schmidt, Helmut, 397
Schmuskii, Jack, 787
Schneck, R.E., 387
Schon, D.A., 62, 424
Schulhof, Michael (Mickey), 784, 785, 786, 787, 788, 790, 795, 797
Schwarzer, Judge, 198
Scott, Michael, 170
Scott, Walter D., 872, 874, 875
Sculley, John, 173, 180-82, 192, 199, 759
Segel, Joseph, 823
Selznick, P., 14, 375, 376, 419
Senge, P., 410, 417, 423
Shaheen, George, 552, 553
Shamsie, Jamal, 679
Shanken, Marvin, 214
Sheean, Vincent, 132
Sheridan, Robert, 447
Sherman, Willie, 616
Sherwood, Robert, 792, 795
Shimazu, Misanaga, 787
Shirley, Jon, 503
Shockley, William, 149, 154
Shook, R., 849
Shubik, M., 4
Siegal, Allan, 447
Siegel, Marvin, 447
Silberman, Samuel J., 848
Silver, Julius, 562, 572, 575
Simon, H.A., 356, 366
Simon, M.A., 3
Simons, R., 28
Sinatra, Frank, 783
Singh, Baldev, 951
Singh, Yadavindra, 945
Singleton, Henry, 168
Slater, P.L., 355, 366, 680
Small, Lawrence M., 848
Smith, Adam, 406
Smith, D., 424
Smith, Donald N., 875, 876
Smith, Fern, 258

Smith, Fred, 628
Smith, J., 552
Smith, L., 406, 714
Smith, Raymond, 829
Smith, W.R., 90
Snell, E.M., 7
Snow, C., 65, 354, 366
Snyder, Richard, 821
Solzhenitsyn, A., 403
Sommer, Steven, 213
Spaulding, Don, 224
Speer, A., 618
Spencer, F.C., 659, 668
Spender, J.C., 719
Spielberg, Stephen, 782, 789
Spindler, Michael, 181, 922
Spoor, William, 98-99, 867, 868-78, 880
Springsteen, Bruce, 782, 795
Stafford, Jack, 867, 876, 878
Stalin, Joseph, 137, 139
Stalk, G., Jr., 418
Stalker, G.M., 355, 366, 691
Staniforth, D., 894
Steinberg, Jack, 616
Steinberg, Max, 616
Steinberg, Nathan, 616
Steinberg, Sam, 618, 619, 642-43
Steiner, Gary, 39
Sterne, Michael, 447
Stevenson, W., 7, 52
Stewart, R., 20, 21
Stewart, Tim, 247
Stimson, Henry Lewis, 138
Stix, G., 275
Stopford, John, 757
Strebel, ?., 87
Streisand, Barbra, 782, 785
Suchard, Jacob, 891, 892
Suffrin, Harry, 616
Sullivan, Kevin, 181
Sultan, R.G.M., 649
Sulzberger, Arthur, Jr., 444
Sulzberger, Arthur, Sr., 432-33, 438, 440, 444
Sun Lin Chou, 156, 159
Sun Tzu, 5
Sutherland, 127, 135, 137, 140
Suzuki, Sosaku, 132
Swanson, Robert, 121
Swindell, 574

Taguchi, Genichi, 293
Takahashi, Masahiro, 787
Takano, Masayuki, 787
Takeda, 923
Tamiya, Kenji, 787
Taylor, Frederick, 640-41
Taylor, W.H., 665
Telnack, John, 294, 295
Templeman, J., 892
Terk, David, 209, 211
Terkel, 637

Terry, Bill, 479
Thayer, Harvey H., 572, 574
Thompson, J.D., 14, 752
Thompson, V.A., 641
Thorndike, Nick, 805
Tilles, S., 9
Tisch, Lauren, 781, 795
Toffler, A., 352, 686
Tojo Hideki, 132
Towne, James, 503
Townes, Charles, 702
Toyoda, 134
Tregoe, B., 14, 327
Trotman, Alex, 300, 304-7
Truman, Harry S., 22, 139
Tsurushima, Katsuyki, 787
Tuchman, B.W., 7
Turner, D., 68
Turner, Ted, 828
Tushman, M.L., 765
Tushman, Michael, 756
Tyrwhitt, David, 316

Uemura, Masayuki, 255, 257, 923
Uhga, Norio, 787
Urban, G.L., 60
Urwick, Lyndell, 19
Utterback, Jim, 678

Vadasz, Les, 161
van Bronkborst, Ed, 478
Vancil, R.F., 8
Van Kemmel, Gerard, 547
Var, 742
Varner, V.J., 5
Vecchione, Joseph, 447
Veraldi, Lewis, 290, 294, 295, 297, 298
Vidal, Gore, 128
Von Bolow, D.F., 7
Von Clausewitz, C., 5, 7, 10, 12
Von Hippel, E., 694
Von Neumann, J., 4, 10, 365
Voss, 574
Voyer, John, 93

Wachtell, Herbert, 831
Wack, P., 420
Wainwright, Jonathan M., 140
Walker, Judge, 198
Wallin, Winston R., 869, 874, 875, 877
Walner, 497
Ward, R.G., 536
Wareham, 574
Warwick, Bill, 248
Washington, George, 128
Watanabe, Seiichi, 787
Waterman, R.H., 371, 762, 765, 779

Waterman, R.H.Jr., 326
Waters, J.A., 11, 13, 614, 635, 719
Waters, James A., 679
Watson, A.K., 224, 225, 229
Watson, Tom, Jr., 221, 222, 223, 224, 225, 226-27, 229, 230, 231, 232, 233
Watson, Tom, Sr., 221
Wavell, Archibald, 936
Wayne, K., 653, 656
Weber, J., 891
Weber, M., 374-75
Weick, K.E., 34, 660
Weinbach, L., 552
Weinhold, W.A., 728
Weissman, George, 848
Wellington, Duke of, 128
Welty, G., 284, 285
Wensberg, Peter, 562, 565, 572, 574
Westley, F., 614, 617
White, T.H., 8
Wholey, Bruce, 478
Williams, Albert, 224, 225, 230
Williamson, O.E., 712
Willoughby, 127
Wilner, Judith, 447
Wind, Y., 738
Wingate, Edwin H., 874-75
Wolf, 574
Worthy, J.C., 640
Wozniak, Steve, 68, 168, 173
Wrapp, Edward, 18
Wrigley, L., 714
Wyman, Thomas H., 875
Wyman, Tom, 876
Wyser-Pratte, Guy, 828

Yamada, Toshiyuki, 787
Yamakawa, Kiyoshi, 787
Yamashita, Tomoyuki, 132, 136, 137, 138, 463
Yamauchi, Fusagiro, 254
Yamauchi, Hiroshi, 254-55, 256, 257, 258, 265, 923, 924, 928, 931
Yansouni, Cyril, 478
Yetnikoff, Walter, 781, 782, 792
Yip, George, 737
Yokoi, Gunpei, 254, 923
Young, D., 8
Young, John, 475, 477
Young, Richard, 562, 563, 565, 572, 574

Zacharkiw, Peter, 629
Zald, M.N., 387
Zaleznik, A., 19, 33
Zhukov, Georgy K., 137
Zimmerman, I., 14, 327

Abstraction, leaps of, 424
Accountability, 758
Accounting practices, innovation and, 696-97
Acquisitions, 718
  cross-border, 366-70
Action-analysis integration, 631-33
Action planning systems, 342
Action sequences (programs), 8
Activity concentration, global strategy and, 742
Adaptive learning and generative learning, 417-18
Adhocracy, 351-52, 758
  administrative adhocracy, 681-84
  conditions of environment and, 685-87
  environment taking precedence in, 691
  human reactions to, 691-92
  operating adhocracy, 681, 687
  problems of
    ambiguity problems, 691-92
    efficiency problems, 692
    transition problems, 692-93
  strategy making, grass-roots model of, 689-90
  structure of, 680-85
Adjustment, mutual, 337
Administrative adhocracy, 681-84
  strategy formation in, 687-88
Administrative style of management, 34
Administrative systems. See Systems, administrative
Administrators, 26
Advanced Micro Devices (AMD), 158-59
Advance Publications, multimedia assets, 844-45
Advantage, competitive, 59-61
  strategic outsourcing and, 69-70
Advocacy, inquiry vs., 424
Agenda of managerial work, 23-24
Age of organization, design parameters and, 343-45
Airline industry, European, 905-14. See also Scandinavian Airlines System (SAS)
  air traffic market data, 912
  air traffic vs. economic trends, 913
  comparative data, 905
  competition, 907-9
  fare structure example, 914
  market environment, 905-7
  new developments, 911
  oil price changes and, 914
  operating data, 907
  regulation/deregulation, 909-11
  route structures, 913
Alcoa, 331
Alliance-building game, 386
Alliances, 325
  as arbitrage, 367-68
  cross-border, 366-70
  shaky, 388, 389
ALR, 177
Altair, 193-94
AMD, 158-59
Amiga, 259
Amtrak, 396, 397

Analytical tasks, handling in stages, 632
Andersen Consulting (Europe), 325, 541-57
  building personnel capabilities, 543-45
    meritocracy, 544
    partners' roles, 545
    project teams, 544-45
  business integration business, 545-47, 556
    entry into, 547
    from systems integration to, 546
  competitors, 555
  economics for professional service firm, 554
  EMEA1 organization, 553
  financial summary, 552
  history, 541-43
  managing complexity, 547-48
  national differences, 548-50
    cultural differences, 549-50
    developing new capabilities and, 549
    France, 548, 557
    multinational network integration, 550
    United Kingdom, 548-49, 556
  software process, 551
  training sequence, 554
  worldwide organization, 552
Anzio, Battle of, 128
Apollo, 41
Apple Computer, Inc., 64, 168-92, 325, 614
  alliances with Japanese firms, 182
  Apple II computer, 169
  Claris, 182
  distribution channels, 170
  finance and manufacturing, 180-81
  history, 173-74
  Macintosh computer, 174, 197
  manufacturing, 169-70
  marketing mix, 180
  personal computer industry and, 174-75
    alternative technologies, 179
    distribution and buyers, 176-77
    manufacturing and R&D, 175-76
    PC manufacturers, 177-79
    suppliers, 177
  position, 179-80
  Powerbooks, 180
  Power Macs, 198-99
  relationships with other companies, 181
    IBM, 173, 174-75, 181-82, 198-99
    Microsoft, 196-99
  start, 168-69
  statistical tables, 171-72, 184-92
Appleton, 330
Apprenticeship, 673
Arbitrage, alliances as, 367-68
Architecture, social, 419
Argyle Diamond Sales (ADS), 309-18, 325, 614
  Argyle Diamond Mines Joint Venture, 310
  background, 309
  cutting and distribution, 315-16
  diamond product development, 315
  expansion, 316
  marketing, 315
  mining operations, 317-18
  negotiations with De Beers, 316
  pilot strike (1989) and, 311
  production and operations, 310-11

  security issues, 311
  staff development and training, 311
  work force arrangements, 310
  world diamond industry, 311-15
    Central Selling Organization (CSO) and, 309, 311-13
    cutting, polishing, and trading centers, 314
    diamond grading, 314
    industrial diamonds, 313-14
    investment market, 313
    jewelry manufacturers and retailers, 315
    polished diamond traders, 314-15
Arrogance, smart, 633
Artists, 411-12, 413, 416
Ashton Joint Venture, 310
Assimilation of missionary organizations, 378
Atari, 258-59
AT&T, 239-53
  Bell Laboratories, 240-41
  Business Units, 240, 241-43, 246
  cross-business unit initiatives, 246-47
  divestiture, 239
  domestic industry leadership, 244-45
  history, 239-40
  integrating diversity, 246
  international expansion, 245-46
  leadership team, 241-42
  management challenge, 248
  personal communications services (PCS), 244
  preparing for future, 243-48
  rationalizing the business, 240-41
  regional governance, 247-48
  staff functions, 240
  statistical tables and exhibits, 249-53
  strategic framework, 244
  Strategy Forum meetings, 242, 246
  team management, 247
  Universal Card, 244
  values state (Our Common Bond), 242-43, 246, 252
Attractiveness test, 729
Authority, system of, 390
Autogestion, 398
Automakers, Japanese. See also Honda Motor Company
  investments in U.S. (1992), 857
  partnerships with U.S. automakers (1992), 858
Automobile industry, innovation in, 537-38

Baldwin, 110
Barriers to entry, 76, 77-78
Bartles & Jaymes, 213-14
BASIC, 193-94
Bataan, 137
Bear Stearns, 68
Behavior
  formalization of, 339
  patterns of, 421-22
  size or organization and, 345
Bell Laboratories, 154
Better-off test, 729, 730

Big Business and Free Men (Worthy), 640
Billing multiple, 672-73
Blame, moving beyond, 425
Blockbuster, 259, 833
  multimedia assets, 844-45
Board of directors, power of, 399
Borland International, Inc., 207
Boston Consulting Group (BCG), 91, 111-12
"Bottom line" approach to management, 26
Brinkmanship in business, 391-94
Budgeting game, 387
Bundling, 720
Bureaucracy
  excessive, 697
  network organization and, 355
Bureaucratic politics model, 372
Bureaucratic structures, 339
  automation of operating core and, 345-46
Bureaupathologies, 641
Busicom, 152
Business recombination strategies, 720
Business redefinition strategy, 719
Business unit(s)
  competition at level of, 728
  diversification and, 728
Buyer power, 75, 79-80
  determinants of, 76
By-product diversification, 331, 710, 718
By-product seller, vertically integrated, 333, 334-35

Cadbury Schweppes, P.L.C., 887-93
  brand names, 888
  comparative data, 890, 891, 892
  competitors, 888
  contemporary challenges, 890-92
  environment, 888-89
  financial data, 893
  history, 887-88
  modern operations, 889-90
  sales, 892
Canadelle, 620
Canon, 41, 42
Capitalism and Freedom (Freidman), 405
Capital requirements, as entry barrier, 77-78
Career advancement in infinitely flat organizations, 359
Career-path management, 384-85
Case studies
  Andersen Consulting (Europe), 541-57
  Apple Computer, Inc., 168-92
  Argyle Diamond Sales (ADS), 309-18
  AT&T, 239-53
  Cadbury Schweppes, P.L.C., 887-93
  E & J Gallo Winery, 209-19
  European airline industry, 905-14
  Exxon Corporation, 576-94
  Ford: Team Taurus, 289-308
  Ford Motor Co., 288-308
  Genentech, Inc., 121-26
  Hewlett Packard Company, 469-88
  Honda Motor Company, 849-66
  IBM, 220-38
  Intel Corporation, 149-67
  MacArthur and the Philippines, 127-41
  magnetic levitation train, 272-88

Matsushita Electric Industrial Company 1994, 457-68
Microsoft Corporation, 193-208, 503-16
New Steel Corporation, 142-48
New York Times Company, 432-56
Nintendo Co., Ltd., 254-71
Nintendo of America, 922-34
Novacare, inc., 517-29
Orbital Engine Company, 530-40
Paramount Communications, Inc., battle for, 819-48
Peet, Russ, Anderson, & Detroit, 915-21
Pillsbury Company, 867-86
Polaroid Corporation, 558-75
Scandinavian Airlines System (SAS), 894-906
Sony Corporation, 595-609, 781-803
TCG, Ltd., 489-98
Thermo Electron Corporation, 498-502
Vanguard Group, Inc. (A), 804-18
Cash cows, 91
CBS Records, 781
C&C, 753
Center of gravity, 327
  change in, 332-35
  of paper industry, 329-30
  related diversification and, 331
Centralization
  environment and, 346
  power and, 346-47
Cerebral style of managing, 34
Chaeronea, Battle of (338 B.C.), 5-7
Chain integration strategies, 771
Change
  in center of gravity, 332-35
  constancy of, 427-28
  exploiting, 82
  leverage provided by external, 629
  managing, 755-80
    forces/forms in effective organizations, 757-59
    organizational evolution, 764-70
  politics and, 390
  reconciling continuity and, 109-10
  strategy and, 51
  strategy for, 3-10
Channels
  changing role of, 625
  global, 743-44
Charisma, 374-75
Chief executives
  communicating role of, 27-28
  work pace for, 20
"Chunks," managerial, 24
CISC, 160
City of Hope National Medical Center, 122
Claris, 182
Clarity in corporate vision, 381-82
Class action suit, 401
Cleavage
  in combinations, 759-60
  in conversion, 760
Cloister missionaries, 378
Closed system, machine organization as, 639-40
Cluster organization, 325, 362-63
Coalition management, 101
Coalitions, 347

internal and external, 337
Coca-Cola, Co., 41, 890
Coherence, organizational, 428
"Cold War" tactics, 392
Collaboration, 366-70
  alliances as arbitrage, 367-68
  Ohmae's tips for, 368
  as sequence of actions, 369
  willingness to rethink during, 369
Collective strategy, 14
Columbia Pictures Entertainment, 781-82
  financials, 782
  segment data, 783
Combinations, 759-60
Commitment, pockets of, 100
Communicating, 26-27
Compaq, 174, 176-77
Compensation, in infinitely flat organizations, 359
Competence, 762-70
  configuration hypothesis, 763
  congruence hypothesis, 763
  contradiction hypothesis, 763
  convergence hypothesis, 672
  corporate, 52-55
  creation hypothesis, 763-64
  matching opportunity and, 54-55
Competencies, core, 63-69, 427
  defined, 64-65
  essence of, 66-68
  preeminence in, 68-69
Competition, 758
  basis of, 629-30
  benefits of, 762
  at business unit level, 728
  combining with cooperation, 762
  globalized, 746
  head-on, 14
  through politics, 761
  predatory, 366
  restraint of, 393
  strategy evaluation and, 63
  strategy formulation and, 75
  in upstream vs. downstream environments, 328
Competitive advantage, 59-61
  strategic outsourcing and, 69-70
Competitive forces, 74, 75-83
  formulating strategy and, 82-83
  jockeying for position, 81-82
  powerful suppliers and buyers, 75, 79-80
  substitute products, 75, 81
  threat of entry, 75, 77-78
Competitive innovation, 43-44
Competitive leverage, global strategy and, 742
Competitive maneuvering, 373, 391-94
  "Cold War" tactics, 392
  consequences of, 392-93
  friendly, 391-92
  integrated, 743
  nonlogical strategy for, 393-94
  rules for, 394
Competitive strategy, 58
  in emerging industries, 623-26
Competitive Strategy (Porter), 11, 614
Complete political arena (political organization), 388-89

Complex instruction set computer design (CISC), 160
Complexity, detail vs. dynamic, 425
Complex portfolio planning, 702
Computerland, 170
Conceiving, 23
Conceptual horseshoe model of corporate control, 394-409
  democratize it, 397-400, 408
  ignore it, 403-4, 409
  induce it, 404-5, 408
  nationalize it, 396-97, 408
  pressure it, 401-3, 407
  regulate it, 400-401, 407, 408
  restore it, 405-7, 408-9
Conceptual style of management, 34
Confectionary market, 891
Confederation, 723
Configuration approach to organizational structure, 335-53
  coordinating mechanisms and, 337-39
  design parameters and, 339-43
  diversified organization, 350-51
  entrepreneurial organization, 348-49
  innovative organization, 351-52
  machine organization, 349
  missionary organization, 352-53
  parts of organization and, 336-37
  political organization, 353
  professional organization, 349-50
  situational factors and, 343-47
Configuration hypothesis of competence, 763
Configurations, 325, 612, 757-64
  containment of, 759
  contamination by, 758
  out of control, 758-59
  forms and forces, 757-59
Conflict, 386. See also Politics
  dimensions of, 388
Confrontational form of organization, 388, 389
Conglomerate(s)
  entrepreneurial, 722, 724
  financial, 721, 724
  related, 65
  starburst organizations vs., 364
Conglomerate (unrelated) diversification, 65, 332, 710, 711, 717
  congruence hypothesis, 763
Connexion type of organization, 723
Consensus strategy, 13
Consistency
  of strategy, 56, 57
  in vision, 382
Consolidation, market, 92
Consonance of strategy, 56, 57-59
Constellation, 723
Contact personnel, in inverted organizations, 360-61
Container Corporation, 329-30
Context, 325
  diversified context, 612, 704-36
  entrepreneurial context, 612-33
  innovation context, 612, 678-763
  international context, 613, 737-54
  managing change, 755-80
  mature context, 612, 634-56
  professional context, 612, 657-77
Contingency (situational) factors, 343-47

age and size, 343-45
environment, 346
power, 346-47
technical system, 345-46
Contingency theory, 335
Continuity, 415-16
  reconciling change and, 109-10
  in vision, 382
Continuous learning, 415
Contradiction, 761-62
Contradiction hypothesis of competence, 763
Control(s), 415-16
  conceptual horseshoe model of, 394-409
    democratize it, 397-400, 408
    ignore it, 403-4, 409
    induce it, 404-5, 408
    nationalize it, 396-97, 408
    pressure it, 401-3, 407
    regulate it, 400-401, 407, 408
    restore it, 405-7, 408-9
  in diversified context, 723-24
  financial, 724
  ideological, 724
  in missionary organizations, 377
  personalized, 724
  shareholder, 405-6
  strategies of, 718
  by strategy, 724
  by systems, 724
  systems of, 342
Controlling role of managers, 28
Convergence hypothesis, 672, 762, 763
Converging change, 765-66
  fine-tuning, 765
  incremental adjustments to environmental shift, 765
Conversion, 760
Converter missionaries, 378
Conzinc Riotinto of Australia (CRA), 309
Cooperation, 758
  combining with competition, 762
  with competitors, 391-92
  through ideology, 761
  limits to, 761
Coordinating mechanisms, 337-39
Core business
  distinguishing, 85-91
    differentiation strategies, 88-90
    functional areas, 85-86
    Porter's generic strategies, 87-88
    scope strategies, 90-91
  elaborating, 91-92
  generic strategies, 87-88
    for extending, 717-19
    for reconceiving, 719-20
  locating, 84-85
Core competencies, 63-69, 427
  defined, 64-65
  essence of, 66-68
  preeminence in, 68-69
Core of manager's job, 24-25
Core relocation strategies, 720
Corporate control in diversified context, 723-24
Corporate strategy. See Strategy(ies)
Corregidor, 137
Cost(s)
  as barrier to entry, 78
  of diversification, 728

experience and, 651
product development, 745
reductions in, global strategy and, 741-42
Cost dynamics, 649-56
  efficiency vs. effectiveness, 655-56
  experience effect, 650-54, 655-56
    prices and, 654
    sources of, 653
  scale effect, 650, 655-56
  strategic implications, 654-55
Cost Dynamics: Scale and Experience Effects (Abell/Hammond), 634
Cost-of-entry test, 729-30
Counterinsurgency game, 386
Cox Enterprises Comcast, multimedia assets, 844-45
CP/M, 194, 195
CRA Exploration (CRAE), 309
Craftsmen, 412-14, 416
Creation hypothesis of competence, 763-64
Creative tension, 418-19
Creativity, strategic intent and, 42
Credibility, building, 98
Cross-border linkages, 367
Cross-border management, 748-54
  coordination and cooptation, 752-53
  differentiation, 750
  independence, 750-52
  mind matrix, 754
  multidimensional capabilities, 748-49
  simplifying assumptions, 749-50
Crown Cork & Seal, 80
Crystalline diversification, 718
Cuban Missile Crisis, 372
Culture, 324, 371-85
  building structure in managers' minds, 379-85
    building an organization, 380-81
    building shared vision, 381-82
    co-opting management efforts, 385
    human resources development, 382-85
    matrix in manager's mind, 385
  ideology, 371, 374-79
    defined, 374
    development of, 374-76
    missionary organization and, 376-78
    as overlay on conventional organizations, 378-79
  industry supply chain and, 328
  strategy and, 372
Customer needs, homogeneous, 743
Customer preference, global strategy and, 742
Customers, global, 743
Customer service, total, 44
Customizing strategies, 91

Daily learning, 415
Datsun, 117
De Beers, 311-12, 313, 315
Decentralization, 342-43
  environment and, 346
  indoctrination and, 352
Decision making
  in the entrepreneurial organization, 615
  models of, 372-73
  power and, 372
  in professional organizations, 663-67

by administrative fiat, 664-65
by collective choice, 665-66
by professional judgment, 664
Decisions
  politics and, 390
  strategic, 4
Defensive routines, 424
Delegating, 28
Deliberate strategies, 12
Dell Computer, 176, 177
Democratization of corporations, 397-400, 408
Design, organization, 339-43, 419
  situational factors affecting, 343-47
    age and size, 343-45
    environment, 346
    power, 346-47
    technical system, 345-46
Design differentiation strategy, 90
Designer, leader as, 419-20
Development, 383-84
Developmental shoot-outs, 699
Diamond industry, 311-15. See also Argyle Diamond Sales (ADS)
  Central Selling Organization (CSO), 309, 311-13
  cutting, polishing, and trading centers, 314
  diamond grading, 314
  industrial diamonds, 313-14
  investment market, 313
  jewelry manufacturers and retailers, 315
  polished diamond traders, 314-15
Differentiation, generic strategies of, 88-90
Digital Research, 194
Diplomacy, 394
Direction, 757
Directives
  from managers, 28
  top-down, 778
Direct random access memory (DRAM) market, 155-56
Direct supervision, 337
Disconnected strategy, 13
Discontinuity, detecting, 108-9
Discontinuous learning, 415
Distribution channels, access to, 78
Distributors, 327
Diversification, 329-35
  by-product, 331, 718
  conglomerate, 710, 711, 717
  costs and constraints to business units from, 728
  crystalline, 718
  linked, 332, 718
  related, 331
  by shareholders, 728
  strategies for, 96-97, 717-18
  unrelated (conglomerate), 65, 332, 710, 711, 717
Diversified context, 612, 704-36
  corporate strategy, 727-36
    choosing, 734-36
    concepts of, 730-34
    portfolio management, 731
    premises of, 728
    restructuring, 731-32
    sharing activities, 734
    tests of, 728-30

  transferring skills, 732-34
  diversified organization, 705-16
  generic corporate strategies, 717-20
    for extending core business, 717-19
    for reconceiving core business, 719-20
  group management, 721-27
    Asian corporate archetypes, 722
    comparison of, 722-26
    decoding Asian firms, 726-27
    European and Asian groups compared, 724-26
    European corporate archetypes, 721-22
Diversified organization, 350-51, 705-16, 758
  conditions of, 708-9
  divisionalized structure, 705-8
    coordinating mechanisms, 707
    economic advantages of, 711-13
    headquarters, 706-7, 713-14
  performance control system, social performance of, 714-15
  in the public sphere, 715-16
  transitional stages, 709-11
    by-product form, 710
    conglomerate form, 710-11
    integrated form, 709-10
    related-product form, 710-11
Divestiture, 407
Division of labor, 337
Divisions, 350
DNA, recombinant, 121, 125
Dr Pepper, 890
Doers, 26
Doing role of managers, 31-33, 34
Double-loop learning, 62
Downstream business strategy, 85
Downstream companies, 327-29
Driving force, 327
Duties of managers, 20-21

Ecology, strategy formulation and, 50-51
Economics, strategy formulation and, 51
Economic strategy, 48
Economies
  of scale, 650, 655-56, 744
    as entry barrier, 77
  of scope, 744
Edward Marshall Boehm, Inc., 119
Efficiency, 757
  effectiveness vs., 655-56
E & J Gallo Winery, 209-19, 614
  distribution system, 211-12
  as divided kingdom, 210-11
  earnings, 210
  generation gap at, 214
  growing for, 213-14
  statistical tables, 217-19
  wine market, 214-16
Eli Lilly Co., 122
Emergent strategies, 3, 12, 15, 18
Emerging industries, 623-26
  competitive strategy in, 623-26
    early mobility barriers, 624
    embryonic companies/spin-offs, 624
    entry, timing of, 626
    first-time buyers, 624

    high initial costs/steep cost reduction, 624
    short time horizon, 624
    strategic choices, 625
    strategic uncertainty, 623
    structural characteristics, 623-26
    subsidies, 624
    tactical moves, 626
    technological uncertainty, 623
  shaping industry structure, 625
Empire-building game, 387
Energy management, 36
Enlightened self-interest, 404
Entertainment industry. See also Sony Corporation
  box office market shares (1993), 800
  conglomerate revenues, 791
  growth and spending (1986-1991), 797
  market share of top rental films (1992), 800
  MPAA average production costs vs. box office revenue (1980-1992), 798-99
  music business, 794, 795
  North American film rental market shares (1980-1992), 801
  personal consumption expenditures (1980-1992), 798-99
  segments, 792-93
  theatrical revenues, 802
  U.S. consumer spending on (1993), 790
Entrepreneurial conglomerate, 722, 724
Entrepreneurial context, 612-33
Entrepreneurial fanatics, 696
Entrepreneurial organization, 348-49, 614-23, 757
  basic structure, 615
  conditions of, 615-17
  issues associated with, 622-23
  riskiness of, 622
  sense of mission, 622
  simple structure, 615
  start-up, 616
  strategy formation, 617-22
    in a garment firm, 620-21
    leadership and, 621-22
    in a supermarket chain, 618-20
    visionary leadership, 617-18
Entrepreneurial strategy, 13
Entrepreneurs, strategy formation by, 626-33
  action-analysis integration, 631-33
  gauging attractiveness, 630
  parsimonious planning and analysis, 630-31
  screening out losers, 627-30
Entry
  barriers to, 76, 77-78
  cost of, 729-30
  strategies of, 718
  threat of, 75, 77-78
  timing of, 626
Environment
  in adhocracy, 685-87, 691
  design parameters and, 346
  organic organizational forms and, 355
  strategy formulation and, 49-52
EPROM business, 157
European Airline Industry, 325
European Economic Community, U.S. compared to, 891
Evangelical investigation, 632-33

Event explanations, 422
Evolution, organizational, 764-70
  executive leadership and, 769-70
  patterns in, 765-69
    converging change, 765-66
    frame-breaking change, 767-69
Executive leadership, and organizational evolution, 769-70
Expansion, 91
Experience, costs and, 651
Experience curve, 651-53
Expertise game, 387
Extension, product, 92
External coalitions, 337, 347
Externalities in industry development, 625
Exxon Corporation, 325, 420, 576-94
  current operations, 586-87
  developing-country energy demands, 584-86
  Exxon Research and Engineering (ER&E), 586-87
  financial data, 592-94
  national interests, 578-84
    Britain, 579
    China, 579-83
    Indonesia, 583
    Japan, 579
    Nigeria, 584
    Norway, 578
    OPEC, 584
    Venezuela, 583-84
  natural gas production and sales, 590
  1980s glut and, 577
  oil and gas exploration and production earnings, 589
  organization and philosophy, 576-77
  petroleum products sales, 588
  proved reserves, 591
  Saudi pricing vs. worldwide petroleum industry capital spending, 585
  shocks to oil industry and, 577
  world energy consumption, 585
  world oil reserves and production, 580-81, 584-86
  world petroleum supply and disposition, 582-83

Fabrication stage, 327
Fairchild Camera and Instrument Corporation, 149, 150
Fairchild semiconductor, 149
Fanatics, entrepreneurial, 696
Feasibility of strategy, 61-62
Federal Express, 631
Federation, 723
Fifth Discipline, The (Senge), 410
Financial conglomerates, 721, 724
Financial controls, 724
First mover advantage, 60
Flash technology, 157-58
Flexibility, consciously structured, 99
Focus, crystallizing the, 100
Forces and forms, 757-59
Ford Motor Co., 11, 288-308
  emerging talents, 290-92
  employee involvement, 292
  management, 292

mission statement, 293
Model T, 656
Mondeo, 304
outsourcing by, 70
power structure, 289-91
product development cycle, 291
quality improvement, 293-94
rise and fall, 288-90
statistical tables, 307-8
  comparative, 303, 305, 308
  financial summary (1985-1993), 301
  sales (1983-1993), 302, 305, 306
Team Taurus, 289-308, 325, 614
  late '80s doldrums, 300-304
  launch of Taurus, 299-300
  management approach, 297
  manufacturing process, 298
  market concentration, 295-97
  mid-1990s situation, 300
  organizational chart, 296
  rise, 294-97
  stamping and vehicle assembly, 299
  systematic planning, 295
Trotman era, 304-6
world scene, 306-7
Foremen, work pace for, 20
Formal planning, 95
  in corporate strategy, 97
  in the machine organization, 642-49
Formosa, 129
Foster's, 65
Frame-breaking change, 767-69
  and executive leadership, 769-70
  forces leading to, 767
  rapidity of, 768-69
  scope of, 767
Frame of managerial job, 23, 24
Free markets, economic assumptions of, 406
Frei Brothers winery, 213
Function, grouping by, 340
Functional management, 749
Future Shock (Toffler), 352

Game over (Sheff), 257
Genentech, Inc., 121-26, 614
  formation, 121
  goals, 121-22
  human insulin, 122-23
  potential gene-splicer market, 124
  product development process, 126
  recombinant DNA, 125
General Electric, 44, 230-31, 382
  industrial diamonds, 313
General Mills, 335
General Motors, 11, 656
Generative learning, adaptive learning and, 417-18
Generic strategies, 58, 83-92, 717-20
  of differentiation, 88-90
  distinguishing core business, 85-91
  elaborating core business, 91-92
  for extending core business, 717-19
  locating core business, 84-85
  for reconceiving core business, 719-20
  of scope, 90-91
Generic value chain, 85-87
Gene splicing, 121, 125

Geographic expansion strategies, 92
Geographic management, 748
Goals (objectives), 3, 8
  imprecision in statement of, 37-38
GO Corp, 198
Government policy, as barrier to entry, 78
Grass-roots strategy making, 105-6
Gravity, center of. See Center of gravity
Grey Advertising, 116
Grouping, 340-41
Group management, 721-27
  Asian corporate archetypes, 722
  comparison of, 722-26
    corporate control, 723-24
    organizational setting, 723
  decoding Asian firms, 726-27
  European and Asian groups compared, 724-26
  European corporate archetypes, 721-22
Growth, accommodating rapid, 673-74

Harley-Davidson of U.S.A., 110, 111
Harvard Business School, 111-12
Head-on competition, 14
Hewlett Packard Company, 14, 179, 364, 469-88, 614
  cofounders, 469
  comparative financials, 486-87
  computer problems, 475
  corporate objectives, 475-77
  financial data, 481-83
  history, 469-73
    corporate culture and organization, 471-72
    expansion and diversification, 472-73
    HP Way, 470-71
    management by objectives and involvement, 472
    product line, 470
  management by walking around (MBWA), 472
  manufacturing productivity network (MPN), 480
  market share data, 488
  organization charts, 476, 478-79
  products and business segments, 483, 484
  program manager concept, 477-80
  restructuring, 473-75
    loss of control and regaining direction, 474-75
    product groups, 474
  sales breakdown, 485
  Young era, 475-80
Hierarchy, network organization and, 355-56
Hiring process, 673
Honda Motor Company, 41, 110, 614, 849-66
  American Honda, 112, 851-52
  beginning, 850-51
  early vehicles, 852-53
  European market, 856-57
  expansion, 851-52
  history, 849-50
  Honda effect, 110-18
    defined, 117-18
    organizational process perspective on, 113-17

strategy model and, 111-13
issues in mid-1990s, 857-60
  cultural realignment, 859
  curing "big company disease," 859
  reorganization, 857-58
in 1980s, 853-54
strategy, 851
technology organization, 854-57
  integrated designs, 854-55
  production organization, 855
  structure of, 855-56
Honeywell Corp., 229
Horizontal corporation, 355
Horizontal decentralization, 342-43
Human resources development, 382-85
Hybrid, 759
Hypercompetition, 325
  infinitely flat organizations and, 358
  organizational structure and, 354-55
  polymorphism and, 365
  spider's web networks and, 361-62

IBM, 160, 170, 220-38
  Apple and, 173, 174-75, 181-82, 198-99
  chip developments and, 233
  divisional rivalry, 222-23
  8000 series computer, 223-24
  4300 series computer, 232-33
  IBM PC, 59
  Microsoft and, 194-95, 197-99
  mini-market and linkages, 232-33
  missionaries and scientists at, 221-22
  organizing for future, 233-34
  in PC market, 177-79
  Scamp computer, 224-25
  7000 series computer, 224, 225
  statistical tables and exhibits, 235-38
  Stretch computer, 223
  System/360 computers, 98
    competitors' reactions to, 230-31
    development cost, 221
    management challenge, 220-21, 229-31
    organizational issues, 228-29
    programming, 226-27
    public announcement of, 226
    SPREAD Committee, 225-26
    success of, 231-32
    technology issues, 227
  System/370 computers, 332
  System/3 computers, 232
  TopView, 197-98
  World Trade Corp., 224-25
Identification, ideology reinforced through, 375-76
Ideological control, 724
Ideological strategy, 13
Ideology, 336, 371, 374-79
  cooperation through, 761
  defined, 374
  development of, 374-76
  missionary organization and, 376-78
  as overlay on conventional organizations, 378-79
IKEA, 92
Image differentiation strategy, 89
Imposed strategy, 13

Incentives, 695, 697
Incrementalism, 93, 95-101
  critical strategic issues, 96-97
  formal planning in corporate strategy, 97
  formal systems planning approach, 95
  innovation and, 702-3
  integrating strategy of, 100-101
  management of, 98-100
  power-behavioral approach, 95
  summary findings, 95-96
Indoctrination, 339, 376
  decentralization and, 352
Industrial groups, 721
Industrial holdings, 721
Industry
  strategies of, 85
  strategy formulation and, 51
  structural elements of, 76
Industry development, externalities in, 625
Infinitely flat organization, 325, 357-59
Influencers, 337
Information
  flow to managers, 21-22
  managers' sources of, 35-36
  managing by, 26-28
Information systems, in infinitely flat organizations, 359
Information technology, polymorphism and, 365
Innovation
  in automobile industry, 537-38
  capital availability for, 696
  competitive, 43-44
  definition, 680
  experts/fanatics, 694
  flexibility/quickness, 695
  fostering
    atmosphere/vision, 697-98
    developmental shoot-outs, 699
    incentives, 695, 697
    interactive learning, 700
    multiple approaches, 698
    skunkworks, 699-700
  incrementalist approach, 702-3
  large companies
    innovation barriers, 696-97
    orientation to market, 698
  long time horizons, 694-95
  low early costs, 695
  managing, 693-703
  need orientation, 694
  matching management to process, 703
  "Silicon Valley" approach to, 42
  strategy for, 700-702
    complex portfolio planning, 702
  and technology, 694-96
Innovation context, 612, 678-763
  innovative organization, 679-93
  managing innovation, 693-703
Innovative organization, 351-52, 679-93
  administrative adhocracy, 681-84
    operating core, 681-82
    strategy formation in, 687-88
  conditions of, 685-87
  environment taking precedence in, 691
  issues associated with, 691-93
    ambiguity, human reactions to, 691-92
    efficiency problems, 692

inappropriate transition, dangers of, 692-93
operating adhocracy, 681, 687
  strategy formation in, 687
strategic apex, roles of, 684-85
strategy formation, 687-91
  grass-roots model of, 689-90
structure, 680-85
varied strategies of adhocracy, 688-89
Inquiry vs. advocacy, 424
In Search of Excellence (Peters & Waterman), 371, 472
Insightful style of management, 34
Insurgency game, 386
Integrated form, diversified organization, 709-10
Integrating managers, 342
Integration, vertical, 65
  of paper industry, 329-30
Intel Corporation, 67-68, 149-67, 178
  beginnings, 149-53
  culture, 154-55
  1103 chip, 151
  i860 story, 160-61
  Intel Development Organization (IDO), 161
  management system, 153-54
  microprocessors, 152-53
  microprocessor strategy, 158-60
  in 1990s, 155-56
  Portland Technology Development Group, 159
  statistical tables, 162-67
  Systems Business, 161-62
  technology drivers, 156-58
Intellect, locus of, 357
  of cluster organization, 362
  of inverted organization, 359
  of spider's web organization, 361
  of starburst organization, 363
Intellectual assets, network organizations and, 355, 356
Intellectual property protection, 159
Intended strategy, 12
Intent, strategic, 41-45
  challenge and, 42-43
  competitive innovation and, 43-44
  creativity and, 42
  defined, 41
Interactive learning, 700
Interdependence of countries, 746
Interdependencies, 340-41
  residual, 342
Internal coalition, 347
Internal development, 718
International context, 613, 737-54
  cross-border management, 748-54
    coordination and cooptation, 752-53
    differentiation, 750
    independence, 750-52
    mind matrix, 754
    multidimensional capabilities, 748-49
    simplifying assumptions, 749-50
  global strategy, 738-47
    benefits of, 741-42
    changes over time, 746
    competitive drivers, 745-46
    competitive moves, 741

cost drivers, 744-45
definition, 739-40
drawbacks of, 742-43
government drivers, 745
industry globalization drivers, 743-46
market drivers, 743-44
marketing approach, 740-41
market participation, 740
multiple viable, 747
product offering, 740
value added activities, 740
International Paper, 329, 330
Internet, 361
Interpersonal style of management, 34
Inverted organization, 325, 357-61
Isolation of missionary organizations, 378
ITT, 748, 753
"-ization" practice, 384

J. Walter Thompson, 313
Japan
Apple alliances with Japanese firms, 182
automakers. See also Honda Motor
Company
investments in U.S. (1992), 85
partnerships with U.S. automakers
(1992), 858
industry structure, 458-59
MacArthur and, 139-41
atomic bombing, 139-40
occupation, 140-41
magnetic levitation train program, 274-76,
279-80
Japanese National Railways (JNR), 274
Japan Railways Group (JR), 274
Job specialization, 339

Kaleida, 181
Kalumburu Joint Venture, 309
Keiretsus, 722, 723, 724
Kibbutz, 377-78
Kleiner Perkins, 262
Knowledge sets, core competencies in, 66
Kodak, 78
Komatsu, 41

Labor, division of, 337
Labor efficiency, 653
Lateral hires, 674
Lawsuits, class action, 401
Leadership, 26, 418-26
building shared vision, 423-24
creative tension and, 418-19
executive leadership and organizational
evolution, 769-70
learning and, 415
levels of, 29-30
market share, 41
politics and, 390
product, 655
roles, 29, 418-22
as designer, 419-20
as steward, 422

as teacher, 421-22
skills, 422-26
building shared vision, 423-24
surfacing and testing mental models, 424
systems thinking, 424-26
strategy and, 10
surfacing and testing mental models, 424
systems thinking, 424-26
Learning, 758
adaptive and generative, 417-18
interactive, 700
leadership and, 415
rate of, 651
single-loop vs. double-loop, 62
strategic, 104-5
Learning organizations, 404-16, 417-26
adaptive learning and generative learning,
417-18
leadership in, 418-26
building shared vision, 423-24
creative tension and, 418-19
leader as designer, 419-20
leader as steward, 422
leader as teacher, 421-22
surfacing and testing mental models, 424
systems thinking, 424-26
Left-handed planner, 646
Leverage
areas of high, 425
external change and, 629
sources of, 357
in cluster organization, 362
in inverted organization, 359
in spider's web organization, 361
in starburst organization, 364
Leyte Gulf, Battle of, 135
Liaison devices, 342
Liaison positions, 342
Liberty Media, 844-45
Limited vertical decentralization, 346
Line versus staff game, 387
Linkage(s)
cross-border, 367
mode of, 357
in spider's web organization, 361
Linked companies, 333
Linked diversification, 332, 718
Linking, role of, 30
Local producers, 616
Logical incrementalism, 93, 95-101
critical strategic issues, 96-97
formal planning in corporate strategy, 97
formal systems planning approach, 95
integrating strategy of, 100-101
management of, 98-100
power-behavioral approach, 95
summary findings, 95-96
Lording game, 387
Lotus Development Corporation, 198, 207
Lotus 1-2-3, 195
Lotus Notes, 199
Loyalty, 375
Lumpers, 757

MacArthur, Douglas
Japan and, 139-41
atomic bombing, 139-40

occupation, 140-41
Philippines and, 127-41
"bypass" vs. "island hop" strategy, 127-28
command style, 135-36, 137-38
Hawaiian conference, 128-29
invasion, 130-32
invasion timetable, 130
Leyte, 132-35
liberation of, 138
Luzon target, 129-30
Manila, 137, 138
Surigao Straits, 134-35
McCaw Cellular Communications, 244, 246
McDonald's, 14
Machine Bureaucracies, 398-99
Machine organization, 349, 635-49, 757
administrative center, 635-37
coordination problems in, 641
conditions of, 638-39
control and, 637, 638
formulation/implementation dichotomy,
647-48
as instruments and closed systems, 639-40
issues associated with, 640-42
operating core, 635-37
human problems in, 640-41
organization taking precedence in, 649
strategic apex, 637-38
adaptation problems in, 641-42
strategic revolutions in, 648-49
strategy formation in, 642-49
airline example, 643
automobile firm example, 646
planning/plans/planners, roles of, 643-46
and senior management, 646-47
supermarket chain example, 642-43
structure, 635-37
"McIntel" approach, 151
McKinsey & Co., 355
Macro politics, 373
MCS-4 microprocessor, 152
Magnetic levitation train, 272-88
competitive situation, 276-78
dream of, 272
Japanese program, 274-76, 279-80
national policy analysis, 278-79
politics and, 278
statistical tables and exhibits, 281-88
superconductivity and, 272-73
U.S. lag in, 276-78
Management
coalition, 101
empowering, 776-77
in upstream vs. downstream companies, 329
Management and Machiavelli (Jay), 377
Management by objectives, 38
Manager(s), 35-40
imprecision of, 37-38
information sources of, 35-36
integrating, 342
middle line, tasks of, 635-36
muddling with a purpose, 39-40
policy decisions and, 35-40
power game and, 36-37
roles of, 28-33
controlling role, 28
doing role, 31-33, 34
leading, 29
people role, 28-31

sense of timing of, 37
time and energy management by, 36
Managerial styles, 34, 410-32
  artists, 411-12, 413, 416
  craftsmen, 412-14, 416
  learning organizations and, 414-16, 417-26
    adaptive learning and generative learning, 417-18
    leadership in, 418-26
  middle managers, 426-31
    pivotal position of, 428-29
    as working leaders, 430-31
  teamwork and, 413-14
  technocrats, 411, 412, 413, 414, 416
Managing, 18-25
  action, 31-33
  description of, 23-25
  folklore and facts about, 20-23
  by information, 26-28
  through people, 28-31
  of stability, 108
  strategy for, 107-10
  well-rounded job of, 33-34
Market, grouping by, 341
Market consolidation, 92
Market development strategies, 91-92
Marketers, 327
Marketing
  regulations, 745
  transferable, 744
  uniform, 742-43
"Marketing Success Through
  Differentiation—of Anything" (Levitt),
  89
Market participation, global strategy
  approach to, 742
Market share leadership, 41
Mass production firms, 638
Matching opportunity and competence, 54-55
Matrix structure, 342, 344, 379-80
Matsushita Electric Industrial Company
  1994, 457-68
  company philosophy, 459
  comparative statistics, 459
  competition and cooperation, 461
  decentralization, 460-61
  early history, 457-58
  human resources development at, 383
  Japan's industry structure and, 458-59
  management approach, 462-63
  NTG and, 263
  overseas operations, 464
  performance reviews, 463
  planning and control systems, 463
  pragmatic approach, 464-65
  product group matrix, 461
  product groups, 466
  R&D, 462-63
  statistical tables, 466-68
  technology and manufacturing, 461-62
  250-year strategy, 458
Mature context, 612, 634-56
  cost dynamics, 649-56
    efficiency vs. effectiveness, 655-56
    experience effect, 650-54, 655-56
    scale effect, 650, 655-56
    strategic implications, 654-55

machine organization, 635-49
Mazda, 117
Mental models, 421-22
  surfacing and testing, 424
Merrill Lynch, 358
MicroPro, 196
Microsoft Corporation, 160, 193-208, 325,
  503-16, 614
  alliances and rivalries, 199-201
  Apple and, 196-99
  beginnings, 193-95
  competitors, 195, 196, 199-201, 207
  culture, 507-8
  digital/electronic media, 512
  Excel spreadsheet, 197
  financial data, 516
  graphical user interfaces, 197
  home computer and multimedia markets,
    514
  home marketplace, 200
  human resources, 506-7
  IBM interactions, 194-95, 197-99
  licensing, 194
  motivation system, 508-10
    future direction, 509-10
    performance focus, 508-9
  Multiplan spreadsheet, 195
  networking, 199
  networking market, 513
  operating system dominances, 178
  organization chart, 511
  OS/2, 198
  past management style, 503-4
  software development process, 504-6
    code writing process, 506
    competitive targets, 505
    project management, 505-6
    specification process, 504-5
  statistical tables and exhibits, 206-8
  style, 201-2
  Windows, 178-79, 197-99
  Word software, 196-97
  worldwide software market, 511, 515
Middle line, 336, 635-36
Middle managers, 410, 426-31
  pivotal position of, 428-29
  as working leaders, 430-31
Midstream business strategy, 85
Military-diplomatic strategies, 5, 7-8, 9
Mission
  ideology and, 374-75
  stewardship for, 422
Missionary organization, 352-53
Mitbestimmung ("codetermination"), 397-98
MITS, 193-94
Mobility barriers, shifting, 625
Morgan Stanley, 68
Mountbatten and India, 935-55
  Civil War, 938-39
  division of India
    date of, 954-55
    plan for, 951-52
  Gandhi, 940-42, 948, 949, 952
  governors' input, 946-47
  Indian problem, roots of, 935-36
  Jinnah, 943-45, 949, 951, 952
  Kahuta slaughter, 948-49
  Kashmiri Brahmans, 939-40

Mountbatten Plan, 951-52
Nehru, 949, 950, 951, 952
  Operation Seduction, 937-38
  partition of India, 946-49
  Patel, 942-43
  Peshawar visit, 947-48
  Singh, 945, 951
Multinationals, collaboration among, 366-70
Multiple combinations, 759
Mutual adjustment, 337
Myths, 375

NASA Weather Satellite Program, 344
National Can, 80
National Film Board of Canada (NFB), 103-
  4, 105
National holdings, 722
Nationalization of corporations, 396-97, 408
NEC, 260, 262, 753
  integration of computers and communications, 381
Need orientation, 694
Networking, 30-31
Network organization, 325, 354-55
  cluster organization, 325, 362-63
  "infinitely" flat organization, 325, 357-59
  inverted organization, 325, 357-61
  "spider's web" organization, 325, 361-62
  starburst organization, 325, 363-65
New Steel Corporation, 142-48, 614
  history, 142
  statistical tables, 143-48
New Technologies Group (NTG), 259-65
  choice of future for, 261-62
  electronics firm alliances, 262-65
    Electronic Arts (EA), 263-65
  formation, 259-60
  strategy, 260-61
  technology and, 260
  venture capital for, 262
New York Times Company, 432-56
  acquisitions and divestitures, 433, 434-35
  advertising, 437, 454
  changing times for, 433-38
  comparative data, 453
  competition, 441
    in advertising, 442-43
    niche, 443-44
    statistics on, 452
  financial data, 455-56
  future of, 444
  history, 432-41
  magazine group, 436
  major issues facing, 444-46
  market changes, 441-42
  news gathering and reporting, 440-41
  organization chart, 447
  readership data, 448-52
  technology and, 438-40, 446
NeXt Corp, 198
Nicest People campaign, 116-17
Niche strategy, 90-91
Nike, Inc., 64, 72
Nintendo Co., Ltd., 254-71, 325, 614
  American business, 257
  cartridge protection scheme, 257

copyright battles, 258-59
crash and rebirth, 258
Electronic Arts (EA) threat, 263-65
electronic toys, 254-55
expansions into networks, 257
Family Computer (Famicom) system, 255-56
licensing program, 256-57
New Technologies Group (NTG) threat, 259-65
in 1993, 265-66
statistical tables, 267-71
Nintendo of America, 325, 922-34
action memos, 926-27
budgets, 926
changing environment, 930-31
competition, 928-29
corporate controls, 926-27
decline in profits, 929-30
future, 931
marketing concept, 924-25
nature of video game business, 928
organization, 925-26, 932-33
position, 929
product development, 927
SEGA and, 931
software organization, 923
style of, 924-26
videogames market and trend data, 934
Yamauchi's style, 923-24
Normandy, Battle of, 128
Norms, standardization of, 339, 377
North American Philips (NAP), 382, 385
NovaCare, Inc., 325, 517-29
cluster organization of, 363
competitors, 529
early history, 517-20
company vision, 518-19
professional staffing issues, 519-20
therapists' company, 520
inverted organization, 360, 520-23
clinicians focus, 521
customer complexity, 522
incentive systems, 522-23
quality and revenue control, 523
support organization, 521-22
polymorphism, 365
statistical tables, 524-25
strategy and future markets, 523-28
implementation and questions, 527-28
NovaNet, 365, 526-27
Novell Inc., 199, 207
Novelty, locus of, 357
in cluster organization, 362
in inverted organization, 359
in starburst organization, 363
N-person games, 14

Objectives (goals), 3, 8
imprecision in statement of, 37-38
Object orientation, 365
Operating adhocracy, 681, 687
Operating capabilities, shift to, 426-27
Operating core, 336
Operating turnarounds, 617
Operations, 427-28
Opportunities-resources relationship, 49-55

environment and, 49-52
identifying corporate competence and resources, 52-55
Opportunity orientation, 701
Opposition, overcoming, 99
Oracle, 199
Orbital Engine Company, 325, 530-40, 614
conventional engine compared to orbital engine, 532
engine design and patents or patent applications, 531, 534
exhaust emission standards, 532
finance, 535-37
financial data, 539-40
future and, 538
innovation in automobile industry and, 537-38
intellectual property protection, 533
negotiations and relationships with other firms, 533-35
orbital technologies, 530-33
value adding activities, 533
workforce, 535
Organic structures, 339
automation of operating core and, 345-46
environment and, 346, 355
Organizational awareness, 98
Organizational evolution, 764-70
executive leadership and, 769-70
patterns in, 765-69
converging change, 765-66
frame-breaking change, 767-69
Organizations, forces/forms in, 757-59
Organizations process model, 113-17, 372
Outpacing strategies, 87
Outputs, standardization of, 338
Outside support, 778
Outsourcing, strategic, 64, 65, 69-72
competitive advantage and, 69-70
degree of control over, 71
key considerations in, 69
new management approaches, 72
strategic risks of, 71-72
transaction costs of, 70
vulnerability and, 71

Packard Bell, 177
Paper industry, 329-30
Parallel decentralization, 343
Parallel processing, 365
Paramount Communications, Inc.
battle for, 819-48
Blockbuster and, 833
Chancery Court and Supreme Court rulings, 831-32
final deadline, 834
market value of bids, 847
merger with Viacom, 826, 828
QVC's offers, 826-27, 828, 829-31
share prices during, 847
TCI and, 827-28
TCI-Liberty Media and TCI-Bell Atlantic deals, 829
time line of major events in, 846
Viacom's offers, 828-29, 830, 833-34
board of directors, 848
entertainment business, 820-21

financial data, 835-36, 841-43
multimedia assets, 844-45
multimedia industry and competition, 824-26
publishing business, 821-22
Partial solutions, 99
Participative management, 397
Participatory democracy, 397, 398-400
Pattern(s)
managing, 109
strategy as, 11-12, 15, 16
Peet, Russ, Anderson, & Detroit, 915-21
communication/coordination among groups, 919-20
industry structure, 915-16
major accounting firms, profile of, 920-21
market-driven strategy, 918
organization/incentive issues, 918-19
position, 917-18
trends in the profession, 916-17
Penetration strategies, 91
People management, 431
People roles of managers, 28-31
PepsiCo, 890
Performance, strategy and, 333-35
Performance control systems, 342
Peripheral vision, 110
Personal computer industry, 174-75. See also Apple Computer, Inc.; Microsoft Corporation
alternative technologies, 179
distribution and buyers, 176-77
manufacturing and R&D, 175-76
PC manufacturers, 177-79
suppliers, 177
Personalized control, 724
Personal-service organization, 662-63
Perspective, strategy as, 14-16
"Peter Principle recycling," 152
Petrocan, 397
Philippines, MacArthur and, 127-41
"bypass" vs. "island hop" strategy, 127-28
command style, 135-36, 137-38
Hawaiian conference, 128-29
invasion, 130-32
invasion timetable, 130
Leyte, 132-35
liberation of, 138
Luzon target, 129-30
Manila, 137, 138
Surigao Straits, 134-35
Philips, 381
co-optation of management efforts, 385
corporate vision of, 382
NTG and, 263
training and development at, 383-84
Pillsbury Company, 99, 614, 867-86
Agri-Products, 873, 878
operating profit, 883
balance sheets, 884
Burger King restaurants, 879-80
cash dividends, 881
charitable contributions, 882
comparisons in food industry, 886
Consumer Foods operating profits, 882
consumer group, 872-73
consumer orientation, 879
consumer strategies, 879
corporate objectives, 878

financial performance, 876-78
future of, 877-78
goals/strategies, 868-69
history of, 867-68
industry segment, 885
net earnings, 881
overview of company, 868-69
Pillsbury Farms, 879
presentation highlights, 878-80
reinvestment/diversification, 871-72, 876
reorganization of, 874-76
  consolidation/acquisition, 874
  Green Giant merger, 875-76
  management changes, 875
restaurant operating profit, 883
sales, 880
social responsibility, 880
stabilizing earnings, 869-70
strategic posture, 878-80
Plan, strategy as, 10-11, 15, 16
Planned strategy, 13
Planner, manager as, 20
Planning
  complex portfolio planning, 702
  roles in machine organization, 643-46
  strategic, 108
  strategy and, 326-35
    by-products diversification, 331
    center of gravity change and, 332-33,
      334-35
    linked diversification, 332
    performance and, 333-35
    related diversification, 331
    strategic change and, 329-31
    unrelated diversification, 332
  total posture, 97
Planning systems, 342
Ploy, strategy as, 11, 16
Pluralistic participatory democracy, 400
Polaroid Corporation, 78, 325, 558-75, 614
  comparative data, 571
  competition, 560-61
  consumer camera sales, 570
  consumer film purchases, 568-70
  diversification efforts, 561
  early history, 558
  executive officers, 572
  financial data, 566-67
  imports/exports of equipment and supplies,
    568-69
  instant camera and film data, 567
  instant photography, 558-59
  international division, 563-64
  management and organizational changes,
    561-62
  manufacturer's shipments of photographic
    equipment and supplies, 568-69
  manufacturing division, 562
  marketing division, 562-63
  organization chart, 574-75
  philosophy and culture, 565-66
  production facilities, 573
  project teams, 564-65
  reorganization, 565
  research division, 563
  staff divisions, 564
  SX-70 line, 559-60
Policies

decisions on, 35-40
defined, 4
strategies and, 8
Policy making, 419-20
Political organization, 353
Political support, broadening, 99
Politicized organization, 388, 389
Politics, 373, 386-91
  competition through, 761
  forms of political organizations, 388-89
  functional roles of, 389-91
  in organizations, 386
  political games, 386-88
  strategy and, 62-63
  strategy formulation and, 51
Polymorphism, 365
Portfolio management, 731
  complex, 702
Portfolio theory, 110-11
Position
  competitive advantage in, 59-61
  strategy as, 13-14, 15, 16
Positioning the company, 82
Power, 371-73, 386-409, 615
  of board of directors, 399
  competitive maneuvering, 373, 391-94
    "Cold War" tactics, 392
    consequences of, 392-93
    friendly, 391-92
    integrated, 743
    nonlogical strategy for, 393-94
    rules for, 394
  control of corporation, conceptual horse-
    shoe model of, 394-409
    democratize it, 397-400, 408
    ignore it, 403-4, 409
    induce it, 404-5, 408
    nationalize it, 396-97, 408
    pressure it, 401-3, 407
    regulate it, 400-401, 407, 408
    restore it, 405-7, 408-9
  decision making and, 372
  managers and, 36-37
  politics, 373, 386-91
    forms of political organizations, 388-89
    functional roles of, 389-91
    in organizations, 386
    political games, 386-88
  in professional organizations, 661
  strategy and, 372
  of suppliers and buyers, 75, 76, 79-80
Power-behavioral approach, 95
PowerPC chip, 198
Precipitating events, incremental logic and,
  96
Predatory competition, 366
Pressuring of corporations, 401-3, 407
Price-cost relationship, 654-55
Price differentiation strategy, 89
Prices, experience and, 654
Primary activities, 86, 733
Proactive differentiation, 87
Process reengineering, 779-80
Process strategy, 13, 106
Procter & Gamble, 330, 331, 750-51
Product development costs, 745
Product development strategies, 92
Product differentiation, as entry barrier, 77

Product extension, 92
Production processes, 653
Product leadership, 655
Product line proliferation, 92
Product line rationalization, 92
Product producers, 327
Product quality, global strategy and, 742
Product redesign, 653
Products, substitute, 75, 81
Product standardization, 653, 742
Profession, management as, 22
Professional context, 612, 657-77
  professional organization, 658-69
  professional service firms (PSF), 669-77
Professional jobs, 339
Professional organization, 349-50, 658-69,
  758
  basic structure, 658-62
    administrative structure, 660-61
    administrators of professional work, 661
    pigeonholing process, 659-60
    professional operators, 658-59
  conditions of, 662-63
  issues associated with, 667-69
    coordination problems, 666
    innovation problems, 666-69
    public responses to problems, 669
  strategy formation in, 663-67
    by administrative fiat, 664-65
    by collective choice, 665-66
    by professional judgment, 664
Professional service firms (PSF), 669-77
  balancing, 676-77
  capacity planning, 672
  economics of, 672
  framework for analyzing, 670-71
  market for professional labor and, 673-74
  market for services, 674-76
  organizational structure, 670-71
  project team structure, 671-72, 675-76
  project types, 675
  revenue generation, 672-73
Proficiency, 758
Programs, defined, 4
Proliferation, product line, 92
Promotion policy, 673
Pure customization, 91

Quality circles, 44
Quality differentiation strategy, 90
Quasi-market relationships, 355
QVC Network, Inc., 823-24
  battle for Paramount, 826-27, 828, 829-31
  financial statements, 839-40
  leadership, 848
  multimedia assets, 844-45

Rabaul, 127-28
Railway Technical Research Institute
  (RTRI), 274, 279-80
Rational actor model, 372
Rationalism, excessive, 697
Rationalization, product line, 92
Raw material extraction stage, 327

Raychem, 67-68
RCA, 231
R&D, by upstream and downstream companies, 329
Realized strategy, 12
Reciprocal responsibility, 43
Recombinant DNA, 121, 125
Recombination strategies, business, 720
Recruitment, 383
Redefinition strategy, business, 719
Redesign, product, 653
Reduced instruction set computer (RISC), 160-61, 178
Reengineering, process, 779-80
Reformer missionaries, 378
Refreezing process, 621
Regis McKenna, 168-69
Regulation, 400-401, 408
Reinforcers, 60
Related businesses, 333, 334, 335
Related conglomerates, 65
Related diversification, 331
Related-product form of diversified organization, 710-11
Relocation strategies, core, 720
Reminiscences (MacArthur), 127
Reorganization
    Honda, 857-58
    logical incrementalism and, 97
    Pillsbury Company, 874-76
    Polaroid, 565
    SAS, 902
Reorientations, strategic, 106-7
Representative democracy, 397-98, 399
Research and development (R&D), by upstream and downstream companies, 329
Residual interdependencies, 342
Resource mix, changes in, 653
Resources, competitive advantage in, 59
Resources-opportunities relationship, 49-55
    environment and, 49-52
    identifying corporate competence and resources, 52-55
Responsibility
    reciprocal, 43
    social, 343, 401-3, 405, 407
Restructuring, in diversified context, 731-32
Retailers, 327
RISC chips, 160-61, 178
Rival camps game, 387
Rivalry, 81-82
    determinants of, 76
Routines, defensive, 424

Sagas, development of ideology through, 375
Scale, economies of, 650, 655-56, 744
    as entry barrier, 77
Scandinavian Airlines System (SAS), 325, 894-906
    advertisement, 904
    Carlzon's Little Red Books, 898, 906
    comparative data, 902, 905
    corporate culture, 897-98
    credit cards and service partners, 900-901
    early postwar history, 895
    evolution of fleet, 904

financial and operating results, 900-901
future, 902-5
group structure, 902, 908
international hotels (SIH), 899
milestones, 903
in 1988, 894
problems in 1981, 895-96
publisher services, 901
reorganization, 902
reservation system, 899-900
strategy, 896-97
Vingresor, 901-2
Scenario analysis, 420
Scheduling, 23-24
Science, management as, 22
Scope, economies of, 744
Scope strategies, 90-91
SEGA Enterprises, Ltd., 260, 262-63, 265, 931
    historical financial summary, 268
Segmentation strategies, 90
Selection, 383
Selective decentralization, 343
Self-interest, enlightened, 404
Seller, by-product, 333, 334-35
Servant Leadership (Greenleaf), 422
Seven-Up, 890
Shaky alliance, 388, 389
Shareholders
    diversification by, 728
    fallacy of control by, 405-6
Sharp, 179
Shell, 420
Shifts, tactical, 99
Shoot-outs, developmental, 699
"Silicon Valley" approach to innovation, 42
Simple structure, 615
Single-loop learning, 62
Situational factors, 343-47
    age and size, 343-45
    environment, 346
    power, 346-47
    technical system, 345-46
Size or organization, design parameters and, 343-45
Skill(s)
    competitive advantage in, 59
    core competencies in, 66
    outsourcing and, 71-72
    standardization of, 338
    transfer of, in diversified context, 732-34
Skunkworks, 699-700
SMILE, 383
Social architecture, 419
Socialization, 376
Social responsibility, 343, 401-3, 405, 407
Society, strategy formulation and, 51
Soft drink companies, 890. See also Cadbury Schweppes, P.L.C.
Software design, object oriented, 365
Solutions
    partial, 99
    symptomatic, 425
Sony Corporation, 595-609, 614, 781-803
    acquisitions, 781-82, 783-85
    beginnings, 595-97
    cell system, 599
    creative artists management, 792-95
    design approach, 601-2

early problems and successes, 782-83
entertainment and software businesses, 786-95
entertainment conglomerates, 785
expansion, 596-97
financial data, 608-9, 797, 802-3
future vision, 795-97
income and cash flows, 784
laser diode costs, 609
market data, 798-801
Mavica system, 603-6
media mergers, 790-92
movie economics, 789-90
music industry and, 794, 795
NTG and, 263
organization, 785-86, 788
personnel policies, 598-99
purposes of incorporation, 596
segment data, 608, 796
SEMA, 786
SMPGA, 786
Sony Entertainment, 325
spirit of, 598
tape recorder, 597
televisions, 599-600
transistor radios, 597-98
U.S. consumer electronics markets data, 607
videotape recorders, 600-602
Walkman, 602-3
Span of control, 341
SPARC chip, 160
Specialization, 653
    job, 339
Spider's web organization, 325, 361-62
Splitters, 757
Sponsorship game, 386
Stability, managing, 108
Standardization
    of norms, 339, 377
    of outputs, 338
    product, 653
    of skills, 338
    of work, 337-38
Standardized customization, 91
Standing committees, 342
Starburst organization, 325, 363-65
Star Electronics, 200
Start-up, entrepreneurial organization, 616
State Street Boston, 66
Steinberg, Inc., 106
Steward, leader as, 422
Strategic apex, 336, 637-38
    innovative organization, roles in, 684-85
    machine organization, adaptation problems in, 641-42
Strategic candidates game, 387
Strategic change, 621
Strategic decisions, defined, 4
Strategic goals, 3
Strategic intent, 41-45
    challenge and, 42-43
    competitive innovation and, 43-44
    creativity and, 42
    defined, 41
Strategic learning, 104-5
Strategic planning, 108
Strategic policies, 4
Strategic programming, 4, 644

Strategic turnarounds, 617
Strategic vision, 616
Strategies for Change: Logical
    Incrementalism (Quinn), 2, 93
Strategists. See Manager(s); Managing
Strategy(ies), 1-17. See also Generic strate-
    gies
  for change, 3-10
  change and, 51
  classical approach to, 5-7
  collective, 14
  competitive, 58
  as concept, 15
  concept of, 47-49
  consensus, 13
  control by, 724
  criteria for effective, 9-10
  culture and, 372
  definitions of, 2-4, 10-17
  deliberate, 12
  dimensions of, 8-9
  disconnected, 13
  for diversification, 96-97
  in diversified context, 727-36
    choosing, 734-36
    concepts of, 730-34
    portfolio management, 731
    premises of, 728
    restructuring, 731-32
    sharing activities, 734
    tests of, 728-30
    transferring skills, 732-34
  economic, 48
  emergent, 3, 12, 15, 18
  entrepreneurial, 13
  evaluating, 55-63
    challenge of, 56
    competitive advantage, 59-61
    consistency, 56, 57
    consonance, 56, 57-58
    feasibility, 61-62
    process of, 62-63
  formal, 8-9
  formal planning in, 97
  generic, 58
  global, 738-47
    benefits of, 741-42
    changes over time, 746
    competitive drivers, 745-46
    competitive moves, 741
    cost drivers, 744-45
    definition, 739-40
    drawbacks of, 742-43
    government drivers, 745
    industry globalization drivers, 743-46
    market drivers, 743-44
    marketing approach, 740-41
    market participation, 740
    multiple viable, 747
    product offering, 740
    value added activities, 740
  ideological, 13
  implementation of, 48, 49
  imposed, 13
  of industry, 85
  intended vs. realized, 12
  military-diplomatic, 5, 7-8, 9
  modern, 7-9

organizational planning and, 326-35
  by-products diversification, 331
  center of gravity change and, 332-33,
    334-35
  linked diversification, 332
  performance and, 333-35
  related diversification, 331
  strategic change and, 329-31
  unrelated diversification, 332
organizational structure and, 324, 327-29,
    333-35
as pattern, 11-12, 15, 16
as perspective, 14-16
as plan, 10-11, 15, 16
  planned, 13
as ploy, 11, 16
  politics and, 62-63
as position, 13-14, 15, 16
  power and, 371-73, 386-409
  process, 13, 106
  of stage of operations, 84-85
  summary statements of, 48
  tactics vs., 4-5, 12-13
  umbrella, 13, 105-6
  uniqueness of, 55
Strategy Alternatives for the British
    Motorcycle Industry, 111
Strategy analysis, 74-92
  competitive forces, 74, 75-83
    formulating strategy and, 82-83
    jockeying for position, 81-82
    powerful suppliers and buyers, 75, 79-80
    substitute products, 75, 81
    threat of entry, 75, 77-78
  generic strategies, 83-92
    of differentiation, 88-90
    distinguishing core business, 85-91
    elaborating core business, 91-92
    locating core business, 84-85
    of scope, 90-91
Strategy and Structure (Chandier), 326, 327
Strategy formation, 93-118
  crafting strategy, 101-10
    emergent nature of, 103-5
    grass-roots strategy making, 105-6
    managing, 107-10
    as plans for future and patterns from the
      past, 102-3
    strategic reorientations, 106-7
  of entrepreneurial organization, 617-22
  by entrepreneurs, 626-33
    action-analysis integration, 631-33
    gauging attractiveness, 630
    parsimonious planning and analysis, 630-
      31
    screening out losers, 627-30
  Honda effect, 110-18
    defined, 117-18
    organizational process perspective on,
      113-17
    strategy model and, 111-13
  logical incrementalism, 93, 95-101
    critical strategic issues, 96-97
    formal planning in corporate strategy, 97
    formal systems planning approach, 95
    integrating strategy of, 100-101
    management of, 98-100
    power-behavioral approach, 95

summary findings, 95-96
  in the machine organization, 642-49
Strategy formulation, 46-73
  competition and, 75
  competitive forces and, 82-83
  consensuses on, 46
  core competencies and, 63-69
  relating opportunities to resources in, 49-55
    environment, 49-52
    identifying corporate competence and
      resources, 52-55
  strategic outsourcing and, 64, 65, 69-72
  subactivities of, 48
Strategy hierarchy, 44
Strategy of Conflict, The (Schelling), 11
Strengths, identifying, 53-54
Structural explanations, 422
Structure, organizational, 324-70, 379-85
  building an organization, 380-81
  building shared vision, 381-82
  collaboration (alliances), 366-70
  configuration approach to, 335-53
    coordinating mechanisms and, 337-39
    design parameters and, 339-43
    diversified organization, 350-51
    entrepreneurial organization, 348-49
    innovative organization, 351-52
    machine organization, 349
    missionary organization, 352-53
    parts or organization and, 336-37
    political organization, 353
    professional organization, 349-50
    situational factors and, 343-47
  co-opting management efforts, 385
  design by managers, 28
  forms of, 325
  human resources development, 382-85
  hypercompetition and, 354-55
  matrix, 379-80
  matrix in manager's mind, 385
  network organization, 354-56
    cluster organization, 325, 362-63
    "infinitely" flat organization, 325, 357-59
    inverted organization, 325, 357-61
    "spider's web" organization, 325, 361-62
    starburst organization, 325, 363-65
  strategy and, 324, 327-29, 333-35
Structuring of Organizations (Mintzberg),
    614
Styles, managerial. See Managerial styles
Substitute products, 75, 81
Substitution threat, determinants of, 76
Sun Microsystems, 160
Supercub (Honda), 114, 116
Supermarket chain, 59
Supervision, direct, 337
Suppliers
  changing role of, 625
  outsourcing and, 72
  power of, 75, 76, 79-80
Supply chain, industry, 327, 328
Support, outside, 778
Support activities, 86, 733
Support differentiation strategy, 89
Support staff, 336
Symbolic actions, 98
Symptomatic solutions, 425
Systematic waiting, 99

Systems, administrative, 324
Systems development by managers, 28
Systems thinking, 424-26

Tactical shifts, 99
Tactics, strategy vs., 4-5, 12-13
Tailored customization, 91
Takeover, 91
Taligent, 181
Talon, 110
Task forces, 342
TCG, Ltd., 325, 489-98
　financial data, 490, 491
　group formation chronology, 495
　history, 494-95
　incubator concept, 497
　internal management techniques, 495-96
　network system, 490-91, 493-94
　new product development, 493
　1993 situation, 489-90
　operating problems, 496-97
　organization, 491-93
　public offering, 497-98
TCI, 199, 827-28
　multimedia assets, 844-45
Teacher, leader as, 421-22
Teamwork, managerial styles and, 413-14
TechComm Group. See TCG, Ltd.
Technical standards, 745
Technical system, 345-46
Technocrats, 411, 412, 413, 414, 416, 431
Technology
　middle managers and, 430
　strategy formulation and, 50
Technostructure, 336
　machine organization, 635, 636-37
Teledyne, 332
Textron, 332
Theory, espoused vs. in-use, 424
Thermo Electron Corporation, 498-502
　critical success factors, 499-500
　financial data, 499
　performance of public subsidiaries, 502
　spin offs, 500-501
　starburst organization, 498-99
　strategic acquisitions, 501-2
Thordike, Doran, Paine & Lewis, Inc.
　(TDP&L), 805
3M Company, 66, 331
3DO, 939
Time management, 36
Time Warner, 199
Timing, manager's sense of, 37
Tokyo Telecommunications Engineering Co.
　(TTK), 595-98
Top-down directives, 778
Total customer service, 44
Total posture planning, 97
Total quality management (TQM), 779-80
Toyota, 11, 115, 117
　as Type J corporation, 378-79

Toys "R" Us, 66
Trade-offs, evaluation of, 430
Trade policies, 745
Traditions, development of ideology through,
　375
Training, 339, 383-84
　in infinitely flat organizations, 359
Trains, magnetic levitation. See Magnetic
　levitation train
Transaction costs, of strategic outsourcing, 70
Transrapid International, 276
Trend analysis, 421-22
Trial balloons, 99
Turnarounds
　operating turnarounds, 617
　strategic, 617
Turnover, in PSF industries, 674
Two-person game, 14
Type Z corporation, 379

Umbrella strategy, 13, 105-6
Unbundling, 720
Undifferentiation strategy, 90
Unfreezing process, 620-21
Unilever, 382, 750
　human resources development at, 383-85
Union Camp, 332
U.S. motorcycle industry, 110-12
Unit grouping, 340-41
Unit size, 341-42
　size of organization and, 345
Unrelated business company, 333, 334
Unrelated (conglomerate) diversification, 65,
　332, 710, 711, 717
Unsegmentation strategy, 90
Unskilled jobs, 339
Upstream business strategy, 85
Upstream companies, 327-29

Value activities, 732-33
Value added activities, 740
Vanguard Group, Inc., 325, 804-18
　client service, 809-10
　competitors, 812-13
　cost advantage, 818
　direct marketing share, 817, 818
　funds, 815-16
　　bond, 812
　　equity, 812-13
　　fixed-income, 806-7, 810-11
　　index, 806
　　market share, 814
　　no-load strategy, 806
　funds management, 810-11
　future, 813-14
　history, 804-7
　money market wars, 812
　organization and culture, 807-9
　pension market, 810

　quantitative equity group, 811
　savings to shareholders, 818
　strategy, 809-10
Variety-reducing stage, 327
Venrock Associates, 168
Verbal media, manager's emphasis on, 21-22
Vertical decentralization, 342-43
Vertical integration, 65
　of paper industry, 329-30
Viacom International, Inc., 822-23
　battle for Paramount, 828-29, 830, 833-34
　financial statements, 837-38
　line of business financial data for, 841-42
　multimedia assets, 844-45
Vingresor, 901-2
VisiCalc, 169, 195
VisiCorp, 197
Vision, 415-16
　company, 381-82
　creative tension and, 418
　extrinsic and intrinsic, 423
　personal, 423
　positive vs. negative, 423
　shared, 423-24
　strategic, 616
Volkswagenwerk, 106, 107
Vulnerability, strategic outsourcing and, 71

WA Diamond Trust (WADT), 310
Waiting, systematic, 99
Walt Disney Company, 929
Weiden and Kennedy, 64
Wellington Fund, 804-5
Western Digital, 158
Weyerhauser, 329, 330
Whistle-blowing game, 387
Withdrawal strategies, 718
WordPerfect, 196-97
WordStar, 196
Work, standardization of, 337-38
Worker participatory democracy, 398-99
Worker representative democracy, 397-98
Workflow linkages, 340-41
Working Leader, The (Sayles), 31
Working leaders, middle managers as, 430-31
Wrigley Chewing Gum, 333

Xerox, 42

Yamaha, 110
YKK, 110
Young Turks game, 387
Yuino, 313

Zero-base budgeting, 63